3 × 33

Short Fiction by 33 Writers

Mark Winegardner

Florida State University

THOMSON
WADSWORTH

Australia Canada Mexico Singapore Spain United Kingdom United States

THOMSON

WADSWORTH

3 × 33: Short Fiction by 33 Writers

Mark Winegardner

Publisher, Acquisitions Editor: *Michael Rosenberg*
Development Editor: *Cathy Richard Dodson*
Production Project Manager: *Diana Baczynskyj*
Executive Marketing Manager: *Carrie Brandon*
Marketing Manager: *Katrina Byrd*
Senior Print Buyer: *Mary Beth Hennebury*
Compositor: *ATLIS Graphics & Design*
Project Manager: *Laura Horowitz*

Cover Image: © *CNAC/MNAM/Dist. Réunion des Musées Nationaux / Art Resource, NY*

Printed in the United States of America.
1 2 3 4 5 6 – 07 06 05 04

For more information contact Thomson Wadsworth, 25 Thomson Place, Boston, Massachusetts 02210 USA, or you can visit our Internet site at http://www.thomson.com

Photography Manager: *Sheri Blaney*
Text Permissions Manager: *Bob Kauser*
Text Designer: *Hearthside Publishing Services*
Cover Designer: *Brian Salisbury*
Printer: *Malloy*

ISBN: 0-15-510480-2

Library of Congress Control Number 2004105079

Credits appear on pages 1133–1136, which constitute a continuation of the copyright page.

Contents

Preface

3 × 33: Short Fiction by 33 Writers—an anthology of ninety-nine short stories, three stories apiece by thirty-three North American writers born after 1900—proceeds from a simple idea: Read one story by a writer and you're studying the story. Only if you read a group of stories by the writer are you studying both the stories *and* the writer. A single story by a writer can't begin to take the measure of that writer's development, range, and career, but a small group of stories—even three apiece—often can.

By the end of a typical term, students may have read, say, forty of a typical anthology's hundred stories. These stories will have come at the students in such a blur that the mention of a particular assigned writer might elicit no more than a blank stare. Because students typically read only one story per writer, any sense they have of what a particular writer is really about—in terms of the writer's craft, the writer's preoccupations, the writer's contributions to literature and culture—will have been gleaned largely from outside reading or the instructor's lectures.

In twenty-some years of college teaching, I've taught about a hundred courses—first-year writing, short story lit classes, fiction workshops to inexperienced sophomores and to extremely advanced graduate students—where what I really needed was *one book* in which, for a reasonable cost, my students would have at their fingertips a group of stories by any and all writers I was teaching. The stories would be a healthy mix of both widely anthologized stories *and* more unexpected picks. In a perfect world, each writer would be introduced by another writer, one who could give a practitioner's-eye view of the writer and the stories in question, one that would be of use to those reading the stories for the first time as well as those who have loved them for years.

This is most assuredly not yet a perfect world.

But this *is* that book.

In a Nutshell, What's Special About This Book?

1. It allows students to read multiple stories from each writer.
2. It provides instructors with a refreshing blend of commonly anthologized short stories and undiscovered gems.
3. All thirty-three writers are introduced by brief, lively essays by other accomplished fiction writers commissioned specifically for this anthology.

And Those Things Are Special Because . . . ?

There is a degree to which readers, at any level of experience or sophistication, can learn about the same amount—*on their own,* without the need for extensive lectures (however helpful those would undoubtedly be) or outside reading (ditto)—from reading a group of a writer's short stories as from reading a group of a writer's novels. In either case, a short story or something much longer, the writer has to (again with the threes—forgive me):

1. Stir up some trouble that disturbs a preexisting and often fragile equilibrium and thereby get a fictional world up and running;
2. Develop that trouble and that world, upping the ante along the way;
3. Make the whole thing pay off and show at least some repercussions of the characters' decision making.

Simply watching a writer do at least those three things repeatedly is going to help any reader learn things about what a given writer does and how he or she does it: an understanding that is the bedrock of even the most elementary of stories *and* their writers (and *that* is the foundation of any story: something central in any class that's reading stories, whether it's first-year writing, a short-story lit class, a contemporary writers class, or a fiction workshop).

3 × 33—alone among all the anthologies of short fiction available—allows any careful reader to be dazzled by having a slightly broader sampling of every writer's work at one's fingertips. It's fairly easy to consider the stories as a group, to see patterns emerge, to experience the magic, yes, but also to have a sporting chance to spot the mirrors and trapdoors, to study every wave of the wand, every flourish of the cape.

Why three?

There's no magic per se to that number. But anything more would be impossible to include within the covers of a single book Anything less than three is not a group. A band with two people in it is a duo, not a group. Two kids standing on a street corner aren't a group, they're just a couple of kids. Three is the minimum number necessary to constitute a group, the smallest number needed to create a pattern of anything.

3 × 33 includes *both* the must-have stories from every writer included *and* a host of brilliant stories that aren't in every table of contents of every anthology of short fiction on your bookshelf. Also not present in any other book are the useful, eye-opening, and delightful essays that introduce each of the thirty-three writers. The introducers are all widely admired writers themselves, authors, collectively, of about two hundred works of fiction and the winners of nearly every worthwhile literary award there is. Several of the essays are by writers whose own stories appear here. Some were written by people who were once the student of the writer they're now introducing. Several writers introduce their heroes. One even introduces his twin brother. What all the essays have in common is that, in them, the writers talk about what they have learned from the stories they're writing about. They share their passion for stories they love, trying to show you—someone who is perhaps unfamiliar with some of the stories you're about to read—what, from the perspective of a good working writer, is so special about the writer in question, why that writer's work is admired, why people read it again and again, how and why it has influenced other writers, why it's worthy of your time.

After extensive consultation, I decided to focus on American writers born after 1900 (both *The Best American Short Stories* and *Prize Stories: The O. Henry Awards* have been defining "American" as "North American" for decades, and we quite naturally followed suit). So that's what is represented here. The year 1900 is a logical birth-year cutoff point, and not merely because neither the estate of F. Scott Fitzgerald (born in 1896) nor that of Ernest Hemingway (born in 1899) allows textbooks to reprint three of the writer's stories. The first two giants of the form born after the turn of what, after all, was widely known as the American century were Eudora Welty (born in 1909) and John Cheever (born in 1912)—not incidentally, the two writers whose best-selling, highly honored career-spanning collections (*The Stories of John Cheever* in 1979, *The Collected Stories of Eudora Welty* in 1980) were instrumental in triggering a broader readership for the American short story.

Is There an Instructor's Manual?

Yes. The Instructor's Manual for *3 × 33* provides pedagogical tools for instructors to use with the stories included in the anthology, as well as print and online resources for each author. Because one strength of *3 × 33* is that it appeals to instructors of both literature and creative writing classes, the Instructor's Manual contains resources for both courses. The Manual includes questions that ask students to consider all three of the author's stories in context, because another strength of *3 × 33* is that students are given a broader view of an author's work than just a single story.

The Instructor's Manual consists of the following elements:

- **Summaries** provide instructors with an overview of the plot, characters, and setting of each story, as well as cues for possible areas to focus on (for example, interesting uses of point of view, and ways in which the story draws on classical plot structures).
- There are three to five **Discussion questions** for each story. These questions focus on analysis and close reading of the stories. In the discussion questions, students are asked to perform a close reading of a passage from the story, react to commentary from an interview with the author concerning a specific story, trace the development of a character, and so on. In addition to providing discussion questions for each story, additional questions ask students to consider the three stories in context.
- **The Writer's Craft questions** are designed especially for creative writing classes, although literature instructors will also find them valuable. These questions focus on the craft of writing and the way stories are put together. Students are quizzed about the way the author uses dialogue, the structure of the plot, and techniques of characterization, among other aspects.
- **Classroom writing activities** give instructors ideas for writing activities based on each story and on all three stories by one author. There are a variety of kinds of activities in order to appeal to both literature and creative writing instructors. Activities include copying the style of the writer, rewriting scenes from different points of view, and applying techniques the writer uses to students' own writing.
- The Manual includes a **Bibliography** for each author. The bibliographies are not meant to be extensive; the focus is on ten to fifteen resources especially useful to literature and creative writing teachers, such as books of interviews (like the *Conversations* series), collections of letters, and books that provide a broad critical overview of the author.
- **Gale and other online resources** are offered for each author. In addition to Gale resources, the list includes Web sites such as PAL (Perspective in American Literature) and Web sites dedicated to specific authors.

- An **Alternative Table of Contents** provides listings of stories according to the following categories:

  Stories by Story Shape
  Stories by Point of View
  Stories by Relationships

In addition to the Instructor's Manual, *Three by Thirty-Three* is accompanied by *The Wadsworth Original Film Series in Literature.* This DVD contains a collection of three short films and interviews:

- ***A Worn Path*** includes an interview with **Eudora Welty,** conducted by Pulitzer Prize–winning playwright **Beth Henley.**
- ***A&P*** includes an interview with **John Updike,** conducted by Pulitzer Prize–winning writer and Wadsworth author **Donald Murray.**
- ***Cathedral*** includes an interview with Raymond Carver's widow **Tess Gallagher,** conducted by Carver scholars **William Stull** and **Maureen P. Carroll.**

Acknowledgments

The ninety-nine stories in this book got here after a truly exhaustive study of other textbooks and anthologies and after consultation with dozens of reviewers and other writers. Particularly helpful on this count, and generous with their time and resources, were Janet Burroway, Dan Chaon, Junot Diaz, Ken Foster, Jonathan Lethem, Michael Martone, Claire Messud, Lorrie Moore, Stewart O'Nan, Elwood Reid, Richard Russo, Lee Smith, and Elizabeth Stuckey-French. In addition, all thirty-three of the writers who wrote introductions helped to shape the selections.

Thanks to Claire Wachtel and Bill Hoffman, the editors at Harcourt who bought this book and who convinced me that it was also a really good idea, one utterly different from everything else out there. Thanks, too, to Cathy Richard Dodson, Karen Judd, and Michael Rosenberg at Wadsworth, whose editorial guidance brought this book to fruition (and who talked me into doing it yet again, after I was picked to write the sequel to Mario Puzo's novel *The Godfather* and didn't think I would be able to find time to do anything else).

I would like to thank Karyn Morrison, who secured permissions for these ninety-nine stories, as well as all the reviewers who made valuable contributions during the development of this book:

Edward Allen	*University of South Dakota*
Greg Bills	*University of Redlands*
Scott Blackwood	*University of Texas at Austin*
Janet Burroway	*Florida State University*
Jim Clark	*University of North Carolina at Greensboro*
Emily Dziuban	*University of Tennessee, Knoxville*
Tom Grimes	*Southwest Texas State University*
Tom Huminski	*Portland Community College*
Wai-Leung Kwok	*San Francisco State University*
Andrew Levy	*Butler University*

Beth Lordan	*Southern Illinois University*
Joe Lostracco	*Austin Community College*
Marilyn Patton	*De Anza College*
Wendy Rawlings	*University of Alabama*
Brian Smyth	*Hofstra University*
John Stoler	*University of Texas at San Antonio*
Paula Uruburu	*Hofstra University*

I want to thank my students—all of them, really, a true cast of thousands who, over the past twenty-some years, collectively taught me the best things I know about teaching. I'm especially grateful to the graduate students in my fall 2002 fiction workshop, in which (aided by the assistance of Tricia Whittemore, who scanned many of these stories) I tested and refined an early beta version of this book: Andrew Cohen, Jocelyn Cullity, Rob Dennis, Kimberly Elkins, Sandra Giles, Charley Henley, Tom C. Hunley, Danielle Kotaska, Nikki Louis, Amy Smith, Lauren Spohrer, Jack Steinbrink, Ed Tarkington, Misty Urban, and Joel Weinbrot.

I'm willing to bet that no Instructor's Manual in the history of textbooks was ever written by a better fiction writer than Dan Melzer of California State University, Sacramento. I'm humbled that someone so smart and talented would take on such a thankless job. Thank you, Dan.

The thirty-three distinguished writers who wrote these introductions certainly didn't do it for the meager amount of money we paid them. Thank you, one and all, for sharing and airing your passions, for helping to pick the stories included here, and for making this book truly, deeply like no other.

There are many debts—in the production of this manuscript and otherwise—that I owe to my wife Jennifer. I'll never repay them adequately, but for her help on this book per se: *molte grazie.*

Finally, there's not a chance that you would be holding this in your hands now if it weren't for the indispensable contributions of my two associate editors, Tom Bligh and Ken Foster. Ken was a brainstorming partner extraordinaire and, among many other tasks, did an excellent job of coordinating and editing all the introductions. Tom was a marvel: an all-purpose troubleshooter, editor, and proofreader.

Mark Winegardner
July 2004

Sherman Alexie (1966–)

grew up on the Spokane Indian Reservation in Wellpinit, Washington. Born hydrocephalic (with water on the brain), Alexie underwent a brain operation at the age of six months and was not expected to survive. When he did, doctors predicted that he would live with severe mental retardation. Instead, Alexie learned to read by age three and read John Steinbeck's The Grapes of Wrath *by age five. He went to a high school off the reservation (where, he says, he was "the only Indian . . . except for the school mascot") and graduated from Washington State University. A year later, he published two collections of his poetry; a year after that, he won a grant from the National Endowment for the Arts; the following year, he published his first collection of short stories,* The Lone Ranger and Tonto Fistfight in Heaven, *which received the PEN/Hemingway Award for Best First Book of Fiction. A story from that book, "This Is What It Means to Say Phoenix, Arizona," was the basis for the film* Smoke Signals, *for which Alexie wrote the screenplay. He has gone on to write several more collections of poems, two novels, and the short story collections* The Toughest Indian in the World *and* Ten Little Indians. *He also continues to write screenplays, perform in poetry slams, sing (he once opened for Indigo Girls), and do stand-up comedy. He lives in Seattle with his wife and children.*

Introduction by **Junot Diaz**

Since the appearance in 1992 of his first books, *The Business of Fancydancing* and *I Would Steal Horses,* Sherman Alexie has been an indefatigable chronicler of American Indian life. In slightly over a decade's time, he has produced a formidable corpus of work: publishing three collections of short stories, two novels, nine books of poetry, writing two screenplays, directing one movie and in the process has garnered extraordinary praise, hailed as one of the best young American fiction writers by both *Granta* and *The New Yorker.*

From the first, Alexie has confounded all expectations. Setting his early work almost entirely in or around the Spokane Indian Reservation (a fourth-world chunk of real estate where phones don't work, cars break down, houses burn, and alcoholism is more prevalent than medicine) and consciously eschewing both the White Man's Indian—that stoic (as in never speaking) savage (as in perfect candidate for a genocide) who is perpetually ambered in the past (as in denied a presence in the Now)—and his modern retread, the valorized New Age Indian (that eagle feather and corn pollen mystic who is a natural-born environmentalist and speaks constantly to the Great Spirit), Alexie's hard-luck characters are complex, flawed, and, even when they're residing in alternative realities (such as the ones described in the stories "Distances" and "The Sin Eaters"), unfailingly contemporary. They fall in love, they lie to themselves, they lose jobs, they sleep with people they probably shouldn't—and like the narrator in "The Lone Ranger and Tonto Fistfight in Heaven" are more likely to be in a 7-11 buying a Creamsicle than participating in a sweat lodge.

And that, I would argue, seems to be the point. Alexie is interested not in the Historical Suffering of Native Peoples or the Remarkable Story of Their Survival, but in something far humbler, far more elusive, that appears all too infrequently in the public consciousness—what Alexie himself has called "the day-to-day lives of Indians."

In "This Is What It Means to Say Phoenix, Arizona," the protagonist's father has died, yet the story focuses on neither the father nor the death but on the mundane business of flying down to Arizona to recover the father's remains and the last of his belongings (a deceptively simple premise that in Alexie's capable hands expands into a rumination on the limits of friendship). "The Lone Ranger and Tonto Fistfight in Heaven" details the aftermath of the narrator's disastrous breakup with his white girlfriend—"'I love you,' she said as I left her. 'And don't ever come back.'"—and the slow roads taken to forgetting and ultimately forgiveness. It's in stories like these where Alexie's abundant gifts are best displayed: the spare, honest, antisentimental prose, the exhilarating flights of lyricism, his characters' ability, even in the midst of tragedy and lost history, never to lose their sense of humor. ("'We've come a long ways,' Thomas said. 'We have outdoor lighting.'") Alexie is never more powerful, though, than when he's exploring that dense, wounding thicket called manhood, the ties between male friends, between fathers and sons, and between a man and his own sense of self. "The Toughest Indian in the World," labeled by one critic as a "a graphic act of pornography," can be read strictly as a story about the narrator's homosexual encounter with an itinerant fighter, but it can be read simultaneously as a story about the narrator's nostalgia for an idealized masculine self. ("'You'd have been a warrior in the old days, enit?' the journalist says. 'You would've been a killer. You would've stolen everybody's goddamn horses.'") The longing for the mythical is strong in Alexie's work—there are, after all, characters who fly, who give birth to salmon, ancestors who return—but Alexie never fails to undercut this longing, to foreground the real-world conditions that compel people to produce such dreams.

And this, at last, is what most awes me about Alexie's work: More than almost any writer before him, of color or otherwise, he has figured out a way to dramatize the profound hammerlock that history has on all of us while simultaneously and improbably arguing its very irrelevancy.

But enough. Time for you to turn the page, to judge for yourself.

For Junot Diaz's bio, see page 409.

Sherman Alexie

The Lone Ranger and Tonto Fistfight in Heaven

Too hot to sleep so I walked down to the Third Avenue 7-11 for a Creamsicle and the company of a graveyard-shift cashier. I know that game. I worked graveyard for a Seattle 7-11 and got robbed once too often. The last time the bastard locked me in the cooler. He even took my money and basketball shoes.

The graveyard-shift worker in the Third Avenue 7-11 looked like they all do. Acne scars and a bad haircut, work pants that showed off his white socks, and those cheap black shoes that have no support. My arches still ache from my year at the Seattle 7-11.

"Hello," he asked when I walked into his store. "How you doing?"

I gave him a half-wave as I headed back to the freezer. He looked me over so he could describe me to the police later. I knew the look. One of my old girlfriends said I started to look at her that way, too. She left me not long after that. No, I left her and don't blame her for anything. That's how it happened. When one person starts to look at another like a criminal, then the love is over. It's logical.

"I don't trust you," she said to me. "You get too angry."

She was white and I lived with her in Seattle. Some nights we fought so bad that I would just get in my car and drive all night, only stop to fill up on gas. In fact, I worked the graveyard shift to spend as much time away from her as possible. But I learned all about Seattle that way, driving its back ways and dirty alleys.

Sometimes, though, I would forget where I was and get lost. I'd drive for hours, searching for something familiar. Seems like I'd spent my whole life that way, looking for anything I recognized. Once, I ended up in a nice residential neighborhood and somebody must have been worried because the police showed up and pulled me over.

"What are you doing out here?" the police officer asked me as he looked over my license and registration.

"I'm lost."

"Well, where are you supposed to be?" he asked me, and I knew there were plenty of places I wanted to be, but none where I was supposed to be.

"I got in a fight with my girlfriend," I said. "I was just driving around, blowing off steam, you know?"

"Well, you should be more careful where you drive," the officer said. "You're making people nervous. You don't fit the profile of the neighborhood."

I wanted to tell him that I didn't really fit the profile of the country but I knew it would just get me into trouble.

"Can I help you?" the 7-11 clerk asked me loudly, searching for some response that would reassure him that I wasn't an armed robber. He knew this dark skin and long, black hair of mine were dangerous. I had potential.

"Just getting a Creamsicle," I said after a long interval. It was a sick twist to pull on the guy, but it was late and I was bored. I grabbed my Creamsicle and walked back to the counter slowly, scanned the aisles for effect. I wanted to whistle low and menacingly but I never learned to whistle.

"Pretty hot out tonight?" he asked, that old rhetorical weather bullshit question designed to put us both at ease.

"Hot enough to make you go crazy," I said and smiled. He swallowed hard like a white man does in those situations. I looked him over. Same old green, red, and white 7-11 jacket and thick glasses. But he wasn't ugly, just misplaced and marked by loneliness. If he wasn't working there that night, he'd be at home alone, flipping through channels and wishing he could afford HBO or Showtime.

"Will this be all?" he asked me, in that company effort to make me do some impulse shopping. Like adding a clause onto a treaty. *We'll take Washington and Oregon, and you get six pine trees and a brand-new Chrysler Cordoba.* I knew how to make and break promises.

"No," I said and paused. "Give me a Cherry Slushie, too."

"What size?" he asked, relieved.

"Large," I said, and he turned his back to me to make the drink. He realized his mistake but it was too late. He stiffened, ready for the gunshot or the blow behind the ear. When it didn't come, he turned back to me.

"I'm sorry," he said. "What size did you say?"

"Small," I said and changed the story.

"But I thought you said large."

"If you knew I wanted a large, then why did you ask me again?" I asked him and laughed. He looked at me, couldn't decide if I was giving him serious shit or just goofing. There was something about him I liked, even if it was three in the morning and he was white.

"Hey," I said. "Forget the Slushie. What I want to know is if you know all the words to the theme from 'The Brady Bunch'?"

He looked at me, confused at first, then laughed.

"Shit," he said. "I was hoping you weren't crazy. You were scaring me."

"Well, I'm going to get crazy if you don't know the words."

He laughed loudly then, told me to take the Creamsicle for free. He was the graveyard-shift manager and those little demonstrations of power tickled him. All seventy-five cents of it. I knew how much everything cost.

"Thanks," I said to him and walked out the door. I took my time walking home, let the heat of the night melt the Creamsicle all over my hand. At three in the morning I could act just as young as I wanted to act. There was no one around to ask me to grow up.

In Seattle, I broke lamps. She and I would argue and I'd break a lamp, just pick it up and throw it down. At first she'd buy replacement lamps, expensive and beautiful. But after a while she'd buy lamps from Goodwill or garage sales. Then she just gave up the idea entirely and we'd argue in the dark.

"You're just like your brother," she'd yell. "Drunk all the time and stupid."

"My brother don't drink that much."

She and I never tried to hurt each other physically. I did love her, after all, and she loved me. But those arguments were just as damaging as a fist. Words can be like that, you know? Whenever I get into arguments now, I remember her and I also remember Muhammad Ali. He knew the power of his fists but, more importantly, he knew the power of his words, too. Even though he only had an IQ of 80 or so, Ali was a genius. And she was a genius, too. She knew exactly what to say to cause me the most pain.

But don't get me wrong. I walked through that relationship with an executioner's hood. Or more appropriately, with war paint and sharp arrows. She was a kindergarten teacher and I continually insulted her for that.

"Hey, schoolmarm," I asked. "Did your kids teach you anything new today?"

And I always had crazy dreams. I always have had them, but it seemed they became nightmares more often in Seattle.

In one dream, she was a missionary's wife and I was a minor war chief. We fell in love and tried to keep it secret. But the missionary caught us fucking in the barn and shot me. As I lay dying, my tribe learned of the shooting and attacked the whites all across the reservation. I died and my soul drifted above the reservation.

Disembodied, I could see everything that was happening. Whites killing Indians and Indians killing whites. At first it was small, just my tribe and the few whites who lived there. But my dream grew, intensified. Other tribes arrived on horseback to continue the slaughter of whites, and the United States Cavalry rode into battle.

The most vivid image of that dream stays with me. Three mounted soldiers played polo with a dead Indian woman's head. When I first dreamed it, I thought it was just a product of my anger and imagination. But since then, I've read similar accounts of that kind of evil in the old West. Even more terrifying, though, is the fact that those kinds of brutal things are happening today in places like El Salvador.

All I know for sure, though, is that I woke from that dream in terror, packed up all my possessions, and left Seattle in the middle of the night.

"I love you," she said as I left her. "And don't ever come back."

I drove through the night, over the Cascades, down into the plains of central Washington, and back home to the Spokane Indian Reservation.

When I finished the Creamsicle that the 7-11 clerk gave me, I held the wooden stick up into the air and shouted out very loudly. A couple lights flashed on in windows and a police car cruised by me a few minutes later. I waved to the men in blue and they waved back accidentally. When I got home it was still too hot to sleep so I picked up a week-old newspaper from the floor and read.

There was another civil war, another terrorist bomb exploded, and one more plane crashed and all aboard were presumed dead. The crime rate was rising in every city with populations larger than 100,000, and a farmer in Iowa shot his banker after foreclosure on his 1,000 acres.

A kid from Spokane won the local spelling bee by spelling the word *rhinoceros.*

When I got back to the reservation, my family wasn't surprised to see me. They'd been expecting me back since the day I left for Seattle. There's an old Indian poet who said that Indians can reside in the city, but they can never live there. That's as close to truth as any of us can get.

Mostly I watched television. For weeks I flipped through channels, searched for answers in the game shows and soap operas. My mother would circle the want ads in red and hand the paper to me.

"What are you going to do with the rest of your life?" she asked.

"Don't know," I said, and normally, for almost any other Indian in the country, that would have been a perfectly fine answer. But I was special, a former college student, a smart kid. I was one of those Indians who was supposed to make it, to rise above the rest of the reservation like a fucking eagle or something. I was the new kind of warrior.

For a few months I didn't even look at the want ads my mother circled, just left the newspaper where she had set it down. After a while, though, I got tired of television and started to play basketball again. I'd been a good player in high school, nearly great, and almost played at the college I attended for a couple years. But I'd been too out of shape from drinking and sadness to ever be good again. Still, I liked the way the ball felt in my hands and the way my feet felt inside my shoes.

At first I just shot baskets by myself. It was selfish, and I also wanted to learn the game again before I played against anybody else. Since I had been good before and embarrassed fellow tribal members, I knew they would want to take revenge on me. Forget about the cowboys versus Indians business. The most intense competition on any reservation is Indians versus Indians.

But on the night I was ready to play for real, there was this white guy at the gym, playing with all the Indians.

"Who is that?" I asked Jimmy Seyler.

"He's the new BIA chief's kid."

"Can he play?"

"Oh, yeah."

And he could play. He played Indian ball, fast and loose, better than all the Indians there.

"How long's he been playing here?" I asked.

"Long enough."

I stretched my muscles, and everybody watched me. All these Indians watched one of their old and dusty heroes. Even though I had played most of my ball at the white high school I went to, I was still all Indian, you know? I was Indian when it counted, and this BIA kid needed to be beaten by an Indian, any Indian.

I jumped into the game and played well for a little while. It felt good. I hit a few shots, grabbed a rebound or two, played enough defense to keep the other team honest. Then that white kid took over the game. He was too good. Later, he'd play college ball back East and would nearly make the Knicks team a couple years on. But we didn't know any of that would happen. We just knew he was better that day and every other day.

The next morning I woke up tired and hungry, so I grabbed the want ads, found a job I wanted, and drove to Spokane to get it. I've been working at the high school exchange program ever since, typing and answering phones. Sometimes I wonder if the people on the other end of the line know that I'm Indian and if their voices would change if they did know.

One day I picked up the phone and it was her, calling from Seattle.

"I got your number from your mom," she said. "I'm glad you're working."

"Yeah, nothing like a regular paycheck."

"Are you drinking?"

"No, I've been on the wagon for almost a year."

"Good."

The connection was good. I could hear her breathing in the spaces between our words. How do you talk to the real person whose ghost has haunted you? How do you tell the difference between the two?

"Listen," I said. "I'm sorry for everything."

"Me, too."

"What's going to happen to us?" I asked her and wished I had the answer for myself.

"I don't know," she said. "I want to change the world."

These days, living alone in Spokane, I wish I lived closer to the river, to the falls where ghosts of salmon jump. I wish I could sleep. I put down my paper or book and turn off all the lights, lie quietly in the dark. It may take hours, even years, for me to sleep again. There's nothing surprising or disappointing in that.

I know how all my dreams end anyway.

SHERMAN ALEXIE

This Is What It Means to Say Phoenix, Arizona

Just after Victor lost his job at the Bureau of Indian Affairs, he also found out that his father had died of a heart attack in Phoenix, Arizona. Victor hadn't seen his father in a few years, had only talked to him on the telephone once or twice, but there still was a genetic pain, which was as real and immediate as a broken bone. Victor didn't have any money. Who does have money on a reservation, except the cigarette and fireworks salespeople? His father had a savings account waiting to be claimed, but Victor needed to find a way to get from Spokane to Phoenix. Victor's mother was just as poor as he was, and the rest of his family didn't have any use at all for him. So Victor called the tribal council.

"Listen," Victor said. "My father just died. I need some money to get to Phoenix to make arrangements."

"Now, Victor," the council said, "you know we're having a difficult time financially."

"But I thought the council had special funds set aside for stuff like this."

"Now, Victor, we do have some money available for the proper return of tribal members' bodies. But I don't think we have enough to bring your father all the way back from Phoenix."

"Well," Victor said. "It ain't going to cost all that much. He had to be cremated. Things were kind of ugly. He died of a heart attack in his trailer and nobody found him for a week. It was really hot, too. You get the picture."

"Now, Victor, we're sorry for your loss and the circumstances. But we can really only afford to give you one hundred dollars."

"That's not even enough for a plane ticket."

"Well, you might consider driving down to Phoenix."

"I don't have a car. Besides, I was going to drive my father's pickup back up here."

"Now, Victor," the council said, "we're sure there is somebody who could drive you to Phoenix. Or could anybody lend you the rest of the money?"

"You know there ain't nobody around with that kind of money."

"Well, we're sorry, Victor, but that's the best we can do."

Victor accepted the tribal council's offer. What else could he do? So he signed the proper papers, picked up his check, and walked over to the Trading Post to cash it.

While Victor stood in line, he watched Thomas Builds-the-Fire standing near the magazine rack talking to himself. Like he always did. Thomas was a storyteller whom nobody wanted to listen to. That's like being a dentist in a town where everybody has false teeth.

Victor and Thomas Builds-the-Fire were the same age, had grown up and played in the dirt together. Ever since Victor could remember, it was Thomas who had always had something to say.

Once, when they were seven years old, when Victor's father still lived with the family, Thomas closed his eyes and told Victor this story: "Your father's heart is weak. He is afraid of his own family. He is afraid of you. Late at night, he sits in the dark. Watches the television until there's nothing but that white noise. Sometimes he feels like he wants to buy a motorcycle and ride away. He wants to run and hide. He doesn't want to be found."

Thomas Builds-the-Fire had known that Victor's father was going to leave, known it before anyone. Now Victor stood in the Trading Post with a one-hundred-dollar check in his hand, wondering if Thomas knew that Victor's father was dead, if he knew what was going to happen next.

Just then, Thomas looked at Victor, smiled, and walked over to him.

"Victor, I'm sorry about your father," Thomas said.

"How did you know about it?" Victor asked.

"I heard it on the wind. I heard it from the birds. I felt it in the sunlight. Also, your mother was just in here crying."

"Oh," Victor said and looked around the Trading Post. All the other Indians stared, surprised that Victor was even talking to Thomas. Nobody talked to Thomas anymore because he told the same damn stories over and over again. Victor was embarrassed, but he thought that Thomas might be able to help him. Victor felt a sudden need for tradition.

"I can lend you the money you need," Thomas said suddenly. "But you have to take me with you."

"I can't take your money," Victor said. "I mean, I haven't hardly talked to you in years. We're not really friends anymore."

"I didn't say we were friends. I said you had to take me with you."

"Let me think about it."

Victor went home with his one hundred dollars and sat at the kitchen table. He held his head in his hands and thought about Thomas Builds-the-Fire, remembered little details, tears and scars, the bicycle they shared for a summer, so many stories.

Thomas Builds-the-Fire sat on the bicycle, waiting in Victor's yard. He was ten years old and skinny. His hair was dirty because it was the Fourth of July.

"Victor," Thomas yelled. "Hurry up. We're going to miss the fireworks."

After a few minutes, Victor ran out of his family's house, vaulted over the porch railing, and landed gracefully on the sidewalk.

Thomas gave him the bike and they headed for the fireworks. It was nearly dark and the fireworks were about to start.

"You know," Thomas said, "It's strange how us Indians celebrate the Fourth of July. It ain't like it was our independence everybody was fighting for."

"You think about things too much," Victor said. "It's just supposed to be fun. Maybe Junior will be there."

"Which Junior? Everybody on this reservation is named Junior."

The fireworks were small, hardly more than a few bottle rockets and a fountain. But it was enough for two Indian boys. Years later, they would need much more.

Afterward, sitting in the dark, fighting off mosquitoes, Victor turned to Thomas Builds-the-Fire.

"Hey," Victor said. "Tell me a story."

Thomas closed his eyes and told this story: "There were these two Indian boys who wanted to be warriors. But it was too late to be warriors in the old way. All the horses were gone. So the two Indian boys stole a car and drove to the city. They parked the stolen car in the front of the police station and then hitchhiked back home to the reservation. When they got back, all their friends cheered and their parents' eyes shone with pride. 'You were very brave,' everybody said to the two Indian boys. 'Very brave.'"

"Ya-hey," Victor said. "That's a good one. I wish I could be a warrior."

"Me too," Thomas said.

Victor sat at his kitchen table. He counted his one hundred dollars again and again. He knew he needed more to make it to Phoenix and back. He knew he needed Thomas Builds-the-Fire. So he put his money in his wallet and opened the front door to find Thomas on the porch.

"Ya-hey, Victor," Thomas said. "I knew you'd call me."

Thomas walked into the living room and sat down in Victor's favorite chair.

"I've got some money saved up," Thomas said. "It's enough to get us down there, but you have to get us back."

"I've got this hundred dollars," Victor said. "And my dad had a savings account I'm going to claim."

"How much in your dad's account?"

"Enough. A few hundred."

"Sounds good. When we leaving?"

When they were fifteen and had long since stopped being friends, Victor and Thomas got into a fistfight. That is, Victor was really drunk and beat Thomas up for no reason at all. All the other Indian boys stood around and watched it happen. Junior was there and so were Lester, Seymour, and a lot of others.

The beating might have gone on until Thomas was dead if Norma Many Horses hadn't come along and stopped it.

"Hey, you boys," Norma yelled and jumped out of her car. "Leave him alone."

If it had been someone else, even another man, the Indian boys would've just ignored the warnings. But Norma was a warrior. She was powerful. She could have picked up any two of the boys and smashed their skulls together. But worse than that, she would have dragged them all over to some tepee and made them listen to some elder tell a dusty old story.

The Indian boys scattered, and Norma walked over to Thomas and picked him up.

"Hey, little man, are you O.K.?" she asked.

Thomas gave her a thumbs-up.

"Why they always picking on you?"

Thomas shook his head, closed his eyes, but no stories came to him, no words or music. He just wanted to go home, to lie in his bed and let his dreams tell the stories for him.

Thomas Builds-the-Fire and Victor sat next to each other in the airplane, coach section. A tiny white woman had the window seat. She was busy twisting her body into pretzels. She was flexible.

"I have to ask," Thomas said, and Victor closed his eyes in embarrassment.

"Don't," Victor said.

"Excuse me, miss," Thomas asked. "Are you a gymnast or something?"

"There's no something about it," she said. "I was first alternate on the 1980 Olympic team."

"Really?" Thomas asked.

"Really."

"I mean, you used to be a world-class athlete?" Thomas asked.

"My husband thinks I still am."

Thomas Builds-the-Fire smiled. She was a mental gymnast too. She pulled her leg straight up against her body so that she could've kissed her kneecap.

"I wish I could do that," Thomas said.

Victor was ready to jump out of the plane. Thomas, that crazy Indian storyteller with ratty old braids and broken teeth, was flirting with a beautiful Olympic gymnast. Nobody back home on the reservation would ever believe it.

"Well," the gymnast said. "It's easy. Try it."

Thomas grabbed at his leg and tried to pull it up into the same position as the gymnast's. He couldn't even come close, which made Victor and the gymnast laugh.

"Hey," she asked. "You two are Indian, right?"

"Full-blood," Victor said.

"Not me," Thomas said. "I'm half magician on my mother's side and half clown on my father's."

They all laughed.

"What are your names?" she asked.

"Victor and Thomas."

"Mine is Cathy. Pleased to meet you all."

The three of them talked for the duration of the flight. Cathy the gymnast complained about the government, how they screwed the 1980 Olympic team by boycotting the games.

"Sounds like you all got a lot in common with Indians," Thomas said.

Nobody laughed.

After the plane landed in Phoenix and they had all found their way to the terminal, Cathy the gymnast smiled and waved goodbye.

"She was really nice," Thomas said.

"Yeah, but everybody talks to everybody on airplanes," Victor said.

"You always used to tell me I think too much," Thomas said. "Now it sounds like you do."

"Maybe I caught it from you."

"Yeah."

Thomas and Victor rode in a taxi to the trailer where Victor's father had died.

"Listen," Victor said as they stopped in front of the trailer. "I never told you I was sorry for beating you up that time."

"Oh, it was nothing. We were just kids and you were drunk."

"Yeah, but I'm still sorry."

"That's all right."

Victor paid for the taxi, and the two of them stood in the hot Phoenix summer. They could smell the trailer.

"This ain't going to be nice," Victor said. "You don't have to go in."

"You're going to need help."

Victor walked to the front door and opened it. The stink rolled out and made them both gag. Victor's father had lain in that trailer for a week in hundred-degree temperatures before anyone had found him. And the only reason anyone found him was the smell. They needed dental records to identify him. That's exactly what the coroner said. They needed dental records.

"Oh, man," Victor said. "I don't know if I can do this."

"Well, then don't."

"But there might be something valuable in there."

"I thought his money was in the bank."

"It is. I was talking about pictures and letters and stuff like that."

"Oh," Thomas said as he held his breath and followed Victor into the trailer.

When Victor was twelve, he stepped into an underground wasps' nest. His foot was caught in the hole and no matter how hard he struggled, Victor couldn't pull free. He might have died there, stung a thousand times, if Thomas Builds-the-Fire had not come by.

"Run," Thomas yelled and pulled Victor's foot from the hole. They ran then, hard as they ever had, faster than Billy Mills, faster than Jim Thorpe, faster than the wasps could fly.

Victor and Thomas ran until they couldn't breathe, ran until it was cold and dark outside, ran until they were lost and it took hours to find their way home. All the way back, Victor counted his stings.

"Seven," Victor said. "My lucky number."

Victor didn't find much to keep in the trailer. Only a photo album and a stereo. Everything else had that smell stuck in it or was useless anyway. "I guess this is all," Victor said. "It ain't much."

"Better than nothing," Thomas said.

"Yeah, and I do have the pickup."

"Yeah," Thomas said. "It's in good shape."

"Dad was good about that stuff."

"Yeah, I remember your dad."

"Really?" Victor asked. "What do you remember?"

Thomas Builds-the-Fire closed his eyes and told this story: "I remember when I had this dream that told me to go to Spokane, to stand by the falls in the middle of the city and wait for a sign. I knew I had to go there but I didn't have a car. Didn't have a license. I was only thirteen. So I walked all the way, took me all day, and I finally made it to the falls. I stood there for an hour waiting. Then your dad came walking up. 'What the hell are you doing here?' he asked me. I said, 'Waiting for a vision.' Then your father said, 'All you're going to get here is mugged.' So he drove me over to Denny's, bought me dinner, and then drove me home to the reservation. For a long time, I was mad because I thought my dreams had lied to me. But they hadn't. Your dad was my vision. *Take care of each other* is what my dreams were saying. *Take care of each other.*"

Victor was quiet for a long time. He searched his mind for memories of his father, found the good ones, found a few bad ones, added it all up, and smiled.

"My father never told me about finding you in Spokane," Victor said.

"He said he wouldn't tell anybody. Didn't want me to get in trouble. But he said I had to watch out for you as part of the deal."

"Really?"

"Really. Your father said you would need the help. He was right."

"That's why you came down here with me, isn't it?" Victor asked.

"I came because of your father."

Victor and Thomas climbed into the pickup, drove over to the bank, and claimed the three hundred dollars in the savings account.

Thomas Builds-the-Fire could fly.

Once, he jumped off the roof of the tribal school and flapped his arms like a crazy eagle. And he flew. For a second he hovered, suspended above all the other Indian boys, who were too smart or too scared to jump too.

"He's flying," Junior yelled, and Seymour was busy looking for the trick wires or mirrors. But it was real. As real as the dirt when Thomas lost altitude and crashed to the ground.

He broke his arm in two places.

"He broke his wing, he broke his wing, he broke his wing," all the Indian boys chanted as they ran off, flapping their wings, wishing they could fly too. They hated Thomas for his courage, his brief moment as a bird. Everybody has dreams about flying. Thomas flew.

One of his dreams came true for just a second, just enough to make it real.

Victor's father, his ashes, fit in one wooden box with enough left over to fill a cardboard box.

"He always was a big man," Thomas said.

Victor carried part of his father out to the pickup, and Thomas carried the rest. They set him down carefully behind the seats, put a cowboy hat on the wooden box and a Dodgers cap on the cardboard box. That was the way it was supposed to be.

"Ready to head back home?" Victor asked.

"It's going to be a long drive."

"Yeah, take a couple days, maybe."

"We can take turns," Thomas said.

"O.K.," Victor said, but they didn't take turns. Victor drove for sixteen hours straight north, made it halfway up Nevada toward home before he finally pulled over.

"Hey, Thomas," Victor said. "You got to drive for a while."

"O.K."

Thomas Builds-the-Fire slid behind the wheel and started off down the road. All through Nevada, Thomas and Victor had been amazed at the lack of animal life, at the absence of water, of movement.

"Where is everything?" Victor had asked more than once.

Now, when Thomas was finally driving, they saw the first animal, maybe the only animal in Nevada. It was a long-eared jackrabbit.

"Look," Victor yelled. "It's alive."

Thomas and Victor were busy congratulating themselves on their discovery when the jackrabbit darted out into the road and under the wheels of the pickup.

"Stop the goddamn car," Victor yelled, and Thomas did stop and backed the pickup to the dead jackrabbit.

"Oh, man, he's dead," Victor said as he looked at the squashed animal.

"Really dead."

"The only thing alive in this whole state and we just killed it."

"I don't know," Thomas said. "I think it was suicide."

Victor looked around the desert, sniffed the air, felt the emptiness and loneliness, and nodded his head.

"Yeah," Victor said. "It had to be suicide."

"I can't believe this," Thomas said. "You drive for a thousand miles and there ain't even any bugs smashed on the windshield. I drive for ten seconds and kill the only living thing in Nevada."

"Yeah," Victor said. "Maybe I should drive."

"Maybe you should."

Thomas Builds-the-Fire walked through the corridors of the tribal school by himself. Nobody wanted to be anywhere near him because of all those stories. Story after story.

Thomas closed his eyes and this story came to him: "We are all given one thing by which our lives are measured, one determination. Mine are the stories that can change or not change the world. It doesn't matter which, as long as I continue to tell the stories. My father, he died on Okinawa in World War II, died fighting for this country, which had tried to kill him for years. My mother, she died giving birth to me, died while I was still inside her. She pushed me out into the world with her last breath. I have no brothers or sisters. I have only my stories, which came to me before I even had the words to speak. I learned a thousand stories before I took my first thousand steps. They are all I have. It's all I can do."

Thomas Builds-the-Fire told his stories to all those who would stop and listen. He kept telling them long after people had stopped listening.

Victor and Thomas made it back to the reservation just as the sun was rising. It was the beginning of a new day on earth, but the same old shit on the reservation.

"Good morning," Thomas said.

"Good morning."

The tribe was waking up, ready for work, eating breakfast, reading the newspaper, just like everybody else does. Willene LeBret was out in her garden, wearing a bathrobe. She waved when Thomas and Victor drove by.

"Crazy Indians made it," she said to herself and went back to her roses.

Victor stopped the pickup in front of Thomas Builds-the-Fire's HUD house. They both yawned, stretched a little, shook dust from their bodies.

"I'm tired," Victor said.

"Of everything," Thomas added.

They both searched for words to end the journey. Victor needed to thank Thomas for his help and for the money, and to make the promise to pay it all back.

"Don't worry about the money," Thomas said. "It don't make any difference anyhow."

"Probably not, enit?"

"Nope."

Victor knew that Thomas would remain the crazy storyteller who talked to dogs and cars, who listened to the wind and pine trees. Victor knew that he couldn't really be friends with Thomas, even after all that had happened. It was cruel but it was real. As real as the ash, as Victor's father, sitting behind the seats.

"I know how it is," Thomas said. "I know you ain't going to treat me any better than you did before. I know your friends would give you too much shit about it."

Victor was ashamed of himself. Whatever happened to the tribal ties, the sense of community? The only real thing he shared with anybody was a bottle and broken dreams. He owed Thomas something, anything.

"Listen," Victor said and handed Thomas the cardboard box that contained half of his father. "I want you to have this."

Thomas took the ashes and smiled, closed his eyes, and told this story: "I'm going to travel to Spokane Falls one last time and toss these ashes into the water. And your father will rise like a salmon, leap over the bridge, over me, and find his way home. It will be beautiful. His teeth will shine like silver, like a rainbow. He will rise, Victor, he will rise."

Victor smiled.

"I was planning on doing the same thing with my half," Victor said. "But I didn't imagine my father looking anything like a salmon. I thought it'd be like cleaning the attic or something. Like letting things go after they've stopped having any use."

"Nothing stops, cousin," Thomas said. "Nothing stops."

Thomas Builds-the-Fire got out of the pickup and walked up his driveway. Victor started the pickup and began the drive home.

"Wait," Thomas yelled suddenly from his porch. "I just got to ask one favor."

Victor stopped the pickup, leaned out the window, and shouted back.

"What do you want?" he asked.

"Just one time when I'm telling a story somewhere, why don't you stop and listen?" Thomas asked.

"Just once?"

"Just once."

Victor waved his arms to let Thomas know that the deal was good. It was a fair trade. That's all Thomas had ever wanted from his whole life. So Victor drove his father's pickup toward home while Thomas went into his house, closed the door behind him, and heard a new story come to him in the silence afterward.

SHERMAN ALEXIE

The Toughest Indian in the World

Being a Spokane Indian, I only pick up Indian hitchhikers. I learned this particular ceremony from my father, a Coeur d'Alene, who always stopped for those twentieth-century aboriginal nomads who refused to believe the salmon were gone. I don't know what they believed in exactly, but they wore hope like a bright shirt.

My father never taught me about hope. Instead, he continually told me that our salmon—our hope—would never come back, and though such lessons may seem cruel, I know enough to cover my heart in any crowd of white people.

"They'll kill you if they get the chance," my father said. "Love you or hate you, white people will shoot you in the heart. Even after all these years, they'll still smell the salmon on you, the dead salmon, and that will make white people dangerous."

All of us, Indian and white, are haunted by salmon.

When I was a boy, I leaned over the edge of one dam or another—perhaps Long Lake or Little Falls or the great gray dragon known as the Grand Coulee—and watched the ghosts of the salmon rise from the water to the sky and become constellations.

For most Indians, stars are nothing more than white tombstones scattered across a dark graveyard.

But the Indian hitchhikers my father picked up refused to admit the existence of sky, let alone the possibility that salmon might be stars. They were common people who believed only in the thumb and the foot. My father envied those simple Indian hitchhikers. He wanted to change their minds about salmon; he wanted to break open their hearts and see the future in their blood. He loved them.

In 1975 or '76 or '77, driving along one highway or another, my father would point out a hitchhiker standing beside the road a mile or two in the distance.

"Indian," he said if it was an Indian, and he was never wrong, though I could never tell if the distant figure was male or female, let alone Indian or not.

If a distant figure happened to be white, my father would drive by without comment.

That was how I learned to be silent in the presence of white people.

The silence is not about hate or pain or fear. Indians just like to believe that white people will vanish, perhaps explode into smoke, if they are ignored enough times. Perhaps a thousand white families are still waiting for their sons and daughters to return home, and can't recognize them when they float back as morning fog.

"We better stop," my mother said from the passenger seat. She was one of those Spokane women who always wore a purple bandanna tied tightly around her head.

These days, her bandanna is usually red. There are reasons, motives, traditions behind the choice of color, but my mother keeps them secret.

"Make room," my father said to my siblings and me as we sat on the floor in the cavernous passenger area of our blue van. We sat on carpet samples because my father had torn out the seats in a sober rage not long after he bought the van from a crazy white man.

I have three brothers and three sisters now. Back then, I had four of each. I missed one of the funerals and cried myself sick during the other one.

"Make room," my father said again—he said everything twice—and only then did we scramble to make space for the Indian hitchhiker.

Of course, it was easy enough to make room for one hitchhiker, but Indians usually travel in packs. Once or twice, we picked up entire all-Indian basketball teams, along with their coaches, girlfriends, and cousins. Fifteen, twenty Indian strangers squeezed into the back of a blue van with nine wide-eyed Indian kids.

Back in those days, I loved the smell of Indians, and of Indian hitchhikers in particular. They were usually in some stage of drunkenness, often in need of soap and a towel, and always ready to sing.

Oh, the songs! Indian blues bellowed at the highest volumes. We called them "49s," those cross-cultural songs that combined Indian lyrics and rhythms with country-and-western and blues melodies. It seemed that every Indian knew all the lyrics to every Hank Williams song ever recorded. Hank was our Jesus, Patsy Cline was our Virgin Mary, and Freddy Fender, George Jones, Conway Twitty, Loretta Lynn, Tammy Wynette, Charley Pride, Ronnie Milsap, Tanya Tucker, Marty Robbins, Johnny Horton, Donna Fargo, and Charlie Rich were our disciples.

We all know that nostalgia is dangerous, but I remember those days with a clear conscience. Of course, we live in different days now, and there aren't as many Indian hitchhikers as there used to be.

Now, I drive my own car, a 1998 Toyota Camry, the best-selling automobile in the United States, and therefore the one most often stolen. *Consumer Reports* has named it the most reliable family sedan for sixteen years running, and I believe it.

In my Camry, I pick up three or four Indian hitchhikers a week. Mostly men. They're usually headed home, back to their reservations or somewhere close to their reservations. Indians hardly ever travel in a straight line, so a Crow Indian might hitchhike west when his reservation is back east in Montana. He has some people to see in Seattle, he might explain if I ever asked him. But I never ask Indians their reasons for hitchhiking. All that matters is this: They are Indians walking, raising their thumbs, and I am there to pick them up.

At the newspaper where I work, my fellow reporters think I'm crazy to pick up hitchhikers. They're all white and never stop to pick up anybody, let alone an Indian. After all, we're the ones who write the stories and headlines: HITCHHIKER KILLS HUSBAND AND WIFE, MISSING GIRL'S BODY FOUND, RAPIST STRIKES AGAIN. If I really tried, maybe I could explain to them why I pick up any Indian, but who wants to try? Instead, if they ask I just give them a smile and turn back to my computer. My coworkers smile back and laugh loudly. They're always laughing loudly at me, at one another, at themselves, at goofy typos in the newspapers, at the idea of hitchhikers.

I dated one of them for a few months. Cindy. She covered the local courts: speeding tickets and divorces, drunk driving and embezzlement. Cindy firmly believed in the who-what-where-when-why-and-how of journalism. In daily conversation, she talked like she was writing the lead of her latest story. Hell, she talked like that in bed.

"How does that feel?" I asked, quite possibly the only Indian man who has ever asked that question.

"I love it when you touch me there," she answered. "But it would help if you rubbed it about thirty percent lighter and with your thumb instead of your middle finger. And could you maybe turn the radio to a different station? KYZY would be good. I feel like soft jazz will work better for me right now. A minor chord, a C or G-flat, or something like that. Okay, honey?"

During lovemaking, I would get so exhausted by the size of her erotic vocabulary that I would fall asleep before my orgasm, continue pumping away as if I were awake, and then regain consciousness with a sudden start when I finally did come, more out of reflex than passion.

Don't get me wrong. Cindy is a good one, cute and smart, funny as hell, a good catch no matter how you define it, but she was also one of those white women who date only brown-skinned guys. Indians like me, black dudes, Mexicans, even a few Iranians. I started to feel like a trophy, or like one of those entries in a personal ad. I asked Cindy why she never dated pale boys.

"White guys bore me," she said. "All they want to talk about is their fathers."

"What do brown guys talk about?" I asked her.

"Their mothers," she said and laughed, then promptly left me for a public defender who was half Japanese and half African, a combination that left Cindy dizzy with the interracial possibilities.

Since Cindy, I haven't dated anyone. I live in my studio apartment with the ghosts of two dogs, Felix and Oscar, and a laptop computer stuffed with bad poems, the aborted halves of three novels, and some three-paragraph personality pieces I wrote for the newspaper.

I'm a features writer, and an Indian at that, so I get all the shit jobs. Not the dangerous shit jobs or the monotonous shit jobs. No. I get to write the articles designed to please the eye, ear, and heart. And there is no journalism more soul-endangering to write than journalism that aims to please.

So it was with reluctance that I climbed into my car last week and headed down Highway 2 to write some damn pleasant story about some damn pleasant people. Then I saw the Indian hitchhiker standing beside the road. He looked the way Indian hitchhikers usually look. Long, straggly black hair. Brown eyes and skin. Missing a couple of teeth. A bad complexion that used to be much worse. Crooked nose that had been broken more than once. Big, misshapen ears. A few whiskers masquerading as a mustache. Even before he climbed into my car I could tell he was tough. He had some serious muscles that threatened to rip through his blue jeans and denim jacket. When he was in the car, I could see his hands up close, and they told his whole story. His fingers were twisted into weird, permanent shapes, and his knuckles were covered with layers of scar tissue.

"Jeez," I said. "You're a fighter, enit?"

I threw in the "enit," a reservation colloquialism, because I wanted the fighter to know that I had grown up on the rez, in the woods, with every Indian in the world.

The hitchhiker looked down at his hands, flexed them into fists. I could tell it hurt him to do that.

"Yeah," he said. "I'm a fighter."

I pulled back onto the highway, looking over my shoulder to check my blind spot.

"What tribe are you?" I asked him, inverting the last two words in order to sound as aboriginal as possible.

"Lummi," he said. "What about you?"

"Spokane."

"I know some Spokanes. Haven't seen them in a long time."

He clutched his backpack in his lap like he didn't want to let it go for anything. He reached inside a pocket and pulled out a piece of deer jerky. I recognized it by the smell.

"Want some?" he asked.

"Sure."

It had been a long time since I'd eaten jerky. The salt, the gamy taste. I felt as Indian as Indian gets, driving down the road in a fast car, chewing on jerky, talking to an indigenous fighter.

"Where you headed?" I asked.

"Home. Back to the rez."

I nodded my head as I passed a big truck. The driver gave us a smile as we went by. I tooted the horn.

"Big truck," said the fighter.

I haven't lived on my reservation for twelve years. But I live in Spokane, which is only an hour's drive from the rez. Still, I hardly ever go home. I don't know why not. I don't think about it much, I guess, but my mom and dad still live in the same house where I grew up. My brothers and sisters, too. The ghosts of my two dead siblings share an apartment in the converted high school. It's just a local call from Spokane to the rez, so I talk to all of them once or twice a week. Smoke signals courtesy of U.S. West Communications. Sometimes they call me up to talk about the stories they've seen that I've written for the newspaper. Pet pigs and support groups and science fairs. Once in a while, I used to fill in for the obituaries writer when she was sick. Then she died, and I had to write her obituary.

"How far are you going?" asked the fighter, meaning how much closer was he going to get to his reservation than he was now.

"Up to Wenatchee," I said. "I've got some people to interview there."

"Interview? What for?"

"I'm a reporter. I work for the newspaper."

"No," said the fighter, looking at me like I was stupid for thinking he was stupid. "I mean, what's the story about?"

"Oh, not much. There's two sets of twins who work for the fire department. Human-interest stuff, you know?"

"Two sets of twins, enit? That's weird."

He offered me more deer jerky, but I was too thirsty from the salty meat, so I offered him a Pepsi instead.

"Don't mind if I do," he said.

"They're in a cooler on the backseat," I said. "Grab me one, too."

He maneuvered his backpack carefully and found room enough to reach into the backseat for the soda pop. He opened my can first and handed it to me. A friendly gesture for a stranger. I took a big mouthful and hiccupped loudly.

"That always happens to me when I drink cold things," he said.

We sipped slowly after that. I kept my eyes on the road while he stared out the window into the wheat fields. We were quiet for many miles.

"Who do you fight?" I asked as we passed through another anonymous small town.

"Mostly Indians," he said. "Money fights, you know? I go from rez to rez, fighting the best they have. Winner takes all."

"Jeez, I never heard of that."

"Yeah, I guess it's illegal."

He rubbed his hands together. I could see fresh wounds.

"Man," I said. "Those fights must be rough."

The fighter stared out the window. I watched him for a little too long and almost drove off the road. Car horns sounded all around us.

"Jeez," the fighter said. "Close one, enit?"

"Close enough," I said.

He hugged his backpack more tightly, using it as a barrier between his chest and the dashboard. An Indian hitchhiker's version of a passenger-side air bag.

"Who'd you fight last?" I asked, trying to concentrate on the road.

"Some Flathead," he said. "In Arlee. He was supposed to be the toughest Indian in the world."

"Was he?"

"Nah, no way. Wasn't even close. Wasn't even tougher than me."

He told me how big the Flathead kid was, way over six feet tall and two hundred and some pounds. Big buck Indian. Had hands as big as this and arms as big as that. Had a chin like a damn buffalo. The fighter told me that he hit the Flathead kid harder than he ever hit anybody before.

"I hit him like he was a white man," the fighter said. "I hit him like he was two or three white men rolled into one."

But the Flathead kid would not go down, even though his face swelled up so bad that he looked like the Elephant Man. There were no referees, no judge, no bells to signal the end of the round. The winner was the Indian still standing. Punch after punch, man, and the kid would not go down.

"I was so tired after a while," said the fighter, "that I just took a step back and watched the kid. He stood there with his arms down, swaying from side to side like some toy, you know? Head bobbing on his neck like there was no bone at all. You couldn't even see his eyes no more. He was all messed up."

"What'd you do?" I asked.

"Ah, hell, I couldn't fight him no more. That kid was planning to die before he ever went down. So I just sat on the ground while they counted me out. Dumb Flathead kid didn't even know what was happening. I just sat on the ground while they raised his hand. While all the winners collected their money and all the losers cussed me out. I just sat there, man."

"Jeez," I said. "What happened next?"

"Not much. I sat there until everybody was gone. Then I stood up and decided to head for home. I'm tired of this shit. I just want to go home for a while. I got enough money to last me a long time. I'm a rich Indian, you hear? I'm a rich Indian."

The fighter finished his Pepsi, rolled down his window, and pitched the can out. I almost protested, but decided against it. I kept my empty can wedged between my legs.

"That's a hell of a story," I said.

"Ain't no story," he said. "It's what happened."

"Jeez," I said. "You would've been a warrior in the old days, enit? You would've been a killer. You would have stolen everybody's goddamn horses. That would've been you. You would've been it."

I was excited. I wanted the fighter to know how much I thought of him. He didn't even look at me.

"A killer," he said. "Sure."

We didn't talk much after that. I pulled into Wenatchee just before sundown, and the fighter seemed happy to be leaving me.

"Thanks for the ride, cousin," he said as he climbed out. Indians always call each other cousin, especially if they're strangers.

"Wait," I said.

He looked at me, waiting impatiently.

I wanted to know if he had a place to sleep that night. It was supposed to get cold. There was a mountain range between Wenatchee and his reservation. Big mountains that were dormant volcanoes, but that could all blow up at any time. We wrote about it once in the newspaper. Things can change so quickly. So many emergencies and disasters that we can barely keep track. I wanted to tell him how much I cared about my job, even if I had to write about small-town firemen. I wanted to tell the fighter that I pick up all Indian hitchhikers, young and old, men and women, and get them a little closer to home, even if I can't get them all the way. I wanted to tell him that the night sky was a graveyard. I wanted to know if he was the toughest Indian in the world.

"It's late," I finally said. "You can crash with me, if you want."

He studied my face and then looked down the long road toward his reservation.

"Okay," he said. "That sounds good."

We got a room at the Pony Soldier Motel, and both of us laughed at the irony of it all. Inside the room, in a generic watercolor hanging above the bed, the U.S. Cavalry was kicking the crap out of a band of renegade Indians.

"What tribe you think they are?" I asked the fighter.

"All of them," he said.

The fighter crashed on the floor while I curled up in the uncomfortable bed. I couldn't sleep for the longest time. I listened to the fighter talk in his sleep. I stared up at the water-stained ceiling. I don't know what time it was when I finally drifted off, and I don't know what time it was when the fighter got into bed with me. He was naked and his penis was hard. I felt it press against my back as he snuggled up close to me, reached inside my underwear, and took my penis in his hand. Neither of us said a word. He continued to stroke me as he rubbed himself against my back. That went on for a long time. I had never been that close to another man, but the fighter's callused fingers felt better than I would have imagined if I had ever allowed myself to imagine such things.

"This isn't working," he whispered. "I can't come."

Without thinking, I reached around and took the fighter's penis in my hand. He was surprisingly small.

"No," he said. "I want to be inside you."

"I don't know," I said. "I've never done this before."

"It's okay," he said. "I'll be careful. I have rubbers."

Without waiting for my answer, he released me and got up from the bed. I turned to look at him. He was beautiful and scarred. So much brown skin marked with bruises, badly healed wounds, and tattoos. His long black hair was unbraided and hung down to his thin waist. My slacks and dress shirt were folded and draped over the chair near the window. My shoes were sitting on the table. Blue light filled the room. The fighter bent down to his pack and searched for his condoms. For reasons I could not explain then and cannot explain now, I kicked off my underwear and rolled over on my stomach. I could not see him, but I could hear him breathing heavily as he found the condoms, tore open a package, and rolled one over his penis. He crawled onto the bed, between my legs, and slid a pillow beneath my belly.

"Are you ready?" he asked.

"I'm not gay," I said.

"Sure," he said as he pushed himself into me. He was small but it hurt more than I expected, and I knew that I would be sore for days afterward. But I wanted him to save me. He didn't say anything. He just pumped into me for a few minutes, came with a loud sigh, and then pulled out. I quickly rolled off the bed and went into the bathroom. I locked the door behind me and stood there in the dark. I smelled like salmon.

"Hey," the fighter said through the door. "Are you okay?"

"Yes," I said. "I'm fine."

A long silence.

"Hey," he said. "Would you mind if I slept in the bed with you?"

I had no answer to that.

"Listen," I said. "That Flathead boy you fought? You know, the one you really beat up? The one who wouldn't fall down?"

In my mind, I could see the fighter pummeling that boy. Punch after punch. The boy too beaten to fight back, but too strong to fall down.

"Yeah, what about him?" asked the fighter.

"What was his name?"

"His name?"

"Yeah, his name."

"Elmer something or other."

"Did he have an Indian name?"

"I have no idea. How the hell would I know that?"

I stood there in the dark for a long time. I was chilled. I wanted to get into bed and fall asleep.

"Hey," I said. "I think, I think maybe—well, I think you should leave now."

"Yeah," said the fighter, not surprised. I heard him softly singing as he dressed and stuffed all of his belongings into his pack. I wanted to know what he was singing, so I opened the bathroom door just as he was opening the door to leave. He stopped, looked at me, and smiled.

"Hey, tough guy," he said. "You were good."

The fighter walked out the door, left it open, and walked away. I stood in the doorway and watched him continue his walk down the highway, past the city limits. I watched him rise from earth to sky and become a new constellation. I closed the door and wondered what was going to happen next. Feeling uncomfortable and cold, I went back into the bathroom. I ran the shower with the hottest water possible. I stared at myself in the mirror. Steam quickly filled the room. I threw a few shadow punches. Feeling stronger, I stepped into the shower and searched my body for changes. A middle-aged man needs to look for tumors. I dried myself with a towel too small for the job. Then I crawled naked into bed. I wondered if I was a warrior in this life and if I had been a warrior in a previous life. Lonely and laughing, I fell asleep. I didn't dream at all, not one bit. Or perhaps I dreamed but remembered none of it. Instead, I woke early the next morning, before sunrise, and went out into the world. I walked past my car. I stepped onto the pavement, still warm from the previous day's sun. I started walking. In bare feet, I traveled upriver toward the place where I was born and will someday die. At that moment, if you had broken open my heart you could have looked inside and seen the thin white skeletons of one thousand salmon.

Margaret Atwood (*1939–)*

a true woman of letters, is the author of more than thirty books, including several volumes of poetry and of essays and criticism, four children's books, eleven novels (including the widely read dystopian novels The Handmaid's Tale *and* Oryx and Crake *and the Booker Prize winner* The Blind Assassin*), and five collections of short stories. Born in Ottawa, Ontario, Atwood didn't attend school until eighth grade; before that, she was taught, along with her precocious older brother and younger sister, by her mother, an avid reader, and her father, a naturalist and professor of zoology. She attended the University of Toronto, Radcliffe, and Harvard and studied with the eminent literary critic Northrop Frye. She published her first book of poetry while still in graduate school and her first novel* (The Edible Woman) *two years after she finished. As a short story writer, she has written stories that experimented with structure, point of view, and metafiction and yet are still utterly concerned with telling a good story (of which "Happy Endings" is a good example). She has also written dozens of realistic stories that quietly deploy daring leaps of innovation. She lives in Toronto with writer Graeme Gibson.*

INTRODUCTION BY **Percival Everett**

These three stories of Margaret Atwood's are scary. I don't mean a little scary. They're scary not only because of what they tell us about ourselves, but also because of what they tell us about how we make sense of the world and about how we make and understand fiction. Instead of addressing these stories individually, I will talk about them at once; they fit together surprisingly well.

The first thing one detects at work in these stories is a certainty of hand, an assuredness, a fast control of the medium—that medium being language. There is at work a profound, undeniable intelligence that is expressed by the construction of the story and not by the words chosen to deliver it. In fact, the language is simple, beautifully simple. It is the meaning that is layered, filtered, and reapplied, and so the stories are sneaky—sneaky but not covert; their mission is clear, forthright, driven, and there is nothing we can do about it. But still, they surprise. Not by twists in story, the tail wagging the dog and all that, but by revelations about human experience, relationships, love, and story. And there is more work than this afoot.

"Happy Endings" appears to be a brief fable, but it is the longest of stories. Atwood takes our most basic story, "girl meets boy," and renders it helpless, meaningless, yet stuffed with import. In doing so, she not only challenges the story we all know but also explores the nature of "story" as well and the business of making story. The story wonders just what a story is, and it can mean anything for us. In different ways, each of these stories performs this same work. There is not only a layering of meaning, but also a sequencing of story lines that lead us away from what we might take as the central story, stepwise, until we realize that we have been on one course all along. This is especially true of "True Trash." The title is a busy one. The story shifts point of view, the way we are always told doesn't work, and it does so with abandon. But the hand at work is so sure that we follow, from the boys watching the waitresses to the waitresses reading the romance stories to Miss Fisk to Donny and Monty to Joanne. We trust the story, and the story turned out to be true.

"Wilderness Tips" is an unsettling and subtle study of the nature of relationships and just nature itself. The story itself comments on the meaning of its title, asking whether "Tips" is a noun or a verb. The vacuity of the lives of the characters is as much the story as the so-called plot. The sisters in this story compete in the wildness of Wacousta Lodge, taking shots at each other, each knowing the other's moves. As in Atwood's other stories, point of view is a shifting and fleeting thing, so we can never know just whose story we're reading, and this too becomes something for which these characters compete. But then it becomes clear again that any story belongs to several characters, never only one, and that we are finally dependent on each other for any meaning that any story of life itself can hold for us. One might view this story as a sort of recasting of a few fairy tales: "The Three Little Pigs," Prue, Pamela, and Portia being playfully monogrammed and George being the wolf; "The Three Bears," George being our Goldilocks, finding one bed too hard, another too soft, and the third just right; and finally "Little Red Riding Hood," Roland being the frustrated woodchopper, unable to save anyone, even if he knew who needed saving. The story spans fifty years with broad strokes, dipping into the past on occasion, but only to establish the depth and shallowness of these relationships.

These stories are bigger than the spaces they occupy. This is partly because they are as much about the form of the short story and the art of fiction as they are about the people that populate them. And also because they are novelistic in sensibility. From the stilted presentation of "Wilderness Tips," its halting present tense, a reflection of the actors, to the rapid-fire, loose "Happy Endings," whose people are ostensibly pieces, types, the stories expand with every sentence. The stories continue to expand long after the last sentence has been read. It is not the story that is an experiment for Atwood, but rather how we understand story and how we receive and process story. This is her experiment. The twist is never in the story but always in the conception of the story and in our own expectations of stories that Atwood has chosen to exploit.

Percival Everett is the author of fifteen books, among them Erasure, Glyph, God's Country, *and* Watershed. *He is Professor of English at the University of Southern California. He lives on a ranch outside Los Angeles and on Vancouver Island, British Columbia.*

MARGARET ATWOOD

Happy Endings

John and Mary meet.
What happens next?
If you want a happy ending, try A.

A.

John and Mary fall in love and get married. They both have worthwhile and remunerative jobs which they find stimulating and challenging. They buy a charming house. Real estate values go up. Eventually, when they can afford live-in help, they have two children, to whom they are devoted. The children turn out well. John and Mary have a stimulating and challenging sex life and worthwhile friends. They go on fun vacations together. They retire. They both have hobbies which they find stimulating and challenging. Eventually they die. This is the end of the story.

B.

Mary falls in love with John but John doesn't fall in love with Mary. He merely uses her body for selfish pleasure and ego gratification of a tepid kind. He comes to her apartment twice a week and she cooks him dinner, you'll notice that he doesn't even consider her worth the price of a dinner out, and after he's eaten the dinner he fucks her and after that he falls asleep, while she does the dishes so he won't think she's untidy, having all those dirty dishes lying around, and puts on fresh lipstick so she'll look good when he wakes up, but when he wakes up he doesn't even notice, he puts on his socks and his shorts and his pants and his shirt and his tie and his shoes, the reverse order from the one in which he took them off. He doesn't take off Mary's clothes, she takes them off herself, she acts as if she's dying for it every time, not because she likes sex exactly, she doesn't, but she wants John to think she does because if they do it often enough surely he'll get used to her, he'll come to depend on her and they will get married, but John goes out the door with hardly so much as a goodnight and three days later he turns up at six o'clock and they do the whole thing over again.

Mary gets run-down. Crying is bad for your face, everyone knows that and so does Mary but she can't stop. People at work notice. Her friends tell her John is a rat, a pig, a dog, he isn't good enough for her, but she can't believe it. Inside John, she thinks, is another John, who is much nicer. This other John will emerge like a butterfly from a cocoon, a Jack from a box, a pit from a prune, if the first John is only squeezed enough.

One evening John complains about the food. He has never complained about the food before. Mary is hurt.

Her friends tell her they've seen him in a restaurant with another woman, whose name is Madge. It's not even Madge that finally gets to Mary; it's the restaurant. John has never taken Mary to a restaurant. Mary collects all the sleeping pills and aspirins she can find, and takes them and half a bottle of sherry. You can see what kind of a woman she is by the fact that it's not even whiskey. She leaves a note for John. She hopes he'll discover her and get her to the hospital in time and repent and then they can get married, but this fails to happen and she dies.

John marries Madge and everything continues as in A.

C.

John, who is an older man, falls in love with Mary, and Mary, who is only twenty-two, feels sorry for him because he's worried about his hair falling out. She sleeps with him even though she's not in love with him. She met him at work. She's in love with someone called James, who is twenty-two also and not yet ready to settle down.

John on the contrary settled down long ago: this is what is bothering him. John has a steady respectable job and is getting ahead in his field, but Mary isn't impressed by him, she's impressed by James, who has a motorcycle and a fabulous record collection. But James is often away on his motorcycle, being free. Freedom isn't the same for girls, so in the meantime Mary spends Thursday evenings with John. Thursdays are the only days John can get away.

John is married to a woman called Madge and they have two children, a charming house which they bought just before the real estate values went up, and hobbies which they find stimulating and challenging, when they have the time. John tells Mary how important she is to him, but of course he can't leave his wife because a commitment is a commitment. He goes on about this more than is necessary and Mary finds it boring, but older men can keep it up longer so on the whole she has a fairly good time.

One day James breezes in on his motorcycle with some top-grade California hybrid and James and Mary get higher than you'd believe possible and they climb into bed. Everything becomes very underwater, but along comes John, who has a key to Mary's apartment. He finds them stoned and entwined. He's hardly in any position to be jealous, considering Madge, but nevertheless he's overcome with despair. Finally he's middle-aged, in two years he'll be bald as an egg, and he can't stand it. He purchases a handgun, saying he needs it for target practice—this is the thin part of the plot, but it can be dealt with later—and shoots the two of them and himself.

Madge, after a suitable period of mourning, marries an understanding man called Fred and everything continues as in A, but under different names.

D.

Fred and Madge have no problems. They get along exceptionally well and are good at working out any little difficulties that may arise. But their charming house is by the seashore and one day a giant tidal wave approaches. Real estate values go down. The rest of the story is about what caused the tidal wave and how they escape from it. They do, though thousands drown. Some of the story is about how the thousands drown, but Fred and Madge are virtuous and lucky. Finally on high ground they clasp each other, wet and dripping and grateful, and continue as in A.

E.

Yes, but Fred has a bad heart. The rest of the story is about how kind and understanding they both are until Fred dies. Then Madge devotes herself to charity work until the end of A. If you like, it can be "Madge," "cancer," "guilty and confused," and "bird watching."

F.

If you think this is all too bourgeois, make John a revolutionary and Mary a counterespionage agent and see how far that gets you. Remember, this is Canada. You'll still end up with A, though in between you may get a lustful brawling saga of passionate involvement, a chronicle of our times, sort of.

You'll have to face it, the endings are the same however you slice it. Don't be deluded by any other endings, they're all fake, either deliberately fake, with malicious intent to deceive, or just motivated by excessive optimism if not by downright sentimentality.

The only authentic ending is the one provided here:

John and Mary die. John and Mary die. John and Mary die.

So much for endings. Beginnings are always more fun. True connoisseurs, however, are known to favor the stretch in between, since it's the hardest to do anything with.

That's about all that can be said for plots, which anyway are just one thing after another, a what and a what and a what.

Now try How and Why.

Margaret Atwood

Wilderness Tips

Prue has folded two red bandanna handkerchiefs into triangles and tied them together at one set of corners. The second set of corners is tied behind her back, the third around her neck. She's wrapped another bandanna, a blue one, around her head and made a little reef knot at the front. Now she's strutting the length of the dock, in her improvised halter top and her wide-legged white shorts, her sunglasses with the white plastic frames, her platform sandals.

"It's the forties look," she says to George, hand on her hip, doing a pirouette. "Rosie the Riveter. From the war. Remember her?"

George, whose name is not really George, does not remember. He spent the forties rooting through garbage heaps and begging, and doing other things unsuitable for a child. He has a dim memory of some film star posed on a calendar tattering on a latrine wall. Maybe this is the one Prue means. He remembers for an instant his intense resentment of the bright, ignorant smile, the well-fed body. A couple of buddies had helped him take her apart with the rusty blade from a kitchen knife they'd found somewhere in the rubble. He does not consider telling any of this to Prue.

George is sitting in a green-and-white striped canvas deck chair, reading *The Financial Post* and drinking Scotch. The ashtray beside him overflows with butts: many women have tried to cure him of smoking; many have failed. He looks up at Prue from behind his paper and smiles his foxy smile. This is a smile he does with the cigarette held right in the center of his mouth: on either side of it his lips curl back, revealing teeth. He has long canines, miraculously still his.

"You weren't born then," he says. This isn't true, but he never misses the chance to bestow a compliment when there's one just lying around. What does it cost? Not a cent, which is something the men in this country have never figured out. Prue's tanned midriff is on a level with his face; it's still firm, still flexible and lithe. At that age his mother had gone soft—loose-fleshed and velvety, like an aging plum. These days they eat a lot of vegetables, they work out, they last longer.

Prue lowers the sunglasses to the end of her nose and looks at him over the plastic rims. "George, you are totally shameless," she says. "You always were." She gives him an innocent smile, a mischievous smile, a smile with a twist of real evil in it. It's a smile that wavers like a gasoline slick on water, shining, changing tone.

This smile of Prue's was the first interesting thing George stumbled over when he hit Toronto, back in the late fifties. It was at a party thrown by a real-estate developer with Eastern European connections. He'd been invited because refugees from Hungary were considered noteworthy back then, right after the uprising. At that time he was young, thin as a snake, with a dangerous-looking scar over one eye and a few bizarre stories. A collectible. Prue had been there in an off-the-shoulder black dress. She'd raised her glass to him, looked over the rim, hoisted the smile like a flag.

The smile is still an invitation, but it's not something George will follow up on—not here, not now. Later, in the city, perhaps. But this lake, this peninsula, Wacousta Lodge itself, are his refuge, his monastery, his sacred ground. Here he will perform no violations.

"Why is it you cannot bear to accept a gift?" says George. Smoke blows into his eyes; he squints. "If I were younger, I would kneel. I would kiss both your hands. Believe me."

Prue, who has known him to do these things back in more impetuous times, turns on her heel. "It's lunchtime," she says. "That's what I came to tell you." She has heard refusal.

George watches her white shorts and her still shapely thighs (with, however, their faint stippling of dimpled fat) going wink, wink, wink through the clear sunlight, past the boathouse, along the stone path, up the hill to the house. From up there a bell is ringing: the lunch bell. For once in her life, Prue is telling the truth.

George takes one more look at the paper. Quebec is talking Separatism; there are Mohawks behind the barricades near Montreal, and people are throwing stones at them; word is the country is falling apart. George is not worried: he's been in countries that were falling apart before. There can be opportunities. As for the fuss people here make about language, he doesn't understand it. What's a second language, or a third, or a fourth? George himself speaks five, if you count Russian, which he would prefer not to. As for the stone-throwing, it's typical. Not bombs, not bullets: just stones. Even the uproar here is muted.

He scratches his belly under the loose shirt he wears; he's been gaining a little too much around the middle. Then he stubs out his cigarette, downs the heel of his Scotch, and hauls himself out of his deck chair. Carefully, he folds the chair and places it inside the boathouse: a wind could come up, the chair could be sent sailing into the lake. He treats the possessions and rituals of Wacousta Lodge with a tenderness, a reverence, that would baffle those who know him only in the city. Despite what some would call his unorthodox business practices, he is in some ways a conservative man; he loves traditions. They are thin on the ground in this country, but he knows one when he sees one, and does it homage. The deck chairs here are like the escutcheons elsewhere.

As he walks up the hill, more slowly than he used to, he hears the sound of wood being split behind the kitchen wing. He hears a truck on the highway that runs along the side of the lake; he hears wind in the white pines. He hears a loon. He remembers the first time he heard one, and hugs himself. He has done well.

Wacousta Lodge is a large, oblong, one-story structure with board-and-batten walls stained a dark reddish brown. It was built in the first years of the century by the family's great-grandfather, who made a bundle on the railways. He included a maid's room and a cook's room at the back, although no maid or cook had ever been induced to stay in them, not to George's knowledge, certainly not in recent years. The great-grandfather's craggy, walrus-whiskered face, frowning above the constriction of a stiff collar, hangs oval-framed in the washroom, which is equipped only with a sink and a ewer. George can remember a zinc bathtub, but it's been retired. Baths take place in the lake. For the rest, there's an outhouse, placed discreetly behind a clump of spruce.

What a lot of naked and semi-naked bodies the old man must have seen over the years, thinks George, lathering his hands, and how he must have disapproved of them. At least the old boy isn't condemned to the outhouse: that would be too much for him. George makes a small, superstitious, oddly Japanese bow towards the great-grandfather as he goes out the door. He always does this. The presence of this scowling ancestral totem is one of the reasons he behaves himself, more or less, up here.

The table for lunch is set on the wide, screened-in veranda at the front of the house, overlooking the lake. Prue is not sitting at it, but her two sisters are: dry-faced Pamela, the eldest, and soft Portia, the youngest of the three and George's own wife. There is also Roland, the brother, large, rounded, and balding. George, who is not all that fond of men on purely social occasions because there are few ways he can manipulate them, gives Roland a polite nod and turns the full force of his vulpine smile upon the two women. Pamela, who distrusts him, sits up straight and pretends not to notice. Portia smiles at him, a wistful, vague smile, as if he were a cloud. Roland ignores him, though not on purpose, because Roland has the inner life of a tree, or possibly of a stump. George can never tell what Roland is thinking, or even if he is thinking at all.

"Isn't the weather marvelous?" George says to Pamela. He has learned over the years that the weather is the proper opening topic here for any conversation at all. Pamela is too well brought up to refuse an answer to a direct question.

"If you like postcards," she says. "At least it's not snowing." Pamela has recently been appointed a Dean of Women, a title George has not yet figured out completely. The Oxford dictionary has informed him that a dean might be the head of ten monks in a monastery, or "as tr. med. L. *decanus,* applied to the *teôingealdor,* the headman of a *tenmannetale.*" Much of what Pamela says sounds more or less like this: incomprehensible, though it might turn out to have a meaning if studied.

George would like to go to bed with Pamela, not because she is beautiful—she is much too rectilinear and slab-shaped for his tastes, she has no bottom at all, and her hair is the color of dried grass—but because he has never done it. Also, he wants to know what she would say. His interest in her is anthropological. Or perhaps geological: she would have to be scaled, like a glacier.

"Did you have a nice read?" says Portia. "I hope you didn't get sunburned. Is there any news?"

"If you can call it news," says Pamela. "That paper's a week old. Why is 'news' plural? Why don't we say 'olds'?"

"George likes old stuff," says Prue, coming in with a platter of food. She's put on a man's white shirt over her kerchief arrangement but hasn't done it up. "Lucky for us ladies, eh? Gobble up, everyone. It's yummy cheese-and-chutney sandwiches and yummy sardines. George? Beer or acid rain?"

George drinks a beer, and eats and smiles, eats and smiles, while the family talks around him—all but Roland, who absorbs his nutriments in silence, gazing out at the lake through the trees, his eyes immobile. George sometimes thinks Roland can change color slightly to blend in with his backgrounds; unlike George himself, who is doomed to stand out.

Pamela is complaining again about the stuffed birds. There are three of them, kept under glass bells in the living room: a duck, a loon, a grouse. These were the bright ideas of the grandfather, meant to go with the generally lodge-like décor: the mangy bearskin rug, complete with claws and head; the miniature birchbark canoe on the mantelpiece; the snowshoes, cracked and drying, crossed above the fireplace; the Hudson's Bay blanket nailed to the wall and beset by moths. Pamela is sure the stuffed birds will get moths too.

"They're probably a sea of maggots, inside," she says, and George tries to picture what a sea of maggots would look like. It's her metaphoric leaps, her tangled verbal stringworks, that confuse him.

"They're hermetically sealed," says Prue. "You know: nothing goes in, nothing comes out. Like nuns."

"Don't be revolting," says Pamela. "We should check them for frass."

"Who, the nuns?" says Prue.

"What is frass?" says George.

"Maggot excrement," says Pamela, not looking at him. "We could have them freeze-dried."

"Would it work?" says Prue.

Prue, who in the city is the first with trends—the first white kitchen, the first set of giant shoulder pads, the first leather pants suit have been hers over the years—is here as resistant to change as the rest of them. She wants everything on this peninsula to stay exactly the way it always has been. And it does, though with a gradual decline into shabbiness. George doesn't mind the shabbiness, however. Wacousta Lodge is a little slice of the past, an alien past. He feels privileged.

A motorboat goes by, one of the plastic-hulled, high-speed kind, far too close. Even Roland flinches. The wake jostles the dock.

"I hate those," says Portia, who hasn't shown much interest in the stuffed-bird question. "Another sandwich, dear?"

"It was so lovely and quiet here during the war," says Pamela. "You should have been here, George." She says this accusingly, as if it's his fault he wasn't. "Hardly any motorboats, because of the gas rationing. More canoes. Of course, the road wasn't built then, there was only the train. I wonder why we say 'train of thought' but never 'car of thought'?"

"And rowboats," says Prue. "I think all those motorboat people should be taken out and shot. At least the ones who go too fast." Prue herself drives like a maniac, but only on land.

George, who has seen many people taken out and shot, though not for driving motorboats, smiles, and helps himself to a sardine. He once shot three men himself, though only two of them were strictly necessary. The third was a precaution. He still feels uneasy about that, about the possibly harmless one with his too-innocent informer's eyes, his shirtfront dappled with blood. But there would be little point in mentioning that, at lunch or at any other time. George has no desire to be startling.

It was Prue who brought him north, brought him here, during their affair, the first one. (How many affairs have there been? Can they be separated, or are they really one long affair, with interruptions, like a string of sausages? The interruptions were Prue's marriages, which never lasted long, possibly because she was monogamous during them. He would know when a marriage was nearing its end: the phone at his office would ring and it would be Prue, saying, "George. I can't do it. I've been so good, but I just can't go on. He comes into the bathroom when I'm flossing my teeth. I long to be in an elevator with you, stuck between floors. Tell me something *filthy.* I hate love, don't you?")

His first time here he was led in chains, trailed in Prue's wake, like a barbarian in a Roman triumph. A definite capture, also a deliberate outrage. He was supposed to alarm Prue's family, and he did, though not on purpose. His English was not good, his hair was too glossy, his shoes too pointed, his clothes too sharply pressed. He wore dark glasses, kissed hands. The mother was alive then, though not the father; so there were four women ranged against him, with no help at all from the impenetrable Roland.

"Mother, this is George," said Prue, on the dock where they were all sitting in their ancestral deck chairs, the daughters in bathing suits with shirts over them, the mother in striped pastels. "It's not his real name, but it's easier to pronounce. He's come up here to see wild animals."

George leaned over to kiss the mother's sun-freckled hand, and his dark glasses fell off into the lake. The mother made cooing sounds of distress, Prue laughed at him, Roland ignored him, Pamela turned away in irritation. But Portia—lovely, small-boned Portia, with her velvet eyes—took off her shirt without a word and dove into the lake. She retrieved his dark glasses for him, smiling diffidently, handing them up to him out of the water, her wet hair dripping down over her small breasts like a water nymph's on an Art Nouveau fountain, and he knew then that she was the one he would marry. A woman of courtesy and tact and few words, who would be kind to him, who would cover up for him; who would pick up the things he had dropped.

In the afternoon, Prue took him for a paddle in one of the leaking canvas-covered canoes from the boathouse. He sat in the front, jabbing ineptly at the water with his paddle, thinking about how he would get Portia to marry him. Prue landed them on a rocky point, led him up among the trees. She wanted him to make his usual rakish, violent, outlandish brand of love to her on the reindeer moss and pine needles; she wanted to break some family taboo. Sacrilege was what she had in mind: that was as clear to him as if he'd read it. But George already had his plan of attack worked out, so he put her off. He didn't want to desecrate Wacousta Lodge: he wanted to marry it.

That evening at dinner he neglected all three of the daughters in favor of the mother: the mother was the guardian; the mother was the key. Despite his limping vocabulary he could be devastatingly charming, as Prue had announced to everyone while they ate their chicken-noodle soup.

"Wacousta Lodge," he said to the mother, bending his scar and his glinting marauder's eyes towards her in the light from the kerosene lamp. "That is so romantic. It is the name of an Indian tribe?"

Prue laughed. "It's named after some stupid book," she said. "Great-grandfather liked it because it was written by a general."

"A major," said Pamela severely. "In the nineteenth century. Major Richardson."

"Ah?" said George, adding this item to his already growing cache of local traditions. So there were books here, and houses named after them! Most people were touchy on the subject of their books; it would be as well to show some interest. Anyway, he *was* interested. But when he asked about the subject of this book it turned out that none of the women had read it.

"I've read it," said Roland, unexpectedly.

"Ah?" said George.

"It's about war."

"It's on the bookshelf in the living room," the mother said indifferently. "After dinner you can have a look, if you're all that fascinated."

It was the mother (Prue explained) who had been guilty of the daughters' alliterative names. She was a whimsical woman, though not sadistic; it was simply an age when parents did that—named their children to match, as if they'd come out of an alphabet book. The bear, the bumblebee, the bunny. Mary and Marjorie Murchison. David and Darlene Daly. Nobody did that anymore. Of course, the mother hadn't stopped at the names themselves but had converted them into nicknames: Pam, Prue, Porsh. Prue's is the only nickname that has stuck. Pamela is now too dignified for hers, and Portia says it's already bad enough, being confused with a car, and why can't she be just an initial?

Roland had been left out of the set, at the insistence of the father. It was Prue's opinion that he had always resented it. "How can you tell?" George asked her, running his tongue around her navel as she lay in her half-slip on the Chinese carpet in his office, smoking a cigarette and surrounded by sheets of paper that had been knocked off the desk during the initial skirmish. She'd made sure the door was unlocked: she liked to run the risk of intrusion, preferably by George's secretary, whom she suspected of being the competition. Which secretary, and when was that? The spilled papers were part of a take-over plan—the Adams group. This is how George keeps track of the various episodes with Prue: by remembering what other skulduggery he was up to at the time. He'd made his money quickly, and then he'd made more. It had been much easier than he'd thought; it had been like spearing fish by lamplight. These people were lax and trusting, and easily embarrassed by a hint of their own intolerance or lack of hospitality to strangers. They weren't ready for him. He'd been as happy as a missionary among the Hawaiians. A hint of opposition and he'd thicken his accent and refer darkly to Communist atrocities. Seize the moral high ground, then grab what you can get.

After that first dinner, they'd all gone into the living room, carrying their cups of coffee. There were kerosene lamps in there, too—old ones, with globe shades. Prue took George flagrantly by the hand and led him over to the bookcase, which was topped with a collection of clam shells and pieces of driftwood from the girls' childhoods. "Here it is," she said. "Read it and weep." She went to refill his coffee. George opened the book, an old edition that had, as he'd hoped, a frontispiece of an angry-looking warrior with tomahawk and paint. Then he scanned the shelves. *From Sea to Sea. Wild Animals I Have Known. The Collected Poems of Robert Service. Our Empire Story. Wilderness Tips.*

"Wilderness Tips" puzzled him. "Wilderness" he knew, but "tips"? He was not immediately sure whether this word was a verb or a noun. There were asparagus tips, as he knew from menus, and when he was getting into the canoe that afternoon in his slippery leather-soled city shoes Prue had said, "Be careful, it tips." Perhaps it was another sort of tip, as in the "Handy Tips for Happy Homemakers" columns in the women's magazines he had taken to reading in order to improve his English—the vocabularies were fairly simple and there were pictures, which was a big help.

When he opened the book he saw he'd guessed right. *Wilderness Tips* was dated 1905. There was a photo of the author in a plaid wool jacket and a felt hat, smoking a pipe and paddling a canoe, against a backdrop that was more or less what you could see out the window: water, islands, rocks, trees. The book itself told how to do useful things, like snaring small animals and eating them—something George himself had done, though not in forests—or lighting a fire in a rainstorm. These instructions were interspersed with lyrical passages about the joys of independence and the open air, and descriptions of fish-catching and sunsets. George took the book over to a chair near one of the globed lamps; he wanted to read about skinning knives, but Prue came back with his coffee, and Portia offered him a chocolate, and he did not want to run the risk of displeasing either of them, not at this early stage. That could come later.

Now George again walks into the living room, again carrying a cup of coffee. By this time he's read all of the books in the great-grandfather's collection. He's the only one who has.

Prue follows him in. The women take it in turns to clear and do the dishes, and it isn't her turn. Roland's job is the wood-splitting. There was an attempt once to press George into service with a tea towel, but he jovially broke three wineglasses, exclaiming over his own clumsiness, and since then he has been left in peace.

"You want more coffee?" Prue says. She stands close to him, proffering the open shirt, the two bandannas. George isn't sure he wants to start anything again, but he sets his coffee down on the top of the bookcase and puts his hand on her hip. He wants to check out his options, make sure he's still welcome. Prue sighs—a long sigh of desire or exasperation, or both.

"Oh, George," she says. "What should I do with you?"

"Whatever you like," says George, moving his mouth close to her ear. "I am merely a lump of clay in your hands." Her earlobe holds a tiny silver earring in the form of a shell. He represses an impulse to nibble.

"Curious George," she says, using one of her old nicknames for him. "You used to have the eyes of a young goat. Lecher eyes."

And now I'm an old goat, thinks George. He can't resist, he wants to be young again; he runs his hand up under her shirt.

"Later," Prue says triumphantly. She steps back from him and aims her wavering smile, and George upsets his cup of coffee with his elbow.

"Fene egye meg," he says, and Prue laughs. She knows the meaning of these swear-words, and worse ones, too.

"Clumsy bugger," she says. "I'll get a sponge."

George lights a cigarette and awaits her return. But it is Pamela who appears, frowning, in the doorway, with a deteriorating scrub cloth and a metal bowl. Trust Prue to have found some other urgent thing to do. She is probably in the outhouse, leafing through a magazine and plotting, deciding when and where she will next entice him.

"So, George, you've made a mess," says Pamela, as if he were a puppy. If she had a rolled-up newspaper, thinks George, she'd give me a swat on the nose.

"It's true, I'm an oaf," says George amiably. "But you've always known that."

Pamela gets down on her knees and begins to wipe. "If the plural of 'loaf' is 'loaves,' what's the plural of 'oaf'?" she says. "Why isn't it 'oaves'?" George realizes that a good deal of what she says is directed not to him or to any other listener but simply to herself. Is that because she thinks no one can hear her? He finds the sight of her down on her knees suggestive—stirring, even. He catches a whiff of her: soap flakes, a tinge of something sweet. Hand lotion? She has a graceful neck and throat. He wonders if she's ever had a lover, and, if so, what he was like. An insensitive man, lacking in skill. An oaf.

"George, you smoke like a furnace," she says, without turning around. "You really should stop, or it'll kill you."

George considers the ambiguity of the phrase. "Smoking like a furnace." He sees himself as a dragon, fumes and red flames pouring out of his ravenous maw. Is this really her version of him? "That would make you happy," he says, deciding on impulse to try a frontal attack. "You'd love to see me six feet underground. You've never liked me."

Pamela stops wiping and looks at him over her shoulder. Then she stands up and wrings the dirty cloth out into the bowl. "That's juvenile," she says calmly, "and unworthy of you. You need more exercise. This afternoon I'll take you canoeing."

"You know I'm hopeless at that," says George truthfully. "I always crash into rocks. I never see them."

"Geology is destiny," says Pamela, as if to herself. She scowls at the stuffed loon in its glass bell. She is thinking. "Yes," she says at last. "This lake is full of hidden rocks. It can be dangerous. But I'll take care of you."

Is she flirting with him? Can a crag flirt? George can hardly believe it, but he smiles at her, holding the cigarette in the center of his mouth, showing his canines, and for the first time in their lives Pamela smiles back at him. Her mouth is quite different when the corners turn up; it's as if he were seeing her upside down. He's surprised by the loveliness of her smile. It's not a knowing smile, like Prue's, or saintly, like Portia's. It's the smile of an imp, of a mischievous child, mixed in with something he'd never expected to find in her. A generosity, a carelessness, a largesse. She has something she wishes to give him. What could it be?

After lunch and a pause for digestion, Roland goes back to his chopping, beside the woodshed out behind the kitchen. He's splitting birch—a dying tree he cut down a year ago. The beavers had made a start on it, but changed their minds. White birch don't live long anyway. He'd used the chain saw, slicing the trunk neatly into lengths, the blade going through the wood like a knife through butter, the noise blotting out all other noises—the wind and waves, the whining of the trucks from the highway across the lake. He dislikes machine noises, but they're easier to tolerate when you're making them yourself, when you can control them. Like gunshot.

Not that Roland shoots. He used to: he used to go out for a deer in season, but now it's unsafe, there are too many other men doing it—Italians and who knows what—who'll shoot at anything moving. In any case, he's lost the taste for the end result, the antlered carcasses strapped to the fronts of cars like grotesque hood ornaments, the splendid, murdered heads peering dull-eyed from the tops of mini-vans. He can see the point of venison, of killing to eat, but to have a cut-off head on your wall? What does it prove, except that a deer can't pull a trigger?

He never talks about these feelings. He knows they would be held against him at his place of work, which he hates. His job is managing money for other people. He knows he is not a success, not by his great-grandfather's standards. The old man sneers at him every morning from that rosewood frame in the washroom, while he is shaving. They both know the same thing: if Roland were a success he'd be out pillaging, not counting the beans. He'd have some gray, inoffensive, discontented man counting the beans for him. A regiment of them. A regiment of men like himself.

He lifts a chunk of birch, stands it on end on the chopping block, swings the axe. A clean split, but he's out of practice. Tomorrow he will have blisters. In a while he'll stop, stoop and pile, stoop and pile. There's already enough wood, but he likes doing this. It's one of the few things he does like. He feels alive only up here.

Yesterday, he drove up from the center of the city, past the warehouses and factories and shining glass towers, which have gone up, it seems, overnight; past the subdivisions he could swear weren't there last year, last month. Acres of treelessness, of new townhouses with little pointed roofs—like tents, like an invasion. The tents of the Goths and the Vandals. The tents of the Huns and the Magyars. The tents of George.

Down comes his axe on the head of George, which splits in two. If Roland had known George would be here this weekend, he wouldn't have come. Damn Prue and her silly bandannas and her open shirt, her middle-aged breasts offered like hot, freckled muffins along with the sardines and cheese, George sliding his oily eyes all over her, with Portia pretending not to notice. Damn George and his shady deals and his pay-offs to town councillors; damn George and his millions, and his spurious, excessive charm. George should stay in the city where he belongs. He's hard to take even there, but at least Roland can keep out of his way. Here at Wacousta Lodge he's intolerable, strutting around as if he owned the place. Not yet. Probably he'll wait for them all to croak, and then turn it into a lucrative retirement home for the rich Japanese. He'll sell them Nature, at a huge margin. That's the kind of thing George would do.

Roland knew the man was a lizard the first time he saw him. Why did Portia marry him? She could have married somebody decent, leaving George to Prue, who'd dredged him up from God knows where and was flaunting him around like a prize fish. Prue deserved him; Portia didn't. But why did Prue give him up without a struggle? That wasn't like her. It's as if there had been some negotiation, some invisible deal between them. Portia got George, but what did she trade for him? What did she have to give up?

Portia has always been his favorite sister. She was the youngest, the baby. Prue, who was the next youngest, used to tease her savagely, though Portia was remarkably slow to cry. Instead, she would just look, as if she couldn't quite figure out what Prue was doing to her or why. Then she would go off by herself. Or else Roland would come to her defense and there would be a fight, and Roland would be accused of picking on his sister and be told he shouldn't behave that way because he was a boy. He doesn't remember what part Pamela used to take in all this. Pamela was older than the rest of them and had her own agenda, which did not appear to include anyone else at all. Pamela read at the dinner table and went off by herself in the canoe. Pamela was allowed.

In the city they were in different schools or different grades; the house was large and they had their own pathways through it, their own lairs. It was only here that the territories overlapped. Wacousta Lodge, which looks so peaceful, is for Roland the repository of the family wars.

How old had he been—nine? ten?—the time he almost killed Prue? It was the summer he wanted to be an Indian, because of *Wilderness Tips*. He used to sneak that book off the shelf and take it outside, behind the woodshed, and turn and re-turn the pages. *Wilderness Tips* told you how to survive by yourself in the woods—a thing he longed to do. How to build shelters, make clothing from skins, find edible plants. There were diagrams too, and pen-and-ink drawings—of animal tracks, of leaves and seeds. Descriptions of different kinds of animal droppings. He remembers the first time he found some bear scat, fresh and reeking, and purple with blueberries. It scared the hell out of him.

There was a lot about the Indians, about how noble they were, how brave, faithful, clean, reverent, hospitable, and honorable. (Even these words sound outmoded now, archaic. When was the last time Roland heard anyone praised for being *honorable?*) They attacked only in self-defense, to keep their land from being stolen. They walked differently too. There was a diagram, on page 208, of footprints, an Indian's and a white man's: the white wore hobnailed boots, and his toes pointed outward; the Indian wore moccasins, and his feet went straight ahead. Roland has been conscious of his feet ever since. He still turns his toes in slightly, to counteract what he feels must be a genetically programmed waddle.

That summer he ran around with a tea towel tucked into the front of his bathing suit for a loincloth and decorated his face with charcoal from the fireplace, alternating with red paint swiped from Prue's paintbox. He lurked outside windows, listening in. Trying to make smoke signals, he set fire to a small patch of undergrowth down near the boathouse, but put it out before he was caught. He lashed an oblong stone to a stick handle with a leather lace borrowed from one of his father's boots; his father was alive then. He snuck up on Prue, who was reading comic books on the dock, dangling her legs in the water.

He had his stone axe. He could have brained her. She was not Prue, of course: she was Custer, she was treachery, she was the enemy. He went as far as raising the axe, watching the convincing silhouette his shadow made on the dock. The stone fell off, onto his bare foot. He shouted with pain. Prue turned around, saw him there, guessed in an instant what he was doing, and laughed herself silly. That was when he'd almost killed her. The other thing, the stone axe, had just been a game.

The whole thing had just been a game, but it wounded him to let go of it. He'd wanted so badly to believe in that kind of Indian, the kind in the book. He'd needed them to exist.

Driving up yesterday, he'd passed a group of actual Indians, three of them, at a blueberry stand. They were wearing jeans and T-shirts and running shoes, the same as everybody else. One of them had a transistor radio. A neat maroon mini-van was parked beside the stand. So what did he expect from them, feathers? All that was gone, lost, ruined, years and years before he was born.

He knows this is nonsense. He's a bean counter, after all; he deals in the hard currency of reality. How can you lose something that was never yours in the first place? (But you can, because *Wilderness Tips* was his once, and he's lost it. He opened the book today, before lunch, after forty years. There was the innocent, fusty vocabulary that had once inspired him: Manhood with a capital M, courage, honor. The Spirit of the Wild. It was naive, pompous, ridiculous. It was dust.)

Roland chops with his axe. The sound goes out through the trees, across the small inlet to the left of him, bounces off a high ridge of rock, making a faint echo. It's an old sound, a sound left over.

★ ★ ★

Portia lies on her bed, listening to the sound of Roland chopping wood, having her nap. She has her nap the way she always has, without sleeping. The nap was enforced on her once, by her mother. Now she just does it. When she was little she used to lie here—tucked safely away from Prue—in her parents' room, in her parents' double bed, which is now hers and George's. She would think about all kinds of things; she would see faces and animal shapes in the knots of the pine ceiling and make up stories about them.

Now the only stories she ever makes up are about George. They are probably even more unrealistic than the stories he makes up about himself, but she has no way of really knowing. There are those who lie by instinct and those who don't, and the ones who don't are at the mercy of the ones who do.

Prue, for instance, is a blithe liar. She always has been; she enjoys it. When they were children she'd say, "Look, there's a big snot coming out of your nose," and Portia would run to the washroom mirror. Nothing was there, but Prue's saying it made it somehow true, and Portia would scrub and scrub, trying to wash away invisible dirt, while Prue doubled over with laughter. "Don't believe her," Pamela would say. "Don't be such a sucker." (One of her chief words then—she used it for lollipops, for fish, for mouths.) But sometimes the things Prue said were true, so how could you ever know?

George is the same way. He gazes into her eyes and lies with such tenderness, such heartfelt feeling, such implicit sadness at her want of faith in him, that she can't question him. To question him would turn her cynical and hard. She would rather be kissed; she would rather be cherished. She would rather believe.

She knew about George and Prue at the beginning, of course. It was Prue who brought him up here first. But after a while George swore to her that the thing with Prue hadn't been serious, and, anyway, it was over; and Prue herself seemed not to care. She'd already had George, she implied; he was used, like a dress. If Portia wanted him next it was nothing to her. "Help yourself," she said. "God knows there's enough of George to go around."

Portia wanted to do things the way Prue did; she wanted to get her hands dirty. Something intense, followed by careless dismissal. But she was too young; she didn't have the knack. She'd come up out of the lake and handed George's dark glasses to him, and he'd looked at her in the wrong way: with reverence, not with passion—a clear gaze with no smut in it. After dinner that evening he'd said, with meticulous politeness, "Everything here is so new to me. I'd like you to be my guide, to your wonderful country."

"Me?" Portia said. "I don't know. What about Prue?" She was already feeling guilty.

"Prue does not understand obligations," he said (which was true enough, she didn't, and this insight of George's was impressive). "You understand them, however. I am the guest; you are the host."

"Hostess," said Pamela, who had not seemed to be listening. "A 'host' is male, like 'mine host' in an inn, or else it's the wafer you eat at Communion. Or the caterpillar that all the parasites lay their eggs on."

"You have a very intellectual sister, I think," said George, smiling, as if this quality in Pamela were a curiosity, or perhaps a deformity. Pamela shot him a look of pure resentment, and ever since that time she has not made any effort with him. He might as well be a bump on a log as far as she's concerned.

But Portia doesn't mind Pamela's indifference; rather, she cherishes it. Once she wanted to be more like Prue, but now it's Pamela. Pamela, considered so eccentric and odd and plain in the fifties, now seems to be the only one of them who got it right. Freedom isn't having a lot of men, not if you think you have to. Pamela does what she wants, nothing more and nothing less.

It's a good thing there's one woman in the universe who can take George or leave him alone. Portia wishes she herself could be so cool. Even after thirty-two years, she's still caught in the breathlessness, the airlessness of love. It's no different from the first night, when he'd bent to kiss her (down by the boathouse, after an evening paddle) and she'd stood there like a deer in the glare of headlights, paralyzed, while something huge and unstoppable bore down on her, waiting for the scream of brakes, the shock of collision. But it wasn't that kind of kiss: it wasn't sex George wanted out of her. He'd wanted the other thing—the wifely white cotton blouses, the bassinets. He's sad they never had children.

He was such a beautiful man then. There were a lot of beautiful men, but the others seemed blank, unwritten on, compared to him. He's the only one she's ever wanted. She can't have him, though, because nobody can. George has himself, and he won't let go.

This is what drives Prue on: she wants to get hold of him finally, open him up, wring some sort of concession out of him. He's the only person in her life she's never been able to bully or ignore or deceive or reduce. Portia can always tell when Prue's back on the attack: there are telltale signs; there are phone calls with no voice attached; there are flights of sincere, melancholy lying from George—a dead giveaway. He knows she knows; he treasures her for saying nothing; she allows herself to be treasured.

There's nothing going on now, though. Not at the moment, not up here, not at Wacousta Lodge. Prue wouldn't dare, and neither would George. He knows where she draws the line; he knows the price of her silence.

Portia looks at her watch: her nap is over. As usual, it has not been restful. She gets up, goes into the washroom, splashes her face. She applies cream lightly, massaging it in around her fallen eyes. The question at this age is what kind of dog you will shortly resemble. She will be a beagle, Prue a terrier. Pamela will be an Afghan, or something equally unearthly.

Her great-grandfather watches her in the mirror, disapproving of her as he always has, although he was dead long before she was born. "I did the best I could," she tells him. "I married a man like you. A robber king." She will never admit to him or to anyone else that this might possibly have been a mistake. (Why does her father never figure in her inner life? Because he wasn't there, not even as a picture. He was at the office. Even in the summers—especially in the summers—he was an absence.)

Outside the window, Roland has stopped chopping and is sitting on the chopping block, his arms on his knees, his big hands dangling, staring off into the trees. He is her favorite; he was the one who always came to her defense. That stopped when she married George. Faced with Prue, Roland had been effective, but George baffled him. No wonder. It's Portia's love that protects George, walls him around. Portia's stupid love.

Where is George? Portia wanders the house, looking for him. Usually at this time of day he'd be in the living room, extended on the couch, dozing; but he isn't there. She looks around the empty room. Everything is as usual: the snowshoes on the wall, the birchbark canoe she always longed to play with but couldn't because it was a souvenir, the rug made out of a bearskin, dull-haired and shedding. That bear was a friend once, it even had a name, but she's forgotten it. On the bookcase there's an empty coffee cup. That's a slip, an oversight; it shouldn't be there. She has the first stirrings of the feeling she gets when she knows George is with Prue, a numbness that begins at the base of the spine. But no, Prue is in the hammock on the screened veranda, reading a magazine. There can't be two of her.

"Where's George?" Portia asks, knowing she shouldn't.

"How the hell should I know?" says Prue. Her tone is peevish, as if she's wondering the same thing. "What's the matter—he slipped his leash? Funny, there's no bimbo secretaries up here." In the sunlight she has a disorderly look: her too-orange lipstick is threading into the tiny wrinkles around her mouth; her bangs are brazen; things are going askew.

"There's no need to be nasty," says Portia. This is what their mother used to say to Prue, over the body of some dismembered doll, some razed sandbox village, a bottle of purloined nail polish hurled against the wall; and Prue never had an answer then. But now their mother isn't here to say it.

"There *is,*" says Prue with vehemence. "There is a need."

Ordinarily, Portia would just walk away, pretending she hadn't heard. Now she says, "Why?"

"Because you always had the best of everything," says Prue.

Portia is astounded. Surely she is the mute one, the shadow; hasn't she always played wallflower to Prue's frantic dancer? "What?" she says. "What did I always have?"

"You've always been too good for words," says Prue with rancor. "Why do you stay with him, anyway? Is it the money?"

"He didn't have a bean when I married him," says Portia mildly. She's wondering whether or not she hates Prue. She isn't sure what real hatred would feel like. Anyway, Prue is losing that taut, mischievous body she's done such damage with, and, now that's going, what will she have left? In the way of weapons, that is.

"When *he* married *you,* you mean," says Prue. "When Mother married you off. You just stood there and let the two of them do it, like the little suck you were."

Portia wonders if this is true. She wishes she could go back a few decades, grow up again. The first time, she missed something; she missed a stage, or some vital information other people seemed to have. This time she would make different choices. She would be less obedient; she would not ask for permission. She would not say "I do" but "I am."

"Why didn't you ever fight back?" says Prue. She sounds genuinely aggrieved.

Portia can see down the path to the lake, to the dock. There's a canvas deck chair down there with nobody in it. George's newspaper, tucked underneath, is fluttering: there's a wind coming up. George must have forgotten to put his chair away. It's unlike him.

"Just a minute," she says to Prue, as if they're going to take a short break in this conversation they've been having in different ways for fifty years now. She goes out the screen door and down the path. Where has George got to? Probably the outhouse. But his canvas chair is rippling like a sail.

She stoops to fold up the chair, and hears. There's someone in the boathouse; there's a scuffling, a breathing. A porcupine, eating salt off the oar handles? Not in broad daylight. No, there's a voice. The water glitters, the small waves slap against the dock. It can't be Prue; Prue is up on the veranda. It sounds like her mother, like her mother opening birthday presents—that soft crescendo of surprise and almost pained wonder. Oh. Oh. *Oh.* Of course, you can't tell what age a person is, in the dark.

Portia folds the chair, props it gently against the wall of the boathouse. She goes up the path, carrying the paper. No sense in having it blow all over the lake. No sense in having the clear waves dirtied with stale news, with soggy human grief. Desire and greed and terrible disappointments, even in the financial pages. Though you had to read between the lines.

She doesn't want to go into the house. She skirts around behind the kitchen, avoiding the woodshed where she can hear the *chock, chock* of Roland piling wood, goes back along the path that leads to the small, sandy bay where they all swam as children, before they were old enough to dive in off the dock. She lies down on the ground there and goes to sleep. When she wakes up there are pine needles sticking to her cheek and she has a headache. The sun is low in the sky; the wind has fallen; there are no more waves. A dead flat calm. She takes off her clothes, not bothering even to listen for motorboats. They go so fast anyway she'd just be a blur.

She wades into the lake, slipping into the water as if between the layers of a mirror: the glass layer, the silver layer. She meets the doubles of her own legs, her own arms, going down. She floats with only her head above water. She is herself at fifteen, herself at twelve, herself at nine, at six. On the shore, attached to their familiar reflections, are the same rock, the same white stump that have always been there. The cold hush of the lake is like a long breathing-out of relief. It's safe to be this age, to know that the stump is her stump, the rock is hers, that nothing will ever change.

There's a bell, ringing faintly from the distant house. The dinner bell. It's Pamela's turn to cook. What will they have? A strange concoction. Pamela has her own ideas about food.

The bell rings again, and Portia knows that something bad is about to happen. She could avoid it; she could swim out further, let go, and sink.

She looks at the shore, at the water line, where the lake ends. It's no longer horizontal: it seems to be on a slant, as if there'd been a slippage in the bedrock; as if the trees, the granite outcrops, Wacousta Lodge, the peninsula, the whole mainland were sliding gradually down, submerging. She thinks of a boat—a huge boat, a passenger liner—tilting, descending, with the lights still on, the music still playing, the people talking on and on, still not aware of the disaster that has already overcome them. She sees herself running naked through the ballroom—an absurd, disturbing figure with dripping hair and flailing arms, screaming at them, "Don't you see? It's coming apart, everything's coming apart, you're sinking. You're finished, you're over, you're dead!"

She would be invisible, of course. No one would hear her. And nothing has happened, really, that hasn't happened before.

MARGARET ATWOOD

True Trash

The waitresses are basking in the sun like a herd of skinned seals, their pinky-brown bodies shining with oil. They have their bathing suits on because it's the afternoon. In the early dawn and the dusk they sometimes go skinny-dipping, which makes this itchy crouching in the mosquito-infested bushes across from their small private dock a great deal more worthwhile.

Donny has the binoculars, which are not his own but Monty's. Monty's dad gave them to him for bird-watching but Monty isn't interested in birds. He's found a better use for the binoculars: he rents them out to the other boys, five minutes maximum, a nickel a look or else a chocolate bar from the tuck shop, though he prefers the money. He doesn't eat the chocolate bars; he resells them, black market, for twice their original price; but the total supply on the island is limited, so he can get away with it.

Donny has already seen everything worth seeing, but he lingers on with the binoculars anyway, despite the hoarse whispers and the proddings from those next in line. He wants to get his money's worth.

"Would you look at that," he says, in what he hopes is a tantalizing voice. "Slobber, slobber." There's a stick poking into his stomach, right on a fresh mosquito bite, but he can't move it without taking one hand off the binoculars. He knows about flank attacks.

"Lessee," says Ritchie, tugging at his elbow.

"Piss off," says Donny. He shifts the binoculars, taking in a slippery bared haunch, a red-polka-dotted breast, a long falling strand of bleach-blond hair: Ronette the tartiest, Ronette the most forbidden. When there are lectures from the masters at St. Jude's during the winter about the dangers of consorting with the town girls, it's those like Ronette they have in mind: the ones who stand in line at the town's only movie theater, chewing gum and wearing their boyfriends' leather jackets, their ruminating mouths glistening and deep red like mushed-up raspberries. If you whistle at them or even look, they stare right through you.

Ronette has everything but the stare. Unlike the others, she has been known to smile. Every day Donny and his friends make bets over whether they will get her at their table. When she leans over to clear the plates, they try to look down the front of her sedate but V-necked uniform. They angle towards her, breathing her in: she smells of hair spray, nail polish, something artificial and too sweet. Cheap, Donny's mother would say. It's an enticing word. Most of the things in his life are expensive, and not very interesting.

Ronette changes position on the dock. Now she's lying on her stomach, chin propped on her hands, her breasts pulled down by gravity. She has a real cleavage, not like some of them. But he can see her collar-bone and some chest ribs, above the top of her suit. Despite the breasts, she's skinny, scrawny; she has little stick arms and a thin, sucked-in face. She has a missing side tooth, you can see it when she smiles, and this bothers him.

He knows he's supposed to feel lust for her, but this is not what he feels.

The waitresses know they're being looked at: they can see the bushes jiggling. The boys are only twelve or thirteen, fourteen at most, small fry. If it was counselors, the waitresses would giggle more, preen more, arch their backs. Or some of them would. As it is, they go on with their afternoon break as if no one is there. They rub oil on one another's backs, toast themselves evenly, turning lazily this way and that and causing Ritchie, who now has the binoculars, to groan in a way that is supposed to madden the other boys, and does. Small punches are dealt out, mutterings of "Jerk" and "Asshole." "Drool, drool," says Ritchie, grinning from ear to ear.

The waitresses are reading out loud. They are taking turns: their voices float across the water, punctuated by occasional snorts and barks of laughter. Donny would like to know what they're reading with such absorption, such relish; but it would be dangerous for him to admit it. It's their bodies that count. Who cares what they read?

"Time's up, shitface," he whispers to Ritchie.

"Shitface yourself," says Ritchie. The bushes thrash.

What the waitresses are reading is a *True Romance* magazine. Tricia has a whole stash of them, stowed under her mattress, and Sandy and Pat have each contributed a couple of others. Every one of these magazines has a woman on the cover, with her dress pulled down over one shoulder or a cigarette in her mouth or some other evidence of a messy life. Usually these women are in tears. Their colors are odd: sleazy, dirt-permeated, like the hand-tinted photos in the five-and-ten. Knee-between-the-legs colors. They have none of the cheerful primaries and clean, toothy smiles of the movie magazines: these are not success stories. True Trash, Hilary calls them. Joanne calls them Moan-o-dramas.

Right now it's Joanne reading. She reads in a serious, histrionic voice, like someone on the radio; she's been in a play, at school. *Our Town.* She's got her sunglasses perched on the end of her nose, like a teacher. For extra hilarity she's thrown in a fake English accent.

The story is about a girl who lives with her divorced mother in a cramped, rundown apartment above a shoe store. Her name is Marleen. She has a part-time job in the store, after school and on Saturdays, and two of the shoe clerks are chasing around after her. One is dependable and boring and wants them to get married. The other one, whose name is Dirk, rides a motorcycle and has a knowing, audacious grin that turns Marleen's knees to jelly. The mother slaves over Marleen's wardrobe, on her sewing machine—she makes a meager living doing dressmaking for rich ladies who sneer at her, so the wardrobe comes out all right—and she nags Marleen about choosing the right man and not making a terrible mistake, the way she did. The girl herself has planned to go to trade school and learn hospital management, but lack of money makes this impossible. She is in her last year of high school and her grades are slipping, because she is discouraged and also she can't decide between the two shoe clerks. Now the mother is on her case about the slipping grades as well.

"Oh God," says Hilary. She is doing her nails, with a metal file rather than an emery board. She disapproves of emery boards. "Someone please give her a double Scotch."

"Maybe she should murder the mother, collect the insurance, and get the hell out of there," says Sandy.

"Have you heard one word about any insurance?" says Joanne, peering over the tops of her glasses.

"You could put some in," says Pat.

"Maybe she should try out both of them, to see which one's the best," says Liz brazenly.

"We know which one's the best," says Tricia. "Listen, with a name like *Dirk!* How can you miss?"

"They're both creeps," says Stephanie.

"If she does that, she'll be a Fallen Woman, capital F, capital W," says Joanne. "She'd have to Repent, capital R."

The others hoot: Repentance! The girls in the stories make such fools of themselves. They are so weak. They fall helplessly in love with the wrong men, they give in, they are jilted. Then they cry.

"Wait," says Joanne. "Here comes the big night." She reads on, breathily. *"My mother had gone out to deliver a cocktail dress to one of her customers. I was all alone in our shabby apartment."*

"Pant, pant," says Liz.

"No, that comes later. *I was all alone in our shabby apartment. The evening was hot and stifling. I knew I should be studying, but I could not concentrate. I took a shower to cool off. Then, on impulse, I decided to try on the graduation formal my mother had spent so many late-night hours making for me."*

"That's right, pour on the guilt," says Hilary with satisfaction. "If it was me I'd axe the mother."

"It was a dream of pink—"

"A dream of pink what?" says Tricia.

"A dream of pink, period, and shut up. *I looked at myself in the full-length mirror in my mother's tiny bedroom. The dress was just right for me. It fitted my ripe but slender body to perfection. I looked different in it, older, beautiful, like a girl used to every luxury. Like a princess. I smiled at myself. I was transformed.*

"I had just undone the hooks at the back, meaning to take the dress off and hang it up again, when I heard footsteps on the stairs. Too late I remembered that I'd forgotten to lock the door on the inside, after my mother's departure. I rushed to the door, holding up my dress—it could be a burglar, or worse! But instead it was Dirk."

"Dirk the jerk," says Alex, from underneath her towel.

"Go back to sleep," says Liz.

Joanne drops her voice, does a drawl. *"'Thought I'd come up and keep you company,' he said mischievously. 'I saw your mom go out.' He knew I was alone! I was blushing and shivering. I could hear the blood pounding in my veins. I couldn't speak. Every instinct warned me against him—every instinct but those of my body, and my heart."*

"So what else is there?" says Sandy. "You can't have a mental instinct."

"You want to read this?" says Joanne. "Then shush. *I held the frothy pink lace in front of me like a shield. 'Hey, you look great in that,' Dirk said. His voice was rough and tender. 'But you'd look even greater out of it.' I was frightened of him. His eyes were burning, determined. He looked like an animal stalking its prey."*

"Pretty steamy," says Hilary.

"What kind of animal?" says Sandy.

"A weasel," says Stephanie.

"A skunk," says Tricia.

"Shh," says Liz.

"I backed away from him," Joanne reads. *"I had never seen him look that way before. Now I was pressed against the wall and he was crushing me in his arms. I felt the dress slipping down . . ."*

"So much for all that sewing," says Pat.

". . . and his hand was on my breast, his hard mouth was seeking mine. I knew he was the wrong man for me but I could no longer resist. My whole body was crying out to his."

"What did it say?"

"It said, *Hey, body, over here!*"

"Shh."

"I felt myself lifted. He was carrying me to the sofa. Then I felt the length of his hard, sinewy body pressing against mine. Feebly I tried to push his hands away, but I didn't really want to. And then—dot dot dot—*we were One,* capital O, exclamation mark."

There is a moment of silence. Then the waitresses laugh. Their laughter is outraged, disbelieving. *One.* Just like that. There has to be more to it.

"The dress is a wreck," says Joanne in her ordinary voice. "Now the mother comes home."

"Not today, she doesn't," says Hilary briskly. "We've only got ten more minutes. I'm going for a swim, get some of this oil off me." She stands up, clips back her honey-blond hair, stretches her tanned athlete's body, and does a perfect swandive off the end of the dock.

"Who's got the soap?" says Stephanie.

Ronette has not said anything during the story. When the others have laughed, she has only smiled. She's smiling now. Hers is an off-center smile, puzzled, a little apologetic.

"Yeah, but," she says to Joanne, "why is it funny?"

The waitresses stand at their stations around the dining hall, hands clasped in front of them, heads bowed. Their royal-blue uniforms come down almost to the tops of their white socks, worn with white bucks or white-and-black saddle shoes or white sneakers. Over their uniforms they wear plain white aprons. The rustic log sleeping cabins at Camp Adanaqui don't have electric lights, the toilets are outhouses, the boys wash their own clothes, not even in sinks but in the lake; but there are waitresses, with uniforms and aprons. Roughing it builds a boy's character, but only certain kinds of roughing it.

Mr. B. is saying grace. He owns the camp, and is a master at St. Jude's as well, during the winters. He has a leathery, handsome face, the gray, tailored hair of a Bay Street lawyer, and the eyes of a hawk: he sees all, but pounces only sometimes. Today he's wearing a white V-necked tennis sweater. He could be drinking a gin and tonic, but is not.

Behind him on the wall, above his head, there's a weathered plank with a motto painted on it in black Gothic lettering: *As the Twig Is Bent.* A piece of bleached driftwood ornaments each end of the plank, and beneath it are two crossed paddles and a gigantic pike's head in profile, its mouth open to show its needle teeth, its one glass eye fixed in a ferocious maniac's glare.

To Mr. B.'s left is the end window, and beyond it is Georgian Bay, blue as amnesia, stretching to infinity. Rising out of it like the backs of whales, like rounded knees, like the calves and thighs of enormous floating women, are several islands of pink rock, scraped and rounded and fissured by glaciers and lapping water and endless weather, a few jack pines clinging to the larger ones, their twisted roots digging into the cracks. It was through these archipelagos that the waitresses were ferried here, twenty miles out from shore, by the same cumbersome mahogany inboard launch that brings the mail and the groceries and everything else to the island. Brings, and takes away. But the waitresses will not be shipped back to the mainland until the end of summer: it's too far for a day off, and they would never be allowed to stay away overnight. So here they are, for the duration. They are the only women on the island, except for Mrs. B. and Miss Fisk, the dietitian. But those two are old and don't count.

There are nine waitresses. There are always nine. Only the names and faces change, thinks Donny, who has been going to this camp ever since he was eight. When he was eight he paid no attention to the waitresses except when he felt homesick. Then he would think of excuses to go past the kitchen window when they were washing the dishes. There they would be, safely aproned, safely behind glass: nine mothers. He does not think of them as mothers anymore.

Ronette is doing his table tonight. From between his half-closed eyelids Donny watches her thin averted face. He can see one earring, a little gold hoop. It goes right through her ear. Only Italians and cheap girls have pierced ears, says his mother. It would hurt to have a hole put through your ear. It would take bravery. He wonders what the inside of Ronette's room looks like, what other cheap, intriguing things she's got in there. About someone like Hilary he doesn't have to wonder, because he already knows: the clean bedspread, the rows of shoes in their shoe-trees, the comb and brush and manicure set laid out on the dresser like implements in a surgery.

Behind Ronette's bowed head there's the skin of a rattlesnake, a big one, nailed to the wall. That's what you have to watch out for around here: rattlesnakes. Also poison ivy, thunderstorms, and drowning. A whole war canoe full of kids drowned last year, but they were from another camp. There's been some talk of making everyone wear sissy life-jackets; the mothers want it. Donny would like a rattlesnake skin of his own, to nail up over his bed; but even if he caught the snake himself, strangled it with his bare hands, bit its head off, he'd never be allowed to keep the skin.

Mr. B. winds up the grace and sits down, and the campers begin again their three-times-daily ritual of bread-grabbing, face-stuffing, under-the-table kicking, whispered cursing. Ronette comes from the kitchen with a platter: macaroni and cheese. "There you go, boys," she says, with her good-natured, lopsided smile.

"Thank you kindly, ma'am," says Darce the counselor, with fraudulent charm. Darce has a reputation as a make-out artist; Donny knows he's after Ronette. This makes him feel sad. Sad, and too young. He would like to get out of his own body for a while; he'd like to be somebody else.

The waitresses are doing the dishes. Two to scrape, one to wash, one to rinse in the scalding-hot rinsing sink, three to dry. The other two sweep the floors and wipe off the tables. Later, the number of dryers will vary because of days off—they'll choose to take their days off in twos, so they can double-date with the counselors—but today all are here. It's early in the season, things are still fluid, the territories are not yet staked out.

While they work they sing. They're missing the ocean of music in which they float during the winter. Pat and Liz have both brought their portables, though you can't pick up much radio out here, it's too far from shore. There's a record player in the counselors' rec hall, but the records are out of date. Patti Page, The Singing Rage. "How Much Is That Doggie in the Window." "The Tennessee Waltz." Who waltzes anymore?

"'Wake up, little Susie,'" trills Sandy. The Everly Brothers are popular this summer; or they were, on the mainland, when they left.

"'What're we gonna tell your mama, what're we gonna tell your pa,'" sing the others. Joanne can improvise the alto harmony, which makes everything sound less screechy.

Hilary, Stephanie, and Alex don't sing this one. They go to a private school, all girls, and are better at rounds, like "Fire's Burning" and "White Coral Bells." They are good at tennis though, and sailing, skills that have passed the others by.

It's odd that Hilary and the other two are here at all, waitressing at Camp Adanaqui; it's not as if they need the money. (Not like me, thinks Joanne, who haunts the mail desk every noon to see if she got her scholarship.) But it's the doing of their mothers. According to Alex, the three mothers banded together and jumped Mrs. B. at a charity function, and twisted her arm. Naturally Mrs. B. would attend the same functions as the mothers: they've seen her, sunglasses pushed up on her forehead, a tall drink in her hand, entertaining on the veranda of Mr. B.'s white hilltop house, which is well away from the camp proper. They've seen the guests, in their spotless, well-pressed sailing clothes. They've heard the laughter, the voices, husky and casual. *Oh God don't tell me.* Like Hilary.

"We were kidnapped," says Alex. "They thought it was time we met some boys."

Joanne can see it for Alex, who is chubby and awkward, and for Stephanie, who is built like a boy and walks like one; but Hilary? Hilary is classic. Hilary is like a shampoo ad. Hilary is perfect. She ought to be sought after. Oddly, here she is not.

Ronette is scraping, and drops a plate. "Shoot," she says. "What a stunned broad." Nobody bawls her out or even teases her as they would anyone else. She is a favorite with them, though it's hard to put your finger on why. It isn't just that she's easygoing: so is Liz, so is Pat. She has some mysterious, extra status. For instance, everyone else has a nickname: Hilary is Hil, Stephanie is Steph, Alex is Al, Joanne is Jo, Tricia is Trish, Sandy is San. Pat and Liz, who cannot be contracted any further, have become Pet and Lizard. Only Ronette has been accorded the dignity of her full, improbable name.

In some ways she is more grown-up than the rest of them. But it isn't because she knows more things. She knows fewer things; she often has trouble making her way through the vocabularies of the others, especially the offhand slang of the private-school trio. "I don't get that" is what she says, and the others take a delight in explaining, as if she's a foreigner, a cherished visitor from some other country. She goes to movies and watches television like the rest of them but she has few opinions about what she has seen. The most she will say is "Crap" or "He's not bad." Though friendly, she is cautious about expressing approval in words. "Fair" is her best compliment. When the others talk about what they've read or what subjects they will take next year at university, she is silent.

But she knows other things, hidden things. Secrets. And these other things are older, and on some level more important. More fundamental. Closer to the bone.

Or so thinks Joanne, who has a bad habit of novelizing.

Outside the window Darce and Perry stroll by, herding a group of campers. Joanne recognizes a few of them: Donny, Monty. It's hard to remember the campers by name. They're just a crowd of indistinguishable, usually grimy young boys who have to be fed three times a day, whose crusts and crumbs and rinds have to be cleaned up afterwards. The counselors call them Grubbies.

But some stand out. Donny is tall for his age, all elbows and spindly knees, with huge deep-blue eyes; even when he's swearing—they all swear during meals, furtively but also loudly enough so that the waitresses can hear them—it's more like a meditation, or more like a question, as if he's trying the words out, tasting them. Monty on the other hand is like a miniature forty-five-year-old: his shoulders already have a businessman's slump, his paunch is fully formed. He walks with a pompous little strut. Joanne thinks he's hilarious.

Right now he's carrying a broom with five rolls of toilet paper threaded onto the handle. All the boys are: they're on Bog Duty, sweeping out the outhouses, replacing the paper. Joanne wonders what they do with the used sanitary napkins in the brown paper bag in the waitresses' private outhouse. She can imagine the remarks.

"Company . . . halt!" shouts Darce. The group shambles to a stop in front of the window. "Present . . . arms!" The brooms are raised, the ends of the toilet-paper tolls fluttering in the breeze like flags. The girls laugh and wave.

Monty's salute is half-hearted: this is well beneath his dignity. He may rent out his binoculars—that story is all over camp, by now—but he has no interest in using them himself. He has made that known. *Not on these girls,* he says, implying higher tastes.

Darce himself gives a comic salute, then marches his bunch away. The singing in the kitchen has stopped; the topic among the waitresses is now the counselors. Darce is the best, the most admired, the most desirable. His teeth are the whitest, his hair the blondest, his grin the sexiest. In the counselors' rec hall, where they go every night after the dishes are done, after they've changed out of their blue uniforms into their jeans and pullovers, after the campers have been inserted into their beds for the night, he has flirted with each one of them in turn. So who was he really saluting?

"It was me," says Pat, joking. "Don't I wish."

"Dream on," says Liz.

"It was Hil," says Stephanie loyally. But Joanne knows it wasn't. It wasn't her, either. It was Ronette. They all suspect it. None of them says it.

"Perry likes Jo," says Sandy.

"Does not," says Joanne. She has given out that she has a boyfriend already and is therefore exempt from these contests. Half of this is true: she has a boyfriend. This summer he has a job as a salad chef on the Canadian National, running back and forth across the continent. She pictures him standing at the back of the train, on the caboose, smoking a cigarette between bouts of salad-making, watching the country slide away behind him. He writes her letters, in blue ball-point pen, on lined paper. *My first night on the Prairies,* he writes. *It's magnificent—all that land and sky. The sunsets are unbelievable.* Then there's a line across the page and a new date, and he gets to the Rockies. Joanne resents it a little that he raves on about places she's never been. It seems to her a kind of male showing-off: he's footloose. He closes with *Wish you were here* and several X's and O's. This seems too formal, like a letter to your mother. Like a peck on the cheek.

She put the first letter under her pillow, but woke up with blue smears on her face and the pillowcase both. Now she keeps the letters in her suitcase under the bed. She's having trouble remembering what he looks like. An image flits past, his face close up, at night, in the front seat of his father's car. The rustle of cloth. The smell of smoke.

Miss Fisk bumbles into the kitchen. She's short, plump, flustered; what she wears, always, is a hairnet over her gray bun, worn wool slippers—there's something wrong with her toes—and a faded blue knee-length sweater-coat, no matter how hot it is. She thinks of this summer job as her vacation. Occasionally she can be seen bobbing in the water in a droopy-chested bathing suit and a white rubber cap with the earflaps up. She never gets her head wet, so why she wears the cap is anyone's guess.

"Well, girls. Almost done?" She never calls the waitresses by name. To their faces they are *girls,* behind their backs *My girls.* They are her excuse for everything that goes wrong: *One of the girls must have done it.* She also functions as a sort of chaperon: her cabin is on the pathway that leads to theirs, and she has radar ears, like a bat.

I will never be that old, thinks Joanne. I will die before I'm thirty. She knows this absolutely. It's a tragic but satisfactory thought. If necessary, if some wasting disease refuses to carry her off, she'll do it herself, with pills. She is not at all unhappy but she intends to be, later. It seems required.

This is no country for old men, she recites to herself. One of the poems she memorized, though it wasn't on the final exam. Change that to old women.

When they're all in their pajamas, ready for bed, Joanne offers to read them the rest of the True Trash story. But everyone is too tired, so she reads it herself, with her flashlight, after the one feeble bulb has been switched off. She has a compulsion about getting to the ends of things. Sometimes she reads books backwards.

Needless to say, Marleen gets knocked up and Dirk takes off on his motorcycle when he finds out. *I'm not the settling-down type, baby. See ya round.* Vroom. The mother practically has a nervous breakdown, because she made the same mistake when young and blew her chances and now look at her. Marleen cries and regrets, and even prays. But luckily the other shoe clerk, the boring one, still wants to marry her. So that's what happens. The mother forgives her, and Marleen herself learns the true value of quiet devotion. Her life isn't exciting maybe, but it's a good life, in the trailer park; the three of them. The baby is adorable. They buy a dog. It's an Irish setter, and chases sticks in the twilight while the baby laughs. This is how the story ends, with the dog.

Joanne stuffs the magazine down between her narrow little bed and the wall. She's almost crying. She will never have a dog like that, or a baby either. She doesn't want them, and anyway how would she have time, considering everything she has to get done? She has a long, though vague, agenda. Nevertheless she feels deprived.

Between two oval hills of pink granite there's a small crescent of beach. The boys, wearing their bathing suits (as they never do on canoe trips but only around the camp where they might be seen by girls), are doing their laundry, standing up to their knees and swabbing their wet T-shirts and underpants with yellow bars of Sunlight soap. This only happens when they run out of clothes, or when the stench of dirty socks in the cabin becomes too overpowering. Darce the counselor is supervising, stretched out on a rock, taking the sun on his already tanned torso and smoking a fag. It's forbidden to smoke in front of the campers but he knows this bunch won't tell. To be on the safe side he's furtive about it, holding the cigarette down close to the rock and sneaking quick puffs.

Something hits Donny in the side of the head. It's Ritchie's wet underpants, squashed into a ball. Donny throws them back and soon there's an underpants war. Monty refuses to join in, so he becomes the common target. "Sod off!" he yells.

"Cut it out, you pinheads," Darce says. But he isn't really paying attention: he's seen something else, a flash of blue uniform, up among the trees. The waitresses aren't supposed to be over here on this side of the island. They're supposed to be on their own dock, having their afternoon break.

Darce is up among the trees now, one arm braced against a trunk. A conversation is going on; there are murmurs. Donny knows it's Ronette, he can tell by the shape, by the color of the hair. And here he is, with his wash-board ribs exposed, his hairless chest, throwing underpants around like a kid. He's disgusted with himself.

Monty, outnumbered but not wanting to admit defeat, says he needs to take a crap and disappears along the path to the outhouse. By now Darce is nowhere in sight. Donny captures Monty's laundry, which is already finished and wrung out and spread neatly on the hot rock to dry. He starts tossing it up into a jack pine, piece by piece. The others, delighted, help him. By the time Monty gets back, the tree is festooned with Monty's underpants and the other boys are innocently rinsing.

They're on one of the pink granite islands, the four of them: Joanne and Ronette, Perry and Darce. It's a double date. The two canoes have been pulled half out of the water and roped to the obligatory jack pines, the fire has done its main burning and is dying down to coals. The western sky is still peach-toned and luminous, the soft ripe juicy moon is rising, the evening air is warm and sweet, the waves wash gently against the rocks. It's the Summer Issue, thinks Joanne. *Lazy Daze. Tanning Tips. Shipboard Romance.*

Joanne is toasting a marshmallow. She has a special way of doing it: she holds it close to the coals but not so close that it catches fire, just close enough so that it swells up like a pillow and browns gently. Then she pulls off the toasted skin and eats it, and toasts the white inside part the same way, and peeling it down to the core. She licks marshmallow goo off her fingers and stares pensively into the shifting red glow of the coal bed. All of this is a way of ignoring or pretending to ignore what is really going on.

There ought to be a teardrop, painted and static, on her cheek. There ought to be a caption: *Heartbreak.* On the spread-out groundsheet right behind her, his knee touching her back, is Perry, cheesed off with her because she won't neck with him. Off behind the rocks, out of the dim circle of firelight, are Ronette and Darce. It's the third week in July and by now they're a couple, everyone knows it. In the rec hall she wears his sweatshirt with the St. Jude's crest; she smiles more these days, and even laughs when the other girls tease her about him. During this teasing Hilary does not join in. Ronette's face seems rounder, healthier, its angles smoothed out as if by a hand. She is less watchful, less diffident. She ought to have a caption too, thinks Joanne. *Was I Too Easy?*

There are rustlings from the darkness, small murmurings, breathing noises. It's like a movie theater on Saturday night. Group grope. *The young in one another's arms.* Possibly, thinks Joanne, they will disturb a rattlesnake.

Perry puts a hand, tentatively, on her shoulder. "Want me to toast you a marshmallow?" she says to him politely. The frosty freeze. Perry is no consolation prize. He merely irritates her, with his peeling sunburnt skin and begging spaniel's eyes. Her so-called real boyfriend is no help either, whizzing on his train tracks back and forth across the prairies, writing his by-now infrequent inky letters, the image of his face all but obliterated, as if it's been soaked in water.

Nor is it Darce she wants, not really. What she wants is what Ronette has: the power to give herself up, without reservation and without commentary. It's that languor, that leaning back.

Voluptuous mindlessness. Everything Joanne herself does is surrounded by quotation marks.

"Marshmallows. Geez," says Perry, in a doleful, cheated voice. All that paddling, and what for? Why the hell did she come along, if not to make out?

Joanne feels guilty of a lapse of manners. Would it hurt so much to kiss him?

Yes. It would.

Donny and Monty are on a canoe trip, somewhere within the tangled bush of the mainland. Camp Adanaqui is known for its tripping. For five days they and the others, twelve boys in all, have been paddling across lake after lake, hauling the gear over wave-rounded boulders or through the suck and stench of the moose-meadows at the portage entrances, grunting uphill with the packs and canoes, slapping the mosquitoes off their legs. Monty has blisters, on both his feet and his hands. Donny isn't too sad about that. He himself has a festering sliver. Maybe he will get blood-poisoning, become delirious, collapse and die on a portage, among the rocks and pine needles. That will serve someone right. Someone ought to be made to pay for the pain he's feeling.

The counselors are Darce and Perry. During the days they crack the whip; at night they relax, backs against a rock or tree, smoking and supervising while the boys light the fire, carry the water, cook the Kraft Dinners. They both have smooth large muscles which ripple under their tans, they both—by now—have stubbly beards. When everyone goes swimming Donny sneaks covert, envious looks at their groins. They make him feel spindly, and infantile in his own desires.

Right now it's night. Perry and Darce are still up, talking in low voices, poking the embers of the dying fire. The boys are supposed to be asleep. There are tents in case of rain, but nobody's suggested putting them up since the day before yesterday. The smell of grime and sweaty feet and wood smoke is getting too potent at close quarters; the sleeping bags are high as cheese. It's better to be outside, rolled up in the bag, a groundsheet handy in case of a deluge, head under a turned-over canoe.

Monty is the only one who has voted for a tent. The bugs are getting to him; he says he's allergic. He hates canoe trips and makes no secret of it. When he's older, he says, and can finally get his hands on the family boodle, he's going to buy the place from Mr. B. and close it down. "Generations of boys unborn will thank me," he says. "They'll give me a medal." Sometimes Donny almost likes him. He's so blatant about wanting to be filthy rich. No hypocrisy about him, not like some of the other millionaire offshoots, who pretend they want to be scientists or something else that's not paid much.

Now Monty is twisting around, scratching his bites. "Hey Finley," he whispers.

"Go to sleep," says Donny.

"I bet they've got a flask."

"What?"

"I bet they're drinking. I smelled it on Perry's breath yesterday."

"So?" says Donny.

"So," says Monty. "It's against the rules. Maybe we can get something out of them."

Donny has to hand it to him. He certainly knows the angles. At the very least they might be able to share the wealth.

The two of them inch out of their sleeping bags and circle around behind the fire, keeping low. Their practice while spying on the waitresses stands them in good stead. They crouch behind a bushy spruce, watching for lifted elbows or the outlines of bottles, their ears straining.

But what they hear isn't about booze. Instead it's about Ronette. Darce is talking about her as if she's a piece of meat. From what he's implying, she lets him do anything he wants. "Summer sausage" is what he calls her. This is an expression Donny has never heard before, and ordinarily he would think it was hilarious.

Monty sniggers under his breath and pokes Donny in the ribs with his elbow. Does he know how much it hurts, is he rubbing it in? *Donny loves Ronette.* The ultimate grade six insult, to be accused of loving someone. Donny feels as if it's he himself who's been smeared with words, who's had his face rubbed in them. He knows Monty will repeat this conversation to the other boys. He will say Darce has been porking Ronette. Right now Donny detests this word, with its conjuring of two heaving pigs, or two dead but animate uncooked Sunday roasts; although just yesterday he used it himself, and found it funny enough.

He can hardly charge out of the bushes and punch Darce in the nose. Not only would he look ridiculous, he'd get flattened.

He does the only thing he can think of. Next morning, when they're breaking camp, he pinches Monty's binoculars and sinks them in the lake.

Monty guesses, and accuses him. Some sort of pride keeps Donny from denying it. Neither can he say why he did it. When they get back to the island there's an unpleasant conversation with Mr. B. in the dining hall. Or not a conversation: Mr. B. talks, Donny is silent. He does not look at Mr. B. but at the pike's head on the wall, with its goggling voyeur's eye.

The next time the mahogany inboard goes back into town, Donny is in it. His parents are not pleased.

It's the end of summer. The campers have already left, though some of the counselors and all of the waitresses are still here. Tomorrow they'll go down to the main dock, climb into the slow launch, thread their way among the pink islands, heading towards winter.

It's Joanne's half-day off so she isn't in the dining hall, washing the dishes with the others. She's in the cabin, packing up. Her duffle bag is finished, propped like an enormous canvas wiener against her bed; now she's doing her small suitcase. Her paycheck is already tucked inside: two hundred dollars, which is a lot of money.

Ronette comes into the cabin, still in her uniform, shutting the screen door quietly behind her. She sits down on Joanne's bed and lights a cigarette. Joanne is standing there with her folded-up flannelette pajamas, alert: something's going on. Lately, Ronette has returned to her previous taciturn self; her smiles have become rare. In the counselors' rec hall, Darce is again playing the field. He's been circling around Hilary, who's pretending—out of consideration for Ronette—not to notice. Maybe, now, Joanne will get to hear what caused the big split. So far Ronette has not said anything about it.

Ronette looks up at Joanne, through her long yellow bangs. Looking up like that makes her seem younger, despite the red lipstick. "I'm in trouble," she says.

"What sort of trouble?" says Joanne.

Ronette smiles sadly, blows out smoke. Now she looks old. "You know. Trouble."

"Oh," says Joanne. She sits down beside Ronette, hugging the flannelette pajamas. She feels cold. It must be Darce. *Caught in that sensual music.* Now he will have to marry her. Or something. "What're you going to do?"

"I don't know," says Ronette. "Don't tell, okay? Don't tell the others."

"Aren't you going to tell *him?*" says Joanne. She can't imagine doing that, herself. She can't imagine any of it.

"Tell who?" Ronette says.

"Darce."

Ronette blows out more smoke. "Darce," she says. "Mr. Chickenshit. It's not *his.*"

Joanne is astounded, and relieved. But also annoyed with herself: what's gone past her, what has she missed? "It's not? Then whose is it?"

But Ronette has apparently changed her mind about confiding. "That's for me to know and you to find out," she says, with a small attempt at a laugh.

"Well," says Joanne. Her hands are clammy, as if it's her that's in trouble. She wants to be helpful, but has no idea how. "Maybe you could—I don't know." She doesn't know. An abortion? That is a dark and mysterious word, connected with the States. You have to go away. It costs a lot of money. A home for unwed mothers, followed by adoption? Loss washes through her. She foresees Ronette, bloated beyond recognition, as if she's drowned—a sacrifice, captured by her own body, offered up to it. Truncated in some way, disgraced. Unfree. There is something nun-like about this condition. She is in awe. "I guess you could get rid of it, one way or another," she says; which is not at all what she feels. *Whatever is begotten, born, and dies.*

"Are you kidding?" says Ronette, with something like contempt. "Hell, not me." She throws her cigarette on the floor, grinds it out with her heel. "I'm keeping it. Don't worry, my mom will help me out."

"Yeah," says Joanne. Now she has caught her breath; now she's beginning to wonder why Ronette has dumped all this on her, especially since she isn't willing to tell the whole thing. She's beginning to feel cheated, imposed upon. So who's the guy, so which one of them? She shuffles through the faces of the counselors, trying to remember hints, traces of guilt, but finds nothing.

"Anyways," says Ronette, "I won't have to go back to school. Thank the Lord for small mercies, like they say."

Joanne hears bravado, and desolation. She reaches out a hand, gives Ronette's arm a small squeeze. "Good luck," she says. It comes out sounding like something you'd say before a race or an exam, or a war. It sounds stupid.

Ronette grins. The gap in her teeth shows, at the side. "Same to you," she says.

Eleven years later Donny is walking along Yorkville Avenue, in Toronto, in the summer heat. He's no longer Donny. At some point, which even he can't remember exactly, he has changed into Don. He's wearing sandals, and a white Indian-style shirt over his cut-off jeans. He has longish hair and a beard. The beard has come out yellow, whereas the hair is brown. He likes the effect: WASP Jesus or Hollywood Viking, depending on his mood. He has a string of wooden beads around his neck.

This is how he dresses on Saturdays, to go to Yorkville; to go there and just hang around, with the crowds of others who are doing the same. Sometimes he gets high, on the pot that circulates as freely as cigarettes did once. He thinks he should be enjoying this experience more than he actually does.

During the rest of the week he has a job in his father's law office. He can get away with the beard there, just barely, as long as he balances it with a suit. (But even the older guys are growing their sideburns and wearing colored shirts, and using words like "creative" more than they used to.) He doesn't tell the people he meets in Yorkville about this job, just as he doesn't tell the law office about his friends' acid trips. He's leading a double life. It feels precarious, and brave.

Suddenly, across the street, he sees Joanne. He hasn't even thought about her for a long time, but it's her all right. She isn't wearing the tie-dyed or flowing-shift uniform of the Yorkville girls; instead she's dressed in a brisk, businesslike white miniskirt, with matching suit-jacket top. She's swinging a briefcase, striding along as if she has a purpose. This makes her stand out: the accepted walk here is a saunter.

Donny wonders whether he should run across the street, intercept her, reveal what he thinks of as his true but secret identity. Now all he can see is her back. In a minute she'll be gone.

"Joanne," he calls. She doesn't hear him. He dodges between cars, catches up to her, touches her elbow. "Don Finley," he says. He's conscious of himself standing there, grinning like a fool. Luckily and a little disappointingly, she recognizes him at once.

"Donny!" she says. "My God, you've grown!"

"I'm taller than you," he says, like a kid, an idiot.

"You were then," she says, smiling. "I mean you've grown *up*."

"So have you," says Donny, and they find themselves laughing, almost like equals. Three years, four years between them. It was a large difference, then. Now it's nothing.

So, thinks Joanne, Donny is no longer Donny. That must mean Ritchie is now Richard. As for Monty, he has become initials only, and a millionaire. True, he inherited some of it, but he's used it to advantage; Joanne has tuned in on his exploits now and then, in the business papers. And he got married to Hilary, three years ago. Imagine that. She saw that in the paper too.

They go for coffee and sit drinking it at one of the new, daring, outside tables, under a large, brightly painted wooden parrot. There's an intimacy between them, as if they are old friends. Donny asks Joanne what she's doing. "I live by my wits," she says. "I freelance." At the moment she's writing ad copy. Her face is thinner, she's lost that adolescent roundness; her once nondescript hair has been shaped into a stylish cap.

Good enough legs too. You have to have good legs to wear a mini. So many women look stumpy in them, hams in cloth, their legs bulging out the bottom like loaves of white bread. Joanne's legs are out of sight under the table, but Donny finds himself dwelling on them as he never did when they were clearly visible, all the way up, on the waitresses' dock. He'd skimmed over those legs then, skimmed over Joanne altogether. It was Ronette who had held his attention. He is more of a connoisseur, by now.

"We used to spy on you," he says. "We used to watch you skinny-dipping." In fact they'd never managed to see much. The girls had held their towels around their bodies until the last minute, and anyway it was dusk. There would be a blur of white, some shrieking and splashing. The great thing would have been pubic hair. Several boys claimed sightings, but Donny had felt they were lying. Or was that just envy?

"Did you?" says Joanne absently. Then, "I know. We could see the bushes waving around. We thought it was so cute."

Donny feels himself blushing. He's glad he has the beard; it conceals things. "It wasn't cute," he says. "Actually we were pretty vicious." He's remembering the word *pork.* "Do you ever see the others?"

"Not anymore," says Joanne. "I used to see a few of them, at university. Hilary and Alex. Pat sometimes."

"What about Ronette?" he says, which is the only thing he really wants to ask.

"I used to see Darce," says Joanne, as if she hasn't heard him.

Used to see is an exaggeration. She saw him once.

It was in the winter, a February. He phoned her, at *The Varsity* office: that was how he knew where to find her, he'd seen her name in the campus paper. By that time Joanne scarcely remembered him. The summer she'd been a waitress was three years, light-years, away. The railroad-chef boyfriend was long gone; nobody so innocent had replaced him. She no longer wore white bucks, no longer sang songs. She wore turtlenecks and drank beer and a lot of coffee, and wrote cynical exposés of such things as the campus dining facilities. She'd given up the idea of dying young, however. By this time it seemed overly romantic.

What Darce wanted was to go out with her. Specifically, he wanted her to go to a fraternity party with him. Joanne was so taken aback that she said yes, even though fraternities were in political disfavor among the people she traveled with now. It was something she would have to do on the sly, and she did. She had to borrow a dress from her roommate, however. The thing was a semi-formal, and she had not deigned to go to a semi-formal since high school.

She had last seen Darce with sun-bleached hair and a deep glowing tan. Now, in his winter skin, he looked wan and malnourished. Also, he no longer flirted with everyone. He didn't even flirt with Joanne. Instead he introduced her to a few other couples, danced her perfunctorily around the floor, and proceeded to get very drunk on a mixture of grape juice and straight alcohol that the fraternity brothers called Purple Jesus. He told her he'd been engaged to Hilary for over six months, but she'd just ditched him. She wouldn't even say why. He said he'd asked Joanne out because she was the kind of girl you could talk to, he knew she would understand. After that he threw up a lot of Purple Jesus, first onto her dress, then—when she'd led him outside, to the veranda—onto a snowdrift. The color scheme was amazing.

Joanne got some coffee into him and hitched a lift back to the residence, where she had to climb up the icy fire escape and in at a window because it was after hours.

Joanne was hurt. All she was for him was a big flapping ear. Also she was irritated. The dress she'd borrowed was pale blue, and the Purple Jesus would not come out with just water. Darce called the next day to apologize—St. Jude's at least taught manners, of a sort—and Joanne stuck him with the cleaning bill. Even so there was a faint residual stain.

While they were dancing, before he started to slur and reel, she said, "Do you ever hear from Ronette?" She still had the narrative habit, she still wanted to know the ends of stories. But he'd looked at her in complete bewilderment.

"Who?" he said. It wasn't a put-down, he really didn't remember. She found this blank in his memory offensive. She herself might forget a name, a face even. But a body? A body that had been so close to your own, that had generated those murmurings, those rustlings in the darkness, that aching pain—it was an affront to bodies, her own included.

After the interview with Mr. B. and the stuffed pike's head, Donny walks down to the small beach where they do their laundry. The rest of his cabin is out sailing, but he's free now of camp routine, he's been discharged. A dishonorable discharge. After seven summers of being under orders here he can do what he wants. He has no idea what this might be.

He sits on a bulge of pink rock, feet on the sand. A lizard goes across the rock, near his hand, not fast. It hasn't spotted him. Its tail is blue and will come off if grabbed. Skinks, they're called. Once he would have taken joy from this knowledge. The waves wash in, wash out, the familiar heartbeat. He closes his eyes and hears only a machine. Possibly he is very angry, or sad. He hardly knows.

Ronette is there without warning. She must have come down the path behind him, through the trees. She's still in her uniform, although it isn't close to dinner. It's only late afternoon, when the waitresses usually leave their dock to go and change.

Ronette sits down beside him, takes out her cigarettes from some hidden pocket under her apron. "Want a cig?" she says.

Donny takes one and says "Thank you." Not *thanks,* not wordlessly like leather-jacketed men in movies, but "Thank you," like a good boy from St. Jude's, like a suck. He lets her light it. What else can he do? She's got the matches. Gingerly he inhales. He doesn't smoke much really, and is afraid of coughing.

"I heard they kicked you out," Ronette says. "That's really tough."

"It's okay," says Donny. "I don't care." He can't tell her why, how noble he's been. He hopes he won't cry.

"I heard you tossed Monty's binoculars," she says. "In the lake."

Donny can only nod. He glances at her. She's smiling; he can see the heartbreaking space at the side of her mouth: the missing tooth. She thinks he's funny.

"Well, I'm with you," she says. "He's a little creep."

"It wasn't because of him," says Donny, overcome by the need to confess, or to be taken seriously. "It was because of Darce." He turns, and for the first time looks her straight in the eyes. They are so green. Now his hands are shaking. He drops the cigarette into the sand. They'll find the butt tomorrow, after he's gone. After he's gone, leaving Ronette behind, at the mercy of other people's words. "It was because of you. What they were saying about you. Darce was."

Ronette isn't smiling anymore. "Such as what?" she says.

"Never mind," says Donny. "You don't want to know."

"I know anyhow," Ronette says. "That shit." She sounds resigned rather than angry. She stands up, puts both her hands behind her back. It takes Donny a moment to realize she's untying her apron. When she's got it off she takes him by the hand, pulls gently. He allows himself to be led around the hill of rock, out of sight of anything but the water. She sits down, lies down, smiles as she reaches up, arranges his hands. Her blue uniform unbuttons down the front. Donny can't believe this is happening, to him, in full daylight. It's like sleepwalking, it's like running too fast, it's like nothing else.

"Want another coffee?" Joanne says. She nods to the waitress. Donny hasn't heard her.

"She was really nice to me," he is saying. "Ronette. You know, when Mr. B. turfed me out. That meant a lot to me at the time." He's feeling guilty, because he never wrote her. He didn't know where she lived, but he didn't take any steps to find out. Also, he couldn't keep himself from thinking: *They're right. She's a slut.* Part of him had been profoundly shocked by what she'd done. He hadn't been ready for it.

Joanne is looking at him with her mouth slightly open, as if he's a talking dog, a talking stone. He fingers his beard nervously, wondering what he's said wrong, or given away.

Joanne has just seen the end of the story, or one end of one story. Or at least a missing piece. So that's why Ronette wouldn't tell: it was Donny. She'd been protecting him; or maybe she'd been protecting herself. A fourteen-year-old boy. Ludicrous.

Ludicrous then, possible now. You can do anything now and it won't cause a shock. Just a shrug. Everything is *cool.* A line has been drawn and on the other side of it is the past, both darker and more brightly intense than the present.

She looks across the line and sees the nine waitresses in their bathing suits, in the clear blazing sunlight, laughing on the dock, herself among them; and off in the shadowy rustling bushes of the shoreline, sex lurking dangerously. It had been dangerous, then. It had been sin. Forbidden, secret, sullying. *Sick with desire.* Three dots had expressed it perfectly, because there had been no ordinary words for it.

On the other hand there had been marriage, which meant wifely checked aprons, play-pens, a sugary safety.

But nothing has turned out that way. Sex has been domesticated, stripped of the promised mystery, added to the category of the merely expected. It's just what is done, mundane as hockey. It's celibacy these days that would raise eyebrows.

And what has become of Ronette, after all, left behind in the past, dappled by its chiaroscuro, stained and haloed by it, stuck with other people's adjectives? What is she doing, now that everyone else is following in her footsteps? More practically: did she have the baby, or not? Keep it or not? Donny, sitting sweetly across the table from her, is in all probability the father of a ten-year-old child, and he knows nothing about it at all.

Should she tell him? The melodrama tempts her, the idea of a revelation, a sensation, a neat ending.

But it would not be an ending, it would only be the beginning of something else. In any case, the story itself seems to her outmoded. It's an archaic story, a folk-tale, a mosaic artifact. It's a story that would never happen now.

James Baldwin (1924–1987)

was the grandson of a slave and the oldest of nine children, born of a father he never knew and raised by his mother and stepfather, a storefront preacher. Baldwin took his own place behind the pulpit of Harlem's Fireside Pentecostal Church at the age of fourteen, a formative experience not just for the man but for his writing as well, helping to forge a prose style that often had the cadence—as well as the righteous indignation and sense of moral urgency—of a revival meeting. His stepfather "was a righteous man in the pulpit," Baldwin once said, "and a monster in the house. . . . I've hated only one person and that was my father." After his stepfather died (in a mental hospital, on the author's nineteenth birthday), Baldwin abandoned first Christianity and soon thereafter the United States, moving to Paris, where he spent the better part of his life. In 1953, he published his first novel, Go Tell It on the Mountain, *which was an instant sensation. His impassioned essays made him an important and influential voice in the civil rights movement and, later in life, in the fight against discrimination toward gays and lesbians. In addition, he wrote six novels and two plays. Though he published only a single collection of short fiction,* Going to Meet the Man, *its masterpiece, "Sonny's Blues," is among the most widely admired and anthologized stories ever written.*

INTRODUCTION BY **Ben Neihart**

James Baldwin was an illegitimate eldest son born in 1924, a celebrated child preacher in Harlem, a homosexual, an expatriate member of Paris's artistic milieu, an insatiable reader. He was what the French call a "sauvage" (a more sophisticated version of what we Americans call a "party animal.") He was a world-famous novelist, essayist, and political activist. His influences were as varied as Henry James, the epicene 19th century novelist of consciousness, and the Black Panthers, who, in the 1960s, fought on socialist principles for the liberation of black people in the United States. So James Baldwin can teach you nothing about acquiring the raw materials, the personal biography you must mine to write your own compelling stories. He had his life; you have yours. You will have to call up your own heritage, your own obsessions and empathies, your own paternal instincts and ingrained artistic prejudices. Like Baldwin, you will have to engage with the past as passionately as you engage with the present.

In Baldwin's short stories, the past arrives unbidden in the present. Memories are an opportunity for characters to confront the choices they have made, and memories are an opportunity for Baldwin, the author, to ground background material in the current action of his story. In "Going to Meet the Man," Baldwin lets the past slowly fill the poisoned room where Jesse, a violently deranged white deputy sheriff, is telling his wife, Grace, about the day he's had, beating a jailed young black civil rights worker. With a film director's or poet's sense of when to cut a line and how to shift time, Baldwin uses a line of dialogue or the refrain of a song to pull the past forward. He cuts paragraphs like a frame of film, a foot of poetry. For instance, Jesse the sheriff, in bed, hears a song from his past that fills him with "an overwhelming fear, which yet contained a curious and dreadful pleasure."

The song is one he'd heard long ago, driving home with his family from a lynching, which Baldwin has described in such graphic detail that we glimpse the roots of Jesse's pathology. Not an explanation, the solution to a puzzle, but one searing scene that the reader shares with a monster before he became a monster.

To use the complicated effects in his arsenal, to shift time, to illuminate character without being limited by character, Baldwin needs a sophisticated instrument. His fictional voice combines a superarticulate, liturgical prose with casually devastating, infallibly realistic dialogue. It is a highly flexible voice that allows Baldwin to surround some of his characters with insights they would not themselves be able to articulate so clearly. For instance, when Florence, the uneducated daughter of a former slave in "Exodus," tells her sobbing mother that she is leaving the South and moving to New York, her dialogue is plain-spoken: "Ma, don't be like that. Ain't a blessed thing for you to cry about so. Ain't a thing can happen to me up North can't happen to me here. God's everywhere, Ma. Ain't no need to worry." But Baldwin does not stick to Florence's way of speaking when he delineates her thoughts: "She knew that she was mouthing words; and she realized suddenly that her mother scorned to dignify these words with her attention."

In his 1949 essay "Everybody's Protest Novel," Baldwin argued that he was under no obligation, as a black man, to create art that delineated a particular ideology. That was the job of a propagandist. The artist's job was to persuade readers that stories were full of real life, "this web of ambiguity, paradox, this hunger, danger, darkness." By making readers believe that a man is being killed before their eyes in "Going to Meet the Man," that a daughter will walk out on her feeble, sobbing mother in "Exodus," that two brothers will make peace with one another from across a crowded jazz club in "Sonny's Blues," Baldwin taps directly into the inner life—however humble, exalted, or poisoned—that turns a stereotype into a person.

"Sonny's Blues" is as close as you'll get to a fictional autobiography of Baldwin the artist. In its final moments, as one buttoned-up, "responsible" brother watches his artist brother play the piano onstage, the story explodes the cliché of the artist as an unknowable stranger. The artist is telling a story for everyone to listen to, he writes, and "while the tale of how we suffer, and how we are delighted, and how we may triumph is never new, it must always be heard. There isn't any other tale to tell, it's the only light we've got in all this darkness."

Ben Neihart is the author of two novels, Hey, Joe *and* Burning Girl, *and a work of nonfiction,* Rough Amusements. *His fiction has appeared in* The New Yorker, Nerve, Mississippi Review, *and elsewhere.*

JAMES BALDWIN

Sonny's Blues

I read about it in the paper, in the subway, on my way to work. I read it, and I couldn't believe it, and I read it again. Then perhaps I just stared at it, at the newsprint spelling out his name, spelling out the story. I stared at it in the swinging lights of the subway car, and in the faces and bodies of the people, and in my own face, trapped in the darkness which roared outside.

It was not to be believed and I kept telling myself that, as I walked from the subway station to the high school. And at the same time I couldn't doubt it. I was scared, scared for Sonny. He became real to me again. A great block of ice got settled in my belly and kept melting there slowly all day long, while I taught my classes algebra. It was a special kind of ice. It kept melting, sending trickles of ice water all up and down my veins, but it never got less. Sometimes it hardened and seemed to expand until I felt my guts were going to come spilling out or that I was going to choke or scream. This would always be at a moment when I was remembering some specific thing Sonny had once said or done.

When he was about as old as the boys in my classes his face had been bright and open, there was a lot of copper in it; and he'd had wonderfully direct brown eyes, and great gentleness and privacy. I wondered what he looked like now. He had been picked up, the evening before, in a raid on an apartment downtown, for peddling and using heroin.

I couldn't believe it: but what I mean by that is that I couldn't find any room for it anywhere inside me. I had kept it outside me for a long time. I hadn't wanted to know. I had had suspicions, but I didn't name them, I kept putting them away. I told myself that Sonny was wild, but he wasn't crazy. And he'd always been a good boy, he hadn't ever turned hard or evil or disrespectful, the way kids can, so quick, so quick, especially in Harlem. I didn't want to believe that I'd ever see my brother going down, coming to nothing, all that light in his face gone out, in the condition I'd already seen so many others. Yet it had happened and here I was, talking about algebra to a lot of boys who might, every one of them for all I knew, be popping off needles every time they went to the head. Maybe it did more for them than algebra could.

I was sure that the first time Sonny had ever had horse, he couldn't have been much older than these boys were now. These boys, now, were living as we'd been living then, they were growing up with a rush and their heads bumped abruptly against the low ceiling of their actual possibilities. They were filled with rage. All they really knew were two darknesses, the darkness of their lives, which was now closing in on them, and the darkness of the movies, which had blinded them to that other darkness, and in which they now, vindictively, dreamed, at once more together than they were at any other time, and more alone.

When the last bell rang, the last class ended, I let out my breath. It seemed I'd been holding it for all that time. My clothes were wet—I may have looked as though

I'd been sitting in a steam bath, all dressed up, all afternoon. I sat alone in the classroom a long time. I listened to the boys outside, downstairs, shouting and cursing and laughing. Their laughter struck me for perhaps the first time. It was not the joyous laughter which—God knows why—one associates with children. It was mocking and insular, its intent to denigrate. It was disenchanted, and in this, also, lay the authority of their curses. Perhaps I was listening to them because I was thinking about my brother and in them I heard my brother. And myself.

One boy was whistling a tune, at once very complicated and very simple, it seemed to be pouring out of him as though he were a bird, and it sounded very cool and moving through all that harsh, bright air, only just holding its own through all those other sounds.

I stood up and walked over to the window and looked down into the courtyard. It was the beginning of the spring and the sap was rising in the boys. A teacher passed through them every now and again, quickly, as though he or she couldn't wait to get out of that courtyard, to get those boys out of their sight and off their minds. I started collecting my stuff. I thought I'd better get home and talk to Isabel.

The courtyard was almost deserted by the time I got downstairs. I saw this boy standing in the shadow of a doorway, looking just like Sonny. I almost called his name. Then I saw that it wasn't Sonny, but somebody we used to know, a boy from around our block. He'd been Sonny's friend. He'd never been mine, having been too young for me, and, anyway, I'd never liked him. And now, even though he was a grown-up man, he still hung around that block, still spent hours on the street corners, was always high and raggy. I used to run into him from time to time and he'd often work around to asking me for a quarter or fifty cents. He always had some real good excuse, too, and I always gave it to him, I don't know why.

But now, abruptly, I hated him. I couldn't stand the way he looked at me, partly like a dog, partly like a cunning child. I wanted to ask him what the hell he was doing in the school courtyard.

He sort of shuffled over to me, and he said, "I see you got the papers. So you already know about it."

"You mean about Sonny? Yes, I already know about it. How come they didn't get you?"

He grinned. It made him repulsive and it also brought to mind what he'd looked like as a kid. "I wasn't there. I stay away from them people."

"Good for you." I offered him a cigarette and I watched him through the smoke. "You come all the way down here just to tell me about Sonny?"

"That's right." He was sort of shaking his head and his eyes looked strange, as though they were about to cross. The bright sun deadened his damp dark brown skin and it made his eyes look yellow and showed up the dirt in his kinked hair. He smelled funky. I moved a little away from him and I said, "Well, thanks. But I already know about it and I got to get home."

"I'll walk you a little ways," he said. We started walking. There were a couple of kids still loitering in the courtyard and one of them said goodnight to me and looked strangely at the boy beside me.

"What're you going to do?" he asked me. "I mean, about Sonny?"

"Look. I haven't seen Sonny for over a year. I'm not sure I'm going to do anything. Anyway, what the hell *can* I do?"

"That's right," he said quickly, "ain't nothing you can do. Can't much help old Sonny no more, I guess."

It was what I was thinking and so it seemed to me he had no right to say it.

"I'm surprised at Sonny, though," he went on—he had a funny way of talking, he looked straight ahead as though he were talking to himself—"I thought Sonny was a smart boy, I thought he was too smart to get hung."

"I guess he thought so too," I said sharply, "and that's how he got hung. And how about you? You're pretty goddamn smart, I bet."

Then he looked directly at me, just for a minute. "I ain't smart," he said. "If I was smart, I'd have reached for a pistol a long time ago."

"Look. Don't tell *me* your sad story, if it was up to me, I'd give you one." Then I felt guilty—guilty, probably, for never having supposed that the poor bastard *had* a story of his own, much less a sad one, and I asked, quickly, "What's going to happen to him now?"

He didn't answer this. He was off by himself some place. "Funny thing," he said, and from his tone we might have been discussing the quickest way to get to Brooklyn, "when I saw the papers this morning, the first thing I asked myself was if I had anything to do with it. I felt sort of responsible."

I began to listen more carefully. The subway station was on the corner, just before us, and I stopped. He stopped, too. We were in front of a bar and he ducked slightly, peering in, but whoever he was looking for didn't seem to be there. The juke box was blasting away with something black and bouncy and I half watched the barmaid as she danced her way from the juke box to her place behind the bar. And I watched her face as she laughingly responded to something someone said to her, still keeping time to the music. When she smiled one saw the little girl, one sensed the doomed, still-struggling woman beneath the battered face of the semi-whore.

"I never *give* Sonny nothing," the boy said finally, "but a long time ago I come to school high and Sonny asked me how it felt." He paused, I couldn't bear to watch him, I watched the barmaid, and I listened to the music which seemed to be causing the pavement to shake. "I told him it felt great." The music stopped, the barmaid paused and watched the juke box until the music began again. "It did."

All this was carrying me some place I didn't want to go. I certainly didn't want to know how it felt. It filled everything, the people, the houses, the music, the dark, quicksilver barmaid, with menace; and this menace was their reality.

"What's going to happen to him now?" I asked again.

"They'll send him away some place and they'll try to cure him." He shook his head. "Maybe he'll even think he's kicked the habit. Then they'll let him loose"—he gestured, throwing his cigarette into the gutter. "That's all."

"What do you mean, that's *all?*"

But I knew what he meant.

"I *mean,* that's *all.*" He turned his head and looked at me, pulling down the corners of his mouth. "Don't you know what I mean?" he asked, softly.

"How the hell *would* I know what you mean?" I almost whispered it, I don't know why.

"That's right," he said to the air, "how would *he* know what I mean?" He turned toward me again, patient and calm, and yet I somehow felt him shaking, shaking as though he were going to fall apart. I felt that ice in my guts again; the dread I'd felt all afternoon; and again I watched the barmaid, moving about the bar, washing glasses, and singing. "Listen. They'll let him out and then it'll just start all over again. That's what I mean."

"You mean—they'll let him out. And then he'll just start working his way back in again. You mean he'll never kick the habit. Is that what you mean?"

"That's right," he said, cheerfully. "*You* see what I mean."

"Tell me," I said at last, "why does he want to die? He must want to die, he's killing himself, why does he want to die?"

He looked at me in surprise. He licked his lips. "He don't want to die. He wants to live. Don't nobody want to die, ever."

Then I wanted to ask him—too many things. He could not have answered, or if he had, I could not have borne the answers. I started walking. "Well, I guess it's none of my business."

"It's going to be rough on old Sonny," he said. We reached the subway station. "This is your station?" he asked. I nodded. I took one step down. "Damn!" he said, suddenly. I looked up at him. He grinned again. "Damn it if I didn't leave all my money home. You ain't got a dollar on you, have you? Just for a couple of days, is all."

All at once something inside gave and threatened to come pouring out of me. I didn't hate him any more. I felt that in another moment I'd start crying like a child.

"Sure," I said. "Don't sweat." I looked in my wallet and didn't have a dollar, I only had a five. "Here," I said. "That hold you?"

He didn't look at it—he didn't want to look at it. A terrible closed look came over his face, as though he were keeping the number on the bill a secret from him and me. "Thanks," he said, and now he was dying to see me go. "Don't worry about Sonny. Maybe I'll write him or something."

"Sure," I said. "You do that. So long."

"Be seeing you," he said. I went on down the steps.

And I didn't write Sonny or send him anything for a long time. When I finally did it was just after my little girl died, he wrote me back a letter which made me feel like a bastard.

Here's what he said:

Dear brother,

> You don't know how much I needed to hear from you. I wanted to write you many a time but I dug how much I must have hurt you and so I didn't write. But now I feel like a man who's been trying to climb up out of some deep, real deep and funky hole and just saw the sun up there, outside. I got to get outside.
>
> I can't tell you much about how I got here. I mean I don't know how to tell you. I guess I was afraid of something or I was trying to escape from something and you know I have never been very strong in the head (smile). I'm glad Mama and Daddy are dead and can't see what's happened to their son and I swear if I'd known what I was doing I would never have hurt you so, you and a lot of other fine people who were nice to me and who believed in me.
>
> I don't want you to think it had anything to do with me being a musician. It's more than that. Or maybe less than that. I can't get anything straight in my head down here and I try not to think about what's going to happen to me when I get outside again. Sometime I think I'm going to flip and *never* get outside and

sometime I think I'll come straight back. I tell you one thing, though, I'd rather blow my brains out than go through this again. But that's what they all say, so they tell me. If I tell you when I'm coming to New York and if you could meet me, I sure would appreciate it. Give my love to Isabel and the kids and I was sure sorry to hear about little Gracie. I wish I could be like Mama and say the Lord's will be done, but I don't know it seems to me that trouble is the one thing that never does get stopped and I don't know what good it does to blame it on the Lord. But maybe it does some good if you believe it.

Your brother,
Sonny

Then I kept in constant touch with him and I sent him whatever I could and went to meet him when he came back to New York. When I saw him many things I thought I had forgotten came flooding back to me. This was because I had begun, finally, to wonder about Sonny, about the life that Sonny lived inside. This life, whatever it was, had made him older and thinner and it had deepened the distant stillness in which he had always moved. He looked very unlike my baby brother. Yet, when he smiled, when we shook hands, the baby brother I'd never known looked out from the depths of his private life, like an animal waiting to be coaxed into the light.

"How you been keeping?" he asked me.

"All right. And you?"

"Just fine." He was smiling all over his face. "It's good to see you again."

"It's good to see you."

The seven years' difference in our ages lay between us like a chasm: I wondered if these years would ever operate between us as a bridge. I was remembering, and it made it hard to catch my breath, that I had been there when he was born; and I had heard the first words he had ever spoken. When he started to walk, he walked from our mother straight to me. I caught him just before he fell when he took the first steps he ever took in this world.

"How's Isabel?"

"Just fine. She's dying to see you."

"And the boys?"

"They're fine, too. They're anxious to see their uncle."

"Oh, come on. You know they don't remember me."

"Are you kidding? Of course they remember you."

He grinned again. We got into a taxi. We had a lot to say to each other, far too much to know how to begin.

As the taxi began to move, I asked, "You still want to go to India?"

He laughed. "You still remember that. Hell, no. This place is Indian enough for me."

"It used to belong to them," I said.

And he laughed again. "They damn sure knew what they were doing when they got rid of it."

Years ago, when he was around fourteen, he'd been all hipped on the idea of going to India. He read books about people sitting on rocks, naked, in all kinds of weather, but mostly bad, naturally, and walking barefoot through hot coals and arriving at wisdom. I used to say that it sounded to me as though they were getting away from wisdom as fast as they could. I think he sort of looked down on me for that.

"Do you mind," he asked, "if we have the driver drive alongside the park? On the west side—I haven't seen the city in so long."

"Of course not," I said. I was afraid that I might sound as though I were humoring him, but I hoped he wouldn't take it that way.

So we drove along, between the green of the park and the stony, lifeless elegance of hotels and apartment buildings, toward the vivid, killing streets of our childhood. These streets hadn't changed, though housing projects jutted up out of them now like rocks in the middle of a boiling sea. Most of the houses in which we had grown up had vanished, as had the stores from which we had stolen, the basements in which we had first tried sex, the rooftops from which we had hurled tin cans and bricks. But houses exactly like the houses of our past yet dominated the landscape, boys exactly like the boys we once had been found themselves smothering in these houses, came down into the streets for light and air and found themselves encircled by disaster. Some escaped the trap, most didn't. Those who got out always left something of themselves behind, as some animals amputate a leg and leave it in the trap. It might be said, perhaps, that I had escaped, after all, I was a school teacher; or that Sonny had, he hadn't lived in Harlem for years. Yet, as the cab moved uptown through streets which seemed, with a rush, to darken with dark people, and as I covertly studied Sonny's face, it came to me that what we both were seeking through our separate cab windows was that part of ourselves which had been left behind. It's always at the hour of trouble and confrontation that the missing member aches.

We hit 110th Street and started rolling up Lenox Avenue. And I'd known this avenue all my life, but it seemed to me again, as it had seemed on the day I'd first heard about Sonny's trouble, filled with a hidden menace which was its very breath of life.

"We almost there," said Sonny.

"Almost." We were both too nervous to say anything more.

We live in a housing project. It hasn't been up long. A few days after it was up it seemed uninhabitably new, now, of course, it's already rundown. It looks like a parody of the good, clean, faceless life—God knows the people who live in it do their best to make it a parody. The beat-looking grass lying around isn't enough to make their lives green, the hedges will never hold out the streets, and they know it. The big windows fool no one, they aren't big enough to make space out of no space. They don't bother with the windows, they watch the TV screen instead. The playground is most popular with the children who don't play at jacks, or skip rope, or roller skate, or swing, and they can be found in it after dark. We moved in partly because it's not too far from where I teach, and partly for the kids; but it's really just like the houses in which Sonny and I grew up. The same things happen, they'll have the same things to remember. The moment Sonny and I started into the house I had the feeling that I was simply bringing him back into the danger he had almost died trying to escape.

Sonny has never been talkative. So I don't know why I was sure he'd be dying to talk to me when supper was over the first night. Everything went fine, the oldest boy remembered him, and the youngest boy liked him, and Sonny had remembered to bring something for each of them; and Isabel, who is really much nicer than I am, more open and giving, had gone to a lot of trouble about dinner and was genuinely glad to see him. And she's always been able to tease Sonny in a way that I haven't. It was nice to see her face so vivid again and to hear her laugh and watch her make Sonny laugh. She wasn't, or, anyway, she didn't seem to be, at all uneasy or embarrassed. She chatted as though there were no subject which had to be avoided and she got Sonny past his first, faint stiffness. And thank God she was there, for I was filled with that icy dread again. Everything I did seemed awkward to me, and everything I said sounded freighted with hidden meaning. I was trying to remember everything I'd heard about dope addiction and I couldn't help watching Sonny for signs. I wasn't doing it out of malice. I was trying to find out something about my brother. I was dying to hear him tell me he was safe.

"Safe!" my father grunted, whenever Mama suggested trying to move to a neighborhood which might be safer for children. "Safe, hell! Ain't no place safe for kids, nor nobody."

He always went on like this, but he wasn't, ever, really as bad as he sounded, not even on weekends, when he got drunk. As a matter of fact, he was always on the lookout for "something a little better," but he died before he found it. He died suddenly, during a drunken weekend in the middle of the war, when Sonny was fifteen. He and Sonny hadn't ever got on too well. And this was partly because Sonny was the apple of his father's eye. It was because he loved Sonny so much and was frightened for him, that he was always fighting with him. It doesn't do any good to fight with Sonny. Sonny just moves back, inside himself, where he can't be reached. But the principal reason that they never hit it off is that they were so much alike. Daddy was big and rough and loud-talking, just the opposite of Sonny, but they both had—that same privacy.

Mama tried to tell me something about this, just after Daddy died. I was home on leave from the army.

This was the last time I ever saw my mother alive. Just the same, this picture gets all mixed up in my mind with pictures I had of her when she was younger. The way I always see her is the way she used to be on a Sunday afternoon, say, when the old folks were talking after the big Sunday dinner. I always see her wearing pale blue. She'd be sitting on the sofa. And my father would be sitting in the easy chair, not far from her. And the living room would be full of church folks and relatives. There they sit, in chairs all around the living room, and the night is creeping up outside, but nobody knows it yet. You can see the darkness growing against the windowpanes and you hear the street noises every now and again, or maybe the jangling beat of a tambourine from one of the churches close by, but it's real quiet in the room. For a moment nobody's talking, but every face looks darkening, like the sky outside. And my mother rocks a little from the waist, and my father's eyes are closed. Everyone is looking at something a child can't see. For a minute they've forgotten the children. Maybe a kid is lying on the rug, half asleep. Maybe somebody's got a kid in his lap and is absent-mindedly stroking the kid's head. Maybe there's a kid, quiet and big-eyed, curled up in a big chair in the corner. The silence, the darkness coming, and the darkness in the faces frightens the child obscurely. He hopes that the hand which strokes his forehead will never stop—will never die. He hopes that there will never come a time when the old folks won't be sitting around the living room, talking about where they've come from, and what they've seen, and what's happened to them and their kinfolk.

But something deep and watchful in the child knows that this is bound to end, is already ending. In a moment someone will get up and turn on the light. Then the old folks will remember the children and they won't talk any more that day. And when light fills the room, the child is filled with darkness. He knows that every time this happens he's moved just a little closer to that darkness outside. The darkness outside is what the old folks have been talking about. It's what they've come from. It's what they endure. The child knows that they won't talk any more because if he knows too much about what's happened to *them,* he'll know too much too soon, about what's going to happen to *him.*

The last time I talked to my mother, I remember I was restless. I wanted to get out and see Isabel. We weren't married then and we had a lot to straighten out between us.

There Mama sat, in black, by the window. She was humming an old church song, *Lord, you brought me from a long ways off.* Sonny was out somewhere. Mama kept watching the streets.

"I don't know," she said, "if I'll ever see you again, after you go off from here. But I hope you'll remember the things I tried to teach you."

"Don't talk like that," I said, and smiled. "You'll be here a long time yet."

She smiled, too, but she said nothing. She was quiet for a long time. And I said, "Mama, don't you worry about nothing. I'll be writing all the time, and you be getting the checks. . . ."

"I want to talk to you about your brother," she said, suddenly. "If anything happens to me he ain't going to have nobody to look out for him."

"Mama," I said, "ain't nothing going to happen to you or Sonny. Sonny's all right. He's a good boy and he's got good sense."

"It ain't a question of his being a good boy," Mama said, "nor of his having good sense. It ain't only the bad ones, nor yet the dumb ones that gets sucked under." She stopped, looking at me. "Your Daddy once had a brother," she said, and she smiled in a way that made me feel she was in pain. "You didn't never know that, did you?"

"No," I said, "I never knew that," and I watched her face.

"Oh, yes," she said, "your Daddy had a brother." She looked out of the window again. "I know you never saw your Daddy cry. But *I* did—many a time, through all these years."

I asked her, "What happened to his brother? How come nobody's ever talked about him?"

This was the first time I ever saw my mother look old.

"His brother got killed," she said, "when he was just a little younger than you are now. I knew him. He was a fine boy. He was maybe a little full of the devil, but he didn't mean nobody no harm."

Then she stopped and the room was silent, exactly as it had sometimes been on those Sunday afternoons. Mama kept looking out into the streets.

"He used to have a job in the mill," she said, "and, like all young folks, he just liked to perform on Saturday nights. Saturday nights, him and your father would drift around to different places, go to dances and things like that, or just sit around with people they knew, and your father's brother would sing, he had a fine voice, and play along with himself on his guitar. Well, this particular Saturday night, him and your father was coming home from some place, and they were both a little drunk and there was a moon that night, it was bright like day. Your father's brother was feeling kind of good, and he was whistling to himself, and he had his guitar slung over his shoulder. They was coming down a hill and beneath them was a road that turned off from the highway. Well, your father's brother, being always kind of frisky, decided to run down this hill, and he did, with that guitar banging and clanging behind him, and he ran across the road, and he was making water behind a tree. And your father was sort of amused at him and he was still coming down the hill, kind of slow. Then he heard a car motor and that same minute his brother stepped from behind the tree, into the road, in the moonlight. And he started to cross the road. And your father started to run down the hill, he says he don't know why. This car was full of white men. They was all drunk, and when they seen your father's brother they let out a great whoop and holler and they aimed the car straight at him. They was having fun, they just wanted to scare him, the way they do sometimes, you know. But they was drunk. And I guess the boy, being drunk, too, and scared, kind of lost his head. By the time he jumped it was too late. Your father says he heard his brother scream when the car rolled over him, and he heard the wood of that guitar when it give, and he heard them strings go flyng, and he heard them white men shouting, and the car kept on a-going and it ain't stopped till this day. And, time your father got down the hill, his brother weren't nothing but blood and pulp."

Tears were gleaming on my mother's face. There wasn't anything I could say.

"He never mentioned it," she said, "because I never let him mention it before you children. Your Daddy was like a crazy man that night and for many a night thereafter. He says he never in his life seen anything as dark as that road after the lights of that car had gone away. Weren't nothing, weren't nobody on that road, just your Daddy and his brother and that busted guitar. Oh, yes. Your Daddy never did really get right again. Till the day he died he weren't sure but that every white man he saw was the man that killed his brother."

She stopped and took out her handkerchief and dried her eyes and looked at me.

"I ain't telling you all this," she said, "to make you scared or bitter or to make you hate nobody. I'm telling you this because you got a brother. And the world ain't changed."

I guess I didn't want to believe this. I guess she saw this in my face. She turned away from me, toward the window again, searching those streets.

"But I praise my Redeemer," she said at last, "that He called your Daddy home before me. I ain't saying it to throw no flowers at myself, but, I declare, it keeps me from feeling too cast down to know I helped your father get safely through this world. Your father always acted like he was the roughest, strongest man on earth. And everybody took him to be like that. But if he hadn't had *me* there—to see his tears!"

She was crying again. Still, I couldn't move. I said, "Lord, Lord, Mama, I didn't know it was like that."

"Oh, honey," she said, "there's a lot that you don't know. But you are going to find it out." She stood up from the window and came over to me. "You got to hold on to your brother," she said, "and don't let him fall, no matter what it looks like is happening to him and no matter how evil you gets with him. You going to be evil with him many a time. But don't you forget what I told you, you hear?"

"I won't forget," I said. "Don't you worry, I won't forget. I won't let nothing happen to Sonny."

My mother smiled as though she were amused at something she saw in my face. Then, "You may not be able to stop nothing from happening. But you got to let him know you's *there.*"

★ ★ ★

Two days later I was married, and then I was gone. And I had a lot of things on my mind and I pretty well forgot my promise to Mama until I got shipped home on a special furlough for her funeral.

And, after the funeral, with just Sonny and me alone in the empty kitchen, I tried to find out something about him.

"What do you want to do?" I asked him.

"I'm going to be a musician," he said.

For he had graduated, in the time I had been away, from dancing to the juke box to finding out who was playing what, and what they were doing with it, and he had bought himself a set of drums.

"You mean, you want to be a drummer?" I somehow had the feeling that being a drummer might be all right for other people but not for my brother Sonny.

"I don't think," he said, looking at me very gravely, "that I'll ever be a good drummer. But I think I can play a piano."

I frowned. I'd never played the role of the older brother quite so seriously before, had scarcely ever, in fact, *asked* Sonny a damn thing. I sensed myself in the presence of something I didn't really know how to handle, didn't understand. So I made my frown a little deeper as I asked: "What kind of musician do you want to be?"

He grinned. "How many kinds do you think there are?"

"Be serious," I said.

He laughed, throwing his head back, and then looked at me. "I am serious."

"Well, then, for Christ's sake, stop kidding around and answer a serious question. I mean, do you want to be a concert pianist, you want to play classical music and all that, or—or what?" Long before I finished he was laughing again. "For Christ's *sake,* Sonny!"

He sobered, but with difficulty. "I'm sorry. But you sound so—*scared!*" and he was off again.

"Well, you may think it's funny now, baby, but it's not going to be so funny when you have to make your living at it, let me tell you *that.*" I was furious because I knew he was laughing at me and I didn't know why.

"No," he said, very sober now, and afraid, perhaps, that he'd hurt me, "I don't want to be a classical pianist. That isn't what interests me. I mean"—he paused, looking hard at me, as though his eyes would help me to understand, and then gestured helplessly, as though perhaps his hand would help—"I mean, I'll have a lot of studying to do, and I'll have to study *everything,* but, I mean, I want to play *with*—jazz musicians." He stopped. "I want to play jazz," he said.

Well, the word had never before sounded as heavy, as real, as it sounded that afternoon in Sonny's mouth. I just looked at him and I was probably frowning a real frown by this time. I simply couldn't see why on earth he'd want to spend his time hanging around nightclubs, clowning around on bandstands, while people pushed each other around a dance floor. It seemed—beneath him, somehow. I had never thought about it before, had never been forced to, but I suppose I had always put jazz musicians in a class with what Daddy called "good-time people."

"Are you *serious?*"

"Hell, *yes,* I'm serious."

He looked more helpless than ever, and annoyed, and deeply hurt.

I suggested, helpfully: "You mean—like Louis Armstrong?"

His face closed as though I'd struck him. "No. I'm not talking about none of that old-time, down home crap."

"Well, look, Sonny, I'm sorry, don't get mad. I just don't altogether get it, that's all. Name somebody—you know, a jazz musician you admire."

"Bird."

"Who?"

"Bird! Charlie Parker! Don't they teach you nothing in the goddamn army?"

I lit a cigarette. I was surprised and then a little amused to discover that I was trembling. "I've been out of touch," I said. "You'll have to be patient with me. Now. Who's this Parker character?"

"He's just one of the greatest jazz musicians alive," said Sonny, sullenly, his hands in his pockets, his back to me. "Maybe *the* greatest," he added, bitterly, "that's probably why you never heard of him.

"All right," I said, "I'm ignorant. I'm sorry. I'll go out and buy all the cat's records right away, all right?"

"It don't," said Sonny, with dignity, "make any difference to me. I don't care what you listen to. Don't do me no favors."

I was beginning to realize that I'd never seen him so upset before. With another part of my mind I was thinking that this would probably turn out to be one of those things kids go through and that I shouldn't make it seem important by pushing it too hard. Still, I didn't think it would do any harm to ask: "Doesn't all this take a lot of time? Can you make a living at it?"

He turned back to me and half leaned, half sat, on the kitchen table. "Everything takes time," he said, "and—well, yes, sure, I can make a living at it. But what I don't seem to be able to make you understand is that it's the only thing I want to do."

"Well, Sonny," I said, gently, "you know people can't always do exactly what they *want* to do—"

"*No,* I don't know that," said Sonny, surprising me. "I think people ought to do what they want to do, what else are they alive for?"

"You getting to be a big boy," I said desperately, "it's time you started thinking about your future."

"I'm thinking about my future," said Sonny, grimly. "I think about it all the time."

I gave up. I decided, if he didn't change his mind, that we could always talk about it later. "In the meantime," I said, "you got to finish school." We had already decided that he'd have to move in with Isabel and her folks. I knew this wasn't the ideal arrangement because Isabel's folks are inclined to be dicty and they hadn't especially wanted Isabel to marry me. But I didn't know what else to do. "And we have to get you fixed up at Isabel's."

There was a long silence. He moved from the kitchen table to the window. "That's a terrible idea. You know it yourself."

"Do you have a *better* idea?"

He just walked up and down the kitchen for a minute. He was as tall as I was. He had started to shave. I suddenly had the feeling that I didn't know him at all.

He stopped at the kitchen table and picked up my cigarettes. Looking at me with a kind of mocking, amused defiance, he put one between his lips. "You mind?"

"You smoking already?"

He lit the cigarette and nodded, watching me through the smoke. "I just wanted to see if I'd have the courage to smoke in front of you." He grinned and blew a great cloud of smoke to the ceiling. "It was easy." He looked at my face. "Come on, now. I bet you was smoking at my age, tell the truth."

I didn't say anything but the truth was on my face, and he laughed. But now there was something very strained in his laugh. "Sure. And I bet that ain't all you was doing."

He was frightening me a little. "Cut the crap," I said. "We already decided that you was going to go and live at Isabel's. Now what's got into you all of a sudden?"

"*You* decided it," he pointed out. "*I* didn't decide nothing." He stopped in front of me, leaning against the stove, arms loosely folded. "Look, brother. I don't want to stay in Harlem no more, I really don't." He was very earnest. He looked at me, then over toward the kitchen window. There was something in his eyes I'd never seen before, some thoughtfulness, some worry all his own. He rubbed the muscle of one arm. "It's time I was getting out of here."

"Where do you want to *go,* Sonny?"

"I want to join the army. Or the navy, I don't care. If I say I'm old enough, they'll believe me."

Then I got mad. It was because I was so scared. "You must be crazy. You goddamn fool, what the hell do you want to go and join the *army* for?"

"I just told you. To get out of Harlem."

"Sonny, you haven't even finished *school.* And if you really want to be a musician, how do you expect to study if you're in the *army?*"

He looked at me, trapped, and in anguish. "There's ways. I might be able to work out some kind of deal. Anyway, I'll have the G.I. Bill when I come out."

"*If* you come out." We stared at each other. "Sonny, please. Be reasonable. I know the setup is far from perfect. But we got to do the best we can."

"I ain't learning nothing in school," he said. "Even when I go." He turned away from me and opened the window and threw his cigarette out into the narrow alley. I watched his back. "At least, I ain't learning nothing you'd want me to learn." He slammed the window so hard I thought the glass would fly out, and turned back to me. "And I'm sick of the stink of these garbage cans!"

"Sonny," I said, "I know how you feel. But if you don't finish school now, you're going to be sorry later that you didn't." I grabbed him by the shoulders. "And you only got another year. It ain't so bad. And I'll come back and I swear I'll help you do *whatever* you want to do. Just try to put up with it till I come back. Will you please do that? For me?"

He didn't answer and he wouldn't look at me.

"Sonny. You hear me?"

He pulled away. "I hear you. But you never hear anything I say."

I didn't know what to say to that. He looked out of the window and then back at me. "OK," he said, and sighed. "I'll try."

Then I said, trying to cheer him up a little, "They got a piano at Isabel's. You can practice on it."

And as a matter of fact, it did cheer him up for a minute. "That's right," he said to himself. "I forgot that." His face relaxed a little. But the worry, the thoughtfulness, played on it still, the way shadows play on a face which is staring into the fire.

But I thought I'd never hear the end of that piano. At first, Isabel would write me, saying how nice it was that Sonny was so serious about his music and how, as soon as he came in from school, or wherever he had been when he was supposed to be at school, he went straight to that piano and stayed there until suppertime. And, after supper, he went back to that piano and stayed there until everybody went to bed. He was at the piano all day Saturday and all day Sunday. Then he bought a record player and started playing records. He'd play one record over and over again, all day long sometimes, and he'd improvise along with it on the piano. Or he'd play one section of the record, one chord, one change, one progression, then he'd do it on the piano. Then back to the record. Then back to the piano.

Well, I really don't know how they stood it. Isabel finally confessed that it wasn't like living with a person at all, it was like living with sound. And the sound didn't make any sense to her, didn't make any sense to any of them—naturally. They began, in a way, to be afflicted by this presence that was living in their home. It was as though Sonny were some sort of god, or monster. He moved in an atmosphere which wasn't like theirs at all. They fed him and he ate, he washed himself, he walked in and out of their door; he certainly wasn't nasty or unpleasant or rude, Sonny isn't any of those things; but it was as though he were all wrapped up in some cloud, some fire, some vision all his own; and there wasn't any way to reach him.

At the same time, he wasn't really a man yet, he was still a child, and they had to watch out for him in all kinds of ways. They certainly couldn't throw him out. Neither did they dare to make a great scene about that piano because even they dimly sensed, as I sensed, from so many thousands of miles away, that Sonny was at that piano playing for his life.

But he hadn't been going to school. One day a letter came from the school board and Isabel's mother got it—there had, apparently, been other letters but Sonny had torn them up. This day, when Sonny came in, Isabel's mother showed him the letter and asked where he'd been spending his time. And she finally got it out of him that he'd been down in Greenwich Village, with musicians and other characters, in a white girl's apartment. And this scared her and she started to scream at him and what came up, once she began—though she denies it to this day—was what sacrifices they were making to give Sonny a decent home and how little he appreciated it.

Sonny didn't play the piano that day. By evening, Isabel's mother had calmed down but then there was the old man to deal with, and Isabel herself. Isabel says she did her best to be calm but she broke down and started crying. She says she just watched Sonny's face. She could tell, by watching him, what was happening with him. And what was happening was that they penetrated his cloud, they had reached him. Even if their fingers had been a thousand times more gentle than human fingers ever are, he could hardly help feeling that they had stripped him naked and were spitting on that nakedness. For he also had to see that his presence, that music, which was life or death to him, had been torture for them and that they had endured it, not at all for his sake, but only for mine. And Sonny couldn't take that. He can take it a little better today than he could then but he's still not very good at it and, frankly, I don't know anybody who is.

The silence of the next few days must have been louder than the sound of all the music ever played since time began. One morning, before she went to work, Isabel was in his room for something and she suddenly realized that all of his records were gone. And she knew for certain that he was gone. And he was. He went as far as the navy would carry him. He finally sent me a postcard from some place in Greece and that was the first I knew that Sonny was still alive. I didn't see him any more until we were both back in New York and the war had long been over.

He was a man by then, of course, but I wasn't willing to see it. He came by the house from time to time, but we fought almost every time we met. I didn't like the way he carried himself, loose and dreamlike all the time, and I didn't like his friends, and his music seemed to be merely an excuse for the life he led. It sounded just that weird and disordered.

Then we had a fight, a pretty awful fight, and I didn't see him for months. By and by I looked him up, where he was living, in a furnished room in the Village, and I tried to make it up. But there were lots of people in the room and Sonny just lay on his bed, and he wouldn't come downstairs with me, and he treated these other people as though they were his family and I weren't. So I got mad and then he got mad, and then I told him that he might just as well be dead as live the way he was living. Then he stood up and he told me not to worry about him any more in life, that he was dead as far as I was concerned. Then he pushed me to the door and the other people looked on as though nothing were happening, and he slammed the door behind me. I stood in the hallway, staring at the door. I heard somebody laugh in the room and then the tears came to my eyes. I started down the steps, whistling to keep from crying, I kept whistling to myself, *You going to need me, baby, one of these cold, rainy days.*

I read about Sonny's trouble in the spring. Little Grace died in the fall. She was a beautiful little girl. But she only lived a little over two years. She died of polio and she suffered. She had a slight fever for a couple of days, but it didn't seem like anything and we just kept her in bed. And we would certainly have called the doctor, but the fever dropped, she seemed to be all right. So we thought it had just been a cold. Then, one day, she was up, playing, Isabel was in the kitchen fixing lunch for the two boys when they'd come in from school, and she heard Grace fall down in the living room. When you have a lot of children you don't always start running when one of them falls, unless they start screaming or something. And, this time, Grace was quiet. Yet, Isabel says that when she heard that thump and then that silence, something happened in her to make her afraid. And she ran to the living room and there was little Grace on the floor, all twisted up, and the reason she hadn't screamed was that she couldn't get her breath. And when she did scream, it was the worst sound, Isabel says, that she'd ever heard in all her life, and she still hears it sometimes in her dreams. Isabel will sometimes wake me up with a low, moaning, strangled sound and I have to be quick to awaken her and hold her to me and where Isabel is weeping against me seems a mortal wound.

I think I may have written Sonny the very day that little Grace was buried. I was sitting in the living room in the dark, by myself, and I suddenly thought of Sonny. My trouble made his real.

One Saturday afternoon, when Sonny had been living with us, or, anyway, been in our house, for nearly two weeks, I found myself wandering aimlessly about the living room, drinking from a can of beer, and trying to work up the courage to search Sonny's room. He was out, he was usually out whenever I was home, and Isabel had taken the children to see their grandparents. Suddenly I was standing still in front of the living room window, watching Seventh Avenue. The idea of searching Sonny's room made me still. I scarcely dared to admit to myself what I'd be searching for. I didn't know what I'd do if I found it. Or if I didn't.

On the sidewalk across from me, near the entrance to a barbecue joint, some people were holding an old-fashioned revival meeting. The barbecue cook, wearing a dirty white apron, his conked hair reddish and metallic in the pale sun, and a cigarette between his lips, stood in the doorway, watching them. Kids and older people paused in their errands and stood there, along with some older men and a couple of very tough-looking women who watched everything that happened on the avenue, as though they owned it, or were maybe owned by it. Well, they were watching this, too. The revival was being carried on by three sisters in black, and a brother. All they had were their voices and their Bibles and a tambourine. The brother was testifying and while he testified two of the sisters stood together, seeming to say, amen, and the third sister walked around with the tambourine outstretched and a couple of people dropped coins into it. Then the brother's testimony ended and the sister who had been taking up the collection dumped the coins into her palm and transferred them to the pocket of her long black robe. Then she raised both hands, striking the tambourine against the air, and then against one hand, and she started to sing. And the two other sisters and the brother joined in.

It was strange, suddenly, to watch, though I had been seeing these street meetings all my life. So, of course, had everybody else down there. Yet, they paused and watched and listened and I stood still at the window. *"Tis the old ship of Zion,"* they sang, and the sister with the tambourine kept a steady, jangling beat, *"it has rescued many a thousand!"* Not a soul under the sound of their voices was hearing this song for the first time, not one of them had been rescued. Nor had they seen much in the way of rescue work being done around them. Neither did they especially believe in the holiness of the three sisters and the brother, they knew too much about them, knew where they lived, and how. The woman with the tambourine, whose voice dominated the air, whose face was bright with joy, was divided by very little from the woman who stood watching her, a cigarette between her heavy, chapped lips, her hair a cuckoo's nest, her face scarred and swollen from many beatings, and her black eyes glittering like coal. Perhaps they both knew this, which was why, when, as rarely, they addressed each other, they addressed each other as Sister. As the singing filled the air the watching, listening faces underwent a change, the eyes focusing on something within; the music seemed to soothe a poison out of them; and time seemed, nearly, to fall away from the sullen, belligerent, battered faces, as though they were fleeing back to their first condition, while dreaming of their last. The barbecue cook half shook his head and smiled, and dropped his cigarette and disappeared into his joint. A man fumbled in his pockets for change and stood holding it in his hand impatiently, as though he had just remembered a pressing appointment further up the avenue. He looked furious. Then I saw Sonny, standing on the edge of the crowd. He was carrying a wide, flat notebook with a green cover, and it made him look, from where I was standing, almost like a schoolboy. The coppery sun brought out the copper in his skin, he was very faintly smiling, standing very still. Then the singing stopped, the tambourine turned into a collection plate again. The furious man dropped in his coins and vanished, so did a couple of the women, and Sonny dropped some change in the plate, looking directly at the woman with a little smile. He started across the avenue, toward the house. He has a slow, loping walk, something like the way Harlem hipsters walk, only he's imposed on this his own half-beat. I had never really noticed it before.

I stayed at the window, both relieved and apprehensive. As Sonny disappeared from my sight, they began singing again. And they were still singing when his key turned in the lock.

"Hey," he said.

"Hey, yourself. You want some beer?"

"No. Well, maybe." But he came up to the window and stood beside me, looking out. "What a warm voice," he said.

They were singing *If I could only hear my mother pray again!*

"Yes," I said, "and she can sure beat that tambourine."

"But what a terrible song," he said, and laughed. He dropped his notebook on the sofa and disappeared into the kitchen. "Where's Isabel and the kids?"

"I think they went to see their grandparents. You hungry?"

"No." He came back into the living room with his can of beer. "You want to come some place with me tonight?"

I sensed, I don't know how, that I couldn't possibly say no. "Sure. Where?"

He sat down on the sofa and picked up his notebook and started leafing through it. "I'm going to sit in with some fellows in a joint in the Village."

"You mean, you're going to play, tonight?"

"That's right." He took a swallow of his beer and moved back to the window. He gave me a sidelong look. "If you can stand it."

"I'll try," I said.

He smiled to himself and we both watched as the meeting across the way broke up. The three sisters and the brother, heads bowed, were singing *God be with you till we meet again.* The faces around them were very quiet. Then the song ended. The small crowd dispersed. We watched the three women and the lone man walk slowly up the avenue.

"When she was singing before," said Sonny, abruptly, "her voice reminded me for a minute of what heroin feels like sometimes—when it's in your veins. It makes you feel sort of warm and cool at the same time. And distant. And—and sure." He sipped his beer, very deliberately not looking at me. I watched his face. "It makes you feel—in control. Sometimes you've got to have that feeling."

"Do you?" I sat down slowly in the easy chair.

"Sometimes." He went to the sofa and picked up his notebook again. "Some people do."

"In order," I asked, "to play?" And my voice was very ugly, full of contempt and anger.

"Well"—he looked at me with great, troubled eyes, as though, in fact, he hoped his eyes would tell me things he could never otherwise say—"they *think* so. And *if* they think so—!"

"And what do *you* think?" I asked.

He sat on the sofa and put his can of beer on the floor. "I don't know," he said, and I couldn't be sure if he were answering my question or pursuing his thoughts. His face didn't tell me. "It's not so much to *play.* It's to *stand* it, to be able to make it at all. On any level." He frowned and smiled: "In order to keep from shaking to pieces."

"But these friends of yours," I said, "they seem to shake themselves to pieces pretty goddamn fast."

"Maybe." He played with the notebook. And something told me that I should curb my tongue, that Sonny was doing his best to talk, that I should listen. "But of course you only know the ones that've gone to pieces. Some don't—or at least they haven't *yet* and that's just about all *any* of us can say." He paused. "And then there are some who just live, really, in hell, and they know it and they see what's happening and they go right on. I don't know." He sighed, dropped the notebook, folded his arms. "Some guys, you can tell from the way they play, they on something *all* the time. And you can see that, well, it makes something real for them. But of course," he picked up his beer from the floor and sipped it and put the can down again, "they *want* to, too, you've got to see that. Even some of them that say they don't—*some,* not all."

"And what about you?" I asked—I couldn't help it. "What about you? Do *you* want to?"

He stood up and walked to the window and remained silent for a long time. Then he sighed. "Me," he said. Then: "While I was downstairs before, on my way here, listening to that woman sing, it struck me all of a sudden how much suffering she must have had to go through—to sing like that. It's *repulsive* to think you have to suffer that much."

I said: "But there's no way not to suffer—is there, Sonny?"

"I believe not," he said and smiled, "but that's never stopped anyone from trying." He looked at me. "Has it?" I realized, with this mocking look, that there stood between us, forever, beyond the power of time or forgiveness, the fact that I had held silence—so long!—when he had needed human speech to help him. He turned back to the window. "No, there's no way not to suffer. But you try all kinds of ways to keep from drowning in it, to keep on top of it, and to make it seem. well, like *you.* Like you did something, all right, and now you're suffering for it. You know?" I said nothing. "Well you know," he said, impatiently, "why *do* people suffer? Maybe it's better to do something to give it a reason, any reason."

"But we just agreed," I said, "that there's no way not to suffer. Isn't it better, then, just to—take it?"

"But nobody just takes it," Sonny cried, "that's what I'm telling you! *Everybody* tries not to. You're just hung up on the *way* some people try—it's not your way!"

The hair on my face began to itch, my face felt wet. "That's not true," I said, "that's not true. I don't give a damn what other people do, I don't even care how they suffer. I just care how *you* suffer." And he looked at me. "Please believe me," I said, "I don't want to see you—die—trying not to suffer."

"I won't," he said, flatly, "die trying not to suffer. At least, not any faster than anybody else."

"But there's no need," I said, trying to laugh, "is there? in killing yourself."

I wanted to say more, but I couldn't. I wanted to talk about will power and how life could be—well, beautiful. I wanted to say that it was all within; but was it? or, rather, wasn't that exactly the trouble? And I wanted to promise that I would never fail him again. But it would all have sounded—empty words and lies.

So I made the promise to myself and prayed that I would keep it.

"It's terrible sometimes, inside," he said, "that's what's the trouble. You walk these streets, black and funky and cold, and there's not really a living ass to talk to, and there's nothing shaking, and there's no way of getting it out—that storm inside. You can't talk it and you can't make love with it, and when you finally try to get with it and play it, you realize *nobody's* listening. So *you've* got to listen. You got to find a way to listen."

And then he walked away from the window and sat on the sofa again, as though all the wind had suddenly been knocked out of him. "Sometimes you'll do *anything* to play, even cut your mother's throat." He laughed and looked at me. "Or your brother's." Then he sobered. "Or your own." Then: "Don't worry. I'm all right now and I think I'll *be* all right. But I can't forget—where I've been. I don't mean just the physical place I've been, I mean where I've *been.* And *what* I've been."

"What have you been, Sonny?" I asked.

He smiled—but sat sideways on the sofa, his elbow resting on the back, his fingers playing with his mouth and chin, not looking at me. "I've been something I didn't recognize, didn't know I could be. Didn't know anybody could be." He stopped, looking inward, looking helplessly young, looking old. "I'm not talking about it now because I feel *guilty* or anything like that—maybe it would be better if I did, I don't know. Anyway, I can't really talk about it. Not to you, not to anybody," and now he turned and faced me. "Sometimes, you know, and it was actually when I was most *out* of the world, I felt that I was in it, that I was *with* it, really; and I could play or I didn't really have to *play,* it just came out of me, it was there. And I don't know how I played, thinking about it now, but I know I did awful things, those times, sometimes, to people. Or it wasn't that I *did* anything to them—it was that they weren't real." He picked up the beer can; it was empty; he rolled it between his palms: "And other times—well, I needed a fix, I needed to find a place to lean, I needed to clear a space to *listen*—and I couldn't find it, and I—went crazy, I did terrible things to *me,* I was terrible *for* me." He began pressing the beer can between his hands, I watched the metal begin to give. It glittered, as he played with it, like a knife, and I was afraid he would cut himself, but I said nothing. "Oh well. I can never tell you. I was all by myself at the bottom of something, stinking and sweating and crying and shaking, and I smelled it, you know? *my* stink, and I thought I'd die if I couldn't get away from it and yet, all the same, I knew that everything I was doing was just locking me in with it. And I didn't know," he paused, still flattening the beer can, "I didn't know, I *still* don't know, something kept telling me that maybe it was good to smell your own stink, but I didn't think that *that* was what I'd been trying to do—and—who can stand it?" and he abruptly dropped the ruined beer can, looking at me with a small, still smile, and then rose, walking to the window as though it were the lodestone rock. I watched his face, he watched the avenue. "I couldn't tell you when Mama died—but the reason I wanted to leave Harlem so bad was to get away from drugs. And then, when I ran away, that's what I was running from—really. When I came back, nothing had changed, *I* hadn't changed, I was just—older." And he stopped, drumming with his fingers on the windowpane. The sun had vanished, soon darkness would fall. I watched his face. "It can come again," he said, almost as though speaking to himself. Then he turned to me. "It can come again," he repeated. "I just want you to know that."

"All right," I said, at last. "So it can come again. All right."

He smiled, but the smile was sorrowful. "I had to try to tell you," he said.

"Yes," I said. "I understand that."

"You're my brother," he said, looking straight at me, and not smiling at all.

"Yes," I repeated, "yes. I understand that."

He turned back to the window, looking out. "All that hatred down there," he said, "all that hatred and misery and love. It's a wonder it doesn't blow the avenue apart."

We went to the only nightclub on a short, dark street, downtown. We squeezed through the narrow, chattering, jam-packed bar to the entrance of the big room, where the bandstand was. And we stood there for a moment, for the lights were very dim in this room and we couldn't see. Then, "Hello, boy," said a voice and an enormous black man, much older than Sonny or myself, erupted out of all that atmospheric lighting and put an arm around Sonny's shoulder. "I been sitting right here," he said, "waiting for you."

He had a big voice, too, and heads in the darkness turned toward us.

Sonny grinned and pulled a little away, and said, "Creole, this is my brother. I told you about him."

Creole shook my hand. "I'm glad to meet you, son," he said, and it was clear that he was glad to meet me *there,* for Sonny's sake. And he smiled, "You got a real musician in *your* family," and he took his arm from Sonny's shoulder and slapped him, lightly, affectionately, with the back of his hand.

"Well. Now I've heard it all," said a voice behind us. This was another musician, and a friend of Sonny's, a coal-black, cheerful-looking man, built close to the ground. He immediately began confiding to me, at the top of his lungs, the most terrible things about Sonny, his teeth gleaming like a lighthouse and his laugh coming up out of him like the beginning of an earthquake. And it turned out that everyone at the bar knew Sonny, or almost everyone; some were musicians, working there, or nearby, or not working, some were simply hangers-on, and some were there to hear Sonny play. I was introduced to all of them and they were all very polite to me. Yet, it was clear that, for them, I was only Sonny's brother. Here, I was in Sonny's world. Or, rather: his kingdom. Here, it was not even a question that his veins bore royal blood.

They were going to play soon and Creole installed me, by myself, at a table in a dark corner. Then I watched them, Creole, and the little black man, and Sonny, and the others, while they horsed around, standing just below the bandstand. The light from the bandstand spilled just a little short of them and, watching them laughing and gesturing and moving about, I had the feeling that they, nevertheless, were being most careful not to step into that circle of light too suddenly: that if they moved into the light too suddenly, without thinking, they would perish in flame. Then, while I watched, one of them, the small, black man, moved into the light and crossed the bandstand and started fooling around with his drums. Then—being funny and being, also, extremely ceremonious—Creole took Sonny by the arm and led him to the piano. A woman's voice called Sonny's name and a few hands started clapping. And Sonny, also being funny and being ceremonious, and so touched, I think, that he could have cried, but neither hiding it nor showing it, riding it like a man, grinned, and put both hands to his heart and bowed from the waist.

Creole then went to the bass fiddle and a lean, very bright-skinned brown man jumped up on the bandstand and picked up his horn. So there they were, and the atmosphere on the bandstand and in the room began to change and tighten. Someone stepped up to the microphone and announced them. Then there were all kinds of murmurs. Some people at the bar shushed others. The waitress ran around, frantically getting in the last orders, guys and chicks got closer to each other, and the lights on the bandstand, on the quartet, turned to a kind of indigo. Then they all looked different there. Creole looked about him for the last time, as though he were making certain that all his chickens were in the coop, and then he—jumped and struck the fiddle. And there they were.

All I know about music is that not many people ever really hear it. And even then, on the rare occasions when something opens within, and the music enters, what we mainly hear, or hear corroborated, are personal, private, vanishing evocations. But the man who creates the music is hearing something else, is dealing with the roar rising from the void and imposing order on it as it hits the air. What is evoked in him, then, is of another order, more terrible because it has no words, and triumphant, too, for that same reason. And his triumph, when he triumphs, is ours. I just watched Sonny's face. His face was troubled, he was working hard, but he wasn't with it. And I had the feeling that, in a way, everyone on the bandstand was waiting for him, both waiting for him and pushing him along. But as I began to watch Creole, I realized that it was Creole who held them all back. He had them on a short rein. Up there, keeping the beat with his whole body, wailing on the fiddle, with his eyes half closed, he was listening to everything, but he was listening to Sonny. He was having a dialogue with Sonny. He wanted Sonny to leave the shoreline and strike out for the deep water. He was Sonny's witness that deep water and drowning were not the same thing—he had been there, and he knew. And he wanted Sonny to know. He was waiting for Sonny to do the things on the keys which would let Creole know that Sonny was in the water.

And, while Creole listened, Sonny moved, deep within, exactly like someone in torment. I had never before thought of how awful the relationship must be between the musician and his instrument. He has to fill it, this instrument, with the breath of life, his own. He has to make it do what he wants it to do. And a piano is just a piano. It's made out of so much wood and wires and little hammers and big ones, and ivory. While there's only so much you can do with it, the only way to find this out is to try; to try and make it do everything.

And Sonny hadn't been near a piano for over a year. And he wasn't on much better terms with his life, not the life that stretched before him now. He and the piano stammered, started one way, got scared, stopped; started another way, panicked, marked time, started again; then seemed to have found a direction, panicked again, got stuck. And the face I saw on Sonny I'd never seen before. Everything had been burned out of it, and, at the same time, things usually hidden were being burned in, by the fire and fury of the battle which was occurring in him up there.

Yet, watching Creole's face as they neared the end of the first set, I had the feeling that something had happened, something I hadn't heard. Then they finished, there was scattered applause, and then, without an instant's warning, Creole started into something else, it was almost sardonic, it was *Am I Blue.* And, as though he commanded, Sonny began to play. Something began to happen. And Creole let out the reins. The dry, low, black man said something awful on the drums, Creole answered, and the drums talked back. Then the horn insisted, sweet and high, slightly detached perhaps, and Creole listened, commenting now and then, dry, and driving, beautiful and calm and old. Then they all came together again, and Sonny was part of the family again. I could tell this from his face. He seemed to have found, right there beneath his fingers, a damn brand-new piano. It seemed that he couldn't get over it. Then, for awhile, just being happy with Sonny, they seemed to be agreeing with him that brand-new pianos certainly were a gas.

Then Creole stepped forward to remind them that what they were playing was the blues. He hit something in all of them, he hit something in me, myself, and the music tightened and deepened, apprehension began to beat the air. Creole began to tell us what the blues were all about. They were not about anything very new. He and his boys up there were keeping it new, at the risk of ruin, destruction, madness, and death, in order to find new ways to make us listen. For, while the tale of how we suffer, and how we are delighted, and how we may triumph is never new, it always must be heard. There isn't any other tale to tell, it's the only light we've got in all this darkness.

And this tale, according to that face, that body, those strong hands on those strings, has another aspect in every country, and a new depth in every generation. Listen, Creole seemed to be saying, listen. Now these are Sonny's blues. He made the little black man on the drums know it, and the bright, brown man on the horn. Creole wasn't trying any longer to get Sonny in the water. He was wishing him Godspeed. Then he stepped back, very slowly, filling the air with the immense suggestion that Sonny speak for himself.

Then they all gathered around Sonny and Sonny played. Every now and again one of them seemed to say, amen. Sonny's fingers filled the air with life, his life. But that life contained so many others. And Sonny went all the way back, he really began with the spare, flat statement of the opening phrase of the song. Then he began to make it his. It was very beautiful because it wasn't hurried and it was no longer a lament. I seemed to hear with what burning he had made it his, with what burning we had yet to make it ours, how we could cease lamenting. Freedom lurked around us and I understood, at last, that he could help us to be free if we would listen, that he would never be free until we did. Yet, there was no battle in his face now. I heard what he had gone through, and would continue to go through until he came to rest in earth. He had made it his: that long line, of which we knew only Mama and Daddy. And he was giving it back, as everything must be given back, so that, passing through death, it can live forever. I saw my mother's face again, and felt, for the first time, how the stones of the road she had walked on must have bruised her feet. I saw the moon-lit road where my father's brother died. And it brought something else back to me, and carried me past it. I saw my little girl again and felt Isabel's tears again, and I felt my own tears begin to rise. And I was yet aware that this was only a moment, that the world waited outside, as hungry as a tiger, and that trouble stretched above us, longer than the sky.

Then it was over. Creole and Sonny let out their breath, both soaking wet, and grinning. There was a lot of applause and some of it was real. In the dark, the girl came by and I asked her to take drinks to the bandstand. There was a long pause, while they talked up there in the indigo light and after awhile I saw the girl put a Scotch and milk on top of the piano for Sonny. He didn't seem to notice it, but just before they started playing again, he sipped from it and looked toward me, and nodded. Then he put it back on top of the piano. For me, then, as they began to play again, it glowed and shook above my brother's head like the very cup of trembling.

James Baldwin

Going to Meet the Man

"What's the matter?" she asked.

"I don't know," he said, trying to laugh, "I guess I'm tired."

"You've been working too hard," she said. "I keep telling you."

"Well, goddammit woman," he said, "it's not my fault!" He tried again; he wretchedly failed again. Then he just lay there, silent, angry, and helpless. Excitement filled him just like a toothache, but it refused to enter his flesh. He stroked her breast. This was his wife. He could not ask her to do just a little thing for him, just to help him out, just for a little while, the way he could ask a nigger girl to do it. He lay there, and he sighed. The image of a black girl caused a distant excitement in him, like a far-away light; but, again, the excitement was more like pain; instead of forcing him to act, it made action impossible.

"Go to sleep," she said, gently, "you got a hard day tomorrow."

"Yeah," he said, and rolled over on his side, facing her, one hand still on one breast. "Goddamn the niggers. The black stinking coons. You'd think they'd learn. Wouldn't you think they'd learn? I mean, *wouldn't* you?"

"They going to be out there tomorrow," she said, and took his hand away, "get some sleep."

He lay there, one hand between his legs, staring at the frail sanctuary of his wife. A faint light came from the shutters; the moon was full. Two dogs, far away, were barking at each other, back and forth, insistently, as though they were agreeing to make an appointment. He heard a car coming north on the road and he half sat up, his hand reaching for his holster, which was on a chair near the bed, on top of his pants. The lights hit the shutters and seemed to travel across the room and then went out. The sound of the car slipped away, he heard it hit gravel, then heard it no more. Some liver-lipped students, probably, heading back to that college—but coming from where? His watch said it was two in the morning. They could be coming from anywhere, from out of state most likely, and they would be at the courthouse tomorrow. The niggers were getting ready. Well, they would be ready, too.

He moaned. He wanted to let whatever was in him out; but it wouldn't come out. Goddamn! he said aloud, and turned again, on his side, away from Grace, staring at the shutters. He was a big, healthy man and he had never had any trouble sleeping. And he wasn't old enough yet to have any trouble getting it up—he was only forty-two. And he was a good man, a God-fearing man, he had tried to do his duty all his life, and he had been a deputy sheriff for several years. Nothing had ever bothered him before, certainly not getting it up. Sometimes, sure, like any other man, he knew that he wanted a little more spice than Grace could give him and he would drive over yonder and pick up a black piece or arrest her, it came to the same thing, but he couldn't do that now, no more. There was no telling what might happen once your ass was in the air. And they were low enough to kill a man then, too, everyone of them, or the girl herself might do it, right while she was making believe you made her feel so good. The niggers. What had the good Lord Almighty had in mind when he made the niggers? Well. They were pretty good at that, all right. Damn. Damn. Goddamn.

This wasn't helping him to sleep. He turned again, toward Grace again, and moved close to her warm body. He felt something he had never felt before. He felt that he would like to hold her, hold her, hold her, and be buried in her like a child and never have to get up in the morning again and go downtown to face those faces, good Christ, they were ugly! and never have to enter that jail house again and smell that smell and hear that singing; never again feel that filthy, kinky, greasy hair under his hand, never again watch those black breasts leap against the leaping cattle prod, never hear those moans again or watch that blood run down or the fat lips split or the sealed eyes struggle open. They were animals, they were no better than animals, what could be done with people like that? Here they had been in a civilized country for years and they still lived like animals. Their houses were dark, with oil cloth or cardboard in the windows, the smell was enough to make you puke your guts out, and there they sat, a whole tribe, pumping out kids, it looked like, every damn five minutes, and laughing and talking and playing music like they didn't have a care in the world, and he reckoned they didn't, neither, and coming to the door, into the sunlight, just standing there, just looking foolish, not thinking of anything but just getting back to what they were doing, saying, Yes suh, Mr. Jesse. I surely will, Mr. Jesse. Fine weather, Mr. Jesse. Why, I thank you, Mr. Jesse. He had worked for a mail-order house for a while and it had been his job to collect the payments for the stuff they bought. They were too dumb to know that they were being cheated blind, but that was no skin off his ass—he was supposed to do his job. They would be late—they didn't have the sense to put money aside; but it was easy to scare them, and he never really had any trouble. Hell, they all liked him, the kids used to smile when he came to the door. He gave them candy, sometimes, or chewing gum, and rubbed their rough bullet heads—maybe the candy should have been poisoned. Those kids were grown now. He had had trouble with one of them today.

"There was this nigger today," he said; and stopped; his voice sounded peculiar. He touched Grace. "You awake?" he asked. She mumbled something, impatiently, she was probably telling him to go to sleep. It was all right. He knew that he was not alone.

"What a funny time," he said, "to be thinking about a thing like that—you listening?" She mumbled something again. He rolled over on his back. "This nigger's one of the ringleaders. We had trouble with him before. We must have had him out there at the work farm three or four times. Well, Big Jim C. and some of the boys really had to whip that nigger's ass today." He looked over at Grace; he could not tell whether she was listening or not; and he was afraid to ask again. "They had this line you know, to register"—he laughed, but she did not—"and they wouldn't stay where Big Jim C. wanted them, no, they had to start blocking traffic all around the court house so couldn't nothing or nobody get through, and Big Jim C. told them to disperse and they wouldn't move, they just kept up that singing, and Big Jim C. figured that the others would move if this nigger would move, him being the ringleader, but he wouldn't move and he wouldn't let the others move, so they had to beat him and a couple of the others and they threw them in the wagon—but *I* didn't see this nigger till I got to the jail. They were still singing and I was supposed to make them stop. Well, I couldn't make them stop for me but I knew he could make them stop. He was lying on the ground jerking and moaning, they had threw him in a cell by himself, and blood was coming out his ears from where Big Jim C. and his boys had whipped him. Wouldn't you think they'd learn? I put the prod to him and he jerked some more and he kind of screamed—but he didn't have much voice left. "You make them stop that singing," I said to him, "you hear me? You make them stop that singing." He acted like he didn't hear me and I put it to him again, under his arms, and he just rolled around on the floor and blood started coming from his mouth. He'd pissed his pants already." He paused. His mouth felt dry and his throat was as rough as sandpaper; as he talked, he began to hurt all over with that peculiar excitement which refused to be released. "You all are going to stop your singing, I said to him, and you are going to stop coming down to the court house and disrupting traffic and molesting the people and keeping us from our duties and keeping doctors from getting to sick white women and getting all them Northerners in this town to give our town a bad name—!" As he said this, he kept prodding the boy, sweat pouring from beneath the helmet he had not yet taken off. The boy rolled around in his own dirt and water and blood and tried to scream again as the prod hit his testicles, but the scream did not come out, only a kind of rattle and a moan. He stopped. He was not supposed to kill the nigger. The cell was filled with a terrible odor. The boy was still. "You hear me?" he called. "You had enough?" The singing went on. "You had enough?" His foot leapt out, he had not known it was going to, and caught the boy flush on the jaw. *Jesus,* he thought, *this ain't no nigger, this is a goddamn bull,* and he screamed again, "You had enough? You going to make them stop that singing now?"

But the boy was out. And now he was shaking worse than the boy had been shaking. He was glad no one could see him. At the same time, he felt very close to a very peculiar, particular joy; something deep in him and deep in his memory was stirred, but whatever was in his memory eluded him. He took off his helmet. He walked to the cell door.

"White man," said the boy, from the floor, behind him.

He stopped. For some reason, he grabbed his privates.

"You remember Old Julia?"

The boy said, from the floor, with his mouth full of blood, and one eye, barely open, glaring like the eye of a cat in the dark, "My grandmother's name was Mrs. Julia Blossom. *Mrs.* Julia Blossom. You going to call our women by their right names yet. —And those kids ain't going to stop singing. We going to keep on singing until every one of you miserable white mothers go stark raving out of your minds." Then he closed the one eye; he spat blood; his head fell back against the floor.

He looked down at the boy, whom he had been seeing, off and on, for more than a year, and suddenly remembered him: Old Julia had been one of his mail-order customers, a nice old woman. He had not seen her for years, he supposed that she must be dead.

He had walked into the yard, the boy had been sitting in a swing. He had smiled at the boy, and asked, "Old Julia home?"

The boy looked at him for a long time before he answered. "Don't no Old Julia live here."

"This is her house. I know her. She's lived here for years."

The boy shook his head. "You might know a Old Julia someplace else, white man. But don't nobody by that name live here."

He watched the boy; the boy watched him. The boy certainly wasn't more than ten. *White man.* He didn't have time to be fooling around with some crazy kid. He yelled, "Hey! Old Julia!"

But only silence answered him. The expression on the boy's face did not change. The sun beat down on them both, still and silent; he had the feeling that he had been caught up in a nightmare, a nightmare dreamed by a child; perhaps one of the nightmares he himself had dreamed as a child. It had that feeling—everything familiar, without undergoing any other change, had been subtly and hideously displaced: the trees, the sun, the patches of grass in the yard, the leaning porch and the weary porch steps and the cardboard in the windows and the black hole of the door which looked like the entrance to a cave, and the eyes of the pickaninny, all, all, were charged with malevolence. *White man.* He looked at the boy. "She's gone out?"

The boy said nothing.

"Well," he said, "tell her I passed by and I'll pass by next week." He started to go; he stopped. "You want some chewing gum?"

The boy got down from the swing and started for the house. He said, "I don't want nothing you got, white man." He walked into the house and closed the door behind him.

Now the boy looked as though he were dead. Jesse wanted to go over to him and pick him up and pistol whip him until the boy's head burst open like a melon. He began to tremble with what he believed was rage, sweat, both cold and hot, raced down his body, the singing filled him as though it were a weird, uncontrollable, monstrous howling rumbling up from the depths of his own belly, he felt an icy fear rise in him and raise him up, and he shouted, he howled, "You lucky we *pump* some white blood into you every once in a while—your women! Here's what I got for all the black bitches in the world—!" Then he was, abruptly, almost too weak to stand; to his bewilderment, his horror, beneath his own fingers, he felt himself violently stiffen—with no warning at all; he dropped his hands and he stared at the boy and he left the cell.

"All that singing they do," he said. "All that singing." He could not remember the first time he had heard it; he had been hearing it all his life. It was the sound with which he was most familiar—though it was also the sound of which he had been least conscious—and it had always contained an obscure comfort. They were singing to God. They were singing for mercy and they hoped to go to heaven, and he had even sometimes felt, when looking into the eyes of some of the old women, a few of the very old men, that they were singing for mercy for his soul, too. Of course he had never thought of their heaven or of what God was, or could be, for them; God was the same for everyone, he supposed, and heaven was where good people went—he supposed. He had never thought much about what it meant to be a good person. He tried to be a good person and treat everybody right: it wasn't his fault if the niggers had taken it into their heads to fight against God and go against the rules laid down in the Bible for everyone to read! Any preacher would tell you that. He was only doing his duty: protecting white people from the niggers and the niggers from themselves. And there were still lots of good niggers around—he had to remember that; they weren't all like that boy this afternoon; and the good niggers must be mighty sad to see what was happening to their people. They would thank him when this was over. In that way they had, the best of them, not quite looking him in the eye, in a low voice, with a little smile: We surely thanks you, Mr. Jesse. From the bottom of our hearts, we thanks you. He smiled. They hadn't all gone crazy. This trouble would pass. He knew that the young people had changed some of the words to the songs. He had scarcely listened to the words before and he did not listen to them now; but he knew that the words were different; he could hear that much. He did not know if the faces were different, he had never, before this trouble began, watched them as they sang, but he certainly did not like what he saw now. They hated him, and this hatred was blacker than their hearts, blacker than their skins, redder than their blood, and harder, by far, than his club. Each day, each night, he felt worn out, aching, with their smell in his nostrils and filling his lungs, as though he were drowning—drowning in niggers; and it was all to be done again when he awoke. It would never end. It would never end. Perhaps—this was what the singing had meant all along. They had not been singing black folks into heaven, they had been singing white folks into hell.

Everyone felt this black suspicion in many ways, but no one knew how to express it. Men much older than he, who had been responsible for law and order much longer than he, were now much quieter than they had been, and the tone of their jokes, in a way that he could not quite put his finger on, had changed. These men were his models, they had been friends to his father, and they had taught him what it meant to be a man. He looked to them for courage now. It wasn't that he didn't know that what he was doing was right—he knew that, nobody had to tell him that; it was only that he missed the ease of former years. But they didn't have much time to hang out with each other these days. They tended to stay close to their families every free minute because nobody knew what might happen next. Explosions rocked the night of their tranquil town. Each time each man wondered silently if perhaps this time the dynamite had not fallen into the wrong hands. They thought that they knew where all the guns were; but they could not possibly know every move that was made in that secret place where the darkies lived. From time to time it was suggested that they form a posse and search the home of every nigger, but they hadn't done it yet. For one thing, this might have brought the bastards from the North down on their backs; for another, although the niggers were scattered throughout the town—down in the hollow near the railroad tracks, way west near the mills, up on the hill, the well-off ones, and some out near the college—nothing seemed to happen in one part of town without the niggers immediately knowing it in the other. This meant that they could not take them by surprise. They rarely mentioned it, but they knew that some of the niggers had guns. It stood to reason, as they said, since, after all, some of them had been in the Army. There were niggers in the Army right now and God knows they wouldn't have had any trouble stealing this half-assed government blind—the whole world was doing it, look at the European countries and all those countries in Africa. They made jokes about it—bitter jokes; and they cursed the government in Washington, which had betrayed them; but they had not yet formed a posse. Now, if their town had been laid out like some towns in the North, where all the niggers lived together in one locality, they could have gone down and set fire to the houses and brought about peace that way. If the niggers had all lived in one place, they could have kept the fire in one place. But the way this town was laid out, the fire could hardly be controlled. It would spread all over town—and the niggers would probably be helping it to spread. Still, from time to time, they spoke of doing it, anyway; so that now there was a real fear among them that somebody might go crazy and light the match.

They rarely mentioned anything not directly related to the war that they were fighting, but this had failed to establish between them the unspoken communication of soldiers during a war. Each man, in the thrilling silence which sped outward from their exchanges, their laughter, and their anecdotes, seemed wrestling, in various degrees of darkness, with a secret which he could not articulate to himself, and which, however directly it related to the war, related yet more surely to his privacy and his past. They could no longer be sure, after all, that they had all done the same things. They had never dreamed that their privacy could contain any element of terror, could threaten, that is, to reveal itself to the scrutiny of a judgment day, while remaining unreadable and inaccessible to themselves; nor had they dreamed that the past, while certainly refusing to be forgotten, could yet so stubbornly refuse to be remembered. They felt themselves mysteriously set at naught, as no longer entering into the real concerns of other people—while here they were, out-numbered, fighting to save the civilized world. They had thought that people would care—people didn't care; not enough, anyway, to help them. It would have been a help, really, or at least a relief, even to have been forced to surrender. Thus they had lost, probably forever, their old and easy connection with each other. They were forced to depend on each other more and, at the same time, to trust each other less. Who could tell when one of them might not betray them all, for money, or for the ease of confession? But no one dared imagine what there might be to confess. They were soldiers fighting a war, but their relationship to each other was that of accomplices in a crime. They all had to keep their mouths shut.

I stepped in the river at Jordan.

Out of the darkness of the room, out of nowhere, the line came flying up at him, with the melody and the beat. He turned wordlessly toward his sleeping wife. *I stepped in the river at Jordan.* Where had he heard that song?

"Grace," he whispered. "You awake?"

She did not answer. If she was awake, she wanted him to sleep. Her breathing was slow and easy, her body slowly rose and fell.

I stepped in the river at Jordan.
The water came to my knees.

He began to sweat. He felt an overwhelming fear, which yet contained a curious and dreadful pleasure.

I stepped in the river at Jordan.
The water came to my waist.

It had been night, as it was now, he was in the car between his mother and his father, sleepy, his head in his mother's lap, sleepy, and yet full of excitement The singing came from far away, across the dark fields. There were no lights anywhere. They had said good-bye to all the others and turned off on this dark dirt road. They were almost home.

I stepped in the river at Jordan,
The water came over my head,
I looked way over to the other side,
He was making up my dying bed!

"I guess they singing for him," his father said, seeming very weary and subdued now. "Even when they're sad, they sound like they just about to go and tear off a piece." He yawned and leaned across the boy and slapped his wife lightly on the shoulder, allowing his hand to rest there for a moment. "Don't they?"

"Don't talk that way," she said.

"Well, that's what we going to do," he said, "you can make up your mind to that." He started whistling. "You see? When I begin to feel it, I gets kind of musical, too."

Oh, Lord! Come on and ease my troubling mind!

He had a black friend, his age, eight, who lived nearby. His name was Otis. They wrestled together in the dirt. Now the thought of Otis made him sick. He began to shiver. His mother put her arm around him.

"He's tired," she said.

"We'll be home soon," said his father. He began to whistle again.

"We didn't see Otis this morning," Jesse said. He did not know why he said this. His voice, in the darkness of the car, sounded small and accusing.

"You haven't seen Otis for a couple of mornings," his mother said.

That was true. But he was only concerned about *this* morning.

"No," said his father, "I reckon Otis's folks was afraid to let him show himself this morning."

"But Otis didn't do nothing!" Now his voice sounded questioning.

"Otis *can't* do nothing," said his father, "he's too little." The car lights picked up their wooden house, which now solemnly approached them, the lights falling around it like yellow dust. Their dog, chained to a tree, began to bark.

"We just want to make sure Otis *don't* do nothing," said his father, and stopped the car. He looked down at Jesse. "And you tell him what your Daddy said, you hear?"

"Yes, sir," he said.

His father switched off the lights. The dog moaned and pranced, but they ignored him and went inside. He could not sleep. He lay awake, hearing the night sounds, the dog yawning and moaning outside, the sawing of the crickets, the cry of the owl, dogs barking far away, then no sounds at all, just the heavy, endless buzzing of the night. The darkness pressed on his eyelids like a scratchy blanket. He turned, he turned again. He wanted to call his mother, but he knew his father would not like this. He was terribly afraid. Then he heard his father's voice in the other room, low, with a joke in it; but this did not help him, it frightened him more, he knew what was going to happen. He put his head under the blanket, then pushed his head out again, for fear, staring at the dark window. He heard his mother's moan, his father's sigh; he gritted his teeth. Then their bed began to rock. His father's breathing seemed to fill the world.

That morning, before the sun had gathered all its strength, men and women, some flushed and some pale with excitement, came with news. Jesse's father seemed to know what the news was before the first jalopy stopped in the yard, and he ran out, crying, "They got him, then? They got him?"

The first jalopy held eight people, three men and two women and three children. The children were sitting on the laps of the grown-ups. Jesse knew two of them, the two boys; they shyly and uncomfortably greeted each other. He did not know the girl.

"Yes, they got him," said one of the women, the older one, who wore a wide hat and a fancy, faded blue dress. "They found him early this morning."

"How far had he got?" Jesse's father asked.

"He hadn't got no further than Harkness," one of the men said. "Look like he got lost up there in all them trees—or maybe he just got so scared he couldn't move." They all laughed.

"Yes, and you know it's near a graveyard, too," said the younger woman, and they laughed again.

"Is that where they got him now?" asked Jesse's father.

By this time there were three cars piled behind the first one, with everyone looking excited and shining, and Jesse noticed that they were carrying food. It was like a Fourth of July picnic.

"Yeah, that's where he is," said one of the men, "declare, Jesse, you going to keep us here all day long, answering your damn fool questions. Come on, we ain't go no time to waste."

"Don't bother putting up no food," cried a woman from one of the other cars, "we got enough. Just come on."

"Why, thank you," said Jesse's father, "we be right along then."

"I better get a sweater for the boy," said his mother, "in case it turns cold."

Jesse watched his mother's thin legs cross the yard. He knew that she also wanted to comb her hair a little and maybe put on a better dress, the dress she wore to church. His father guessed this, too, for he yelled behind her, "Now don't you go trying to turn yourself into no movie star. You just come on." But he laughed as he said this, and winked at the men; his wife was younger and prettier than most of the other women. He clapped Jesse on the head and started pulling him toward the car. "You all go on," he said. "I'll be right behind you. Jesse, you go tie up that there dog while I get this car started."

The cars sputtered and coughed and shook; the caravan began to move; bright dust filled the air. As soon as he was tied up, the dog began to bark. Jesse's mother came out of the house, carrying a jacket for his father and a sweater for Jesse. She had put a ribbon in her hair and had an old shawl around her shoulders.

"Put these in the car, son," she said, and handed everything to him. She bent down and stroked the dog, looked to see if there was water in his bowl, then went back up the three porch steps and closed the door.

"Come on," said his father, "ain't nothing in there for nobody to steal." He was sitting in the car, which trembled and belched. The last car of the caravan had disappeared but the sound of singing floated behind them.

Jesse got into the car, sitting close to his father, loving the smell of the car, and the trembling, and the bright day, and the sense of going on a great and unexpected journey. His mother got in and closed the door and the car began to move. Not until then did he ask, "Where are we going? Are we going on a picnic?"

He had a feeling that he knew where they were going, but he was not sure.

"That's right," his father said, "we're going on a picnic. You won't ever forget *this* picnic!"

"Are we," he asked, after a moment, "going to see the bad nigger—the one that knocked down old Miss Standish?"

"Well, I reckon," said his mother, "that we might see him."

He started to ask, *Will a lot of niggers be there? Will Otis be there?*—but he did not ask his question, to which, in a strange and uncomfortable way, he already knew the answer. Their friends, in the other cars, stretched up the road as far as he could see; other cars had joined them; there were cars behind them. They were singing. The sun seemed suddenly very hot, and he was, at once very happy and a little afraid. He did not quite understand what was happening, and he did not know what to ask—he had no one to ask. He had grown accustomed, for the solution of such mysteries, to go to Otis. He felt that Otis knew everything. But he could not ask Otis about this. Anyway, he had not seen Otis for two days; he had not seen a black face anywhere for more than two days; and he now realized, as they began chugging up the long hill which eventually led to Harkness, that there were no black faces on the road this morning, no black people anywhere. From the houses in which they lived, all along the road, no smoke curled, no life stirred—maybe one or two chickens were to be seen, that was all. There was no one at the windows, no one in the yard, no one sitting on the porches, and the doors were closed. He had come this road many a time and seen women washing in the yard (there were no clothes on the clotheslines), men working in the fields, children playing in the dust; black men passed them on the road other mornings, other days, on foot, or in wagons, sometimes in cars, tipping their hats, smiling, joking, their teeth a solid white against their skin, their eyes as warm as the sun, the blackness of their skin like dull fire against the white or the blue or the grey of their torn clothes. They passed the nigger church—dead-white, desolate, locked up; and the graveyard, where no one knelt or walked, and he saw no flowers. He wanted to ask, *Where are they? Where are they all?* But he did not dare. As the hill grew steeper, the sun grew colder. He looked at his mother and his father. They looked straight ahead, seeming to be listening to the singing which echoed and echoed in this graveyard silence. They were strangers to him now. They were looking at something he could not see. His father's lips had a strange, cruel curve, he wet his lips from time to time, and swallowed. He was terribly aware of his father's tongue, it was as though he had never seen it before. And his father's body suddenly seemed immense, bigger than a mountain. His eyes, which were grey-green, looked yellow in the sunlight; or at least there was a light in them which he had never seen before. His mother patted her hair and adjusted the ribbon, leaning forward to look into the car mirror. "You look all right," said his father, and laughed. "When that nigger looks at you, he's going to swear he throwed his life away for nothing. Wouldn't be surprised if he don't come back to haunt you." And he laughed again.

The singing now slowly began to cease; and he realized that they were nearing their destination. They had reached a straight, narrow, pebbly road, with trees on either side. The sunlight filtered down on them from a great height, as though they were under-water; and the branches of the trees scraped against the cars with a tearing sound. To the right of them, and beneath them, invisible now, lay the town; and to the left, miles of trees which led to the high mountain range which his ancestors had crossed in order to settle in this valley. Now, all was silent, except for the bumping of the tires against the rocky road, the sputtering of motors, and the sound of a crying child. And they seemed to move more slowly. They were beginning to climb again. He watched the cars ahead as they toiled patiently upward, disappearing into the sunlight of the clearing. Presently, he felt their vehicle also rise, heard his father's changed breathing, the sunlight hit his face, the trees moved away from them, and they were there. As their car crossed the clearing, he looked around. There seemed to be millions, there were certainly hundreds of people in the clearing, staring toward something he could not see. There was a fire. He could not see the flames, but he smelled the smoke. Then they were on the other side of the clearing, among the trees again. His father drove off the road and parked the car behind a great many other cars. He looked down at Jesse.

"You all right?" he asked.

"Yes, sir," he said.

"Well, come on, then," his father said. He reached over and opened the door on his mother's side. His mother stepped out first. They followed her into the clearing. At first he was aware only of confusion, of his mother and father greeting and being greeted, himself being handled, hugged, and patted, and told how much he had grown. The wind blew the smoke from the fire across the clearing into his eyes and nose. He could not see over the backs of the people in front of him. The sounds of laughing and cursing and wrath—and something else—rolled in waves from the front of the mob to the back. Those in front expressed their delight at what they saw, and this delight rolled backward, wave upon wave, across the clearing, more acrid than the smoke. His father reached down suddenly and sat Jesse on his shoulders.

Now he saw the fire—of twigs and boxes, piled high; flames made pale orange and yellow and thin as a veil under the steadier light of the sun; grey-blue smoke rolled upward and poured over their heads. Beyond the shifting curtain of fire and smoke, he made out first only a length of gleaming chain, attached to a great limb of the tree; then he saw that this chain bound two black hands together at the wrist, dirty yellow palm facing dirty yellow palm. The smoke poured up; the hands dropped out of sight; a cry went up from the crowd. Then the hands slowly came into view again, pulled upward by the chain. This time he saw the kinky, sweating, bloody head—he had never before seen a head with so much hair on it, hair so black and so tangled that it seemed like another jungle. The head was hanging. He saw the forehead, flat and high, with a kind of arrow of hair in the center, like he had, like his father had; they called it a widow's peak; and the mangled eye brows, the wide nose, the closed eyes, and the glinting eye lashes and the hanging lips, all streaming with blood and sweat. His hands were straight above his head. All his weight pulled downward from his hands; and he was a big man, a bigger man than his father, and black as an African jungle cat, and naked. Jesse pulled upward; his father's hands held him firmly by the ankles. He wanted to say something, he did not know what, but nothing he said could have been heard, for now the crowd roared again as a man stepped forward and put more wood on the fire. The flames leapt up. He thought he heard the hanging man scream, but he was not sure. Sweat was pouring from the hair in his armpits, poured down his sides, over his chest, into his navel and his groin. He was lowered again; he was raised again. Now Jesse knew that he heard him scream. The head went back, the mouth wide open, blood bubbling from the mouth; the veins of the neck jumped out; Jesse clung to his father's neck in terror as the cry rolled over the crowd. The cry of all the people rose to answer the dying man's cry. He wanted death to come quickly. They wanted to make death wait; and it was they who held death, now, on a leash which they lengthened little by little. *What did he do?* Jesse wondered. *What did the man do? What did he do?*—but he could not ask his father. He was seated on his father's shoulders, but his father was far away. There were two older men, friends of his father's, raising and lowering the chain; everyone, indiscriminately, seemed to be responsible for the fire. There was no hair left on the nigger's privates, and the eyes, now, were wide open, as white as the eyes of a clown or a doll. The smoke now carried a terrible odor across the clearing, the odor of something burned which was both sweet and rotten.

He turned his head a little and saw the field of faces. He watched his mother's face. Her eyes were very bright, her mouth was open: she was more beautiful than he had ever seen her, and more strange. He began to feel a joy he had never felt before. He watched the hanging, gleaming body, the most beautiful and terrible object he had ever seen till then. One of his father's friends reached up and in his hands he held a knife: and Jesse wished that he had been that man. It was a long, bright knife and the sun seemed to catch it, to play with it, to caress it—it was brighter than the fire. And a wave of laughter swept the crowd. Jesse felt his father's hands on his ankles slip and tighten. The man with the knife walked toward the crowd, smiling slightly; as though this were a signal, silence fell; he heard his mother cough. Then the man with the knife walked up to the hanging body. He turned and smiled again. Now there was a silence all over the field. The hanging head looked up. It seemed fully conscious now, as though the fire had burned out terror and pain. The man with the knife took the nigger's privates in his hand, one hand, still smiling, as though he were weighing them. In the cradle of the one white hand, the nigger's privates seemed as remote as meat being weighed in the scales; but seemed heavier, too, much heavier, and Jesse felt his scrotum tighten; and huge, huge, much bigger than his father's, flaccid, hairless, the largest thing he had ever seen till then, and the blackest. The white hand stretched them, cradled them, caressed them. Then the dying man's eyes looked straight into Jesse's eyes—it could not have been as long as a second, but it seemed longer than a year. Then Jesse screamed, and the crowd screamed as the knife flashed, first up, then down, cutting the dreadful thing away, and the blood came roaring down. Then the crowd rushed forward, tearing at the body with their hands, with knives, with rocks, with stones, howling and cursing. Jesse's head, of its own weight, fell downward toward his father's head. Someone stepped forward and drenched the body with kerosene. Where the man had been, a great sheet of flame appeared. Jesse's father lowered him to the ground.

"Well, I told you," said the father, "you wasn't never going to forget *this* picnic." His father's face was full of sweat, his eyes were very peaceful. At that moment Jesse loved his father more than he had ever loved him. He felt that his father had carried him through a mighty test, had revealed to him a great secret which would be the key to his life forever.

"I reckon," he said. "I reckon."

Jesse's father took him by the hand and, with his mother a little behind them, talking and laughing with the other women, they walked through the crowd, across the clearing. The black body was on the ground, the chain which had held it was being rolled up by one of his father's friends. Whatever the fire had left undone, the hands and the knives and the stones of the people accomplished. The head was caved in, one eye was torn out, one ear was hanging. But one had to look carefully to realize this, for it was, now, merely, a black charred object on the black, charred ground. He lay spread-eagled with what had been a wound between what had been his legs.

"They going to leave him there, then?" Jesse whispered.

"Yeah," said his father, "they'll come and get him by and by. I reckon we better get over there and get some of that food before it's all gone."

"I reckon," he muttered now to himself; "I reckon." Grace stirred and touched him on the thigh: the moonlight covered her like glory. Something bubbled up in him, his nature again returned to him. He thought of the boy in the cell; he thought of the man in the fire; he thought of the knife and grabbed himself and stroked himself and a terrible sound, something between a high laugh and a howl, came out of him and dragged his sleeping wife up on one elbow. She stared at him in the moonlight which had now grown cold as ice. He thought of the morning and grabbed her, laughing and crying, crying and laughing, and he whispered, as he stroked her, as he took her, "Come on, sugar, I'm going to do you like a nigger, just like a nigger, come on, sugar, and love me just like you'd love a nigger." He thought of the morning as he labored and she moaned, thought of morning as he labored harder than he ever had before, and before his labors had ended, he heard the first cock crow and the dogs begin to bark, and the sound of tires on the gravel road.

JAMES BALDWIN

Exodus

I

She had always seemed to Florence the oldest woman in the world—for she often spoke of Florence and Gabriel as the children of her old age; and she had been born, innumerable years ago, during slavery, on a plantation in another state. On this plantation she had grown up one of the field workers, for she was very tall and strong; and by-and-by she had married, and raised children, all of whom had been taken from her, one by sickness, and two by auction, and one whom she had not been allowed to call her own, who had been raised in the master's house. When she was a woman grown, well past thirty as she reckoned it, with one husband buried—but the master had given her another—armies, plundering and burning, had come from the North to set them free. This was in answer to the prayers of the faithful, who had never ceased, both day and night, to cry out for deliverance.

For it had been the will of God that they should hear, and pass it, thereafter, one to another, the story of the Hebrew children, who had been held in bondage in the land of Egypt; and how the Lord had heard their groaning, and how His heart was moved; and how He bid them wait but a little season till He should send deliverance. She had known this story, so it seemed, from the day that she was born. And while life ran, rising in the morning before the sun came up, standing and bending in the fields when the sun was high, crossing the fields homeward while the sun went down at the gates of heaven far away—hearing the whistle of the foreman, and his eerie cry across the fields; in the whiteness of winter when hogs and turkeys and geese were slaughtered, and lights burned bright in the big house, and Bathsheba, the cook, sent over in a napkin bits of ham and chicken and cakes left over by the white folks; in all that befell, in her joys—her pipe in the evening, her man at night, the children she suckled, and guided on their first short steps—and in her tribulations, death, and parting, and the lash; she did not forget that deliverance was promised, and would surely come. She had only to endure and trust in God. She knew that the big house, the house of pride where the white folks lived, would come down: it was written in the Word of God. And they who walked so proudly now, yet had not fashioned, for themselves, or their children, so sure a foundation as was hers. They walked on the edge of a steep place and their eyes were sightless—God would cause them to rush down, as the herd of swine had once rushed down, into the sea. For all that they were so beautiful, and took their ease, she knew them, and she pitied them, who would have no covering in the great day of His wrath.

Yet, she told her children, God was just, and He struck no people without first giving many warnings. God gave men time, but all the times were in His hand, and, one day the time to forsake evil and do good would all be finished: then only the whirlwind, death riding on the whirlwind, awaited those people who had forgotten

God. In all the days that she was growing up, signs failed not, but none heeded. *Slaves done riz,* was whispered in the cabin, and at the master's gate: slaves in another county had fired the master's house and fields, and dashed their children to death against the stones. *Another slave in hell,* Bathsheba might say one morning, shooing the pickaninnies away from the great porch: a slave had killed his master, or his overseer, and had gone down to hell to pay for it. *I ain't got long to stay here,* someone crooned beside her in the fields: who would be gone by morning on his journey North. All these signs, like the plagues with which the Lord had afflicted Egypt, only hardened the hearts of these people against the Lord. They thought the lash would save them, and they used the lash; or the knife, or the gallows, or the auction block; they thought that kindness would save them, and the master and mistress came down, smiling, to the cabins, making much of the pickaninnies, and bearing gifts. These were great days, and they all, black and white, seemed happy together. But when the Word has gone forth from the mouth of God nothing can turn it back.

The word was fulfilled one morning before she was awake. Many of the stories her mother told meant nothing to Florence, she knew them for what they were, tales told by an old black woman in a cabin in the evening to distract her children from their cold and hunger. But the story of this day she was never to forget, it was a day like the day for which she lived. There was a great running and shouting, said her mother, everywhere outside, and, as she opened her eyes to the light of that day so bright, she said, and cold, she was certain that the judgment trump had sounded. While she still sat, amazed, and wondering what, on the judgment day would be the best behavior, in rushed Bathsheba, and behind her many tumbling children, and field hands, and house niggers, all together, and Bathsheba shouted, "Rise up, rise up, Sister Rachel, and see the Lord's deliverance! He done brought us out of Egypt, just like He promised, and we's free at last!"

Bathsheba grabbed her, tears running down her face; she, dressed in the clothes in which she had slept, walked to the door to look out on the new day God had given them.

On that day she saw the proud house humbled, green silk and velvet blowing out of windows, and the garden trampled by many horsemen, and the big gates open. The master and mistress, and their kin, and one child she had borne were in that house—which she did not enter. Soon it occurred to her that there was no reason any more to tarry here. She tied her things in a cloth, which she put on her head, and walked out through the big gate, never to see that country any more.

And this, as Florence grew, became her deep ambition: to walk out one morning through the cabin door, never to return. . . .

II

In 1900, when she was twenty-six, Florence walked out through the cabin door. She had thought to wait until her mother, who was so ill now that she no longer stirred out of bed, should be buried—but suddenly she knew that she would wait no longer, the time had come. She had been working as cook and serving girl for a large white family in town, and it was on the day that her master proposed that she become his concubine that she knew that her life among these wretched had come to its destined end. She left her employment that same day (leaving behind her a most vehement conjugal bitterness) and with part of the money which, with cunning, cruelty, and sacrifice, she had saved over a period of years, bought a railroad ticket to New York. When she bought it, in a kind of scarlet rage, she held, like a talisman at the back of her mind, the thought: "I can give it back, I can sell it. This doesn't mean I got to go." But she knew that nothing could stop her.

And it was this leave-taking which came to stand, in Florence's latter days, and with many another witness, at her bedside. Gray clouds obscured the sun that day and outside the cabin window she saw that mist still covered the ground. Her mother lay in bed, awake; she was pleading with Gabriel, who had been out drinking the night before, and who was not really sober now, to mend his ways and come to the Lord. And Gabriel, full of the confusion, and pain, and guilt which were his whenever he thought of how he made his mother suffer, but which became nearly insupportable when she taxed him with it, stood before the mirror, head bowed, buttoning his shirt. Florence knew that he could not unlock his lips to speak; he could not say Yes to his mother, and to the Lord; and he could not say No.

"Honey," their mother was saying, "don't you *let* your old mother die without you look her in the eye and tell her she going to see you in glory. You hear me, boy?"

In a moment, Florence thought with scorn, tears would fill his eyes, and he would promise to "do better." He had been promising to "do better" since the day he had been baptized.

She put down her bag in the center of the hateful room.

"Ma," she said, "I'm going. I'm a-going this morning."

Now that she had said it, she was angry with herself for not having said it the night before, so that they would have had time to be finished with their weeping and their arguments. She had not trusted herself to withstand, the night before; but now there was almost no time left. The center of her mind was filled with the image of the great, white clock at the railway station, on which the hands did not cease to move.

"You going where?" her mother asked, sharply. But she knew that her mother had understood, had, indeed, long before this moment, known that this moment would come. The astonishment with which she stared at Florence's bag was not altogether astonishment, but a startled, wary attention. A danger imagined had become present and real, and her mother was already searching for a way to break Florence's will. All this Florence, in a moment, knew, and it made her stronger. She watched her mother, waiting.

But at the tone of his mother's voice, Gabriel, who had scarcely heard Florence's announcement, so grateful had he been that something had occurred to distract from him his mother's attention, dropped his eyes, and saw Florence's traveling bag. And he repeated his mother's question in a stunned, angry voice, understanding it only as the words hit the air:

"Yes, girl. Where you think you going?"

"I'm going," she said, "to New York. I got my ticket."

And her mother watched her. For a moment no one said a word. Then, Gabriel, in a changed and frightened voice, asked:

"And when you done decide that?"

She did not look at him, nor answer his question. She continued to watch her mother. "I got my ticket," she repeated. "I'm going on the morning train."

"Girl," asked her mother, quietly, "is you sure you know what you's doing?"

She stiffened, seeing in her mother's eyes a mocking pity. "I'm a woman grown," she said. "I know what I'm doing."

"And you going," cried Gabriel, "this morning—just like that? And you going to walk off and leave your mother—just like that?"

"You hush," she said, turning to him for the first time; "she got you, ain't she?"

This was indeed, she realized, as he dropped his eyes, the bitter, troubling point. He could not endure the thought of being left alone with his mother, with nothing whatever to put between himself and his guilty love. With Florence gone, time would have swallowed up all his mother's children, except himself, and *he,* then, must make amends for all the pain that she had borne, and sweeten her last moments with all his proofs of love. And his mother required of him one proof only that he tarry no longer in sin. With Florence gone, his stammering time, his playing time, contracted with a bound to the sparest interrogative second; when he must stiffen himself, and answer to his mother, and all the host of heaven, Yes, or No.

Florence smiled inwardly a small, malicious smile, watching his slow bafflement and panic, and rage; and she looked at her mother again. "She got you," she repeated. "She don't need me."

"You going North," her mother said, then. "And when you reckon on coming back?"

"I don't reckon on coming back," she said.

"You come crying back soon enough," said Gabriel, with malevolence, "soon as they whip your butt up there four or five times."

She looked at him again. "Just don't you try to hold your breath till then, you hear?"

"Girl," said her mother, "you mean to tell me the devil's done made your heart so hard you can just leave your mother on her dying bed, and you don't care if you don't never see her in this world no more? Honey you can't tell me you done got so evil as all that?"

She felt Gabriel watching her to see how she would take this question—the question, which, for all her determination, she had dreaded most to hear. She looked away from her mother, and straightened, catching her breath, looking outward through the small, cracked window. There, outside, beyond the slowly rising mist, and farther off than her eyes could see, her life awaited her. The woman on the bed was old, her life was fading as the mist rose. She thought of her mother as already in the grave; and she would not let herself be strangled by the hands of the dead.

"I'm going, Ma," she said. "I got to go."

Her mother leaned back, face upward to the light, and began to cry. Gabriel moved to Florence's side and grabbed her arm. She looked up into his face and saw that his eyes were full of tears.

"You can't go," he said. "You can't go. You can't go and leave your mother this-away. She need a woman, Florence, to help look after her. What she going to do here, all alone with me?"

She pushed him from her and moved to stand over her mother's bed.

"Ma," she said, "don't be like that. Ain't a blessed thing for you to cry about so. Ain't a thing can happen to me up North can't happen to me here. God's everywhere, Ma. Ain't no need to worry."

She knew that she was mouthing words; and she realized suddenly that her mother scorned to dignify these words with her attention. She had granted Florence the victory—with a promptness which had the effect of making Florence, however dimly and unwillingly, wonder if her victory was real; and she was not weeping for her daughter's future; she was weeping for the past, and weeping in an anguish in which Florence had no part. And all of this filled Florence with a terrible fear, which was immediately transformed into anger.

"Gabriel can take care of you," she said, her voice shaking with malice; "Gabriel ain't never going to leave you. Is you, boy?" and she looked at him. He stood, stupid with bewilderment and grief, a few inches from the bed. "But me," she said, "I got to go." She walked to the center of the room again, and picked up her bag.

"Girl," Gabriel whispered, "ain't you got no feelings at *all?*"

"Lord!" her mother cried; and at the sound her heart turned over; she and Gabriel, arrested, stared at the bed. "Lord, Lord, Lord! Lord, have mercy on my sinful daughter! Stretch out your hand and hold her back from the lake that burns forever! Oh, my Lord, my Lord!" and her voice dropped, and broke, and tears ran down her face. "Lord, I done my best with all the children what you give me. Lord, have mercy on my children, and my children's children."

"Florence," said Gabriel, "please don't go. Please don't go. You ain't really fixing to go and leave her like this?"

Tears stood suddenly in her own eyes, though she could not have said what she was crying for. "Leave me be," she said to Gabriel, and picked up her bag again. She opened the door; the cold morning air came in. "Good-by," she said. And then to Gabriel: "Tell her I said good-by." She walked through the cabin door and down the short steps into the frosty yard. Gabriel watched her, standing magnetized between the door and the weeping bed. Then, as her hand was on the gate, he ran before her, and slammed the gate shut.

"Girl, where you going? What you doing? You reckon on finding some men up North to dress you in pearls and diamonds?"

Violently, she opened the gate and moved out into the road. He watched her with his jaw hanging, until the dust and the distance swallowed her up.

Toni Cade Bambara *(1939–1995)*

was born and raised in New York's Harlem and Bedford-Stuyvesant neighborhoods. She graduated from Queens College in 1959 and studied abroad at the University of Florence and the École de Mme. Étienne Decroux in Paris; she then came back to New York to study screenwriting and dance. Though she worked as a recreation director and as a social worker for the New York State Department of Welfare, throughout all this she was publishing short stories, debuting in 1972 with the widely praised collection Gorilla, My Love. *She was a staunch civil rights advocate and a teacher at a number of colleges and universities. She moved to Atlanta and spent the last twelve years of her life writing a massive novel based on the 1979–1981 murders of more than forty African-American children in Atlanta. When Bambara died of cancer at the age of fifty-six, the book was unfinished. Toni Morrison, who called the book Bambara's magnum opus, edited the manuscript for its publication in 1999.*

INTRODUCTION BY **David Haynes**

Three of the twentieth century's essential literary phenomena merge in the writing of Toni Cade Bambara (born Miltona Mirkin Cade): the Black Arts movement's embrace of the core realities of African-American life; feminism's celebration of women's stories; and, leaping forward from the Harlem Renaissance, the recognition by Zora Neale Hurston and others of the power and strength of the language and voices of ordinary men and women.

Her two novels and many short stories reflect the lives of the men and women Bambara met and worked with as she traveled the world as a teacher, activist, filmmaker, and scholar, although her work is—as she insists in the short preface to the collection *Gorilla, My Love*—"straight up fiction." Her characters, many of them working-class black women, move through life with extraordinary insight and, often enough, rich and warm comic intensity. It is the author's adherence to universal truths and to the specificity of individual behavior (and misbehavior) that infuse her fictions with the texture of lives being lived and make many of her stories laugh-out-loud funny.

Bambara's short stories have become a standard feature of the performance repertoire, and one need look no further than "My Man Bovanne" to understand why. In this story, Bambara demonstrates her mastery of first-person storytelling. Widowed Hazel, mother of grown children and keen observer of the goings-on within her family and in her community, becomes the eyes of a blind man in this commentary on seeing oneself afresh. Through cadence, syntax, word choice, and the occasional transliteration, Bambara creates a voice that is all Hazel's own and then, through dialogue, plays this voice off of those of Bovanne and of Hazel's overprotective children. After her son invites the clan home for a family dinner meeting about their mother's "shameful" behavior in public, Hazel hustles Bovanne from the party, where she and the blind man had been quite enjoying themselves on the dance floor.

> "Where we goin, Miss Hazel?" Him knowin all the time.
>
> "First we buying you some dark sunglasses. Then you comin with me to the supermarket so I can pick up tomorrow's dinner, which is goin to be a grand thing and you invited. Then we goin to my house."

> "That be fine. I surely would like to rest my feet." Bein cute, but you got to let men play out they little show, blind or not.

No, we don't get to see the showdown at dinner, but the rich evocation of character achieved through this voice and through the way it plays against its counterpoints tells us as much as we need to know about the comic fiasco that's to come.

Contrast Hazel's voice with that of the tough-exteriored Sylvia in "The Lesson." Augmenting her technique with run-ons, fragments, and a flow of sentences that often begin with conjunctions, Bambara evokes the rambling but sensible sensibility of a girl trying to reason her way through an unreasonable world. Mentor and activist Miss Moore rounds up the young people of the neighborhood and takes them on a field trip to the big bad world, which has by custom and habit excluded the likes of them.

> Only she don't lead the way. So me and Sugar turn the corner to where the entrance is, but when we get there I kinda hang back. Not that I'm scared, what's there to be afraid of, just a toy store. But I feel funny, shamed. But what I got to be shamed about? Got as much right to go in as anybody. But somehow I can't seem to get hold of the door, so I step away for Sugar to lead.

The surface of the story hypnotizes us with a nonstop stream of language, including Sylvia's sharp and cynical observations about the tour as well as her trenchant commentary on the ever-so-proper Miss Moore. But it's what Sylvia can't or doesn't see that teaches most profoundly here. As is typical for Bambara, she infuses the story with an almost strident didacticism, all leavened gracefully through the use of the jaded eye of the young narrator.

Like many of the stories in her second collection *The Sea Birds Are Still Alive,* "The Organizer's Wife" moves away from voice-driven narrative and into the third person, observing the story closely and as if from just outside the troubled but determined consciousness of its central character, Virginia. An almost archetypal feminist heroine, Virginia just might be the only person with any backbone in a community wrestling Jim Crow and trying to ignite its own struggle for civil rights. While maintaining enough distance to fully evoke this larger world and its tribulations, Bambara also moves daringly close to Virginia's own voice to evoke her bewilderment and her outrage.

> And how to explain to Graham so many things. About this new growth she was experiencing, was thinking on at night wrapped in his quilt. Not like the dread growing up out of her clothes as though she'd never stop 'fore she be freak, 'cause she had stopped. And not like the new growth that was the baby, for she'd expected that, had been prepared. More like the toenail smashed the day the work brigade had stacked the stones to keep the road from splitting apart. The way the new nail pushed up against the old turning blue, against the gauze and the tape, stubborn to establish itself. A chick pecking through the shell, hard-headed and hasty and wobbly.

Here the inimitable Bambara voice—its trademark imagery of motherhood and birth and struggle against pain—reprocesses itself through an alternative perspective without losing any of its intimacy or immediacy.

At the time of her death in 1995, Toni Cade Bambara had influenced a generation of writers and had established herself as one of the leading voices in American literature. She will be remembered for her activism and commitment as well as for being the writer whose work perhaps most artfully built a bridge from the African-American oral tradition to the printed page.

David Haynes has written several novels, including Live at Five, Somebody Else's Mama, Heathens, *and* All American Dream Dolls. *The American Library Association named* Right By My Side *one of their Best Books of the Year for Young Adults. Two of his short stories have been performed on the "Selected Shorts" program on National Public Radio. In 1996, Haynes was selected as one of* Granta's *Best of the Young American Novelists. He also writes novels for juveniles in* The West 7th Wildcats *series.*

TONI CADE BAMBARA

My Man Bovanne

Blind people got a hummin jones if you notice. Which is understandable completely once you been around one and notice what no eyes will force you into to see people, and you get past the first time, which seems to come out of nowhere, and it's like you in church again with fat-chest ladies and old gents gruntin a hum low in the throat to whatever the preacher be saying. Shakey Bee bottom lip all swole up with Sweet Peach and me explainin how come the sweet-potato bread was a dollar-quarter this time stead of dollar regular and he say uh hunh he understand, then he break into this thizzin kind of hum which is quiet, but fiercesome just the same, if you ain't ready for it. Which I wasn't. But I got used to it and the onliest time I had to say somethin bout it was when he was playin checkers on the stoop one time and he commenst to hummin quite churchy seem to me. So I says, "Look here Shakey Bee, I can't beat you and Jesus too." He stop.

So that's how come I asked My Man Bovanne to dance. He ain't my man mind you, just a nice ole gent from the block that we all know cause he fixes things and the kids like him. Or used to fore Black Power got hold their minds and mess em around till they can't be civil to ole folks. So we at this benefit for my niece's cousin who's runnin for somethin with this Black party somethin or other behind her. And I press up close to dance with Bovanne who blind and I'm hummin and he hummin, chest to chest like talkin. Not jammin my breasts into the man. Wasn't bout tits. Was about vibrations. And he dug it and asked me what color dress I had on and how my hair was fixed and how I was doin without a man, not nosy but nice-like, and who was at this affair and was the canapes dainty-stingy or healthy enough to get hold of proper. Comfy and cheery is what I'm tryin to get across. Touch talkin like the heel of the hand on the tambourine or on a drum.

But right away Joe Lee come up on us and frown for dancin so close to the man. My own son who knows what kind of warm I am about; and don't grown men call me long distance and in the middle of the night for a little Mama comfort? But he frown. Which ain't right since Bovanne can't see and defend himself. Just a nice old man who fixes toasters and busted irons and bicycles and things and changes the lock on my door when my men friends get messy. Nice man. Which is not why they invited him. Grass roots you see. Me and Sister Taylor and the woman who does heads at Mamies and the man from the barber shop, we all there on account of we grass roots. And I ain't never been souther than Brooklyn Battery and no more country than the window box on my fire escape. And just yesterday my kids tellin me to take them countrified rags off my head and be cool. And now can't get Black enough to suit em. So everybody passin sayin My Man Bovanne. Big deal, keep steppin and don't even stop a minute to get the man a drink or one of them cute sandwiches or tell him what's goin on. And him standin there with a smile ready case someone do speak he want to be ready. So that's how come I pull him on the dance floor and we dance squeezin past the tables and chairs and all them coats and people standin round up in each other face talkin bout this and that but got no use for this blind man who mostly fixed skates and scooters for all these folks when they was just kids. So I'm pressed up close and we touch talkin with the hum. And here come my daughter cuttin her eye at me like she do when she tell me about my "apolitical" self like I got hoof and mouf disease and there ain't no hope at all. And I don't pay her no mind and just look up in Bovanne shadow face and tell him his stomach like a drum and he laugh. Laugh real loud. And here come my youngest, Task, with a tap on my elbow like he the third-grade monitor and I'm cuttin up on the line to assembly.

"I was just talkin on the drums," I explained when they hauled me into the kitchen. I figured drums was my best defense. They can get ready for drums what with all this heritage business. And Bovanne stomach just like that drum Task give me when he come back from Africa. You just touch it and it hum thizzm, thizzm. So I stuck to the drum story. "Just drummin that's all."

"Mama, what are you talkin about?"

"She had too much to drink," say Elo to Task cause she don't hardly say nuthin to me direct no more since that ugly argument about my wigs.

"Look here Mama," say Task, the gentle one. "We just tryin to pull your coat. You were makin a spectacle of yourself out there dancing like that."

"Dancin like what?"

Task run a hand over his left ear like his father for the world and his father before that.

"Like a bitch in heat," say Elo.

"Well uhh, I was goin to say like one of them sex-starved ladies gettin on in years and not too discriminating. Know what I mean?"

I don't answer cause I'll cry. Terrible thing when your own children talk to you like that. Pullin me out the party and hustlin me into some stranger's kitchen in the back of a bar just like the damn police. And ain't like I'm old old. I can still wear me some sleeveless dresses without the meat hangin off my arm. And I keep up with some things through my kids. Who ain't kids no more. To hear them tell it. So I don't say nuthin.

"Dancin with that tom," say Elo to Joe Lee, who leanin on the folks' freezer. "His feet can smell a cracker a mile away and go into their shuffle number post haste. And them eyes. He could be a little considerate and put on some shades. Who wants to look into them blown-out fuses that—"

"Is this what they call the generation gap?" I say.

"Generation gap," spits Elo, like I suggested castor oil and fricassee possum in the milk-shakes or somethin. "That's a white concept for a white phenomenon. There's no generation gap among Black people. We are a col—"

"Yeh, well never mind," says Joe Lee. "The point is Mama . . . well, it's pride. You embarrass yourself and us too dancin like that."

"I wasn't shame." Then nobody say nuthin. Them standin there in they pretty clothes with drinks in they hands and gangin up on me, and me in the third-degree chair and nary a olive to my name. Felt just like the police got hold to me.

"First of all," Task say, holding up his hand and tickin off the offenses, "the dress. Now that dress is too short, Mama, and too low-cut for a woman your age. And Tamu's going to make a speech tonight to kick off the campaign and will be introducin you and expecting you to organize the council of elders—"

"Me? Didn nobody ask me nuthin. You mean Nisi? She change her name?"

"Well, Norton was supposed to tell you about it. Nisi wants to introduce you and then encourage the older folks to form a Council of the Elders to act as an advisory—"

"And you going to be standing there with your boobs out and that wig on your head and that hem up to your ass. And people'll say, 'Ain't that the horny bitch that was grindin with the blind dude?"

"Elo, be cool a minute," say Task, gettin to the next finger. "And then there's the drinkin. Mama, you know you can't drink cause next thing you know you be laughin loud and carryin on," and he grab another finger for the loudness. "And then there's the dancin. You been tattooed on the man for four records straight and slow draggin even on the fast numbers. How you think that look for a woman your age?"

"What's my age?"

"What?"

"I'm axin you all a simple question. You keep talkin bout what's proper for a woman my age. How old am I anyhow?" And Joe Lee slams his eyes shut and squinches up his face to figure. And Task run a hand over his ear and stare into his glass like the ice cubes goin calculate for him. And Elo just starin at the top of my head like she goin rip the wig off any minute now.

"Is your hair braided up under that thing? If so, why don't you take it off? You always did do a neat cornroll."

"Uh huh," cause I'm thinkin how she couldn't undo her hair fast enough talking bout cornroll so countrified. None of which was the subject. "How old, I say?"

"Sixtee-one or—"

"You a damn lie Joe Lee Peoples."

"And that's another thing," say Task on the fingers.

"You know what you can all kiss," I said, gettin up and brushin the wrinkles out my lap.

"Oh, Mama," Elo say, puttin a hand on my shoulder like she hasn't done since she left home and the hand landin light and not sure it supposed to be there. Which hurt me to my heart. Cause this was the child in our happiness fore Mr. Peoples die. And I carried that child strapped to my chest till she was nearly two. We was close is what I'm tryin to tell you. Cause it was more me in the child than the others. And even after Task it was the girlchild I covered in the night and wept over for no reason at all less it was she was a chub-chub like me and not very pretty, but a warm child. And how did things get to this, that she can't put a sure hand on me and say Mama we love you and care about you and you entitled to enjoy yourself cause you a good woman?

"And then there's Reverend Trent," say Task, glancin from left to right like they hatchin a plot and just now lettin me in on it. "You were suppose to be talking with him tonight, Mama, about giving us his basement for campaign headquarters and—"

"Didn nobody tell me nuthin. If grass roots mean you kept in the dark I can't use it. I really can't. And Reven Trent a fool anyway the way he tore into the widow man up there on Edgecomb cause he wouldn't take in three of them foster children and the woman not even comfy in the ground yet and the man's mind messed up and—"

"Look here," say Task. "What we need is a family conference so we can get all this stuff cleared up and laid out on the table. In the meantime I think we better get back into the other room and tend to business. And in the meantime, Mama, see if you can't get to Reverend Trent and—"

"You want me to belly rub with the Reven, that it?"

"Oh damn," Elo say and go through the swingin door.

"We'll talk about all this at dinner. How's tomorrow night, Joe Lee?" While Joe Lee being self-important I'm wonderin who's doin the cookin and how come no body ax me if I'm free and do I get a corsage and things like that. Then Joe nod that it's O.K. and he go through the swingin door and just a little hubbub come through from the other room. Then Task smile his smile, lookin just like his daddy, and he leave. And it just me in this stranger's kitchen, which was a mess I wouldn't never let my kitchen look like. Poison you just to look at the pots. Then the door swing the other way and it's My Man Bovanne standin there sayin Miss Hazel but lookin at the deep fry and then at the steam table, and most surprised when I come up on him from the other direction and take him on out of there. Pass the folks pushin up towards the stage where Nisi and some other people settin and ready to talk, and folks gettin to the last of the sandwiches and the booze fore they settle down in one spot and listen serious. And I'm thinkin bout tellin Bovanne what a lovely long dress Nisi got on and the earrings and her hair piled up in a cone and the people bout to hear how we all gettin screwed and gotta form our own party and everybody there listenin and lookin. But instead I just haul the man on out of there, and Joe Lee and his wife look at me like I'm terrible, but they ain't said boo to the man yet. Cause he blind and old and don't nobody there need him since they grown up and don't need they skates fixed no more.

"Where we goin, Miss Hazel?" Him knowin all the time.

"First we gonna buy you some dark sunglasses. Then you comin with me to the supermarket so I can pick up tomorrow's dinner, which is goin to be a grand thing proper and you invited. Then we goin to my house."

"That be fine. I surely would like to rest my feet." Bein cute, but you got to let men play out they little show, blind or not. So he chat on bout how tired he is and how he appreciate me takin him in hand this way. And I'm thinkin I'll have him change the lock on my door first thing. Then I'll give the man a nice warm bath with jasmine leaves in the water and a little Epsom salt on the sponge to do his back. And then a good rubdown with rose water and olive oil. Then a cup of lemon tea with a taste in it. And a little talcum, some of that fancy stuff Nisi mother sent over last Christmas. And then a massage, a good face massage round the forehead which is the worryin part. Cause you gots to take care of the older folks. And let them know they still needed to run the mimeo machine and keep the spark plugs clean and fix the mailboxes for folks who might help us get the breakfast program goin, and the school for the little kids and the campaign and all. Cause old folks is the nation. That what Nisi was sayin and I mean to do my part.

"I imagine you are a very pretty woman, Miss Hazel."

"I surely am," I say just like the hussy my daughter always say I was.

Toni Cade Bambara

The Lesson

Back in the days when everyone was old and stupid or young and foolish and me and Sugar were the only ones just right, this lady moved on our block with nappy hair and proper speech and no makeup. And quite naturally we laughed at her, laughed the way we did at the junk man who went about his business like he was some big-time president and his sorry-ass horse his secretary. And we kinda hated her too, hated the way we did the winos who cluttered up our parks and pissed on our handball walls and stank up our hallways and stairs so you couldn't halfway play hide-and-seek without a goddamn gas mask. Miss Moore was her name. The only woman on the block with no first name. And she was black as hell, cept for her feet, which were fish-white and spooky. And she was always planning these boring-ass things for us to do, us being my cousin, mostly, who lived on the block cause we all moved North the same time and to the same apartment then spread out gradual to breathe. And our parents would yank our heads into some kinda shape and crisp up our clothes so we'd be presentable for travel with Miss Moore, who always looked like she was going to church, though she never did. Which is just one of the things the grownups talked about when they talked behind her back like a dog. But when she came calling with some sachet she'd sewed up or some gingerbread she'd made or some book, why then they'd all be too embarrassed to turn her down and we'd get handed over all spruced up. She'd been to college and said it was only right that she should take responsibility for the young ones' education, and she not even related by marriage or blood. So they'd go for it. Specially Aunt Gretchen. She was the main gofer in the family. You got some ole dumb shit foolishness you want somebody to go for, you send for Aunt Gretchen. She been screwed into the go-along for so long, it's a blood-deep natural thing with her. Which is how she got saddled with me and Sugar and Junior in the first place while our mothers were in a la-de-da apartment up the block having a good ole time.

So this one day Miss Moore rounds us all up at the mailbox and it's puredee hot and she's knockin herself out about arithmetic. And school suppose to let up in summer I heard, but she don't never let up. And the starch in my pinafore scratching the shit outta me and I'm really hating this nappy-head bitch and her goddamn college degree. I'd much rather go to the pool or to the show where it's cool. So me and Sugar leaning on the mailbox being surly, which is a Miss Moore word. And Flyboy checking out what everybody brought for lunch. And Fat Butt already wasting his peanut-butter-and-jelly sandwich like the pig he is. And Junebug punchin on Q.T.'s arm for potato chips. And Rosie Giraffe shifting from one hip to the other waiting for somebody to step on her foot or ask her if she from Georgia so she can kick ass, preferably Mercedes'. And Miss Moore asking us do we know what money is, like we a bunch of retards. I mean real money, she say, like it's only poker chips or monopoly papers we lay on the grocer. So right away I'm tired of this and say so. And would much rather snatch Sugar and go to the Sunset and terrorize the West Indian kids and take their hair ribbons and their money too. And Miss Moore files that remark away for next week's lesson on brotherhood, I can tell. And finally I say we oughta get to the subway cause it's cooler and besides we might meet some cute boys. Sugar done swiped her mama's lipstick, so we ready.

So we heading down the street and she's boring us silly about what things cost and what our parents make and how much goes for rent and how money ain't divided up right in this country. And then she gets to the part about we all poor and live in the slums, which I don't feature. And I'm ready to speak on that, but she steps out in the street and hails two cabs just like that. Then she hustles half the crew in with her and hands me a five-dollar bill and tells me to calculate 10 percent tip for the driver. And we're off Me and Sugar and Junebug and Flyboy hangin out the window and hollering to everybody, putting lipstick on each other cause Flyboy a faggot anyway, and making farts with our sweaty armpits. But I'm mostly trying to figure how to spend this money. But they all fascinated with the meter ticking and Junebug starts laying bets as to how much it'll read when Flyboy can't hold his breath no more. Then Sugar lays bets as to how much it'll be when we get there. So I'm stuck. Don't nobody want to go for my plan, which is to jump out at the next light and run off to the first bar-b-que we can find. Then the driver tells us to get the hell out cause we there already. And the meter reads eighty five cents. And I'm stalling to figure out the tip and Sugar say give him a dime. And I decide he don't need it bad as I do, so later for him. But then he tries to take off with Junebug foot still in the door so we talk about his mama something ferocious. Then we check out that we on Fifth Avenue and everybody dressed up in stockings. One lady in a fur coat, hot as it is. White folks crazy.

"This is the place," Miss Moore say, presenting it to us in the voice she uses at the museum. "Let's look in the windows before we go in."

"Can we steal?" Sugar asks very serious like she's getting the ground rules squared away before she plays. "I beg your pardon," say Miss Moore, and we fall out. So she leads us around the windows of the toy store and me and Sugar screamin, "This is mine, that's mine, I gotta have that, that was made for me, I was born for that," till Big Butt drowns us out.

"Hey, I'm goin to buy that there."

"That there? You don't even know what it is, stupid."

"I do so," he say punchin on Rosie Giraffe. "It's a microscope."

"Whatcha gonna do with a microscope, fool?"

"Look at things."

"Like what, Ronald?" ask Miss Moore. And Big Butt ain't got the first notion. So here go Miss Moore gabbing about the thousands of bacteria in a drop of water and the somethinorother in a speck of blood and the million and one living things in the air around us is invisible to the naked eye. And what she say that for? Junebug go to town on that "naked" and we rolling. Then Miss Moore ask what it cost. So we all jam into the window smudgin it up and the price tag say $300. So then she ask how long'd take for Big Butt and Junebug to save up their allowances. "Too long," I say. "Yeh," adds Sugar, "outgrown it by that time." And Miss Moore say no, you never outgrow learning instruments. "Why, even medical students and interns and," blah, blah, blah. And we ready to choke Big Butt for bringing it up in the first damn place.

"This here costs four hundred eighty dollars," say Rosie Giraffe. So we pile up all over her to see what she pointin out. My eyes tell me it's a chunk of glass cracked with something heavy, and different-color inks dripped into the splits, then the whole thing put into a oven or something. But for $480 it don't make sense.

"That's a paperweight made of semi-precious stones fused together under tremendous pressure," she explains slowly, with her hands doing the mining and all the factory work.

"So what's a paperweight?" asks Rosie Giraffe.

"To weigh paper with, dumbbell," say Flyboy, the wise man from the East.

"Not exactly," say Miss Moore, which is what she say when you warm or way off too. "It's to weigh paper down so it won't scatter and make your desk untidy." So right away me and Sugar curtsy to each other and then to Mercedes who is more the tidy type.

"We don't keep paper on top of the desk in my class," say Junebug, figuring Miss Moore crazy or lyin one.

"At home, then," she say. "Don't you have a calendar and a pencil case and a blotter and a letter-opener on your desk at home where you do your homework?" And she know damn well what our homes look like cause she nosys around in them every chance she gets.

"I don't even have a desk," say Junebug. "Do we?"

"No. And I don't get no homework neither," says Big Butt.

"And I don't even have a home," say Flyboy like he do at school to keep the white folks off his back and sorry for him. Send this poor kid to camp posters, is his specialty.

"I do," says Mercedes. "I have a box of stationery on my desk and a picture of my cat. My godmother bought the stationery and the desk. There's a big rose on each sheet and the envelopes smell like roses."

"Who wants to know about your smelly-ass stationery," say Rosie Giraffe fore I can get my two cents in.

"It's important to have a work area all your own so that . . ."

"Will you look at this sailboat, please," say Flyboy, cuttin her off and pointin to the thing like it was his. So once again we tumble all over each other to gaze at this magnificent thing in the toy store which is just big enough to maybe sail two kittens across the pond if you strap them to the posts tight. We all start reciting the price tag like we in assembly. "Handcrafted sailboat of fiberglass at one thousand one hundred ninety-five dollars."

"Unbelievable," I hear myself say and am really stunned. I read it again for myself just in case the group recitation put me in a trance. Same thing. For some reason this pisses me off. We look at Miss Moore and she lookin at us, waiting for I dunno what.

"Who'd pay all that when you can buy a sailboat set for a quarter at Pop's, a tube of glue for a dime, and a ball of string for eight cents? It must have a motor and a whole lot else besides," I say. "My sailboat cost me about fifty cents."

"But will it take water?" say Mercedes with her smart ass.

"Took mine to Alley Pond Park once," say Flyboy. "String broke. Lost it. Pity."

"Sailed mine in Central Park and it keeled over and sank. Had to ask my father for another dollar."

"And you got the strap," laugh Big Butt. "The jerk didn't even have a string on it. My old man wailed on his behind."

Little Q.T. was staring hard at the sailboat and you could see he wanted it bad. But he too little and somebody'd just take it from him. So what the hell. "This boat for kids, Miss Moore?"

"Parents silly to buy something like that just to get all broke up," say Rosie Giraffe.

"That much money it should last forever," I figure.

"My father'd buy it for me if I wanted it."

"Your father, my ass," say Rosie Giraffe getting a chance to finally push Mercedes.

"Must be rich people shop here," say Q.T.

"You are a very bright boy," say Flyboy. "What was your first clue?" And he rap him on the head with the back of his knuckles, since Q.T. the only one he could get away with. Though Q.T. liable to come up behind you years later and get his licks in when you half expect it.

"What I want to know is," I says to Miss Moore though I never talk to her, I wouldn't give the bitch that satisfaction, "is how much a real boat costs? I figure a thousand'd get you a yacht any day."

"Why don't you check that out," she says, "and report back to the group?" Which really pains my ass. If you gonna mess up a perfectly good swim day least you could do is have some answers. "Let's go in," she say like she got something up her sleeve. Only she don't lead the way. So me and Sugar turn the corner to where the entrance is, but when we get there I kinda hang back. Not that I'm scared, what's there to be afraid of, just a toy store. But I feel funny, shame. But what I got to be shamed about? Got as much right to go in as anybody. But somehow I can't seem to get hold of the door, so I step away for Sugar to lead. But she hangs back too. And I look at her and she looks at me and this is ridiculous. I mean, damn, I have never ever been shy about doing nothing or going nowhere. But then Mercedes steps up and then Rosie Giraffe and Big Butt crowd in behind and shove, and next thing we all stuffed into the doorway with only Mercedes squeezing past us, smoothing out her jumper and walking right down the aisle. Then the rest of us tumble in like a glued together jigsaw done all wrong. And people lookin at us. And it's like the time me and Sugar crashed into the Catholic church on a dare. But once we got in there and everything so hushed and holy and the candles and the bowin and the handkerchiefs on all the drooping heads, I just couldn't go through with the plan. Which was for me to run up to the altar and do a tap dance while Sugar played the nose flute and messed around in the holy water. And Sugar kept givin me the elbow. Then later teased me so bad I tied her up in the shower and turned it on and locked her in. And she'd be there till this day if Aunt Gretchen hadn't finally figured I was lyin about the boarder takin a shower.

Same thing in the store. We all walkin on tiptoe and hardly touchin the games and puzzles and things. And I watched Miss Moore who is steady watchin us like she waitin for a sign. Like Mama Drewery watches the sky and sniffs the air and takes note of just how much slant is in the bird formation. Then me and Sugar bump smack into each other, so busy gazing at the toys, 'specially the sailboat. But we don't laugh and go into our fat-lady bump-stomach routine. We just stare at that price tag. Then Sugar run a finger over the whole boat. And I'm jealous and want to hit her. Maybe not her, but I sure want to punch somebody in the mouth.

"Watcha bring us here for, Miss Moore?"

"You sound angry, Sylvia. Are you mad about something?" Givin me one of them grins like she tellin a grown-up joke that never turns out to be funny. And she's lookin very closely at me like maybe she plannin to do my portrait from memory. I'm mad, but I won't give her that satisfaction. So I slouch around the store bein very bored and say, "Let's go."

Me and Sugar at the back of the train watchin the tracks whizzin by large then small then gettin gobbled up in the dark. I'm thinkin about this tricky toy I saw in the store. A clown that somersaults on a bar then does chin-ups just cause you yank lightly at his leg. Cost $35. I could see me askin my mother for a $35 birthday clown. "You wanna who that costs what?" she'd say, cocking her head to the side to get a better view of the hole in my head. Thirty-five dollars could buy new bunk beds for Junior and Gretchen's boy. Thirty-five dollars and the whole household could go visit Granddaddy Nelson in the country. Thirty-five dollars would pay for the rent and the piano bill too. Who are these people that spend that much for performing clowns and $1000 for toy sailboats? What kinda work they do and how they live and how come we ain't in on it? Where we are is who we are, Miss Moore always pointin out. But it don't necessarily have to be that way, she always adds then waits for somebody to say that poor people have to wake up and demand their share of the pie and don't none of us know what kind of pie she talkin about in the first damn place. But she ain't so smart cause I still got her four dollars from the taxi and she sure ain't gettin it. Messin up my day with this shit. Sugar nudges me in my pocket and winks.

Miss Moore lines us up in front of the mailbox where we started from, seem like years ago, and I got a headache for thinkin so hard. And we lean all over each other so we can hold up under the draggy-ass lecture she always finishes us off with at the end before we thank her for borin us to tears. But she just looks at us like she readin tea leaves. Finally she say, "Well, what did you think of F.A.O. Schwarz?"

Rosie Giraffe mumbles, "White folks crazy."

"I'd like to go there again when I get my birthday money," says Mercedes, and we shove her out the pack so she has to lean on the mailbox by herself.

"I'd like a shower. Tiring day," say Flyboy.

Then Sugar surprises me by saying, "You know, Miss Moore, I don't think all of us here put together eat in a year what that sailboat costs." And Miss Moore lights up like somebody goosed her. "And?" she say, urging Sugar on. Only I'm standin on her foot so she don't continue.

"Imagine for a minute what kind of society it is in which some people can spend on a toy what it would cost to feed a family of six or seven. What do you think?"

"I think," say Sugar pushing me off her feet like she never done before, cause I whip her ass in a minute, "that this is not much of a democracy if you ask me. Equal chance to pursue happiness means an equal crack at the dough, don't it?" Miss Moore is besides herself and I am disgusted with Sugar's treachery. So I stand on her foot one more time to see if she'll shove me. She shuts up, and Miss Moore looks at me, sorrowfully I'm thinkin. And somethin weird is going on, I can feel it in my chest.

"Anybody else learn anything today?" lookin dead at me. I walk away and Sugar has to run to catch up and don't even seem to notice when I shrug her arm off my shoulder.

"Well, we got four dollars anyway," she says.

"Uh hunh."

"We could go to Hascombs and get half a chocolate layer and then go to the Sunset and still have plenty money for potato chips and ice cream sodas."

"Uh hunh."

"Race you to Hascombs," she say.

We start down the block and she gets ahead which is O.K. by me cause I'm going to the West End and then over to the Drive to think this day through. She can run if she want to and even run faster. But ain't nobody gonna beat me at nuthin.

TONI CADE BAMBARA

The Organizer's Wife

The men from the co-op school were squatting in her garden. Jake, who taught the day students and hassled the town school board, was swiping at the bushy greens with his cap, dislodging slugs, raising dust. The tall gent who ran the graphics workshop was pulling a penknife open with his teeth, scraping rust from the rake she hadn't touched in weeks. Old Man Boone was up and down. Couldn't squat too long on account of the ankle broken in last spring's demonstration when the tobacco weights showed funny. Jack-in-the-box up, Boone snatched at a branch or two and stuffed his pipe—crumblings of dry leaf, bits of twig. Down, he eased string from the seams of his overalls, up again, thrumbling up tobacco from the depths of his pockets.

She couldn't hear them. They were silent. The whole morning stock-still, nothing stirring. The baby quiet too, drowsing his head back in the crook of her arm as she stepped out into the sun already up and blistering. The men began to unbend, shifting weight to one leg then the other, watching her move about the jumbled yard. But no one spoke.

She bathed the baby with the little dew that had gathered on what few leaves were left on the branches crackling, shredding into the empty rain barrels. The baby gurgled, pinching her arms. Virginia had no energy for a smile or a wince. All energy summoned up at rising was focused tightly on her two errands of the day. She took her time going back in, seeing the men shift around in the heaps of tomatoes, in the snarl of the strawberry runners. Stamped her shoe against each step, carrying the baby back in. Still no one spoke, though clearly, farmers all their lives, they surely had some one thing to say about the disarray of her garden.

The young one, whose voice she well knew from the sound truck, had his mouth open and his arm outstretched as though to speak on the good sense of turning every inch of ground to food, or maybe to rant against the crime of letting it just go. He bent and fingered the brown of the poke salad that bordered the dry cabbages, his mouth closing again. Jake rose suddenly and cleared his throat, but turned away to light Old Man Boone's pipe, lending a shoulder for the old one to bunch against, cupping the bowl and holding the match, taking a long lingering time, his back to her. She sucked her teeth and went in.

When she came out again, banding the baby's carry straps around her waist, she moved quickly, stepping into the radishes, crushing unidentifiable shoots underfoot. Jake stepped back out of the way and caught his cuffs in the rake. Jake was the first in a long line to lose his land to unpaid taxes. The bogus receipts were pinned prominently as always to his jacket pocket. Signed by someone the county said did not exist, but who'd managed nonetheless to buy up Jake's farm at auction and turn it over swiftly to the granite company. She looked from the huge safety pin to the hot, brown eyes that quickly dropped. The other men rose up around her, none taller than she, though all taller than the corn bent now, grit-laden with neglect. Out of the comer of her eye, she saw a white worm work its way into the once-silky tufts turned straw, then disappear.

"Mornin," she said, stretching out her hand.

The men mumbled quickly, clearing their throats again. Boone offering a hand in greeting, then realizing she was extending not her hand but the small, round tobacco tin in it. Graham's red tobacco tin with the boy in shiny green astride an iron horse. It was Graham's habit, when offering a smoke, to spin some tale or other about the boy on the indestructible horse, a tale the smoker would finish. The point always the same—the courage of the youth, the hope of the future. Boone drew his hand back quickly as though the red tin was aflame. She curled her hand closed and went out the gate, slowly, deliberately, fixing her tall, heavy image indelibly on their eyes.

"Good-for-nuthin."

They thought that's what they heard drift back over her shoulder. Them? The tin? The young one thought he saw her pitch it into the clump of tomatoes hanging on by the gate. But no one posed the question.

"Why didn't you say somethin?" Jake demanded of his star pupil, the orator, whose poems and tales and speeches delivered from the sound truck had done more to pull the districts together, the women all said, than all the leaflets the kids cluttered the fields with, than all the posters from the co-op's graphic workshop masking the road signs, than all the meetings which not all the folk could get to.

"Why didn't you speak?" Jake shoved the young one, and for a minute they were all stumbling, dancing nimbly to avoid destroying food that could still be salvaged.

"Watch it, watch it now," Old Boone saying, checking his foot brace and grabbing the young one up, a fistful of sleeve.

"You shoulda said somethin," the tall gent spat.

"Why me?" The young one whined—not in the voice he'd cultivated for the sound truck. "I don't know her no better than yawl do."

"One of the women shoulda come," said the tall gent.

The men looked at each other, then stared down the road. It was clear that no one knew any more how to talk to the bristling girl-woman, if ever any had.

It wasn't a shift in breeze that made the women look up, faces stuck out as if to catch the rain. 'Cause there was no breeze and there'd been no rain. And look like, one of them said, there'd be no bus either. The strained necks had more to do with sound than weather. Someone coming. A quick check said all who worked in town were already gathered at the bus stop. Someone coming could only mean trouble—fire broke out somewhere, riot in town, one of the children hurt, market closed down, or maybe another farm posted. The women standing over their vegetable baskets huddled together for conference, then broke apart to jut their bodies out over the road for a look-see. The women seated atop the bags of rags or uniforms, clustered to question each other, then scattered, some standing tiptoe, others merely leaning up from the rocks to question the market women. And in that brief second, as bodies pulled upward, the rocks blotted up more sun to sear them, sting them, sicken them with. These stones, stacked generations ago to keep the rain from washing the road away, banked higher and broader by the young folk now to keep the baking earth from breaking apart.

Virginia nodded to the women, her earrings tinkling against her neck. The "Mornins" and "How do's" came scraggly across the distance. The bus-stop plot was like an island separated from the mainland road by shimmering sheets of heat, by arid moats and gullies that had once been the drainage system, dried-out craters now misshapen, as though pitted and gouged by war.

One clear voice rising above the scattered sopranos, calling her by name, slowed Virginia down. Frankie Lee Taylor, the lead alto in the choir, was standing on the rocks waving, out of her choir robes and barely recognizable but for that red-and-yellow jumper, the obligatory ugly dress just right for the kitchens in town. "Everything all right?" the woman asked for everyone there. And not waiting for a word once Virginia's face could be read by all, she continued: "Bus comin at all, ever?"

Virginia shrugged and picked up her pace. If the six-thirty bus was this late coming, she thought, she could make the first call and be back on the road in time for the next bus to town. She wouldn't have to borrow the church station wagon after all. She didn't want to have to ask for nothing. When she saw Graham that afternoon she wanted the thing stitched up, trimmed, neat, finished. Wanted to be able to say she asked for "nuthin from nobody and didn't nobody offer up nuthin." It'd be over with. They'd set bail and she'd pay it with the money withheld from the seed and the fertilizer, the wages not paid to the two students who used to help in the garden, the money saved 'cause she was too cranky to eat, to care. Pay the bail and unhook them both from this place. Let some other damn fool break his health on this place, the troubles.

She'd been leaving since the first day coming, the day her sister came home to cough herself to death and leave her there with nobody to look out for her 'cept some hinkty cousins in town and Miz Mama Mae, who shook her head sadly whenever the girl spoke of this place and these troubles and these people and one day soon leaving for some other place. She'd be going now for sure. Virginia was smiling now and covering a whole lotta ground.

Someone was coming up behind her, churning up the loose layers of clay, the red-and-yellow jumper a mere blur in the haze of red dust. Everyone these dry, hot days looked like they'd been bashed with a giant powder puff of henna. Virginia examined her own hands, pottery-red like the hands of her cousins seen through the beauty-parlor windows in town, hands sunk deep in the pots, working up the mud packs for the white women lounging in the chairs. She looked at her arms, her clothes, and slowed down. Not even well into the morning and already her skimpy bath ruined. The lime-boiled blouse no longer white but pink.

"Here, Gin," the woman was saying. "He a good man, your man. He share our hardships, we bear his troubles, our troubles." She was stuffing money in between the carry straps, patting the chubby legs as the baby lolled in his cloth carriage. "You tell Graham we don't forget that he came back. Lots of the others didn't, forgot. You know, Gin, that you and me and the rest of the women . . ." She was going to say more but didn't. Was turning with her mouth still open, already trotting up the road, puffs of red swirling about her feet and legs, dusting a line in that red-and-yellow jumper the way Miz Mama Mae might do making hems in the shop.

Virginia hoisted the baby higher on her back and rewound the straps, clutching the money tight, flat in her fist. She thought about Miz Mama Mae, pins in her mouth, fussing at her. "What's them hanky-type hems you doin, Gin?" she'd say, leaning over her apprentice. "When ya sew for the white folks you roll them kinda stingy hems. And you use this here oldish thread to insure a quick inheritance. But when you sew for us folks, them things got to last season in and season out and many a go-round exchange. Make some hefty hems, girl, hefty."

And Virginia had come to measure her imprisonment by how many times that same red-and-yellow jumper met her on the road, faded and fading some more, but the fairly bright hem getting wider and wider, the telltale rim recording the seasons past, the owners grown. While she herself kept busting out of her clothes, straining against the good thread, outdistancing the hefty hems. Growing so fast from babe to child to girl to someone, folks were always introducing and reintroducing themselves to her. It seemed at times that the walls wouldn't contain her, the roof wouldn't stop her. Busting out of childhood, busting out her clothes, but never busting out the place.

And now the choir woman had given her the money like that and spoken, trying to attach her all over again, root her, ground her in the place. Just when there was a chance to get free. Virginia clamped her jaws tight and tried to go blank. Tried to blot out all feelings and things—the farms, the co-op sheds, the lone gas pump, a shoe left in the road, the posters promising victory over the troubles. She never wanted these pictures called up on some future hot, dry day in some other place. She squinted, closed her eyes even, 'less the pictures cling to her eyes, store in the brain, to roll out later and crush her future with the weight of this place and its troubles.

Years before when there'd been rain and ways to hold it, she'd trotted along this road not seeing too much, trotting and daydreaming, delivering parcels to and from Miz Mama Mae's shop. She could remember that one time, ducking and dodging the clods of earth chucked up by the horse's hooves. Clods spinning wet and heavy against her skirts, her legs, as she followed behind, seeing nothing outside her own pictures but that horse and rider. Trying to keep up, keep hold of the parcel slipping all out of shape in the drizzle, trying to piece together the things she would say to him when he finally turned round and saw her. She had lived the scene often enough in bed to know she'd have to speak, say something to make him hoist her up behind him in the saddle, to make him gallop her off to the new place. She so busy dreaming, she let the curve of the road swerve her off toward the edge. Mouthing the things to say and even talking out loud with her hands and almost losing the slippery bundle, not paying good enough attention. And a ball of earth shot up and bit her square in the chest and sent her stumbling over the edge into the gully. The choir organist's robe asprawl in the current that flushed the garbage down from the hill where the townies lived, to the bottom where the folks lived, to the pit where the co-op brigade made compost heaps for independence, laughing.

Graham had pulled her up and out by the wrists, pulled her against him and looked right at her. Not at the cabbage leaves or chicory on her arms, a mango sucked hairy to its pit clinging to her clothes. But looked at her. And no screen door between them now. No glass or curtain, or shrub peeked through.

"You followin me." He grinned. And she felt herself swimming through the gap in his teeth.

And now she would have to tell him. 'Cause she had lost three times to the coin flipped on yesterday morning. Had lost to the icepick pitched in the afternoon in the dare-I-don't-I boxes her toe had sketched in the yard. Had lost at supper to the shadow slanting across the tablecloth that reached her wrist before Miz Mama Mae finished off the corn relish. Had lost that dawn to the lazy lizard, suddenly quickened in his journey on the ceiling when the sun came up. Lost against doing what she'd struggled against doing in order to win one more day of girlhood before she jumped into her womanstride and stalked out on the world. I want to come to you. I want to come to you and be with you. I want to be your woman, she did not say after all.

"I want to come to the co-op school," she said. "I want to learn to read better and type and figure and keep accounts so I can get out of . . ."—this place, she didn't say—"my situation."

He kept holding her and she kept wanting and not wanting to ease out of his grip and rescue the choir robe before it washed away.

"I had five years schooling 'fore I came here," she said, talking way too loud. "Been two years off and on at the church school . . . before you came."

"You do most of Miz Mama Mae's cipherin I hear? Heard you reading the newspapers to folks in the tobacco shed. You read well."

She tried to pull away then, thinking he was calling her a liar or poking fun some way. "Cipherin" wasn't how he talked. But he didn't let go. She expected to see her skin twisted and puckered when she looked at where he was holding her. But his grip was soft. Still she could not step back.

"You been watchin me," he said with the grin again. And looking into his face, she realized he wasn't at all like she'd thought. Was older, heavier, taller, smoother somehow. But then looking close up was not like sneaking a look from the toolshed as he'd come loping across the fields with his pigeon-toed self and in them soft leather boots she kept waiting to see fall apart from rough wear till she finally decided he must own pairs and pairs of all the same kind. Yes, she'd watched him on his rounds, in and out of the houses, the drying sheds, down at the docks, after fellowship in the square. Talking, laughing, teaching, always moving. Had watched him from the trees, through windows as he banged tables, arguing about deeds, urging, coaxing, pleading, hollering, apologizing, laughing again. In the early mornings, before Miz Mama Mae called the girls to sew, she had watched him chinning on the bar he'd slammed between the portals of the co-op school door. Huffing, puffing, cheeks like chipmunks. The dark circle of his gut sucking in purple, panting out blue. Yes, she watched him. But she said none of this or of the other either. Not then.

"I want to come to night school" was how she put it. "I don't know yet what kinda work I can do for the co-op. But I can learn."

"That's the most I ever heard you talk," he was saying, laughing so hard, he loosened his grip. "In the whole three years I've been back, that's the most—" He was laughing again. And he was talking way too loud himself.

She hadn't felt the least bit foolish standing there in the drizzle, in the garbage, tall up and full out of her clothes nearly, and Graham laughing at her. Not the least bit foolish 'cause he was talking too loud and laughing too hard. And she was going to go to his school. And whether he knew it or not, he was going to take her away from this place.

Wasn't but a piece of room the school, with a shed tacked on in back for storage and sudden meetings. The furniture was bandaged but brightly painted. The chemistry equipment was old but worked well enough. The best thing was the posters. About the co-op, about Malcolm and Harriet and Fannie Lou, about Guinea-Bissau and Vietnam. And the posters done by the children, the pictures cut from magazines, the maps—all slapped up as though to hold the place together, to give an identity to the building so squat upon the land. The identity of the place for her was smells. The smell of mortar vibrating from the walls that were only wood. The smell of loam that curled up from the sink, mostly rusted metal. The green-and-brown smell rising up over heads sunk deep into palms as folks leaned over their papers, bearing down on stumps of pencil or hunks of charcoal, determined to get now and to be what they'd been taught was privilege impossible, what they now knew was their right, their destiny.

"Season after season," Graham was dictating that first night, leaning up against the maps with the ruler, "we have pulled gardens out of stones, creating something from nothing—creators."

Sweat beading on a nose to her left, a temple to her right. Now and then a face she knew from fellowship looking up as Graham intoned the statements, tapping the ruler against the table to signal punctuation traps. And she working hard, harder than some, though she never ever did learn to speak her speak as most folks finally did. But grateful just to be there, and up in front, unlike the past when, condemned by her size, she'd been always exiled in the rear with the goldfish tanks or the rabbits that always died, giving her a suspect reputation.

"The first step toward getting the irrigation plant," he continued, crashing the ruler down, "is to organize."

"Amen," said one lady by the window, never looking up from her paper, certain she would finally train herself and be selected secretary of the church board. "That way us folks can keep track of them folks" was how she'd said it when she rose to speak her speak one summer night.

"What can defeat greed, technological superiority, and legal lawlessness," Graham had finished up, "is discipline, consciousness, and unity."

Always three sentences that folks would take home for discussion, for transformation into well-ordered paragraphs that wound up, some of them, in the co-op newsletter or on the posters or in the church's bulletin. Many became primers for the children.

Graham had been wearing the denim suit with the leather buckles the first night in class. Same fancy suit she'd caught sight of through the screen door when he'd come calling on Miz Mama Mae to buy the horse. A denim suit not country-cut at all—in fact, so *not* she was sure he would be leaving. Dudes in well-cut denim'd been coming and leaving since the days she wore but one yard of cloth. It was his would-be-moving-on clothes that had pulled her to him. But then the pull had become too strong to push against once his staying-on became clear.

She often fixed him supper in a metal cake tin once used for buttons. And Miz Mama Mae joked with the pin cushion, saying the girl weren't fooling nobody but herself sneaking around silly out there in the pantry with the button box. Telling the bobbins it was time certain folk grew up to match they size. And into the night, treadling away on the machine, the woman addressed the dress form, saying a strong, serious-type schoolteacher man had strong, serious work to do. Cutting out the paper patterns, the woman told the scissors that visiting a man in his rooms at night could mean disaster or jubilee one. And Virginia understood she would not be stopped by the woman. But some felt she was taking up too much of his time, their time. He was no longer where they could find him for homework checks or questions about the law. And Jake and Old Man Boone sullen, nervous that the midnight strategy meetings were too few now and far between. The women of the nearby district would knock and enter with trapped firefly lanterns, would shove these on the table between the couple, and make their point as Graham nodded and Virginia giggled or was silent, one.

His quilt, Graham explained, leaving the earrings on the table for her to find, was made from patches from his daddy's overalls, and scraps from Boone's wedding cutaway, white remnants from his mother's shroud, some blue from a sister's graduation, and khaki, too, snatched from the uniform he'd been proud of killing in in Korea a hundred lives ago. The day students had stitched a liberation flag in one corner. The night students had restuffed it and made a new border. She and Miz Mama Mae had stitched it and aired it. And Virginia had brought it back to him, wrapped in it. She had rolled herself all in it, to hide from him in her new earrings, childish. But he never teased that she was too big for games, and she liked that. He found her in it, his tongue finding the earrings first. Careful, girl, she'd warned herself. This could be a trap, she murmured under him.

"Be my woman," he whispered into her throat.

You don't have time for me, she didn't say, lifting his tikis and medallions up over his head. And there'd never be enough time here with so many people, so much land to work, so much to do, and the wells not even dug, she thought, draping the chains around his bedpost.

"Be my woman, Gin," he said again. And she buried her fingers in his hair and he buried his hair inside her clothes and she pulled the quilt close and closed him in, crying.

She was leaking. The earrings tinkling against her neck. The medallions clinking against the bedpost in her mind. Cray splotches stiffened in her new pink blouse, rubbing her nipples raw. But other than a dribble that oozed momentarily down her back, there was no sign of the baby aroused and hungry. If the baby slept on, she'd keep on. She wanted to reach Revun Michaels before the white men came. Came this time brazenly with the surveyors and the diggers, greedy for the granite under the earth. Wanted to catch Revun Michaels before he showed them his teeth and wouldn't hear her, couldn't, too much smiling. Wanted to hear him say it—the land's been sold. The largest passel of land in the district, the church holdings where the co-op school stood, where two storage sheds of the co-op stood, where the graphics workshop stood, where four families had lived for generations working the land. The church had sold the land. He'd say it, she'd hear it, and it'd be over with. She and Graham could go.

She was turning the bend now, forgetting to not look, and the mural the co-op had painted in eye-stinging colors stopped her. FACE UP TO WHAT'S KILLING YOU, it demanded. Below the statement a huge triangle that from a distance was just a triangle, but on approaching, as one muttered 'how deadly can a triangle be?' turned into bodies on bodies. At the top, fat, fanged beasts in smart clothes, like the ones beneath it laughing, drinking, eating, bombing, raping, shooting, lounging on the backs of, feeding off the backs of, the folks at the base, crushed almost flat but struggling to get up and getting up, topple the structure. She passed it quickly. All she wanted to think about was getting to Revun Michaels quick to hear it. Sold the land. Then she'd be free to string together the bits and scraps of things for so long bobbing about in her head. Things that had to be pieced together well, with strong thread so she'd have a whole thing to shove through the mesh at Graham that afternoon.

And would have to shove hard or he'd want to stay, convinced that folks would battle for his release, would battle for themselves, the children, the future, would keep on no matter how powerful the thief, no matter how little the rain, how exhausted the soil, 'cause this was home. Not a plot of earth for digging in or weeping over or crawling into, but home. Near the Ethiopic where the ancestral bones spoke their speak on certain nights if folks stamped hard enough, sang long enough, shouted. Home. Where "America" was sung but meant something altogether else than it had at the old school. Home in the future. The future here now developing. Home liberated soon. And the earth would recover. The rain would come. The ancient wisdoms would be revived. The energy released. Home a human place once more. The bones spoke it. The spirit spoke, too, through flesh when the women gathered at the altar, the ancient orishas still vibrant beneath the ghostly patinas some thought right to pray to, but connected in spite of themselves to the spirits under the plaster.

WE CANNOT LOSE, the wall outside the church said. She paused at the bulletin board, the call-for-meeting flyers limp in the heat. She bent to spit but couldn't raise it. She saw Revun Michaels in the schoolhouse window watching her. He'd say it. Sold the land.

Virginia wondered what the men in her ruined garden were telling themselves now about land as power and land and man tied to the future, not the past. And what would they tell the women when the bulldozers came to claim the earth, to maim it, rape it, plunder it all with that bone-deep hatred for all things natural? And what would the women tell the children dangling in the tires waiting for Jake to ring the bell? Shouting from the clubhouses built in the trees? The slashed trees oozing out money into the white man's pails, squeezing hard to prolong a tree life, forestalling the brutal cut down to stump. Then stump wasting, no more money to give, blown up out of the earth, the iron claw digging deep and merciless to rip out the taproots, leaving for the children their legacy, an open grave, gouged out by a gene-deep hatred for all things natural, for all things natural that couldn't turn a quick penny quick enough to dollar. She spit.

Revun Michaels, small and balding, was visible in the schoolhouse window. His expression carried clear out the window to her, watching her coming fast, kicking himself for getting caught in there and only one door, now that the shed was nailed on fast in back.

"Did you sell the land as well?" she heard herself saying, rushing in the doorway much too fast. "You might have waited like folks asked you. You didn't have to. Enough granite under this schoolhouse alone"—she stamped, frightening him—"to carry both the districts for years and years, if we developed it ourselves." She heard the "we ourselves" explode against her teeth and she fell back.

"Wasn't me," he stammered. "The church board saw fit to—"

"Fit!" She was advancing now, propelled by something she had no time to understand. "Wasn't nuthin fitten about it." She had snatched the ruler from its book. The first slam hard against the chair he swerved around, fleeing. The next cracked hard against his teeth. His legs buckled under and he slid down, his face frozen in disbelief. But nothing like the disbelief that swept through her the moment "we ourselves" pushed past clenched teeth and nailed her to the place, a woman unknown. She saw the scene detached, poster figures animated: a hefty woman pursuing a scrambling man in and out among the tables and chairs in frantic games before Jake rang the bell for lessons to commence.

"And what did the white folks pay you to turn Graham in and clear the way? Disturber of the peace. What peace? Racist trying to incite a riot. Ain't that how they said it? Outside agitator, as you said. And his roots put down here long before you ever came. When you were just a twinkle in Darwin's eye." Virginia heard herself laughing. It was a good, throaty laugh and big. The man was turning round now on the floor, staring at her in amazement.

"Thirty pieces of silver, maybe? That's what you preach, tradition. Thirty pieces 'bout as traditional as—"

"Just hold on. It wasn't me that—The board of trustees advised me that this property could not be used for—"

The ruler came down on the stiff of his arm and broke. Michaels dropped between two rickety chairs that came apart on top of him. The baby cried, the woman shushed, as much to quiet the woman that was her. Calm now, she watched the man try to get up, groping the chairs the folks had put together from cast-offs for the school. Her shoe caught him at the side of his head and he went under.

The station wagon was pulling up as she was coming out, flinging the piece of ruler into the bushes. She realized then that the men had come in it, that the station wagon had been sitting all morning in her garden. That they had come to take her to see Graham. She bit her lip. She never gave folk a chance, just like Miz Mama Mae always fussed. Never gave them or herself a chance to speak the speak.

"We'll take you to him," Jake was saying, holding the door open and easing the baby off her back.

The young one shoved over. "Mother Lee who's secretarying for the board has held up the papers for the sale. We came to tell you that." He waited till she smiled to laugh. "We're the delegation that's going to confront the board this evening. Us and Frankie Lee Taylor and—"

"Don't talk the woman to death," said Boone, turning in his seat and noting her daze. He was going to say more, but the motor drowned him out. Virginia hugged the baby close and unbuttoned her blouse.

"That's one sorry piece of man," drawled Boone as they pulled out. All heads swung to the right to see the short, fat, balding preacher darting in and out among the gravestones for the sanctuary of the church. To the phone, Virginia figured. And would they jail her too, she and the baby?

Then everyone was silent before the naked breast and the sucking. Silence was what she needed. And time, to draw together tight what she'd say to Graham. How blood had spurted from Revun Michaels's ear, for one thing. Graham might not want to hear it, but there was no one else to tell it to, to explain how it was when all she thought she wanted was to hear it said flat out—land's been sold, school's no more. Not that a school's a building, she argued with herself, watching the baby, playing with the image of herself speaking her speak finally in the classroom, then realizing that she already had. By tomorrow the women would have burrowed beneath the tale of some swinging door or however Revun Michaels would choose to tell it. But would the women be able to probe and sift and explain it to her? Who could explain her to her?

And how to explain to Graham so many things. About this new growth she was experiencing, was thinking on at night wrapped in his quilt. Not like the dread growing up out of her clothes as though she'd never stop 'fore she be freak, 'cause she had stopped. And not like the new growth that was the baby, for she'd expected that, had been prepared. More like the toenail smashed the day the work brigade had stacked the stones to keep the road from splitting apart. The way the new nail pushed up against the old turning blue, against the gauze and the tape, stubborn to establish itself. A chick pecking through the shell, hard-headed and hasty and wobbly. She might talk of it this time. She was convinced she could get hold of it this time.

She recalled that last visiting time trying to speak on what was happening to her coming through the shell. But had trouble stringing her feelings about so many things together, words to drape around him, to smother all those other things, things she had said, hurled unstrung, flung out with tantrum heat at a time when she thought there would always be time enough to coolly take them back, be woman warm in some elsewhere place and make those hurtful words forgettable. But then they had come for him in the afternoon, came and got him, took him from the schoolhouse in handcuffs. And when she had visited him in the jail, leaning into the mesh, trying to push past the barrier, she could tell the way the guards hovered around her and baby that clearly they thought she could do, would do, what they had obviously tried over and over to do, till Graham was ashy and slow, his grin lax. That she could break him open so they could break him down. She almost had, not knowing it, leaking from the breast as she always did not keeping track of the time. Stuttering, whining, babbling, hanging on to the mesh with one hand, the other stuffed in her mouth, her fingers ensnarled in the skein of words coming out all tangled, knotted.

"I don't mind this so much," he'd cut in. "Time to think."

And when she pulled her fingers from her mouth, the thread broke and all her words came bouncing out in a hopeless scatter of tears and wails until something—her impatience with her own childishness, or maybe it was the obvious pleasure of the guards—made her grab herself up. She grabbed herself up abrupt, feeling in that moment what it was she wanted to say about her nights wrapped up in the quilt smelling him in it, hugging herself, grabbing herself up and trying to get to that place that was beginning to seem more of a when than a where. And the when seemed to be inside her if she could only connect.

"I kinda like the quiet," he had said. "Been a while since I've had so much time to think." And then he grinned and was ugly. Was that supposed to make her hate him? To hate and let go? That had occurred to her on the bus home. But roaming around the house, tripping on the edges of the quilt, she had rejected it. That was not the meaning of his words or that smile that had torn his face. She'd slumped in the rocking chair feeding the baby, examining her toenail for such a time.

"They never intended to dig the wells, that's clear," Old Man Boone was saying. "That was just to get into the district, get into our business, check out our strength. I was a fool," he muttered, banging his pipe against his leg remembering his hopefulness, his hospitality even. "A fool."

"Well, gaddamn, Boone," the tall gent sputtered. "Can't you read? That's what our flyers been saying all along. Don't you read the stuff we put out? Gaddamnit, Boone."

"If you don't read the flyers, you leastways knows history," the young one was saying. "When we ever invited the beast to dinner he didn't come in and swipe the napkins and start taking notes on the tablecloth 'bout how to take over the whole house?"

"Now that's the truth," Jake said, laughing. His laughter pulled Virginia forward, and she touched his arm, moved. That he could laugh. His farm stolen and he could laugh. But that was one of the three most moving things about Jake, she was thinking. The way he laughed. The way he sweated. The way he made his body comfy for the children to lean against.

"Yeh, they sat right down to table and stole the chicken," said Jake.

"And took the table. And the deed." The tall gent smacked Jake on his cap.

"Yeh," Old Man Boone muttered, thinking of Graham.

"We ain't nowhere's licked yet though, huhn?"

The men looked quickly at Virginia, Jake turning clear around, so that Boone leaned over to catch the steering wheel.

"Watch it, watch it now, young feller."

"There's still Mama Mae's farm," Virginia continued, patting the baby. "Enough granite under there even if the church do—"

"But they ain't," said the young one. "Listen, we got it all figured out. We're going to bypass the robbers and deal directly with the tenant councils in the cities, and we're—"

"Don't talk the woman to death," soothed Boone. "You just tell Graham his landlady up there in the North won't have to eat dog food no more. No more in life. New day coming."

"And you tell him . . ."—Jake was turning around again—"just tell him to take his care."

By the time the bolt had lifted and she was standing by the chair, the baby fed and alert now in her arms, she had done with all the threads and bits and shards of the morning. She knew exactly what to tell him, coming through the steel door now, reaching for the baby he had not held yet, could not hold now, screened off from his father. All she wished to tell him was the bail'd been paid, her strength was back, and she sure as hell was going to keep up the garden. How else to feed the people?

Andrea Barrett (1954–)

described her fiction to Publishers Weekly *as "strangely of a piece, in the sense that I've always relied quite heavily on research to provide both the plot of my novels and the stuff that is the background of the character's lives." Barrett grew up on Cape Cod and graduated from Union College in Schenectady, New York, where she studied biology and hoped to become "Darwin in a skirt wandering through the Galapagos or the Amazon naming birds and trees." But in her first ten years out of college, she held thirteen different jobs, all of them bad; "the worst one," she once said, "was three days as assistant to a dental surgeon, pulling people's teeth and getting sprayed with their blood. . . . I fainted so many times I had to quit." She returned to school, studying medieval and Reformation theological history at the University of Massachusetts, where, in writing her papers, she would "go to the library and pull out everything, fill my room and become obsessed with the shape and the texture of the paper, and the way the words look, trying to make it all dramatic"—the same process she now uses to write her fiction. She has written several novels as well as two collections of short stories:* Ship Fever *(which won the 1996 National Book Award) and* Servants of the Map *(a finalist for the 2003 Pulitzer Prize). The recipient of a MacArthur "genius" grant, Barrett lives with her husband (a biologist) in Rochester, New York.*

INTRODUCTION BY **Frederick Reiken**

Many of Andrea Barrett's short stories either refer to or take place during the mid- to late-nineteenth century, a time when much of the world's geography was still uncharted and when countless species of plants, insects, and birds had not yet been named, particularly those endemic to uncharted regions. It was a time of scientific romance and wonder, a time when almost all categories of scientific theory were still in their nascent stages and when the world's natural resources were thought to be endless. Barrett herself majored in biology in college, and although, as she has stated publicly, she proved to be a poor science student, her fascination with nineteenth-century natural history—as well as the indomitable and at times misguided spirit of those who pursued it—lies at the core of her two story collections, *Ship Fever* and more recently *Servants of the Map.* Her 1998 novel *The Voyage of the Narwhal,* which chronicles a mid-nineteenth-century Arctic expedition, incorporates several of the characters included in her story collections and offers an extensive exploration of these same themes.

A trademark of Barrett's work is the careful research that goes into her stories. Unlike most contemporary fiction, her stories often make use of precise, specific factual knowledge, much of which she acquires from outdated science texts. She has made an art of finding arcane anecdotes or details and building fictional worlds around them. One of the stories included here is "The Behavior of the Hawkweeds," which recounts the somewhat tragic life of Gregor Mendel, whose famous experiments with peas posthumously became the foundation for the science of genetics, but who, unbeknownst to most, wasted many years trying but failing to duplicate the results of his pea experiments using hawkweeds (a plant that much later was discovered to have atypical genetic mechanisms) and died believing that all his work on peas had been useless. One of the delights of reading this particular story is, quite simply, the reader's own discovery of a fascinating and lesser-known piece of scientific history.

Yet what is most distinct and satisfying about Barrett's fiction is the manner in which precise scientific and historical fact intersects with fictional invention. As much as we may be interested in Gregor Mendel, the anecdote would be nothing more than an interesting tidbit if not for the larger fictional context in which Barrett places it. That is, the true story of Mendel comes to life because of our connection with the fictional Tati, who in Barrett's tale scales the wall into Mendel's garden and for a time becomes Mendel's assistant. The fictional invention of Tati's life also becomes the touchstone for our interest in the story's narrator, Tati's granddaughter, whose childhood relationship with her grandfather becomes a singular point of focus in her uncertain relationship with her biology professor husband.

Barrett's stories are often focused on the obsessive scientific mind, particularly that of the wandering naturalist, and the aspects of temperament that go with it. The two other stories included here exemplify this proclivity. Both are set in the mid-1800s, and in each, we witness the private saga of a naturalist who has journeyed to the very frontier of human imagination in that era. The protagonist of "Birds with No Feet" is seeking fame and fortune, whereas the protagonist of "Servants of the Map" seems to be searching for something more akin to spiritual renewal. It is this frontier between known and unknown, between what has been recorded and that which can only be imagined, that seems to animate all of Barrett's stories. In this regard, the art of scientific inquiry and that of storytelling are never far apart in Barrett's work. The known facts of science and history become transmuted from objective certainty into something that is mercurial, tenuous, and fleeting—something that points us back to the nature of humanity, to the limitations of our capacity for understanding the universe, despite our unceasing desire to know all things.

Frederick Reiken teaches writing and literature at Emerson College. He is the author of two novels, The Odd Sea *and* The Lost Legends of New Jersey. *His stories have appeared in* The New Yorker *and other publications.*

ANDREA BARRETT

The Behavior of the Hawkweeds

For thirty years, until he retired, my husband stood each fall in front of his sophomore genetics class and passed out copies of Gregor Mendel's famous paper on the hybridization of edible peas. This paper was a model of clarity, Richard told his students. It represented everything that science should be.

Richard paced in front of the chalkboard, speaking easily and without notes. Like the minor evolutionist Robert Chambers, he had been born hexadactylic; he was sensitive about his left hand, which was somewhat scarred from the childhood operation that had removed his extra finger. And so, although Richard gestured freely, he used only his right hand and kept his left in his pocket. From the back of the room, where I sat when I came each fall to hear him lecture, I could watch the students listen to him.

After he passed out the paper, Richard told the students his first, conventional version of Gregor Mendel's life. Mendel, he said, grew up in a tiny village in the northwestern corner of Moravia, which was then a part of the Hapsburg Empire and later became part of Czechoslovakia. When he was twenty-one, poor and desperate for further education, he entered the Augustinian monastery in the capital city of Brünn, which is now called Brno. He studied science and later taught at a local high school. In 1856, at the age of thirty-four, he began his experiments in the hybridization of the edible pea. For his laboratory he used a little strip of garden adjoining the monastery wall.

Over the next eight years Mendel performed hundreds of experiments on thousands of plants, tracing the ways in which characteristics were passed through generations. Tall and short plants, with white or violet flowers; peas that were wrinkled or smooth; pods that were arched or constricted around the seeds. He kept meticulous records of his hybridizations in order to write the paper the students now held in their hands. On a clear, cold evening in 1865, he read the first part of this paper to his fellow members of the Brünn Society for the Study of Natural Science. About forty men were present, a few professional scientists and many serious amateurs. Mendel read to them for an hour, describing his experiments and demonstrating the invariable ratios with which traits appeared in his hybrids. A month later, at the Society's next meeting, he presented the theory he'd formulated to account for his results.

Right there, my husband said, right in that small, crowded room, the science of genetics was born. Mendel knew nothing of genes or chromosomes or DNA, but he'd discovered the principles that made the search for those things possible.

"Was there applause?" Richard always asked at this point. "Was there a great outcry of approval or even a mutter of disagreement?" A rhetorical question; the students knew better than to answer.

"There was not. The minutes of that meeting show that no questions were asked and no discussion took place. Not one person in that room understood the significance of what Mendel had presented. A year later, when the paper was published, no one noticed it."

The students looked down at their papers and Richard finished his story quickly, describing how Mendel went back to his monastery and busied himself with other things. For a while he continued to teach and do other experiments; he raised grapes and fruit trees and all kinds of flowers, and he kept bees. Eventually he was elected abbot of his monastery, and from that time until his death he was occupied with his administrative duties. Only in 1900 was his lost paper rediscovered and his work appreciated by a new generation of scientists.

When Richard reached this point, he would look toward the back of the room and catch my eye and smile. He knew that I knew what was in store for the students at the end of the semester. After they'd read the paper and survived the labs where fruit flies bred in tubes and displayed the principles of Mendelian inheritance, Richard would tell them the other Mendel story. The one I told him, in which Mendel is led astray by a condescending fellow scientist and the behavior of the hawkweeds. The one in which science is not just unappreciated, but bent by loneliness and longing.

I had a reason for showing up in that classroom each fall, and it was not just that I was so dutiful, so wifely. Richard was not the one who introduced Mendel into my life.

When I was a girl, during the early years of the Depression, my grandfather, Anton Vaculik, worked at a nursery in Niskayuna, not far from where Richard and I still live in Schenectady. This was not the only job my grandfather had ever had, but it was the one he liked the best. He had left Moravia in 1891 and traveled to the city of Bremen with his pregnant wife. From there he'd taken a boat to New York and then another to Albany. He'd meant to journey on to one of the large Czech settlements in Minnesota or Wisconsin, but when my mother was born six weeks early he settled his family here instead. A few other Czech families lived in the area, and one of those settlers hired my grandfather to work in a small factory that made mother-of-pearl buttons for women's blouses.

Later, after he learned more English, he found the nursery job that he liked so much. He worked there for thirty years; he was so skilled at propagating plants and grafting trees that his employers kept him on part-time long past the age when he should have retired. Everyone at the nursery called him Tony, which sounded appropriately American. I called him Tati, a corruption of *tatínek,* which is Czech for "dad" and was what my mother called him. I was named Antonia after him.

We were never hungry when I was young; we were better off than many, but our daily life was a web of small economies. My mother took in sewing, making over jackets and mending pants; when she ironed she saved the flat pieces for last, to be pressed while the iron was cooling and the electricity was off. My father's wages had been cut at the GE plant and my older brothers tried to help by scrounging for odd jobs. I was the only idle member of the family, and so on weekends and during the summer my mother sometimes let me go with Tati. I loved it when Tati put me to work.

At the nursery there were fields full of fruit trees, peach and apple and pear, and long, low glass houses full of seedlings. I followed Tati around and helped him as he transplanted plants or worked with his sharp, curved knife and his grafting wax. I sat next to him on a tall wooden stool, holding his forceps or the jar of methylated spirits as he emasculated flowers. While we worked he talked, which is how I learned about his early days in America.

The only time Tati frowned and went silent was when his new boss appeared. Sheldon Hardy, the old chief horticulturalist, had been our friend; he was Tati's age and had worked side by side with Tati for years, cutting scions and whip-grafting fruit trees. But in 1931, the year I was ten, Mr. Hardy had a heart attack and went to live with his daughter in Ithaca. Otto Leiniger descended on us shortly after that, spoiling part of our pleasure every day.

Leiniger must have been in his late fifties. He lost no time telling Tati that he had a master's degree from a university out west, and it was clear from his white lab coat and the books in his office that he thought of himself as a scholar. In his office he sat at a big oak desk, making out lists of tasks for Tati with a fancy pen left over from better days; once he had been the director of an arboretum. He tacked the lists to the propagating benches, where they curled like shavings of wood from the dampness, and when we were deep in work he'd drift into the glass house and hover over us. He didn't complain about my presence, but he treated Tati like a common laborer. One day he caught me alone in a greenhouse filled with small begonias we'd grown from cuttings.

Tati had fitted a misting rose to a pot small enough for me to handle, and I was watering the tiny plants. It was very warm beneath the glass roof. I was wearing shorts and an old white shirt of Tati's, with nothing beneath it but my damp skin; I was only ten. There were benches against the two side walls and another, narrower, propagating bench running down the center of the house. On one side of this narrow bench I stood on an overturned crate to increase my reach, bending to mist the plants on the far side. When I looked up Leiniger was standing across from me. His face was round and heavy, with dark pouches beneath his eyes.

"You're a good little helper," he said. "You help your grandpapa out." Tati was in the greenhouse next door, examining a new crop of fuchsias.

"I like it here," I told Leiniger. The plants beneath my hands were Rex begonias, grown not for their flowers but for their showy, ruffled leaves. I had helped Tati pin the mother leaves to the moist sand and then transplant the babies that rooted from the ribs.

Leiniger pointed at the row of begonias closest to him, farthest from me. "These seem a little dry," he said. "Over here."

I didn't want to walk around the bench and stand by his side. "You can reach," he said. "Just lean over a little farther."

I stood up on my toes and bent across the bench, stretching the watering pot to reach those farthest plants. Leiniger flushed. "That's right," he said thickly. "Lean towards me."

Tati's old white shirt gaped at the neck and fell away from my body when I bent over. I stretched out my arm and misted the begonias. When I straightened I saw that Leiniger's face was red and that he was pressed against the wooden bench.

"Here," he said, and he made a shaky gesture at another group of plants to the right of him. "These here, these are also very dry."

I was afraid of him, and yet I also wanted to do my job and feared that any sloppiness on my part might get Tati in trouble. I leaned over once again, the watering pot in my hand. This time Leiniger reached for my forearm with his thick fingers. "Not those," he said, steering my hand closer to the edge of the bench, which he was still pressed against. "These, here, these are very dry."

Just as the pot brushed the front of his lab coat, Tati walked in. I can imagine, now, what that scene must have looked like to him. Me bent over that narrow bench, my toes barely touching the crate and the white shirt hanging down like a sheet to the young begonias below; Leiniger red-faced, sweating, grinding into the wooden bench. And his hand, that guilty hand, forcing me toward him. I dropped the pot when I heard Tati shout my name.

Who can say what Leiniger had in mind? To Tati it must have looked as though Leiniger was dragging me across the begonias to him. But Leiniger was just a lonely old man and it seems possible to me, now, that he wanted only the view down my shirt and that one small contact with the skin of my inner arm. Had Tati not entered the greenhouse just then, nothing more might have happened.

But Tati saw the worst in what was there. He saw that fat hand on my arm and those eyes fixed on my childish chest. He had a small pruning knife in his hand. When he called my name and I dropped the pot, Leiniger clamped down on my arm. As I was tearing myself away, Tati flew over and jabbed his knife into the back of Leiniger's hand.

"Nêmecky!" he shouted. *"Prase!"*

Leiniger screamed and stumbled backward. Behind him was the concrete block on which I stood to water the hanging plants, and that block caught Leiniger below the knees. He went down slowly, heavily, one hand clutching the wound on the other and a look of disbelief on his face. Tati was already reaching out to catch him when Leiniger cracked his head against a heating pipe.

But of course this is not what I told Richard. When we met, just after the war, I was working at the GE plant that had once employed my father and Richard was finishing his thesis. After my father died I had dropped out of junior college; Richard had interrupted his Ph.D. program to join the Navy, where he'd worked for three years doing research on tropical fungi. We both had a sense of urgency and a need to make up for lost time. During our brief courtship, I told Richard only the things that I thought would make him love me.

On our second date, over coffee and Italian pastries, I told Richard that my grandfather had taught me a little about plant breeding when I was young, and that I was fascinated by genetics. "Tati lived with us for a while, when I was a girl," I said. "He used to take me for walks through the empty fields of Niskayuna and tell me about Gregor Mendel. I still know a pistil from a stamen."

"Mendel's my hero," Richard said. "He's always been my ideal of what a scientist should be. It's not so often I meet a woman familiar with his work."

"I know a lot about him," I said. "What Tati told me—you'd be surprised." I didn't say that Tati and I had talked about Mendel because we couldn't stand to talk about what we'd both lost.

Tati slept in my room during the months before the trial; he was released on bail on the condition that he leave his small house in Rensselaer and stay with us. I slept on the couch in the living room and Leiniger lay unconscious in the Schenectady hospital. We were quiet, Tati and I. No one seemed to want to talk to us. My brothers stayed away from the house as much as possible and my father worked long hours. My mother was around, but she was so upset by what had happened that she could hardly speak to either Tati or myself. The most she could manage to do was to take me aside, a few days after Tati's arrival, and say, "What happened to Leiniger wasn't your fault. It's an old-country thing, what's between those men."

She made me sit with her on the porch, where she was turning mushrooms she'd gathered in the woods and laid out to dry on screens. Red, yellow, violet, buff. Some pieces were drier than others. While she spoke she moved from screen to screen, turning the delicate fragments.

"What country?" I said. "What are you talking about?"

"Tati is Czech," my mother said. "Like me. Mr. Leiniger's family is German, from a part of Moravia where only Germans live. Tati and Mr. Leiniger don't like each other because of things that happened in the Czech lands a long time ago."

"Am I Czech, then?" I said. "This happened because I am Czech?"

"You're American," my mother said. "American first. But Tati hates Germans. He and Leiniger would have found some way to quarrel even if you hadn't been there." She told me a little about the history of Moravia, enough to help me understand how long the Czechs and Germans had been quarreling. And she told me how thrilled Tati had been during the First World War, when the Czech and Slovak immigrants in America had banded together to contribute funds to help in the formation of an independent Czechoslovak state. When she was a girl, she said, Tati and her mother had argued over the donations Tati made and the meetings he attended.

But none of this seemed important to me. In the greenhouse, a policeman had asked Tati what had happened, and Tati had said, "I stuck his hand with my knife. But the rest was an accident—he tripped over that block and fell."

"Why?" the policeman had said. "Why did you do that?"

"My granddaughter," Tati had said. "He was . . . feeling her."

The policeman had tipped my chin up with his hand and looked hard at me. "Is that right?" he'd asked. And I had nodded dumbly, feeling both very guilty and very important. Now my mother was telling me that I was of no consequence.

"Am *I* supposed to hate Germans?" I asked.

A few years later, when Tati was dead and I was in high school and Hitler had dismembered Czechoslovakia, my mother would become loudly anti-German. But now all she said was, "No. Mr. Leiniger shouldn't have bothered you, but he's only one man. It's not right to hate everyone with a German last name."

"Is that what Tati does?"

"Sometimes."

I told my mother what Tati had shouted at Leiniger, repeating the foreign sounds as best as I could. My mother blushed. "*Nêmecky* means 'German,'" she said reluctantly. "*Prase* means 'pig.' You must never tell anyone you heard your grandfather say such things."

I did not discuss this conversation with Tati. All during that fall, but especially after Leiniger died, I'd come home from school to find Tati waiting for me on the porch, his knobby walking stick in his hands and his cap on his head. He wanted to walk, he was desperate to walk. My mother wouldn't let him leave the house alone but she seldom found the time to go out with him; my brothers could not be bothered. And so Tati waited for me each afternoon like a restless dog.

While we walked in the fields and woods behind our house, we did not talk about what had happened in the greenhouse. Instead, Tati named the ferns and mosses and flowers we passed. He showed me the hawkweeds—Canada hawkweed, spotted hawkweed, poor-Robin's hawkweed, orange hawkweed, also called devil's paintbrush, creeping into abandoned fields. The plants had long stems, rosettes of leaves at the base, small flowerheads that resembled dandelions. Once Tati opened my eyes to them I realized they were everywhere.

"Hieracium," Tati said. "That is their real name. It comes from the Greek word for hawk. The juice from the stem is supposed to make your vision very sharp." They were weeds, he said: extremely hardy. They grew wherever the soil was too poor to support other plants. They were related to asters and daisies and dahlias—all plants I'd seen growing at the nursery—but also to thistles and burdocks. I should remember them, he said. They were important. With his own eyes he had watched the hawkweeds ruin Gregor Mendel's life.

Even now this seems impossible: how could I have known someone of an age to have known Mendel? And yet it was true: Tati had grown up on the outskirts of Brno, the city where Mendel spent most of his life. In 1866, when they first met, there was cholera in Brno and Prussian soldiers passing through after the brief and nasty war. Tati was ten then, and those things didn't interest him. He had scaled the white walls of the Augustinian monastery of St. Thomas one afternoon, for a lark. As he'd straddled the wall he'd seen a plump, short-legged man with glasses looking up at him.

"He looked like my mother's uncle," Tati said. "A little bit."

Mendel had held out a hand and helped Tati jump down from the wall. Around him were fruit trees and wild vines; in the distance he saw a clocktower and a long, low building. Where Tati had landed, just where his feet touched ground, there were peas. Not the thousands of plants that would have been there at the height of Mendel's investigations, but still hundreds of plants clinging to sticks and stretched strings.

The place was magical, Tati said. Mendel showed him the tame fox he tied up during the day but allowed to run free at night, the hedgehogs and the hamsters and the mice he kept, the beehives and the cages full of birds. The two of them, the boy and the middle-aged man, made friends. Mendel taught Tati most of his horticultural secrets and later he was responsible for getting him a scholarship to the school where he taught. But Tati said that the first year of their friendship, before the hawkweed experiments, was the best. He and Mendel, side by side, had opened pea flowers and transferred pollen with a camel-hair brush.

On the last day of 1866, Mendel wrote his first letter to Carl Nägeli of Munich, a powerful and well-known botanist known to be interested in hybridization. He sent a copy of his pea paper along with the letter, hoping Nägeli might help it find the recognition it deserved. But he also, in his letter, mentioned that he had started a few experiments with hawkweeds, which he hoped would confirm his results with peas.

Nägeli was an expert on the hawkweeds, and Tati believed that Mendel had only mentioned them to pique Nägeli's interest in his work. Nägeli didn't reply for several months, and when he finally wrote back he said almost nothing about the peas. But he was working on the hawkweeds himself, and he proposed that Mendel turn his experimental skills to them. Mendel, desperate for recognition, ceased to write about his peas and concentrated on the hawkweeds instead.

"Oh, that Nägeli!" Tati said. "Month after month, year after year, I watched Mendel writing his long, patient letters and getting no answer or slow answers or answers off the point. Whenever Nägeli wrote to Mendel, it was always about the hawkweeds. Later, when I learned why Mendel's experiments with them hadn't worked, I wanted to cry."

The experiments that had given such tidy results with peas gave nothing but chaos with hawkweeds, which were very difficult to hybridize. Experiment after experiment failed; years of work were wasted. The inexplicable behavior of the hawkweeds destroyed Mendel's belief that the laws of heredity he'd worked out with peas would be universally valid. By 1873, Mendel had given up completely. The hawkweeds, and Nägeli behind them, had convinced him that his work was useless.

It was bad luck, Tati said. Bad luck in choosing Nägeli to help him, and letting Nägeli steer him toward the hawkweeds. Mendel's experimental technique was fine, and his laws of heredity were perfectly true. He could not have known—no one knew for years—that his hawkweeds didn't hybridize in rational ways because they frequently formed seeds without fertilization. "Parthenogenesis," Tati told me—a huge, knobby word that I could hardly get my mouth around. Still, it sounds to me like a disease. "The plants grown from seeds formed this way are exact copies of the mother plant, just like the begonias we make from leaf cuttings."

Mendel gave up on science and spent his last years, after he was elected abbot, struggling with the government over the taxes levied on his monastery. He quarreled with his fellow monks; he grew bitter and isolated. Some of the monks believed he had gone insane. In his quarters he smoked heavy cigars and gazed at the ceiling, which he'd had painted with scenes of saints and fruit trees, beehives and scientific equipment. When Tati came to visit him, his conversation wandered.

Mendel died in January 1884, on the night of Epiphany, confused about the value of his scientific work. That same year, long after their correspondence had ceased, Nägeli published an enormous book summarizing all his years of work. Although many of his opinions and observations seemed to echo Mendel's work with peas, Nägeli made no mention of Mendel or his paper.

That was the story I told Richard. Torn from its context, stripped of the reasons why it was told, it became a story about the beginnings of Richard's discipline. I knew that Richard would have paid money to hear it, but I gave it to him as a gift.

"And your grandfather saw all that?" he said. This was later on in our courtship; we were sitting on a riverbank, drinking Manhattans that Richard had mixed and enjoying the cold spiced beef and marinated vegetables and lemon tart I had brought in a basket. Richard liked my cooking quite a bit. He liked me too, but apparently not enough; I was longing for him to propose but he still hadn't said a word. "Your grandfather saw the letters," he said. "He watched Mendel assembling data for Nägeli. That's remarkable. That's extraordinary. I can't believe the things you know."

There was more, I hinted. What else did I have to offer him? Now it seems to me that I had almost everything: youth and health and an affectionate temperament; the desire to make a family. But then I was more impressed than I should have been by Richard's education.

"More?" he said.

"There are some papers," I said. "That Tati left behind."

★ ★ ★

Of course I was not allowed in the courtroom, I was much too young. After Leiniger died, the date of the trial was moved forward. I never saw Tati sitting next to the lawyer my father had hired for him; I never saw a judge or a jury and never learned whether my testimony might have helped Tati. I never even learned whether, in that long-ago time, the court would have accepted the testimony of a child, because Tati died on the evening before the first day of the trial.

He had a stroke, my mother said. In the night she heard a loud, garbled cry and when she ran into the room that had once been mine she found Tati tipped over in bed, with his head hanging down and his face dark and swollen. Afterwards, after the funeral, when I came home from school I no longer went on walks through the woods and fields. I did my homework at the kitchen table and then I helped my mother around the house. On weekends I no longer went to the nursery.

Because there had been no trial, no one in town learned of my role in Leiniger's death. There had been a quarrel between two old men, people thought, and then an accident. No one blamed me or my family. I was able to go through school without people pointing or whispering. I put Tati out of my mind, and with him the nursery and Leiniger, Mendel and Nägeli, and the behavior of the hawkweeds. When the war came I refused to listen to my mother's rantings. After my father died she went to live with one of my married brothers, and I went off on my own. I loved working in the factory; I felt very independent.

Not until the war was over and I met Richard did I dredge up the hawkweed story. Richard's family had been in America for generations and seemed to have no history; that was one of the things that drew me to him. But after our picnic on the riverbank I knew for sure that part of what drew him to me was the way I was linked so closely to other times and places. I gave Richard the yellowed sheets of paper that Tati had left in an envelope for me.

This is a draft of one of Mendel's letters to Nägeli, Tati had written, on a note attached to the manuscript. *He showed it to me once, when he was feeling sad. Later he gave it to me. I want you to have it.*

Richard's voice trembled when he read that note out loud. He turned the pages of Mendel's letter slowly, here and there reading a line to me. The letter was an early one, or perhaps even the first. It was all about peas.

Richard said, "I can't believe I'm holding this in my hand."

"I could give it to you," I said. In my mind this seemed perfectly reasonable. Mendel had given the letter to Tati, the sole friend of his last days; then Tati had passed it to me, when he was no longer around to protect me himself. Now it seemed only right that I should give it to the man I wanted to marry.

"To me?" Richard said. "You would give it to me?"

"Someone who appreciates it should have it."

Richard cherished Tati's letter like a jewel. We married, we moved to Schenectady, Richard got a good job at the college, and we had our two daughters. During each of my pregnancies Richard worried that our children might inherit his hexadactyly, but Annie and Joan were both born with regulation fingers and toes. I stayed home with them, first in the apartment on Union Street and then later, after Richard's promotion, in the handsome old house on campus that the college rented to us. Richard wrote papers and served on committees; I gave monthly dinners for the departmental faculty, weekly coffee hours for favored students, picnics for alumni on homecoming weekends. I managed that sort of thing rather well: it was a job, if an unpaid one, and it was expected of me.

Eventually our daughters grew up and moved away. And then, when I was nearly fifty, after Richard had been tenured and won his awards and grown almost unbearably self-satisfied, there came a time when the world went gray on me for the better part of a year.

I still can't explain what happened to me then. My doctor said it was hormones, the beginning of my change of life. My daughters, newly involved with the women's movement, said my years as a housewife had stifled me and that I needed a career of my own. Annie, our oldest, hemmed and hawed and finally asked me if her father and I were still sharing a bed; I said we were but didn't have the heart to tell her that all we did was share it. Richard said I needed more exercise and prescribed daily walks in the college gardens, which were full of exotic specimen trees from every corner of the earth.

He was self-absorbed, but not impossible; he hated to see me suffer. And I suppose he also wanted back the wife who for years had managed his household so well. But I could no longer manage anything. All I knew was that I felt old, and that everything had lost its savor. I lay in the windowseat in our bedroom with an afghan over my legs, watching the students mass and swirl and separate in the quad in front of the library.

This was 1970, when the students seemed to change overnight from pleasant boys into uncouth and hairy men. Every week brought a new protest. Chants and marches and demonstrations; bedsheets hanging like banners from the dormitory windows. The boys who used to come to our house for tea dressed in blue blazers and neatly pressed pants now wore vests with dangling fringes and jeans with holes in them. And when I went to Richard's genetics class that fall, to listen to his first Mendel lecture, I saw that the students gazed out the window while he spoke or tipped back in their chairs with their feet on the desks: openly bored, insubordinate. A girl encased in sheets of straight blonde hair—there were girls in class, the college had started admitting them—interrupted Richard mid-sentence and said, "But what's the *relevance* of this? Science confined to the hands of the technocracy produces nothing but destruction."

Richard didn't answer her, but he hurried through the rest of his lecture and left the room without looking at me. That year, he didn't give his other Mendel lecture. The students had refused to do most of the labs; there was no reason, they said, why harmless fruit flies should be condemned to death just to prove a theory that everyone already acknowledged as true. Richard said they didn't deserve to hear about the hawkweeds. They were so dirty, so destructive, that he feared for the safety of Mendel's precious letter.

I was relieved, although I didn't say that; I had no urge to leave my perch on the windowseat and no desire to hear Richard repeat that story again. It seemed to me then that he told it badly. He muddled the dates, compressed the years, identified himself too closely with Mendel and painted Nägeli as too black a villain. By then I knew that he liked to think of himself as another Mendel, unappreciated and misunderstood. To me he looked more like another Nägeli. I had seen him be less than generous to younger scientists struggling to establish themselves. I had watched him pick, as each year's favored student, not the brightest or most original but the most agreeable and flattering.

That year all the students seemed to mutate, and so there was no favorite student, no obsequious well-dressed boy to join us for Sunday dinner or cocktails after the Wednesday seminars. As I lay in my windowseat, idly addressing envelopes and stuffing them with reprints of Richard's papers, I hardly noticed that the house was emptier than usual. But at night, when I couldn't sleep, I rose from Richard's side and went down to the couch in the living room, where I lay midway between dream and panic. I heard Tati's voice then, telling me about Mendel. I heard Mendel, frantic over those hawkweeds, trying out draft after draft of his letters on the ears of an attentive little boy who sat in a garden next to a fox. *Highly esteemed sir, your honor. I beg you to allow me to submit for your kind consideration the results of these experiments.* How humble Mendel had been in his address, and yet how sure of his science. How kind he had been to Tati.

Some nights I grew very confused. Mendel and Nägeli, Mendel and Tati; Tati and Leiniger, Tati and me. Pairs of men who hated each other and pairs of friends passing papers. A boy I saw pruning shrubs in the college garden turned into a childish Tati, leaping over a white wall. During a nap I dreamed of Leiniger's wife. I had seen her only once; she had come to Tati's funeral. She stood in the back of the church in a brown dress flecked with small white leaves, and when my family left after the service she turned her face from us.

That June, after graduation, Sebastian Dunitz came to us from his lab in Frankfurt. He and Richard had been corresponding and they shared common research interests; Richard had arranged for Sebastian to visit the college for a year, working with Richard for the summer on a joint research project and then, during the fall and spring semesters, as a teaching assistant in the departmental laboratories. He stayed with us, in Annie's old bedroom, but he was little trouble. He did his own laundry and cooked his own meals except when we asked him to join us.

Richard took to Sebastian right away. He was young, bright, very well educated; although speciation and evolutionary relationships interested him more than the classical Mendelian genetics Richard taught, his manner toward Richard was clearly deferential. Within a month of his arrival, Richard was telling me how, with a bit of luck, a permanent position might open up for his new protegé. Within a month of his arrival, I was up and about, dressed in bright colors, busy cleaning the house from basement to attic and working in the garden. It was nice to have some company around.

Richard invited Sebastian to a picnic dinner with us on the evening of the Fourth of July. This was something we'd done every year when the girls were growing up; we'd let the custom lapse but Richard thought Sebastian might enjoy it. I fried chicken in the morning, before the worst heat of the day; I dressed tomatoes with vinegar and olive oil and chopped fresh basil and I made potato salad and a chocolate cake. When dusk fell, Richard and I gathered a blanket and the picnic basket and our foreign guest and walked to the top of a rounded hill not far from the college grounds. In the distance, we could hear the band that preceded the fireworks.

"This is wonderful," Sebastian said. "Wonderful food, a wonderful night. You have both been very kind to me."

Richard had set a candle in a hurricane lamp in the center of our blanket, and in the dim light Sebastian's hair gleamed like a helmet. We all drank a lot of the sweet white wine that Sebastian had brought as his offering. Richard lay back on his elbows and cleared his throat, surprising me when he spoke.

"Did you know," he said to Sebastian, "that I have an actual draft of a letter that Gregor Mendel wrote to the botanist Nägeli? My dear Antonia gave it to me."

Sebastian looked from me to Richard and back. "Where did you get such a thing?" he asked. "How . . . ?"

Richard began to talk, but I couldn't bear to listen to him tell that story badly one more time. "My grandfather gave it to me," I said, interrupting Richard. "He knew Mendel when he was a little boy." And without giving Richard a chance to say another word, without even looking at the hurt and puzzlement I knew must be on his face, I told Sebastian all about the behavior of the hawkweeds. I told the story slowly, fully, without skipping any parts. In the gathering darkness I moved my hands and did my best to make Sebastian see the wall and the clocktower and the gardens and the hives, the spectacles on Mendel's face and Tati's bare feet. And when I was done, when my words hung in the air and Sebastian murmured appreciatively, I did something I'd never done before, because Richard had never thought to ask the question Sebastian asked.

"How did your grandfather come to tell you that?" he said. "It is perhaps an unusual story to tell a little girl."

"It gave us something to talk about," I said. "We spent a lot of time together, the fall that I was ten. He had killed a man—accidentally, but still the man was dead. He lived with us while we were waiting for the trial."

Overhead, the first fireworks opened into blossoms of red and gold and green. "Antonia," Richard said, but he caught himself. In front of Sebastian he would not admit that this was something his wife of twenty-five years had never told him before. In the light of the white cascading fountain above us I could see him staring at me, but all he said was, "An amazing story, isn't it? I used to tell it to my genetics students every year, but this fall everything was so deranged—I left it out, I knew they wouldn't appreciate it."

"Things are different," Sebastian said. "The world is changing." He did not ask me how it was that my grandfather had killed a man.

The pace and intensity of the fireworks increased, until all of them seemed to be exploding at once; then there was one final crash and then silence and darkness. I had been rude, I knew. I had deprived Richard of one of his great pleasures simply for the sake of hearing that story told well once.

We gathered up our blanket and basket and walked home quietly. The house was dark and empty. In the living room I turned on a single light and then went to the kitchen to make coffee; when I came in with the tray the men were talking quietly about their work. "I believe what we have here is a *Rassenkreis,*" Sebastian said, and he turned to include me in the conversation. In his short time with us, he had always paid me the compliment of assuming I understood his and Richard's work. "A German word," he said. "It means 'race-circle'—it is what we call it when a species spread over a large area is broken into a chain of subspecies, each of which differs slightly from its neighbors. The neighboring subspecies can interbreed, but the subspecies at the two ends of the chain may be so different that they cannot. In the population that Richard and I are examining. . . ."

"I am very tired," Richard said abruptly. "If you'll excuse me, I think I'll go up to bed."

"No coffee?" I said.

He looked at a spot just beyond my shoulder, as he always did when he was upset. "No," he said. "Are you coming?"

"Soon," I said.

And then, in that dim room, Sebastian came and sat in the chair right next to mine. "Is Richard well?" he said. "Is something wrong?"

"He's fine. Only tired. He's been working hard."

"That was a lovely story you told. When I was a boy, at university, our teachers did not talk about Nägeli, except to dismiss him as a Lamarckian. They would skip from Mendel's paper on the peas to its rediscovery, later. Nägeli's student, Correns, and Hugo de Vries—do you know about the evening primroses and de Vries?"

I shook my head. We sat at the dark end of the living room, near the stairs and away from the windows. Still, occasionally, came the sound of a renegade firecracker.

"No? You will like this."

But before he could tell me his anecdote I leaned toward him and rested my hand on his forearm. His skin was as smooth as a flower. "Don't tell me any more science," I said. "Tell me about yourself."

There was a pause. Then Sebastian pulled his arm away abruptly and stood up. "Please," he said. "You're an attractive woman, still. And I am flattered. But it's quite impossible, anything between us." His accent, usually almost imperceptible, thickened with those words.

I was grateful for the darkness that hid my flush. "You misunderstood," I said. "I didn't mean . . ."

"Don't be embarrassed," he said. "I've seen the way you watch me when you think I am not looking. I appreciate it."

A word came back to me, a word I thought I'd forgotten. *"Prase,"* I muttered.

"What?" he said. Then I heard a noise on the stairs behind me, and a hand fell on my shoulder. I reached up and felt the knob where Richard's extra finger had once been.

"Antonia," Richard said. His voice was very gentle. "It's so late—won't you come up to bed?" He did not say a word to Sebastian; upstairs, in our quiet room, he neither accused me of anything nor pressed me to explain the mysterious comment I'd made about my grandfather. I don't know what he said later to Sebastian, or how he arranged things with the Dean. But two days later Sebastian moved into an empty dormitory room, and before the end of the summer he was gone.

Německy, prase; secret words. I have forgotten almost all the rest of Tati's language, and both he and Leiniger have been dead for sixty years. Sebastian Dunitz is back in Frankfurt, where he has grown very famous. The students study molecules now, spinning models across their computer screens and splicing the genes of one creature into those of another. The science of genetics is utterly changed and Richard has been forgotten by everyone. Sometimes I wonder where we have misplaced our lives.

Of course Richard no longer teaches. The college retired him when he turned sixty-five, despite his protests. Now they trot him out for dedications and graduations and departmental celebrations, along with the other emeritus professors who haunt the library and the halls. Without his class, he has no audience for his treasured stories. Instead he corners people at the dim, sad ends of parties when he's had too much to drink. Young instructors, too worried about their jobs to risk being impolite, turn their ears to Richard like flowers. He keeps them in place with a knobby hand on a sleeve or knee as he talks.

When I finally told him what had happened to Tati, I didn't really tell him anything. Two old men had quarreled, I said. An immigrant and an immigrant's son, arguing over some plants. But Tati and Leiniger, Richard decided, were Mendel and Nägeli all over again; surely Tati identified with Mendel and cast Leiniger as another Nägeli? Although he still doesn't know of my role in the accident, somehow the equation he's made between these pairs of men allows him to tell his tale with more sympathy, more balance. As he talks he looks across the room and smiles at me. I nod and smile back at him, thinking of Annie, whose first son was born with six toes on each foot.

Sebastian sent me a letter the summer after he left us, in which he finished the story I'd interrupted on that Fourth of July. The young Dutch botanist Hugo de Vries, he wrote, spent his summers searching the countryside for new species. One day, near Hilversum, he came to an abandoned potato field glowing strangely in the sun. The great evening primrose had been cultivated in a small bed in a nearby park; the plants had run wild and escaped into the field, where they formed a jungle as high as a man. From 1886 through 1888, de Vries made thousands of hybridization experiments with them, tracing the persistence of mutations. During his search for a way to explain his results, he uncovered Mendel's paper and found that Mendel had anticipated all his theories. Peas and primroses, primroses and peas, passing their traits serenely through generations.

I still have this letter, as Richard still has Mendel's. I wonder, sometimes, what Tati would have thought of all this. Not the story about Hugo de Vries, which he probably knew, but the way it came to me in a blue airmail envelope, from a scientist who meant to be kind. I think of Tati when I imagine Sebastian composing his answer to me.

Because it was an answer, of sorts; in the months after he left I mailed him several letters. They were, on the surface, about Mendel and Tati, all I recalled of their friendship. But I'm sure Sebastian read them for what they were. In 1906, Sebastian wrote, after Mendel's work was finally recognized, a small museum was opened in the Augustinian monastery. Sebastian visited it, when he passed through Brno on a family holiday.

"I could find no trace of your Tati," he wrote. "But the wall is still here, and you can see where the garden was. It's a lovely place. Perhaps you should visit someday."

ANDREA BARRETT

Birds with No Feet

[Fire—1853]

There was no breeze that night. The sea, lit by the full moon, shone smooth and silver; the Southern Cross turned above the ship and below it squid slipped invisibly through the depths. Between sky and sea lay Alec Carrière, sprawled like a starfish in his hammock and imagining how the treasures packed in the holds were about to change his life.

Beetles and butterflies and spiders and moths, bird skins and snakeskins and bones: these were what he'd collected along the Amazon and then guarded against the omnivorous ants. Mr. Barton, his agent back home in Philadelphia, had sold Alec's first specimens for a good price, and Alec expected this shipment would finally set him free to pursue his studies in peace. He was a few months shy of twenty-one, and dreaming a young man's dreams.

Until he'd sailed for the Amazon, he'd worked in a shop making leather valises, not far from the tavern his parents ran in Germantown. But like the young English collector he'd met in Barra, near the flooded islands of the Rio Negro, he'd been saved from a squalid and unremarkable life by a few kind men and a book. With his uncle's ornithology text in his pocket he'd wandered the banks of the Wissahickon, teaching himself the names of birds and imagining wild places. His brother Frank had taught him to shoot, and behind the outhouse he'd prepared his first clumsy skins and mounts. Even then he'd known that other naturalists had taught themselves their trade. Others had risen from just such humble beginnings, and he'd seen nothing extraordinary in his ambitions.

Once every few months he went into downtown Philadelphia to visit the Academy of Natural Sciences, where a few of the members corrected his malformed preparations and taught him what they could. His interests spread from birds to other species. Titian Peale showed him an excellent way to pin and display his moths. Two of the Wells brothers, Copernicus and Erasmus, taught him how to prepare skeletons. All this gave Alec great pleasure but annoyed his father; by the time he was sixteen his father was pressing him to abandon this childish hobby and take his work more seriously. He almost gave up. But in 1850 Peale made him a gift of William Edwards's small and wonderful book, *A Voyage Up the River Amazon.*

When Alec read it a door seemed to open. What was there to keep him in Philadelphia? Edwards had been only a few years older than him when he'd set off; Alec was strong and healthy and his three brothers could look after their parents. And he had a most earnest desire to behold the luxuriant life of the tropics. Mr. Barton, a natural history auctioneer whom he'd met at the Academy, assured him that all of northern Brazil was little known, that Edwards had brought back only small collections, and that Alec might easily pay the expenses of his trip by gathering birds, small mammals, land-shells, and all the orders of insects. Among the wealthy, Mr. Barton said, glass cases filled with tropical creatures arranged by genus or poised in tableaux were wildly fashionable. And so few specimens had reached North America from the Amazon that high prices were guaranteed.

With the brashness of youth Alec wrote to Mr. Edwards himself, who provided him with letters of introduction to several traders. Then he packed his things and used his small savings to book passage on a merchant ship. His father was angry with him; his mother wept. But he saw miracles. The mouth of the Amazon was like a sea, and could be distinguished from the ocean only by its extraordinary deep yellow color. The Rio Negro was as black as the river Styx. Jet-black jaguars and massive turtle's nests, agoutis and giant serpents; below Baião, a crowd of Indians gathered, laughing and curious, to watch Alec skinning parrots. Driven to gather as much as he could, Alec shrugged off the heat and the poor food and the fevers that plagued him intermittently. His persistence was rewarded in Barra, where Alfred Wallace greeted him like a brother.

Wallace wasn't famous then. Except for the light that burned in him and lit a similar flame in Alec, he was just another collector, exceedingly tall, with a thatch of yellow hair and clothes as shabby as Alec's own. On the day they met the sun dropped like a shot bird, and in the sudden tropical night they compared skins and guns.

Alec was lonely, and glad for the company after months among Indians whose language he couldn't speak. He talked too much the night he met Wallace, he knew he did. But although Wallace was a decade older, wracked with fever and ready to leave for home after three hard years in the jungle, he never laughed at Alec's chatter or made him feel less than an equal. He showed Alec the blow-pipes his Indian hunters used, and the bitter vegetable oil with which he coated the ropes of his specimen-drying racks. Alec showed him the glorious umbrella-birds he'd captured in the flooded forest of the *igapo.* Standing by the side of this long, lean, wasted man, Alec took pleasure in his own youth and compact sturdiness; how his hands, next to Wallace's fine bones, were all broad palm and spatulate thumb. Around them the toucans yelped and the parrots chattered and the palms went *swish, swish* in the evening breeze. They ate fish and farinha and turtle. Later they traded stories about the books that had saved them. When Alec learned that Wallace was no gentleman scientist but was, like Alec himself, solely dependent on selling specimens to pay his way, he felt an immediate bond.

After they parted, Alec collected with even more fervor. Now the results lay snugly packed below him, and as the ship rocked sluggishly he was imagining how he'd drive up to his parents' tavern, dressed in a new suit and laden with more money than they'd ever seen.

They would be thrilled, Alec thought. As would everyone who'd helped him. How surprised the Wells brothers and Titian Peale would be, when Alec made them gifts of the especially amazing butterflies he'd set aside for them! And then the hush inside the Academy, as he lectured to the men who'd taught him. Holding up a perfect skin from one of those rare umbrella-birds, he would point out the glossy blue tufts on the crest-feathers. "When the bird is resting," he would say, "the raised crest forms a deep blue dome, which completely hides the head and beak." The men would give him a desk, Alec thought, where he might catalogue his treasures. And he might marry, were he to meet someone appealing.

He was happy; he was half-asleep. Then the cabin-boy ran up to Alec's hammock and shook him and said, "Mr. Carrière! The captain says to come immediately. There seems to be a fire!" And Alec, still dreaming of his wonderful future, stumbled from his cabin with only the most recent volume of his journal and the clothes on his back.

The scene on deck was pure chaos: smoke rising through the masts, a sheet of flame shooting up from the galley, crew members hurling water along the deck and onto the sails. Captain Longwood was shouting orders and several of the men were unlashing the boats and preparing to lower them, while others hurriedly gathered casks of water and biscuit.

"What's happened?" Alec shouted. "What can I do?"

"Save what you can!" Captain Longwood shouted back. "I fear we may lose the ship."

Even as Alec headed for the forecastle, he could not believe this was happening. Some months after his meeting with Wallace, he'd heard that the brig carrying Wallace home had burned to the waterline, destroying all his collections and casting him adrift on the sea for several weeks. This news had filled Alec with genuine horror. Yet at the same time he'd also felt a small, mean sense of superstitious relief: such a disaster, having happened once, could surely never happen again. Although Alec's own collections were not insured, since he could not afford the fees, Wallace's bad luck had seemed to guarantee Alec's safe passage home.

All this passed through his mind as he fought his way forward. Then every thought but panic was driven away when he saw the plight of his animals.

In the holds below him was a fortune in things dead and preserved—but in the forecastle was the living menagerie he was also bringing home. His sweet sloth, no bigger than a rabbit, with his charming habit of hanging upside down on the back of a chair and his melancholy expression; the parrots and parakeets and the forest-dog; the toucans; the monkeys: already they were calling through the smoke. And before Alec could reach them a spout of flame rose like a wall through the hatchway in front of him. Wallace's ship, he knew, had caught fire through the spontaneous combustion of kegs of balsam-capivi, but their own fire had no such exotic cause. The cook had knocked over a lamp, which had ignited a keg of grease, which had dripped, burning, through the floorboards and set fire to the cargo of rubber and lumber just below. From there the fire licked forward, downward, upward; and when the hatches were opened the draft made the fire jump and sing.

Alec was driven back to the quarterdeck and stood there, helpless, while the men prepared the boats and hurriedly gathered spars and oars and sails. The captain flew by, still shouting, his hands bristling with charts and compasses; they were five days out of Para and no longer within sight of land. The skylight exploded with a great roar, and the burning berths crackled below them. Terrible noises rose from the bow where the animals were confined. His lovely purple-breasted cotingas, roasting; the handsome pair of big-bellied monkeys, which the Brazilians called *barraidugo*—his entire life, until that moment, had contained nothing so distressing.

For a moment he thought the birds at least might be saved. One of the men dropped from his perch on the cross-trees and smashed in the forecastle door with an axe. Then the toucans, kept unconfined, flew out, and also a flock of parakeets. The cloud of birds seemed to head for the cloud of smoke but then swooped low and settled on the bowsprit, as far from the fire as they could get. They were joined by the sloth, who had magically crept up the ironwork. But meanwhile the mate was shouting, "Go! *Now!*" and hands were pushing against Alec's back, men were tumbling over the stern and he tumbled with them, falling into one of the leaky boats. Someone thrust a dipper into his hands and he began to bail, while men he had never noticed before barked and struggled to fit the oars in the oarlocks. The man pressed against his knee dripped blood from a scratch on his check and gagged, as did Alec, on the smoke from the rubber seething in the wreck.

The shrouds and sails burned briskly; then the masts began to catch. Soon enough the main-mast toppled and the moon-lit water filled with charred remains.

"Please," Alec begged Captain Longwood. "Can we row toward the bow? Can we try to save some of them?" His animals were lined along the last scrap of solid wood.

Captain Longwood hesitated, but then agreed. "Two minutes," he said sternly.

But when they approached the bow Alec found that the creatures would not abandon their perches. As the flames advanced, the birds seemed to dive into them, disappear in sudden brilliant puffs that hung like stars. Only the sloth escaped; and he only because the section of bowsprit from which he hung upside down burned at the base and plopped into the water. When Alec picked him up, his feet still clung to the wood.

They were three days drifting in their leaky boats before they saw a sail in the distance: the *Alexandra,* headed for New Orleans. A fortunate rescue. Alec was grateful. But a year and a half of hard work, on which his whole future depended, was destroyed; as was the sloth, who died on the voyage. Alec reached home in one piece, but with hardly more to his name than when he'd left. As a souvenir he was given nightmares, in which the smell of singeing feathers filled his nostrils and his sloth curled smaller and smaller, and closed his eyes, and died again and again.

In November, recuperating at his uncle's house as his father would not have him at his, Alec learned that his acquaintance from Barra had written two books, one about his travels and the other about the exotic palms. Alec read both and liked them very much. They had shared a rare and terrible thing, Alec thought: all they'd gathered of the astonishing fauna of the Amazon, both quick and dead, turned into ash on the sea. Alec wrote to him, in England.

> *Dear Mr. Wallace: I expect you will not remember me, but we passed a pleasant evening together in Barra in September 1851. I was the young American man heading up the Rio Negro in search of specimens. I write both to express my admiration for your recent books, and to record an astonishing coincidence. You will hardly believe what happened to me on my journey home. . . .*

Wallace wrote back.

> *Dear Alec: My sympathies on the distressing loss of your collections. No one who has not been through this himself can understand. Beyond the horrors of the fire itself, the terrible loss of animal life, and the substantial financial blow is this fact, so difficult to explain: That each specimen lost represents a double death. Our hunting always had a point; each bird we shot and butterfly we netted was in the service of science. But burnt, they now serve no one. It is very hard. I thank you for your kind words about my books. I plan to head, this coming spring, for the Malay Archipelago: an area hardly explored at all, which should prove extremely rich for our purposes. Perhaps you might like to consider this yourself?*

Alec's mother, who had faithfully written to him during his absence, without understanding that he would get her letters only in one great batch when he returned to Para, was during this hard time very kind to him. She visited Alec weekly at his uncle's. And when he told her what he planned to do next, she encouraged him and secretly bought him two suits of clothes.

[Ague—1855]

It was not as if Wallace and Alec traveled together throughout the Malay Archipelago, nor as if Wallace took Alec under his wing in any practical way. Alec was in Macassar when Wallace was in Ball; Wallace was in Lombok when Alec was in Timor; they both visited the Aru Islands, but in different years. And their situations were no longer as similar as they'd been in the Amazon. Wallace was still strapped for money, but his books had made him a reputation and the Royal Geographical Society had paid his first-class passage to Singapore aboard a fast steamer. Alec made a slow and uncomfortable voyage on three merchant ships and a filthy whaler. Wallace had with him an assistant, 16-year-old Charles, who helped capture, preserve, and catalog specimens, whereas Alec was all alone, and often overcome by details.

During the wet season of 1855, Alec was in Sarawak, in northwestern Borneo. He'd heard tales of a lively Christmas house-party at the bungalow of Sir John Brooke, the English Rajah of the territory—all the Europeans in the out-stations being invited to enjoy the Rajah's fabled hospitality, and so forth. But he had not been asked to join the party, and he never suspected that Wallace was there. Over that Christmas, and into January, Alec was miles east of the Rajah's bungalow, collecting beetles and hunting orangutans in the swamps along the Sadong River.

For some weeks he'd been blessed with astonishing luck. Moving through the dense foliage he would hear a rustling overhead, then glimpse one of the reddish-brown apes swinging. Branch to branch, tree to tree, never touching the ground. His desire for possession seemed to carve a line in the air between his gun and his target; he aimed and a moment later the orangutan was his. Retrieving the body was more difficult, but here the native Dyaks helped him. As the orangutans fed on the fruit of the durian tree, of which the Dyaks were very fond, the Dyaks were happy to guide Alec to them and then, after the shooting, to fell the trees in which the bodies were trapped, or climb the trunks and lower the bodies down. With their help Alec obtained four full-grown males, three females, and several juveniles. Just before the ague hit again, he also shot another female high in a giant tree. While lashing the body to the carrying poles, one of his Dyak hunters found the orangutan's little infant face-down in the swamp, crying piteously.

This orphan Alec brought back to camp with him. He could not feel guilty about shooting the infant's mother; this was part of his work, what he was meant to do. But neither could he abandon the small creature who'd become his responsibility. While he lay on his cot, alternately burning and chilled, the infant orangutan clung to his clothes and beard and sucked on his fingers as he might at his mother's breast. For a long time no one had touched Alec. He gave the infant sugar-water and rice-water and coconut milk through a quill, and later offered bits of fruit and sweet potato. The orangutan insisted on clinging to some part of his body at all times. And Alec found this peculiarly touching, despite the weakness and lassitude brought on by his fever.

When a pair of strangers walked into his hut, he was flat on his back, in a violent sweat, with the infant curled like a cap around his head.

Wallace, Alec learned from the strangers, had been at the Rajah's bungalow this whole time, staying on alone but for Charles and a Malay cook after the holidays had passed and the Rajah and his entourage had left. Having heard of Alec's plight through some visiting Dyaks, Wallace had sent these two back to fetch him. The pair carried Alec through the swamp and the forest, on a litter made of bamboo poles. Some of his helpers followed with his belongings, including all his crates of insect specimens and the skins and skeletons of the orangutans. The infant rode on his chest.

Wallace had the ague as well. When Alec arrived at the Rajah's bungalow, and first caught sight of the veranda and the huge teak beams, the wicker chairs and the spacious library, Wallace was desperately ill, and in bed. A few days later, when Wallace could get up, Alec was delirious. For ten days the men alternated bouts of fever as if they were playing lawn-tennis, but then finally, after large doses of quinine, both were well at the same time. In their weakened state they sat on the veranda, sipping arrack from narrow bamboos and talking. Wallace claimed that the bouts of ague stimulated his brain.

"Aren't these beetles astonishing?" Alec said, pawing through the box at his feet. His clothes and person were clean, he had had a good dinner, he'd slept on a real bed. He felt wonderful. This Brooke, he thought, truly lived like a king. And even though the Rajah had welcomed Wallace and not Alec, Alec was consoled by the beautiful things he had to show for his isolation.

"In two weeks I collected more than 600 different kinds, sometimes a dozen new species a day—it's bewildering," Alec said. He held out a beetle with horns twice the length of its body. "Have you come across this one? And what do you make of the remarkable multitude of species here?"

Wallace smiled and turned the beetle delicately on its back. He said, "I have several of these; they're charming. I do not see how a reasonable man can believe any longer in the permanence of species. All species, as you have seen yourself, constantly produce varieties. If this process goes on indefinitely, the varieties must move farther and farther from the original species, and some of these *must,* in time, develop into new species—but how and when does this happen? What is the method by which species undergo a natural process of gradual extinction and creation?"

"The method?" Alec said. Wallace passed the beetle back to Alec and Alec held it cupped in his palm. Since his first day in the archipelago he'd been haunted, vaguely, by the question Wallace now posed clearly: where had all these creatures come from? But Alec had had no time to theorize, caught up as he was in the urgency of trying to capture and name everything he saw.

"There must be a *mechanism,*" Wallace said.

The rain was falling steadily. From the trees three Dyaks emerged and joined the men on the veranda; Wallace produced a piece of string and tried to show them how to play the child's game of cat's cradle. Much to Alec's astonishment the Dyaks knew it better than he did. The three of them stood in a close circle, weaving figures he'd never seen before on each other's hands and passing the cradle back and forth. When Alec joined them they netted his fingers together.

Later Wallace showed Alec the lone specimen he'd found of a huge new butterfly, which had brilliant green spots arrayed against the black velvet of its wings. "I have named it *Ornithoptera Brookeana,*" Wallace said. "After our host." In return Alec showed Wallace how happily his little orangutan, whom he'd named Ali, lay in his arms as he brushed its long brown hair. He tried not to feel jealous when Ali leapt into Wallace's lap, and licked his cheek. Wallace was Alec's friend, but also his rival, and sometimes Alec longed for Wallace to have some failing. A certain coldness, say. Or an absent-mindedness, brought on by deep thinking. But it seemed there was no part of their lives in which Wallace could not surpass him.

The ague struck them both again on the following day—and to their great sorrow, it also struck Ali. Wallace, too weak himself to rise from bed, had Charles give the infant castor-oil to cure its diarrhea, but although this worked the other symptoms of fever continued; Ali's head and feet swelled; and then he died. Everyone at the bungalow much regretted the loss of the little pet. When Alec's own strength returned, he wept over Ali's body and then decided to bring the skin and skeleton home with him. Ali was sixteen inches tall, four pounds in weight, with an arm-spread of twenty-four inches. Alec made these measurements, but he shrank from the task of preparing the specimen and thought to have Wallace's Charles help him out. Wallace discouraged that.

"Charles is a nice boy," he said. "But quite incapable—look what he has done with this bird." He showed Alec a bee-eater Charles had been putting up, which resembled Alec's own first specimens. The head was crooked, a lump of cotton bulged from the breast, and the bird's feet had somehow been twisted soles uppermost. Alec looked at this, sighed, and steeled himself to prepare Ali's remains alone. Separating the skin from the bone and muscle beneath, he reminded himself that, in so doing, he served science. Was this science? That night he was unable to sleep. Some hours after the bungalow had lapsed into silence, he found himself outside, in the dripping forest, slashing savagely at a tangle of lianas.

Not until later did he learn that somewhere during this long run of fever-soaked days, Wallace had written a paper on the possible origin of species by, as he put it, *natural succession and descent—one species becoming changed either slowly or rapidly into another. . . . Every species has come into existence coincident both in time and space with a pre-existing closely allied species.* His paper caused a stir when it was published in England that September, bringing him to the notice of such eminent men as Lyell and Darwin.

What was Alec doing while Wallace was writing? Tossing on his sweaty bed; mourning his little orangutan as he sorted and arranged his insect collections. He prepared a shipment for Mr. Barton, with a long anxious letter about the difficulty of his finances, and how much he needed to receive a good price for this batch of specimens. He wrote,

Enclosed please find:

Beetles	*600 species*
Moths	*520 species*
Butterflies	*500 species*
Bees and wasps	*480 species*
Flies	*470 species*
Locusts, etc.	*450 species*
Dragonflies, etc.	*90 species*
Earwigs, etc.	*45 species*
Total:	*3155 species of insects*

(note: multiple specimens enclosed of many species)

Alec never claimed that his financial difficulties kept him from such fruitful speculations as Wallace made; he knew that Wallace, like himself, spent precious hours sorting and crating specimens and was largely dependent on the income from the sale of same. Alec merely noted that Wallace had Charles, however incapable; a bungalow-palace where he might return from time to time to regain his strength; and powerful friends.

[Theories—1862]

Here is one: Two human beings, coincident in time and space, cannot simultaneously think the same thought; one always precedes the other. As Wallace always preceded Alec, except in a single case. For consolation Alec had this: that *he* was the first to bring living specimens of paradise birds to the western world. And he believed he was the first American to see these creatures in their native forests. Although Alec thought of Wallace often, and longed to see him, the Malay Archipelago is a very big place and they never crossed paths again. Not until the winter of 1860, while Alec was on Sumatra plowing stupefied through a year's accumulation of letters—his mother was ill, or had been the previous May; his brother Frank had married; Mr. Barton had sold his last shipment of insect specimens for a gratifying sum, but had advanced all the money save for a pittance to his father, at his father's request—did he again hear news of Wallace.

In a letter Mr. Barton, who kept up with the natural history journals in both England and America, recounted to Alec how at Ternate, while suffering again from the ague, Wallace had written a further essay on the origin of species and mailed it to Darwin for comments. The essay had caused a sensation, Mr. Barton said, summarizing its main points for Alec. It had been read at a meeting of the Linnaean Society, along with some notes of Darwin's expressing a similar idea.

Genius, Alec thought, sitting stunned on his wooden stool. That's what had come of Wallace's ague. Of his own, which was upon him again, there were only incoherent letters begging to know the true state of his finances. He would not repeat to anyone what he wrote to his family. To Mr. Barton he wrote,

> *Thank you for your last, and for the most interesting news of Wallace's essay. You cannot imagine how tired I am after my last year's voyages. During the recent months, when I might have been resting, I have been cleaning, labeling, arranging and packing the enclosed: some 10,000 insects, shells, birds, and skeletons. Also hiring men and obtaining stores for my trip to Celebes and the Aru Islands—none of this made any easier by the fact that you have sent me hardly enough money to live on. Do not give the proceeds of this shipment to my family, but forward a full statement directly to me.*

Perhaps this is when Alec first wondered why his journal had deteriorated into little more than a tally of species, interspersed with fumbling descriptions of places and people. Why all he'd observed and learned had not crystallized in his mind into some shimmering structure. Certainly he'd never lacked for facts—but he was caught like a fly in the richness around him, drowning in detail, spread too thin. If he were to narrow his gaze, perhaps? Focus on one small group of species, contemplate only them? Then he might make both his reputation and his fortune.

As a boy he'd spent hours in the Philadelphia museum staring at a skin labeled *Magnificent Bird of Paradise:* red wings, dark green breast-plumes, cobalt-blue head, a stunning yellow ruff or mantle, and behind that a second mantle of glossy pure red. Sprouting from the tail were two long spires of steely blue. He had stared not only because the skin was so beautiful, but because it had no wings or feet. Birds with no feet—could there be such a thing? From a book in the museum's library, he'd learned that Linnaeus had labeled the skin he'd seen *Paradisea apoda,* or the footless paradise bird. A Dutch naturalist wrote that the paradise birds, wingless and footless, were buoyed up by the beams of the sun and never touched the earth till they died. How tantalizing, Alec thought now, looking up from his papers and crates. They were elusive, irresistible; and their skins were so rare as to be very valuable. Money crossed his mind, as it always had. Nearly penniless, and still without a wife or any possibility of supporting one, he seized on the prospect that the paradise birds might save him. Had Wallace married yet? He thought not. Once more he gathered the necessary supplies and prepared to disappear from sight.

After a long journey in a native *prau* from Celebes, during which his life was often in grave danger, he arrived in the Aru Islands. He shut his eyes to the fabulous trees, the astonishing moths and ants, and sought singlemindedly the Great Paradise Bird, with its dense tufts of long golden plumes raised to hide the whole body; the King Paradise Bird, so small and red, with its beautiful, emerald-green, spiral disks lifted high on slender paired shafts. The islanders with whom he was staying took him to see the *sacaleli,* or dancing-party, of the Great Paradise Birds.

In a huge tree, deep in the forest, he saw several dozen gather together. They raised their wings, they arched their necks, they lifted their long, flowing plumes and shivered them as if to music, darting now and then between the branches in great excitement. Their beauty and strangeness beggared even that of the lyre-tailed drongo-shrike or the Amazonian umbrella-bird. Above the crouching, glossy bodies the plumes formed golden fans. The islanders taught Alec to use a bow, and arrows tipped with blunt knobs. He sat in the trees, dazed by the beauty surrounding him, and shot strongly, so as to stun the birds without rending the skins or staining the plumage with blood. On the ground below him, boys wrung the birds' necks as they fell.

And of course they had feet, strong and pink and sturdy. The theories about them, Alec learned, had only been misinformation. He was one of the first to see how the islanders, preparing skins for traders, cut off the wings and feet, skinned the body up to the beak and removed the skull, then wrapped the skin around a sturdy stick and a stuffing of leaves and smoked the whole over a fire. This shrank the head and body very much and made the flowing plumage more prominent. Alec prepared his own specimens differently, so that the natural characteristics were preserved. And this absorbed him so completely that only in brief moments, as he fell into sleep, would he wonder about such things as how the golden plumes were related to the emerald disks.

Rain, fungus, aggressive ants, and the ever-ravenous dogs of the region all plagued him. Still, before the fever overcame him and he had to declare his journey at an end, he salvaged four crates of excellent skins and also captured three living specimens. He might not have an hypothesis about the divergence of species, but he knew how these birds lived. At the Smithsonian Institution, where he thought to donate them, he could point to their sturdy pink feet and say, "Look. *I* was the first to bring these back."

As he hop-scotched his way across the archipelago to Singapore, he easily found fruit and insects his birds would eat. Little figs they particularly enjoyed, also grasshoppers, locusts, and caterpillars. From Singapore to Bombay he fed the birds boiled rice and bananas, but they drooped in the absence of insect food and after Bombay even the fruit ran out. It was Alec's good fortune to discover they savored cockroaches, and for him to be aboard a battered old barkentine that swarmed with them. Each morning he scoured the hold and the store-rooms until he'd filled several biscuit-tins, and during the afternoon and evening he doled them out to the birds, a dozen at a time. As the ship headed south to round the Cape he worried that the increasing cold would bother them, but they did fine.

And if, as he learned after being back in Philadelphia for only a month, Wallace had been making his way to England simultaneously, carrying his own birds of paradise; and if Wallace's trip was shaped by the same quest for cockroaches—what did that matter? Wallace had traveled once more on a comfortable British steamer, aboard which cockroaches were rare; from his forced stops to gather them on land he made amusing anecdotes. But *I* was the one, Alec thought, who first solved the problem of keeping the birds alive.

From a London paper Alec learned that Wallace had returned to fame, as a result of his Ternate essay. His birds had taken up residence in the Zoological Gardens, where they were much admired. Meanwhile Alec had himself returned, unknown, to a country at war. To a half-country, he thought, which might soon be at war with England. His crates of skins lay uncatalogued at the Academy of Sciences. And the curators at the Smithsonian seemed less than grateful for his beautiful birds. No one had time to look at birds, their eyes were fixed on battles.

Alec wrote to Wallace once more—inappropriately, he knew; their stations had altered, their friendship had lapsed. Still he felt closer to Wallace than to anyone else in the world, and he could not keep from trying to explain himself to this man he'd meant to emulate. After giving the details of his voyage, of his birds and their fate, he wrote:

> *All of this may be blamed on the war. I cannot explain how bewildering it has been to return, after my long absence, to see what's become of my country. My mother died during my journey home. All three of my brothers have married, and my father has gone to live with my brother Frank, having lost through improvidence both the tavern and much of the money rightfully mine, which he obtained through trickery from Mr. Barton. Mr. Barton himself is gone, enlisted in the Army. The weather is cold and grey; the streets swarm with pallid people lost in their clothes; the air rings with boys shouting newspaper headlines, over and over again. In the Dyak longhouses, the heads of their enemies hung from the rafters, turning gently as we ate: and I felt more at home with them than here. Do you feel this? When you walk into a drawing-room, do you not feel yourself a stranger?*
>
> *What I meant to do, what I wanted to do, was to visit Mr. Edwards, whose book sent me off on my life's work. He is no great thinker himself; only a man who traveled like me, and described what he saw as I have failed to do. I thought he might help me gather some of my impressions into a book. But now I find that what I must do is abandon my collections, leave home once more, and enlist. The Potomac swarms with a great armada, ready to transport 100,000 men for an attack on Richmond.*

As he mailed his letter, he thought about the legend that seemed—even before he left—to be growing up around his presence in the Aru Islands. He'd learned some of the islanders' language, and had occasionally entertained his companions by lighting fires with a hand-lens, or picking up bits of iron with a magnet, which acts they regarded as magic. And because he asked questions, even laughable questions, about the birds with no feet before he ever saw them; because he knew where beetles might be found and how to lure butterflies to a bit of dried dung; and most of all because he walked alone through the forests, for hours and days, and was comfortable there, and at peace, the islanders ascribed mystical powers to him. The birds, they claimed, came down from the trees to meet him.

One of the boys he hunted with said, "You know everything. You know our birds and animals as well as we do, and the ways of the forest. You are not afraid to walk alone at night. We believe that all the animals you kill and keep will come to life again."

Alec denied this strenuously. "These animals are *dead,*" he said, pointing at a cluster of ants preserved in spirits. "Truly, truly dead."

The boy looked serenely into a golden glade dense with fallen trees. "They will rise," he said. "When the forest is empty and needs new animals."

Alec remembers staring at him; how the jar of ants dropped from his hand and rolled into the leafy litter. The suggestion seemed, in that moment, no more likely or unlikely than what Wallace had proposed for the origin of species: another theory of evolution; another theory. In that instant a line from Wallace's first letter to him returned and pierced like a bamboo shaft through his heart: *Each bird we shot and butterfly we netted was in the service of science.*

But this was only ever true for Wallace, not for him, he thinks; he has never been the scientist he'd believed himself to be, perhaps is no scientist at all. And that legend is as false as the moment, on the first leg of his first voyage home, when he hung suspended in joy. All the animals he's collected, sure that more would spring forth from the earth, are gone and will not rise. But as he packs his bags and readies himself for another murderous journey, they are what he thinks of now. The objects of his desire along the Amazon, in Borneo and Sumatra and Celebes, on the Aru Islands; his sloth, his orangutan, his birds with no feet.

ANDREA BARRETT

Servants of the Map

I.

He does not write to his wife about the body found on a mountain that is numbered but still to be named: not about the bones, the shreds of the tent, the fragile, browning skull. He says nothing about the diary wedged beneath the rock, or about how it felt to turn the rippled pages. Unlike himself, the surveyor thinks, the lost man traveled alone. Not attached to a branch, however small and insignificant, of the Great Trigonometrical Survey of India. On this twig charged to complete the Kashmir Series, he is nothing. A leaf, an apricot, easily replaced; a Civil Junior Sub-Assistant in the Himalayan Service.

The surveyor, whose name is Max Vigne, reads through the diary before relinquishing it to his superiors. The handwriting trembled in the final pages, the entries growing shorter and more confused. Hail storms, lightning storms, the loss of a little shaving mirror meant to send a glinting signal from the summit to the admiring crowds below—after noting these, the lost man wrote:

> I have been fasting. Several weeks—the soul detaches from the flesh. The ills of spirit and body are washed away and here on the roof of the world, in the abode of snow, one becomes greatly strengthened yet as fresh as a child.

Although Max pauses in wonder over these lines, he still doesn't share them with his wife. Instead he writes:

April 13, 1863

Dear Clara—

I can hardly understand where I am myself; how shall I explain it to you? Try to imagine the whole chain of the Himalaya, as wide as England and four times its length. Then imagine our speck of a surveying party tucked in the northwest corner, where the Great Himalaya tangles into the Karakoram—or not quite there, but almost there. We are at the edge of the land called Baltistan, or Little Tibet: Ladakh and Greater Tibet lie to the east. And it is so much more astonishing than we imagined. The mountains I wrote you about earlier, which we crossed to enter the Vale of Kashmir—everything I said about them was true, they dwarf the highest peaks I saw at home. But the land I am headed toward dwarfs in turn the range that lies behind me. Last Wednesday, after breakfast, the low clouds lifted and the sun came out. To the north a huge white mass remained, stretching clear across the horizon. I was worried about an approaching storm. Then I realized those improbable masses were mountains, shimmering and seeming to float over the plains below.

How I wish you could see this for yourself. I have had no mail from you since Srinagar, but messengers do reach us despite our frequent moves and I am hopeful. This morning I opened an envelope from the little trunk you sent with me. Have any of my letters reached you yet? If they have, you will know how much your messages have cheered me. No one but you, my love, would have thought to do this. On the ship, then during our tedious journey across the plains to the Pir Panjal; and even more throughout the weeks of preparation and training in Srinagar, your words have been my great consolation. I wait like a child on Christmas Eve for the dates you have marked on each envelope to arrive: I obey you, you see; I have not cheated. Now that the surveying season has finally begun and we're on the move, I treasure these even more. I wish I had thought to leave behind a similar gift for you. The letters I wrote you from Srinagar—I know the details about my work could not have been of much interest to you. But I mean to do better, now that we're entering this astonishing range. If I share with you what I see, what I feel: will that be a kind of gift?

Yours marked to be opened today, the anniversary of that wonderful walk along the Ouse when I asked you to marry me and, against a background of spinning windmills and little boys searching for eels, you stood so sleek and beautiful and you said "yes"—it made me remember the feel of your hand in mine, it was like holding you. I am glad you plan to continue with your German. By now you must have opened the birthday gifts I left for you. Did you like the dictionary? And the necklace?

I should try to catch you up on our journeys of these last few weeks. From Srinagar we labored over the Gurais pass, still knee-deep in snow: my four fellow plane-tablers, the six Indian chainmen, a crowd of Kashmiri and Balti porters, and Michaels, who has charge of us for the summer. Captain Montgomerie of the Bengal Engineers, head of the entire Kashmir Series, we have not seen since leaving Srinagar. I am told it is his habit to tour the mountains from April until October, inspecting the many small parties of triangulators and plane-tablers, of which we are only one. The complexities of the Survey's organization are beyond explaining: a confusion of military men and civilians, Scots and Irish and English; and then the assistants and porters, all races and castes. All I can tell you is that, although we civilians may rise in the ranks of the Survey, even the most senior of us may never have charge of the military officers. And I am the most junior of all.

From the top of the pass I saw the mountain called Nanga Parbat, monstrous and beautiful, forty miles away. Then we were in the village of Gurais, where we gathered more provisions and porters to replace those returning to Srinagar. Over the Burzil Pass and across the Deosai Plateau—it is from here that I write to you, a grassy land populated by chattering rodents called marmots. The air is clear beyond clearness today and to the north rises that wall of snowy summits I first mistook for a cloud: the Karakoram range, which we are to map. Even this far away I can see the massive glaciers explored by Godfrey Vigne, to whom I am so tangentially related.

I wonder what he would have thought of me ending up here? Often people ask if I'm related to that famous man but I deny it; it would be wrong of me, even now that he's dead, to claim such a distant connection. My eccentric, sometimes malicious supervisor, Michaels (an Irishman and former soldier of the Indian Army), persists in calling me "Mr. Vaahnya," in an atrocious French accent. This although I have reminded him repeatedly that ours is a good East Anglian family, even if we do have Huguenot ancestors, and that we say the name "Vine."

All the men who've explored these mountains—what a secret, isolated world this is! A kind of archipelago, sparsely populated, visited now and again by passing strangers; each hidden valley an island unto itself, inhabited by small groups of people wildly distinct from each other—it is as if, at home, a day's journey in one direction brought us to Germany, another's to Africa. As if, in the distance between the fens and the moors, there were twenty separate kingdoms. I have more to tell you, so much more, but it is late and I must sleep.

What doesn't he tell Clara? So much, so much. The constant discomforts of the body, the hardships of the daily climbs, the exhaustion, the loneliness: he won't reveal the things that would worry her. He restrains himself, a constant battle; the battle itself another thing he doesn't write about. He hasn't said a word about the way his fellow surveyors tease him. His youth, his chunky, short-legged frame and terribly white skin; the mop of bright yellow hair on his head and the paucity of it elsewhere: although he keeps up with the best of them, and is often the last to tire, he is ashamed each time they strip their clothes to bathe in a freezing stream or a glacial tarn. His British companions are tall and hairy, browning in the sun; the Indians and Kashmiris and Baltis smoother and slighter but dark; he alone looks like a figure made from snow. The skin peels off his nose until he bleeds. When he extends his hat brim with strips of bark, in an effort to fend off the burning rays, Michaels asks him why he doesn't simply use a parasol.

Michaels himself is thickly pelted, fleshy and sweaty, strong-smelling and apparently impervious to the sun. They have all grown beards, shaving is impossible; only Max's is blonde and sparse. He gets teased for this, for the ease with which he burns, and sometimes, more cruelly, for the golden curls around his genitals. Not since he was fourteen, when he first left school and began his apprenticeship on the railway survey, has he been so mocked. Then he had his older brother, Laurence, to protect him. But here he is on his own.

The men are amused not only by his looks, but by his box of books and by the pretty, brass-bound trunk that holds Clara's precious gift to him: a long series of letters, some written by her and others begged from their family and friends. The first is dated the week after he left home, the last more than a year hence; all are marked to be opened on certain dates and anniversaries. Who but Clara would have thought of such a gift? Who else would have had the imagination to project herself into the future, sensing what he might feel like a week, a month, a year from leaving home and writing what might comfort him then?

His companions have not been so lucky. Some are single; others married but to wives they seem not to miss or perhaps are even relieved to have left behind. A Yorkshireman named Wyatt stole one of Clara's missives from Max's campstool, where he'd left it while fetching a cup of tea. "Listen to this," Wyatt said—laughing, holding the letter above Max's head and reading aloud to the entire party. "Max, you must wear your woolly vest, you know how cold you get." Now the men ask tauntingly, every day, what he's read from the trunk. He comforts himself by believing that they're jealous.

A more reliable comfort is his box of books. In it, beyond the mathematical and cartographical texts he needs for his work, are three other gifts. With money she'd saved from the household accounts, Clara bought him a copy of Joseph Hooker's *Himalayan Journals.* This Max cherishes for the thought behind it, never correcting her misapprehension that Sikkim, where Hooker traveled in 1848, is only a stone's throw from where Max is traveling now. At home, with a map, he might have put his left thumb on the Karakoram range and his right, many inches away to the east, on the lands that Hooker explored: both almost equally far from England, yet still far apart themselves. Clara might have smiled—despite her interest in Max's work, geography sometimes eludes her—but that last evening passed in such a flurry that all he managed to do was to thank her. For his brother Laurence, who gave him a copy of Charles Darwin's *Origin of Species,* he'd had only the same hurried thanks. On the flyleaf, Laurence had written: "New ideas, for your new life. Think of me as you read this; I will be reading my own copy in your absence and we can write to each other about what we learn."

Repeatedly Max has tried to keep up his end of this joint endeavor, only to be frustrated by the book's difficulty. For now he has set it aside in favor of a more unexpectedly useful gift. Clara's brother, far away in the city of New York, works as an assistant librarian and sometimes sends extra copies of the books he receives to catalog. "Not of much interest to me," he wrote to Max, forwarding Asa Gray's *Lessons in Botany and Vegetable Physiology.* "But I know you and Clara like to garden, and to look at flowers in the woods—and I thought perhaps you would enjoy this."

At first, finding his companions uncongenial, Max read out of boredom and loneliness. Later he fell under the spell of the books themselves. The drawings at the back of Gray's book, the ferns and grasses and seed-pods and spore capsules: how lovely these are! As familiar as his mother's eyes; as distant as the fossilized ferns found by a British explorer on the shores of Melville Island. As a boy he'd had a passion for botany: a charmed few years of learning plants and their names before the shock of his mother's death, his father's long decline, the necessity of going out, so young, to earn a living and help care for his family. Now he has a family of his own. Work of his own, as well, which he is proud of. But the illustrations draw him back to a time when the differences between a hawkweed and a dandelion could fascinate him for hours.

Charmed by the grasses of the Deosai Plateau, he begins to dip into Dr. Hooker's book as well. Here too he finds much of interest. When he feels lost, when all he's forgotten or never knew about simple botany impedes his understanding, he marks his place with a leaf or a stem and turns back to Gray's manual. At home, he thinks, after he's safely returned, he and Clara can wander the fields as they did in the days of their courtship, this time understanding more clearly what they see and teaching these pleasures to their children. He copies passages into his notebook, meaning to share them with her:

Lesson I. Botany as a Branch of Natural History

The Organic World is the world of organized beings. These consist of *organs;* of parts which go to make up an *individual,* a *being.* And each individual owes its existence to a preceding one like itself, that is, to a parent. It was not merely formed, but *produced.* At first small and imperfect, it grows and develops by powers of its own; it attains maturity, becomes old, and finally dies. It was formed of inorganic or mineral matter, that is, of earth and air, indeed; but only of this matter under the influence of life; and after life departs, sooner or later, it is decomposed into earth and air again.

He reads, and makes notes, and reads some more. The *Himalayan Journals,* he has noticed, are "Dedicated to Charles Darwin by his affectionate friend, Joseph Dalton Hooker." What lives those men lead: far-flung, yet always writing to each other and discussing their ideas. Something else he hasn't told Clara is this: Before leaving Srinagar, in a shop he entered meaning only to buy a new spirit level, he made an uncharacteristically impulsive purchase. A botanical collecting outfit, charming and neat; he could not resist it although he wasn't sure, then, what use he'd make of it. But on the Deosai Plateau he found, after a windstorm, an unusual primrose flowering next to a field of snow. He pressed it, mounted it—not very well, he's still getting the hang of this—and drew it; then, in a fit of boldness, wrote about it to Dr. Hooker, care of his publisher in England. "The willows and stonecrops are remarkable," he added. "And I am headed higher still; might the lichens and mosses here be of some interest to you?" He doesn't expect that Dr. Hooker will write him back.

In his tent made from blankets, with a candle casting yellow light on the pages, Max pauses over a drawing of a mallow. About his mother, who died when he was nine, he remembers little. In a coffin she lay, hands folded over her black bombazine dress, face swollen and unrecognizable. When he was five or six, still in petticoats, she guided him through the marshes. Her pale hands, so soon to be stilled, plucked reeds and weeds and flowers. *You must remember these,* she said. *You must learn the names of the wonderful things surrounding us.* Horsetails in her hands, and then in his; the ribbed walls and the satisfying way the segments popped apart at the swollen joints. Pickerel rush and mallow and cattail and reed; then she got sick, and then she died. After that, for so many years, there was never time for anything but work.

2.

May 1, 1863

Dearest Clara—

A great day: as I was coming down an almost vertical cliff, on my way back to camp, a Balti coming up from the river met me and handed me a greasy, dirty packet. Letters from you, Laurence, and Zoe—yours were marked "Packet #12," which I had thought lost after receiving #13 and #14 back in Srinagar. From those earlier letters I knew you had been delivered safely of our beloved Joanna, and that Elizabeth had welcomed her new sister and all three of you were well: but I had no details, and to have missed not only this great event but your account of it made me melancholy. How wonderful then, after five long months, to have your description of the birth. All our family around you, the dawn just breaking as Joanna arrived and Elizabeth toddling in, later, to peer at the infant in your arms: how I wish I had been with you, my love.

And how I wish I knew what that long night and its aftermath had really been like; you spare my feelings, I know. You say not a word about your pains and trials. In #13 you mentioned recovering completely from the milk fever, but in #12 you did not tell me you had it, though you must have been suffering even then. Did we understand, when I took this position, how hard it would be? So many months elapse between one of us speaking, the other hearing; so many more before a response arrives. Our emotions lag so far behind the events. For me, it was as if Joanna had been born today. Yet she is five months old, and I have no idea of what those months have brought. Zoe says Elizabeth is growing like a cabbage, and Laurence says he heard from your brother in New York and that the family is thriving; how fortunate that the wound to his foot, which we once so regretted, has saved him from conscription.

I am well too, though terribly busy. But what I want, even more than sleep, is to talk to you. Everything I am seeing and doing is so new it is nothing, really, like the work I did in England—so much is rushing into me all at once—I get confused. When I lie down to sleep everything spins in my brain. I can only make sense of my new life the way I have made sense of everything, since we first met: by describing it to you. That great gift you have always had of listening, *asking such excellent questions when I tell you enough to let you imagine me clearly, then I can imagine myself.*

So, my dearest: imagine this. If this were an army (it almost is; three of Montgomerie's assistants are military officers, while others, like Michaels and his friends, served in the military forces of the East India Company until the Mutiny, then took their discharge rather than accept transfer to the British Army), I'd be a foot-soldier, far behind the dashing scouts of the triangulating parties who precede us up the summits. It is they who measure, with the utmost accuracy, the baseline between two vantage points, which becomes the first side of a triangle. They who with their theodolites measure the angles between each end of that line and a third high point in the distance: and they who calculate by trigonometry the two other sides of the triangle, thus fixing the distance to the far point and the point's exact position. One of the sides of that triangle then becomes the base for a new triangle—and so the chain slowly grows, easy enough to see on paper but dearly won in life. In the plains these triangles are small and neat. Out here the sides of a triangle may be a hundred miles or more.

Is this hard to follow? Try to imagine how many peaks must be climbed. And how high they are: 15,000 and 17,000 and 19,000 feet. My companions and I see the results of the triangulators' hard work when we follow them to the level platforms they've exposed by digging through feet of snow, and the supporting pillars they've constructed from rocks. Imagine a cold, weary man on the top of a mountain, bent over his theodolite and waiting for a splash of light. Far from him, on another peak, a signal squad manipulates a heliotrope (which is a circular mirror, my dear, mounted on a staff so it may be turned in any direction). On a clear day it flashes bright with reflected sunlight. At night it beams back the rays of a blue-burning lamp.

The triangulators leap from peak to peak; if they are the grasshoppers, we plane-tablers are the ants. At their abandoned stations we camp for days, collecting topographical details and filling in their sketchy outline maps. You might imagine us as putting muscle and sinew on the bare bones they have made. Up through the snow we go, a little file of men; and then at the station I draw and draw until I've replicated all I see. I have a new plane-table, handsome and strong. The drawing-board swivels on its tripod, the spirit level guides my position; I set the table directly over the point corresponding to the plotted site of my rough map. Then I rotate the board with the sheet of paper pinned to it until the other main landscape features I can see—those the triangulators have already plotted—are positioned correctly relative to the map.

As I fill in the blank spaces with the bends and curves of a river valley, the dips and rises of a range, the drawing begins to resemble a map of home. For company I have the handful of porters who've carried the equipment, and one or two of the Indian chainmen who assist us—intelligent men, trained at Dehra Dun in the basics of mapping and observation. Some know almost as much as I do, and have the additional advantage of speaking the local languages as well as some English. When we meet to exchange results with those who work on the nearby peaks and form the rest of our group, the chainmen gather on one side of the fire, sharing food and stories. In their conversations a great idea called "the Survey" looms like a disembodied god to whom they—we—are all devoted. Proudly, they refer to both themselves and us as "Servants of the Map."

I will tell you what your very own Servant of the Map saw a few days ago. On the edge of the Deosai Plateau, overlooking Skardu, I saw two far-away peaks towering above the rest of the Karakoram, the higher gleaming brilliant blue and the lower yellow. These are the mountains which Montgomerie, seven years ago, designated K1 and K2. K2 the triangulators have calculated at over 28,000 feet: imagine, the second highest mountain in the world, and I have seen it! The sky was the deepest blue, indescribable, sparkling with signals, the heliotropes of the triangulating parties twinkled at one another. Do you remember our visit to Ely Cathedral? The way the stone rose up so sharply from the flat plain, an explosion of height—it was like our first glimpse of that, magnified beyond reason and lit all about by fireflies.

We have thunderstorms almost every day, they are always terrifying; the one that shook us the afternoon I saw K2 brought hail, and lightning so close that sparks leapt about the rocks at my feet and my hair bristled and crackled. The wind tore my map from the drawing board and sent it spinning over the edge of the plain, a white bird flying into the Indus Valley below. But I do not mean to frighten you. I take care of myself, I am as safe as it is possible to be in such a place, I think of you constantly. Even the things I read remind me of you.

In Asa Gray's book, I read this today, from "Lesson VII: Morphology of Leaves":

> We may call foliage the *natural form* of leaves, and look upon the other sorts as *special forms,*—as *transformed* leaves . . . the Great Author of Nature, having designed plants upon one simple plan, just adapts this plan to all cases. So, whenever any special purpose is to be accomplished, no new instruments or organs are created for it, but one of the three general organs of the vegetable, *root, stem,* or *leaf,* is made to serve the purpose, and is adapted by taking some peculiar form.

Have I told you I have been working my way through this manual, lesson by lesson? I forget sometimes what I have written to you and what I have not. But I study whenever I can and use what I learn to help make sense both of my surroundings and of what I read in the Himalayan Journals, *which I treasure, because it's from you. As the book Laurence gave me requires more concentration than I can summon I've set it aside for now (my guilty secret; don't tell him this): but Dr. Hooker I think even more highly of since my arrival here. The rhododendron that Zoe, my thoughtful sister, gave us as a wedding present—do you remember how, when it first flowered, we marveled at the fragrant, snowy blossoms with their secret gold insides? It was raised in a greenhouse in St. John's Wood, from seeds sent back by Dr. Hooker. I wish I could have been with you this spring to watch it bloom.*

I am drifting from my point, I see. Forgive me. The point, *the reason I copy this passage, is not to teach you about leaves but to say these words brought tears to my eyes; they made me think of our marriage. When we were together our lives were shaped like our neighbors', as simple as the open leaves of the maple. Now we are apart, trying to maintain our connection over this im-*

mense distance. Trying to stay in touch without touch; which effort changes us deeply, perhaps even deforms us.

To an outsider we might now look like the thick seed leaves of the almond or the bean, or the scales of buds or bulbs; like spines or tendrils, sepals or petals, which are also altered leaves. Do you know that, in certain willows, pistils and stamens can sometimes change into each other? Or that pistils often turn into petals in cultivated flowers? Only now do I begin to grasp the principles of growth and change in the plants I learned to name in the woods, those we have grown at home—there is a science to this. Something that transcends mere identification.

I wander, I know. Try to follow me. The point, dear heart, is that through all these transformations one can still discern the original morphology; the original character is altered yet not lost. In our separation our lives are changing, our bond to each other is changing. Yet still we are essentially the same.

I love you. So much. Do you know this?

It is raining again, we are damp and cold. I miss you. All the time.

Max regards the last page of his letter doubtfully. That business about the alteration of leaves; before he sends it, he scratches out the line about the effects of his and Clara's separation. *Deform:* such a frightening word.

His days pass in promiscuous chatter, men eating and drinking and working and snoring, men sick and wounded and snow-blind and wheezing; always worries about supplies and medicines and deadlines. He is never alone. He has never felt lonelier. There are quarrels everywhere: among the Indian chainmen, between the chainmen and the porters, the porters and his fellow plane-tablers; between the plane-tablers and the triangulators; even, within his own group, among the parties squatting on the separate peaks. Michaels, their leader, appears to enjoy setting one team against another. Michaels takes the youngest of the porters into his tent at night; Michaels has made advances toward Max and, since Max rebuffed him, startled and furious, has ceased speaking with him directly and communicates by sarcastic notes.

Wyatt has approached Max as well; and a man from another party—the only one as young as Max—with a shock of red hair as obtrusive as a kingfisher's crest. Now all three are aligned against him. When the whole group meets he has seen, in the shadows just beyond the ring of light sent out by the campfire, men kneeling across from each other, britches unbuttoned, hands on each other . . . He closed his eyes and turned his back and blocked his ears to the roar of laughter following his hasty departure. Yet who is he to judge them? So starved for love and touch is he that he has, at different times, found himself attracted to the middle-aged, stiff-necked wife of an English official in Srinagar, a Kashmiri flower-seller, a Tibetan herdsman, the herdsman's dog. He has felt such lust that his teeth throb, and the roots of his hair; the skin of his whole body itching as if about to explode in a giant sneeze.

In the act of writing to Clara, Max makes for himself the solitude he so desperately needs. He holds two strands of her life: one the set of letters she writes to him now—or not *now,* but as close to now as they can get, four months earlier, five, six—and the other the set of letters she wrote secretly in the months before he left, trying to imagine what he might need to hear. Occasionally he has allowed himself the strange pleasure of opening one letter from each set on the same day. A rounded image of Clara appears when he reads them side by side: she is with him. And this fills him with a desire to offer back to her, in his letters, his truest self. He wants to give her everything: what he is seeing, thinking, feeling; who he truly is. Yet these days he scarcely recognizes himself. How can he offer these aberrant knots of his character to Clara?

He tries to imagine himself into the last days of her pregnancy, into the events of Joanna's birth, the fever after that. He tries to imagine his family's daily life, moving on without him. Clara is nursing Joanna, teaching Elizabeth how to talk, tending the garden, watching the flowers unfold; at night, if she is not too weary, she is bending over her dictionary and her German texts, and then . . . He wonders what would happen if he wrote, *Tell me what it feels like to lie in our bed, in the early morning light, naked and without me. Tell me what you do when you think of me. What your hands do, what you imagine me doing.*

He doesn't write that; he doesn't write about what he does to himself on a narrow cot, in a tent made from a blanket strung over a tree limb, the wind whistling as he stifles his groans with a handkerchief. Even then he doesn't feel alone. Close by, so near, his companions stifle noises of their own. His only truly private moments are these: bent over a blank page, dreaming with his pen.

3.

June 11, 1863

Dearest, dearest Clara:

The packet containing this letter will follow a very zigzag course on its way to you; a miracle that my words reach you at all. Or that yours reach me—how long it has been since the last! A ship that sailed from Bordeaux in March is rumored to have arrived at Bombay and will, I hope, have letters from you. Others from England have reached me—yet none from you—which is why I worry so. But already I hear your voice, reminding me that the fate of mail consigned to one ship may differ so from that consigned to another. I know you and the girls are well.

I am well too, although worried about you. I do what I can to keep busy. Did I tell you that I received, in response to some modest botanical observations I had sent to Dr. Hooker, a brief reply? He corrected my amateur mistakes, suggested I gather some specimens for him, and told me his great love of mosses dated from the time he was five or six. His mother claims that when he was very tiny he was found grubbing in a wall, and that when she asked what he was doing, he cried that he had found Bryam argenteum *(not true, he notes now), a pretty moss he'd admired in his father's collection. At any age, he says—even mine—the passion for botany may manifest itself.*

I found this touching and thought you would too. And I'm honored that he would answer me at all. In the hope of being of further use to him, I plan to continue my observations. Where I am now—deep in the heart of the Karakoram—nothing grows but the tiny lichens and mosses that are Dr. Hooker's greatest love. I can do little with them yet, they're extremely difficult. Except for them the landscape is barren. No one lives here: how would they live? Yet people do pass through from the neighboring valleys, the glaciers serving as highways through the mountains: I have met Hunzakuts, Baltis, Ladakhis and Nagiris and Turkis. But so far no travelers from home, although I hear rumors of solitary wanderers, English and German and French. One elderly adventurer has apparently haunted these mountains for decades, staying at times in Askole and Skardu; traveling even on the Baltoro Glacier and its branches—can this be true? If he exists, no one will tell me his name.

Around me is a confused mass of rock and glacier and mist, peaks appearing then disappearing beyond the curtains of clouds. The glaciers, covered with rocks and striated like frozen rivers, you would never mistake for snowfields or for anything else; the porters fear them and have their own names for them, while the chainmen claim that, deep within them, are the bodies of men who died in the mountains and are now being slowly carried down the stream of ice. Some decades from now, at the foot of the glacier, a glove or a couple of bones may be spit out.

I have seen wild sheep the size of ponies. I have slept ten nights at a stretch above 15,000 feet; I have woken buried in snow, lost in clouds; days have passed when I could make no sightings and sketch no maps, when we have nothing to eat and huddle together forlornly, watching avalanches peel down the side of the peaks. The weather here is beastly. At the snout of the Baltoro we were nearly swept away by a river leaping from an ice cave. There are no vistas when one travels the glaciers, more a sense of walking along a deep corridor, framed by perpendicular walls. I have a headache nearly all the time, and my neck aches from always gazing upward. The mornings are quiet, everything frozen in place by the frosts of the night. By afternoon the landscape has come alive, moving and shifting as rocks fall, walls of mud slide down, hidden streams dammed by the ice break free with a shout. No place for men.

I travel now in a party of six. Me in charge, the sole Englishman (the others lead similar parties, on other glaciers, on their way to other peaks); two Indian assistants who aid me with the measurements and mapping; three porters. We are on the Baltoro itself as I write. So frequent are the crevasses, and so deceitfully covered with snow, that we tie ourselves together with ropes and move like a single long caterpillar. Yesterday we stopped by the edge of a huge open fissure and, while the other men rested, I tied all our ropes together and sounded the depth; 170 feet of rope failed to reach bottom. Framing us, on both sides of the glacier, are some of the world's highest peaks.

My task has been to map where Montgomerie's K2 lies in relation to the Karakoram watershed. And this I have done, though there is no clear sight of it from the glacier itself. With my men I climbed the flank of an enormous mountain called Masherbrum. My men—I ought to try and tell you what it's like to live in such enforced companionship. They . . . I will save this for another letter. You know how awkward I have always been. With my own family, with you, I can be myself but here, with strangers it is terrible, the old shyness seizes me. Without you by my side, to start the conversation and set everyone at ease, I am so clumsy. I do try, but it does no good. Especially with the porters and the chainmen I am at a loss. The barriers of language and our very different circumstances and habits and religions—I ought to be able to break through these, given the bonds of our shared work. Somewhere they too have wives and children, families and homes, but I can't imagine them, I can't see these men in any other setting and I think they can't see me any more clearly. For them, I am simply the person who gives orders. In my early days surveying seemed like a perfect career for such a solitary creature as myself. I didn't understand that, out here, I would be accompanied ceaselessly by strangers.

Yet one does not need to talk all the time. And some things are beyond conversation—several thousand feet up the flank of Masherbrum, as we were perched on a sharp bleak shoulder, there it suddenly rose: K2, sixteen or seventeen miles away, separating one system of glaciers from another. We believe the reason it has no local name is that it isn't visible from any inhabited place; the nearest village is six days' march away and the peak is hidden by others, almost as large. I cannot tell you how it felt to see it clearly. I have spent two days here, mapping all the visible peaks and their relationships to each other and the glaciers.

I will entrust this to the herdsman I met, who is on his way to Skardu; may it find its way to you. One of our porters speaks a language somewhat familiar to this herdsman. The pair had a discussion involving much pointing at Masherbrum, an insistent tone on the part of the porter, violent head-shakings from the herdsman. Later I asked the porter what they'd been talking about. The herdsman had asked where we'd been; the porter had shown him the shoulder from which we saw K2. "You have never been there," the herdsman apparently said. "No one can go there. It is not for men."

He does not write to Clara about his glacial misadventures. Walking along on a hazy day with his party strung out behind him, he had seen what resembled a small round rock perched on the ice in the distance. Fresh snow had fallen the night before and the glare was terrible; over his eyes he'd drawn a piece of white muslin, like a beekeeper's veil, which cut the worst of the blinding light but dimmed the outlines of everything. One of his companions had bound a sheet of slit paper over his eyes, while others had woven shades from the hair of yaks' tails or had unbound their own hair and combed it forward until it screened their eyes. Max was nearly upon the round rock before he recognized it as a head.

A narrow crevasse, its opening covered by drifted snow; a wedge-shaped crack the width of a man at the top, tapering swiftly to a crease: inspecting it, with his veil raised, Max could imagine what had happened. The testing step forward, the confident placement of the second foot; and then one last second of everyday life before the deceitful bridge crumbled and the man plunged down, leaving his head and neck above the surface. The slit would have fit as intimately as a shroud, trapping the man's feet with his toes pointed down. No room to flex his knees or elbows and gain some purchase—but his head was free, he was breathing, he wasn't that cold and surely—surely?—he could pull himself out.

The man had a name, although it would take a while to determine it: Bancroft, whom Max had met only once, a member of one of the triangulating parties, disappeared three days before Max arrived. The ice inside the crevasse, warmed by the heat it stole from Bancroft's body, would have melted and pulled him inch by inch farther down, chilling him and slowing his blood, stealing his breath as fluid pooled in his feet and legs and his heart struggled to push it back up. By nightfall, with the cold pouring down from the stars, the cold wind pouring down from the peaks, the slit which had parted and shaped itself to Bancroft's body would have frozen solid around him. After hours of fruitless work, Max and his companions had reluctantly left Bancroft in a grave that would move until someone, a lifetime away, would puzzle over the boots and bones deposited in a moraine.

Max had not told Clara any of this: it would have frightened her. It frightened him. And yet despite that he went walking alone, ten days later. The sun was out, the sky was clear; the men had stopped in the middle of the afternoon, refused to go farther without a rest, and set up camp against his wishes. Irritated, he'd refused to waste the day. He'd mapped this section already, but wanted more detail for his sketches: how the ice curved and cracked as it ground past the embracing wall of the mountain. In Wales, when he was being trained, he and Laurence had seen erratic boulders and mountains with deeply scored flanks which were caused, said the bookish young man who led them, by a glacial period that covered all Europe with ice. Now it was as if he'd walked backward into that earlier time.

He fell into a fissure, forty feet deep. A leaf of ice, like the recalcitrant piece of heartwood bridging two halves of a split log, stretched between the uphill and downhill walls of the crevasse and broke his fall. He landed face down, embracing a narrow slab, calling himself back to life and aware of his arms and legs dangling into space. Above him was a ceiling of snow, with a narrow slit of blue sky where his body had broken through. He could move his feet, his hands, his shoulders; apparently nothing was broken. Slowly, hugging the ice with his thighs, he sat upright. Before him the uphill wall of the crevasse glimmered smooth in the blue shadows. Slim ribs of ice, bulges and swellings reminiscent of Clara's back and belly. Behind him the downhill wall was jagged and white and torn. To his right the crevasse stretched without end, parallel faces disappearing into darkness. But to his left the walls appeared to taper together.

He might make of himself a bridge, he thought. A bridge of flesh, like the bridge of ice. With his back pressed against the wet uphill wall, his legs extended and his boots pressed into the crunching, jagged downhill wall, he suspended himself. He moved his right foot a few inches, then his left; sent all his strength into the soles of his feet and then slid his back a few inches, ignoring the icy stream that chattered so far below. Again and again, right foot, left foot, heave. Time stopped, thinking stopped, everything stopped but these small painful motions. The walls drew closer together and he folded with them, his legs bending at the knees, then doubled, until finally he was hung in a sideways crouch.

He reached the corner without knowing what he'd do when he got there. The crevasse was shaped like a smile; where the two lips met, the bottom also curved up. He released his right leg and let it slide down, touching some rubble on which he might balance. He stood, he straightened partway. Soaked, scared, exhausted, and so cold. Above him was not the sky, but a roof of snow. Like a mole he scratched at the bottom surface. He tore his fingernails and ripped his hands. When he realized what was happening he stopped digging with his right hand and dug only with his left.

He dug himself out. He hauled himself up. How many hours did this take? His left hand was bloody and blue, his right torn but still working; how lucky he had been. On the surface of the glacier, under the setting sun, he closed his eyes and fixed in his mind the dim, shadowed, silent grave he'd known for a few hours. Among the things he would not write Clara—he would never write a word of this—was how seductive he'd found the cold and quiet. How easy he would have found it to sleep on the leaf of ice, his head pillowed on his arm while snow drifted over the broken roof, sealing him in silent darkness. Nothing would have been left of him but his books and maps, and the trunk with Clara's letters. So many still unopened, dated months in the future, a year in the future. It was the thought of not getting to read them that made him wake up.

4.

July 21, 1863

Dear heart—

This week I received your Packet #15, from March; you cannot know what a relief it is to hear from you. But why do I say that when I know you suffer the same torments? It is very upsetting to hear that none of my letters have reached you, and that you have as yet no news of my travels across the country to Kashmir, never mind news of my journeys in the mountains. Although perhaps by now you do: it was still March, *I remind myself, when you hadn't heard from me. It may be September or December before you receive this, and you will be in possession of all my other letters by then, smiling to see me worry in this.*

We heard a ship leaving Calcutta was burnt down to the waterline just after it embarked; all the passengers were saved but everything else on board was lost and I wonder if some of my letters were on it, now bits of ash on the sea. When I think about the hands through which these must pass, to find their way to you: a passing herdsmen to another party of the Survey, to another messenger, to some official in Srinagar; perhaps to Calcutta, perhaps to Bombay; through a merchant's hands, or a branch of the military—hand to hand to hand, to a ship, or several ships: and the hazards of weather and human carelessness every inch of the way. . . . My dear, you must keep these accidents in mind, when you worry about me. It grieves me to think of your suffering. Remember the promise we made to each other, to consider not just the accidents that might happen to us, but to our correspondence. Remember how tough I am. How prudent.

Thank you for the story about Elizabeth and the garden. I love to think about the three of you, bundled up and watching the birds as they flick within the branches on the hedgerow. Joanna in your arms, Elizabeth darting along the hawthorns, pursuing the sparrows: these glimpses of your life together keep me going. If you knew how much I miss you . . . but I have promised myself I will write sensibly. *I want you to think of me as I am, as you have always known me, and not as a stranger perpetually complaining. I'm glad Mrs. Moore's nephew—Gideon?—has been so helpful during his stay with his aunt and has been able to solve the problem with the drains. When next you see him, please tell him I am grateful. Do you see him often?*

I received with the letters from you and our family two more letters from Dr. Hooker. He has *received mail from me, from as late as April; how is it my letters are reaching him but not you? When I get home I will let you read what he writes, you will find it fascinating. He is in touch with botanists and collectors all over the world; involved with so many projects and yet still he takes the time to encourage an amateur such as myself. On his own journey, he said, as he climbed from the terai to the snowline he traversed virtually the entire spectrum of the world's flora, from the leech-infested, dripping jungle to the tiny lichens of the Tibetan plateau. I have a similar opportunity, he says. If I am wise enough to take it. I copy for you here a little paragraph, which he included with questions about what is growing where, and requests for a series of measurements of temperature and altitude.*

"When still a child," he writes, "my father used to take me on excursions in the Highlands, where I fished a good deal, but also botanized; and well I remember on one occasion, that, after returning home, I built up by a heap of stones a representation of one of the mountains I had ascended, and stuck upon it specimens of the mosses I had collected, at heights relative to those at which I had gathered them. This was the dawn of my love for geographical botany. It pleases me greatly that, though you have started your botanizing as a grown man, you may come to share a similar passion."

Is that not a lovely tale? The mountain was a little one, by our standards here, less than 4,000 feet. He has been very encouraging of my efforts and with his help I have set myself a study plan, as if I'm at university. I would like to make myself worthy; *worthy to write to such a man as Dr. Hooker, and receive a response. Worthy of seeking an answer to the question that now occupies everyone: how the different forms of life have reached their present habitats. When else will I have a chance like this?*

What draws me to these men and their writings is not simply their ideas but the way they defend each other so vigorously and are so firmly bound. Hooker, standing up for Darwin at Oxford and defending his dear friend passionately. Gray, in America, championing Darwin in a series of public debates and converting the world of American science one resistant mind at a time. Our group here is very different. Although the work gets done—the work always gets done, the maps accumulate—I have found little but division and quarrels and bad behavior.

You may find my handwriting difficult to decipher; I have suffered much from snow blindness. And a kind of generalized mountain sickness as well. We are so high, almost all the time; the smallest effort brings on fatigue and nausea and the most piercing of headaches. I sleep only with difficulty; it is cold at night, and damp. Our fires will not stay lit. But every day brings new additions to our map, and new sketches of the topography: you will be proud of me, I am becoming quite the draftsman. And I manage to continue with my other work as well. I keep in mind Hooker's travails in Nepal and Sikkim: how, in the most difficult of circumstances, he made excellent and detailed observations of his surroundings. I keep in mind Godfrey Vigne, and all he managed to note. Also a man I did not tell you about before, whose diary passed through my hands: how clearly he described his travels, despite his difficulties! By this discipline, and by my work, I hold myself together.

This week my party climbed a peak some 21,000 feet high. We were not the first ones here: awaiting us was the station the strongest and most brilliant of the triangulators built last season. I have not met him; he remains an almost mythical creature. But I occupied his heap of stones with pride. He triangulated all the high peaks visible from here and the map I have made from this outline, the curves of the glaciers and the jagged valleys, the passes and the glacial lakes—Clara, how I wish you could see it! It is the best thing I have ever done and the pains of my body are nothing.

I have learned something, these past few months. Something important. On the descent from such a peak, I have learned, I can see almost nothing: by then I am so worn and battered that my eyes and mind no longer work correctly; often I have a fever, I can maintain no useful train of thought, I might as well be blind.

On my first ascents, before I grasped this, I would make some notes on the way up but often I would skip things, thinking I would observe more closely on the way down. Now I note everything *on the way up. As we climbed this giant peak I kept a notebook and pencil tied to my jacket pocket and most of the time had them right in my hand: I made note of every geological feature, every bit of vegetation or sign of a passing animal; I noted the weather as it changed over the climb, the depth of the snow, the movements of the clouds. This record—these records, I do this now with every ascent—will I think be invaluable to subsequent travelers. When I return I plan to share them with Dr. Hooker and whoever else is interested.*

It's an odd thing, though, that there is not much pleasure in the actual recording. Although I am aware, distantly, that I often move through scenes of great beauty, I can't feel *that as I climb; all is lost in giddiness and headache and the pain of moving my limbs and drawing breath. But a few days after I descend to a lower altitude, when my body has begun to repair itself—then I look at the notes I made during my hours of misery and find great pleasure in them. It is odd, isn't it? That all one's pleasures here are retrospective; in the moment itself, there is only the moment, and the pain.*

I must go. A messenger from Michaels came by the camp this morning with new instructions and leaves soon to contact three other parties; if I put this into his hands it will find its way down the glacier, out of the mountains, over the passes. To you.

After relinquishing the letter to Michaels' messenger, he thinks: What use was that? For all those words about his work, he has said little of what he really meant. How will Clara know who he is these days, if he hides both his worries, and his guilty pleasures? He still hasn't told her about the gift he bought for himself. A collecting box, like a candle-box only flatter, in which to place fresh specimens. A botanical press, with a heap of soft drying-paper, to prepare the best of his specimens for an herbarium; and a portfolio in which to lay them out, twenty inches by twelve, closed with a sturdy leather strap and filled with sheets of thin, smooth, unsized paper. Always he has been a man of endless small economies, saving every penny of his pay, after the barest necessities, for Clara in England. He has denied himself warm clothes, extra blankets, the little treats of food and drink on which the other surveyors squandered their money in Srinagar, and before. But this one extravagance he couldn't resist: not a dancing-girl, not a drunken evening's carouse, but still he is ashamed.

A different kind of shame has kept him from writing about the doubts that plague his sleepless nights. He knows so little, really—why does he think his observations might be useful? He ought to be content with the knowledge that the work he does each day is solid, practical, strong; these maps will stand for years. In Dehra Dun, and in Calcutta and back in England, copyists and engravers will render from his soiled rough maps clean and permanent versions. In a year the Series will be complete: Jammu and Kashmir, Khagan, Ladakh and Baltistan, caught in a net of lines; a topographical triumph. Still he longs to make some contribution more purely his.

He dreams of a different kind of map, in shades of misty green. Where the heads of the Survey see the boundaries of states and tribes, here the watershed between India and China, there a plausible boundary for Kashmir, he sees plants, each kind in a range bounded by soil and rainfall and altitude and temperature. And it is this—the careful delineation of the boundaries of those ranges, the subtle links between them—that has begun to interest him more than anything else. *Geographical botany,* Dr. Hooker said. What grows where. Primulas up to this level, no higher; deodar here, stonecrops and rock jasmines giving way to lichens . . . Why do rhododendrons grow in Sikkim, and not here? He might spend his life in the search for an answer.

Part of the reason he has formed no close ties to either the men with whom he daily climbs and maps, nor those who lead the other small parties, is that when they gather at night they argue about the ebb and flow not of plant life, but of politics. The Sikh Wars and the annexation of the Punjab, the administration of Lord Dalhousie, the transfer of power from the East India Company to the Crown, the decisions of the regional revenue officers—it is embarrassing, how little all this interests him. Among the surveyors are military men who have served in the Burmese War, or in Peshawar; who survived the Mutiny or, in various mountains, that stormy year when supplies to the Survey were interrupted and bands of rebels entered Kashmir. He ought to find their stories fascinating. Germans and Russians and Turks and Chinese, empires clashing; Dogras and Sikhs, spies and informants—currents no one understands, secrets it might take a lifetime to unravel. Yet of all this, two stories only have stayed with him.

The first he heard on a snow bench carved in a drift on a ridge, from an Indian chainman who'd served for a while in the Bengal Army, and who worked as Max's assistant for two weeks, and then disappeared. They were resting. The chainman was brewing tea. At Lahore, he said, his regiment had been on the verge of mutiny. On a June night in 1857, one of the spies the suspicious British officers had planted within the regiment reported to the Brigadier that the sepoys planned an uprising the following day. That night, when the officers ordered a regimental inspection, they found two sepoys with loaded muskets.

There was a court-martial, the chainman said. He told the story quietly, as if he'd played no part in it; he had been loyal, he said. He had been simply an observer. Indian officers had convicted the two sepoys and sentenced them to death. "There was a parade," the chainman said. His English was very good, the light lilting accent at odds with the tale he told. "A formal parade. We stood lined up on three sides of a square. On the fourth side were two cannon. The sepoys—"

"Did you know them?" Max had asked.

"I knew both of them—I had tried to talk them out of their plan. They were . . . the officers lashed those two men over the muzzles of the cannons. Then they fired."

Below them the mountains shone jagged and white, clean and untenanted. Nearby were other Englishmen, and other Indians, working in apparent harmony in this landscape belonging to neither. Yet all this had happened only six years ago.

"There was nothing left of them," the chainman said. He rose and kicked snow into the fire; the kettle he emptied and packed tidily away. "Parts of them came down like rain, bits of bone and flesh, shreds of uniforms. Some of us were sprinkled with their blood."

"I . . ." Max had murmured. What could he say? "A terrible thing," he said. The chainman returned to work, leaving Max haunted and uneasy.

The other story was this, which Michaels encouraged a triangulator to tell one night when three different surveying teams gathered in a valley to plan their tasks for the next few weeks. An Indian atrocity to match the British one: Cawnpore, a month after the incident reported by the chainman. Of course Max had heard of the massacre of women and children there. No one in England had escaped that news, nor the public frenzy that followed. But Michaels' gruff, hard-drinking companion, who in 1857 had been with a unit of the Highlanders, told with relish certain details the newspaper hadn't printed.

"If you had seen the huts," said Michaels' friend: Archdale, Max thought his name was. Or maybe Archvale. "A hundred and twenty women and children escaped the first massacre on the river boats—the mutineers rounded them up and kept them in huts. We arrived not long after they were butchered. I saw those huts, they looked like cages where a pack of wild animals had been set loose among their prey."

"Tell about the shoes," Michaels had called from the other side of the fire. All the men were drinking; Michaels had had a case of brandy carried in from Srinagar. His face was dark red, sweating, fierce. That night, as always, he ignored Max almost completely.

"The shoes," Archdale said. He emptied his glass and leaned forward, face shining in the firelight. "Picture this," he said. "I go into one hut and the walls are dripping with blood, the floor smeared, the smell unthinkable. Flies buzzing so loudly I thought I'd go mad. Against one wall is a row of women's shoes, running with blood, draped with bits of clothing." The Indian chainmen and the Balti porters were gathered around their separate fires, not far away: could they hear Archdale? Max wondered. Was it possible Archdale would say these things within earshot of them? "Against the other wall, a row of children's shoes, so small, just like those our children wear at home. And"—he leaned further forward here—"do you know what was in them?"

No one answered. Was Joanna wearing shoes yet? Max wondered. "What?" he'd said, unable to stop himself.

"Feet!" Archdale roared. "*Feet!* Those filthy animals, those swine, they had lopped off the children's feet. We found the bodies in the well."

That terrible story had set off others; the night had been like a night in hell; Max had fled the campfire soon after Archdale's tirade and rolled himself in a blanket in a hollow, far from everyone, carved into the rocky cliffs. When he woke he'd been surprised not to find the campground littered with bodies.

Since hearing those tales he has wondered how there could be so much violence on both sides; and how, after that, Englishmen and Indians could be up in these mountains, working so calmly together. How can he make sense of an empire founded on such things? *Nothing,* he thought after hearing those stories. And still thinks. *I understand nothing.*

Dr. Hooker wrote at great length, in a letter Max didn't mention to Clara, about the problems of packing botanical collections for the journey home: the weight, the costs; the necessity of using Ward's cases; the crating of tree-ferns and the boats to be hired. How kind he was, to take such trouble in writing Max, and to warn him of these potential hazards! And yet how little Dr. Hooker understands Max's own situation. There is no possibility of paying for such things, without depriving Clara and his daughters. His collections are limited to the scraps he can dry and preserve in his small press—bad enough he spent money on that—the herbarium sheets he can carry; the sketches and observations in his notebook. He can offer Dr. Hooker only these, but they are nothing, and he hopes his gifts will be received without disappointment.

The lost man whose skull he found when he first entered these mountains: at least that solitary explorer left behind a record of the movements of his soul. What is he doing, himself? Supporting his family, advancing his career; when he returns to England, he'll have no trouble finding a good position. But he would like also to feel that he has *broadened* himself. Hunched over his plane-table, his temples pounding as he draws the lateral moraines of the glacier below him, he hears his mother's voice.

Look. Remember this. The ribbon of ice below him turns into a snow-covered path that curves through the reeds along the river and vanishes at the horizon; across it a rabbit is moving and his mother stands, her hand in his, quietly keeping him company. They watch, and watch, until the path seems not to be moving away from them, but toward them; the stillness of the afternoon pouring into their clasped hands. *There is something special in you,* she said. *In the way you see.*

A few days ago, on his twenty-eighth birthday, he opened the birthday greeting Clara had tucked in his trunk. She had written about the earlier birthdays they'd shared. And about this one, as she imagined it: *Your companions, I know, will have made you a special birthday meal. Perhaps you'll all share a bottle of brandy, or whatever you drink there. I am thinking of you, and of the birthdays in the future we will once more spend together.*

Reading this, he'd felt for the first time that Clara's project might fail. He is no longer the person she wrote to, almost a year ago now. She may have turned into someone else as well. That Gideon she mentions, that nice young man who prunes the trees and brings her wood and does the tasks Max ought to be doing himself: what other parts of Max's life is he usurping? Max conjures up someone broad-shouldered, very tall—Max and Clara are almost the same height—unbuttoning his shirt and reaching out for Clara . . . Impossible, it makes him want to howl. Surely she wouldn't have mentioned him if their friendship were anything but innocent. Yet even if it is, it will have changed her.

He himself has changed so much, he grows further daily from her picture of him. There was no birthday celebration; he told no one of this occasion. If he had, there would have been no response. It is his mother, dead so many years, who seems to speak most truly to the new person he is becoming. As if the years between her death and now were only a detour, his childhood self emerging from a long uneasy sleep. Beyond his work, beyond the mapping and recording, he is *seeing;* and this—it is terrifying—is becoming more important to him than anything,

5.

October 1, 1863

Dearest Clara—

Forgive me for not writing in so long. Until I received your Packets #17, 18, and 19, all in a wonderful clump last week (#16, though, has gone astray), I had almost given up hope of us being in touch before winter. I should have realized your letters couldn't find me while we were among the glaciers. We are in the valley of the Shighar now, and from here will make our way back to Srinagar. I don't yet know what my winter assignment will be. The triangulating parties will winter at the headquarters in Dehra Dun, recalibrating the instruments and checking their calculations and training new assistants. There is talk of leaving a small group of planetablers in Srinagar, to complete topographical maps of the city and the outlying areas and lakes. I will let you know my orders as soon as I get them.

At least you know I am alive now. Though how can you make sense of my life here on the evidence of one letter from when I first arrived in Kashmir, and one from deep in the mountains? The others—I must have faith they will find their way to you. Your description of your journey to London, trudging through those government offices as you tried to get some word of me—this filled me with sadness, and with shame. You are generous to say it is not my fault that you went so long without word of me, that you blame a careless ship's captain, clumsy clerks and accidents: but it is my fault, still. I am the one who left home. And that I have not written these last weeks—can you forgive me? I console myself with the thought that, since my earlier letters were so delayed, perhaps a trickle of them will continue to reach you during the gap between then and now. But really my only excuse is the hardships of these last weeks. I am so weary; the cold and the altitude make it hard to sleep. And when I do catch a few brief hours I am plagued by nightmares. The men I work with tell me stories, things I would never repeat to you; and though I try not to think about them they haunt me at night.

The season in the mountains is already over; we stayed too long. We crossed one high pass after another during our retreat. And Clara, you can't imagine the weather. I couldn't work on my maps, or keep up my notes, or even—my most cherished task—write to you; when I heated the inkpot, the ink still froze on its short journey to the paper. My hands were frozen, my beard a mass of icicles. I wore everything you packed for me, all at once, and still couldn't stay warm. Lamb's wool vest and drawers, heavy flannel shirt and lined chamois vest, wool trousers and shirt, three pairs of stockings and my fur-lined boots, thick woolen hat, flannel-lined kidskin jacket, over that my big sheepskin coat and then a Kashmir shawl wrapped twice about me, binding the whole mass together—I sweated under the weight of all this, yet grew chilled the instant we stopped moving. Nights were the worst, there is no firewood in the mountains and we had already used up all we'd carried. Food was short as well.

I shouldn't tell you these things; never mind. Now that we are down in the valleys things are easier. And I am fine. Soon enough we'll reach Srinagar, and whether I stay there or move on to Debra Dun I am looking forward to the winter. Long quiet months of cleaning up my sketch maps, improving my drawings, fitting together the sections into the larger picture of the Himalayan system. From either place I may write to you often, knowing the chances of you getting my letters in just a few months are good: and I may look forward to receiving yours with some regularity. Still I have some of the letters in your trunk to look forward to, as well: I ration these now, I open one only every few weeks, sometimes ignoring the dates with which you marked them. Forgive me—I save them for when I most need them. This evening, before I began to write to you, I opened one intended for Elizabeth's birthday. How lovely to be reminded of that happy time when you leaned on my arm, plump and happy as we walked in the garden and waited for her birth. The lock of Elizabeth's hair you enclosed I have sewn into a pouch, which I wear under my vest.

What else do I have to tell you? So much has happened these last weeks that I don't know how to describe it all; and perhaps it wouldn't interest you, it is just my daily work. Yesterday I had a strange encounter, though. Camped by the edge of a river, trying to restore some order to my papers while my companions were off in search of fuel, I looked up to see a stranger approaching; clearly a European although he wore clothes of Kashmiri cut. When I invited him to take tea with me he made himself comfortable and told me about himself. A doctor and an explorer, elderly; he calls himself Dr. Chouteau and says he is of French birth, though his English is indistinguishable from mine. This he explains by claiming to have left home as a boy of fourteen; claiming also to have been exploring in these mountains for over forty years. We did not meet in Srinagar, he told me, because he lives in a native quarter there. I think he may be the solitary traveler of whom I heard such odd rumors earlier in the season, though when I asked him this he shrugged and said, "There are a few of us."

We passed together the most interesting afternoon I've had in weeks. My own companions and I have grown weary of each other, we seldom speak at all; but Dr. Chouteau talked without stopping for several hours. A great liar, I would have to say. Even within those hours he began to contradict himself. But how intriguing he was. He is very tall, thin and hawk-nosed, with a skin burnt dark brown by years in the sun and deeply lined. His ragtag outfit he tops with a large turban, from which sprout the plumes of some unidentifiable bird. He showed me his scars: a round one, like a coin, on the back of one hand, and another to match on the front—here a bullet passed through, he said, when he was fighting in Afghanistan. A hollow in his right calf, where, in Kabul, a bandit hacked at him with a sword as he escaped by horse. For some time he lived among a Kafir tribe, with a beautiful black-eyed mistress; the seam running from eyebrow to cheekbone to chin he earned, he says, in a fight to win her. He has been in Jalalabad and the Kabul river basin; in the Pamirs among the Kirghiz nomads; in Yarkand and Leh, Chitral and Gilgit.

Or so he says. Myself, I cannot quite credit this; he is elusive regarding his travel routes, and about dates and seasons and companions. But perhaps he truly did all these things, at one time or another, and erases the details and connections out of necessity: I think perhaps he has been a spy. For whom?

I try to forget what you have said about the way you gather with our families and friends and pass these letters around, or read them out loud; if I thought of that I would grow too self-conscious to write to you at all. But I will tell you one peculiar thing about Dr. Chouteau if you promise to keep this to yourself. He has lived to such a robust old age, he swears, by the most meticulous attention to personal hygiene. And how has he avoided the gastric complaints that afflict almost all of us when we eat the local foods? A daily clyster, he says. The cleansing enema he administers to himself, with a special syringe. I have seen this object with my own eyes, he carries it with him and showed it to me. It looked rather like a hookah. Far better this, he said, looking at my bewildered countenance, than the calomel and other purgatives on which less wise travelers rely.

Some of the other things he told me I can't repeat, even to you: they have to do with princes and dancing-girls, seraglios and such-like: when I am home again I will share these with you, in the privacy of our own bed.

Clara, I am so confused. Meeting this stranger made me realize with more than usual sharpness how lonely I am, how cut off I feel from all that is important to me. My past life seems to be disappearing, my memories grow jumbled. Who was the Max Vigne who went here or there, did this or that? It's as if I am dissolving and reforming; I am turning into someone I don't recognize. If I believed in the doctrine of the transmigration of souls, I might suspect that the wind is blowing someone else's soul in through my nostrils, while my old soul flies out my ears. In the mountains I lay awake in the cold, frozen despite my blankets, and my life in England—my boyhood, even my life with you—passed by my eyes as if it had been lived by someone else. Forgive these wanderings. The household details of which you wrote, the problems with the roof, the chimney, the apple trees—I know I should offer some answers in response to your questions but it feels pointless. You will have long since had to resolve these things before you receive my advice. I trust your judgment completely.

Good night; the wind is blowing hard. What a fine thing a house is. In my tent I think of you and the girls, snug inside the walls.

After that, he does not write to Clara for a while.

The river valleys, the high plains, the dirt and crowds and smells and noise of Srinagar, where the surveying parties are reshuffled and he finds himself, with three other plane-tablers, left behind in makeshift quarters, with preliminary maps of the city and the valley and vague instructions to fill in the details while everyone else (Michaels, too; at least he is finally free of Michaels!) moves on to Dehra Dun, not to return until spring: and still, he does not write Clara. He does not write to anyone, he does not keep up his botanical notes, he makes no sketches other than those required for the maps. He does his work, because he must. But he does no more. He cannot remember ever feeling like this.

6.

If he could make himself write, he might say this:

Dearest Clara—

Who am I? Who am I meant to be? I imagine a different life for myself, but how can I know, how can anyone know, if this is a foolish dream or a sensible goal? Have I any scientific talent at all? Dr. Hooker says I do, he has been most encouraging. If he is right, then my separation from you means something, and the isolation I've imposed on myself, and the long hours of extra work. But if I have no real gift, if I am only deluding myself . . . then I am wasting everything.

There is something noble, surely, in following the path of one's gifts; don't we have a duty to use our talents to the utmost? Isn't any sacrifice, in the pursuit of that, worthwhile? In these past months I have often felt that the current which is most truly me, laid aside when I was still a boy and had to face the responsibilities of family life, has all this time continued to flow the way water moves unseen beneath the glaciers. When I am alone, with my notes and plants and the correlations of weather and geology and flora springing clear before me, I feel: This is who I am. This is what I was born to do. *But if in fact I have no real capacity for this work, if it is only my vanity leading me down this path—what then?*

He has grown morose, he knows. Worse than morose. Maudlin, self-pitying. And self-deluding: not just about his possible talents, but in the very language with which he now contemplates writing Clara. Nobility, duty, sacrifice—whose words are those? Not his. He is using them to screen himself from the knowledge of whatever is shifting in him.

On the journey back to Srinagar, among the triangulators and plane-tablers led by Michaels and eventually joined by Captain Montgomerie himself, he was silent, sullen, distant. If he could, he would have talked to no one. In Srinagar, once the crowd of officers and triangulators left for Dehra Dun, he felt still worse. Investigating the streets and alleys, the outlying villages and the limestone springs, he was charmed by what he saw and wished it would stay the same. But meanwhile he couldn't help hearing talk of his government annexing Kashmir and turning the valley into another Simla: a retreat for soldiers and government officials, people he would prefer to avoid.

When he returns at night to the room he shares with three other plane-tablers, he flops on his cot and can't understand why he feels so trapped. The walls that shelter him from the cold and the wind—didn't he miss these? Perhaps it isn't the dark planks and the stingy windows that make him grind his teeth, but his companions' self-important chatter about measurements and calculations, possibilities for promotion. He shuts his ears to them and imagines, instead, talking with the vainglorious old explorer whose tales left him feeling lost, and full of questions.

The stories he wrote to Clara were the least of what happened that afternoon. Dr. Chouteau had been everywhere, Max learned. Without a map; maps meant nothing to him. Max's work he'd regarded with detached interest, almost amusement. Looking down at the sheets of paper, the carefully drawn cliffs and rivers and glaciers, Dr. Chouteau had said, *I have been here. And here. Here. And so many other places.* He spoke of the gravestone, seen in Kabul, that marked the resting place of an Englishman who'd passed through there a century and a half ago. Of wandering Russians, Austrians, Chinese, Turks, the twists and turns of the Great Game, the nasty little wars. Godfrey Vigne, he'd said—*Isn't it odd, that you share that last name?*—had been no simple traveler, but a British spy. Those forays into Baltistan a way of gathering information; and his attempts to reach Central Asia a way of determining that the only routes by which the Russians might enter India lay west of the Karakoram. *I knew him,* Dr. Chouteau said. *We were in Afghanistan together. He was the one who determined that Baltistan has no strategic importance to the British plans for India.*

More than anyone else, Dr. Chouteau made Max understand the purpose of his work. *I never make maps,* Dr. Chouteau said. *Or not maps anyone else could read. They might fall into the wrong hands.* Max's maps, he pointed out, would be printed, distributed to governments, passed on to armies and merchants and travelers. Someone, someday, would study them as they planned an invasion, or planned to stop one. What can Max's insignificant hardships matter, when compared to the adventures of such solitary travelers as Dr. Chouteau, or the lost man he saw when he first arrived in the mountains; of Godfrey Vigne or of Dr. Hooker? In Srinagar, Max understands that his journeys have been only the palest imitations of theirs.

He hasn't heard from Dr. Hooker in months. And although he knows he ought to understand, from Clara's trials, that accident may have been at work, he interprets this as pure rejection. The observations he sent weren't worthy; Hooker has ceased to reply because Max's work is of no interest. All he will leave behind are maps, which will be merged with all the other maps, on which he will be nameless: small contributions to the great *Atlas of India,* which has been growing for almost forty years. In London a faceless man collates the results of the triangulations into huge unwieldy sheets, engraved on copper or lithographed: two miles to an inch, four miles to an inch—what will become of them? He knows, or thinks he knows, though his imagination is colored by despair: they will burn, or be eaten by rats and cockroaches, or obliterated by fungus. Frayed and dust-stained, uncatalogued, they'll be sold as waste paper, or burned. Those that survive will be shared with allies, or hidden from enemies.

Max might write to Dr. Hooker about this; in Sikkim, he knows, Dr. Hooker and a companion had been seized while botanizing and held as political hostages. That event had served as excuse for an invasion by the British army and the annexation of southern Sikkim. Although Dr. Hooker refused to accompany the troops, he gave the general in charge of the invasion the topographical map he'd drawn. That map was copied at the Surveyor General's office; another map, of the Khasia Hills, made its way into the *Atlas of India,* complimented by all for its geological, botanical, and meteorological notes. Max has seen this one himself, though its import escaped him at the time. Dr. Hooker did it in his spare time, tossing off what cost Max so much labor.

But what is the point of tormenting himself? In the increasing cold he reads over Dr. Hooker's letters to him, looking for the first signs of disfavor. The letters are imperturbably kind, he can find no hint of where he failed. For comfort he turns, not to the remaining letters in Clara's trunk—those forward-casting, hopeful exercises make him feel too sad—but instead to the first of her letters to reach him. From those, still brave and cheerful, he works his way into the later ones. A line about Joanna's colic, and how it lingered; a line about the bugs in the rhubarb: unsaid, all the difficulties that must have surrounded each event. The roof is leaking, the sink is broken, *Elizabeth has chickenpox,* Clara wrote. *Zoe is bearing bravely her broken engagement, but we are all worried about her.* What she means is: *Where are you, where are you? Why have you left me to face this all alone?*

Her packet #16, which failed to reach him in October with the rest of that batch, has finally arrived along with other, more recent letters. In early April she described the gardens, the plague of slugs, the foundling sparrow Elizabeth had adopted and Joanna's avid, crawling explorations; the death of a neighbor and the funeral, which she attended with Gideon. Gideon, again. Then something broke through and she wrote what she'd never permitted herself before:

> Terrible scenes rise up before my eyes and they are as real as the rest of my life. I look out the window and I see a carriage pull up to the door, a man steps out, he is bearing a black-bordered envelope; I know what is in it, I know. He walks up to the door and I am already crying. He looks down at his shoes. I take the letter from him, I open it; it is come from the government offices in London and I skip over the sentences which attempt to prepare me for the news. I skip to the part in which it says you have died. In the mountains, of an accident. In the plains, of some terrible fever. On a ship which has sunk—I read the sentences again and again—they confirm my worst fears and I grow faint—hope expires in me and yet I will not believe. In the envelope, too, another sheet: The words of someone I have never met, who witnessed your last days. *Though I am a stranger to you, it is my sad duty to inform you of a most terrible event.* And then a description of whatever befell you; and one more sheet, which is your last letter to me.
>
> You see how I torment myself. I imagine all the things you might write. I imagine, on some days, that you tell me the truth; on others that you lie, to spare my feelings. I imagine you writing, *Do not grieve too long, dearest Clara. The cruelest thing, when we think of our loved ones dying in distant lands, is the thought of them dying alone and abandoned, uncared for—but throughout my illness I have had the attentions of kind men.* I imagine, I imagine . . . how can I imagine you alive and well, when I have not heard from you for so long?
>
> I am ashamed of myself for writing this. All over Britain other women wait, patiently, for soldiers and sailors and explorers and merchants—why can't I? I will try to be stronger. When you read this page, know that it was written by Clara who loves you, in a moment of weakness and despair.

At least that is past now, for her; from her other letters he knows she was finally reassured. But that she suffered like this; that he is only hearing about it now . . . To whom is she turning for consolation?

Winter drags on. Meetings and work; official appearances and work; squabbles and work. Work. He does what he can, what he must. Part of him wants to rush home to Clara. To give up this job, this place, these ambitions; to sail home at the earliest opportunity and never to travel again. It has all been too much: the complexities and politics, the secrets underlying everything. Until he left England, he thinks now, he had lived in a state of remarkable innocence. Never, not even as a boy, had he been able to fit himself into the world. But he had thought, until recently, that he might turn his back on what he didn't understand and make his own solitary path. Have his own heroes, pursue his own goals. But if his heroes are spies; if his work is in service of men whose goals led to blood-stained rooms and raining flesh—nothing is left of the world as he once envisioned it.

He wanders the city and its outskirts, keeping an eye out, as he walks, for Dr. Chouteau. He must be here; where else would he spend the winter? Stories of that irascible old man, or of someone like him, surface now and then; often Max has a sense that Dr. Chouteau hides down the next alley, across the next bridge. He hears tales of other travelers as well—Jacquemont and Moorcroft, the Schlagintweit brothers, Thomas Thomson and the Baron von Hugel. The tales contradict each other, as do those about Dr. Chouteau himself. In one story he is said to be an Irish mercenary, in another an American businessman. Through these distorted lenses Max sees himself as if for the first time, and something happens to him.

That lost man, whose skull he found when he first arrived in the mountains—is this what befell him? As an experiment, Max stops eating. He fasts for three days and confirms what the lost man wrote in his diary: his spirit soars free, everything looks different. His mother is with him often, during that airy, delirious time. Dr. Chouteau strolls through his imagination as well. In a brief break in the flow of Dr. Chouteau's endless, self-regarding narrative, Max had offered an account of his own experiences up on the glacier. His cold entombment, his lucky escape; he'd been humiliated when Dr. Chouteau laughed and patted his shoulder. *A few hours,* he said. *You barely tasted the truth. I was caught for a week on the Siachen Glacier, in a giant blizzard. There is no harsher place on this earth; it belongs to no one. Which won't keep people from squabbling over it someday. The men I traveled with died.*

When Max hallucinates Dr. Chouteau's voice emerging from the mouth of a boatwoman arguing with her neighbor, he starts eating again, moving again. The old maps he's been asked to revise are astonishingly inaccurate. He wanders through narrow lanes overhung by balconies, in and out of a maze of courtyards. The air smells of stale cooking oil, burning charcoal, human excrement. He makes his way back and forth across the seven bridges of Srinagar so often he might be weaving a web. Temples, mosques, the churches of the missionaries; women carrying earthenware pots on their heads; barges and bakeshops and markets piled with rock salt and lentils, bottles of ghee—his wanderings he justifies as being in service to the map, although he also understands that part of what drives him into the biting air is a search for Dr. Chouteau. If Max could find him, if he could ask him some questions, perhaps this unease that has settled over him might lift.

As winter turns into early spring, as he does what he can with his map of the valley and, in response to letters from Dehra Dun, begins preparations for another season up in the mountains, his life spirals within him like the tendril of a climbing plant. One day he sits down, finally, with Laurence's gift to him and begins working slowly through the lines of Mr. Darwin's argument. The ideas aren't unfamiliar to him; as with the news of Cawnpore and the Mutiny, he has heard them summarized, read accounts in the newspapers, discussed the outlines of the theory of descent with modification with Laurence and others. But when he confronts the details and grasps all the strands of the theory, it hits him like the knowledge of the use made of Dr. Hooker's maps, or the uses that will be made of his own. He scribbles all over the margins. At first he writes Laurence simply to say: *I am reading it. Have you read it? It is marvelous. The world is other than we thought.* But a different, more complicated letter begins to unfurl in his mind.

A mountain, he reads, *is an island on the land. The identity of many plants and animals, on mountain-summits, separated from each other by hundreds of miles of lowlands, where the alpine species could not possibly exist, is one of the most striking cases known of the same species living at distant points, without the apparent possibility of their having migrated from one to another . . . The glacial period affords a simple explanation of these facts.*

He closes his eyes and sees the cold sweeping south and covering the land with snow and ice, arctic plants and animals migrating into the temperate regions. Then, centuries later, the warmth returning and the arctic forms retreating northward with the glaciers, leaving isolated representatives stranded on the icy summits. *Along the Himalaya,* Mr. Darwin writes, *at points 900 miles apart, glaciers have left the marks of their former low descent, and in Sikkim, Dr. Hooker saw maize growing on gigantic ancient moraines.* The point of Dr. Hooker's work, Max sees, is not just to map the geographical distribution of plants but to use that map in service of a broader theory. Not just *The same genus of lichen appears in Baltistan and in Sikkim,* but, *The lichens of the far ends of the Himalaya are related, descending from a common ancestor.*

It is while his head is spinning with these notions that, on the far side of the great lake called the Dal, near a place where, if it was summer, the lotus flowers would be nodding their heads above their enormous circular leaves, by a chenar tree in which herons have nested for generations, he meets at last not Dr. Chouteau, but a woman. Dark-haired, dark-eyed: Dima. At first he speaks to her simply to be polite, and to conceal his surprise that she'd address him without being introduced. Then he notices, in her capable hands, a sheaf of reeds someone else might not consider handsome, but which she praises for the symmetry of their softly drooping heads. Although she wears no wedding ring, she is here by the lake without a chaperone.

The afternoon passes swiftly as they examine other reeds, the withered remains of ferns, lichens clustered on the rocks. Her education has come, Max learns, from a series of tutors and travelers and missionaries; botanizing is her favorite diversion. He eyes her dress, which is well cut although not elaborate; her boots, which are sturdy and look expensive. From what is she seeking diversion? She speaks of plants and trees and gardens, a stream of conversation that feels intimate yet reveals nothing personal. In return he tells her a bit about his work. When they part, and she invites him to call on her a few days later, he accepts. Such a long time since he has spoken with anyone congenial.

Within the week, she lets him know that he'd be welcome in her bed; and, gently, that he'd be a fool to refuse her. Max doesn't hide from her the fact that he's married, nor that he must leave this place soon. But the relief he finds with her—not just her body, the comforts of her bed, but her intelligence, her hands on his neck, the sympathy with which she listens to his hopes and longings—the relief is so great that sometimes, after she falls asleep, he weeps.

"I have been lonely," she tells him. "I have been without company for a while." She strokes his thighs and his sturdy smooth chest and slips down the sheets until their hipbones are aligned. Compactly built, she is several inches shorter than him but points out that their legs are the same length; his extra height is in his torso. Swiftly he pushes away a memory of his wedding night with long-waisted Clara. The silvery filaments etched across Dima's stomach he tries not to recognize as being like those that appeared on Clara, after Elizabeth's birth.

He doesn't insult her by paying her for their time together; she isn't a prostitute, simply a woman grown used, of necessity, to being kept by men. Each time he arrives at her bungalow he brings gifts: little carved boxes and bangles and lengths of cloth; for her daughter, who is nearly Elizabeth's age, toy elephants and camels. Otherwise he tries to ignore the little girl. Who is her father, what is her name? He can't think about that, he can't look at her. Dima, seeming somehow to understand, sends her daughter off to play with the children of her servants when he arrives. Through the open window over her bed he sometimes hears them laughing.

Dima has lived with her father in Leh and Gilgit and here, in a quarter of Srinagar seldom visited by Europeans; she claims to be the daughter of a Russian explorer and a woman, now dead, from Skardu. For some years she was the mistress of a Scotsman who fled his job with the East India Company, explored in Ladakh, and ended up in Kashmir; later she lived with a German geologist. Or so she says. In bed she tells Max tales of her lovers, their friends, her father's friends—a secret band of wanderers, each with a story as complicated as Dr. Chouteau's. Which one taught her botany? In those stories, and the way that she appears to omit at least as much as she reveals, she resembles Dr. Chouteau himself, whom she claims to know. A friend of her father's, she says. A cartographer (but didn't he tell Max he never made maps?) and advisor to obscure princes; a spendthrift and an amateur geologist. Bad with his servants but excellent with animals; once he kept falcons. She knows a good deal about him but not, she claims, where he is now.

One night, walking back from her bungalow, a shadowy figure resembling Dr. Chouteau appears on the street before Max and then disappears into an alley. Although the night is dark, Max follows. The men crouched around charcoal braziers and leaning in doorways regard him quietly. Not just Kashmiris: Tibetans and Ladakhis, Yarkandis, Gujars, Dards—are those Dards?—and Baltis and fair-haired men who might be Kafirs. During this last year, he has learned to recognize such men by their size and coloring and the shape of their eyes, their dress and weapons and bearing. As they have no doubt learned to recognize Englishmen. If Dr. Chouteau is among them, he hides himself. For a moment, as Max backs away with his hands held open and empty before him, he realizes that anything might happen to him. He is no one here. No one knows where he is. In the Yasin Valley, Dr. Chouteau said, he once stumbled across a pile of stones crowned by a pair of hands. The hands were white, desiccated, bound together at the wrists. Below the stones was the remainder of the body.

When he leaves the alley, all Max can see for a while are the stars and the looming blackness of the mountains. How clear the sky is! His mind feels equally clear, washed out by that moment of darkness.

During his next weeks with Dima, Clara recedes—a voice in his ear, words on paper; mysterious, as she was when he first knew her. Only when Dima catches a cold and he has to tend her, bringing basins and handkerchiefs and cups of tea, does he recollect what living with Clara was really like. Not the ardent, long-distance exchange of words, on which they've survived for more than a year, but the grit and weariness of everyday life. Household chores and worries over money, a crying child, a smoking stove; relatives coming and going, all needing things, and both of them stretched so thin; none of it Clara's fault, it is only life. Now it is Dima who is sick, and who can no longer maintain her enchanting deceits. The carefully placed candles, the painted screen behind which she undoes her ribbons and laces to emerge in a state of artful undress, the daughter disposed of so she may listen with utmost attention to him, concentrate on him completely—all that breaks down. One day there is a problem with her well, which he must tend to. On another her daughter—her name is Kate—comes into Dima's bedroom in tears, her dress torn by some children who've been teasing her. He has to take Kate's hand. He has to find the other children and scold them and convince them all to play nicely together, then report back to Dima how this has been settled. He is falling, he thinks. Headfirst, into another crevasse.

During Dima's illness it is with some relief—he knows it is shameful—that he returns at night to his spartan quarters. Through the gossip that flies so swiftly among the British community, the three other surveyors have heard about Dima. Twice Max was spotted with her, and this was all it took; shunned alike by Hindus and Moslems, Christians and Sikhs, she has a reputation. That it is Max she's taken up with, Max she's chosen: to Max's amazement and chagrin, his companions find this glamorous. They themselves have found solace in the brothels; Srinagar is filled with women and they no longer turn to each other for physical relief. But to them, unaware of Dima's illness and her precarious household, Max's situation seems exotic. The knowledge that he shares their weaknesses, despite the way he has kept to himself—this, finally, is what makes Max's companions accept him.

They stop teasing him. They ask him to drink with them, to dine with them; which, on occasion, he does. They ask for details, which he refuses. But despite his reticence, his connection to Dima has made his own reputation. When the rest of the surveyors return from Dehra Dun and they all head back to the mountains, Max knows he will occupy a different position among them. Because of her, everything will be different, and easier, than during the last season. It is this knowledge that breaks the last piece of his heart.

April arrives; the deep snow mantling the Pir Panjal begins to shrink back from the black rock. Max writes long letters to Laurence, saying nothing about Dima but musing about what he reads. Into Srinagar march triangulators in fresh tidy clothes, newly trained Indian assistants, new crowds of porters bearing glittering instruments, and the officers: Michaels among them. But Michaels can no longer do Max any harm. Max and his three companions present their revised map of Srinagar, and are praised. Then it is time to leave. Still Max has no answers. Dr. Chouteau has continued to elude him; Dima, fully recovered now, thanks him for all his help, gives him some warm socks, and wishes him well with his work.

Which work? Even to her he has not admitted what he is thinking about doing these next months. He holds her right hand in both of his and nods numbly when she says she will write him, often, and hopes that he'll write her. Hopes that they'll see each other again, when the surveying party returns to Srinagar.

More letters. Another person waiting for him. "Don't write," he says, aware the instant he does so of his cruelty. The look on her face—but she has had other lovers (how many lovers?), and she doesn't make a scene. Perhaps this is why he chose her. When they part, he knows he will become simply a story she tells to the next stranger she welcomes into her life.

And still he does not write Clara. Other letters from her have arrived, which he hasn't answered: six months, what is he thinking? Not about her, the life she is leading in his absence, the way her days unfold; not what she and their children are doing, their dreams and daily duties and aspirations and disappointments. Neither is he thinking about Dima; it is not as if his feelings for her have driven out those he has for Clara. He isn't thinking about either of them. This is his story, his life unfolding. The women will tell the tale of these months another way.

7.

April 21, 1864

My dearest, my beloved Clara—

Forgive me for not writing in so long. I have been sick—nothing serious, nothing you need worry about, although it did linger. But I am fully recovered now, in time to join the rest of the party on our march back into the mountains. This season, I expect, will be much like the last. Different mountains, similar work; in October I will be done with the services I contracted for and the Survey will be completed. From my letters of last season you will have a good idea of what I'll be doing. But Clara . . .

Max pauses, then crosses out the last two words. What he should say is what he knows she wants to hear: that when October comes he'll be on his way back to her, as they agreed. But he doesn't want to lie to her. Not yet.

His party is camped by a frozen stream. The porters are butchering a goat. Michaels, in a nearby tent, has just explained to the men their assignments for the coming week; soon it will be time to eat; Max has half an hour to finish this letter and no way to say what he really means: that after the season is finished, he wants to stay on.

Everything has changed for me, he wants to say. *I am changed, I know now who I am and what I want and I can only hope you accept this, and continue to wait for me. I want to stay a year longer. When the Survey ends, in October, I want to wait out the winter in Srinagar, writing up all I have learned and seen so far; and then I want to spend next spring and summer traveling by myself. If I had this time to explore, to test myself, discover the secrets of these mountains—it would be enough, I could be happy with this, it would last me the rest of my life. When I come home, I mean to try to establish myself as a botanist. I have no hope of doing so without taking this time and working solely on my studies.*

But he can't write any of that. Behind him men are laughing, a fire is burning, he can smell the first fragrance of roasting meat. He is off again, to the cold bare brilliance of a place like the moon, and what he can't explain, yet, to Clara is that he needs other time, during the growing season, to study the plants in the space between the timberline and the line of permanent snow. How do the species that have arisen here differ from those in other places? How do they make a life for themselves, in such difficult circumstances?

But how could Clara possibly understand this? He will break it to her gently, he thinks. A hint, at first; a few more suggestions in letters over the coming months; in September he'll raise the subject. Perhaps by then he'll have more encouragement from Dr. Hooker, which he can offer to Clara as evidence that his work is worthwhile. Perhaps by then he'll understand how he might justify his plans to her. For now—what else can he say in this letter? He has kept too much from her, these last months. If his letters were meant to be a map of his mind, a way for her to follow his trail, then he has failed her. Somehow, as summer comes to these peaks and he does his job for the last time, he must find a way to let her share in his journey. But for now all he can do is triangulate the first few points.

. . . I have so much to tell you, Clara. And no more time today; what will you think, after all these months, when you receive such a brief letter? Know that I am thinking of you and the girls, no matter what I do. I promise we'll do whatever you want when I return: I know how much you miss your brother, perhaps we will join him in New York. *I would like that, I think. I would like to start over, all of us, someplace new. Somewhere I can be my new self, live my new life, in your company.*

Next to my heart, in an oilskin pouch, I keep the lock of Elizabeth's hair and your last unopened letter to me, with your solemn instruction on the envelope: To Be Opened if You Know You Will Not Return to Me. *If the time comes, I will open it. But the time won't come; I will make it back, I will be with you again.*

This comes to you with all my love, from your dearest

Max

Donald Barthelme (1931–1989)

was born in Philadelphia and grew up in Houston, where his father, a modernist architect and professor at the University of Houston, built a home for the family so unusual—at least for Houston in the 1930s—that strangers parked their cars in front of it to stare. When enough gathered, the five Barthelme children often ran out into the front yard and entertained the gawkers by forming a chorus line. (Two of Donald's brothers—Frederick and Steven—also grew up to become fiction writers.) After graduating from the University of Houston as a journalism major, he worked as a reporter for the Houston Post *(interrupted when he was drafted into the army during the Korean conflict) and for a year directed Houston's Contemporary Arts Museum. In the 1960s, he moved to New York to edit* Location *and began publishing short stories regularly in* The New Yorker. *He published eight collections of stories (most of which are collected in 1981's* Sixty Stories *and 1987's* Forty Stories*), four novels, and a children's book—*The Slightly Irregular Fire Engine: or, The Hithering Thithering Djinn*—which won the National Book Award. Critics have variously tried to pigeonhole his stories as postmodern or minimalist or metafictional; to resort to further name-calling, he was an American original, one of the wildest, funniest writers in our literature. Barthelme returned to Houston as a professor of creative writing at—yes—the University of Houston.*

INTRODUCTION BY **Jonathan Lethem**

Welcome to the wacky world of.

Donald Barthelme is the consummate jester of the American short story, but to say that is perhaps to risk a slight. For it is Barthelme's great achievement that during his heyday (and perhaps no American writer has ever had so hey a day as Barthelme, if you wish to go back and study the record of his prolificity and consistency in the decades of the 1960s and 1970s), his "jesting" made as essential a contribution to the literary life of his times as any story writer ever has—Hemingway, Beattie, Carver, anybody.

The three stories here show wonderful evidence of the things Barthelme did well—though it is odd to speak of "doing well" at things that, especially at the time they were done, nobody else had ever dreamed of or dared to do. Barthelme is a demon of compression and surprise. He never bothers with dull transitions, rote explanations, or any kind of apology for what interests or amuses him. Instead, the man made an art of letting his writerly attention drift into silliness, gloom, parody, restlessness, self-mocking, all within the space of stories that were each relentlessly well conceived, each a kind of formal proposal for a new kind of story.

Barthelme is in love with voice, as any story writer ought to be, but the voices he loves are unexpected ones: the tedious complainer, the pompous aesthete or windy literary professor, the writers of bureaucratic press releases or technical manuals. He finds the hidden beauty and hilarity and sadness in the sound of the human voice pretending and failing to know what the hell it is talking about or to admit what's really on its mind. The result is that if the word "postmodern" didn't need to exist before Barthelme, it sure did after—though by the time you're done struggling over a definition for that silly word, you'll wish you'd just pointed to Barthelme instead: he single-handedly authenticates and exhausts "the postmodern short story"; he corners the market.

"Robert Kennedy Saved from Drowning" (which as it is collected in Barthelme's *Sixty Stories* is touchingly dated "April 1968" so that the reader will know that it anticipates Kennedy's assassination rather than being a commentary after the fact) is the story among these three that most shows evidence of Barthelme's "laboratory" techniques (the word is Barthelme's—he spoke often in interviews of the laboratory of his fiction). The partitioned structure frees the ventriloquizing voice to wander in and out of the language of recounted dreams, of bureaucratic hagiography, and of corny anecdotes. Nevertheless, the story is unified by an underlying voice—would it be foolish to call it Barthelme's?—that ultimately confesses a tender feeling, a perhaps grandiosely tender feeling, toward the depressive Kennedy.

"A City of Churches" and "The School" play more at the conventions of the traditional story. Still the restless absurdities and ghoulish irreverence of "The School" and the unembarrassed fascination with lists and the metafictional aside about a CBS news story with the title "A City of Churches" in "A City of Churches"—as well as the frank sexual fantasizing in both stories—all reveal Barthelme's impatience with the consistency and earnestness of slice-of-life fiction, even when he briefly arouses more conventional expectations in the reader. Both stories read partly like fables or allegories, except that they resist any easy diagrammatical interpretation. Barthelme loves to tease at moralizing, but his universe is often one of cheery horror.

Barthelme has had many imitators, and not only in his own medium. His work connects literature to performance art and to comic routines and *Saturday Night Live* skits. What makes it literature, however, and irreplaceable, no matter how complete its subsequent assimilation into the culture, is the immaculate and luminous quality of his sentences, of his paragraphs. His attention drifts *beautifully.* Donald Barthelme might seem to throw the baby out with the bathwater and from a very high window. But when you rush downstairs to look, both baby and bathwater have come to a gentle and happy landing in the garden.

Jonathan Lethem is the author of several novels, including Motherless Brooklyn, *winner of the 2001 National Book Critics Circle Award for Fiction, and* The Fortress of Solitude. *His work has appeared in* The New Yorker, Rolling Stone, McSweeney's, *and many other magazines. He lives in Brooklyn, New York.*

DONALD BARTHELME

A City of Churches

"Yes," Mr. Phillips said, "ours is a city of churches all right."

Cecelia nodded, following his pointing hand. Both sides of the street were solidly lined with churches, standing shoulder to shoulder in a variety of architectural styles. The Bethel Baptist stood next to the Holy Messiah Free Baptist, St. Paul's Episcopal next to Grace Evangelical Covenant. Then came the First Christian Science, the Church of God, All Souls, Our Lady of Victory, the Society of Friends, the Assembly of God, and the Church of the Holy Apostles. The spires and steeples of the traditional buildings were jammed in next to the broad imaginative flights of the "contemporary" designs.

"Everyone here takes a great interest in church matters," Mr. Phillips said.

Will I fit in? Cecelia wondered. She had come to Prester to open a branch office of a car-rental concern.

"I'm not especially religious," she said to Mr. Phillips, who was in the real-estate business.

"Not *now,* " he answered. "Not *yet.* But we have many fine young people here. You'll get integrated into the community soon enough. The immediate problem is, where are you to live? Most people," he said, "live in the church of their choice. All of our churches have many extra rooms. I have a few belfry apartments that I can show you. What price range were you thinking of?"

They turned a corner and were confronted with more churches. They passed St. Luke's, the Church of the Epiphany, All Saints Ukrainian Orthodox, St. Clement's, Fountain Baptist, Union Congregational, St. Anargyri's, Temple Emanuel, the First Church of Christ Reformed. The mouths of all the churches were gaping open. Inside, lights could be seen dimly.

"I can go up to a hundred and ten," Cecelia said. "Do you have any buildings here that are *not* churches?"

"None," said Mr. Phillips. "Of course many of our fine church structures also do double duty as something else." He indicated a handsome Georgian facade. "That one," he said, "houses the United Methodist and the Board of Education. The one next to it, which is Antioch Pentecostal, has the barbershop."

It was true. A red-and-white striped barber pole was attached inconspicuously to the front of the Antioch Pentecostal.

"Do many people rent cars here?" Cecelia asked. "Or would they, if there was a handy place to rent them?"

"Oh, I don't know," said Mr. Phillips. "Renting a car implies that you want to go somewhere. Most people are pretty content right here. We have a lot of activities. I don't think I'd pick the car-rental business if I was just starting out in Prester. But you'll do fine." He showed her a small, extremely modern building with a severe brick, steel, and glass front. "That's St. Barnabas. Nice bunch of people over there. Wonderful spaghetti suppers."

Cecelia could see a number of heads looking out of the windows. But when they saw that she was staring at them, the heads disappeared.

"Do you think it's healthy for so many churches to be gathered together in one place?" she asked her guide. "It doesn't seem . . . *balanced,* if you know what I mean."

"We are famous for our churches," Mr. Phillips replied. "They are harmless. Here we are now."

He opened a door and they began climbing many flights of dusty stairs. At the end of the climb they entered a good-sized room, square, with windows on all four sides. There was a bed, a table, and two chairs, lamps, a rug. Four very large bronze bells hung in the exact center of the room.

"What a view!" Mr. Phillips exclaimed. "Come here and look."

"Do they actually ring these bells?" Cecelia asked.

"Three times a day," Mr. Phillips said, smiling. "Morning, noon, and night. Of course when they're rung you have to be pretty quick at getting out of the way. You get hit in the head by one of these babies and that's all she wrote."

"God Almighty," said Cecelia involuntarily. Then she said, "Nobody lives in the belfry apartments. That's why they're empty."

"You think so?" Mr. Phillips said.

"You can only rent them to new people in town," she said accusingly.

"I wouldn't do that," Mr. Phillips said. "It would go against the spirit of Christian fellowship."

"This town is a little creepy, you know that?"

"That may be, but it's not for you to say, is it? I mean, you're new here. You should walk cautiously, for a while. If you don't want an upper apartment I have a basement over at Central Presbyterian. You'd have to share it. There are two women in there now."

"I don't want to share," Cecelia said. "I want a place of my own."

"Why?" the real-estate man asked curiously. "For what purpose?"

"Purpose?" asked Cecelia. "There is no particular purpose. I just want—"

"That's not usual here. Most people live with other people. Husbands and wives. Sons with their mothers. People have roommates. That's the usual pattern."

"Still, I prefer a place of my own."

"It's very unusual."

"Do you have any such places? Besides bell towers, I mean?"

"I guess there are a few," Mr. Phillips said, with clear reluctance. "I can show you one or two, I suppose."

He paused for a moment.

"It's just that we have different values, maybe, from some of the surrounding communities," he explained. "We've been written up a lot. We had four minutes on the CBS Evening News one time. Three or four years ago. *A City of Churches,* it was called."

"Yes, a place of my own is essential," Cecelia said, "if I am to survive here."

"That's kind of a funny attitude to take," Mr. Phillips said. "What denomination are you?"

Cecelia was silent. The truth was, she wasn't anything.

"I said, what denomination are you?" Mr. Phillips repeated.

"I can will my dreams," Cecelia said. "I can dream whatever I want. If I want to dream that I'm having a good time, in Paris or some other city, all I have to do is go to sleep and I will dream that dream. I can dream whatever I want."

"What do you dream, then, mostly?" Mr. Phillips said, looking at her closely.

"Mostly sexual things," she said. She was not afraid of him.

"Prester is not that kind of a town," Mr. Phillips said, looking away.

They went back down the stairs.

The doors of the churches were opening, on both sides of the street. Small groups of people came out and stood there, in front of the churches, gazing at Cecelia and Mr. Phillips.

A young man stepped forward and shouted, *"Everyone in this town already has a car! There is no one in this town who doesn't have a car!"*

"Is that true?" Cecelia asked Mr. Phillips.

"Yes," he said. "It's true. No one would rent a car here. Not in a hundred years."

"Then I won't stay," she said. "I'll go somewhere else."

"You must stay," he said. "There is already a car-rental office for you. In Mount Moriah Baptist, on the lobby floor. There is a counter and a telephone and a rack of car keys. And a calendar."

"I won't stay," she said. "Not if there's not any sound business reason for staying."

"We want you," said Mr. Phillips. "We want you standing behind the counter of the car-rental agency, during regular business hours. It will make the town complete."

"I won't," she said. "Not me."

"You must. It's essential."

"I'll dream," she said. "Things you won't like."

"We are discontented," said Mr. Phillips. "Terribly, terribly discontented. Something is wrong."

"I'll dream the Secret," she said. "You'll be sorry."

"We are like other towns, except that we are perfect," he said. "Our discontent can only be held in check by perfection. We need a car-rental girl. Someone must stand behind that counter."

"I'll dream the life you are most afraid of," Cecelia threatened.

"You are ours," he said, gripping her arm. "Our car-rental girl. Be nice. There is nothing you can do."

"Wait and see," Cecelia said.

Donald Barthelme

The School

Well, we had all these children out planting trees, see, because we figured that . . . that was part of their education, to see how, you know, the root systems . . . and also the sense of responsibility, taking care of things, being individually responsible. You know what I mean. And the trees all died. They were orange trees. I don't know why they died, they just died. Something wrong with the soil possibly or maybe the stuff we got from the nursery wasn't the best. We complained about it. So we've got thirty kids there, each kid had his or her own little tree to plant, and we've got these thirty dead trees. All these kids looking at these little brown sticks, it was depressing.

It wouldn't have been so bad except that just a couple of weeks before the thing with the trees, the snakes all died. But I think that the snakes—well, the reason that the snakes kicked off was that . . . you remember, the boiler was shut off for four days because of the strike, and that was explicable. It was something you could explain to the kids because of the strike. I mean, none of their parents would let them cross the picket line and they knew there was a strike going on and what it meant. So when things got started up again and we found the snakes they weren't too disturbed.

With the herb gardens it was probably a case of overwatering, and at least now they know not to overwater. The children were very conscientious with the herb gardens and some of them probably . . . you know, slipped them a little extra water when we weren't looking. Or maybe . . . well, I don't like to think about sabotage, although it did occur to us. I mean, it was something that crossed our minds. We were thinking that way probably because before that the gerbils had died, and the white mice had died, and the salamander . . . well, now they know not to carry them around in plastic bags.

Of course we *expected* the tropical fish to die, that was no surprise. Those numbers, you look at them crooked and they're belly-up on the surface. But the lesson plan called for a tropical-fish input at that point, there was nothing we could do, it happens every year, you just have to hurry past it.

We weren't even supposed to have a puppy.

We weren't even supposed to have one, it was just a puppy the Murdoch girl found under a Gristede's truck one day and she was afraid the truck would run over it when the driver had finished making his delivery, so she stuck it in her knapsack and brought it to school with her. So we had this puppy. As soon as I saw the puppy I thought, Oh Christ, I bet it will live for about two weeks and then . . . And that's what it did. It wasn't supposed to be in the classroom at all, there's some kind of regulation about it, but you can't tell them they can't have a puppy when the puppy is already there, right in front of them, running around on the floor and yap yap yapping. They named it Edgar—that is, they named it after me. They had a lot of fun running after it and yelling, "Here, Edgar! Nice Edgar!" Then they'd laugh like hell. They enjoyed the ambiguity. I enjoyed it myself. I don't mind being kidded. They made a little house for it in the supply closet and all that. I don't know what it died of. Distemper, I guess. It probably hadn't had any shots. I got it out of there before the kids got to school. I checked the supply closet each morning, routinely, because I knew what was going to happen. I gave it to the custodian.

And then there was this Korean orphan that the class adopted through the Help the Children program, all the kids brought in a quarter a month, that was the idea. It was an unfortunate thing, the kid's name was Kim and maybe we adopted him too late or something. The cause of death was not stated in the letter we got, they suggested we adopt another child instead and sent us some interesting case histories, but we didn't have the heart. The class took it pretty hard, they began (I think, nobody ever said anything to me directly) to feel that maybe there was something wrong with the school. But I don't think there's anything wrong with the school, particularly, I've seen better and I've seen worse. It was just a run of bad luck. We had an extraordinary number of parents passing away, for instance. There were I think two heart attacks and two suicides, one drowning, and four killed together in a car accident. One stroke. And we had the usual heavy mortality rate among the grandparents, or maybe it was heavier this year, it seemed so. And finally the tragedy.

The tragedy occurred when Matthew Wein and Tony Mavrogordo were playing over where they're excavating for the new federal office building. There were all these big wooden beams stacked, you know, at the edge of the excavation. There's a court case coming out of that, the parents are claiming that the beams were poorly stacked. I don't know what's true and what's not. It's been a strange year.

I forgot to mention Billy Brandt's father, who was knifed fatally when he grappled with a masked intruder in his home.

One day, we had a discussion in class. They asked me, where did they go? The trees, the salamander, the tropical fish, Edgar, the poppas and mommas, Matthew and Tony, where did they go? And I said, I don't know, I don't know. And they said, who knows? and I said, nobody knows. And they said, is death that which gives meaning to life? And I said, no, life is that which gives meaning to life. Then they said, but isn't death, considered as a fundamental datum, the means by which the taken-for-granted mundanity of the everyday may be transcended in the direction of—

I said, yes, maybe.

They said, we don't like it.

I said, that's sound.

They said, it's a bloody shame!

I said, it is.

They said, will you make love now with Helen (our teaching assistant) so that we can see how it is done? We know you like Helen.

I do like Helen but I said that I would not.

We've heard so much about it, they said, but we've never seen it.

I said I would be fired and that it was never, or almost never, done as a demonstration. Helen looked out of the window.

They said, please, please make love with Helen, we require an assertion of value, we are frightened.

I said that they shouldn't be frightened (although I am often frightened) and that there was value everywhere. Helen came and embraced me. I kissed her a few times on the brow. We held each other. The children were excited. Then there was a knock on the door, I opened the door, and the new gerbil walked in. The children cheered wildly.

DONALD BARTHELME

Robert Kennedy Saved from Drowning

K. at His Desk

He is neither abrupt with nor excessively kind to associates. Or he is both abrupt and kind.

The telephone is, for him, a whip, a lash, but also a conduit for soothing words, a sink into which he can hurl gallons of syrup if it comes to that.

He reads quickly, scratching brief comments ("Yes," "No") in corners of the paper. He slouches in the leather chair, looking about him with a slightly irritated air for new visitors, new difficulties. He spends his time sending and receiving messengers.

"I spend my time sending and receiving messengers," he says. "Some of these messages are important. Others are not."

Described by Secretaries

A: "Quite frankly I think he forgets a lot of things. But the things he forgets are those which are inessential. I even think he might forget deliberately, to leave his mind free. He has the ability to get rid of unimportant details. And he does."

B: "Once when I was sick, I hadn't heard from him, and I thought he had forgotten me. You know usually your boss will send flowers or something like that. I was in the hospital, and I was mighty blue. I was in a room with another girl, and *her* boss hadn't sent her anything either. Then suddenly the door opened and there he was with the biggest bunch of yellow tulips I'd ever seen in my life. And the other girl's boss was with him, and he had tulips too. They were standing there with all those tulips, smiling."

Behind the Bar

At a crowded party, he wanders behind the bar to make himself a Scotch and water. His hand is on the bottle of Scotch, his glass is waiting. The bartender, a small man in a beige uniform with gilt buttons, politely asks K. to return to the other side, the guests' side, of the bar. "You let one behind here, they all be behind here," the bartender says.

K. Reading the Newspaper

His reactions are impossible to catalogue. Often he will find a note that amuses him endlessly, some anecdote involving, say, a fireman who has propelled his apparatus at record-breaking speed to the wrong address. These small stories are clipped, carried about in a pocket, to be produced at appropriate moments for the pleasure of friends.

Other manifestations please him less. An account of an earthquake in Chile, with its thousands of dead and homeless, may depress him for weeks. He memorizes the terrible statistics, quoting them everywhere and saying, with a grave look: "We must do something." Important actions often follow, sometimes within a matter of hours. (On the other hand, these two kinds of responses may be, on a given day, inexplicably reversed.)

The more trivial aspects of the daily itemization are skipped. While reading, he maintains a rapid drumming of his fingertips on the desktop. He receives twelve newspapers, but of these, only four are regarded as serious.

Attitude Toward His Work

"Sometimes I can't seem to do anything. The work is there, piled up, it seems to me an insurmountable obstacle, really out of reach. I sit and look at it, wondering where to begin, how to take hold of it. Perhaps I pick up a piece of paper, try to read it but my mind is elsewhere, I am thinking of something else, I can't seem to get the gist of it, it seems meaningless, devoid of interest, not having to do with human affairs, drained of life. Then, in an hour, or even a moment, everything changes suddenly: I realize I only have to *do* it, hurl myself into the midst of it, proceed mechanically, the first thing and then the second thing, that it is simply a matter of moving from one step to the next, plowing through it. I become interested, I become excited, I work very fast, things fall into place, I am exhilarated, amazed that these things could ever have seemed dead to me."

Sleeping on the Stones of Unknown Towns (Rimbaud)

K. is walking, with that familiar slight dip of the shoulders, through the streets of a small city in France or Germany. The shop signs are in a language which alters when inspected closely, MÖBEL becoming MEUBLES for example, and the citizens mutter to themselves with dark virtuosity a mixture of languages. K. is very interested, looks closely at everything, at the shops, the goods displayed, the clothing of the people, the tempo of street life, the citizens themselves, wondering about them. What are their water needs?

> "In the West, wisdom is mostly gained at lunch. At lunch, people tell you things."
> The nervous eyes of the waiters.
> The tall bald cook, white apron, white T-shirt, grinning through an opening in the wall.
> "Why is that cook looking at me?"

Urban Transportation

"The transportation problems of our cities and their rapidly expanding suburbs are the most urgent and neglected transportation problems confronting the country. In these heavily populated and industrialized areas, people are dependent on a system of transportation that is at once complex and inadequate. Obsolete facilities and growing demands have created seemingly insoluble difficulties and present methods of dealing with these difficulties offer little prospect of relief."

★ ★ ★

K. Penetrated with Sadness

He hears something playing on someone else's radio, in another part of the building.

The music is wretchedly sad; now he can (barely) hear it, now it fades into the wall.

He turns on his own radio. There it is, on his own radio, the same music. The sound fills the room.

Karsh of Ottawa

"We sent a man to Karsh of Ottawa and told him that we admired his work very much. Especially, I don't know, the Churchill thing and, you know, the Hemingway thing, and all that. And we told him we wanted to set up a sitting for K. sometime in June, if that would be convenient for him, and he said yes, that was okay, June was okay, and where did we want to have it shot, there or in New York or where. Well, that was a problem because we didn't know exactly what K's schedule would be for June, it was up in the air, so we tentatively said New York around the fifteenth. And he said, that was okay, he could do that. And he wanted to know how much time he could have, and we said, well, how much time do you need? And he said he didn't know, it varied from sitter to sitter. He said some people were very restless and that made it difficult to get just the right shot. He said there was one shot in each sitting that was, you know, the key shot, the right one. He said he'd have to see, when the time came."

Dress

He is neatly dressed in a manner that does not call attention to itself. The suits are soberly cut and in dark colors. He must at all times present an aspect of freshness difficult to sustain because of frequent movements from place to place under conditions which are not always the most favorable. Thus he changes clothes frequently, especially shirts. In the course of a day he changes his shirt many times. There are always extra shirts about, in boxes.

"Which of you has the shirts?"

A Friend Comments: K.'s Aloneness

"The thing you have to realize about K. is that essentially he's absolutely alone in the world. There's this terrible loneliness which prevents people from getting too close to him. Maybe it comes from something in his childhood, I don't know. But he's very hard to get to know, and a lot of people who think they know him rather well don't really know him at all. He says something or does something that surprises you, and you realize that all along you really didn't know him at all.

"He has surprising facets. I remember once we were out in a small boat. K. of course was the captain. Some rough weather came up and we began to head back in. I began worrying about picking up a landing and I said to him that I didn't think the anchor would hold, with the wind and all. He just looked at me. Then he said: 'Of course it will hold. That's what it's for.'"

★ ★ ★

K. on Crowds

"There are exhausted crowds and vivacious crowds.

"Sometimes, standing there, I can sense whether a particular crowd is one thing or the other. Sometimes the mood of the crowd is disguised, sometimes you only find out after a quarter of an hour what sort of crowd a particular crowd is.

"And you can't speak to them in the same way. The variations have to be taken into account. You have to say something to them that is meaningful to them *in that mood.*"

Gallery-going

K. enters a large gallery on Fifty-seventh Street, in the Fuller Building. His entourage includes several ladies and gentlemen. Works by a geometricist are on show. K. looks at the immense, rather theoretical paintings.

"Well, at least we know he has a ruler."

The group dissolves in laughter. People repeat the remark to one another, laughing.

The artist, who has been standing behind a dealer, regards K. with hatred.

K. Puzzled by His Children

The children are crying. There are several children, one about four, a boy, then another boy, slightly older, and a little girl, very beautiful, wearing blue jeans, crying. There are various objects on the grass, an electric train, a picture book, a red ball, a plastic bucket, a plastic shovel.

K. frowns at the children whose distress issues from no source immediately available to the eye, which seems indeed uncaused, vacant, a general anguish. K. turns to the mother of these children who is standing nearby wearing hip-huggers which appear to be made of linked marshmallows studded with diamonds but then I am a notoriously poor observer.

"Play with them," he says.

This mother of ten quietly suggests that K. himself "play with them."

K. picks up the picture book and begins to read to the children. But the book has a German text. It has been left behind, perhaps, by some foreign visitor. Nevertheless K. perseveres.

"A ist der Affe, er isst mit der Pfote." ("A is the Ape, he eats with his Paw.")

The crying of the children continues.

A Dream

Orange trees.

Overhead, a steady stream of strange aircraft which resemble kitchen implements, bread boards, cookie sheets, colanders.

The shiny aluminum instruments are on their way to complete the bombings of Sidi-Madani.

A farm in the hills.

★ ★ ★

Matters (from an Administrative Assistant)

"A lot of matters that had been pending came to a head right about that time, moved to the front burner, things we absolutely had to take care of. And we couldn't find K. Nobody knew where he was. We had looked everywhere. He had just withdrawn, made himself unavailable. There was this one matter that was probably more pressing than all the rest put together. Really crucial. We were all standing around wondering what to do. We were getting pretty nervous because this thing was really. . . . Then K. walked in and disposed of it with a quick phone call. A quick phone call!"

Childhood of K. as Recalled by a Former Teacher

"He was a very alert boy, very bright, good at his studies, very thorough, very conscientious. But that's not unusual; that describes a good number of the boys who pass through here. It's not unusual, that is, to find these qualities which are after all the qualities that we look for and encourage in them. What was unusual about K. was his compassion, something very rare for a boy of that age—even if they have it, they're usually very careful not to display it for fear of seeming soft, girlish. I remember, though, that in K. this particular attribute was very marked. I would almost say that it was his strongest characteristic."

Speaking to No One but Waiters, He—

"The dandelion salad with bacon, I think."

"The *rysstafel.*"

"The poached duck."

"The black bean purée."

"The cod fritters."

K. Explains a Technique

"It's an expedient in terms of how not to destroy a situation which has been a long time gestating, or, again, how *to* break it up if it appears that the situation has changed, during the gestation period, into one whose implications are not quite what they were at the beginning. What I mean is that in this business things are constantly altering (usually for the worse) and usually you want to give the impression that you're not watching this particular situation particularly closely, that you're paying no special attention to it, until you're ready to make your move. That is, it's best to be sudden, if you can manage it. Of course you can't do that all the time. Sometimes you're just completely wiped out, cleaned out, totaled, and then the only thing to do is shrug and forget about it."

K. on His Own Role

"Sometimes it seems to me that it doesn't matter what I do, that it is enough to exist, to sit somewhere, in a garden for example, watching whatever is to be seen there, the small events. At other times, I'm aware that other people, possibly a great number of other people, could be affected by what I do or fail to do, that I have a responsibility, as we all have, to make the best possible use of whatever talents I've been given, for the common good. It is not enough to sit in that garden, however restful or pleasurable it might be. The world is full of unsolved problems, situations that demand careful, reasoned and intelligent action. In Latin America, for example."

As Entrepreneur

The original cost estimates for burying the North Sea pipeline have been exceeded by a considerable margin. Everyone wonders what he will say about this contretemps which does not fail to have its dangers for those responsible for the costly miscalculations, which are viewed in many minds as inexcusable.

He says only: "Exceptionally difficult rock conditions."

With Young People

K., walking the streets of unknown towns, finds himself among young people. Young people line these streets, narrow and curving, which are theirs, dedicated to them. They are everywhere, resting on the embankments, their guitars, small radios, long hair. They sit on the sidewalks, back to back, heads turned to stare. They stand implacably on street corners, in doorways, or lean on their elbows in windows, or squat in small groups at that place where the sidewalk meets the walls of buildings. The streets are filled with these young people who say nothing, reveal only a limited interest, refuse to declare themselves. Street after street contains them, a great number, more displayed as one turns a corner, rank upon rank stretching into the distance, drawn from the arcades, the plazas, staring.

He Discusses the French Writer, Poulet

"For Poulet, it is not enough to speak of *seizing the moment.* It is rather a question of, and I quote, 'recognizing in the instant which lives and dies, which surges out of nothingness and which ends in dream, an intensity and depth of significance which ordinarily attaches only to the whole of existence.'

"What Poulet is describing is neither an ethic nor a prescription but rather what he has discovered in the work of Marivaux. Poulet has taken up the Marivaudian canon and squeezed it with both hands to discover the essence of what may be called the Marivaudian being, what Poulet in fact calls the Marivaudian being.

"The Marivaudian being is, according to Poulet, a pastless futureless man, born anew at every instant. The instants are points which organize themselves into a line, but what is important is the instant, not the line. The Marivaudian being has in a sense no history. Nothing follows from what has gone before. He is constantly surprised. He cannot predict his own reaction to events. He is constantly being *overtaken* by events. A condition of breathlessness and dazzlement surrounds him. In consequence he exists in a certain freshness which seems, if I may say so, very desirable. This freshness Poulet, quoting Marivaux, describes very well."

K. Saved from Drowning

K. in the water. His flat black hat, his black cape, his sword are on the shore. He retains his mask. His hands beat the surface of the water which tears and rips about him. The white foam, the green depths. I throw a line, the coils leaping out over the surface of the water. He has missed it. No, it appears that he has it. His right hand (sword arm) grasps the line that I have thrown him. I am on the bank, the rope wound round my waist, braced against a rock. K. now has both hands on the line. I pull him out of the water. He stands now on the bank, gasping.

"Thank you."

Richard Bausch (1945–)

grew up in Virginia, wanting to become a priest until he met the woman who is now his wife, "and that was the end of that." He spent time in the Air Force and as a singer/songwriter (his band once opened for Janis Joplin at the Aragon Ballroom in Chicago) before receiving his MFA from the Iowa Writers' Workshop, where his classmates included John Irving and Jane Smiley. One day, mired in the writing of a novel that would have been his fourth, a book he had worked on for years, Bausch decided that the book was "crap," went out into his back yard and burned it, page by page, savoring the wave of relief that washed over him. The next day, he started writing short stories again (he had only occasionally written them since graduate school, with modest success), and the stories got snapped up by the likes of The Atlantic Monthly *and* The New Yorker; *not long after that, his stories began to appear regularly in* The Best American Stories *and* Prize Stories: The O. Henry Awards. *A career retrospective,* The Stories of Richard Bausch, *was published in 2003. Bausch is a member of the Fellowship of Southern Writers and a recipient of the Lila Wallace–Reader's Digest Writer's Award and the Award in Literature from the American Academy of Arts and Letters. His nine novels include* Hello to the Cannibals, The Last Good Time, *and the PEN/Faulkner nominee* Take Me Back. *He and his twin brother Robert (author of five books of fiction, including* A Hole in the Earth*) are perhaps the only identical twin novelists in history. Richard Bausch teaches at George Mason University, where he holds the Heritage Chair in Writing.*

INTRODUCTION BY **Robert Bausch**

First, the three stories in this collection are not by any means representative of the range, variety, or deftness of my brother's body of work. They are, however, great examples of his artistry—of the way in which he makes the art of the short story behave itself. To clearly understand what he's up to in these stories, it is important to remember a few basic principles about the difference between literature and entertainment. Literature has at its core a serious intent. When I say serious, I don't mean somber. I mean not frivolous. Literature is concerned with what John Updike has called "the human news." What I think he means is the truth—pure and simple. This does not mean facts, or any allegiance to logic, or even what is possible in human events. It means only that whatever situations in which you find human characters, those characters should be recognizably human, and what you reveal about them should be recognizably true. Entertainment's main purpose is not to provide the truth about anything important, but rather to divert us from the truth. In this regard, all entertainment is a delightful and diverting lie—pure and simple. There's nothing wrong with that, except that a steady diet of it can distort what is true and provide virtually nothing in the way of human news that matters.

In entertainment, most often, you get conflicts and trouble where action makes a difference, and then you get powerful, super capable characters who provide the action. Things get solved in the end. Everybody's happy.

In literature, most often, you get conflicts and trouble where action makes no difference; where it *cannot* make a difference, and then you get less than powerful, ordinary people who provide the action. Things don't get solved in the end. Everybody's not necessarily happy. What has to get resolved in a work of literature is the story, not the conflict. If the conflict is resolved, you have a story that does not deal with much more than a conflict where action makes a difference, so you probably don't have a work of literature. If you're totally concerned with "the end" and how it comes out "in the end" and if you're telling people, "Don't tell me how it ends," you are coming to books and reading for entertainment only. There are older and better reasons for reading literature. You don't go to a rock concert to find out what the last song will be. You go to hear the music and enjoy it all along the way, and that is also why you read literature. To hear the language and enjoy it all along the way.

This one distinction is the very thing that makes the work of Richard Bausch so satisfying and so clearly literature. His characters are indelible, they are totally human—with weaknesses, flaws, strengths and talents, hopes, lies and dreams. What you find in the stories of Richard Bausch is the human news—in spades. And you also find an exquisite use of the language—a kind of poetic vision that is always intriguing and always staggeringly accurate.

The mistake that students most often make about reading literature and perhaps especially the short story is the belief that plot is the story. Plot is no more the story than a map is a journey. Plot is the map, but the story is something else, has to be something else or the whole enterprise isn't worthy of our attention. If you've heard a joke, it isn't funny anymore, and if you've heard a story or anecdote where the only thing that stands out is the plot, after a while it isn't interesting anymore either. The key to studying literature and to creating literature is character. Too often, students misunderstand what is going on in a short story when they latch onto the plot or the crisis that causes the conflict to come to the fore and mistake that crisis for the conflict. They are often disappointed when they get to the end of a story and the crisis is not resolved the way they had hoped.

For example, in the story "What Feels Like the World," students frequently want the character's problems to be resolved in the end of the story. The question becomes, in a misreading of the story, "Does Brenda, who is overweight and desperately trying to slim down, make it over the vault box in the gymnastics demonstration the fifth and sixth grades will put on at the last PTA meeting of the year?" The story opens with her grandfather watching her from his bedroom window. She has gotten up "very early in the morning, too early," and he hears her jumping rope on the sidewalk below. We learn in the second paragraph that she is the "unfortunate inheritor of [the grandfather's] big-boned genes, his tendency toward bulk, and she is on a self-induced program of exercise and dieting, to lose weight." Gradually, you come to see that she can't do it now, and she won't be able to do it. She has not succeeded in losing weight, and now it's too late. When you look for the ending with this problem in mind, you of course misunderstand what the story is doing. The conflict isn't about the vault box. That's just the crisis that brings the conflict to its terrible and beautiful fruition; what makes the story the human news. Look at the opening of the story again. Study the grandfather's approach to his daughter's child—his dead daughter's child. In the first paragraph, the narrator tells us, "he thinks of the heartless way children tease the imperfect among them." There is great truth in what the grandfather wants—what he is hoping for in his granddaughter. Look at what has happened to her. She has lost her mother in death, and her father has just gone away—he keeps up payments for the child but "he never visits or calls."

Brenda's parents divorced when she was a baby, and her mother moved back to live with the grandfather. But at the school, Brenda's teacher says to the grandfather, "I got the impression it was recent for her. I mean, you know, that she had just come from it all. It was all very vivid for her, I remember that."

Look at the title of the story: "What Feels Like the World." Then examine what is going on with Brenda and her grandfather—what is being "put on the child," and I submit it doesn't have very much to do with a vault box or a gymnastics demonstration. In the last analysis, it is irrelevant whether she makes it over the vault box. Whether she does or doesn't, nothing in her life will change. To suggest that her life is changed by an action such as that would be a lie—would not be the human news, would be, in short, entertainment. The story goes beyond simple entertainment, although the language of it, the way the characters are drawn and the way the story unfolds, is beautiful and in its own way entertaining.

When it comes to the moment and Brenda is about to make the effort, you know she has not lost the weight, she has not been successful at what she set out to do, and she probably won't make it over the vault box. But you should be thinking that it doesn't matter if she does. Her grandfather says, too loud, "They shouldn't make them do these things . . . it's too hard." It astonishes him that he seems to be addressing everyone and he says, "They shouldn't have to go through a thing like this . . . It's too much, . . . Too much to put on a child. There's just so much a child can take."

He's not talking about the vault box.

So the story has its crisis—the thing that moves the conflict to a kind of fruition—but the crisis is not resolved. We don't even have what happens when she tries to leap over the vault box in the story. Since it is irrelevant, it is not there—a good rule of thumb for any writer to follow. Examine the other two stories in this collection, "The Man Who Knew Belle Starr" and "Tandolfo the Great," and ask yourself: What is the crisis? Then go deeper. *Why* is this birthday party with the misbehaving little boy a crisis for Tandolfo? *Why* is McRae's run in with "Belle Starr" a crisis? What you are looking for is the conflict that is deeper, that runs beneath, that drives the story and carries with it the human news. Doing so will provide a much richer understanding of the art of the short story and of what it means to be human.

Virtually all of Richard Bausch's stories proceed like this. What drives them is character, people of all stripes and kinds, and there is always something that is mute in each human heart but that manages to speak to us anyway. And that is why I can confidently say that my brother is—and I say this without bias but rather with more than a tad of envy—a master of the short story.

Read the others.

You'll see.

Robert Bausch, Richard's twin brother, is also a novelist and short story writer. His most recent book is The Gypsy Man, *a novel. A new novel,* Out of Season, *is forthcoming from Harcourt in 2005.*

RICHARD BAUSCH

The Man Who Knew Belle Starr

On his way west McRae picked up a hitcher, a young woman carrying a paper bag and a leather purse, wearing jeans and a shawl—which she didn't take off, though it was more than ninety degrees out and McRae had no air-conditioning. He was driving an old Dodge Charger with a bad exhaust system and one long crack in the wraparound windshield. He pulled over for her, and she got right in, put the leather purse on the seat between them, and settled herself with the paper bag on her lap between her hands. He had just crossed into Texas from Oklahoma. This was the third day of the trip.

"Where you headed?" he asked.

She said, "What about you?"

"Nevada, maybe."

"Why maybe?"

And that fast he was answering *her* questions. "I just got out of the Air Force," he told her, though this wasn't exactly true. The Air Force had given him a dishonorable discharge, after four years at Leavenworth for assaulting a staff sergeant. He was a bad character. He had a bad temper that had got him into a load of trouble already, and he just wanted to get out west, out to the wide open spaces. Just to see it, really. He had the feeling that people didn't require as much from a person way out where there was that kind of room. He didn't have any family now. He had five thousand dollars from his father's insurance policy, and he was going to make the money last a while. He said, "I'm sort of undecided about a lot of things."

"Not me," she said.

"You figured out where you're going?"

"You could say that."

"So where might that be?"

She made a fist and then extended her thumb, and turned it over. "Under," she said. "Down."

"Excuse me?"

"Does the radio work?" she asked, reaching for it.

"It's on the blink," he said.

She turned the knob anyway. Then she sat back and folded her arms over the paper bag.

He took a glance at her. She was skinny and long-necked, and her hair was the color of water in a metal pail. She looked just old enough for high school.

"What's in the bag?" he said.

She sat up a little. "Nothing. Another blouse."

"Well, so what did you mean back there?"

"Back where?"

"Look," he said, "we don't have to do any talking if you don't want to."

"Then what will we do?"

"Anything you want," he said.

"What if I just want to sit here and let you drive me all the way to Nevada?"

"That's fine," he said. "That's just fine."

"Well, I won't do that. We can talk."

"Are you going to Nevada?" he asked.

She gave a little shrug of her shoulders. "Why not?"

"All right," he said, and for some reason he offered her his hand. She looked at it and then smiled at him, and he put his hand back on the wheel.

It got a little awkward almost right away. The heat was awful, and she sat there sweating, not saying much. He never thought he was very smooth or anything, and he had been in prison; it had been a long time since he had found himself in the company of a woman. Finally she fell asleep, and for a few miles he could look at her without worrying about anything but staying on the road. He decided that she was kind of good-looking around the eyes and mouth. If she ever filled out, she might be something. He caught himself wondering what might happen, thinking of sex. A girl who traveled alone like this was probably pretty loose. Without quite realizing it, he began to daydream about her, and when he got aroused by the daydream he tried to concentrate on figuring his chances, playing his cards right, not messing up any opportunities—but being gentlemanly, too. He was not the sort of man who forced himself on young women. She slept very quietly, not breathing loudly or sighing or moving much; and then she simply sat up and folded her arms over the bag again and stared out at the road.

"God," she said. "I went out."

"You hungry?" he asked.

"No."

"What's your name? I never got your name."

"Belle Starr," she said, and, winking at him, she made a clicking sound out of the side of her mouth.

"Belle Starr," he said.

"Don't you know who Belle Starr was?"

All he knew was that it was a familiar-sounding name. "Belle Starr."

She put her index finger to the side of his head and said, "Bang."

"Belle Starr," he said.

"Come on," she said. "Annie Oakley. Wild Bill Hickok."

"Oh," McRae said. "Okay."

"That's me," she said, sliding down in the seat. "Belle Starr."

"That's not your real name."

"It's the only one I go by these days."

They rode on in silence for a time.

"What's *your* name?" she asked.

He told her.

"Irish?"

"I never thought about it."

"Where you from, McRae?"

"Washington, D.C."

"Long way from home."

"I haven't been there in years."

"Where *have* you been?"

"Prison," he said. He hadn't known he would say it, and now that he had, he kept his eyes on the road. He might as well have been posing for her; he had an image of himself as he must look from the side, and he shifted his weight a little, sucked in his belly. When he stole a glance at her, he saw that she was simply gazing out at the Panhandle, one hand up like a visor to shade her eyes.

"What about you?" he asked, and felt like somebody in a movie—two people with a past come together on the open road. He wondered how he could get the talk around to the subject of love.

"What *about* me?"

"Where you from?"

"I don't want to bore you with all the facts," she said.

"I don't mind," McRae said. "I got nothing else to do."

"I'm from way up north."

"Okay," he said, "you want me to guess?"

"Maine," she said. "Land of moose and lobster."

He said, "Maine. Well, now."

"See?" she said. "The facts are just a lot of things that don't change."

"Unless you change them," McRae said.

She reached down and, with elaborate care, as if it were fragile, put the paper bag on the floor. Then she leaned back and put her feet up on the dash. She was wearing low-cut tennis shoes.

"You going to sleep?" he asked.

"Just relaxing," she said. But a moment later, when he asked if she wanted to stop and eat, she didn't answer. He looked over and saw that she was sound asleep.

His father had died while he was at Leavenworth. The last time McRae saw him, he was lying on a gurney in one of the bays of D.C. General's emergency ward, a plastic tube in his mouth, an IV set into an ugly yellow-blue bruise on his wrist. McRae had come home on leave from the Air Force—which he had joined on the suggestion of a juvenile judge—to find his father on the floor in the living room, in a pile of old newspapers and bottles, wearing his good suit, with no socks or shoes and no shirt. He looked like he was dead. But the ambulance drivers found a pulse and rushed him off to the hospital. McRae cleaned the house up a little and then followed in the Charger. The old man had been going steadily downhill from the time McRae was a boy, so this latest trouble wasn't new. In the hospital they got the tube in his mouth and hooked him to the IV, and then left him there on the gurney. McRae stood at his side, still in uniform, and when the old man opened his eyes and looked at him, it was clear that he didn't know who it was. The old man blinked, stared, and then sat up, took the tube out of his mouth, and spit something terrible-looking into a small metal dish that was suspended from the complicated apparatus of the room, which made a continual water-dropping sound, like a leaking sink. He looked at McRae again, and then he looked at the tube.

"Jesus Christ," he said.

"Hey," McRae said.

"What."

"It's me."

The old man put the tube back in his mouth and looked away.

"Pops," McRae said. He didn't feel anything.

The tube came out. "Don't look at me, boy. You got yourself into it. Getting into trouble, stealing and running around. You got yourself into it."

"I don't mind it, Pops. It's three meals a day and a place to sleep."

"Yeah," the old man said, and then seemed to gargle something. He spit into the little metal dish again.

"I got thirty days of leave, Pops."

"Eh?"

"I don't have to go back for a month."

"Where you going?"

"Around," McRae said.

The truth was that he hated the Air Force, and he was thinking of taking the Charger and driving to Canada or someplace like that, and hiding out for the rest of his life. The Air Force felt like punishment—it *was* punishment—and he had already been in trouble for his quick temper and his attitude. That afternoon he left his father to whatever would happen, got in the Charger, and started north. But he didn't make it. He lost heart a few miles south of New York City, and he turned around and came back. The old man had been moved to a room in the alcoholic ward, but McRae didn't go to see him. He stayed in the house, watching television and drinking beer, and when old high school buddies came by he went around with them a little. Mostly he stayed home, though, and at the end of his leave he locked the place and drove back to Chanute, in Illinois, where he was stationed. He hadn't been there two months before he got into the scrape that landed him in prison. A staff sergeant caught him drinking beer in the dayroom of one of the training barracks and asked for his name. McRae walked over to him, said, "My name is trouble," and, at the word *trouble,* struck the other man in the face. He'd had a lot of beer, and he had been sitting there in the dark, going over everything in his mind, and the staff sergeant, a baby-faced man with a spare tire of flesh around his waist and an attitude about the stripes on his sleeves, had just walked into it. McRae didn't even know him. Yet he stood over the sergeant where he had fallen and started kicking him. The poor man wound up in the hospital with a broken jaw (the first punch had done it), a few cracked ribs, and multiple lacerations and bruises. The court-martial was swift. The sentence was four years at hard labor, along with a dishonorable discharge. He'd had less than a month on the sentence when he got the news about his father. He felt no surprise, nor, really, any grief, yet there was a little thrill of something like fear; he was in his cell, and for an instant some part of him actually wanted to remain there, inside walls, where things were certain and no decisions had to be made. A week later he learned of the money from the insurance, which would have been more than the five thousand except that his father had been a few months behind on the rent and on other payments. McRae settled what he had to of those things, and kept the rest. He had started to feel like a happy man, out of Leavenworth and the Air Force. And now he was on his way to Nevada, or someplace like that—and he had picked up a girl.

★ ★ ★

He drove on until dusk, stopping only for gas, and the girl slept right through. Just past the line into New Mexico he pulled off the interstate and went north for a mile or so, looking for some place other than a chain restaurant to eat. She sat up straight and pushed the hair back from her face. "Where are we?"

"New Mexico," he said. "I'm looking for a place to eat."

"I'm not hungry."

"Well," he said, "you might be able to go all day without eating, but I got a three-meal-a-day habit to support."

She brought the paper bag up from the floor and held it in her lap.

"You got food in there?"

"No."

"You're very pretty—childlike, sort of, when you sleep."

"I didn't snore?"

"You were quiet as a mouse."

"And you think I'm pretty."

"I guess you know a thing like that. I hope I didn't offend you."

"I don't like dirty remarks," she said. "But I guess you don't mean to be dirty."

"Dirty."

"Sometimes people can say a thing like that and mean it very dirty, but I could tell you didn't."

He pulled in at a roadside diner and turned the ignition off. "Well?" he said.

She sat there with the bag on her lap. "I don't think I'll go in with you."

"You can have a cold drink or something," he said.

"You go in. I'll wait out here."

"Come on in there with me and have a cold drink," McRae said. "I'll buy it for you. I'll buy you dinner, if you want."

"I don't want to," she said.

He got out and started for the entrance, and before he reached it, he heard her door open and close, and turned to watch her come toward him, thin and waiflike in the shawl, which hid her arms and hands.

The diner was empty. A long, low counter ran along one side, with soda fountains and glass cases in which pies and cakes were set. There were booths along one wall. Everything seemed in order, except that no one was around. McRae and the girl stood in the doorway for a moment and waited, and finally she stepped in and took a seat in the first booth. "I guess we're supposed to seat ourselves," she said.

"This is weird," McRae said.

"Hey," she said, rising. "A jukebox." She strode over to it and leaned on it, crossing one leg behind the other at the ankle, her hair falling down to hide her face.

"Hello?" McRae said. "Anybody here?"

"Got any change?" the girl asked.

He gave her a quarter and then sat at the counter. A door at the far end of the diner swung in and a big, red-faced man entered, wearing a white cook's apron over a sweat-stained baby-blue shirt, the sleeves of which he had rolled up past the meaty curve of his elbows. "Yeah?" he said.

"You open?" McRae asked.

"That jukebox don't work, honey," the man said.

"You open?" McRae said, as the girl came and sat down beside him.

"I guess maybe I am."

"Place is kind of empty."

"What do you want to eat?"

"You got a menu?"

"You want a menu?"

"Sure," McRae said. "Why not."

"Truth is," the big man said, "I'm selling this place. I don't have menus anymore. I make hamburgers and breakfast stuff. Some french fries and cold drinks. A hot dog, maybe. I'm not keeping track."

"Let's go somewhere else," the girl said.

"Yeah," the big man said, "why don't you do that."

"Look," McRae said, "what's the story here?"

The other man shrugged. "You came in at the end of the run, you know what I mean? I'm going out of business. Sit down and I'll make you a hamburger, on the house."

McRae looked at the girl.

"Okay," she said, in a tone that made it clear that she would've been happier to leave.

The big man put his hands on the bar and leaned toward her. "Miss, if I were you, I wouldn't look a gift horse in the mouth."

"I don't like hamburger," she said.

"You want a hot dog?" the man said. "I got a hot dog for you. Guaranteed to please."

"I'll have some french fries," she said.

The big man turned to the grill and opened the metal drawer under it. He was very wide at the hips, and his legs were like tree trunks. "I get out of the Army after twenty years," he said, "and I got a little money put aside. The wife and I decide we want to get into the restaurant business. The government's going to be paying me a nice pension, and we got the savings, so we sink it all in this Goddamn diner. Six and a half miles from the interstate. You get the picture? The guy's selling us this diner at a great price, you know? A terrific price. For a song, I'm in the restaurant business. The wife will cook the food and I'll wait tables, you know, until we start to make a little extra, and then we'll hire somebody—a high school kid, or somebody like that. We might even open another restaurant, if the going gets good enough. But, of course, this is New Mexico. This is six and a half miles from the interstate. You know what's up the road? Nothing." He had put the hamburger on, and a basket of frozen french fries. "Now the wife decides she's had enough of life on the border, and off she goes to Seattle to sit in the rain with her mother, and here I am trying to sell a place nobody else is dumb enough to buy. You know what I mean?"

"That's rough," McRae said.

"You're the second customer I've had all *week,* bub."

The girl said, "I guess that cash register's empty, then, huh."

"It ain't full, honey."

She got up and wandered across the room. For a while she stood gazing out the windows over the booths, her hands invisible under the woolen shawl. When she came back to sit next to McRae again, the hamburger and french fries were ready.

"On the house," the big man said.

And the girl brought a gun out from under the shawl—a pistol that looked like a toy. "Suppose you open up that register, Mr. Poor Mouth," she said.

The big man looked at her, then at McRae, who had taken a large bite of his hamburger and had it bulging in his cheeks.

"This thing is loaded, and I'll use it."

"Well, for Christ's sake," the big man said.

McRae started to get off the stool. "Hold on a minute," he said to them both, his words garbled by the mouthful of food, and then everything started happening at once. The girl aimed the pistol. There was a popping sound—a single small pop, not much louder than the sound of a cap gun—and the big man took a step back, into the dishes and pans. He stared at the girl, wide-eyed, for what seemed like a long time, and then went down, pulling dishes with him in a tremendous shattering.

"Jesus Christ," McRae said, swallowing, standing back far from her, raising his hands.

She put the pistol back in her jeans, under the shawl, and then went around the counter and opened the cash register. "Damn," she said.

McRae said, low, "Jesus Christ."

And now she looked at him; it was as if she had forgotten he was there. "What're you standing there with your hands up like that?"

"God," he said, "oh, God."

"Stop it," she said. "Put your hands down."

He did so.

"Cash register's empty." She sat down on one of the stools and gazed over at the body of the man where it had fallen. "Damn."

"Look," McRae said, "take my car. You can have my car."

She seemed puzzled. "I don't want your car. What do I want your car for?"

"You—" he said. He couldn't talk, couldn't focus clearly, or think. He looked at the man, who lay very still, and then he began to cry.

"Will you stop it?" she said, coming off the stool, reaching under the shawl and bringing out the pistol again.

"Jesus," he said. "Good Jesus."

She pointed the pistol at his forehead. "Bang," she said. "What's my name?"

"Your—name?"

"My name."

"Belle—" he managed.

"Come on," she said. "The whole thing. You remember."

"Belle—Belle Starr."

"Right." She let the gun hand drop to her side, into one of the folds of the shawl. "I like that so much better than Annie Oakley."

"Please," McRae said.

She took a few steps away from him and then whirled and aimed the gun. "I think we better get out of here. What do you think?"

"Take the car," he said, almost with exasperation; he was frightened to hear it in his voice.

"I can't drive," she said simply. "Never learned."

"Jesus," he said. It went out of him like a sigh.

"Lordy," she said, gesturing with the pistol for him to move to the door, "it's hard to believe you were ever in *prison.*"

The interstate went on into the dark, beyond the glow of the headlights. He lost track of miles, road signs, other traffic, time; trucks came by and surprised him, and other cars seemed to materialize as they started the lane change that would bring them over in front of him. He saw their taillights grow small in the distance, and all the while the girl sat watching him, her hands somewhere under the shawl. For a long time he heard only the sound of the rushing night air at the windows, and then she moved a little, shifted her weight, bringing one leg up on the seat.

"What were you in prison for, anyway?"

Her voice startled him, and for a moment he couldn't think of an answer.

"Come on," she said. "I'm getting bored with all this quiet. What were you in prison for?"

"I—beat up a guy."

"That's all?"

"Yes, that's all." He couldn't keep the irritation out of his voice.

"Tell me about it."

"It was just—I just beat up a guy. It wasn't anything."

"I didn't shoot that man for money, you know."

McRae said nothing.

"I shot him because he made a nasty remark to me about the hot dog."

"I didn't hear any nasty remark."

"If he hadn't said it, he'd still be alive."

McRae held tight to the wheel.

"Don't you wish it was the Wild West?" she said.

"Wild West," he said. "Yeah." He could barely speak for the dryness in his mouth and the deep ache of his own breathing.

"You know," she said, "I'm not really from Maine."

He nodded.

"I'm from Florida."

"Florida," he managed.

"Yes, only I don't have a southern accent, so people think I'm not from there. Do you hear any trace of a southern accent at all when I talk?"

"No," he said.

"Now you—you've got an accent. A definite southern accent."

He was silent.

"Talk to me," she said.

"What do you want me to say?" he said. "Jesus."

"You could ask me things."

"Ask you things—"

"Ask me what my name is."

Without hesitating, McRae said, "What's your name?"

"You know."

"No, really," he said, trying to play along.

"It's Belle Starr."

"Belle Starr," he said.

"Nobody *but,*" she said.

"Good," he said.

"And I don't care about money, either," she said. "That's not what I'm after."

"No," McRae said.

"What I'm after is adventure."

"Right," McRae said.

"Fast living."

"Fast living, right."

"A good time."

"Good," he said.

"I'm going to live a ton before I die."

"A ton, yes."

"What about you?"

"Yes," he said. "Me too."

"Want to join up with me?"

"Join up," he said. "Right." He was watching the road.

She leaned toward him a little. "Do you think I'm lying about my name?"

"No."

"Good," she said.

He had begun to feel as though he might start throwing up what he'd had of the hamburger. His stomach was cramping on him, and he was dizzy. He might even be having a heart attack.

"Your eyes are as big as saucers," she said.

He tried to narrow them a little. His whole body was shaking now.

"You know how old I am, McRae? I'm nineteen."

He nodded, glanced at her and then at the road again.

"How old are you?"

"Twenty-three."

"Do you believe people go to heaven when they die?"

"Oh, God," he said.

"Look, I'm not going to shoot you while you're driving the car. We'd crash if I did that."

"Oh," he said. "Oh, Jesus, please—look, I never saw anybody shot before—"

"Will you *stop it?*"

He put one hand to his mouth. He was soaked: he felt the sweat on his upper lip, and then he felt the dampness all through his clothes.

She said, "I don't kill everybody I meet, you know."

"No," he said. "Of course not." The absurdity of this exchange almost brought a laugh up out of him. How astonishing, that a laugh could be anywhere in him at such a time, but here it was, rising up in his throat like some loosened part of his anatomy. He held on with his whole mind, and a moment passed before he realized that *she* was laughing.

"Actually," she said, "I haven't killed all that many people."

"How—" he began. Then he had to stop to breathe. "How many?"

"Take a guess."

"I don't have any idea," he said.

"Well," she said, "you'll just have to guess. And you'll notice that I haven't spent any time in prison.

He was quiet.

"Guess," she said.

McRae said, "Ten?"

"No."

He waited.

"Come on, keep guessing."

"More than ten?"

"Maybe."

"More than ten," he said.

"Well, all right. Less than ten."

"Less than ten," he said.

"Guess," she said.

"Nine."

"No."

"Eight."

"No, not eight."

"Six?"

"Not six."

"Five?"

"Five and a half people," she said. "You almost hit it right on the button."

"Five and a half people," McRae said.

"Right. A kid who was hitchhiking, like me; a guy at a gas station; a dog that must've got lost—I count him as the half; another guy at a gas station; a guy that took me to a motel and made an obscene gesture to me; and the guy at the diner. That makes five and a half."

"Five and a half," McRae said.

"You keep repeating everything I say. I wish you'd quit that."

He wiped his hand across his mouth and then feigned a cough to keep from having to speak.

"Five and a half people," she said, turning a little in the seat, putting her knees up on the dash. "Have you ever met anybody like me? Tell the truth."

"No," McRae said, "nobody."

"Just think about it, McRae. You can say you rode with Belle Starr. You can tell your grandchildren."

He was afraid to say anything to, this, for fear of changing the delicate balance of the thought. Yet he knew the worst mistake would be to say nothing at all. He was beginning to sense something of the cunning that he would need to survive, even as he knew that the slightest miscalculation might mean the end of him. He said, with fake wonder, "I knew Belle Starr."

She said, "Think of it."

"Something," he said.

And she sat farther down in the seat. "Amazing."

He kept to fifty-five miles an hour, and everyone else was speeding. The girl sat straight up now, nearly facing him on the seat. For long periods she had been quiet, simply watching him drive. Soon they were going to need gas; they had less than half a tank.

"Look at those people speeding," she said. "We're the only ones obeying the speed limit. Look at them."

"Do you want me to speed up?"

"I think they ought to get tickets for speeding, that's what I think. Sometimes I wish I were a policeman."

"Look," McRae said, "we're going to need gas pretty soon."

"No, let's just run it until it quits. We can always hitch a ride with somebody."

"This car's got a great engine," McRae said. "We might have to outrun the police, and I wouldn't want to do that in any other car."

"This old thing? It's got a crack in the windshield. The radio doesn't work."

"Right. But it's a fast car. It'll outrun a police car."

She put one arm over the seat back and looked out the rear window. "You really think the police are chasing us?"

"They might be," he said.

She stared at him a moment. "No. There's no reason. Nobody saw us."

"But if somebody did—this car, I mean, it'll go like crazy."

"I'm afraid of speeding, though," she said. "Besides, you know what I found out? If you run slow enough, the cops go right past you. Right on past you, looking for somebody who's in a hurry. No, I think it's best if we just let it run until it quits and then get out and hitch."

McRae thought he knew what might happen when the gas ran out: she would make him push the car to the side of the road, and then she would walk him back into the cactus and brush there, and when they were far enough from the road, she would shoot him. He knew this as if she had spelled it all out, and he began again to try for the cunning he would need. "Belle," he said. "Why don't we lay low for a few days in Albuquerque?"

"Is that an obscene gesture?" she asked.

"No!" he said, almost shouted. "No! That's—it's outlaw talk. You know. Hide out from the cops—lay low. It's—it's prison talk."

"Well, I've never been in prison."

"That's all I meant."

"You want to hide out."

"Right," he said.

"You and me?"

"You—you asked if I wanted to join up with you."

"Did I?" She seemed puzzled by this.

"Yes," he said, feeling himself press it a little. "Don't you remember?"

"I guess I do."

"You did," he said.

"I don't know."

"Belle Starr had a gang," he said.

"She did?"

"I could be the first member of your gang."

She sat there thinking this over. McRae's blood moved at the thought that she was deciding whether or not he would live. "Well," she said, "maybe."

"You've got to have a gang, Belle."

"We'll see," she said.

A moment later she said, "How much money do you have?"

"I have enough to start a gang."

"It takes money to start a gang?"

"Well—" He was at a loss.

"How much do you have?"

He said, "A few hundred."

"Really?" she said. "That much?"

"Just enough to—just enough to get to Nevada."

"Can I have it?"

He said, "Sure." He was holding the wheel and looking out into the night.

"And we'll be a gang?"

"Right," he said. "I like the idea. Belle Starr and her gang."

McRae started talking about what the gang could do, making it up as he went along, trying to sound like all the gangster movies he'd seen. He heard himself talking about things like robbery and getaway cars and not getting nabbed and staying out of prison, and then, as she sat there staring at him, he started talking about being at Leavenworth, what it was like. He went on about it, the hours of forced work and the time alone, the harsh day-to-day routines, the bad food. Before he was through, feeling the necessity of deepening her sense of him as her new accomplice—and feeling strangely as though in some way he had indeed, become exactly that—he was telling her everything, all the bad times he'd had: his father's alcoholism, and growing up wanting to hit something for the anger that was in him; the years of getting into trouble; the fighting and the kicking and what it had got him. He embellished it all, made it sound worse than it really was, because she seemed to be going for it and because, telling it to her, he felt oddly sorry for himself; a version of this story of pain and neglect and lonely rage was true. He had been through a lot. And as he finished describing for her the scene at the hospital the last time he saw his father, he was almost certain he had struck a chord in her. He thought he saw it in the rapt expression on her face.

"Anyway," he said, and smiled at her.

"McRae?" she said.

"Yeah?"

"Can you pull over?"

"Well," he said, his voice shaking, "why don't we wait until it runs out of gas?"

She was silent.

"We'll be that much farther down the road," he said.

"I don't really want a gang," she said. "I don't like dealing with other people that much. I mean, I don't think I'm a leader."

"Oh, yes," McRae said. "No—you're a leader. You're definitely a leader. I was in the Air Force and I know leaders, and you are definitely what I'd call a leader."

"Really?"

"Absolutely. You are leadership material all the way."

"I wouldn't have thought so."

"Definitely," he said. "Definitely a leader."

"But I don't really like people around, you know."

"That's a leadership quality. Not wanting people around. It is definitely a leadership quality."

"Boy," she said, "the things you learn."

He waited. If he could only think himself through to the way out. If he could get her to trust him, get the car stopped—be there when she turned her back.

"You want to be in my gang, huh?"

"I sure do," he said.

"Well, I guess I'll have to think about it."

"I'm surprised nobody's mentioned it to you before."

"You're just saying that."

"No, really."

"Were you ever married?" she asked.

"Married?" he said, and then stammered over the answer. "Ah—uh, no."

"You ever been in a gang before?"

"A couple times, but—they never had good leadership."

"You're giving me a line, huh."

"No," he said, "it's true. No good leadership. It was always a problem."

"I'm tired," she said, shifting toward him a little. "I'm tired of talking."

The steering wheel was hurting the insides of his hands. He held tight, looking at the coming-on of the white stripes in the road. There were no other cars now, and not a glimmer of light anywhere beyond the headlights.

"Don't you ever get tired of talking?"

"I never was much of a talker," he said.

"I guess I don't mind talking as much as I mind listening," she said.

He made a sound in his throat which he hoped she took for agreement.

"That's just when I'm tired, though."

"Why don't you take a nap?" he said.

She leaned back against the door and regarded him. "There's plenty of time for that later."

"So," he wanted to say, "you're not going to kill me—we're a gang?"

They had gone for a long time without speaking, an excruciating hour of minutes, during which the gas gauge had sunk to just above empty, and finally she had begun talking about herself, mostly in the third person. It was hard to make sense of most of it, yet he listened as if to instructions concerning how to extricate himself. She talked about growing up in Florida, in the country, and owning a horse; she remembered when she was taught to swim by somebody she called Bill, as if McRae would know who that was; and then she told him how when her father ran away with her mother's sister, her mother started having men friends over all the time. "There was a lot of obscene things going on," she said, and her voice tightened a little.

"Some people don't care what happens to their kids," McRae said.

"Isn't it the truth?" she said. Then she took the pistol out of the shawl. "Take this exit."

He pulled onto the ramp and up an incline to a two-lane road that went off through the desert, toward a glow that burned on the horizon. For perhaps five miles the road was straight as a plumb line, and then it curved into long, low undulations of sand and mesquite and cactus.

"My mother's men friends used to do whatever they wanted to me," she said. "It went on all the time. All sorts of obscene goings-on."

McRae said, "I'm sorry that happened to you, Belle." And for an instant he was surprised by the sincerity of his feeling: it was as if he couldn't feel sorry enough. Yet it was genuine: it had to do with his own unhappy story. The whole world seemed very, very sad to him. "I'm really very sorry," he said.

She was quiet a moment, as if thinking about this. Then she said, "Let's pull over now. I'm tired of riding."

"It's almost out of gas," he said.

"I know, but pull it over anyway."

"You sure you want to do that?"

"See?" she said. "That's what I mean—I wouldn't like being told what I should do all the time, or asked if I was sure of what I wanted or not."

He pulled the car over and slowed to a stop. "You're right," he said. "See? Leadership. I'm just not used to somebody with leadership qualities."

She held the gun a little toward him. He was looking at the small, dark, perfect circle at the end of the barrel. "I guess we should get out," she said.

"I guess so," he said.

"Do you have any relatives left anywhere?"

"No."

"Your folks are both dead?"

"Right, yes."

"Which one died first?"

"I told you," he said. "Didn't I? My mother, my mother died first."

"Do you feel like an orphan?"

He sighed. "Sometimes." The whole thing was slipping away from him.

"I guess I do too." She reached back and opened her door. "Let's get out now."

And when he reached for the door handle, she aimed the gun at his head. "Get out slow."

"Aw, Jesus," he said. "Look, you're not going to do this, are you? I mean, I thought we were friends and all."

"Just get out real slow, like I said to."

"Okay," he said. "I'm getting out." He opened his door, and the ceiling light surprised and frightened him. Some wordless part of him understood that this was it, and all his talk had come to nothing: all the questions she had asked him, and everything he had told her—it was all completely useless. This was going to happen to him, and it wouldn't mean anything; it would just be what happened.

"Real slow," she said. "Come on."

"Why are you doing this?" he asked. "You've got to tell me that before you do it."

"Will you please get out of the car now?"

He just stared at her.

"All right, I'll shoot you where you sit."

"Okay," he said. "Don't shoot."

She said in an irritable voice, as though she were talking to a recalcitrant child, "You're just putting it off."

He was backing himself out, keeping his eyes on the little barrel of the gun, and he could hear something coming, seemed to notice it in the same instant that she said, "Wait." He stood half in and half out of the car, doing as she said, and a truck came over the hill ahead of them, a tractor trailer, all white light and roaring.

"Stay still," she said, crouching, aiming the gun at him.

The truck came fast, was only fifty yards away, and without having to decide about it, without even knowing that he would do it, McRae bolted into the road. He was running; he heard the exhausted sound of his own breath, the truck horn blaring, coming on, louder, the thing bearing down on him, something buzzing past his head. Time slowed. His legs faltered under him, were heavy, all the nerves gone out of them. In the light of the oncoming truck he saw his own white hands outstretched as if to grasp something in the air before him, and then the truck was past him, the blast of air from it propelling him over the side of the road and down an embankment, in high, dry grass, which pricked his skin and crackled like hay.

He was alive. He lay very still. Above him was the long shape of the road, curving off in the distance, the light of the truck going on. The noise faded and was nothing. A little wind stirred. He heard the car door close. Carefully he got to all fours and crawled a few yards away from where he had fallen. He couldn't be sure of which direction—he only knew he couldn't stay where he was. Then he heard what he thought were her footsteps in the road, and he froze. He lay on his side, facing the embankment. When she appeared there he almost cried out.

"McRae?" she said. "Did I get you?" She was looking right at where he was in the dark, and he stopped breathing. "McRae?"

He watched her move along the edge of the embankment.

"McRae?" She put one hand over her eyes and stared at a place a few feet over from him, and then she turned and went back out of sight. He heard the car door again, and again he began to crawl farther away. The ground was cold and rough, sandy.

He heard her put the key in the trunk. He stood up, tried to run, but something went wrong in his leg, something sent him sprawling, and a sound came out of him that seemed to echo, to stay on the air, as if to call her to him. He tried to be perfectly still, tried not to breathe, hearing now the small pop of the gun. He counted the reports: one, two, three. She was standing there at the edge of the road, firing into the dark, toward where she must have thought she heard the sound. Then she was rattling the paper bag. She was reloading—he could hear the click of the gun. He tried to get up and couldn't. He had sprained his ankle, had done something very bad to it. Now he was crawling wildly, blindly, through the tall grass, hearing again the small report of the pistol. At last he rolled into a shallow gully. He lay there with his face down, breathing the dust, his own voice leaving him in a whimpering, animal-like sound that he couldn't stop, even as he held both shaking hands over his mouth.

"McRae?" She sounded so close. "Hey," she said. "McRae?"

He didn't move. He lay there perfectly still, trying to stop himself from crying. He was sorry for everything he had ever done. He didn't care about the money, or the car, or going out west, or anything. When he lifted his head to peer over the lip of the gully and saw that she had started down the embankment with his flashlight, moving like someone with time and the patience to use it, he lost his sense of himself as McRae; he was just something crippled and breathing in the dark, lying flat in a little winding gully of weeds and sand. McRae was gone, was someone far, far away, from ages ago—a man fresh out of prison, with the whole country to wander in and insurance money in his pocket, who had headed west with the idea that maybe his luck, at long last, had changed.

RICHARD BAUSCH

What Feels Like the World

Very early in the morning, too early, he hears her trying to jump rope out on the sidewalk below his bedroom window. He wakes to the sound of her shoes on the concrete, her breathless counting as she jumps—never more than three times in succession—and fails again to find the right rhythm, the proper spring in her legs to achieve the thing, to be a girl jumping rope. He gets up and moves to the window and, parting the curtain only slightly, peers out at her. For some reason he feels he must be stealthy, must not let her see him gazing at her from this window. He thinks of the heartless way children tease the imperfect among them, and then he closes the curtain.

She is his only granddaughter, the unfortunate inheritor of his big-boned genes, his tendency toward bulk, and she is on a self-induced program of exercise and dieting, to lose weight. This is in preparation for the last meeting of the PTA, during which children from the fifth and sixth grades will put on a gymnastics demonstration. There will be a vaulting horse and a mini-trampoline, and everyone is to participate. She wants to be able to do at least as well as the other children in her class, and so she has been trying exercises to improve her coordination and lose the weight that keeps her rooted to the ground. For the past two weeks she has been eating only one meal a day, usually lunch, since that's the meal she eats at school, and swallowing cans of juice at other mealtimes. He's afraid of anorexia but trusts her calm determination to get ready for the event. There seems no desperation, none of the classic symptoms of the disease. Indeed, this project she's set for herself seems quite sane: to lose ten pounds, and to be able to get over the vaulting horse—in fact, she hopes that she'll be able to do a handstand on it and, curling her head and shoulders, flip over to stand upright on the other side. This, she has told him, is the outside hope. And in two weeks of very grown-up discipline and single-minded effort, that hope has mostly disappeared; she's still the only child in the fifth grade who has not even been able to propel herself over the horse, and this is the day of the event. She will have one last chance to practice at school today, and so she's up this early, out on the lawn, straining, pushing herself.

He dresses quickly and heads downstairs. The ritual in the mornings is simplified by the fact that neither of them is eating breakfast. He makes the orange juice, puts vitamins on a saucer for them both. When he glances out the living-room window, he sees that she is now doing somersaults in the dewy grass. She does three of them while he watches, and he isn't stealthy this time but stands in the window with what he hopes is an approving, unworried look on his face. After each somersault she pulls her sweat shirt down, takes a deep breath, and begins again, the arms coming down slowly, the head ducking slowly under; it's as if she falls on her back, sits up, and then stands up. Her cheeks are ruddy with effort. The moistness of the grass is on the sweat suit, and in the ends of her hair. It will rain this morning—there's thunder beyond the trees at the end of the street. He taps on the window, gestures, smiling, for her to come in. She waves at him, indicates that she wants him to watch her, so he watches her. He applauds when she's finished—three hard, slow tumbles. She claps her hands together as if to remove dust from them and comes trotting to the door. As she moves by him, he tells her she's asking for a bad cold, letting herself get wet so early in the morning. It's his place to nag. Her glance at him acknowledges this.

"I can't get the rest of me to follow my head," she says about the somersaults.

They go into the kitchen, and she sits down, pops a vitamin into her mouth, and takes a swallow of the orange juice. "I guess I'm not going to make it over that vaulting horse after all," she says suddenly.

"Sure you will."

"I don't care." She seems to pout. This is the first sign of true discouragement she's shown.

He's been waiting for it. "Brenda—honey, sometimes people aren't good at these things. I mean, I was never any good at it."

"I bet you were," she says. "I bet you're just saying that to make me feel better."

"No," he says, "really."

He's been keeping to the diet with her, though there have been times during the day when he's cheated. He no longer has a job, and the days are long; he's hungry all the time. He pretends to her that he's still going on to work in the mornings after he walks her to school, because he wants to keep her sense of the daily balance of things, of a predictable and orderly routine, intact. He believes this is the best way to deal with grief—simply to go on with things, to keep them as much as possible as they have always been. Being out of work doesn't worry him, really: he has enough money in savings to last awhile. At sixty-one, he's almost eligible for Social Security, and he gets monthly checks from the girl's father, who lives with another woman, and other children, in Oregon. The father has been very good about keeping up the payments, though he never visits or calls. Probably he thinks the money buys him the privilege of remaining aloof, now that Brenda's mother is gone. Brenda's mother used to say he was the type of man who learned early that there was nothing of substance anywhere in his soul, and spent the rest of his life trying to hide this fact from himself. No one was more upright, she would say, no one more honorable, and God help you if you ever had to live with him. Brenda's father was the subject of bitter sarcasm and scorn. And yet, perhaps not so surprisingly, Brenda's mother would call him in those months just after the divorce, when Brenda was still only a toddler, and she would try to get the baby to say things to him over the phone. And she would sit there with Brenda on her lap and cry after she had hung up.

"I had a doughnut yesterday at school," Brenda says now.

"That's lunch. You're supposed to eat lunch."

"I had spaghetti, too. And three pieces of garlic bread. And pie. And a big salad."

"What's one doughnut?"

"Well, and I didn't eat anything the rest of the day."

"I know," her grandfather says. "See?"

They sit quiet for a little while. Sometimes they're shy with each other—more so lately. They're used to the absence of her mother by now—it's been almost a year—but they still find themselves missing a beat now and then, like a heart with a valve almost closed. She swallows the last of her juice and then gets up and moves to the living room, to stand gazing out at the yard. Big drops have begun to fall. It's a storm, with rising wind and, now, very loud thunder. Lightning branches across the sky, and the trees in the yard disappear in sheets of rain. He has come to her side, and he pretends an interest in the details of the weather, remarking on the heaviness of the rain, the strength of the wind. "Some storm," he says finally. "I'm glad we're not out in it." He wishes he could tell what she's thinking, where the pain is; he wishes he could be certain of the harmlessness of his every word. "Honey," he ventures, "we could play hooky today. If you want to."

"Don't you think I can do it?" she says.

"I know you can."

She stares at him a moment and then looks away, out at the storm.

"It's terrible out there, isn't it?" he says. "Look at that lightning."

"You don't think I can do it," she says.

"No. I know you can. Really."

"Well, I probably can't."

"Even if you can't. Lots of people—lots of people never do anything like that."

"I'm the only one who can't that *I* know."

"Well, there's lots of people. The whole thing is silly, Brenda. A year from now it won't mean anything at all—you'll see."

She says nothing.

"Is there some pressure at school to do it?"

"No." Her tone is simple, matter-of-fact, and she looks directly at him.

"You're sure."

She's sure. And of course, he realizes, there *is* pressure; there's the pressure of being one among other children, and being the only one among them who can't do a thing.

"Honey," he says lamely, "it's not that important." When she looks at him this time, he sees something scarily unchildlike in her expression, some perplexity that she seems to pull down into herself. "It is too important," she says.

He drives her to school. The rain is still being blown along the street and above the low roofs of the houses. By the time they arrive, no more than five minutes from the house, it has begun to let up.

"If it's completely stopped after school," she says, "can we walk home?"

"Of course," he says. "Why wouldn't we?"

She gives him a quick wet kiss on the cheek. "Bye, Pops."

He knows she doesn't like it when he waits for her to get inside, and still he hesitates. There's always the apprehension that he'll look away or drive off just as she thinks of something she needs from him, or that she'll wave to him and he won't see her. So he sits here with the car engine idling, and she walks quickly up the sidewalk and into the building. In the few seconds before the door swings shut, she turns and gives him a wave, and he waves back. The door is closed now. Slowly he lets the car glide forward, still watching the door. Then he's down the driveway, and he heads back to the house.

It's hard to decide what to do with his time. Mostly he stays in the house, watches television, reads the newspapers. There are household tasks, but he can't do anything she might notice, since he's supposed to be at work during these hours. Sometimes, just to please himself, he drives over to the bank and visits with his old co-workers, though there doesn't seem to be much to talk about anymore and he senses that he makes them all uneasy. Today he lies down on the sofa in the living room and rests awhile. At the windows the sun begins to show, and he thinks of driving into town, perhaps stopping somewhere to eat a light breakfast. He accuses himself with the thought and then gets up and turns on the television. There isn't anything of interest to watch, but he watches anyway. The sun is bright now out on the lawn, and the wind is the same, gusting and shaking the window frames. On television he sees feasts of incredible sumptuousness, almost nauseating in the impossible brightness and succulence of the food: advertisements from cheese companies, dairy associations, the makers of cookies and pizza, the sellers of seafood and steaks. He's angry with himself for wanting to cheat on the diet. He thinks of Brenda at school, thinks of crowds of children, and it comes to him more painfully than ever that he can't protect her. Not any more than he could ever protect her mother.

He goes outside and walks up the drying sidewalk to the end of the block. The sun has already dried most of the morning's rain, and the wind is warm. In the sky are great stormy Matterhorns of cumulus and wide patches of the deepest blue. It's a beautiful day, and he decides to walk over to the school. Nothing in him voices this decision; he simply begins to walk. He knows without having to think about it that he can't allow her to see him, yet he feels compelled to take the risk that she might; he feels a helpless wish to watch over her, and, beyond this, he entertains the vague notion that by seeing her in her world he might be better able to be what she needs in his.

So he walks the four blocks to the school and stands just beyond the playground, in a group of shading maples that whisper and sigh in the wind. The playground is empty. A bell rings somewhere in the building, but no one comes out. It's not even eleven o'clock in the morning. He's too late for morning recess and too early for the afternoon one. He feels as though she watches him make his way back down the street.

His neighbor, Mrs. Eberhard, comes over for lunch. It's a thing they planned, and he's forgotten about it. She knocks on the door, and when he opens it she smiles and says, "I knew you'd forget." She's on a diet too, and is carrying what they'll eat: two apples, some celery and carrots. It's all in a clear plastic bag, and she holds it toward him in the palms of her hands as though it were piping hot from an oven. Jane Eberhard is relatively new in the neighborhood. When Brenda's mother died, Jane offered to cook meals and regulate things, and for a while she was like another member of the family. She's moved into their lives now, and sometimes they all forget the circumstances under which the friendship began. She's a solid, large-hipped woman of fifty-eight, with clear, young blue eyes and gray hair. The thing she's good at is sympathy; there's something oddly unspecific about it, as if it were a beam she simply radiates.

"You look so worried," she says now, "I think you should be proud of her."

They're sitting in the living room, with the plastic bag on the coffee table before them. She's eating a stick of celery.

"I've never seen a child that age put such demands on herself," she says.

"I don't know what it's going to do to her if she doesn't make it over the damn thing," he says.

"It'll disappoint her. But she'll get over it."

"I don't guess you can make it tonight."

"Can't," she says. "Really. I promised my mother I'd take her to the ocean this weekend. I have to go pick her up tonight."

"I walked over to the school a little while ago."

"Are you sure you're not putting more into this than she is?"

"She was up at dawn this morning, Jane. Didn't you see her?"

Mrs. Eberhard nods. "I saw her."

"Well?" he says.

She pats his wrist. "I'm sure it won't matter a month from now."

"No," he says, "that's not true. I mean, I wish I could believe you. But I've never seen a kid work so hard."

"Maybe she'll make it."

"Yes," he says. "Maybe."

Mrs. Eberhard sits considering for a moment, tapping the stick of celery against her lower lip. "You think it's tied to the accident in some way, don't you?"

"I don't know," he says, standing, moving across the room. "I can't get through somehow. It's been all this time and I still don't know. She keeps it all to herself—all of it. All I can do is try to be there when she wants me to be there. I don't know—I don't even know what to say to her."

"You're doing all you can do, then."

"Her mother and I . . ." he begins. "She—we never got along that well."

"You can't worry about that now."

Mrs. Eberhard's advice is always the kind of practical good advice that's impossible to follow.

He comes back to the sofa and tries to eat one of the apples, but his appetite is gone. This seems ironic to him. "I'm not hungry now," he says.

"Sometimes worry is the best thing for a diet."

"I've always worried. It never did me any good, but I worried."

"I'll tell you," Mrs. Eberhard says. "It's a terrific misfortune to have to be raised by a human being."

He doesn't feel like listening to this sort of thing, so he asks her about her husband, who is with the government in some capacity that requires him to be both secretive and mobile. He's always off to one country or another, and this week he's in India. It's strange to think of someone traveling as much as he does without getting hurt or killed. Mrs. Eberhard says she's so used to his being gone all the time that next year, when he retires, it'll take a while to get used to having him underfoot. In fact, he's not a very likable man; there's something murky and unpleasant about him. The one time Mrs. Eberhard brought him to visit, he sat in the living room and seemed to regard everyone with detached curiosity, as if they were all specimens on a dish under a lens. Brenda's grandfather had invited some old friends over from the bank—everyone was being careful not to let on that he wasn't still going there every day. It was an awkward two hours, and Mrs. Eberhard's husband sat with his hands folded over his rounded belly, his eyebrows arched. When he spoke, his voice was cultivated and quiet, full of self-satisfaction and haughtiness. They had been speaking in low tones about how Jane Eberhard had moved in to take over after the accident, and Mrs. Eberhard's husband cleared his throat, held his fist gingerly to his mouth, pursed his lips, and began a soft-spoken, lecture-like monologue about his belief that there's no such thing as an accident. His considered opinion was that there are subconscious explanations for everything. Apparently, he thought he was entertaining everyone. He sat with one leg crossed over the other and held forth in his calm, magisterial voice, explaining how everything can be reduced to a matter of conscious or subconscious will. Finally his wife asked him to let it alone, please, drop the subject.

"For example," he went on, "there are many collisions on the highway in which no one appears to have applied brakes before impact, as if something in the victims had decided on death. And of course there are the well-known cases of people stopped on railroad tracks, with plenty of time to get off, who simply do not move. Perhaps it isn't being frozen by the perception of one's fate but a matter of decision making, of will. The victim decides on his fate."

"I think we've had enough, now," Jane Eberhard said.

The inappropriateness of what he had said seemed to dawn on him then. He shifted in his seat and grew very quiet, and when the evening was over he took Brenda's grandfather by the elbow and apologized. But even in the apology there seemed to be a species of condescension, as if he were really only sorry for the harsh truth of what he had wrongly deemed it necessary to say. When everyone was gone, Brenda said, "I don't like that man."

"Is it because of what he said about accidents?" her grandfather asked.

She shook her head. "I just don't like him."

"It's not true, what he said, honey. An accident is an accident."

She said, "I know." But she would not return his gaze.

"Your mother wasn't very happy here, but she didn't want to leave us. Not even—you know, without . . . without knowing it or anything."

"He wears perfume," she said, still not looking at him.

"It's cologne. Yes, he does—too much of it."

"It smells," she said.

In the afternoon he walks over to the school. The sidewalks are crowded with children, and they all seem to recognize him. They carry their books and papers and their hair is windblown and they run and wrestle with each other in the yards. The sun's high and very hot, and most of the clouds have broken apart and scattered. There's still a fairly steady wind, but it's gentler now, and there's no coolness in it.

Brenda is standing at the first crossing street down the hill from the school. She's surrounded by other children yet seems separate from them somehow. She sees him and smiles. He waits on his side of the intersection for her to cross, and when she reaches him he's careful not to show any obvious affection, knowing it embarrasses her.

"How was your day?" he begins.

"Mr. Clayton tried to make me quit today."

He waits.

"I didn't get over," she says. "I didn't even get close."

"What did Mr. Clayton say?"

"Oh—you know. That it's not important. That kind of stuff."

"Well," he says gently, "*is* it so important?"

"I don't know." She kicks at something in the grass along the edge of the sidewalk—a piece of a pencil someone else had discarded. She bends, picks it up, examines it, and then drops it. This is exactly the kind of slow, daydreaming behavior that used to make him angry and impatient with her mother. They walk on. She's concentrating on the sidewalk before them, and they walk almost in step.

"I'm sure I could never do a thing like going over a vaulting horse when I was in school," he says.

"Did they have that when you were in school?"

He smiles. "It was hard getting everything into the caves. But sure, we had that sort of thing. We were an advanced tribe. We had fire, too."

"Okay," she's saying, "okay, okay."

"Actually, with me, it was pull-ups. We all had to do pull-ups. And I just couldn't do them. I don't think I ever accomplished a single one in my life."

"I can't do pull-ups," she says.

"They're hard to do."

"Everybody in the fifth and sixth grades can get over the vaulting horse," she says.

How much she reminds him of her mother. There's a certain mobility in her face, a certain willingness to assert herself in the smallest gesture of the eyes and mouth. She has her mother's green eyes, and now he tells her this. He's decided to try this. He's standing, quite shy, in her doorway, feeling like an intruder. She's sitting on the floor, one leg outstretched, the other bent at the knee. She tries to touch her forehead to the knee of the outstretched leg, straining, and he looks away.

"You know?" he says. "They're just the same color—just that shade of green."

"What was my grandmother like?" she asks, still straining.

"She was a lot like your mother."

"I'm never going to get married."

"Of course you will. Well, I mean—if you want to, you will."

"How come you didn't ever get married again?"

"Oh," he says, "I had a daughter to raise, you know."

She changes position, tries to touch her forehead to the other knee.

"I'll tell you, that mother of yours was enough to keep me busy. I mean, I called her double trouble, you know, because I always said she was double the trouble a son would have been. That was a regular joke around here."

"Mom was skinny and pretty."

He says nothing.

"Am I double trouble?"

"No," he says.

"Is that really why you never got married again?"

"Well, no one would have me, either."

"Mom said you liked it."

"Liked what?"

"Being a widow."

"Yes, well," he says.

"Did you?"

"All these questions," he says.

"Do you think about Grandmom a lot?"

"Yes," he says. "That's—you know, we remember our loved ones."

She stands and tries to touch her toes without bending her legs. "Sometimes I dream that Mom's yelling at you and you're yelling back."

"Oh, well," he says, hearing himself say it, feeling himself back down from something. "That's—that's just a dream. You know, it's nothing to think about at all. People who love each other don't agree sometimes—it's—it's nothing. And I'll bet these exercises are going to do the trick."

"I'm very smart, aren't I?"

He feels sick, very deep down. "You're the smartest little girl I ever saw."

"You don't have to come tonight if you don't want to," she says. "You can drop me off if you want, and come get me when it's over."

"Why would I do that?"

She mutters. "*I* would."

"Then why don't we skip it?"

"Lot of good *that* would do," she says.

For dinner they drink apple juice, and he gets her to eat two slices of dry toast. The apple juice is for energy. She drinks it slowly and then goes into her room to lie down, to conserve her strength. She uses the word *conserve,* and he tells her he's so proud of her vocabulary. She thanks him. While she rests, he does a few household chores, trying really just to keep busy. The week's newspapers have been piling up on the coffee table in the living room, the carpets need to be vacuumed, and the whole house needs dusting. None of it takes long enough; none of it quite distracts him. For a while he sits in the living room with a newspaper in his lap and pretends to be reading it. She's restless too. She comes back through to the kitchen, drinks another glass of apple juice, and then joins him in the living room, turns the television on. The news is full of traffic deaths, and she turns to one of the local stations that shows reruns of old situation comedies. They both watch *M*A*S*H* without really taking it in. She bites the cuticles of her nails, and her gaze wanders around the room. It comes to him that he could speak to her now, could make his way through to her grief—and yet he knows that he will do no such thing; he can't even bring himself to speak at all. There are regions of his own sorrow that he simply lacks the strength to explore, and so he sits there watching her restlessness, and at last it's time to go over to the school. Jane Eberhard makes a surprise visit, bearing a handsome good-luck card she's fashioned herself. She kisses Brenda, behaves exactly as if Brenda were going off to some dangerous, faraway place. She stands in the street and waves at them as they pull away, and Brenda leans out the window to shout goodbye. A moment later, sitting back and staring out at the dusky light, she says she feels a surge of energy, and he tells her she's way ahead of all the others in her class, knowing words like *conserve* and *surge.*

"I've always known them," she says.

It's beginning to rain again. Clouds have been rolling in from the east, and the wind shakes the trees. Lightning flickers on the other side of the clouds. Everything seems threatening, relentless. He slows down. There are many cars parked along both sides of the street. "Quite a turnout," he manages.

"Don't worry," she tells him brightly. "I still feel my surge of energy."

It begins to rain as they get out of the car, and he holds his sport coat like a cape to shield her from it. By the time they get to the open front doors, it's raining very hard. People are crowding into the cafeteria, which has been transformed into an arena for the event—chairs set up on four sides of the room as though for a wrestling match. In the center, at the end of the long, bright-red mat, are the vaulting horse and the mini-trampoline. The physical-education teacher, Mr. Clayton, stands at the entrance. He's tall, thin, scraggly-looking, a boy really, no older than twenty-five.

"There's Mr. Clayton," Brenda says.

"I see him."

"Hello, Mr. Clayton."

Mr. Clayton is quite distracted, and he nods quickly, leans toward Brenda, and points to a doorway across the hall. "Go on ahead," he says. Then he nods at her grandfather.

"This is it," Brenda says.

Her grandfather squeezes her shoulder, means to find the best thing to tell her, but in the next confusing minute he's lost her, she's gone among the others and he's being swept along with the crowd entering the cafeteria. He makes his way along the walls behind the chairs, where a few other people have already gathered and are standing. At the other end of the room a man is speaking from a lectern about old business, new officers for the fall. Brenda's grandfather recognizes some of the people in the crowd. A woman looks at him and nods, a familiar face he can't quite place. She turns to look at the speaker. She's holding a baby, and the baby's staring at him over her shoulder. A moment later, she steps back to stand beside him, hefting the baby higher and patting its bottom.

"What a crowd," she says.

He nods.

"It's not usually this crowded."

Again, he nods.

The baby protests, and he touches the miniature fingers of one hand—just a baby, he thinks, and everything still to go through.

"How is—um . . . Brenda?" she says.

"Oh," he says, "fine." And he remembers that she was Brenda's kindergarten teacher. She's heavier than she was then, and her hair is darker. She has a baby now.

"I don't remember all my students," she says, shifting the baby to the other shoulder. "I've been home now for eighteen months, and I'll tell you, it's being at the PTA meeting that makes me see how much I *don't* miss teaching."

He smiles at her and nods again. He's beginning to feel awkward. The man is still speaking from the lectern, a meeting is going on, and this woman's voice is carrying beyond them, though she says everything out of the side of her mouth.

"I remember the way you used to walk Brenda to school every morning. Do you still walk her to school?"

"Yes."

"That's so nice."

He pretends an interest in what the speaker is saying.

"I always thought it was so nice to see how you two got along together—I mean these days it's really rare for the kids even to know who their grandparents *are,* much less have one to walk them to school in the morning. I always thought it was really something." She seems to watch the lectern for a moment, and then speaks to him again, this time in a near whisper. "I hope you won't take this the wrong way or anything, but I just wanted to say how sorry I was about your daughter. I saw it in the paper when Brenda's mother. . . . Well. You know, I just wanted to tell you how sorry.

When I saw it in the paper, I thought of Brenda, and how you used to walk her to school. I lost my sister in an automobile accident, so I know how you feel—it's a terrible thing. Terrible. An awful thing to have happen. I mean it's much too sudden and final and everything. I'm afraid now every time I get into a car." She pauses, pats the baby's back, then takes something off its ear. "Anyway, I just wanted to say how sorry I was."

"You're very kind," he says.

"It seems so senseless," she murmurs. "There's something so senseless about it when it happens. My sister went through a stop sign. She just didn't see it, I guess. But it wasn't a busy road or anything. If she'd come along one second later or sooner nothing would've happened. So senseless. Two people driving two different cars coming along on two roads on a sunny afternoon and they come together like that. I mean—what're the chances, really?"

He doesn't say anything.

"How's Brenda handling it?"

"She's strong," he says.

"I would've said that," the woman tells him. "Sometimes I think the children take these things better than the adults do. I remember when she first came to my class. She told everyone in the first minute that she'd come from Oregon. That she was living with her grandfather, and her mother was divorced.

"She was a baby when the divorce—when she moved here from Oregon."

This seems to surprise the woman. "Really," she says, low. "I got the impression it was recent for her. I mean, you know, that she had just come from it all. It was all very vivid for her, I remember that."

"She was a baby," he says. It's almost as if he were insisting on it. He's heard this in his voice, and he wonders if she has, too.

"Well," she says, "I always had a special place for Brenda. I always thought she was very special. A very special little girl."

The PTA meeting is over, and Mr. Clayton is now standing at the far door with the first of his charges. They're all lining up outside the door, and Mr. Clayton walks to the microphone to announce the program. The demonstration will commence with the mini-trampoline and the vaulting horse: a performance by the fifth- and sixth-graders. There will also be a break dancing demonstration by the fourth-grade class.

"Here we go," the woman says. "My nephew's afraid of the mini-tramp."

"They shouldn't make them do these things," Brenda's grandfather says, with a passion that surprises him. He draws in a breath. "It's too hard," he says, loudly. He can't believe himself. "They shouldn't have to go through a thing like this."

"I don't know," she says vaguely, turning from him a little. He has drawn attention to himself. Others in the crowd are regarding him now—one, a man with a sparse red beard and wild red hair, looking at him with something he takes for agreement.

"It's too much," he says, still louder. "Too much to put on a child. There's just so much a child can take."

Someone asks gently for quiet.

The first child is running down the long mat to the mini-trampoline; it's a girl, and she times her jump perfectly, soars over the horse. One by one, other children follow. Mr. Clayton and another man stand on either side of the horse and help those who go over on their hands. Two or three go over without any assistance at all, with remarkable effortlessness and grace.

"Well," Brenda's kindergarden teacher says, "there's my nephew."

The boy hits the mini-tramp and does a perfect forward flip in the air over the horse, landing upright and then rolling forward in a somersault.

"Yea, Jack!" she cheers. "No sweat! Yea, Jackie boy!"

The boy trots to the other end of the room and stands with the others; the crowd is applauding. The last of the sixth-graders goes over the horse, and Mr. Clayton says into the microphone that the fifth-graders are next. It's Brenda who's next. She stands in the doorway, her cheeks flushed, her legs looking too heavy in the tights. She's rocking back and forth on the balls of her feet, getting ready. It grows quiet. Her arms swing slightly, back and forth, and now, just for a moment, she's looking at the crowd, her face hiding whatever she's feeling. It's as if she were merely curious as to who is out there, but he knows she's looking for him, searching the crowd for her grandfather, who stands on his toes, unseen against the far wall, stands there thinking his heart might break, lifting his hand to wave.

RICHARD BAUSCH

Tandolfo the Great

"Tandolfo," he says to his own image in the mirror over the bathroom sink. "She loves you not, you goddam fool."

He's put the makeup on, packed the bag of tricks—including the rabbit, whom he calls Chi-Chi; and the bird, the attention-getter, which he calls Witch. He's to do a birthday party on the other side of the river. Some five-year-old, and so this is going to be one of those tough ones, a crowd of babies, and all the adults waiting around for him to screw up.

He has fortified himself with something, and he feels ready. He isn't particularly worried about it. But there's a little something else he has to do, first. Something on the order of the embarrassingly ridiculous: he has to make a small delivery.

This morning, at the local bakery, he picked up a big pink wedding cake, with its six tiers and its scalloped edges and its little bride and groom on top. He'd ordered it on his own; he'd taken the initiative, planning to offer it to a young woman of his acquaintance. He managed somehow to set the thing on the backseat of the car and when he got home he found a note from her announcing, all excited and happy, that she's engaged. The man she'd had such trouble with has had a change of heart; he wants to get married after all. She's going to Houston to live. She loves her dear old Tandolfo with a big kiss and a hug always, and she knows he'll have every happiness. She's so thankful for his friendship. Her magic man. He's her sweet clown. She has actually driven over here and, finding him gone, left the note for him, folded under the door knocker—her pink notepaper, with the little tangle of flowers at the top. She wants him to call her, come by as soon as he can to help celebrate. *Please,* she says. *I want to give you a big hug.* He read this and then walked out to stand on the sidewalk and look at the cake in its place on the backseat of the car.

"Good God," he said. He'd thought he would put the clown outfit on, deliver the cake in person in the evening; an elaborate proposal to a girl he's never even kissed. He's a little unbalanced, and he knows it. Over the months of their working together for the county government, he's built up tremendous feelings of loyalty and yearning toward her. He thought she felt something, too. He interpreted gestures—her hand lingering on his shoulder when he made her laugh; her endearments to him, tinged as they seemed to be with a kind of sadness, as if she were afraid for what the world might do to someone so romantic.

"You sweet clown," she said. And she said it a lot. And she talked to him about her ongoing trouble, the guy she'd been in love with who kept waffling about getting married. He wanted no commitments. Tandolfo, aka Rodney Wilbury, told her that he hated men who weren't willing to run the risks of love. Why, he personally was the type who'd always believed in marriage and children, lifelong commitments. He had caused difficulties for himself and life was a disappointment so far, but he believed in falling in love and starting a family. She didn't hear him. It all went right through her like white noise on the radio. For weeks he had come around to visit her, had invited her to watch him perform. She confided in him, and he thought of movies where the friend sticks around and is a good listener, and eventually gets the girl. They fall in love. He put his hope in that. He was optimistic; he'd ordered and bought the cake. Apparently the whole time, all through the listening and being noble with her, she thought of it as nothing more than friendship, accepting it from him because she was accustomed to being offered friendship.

Now he leans close to the mirror to look at his own eyes through the makeup. They look clear enough. "Loves you absolutely not. You must be crazy. You must be the great Tandolfo."

Yes.

Twenty-six-year-old, out-of-luck Tandolfo. In love. With a great oversized cake in the backseat of his car. It's Sunday, a cool April day. He's a little inebriated. That's the word he prefers. It's polite; it suggests something faintly silly. Nothing could be sillier than to be dressed like this in the broad daylight, and to go driving across the bridge into Virginia to put on a magic show. Nothing could be sillier than to have spent all that money on a completely useless purchase—a cake six tiers high. Maybe fifteen pounds of sugar.

When he has made his last check of the clown face in the mirror, and the bag of tricks and props, he goes to his front door and stands at the screen looking out at the architectural shadow of it in the backseat. The inside of the car will smell like icing for days. He'll have to keep the windows open even if it rains; he'll go to work smelling like confectionery delights. The whole thing makes him laugh. A wedding cake. He steps out of the house and makes his way in the late-afternoon sun down the sidewalk to the car. As if they have been waiting for him, three boys come skating down from the top of the hill. He has the feeling that if he tried to sneak out like this at two in the morning, someone would come by and see him anyway. "Hey, Rodney," one boy says. "I mean Tandolfo."

Tandolfo recognizes him. A neighborhood boy, a tough. Just the kind to make trouble, just the kind with no sensitivity to the suffering of others. "Leave me alone or I'll turn you into spaghetti," he says.

"Hey, guys—it's Tandolfo the Great." The boy's hair is a bright blond color, and you can see through it to his scalp.

"Scram," Tandolfo says. "Really."

"Aw, what's your hurry, man?"

"I've just set off a nuclear device," Tandolfo says with grave seriousness. "It's on a timer. Poof."

"Do a trick for us," the blond one says. "Where's that scurvy rabbit of yours?"

"I gave it the week off." Someone, last winter, poisoned the first Chi-Chi. He keeps the cage indoors now. "I'm in a hurry. No rabbit to help with the driving."

But they're interested in the cake now. "Hey, what's that in your car? Is that what I think it is?"

"Just stay back."

"Is that a cake, man? Is that real?"

Tandolfo gets his cases into the trunk, and hurries to the driver's side door. The three boys are peering into the backseat.

"Hey, man. A cake. Can we have a piece of cake?"

"Back off," Tandolfo says.

The white-haired one says, "Come on, Tandolfo."

"Hey, Tandolfo, I saw some guys looking for you, man. They said you owed them money."

He gets in, ignoring them. He starts the car.

"You sucker," one of them says.

"Hey, man. Who's the cake for?"

He drives away, thinks of himself leaving them in a cloud of exhaust. Riding through the green shade, he glances in the rear-view mirror and sees the clown face, the painted smile. It makes him want to laugh. He tells himself he's his own cliché—a clown with a broken heart. Looming behind him is the cake, like a passenger in the backseat.

He drives slow. He has always believed viscerally that gestures mean everything. When he moves his hands and brings about the effects that amaze little children, he feels larger than life, unforgettable. He learned the magic while in high school, as a way of making friends, and though it didn't really make him any friends, he's been practicing it ever since. It's an extra source of income, and lately income has had a way of disappearing too quickly. He's been in some trouble—betting the horses; betting the sports events. He's hungover all the time. There have been several polite warnings at work. He's managed so far to tease everyone out of the serious looks, the cool evaluative study of his face. The fact is, people like him in an abstract way, the way they like distant clownish figures: the comedian whose name they can't remember. He can see it in their eyes. Even the rough characters after his loose change have a certain sense of humor about it. He's a phenomenon, a subject of conversation.

There's traffic on Key Bridge, and he's stuck for a while. It becomes clear that he'll have to go straight to the birthday party. Sitting behind the wheel of the car with his cake on the backseat, he becomes aware of people in other cars noticing him. In the car to his left, a girl stares, chewing gum. She waves, rolls her window down. Two others are with her, one in the backseat. "Hey," she says. He nods. Smiles inside what he knows is the painted smile. His teeth will look dark against the makeup.

"Where's the party?" she says.

But the traffic moves again. He concentrates. The snarl is on the other side of the bridge—construction of some kind. He can see the cars lined up, waiting to go up the hill into Rosslyn and beyond. Time is beginning to be a consideration. In his glove box, he has a flask of bourbon. He reaches over and takes it out, looks around himself. No police anywhere. Just the idling cars and people tuning their radios or arguing or simply staring out as if at some distressing event. The smell of the cake is making him woozy. He takes a swallow of the bourbon, then puts it back. The car with the girls in it goes by him in the left lane, and they are not even looking at him. He watches them go on ahead. He's in the wrong lane again; he can't remember a time when his lane was the only one moving. He told her once that he considered himself in the race of people who gravitate to the nonmoving lanes of highways, and who cause traffic lights to turn yellow by approaching them. She took the idea and carried it out a little—saying she was of the race of people who emitted enzymes which instilled a sense of impending doom in marriageable young men, and made them wary of long-term relationships.

"No," Tandolfo/Rodney said. "I'm living proof that isn't so. I have no such fear, and I'm with you."

"But you're of the race of people who make mine relax all the enzymes."

"You're not emitting the enzymes now, I see."

"No," she said. "It's only with marriageable young men."

"I emit enzymes that prevent people like you from seeing that I'm a marriageable young man."

"I'm too relaxed to tell," she said, and touched his shoulder. A plain affectionate moment that gave him tossing nights and fever.

Because of the traffic, he arrives late at the birthday party. He gets out of the car and two men come down from the house to greet him. He keeps his face turned away, remembering too late the breath mints in his pocket.

"Jesus," one of the men says. "Look at this. Hey—who comes out of the cake? This is a kid's birthday party."

"The cake stays."

"What does he mean, it stays? Is that a trick?"

They're both looking at him. The one spoken to must be the birthday boy's father—he's wearing a party cap that says DAD. He has long dirty-looking strands of blond hair jutting out from the cap, and there are streaks of sweaty grit on the sides of his face. "So you're the Great Tandolfo," he says, extending a meaty red hand. "Isn't it hot in that makeup?"

"No, sir.

"We've been playing volleyball."

"You've exerted yourselves."

They look at him. "What do you do with the cake?" the one in the DAD cap asks.

"Cake's not part of the show, actually."

"You just carry it around with you?"

The other man laughs. He's wearing a T-shirt with a smile face on the chest. "This ought to be some show," he says.

They all make their way across the street and the lawn, to the porch of the house. It's a big party—bunting everywhere and children gathering quickly to see the clown.

"Ladies and gentlemen," says the man in the DAD cap. "I give you Tandolfo the Great."

Tandolfo isn't ready yet. He's got his cases open, but he needs a table to put everything on. The first trick is where he releases the bird. He'll finish with the best trick, in which the rabbit appears as if from a pan of flames: it always draws a gasp, even from the adults; the fire blooms in the pan, down goes the "lid"—it's the rabbit's tight container—the latch is tripped, and the skin of the "lid" lifts off. *Voilà!* Rabbit. The fire is put out by the fireproof cage bottom. He's gotten pretty good at making the switch, and if the crowd isn't too attentive—as children often are not—he can perform certain hand tricks with some style. But he needs a table, and he needs time to set up.

The whole crowd of children is seated in front of the door into the house. He's standing here on the porch, his back to the stairs, and he's been introduced.

"Hello, boys and girls," he says, and bows. "Tandolfo needs a table."

"A table," one of the women says. All the adults are ranged against the porch wall, behind the children. He sees light sweaters, shapely hips, and wild tresses; he sees beer cans in tight fists and heavy jowls, bright ice-blue eyes. A little row of faces, and one elderly face. He feels more inebriated than he likes now, and he tries to concentrate.

"Mommy, I want to touch him," one child says.

"Look at the cake," says another, who's sitting on the railing to Tandolfo's right, with a new pair of shiny binoculars trained on the car. "Do we get some cake?"

"There's cake," says the man in the DAD cap. "But not that cake. Get down, Ethan."

"I want that cake."

"Get down. This is Teddy's birthday."

"Mommy, I want to touch him."

"I need a table, folks. I told somebody that over the telephone."

"He did say he needed a table. I'm sorry," says a woman who is probably the birthday boy's mother. She's quite pretty, leaning in the doorframe with a sweater tied to her waist.

"A table," says another woman. Tandolfo sees the birthmark on her mouth, which looks like a stain. He thinks of this woman as a child in school, with this difference from other children, and his heart goes out to her.

"I need a table," he says to her, his voice as gentle as he can make it.

"What's he going to do, perform an operation?" says DAD.

It amazes Tandolfo how easily people fall into talking about him as though he were an inanimate object, or something on a television screen. "The Great Tandolfo can do nothing until he gets a table," he says, with as much mysteriousness and drama as he can muster under the circumstances.

"I want that cake out there," says Ethan, still perched atop the porch railing. The other children start talking about cake and ice cream, and the big cake Ethan has spotted; there's a lot of confusion, and restlessness. One of the smaller children, a girl in a blue dress, comes forward and stands gazing at Tandolfo. "What's your name?" she says, swaying slightly, her hands behind her. back.

"Go sit down," he says to her. "We have to sit down or Tandolfo can't do his magic."

In the doorway, two of the men are struggling with a folding card table. It's one of those rickety ones with the skinny legs, and it won't do.

"That's kind of rickety, isn't it?" says the woman with the birthmark.

"I said Tandolfo needs a sturdy table, boys and girls."

There's more confusion. The little girl has come forward and taken hold of his pant leg. She's just standing there holding it, looking at him. "We have to go sit down," he says, bending to her, speaking sweetly, clownlike. "We have to do what Tandolfo wants."

Her small mouth opens wide, as if she's trying to yawn, and with pale blue eyes quite calm and staring she emits a screech, an ear-piercing, nonhuman shriek that brings everything to a stop. Tandolfo/Rodney steps back, with his amazement and his inebriate heart, and now everyone's gathering around the girl, who continues to scream, less piercing now, her hands fisted at her sides, those blue eyes closed tight.

"What happened?" the man in the DAD cap wants to know. "Where the hell's the magic tricks?"

"I told you all I needed a *table*."

"Whud you say to her to make her cry?" He indicates the little girl, who is not merely crying but is giving forth a series of broken, grief-stricken howls.

"I want magic tricks," the birthday boy says, loud. "Where's the magic tricks?"

"Perhaps if we moved the whole thing inside," the woman with the birthmark says, fingering her left ear and making a face.

The card table has somehow made its way to Tandolfo, through the confusion and grief. The man in the DAD cap sets it down and opens it.

"There," he says, as if his point is made.

In the next moment, Tandolfo realizes that someone's removed the little girl. Everything's relatively quiet again, though her cries are coming through the walls of one of the rooms inside the house. There are perhaps fifteen children, mostly seated before him; five or six men and women behind them, or kneeling with them. "Okay, now," DAD says. "Tandolfo the Great."

"Hello, little boys and girls," Tandolfo/Rodney says. "I'm happy to be here. Are you glad to see me?" A general uproar goes up. "Well, good," he says. "Because just look what I have in my magic bag." And with a flourish, he brings out the hat from which he will release Witch. The bird is encased inside a fold of shiny cloth, pulsing there. He can feel it. He rambles on, talking fast, or trying to, and when the time comes to reveal the bird, he almost flubs it. But Witch flaps his wings and makes enough of a commotion to distract even the adults, who applaud now, and get the children to applaud. "Isn't that wonderful," Tandolfo hears. "Where did that bird come from?"

"He had it hidden away," says the birthday boy.

"Now," Tandolfo says, "for my next spell, I need a little friend from the audience." He looks right at the birthday boy—round face; short nose; freckles. Bright red hair. Little green eyes. The whole countenance speaks of glutted appetites and sloth. This kid could be on Roman coins, an emperor. He's not used to being compelled to do anything, but he seems eager for a chance to get into the act. "How about you?" Tandolfo says to him.

The others, led by their parents, cheer.

The birthday boy gets to his feet and makes his way over the bodies of the other children to stand with Tandolfo. In order for the trick to work, Tandolfo must get everyone watching the birthday boy, and there's a funny hat he keeps in the bag for this purpose. "Now," he says to the boy, "since you're part of the show, you have to wear a costume." He produces the hat as if from behind the boy's ear. Another cheer goes up. He puts the hat on his head and adjusts it, crouching down. The green eyes stare impassively at him; there's no hint of awe or fascination in them. "There we are," he says. "What a handsome fellow."

But the birthday boy takes the hat off.

"No, no. We have to wear the hat to be onstage."

"Ain't a stage," the boy says.

"Well, but hey," Tandolfo says for the benefit of the adults. "Didn't you know that all the world's a stage?" He tries to put the hat on again, but the boy moves from under his reach and slaps his hand away. "We have to wear the hat," Tandolfo says, trying to control his anger. "We can't do the magic without our magic hats." He tries once more, and the boy waits until the hat is on, then simply removes it and holds it behind him, shying away when Tandolfo tries to retrieve it. The noise of the others now sounds like the crowd at a prizefight; there's a contest going on, and they're enjoying it. "Give Tandolfo the hat now. We want magic, don't we?"

"Do the magic," the boy demands.

"I'll do the magic if you give me the hat."

"I won't."

Nothing. No support from the adults. Perhaps if he weren't a little tipsy, perhaps if he didn't feel ridiculous and sick at heart and forlorn, with his wedding cake and his odd mistaken romance, his loneliness, which he has always borne gracefully and in humor, and his general dismay; perhaps if he were to find it in himself to deny the sudden, overwhelming sense of the unearned affection given this little slovenly version of stupid complacent spoiled satiation standing before him—he might've simply gone on to the next trick.

Instead, he leans down and in the noise of the moment, says to the boy, "Give me the hat, you little prick."

The green eyes widen slightly.

It grows quiet. Even the small children can tell that something's happened to change everything.

"Tandolfo has another trick," Rodney says, "where he makes the birthday boy pop like a balloon. Especially if he's a fat birthday boy."

A stirring among the adults.

"Especially if he's an ugly little slab of flesh like this one here."

"Now just a minute," says DAD.

"Pop," Rodney says to the birthday boy, who drops the hat and then, seeming to remember that defiance is expected, makes a face. Sticks out his tongue. Rodney/Tandolfo is quick with his hands by training, and he grabs the tongue.

"Awk," the boy says. "Aw-aw-aw."

"Abracadabra." Rodney lets go, and the boy falls backward into the lap of one of the older children. "Whoops, time to sit down," says Rodney.

Very quickly, he's being forcibly removed. They're rougher than gangsters. They lift him, punch him, tear at his costume—even the women. Someone hits him with a spoon. The whole scene boils out onto the lawn, where someone has released the case that Chi-Chi was in. Chi-Chi moves about wide-eyed, hopping between running children, evading them, as Tandolfo the Great cannot evade the adults. He's being pummeled, because he keeps trying to return for his rabbit. And the adults won't let him off the curb.

"Okay," he says finally, collecting himself. He wants to let them know he's not like this all the time; wants to say it's circumstances, grief, personal pain hidden inside seeming brightness and cleverness; he's a man in love, humiliated, wrong about everything. He wants to tell them, but he can't speak for a moment, can't even quite catch his breath. He stands in the middle of the street, his funny clothes torn, his face bleeding, all his magic strewn everywhere. "I would at least like to collect my rabbit," he says, and is appalled at the absurd sound of it—its huge difference from what he intended to say. He straightens, pushes the hair out of his eyes, adjusts the clown nose, and looks at them. "I would say that even though I wasn't as patient as I could've been, the adults have not comported themselves well here," he says.

"Drunk," one of the women says.

Almost everyone's chasing Chi-Chi now. One of the older boys approaches him, carrying Witch's case. Witch looks out the air hole, impervious, quiet as an idea. And now one of the men, someone Tandolfo hasn't noticed before, an older man clearly wearing a hairpiece, brings Chi-Chi to him. "Bless you," Rodney says, staring into the man's sleepy, deploring gaze.

"I don't think we'll pay you," the man says. The others are all filing back into the house, herding the children before them.

Rodney speaks to the man. "The rabbit appears out of fire."

The man nods. "Go home and sleep it off, kid."

"Right, thank you."

He puts Chi-Chi in his compartment, stuffs everything in its place in the trunk. Then he gets in and drives away. Around the corner he stops, wipes off what he can of the makeup; it's as if he's trying to remove the grime of bad opinion and disapproval. Nothing feels any different. He drives to the little suburban street where she lives with her parents, and by the time he gets there it's almost dark. The houses are set back in the trees; he sees lighted windows, hears music, the sound of children playing in the yards. He parks the car and gets out. A breezy April dusk.

"I am Tandolfo the soft-hearted," he says. "Hearken to me." Then he sobs. He can't believe it. "Jeez," he says. "Goddam."

He opens the back door of the car, leans in to get the cake. He'd forgotten how heavy it is. Staggering with it, making his way along the sidewalk, intending to leave it on her doorstep, he has an inspiration. Hesitating only for the moment it takes to make sure there are no cars coming, he goes out and sets it down in the middle of the street.

Part of the top sags slightly, from having bumped his shoulder as he pulled it off the backseat of the car. The bride and groom are almost supine, one on top of the other. He straightens them, steps back, and looks at it. In the dusky light, it looks blue. It sags just right, with just the right angle, expressing disappointment and sorrow.

Yes, he thinks. This is the place for it. The aptness of it, sitting out like this, where anyone might come by and splatter it all over creation, actually makes him feel some faint sense of release, as if he were at the end of a story. Everything will be all right if he can think of it that way. He's wiping his eyes, thinking of moving to another town. There are money troubles and troubles at work, and failures beginning to catch up to him, and he's still aching in love. He thinks how he has suffered the pangs of failure and misadventure, but in this painful instance there's symmetry, and he will make the one eloquent gesture—leaving a wedding cake in the middle of the road, like a sugar-icinged pylon. Yes.

He walks back to the car, gets in, pulls it around, and backs into the driveway of the house across the street. Leaving the engine idling, he rolls the window down and rests his arm on the sill, gazing at the incongruous shape of it there in the falling dark. He feels almost glad, almost—in some strange inexpressible way—vindicated, and he imagines what she might do if she saw him here. In a moment he's fantasizing that she comes running from her house, calling his name, looking at the cake and admiring it. This fantasy gives way to something else: images of destruction, flying sugar and candy debris. He's quite surprised to find that he wants her to stay where she is, doing whatever she's doing. He realizes with a feeling akin to elation that what he really wants—and for the moment all he really wants—is what he now has: a perfect vantage point from which to watch oncoming cars.

Turning the engine off, he waits, concentrating on the one thing, full of anticipation—dried blood and grime on his face, his hair all on end, his eyes glazed with rage and humiliation—a man imbued with interest, and happily awaiting the results of his labor.

Charles Baxter (1947–)

was born in Minneapolis and graduated from Macalester College, in St. Paul, where he was the editor of the literary magazine at the same time Tim O'Brien *(see page 860)* *was student-body president. After completing a doctorate in English at the State University of New York at Buffalo (where he opted not to take writing courses, including ones taught by Donald Barthelme and John Barth, because he was afraid of getting harsh criticism—which years later Baxter called "lunacy on my part"), Baxter taught for several years at Wayne State University in Detroit. "What I thought was, 'I'll get a job teaching literature, and write fiction during the summer and my free time in the school year.'" Baxter told Beatrice.com. "The practical result of that is that it took me a long time to learn how to write fiction. It took me a long time to get published. My first book wasn't published until I was thirty-seven," though he had managed to publish two collections of poems by then. Published in 1984 when it won the Associated Writing Programs Award, his first collection was* Harmony of the World; *his second,* Through the Safety Net, *came out the following year. Soon thereafter, he began teaching in the MFA program at the University of Michigan. He has published two more collections of stories, a collection of essays, and four novels, including* First Light, Saul and Patsy, *and the National Book Award–nominated* The Feast of Love. *"When I'm writing a short story," Baxter told* The Atlantic Monthly, *"I like to throw characters together into situations that create stress so that as the story goes forward, something in the situation or the characters is forced to reveal itself. . . . I've always thought that one way to achieve this is to use characters who are strangers—they don't know anything more about themselves than the reader does, so the story has to move itself along from that point on."*

Introduction by **Elwood Reid**

During his long career, Charles Baxter has tirelessly explored the tickings of flyover country. In four collections of short stories and as many novels, Baxter continues to create whole complicated worlds right in his own backyard. He is not a "regional writer" with all the backhanded implications of that term. Much like Alice Munro, he has created a startling and fictionally rich province all his own.

The stories here demonstrate Baxter's killer timing and his uncanny ability to stock his stories with what in a lesser writer's hands would be turgid and pedantic themes. Baxter has that rare and overlooked gift of good timing. Good timing, both comically and dramatically speaking, depends on economy—pile it on or set up easy targets, and you've got slapstick or cruel condescension masquerading as satire. Instead, Baxter's stories are marvels of compression, and he eschews tedious dissertation defense dialogue as well as overbearing simile and metaphor for a cutting plainspoken style. This is not to say that Baxter's style is repressed, laconic, or wry (read "boring")—tags that are often stapled to inscrutable Midwesterners. Baxter, who started as a poet, mints oddly lucid sentences that sneak across the page and explode on a word. He uses space and all that is left unsaid to build characters who are caught by their unspoken desires only to be brought to painful understanding by a character who shoots from the hip, like the nut job substitute teacher, Miss Ferenczi, who blitzes the young narrator's classroom in "Gryphon." She sprinkles her lessons with lies, fabulations, and brutal truths. Miss Ferenczi tells her students that six times eleven is not sixty-six but sixty-eight because "It's more interesting that way." Or "Diamonds are magic and this is why women wear them on their fingers and . . . Men have strength, but not true magic. That is why men fall in love with women but women do not fall in love with men." She also goes on to say that George Washington was not the first president and that "Certain features of the Constitution of the United States are notable for their Egyptian ideals." The students, already suspicious of a world that seems less and less wondrous with each passing year, respond to Miss Ferenczi's whimsical world view with a renewed sense of mystery. The young narrator of "Gryphon," who ends up coming to blows with a disbelieving classmate over the substitute, declares, "She was always right! She told the truth!"

A sense of wonder is similarly restored to Warren, a social worker and therapist who narrates "Westland," when he meets Jaynee, a mixed up teen with a "candy-bar-and-cola complexion" who has spent the night in the zoo. She tells Warren she has a gun and can take care of herself. After buying her a hamburger, he offers to take Jaynee home to Westland, a blighted and poisoned place in the toxic shadows of Detroit. He meets Jaynee's dad, Earl Lampson, who is busy dismantling a huge wooden play set his daughter no longer needs. The two men strike up an unlikely friendship. Warren sums up Earl this way: "Earl had a good heart and didn't know what to do with it, just as he didn't know what to do with that thing [play set] in his backyard. He just had it, and it was no use to him." Eventually, Warren pitches in and helps Earl take apart the play set, but what Earl is really after is a little free counseling from Warren on how to raise his daughter. But it's Warren who needs the help. He admits, "I couldn't keep my mind on ordinary, daily things. I had come to believe that depression was the realism of the future, and phobias a sign of sanity. I was supposed to know better, but didn't." Earl asks Warren to dispose of the gun for him. Instead of dropping it into the lake, Warren quixotically fires at a nuclear power plant. Warren describes the moment:

> There's a kind of architecture that makes you ashamed of human beings, and in my generic rage, my secret craziness that felt completely sensible, I took the gun and held my arm out the window. It felt good to do that. I was John Wayne. I fired four times at that building, once for me, once for Ann [his wife], and once for each of my two boys. I don't know what I hit. I don't care.

But he's not done with the cure for his nameless depression, not until Earl calls up and demands that he bring his family to a shopping center where Earl is participating in a local Jerry Lewis telethon. While watching Earl, who is dressed as a clown, race a bunch of other clowns, Warren experiences the irrational exuberance of a cure.

Cooper, the narrator in "Shelter," is a happily married baker who finds himself sandbagged by the guilt of plenty when confronted by a homeless man. He offers to buy the man a hamburger. Of course, no good deed goes unpunished, and later Cooper seeks out the homeless shelter, where he meets a troubled young man named Billy, who tells Cooper, "My problem, Cooper, my problem is the problem of the month, which is pointlessness and the point of doing anything, which I can't see most of the time. I want to heal people but I can't do that. I'm stalled." Cooper, of course, is stalled. He takes Billy to the bakery where he works and shows him the baker's bench where he spends his days making things that bring "private smiles" to his customers. Then Cooper takes Billy home to meet his wife and young son, with disastrous results. On seeing the house and the life Cooper has made for himself, Billy says,

> I didn't have any dreams until today, but now I do, seeing your cute house and your cute family. Here's what I'd like to do. I want to be *just like all of you.* I'd put on a chef's hat and stand outside in my apron like one of those assholes you see in the Sunday magazine section with a spatula in his hand, and, like, I'll be flipping hamburgers and telling my kids to keep their hands out of the chive dip and go run in the sprinkler or do some shit like that. I'll belong to do-good groups like Save the Rainforests, and I'll ask my wife how she likes her meat, rare or well-done, and she'll say well-done with that pretty smile she has, and that's how I'll do it. A wonderful fucking barbecue, this is, with folding aluminum chairs and paper plates and ketchup all over the goddamn place. Oceans of vodka and floods of beer. Oh, and we've sprayed the yard with that big spray that kills anything that moves, and all the flies and mosquitoes and bunnies are dead at our feet. Talk about the good life. That has got to be it.

Bang—Baxter nails all the rot and magic of Cooper's life in one shot, and he does it not with a cold authorial pronouncement, but instead by channeling this brutal summation through a broken young man. The effect is that we empathize with both Cooper and Billy. And then Baxter ups the ante. Outside, Billy tells Cooper that he looked into a jar sitting on Cooper's counter and says, "That jar was full of pain. I had to close the lid over it immediately. Now tell me something, because I don't have the answer to it. Why does a man like you, a baker, have a jar full of pain in his kitchen?" As Cooper stares into the dusk he thinks, "What was the price one paid for loving one's own life? He felt great tenderness toward existence and toward his own life, and felt guilty for that." And there you have it: a well-earned big moment that doesn't come off as preachy or cloying. Baxter's stories are chock full of big moments that resonate and leave you, like the all of the best fiction does, breathless and wanting more. Oh, and like a pro, he makes it look easy.

Elwood Reid is the author of the short story collection What Salmon Know *and the novels* If I Don't Six, Midnight Sun, *and* D.B.

CHARLES BAXTER

Gryphon

On Wednesday afternoon, between the geography lesson on ancient Egypt's hand-operated irrigation system and an art project that involved drawing a model city next to a mountain, our fourth-grade teacher, Mr. Hibler, developed a cough. This cough began with a series of muffled throat-clearings and progressed to propulsive noises contained within Mr. Hibler's closed mouth. "Listen to him," Carol Peterson whispered to me. "He's gonna blow up." Mr. Hibler's laughter—dazed and infrequent—sounded a bit like his cough, but as we worked on our model cities we would look up, thinking he was enjoying a joke, and see Mr. Hibler's face turning red, his cheeks puffed out. This was not laughter. Twice he bent over, and his loose tie, like a plumb line, hung down straight from his neck as he exploded himself into a Kleenex. He would excuse himself, then go on coughing. "I'll bet you a dime," Carol Peterson whispered, "we get a substitute tomorrow."

Carol sat at the desk in front of mine and was a bad person—when she thought no one was looking she would blow her nose on notebook paper, then crumple it up and throw it into the wastebasket—but at times of crisis she spoke the truth. I knew I'd lose the dime.

"No deal," I said.

When Mr. Hibler stood us in formation at the door just prior to the final bell, he was almost incapable of speech. "I'm sorry, boys and girls," he said. "I seem to be coming down with something."

"I hope you feel better tomorrow, Mr. Hibler," Bobby Kryzanowicz, the faultless brown-noser, said, and I heard Carol Peterson's evil giggle. Then Mr. Hibler opened the door and we walked out to the buses, a clique of us starting noisily to hawk and cough as soon as we thought we were a few feet beyond Mr. Hibler's earshot.

Since Five Oaks was a rural community, and in Michigan, the supply of substitute teachers was limited to the town's unemployed community college graduates, a pool of about four mothers. These ladies fluttered, provided easeful class days, and nervously covered material we had mastered weeks earlier. Therefore it was a surprise when a woman we had never seen came into the class the next day, carrying a purple purse, a checkerboard lunchbox, and a few books. She put the books on one side of Mr. Hibler's desk and the lunchbox on the other, next to the Voice of Music phonograph. Three of us in the back of the room were playing with Heever, the chameleon that lived in a terrarium and on one of the plastic drapes, when she walked in.

She clapped her hands at us. "Little boys," she said, "why are you bent over together like that?" She didn't wait for us to answer. "Are you tormenting an animal? Put it back. Please sit down at your desks. I want no cabals this time of the day." We just stared at her. "Boys," she repeated, "I asked you to sit down."

I put the chameleon in his terrarium and felt my way to my desk, never taking my eyes off the woman. With white and green chalk, she had started to draw a tree on the left side of the blackboard. She didn't look usual. Furthermore, her tree was outsized, disproportionate, for some reason.

"This room needs a tree," she said, with one line drawing the suggestion of a leaf. "A large, leafy, shady, deciduous . . . oak."

Her fine, light hair had been done up in what I would learn years later was called a chignon, and she wore gold-rimmed glasses whose lenses seemed to have the faintest blue tint. Harold Knardahl, who sat across from me, whispered, "Mars," and I nodded slowly, savoring the imminent weirdness of the day. The substitute drew another branch with an extravagant arm gesture, then turned around and said, "Good morning. I don't believe I said good morning to all of you yet."

Facing us, she was no special age—an adult is an adult—but her face had two prominent lines, descending vertically from the sides of her mouth to her chin. I knew where I had seen those lines before: *Pinocchio.* They were marionette lines. "You may stare at me," she said to us, as a few more kids from the last bus came into the room, their eyes fixed on her, "for a few more seconds until the bell rings. Then I will permit no more staring. Looking I will permit. Staring, no. It is impolite to stare, and a sign of bad breeding. You cannot make a social effort while staring."

Harold Knardahl did not glance at me, or nudge, but I heard him whisper "Mars" again, trying to get more mileage out of his single joke with the kids who had just come in.

When everyone was seated, the substitute teacher finished her tree, put down her chalk fastidiously on the phonograph, brushed her hands, and faced us. "Good morning," she said. "I am Miss Ferenczi, your teacher for the day. I am fairly new to your community, and I don't believe any of you know me. I will therefore start by telling you a story about myself."

While we settled back, she launched into her tale. She said her grandfather had been a Hungarian prince; her mother had been born in some place called Flanders, had been a pianist, and had played concerts for people Miss Ferenczi referred to as "crowned heads." She gave us a knowing look. "Grieg," she said, "the Norwegian master, wrote a concerto for piano that was . . ."—she paused—"my mother's triumph at her debut concert in London." Her eyes searched the ceiling. Our eyes followed. Nothing up there but ceiling tile. "For reasons that I shall not go into, my family's fortunes took us to Detroit, then north to dreadful Saginaw, and now here I am in Five Oaks, as your substitute teacher, for today, Thursday, October the eleventh. I believe it will be a good day: all the forecasts coincide. We shall start with your reading lesson. Take out your reading book. I believe it is called *Broad Horizons,* or something along those lines."

Jeannie Vermeesch raised her hand. Miss Ferenczi nodded at her. "Mr. Hibler always starts the day with the Pledge of Allegiance," Jeannie whined.

"Oh, does he? In that case," Miss Ferenczi said, "you must know it *very* well by now, and we certainly need not spend our time on it. No, no allegiance pledging on the premises today, by my reckoning. Not with so much sunlight coming into the room. A pledge does not suit my mood." She glanced at her watch. "Time *is* flying. Take out *Broad Horizons.*"

★ ★ ★

She disappointed us by giving us an ordinary lesson, complete with vocabulary and drills, comprehension questions, and recitation. She didn't seem to care for the material, however. She sighed every few minutes and rubbed her glasses with a frilly handkerchief that she withdrew, magician-style, from her left sleeve.

After reading we moved on to arithmetic. It was my favorite time of the morning, when the lazy autumn sunlight dazzled its way through ribbons of clouds past the windows on the east side of the classroom and crept across the linoleum floor. On the playground the first group of children, the kindergartners, were running on the quack grass just beyond the monkey bars. We were doing multiplication tables. Miss Ferenczi had made John Wazny stand up at his desk in the front row. He was supposed to go through the tables of six. From where I was sitting, I could smell the Vitalis soaked into John's plastered hair. He was doing fine until he came to six times eleven and six times twelve. "Six times eleven," he said, "is sixty-eight. Six times twelve is . . ." He put his fingers to his head, quickly and secretly sniffed his fingertips, and said, ". . . seventy-two." Then he sat down.

"Fine," Miss Ferenczi said. "Well now. That was very good."

"Miss Ferenczi!" One of the Eddy twins was waving her hand desperately in the air. "Miss Ferenczi! Miss Ferenczi!"

"Yes?"

"John said that six times eleven is sixty-eight and you said he was right!"

"*Did* I?" She gazed at the class with a jolly look breaking across her marionette's face. "Did I say that? Well, what *is* six times eleven?"

"It's sixty-six!"

She nodded. "Yes. So it is. But, and I know some people will not entirely agree with me, at some times it is sixty-eight."

"When? When is it sixty-eight?"

We were all waiting.

"In higher mathematics, which you children do not yet understand, six times eleven can be considered to be sixty-eight." She laughed through her nose. "In higher mathematics numbers are . . . more fluid. The only thing a number does is contain a certain amount of something. Think of water. A cup is not the only way to measure a certain amount of water, is it?" We were staring, shaking our heads. "You could use saucepans or thimbles. In either case, the water *would be the same.* Perhaps," she started again, "it would be better for you to think that six times eleven is sixty-eight only when I am in the room."

"Why is it sixty-eight," Mark Poole asked, "when you're in the room?"

"Because it's more interesting that way," she said, smiling very rapidly behind her blue-tinted glasses. "Besides, I'm your substitute teacher, am I not?" We all nodded. "Well, then, think of six times eleven equals sixty-eight as a substitute fact."

"A substitute fact?"

"Yes." Then she looked at us carefully. "Do you think," she asked, "that anyone is going to be hurt by a substitute fact?"

We looked back at her.

"Will the plants on the windowsill be hurt?" We glanced at them. There were sensitive plants thriving in a green plastic tray, and several wilted ferns in small clay pots. "Your dogs and cats, or your moms and dads?" She waited. "So," she concluded, "what's the problem?"

"But it's wrong," Janice Weber said, "isn't it?"

"What's your name, young lady?"

"Janice Weber."

"And you think it's wrong, Janice?"

"I was just asking."

"Well, all right. You were just asking. I think we've spent enough time on this matter by now, don't you, class? You are free to think what you like. When your teacher, Mr. Hibler, returns, six times eleven will be sixty-six again, you can rest assured. And it will be that for the rest of your lives in Five Oaks. Too bad, eh?" She raised her eyebrows and glinted herself at us. "But for now, it wasn't. So much for that. Let us go on to your assigned problems for today, as painstakingly outlined, I see, in Mr. Hibler's lesson plan. Take out a sheet of paper and write your names on the upper left-hand corner."

For the next half hour we did the rest of our arithmetic problems. We handed them in and then went on to spelling, my worst subject. Spelling always came before lunch. We were taking spelling dictation and looking at the clock. "Thorough," Miss Ferenczi said. "Boundary." She walked in the aisles between the desks, holding the spelling book open and looking down at our papers. "Balcony." I clutched my pencil. Somehow, the way she said those words, they seemed foreign, mis-voweled and mis-consonanted. I stared down at what I had spelled. *Balconie.* I turned the pencil upside down and erased my mistake. *Balconey.* That looked better, but still incorrect. I cursed the world of spelling and tried erasing it again and saw the paper beginning to wear away. *Balkony.* Suddenly I felt a hand on my shoulder.

"I don't like that word either," Miss Ferenczi whispered, bent over, her mouth near my ear. "It's ugly. My feeling is, if you don't like a word, you don't have to use it." She straightened up, leaving behind a slight odor of Clorets.

At lunchtime we went out to get our trays of sloppy joes, peaches in heavy syrup, coconut cookies, and milk, and brought them back to the classroom, where Miss Ferenczi was sitting at the desk, eating a brown sticky thing she had unwrapped from tightly rubber-banded waxed paper. "Miss Ferenczi," I said, raising my hand. "You don't have to eat with us. You can eat with the other teachers. There's a teachers' lounge," I ended up, "next to the principal's office."

"No, thank you," she said. "I prefer it here."

"We've got a room monitor," I said. "Mrs. Eddy." I pointed to where Mrs. Eddy, Joyce and Judy's mother, sat silently at the back of the room, doing her knitting.

"That's fine," Miss Ferenczi said. "But I shall continue to eat here, with you children. I prefer it," she repeated.

"How come?" Wayne Razmer asked without raising his hand.

"I talked to the other teachers before class this morning," Miss Ferenczi said, biting into her brown food. "There was a great rattling of the words for the fewness of the ideas. I didn't care for their brand of hilarity. I don't like ditto-machine jokes."

"Oh," Wayne said.

"What's that you're eating?" Maxine Sylvester asked, twitching her nose. "Is it food?"

"It most certainly *is* food. It's a stuffed fig. I had to drive almost down Detroit to get it. I also brought some smoked sturgeon. And this," she said, lifting some green leaves out of her lunchbox, "is raw spinach, cleaned this morning."

"Why're you eating raw spinach?" Maxine asked.

"It's good for you," Miss Ferenczi said. "More stimulating than soda pop or smelling salts." I bit into my sloppy joe and stared blankly out the window. An almost invisible moon was faintly silvered in the daytime autumn sky. "As far as food is concerned," Miss Ferenczi was saying, "you have to shuffle the pack. Mix it up. Too many people eat . . . well, never mind."

"Miss Ferenczi," Carol Peterson said, "what are we going to do this afternoon?"

"Well," she said, looking down at Mr. Hibler's lesson plan, "I see that your teacher, Mr. Hibler, has you scheduled for a unit on the Egyptians." Carol groaned. "Yessss," Miss Ferenczi continued, "that is what we will do: the Egyptians. A remarkable people. Almost as remarkable as the Americans. But not quite." She lowered her head, did her quick smile, and went back to eating her spinach.

After noon recess we came back into the classroom and saw that Miss Ferenczi had drawn a pyramid on the blackboard close to her oak tree. Some of us who had been playing baseball were messing around in the back of the room, dropping the bats and gloves into the playground box, and Ray Schontzeler had just slugged me when I heard Miss Ferenczi's high-pitched voice, quavering with emotions. "Boys," she said, "come to order right this minute and take your seats. I do not wish to waste a minute of class time. Take out your geography books." We trudged to our desks and, still sweating, pulled out *Distant Lands and Their People.* "Turn to page forty-two." She waited for thirty seconds, then looked over at Kelly Munger. "Young man," she said, "why are you still fossicking in your desk?"

Kelly looked as if his foot had been stepped on. "Why am I what?"

"Why are you . . . burrowing in your desk like that?"

"I'm lookin' for the book, Miss Ferenczi."

Bobby Kryzanowicz, the faultless brown-noser who sat in the first row by choice, softly said, "His name is Kelly Munger. He can't ever find his stuff. He always does that."

"I don't care what his name is, especially after lunch," Miss Ferenczi said. *"Where is your book?"*

"I just found it." Kelly was peering into his desk and with both hands pulled at the book, shoveling along in front of it several pencils and crayons, which fell into his lap and then to the floor.

"I hate a mess," Miss Ferenczi said. "I hate a mess in a desk or a mind. It's . . . unsanitary. You wouldn't want your house at home to look like your desk at school, now, would you?" She didn't wait for an answer. "I should think not. A house at home should be as neat as human hands can make it. What were we talking about? Egypt. Page forty-two. I note from Mr. Hibler's lesson plan that you have been discussing the modes of Egyptian irrigation. Interesting, in my view, but not so interesting as what we are about to cover. The pyramids, and Egyptian slave labor. A plus on one side, a minus on the other." We had our books open to page forty-two, where there was a picture of a pyramid, but Miss Ferenczi wasn't looking at the book. Instead, she was staring at some object just outside the window.

"Pyramids," Miss Ferenczi said, still looking past the window. "I want you to think about pyramids. And what was inside. The bodies of the pharaohs, of course, and their attendant treasures. Scrolls. Perhaps," Miss Ferenczi said, her face gleeful but unsmiling, "these scrolls were novels for the pharaohs, helping them to pass the time in their long voyage through the centuries. But then, I am joking." I was looking at the lines on Miss Ferenczi's skin. "Pyramids," Miss Ferenczi went on, "were the repositories of special cosmic powers. The nature of a pyramid is to guide cosmic energy forces into a concentrated point. The Egyptians knew that; we have generally forgotten it. Did you know," she asked, walking to the side of the room so that she was standing by the coat closet, "that George Washington had Egyptian blood, from his grandmother? Certain features of the Constitution of the United States are notable for their Egyptian ideas."

Without glancing down at the book, she began to talk about the movement of souls in Egyptian religion. She said that when people die, their souls return to Earth in the form of carpenter ants or walnut trees, depending on how they behaved—"well or ill"—in life. She said that the Egyptians believed that people act the way they do because of magnetism produced by tidal forces in the solar system, forces produced by the sun and by its "planetary ally," Jupiter. Jupiter, she said, was a planet, as we had been told, but had "certain properties of stars." She was speaking very fast. She said that the Egyptians were great explorers and conquerors. She said that the greatest of all the conquerors, Genghis Khan, had had forty horses and forty young women killed on the site of his grave. We listened. No one tried to stop her. "I myself have been in Egypt," she said, "and have witnessed much dust and many brutalities." She said that an old man in Egypt who worked for a circus had personally shown her an animal in a cage, a monster, half bird and half lion. She said that this monster was called a gryphon and that she had heard about them but never seen them until she traveled to the outskirts of Cairo. She wrote the word out on the blackboard in large capital letters: GRYPHON. She said that Egyptian astronomers had discovered the planet Saturn but had not seen its rings. She said that the Egyptians were the first to discover that dogs, when they are ill, will not drink from rivers, but wait for rain, and hold their jaws open to catch it.

"She lies."

We were on the school bus home. I was sitting next to Carl Whiteside who had bad breath and a huge collection of marbles. We were arguing. Carl thought she was lying. I said she wasn't, probably.

"I didn't believe that stuff about the bird," Carl said, "and what she told us about the pyramids? I didn't believe that, either. She didn't know what she was talking about."

"Oh yeah?" I had liked her. She was strange. I thought I could nail him. "If she was lying," I said, "what'd she say that was a lie?"

"Six times eleven isn't sixty-eight. It isn't ever. It's sixty-six. I know for a fact."

"She said so. She admitted it. What else did she lie about?"

"I don't know," he said. "Stuff."

"What stuff?"

"Well." He swung his legs back and forth. "You ever see an animal that was half lion and half bird?" He crossed his arms. "It sounded real fakey to me."

"It could happen," I said. I had to improvise, to outrage him. "I read in this newspaper my mom bought in the IGA about this scientist, this mad scientist in the Swiss Alps, and he's been putting genes and chromosomes and stuff together in test tubes, and he combined a human being and a hamster." I waited, for effect. "It's called a humster."

"You never." Carl was staring at me, his mouth open, his terrible bad breath making its way toward me. "What newspaper was it?"

"The National Enquirer," I said, "that they sell next to the cash registers." When I saw his look of recognition, I knew I had him. "And this mad scientist," I said, "his name was, um, Dr. Frankenbush." I realized belatedly that this name was a mistake and waited for Carl to notice its resemblance to the name of the other famous mad master of permutations, but he only sat there.

"A man and a hamster?" He was staring at me, squinting, his mouth opening in distaste. "Jeez. What'd it look like?"

When the bus reached my stop, I took off down our dirt road and ran up through the backyard, kicking the tire swing for good luck. I dropped my books on the back steps so I could hug and kiss our dog, Mr. Selby. Then I hurried inside. I could smell brussels sprouts cooking, my unfavorite vegetable. My mother was washing other vegetables in the kitchen sink, and my baby brother was hollering in his yellow playpen on the kitchen floor.

"Hi, Mom," I said, hopping around the playpen to kiss her. "Guess what?"

"I have no idea."

"We had this substitute today, Miss Ferenczi, and I'd never seen her before, and she had all these stories and ideas and stuff."

"Well. That's good." My mother looked out the window in front of the sink, her eyes on the pine woods west of our house. That time of the afternoon her skin always looked so white to me. Strangers always said my mother looked like Betty Crocker, framed by the giant spoon on the side of the Bisquick box. "Listen, Tommy," she said. "Would you please go upstairs and pick your clothes off the floor in the bathroom, and then go outside to the shed and put the shovel and ax away that your father left outside this morning?"

"She said that six times eleven was sometimes sixty-eight!" I said. "And she said she once saw a monster that was half lion and half bird." I waited. "In Egypt."

"Did you hear me?" my mother asked, raising her arm to wipe her forehead with the back of her hand. "You have chores to do."

"I know," I said. "I was just telling you about the substitute."

"It's very interesting," my mother said, quickly glancing down at me, "and we can talk about it later when your father gets home. But right now you have some work to do."

"Okay, Mom." I took a cookie out of the jar on the counter and was about to go outside when I had a thought. I ran into the living room, pulled out a dictionary next to the TV stand, and opened it to the Gs. After five minutes I found it. *Gryphon:* variant of griffin. *Griffin:* "a fabulous beast with the head and wings of an eagle and the body of a lion." Fabulous was right. I shouted with triumph and ran outside to put my father's tools in their proper places.

Miss Ferenczi was back the next day, slightly altered. She had pulled her hair down and twisted it into pigtails, with red rubber bands holding them tight one inch from the ends. She was wearing a green blouse and pink scarf, making her difficult to look at for a full class day. This time there was no pretense of doing a reading lesson or moving on to arithmetic. As soon as the bell rang, she simply began to talk.

She talked for forty minutes straight. There seemed to be less connection between her ideas, but the ideas themselves were, as the dictionary would say, fabulous. She said she had heard of a huge jewel, in what she called the antipodes, that was so brilliant that when light shone into it at a certain angle it would blind whoever was looking at its center. She said the biggest diamond in the world was cursed and had killed everyone who owned it, and that by a trick of fate it was called the Hope Diamond. Diamonds are magic, she said, and this is why women wear them on their fingers, as a sign of the magic of womanhood. Men have strength, Miss Ferenczi said, but no true magic. That is why men fall in love with women but women do not fall in love with men: they just love being loved. George Washington had died because of a mistake he made about a diamond. Washington was not the first *true* President, but she didn't say who was. In some places in the world, she said, men and women still live in the trees and eat monkeys for breakfast. Their doctors are magicians. At the bottom of the sea are creatures thin as pancakes who have never been studied by scientists because when you take them up to air, the fish explode.

There was not a sound in the classroom, except for Miss Ferenczi's voice, and Donna DeShano's coughing. No one even went to the bathroom.

Beethoven, she said, had not been deaf; it was a trick to make himself famous, and it worked. As she talked, Miss Ferenczi's pigtails swung back and forth. There are trees in the world, she said, that eat meat: their leaves are sticky and close up on bugs like hands. She lifted her hands and brought them together, palm to palm. Venus, which most people think is the next closest planet to the sun, is not always closer, and, besides, it is the planet of greatest mystery because of its thick cloud cover. "I know what lies underneath those clouds," Miss Ferenczi said, and waited. After the silence, she said, "Angels. Angels live under those clouds." She said that angels were not invisible to everyone and were in fact smarter than most people. They did not dress in robes as was often claimed but instead wore formal evening clothes, as if they were about to attend a concert. Often angels *do* attend concerts and sit in the aisles, where, she said, most people pay no attention to them. She said the most terrible angel had the shape of the Sphinx. "There is no running away from that one," she said. She said that unquenchable fires burn just under the surface of the earth in Ohio, and that the baby Mozart fainted dead away in his cradle when he first heard the sound of a trumpet. She said that someone named Narzim al Harrardim was the greatest writer who ever lived. She said that planets control behavior, and anyone conceived during a solar eclipse would be born with webbed feet.

"I know you children like to hear these things," she said, "these secrets, and that is why I am telling you all this." We nodded. It was better than doing comprehension questions for the readings in *Broad Horizons.*

"I will tell you one more story," she said, "and then we will have to do arithmetic." She leaned over, and her voice grew soft. "There is no death," she said. "You must never be afraid. Never. That which is, cannot die. It will change into different earthly and unearthly elements, but I know this as sure as I stand here in front of you, and I swear it: you must not be afraid. I have seen this truth with these eyes. I know it because in a dream God kissed me. Here." And she pointed with her right index finger to the side of her head, below the mouth where the vertical lines were carved into her skin.

★ ★ ★

Absentmindedly we all did our arithmetic problems. At recess the class was out on the playground, but no one was playing. We were all standing in small groups, talking about Miss Ferenczi. We didn't know if she was crazy, or what. I looked out beyond the playground, at the rusted cars piled in a small heap behind a clump of sumac, and I wanted to see shapes there, approaching me.

On the way home, Carl sat next to me again. He didn't say much, and I didn't either. At last he turned to me. "You know what she said about the leaves that close up on bugs?"

"Huh?"

"The leaves," Carl insisted. "The meat-eating plants. I know it's true. I saw it on television. The leaves have this icky glue that the plants have got smeared all over them and the insects can't get off 'cause they're stuck. I saw it." He seemed demoralized. "She's tellin' the truth."

"Yeah."

"You think she's seen all those angels?"

I shrugged.

"I don't think she has," Carl informed me. "I think she made that part up."

"There's a tree," I suddenly said. I was looking out the window at the farms along County Road H. I knew every barn, every broken windmill, every fence, every anhydrous ammonia tank, by heart. "There's a tree that's . . . that I've seen . . ."

"Don't you try to do it," Carl said. "You'll just sound like a jerk."

I kissed my mother. She was standing in front of the stove. "How was your day?" she asked.

"Fine."

"Did you have Miss Ferenczi again?"

"Yeah."

"Well?"

"She was fine. Mom," I asked, "can I go to my room?"

"No," she said, "not until you've gone out to the vegetable garden and picked me a few tomatoes." She glanced at the sky. "I think it's going to rain. Skedaddle and do it now. Then you come back inside and watch your brother for a few minutes while I go upstairs. I need to clean up before dinner." She looked down at me. "You're looking a little pale, Tommy." She touched the back of her hand to my forehead and I felt her diamond ring against my skin. "Do you feel all right?"

"I'm fine," I said, and went out to pick the tomatoes.

Coughing mutedly, Mr. Hibler was back the next day, slipping lozenges into his mouth when his back was turned at forty-five-minute intervals and asking us how much of his prepared lesson plan Miss Ferenczi had followed. Edith Atwater took the responsibility for the class of explaining to Mr. Hibler that the substitute hadn't always done exactly what he, Mr. Hibler, would have done, but we had worked hard even though she talked a lot. About what? he asked. All kinds of things, Edith said. I sort of forgot. To our relief, Mr. Hibler seemed not at all interested in what Miss Ferenczi had said to fill the day. He probably thought it was woman's talk: unserious and not suited for school. It was enough that he had a pile of arithmetic problems from us to correct.

For the next month, the sumac turned a distracting red in the field, and the sun traveled toward the southern sky, so that its rays reached Mr. Hibler's Halloween display on the bulletin board in the back of the room, fading the pumpkin head scarecrow from orange to tan. Every three days I measured how much farther the sun had moved toward the southern horizon by making small marks with my black Crayola on the north wall, ant-sized marks only I knew were there.

And then in early December, four days after the first permanent snowfall, she appeared again in our classroom. The minute she came in the door, I felt my heart begin to pound. Once again, she was different: this time, her hair hung straight down and seemed hardly to have been combed. She hadn't brought her lunchbox with her, but she was carrying what seemed to be a small box. She greeted all of us and talked about the weather. Donna DeShano had to remind her to take her overcoat off.

When the bell to start the day finally rang, Miss Ferenczi looked out at all of us and said, "Children, I have enjoyed your company in the past, and today I am going to reward you." She held up the small box. "Do you know what this is?" She waited. "Of course you don't. It is a Tarot pack."

Edith Atwater raised her hand. "What's a Tarot pack, Miss Ferenczi?"

"It is used to tell fortunes," she said. "And that is what I shall do this morning. I shall tell your fortunes, as I have been taught to do."

"What's fortune?" Bobby Kryzanowicz asked.

"The future, young man. I shall tell you what your future will be. I can't do your whole future, of course. I shall have to limit myself to the five-card system, the wands, cups, swords, pentacles, and the higher arcanes. Now who wants to be first?"

There was a long silence. Then Carol Peterson raised her hand.

"All right," Miss Ferenczi said. She divided the pack into five smaller packs and walked back to Carol's desk, in front of mine. "Pick one card from each one of these packs," she said. I saw that Carol had a four of cups and a six of swords, but I couldn't see the other cards. Miss Ferenczi studied the cards on Carol's desk for a minute. "Not bad," she said. "I do not see much higher education. Probably an early marriage. Many children. There's something bleak and dreary here, but I can't tell what. Perhaps just the tasks of a housewife life. I think you'll do very well, for the most part." She smiled at Carol, a smile with a certain lack of interest. "Who wants to be next?"

Carl Whiteside raised his hand slowly.

"Yes," Miss Ferenczi said, "let's do a boy." She walked over to where Carl sat. After he picked his five cards, she gazed at them for a long time. "Travel," she said. "Much distant travel. You might go into the army. Not too much romantic interest here. A late marriage, if at all. But the Sun in your major arcana, that's a very good card." She giggled. "You'll have a happy life."

Next I raised my hand. She told me my future. She did the same with Bobby Kryzanowicz, Kelly Munger, Edith Atwater, and Kim Foor. Then she came to Wayne Razmer. He picked his five cards, and I could see that the Death card was one of them.

"What's your name?" Miss Ferenczi asked.

"Wayne."

"Well, Wayne," she said, "you will undergo a great metamorphosis, a change, before you become an adult. Your earthly element will no doubt leap higher, because you seem to be a sweet boy. This card, this nine of swords, tells me of suffering and desolation. And this ten of wands, well, that's a heavy load."

"What about this one?" Wayne pointed at the Death card.

"It means, my sweet, that you will die soon." She gathered up the cards. We were all looking at Wayne. "But do not fear," she said. "It is not really death. Just change. Out of your earthly shape." She put the cards on Mr. Hibler's desk. "And now, let's do some arithmetic."

At lunchtime Wayne went to Mr. Faegre, the principal, and informed him of what Miss Ferenczi had done. During the noon recess, we saw Miss Ferenczi drive out of the parking lot in her rusting green Rambler American. I stood under the slide, listening to the other kids coasting down and landing in the little depressive bowls at the bottom. I was kicking stones and tugging at my hair right up to the moment when I saw Wayne come out to the playground. He smiled, the dead fool, and with the fingers of his right hand he was showing everyone how he had told on Miss Ferenczi.

I made my way toward Wayne, pushing myself past two girls from another class. He was watching me with his little pinhead eyes.

"You told," I shouted at him. "She was just kidding."

"She shouldn't have," he shouted back. "We were supposed to be doing arithmetic."

"She just scared you," I said. "You're a chicken. You're a chicken, Wayne. You are. Scared of a little card," I singsonged.

Wayne fell at me, his two fists hammering down on my nose. I gave him a good one in the stomach and then I tried for his head. Aiming my fist, I saw that he was crying. I slugged him.

"She was right," I yelled. "She was always right! She told the truth!" Other kids were whooping. "You were just scared, that's all!"

And then large hands pulled at us, and it was my turn to speak to Mr. Faegre.

In the afternoon Miss Ferenczi was gone, and my nose was stuffed with cotton clotted with blood, and my lip had swelled, and our class had been combined with Mrs. Mantei's sixth-grade class for a crowded afternoon science unit on insect life in ditches and swamps. I knew where Mrs. Mantei lived: she had a new house trailer just down the road from us, at the Clearwater Park. She was no mystery. Somehow she and Mr. Bodine, the other fourth-grade teacher, had managed to fit forty-five desks into the room. Kelly Munger asked if Miss Ferenczi had been arrested, and Mrs. Mantei said no, of course not. All that afternoon, until the buses came to pick us up, we learned about field crickets and two-striped grasshoppers, water bugs, cicadas, mosquitoes, flies, and moths. We learned about insects' hard outer shell, the exoskeleton, and the usual parts of the mouth, including the labrum, mandible, maxilla, and glossa. We learned about compound eyes, and the four-stage metamorphosis from egg to larva to pupa to adult. We learned something, but not much, about mating. Mrs. Mantei drew, very skillfully, the internal anatomy of the grasshopper on the blackboard. We learned about the dance of the honeybee, directing other bees in the hive to pollen. We found out about which insects were pests to man, and which were not. On lined white pieces of paper we made lists of insects we might actually see, then a list of insects too small to be clearly visible, such as fleas; Mrs. Mantei said that our assignment would be to memorize these lists for the next day, when Mr. Hibler would certainly return and test us on our knowledge.

CHARLES BAXTER

Westland

Saturday morning at the zoo, facing the lions' cage, overcast sky and a light breeze carrying the smell of peanuts and animal dung, the peacocks making their stilted progress across the sidewalks. I was standing in front of the gorge separating the human viewers from the lions. The lions weren't caged, exactly; they just weren't free to go. One male and one female were slumbering on fake rock ledges. Raw meat was nearby. My hands were in my pockets and I was waiting for a moment of energy so I could leave and do my Saturday morning errands. Then this girl, this teenager, appeared from behind me, hands in *her* pockets, and she stopped a few feet away on my right. In an up-all-night voice, she said, "What would you do if I shot that lion?" She nodded her head: she meant the male, the closer one.

"Shot it?"

"That's right."

"I don't know." Sometimes you have to humor people, pretend as if they're talking about something real. "Do you have a gun?"

"Of course I have a gun." She wore a protective blankness on her thin face. She was fixed on the lion. "I have it here in my pocket."

"I'd report you," I said. "I'd try to stop you. There are guards here. People don't shoot caged animals. You shouldn't even carry a concealed weapon, a girl your age."

"This is Detroit," she explained.

"I know it is," I said. "But people don't shoot caged lions in Detroit or anywhere else."

"It wouldn't be that bad," she said, nodding at the lions again. "You can tell from their faces how much they want to check out."

I said I didn't think so.

She turned to look at me. Her skin was so pale it seemed bleached, and she was wearing a vaudeville-length overcoat and a pair of hightop tennis shoes and jeans with slits at the knees. She looked like a fifteen-year-old bag lady. "It's because you're a disconnected person that you can't see it," she said. She shivered and reached into her pocket and pulled out a crumpled pack of cigarettes. "Lions are so human. Things get to them. They experience everything more than we do. They're romantic." She glanced at her crushed pack of cigarettes, and in a shivering motion she tossed it into the gorge. She swayed back and forth. "They want to kill and feast and feel," she said.

I looked at this girl's bleached skin, that candy-bar-and-cola complexion, and I said, "Are you all right?"

"I slept here last night," she said. She pointed vaguely behind her. "I was sleeping over there. Under those trees. Near the polar bears."

"Why'd you do that?"

"I wasn't alone *all* night." She was answering a question I hadn't asked. "This guy, he came in with me for a while to be nice and amorous but he couldn't see the point in staying. He split around midnight. He said it was righteous coming in here and being solid with the animal world, but he said you had to know when to stop. I told him I wouldn't defend him to his friends if he left, and he left, so as far as I'm concerned, he is over, he is zippo."

She was really shivering now, and she was huddling inside that long overcoat. I don't like to help strangers, but she needed help. "Are you hungry?" I asked. "You want a hamburger?"

"I'll eat it," she said, "but only if you buy it."

I took her to a fast-food restaurant and sat her down and brought her one of their famous giant cheeseburgers. She held it in her hands familiarly as she watched the cars passing on Woodward Avenue. I let my gaze follow hers, and when I looked back, half the cheeseburger was gone. She wasn't even chewing. She didn't look at the food. She ate like a soldier in a foxhole. What was left of her food she gripped in her skinny fingers decorated with flaking pink nail polish. She was pretty in a raw and sloppy way.

"You're looking at me."

"Yes, I am," I admitted.

"How come?"

"A person can look," I said.

"Maybe." Now she looked back. "Are you one of those creeps?"

"Which kind?"

"The kind of old man creep who picks up girls and drives them places, and, like, terrorizes them for days and then dumps them into fields."

"No," I said. "I'm not like that. And I'm not that old."

"Maybe it's the accent," she said. "You don't sound American."

"I was born in England," I told her, "but I've been in this country for thirty years. I'm an American citizen."

"You've got to be born in this country to sound American," she said, sucking at her chocolate shake through her straw. She was still gazing at the traffic. Looking at traffic seemed to restore her peace of mind. "I guess you're okay," she said distantly, "and I'm not worried anyhow, because, like I told you, I've got a gun."

"Oh yeah," I said.

"You're not a real American because you don't *believe!*" Then this child fumbled in her coat pocket and clunked down a small shiny handgun on the table, next to the plastic containers and the french fries. "So there," she said.

"Put it back," I told her. "Jesus, I hope the safety's on."

"I think so." She wiped her hand on a napkin and dropped the thing back into her pocket. "So tell me your name, Mr. Samaritan."

"Warren," I said. "My name's Warren. What's yours?"

"I'm Jaynee. What do you do, Warren? You must do something. You look like someone who does something."

I explained to her about governmental funding for social work and therapy, but her eyes glazed and she cut me off.

"Oh yeah," she said, chewing her french fries with her mouth open so that you could see inside if you wanted to. "One of those professional friends. I've seen people like you."

I drove her home. She admired the tape machine in the car and the carpeting on the floor. She gave me directions on how to get to her house in Westland, one of the suburbs. Detroit has four shopping centers at its cardinal points: Westland, Eastland, Southland, and Northland. A town grew up around Westland, a blue-collar area, and now Westland is the name of both the shopping center and the town.

She took me down fast-food alley and then through a series of right and left ninety-degree turns on streets with bungalows covered by aluminum siding. Few trees, not much green except the lawns, and the half-sun dropped onto those perpendicular lines with nothing to stop it or get in its way. The girl, Jaynee, picked at her knees and nodded, as if any one of the houses would do. The houses all looked exposed to me, with a straight shot at the elements out there on that flat grid.

I was going to drop her off at what she said was her driveway, but there was an old chrome-loaded Pontiac in the way, one of those vintage 1950s cars, its front end up on a hoist and some man working on his back on a rolling dolly underneath it. "That's him," the girl said. "You want to meet him?"

I parked the car and got out. The man pulled himself away from underneath the car and looked over at us. He stood up, wiping his hands on a rag, and scowled at his daughter. He wasn't going to look at me right away. I think he was checking Jaynee for signs of damage.

"What's this?" he asked. "What's this about, Jaynee?"

"This is about nothing," she said. "I spent the night in the zoo and this person found me and brought me home."

"At the zoo. Jesus Christ. At the zoo. Is that what happened?" He was asking me.

"That's where I saw her," I told him. "She looked pretty cold."

He dropped a screwdriver I hadn't noticed he was holding. He was standing there in his driveway next to the Pontiac, looking at his daughter and me and then at the sky. I'd had those moments, too, when nothing made any sense and I didn't know where my responsibilities lay. "Go inside," he told his daughter. "Take a shower. I'm not talking to you here on the driveway. I know that."

We both watched her go into the house. She looked like an overcoat with legs. I felt ashamed of myself for thinking of her that way, but there are some ideas you can't prevent.

We were both watching her, and the man said, "You can't go to the public library and find out how to raise a girl like that." He said something else, but an airplane passed so low above us that I couldn't hear him. We were about three miles from the airport. He ended his speech by saying, "I don't know who's right."

"I don't either."

"Earl Lampson." He held out his hand. I shook it and took away a feel of bone and grease and flesh. I could see a fading tattoo on his forearm of a rose run through with a sword.

"Warren Banks," I said. "I guess I'll have to be going."

"Wait a minute, Warren. Let me do two things. First, let me thank you for bringing my daughter home. Unhurt." I nodded to show I understood. "Second. A question. You got any kids?"

"Two," I said. "Both boys."

"Then you know about it. You know what a child can do to you. I was awake last night. I didn't know what had happened to her. I didn't know if she had planned it. That was the worst. She makes plans. Jesus Christ. The zoo. The lions?"

I nodded.

"She'll do anything. And it isn't an act with her." He looked up and down the street, as if he were waiting for something to appear, and I had the wild idea that I was going to see a float coming our way, with beauty queens on it, and little men dressed up in costumes.

I told him I had to leave. He shook his head.

"Stay a minute, Warren," he said. "Come into the backyard. I want to show you something."

He turned around and walked through the garage, past a pile of snow tires and two rusted-out bicycles. I followed him, thinking of my boys this morning at their Scout meeting, and of my wife, out shopping or maybe home by now and wondering vaguely where I was. I was supposed to be getting groceries. Here I was in this garage. She would look at the clock, do something else, then look back at the clock.

"Now how about this?" Earl pointed an index finger toward a wooden construction that stood in the middle of his yard, running from one side to another: a play structure, with monkey bars and a swing set, a high perch like a ship's crow's nest, a set of tunnels to crawl through and climb on, and a little rope bridge between two towers. I had never seen anything like it, so much human effort expended on a backyard toy, this huge contraption.

I whistled. "It must have taken you years."

"Eighteen months," he said. "And she hasn't played on it since she was twelve." He shook his head. "I bought the wood and put it together piece by piece. She was only three years old when I did it, weekends when I wasn't doing overtime at Ford's. She was my assistant. She'd bring me nails. I told her to hold the hammer when I wasn't using it, and she'd stand there, real serious, just holding the hammer. Of course now she's too old for it. I have the biggest backyard toy in Michigan and a daughter who goes off to the zoo and spends the night there and that's her idea of a good time."

A light rain had started to fall. "What are you going to do with this thing?" I asked.

"Take it apart, I guess." He glanced at the sky. "Warren, you want a beer?"

It was eleven o'clock in the morning. "Sure," I said.

We sat in silence on his cluttered back porch. We sipped our beers and watched the rain fall over things in our line of sight. Neither of us was saying much. It was better being there than being at home, and my morning gloom was on its way out. It wasn't lifting so much as converting into something else, as it does when you're in someone else's house. I didn't want to move as long as I felt that way.

I had been in the zoo that morning because I had been reading the newspaper again, and this time I had read about a uranium plant here in Michigan whose employees were spraying pastureland with a fertilizer recycled from radioactive wastes. They called it treated raffinate. The paper said that in addition to trace amounts of radium and radioactive thorium, this fertilizer spray had at least eighteen poisonous heavy metals in it, including molybdenum, arsenic, and lead. It had been sprayed out into the pastures and was going into the food supply. I was supposed to get up from the table and go out and get the groceries, but I had gone to the zoo instead to stare at the animals. This had been happening more often lately. I couldn't keep my mind on ordinary, daily things. I had come to believe that depression was the realism of the future, and phobias a sign of sanity. I was supposed to know better, but I didn't.

I had felt crazy and helpless, but there, on Earl Lampson's porch, I was feeling a little better. Calm strangers sometimes have that effect on you.

Jaynee came out just then. She'd been in the shower, and I could see why some kid might want to spend a night in the zoo with her. She was in a T-shirt and jeans, and the hot water had perked her up. I stood and excused myself. I couldn't stand to see her just then, breaking my mood. Earl went to a standing position and shook my hand and said he appreciated what I had done for his daughter. I said it was nothing and started to leave when Earl, for no reason that I could see, suddenly said he'd be calling me during the week, if that was all right. I told him that I would be happy to hear from him.

Walking away from there, I decided, on the evidence so far, that Earl had a good heart and didn't know what to do with it, just as he didn't know what to do with that thing in his backyard. He just had it, and it was no use to him.

He called my office on Wednesday. I'd given him the number. There was something new in his voice, of someone wanting help. He repeated his daughter's line about how I was a professional friend, and I said, yes, sometimes that was what I was. He asked me if I ever worked with "bad kids"—that was his phrase—and I said that sometimes I did. Then he asked me if I'd help him take apart his daughter's play structure on the following Saturday. He said there'd be plenty of beer. I could see what he was after: a bit of free counseling, but since I hadn't prepared myself for his invitation, I didn't have a good defense ready. I looked around my office cubicle, and I saw myself in Earl's backyard, a screwdriver in one hand and a beer in the other. I said yes.

The day I came over, it was a fair morning, for Michigan. This state is like Holland. Cold clammy mists mix with freezing rain in autumn, and hard rains in the spring are broken by tropical heat and tornadoes. It's attack weather. The sky covers you over with a metallic blue, watercolor wash over tinfoil. But this day was all right. I worked out there with Earl, pulling the wood apart with our crowbars and screwdrivers, and we had an audience, Jaynee and Earl's new woman. That was how she was introduced to me: Jody. She's the new woman. She didn't seem to have more than about eight or nine years on Jaynee, and she was nearsighted. She had those thick corrective lenses. But she was pretty in the details, and when she looked at Earl, the lenses enlarged those eyes, so that the love was large and naked and obvious.

I was pulling down a support bar for the north end of the structure and observing from time to time the neighboring backyards. My boys had gone off to a Scout meeting again, and my wife was busy, catching up on some office work. No one missed me. I was pulling at the wood, enjoying myself, talking to Earl and Jaynee and Jody about some of the techniques people in my profession use to resolve bad family quarrels; Jaynee and Jody were working at pulling down some of the wood, too. We already had two piles of scrap lumber.

I had heard a little of how Earl raised Jaynee. Her mother had taken off, the way they sometimes do, when Jaynee was three years old. He'd done the parental work. "You've been the dad, haven't you, Earl?" Jody said, bumping her hip at him. She sat down to watch a sparrow. Her hair was in a ponytail, one of those feminine brooms. "Earl doesn't know the first thing about being a woman, and he had to teach it all to

Jaynee here." Jody pointed her cigarette at Jaynee. "Well, she learned it from somewhere. There's not much left she doesn't know."

"Where's the mystery?" Jaynee asked. She was pounding a hammer absentmindedly into a piece of wood lying flat on the ground. "It's easier being a woman than a girl. Men treat you better 'cause they want you."

Earl stopped turning his wrench. "Only if you don't go to the zoo anytime some punk asks you."

"That was once," she said.

Earl aimed himself at me. "I was strict with her. She knows about the laws I laid down. Fourteen laws. They're framed in her bedroom. Nobody in this country knows what it is to be decent anymore, but I'm trying. It sure to hell isn't easy."

Jody smiled at me. "Earl restrained himself until I came along." She laughed. Earl turned away, so I wouldn't see his face.

"I only spent the night in the zoo *once,*" Jaynee repeated, as if no one had been listening. "And besides, I was protected."

"Protected," Earl repeated, staring at her.

"You know." Jaynee pointed her index finger at her father with her thumb in the air and the other fingers pulled back, and she made an explosive sound in her mouth.

"You took that?" her father said. "You took that to the zoo?"

Jaynee shrugged. At this particular moment, Earl turned to me. "Warren, did you see it?"

I assumed he meant the gun. I looked over toward him from the bolt I was unscrewing, and I nodded. I was so involved in the work of this job that I didn't want my peaceful laboring disturbed.

"You shouldn't have said that," Jody said to Jaynee. Earl had disappeared inside the house. "You know your father well enough by now to know that." Jody stood up and walked to the yard's back fence. "Your father thinks that women and guns are a terrible combination."

"He always said I should watch out for myself," Jaynee said, her back to us. She pulled a cookie out of her pocket and began to eat it.

"Not with a gun," Jody said.

"He showed me how to use it," the daughter said loudly. "I'm not ignorant about firearms." She didn't seem especially interested in the way the conversation was going.

"That was just information," Jody said. "It wasn't for you to use." She was standing and waiting for Earl to reappear. I didn't do work like this, and I didn't hear conversations like this during the rest of the week, and so I was the only person still dismantling the play structure when Earl reappeared in the backyard with the revolver in his right hand. He had his shirt sleeve pulled back so anybody could see the tattoo of the rose run through with the saber on his forearm. Because I didn't know what he was going to do with that gun, I thought I had just better continue to work.

"The ninth law in your bedroom," Earl announced, "says you use violence only in self-defense." He stepped to the fence, then held his arm straight up into the air and fired once. That sound, that shattering, made me drop my wrench. It hit the ground with a clank, three inches from my right foot. Through all the backyards of Westland I heard the blast echoing. The neighborhood dogs set up a barking chain; front and back doors slammed.

Earl was breathing hard and staring at his daughter. We were in a valley, I thought, of distinct silence. "That's all the bullets I own for that weapon," he said. He put the gun on the doorstep. Then he made his way over to where his daughter was sitting. There's a kind of walk, a little stiff, where you know every step has been thought about, every step is a decision. This was like that.

Jaynee was munching the last of her cookie. Her father grabbed her by the shoulders and began to shake her. It was like what you see in movies, someone waking up a sleepwalker. Back and forth her head tossed. "Never never never never never," he said. I started to laugh, but it was too crazed and despairing to be funny. He stopped. I could see he wanted to make a parental speech: his face was tightening up, his flesh stiff, but he didn't know how to start it, the right choice for the first word, and his daughter pushed him away and ran into the house. In that run, something happened to me, and I knew I had to get out of there.

I glanced at Jody, the new woman. She stood with her hands in her blue jeans. She looked bored. She had lived here all her life. What had just happened was a disturbance in the morning's activities. Meanwhile, Earl had picked up a board and was tentatively beating the ground with it. He was staring at the revolver on the steps. "I got to take that gun and throw it into Ford Lake," he said. "First thing I do this afternoon."

"Have to go, Earl," I said. Everything about me was getting just a little bit out of control, and I thought I had better get home.

"You're going?" Earl said, trying to concentrate on me for a moment. "You're going now? You're sure you don't want another beer?"

I said I was sure. The new woman, Jody, went over to Earl and whispered something to him. I couldn't see why, right now, out loud, she couldn't say what she wanted to say. Christ, we were all adults, after all.

"She wants you to take that .22 and throw it," Earl said. He went over to the steps, picked up the gun, and returned to where I was standing. He dropped it into my hand. The barrel was warm, and the whole apparatus smelled of cordite.

"Okay, Earl," I said. I held this heavy object in my hand, and I had the insane idea that my life was just beginning. "You have any particular preference about where I should dispose of it?"

He looked at me, his right eyebrow going up. This kind of diction he hadn't heard from me before. "Particular preference?" He laughed without smiling. "Last I heard," he said, "when you throw a gun out, it doesn't matter where it goes so long as it's gone."

"Gotcha," I said. I was going around to the front of the house. "Be in touch, right?"

Those two were back to themselves again, talking. They'd be interested in saying goodbye to me about two hours from now, when they would notice that I wasn't there.

In the story that would end here, I go out to Belle Isle in the city of Detroit and drop Earl's revolver off the Belle Isle Bridge at the exact moment when no one is looking. But this story has a way to go. That's not what I did. To start with, I drove around with that gun in my car, underneath the front seat, like half the other residents of this area. I drove to work and at the end of the day I drove home, a model bureaucrat, and each time I sat in the car and turned on the ignition, I felt better than I should have because that gun was on the floor. After about a week, the only problem I had was not that the gun was there but that it wasn't loaded. So I went to the ammo store—it's actually called the Michigan Rod and Gun Club—about two miles away from my house and bought some bullets for it. This was all very easy. In fact, the various details were getting easier and easier. I hadn't foreseen this. I've read Freud and Heinz Kohut and D. W. Winnicott, and I can talk to you about psychotic breaks and object-relations and fixation on oedipal grandiosity characterized by the admixture of strong object cathexes and the implicitly disguised presence of castration fears, and, by virtue of my being able to talk about those conditions, I have had some trouble getting into gear and moving when the occasion called for it. But now, with the magic wand under the front seat, I was getting ready for some kind of adventure.

Around the house my character was improving rather than degenerating. Knowing my little secret, I was able to sit with Gary, my younger son, as he practiced the piano, and I complimented him on the Czerny passages he had mastered, and I helped him through the sections he hadn't learned. I was a fiery angel of patience. With Sam, my older boy, I worked on a model train layout. I cooked a few more dinners than I usually did: from honey-mustard chicken, I went on to varieties of stuffed fish and other dishes with sauces that I had only imagined. I was attentive to Ann. The nature of our intimacies improved. We were whispering to each other again. We hadn't whispered in years.

I was frontloading a little fantasy. After all, I had tried intelligence. Intelligence was not working, not with me, not with the world. So it was time to try the other thing.

My only interruption was that I was getting calls from Earl. He called the house. He had the impression that I understood the mind and could make his ideas feel better. I told him that nobody could make his ideas feel better, ideas either feel good or not, but he didn't believe me.

"Do you mind me calling like this?" he asked. It was just before dinner. I was in the study, and the news was on. I pushed the MUTE button on the remote control. While Earl talked, I watched the silent coverage of mayhem.

"No, I don't mind."

"I shouldn't do this, I know, 'cause you get paid to listen, being a professional friend. But I have to ask your advice."

"Don't call me a professional friend. Earl, what's your question?" The pictures in front of me showed a boy being shot in the streets of Beirut.

"Well, I went into Jaynee's room to clean up. You know how teenage girls are. Messy and everything."

"Yes." More Beirut carnage, then back to Tom Brokaw.

"And I found her diary. How was I to know she had a diary? She never told me."

"They often don't, Earl. Was it locked?"

"What?"

"Locked. Sometimes diaries have locks."

"Well," Earl said, "this one didn't."

"Sounds as though you read it." Shots now on the TV of Ed Koch, the mayor, then shots of bag ladies in the streets of New York.

Earl was silent. I decided not to get ahead of him again. "I thought that maybe I shouldn't read it, but then I did."

"How much?"

"All of it," he said, "I read all of it."

I waited. He had called *me.* I hadn't called him. I watched the pictures of Gorbachev, then pictures of a girl whose face had been slashed by an ex-boyfriend. "It must be hard, reading your daughter's diary," I said. "And not *right,* if you see what I mean."

"Not the way you think." He took a deep breath. "I don't mind the talk about boys. She's growing up, and you can wish it won't happen, but it does. You know what I'm saying?"

"Yes, I do, Earl." A commercial now, for Toyotas.

"I don't even mind the sex, how she thinks about it. Hey, I was no priest myself when I was that age, and now the women, they want to have the freedom we had, so how am I going to stop it, and maybe why should I?"

"I see what you mean."

"She's very aggressive. *Very* aggressive. The things she does. You sort of wonder if you should believe it."

"Diaries are often fantasies. You probably shouldn't be reading your daughter's diary at all. It's *hers,* Earl. She's writing for herself, not for you."

"She writes about me, sometimes."

"You shouldn't read it, Earl."

Tom Brokaw again, and now pictures of a nuclear reactor, and shots of men in white outer-space protective suits with lead shielding, cleaning up some new mess. I felt my anger rising, as usual.

"I can't help reading it," Earl said. "A person starts prying, he can't stop."

"You shouldn't be reading it."

"You haven't heard what I'm about to say," Earl told me. "It's why I'm calling you. It's what she says."

"What's that?" I asked him.

"Not what I expected," he said. "She pities me."

"Well," I said. More shots of the nuclear reactor. I was getting an idea.

"Well is right." He took another breath. "First she says she loves me. That was shock number one. Then she says she feels sorry for me. That was shock number two. Because I work on the line at Ford's and I drink beer and I live in Westland. Where does she get off? That's what I'd like to know. She mentions the play structure. She feels *sorry* for me! My God, I always hated pity. I could never stand it. It weakens you. I never wanted anybody on earth pitying me, and now here's my punk daughter doing it."

"Earl, put that diary away."

"I hear you," he said. "By the way, what did you do with that gun?"

"Threw it off the Belle Isle Bridge," I said.

"Sure you did," he said. "Well, anyway, thanks for listening, Warren." Then he hung up. On the screen in front of me, Tom Brokaw was introducing the last news story of the evening.

Most landscapes, no matter where you are, manage to keep something wild about them, but the land in southern Michigan along the Ohio border has always looked to me as if it had lost its self-respect some time ago. This goes beyond being tamed. This land has been beaten up. The industrial brass knuckles have been applied to wipe out the trees, and the corporate blackjack has stunned the soil, and what grows there—the grasses and brush and scrub pine—grows tentatively. The plant life looks scared and defeated, but all the other earthly powers are busily at work.

Such were my thoughts as I drove down to the nuclear reactor in Holbein, Michigan, on a clear Saturday morning in August, my loaded gun under my seat. I was in a merry mood. Recently activated madcap joy brayed and sang inside my head. I was speeding. My car was trembling because the front end was improperly aligned and I was doing about seventy-five. One false move on the steering wheel and I'd be permanently combined with a telephone pole. I had an eye out for the constables but knew I would not be arrested. A magic shield surrounded my car, and I was so invincible that Martians could not have stopped me.

Although this was therapy rather than political action, I was taking it very seriously, especially at the moment when my car rose over the humble crest of a humiliated grassy hill, and I saw the infernal dome and cooling towers of the Holbein reactor a mile or so behind a clutch of hills and trees ahead and to my left. The power company had surrounded all this land with high Cyclone fencing, crowned with barbed wire and that new kind of coiled lacerating razor wire they've invented. I slowed down to see the place better.

There wasn't much to see because they didn't want you to see anything; they'd built the reactor far back from the road, and in this one case they had let the trees grow (the usual demoralized silver maples and willows and jack pines) to hide the view. I drove past the main gate and noted that a sign outside the guards' office regretted that the company could not give tours because of the danger of sabotage. Right. I hadn't expected to get inside. A person doesn't always have to get inside.

About one mile down, the fence took a ninety-degree turn to the left, and a smaller county road angled off from the highway I was on. I turned. I followed this road another half mile until there was a break in the trees and I could get a clear view of the building. I didn't want a window. I wanted a wall. I was sweating like an amateur thief. The back of my shirt was stuck to the car seat, and the car was jerking because my foot was trembling with excited shock on the accelerator.

Through the thin trees, I saw the solid wall of the south building, whatever it held. There's a kind of architecture that makes you ashamed of human beings, and in my generic rage, my secret craziness that felt completely sensible, I took the gun and held my arm out of the window. It felt good to do that. I was John Wayne. I fired four times at that building, once for me, once for Ann, and once for each of my two boys. I don't know what I hit. I don't care. I probably hit that wall. It was the only kind of heroism I could imagine, the Don Quixote kind. But I hadn't fired the gun before and wasn't used to the recoil action, with the result that after the last shot, I lost control of the car, and it went off the road. In any other state my Chevy would have flipped, but this is southern Michigan, where the ditches are shallow, and I was bumped around—in my excitement I had forgotten to wear my seat belt—until the engine finally stalled in something that looked like a narrow offroad parking area.

I opened my door, but instead of standing up I fell out. With my head on the ground I opened my eyes, and there in the stones and pebbles in front of me was a shiny penny. I brought myself to a standing position, picked up the penny, a lucky penny, for my purposes, and surveyed the landscape where my car had stopped. I walked around to the other side of the car and saw a small pile of beer cans and a circle of ashes, where some revelers, sometime this summer, had enjoyed their little party of pleasure there in the darkness, close by the inaudible hum of the Holbein reactor. I dropped the penny in my trouser pocket, put the gun underneath the front seat again, and I started the car. After two tries I got it out, and before the constables came to check on the gunshots, I had made my escape.

I felt I had done something in the spirit of Westland. I sang, feeling very good and oddly patriotic. On the way back I found myself behind a car with a green bumpersticker.

CAUTION: THIS VEHICLE
EXPLODES UPON IMPACT!

That's me, I said to myself. I am that vehicle.

There was still the matter of the gun, and what to do with it. Fun is fun, but you have to know when the party's over. Halfway home, I pulled off the road into one of those rest stops, and I was going to discard the gun by leaving it on top of a picnic table or by dropping it into a trash can. What I actually did was to throw it into the high grass. Half an hour later, I walked into our suburban kitchen with a smile on my face. I explained the scratch on my cheek as the result of an accident while playing racquetball at the health club. Ann and the boys were delighted by my mood. That evening we went out to a park, and, sitting on a blanket, ate our picnic dinner until the darkness came on.

Many of the American stories I was assigned to read in college were about anger, a fact that would not have surprised my mother, who was British, from Brighton. "Warren," she used to say to me, "watch your tongue in front of these people." "These people" always meant "these Americans." Among them was my father, who had been born in Omaha and who had married her after the war. "Your father," my mother said, "has the temper of a savage." Although it is true that my mind has retained memories of household shouting, what I now find queer is that my mother thought that anger was peculiar to this country.

Earl called me a few more times, in irate puzzlement over his life. The last time was at the end of the summer, on Labor Day. Usually Ann and I and the boys go out on Labor Day to a Metropark and take the last long swim of the summer, but this particular day was cloudy, with a forecast for rain. Ann and I had decided to pitch a tent on the back lawn for the boys, and to grill some hot dogs and hamburgers. We were hoping that the weather would hold until evening. What we got was drizzle, off and on, so that you couldn't determine what kind of day it was. I resolved to go out and cook in the rain anyway. I often took the weather personally. I was standing there, grim-faced and wet, firing up the coals, when Ann called me to the telephone.

It was Earl. He apologized for bringing me to the phone on Labor Day. I said it was okay, that I didn't mind, although I *did* mind, in fact. We waited. I thought he was going to tell me something new about his daughter, and I was straining for him not to say it.

"So," he said, "have you been watching?"

"Watching what? The weather? Yes, I've been watching that."

"No," he said, "not the sky. The Jerry Lewis telethon."

"Oh, the telethon," I said. "No, I don't watch it."

"It's important, Warren. We need all the money we can get. We're behind this year. You know how it's for Jerry's kids."

"I know it, Earl." Years ago, when I was a bachelor, once or twice I sat inside drinking all weekend and watching the telethon and making drunken pledges of money. I didn't want to remember such entertainment now.

"If we're going to find a cure for this thing, we need for everybody to contribute. It's for the kids."

"Earl," I said, "they won't find a cure. It's a genetic disorder, some scrambling in the genetic code. They might be able to prevent it, but they won't *cure* it."

There was a long silence. "You weren't born in this country, were you?"

"No," I said.

"I didn't think so. You don't sound like it. I can tell you weren't born here. At heart you're still a foreigner. You have a no-can-do attitude. No offense. I'm not criticizing you for it. It's not your fault. You can't help it. I see that now."

"Okay, Earl."

Then his voice brightened up. "What the hell," he said. "Come out anyway. You know where Westland is? Oh, right, you've been here. You know where the shopping center's located?"

"Yes," I said.

"It's the clown races. We're raising money. Even if you don't believe in the cure, you can still come to the clown races. We're giving away balloons, too. Your kids will enjoy it. Bring 'em along. *They'll* love it. It's quite a show. It's all on TV."

"Earl," I said, "this isn't my idea of what a person should be doing on a holiday. I'd rather—"

"I don't want to hear what you'd rather do. Just come out here and bring your money. All right?" He raised his voice after a quick pause. "Are you listening?"

"Yes, Earl," I said. "I'm listening."

Somehow I put out the charcoal fire and managed to convince my two boys and my wife that they should take a quick jaunt to Westland. I told them about Earl, the clown races, but what finally persuaded the boys was that I claimed there'd be a remote TV unit out there, and they might turn up with their faces on Channel 2. Besides, the rain was coming down a little harder, a cool rain, one of those end-of-summer drizzles that make your skin feel the onset of autumn. When you feel like that, it helps to be in a crowd.

They had set up a series of highway detours around the shopping center, but we finally discovered how to get into the north parking lot. They'd produced the balloons, tents, and lights, but they hadn't produced much of a crowd. They had a local TV personality dressed in a LOVE NETWORK raincoat trying to get people to cheer. The idea was, you made a bet for your favorite clown and put your money in his fishbowl. If your clown won, you'd get a certificate for a free cola at a local restaurant. It wasn't much of a prize, I thought; maybe it *was* charity, but I felt that they could do better than that.

Earl was clown number three. We'd brought three umbrellas and were standing off to the side when he came up to us and introduced himself to my wife and the boys.

He was wearing an orange wig and a clown nose, and he had painted his face white, the way clowns do, and he was wearing Bozo shoes, the size eighteens, but one of his sleeves was rolled up, and you could see the tattoo of that impaled rose. The white paint was running off his face a bit in the rain, streaking, but he didn't seem to mind. He shook hands with my children and Ann and me very formally. He had less natural ability as a clown than anyone else I've ever met. It would never occur to you to laugh at Earl dressed up in that suit. What you felt would be much more complicated. It was like watching a family member descend into a weakness like alcoholism. Earl caught the look on my face.

"What's the matter, Warren?" he asked. "You okay?"

I shrugged. He had his hand in a big clown glove and was shaking my hand.

"It's all for a good cause," he said, waving his other hand at the four lanes they had painted on the parking lot for the races. "We've made a lot of money already. It's all for the kids, kids who aren't as lucky as ours." He looked down at my boys. "You have to believe," he said.

"You sound like Jaynee," I told him. My wife was looking at Earl. I had tried to explain him to her, but I wasn't sure I had succeeded.

"Believe what?" she asked.

"You've been married to this guy for too long," he said, laughing his big clown laugh. "Maybe your kids can explain it to you, about what the world needs now." There was a whistle. Earl turned around. "Gotta go," he said. He flopped off in those big shoes.

"What's he talking about?" my wife asked.

They lined up the four clowns, including Earl, at the chalk, and those of us who were spectators stood under the tent and registered our bets while the LOVE NETWORK announcer from Channel 2 stood in front of the cameras and held up his starter's gun. I stared for a long time at that gun. Then I placed my bet on Earl.

The other three clowns were all fat, middle-aged guys, Shriners or Rotarians, and I thought Earl had a good chance. My gaze went from the gun down to the parking lot, where I saw Jaynee. She was standing in the rain and watching her old man. I heard the gun go off, but instead of watching Earl, I watched her.

Her hair was stuck to the sides of her head in that rain, and her cotton jacket was soaked through. She had her eyes fixed on her father. By God, she looked affectionate. If he wanted his daughter's love, he had it. I watched her clench her fists and start to jump up and down, cheering him on. After twenty seconds I could tell by the way she raised her fist in the air that Earl had clumped his way to victory. Then I saw the new woman, Jody, standing behind Jaynee, her big glasses smeared with rain, grinning.

I looked around the parking lot and thought: everyone here understands what's going on better than I do. But then I remembered that I had fired shots at a nuclear reactor. All the desperate remedies. And I remembered my mother's first sentence to me when we arrived in New York harbor when I was ten years old. She pointed down from the ship at the pier, at the crowds, and she said, "Warren, look at all those Americans." I felt then that if I looked at that crowd for too long, something inside my body would explode, not metaphorically but literally: it would blow a hole through my skin, through my chest cavity. And it came back to me in that shopping center parking lot, full of those LOVE NETWORK people, that feeling of pressure of American crowds and exuberance.

We collected our free cola certificates, and then I hustled my wife and kids back into the car. I'd had enough. We drove out of the Westland parking lot, then were directed by a detour sign into a service drive that circled the entire shopping center and reentered the lot on the north side, back at the clown races. I saw Jaynee again, still in the rain, hugging her American dad, and Jody holding on to his elbow, looking up at him, pressing her thigh against him. I took another exit out of the lot but somehow made the same mistake I had made before, and, once again, found myself back in Westland. Every service drive seemed designed to bring us back to this same scene of father, daughter, and second wife. I gave them credit for who they were and what they were doing—I give them credit now—but I had to get out of there immediately. I don't know how I managed to get out of that place, but on the fourth try, I succeeded.

CHARLES BAXTER

Shelter

Cooper had stopped at a red light on his way to work and was adjusting the dial on his radio when he looked up and saw a man in a filthy brown corduroy suit and a three-day growth of beard staring in through the front windshield and picking with his fingernails at Cooper's windshield wiper. Whenever Cooper had seen this man before, on various Ann Arbor street corners, he had felt a wave of uneasiness and unpleasant compassion. Rolling down the window and leaning out, Cooper said, "Wait a minute there. Just wait a minute. If you get out of this intersection and over to that sidewalk, I'll be with you in a minute"—the man stared at him—*"I'll have something for you."*

Cooper parked his car at a meter two blocks up, and when he returned, the man in the corduroy suit was standing under a silver maple tree, rubbing his back against the bark.

"Didn't think you'd come back," the man said, glancing at Cooper. His hair fell over the top of his head in every direction.

"How do you do?" Cooper held his hand out, but the man—who seemed rather old, close up—didn't take it. "I'm Cooper." The man smelled of everything, a bit like a municipal dump. Cooper tried not to notice it.

"It doesn't matter who I am," the man said, standing unsteadily. "I don't care who I am. It's not worth anybody thinking about it." He looked up at the sky and began to pick at his coat sleeve.

"What's your name?" Cooper asked softly. "Tell me your name, please."

The old man's expression changed. He stared at the blue sky, perfectly empty of clouds, and after a moment said, "My mother used to call me James."

"Good. Well, then, how do you do, James?" The man looked dubiously at his own hand, then reached over and shook. "Would you like something to eat?"

"I like sandwiches," the man said.

"Well, then," Cooper said, "that's what we'll get you."

As they went down the sidewalk, the man stumbled into the side of a bench at a bus stop and almost tripped over a fire hydrant. He had a splay-footed walk, as if one of his legs had once been broken. Cooper began to pilot him by touching him on his back.

"Would you like to hear a bit of the Gospels?" the man asked.

"All right. Sure."

He stopped and held on to a light pole. "This is the fourth book of the Gospels. Jesus is speaking. He says, 'I will not leave you desolate; I will come to you. Yet a little while, and the world will see me no more, but you will see me; because I live, you will live also.' That's from John," the man said. They were outside the Ann Arbor Diner, a neon-and-chrome Art Deco hamburger joint three blocks down from the university campus. "There's more," the old man said, "but I don't remember it."

"Wait here," Cooper said. "I'm going to get you a sandwich."

The man was looking uncertainly at his lapel, fingering a funguslike spot.

"James!" Cooper said loudly. "Promise me you won't go away!"

The man nodded.

When Cooper came out again with a bag of french fries, a carton of milk, and a hamburger, the man had moved down the street and was leaning against the plate-glass window of a seafood restaurant with his hands covering his face. "James!" Cooper said. "Here's your meal." He held out the bag.

"Thank you." When the man removed his hands from his face, Cooper saw in his eyes a moment of complete lucidity and sanity, a glance that took in the street and himself, made a judgment about them all, and quickly withdrew from any engagement with them. He took the hamburger out of its wrapping, studied it for a moment, and then bit into it. As he ate, he gazed toward the horizon.

"I have to go to work now," Cooper said.

The man glanced at him, nodded again, and turned his face away.

"What are we going to do?" Cooper said to his wife. They were lying in bed at sunrise, when they liked to talk. His hand was on her thigh and was caressing it absently and familiarly. "What are we going to do about these characters? They're on the street corners. Every month there are more of them. Kids, men, women, everybody. It's a horde. They're sleeping in the arcade, and they're pushing those terrible grocery carts around with all their worldly belongings, and it makes me nuts to watch them. I don't know what I'm going to do, Christine, but whatever it is, I have to do it." With his other hand, he rubbed his eyes. "I dream about them."

"You're such a good person," she said sleepily. Her hand brushed over him. "I've noticed that about you."

"No, that's wrong," Cooper said. "This has nothing to do with good. Virtue doesn't interest me. What this is about is not feeling crazy when I see those people."

"So what's your plan?"

He rose halfway out of bed and looked out the back window at the treehouse he had started for Alexander, their seven-year-old. Dawn was breaking, and the light came in through the slats of the blinds and fell in strips over him.

When he didn't say anything, she said, "I was just thinking. When I first met you, before you dropped out of law school, you always used to have your shirts laundered, with starch, and I remember the neat creases in your trouser legs, from somebody ironing them. You smelled of after-shave in those days. Sexually, you were ambitious. You took notes slowly. Fastidious penmanship. I like you better now."

"I remember," he said. "It was a lecture on proximate cause."

"No," she said. "It was contribution and indemnification."

"Whatever."

He took her hand and led her to the bathroom. Every morning Cooper and his wife showered together. He called it soul-showering. He had picked up the phrase from a previous girlfriend, though he had never told Christine that. Cooper had told his wife that by the time they were thirty they would probably not want to do this anymore, but they were both now twenty-eight, and she still seemed to like it.

Under the sputter of the water, Christine brushed some soap out of her eyes and said, "Cooper, were you ever a street person?"

"No."

"Smoke a lot of dope in high school?"

"No."

"I bet you drank a lot once." She was an assistant prosecutor in the district attorney's office and sometimes brought her professional habits home. "You tapped kegs and lay out on the lawns and howled at the sorority girls."

"Sometimes I did that," he said. He was soaping her back. She had wide flaring shoulders from all the swimming she had done, and the soap and water flowed down toward her waist in a pattern of V's. "I did all those things," he said, "but I never became that kind of person. What's your point?"

She turned around and faced him, the full display of her smile. "I think you're a latent vagrant," she said.

"But I'm not," he said. "I'm here. I have a job. *This* is where I am. I'm a father. How can you say that?"

"Do I love you?" she asked, water pouring over her face. "Stay with me."

"Well, sure," he said. "That's my plan."

The second one he decided to do something about was standing out of the hot summer sun in the shade of a large catalpa tree near a corner newsstand. This one was holding what seemed to be a laundry sack with the words AMERICAN LINEN SUPPLY stenciled on it. She was wearing light summer clothes—a Hawaiian shirt showing a palm tree against a bloody splash of sunset, and a pair of light cotton trousers, and red Converse tennis shoes—and she stood reading a paperback, beads of sweat falling off her face onto the pages.

This time Cooper went first to a fast-food restaurant, bought the hamburger, french fries, and milk, and then came back.

"I brought something for you," Cooper said, walking to the reading woman. "I brought you some lunch." He held out a bag. "I've seen you out here on the streets many times."

"Thank you," the woman said, taking the bag. She opened it, looked inside, and sniffed appreciatively.

"Are you homeless?" Cooper asked.

"They have a place where you can go," the woman said. She put down the bag and looked at Cooper. "My name's Estelle," she said. "But we don't have to talk."

"Oh, that's all right. If you want. Where's this shelter?"

"Over there." The woman gestured with a french fry she had picked out. She lifted the bag and began to eat. Cooper looked down at the book and saw that it was in a foreign language. The cover had fallen off. He asked her about it.

"Oh, that?" she said. She spoke with her mouth full of food, and Cooper felt a moment of superiority about her bad manners. "It's about women—what happens to women in this world. It's in French. I used to be Canadian. My mother taught me French."

Cooper stood uncomfortably. He took a key ring out of his pocket and twirled it around his index finger. "So what happens to women in this world?"

"What *doesn't?*" the woman said. "Everything happens. It's terrible but sometimes it's all right, and, besides, you get used to it."

"You seem so normal," Cooper said. "How come you're out here?"

The woman straightened up and looked at him. "My mind's not quite right," she said, scratching an eyelid. "Mostly it is but sometimes it isn't. They messed up my medication and one thing led to another and here I am. I'm not complaining. I don't have a bad life."

Cooper wanted to say that she *did* have a bad life, but stopped himself.

"If you want to help people," the woman said, "you should go to the shelter. They need volunteers. People to clean up. You could get rid of your guilt over there, mopping the floors."

"What guilt?" he asked.

"All men are guilty," she said. She was chewing but had put her bag of food on the ground and was staring hard and directly into Cooper's face. He turned toward the street. When he looked at the cars, everyone heading somewhere with a kind of fierce intentionality, braking hard at red lights and peeling rubber at the green, he felt as though he had been pushed out of his own life.

"You're still here," the woman said. "What do you want?"

"I was about to leave." He was surprised by how rude she was.

"I don't think you've ever seen the Rocky Mountains or even the Swiss Alps, for that matter," the woman said, bending down to inspect something close to the sidewalk.

"No, you're right. I haven't traveled much."

"We're not going to kiss, if that's what you think," the woman said, still bent over. Now she straightened up again, glanced at him, and looked away.

"No," Cooper said. "I just wanted to give you a meal."

"Yes, thank you," the woman said. "And now you have to go."

"I was . . . I *was* going to go."

"I don't want to talk to you anymore," the woman said. "It's nothing against you personally, but talking to men just tires me out terribly and drains me of all my strength. Thank you very much, and goodbye." She sat down again and opened up her paperback. She took some more french fries out of the sack and began to eat as she read.

"They're polite," Cooper said, lying next to his wife. "They're polite, but they aren't nice."

"Nice? Nice? Jesus, Cooper, I prosecute rapists! Why should they be nice? They'd be crazy to be nice. Who cares about nice except you? This is the 1980s, Cooper. Get real."

He rolled over in bed and put his hand on her hip. "All right," he said.

They lay together for a while, listening to Alexander snoring in his bedroom across the hall.

"I can't sleep, Cooper," she said. "Tell me a story."

"Which one tonight?" Cooper was a good improviser of stories to help his wife relax and doze off. "Hannah, the snoopy cleaning woman?"

"No," Christine said. "I'm tired of Hannah."

"The adventures of Roderick, insurance adjuster?"

"I'm sick of him, too.

"How about another boring day in Paradise?"

"Yeah. Do that."

For the next twenty minutes, Cooper described the beauty and tedium of Paradise—the perfect rainfalls, the parks with roped-off grassy areas, the sideshows and hot-air balloon rides, the soufflés that never fell—and in twenty minutes, Christine was asleep, her fingers touching him. He was aroused. "Christine?" he whispered. But she was sleeping.

The next morning, as Cooper worked at his baker's bench, rolling chocolate-almond croissants, he decided that he would check out the shelter in the afternoon to see if they needed any help. He looked up from his hands, with a trace of dough and sugar under the fingernails, over toward his boss, Gilbert, who was brewing coffee and humming along to some Coltrane coming out of his old radio perched on top of the mixer. Cooper loved the bakery where he worked. He loved the smell and everything they made there. He had noticed that bread made people unusually happy. Customers closed their eyes when they ate Cooper's doughnuts and croissants and danishes. He looked up toward the skylight and saw that the sky had turned from pale blue to dark blue, what the 64 Crayola box called blue-indigo. He could tell from the tint of the sky that it was seven o'clock, time to unlock the front doors to let in the first of the customers. After Gilbert turned the key and the Firestone mechanics from down the street shuffled in to get their morning doughnuts and coffee in Styrofoam cups, Cooper stood behind the counter in his whites and watched their faces, the slow private smiles that always registered when they first caught the scent of the baked dough and the sugared fruit.

The shelter was in a downtown furniture store that had gone out of business during the recession of '79. To provide some privacy, the first volunteers had covered over the front plate-glass window with long strips of paper from giant rolls, with the result that during the daytime the light inside was colored an unusual tint, somewhere between orange and off-white. As soon as he volunteered, he was asked to do odd jobs. He first went to work in the evening ladling out food—stew, usually, with ice-cream-scoop mounds of mashed potatoes.

The director of the shelter was a brisk and slightly overweight woman named Marilyn Adams, who, though tough and efficient, seemed vaguely annoyed about everything. Cooper liked her officious irritability. He didn't want any baths of feeling in this place.

Around five o'clock on a Thursday afternoon—the bakery closed at four—Cooper was making beds near the front window when he heard a voice from behind him. "Hey," the voice said. "I want to get in here."

Cooper turned around. He saw the reddest person he had ever laid eyes on: the young man's hair was red, his face flamed with sunburn and freckles, and, as if to accentuate his skin and hair tone, he was wearing a bright pink Roxy Music T-shirt. He was standing near the window, with the light behind him, and all Cooper could see of him was a still, flat expression and deeply watchful eyes. When he turned, he had the concentrated otherworldliness of figures in religious paintings.

Cooper told the young man about the shelter's regulations and told him which bed he could have. The young man—he seemed almost a boy—stood listening, his right foot thumping against the floor and his right hand shaking in the air as if he were trying to get water off it. When the young man nodded, his head went up and down too fast, and Cooper thought he was being ironic. "Who are you?" he finally asked. "My name's Cooper."

"Billy Bell," the young man said. "That's a real weird name, isn't it?" He shook his head but didn't look at Cooper or wait for him to agree or disagree. "My mother threw me out last week. Why shouldn't she? I'm twenty-three. She thought I was doing drugs. I wasn't doing drugs. Drugs are so boring. Look at those awful capitalist lizards using them and you'll know what I mean. But I *was* a problem. She was right. She had to get on my case. She decided to throw me away for a while. Trash trash. So I've been sleeping in alleys and benches and I slept for a couple of nights in the Arboretum, but there are too many mosquitoes this time of year for that and I've got bites. I was living with a girl but all my desires left me. You live here, Cooper? You homeless yourself, or what?"

"I'm a volunteer," he said. "I just work here. I've got a home."

"I don't," Billy Bell said. "People should have homes. I don't work now. I lost my job. I'm full of energy but I'm apathetic. Very little appeals to me. I guess I'm going to start some of those greasy minimum-wage things if I can stand them. I'm smart. I'm not a loser. I'm definitely not one of these messed-up ghouls who call this place home."

Cooper stood up and walked toward the kitchen, knowing that the young man would follow him. "They aren't ghouls," he said. "Look around. They're more normal than you are, probably. They're down on their luck."

"Of course they are, of course they are," Billy said, his voice floating a few inches behind Cooper's head. Cooper began to wipe off the kitchen counter, as the young man watched him. Then Billy began waving his right hand again. "My problem, Cooper, my problem is the problem of the month, which is pointlessness and the point of doing anything, which I can't see most of the time. I want to heal people but I can't do that. I'm stalled. What happened was, about a year ago, there was this day. I remember it was sunny, I mean the sun was out, and I heard these wings flapping over my head because I was out in the park with my girlfriend feeding Cheerios to the pigeons. Then this noise: *flap flap flap.* Wings, Cooper, *big* wings, taking my soul away. I didn't want to look behind me because I was afraid they'd taken my shadow, too. It could happen, Cooper, it could happen to anybody. Anyhow, after that, what I knew was, I didn't want what everybody else did, I mean I don't have any desires for anything, and at some times of day I *don't* cast a shadow. My desires just went away like that—poof, poor desires. I'm a saint now but I'm not enjoying it one bit. I can bless people but not heal them. Anybody could lose his soul the way I did. Now all I got is that sad robot feeling. You know, that five-o'clock feeling? But all day, with me."

"You mentioned your mother," Cooper said. He dropped some cleanser into the sink and began to scour. "What about your father?"

"Let me do that." Billy nudged Cooper aside and started to clean the sink with agitated, almost frantic hand motions. "I've done a *lot* of this. My father died last year. I did a lot of housecleaning. I'm a man-maid. My father was in the hospital, but we took him out, and I was trying to be, I don't know, a sophomore in college, which is a pretty dumb thing to aspire to, if you think about it. But I was also sitting by my father's bed and taking care of him—he had pancreatic cancer—and I was reading *Popular Mechanics* to him, the home-improvement section, and feeding him when he could eat, and then when he died, the wings flew over me, though that was later, and there wasn't much I wanted to do. What a sink." As he talked, Billy's hand accelerated in its motions around the drain.

"Come on," Cooper said. "I'm going to take you somewhere."

His idea was to lift the young man's spirits, but he didn't know quite how to proceed. He took him to his car and drove him down the river road to a park, where Billy got out of the car, took his shoes off, and waded into the water. He bent down, and, as Cooper watched, cupped his hands in the river before splashing it over his face. Cooper thought his face had a strange expression, something between ecstasy and despair. He couldn't think of a word in English for this expression but thought there might be a word in another language for it. German, for example. When Billy was finished washing his face, he looked up into the sky. Pigeons and killdeer were flying overhead. After he had settled back into the front seat of Cooper's car, drops of water from his face dripping onto the seat, Billy said, "That's a good feeling, Cooper. You should try it. You wash your face in the flowing water and then you hear the cries of the birds. I'd like to think it makes me a new man but I know it doesn't. How old are you, Cooper?"

"I'm twenty-eight."

"Five years older than me. And what did you say you did?"

"I'll show you."

He drove Billy to the bakery and parked in the back alley. It was getting close to twilight. After Cooper had unlocked the back door, Billy walked into the dark bakery kitchen and began to sniff. "I like this place," he said. "I like it very much." He shook some invisible water off his hand, then ran his finger along the bench. "What's this made of?"

"Hardrock maple. It's like the wood they use in bowling alleys. Hardest wood there is. You can't dent it or break it. Look up."

Billy twisted backwards. "A skylight," he said. "Cooper, your life is on the very top of the eggshell. You have grain from the earth and you have the sky overhead. Ever been broken into?"

"No."

Cooper looked at Billy and saw, returning to him, a steady gaze made out of the watchful and flat expression he had first seen on the young man's face when he had met him a few hours before. "No," he repeated, "never have." He felt, suddenly, that he had embarked all at once on a series of misjudgments. "What did your father do, Billy?"

"He was a surgeon," Billy said. "He did surgery on people."

They stood and studied each other in the dark bakery for a moment.

"We'll go one more place," Cooper said. "I'll get you a beer. Then I have to take you back to the shelter."

Cooper's dog, Hugo, came out through the backyard and jumped up on him as he got out of his car. A load of wash, mostly Alexander's shirts, flapped on the clothesline in the evening breeze. Cooper heard children calling from down the street.

"Here we are," Cooper said. "We'll go in through this door."

Inside the house, Christine was sitting at the dining-room table with two legal pads set up in front of her and a briefcase down by the floor. Behind her, in the living room, Alexander was lying on the floor in front of the TV set, his chin cupped in his hands. He was watching a Detroit Tigers game. They both looked up when Cooper knocked on the kitchen doorframe and came into the hallway, followed by Billy, whose hands were in his pockets and who nodded as he walked.

"Christine," Cooper said. "This is Billy. I met him at the shelter." Billy walked quickly around the table and shook Christine's hand. "I brought him here for a beer."

Christine did not change her posture. Behind a smile, she gave Billy a hard look. "Hello," she said. "And welcome, I guess."

"Thank you," Billy said. Cooper went out to the kitchen, opened a beer, and brought it back to him. Billy looked at the bottle, then took a long swig from it. After wiping his mouth, he said, "Well, my goodness. I certainly never expected to be here in your home tonight."

"Well, we didn't expect you either, Mr.—?"

"Bell," Billy said. "Billy Bell."

"We didn't expect you either, Mr. Bell. You're lucky. My husband never does this." She looked now at Cooper. "He never *never* does this."

Cooper pointed toward the living room. "Billy, that's Alexander over there. He's in the Alan Trammell fan club. I guess you can tell."

Alexander turned around, looked at Billy, and said, "Hi," waving quickly. Billy returned the greeting, but Alexander had already returned to the TV set, now showing a commercial for shaving cream.

"So, Mr. Bell," Christine said. "What brings you to Ann Arbor?"

"Oh, I've always lived here," Billy said. "Graduated from Pioneer High and everything." He began a little jumping motion, then quelled it. "How about you?"

"Oh, not me," Christine said. "I'm from Dayton, Ohio. I came here to law school. That's where I met Cooper."

"I thought he was a baker."

"He is now. He dropped out of law school."

"You didn't drop out?" Billy glanced at Christine's legal pads. "You became a lawyer?"

"I became a prosecutor, yes, that's right. In the district attorney's office. That's what I do."

"Do you like it?" Cooper thought Billy was about to explode in some way; he was getting redder and redder.

"Oh yes," Christine said. "I like it very much."

"Why?"

"Why?" She touched her face and her smile faded. "I came from a family of bullies, Mr. Bell. Three brothers. They tied me up and played tricks on me, and they did this for years. Little boy criminals. Every promise they made to me, they broke. Then I discovered the law, when I grew up. It's about limits and enforced regulation and binding agreements. It's a net of words, Mr. Bell. Legal formulas for proscribing behavior. That's what the law is. Now I have a career of putting promise-breakers behind bars. That makes me happy. What makes you happy, Mr. Bell?"

Billy hopped once, then leaned against the counter. "I didn't have any dreams until today," Billy said, "but now I do, seeing your cute house and your cute family. Here's what I'd like to do. I want to be *just like all of you.* I'd put on a chef's hat and stand outside in my apron like one of those assholes you see in the Sunday magazine section with a spatula in his hand, and, like, I'll be flipping hamburgers and telling my kids to keep their hands out of the chive dip and go run in the sprinkler or do some shit like that. I'll belong to do-good groups like Save the Rainforests, and I'll ask my wife how she likes her meat, rare or well-done, and she'll say well-done with that pretty smile she has, and that's how I'll do it. A wonderful fucking barbecue, this is, with folding aluminum chairs and paper plates and ketchup all over the goddamn place. Oceans of vodka and floods of beer. Oh, and we've sprayed the yard with that big spray that kills anything that moves, and all the flies and mosquitoes and bunnies are dead at our feet. Talk about the good life. That has got to be it."

Alexander had turned around and was staring at Billy, and Christine's face had become masklike and rigid. "Finish your beer, Mr. Bell," she said. "I think you absolutely have to go now. Don't let's waste another minute. Finish the beer and back you go."

"Yes," he said, nodding and grinning.

"I suppose you think what you just said was funny," Cooper said, from where he was standing in the back of the kitchen.

"No," Billy said. "I can't be funny. I've tried often. It doesn't work. No gift for that."

"Have you been in prison, Mr. Bell?" Christine asked, looking down at her legal pad and writing something there.

"No," Billy said. "I have not."

"Oh good," Christine said. "I was afraid maybe you had been."

"Do you think that's what will become of me?" Billy asked. His voice had lowered from its previous manic delivery and become soft.

"Oh, who knows?" Christine said, running her hand through her hair. "It could happen, or maybe not."

"Because I think my life is out of my hands," Billy said. "I just don't think I have control over it any longer."

"Back you go," Christine said. "Goodbye. Fare thee well."

"Thank you," Billy said. "That was a nice blessing. And thank you for the beer. Goodbye, Alexander. It was nice meeting you."

"Nice to meet you," the boy said from the floor.

"Let's go," Cooper said, picking at Billy's elbow.

"Back I go," Billy said. "Fare thee well, Billy, goodbye and Godspeed. So long, Mr. Human Garbage. Okay, all right, yes, now I'm gone." He did a quick walk through the kitchen and let the screen door slam behind him. Christine gave Cooper a look, which he knew meant that she was preparing a speech for him, and then he followed Billy out to the car.

On the way to the shelter, Billy slouched down on the passenger side. He said nothing for five minutes. Then he said, "I noticed something about your house, Cooper. I noticed that in the kitchen there were all these glasses and cups and jars out on the counter, and the jars weren't labeled, not the way they usually label them, and so I looked inside one of them, one of those jars, and you know what I saw? I suppose you must know, because it's your kitchen."

"What?" Cooper asked.

"Pain," Billy said, looking straight ahead and nodding. "That jar was full of pain. I had to close the lid over it immediately. Now tell me something, because I don't have the answer to it. Why does a man like you, a baker, have a jar full of pain in his kitchen? Can you explain that?"

Out through the front windows, Cooper saw the reassuring lights of the city, the lamplights shining out through the front windows, and the streetlights beginning to go on. A few children were playing on the sidewalks, hopscotch and tag, and in the sky a vapor trail from a jet was beginning to dissolve into orange wisps. What was the price one paid for loving one's own life? He felt a tenderness toward existence and toward his own life, and felt guilty for that.

At the shelter, he let Billy out without saying good night. He watched the young man do his hop-and-skip walk toward the front door; then he put the car into gear and drove home. As he expected, Christine was waiting up for him and gave him a lecture, in bed, about guilty liberalism and bringing the slime element into your own home.

"That's an exaggeration," Cooper said. He was lying on his side of the bed, his hip touching hers. "That's not what he was. I'm not wrong. I'm not." He felt her lips descending over him and remembered how she always thought that his failures in judgment made him sensual.

Two days later he arrived at work before dawn and found Gilbert standing motionless in front of Cooper's own baker's bench. Cooper closed the door behind him and said, "Hey, Gilbert."

"It's all right," Gilbert said. "I already called the cops."

"What?"

Gilbert pointed. On the wood table were hundreds of pieces of broken glass from the scattered skylight in a slice-of-pie pattern, and, over the glass, a circle of dried blood the width of a teacup. Smaller dots of blood, like afterthoughts, were scattered around the bench and led across the floor to the cash register, which had been jimmied open. Cooper felt himself looking up. A bird of a type he couldn't identify was perched on the broken skylight.

"Two hundred dollars," Gilbert said, overpronouncing the words. "Somewhere somebody's all cut up for a lousy two hundred dollars. I'd give the son of a bitch a hundred not to break in, if he'd asked. But you know what I really mind?"

"The blood," Cooper said.

"Bingo." Gilbert nodded, as he coughed. "I hate the idea of this guy's blood in my kitchen, on the floor, on the table and over there in the mixing pans. I really hate it. A bakery. What a fucking stupid place to break into."

"I TOLD you so," Christine said, washing Cooper's face. Then she turned him around and ran the soapy washcloth down his back and over his buttocks.

August. Three days before Christine's birthday. Cooper and his son were walking down Main Street toward a store called the Peaceable Kingdom to get Christine a present, a small stuffed pheasant that Alexander had had his eye on for many months. Alexander's hand was in Cooper's as they crossed at the corner, after waiting for the WALK sign to go on. Alexander had been asking Cooper for an exact definition of trolls, and how they differ from ghouls. And what, he wanted to know, *what exactly* is a goblin, and how are they born? In forests? Can they be born anywhere, like trolls?

Up ahead, squatting against the window of a sporting-goods store, was the man perpetually dressed in the filthy brown corduroy suit: James. His hands were woven together at his forehead, thumbs at temples, to shade his eyes against the sun. As Cooper and his son passed by, James spoke up. He did not ask for money. He said, "Hello Cooper."

"Hello, James," Cooper said.

"Is this your boy?" He pulled his hands apart and pointed at Alexander.

"Yes."

"Daddy," Alexander said, tugging at his father's hand.

"A fine boy," James said, squinting. "Looks a bit like you." The old man smelled as he had before: like a city dump, like everything.

"Thank you," Cooper said, beaming. "He's a handsome boy, isn't he?"

"Indeed," James said. "Would you like to hear a bit of the Gospels?"

"No, thank you, James," Cooper said. "We're on our way to get this young man's mother a birthday present."

"Well, I won't keep you," the old man said.

As Cooper reached for his wallet, Alexander suddenly spoke: "Daddy, don't."

"What?"

"Don't give him any money," the boy said.

"Why not?"

Alexander couldn't say. He began to shake his head, looking at James, then at his father. He backed away, down the sidewalk, his lower lip beginning to stick out and his eyes starting to grow wet.

"Here, James," Cooper said, watching his son, who had retreated down the block and was hiding in the doorway of a hardware store. He handed the old man five dollars.

"Bless you," James said. "And bless Jesus." He put the money in his pocket, then placed his hands together in front of his chest, lowered himself to his knees, and began to pray.

"Goodbye, James," Cooper said. With his eyes closed, James nodded. Cooper ran down the block to catch up with his son.

After Alexander had finished crying, he told his father that he was afraid—afraid that he was going to bring that dirty man home, the way he did with the red-haired guy, and let him stay, maybe in the basement, in the extra room.

"I wouldn't do that," Cooper said. "Really. I wouldn't do that."

"Wouldn't you?" his wife asked, that night, in bed. "Wouldn't you? I think you might."

"No. Not home. Not again."

But he had been accused, and he rose up and walked down the hall to his son's room. The house was theirs, no one else's; his footsteps were the only audible ones. In Alexander's room, in the dim illumination spread by the Swiss-chalet nightlight, Cooper saw his son's model airplanes and the posters of his baseball heroes, but in looking around the room, he felt that something was missing. He glanced again at his son's dresser. The piggy bank, stuffed with pennies, was gone.

He's frightened of my charity, Cooper thought, looking under the bed and seeing the piggy bank there, next to Alexander's favorite softball.

Cooper returned to bed. "He's hidden his money from me," he said.

"They do that, you know," Christine said. "And they go on doing that."

"You can't sleep," Cooper said, touching his wife.

"No," she said. "But it's all right."

"I can't tell you about Paradise," Cooper told her. "I gave you all the stories I knew."

"Well, what *do* you want?" she asked.

He put his hands over hers.

"Shelter me," he said.

"Oh, Cooper," she said. "Which way this time? Which way?"

To answer her, he rolled over, and, as quietly as he could, so as not to wake their son in the next room, he took her into his arms and held her there.

Ann Beattie (1947–)

grew up in the suburbs of Washington, D.C., attended college at American University, and went on to do graduate work in English literature at the University of Connecticut. She began writing stories out of frustration with her doctoral work. After rejecting twenty-two submissions, The New Yorker *published Beattie's "A Platonic Relationship" in 1974, and Beattie became a regular contributor to the magazine. Her first collection of stories,* Distortions, *and her first novel,* Chilly Scenes of Winter, *appeared simultaneously in 1976 and initiated a long-standing critical debate as to whether Beattie's greater strength is in the story or the novel. All critics agree, however, on the uniqueness of her style and her uncanny ability to expose certain truths about contemporary life, particularly as it lived by those of her own generation and social class (the copyright holder for her fiction is "Irony & Pity, Inc."). "She really did, in some ways, make a generation conscious of itself," said Tobias Wolff. She has published eight novels and several collections of stories, most recently the career-spanning* Park City: New and Selected Stories. *John Updike chose her story "Janus" for inclusion in* The Best American Short Stories of the Century. *Beattie has taught at Harvard University and at the University of Virginia. She lives in Maine and Key West with her husband, the painter Lincoln Perry.*

INTRODUCTION BY **Vendela Vida**

This is What a Confrontation Sounds Like

I recently heard a radio interview with Ann Beattie in which she mentioned that in high school, she had a D average. She told an anecdote about how teachers followed her through the school hallways, snapping. *"Snapping?"* the interviewer asked. Yes, Beattie explained: Without any other explanation for her poor grades, her teachers were checking to see if perhaps she was deaf.

I found this story amusing, yes, but also surprising because Ann Beattie has perhaps the best ear for dialogue—by which I mean a talent for capturing conversation as it really happens—of any living American writer. In fact, one of Beattie's strengths as a writer is her supreme skill at depicting *everything* realistically. But more on this later.

First, two things that Beattie understands about real-life dialogue:

1. *Conversations are often interrupted by the very people having them, and these interruptions, although often inane, occasionally occur at the most crucial, heartbreaking moments of revelation.* In "The Burning House," the narrator, Amy, confides in a friend, Freddy, details about her husband's affair. They're sitting on an outdoor bench, and immediately after Amy makes the disclosure, Freddy says, "I came out here with Mr. Sam [the dog] and he dug up a rock and I put the avocado seed in the hole and packed dirt on top of it . . . ." Amy is the next to speak. She ignores Freddy's aside and says of her husband and his affair, "He's embarrassed." Is Freddy callous? Uncaring? Deaf? Not in the least. Beattie understands that interruptions and asides are an integral part of any conversation—any real conversation.

2. *People repeat themselves during fights.* In "Park City," the narrator tries to break some unwelcome news to her half-sister, Janet. From the start, Janet is reluctant to talk openly. The narrator begs, "Janet, please don't be business-like." A page and a half later, she pleads again, "Please don't sound business-like." What's striking and significant about this scene is that Beattie is aware that the character is repeating herself, but as a writer, she's attentive enough to know that this is what a fight sounds like. Rarely during any confrontation does either party proffer new information or make a progression in attitude; instead, the same invectives and cavils are exchanged over and over.

A Confession

Often, when reading Russian writers such as Tolstoy or Dostoyevsky, I find myself making diagrams to remind me of who is related to whom and how. I do the same thing with many of Beattie's stories.

I love this about Beattie: She writes about the seeds our parents sow and the complicated family trees that are born of them. Her stories are full of half-siblings and children of half-siblings and children of half-sisters' boyfriends. The opening sentence of "Park City" lays it all out for readers:

> For a week, possibly a week and a half, I'm stringing along to Utah with my half sister, Janet, more or less looking after Janet's boyfriend's daughter, Lyric (fourteen), who is in turn looking after Janet's child, my niece, Nell (three): Nell the Bell, Nell from Hell, Bad Smell Nell.

There's no real reason why the sisters have to be half-sisters, and a more fearful writer might have tried to simplify the relationship by thickening the bloodlines. But Beattie is trying to do something else: She's not writing to simplify, she's writing to explore the complications of our relationships to everyone around us.

Fitzgerald's famous adage is "Character is plot." In the world of Beattie's fiction, minor characters are plot. Beattie's stories are full of characters—on the average, many more than most stories—and it's often the minor characters who add a new twist or revelation to the story. In "Park City," it's the Vietnamese resident manager and deep-tissue masseuse, Nguyen ("Nikki") Williams, who discloses an awful truth about Janet's boyfriend. At the end of "Park City," it's a stranger who comes to the narrator's rescue and utters the final potent line of the story: ". . . the one thing you've got to remember next time is to request a slow start."

It's that line, a line stated by a just-introduced bystander, that begs us to surmise how the narrator will interpret it, what she will do next. Beattie's endings are often jolting. At the end of "Janus," the narrator reveals something completely unexpected; you can feel the story switching gears. The result is that the reader feels untethered and thrown back into the story itself, wondering how he or she could have missed all the clues that have built up to the exhilarating ending. Cumulatively, Beattie's stories have a similar yet larger effect: After reading a number of her stories, you are released into reality, looking at everything a little more closely, hearing everything a bit louder. In short, through Beattie's realistic description, your perceptions of the real world around you are that much sharper. It's as though Ann Beattie has been walking behind you, snapping.

Vendela Vida is the author of the nonfiction book Girls on the Verge *and the novel* And Now You Can Go. *She is the coeditor of* Believer *magazine.*

ANN BEATTIE

Janus

The bowl was perfect. Perhaps it was not what you'd select if you faced a shelf of bowls, and not the sort of thing that would inevitably attract a lot of attention at a crafts fair, yet it had real presence. It was as predictably admired as a mutt who has no reason to suspect he might be funny. Just such a dog, in fact, was often brought out (and in) along with the bowl.

Andrea was a real-estate agent, and when she thought that some prospective buyers might be dog lovers, she would drop off her dog at the same time she placed the bowl in the house that was up for sale. She would put a dish of water in the kitchen for Mondo, take his squeaking plastic frog out of her purse and drop it on the floor. He would pounce delightedly, just as he did every day at home, batting around his favorite toy. The bowl usually sat on a coffee table, though recently she had displayed it on top of a pine blanket chest and on a lacquered table. It was once placed on a cherry table beneath a Bonnard still life, where it held its own.

Everyone who has purchased a house or who has wanted to sell a house must be familiar with some of the tricks used to convince a buyer that the house is quite special: a fire in the fireplace in early evening; jonquils in a pitcher on the kitchen counter, where no one ordinarily has space to put flowers; perhaps the slight aroma of spring, made by a single drop of scent vaporizing from a lamp bulb.

The wonderful thing about the bowl, Andrea thought, was that it was both subtle and noticeable—a paradox of a bowl. Its glaze was the color of cream and seemed to glow no matter what light it was placed in. There were a few bits of color in it—tiny geometric flashes—and some of these were tinged with flecks of silver. They were as mysterious as cells seen under a microscope; it was difficult not to study them, because they shimmered, flashing for a split second, and then resumed their shape. Something about the colors and their random placement suggested motion. People who liked country furniture always commented on the bowl, but then it turned out that people who felt comfortable with Biedermeier loved it just as much. But the bowl was not at all ostentatious, or even so noticeable that anyone would suspect that it had been put in place deliberately. They might notice the height of the ceiling on first entering a room, and only when their eye moved down from that, or away from the refraction of sunlight on a pale wall, would they see the bowl. Then they would go immediately to it and comment. Yet they always faltered when they tried to say something. Perhaps it was because they were in the house for a serious reason, not to notice some object.

Once, Andrea got a call from a woman who had not put in an offer on a house she had shown her. That bowl, she said—would it be possible to find out where the owners had bought that beautiful bowl? Andrea pretended that she did not know what the woman was referring to. A bowl, somewhere in the house? Oh, on a table under the window. Yes, she would ask, of course. She let a couple of days pass, then called back to say that the bowl had been a present and the people did not know where it had been purchased.

When the bowl was not being taken from house to house, it sat on Andrea's coffee table at home. She didn't keep it carefully wrapped (although she transported it that way, in a box); she kept it on the table, because she liked to see it. It was large enough so that it didn't seem fragile, or particularly vulnerable if anyone sideswiped the table or Mondo blundered into it at play. She had asked her husband to please not drop his house key in it. It was meant to be empty.

When her husband first noticed the bowl, he had peered into it and smiled briefly. He always urged her to buy things she liked. In recent years, both of them had acquired many things to make up for all the lean years when they were graduate students, but now that they had been comfortable for quite a while, the pleasure of new possessions dwindled. Her husband had pronounced the bowl "pretty," and he had turned away without picking it up to examine it. He had no more interest in the bowl than she had in his new Leica.

She was sure that the bowl brought her luck. Bids were often put in on houses where she had displayed the bowl. Sometimes the owners, who were always asked to be away or to step outside when the house was being shown, didn't even know that the bowl had been in their house. Once—she could not imagine how—she left it behind, and then she was so afraid that something might have happened to it that she rushed back to the house and sighed with relief when the woman owner opened the door. The bowl, Andrea explained—she had purchased a bowl and set it on the chest for safekeeping while she toured the house with the prospective buyers, and she . . . She felt like rushing past the frowning woman and seizing her bowl. The owner stepped aside, and it was only when Andrea ran to the chest that the lady glanced at her a little strangely. In the few seconds before Andrea picked up the bowl, she realized that the owner must have just seen that it had been perfectly placed, that the sunlight struck the bluer part of it. Her pitcher had been moved to the far side of the chest, and the bowl predominated. All the way home, Andrea wondered how she could have left the bowl behind. It was like leaving a friend at an outing—just walking off. Sometimes there were stories in the paper about families forgetting a child somewhere and driving to the next city. Andrea had only gone a mile down the road before she remembered.

In time, she dreamed of the bowl. Twice, in a waking dream—early in the morning, between sleep and a last nap before rising—she had a clear vision of it. It came into sharp focus and startled her for a moment—the same bowl she looked at every day.

She had a very profitable year selling real estate. Word spread, and she had more clients than she felt comfortable with. She had the foolish thought that if only the bowl were an animate object she could thank it. There were times when she wanted to talk to her husband about the bowl. He was a stockbroker, and sometimes told people that he was fortunate to be married to a woman who had such a fine aesthetic sense and yet could also function in the real world. They were a lot alike, really—they had agreed on that. They were both quiet people—reflective, slow to make value judgments, but almost intractable once they had come to a conclusion. They both liked details, but while ironies attracted her, he was more impatient and dismissive when matters became many-sided or unclear. But they both knew this, it was the kind of thing they could talk about when they were alone in the car together, coming home from a party or after a weekend with friends. But she never talked to him about the bowl. When they were at dinner, exchanging their news of the day, or while they lay in bed at night listening to the stereo and murmuring sleepy disconnections, she was often tempted to come right out and say that she thought that the bowl in the living room, the cream-colored bowl, was responsible for her success. But she didn't say it. She couldn't begin to explain it. Sometimes in the morning, she would look at him and feel guilty that she had such a constant secret.

Could it be that she had some deeper connection with the bowl—a relationship of some kind? She corrected her thinking: How could she imagine such a thing, when she was a human being and it was a bowl? It was ridiculous. Just think of how people lived together and love each other. . . . But was that always so clear, always a relationship? She was confused by these thoughts, but they remained in her mind. There was something within her now, something real, that she never talked about.

The bowl was a mystery, even to her. It was frustrating, because her involvement with the bowl contained a steady sense of unrequited good fortune; it would have been easier to respond if some sort of demand were made in return. But that only happened in fairy tales. The bowl was just a bowl. She did not believe that for one second. What she believed was that it was something she loved.

In the past, she had sometimes talked to her husband about a new property she was about to buy or sell—confiding some clever strategy she had devised to persuade owners who seemed ready to sell. Now she stopped doing that, for all her strategies involved the bowl. She became more deliberate with the bowl, and more possessive. She put it in houses only when no one was there, and removed it when she left the house. Instead of just moving a pitcher or a dish, she would remove all the other objects from a table. She had to force herself to handle them carefully, because she didn't really care about them. She just wanted them out of sight.

She wondered how the situation would end. As with a lover, there was no exact scenario of how matters would come to a close. Anxiety became the operative force. It would be irrelevant if the lover rushed into someone else's arms, or wrote her a note and departed to another city. The horror was the possibility of the disappearance. That was what mattered.

She would get up at night and look at the bowl. It never occurred to her that she might break it. She washed and dried it without anxiety, and she moved it often, from coffee table to mahogany corner table or wherever, without fearing an accident. It was clear that she would not be the one who would do anything to the bowl. The bowl was only handled by her, set safely on one surface or another; it was not very likely that anyone would break it. A bowl was a poor conductor of electricity: it would not be hit by lightning. Yet the idea of damage persisted. She did not think beyond that—to what her life would be without the bowl. She only continued to fear that some accident would happen. Why not, in a world where people set plants where they did not belong, so that visitors touring a house would be fooled into thinking that dark corners got sunlight—a world full of tricks?

She had first seen the bowl several years earlier, at a crafts fair she had visited half in secret, with her lover. He had urged her to buy the bowl. She didn't *need* any more things, she told him. But she had been drawn to the bowl, and they had lingered near it. Then she went on to the next booth, and he came up behind her, tapping the rim against her shoulder as she ran her fingers over a wood carving. "You're still insisting that I buy that?" she said. "No," he said. "I bought it for you." He had bought her other things before this—things she liked more, at first—the child's ebony-and-turquoise ring that fitted her little finger; the wooden box, long and thin; beautifully dovetailed, that she used to hold paper clips; the soft gray sweater with a pouch pocket. It was his idea that when he could not be there to hold her hand she could hold her own—clasp her hands inside the lone pocket that stretched across the front. But in time she became more attached to the bowl than to any of his other presents. She tried to talk herself out of it. She owned other things that were more striking or valuable. It wasn't an object whose beauty jumped out at you; a lot of people must have passed it by before the two of them saw it that day.

Her lover had said that she was always too slow to know what she really loved. Why continue with her life the way it was? Why be two-faced, he asked her. He had made the first move toward her. When she would not decide in his favor, would not change her life and come to him, he asked her what made her think she could have it both ways. And then he made the last move and left. It was a decision meant to break her will, to shatter her intransigent ideas about honoring previous commitments.

Time passed. Alone in the living room at night, she often looked at the bowl sitting on the table, still and safe, unilluminated. In its way, it was perfect: the world cut in half, deep and smoothly empty. Near the rim, even in dim light, the eye moved toward one small flash of blue, a vanishing point on the horizon.

ANN BEATTIE

The Burning House

Freddy Fox is in the kitchen with me. He has just washed and dried an avocado seed I don't want, and he is leaning against the wall, rolling a joint. In five minutes, I will not be able to count on him. However: he started late in the day, and he has already brought in wood for the fire, gone to the store down the road for matches, and set the table. "You mean you'd know this stuff was Limoges even if you didn't turn the plate over?" he called from the dining room. He pretended to be about to throw one of the plates into the kitchen, like a Frisbee. Sam, the dog, believed him and shot up, kicking the rug out behind him and skidding forward before he realized his error; it was like the Road Runner tricking Wile E. Coyote into going over the cliff for the millionth time. His jowls sank in disappointment.

"I see there's a full moon," Freddy says. "There's just nothing that can hold a candle to nature. The moon and the stars, the tides and the sunshine—and we just don't stop for long enough to wonder at it all. We're so engrossed in ourselves." He takes a very long drag on the joint. "We stand and stir the sauce in the pot instead of going to the window and gazing at the moon."

"You don't mean anything personal by that, I assume."

"I love the way you pour cream in a pan. I like to come up behind you and watch the sauce bubble."

"No, thank you," I say. "You're starting late in the day."

"My responsibilities have ended. You don't trust me to help with the cooking, and I've already brought in firewood and run an errand, and this very morning I exhausted myself by taking Mr. Sam jogging with me, down at Putnam Park. You're sure you won't?"

"No, thanks," I say. "Not now, anyway."

"I love it when you stand over the steam coming out of a pan and the hairs around your forehead curl into damp little curls."

My husband, Frank Wayne, is Freddy's half brother. Frank is an accountant. Freddy is closer to me than to Frank. Since Frank talks to Freddy more than he talks to me, however, and since Freddy is totally loyal, Freddy always knows more than I know. It pleases me that he does not know how to stir sauce; he will start talking, his mind will drift, and when next you look the sauce will be lumpy, or boiling away.

Freddy's criticism of Frank is only implied. "What a gracious gesture to entertain his friends on the weekend," he says.

"Male friends," I say.

"I didn't mean that you're the sort of lady who doesn't draw the line. I most certainly did not mean that," Freddy says. "I would even have been surprised if you had taken a toke of this deadly stuff while you were at the stove."

"Okay," I say, and take the joint from him. Half of it is left when I take it. Half an inch is left after I've taken two drags and given it back.

"More surprised still if you'd shaken the ashes into the saucepan."

"You'd tell people I'd done it when they'd finished eating, and I'd be embarrassed. You can do it, though. I wouldn't be embarrassed if it was a story you told on yourself."

"You really understand me," Freddy says. "It's moon-madness, but I have to shake just this little bit in the sauce. I have to do it."

He does it.

Frank and Tucker are in the living room. Just a few minutes ago, Frank returned from getting Tucker at the train. Tucker loves to visit. To him, Fairfield County is as mysterious as Alaska. He brought with him from New York a crock of mustard, a jeroboam of champagne, cocktail napkins with a picture of a plane flying over a building on them, twenty egret feathers ("You cannot get them anymore—strictly illegal," Tucker whispered to me), and, under his black cowboy hat with the rhinestone-studded chin strap, a toy frog that hopped when wound. Tucker owns a gallery in SoHo, and Frank keeps his books. Tucker is now stretched out in the living room, visiting with Frank, and Freddy and I are both listening.

". . . so everything I've been told indicates that he lives a purely Jekyll-and-Hyde existence. He's twenty years old, and I can see that since he's still living at home he might not want to flaunt his gayness. When he came into the gallery, he had his hair slicked back—just with water, I got close enough to sniff—and his mother was all but holding his hand. So fresh scrubbed. The stories I'd heard. Anyway, when I called, his father started looking for the number where he could be reached on the Vineyard—very irritated, because I didn't know James, and if I'd just phoned James I could have found him in a flash. He's talking to himself, looking for the number, and I say, 'Oh, did he go to visit friends or—' and his father interrupts and says, 'He was going to a gay pig roast. He's been gone since Monday.' *Just like that.*"

Freddy helps me carry the food out to the table. When we are all at the table, I mention the young artist Tucker was talking about. "Frank says his paintings are really incredible," I say to Tucker.

"Makes Estes look like an Abstract Expressionist," Tucker says. "I want that boy. I really want that boy."

"You'll get him," Frank says. "You get everybody you go after."

Tucker cuts a small piece of meat. He cuts it small so that he can talk while chewing. "Do I?" he says.

Freddy is smoking at the table, gazing dazedly at the moon centered in the window. "After dinner," he says, putting the back of his hand against his forehead when he sees that I am looking at him, "we must all go to the lighthouse."

"If only *you* painted," Tucker says. "I'd want you."

"You couldn't have me," Freddy snaps. He reconsiders. "That sounded half-hearted, didn't it? Anybody who wants me can have me. This is the only place I can be on Saturday night where somebody isn't hustling me."

"Wear looser pants," Frank says to Freddy.

"This is so much better than some bar that stinks of cigarette smoke and leather. Why do I do it?" Freddy says. "Seriously—do you think I'll ever stop?"

"Let's not be serious," Tucker says.

"I keep thinking of this table as a big boat, with dishes and glasses rocking on it," Freddy says.

He takes the bone from his plate and walks out to the kitchen, dripping sauce on the floor. He walks as though he's on the deck of a wave-tossed ship. "Mr. Sam!" he calls, and the dog springs up from the living-room floor, where he had been sleeping; his toenails on the bare wood floor sound like a wheel spinning in gravel. "You don't have to beg," Freddy says. "Jesus, Sammy—I'm just giving it to you."

"I hope there's a bone involved," Tucker says, rolling his eyes to Frank. He cuts another tiny piece of meat. "I hope your brother does understand why I couldn't keep him on. He was good at what he did, but he also might say just *anything* to a customer. You have to believe me that if I hadn't been extremely embarrassed more than once I never would have let him go."

"He should have finished school," Frank says, sopping up sauce on his bread. "He'll knock around a while longer, then get tired of it and settle down to something."

"You think I died out here?" Freddy calls. "You think I can't hear you?"

"I'm not saying anything I wouldn't say to your face," Frank says.

"I'll tell you what I wouldn't say to your face," Freddy says. "You've got a swell wife and kid and dog, and you're a snob, and you take it all for granted."

Frank puts down his fork, completely exasperated. He looks at me.

"He came to work once this stoned," Tucker says. *"Comprenez-vous?"*

"You like me because you feel sorry for me," Freddy says.

He is sitting on the concrete bench outdoors, in the area that's a garden in the springtime. It is early April now—not quite spring. It's very foggy out. It rained while we were eating, and now it has turned mild. I'm leaning against a tree, across from him, glad it's so dark and misty that I can't look down and see the damage the mud is doing to my boots.

"Who's his girlfriend?" Freddy says.

"If I told you her name, you'd tell him I told you."

"Slow down. What?"

"I won't tell you, because you'll tell him that I know."

"He knows you know."

"I don't think so."

"How did you find out?"

"He talked about her. I kept hearing her name for months, and then we went to a party at Garner's, and she was there, and when I said something about her later he said, 'Natalie who?' It was much too obvious. It gave the whole thing away."

He sighs. "I just did something very optimistic," he says. "I came out here with Mr. Sam and he dug up a rock and I put the avocado seed in the hole and packed dirt on top of it. Don't say it—I know: can't grow outside, we'll still have another snow, even if it grew, the next year's frost would kill it."

"He's embarrassed," I say. "When he's home, he avoids me. But it's rotten to avoid Mark, too. Six years old, and he calls up his friend Neal to hint that he wants to go over there. He doesn't do that when we're here alone."

Freddy picks up a stick and pokes around in the mud with it. "I'll bet Tucker's after that painter personally, not because he's the hottest thing since pancakes. That expression of his—it's always the same. Maybe Nixon really loved his mother, but with that expression who could believe him? It's a curse to have a face that won't express what you mean."

"Amy!" Tucker calls. "Telephone."

Freddy waves goodbye to me with the muddy stick. "'I am not a crook,'" Freddy says. "Jesus Christ."

Sam bounds halfway toward the house with me, then turns and goes back to Freddy.

It's Marilyn, Neal's mother, on the phone.

"Hi," Marilyn says. "He's afraid to spend the night."

"Oh, no," I say. "He said he wouldn't be."

She lowers her voice. "We can try it out, but I think he'll start crying."

"I'll come get him."

"I can bring him home. You're having a dinner party, aren't you?"

I lower my voice. "Some party. Tucker's here. J.D. never showed up."

"Well," she says. "I'm sure that what you cooked was good."

"It's so foggy out, Marilyn. I'll come get Mark."

"He can stay. I'll be a martyr," she says, and hangs up before I can object.

Freddy comes into the house, tracking in mud. Sam lies in the kitchen, waiting for his paws to be cleaned. "Come on," Freddy says, hitting his hand against his thigh, having no idea what Sam is doing. Sam gets up and runs after him. They go into the small downstairs bathroom together. Sam loves to watch people urinate. Sometimes he sings, to harmonize with the sound of the urine going into the water. There are footprints and pawprints everywhere. Tucker is shrieking with laughter in the living room. ". . . he says, he says to the other one, 'Then, dearie, have you ever played *spin* the bottle?'" Frank's and Tucker's laughter drowns out the sound of Freddy peeing in the bathroom. I turn on the water in the kitchen sink, and it drowns out all the noise. I begin to scrape the dishes. Tucker is telling another story when I turn off the water: ". . . that it was Onassis in the Anvil, and nothing would talk him out of it. They told him Onassis was dead, and he thought they were trying to make him think he was crazy. There was nothing to do but go along with him, but, God—he was trying to goad this poor old fag into fighting about Stavros Niarchos. You know—Onassis's *enemy.* He thought it was *Onassis.* In the *Anvil.*" There is a sound of a glass breaking. Frank or Tucker puts *John Coltrane Live in Seattle* on the stereo and turns the volume down low. The bathroom door opens. Sam runs into the kitchen and begins to lap water from his dish. Freddy takes his little silver case and his rolling papers out of his shirt pocket. He puts a piece of paper on the kitchen table and is about to sprinkle grass on it, but realizes just in time that the paper has absorbed water from a puddle. He balls it up with his thumb, flicks it to the floor, puts a piece of rolling paper where the table's dry and shakes a line of grass down it. "You smoke this," he says to me. "I'll do the dishes."

"We'll both smoke it. I'll wash and you can wipe."

"I forgot to tell them I put ashes in the sauce," he says.

"I wouldn't interrupt."

"At least he pays Frank ten times what any other accountant for an art gallery would make," Freddy says.

Tucker is beating his hand on the arm of the sofa as he talks, stomping his feet. ". . . so he's trying to feel him out, to see if this old guy with the dyed hair knew *Maria Callas.* Jesus! And he's so out of it he's trying to think what opera singers are called, and instead of coming up with *'diva'* he comes up with *'duenna.'* At this point, Larry Betwell went up to him and tried to calm him down, and he breaks into song—some aria or something that Maria Callas was famous for. Larry told him he was going to lose his *teeth* if he didn't get it together, and . . ."

"He spends a lot of time in gay hangouts, for not being gay," Freddy says.

I scream and jump back from the sink, hitting the glass I'm rinsing against the faucet, shattering green glass everywhere.

"What?" Freddy says. "Jesus Christ, what is it?"

Too late, I realize what it must have been that I saw: J.D. in a goat mask, the puckered pink plastic lips against the window by the kitchen sink.

"I'm sorry," J.D. says, coming through the door and nearly colliding with Frank, who has rushed into the kitchen. Tucker is right behind him.

"Oooh," Tucker says, feigning disappointment, "I thought Freddy smooched her."

"I'm sorry," J.D. says again. "I thought you'd know it was me."

The rain must have started again, because J.D. is soaking wet. He has turned the mask around so that the goat's head stares out from the back of his head. "I got lost," J.D. says. He has a farmhouse upstate. "I missed the turn. I went miles. I missed the whole dinner, didn't I?"

"What did you do wrong?" Frank asks.

"I didn't turn left onto 58. I don't know why I didn't realize my mistake, but I went *miles.* It was raining so hard I couldn't go over twenty-five miles an hour. Your driveway is all mud. You're going to have to push me out."

"There's some roast left over. And salad, if you want it," I say.

"Bring it in the living room," Frank says to J.D. Freddy is holding out a plate to him. J.D. reaches for the plate. Freddy pulls it back. J.D. reaches again, and Freddy is so stoned that he isn't quick enough this time—J.D. grabs it.

"I thought you'd know it was me," J.D. says. "I apologize." He dishes salad onto the plate. "You'll be rid of me for six months, in the morning."

"Where does your plane leave from?" Freddy says.

"Kennedy."

"Come in here!" Tucker calls. "I've got a story for you about Perry Dwyer down at the Anvil last week, when he thought he saw Aristotle Onassis."

"Who's Perry Dwyer?" J.D. says.

"That is not the point of the story, dear man. And when you're in Cassis, I want you to look up an American painter over there. Will you? He doesn't have a phone. Anyway—I've been tracking him, and I know where he is now, and I am *very* interested, if you would stress that with him, to do a show in June that will be *only* him. He doesn't answer my letters."

"Your hand is cut," J.D. says to me.

"Forget it," I say. "Go ahead."

"I'm sorry," he says. "Did I make you do that?"

"Yes, you did."

"Don't keep your finger under the water. Put pressure on it to stop the bleeding."

He puts the plate on the table. Freddy is leaning against the counter, staring at the blood swirling in the sink, and smoking the joint all by himself. I can feel the little curls on my forehead that Freddy was talking about. They feel heavy on my skin. I hate to see my own blood. I'm sweating. I let J.D. do what he does; he turns off the water and wraps his hand around my second finger, squeezing. Water runs down our wrists.

Freddy jumps to answer the phone when it rings, as though a siren just went off behind him. He calls me to the phone, but J.D. steps in front of me, shakes his head no, and takes the dish towel and wraps it around my hand before he lets me go.

"Well," Marilyn says. "I had the best of intentions, but my battery's dead."

J.D. is standing behind me, with his hand on my shoulder.

"I'll be right over," I say. "He's not upset now, is he?"

"No, but he's dropped enough hints that he doesn't think he can make it through the night."

"Okay," I say. "I'm sorry about all of this."

"Six years old," Marilyn says. "Wait till he grows up and gets that feeling."

I hang up.

"Let me see your, hand," J.D. says.

"I don't want to look at it. Just go get me a Band-Aid, please."

He turns and goes upstairs. I unwrap the towel and look at it. It's pretty deep, but no glass is in my finger. I feel funny; the outlines of things are turning yellow. I sit in the chair by the phone. Sam comes and lies beside me, and I stare at his black-and-yellow tail, beating. I reach down with my good hand and pat him, breathing deeply in time with every second pat.

"Rothko?" Tucker says bitterly, in the living room: "Nothing is great that can appear on greeting cards. Wyeth is that way. Would *Christina's World* look bad on a cocktail napkin? You know it wouldn't."

I jump as the phone rings again. "Hello?" I say, wedging the phone against my shoulder with my ear, wrapping the dish towel tighter around my hand.

"Tell them it's a crank call. Tell them anything," Johnny says. "I miss you. How's Saturday night at your house?"

"All right," I say. I catch my breath.

"Everything's all right here, too. Yes indeed. Roast rack of lamb. Friend of Nicole's who's going to Key West tomorrow had too much to drink and got depressed because he thought it was raining in Key West, and I said I'd go in my study and call the National Weather Service. Hello, Weather Service. How are you?"

J.D. comes down from upstairs with two Band-Aids and stands beside me, unwrapping one. I want to say to Johnny, "I'm cut. I'm bleeding. It's no joke."

It's all right to talk in front of J.D., but I don't know who else might overhear me.

"I'd say they made the delivery about four this afternoon," I say.

"This is the church, this is the steeple. Open the door, and see all the people," Johnny says. "Take care of yourself. I'll hang up and find out if it's raining in Key West."

"Late in the afternoon," I say. "Everything is fine."

"Nothing is fine," Johnny says. "Take care of yourself."

He hangs up. I put the phone down, and realize that I'm still having trouble focusing, the sight of my cut finger made me so light-headed. I don't look at the finger again as J.D. undoes the towel and wraps the Band-Aids around my finger.

"What's going on in here?" Frank says, coming into the dining room.

"I cut my finger," I say. "It's okay."

"You did?" he says. He looks woozy—a little drunk. "Who keeps calling?"

"Marilyn. Mark changed his mind about staying all night. She was going to bring him home, but her battery's dead. You'll have to get him. Or I will."

"Who called the second time?" he says.

"The oil company. They wanted to know if we got our delivery today."

He nods. "I'll go get him, if you want," he says. He lowers his voice. "Tucker's probably going to whirl himself into a tornado for an encore," he says, nodding toward the living room. "I'll take him with me."

"Do you want me to go get him?" J.D. says.

"I don't mind getting some air," Frank says. "Thanks, though. Why don't you go in the living room and eat your dinner?"

"You forgive me?" J.D. says.

"Sure," I say. "It wasn't your fault. Where did you get that mask?"

"I found it on top of a Goodwill box in Manchester. There was also a beautiful old birdcage—solid brass."

The phone rings again. I pick it up. "Wouldn't I love to be in Key West with you," Johnny says. He makes a sound as though he's kissing me and hangs up.

"Wrong number," I say.

Frank feels in his pants pocket for the car keys.

J.D. knows about Johnny. He introduced me, in the faculty lounge, where J.D. and I had gone to get a cup of coffee after I registered for classes. After being gone for nearly two years, J.D. still gets mail at the department—he said he had to stop by for the mail anyway, so he'd drive me to campus and point me toward the registrar's. J.D. taught English; now he does nothing. J.D. is glad that I've gone back to college to study art again, now that Mark is in school. I'm six credits away from an M.A. in art history. He wants me to think about myself, instead of thinking about Mark all the time. He talks as though I could roll Mark out on a string and let him fly off, high above me. J.D.'s wife and son died in a car crash. His son was Mark's age. "I wasn't prepared," J.D. said when we were driving over that day. He always says this when he talks about it. "How could you be prepared for such a thing?" I asked him. "I am now," he said. Then, realizing he was acting very hard-boiled, made fun of himself. "Go on," he said, "punch me in the stomach. Hit me as hard as you can." We both knew he wasn't prepared for anything. When he couldn't find a parking place that day, his hands were wrapped around the wheel so tightly that his knuckles turned white.

Johnny came in as we were drinking coffee. J.D. was looking at his junk mail—publishers wanting him to order anthologies, ways to get free dictionaries.

"You are so lucky to be out of it," Johnny said, by way of greeting. "What do you do when you've spent two weeks on *Hamlet* and the student writes about Hamlet's good friend Horchow?"

He threw a blue book into J.D.'s lap. J.D. sailed it back.

"Johnny," he said, "this is Amy."

"Hi, Amy," Johnny said.

"You remember when Frank Wayne was in graduate school here? Amy's Frank's wife."

"Hi, Amy," Johnny said.

J.D. told me he knew it the instant Johnny walked into the room—he knew that second that he should introduce me as somebody's wife. He could have predicted it all from the way Johnny looked at me.

For a long time J.D. gloated that he had been prepared for what happened next—that Johnny and I were going to get together. It took me to disturb his pleasure in himself—me, crying hysterically on the phone last month, not knowing what to do, what move to make next.

"Don't do anything for a while. I guess that's my advice," J.D. said. "But you probably shouldn't listen to me. All I can do myself is run away, hide out. I'm not the learned professor. You know what I believe. I believe all that wicked fairy-tale crap: your heart will break, your house will burn."

Tonight, because he doesn't have a garage at his farm, J.D. has come to leave his car in the empty half of our two-car garage while he's in France. I look out the window and see his old Saab, glowing in the moonlight. J.D. has brought his favorite book, *A Vision,* to read on the plane. He says his suitcase contains only a spare pair of jeans, cigarettes, and underwear. He is going to buy a leather jacket in France, at a store where he almost bought a leather jacket two years ago.

In our bedroom there are about twenty small glass prisms hung with fishing line from one of the exposed beams; they catch the morning light, and we stare at them like a cat eyeing catnip held above its head. Just now, it is 2 A.M. At six-thirty, they will be filled with dazzling color. At four or five, Mark will come into the bedroom and get in bed with us. Sam will wake up, stretch, and shake, and the tags on his collar will clink, and he will yawn and shake again and go downstairs, where J.D. is asleep in his sleeping bag and Tucker is asleep on the sofa, and get a drink of water from his dish. Mark has been coming into our bedroom for about a year. He gets onto the bed by climbing up on a footstool that horrified me when I first saw it—a gift from Frank's mother: a footstool that says TODAY IS THE FIRST DAY OF THE REST OF YOUR LIFE in needlepoint. I kept it in a closet for years, but it occurred to me that it would help Mark get up onto the bed, so he would not have to make a little leap and possibly skin his shin again. Now Mark does not disturb us when he comes into the bedroom, except that it bothers me that he has reverted to sucking his thumb. Sometimes he lies in bed with his cold feet against my leg. Sometimes, small as he is, he snores.

Somebody is playing a record downstairs. It's the Velvet Underground—Lou Reed, in a dream or swoon, singing "Sunday Morning." I can barely hear the whispering and tinkling of the record. I can only follow it because I've heard it a hundred times.

I am lying in bed, waiting for Frank to get out of the bathroom. My cut finger throbs. Things are going on in the house even though I have gone to bed; water runs, the record plays. Sam is still downstairs, so there must be some action.

I have known everybody in the house for years, and as time goes by I know them all less and less. J.D. was Frank's adviser in college. Frank was his best student, and they started to see each other outside of class. They played handball. J.D. and his family came to dinner. We went there. That summer—the summer Frank decided to go to graduate school in business instead of English—J.D.'s wife and son deserted him in a more horrible way, in that car crash. J.D. has quit his job. He has been to Las Vegas, to Colorado, New Orleans, Los Angeles, Paris twice; he tapes postcards to the walls of his living room. A lot of the time, on the weekends, he shows up at our house with his sleeping bag. Sometimes he brings a girl. Lately, not. Years ago, Tucker was in Frank's therapy group in New York, and ended up hiring Frank to work as the accountant for his gallery. Tucker was in therapy at the time because he was obsessed with foreigners. Now he is also obsessed with homosexuals. He gives fashionable parties to which he invites many foreigners and homosexuals. Before the parties he does TM and yoga, and during the parties he does Seconals and isometrics. When I first met him, he was living for the summer in his sister's house in Vermont while she was in Europe, and he called us one night, in New York, in a real panic because there were wasps all over. They were "hatching," he said—big, sleepy wasps that were everywhere. We said we'd come; we drove all through the night to get to Brattleboro. It was true: there were wasps on the undersides of plates, in the plants, in the folds of curtains. Tucker was so upset that he was out behind the house, in the cold Vermont morning, wrapped like an Indian in a blanket, with only his pajamas on underneath. He was sitting in a lawn chair, hiding behind a bush, waiting for us to come.

And Freddy—"Reddy Fox," when Frank is feeling affectionate toward him. When we first met, I taught him to ice-skate and he taught me to waltz; in the summer, at Atlantic City, he'd go with me on a roller coaster that curved high over the waves. I was the one—not Frank—who would get out of bed in the middle of the night and meet him at an all-night deli and put my arm around his shoulders, the way he put his arm around my shoulders on the roller coaster, and talk quietly to him until he got over his latest anxiety attack. Now he tests me, and I retreat: this man he picked up, this man who picked him up, how it feels to have forgotten somebody's name when your hand is in the back pocket of his jeans and you're not even halfway to your apartment. Reddy Fox—admiring my new red silk blouse, stroking his fingertips down the front, and my eyes wide, because I could feel his fingers on my chest, even though I was holding the blouse in front of me on a hanger to be admired. All those moments, and all they meant was that I was fooled into thinking I knew these people because I knew the small things, the personal things.

Freddy will always be more stoned than I am, because he feels comfortable getting stoned with me, and I'll always be reminded that he's more lost. Tucker knows he can come to the house and be the center of attention; he can tell all the stories he knows, and we'll never tell the story we know about him hiding in the bushes like a frightened dog. J.D. comes back from his trips with boxes full of postcards, and I look at all of them, as though they're photographs taken by him, and I know, and he knows, that what he likes about them is their flatness—the unreality of them, the unreality of what he does.

Last summer, I read "The Metamorphosis" and said to J.D., "Why did Gregor Samsa wake up a cockroach?" His answer (which he would have toyed over with his students forever) was "Because that's what people expected of him."

They make the illogical logical. I don't do anything, because I'm waiting, I'm on hold (J.D.); I stay stoned because I know it's better to be out of it (Freddy); I love art because I myself am a work of art (Tucker).

Frank is harder to understand. One night a week or so ago, I thought we were really attuned to each other, communicating by telepathic waves, and as I lay in bed about to speak I realized that the vibrations really existed: they were him, snoring.

Now he's coming into the bedroom, and I'm trying again to think what to say. Or ask. Or do.

"Be glad you're not in Key West," he says. He climbs into bed.

I raise myself up on one elbow and stare at him.

"There's a hurricane about to hit," he says.

"What?" I say. "Where did you hear that?"

"When Reddy Fox and I were putting the dishes away. We had the radio on." He doubles up his pillow, pushes it under his neck. "Boom goes everything," he says. "Bam. Crash. Poof." He looks at me. "You look shocked." He closes his eyes. Then, after a minute or two, he murmurs, "Hurricanes upset you? I'll try to think of something nice."

He is quiet for so long that I think he has fallen asleep. Then he says, "Cars that run on water. A field of flowers, none alike. A shooting star that goes slow enough for you to watch. Your life to do over again." He has been whispering in my ear, and when he takes his mouth away I shiver. He slides lower in the bed for sleep. "I'll tell you something really amazing," he says. "Tucker told me he went into a travel agency on Park Avenue last week and asked the travel agent where he should go to pan for gold, and she told him."

"Where did she tell him to go?"

"I think somewhere in Peru. The banks of some river in Peru."

"Did you decide what you're going to do after Mark's birthday?" I say.

He doesn't answer me. I touch him on the side, finally.

"It's two o'clock in the morning. Let's talk about it another time."

"You picked the house, Frank. They're your friends downstairs. I used to be what you wanted me to be."

"They're your friends, too," he says. "Don't be paranoid."

"I want to know if you're staying or going."

He takes a deep breath, lets it out, and continues to lie very still.

"Everything you've done is commendable," he says. "You did the right thing to go back to school. You tried to do the right thing by finding yourself a normal friend like Marilyn. But your whole life you've made one mistake—you've surrounded yourself with men. Let me tell you something. All men—if they're crazy, like Tucker, if they're gay as the Queen of the May, like Reddy Fox, even if they're just six years old—I'm going to tell you something about them. Men think they're Spider-Man and Buck Rogers and Superman. You know what we all feel inside that you don't feel? That we're going to the stars."

He takes my hand. "I'm looking down on all of this from space," he whispers. "I'm already gone."

ANN BEATTIE

Park City

For a week, possibly a week and a half, I'm stringing along to Utah with my half sister, Janet, more or less looking after Janet's boyfriend's daughter, Lyric (fourteen), who is in turn looking after Janet's child, my niece, Nell (three): Nell the Bell, Nell from Hell, Bad Smell Nell. Nell is the youngest child—in fact, there are only two others I've seen, so far—in the building. Unfortunately, one is a pudgy girl of about ten, who will not reveal her own name and who is obviously jealous that Nell is pretty, petite, and doted upon. She has taken to making up nasty names for Nell. Fortunately, the ten-year-old has in-line skates, so she's gone a lot. We usually only encounter her in the morning, and then again in the evening, when she hangs around eating ice-cream cones with her father, who has a Clint Eastwood squint and therefore the look of someone who wouldn't enjoy hearing anything negative about his child's behavior. Where's the mother? Where's anyone except the run-amok girl who races through the breakfast area as if imitating Pee-wee Herman might be appreciated by real people.

Janet and Damon are renting a unit on the second floor of the Ski Galaxy condo. Lyric and Nell and I share an oddly configured first-floor suite that is laid out like half a spider. There are five corridors leading to five bedrooms, all with their own bathrooms. The central room is a half circle with a big bay window curving around one side that contains many floor cushions silk-screened with pictures of prairie dogs, moose, elk, and—this we don't get—gored bulls. There is a large rear-projection television flanked by deer heads. There is an orange leather sofa that we avoid. It looks like furniture recovering from a chemical peel. We've been here for three days. Settling in, as always, has to do with clothes strewn all over and shoes that get mysteriously separated from their mates.

Each morning an odd spread is put out at one end of the lobby by the resident manager, a Vietnamese lady who, in addition to her care-taking duties, gives something called "deep tissue massage." She is also a would-be chanteuse (so far, the only job she's landed is accompanying herself singing with the Rhythm Ace at the Mexican restaurant on Friday nights those times the owner's nephew has been too high to go on). Each morning, Nguyen ("Nikki") Williams, widow of P.F.C. Theodore Roosevelt Williams, sets out her version of a continental breakfast, which invariably consists of hard-boiled eggs she has dyed pink; blueberry toaster tarts she arranges on the tabletop like carefully laid tiles; Waldorf salad (she told me that's what it is) that is essentially whipped cream and miniature marshmallows amid a few flecks of fruit; and halved bagels with a choice of Kraft grape jelly or I Can't Believe It's Not Butter spray. I stick to a plain bagel, myself, and always wrap an extra bagel for Nell to eat later, and then, before we go back upstairs and change into our swimsuits and ride the free bus over to the big pool at Wasatch Mountain Center, I spritz Nell's hair in a fairly hopeless effort to untangle it before the water does another day's damage, then put in whatever Third World–motif barrette appeals to her that day: the brown farmer with his brown cow; tiny women balancing baskets on their heads. There is also a Pocahontas barrette and there are some ridiculous butterfly barrettes we never use that Lyric has clipped to the rim of the pot containing a red amaryllis that blooms profusely on the shelf above the Jacuzzi in one of our many bathrooms. During the winter, the condo is a ski resort. Off-season, they rent to L.A. burnouts, people who are on vacation or (Nikki has confided to me, with a wink) having "trysts," and conference attendees.

Nell's mother, my older half sister, Janet, is enrolled in a weeklong screenwriting course team-taught by her current love interest: a professor from Cornell who quit his job teaching film theory to experience total immersion in The Industry. For two years, he has had full custody of Lyric, after some incident that is only obliquely referred to, if at all. He and his wife went to Amsterdam when a private detective located their missing twelve-year-old, after which the wife decided to stay on and begin living the life of a man in preparation for a sex-change operation. Come to think of it, references to that trip are not so much oblique as quickly dismissed by Janet, who inevitably begins to fan her face as if smoke were coming at her when any mention of the ex lasts more than ten seconds. Lyric never mentions her mother and rarely mentions Amsterdam, except to say that it was cool to run away and pass as an eighteen-year-old, and that it was a good place to hang out and chill, which is what she prefers to do wherever she is. This means, in part, that she strikes up conversations with random men, and that she watches MTV and paints either her toenails or her fingernails daily. She alternates between being quite talkative and completely silent, and I alternate between relating to her easily and thinking she's a Martian. Nell is a nice child, slightly precocious, entirely predictable in her demands, and, like most children, she doesn't like her hair combed.

Right now, Nell pulls her hair around to one side, pokes her nose in, and breathes deeply. "Stop smelling yourself, Nelly the Smelly," Lyric says. She has picked up the malevolent ten-year-old's way of taunting, which she gets away with because she imitates the fat girl at the same time she says nasty things to her possibly new stepsister-to-be. Nell appreciates my being along on this trip, I know: it provides her with someone who will be reflexively sympathetic when she's made fun of, and it spares her a real babysitter—the sort who phone their boyfriends constantly on their cellular phones and watch TV shows about daughters who pray for the salvation of their mothers who are addicted to body piercing, or priests who battle bulimia. The sitters all assume Nell will love pizza, but actually she's burned out on the pizza-for-dinner routine, and she thinks the trendy ones, like Hawaiian, should be sent back to Hawaii. Recently, she crayoned a picture of a slice of pizza with golden wings, headed in the direction of a large black shape I'm sure was a volcano. Neither is she fond of pineapple pureed into "virgin" drinks, though Janet is; so at the end of her long, hard days we often sit with her at the café outside the Mexican restaurant and watch her sipping through pastel foam, lifting out cherries and pineapple wedges, which Nell does like. Lyric and I stick to Diet Coke, which is always available, especially if you're willing to compromise for Diet Pepsi.

There are five TVs in the five bedrooms, though one is set into the wood headboard of the king-size waterbed I often sprawl out on with Lyric, and it can't be budged, so we watch from the foot of the bed, which has been made from largish tree trunks. Nell's TV is on a glass-topped column that culminates in a flattened plaster cow skull, which she has had us help her wheel around to the side of the bed, close to her pillow. In our adjacent rooms, the shows war with each other: Jay Leno drives through a fast-food drive-in and orders tons of food to give the clerk ample time to notice it's him; Catherine Deneuve, looking classy and scintillating at the same time, seduces someone in *Belle de Jour.* The night before, we all eventually channel surfed to CNN to get stereophonic news about the hurricane that had just started to pound the Carolina coast. The reporter looked like he was ready for liftoff, right there on the scene, holding on to a rope, or whatever it was flapping in his hand as he screamed into his microphone. People were shown nailing plywood to their windows. A roof blew off. There was much screaming on the reporter's part about windsurfers who were out earlier who either went home or drowned, though all we could see was rain pelting the camera lens.

So here I am, in Park City, to—as Lyric would have it—hang and chill with Janet and the gang until approximately the eighteenth of July, give or take a few L.A. minutes, or days. The day when the screenwriting course ends is ambiguously described in the brochure. As best we can make out, it may end on different days for people with different astrological signs. I'm along because even Janet burned out on the babysitters, and she also thought it would be a good idea to get my mind off my former fiancé, Hale Dowd, who didn't so much leave me at the altar as leave *to acquire* altars. Altar gathering in the Southwest; I kid you not. Not that he has a religious bone in his body: it was about procuring altars (sometimes, quite easily; other times, major bribes required; occasionally, an indignant turndown when he genuinely offended the padre). Rich people in L.A. now want altars as additions to their entranceways and as frames for their wet bars. Two months ago, Hale traded his leased BMW for a Ford pickup, his taste in music mutated with no transitions from early Brian Eno to Lyle Lovett all in one trip to Tower Records, and he tried to persuade me to give up my job as a Clinique salesperson so that I could drive around with him and eat *chiles verdes* and help him sweet-talk priests. It wasn't like I'd ever envisioned picket fences, and he'd had a vasectomy, so we weren't going to be a mommy-and-daddy-and-baby family or anything like that, but I did sometimes think about growing herbs and having a dog, though when I think of it, that does seem pretty pathetic. When we broke up, Janet drove over to Silver Lake with a big bottle of Sapporo, a trowel, some rosemary in a tub and some basil in a punch-out six-pack, and a cardboard dog that looked exactly like a perky terrier, and we had some beer and planted the plants and put the dog in among them and backed up and looked, and of course it made us laugh. That night it rained, and that was it for the dog, although I can still see the little assemblage so perfectly that it wasn't a waste of Janet's money at all.

Right now, 10:10 a.m., Lyric is tying the laces of her espadrilles around her shapely ankles. It doesn't matter that we're only going swimming: she doesn't own a pair of crappy shoes. It's her theory that if you have noticeable shoes, you'll get instant respect and admiration, however else you look. I slip into my plastic flip-flops and pull a sleeveless T-shirt size XXL—I barely remember the days of buying T-shirts in my size—over my suit as Lyric teases her hair into an Ivana. She never actually swims at the pool; the most she'll do is sit at the shallow end and dangle her feet in the water while Nell splashes around.

Nell is plopped in the middle of the lumber bed, watching cartoons. A bear peeks into a beehive and is swarmed by bees. Scrambling to right himself, he trips over an alligator and is eaten, headfirst. I watch the cartoon to see the bear regurgitated. Nothing happens. The bees spiral and fly away: a black tornado that is really inconsequential, compared to Hurricane Bertha. The alligator gulps several times and, its sides bulging and its back looking more like it swallowed a camel, slithers into some bushes.

"Turn that off. It's awful," I say.

"She might as well learn the way of the world," Lyric says to me.

Nell takes this as confirmation that she can continue watching. At long last, the wet, exhausted bear reappears, stumbling out of the woods. It slams down into two enormous poles that turn out to be . . . dinosaur legs. This is definitely not a day in the life of Teddy Ruxpin. The dinosaur snatches up the bear. From the woods, the terrible sounds continue—I'm hearing the alligator, right?—as the bear disappears down the escalator-length throat of the dinosaur.

"I wonder if that cute guy will be there again," Lyric says, dotting my Clinique lipstick on her cheeks and rubbing it in. "The guy with the Euro boner," she says, anticipating my "Which one?" question. She means the Frenchman who was walking around displaying his anatomy in little striped briefs. I saw him later in the day reading *GQ,* wearing those half glasses that accountants and gynecologists always peer over, and any curiosity I had about him instantly vanished.

"He was old," I say. "Forty-five, at least," I say, anticipating her "How old?"

"I don't want the fat girl to be there," Nell says, as the now-sopping bear makes another escape, popping out the dinosaur's nostril.

"She's never there. She's a condo rat. She stays here and stuffs her fat face all day and then Rollerblades around until her precious Daddy comes home, and then they stuff themselves with ice cream," Lyric says to Nell. "Give it a break with the anxiety."

"What did she say?" Nell says to me.

"Let's go to the pool," I say. "Come on, Nell. Turn off the TV. Come on, Lyric. Stop preening."

"I swear to God, I think I am getting this spider vein on my throat," she says, her head turned away from the mirror.

Nell gets off the bed with both hands on top of her head, to protect it from my attempts to comb her hair, and runs past me.

"Your suit's on the towel rack," I call after her.

"I don't want to wear my suit," she calls back. Every day, the same thing.

"There are no other girls your age without a swimsuit," I say, with as much solemnity as possible. "You'd be the only one."

"I'm not a girl," she says.

"What are you?"

"A mermaid," she says. I hear the toilet flush. When she returns, she has the suit on. One shoulder strap flops under her armpit. "I want shoes like hers," Nell says.

"These are super-chic shoes made only for people with a minimum shoe size of six," Lyric says, standing on one foot and turning the other foot from side to side, admiringly. "Do you know how much these shoes cost?"

"I want ones like that!" Nell says to me. She looks desperate.

"They cost so much that when you start getting paid for doing chores—when your mom starts quartering you and fifty-centing you for dumping your cruddy clothes in the hamper instead of on the floor, you would have to save for approximately . . ."

"Mommy can buy me shoes like that!" Nell says to me, her voice rising.

"Talk to Mommy about it later," I say, trying to dodge the whole issue.

"Where's Mommy?" Nell says, her eyes clouding with tears.

"Mommy's at her seminar," I say. "You know where Mommy is. She kissed you goodbye."

"I was asleep," Nell says.

There seems no good answer to that. Also, if truth be told, I'm pretty sure it was only Damon who came into the suite this morning, to look at all three of us to make sure we were where we were supposed to be. He walks hard, and it sounded like just one set of footsteps, but it was too early to bother opening my eyes and to possibly risk a conversation. Janet, I know, is not used to rising early, and having to be in class at 9 a.m. is really a struggle for her.

Nell chooses the Pocahontas barrette and I clip it in a clump of hopelessly frizzed curls. Her swimsuit is pink polka dots, with a ruffle bisecting her belly. She's got her mother's pigeon toes and squared shoulders. She looks at once robotically durable and mysteriously frail. Her father is a famous actor who has set up a trust fund for her, in addition to paying monthly child support. This, in an agreement his lawyer made with Janet's lawyer that he would never have to see the child or otherwise participate in her upbringing, and that Janet agree not to tell his wife or to write about their relationship—which lasted all of a month and a half, including the three weeks when she didn't know she was pregnant. We happened to see him on TV a couple of nights ago, and Nell paid less attention to him than to the bear, which I suppose was only natural, since she had no idea he was her father. He was just another guy plotting a crime.

"Are we ready?" I ask. Lyric clips her Walkman to her fanny pack, which she wears pouch forward; she puts on the earphones and turns on the music and does a few dance steps in silent acknowledgment of my question. "I want you to carry me," Nell says, reaching up. This is because she's afraid of encountering the fat girl; she usually hates to be carried. Still, I heft all forty-two pounds of her, shift her to one arm, and with my other hand pick up the sack I've packed with the daily bagel, the *USA Today* Nikki always leaves outside our door, with a photocopied note stapled to it reminding us that she does deep tissue massage "by appointment or even on spur moments," sunblock in two strengths, Evian water in a thermal bottle, Nell's coloring book and crayons. Janet—my father's child of his youth, while I was the child of his old age, and don't I sympathize today, schlepping around a forty-two-pounder . . . my sister, as I think of her, more simply, is in an air-conditioned room at something called the Yarrow, learning how to perfect her screenplay about Sally Hemings, servant to, and alleged lover of, Thomas Jefferson. Originally, the screenplay began in the present day, with the mounted heads of the animal trophies brought back by Lewis and Clark that were hung on the walls at Monticello talking to each other about the odd goings-on at night, but when I lost it entirely and almost died laughing, she was forced to see what she'd written in a new light. I know she's changed the beginning, though she's refused to ever show it to me again. P.O.V. moose. That's my perspective for the day: P.O.V. moose. You can imagine how strange that makes Park City look, as we exit the condo.

★ ★ ★

But it's just a place: yuppified, restored, renovated, repainted, recast. One shop dips perfectly good Oreo cookies into dark chocolate and sells them for a markup that might make simple Oreo fanciers faint. At another store you can have your picture taken by a camera attached to a computer, after which it's put through another machine that fragments the image, then sends it through a tube, and when it emerges, it's been altered into one of those optical-trick pictures. You have to stare at the maze of indecipherable pattern and let your eyes go out of focus until you see a three-dimensional version of yourself. I had one made my first day in Park City, which I intended to send to Hale, back in the nanosecond of sentimentality when I thought we should probably still stay in touch, but it turned out so frightening that I only showed it to Nikki for corroboration of how awful it was (when it came into—or is it out of?—focus, she put her hands over her mouth and inhaled sharply). The thought occurred to me that an enterprising businessperson might realize that small ones might make excellent, repellent business cards. The picture was of me as I was dressed that day, in a baseball cap turned backward. Giggly Nell had painted a cross on my forehead with the zinc oxide I'd applied to her nose, and I'd forgotten about it when I got in front of the camera, so I looked like some deranged cult person or, at the very least, someone making an untimely protest against Ash Wednesday. As the background, I selected rockets being fired, but when you first looked at the picture it seemed to be just nice abstract shades of red and yellow in a sort of herringbone pattern. I apparently selected some other element I didn't realize I was choosing, because when I saw the picture, all the rockets were rising as a maze, and I was above the maze, floating *2001*-ish tipped slightly forward. I ended up looking like some monstrous apparition with weird war paint that had already descended from space while the rockets were wasting their time going exploring.

"Check it out," Lyric says to me from her lounge. Above us, a woman in white and a man are floating in a big balloon. The balloon has descended enough that we can see it's a bride. She's cake-ornament small, but I swear: you can see her smile. The dark, tiny groom stands next to her. There they go, borne on the breezes of optimism.

"Do you think they got married in the air?" Lyric says.

"People get married on cruise ships all the time. I suppose they could have," I say.

"I mean, who's supposed to throw confetti? The angels?"

She lowers the back of her chaise and turns onto her stomach. She reaches back and unties the string of her bikini top. On the other lounge, Nell has fallen asleep clasping the bagel half near her lips like a big pacifier. Fortunately, I slathered her with sunblock before she fell asleep. The curls that have escaped the barrette blow in the breeze, while the painted Pocahontas kneels resolutely, braced for anything.

Someone's beeper goes off.

A waitress passes by carrying a tray with two bowls of salad on it with little state-of-Utah flags stuck in them and two bottles of beer. She exaggerates the swing of her hips. That's because Euro boner is back today, and it turns out he's a big tipper. She almost swooned a while ago when he said, "Keep the change."

In Utah, it seems to be a rule that bartenders can only pour five ounces of wine at a time—enough to intoxicate Thumbelina, but a modest half glass for the rest of us—though it seems they can serve a person an entire bottle of beer, which is curious.

A screenplay about Sally Hemings. Janet's sincere plan for an organizing principle for the rest of her life seems to be completing this screenplay.

Someone is reading a tabloid. Margaux Hemingway, who has died, is depicted on the cover. Her lips are deep pink, her eyebrows penciled dark. She definitely did not strive for the Clinique natural look.

"May you build a ladder to the stars and climb on every rung," Dylan sings. I'm actually hearing the song, not just remembering it. It's floating on the breeze—from where? From somewhere distant.

But oh, Bobecito, we are already no longer young. Which might not be so bad in itself, except that the world doesn't seem young any longer, either. I mean, self-absorption aside, who thought both things would happen simultaneously? The world really seems to be slipping: global warming; the population explosion. What compounds the problem is that once any group starts to be condescended to in the guise of being catered to—once yuppies say yes, and buy the yuppified Oreos they're offered—it's all over. They're taking the bait, they're eating saltpeter, they're becoming impervious to excess, and to surprise. They're just more people trying to keep up the excitement level by having adventure weddings, adventure honeymoons, adventure babies.

This is the way Janet would prefer I not talk when I can be overheard by anyone who might influence her destiny. Meaning: Damon. She's every bit as cynical as I am—haven't we been hearing that heredity explains almost everything?—but she would prefer that I be silent, and that my silence be mistaken for judiciousness. I am, after all, in charge of her most precious possession. I'm her dependable sister whose life has never bottomed out, the slightly introverted, interesting blond counterpart to her extroversion, her slightly horsey, Andie MacDowell-ish beauty. Her looks come from her Brazilian mother: the high cheekbones; the dark, cascading hair. Janet's mother was so beautiful that my own mother never minded the painting of her that hung over my father's desk. Of course, the woman in the painting was dead and was therefore no threat, unless someone was far more neurotic than my mother and thought that the painting was hung because he was still in love with his first wife. My mother didn't think that. All she wondered was whether he ever loved anyone except himself. For a long time in the seventies, it was fashionable for women to think about their husbands that way, though; after a few years of marriage, it came upon them almost the way people get colds when the seasons change.

Lyric turns on her side. "Are you always thinking?" she says.

"What do you mean?"

"Do you have, like, these deep inner thoughts?" She turns sideways, propping herself on an elbow.

"Does something make you think I do?"

"I wish I had them," she says. "Do you like, get them when you get older? Damon"—she calls her father by his first name: none of that "Daddy" stuff—"it's like he's always trying to come down from sensory overload without totally crashing, you know? He calls it brain buzz. Have you ever heard a buzz?"

"No."

"Maybe it's like those diseases that are stored in your nerve cells and they reappear. If you have chicken pox, it can stay dormant for years, and then you might get shingles. But maybe if it's something inside your brain, the stored stuff gets tired of waiting to break out and it starts to rumble, or something."

"Run that by me again," I say.

"You seem, like, really bright. It seems like you're always thinking. Because, I mean, if people are talkative, they're not necessarily thinking, they're just talking, you know? And you don't seem to be a very talkative person."

"I was thinking about my father. He died last year," I say. "While I was sitting here, I heard some music that made me sad. It made me think of him."

"Ooh," she says. "I do this all the time. I go fishing, and then I don't know what to do when I catch a fish."

"I guess you can put it back in the water," I say.

She smiles. "You have an interesting way of talking," she says. "You should talk more."

Is she right about my not being talkative? If so, I realize for the first time why that might be. "Don't take this wrong, but part of the problem might be that while I'm very fond of the people I hang out with, I'm thirty-one and you're fourteen. And Nell is three, and your father is fifty, and my sister is thirty-nine."

"The age thing is what you think it is? I mean, like, I don't have any problem talking to people because of what age they are."

"You're very gregarious. You talk to everybody."

"It comes from being self-involved," she says. "What I'm really doing is projecting my anxiety."

I look at her, surprised.

"He sent me to a psychologist after the Amsterdam thing," she says.

"Oh," I say.

"But you know another thing," she says. "When you do talk, you probably really want to connect with people. I think I just like to talk."

"You're being too hard on yourself," I say.

"No. I've thought about it."

I consider what she's said. "Well, if you're on to yourself, you've got a chance to change," I say.

"I get discouraged, because my limitations all seem to have sorted themselves out while I was sleeping, or something. I mean, I live with Damon, and unless I run away again and he finds me again, I'm going to be living with him until I go to college—right? That's a joke. I do not envision college. But what I'm saying is that Damon's never going to change, is he?"

"People are pretty much the way they're going to be at that age," I say.

"Right. So I'm going to have to watch him bait your sister and then send her flying," she says. "A year from now, no chance I'll know you people."

I look at her, startled.

"What?" she says. "You said you had trouble talking to people who weren't your age, so I'm trying to talk seriously to you."

"Well . . . what exactly are you saying?"

"Don't you know? He's got a violent temper. He scares the shit out of women. He scared my mother so much and he made her feel so powerless that she decided the only thing she could do was get away from him and also become a man for safe measure. I know that sounds funny, but she used to talk to me about it. She'd be lifting weights she kept hidden under her bed, and she'd talk about him through clenched teeth, with the bedroom door closed."

"What did he . . . he has a violent temper?" I shift onto one hip, leaning toward her. "Has he ever hurt you?"

"No," she says. "I've got what's-it-called. I've got immunity. So far, at least, and there have been more than a few times when I've really pushed his buttons."

"But you're not saying he'd do anything to really hurt Janet, are you?"

"He's more a bully than a hitter," Lyric says.

"A hitter? Did he hit your mother?"

"They used to have shoving matches. He didn't really hit her, I don't think. But she always lost. He could stay solid as a sandbag, but the energy would just drain right out of her."

"Jesus. That's horrible," I say.

She waves her hand at me dismissively. "You even get upset by violent cartoons."

My thoughts are bottlenecking; how exactly should I bring this up with Janet? If Lyric was wondering what was going on inside my head, I was naive not to wonder what was going on inside hers.

"He's been that way with women other than your mother?" I say weakly.

"Yeah, he's always that way, eventually," she says.

"I don't suppose it's something you've ever tried to talk to him about? I mean, I guess you wouldn't get very far, being fourteen years old."

"I wouldn't get very far if I was sixty years old, and he was a hundred and ten. You've seen how he shuts down conversation about anything he doesn't want to hear."

In fact, I have. When I was complaining about how the fate of Park City indicated the downward spiral of the modern world, I could see from the way he looked right through me that such observations were not appreciated. I close my eyes and envision my sister just the way Lyric described her: small and snagged on a fishhook. Then I see her spiral out, across choppy water. I immediately open my eyes, and all the people around the pool seem very particular, very distinct, very real.

"I've had girlfriends who've had boyfriends or fathers, or whatever, who've really gotten rough with them. I testified against one girl's stepfather. Some guy came to the house and I gave a deposition. It's not that unusual. I mean, it's a lot more likely that one of those lawyer guys, or whatever they are, are going to show up than that they'll ring your doorbell because you've won the Publishers Clearing House sweepstakes."

"I don't think I know anybody personally who was ever beaten up. But it's so prevalent. It must have happened to someone I know, but no one ever told me that."

"You seem pretty observant," Lyric says. "I mean, you seem like the sort of person who'd put two and two together if a friend said she walked into a wall. Just think about Nicole. I mean, no one with half a brain ever had any doubt about whether he really beat up Nicole, right?"

"Right," I say.

"I don't want to go so far as to say that Damon's a Bruno Magli man," Lyric says.

"But still," I say.

She sighs again. "You're right," she says. "'But still.'"

"I want ice cream," Nell says, touching my arm. I'm so much in another world that when she touches me, I jump. I look at her and think how vulnerable she is. How vulnerable we all are. How long has she been listening?

"Because this bagel got all sweaty, and it tastes like lotion, and I'm tired of bagels, too," she says. That's Nell: always developing her thoughts fully in order to convince you. I smile at her fondly.

"If I give you the money, can you go get it yourself?" I say.

She looks at me, perturbed. "I'm not big enough that they can see me," she says. She looks over at the bar, which is not where she'd go for an ice cream. That's where she'd go for five ounces of wine, if she were my age. And in need of a drink, which I think I might be.

"No, sweetie, you don't go to that window. You just ask the waitress."

"*You* do it," she says.

"When the waitress comes by, we'll get you an ice cream. What kind do you want?"

"Pink," she says.

"If they don't have strawberry, what's the next choice?"

"Find out if they have it!" she says.

"Hel-*lo*? Am I a ghost?" Lyric says.

"Oh," I say. "Sorry. What kind do you want?"

"I want pink, too," she says.

"And I don't suppose you have a backup if they don't have pink?"

"Green," she says.

Great: the alternative is pistachio.

When the waitress does appear, Nell is sitting on the edge of her lounge, like the relative of someone in an operating room, frantic for news. The flavors are: Cherry Garcia (pink with cherries and chocolate, I explain: she'll like it); Swiss almond fudge; and nonfat banana yogurt. I order a Corona, which the man next to Lyric is drinking. Lyric decides on Swiss almond fudge. I cancel my beer and order banana yogurt. Nell, still squinting as she assimilates the information about Cherry Garcia, looks like the doctor has just explained the patient's condition in language too technical to understand. "Does it have coconut?" she says, worrying aloud. "No," the waitress and I say in unison. "Jerry Garcia was only about the greatest musician who ever lived," Lyric says. "I mean, I can understand being a total, absolute Deadhead."

"What does she say is in it?" Nell says to me.

"No coconut. Believe me, you'll like it."

"Okay," Nell says hesitantly.

"Hey, Cindy, let me have another one of these," the man next to Lyric says, holding up his empty bottle. The waitress takes his bottle without comment and walks away, not sashaying a bit.

"It is like so weird to be in a state where almost nobody drinks," Lyric says. "I mean, it's against their religious beliefs to drink, but at the same time, they think stuff that people with the D.T.'s think, like that there are spirit babies floating around in heaven they've got to round up and find a way to give birth to."

"What?" Nell says. Before I can answer, she says, "I'm not going to be floating when Mommy comes home, am I?"

Lyric bursts into laughter. I give her a dirty look.

"No. Why would you think you'd be floating around?" I ask.

"Because that lady in a balloon."

"I thought you were asleep when that went over," I say.

"A bride edging closer to her spirit babies," Lyric says.

This is too much for Nell. She just ignores her. But the man next to Nell has gotten interested. I see him looking at her. I see that she is aware she's being overheard. She adjusts the top of her bikini and looks straight ahead.

The man next to Lyric turns his head. "Here on vacation?" he says.

"No," Lyric says slowly. "This is all work related."

There's a pause.

"May I ask what kind of work you do?" the man asks.

"I work with computers. I set up programs to monitor the way vineyards are run."

This exchange all happens quickly, and Lyric sounds so calm and reasonable, that I'm stunned into silence. Not that the man was flirting with me, in the first place.

"There are vineyards in Utah?"

"I'm here to meet with a client from Sonoma, who's on vacation."

"Really?" the man says. The longer Lyric keeps it up, the more you can see him questioning his perceptions. She might be some sort of prodigy, for all he knows.

"And what about you?" she says.

"I'm one of those people writing the great American novel," he says. "I'm retired from Dow Corning."

"Dow Corning! You know, when I was in my midtwenties, I had breast implants," Lyric says, raising one leg and resting the calf of the other leg on her knee. She looks at me. "Did you hear that? This man is responsible for the money I'm soon going to receive." She turns to the man. "Those implants were responsible for causing me more than a bit of trouble."

"I wasn't a scientist," the man says. "I worked in bookkeeping."

"I was thanking you," Lyric says. "Don't feel defensive."

"Are you . . . are you all in the wine business?" he says to me. I can tell he doubts this highly.

"Who is that man?" Nell says to me.

Lyric answers for me: "It's not that we're in the wine business, per se; we're developmental people, responsible for setting up creative programs that monitor—"

"The little girl, too?" he says.

"I'm a mermaid!" she says.

The man laughs slightly.

"Have you met Jacques?" Lyric says. "He's in a snit today, because we shot down one of his ideas, so he's sulking over there across the pool."

She points to the Frenchman in his little bathing suit. He is reading a magazine.

"I haven't met him," the man says.

"Lyric," I say. She ignores me. I see the waitress approaching. She moves to the man's lounge and gives him a bottle of beer, with a plastic cup turned upside down on the neck. Our three cones stand upright in a metal holder. They are wrapped with napkins absorbing the melting ice cream.

"So here's to great financial settlements!" Lyric says, raising her cone as if to toast him.

"Lyric," I say again. "Give it a rest. Please."

I pay the waitress money for the cones and tell her to keep the change. It might be a lot, it might be a little. Lyric is making me very uncomfortable. From the waitress's "Thank you" I can't tell how I tipped.

There is awkward silence as we lick our cones. For the rest of the time we're there—another half hour or so—the man avoids looking our way, and Lyric loses interest entirely in her game. From her fanny pack, she takes a bottle of nail polish and redoes her toes. It's a big day for ballooning; several others float by, like big, colorful insects. Nell requests her coloring book and crayons and obliterates a picture of a rose garden with wide blue strokes. Before we leave, I take her to the ladies' room to pee. She shrugs her bathing suit to her ankles and jumps backward on the toilet, bracing herself with both hands.

"Don't watch," she says, and I turn and face the door of the stall. I don't hear anything, but in a few seconds she hops off and says, "Flush when I leave," and quickly unlocks the door and rushes out, clutching her half-pulled-up bathing suit, before I hit the handle. She has no fear of flushing a toilet where we live, but she is terrified of flushing toilets in public places.

What a handful Lyric is, I think, following Nell out of the bathroom. Damon has obviously not had an easy time, but I don't even want to look at him, let alone hear his point of view, after what Lyric told me. I wonder how many women there have been; then decide that might be the way to open the discussion with Janet. If she knows. But if she doesn't know, if she hasn't wanted to hear about his past, she's really not going to want to hear my bad news.

Ahead of me, Nell is running back to three empty lounges. Lyric is nowhere in sight, and neither is the man. I see his beer bottle, empty, beside his lounge, and my heart stops for a second; it's like finding a missing person's watch deep in the woods. I look all around. It doesn't help that Nell asks, "Where's Lyric?" The man is nowhere. And then he is somewhere: he's coming out of a telephone booth, walking slowly in our direction, returning to his lounge. Not long afterward, I see Lyric's head break the surface of the water—she never swims!—and she pulls herself onto the rim of the pool, very close to where "Jacques" sits. She sits with her back to him, swishing her legs in the pool. Then she turns sideways, pretending to want to catch the sun on her face. She has Jacques' attention. I go and get her. If it were necessary to take her by the hand and pull her, I would. But she can see from my expression that she's gone as far as she can go. She hops up and skitters toward me, giving me a wet hug.

"Admit it. I was pretty good," she says.

Back at the condo, there's a message on the answering machine. Tom Selleck is paying an unscheduled visit to the seminar; Janet and Damon won't be back until after dinner. We should get dinner on our own. "Jillie Mack is already in the hotel," Janet adds, as if this would matter. But it does matter to Janet: she's decided on a new direction for her life, and Tom Selleck, and even his wife, are beacons. She ends her message by asking, "Who does Mommy love most? Bye."

"It's me," Nell says triumphantly, standing on tiptoe, as if that will bring her closer to her mother, whose voice has been playing from the telephone-answering machine mounted on the kitchen wall.

"To save this message, press one," an automated voice says.

"Press. Press!" Nell says.

I lift her up and let her press it herself.

"Play it again," Nell says.

"Press the replay button," I say, pointing to it. Janet begins to speak again. "Hi, everybody, it's me. Listen, we're going to be late getting home because Tom Selleck is flying in to talk to us. I already saw"—she lowers her voice—"Jillie Mack is in the hotel, and she is *tiny.* I saw her by the Coke machine. There was some rumor that Robert Redford was going to show up and it was like Fantasy Island: somebody who worked at the hotel started pointing to a helicopter and saying it was him, and everybody ran out of the building and stood around, but the thing never landed. I'm not exactly sure what he's going to be doing—Selleck, I mean—but you should get dinner because there's some reception for him at some lodge a friend of Damon's is renting after the talk he's giving, or whatever it is. Anyway: love you all, and I'll see you soon, and I want my dear sister to give a special kiss to Nell if Nell can correctly answer the question: Who does Mommy love most? Bye."

Nell turns in my arms to look at me. "What do I get for a special kiss?" she says.

"Top of the head," I say, kissing her lightly before setting her on the floor.

"I'm not going to take a bath," Nell says. She calls over her shoulder: "I don't have to."

Lyric and I get iced decaf cappuccinos from the store next to the condo. We get an Orangina for Nell. Basically, she likes the bottle. She ate almost no dinner, sulking because Janet didn't come back. In the living room of the condo, when we returned earlier that afternoon, was a green glass vase filled with red roses—a totally unexpected hello (that's all the card said) from Hale. There was also a note:

> *These delivered approx. 1 p.m. Delivery person upset because he was sent to Yarrow House, where they knew where you were. V. upset when he got here, then I heard he had dropped roses and broken vase—had to come back a second time. I left them in an ice bucket in my sink until he returned, and I cleaned up the broken glass. I noticed that there were eleven roses only and suspected they had counted wrong. Had him phone the florist, who he says told him only eleven were ordered, one dozen bad luck, 13 bad luck, therefore rather under. I will be playing Friday night, because the boy is already too sick. Please come! Hope you are enjoying your stay! Remember that I am always available for deep tissue massage.—Nikki*

"So, like, would you consider going back with him?" Lyric says, flopping on the strange-colored sofa.

"I don't know that I should jump to conclusions, when all the card says is 'Hello,'" I say.

"You could send him flowers, too, and let him make the next move," Lyric says.

"I don't know where he is. He's driving around the Southwest."

"So how did he know where you were?"

I think about it a minute. "I had the brochure for this conference lying around the house in Silver Lake for a long time," I say.

"Do you think that maybe he went back there and saw the brochure and missed you?"

"Since when do you have this romantic impulse to get everybody together?" I say.

"I'm meddlesome," she says. "Isn't that a great word? Damon said it about me. Not when I was trying to get him back together with somebody—just when I was putting some decent stuff into the grocery cart."

From Nell's bedroom, we hear the TV. She's channel surfing.

"Please put your nightgown on, Nell, even if you aren't going to bathe," I call out to her.

"I think it was nice of him to send you roses," Lyric says, touching her toes to the edge of the vase. "What was your biggest problem, or was it nothing but problems?"

I'm scanning the *USA Today* I didn't read at the pool. "He was a mechanic when I first met him. Then suddenly he and a guy he worked with started going to Mexico on the weekends and bringing chests back. Chests, chairs, all kinds of stuff. The other guy got a storefront and was selling it in Santa Monica. I thought it was sort of nuts, going to Mexico all the time, but the money was great, and I guess I didn't want to ask questions. Then one night we had the volume control up on the phone by mistake, and in the middle of the night I heard a voice shouting that Hale should stay away, not come anywhere near the store, that it was better to let them do Helter Skelter. He jumped out of bed and took the call. The cops had gone into the store in the middle of the night. They apparently took the door off the hinges and walked in and started axing chair legs off and prying up the bottoms of the chests, or whatever they were doing, looking for drugs. Which they didn't find, but they ended up arresting the other guy. When they didn't find drugs, the stuff suddenly became priceless antiquities, and the other guy got hauled out of his house in the middle of the night, but he never said anything about Hale, and he also got word to his lawyer to tell Hale to stay away. I was *stunned* to realize that a lawyer was calling in the middle of the night, that hysterical."

"Wow," Lyric says. "But I don't get it. Were they smuggling drugs?"

"Hale didn't think so. They didn't find any," I say.

"Yeah, but were they?"

"I don't know," I say.

"So why did you break up?"

"Things hadn't been great before Helter Skelter. We had separate friends, he wanted to move away from L.A. and I didn't. But the week after the phone call was terrible. We got so paranoid we thought people were watching the house."

"Looks like he wants to apologize," Lyric says.

"I wouldn't get back together with him," I say, surprising myself by how suddenly I speak. "I always had an uneasy feeling that he was up to a lot of stuff I didn't know about. I don't want to be with somebody I'd hesitate to ask questions of."

"That's very sensible," Lyric says. "That's a good way of looking at things. I hope I remember that."

I look at her to see if she's mocking me. She isn't. Furthermore, she does me the favor of calling out to Nell to change the channel, so I don't have to be the heavy.

"No! I'm watching!" Nell hollers back.

"You know, if I don't get to hang with you down the line, maybe we could still talk on the phone," Lyric says.

"Sure," I say.

"But you don't know where you'll be living, right?"

"No. I've got to be out of the house by the end of the month. But I know where you are, so I can call you."

"Can you keep a secret?" she says.

"I don't want to," I say, raising my hands as if she's announced a stickup.

"Are you kidding?" she says.

I look at her and suddenly am so self-conscious about my expression that I realize I must look the way Nell did, much earlier, hearing the contents of Cherry Garcia.

"I'm moving to Brooklyn," she says. "He was with this very nice woman before he started going out with Janet. I mean, she was *extremely* nice. When she got away from him, she got a job in New York, and just like she said she would, she kept in touch with me. I'm actually a better person to talk to on the phone than in person, because when I'm not looking right at a person, I tend to have more complex thoughts."

I pick up a pillow and hold it against my stomach, listening.

"The job she got in New York was way below her, but she's waiting for a job in book publishing. She's at one of those brides' magazines right now. I mean, she has a master's degree in history. Did Janet tell you anything about her? Sharon Oglethorpe?"

I shake my head no.

"Well, promise you won't tell. Except that you can tell Janet—you *have* to tell Janet—because it's really important that he doesn't think he can get away with this stuff for all time. But if you tell her all the particulars, and she tells him, he's going to know where she got the information. If that happens, I will not have immunity, I assure you." She slides to the edge of the sofa. "I sort of deemphasized what I said before," she says. "He slapped her one time. Sharon. And she got a detached retina. It was unbelievably awful. But anyway, she was out of there. She filed a complaint with the cops—she did all this stuff that really made him nervous. It ended up with her calling off the cops and with him giving her some money. When she got to New York, she called me, and she said if I'd promise to attend school, I could live with her. And that New York was way cooler than California. Which I'm thinking might not be such a bad change. So the thing is, she's going to send me a plane ticket at my best friend's, and I'm going to do it. If he tries to cause any problems, we're both going to lie and say he pushed me around all the time. Get this: she's *living* with a lawyer."

This is almost too much to take in at one time. I find myself only nodding. She gets up, goes into the other room, and comes back with her fanny pack. From inside one of the zippered pouches she takes a small piece of paper and holds it out. It's a business card, already imprinted with her name, telephone number, and Park Slope address. She says: "So when you land wherever, call me, and that way we can be in touch."

"This is pretty unbelievable," I say. "You're fourteen years old."

"I never think about that," she says. Then she says it again, but the second time, instead of sounding cryptic, she sounds wistful: "It's true," she says. "I never think about that."

Nell skitters through the room, naked. She gets a banana from the kitchen counter and runs back into the bedroom, to the TV.

"If you're going—" I say. I start again: "If you were going to live with her, how come you came to Park City?"

"She's at a spa this week," Lyric says. "And anyway: Who'd miss this?"

We both look around the condo and shake our heads. "I'm with you," Lyric says. "If this is what the Wild West has become, fuck it." She scoots back and leans against the sofa. "Damon had all this stuff from the tourist board about white-water rafting and all this cool stuff I thought I'd gear up to do, but I don't seem to have done it," she says. "You don't seem like somebody who wishes she was out riding horses or shooting the rapids, either."

"No," I say.

"I'd actually say there's something deenergizing about this place. But that's true of any place that seems artificial, I guess," she says.

"Maybe at the very least we should go up by the miniature golf course and get on one of the rides before we leave," I say.

"You scared me," she says. "I thought for a minute you were suggesting miniature golf."

I start slow with Janet. The night before, I put a note under her door telling her it was very important that we talk, alone, and that she had to meet me in the lobby at eight. I don't know what time she got back, but from the circles under her eyes, I'd say it was late.

"Why don't we take the bus down?" I say. "We can get coffee and talk at the Yarrow."

She stands sulkily at the bus stop beside me, more like a pouting little girl than my older sister. She says nothing. In two or three minutes the bus comes, opening its doors for just the two of us.

"If you're going to say anything critical of me, I don't want to hear it," Janet says. She sits in a single seat that faces sideways. I sit down in a two-seater right behind her that faces forward.

"Why don't you give me a little credit for having something I really want to talk to you about?" I say.

"You're not pregnant, are you?" she says, looking right at me.

"No," I say. "What would make you think that?"

"Because I am," she says. "That's why I've been such a bitch."

"What?"

"Well, just because you aren't doesn't mean other people can't be," she says.

"Janet! No!"

She pats my shoulder idly. Then she drops her hand in her lap as if it's made of lead. "I found out in the ladies' room of the Yarrow, on lunch break," she says. "But I knew I was, even before I took the test. I just knew I was."

"Have you told anybody?"

"This bus is making me nauseated," she says.

"Is it really making you sick?" I say, rising to my feet—as if by rushing to her I can do anything about the way her stomach feels. I loom over her, unsteadily. I grab the metal bar and sink back into my seat.

"I told Damon," she says. "Damon, wouldn't you know, is delighted. He's excited about having a second chance to do it right."

"What's wrong with Lyric?" I say.

She raises an eyebrow and lets it sink slowly. "I appreciate your devotion to the child," she says, "but we're not talking about a National Merit Scholar."

"That's not the only way to judge people," I say. "She's very bright."

This time Janet looks at me without the raised eyebrow. First she looks into my eyes, then she drops her eyes when they well with tears. "Oh hell," she says.

"You're upset about this," I say.

Janet nods her head yes. "Or as your friend might say: 'All I wanted to do was hang and chill.'"

"Janet, really, she hasn't had an easy time of it."

"My God, if you're so nuts about her, maybe you could join our little family unit and pal around with her, while I take care of Nell and the baby."

What I know is that there is not going to be any such family unit. But the idea that my sister might be having a baby by a man who knocks women around . . . it's too awful to contemplate.

"He's delighted," she says again. "And then the day after he finds out, who shows up but Selleck, saying that his daughter is the most wonderful thing in his life. Except for his teeny tiny little wife, of course. Who doesn't dance anymore, as far as I know."

"You don't have to do this!" I say urgently.

"My mother was a Catholic," she says. "You don't know about Catholic guilt."

"Janet! That can't seriously be a deciding factor—"

Janet pulls her silver cross out from beneath her T-shirt.

"That's . . . let's not argue about jewelry, Janet. Please. Please. I mean—"

The bus turns the corner and opens its doors to two boys wearing Rollerblades. "In the back and sit down for the duration of the ride," the driver says mechanically. The boys zoom to the back of the bus and start laughing. I look in the rearview mirror and see the bus driver's look of disapproval. It takes me a minute to realize that he's scrutinizing the whole bus, though: he's heard what I've been saying, as well as hearing the boys' silliness. I realize that he's probably a Mormon. Which makes me think of spirit babies, which in turn makes me look upward. I see the ceiling of the bus.

At the Yarrow, we disembark. I get off first and reach back for Janet's hand, as if she's already hugely pregnant. She takes my hand without noticing my odd gentility. She also doesn't drop it as we walk across the circular drive to the hotel. "Okay," she says, taking a deep breath as we walk in the front door. "This is fine. I can deal with this." She walks a slight bit faster. We're going in the direction of the restaurant. Someone says hello and she says hello back. The restaurant is almost empty.

"I don't suppose black coffee has been helping me to feel less nauseous," she says, when we're seated.

"You just got together with Damon," I say. "Don't you think—"

"Not only that, but I already have a three-year-old and a highly evolved Valley Girl stepchild, to say nothing of the fact that he's got a cat I'm allergic to."

"Are you going to let him keep the cat?" I say.

She studies my face. I don't mind meeting her gaze at all. I've got to stand my ground. "No," she says. "I'm going to suggest he get rid of the cat."

She looks at the menu again. When the waitress comes to the table, Janet says, "No coffee for me. Iced tea, if you have it. And the granola with fruit."

"I'll have an English muffin and grapefruit juice," I say. "Coffee with milk, please."

Janet reaches across the table and takes my hand. "I don't know," she says. "I don't know anything."

"That's why we're here," I say. "I have to tell you something."

"Right," she says. "Excuse me for sidetracking you. What is it you wanted to tell me?"

"Janet, please don't be business-like."

"I'm not trying to be business-like. I'm trying to allow you to tell me whatever is so important."

"You're going to have trouble hearing this, because you don't like Lyric."

She starts to say something, then stops. "I've been exaggerating," she says. "Lyric's an easy person to make fun of. I've picked up her father's reservations about her, and I realize that isn't fair. If you say she's intelligent, I'm sure she's intelligent."

The waitress brings the iced tea and juice. She goes to a station and gets a coffee mug and brings it to the table, with the coffeepot and two little plastic containers of milk that she takes out of her apron pocket. We thank her. She says, "You're welcome," and goes away.

"Do you know anything about the woman Damon was involved with before he met you?" I say.

She looks surprised. "A few things. Yes," she says.

"Do you know anything about women—you know—before that?"

"That he's quite a womanizer. Yes," she says slowly.

"But about the women," I say.

"Tell me what you're getting at," she says. "I'm not about to give a recitation of random facts about a bunch of women I've never met."

"He's been physically abusive," I say.

She looks at me. To my surprise, she says: "Once."

"Once?"

"That's what I said. Once. I know about that. Yes. Is that what Lyric told you that you had to tell me?"

"Janet, I don't believe it was just once."

She shifts in her chair. "Well, that's what he told me," she said. "And it flipped him out so much that he was in counseling for a year." She takes the lemon out of her iced tea. Instead of squeezing it, she looks at it, then puts it on the tablecloth. "I realize that once is once too often," she says. "Toward the end, when he had that job he really hated in Ithaca, he was drinking too much. I'm not saying that's an excuse. Just that he doesn't touch alcohol now, as you know. He made a mistake. He told me about it."

I persist: "Do you know about the detached retina?"

"God," she says, "this is so painful. Yes I do. I wish you didn't, because I honestly think he realized that his drinking had gotten out of hand, and I'm entirely certain he regrets it and that he'd never do a thing like that again."

"Listen to yourself. That's the way women who'll let themselves be abused always defend the man."

"He's not 'the man.' He's Damon. He's never hurt me, and he told me about what happened with that other woman. Can we drop the subject now? Please?"

"He shoved Lyric's mother around. The way Lyric described it was that her mother would just get drained of energy, and that he stayed as solid as a bag of sand."

She looks at the floor. She looks back at me. "Why do you believe her?" she says. "There's quite a bit of animosity between them. Maybe what looked to a little child—"

"Listen to yourself!" I say.

She stops talking. "That's what she told you?" she says, finally.

"She's told me more than that."

Janet looks very pale. "She didn't say he hit her, did she?"

"She said he didn't. But come to think of it, I'm not sure I believe her. She might have found it possible to tell me about the others, but not about herself."

"Isn't that a little paranoid?"

"Maybe."

"'Maybe,'" Janet echoes. "So we have for breakfast a big, looming 'maybe' on the table." The waitress is coming our way with a tray. "Why don't we tackle it piece by piece," Janet says. "You eat a bite of muffin, I'll have a spoonful of cereal."

"I'm sure it wasn't," she says.

"Please don't sound business-like," I say, as the waitress puts my plate in front of me.

"What is my alternative? To sound all screwed up and vulnerable? I'm rattled by what you said, okay? It worked. It's made me very nervous. I'm going to have to think about this."

"You've already got a three-year-old. You've only lived with him for a few months. You don't know what it would be like to live with him for years and years. You've got to do your screenplay."

"Are you serious?" she says.

"Sally Hemings."

"Thank you. I don't need prompting to remember what my screenplay is about." She takes another bite of cereal. "Nobody's ever going to unravel the truth about that," she says. "Jefferson either did, or he didn't."

On the last day of the conference, which comes, sure enough, a day earlier than the brochure seemed to indicate, Lyric, Nell, and I decide to buy tickets and ride on the Alpine Slide. I don't know about Janet, but I'm ready to go home—even if all that means is that I'll have to start packing boxes. From time to time, I've thought about Janet's sarcastic suggestion that I move in with her, but what she doesn't know is that Lyric isn't going to be around any time at all, and the prospect of daily life with Nell . . . I adore her, but I don't want to spend all my spare time with a three-year-old. What's this living with other people when you're an adult, anyway? Camping out for six days in Park City has been all I can manage. The second bouquet from Hale didn't bring me around any, either; if anything, it reinforced my resolve to keep away from somebody who so little wanted to express enthusiasm for me that he twice sent flowers with a card that simply said, "Hello."

"I don't know why a pretty girl like you has any trouble finding a fellow," Nikki says to me. She's dunking little tubes in the hot tub, then dropping different chemicals in them with an eyedropper. What happens with each one, which is not discernible to my eye, seems to please her. "Maybe you don't talk enough," she says. "You have to put out some give to get some take."

"You're the second person this week who's told me I'm not very talkative," I say.

"If you were talkative, you'd say who the other person was!" Nikki says. She puts her testing kit on a shelf below the redwood floor and closes the little trapdoor. She wipes her hands on her legs. "Probably the teenager, because she can talk up a storm."

"Lyric," I say.

"Real name Linda," Nikki says.

"It is?"

"Yeah, sure. We traded information a few mornings back. She adopted the name Lyric when she was in grade one to make herself special. I know what she feels like, thinking you've got to have the right name. I could not be in Park City, Utah, and always be Nguyen, you know?"

She goes to the control panel on a small redwood column and turns the dial. The water starts to bubble. "Aah," she says, sitting down, swinging her feet into the water. "Just for a minute. You, too," she says.

"I don't like very hot water," I say.

"Relaxing. Try it," Nikki says. She slowly lowers her legs into the water. Then she pulls them up again. "She could be a real beautician," Nikki says, holding one foot high in the air. "How come if Lyric painted my toenails, you don't have painted toenails?" Nikki says.

"I didn't want them painted."

"You," she says. "You're more fun than you want to let on."

"I doubt it," I say.

"Hey, nobody else got two bouquets here this week," she says, lowering her feet again. The water bubbles close to the hem of her white bermuda shorts.

I sit beside her, cross-legged. Then I change my mind, swing my legs around, and lower them into the water. For a second they sting, then they tingle.

"You know I'm fun, right?" Nikki says.

"What do you mean?"

"Girls know what other girls mean when they talk about fun," she says. "Don't tell me you don't. I talked to Lyric about fun. She guessed something and I said it was right."

A chill goes up my spine. I don't know what I anticipate, but I'm sure it's nothing good. I didn't know Lyric had spent any time with Nikki, let alone that she'd painted her toenails.

"I have been a widow for twelve years. Something has to happen, right?"

"What do you mean?" I say again.

"You know. Fun in bed," Nikki says.

I drop my mouth open. At first, I think she's saying she went to bed with Lyric. She sees my mouth agape, and looks puzzled. She even says, "What's wrong?"

"I'm not following what you're saying," I say.

"I swore her to secrecy, now I swear you," Nikki says. "Just one afternoon. When he scheduled deep tissue massage. There wasn't any. You understand?"

I don't know if I'm relieved or dismayed. This was not a discussion I expected to be having when I took two Tylenols and went out on the deck to get some air.

"He loves your sister," Nikki says. "It doesn't mean anything but that two people had fun. You don't tell her, though, because she doesn't need to know. That would not please anyone."

"You're serious?" I say. "He slept with you?"

"Yeah," she says, giving my shoulder a playful shove. "Lyric had a hunch, from the way he looked at me. She asked me, and I swore her to secrecy. I'm thinking maybe I shouldn't have admitted it, because it was her father, but she's so grown-up,"

Nikki says. "If women aren't honest with other women, there will be no honesty, right?"

"What?" I say, dazed.

"Because the men are not going to be honest! No!" Nikki says.

"Oh, man," I say. "Oh man. I don't believe this."

"You're more surprised than she was!" Nikki says.

"This has been a tough week," I say. "I'm getting tired of being surprised."

"If people weren't willing to be surprised, they'd still think the earth was flat. They wouldn't have tested, right?"

I watch a golden wasp come near the surface of the water and lift off just before it's lapped in. The wasp circles around to buzz behind me and reapproach the water. This time the water gets it, and I watch it wash toward the far end of the whirlpool, where the blue plastic cover is neatly rolled. "Desert rose," Nikki says, lifting her foot to admire it. She looks at me. "If he wasn't nice-looking, I wouldn't have. You can tell when somebody is a nice man."

"Because of the way they look?"

"No, not just looks. Deeper than looks. Some people look at you and let you see inside their soul."

"And he was . . ." I falter. "He was a nice man?"

"Mmmm," Nikki says.

What did I expect? Violence, during the half hour when he was ostensibly getting deep tissue massage? In my imagination, he has become so monstrous I've been assuming he couldn't contain his terrible impulses.

"I like it rough," Nikki whispers. Then she looks to the side, embarrassed.

"Oh no," I say. "Oh no, he didn't do anything to you, did he?"

"When there is real passion, I like it rough," she says again.

"What?" I say. "Nikki, please. What, exactly?"

"Hey, I found a way to get you to talk," Nikki says. When she speaks, though, she sounds more nervous than triumphant.

"Nikki," I say, putting my hand on her elbow. "Nikki, let me level with you. I've been worried that he might do something to my sister. Do you know from Lyric that he's done violent things to women?"

"I was just talking about fun," Nikki says. She looks at my hand clasping her elbow. I remove it. I put my hand on my thigh, spread my fingers, and look at the light circle of skin—much lighter than the rest, in spite of almost a week of tanning—where for years I wore the silver band Hale gave me.

"I don't want to tell," she says, her voice barely audible above the bubbling water. "Too personal."

We sit in silence for a long time. Eventually, extraneously, Nikki says in a very quiet voice: "Don't tell your sister."

To my surprise, when I go downstairs—my headache worse than when I set out—Damon is sprawled on the orange sofa, clicking through channels with the remote.

"There she is!" Nell hollers, jumping off his lap. "Lyric went looking for you!" she squeals.

"Hey—where've you been?" Damon says to me. On the TV screen, there is a shot of Joan Collins, on the witness stand. "Why are they airing old news?" he says, clicking the remote.

"Where's Janet?" I say.

"Mommy has a headache," Nell says.

"Yeah, well, her sister does, too," I say, sitting in a fake-zebra-hide chair.

"What's up with you two? Janet said she was too sick to make it to the last session. You getting sympathetic pains?" Damon says.

"How are we going to find Lyric?" Nell says. "You stay here, and I'll find her."

"No, sweetie," I say. "Just sit here another minute and she'll come back."

"She will come in *one* minute?"

"She definitely will, and if she doesn't, curse me for a fool," I say. I rub my hand over my face. My fingers smell slightly of chlorine.

"We can leave a note for her and go on the ride!" Nell says.

"How would you like it if you went to look for one of us, and when you got back, we'd gone without you?"

"No," Nell says, climbing into my lap. She turns around and puts her thumb in her mouth. She never sucks her thumb.

"You wouldn't like it a bit, would you?" I say. I bounce her slightly on my knees. She is staring at Damon. She continues to suck her thumb.

"Sometimes there are things I sure don't like one bit, either," Damon says. "Like, for instance, one person who will tell another person how she should live her life." He gives me a quick look, then looks back at the TV. "Such as"—he spells—"a-b-o-r-t-i-o-n."

This is not lost on Nell. She looks at me but, surprisingly, does not say, "What did he say?" I jiggle her a little harder on my knees.

"If Lyric goes out to the deck looking for me, Nikki will tell her where I am," I say. Damon shoots me another look, this one much quicker than the last. When he looks away, he looks out the window, not back at the TV. "Because I was up by the hot tub talking to Nikki," I say to Nell, as if she asked to be informed. "She and I were t-a-l-k-i-n-g."

"Tell me!" Nell says. "What did you spell?"

"Talking," I say. "T a-l-k-i-n-g."

Damon turns off the TV, tosses the remote onto the sofa cushion with obvious disgust, and starts down one of the corridors.

"What's he doing?" Nell says.

"Honey, I can't read his mind. I guess he's going to pee."

"I want the TV back on," Nell says, jumping off my lap.

"No you don't, you want to ride on the fabulous Alpine Slide," Lyric says, coming through the front door. She flops down near my feet. "So now that I've made the entire run of the building, including waking up your sister, who looks totally wasted, I'm sorry to say, I find you in our own cozy living room."

"I didn't realize everybody was ready to leave," I say.

"We are ready!" Nell says, beginning to march in a circle. "We are ready! We are ready!"

"Gee, but the question is: Is Nell ready?" Lyric says.

"Yesssssss!" Nell says, crouching and jumping.

"She's perfecting her Ed McMahon imitation," Lyric says to me.

"I am *ready!* I am *ready!*" Nell says.

"So am I! So am I!" Damon says, coming back into the room, tucking his shirt into his jeans. "So is this it? We go have some fun now?"

This is the way he's decided to deal with the information I just gave him. He's going to make me look sulky and strange if I don't get in the swing of things. But the mood is false; it's too put-on, too euphoric, too sudden. What should I believe? That he got happy peeing?

"Do you want to go on the merry-go-round, sweetheart?" he says to Nell.

"No! I want Alpine Slide!"

"Can she go on that?" Damon says. He looks at Lyric. "Is that okay for children?"

"I don't know, Daddy," she says, answering him with a voice as false as his own. "We'll have to go up there and see."

"Yes! I'm going!" Nell says, with the same panic and desire with which she announced, a few days earlier, that her mother would buy her espadrilles. I wonder if she even remembered to ask Janet for them. I wonder when she and Janet last had any real time together. Maternal feelings begin to overwhelm me. Although I'd know better than to do it, some part of me wonders whether Janet might have been half serious about my moving in. Worse, even, than his hurting Janet, if he ever touched a hair on Nell's head. . . .

We ride down together in the elevator. I watch the way Lyric moves closer to the control panel, away from her father. I keep Nell in my arms, but when we reach the lobby, she won't be contained; she kicks free and races for the front door. As fate would have it, the fat girl is coming in at the same time. She's taken off her skates and is walking in her thick brown socks. She's limping, actually. She sees us and looks like she wants to run, but obviously she can't: we're a wall of people coming jaggedly toward her. Damon goes first, taking up so much of the center of the hallway that the girl has to move aside. I go next, not looking at her, holding Nell's hand, which she has backtracked to put in mine. I sense that Nell is looking at the floor.

"Hey, you scuzzes, you might see if you could help me, since I've probably got a broken ankle," the girl says. It stops me in my tracks. I turn around and see her sidling up to the side wall of the hallway. One sock is unrolled almost to her ankle. As I look down, I see blood on it. I'm about to go to her, in spite of how much I dislike her, and in spite of how nastily she spoke to us, when I see her begin to fall. Lyric has hung behind to topple her, hard. I watch in horror as she reaches out and pokes her fingers in the falling girl's chest. "Fuck you," Lyric says. "You're not a human being." I'm stunned. Stunned. I look for Damon, as if, being the oldest, he'll surely do something, but he's already made it out the door.

"Lyric," I gasp. "What did you do?" But I don't stop to find out. Coward that I am—or maybe because I'm so numb I've become robotic—I grab Nell's hand tightly and keep walking. Maybe I just imagined that all that happened. It happened in about six seconds, didn't it? Could I really be hearing the girl, wailing, way back behind the closed door?

"Listen: in this world, you've got to do what you've got to do," Lyric says as she stalks past me, tossing her hair to one side. When she catches up with Damon, she slips her hand into his. He picks up the beat automatically when he takes her hand. Together, they go quickly up the stairs to the next level.

Nell's thumb is back in her mouth. She lags behind, keeping pace with me, while I try to catch my breath. Ahead of us, I see Damon and Lyric stopping at the ticket kiosk. There are a lot of people clustered around, but they don't seem to be in line. They're standing and staring, I see, as we come closer, at a blond girl in a bustier and short-shorts, and her biker boyfriend. A flashbulb goes off. They're movie stars, apparently. But which movie stars? I suddenly feel old and disconnected and—I've felt this since Lyric first confided in me—discouraged and depressed. The man has long, dirty hair, so dark it must be dyed black, and wears boots with spurs and a torn black T-shirt with a heavy chain around the middle. His arms are covered with tattoos. The girl's diamond earrings flash in the sun. "They look just like them," a woman holding a little boy's hand says to me, as I edge nearer.

"Tom Selleck?" Nell says, getting the drift of what's going on. Recently, she's heard Tom Selleck's name mentioned a lot.

The woman looks taken aback. "No. Pamela Anderson and Tommy Lee," she says in a stage whisper. "But they're not really them. They've just made themselves up to look like them."

"The tatts are fake, man," a teenage boy says to his friend. "You can always tell." The boy he speaks to has a tattoo of a coiling serpent that is certainly not fake on his biceps. They stand there, shaking their heads at the impostors. Pamela Anderson has on the brightest pink lipstick I have ever seen. Tommy Lee's boots are made from reptile's skin: some reptile with big, black scales. Meanwhile, Damon and Lyric begin to walk away. Damon drops his arm over Lyric's shoulder. In his other hand, he clasps our tickets.

"That little girl thought Tommy Lee was Tom Selleck," I overhear the woman saying to her son, as we walk away. "Can you imagine that?"

Several Rollerbladers make a path around us, going in the direction of the steps. I keep walking without looking back, but by now there's no wailing: only the sound of wheels receding, and of the breeze. It gets much cooler in Park City about six o'clock. You need a jacket, which I forgot to wear. Nell, too, has hunched her shoulders in the cold. Lyric has on a cotton V-neck sweater over her khakis. Damon has on his leather jacket, which he snatched off the antler coat hook on our way out the front door.

Nell skips ahead as we get closer to the ride. The ski lifts that take passengers to the top are rising. Far in the distance, a few riders on little toboggan-like slides come down a track cut into the mountain. There's almost no line. A group of kids runs into line ahead of us, and a middle-aged man and his gray-haired wife, expressing great doubt about going on the ride, get in line next. The woman is saying exactly what I'm thinking: that she isn't that fond of height; that it looks like a long way up the mountain. Her husband chides her; she'll be fine. Didn't she ride the roller coaster at Coney Island and survive? "They don't make these things so people will get hurt and sue them," the man says, patting his wife's bottom.

"Three to a lift," a teenage boy calls out to the man and woman in front of Lyric and Damon. He stands where the ski lifts round the bend and slow slightly.

"You mean we go with one of them?" the man says to the attendant.

"Not you, them," the attendant hollers, grabbing a car and slowing it ever so slightly for the children to jump on. "Three to a car! No doubles!" he hollers again.

When everyone from their squirmy, excited group is gone, there is one extra boy. He rushes toward the next car and tries to jump on, but a second attendant, in the field, shouts something I can't understand, and the teenage boy puts his arm out, forcing the little boy back in line.

"Step forward! Stand in the footprints!" the attendant says, darting forward to tap his toe on one of three pairs of yellow feet lined up on the mat. He jerks his leg back just before his knee is sideswiped. The boy hesitates, not sure what to do.

"Do we go together?" the middle-aged man says, but before there is any answer, the boy has boarded the lift, sinking in so heavily that it swings wildly from side to side, and the attendant is urging the man into the car, as the man tugs his wife's hand. "Slow it up, okay, open it up again," the attendant hollers. "Oh! My!" I hear the woman exclaim, and then the couple and the boy begin to rise.

So how is it going to work out with four of us? Lyric is already standing soldier-straight in the yellow footprints, but Damon, having heard all the shouting about three to a car; looks over his shoulder at us. "Get in, move!" the attendant says, and suddenly Lyric and Damon are swinging in front of us, being lifted away, the pulley rolling them up the cables. I see Damon put his arm around Lyric. I see her hair float backward. I am, frankly, mesmerized by the sight of the two of them, so that I don't see what's happening with the circling ski lifts, and when the next one comes around, it almost hits me in the head. I duck, and it gets away without either of us in it. Nell is suddenly pulling hard on my hand. What does she want? If she's saying anything, I can't hear her because of the escalating exchange between the two attendants. "Get 'em in! No more empties!" the boy who is farther away hollers, and suddenly I find myself pushed from behind, resting precariously on one hip in the rising lift, scrambling to hold on to the dangling Nell, who is facing me, her belly on the lift, her legs dangling as we rise above the receding green field. "Wait!" I scream hysterically. She seems to weigh twice what she normally does, and I know I'll pitch too far forward myself if I release my grip on the pole on my side of the swaying lift. Suddenly, having leaped an amazing height from the ground, a young man is in our car, pulling—he's got Nell by her waistband at the same time I'm seizing her arm, and he is making good progress in getting her turned forward and seated, though she is screaming so much she can't hear anything he says. At first I think one of the attendants must have jumped on, but when I catch my breath enough to look at the man I see he's just another visitor to the park: a geeky guy in glasses and a baseball cap whose concern seems to be as much about me as about Nell. He is telling me that if the height is bothering me, not to look down. I immediately look down. Someone says, "I don't like height very much," but it's not my voice, it's a little voice inside my head. The ground is bubbling like the hot tub. Some tiny animal zigzags far below. Except for the echo of the little voice, it is preternaturally quiet as we ascend: a swarming, all-enveloping silence. Black specks rise in front of my eyes, like mist. Tears are pouring from my eyes. "Hey, have you ever been on one of these rides before?" the man asks, trying to make light of my near swoon and trying to calm Nell at the same time. "Sit down, honey. We're all taking a ride up the mountain," the man says, reasonably. I see the man's arm tightly around Nell, hooking a seat belt across our car with his free hand. They don't even put seat belts on down there? They didn't even stop the ride when a three-year-old child. . . . But that's it, and then it's blackout. When I come to, I'm lying on the ground at the top of the mountain and people are staring down at me. My hand hurts. I pull it from underneath me and the young man touches my wrist, frowning, then delicately places my hand on my stomach. He continues fanning me, demanding that everyone step back. Nell. Where's Nell? Where is Nell?

Then I see her, in Damon's arms. He's taken off his leather jacket and is holding her in the big black bunting, as she alternately rubs her eyes and struggles to run to my side. She almost died. The kids who run the ride are crazy. What if my reflexes hadn't been as good as they were? What if the man hadn't jumped in the car?

"Jeez, I guess you weren't kidding when you said you didn't like heights," the man says to me. People peer over his shoulder. Aspen leaves rustle behind their heads in the breeze: first green, then silver, then green. I see the cloudless, dark-blue evening sky. I don't even want to think of how I'll get off the mountain. Not by riding the Alpine Slide down, that's for sure. My face is wet with tears and perspiration. Lyric is looking deep enough into my eyes to see her own reflection. Remembering what Nikki said to me, I try to look deep into hers, but she wavers out of focus. "You scared me," she says, cupping her hand over my painful wrist.

"We're even," I say.

The ski lifts dangle going down the mountain like big black spiders. The silence, except for the people's whispered voices, is astonishing. The near crisis has slowed everything down, and everyone on top of the mountain, me among them, is temporarily stranded in the cold and silence. Nell bounces in Damon's arms, stretching one hand toward me. He holds her tight. Is it possible, I wonder hazily, that he only made one mistake, one time? And also: Is it possible that he, too, might love Nell?

The man—my savior; our savior—can't disguise his worry. He is adding to the breeze by fanning me more. It's as if he's enacting some weird ritual. He leans close, and I'm sure he's going to confide in me what it is he's really doing: that he's exorcising demons, or keeping away ghosts. "Next time, remember to ask for a slow start," he says. He has stopped fanning and has decided to try to warm me, instead. "I know right this minute you don't think you'll ever be on it again, but believe me, eventually you will. And the one thing you've got to remember"—he lowers his voice, his lips almost touching my ear—"the one thing you've got to remember next time is to request a slow start."

Robert Olen Butler (1945–)

was born in Granite City, Illinois, attended Northwestern University as a theater major and then switched to playwriting during his master's program at the University of Iowa. In 1969, he joined the military and rose to the rank of sergeant while serving three years in Vietnam, where he became fluent in Vietnamese and served as a translator. After the war, Butler worked in a steel mill and as a taxi driver and a substitute teacher before becoming a writer for trade publications, including a ten-year stint as editor-in-chief of the New York–based Energy User News. *During that time, he rode the Long Island Railroad to and from work every day, and each day on the train, he wrote fiction. The first of the four novels he wrote that way,* The Alleys of Eden, *was rejected twenty-one times before it was finally published. He published seven novels to consistently strong reviews but diminishing sales, a trend that was utterly reversed by the publication of his first book of short stories,* A Good Scent from a Strange Mountain, *which won the 1993 Pulitzer Prize. He has since won a National Magazine Award, the Richard and Hinda Rosenthal Foundation Award from the American Academy of Arts and Letters, and the Tu Do Chinh Kien Award given by the Vietnam Veterans of America for "outstanding contributions to American culture by a Vietnam veteran." His other collections of short fiction include* Tabloid Dreams *and* Had a Good Time. *He holds the Michael Shaara Chair in Creative Writing at Florida State University and is married to novelist and playwright Elizabeth Dewberry.*

INTRODUCTION BY **Ann Patchett**

Years ago, a very successful novelist confided in me that she feared she was writing the same book over and over again. "I only have one story to tell," she said sadly.

I had thought her books were very different from one another, but the more I considered her point, the truer it became. This idea was a revelation to me. I realized that I, too, only had one story but that just about all of the writers I admire only have one story. Probably if you boiled down every plot to its most basic elements, all of the stories there are to tell could be easily catalogued on our fingers. I'm not talking about events or characters or settings. I'm talking about the reason the writer was driven to tell this tale, the statement that he or she has to make about the human condition.

In the same way that some religions extol the freedom that comes with complete spiritual surrender, I would say that there is an enormous creative liberation in recognizing the story that is yours to tell. Once you stop trying to bend yourself into something you're not, you can find all of the depth and variations that exist in what you actually know and understand. I can think of no better example of a writer who has found freedom within his story than Robert Olen Butler.

How is it possible that a man who writes about Americans looking for their history in Vietnam and Vietnamese creating history in America could have one story? A man who writes about a woman auctioneer, and a man who becomes rainwater, and a woman who falls in love with a spaceman, and a spaceman with tender, suctioning fingertips, logically, must have a wealth of stories. But what Butler has is a fearless imagination. There is no character, voice, or feeling that is beyond his ability to capture. Men, women, animals, non-mammals—nothing is off limits to him. But when they are closely observed, his leading characters are nearly all possessed of a striking similarity: They are strangers, outsiders. They are not in the land that they know. Sometimes they are not even in the body they know. But there they are, trying to play the hand they've been dealt as best they can. It is a distinctly American position, as we are a country composed of strangers, foreigners, refugees. Even the venerable members of society stand at the edge of the crowd in Butler's work, as if they are always trying to peer around the shoulders of someone taller. Other people might perceive them as belonging, but they themselves know that this is not the case.

The three stories in this anthology display a range of imagination so wide that they take on the quality of a magic show: See the famous author completely disappear into a set of disparate lives! In "Jealous Husband Returns in Form of Parrot," the plot is laid out completely in the title, but the beauty of the story is in the nuance. The character is not the man he was in a bird's feathered body. He is half himself and half the bird, with both a longing to be with his wife and a longing to fly through the window and sail over the high branches of the trees. He searches for words with a full heart but only a parrot's ability for language. He is home, back in his own living room, but this time hanging from a bar, madly thrashing the dangling toy in his cage.

"A Good Scent from a Strange Mountain," the title story from the collection that won the Pulitzer Prize for Fiction in 1993, is about a beautiful moment in which past, present, life, death, history, and desire all converge in the bedroom of an old man. He is a Vietnamese dying in America while remembering his youth in France. His compassion and understanding for all the people around him, even those involved in actions he knows are wrong, are a flawless testament to his faith and to himself. The layers of displacement include both his dream life, which is real, and his real life, in which he often pretends to be sleeping; yet for all the apparent confusion that surrounds him, the story is told in a voice of absolute peace.

There is no way to create stories like these without complete assuredness. In "This Is Earl Sandt," Butler made his artistic process public by drawing a postcard out of his vast collection and writing a story based on the image on the front of the card and the message on the back. In this case, it was a picture of an airplane along with the words "This is Earl Sandt of Erie Pa in his Aeroplane just before it fell." From this inspiration, Butler sat down to work. His entire process—every keystroke, every sigh of frustration—was shown in real time on the Internet. (It is still archived there, along with hours of Butler's lectures on the writing process, delivered at the end of each day's session; to see it, go to http://www.fsu.edu/~unicomm/butler/.) The story is a suspended moment, the fall of an airplane caught in a photograph by a man who is paralyzed by his life. The narrator is someone who no one would suspect of being a stranger, yet the only person he can identify with is Earl Sandt, the man he captured in the process of crashing to his death.

I expect that making an entire world with all the world watching is something that could be done only by a man who knew what he had to say, not the details of what happened, but the essence of how people live. The resulting stories are beautiful, tender, funny, intelligent, and utterly original works of art.

Ann Patchett is the author of Bel Canto, *winner of the 2002 PEN/Faulkner Award for Fiction. Her other novels include* The Patron Saint of Liars, Taft, *and* The Magician's Assistant. *While attending Sarah Lawrence College, Patchett studied fiction writing with Grace Paley. She sold her first short story to* The Paris Review *when she was 21 years old. She lives in Nashville, Tennessee.*

ROBERT OLEN BUTLER

A Good Scent from a Strange Mountain

Hồ Chí Minh came to me again last night, his hands covered with confectioners' sugar. This was something of a surprise to me, the first time I saw him beside my bed, in the dim light from the open shade. My oldest daughter leaves my shades open, I think so that I will not forget that the sun has risen again in the morning. I am a very old man. She seems to expect that one morning I will simply forget to keep living. This is very foolish. I will one night rise up from my bed and slip into her room and open the shade there. Let *her* see the sun in the morning. She is sixty-four years old and she should worry for herself. I could never die from forgetting.

But the light from the street was enough to let me recognize Hồ when I woke, and he said to me, "Đạo, my old friend, I have heard it is time to visit you." Already on that first night there was a sweet smell about him, very strong in the dark, even before I could see his hands. I said nothing, but I stretched to the nightstand beside me and I turned on the light to see if he would go away. And he did not. He stood there beside the bed—I could even see him reflected in the window—and I knew it was real because he did not appear as he was when I'd known him but as he was when he'd died. This was Uncle Hồ before me, the thin old man with the dewlap beard wearing the dark clothes of a peasant and the rubber sandals, just like in the news pictures I studied with such a strange feeling for all those years. Strange because when I knew him, he was not yet Hồ Chí Minh. It was 1917 and he was Nguyễn Ái Quốc and we were both young men with clean-shaven faces, the best of friends, and we worked at the Carlton Hotel in London, where I was a dishwasher and he was a pastry cook under the great Escoffier. We were the best of friends and we saw snow for the first time together. This was before we began to work at the hotel. We shoveled snow and Hồ would stop for a moment and blow his breath out before him and it would make him smile, to see what was inside him, as if it was the casting of bones to tell the future.

On that first night when he came to me in my house in New Orleans, I finally saw what it was that smelled so sweet and I said to him, "Your hands are covered with sugar."

He looked at them with a kind of sadness.

I have received that look myself in the past week. It is time now for me to see my family, and the friends I have made who are still alive. This is our custom from Vietnam. When you are very old, you put aside a week or two to receive the people of your life so that you can tell one another your feelings, or try at last to understand one another, or simply say good-bye. It is a formal leave-taking, and with good luck you can do this before you have your final illness. I have lived almost a century and perhaps I should have called them all to me sooner, but at last I felt a deep weariness and I said to my oldest daughter that it was time.

They look at me with sadness, some of them. Usually the dull-witted ones, or the insincere ones. But Hồ's look was, of course, not dull-witted or insincere. He considered his hands and said, "The glaze. Maestro's glaze."

There was the soft edge of yearning in his voice and I had the thought that perhaps he had come to me for some sort of help. I said to him, "I don't remember. I only washed dishes." As soon as the words were out of my mouth, I decided it was foolish for me to think he had come to ask me about the glaze.

But Hồ did not treat me as foolish. He looked at me and shook his head. "It's all right," he said. "I remember the temperature now. Two hundred and thirty degrees, when the sugar is between the large thread stage and the small orb stage. The Maestro was very clear about that and I remember." I knew from his eyes, however, that there was much more that still eluded him. His eyes did not seem to move at all from my face, but there was some little shifting of them, a restlessness that perhaps only I could see, since I was his close friend from the days when the world did not know him.

I am nearly one hundred years old, but I can still read a man's face. Perhaps better than I ever have. I sit in the overstuffed chair in my living room and I receive my visitors and I want these people, even the dull-witted and insincere ones—please excuse an old man's ill temper for calling them that—I want them all to be good with one another. A Vietnamese family is extended as far as the bloodline strings us together, like so many paper lanterns around a village square. And we all give off light together. That's the way it has always been in our culture. But these people who come to visit me have been in America for a long time and there are very strange things going on that I can see in their faces.

None stranger than this morning. I was in my overstuffed chair and with me there were four of the many members of my family: my son-in-law Thắng, a former colonel in the Army of the Republic of Vietnam and one of the insincere ones, sitting on my Castro convertible couch; his youngest son, Lợi, who had come in late, just a few minutes earlier, and had thrown himself down on the couch as well, youngest but a man old enough to have served as a lieutenant under his father as our country fell to the communists more than a decade ago; my daughter Lâm, who is Thắng's wife, hovering behind the both of them and refusing all invitations to sit down; and my oldest daughter, leaning against the door frame, having no doubt just returned from my room, where she had opened the shade that I had closed when I awoke.

It was Thắng who gave me the sad look I have grown accustomed to, and I perhaps seemed to him at that moment a little weak, a little distant. I had stopped listening to the small talk of these people and I had let my eyes half close, though I could still see them clearly and I was very alert. Thắng has a steady face and the quick eyes of a man who is ready to come under fire, but I have always read much more there, in spite of his efforts to show nothing. So after he thought I'd faded from the room, it was with slow eyes, not quick, that he moved to his son and began to speak of the killing.

You should understand that Mr. Nguyễn Bích Lê had been shot dead in our community here in New Orleans just last week. There are many of us Vietnamese living in New Orleans and one man, Mr. Lê, published a little newspaper for all of us. He had recently made the fatal error—though it should not be that in America—of writing that it was time to accept the reality of the communist government in Vietnam and begin to talk with them. We had to work now with those who controlled our country. He said that he remained a patriot to the Republic of Vietnam, and I believed him. If anyone had asked an old man's opinion on this whole matter, I would not have been afraid to say that Mr. Lê was right.

But he was shot dead last week. He was forty-five years old and he had a wife and three children and he was shot as he sat behind the wheel of his Chevrolet pickup truck. I find a detail like that especially moving, that this man was killed in his Chevrolet, which I understand is a strongly American thing. We knew this in Saigon. In Saigon it was very American to own a Chevrolet, just as it was French to own a Citroën.

And Mr. Lê had taken one more step in his trusting embrace of this new culture. He had bought not only a Chevrolet but a Chevrolet pickup truck, which made him not only American but also a man of Louisiana, where there are many pickup trucks. He did not, however, also purchase a gun rack for the back window, another sign of this place. Perhaps it would have been well if he had, for it was through the back window that the bullet was fired. Someone had hidden in the bed of his truck and had killed him from behind in his Chevrolet and the reason for this act was made very clear in a phone call to the newspaper office by a nameless representative of the Vietnamese Party for the Annihilation of Communism and for the National Restoration.

And Thắng, my son-in-law, said to his youngest son, Lợi, "There is no murder weapon." What I saw was a faint lift of his eyebrows as he said this, like he was inviting his son to listen beneath his words. Then he said it again, more slowly, like it was code. "There is *no weapon.*" My grandson nodded his head once, a crisp little snap. Then my daughter Lâm said in a very loud voice, with her eyes on me, "That was a terrible thing, the death of Mr. Lê." She nudged her husband and son, and both men turned their faces sharply to me and they looked at me squarely and said, also in very loud voices, "Yes, it was terrible."

I am not deaf, and I closed my eyes further, having seen enough and wanting them to think that their loud talk had not only failed to awake me but had put me more completely to sleep. I did not like to deceive them, however, even though I have already spoken critically of these members of my family. I am a Hòa Hảo Buddhist and I believe in harmony among all living things, especially the members of a Vietnamese family.

After Hồ had reassured me, on that first visit, about the temperature needed to heat Maestro Escoffier's glaze, he said, "Đạo, my old friend, do you still follow the path you chose in Paris?"

He meant by this my religion. It was in Paris that I embraced the Buddha and disappointed Hồ. We went to France in early 1918, with the war still on, and we lived in the poorest street of the poorest part of the Seventeenth Arrondissement. Number nine, Impasse Compoint, a blind alley with a few crumbling houses, all but ours rented out for storage. The cobblestones were littered with fallen roof tiles and Quốc and I each had a tiny single room with only an iron bedstead and a crate to sit on. I could see my friend Quốc in the light of the tallow candle and he was dressed in a dark suit and a bowler hat and he looked very foolish. I did not say so, but he knew it himself and he kept seating and reseating the hat and shaking his head very slowly, with a loudly silent anger. This was near the end of our time together, for I was visiting daily with a Buddhist monk and he was drawing me back to the religion of my father. I had run from my father, gone to sea, and that was where I had met Nguyễn Ái Quốc and we had gone to London and to Paris and now my father was calling me back, through a Vietnamese monk I met in the Tuileries.

Quốc, on the other hand, was being called not from his past but from his future. He had rented the dark suit and bowler and he would spend the following weeks in

Versailles, walking up and down the mirrored corridors of the Palace trying to gain an audience with Woodrow Wilson. Quốc had eight requests for the Western world concerning Indochina. Simple things. Equal rights, freedom of assembly, freedom of the press. The essential things that he knew Wilson would understand, based as they were on Wilson's own Fourteen Points. And Quốc did not even intend to ask for independence. He wanted Vietnamese representatives in the French Parliament. That was all he would ask. But his bowler made him angry. He wrenched out of the puddle of candlelight, both his hands clutching the bowler, and I heard him muttering in the darkness and I felt that this was a bad sign already, even before he had set foot in Versailles. And as it turned out, he never saw Wilson, or Lloyd George either, or even Clemenceau. But somehow his frustration with his hat was what made me sad, even now, and I reached out from my bedside and said, "Uncle Hồ, it's all right."

He was still beside me. This was not an awakening, as you might expect, this was not a dream ending with the bowler in Paris and I awaking to find that Hồ was never there. He was still beside my bed, though he was just beyond my outstretched hand and he did not move to me. He smiled on one side of his mouth, a smile full of irony, as if he, too, was thinking about the night he'd tried on his rented clothes. He said, "Do you remember how I worked in Paris?"

I thought about this and I did remember, with the words of his advertisement in the newspaper "La Vie Ouvrière": "If you would like a lifelong memento of your family, have your photos retouched at Nguyễn Aí Quốc's." This was his work in Paris; he retouched photos with a very delicate hand, the same fine hand that Monsieur Escoffier had admired in London. I said, "Yes, I remember."

Hồ nodded gravely. "I painted the blush into the cheeks of Frenchmen."

I said, "A lovely portrait in a lovely frame for forty francs," another phrase from his advertisement.

"Forty-five," Hồ said.

I thought now of his question that I had not answered. I motioned to the far corner of the room where the prayer table stood. "I still follow the path."

He looked and said, "At least you became a Hòa Hảo."

He could tell this from the simplicity of the table. There was only a red cloth upon it and four Chinese characters: Bảo So'n Kỳ Hu'o'tng. This is the saying of the Hòa Hảo. We follow the teachings of a monk who broke away from the fancy rituals of the other Buddhists. We do not need elaborate pagodas or rituals. The Hòa Hảo believes that the maintenance of our spirits is very simple, and the mystery of joy is simple, too. The four characters mean "A good scent from a strange mountain."

I had always admired the sense of humor of my friend Quốc, so I said, "You never did stop painting the blush into the faces of Westerners."

Hồ looked back to me but he did not smile. I was surprised at this but more surprised at my little joke seeming to remind him of his hands. He raised them and studied them and said, "After the heating, what was the surface for the glaze?"

"My old friend," I said, "you worry me now."

But Hồ did not seem to hear. He turned away and crossed the room and I knew he was real because he did not vanish from my sight but opened the door and went out and closed the door behind him with a loud click.

I rang for my daughter. She had given me a porcelain bell, and after allowing Hồ enough time to go down the stairs and out the front door, if that was where he was headed, I rang the bell, and my daughter, who is a very light sleeper, soon appeared.

"What is it, Father?" she asked with great patience in her voice. She is a good girl. She understands about Vietnamese families and she is a smart girl.

"Please feel the doorknob," I said.

She did so without the slightest hesitation and this was a lovely gesture on her part, a thing that made me wish to rise up and embrace her, though I was very tired and did not move.

"Yes?" she asked after touching the knob.

"Is it sticky?"

She touched it again. "Ever so slightly," she said. "Would you like me to clean it?"

"In the morning," I said.

She smiled and crossed the room and kissed me on the forehead. She smelled of lavender and fresh bedclothes and there are so many who have gone on before me into the world of spirits and I yearn for them all, yearn to find them all together in a village square, my wife there smelling of lavender and our own sweat, like on a night in Saigon soon after the terrible fighting in 1968 when we finally opened the windows onto the night and there were sounds of bombs falling on the horizon and there was no breeze at all, just the heavy stillness of the time between the dry season and the wet, and Saigon smelled of tar and motorcycle exhaust and cordite but when I opened the window and turned to my wife, the room was full of a wonderful scent, a sweet smell that made her sit up, for she sensed it, too. This was a smell that had nothing to do with flowers but instead reminded us that flowers were always ready to fall into dust, while this smell was as if a gemstone had begun to give off a scent, as if a mountain of emerald had found its own scent. I crossed the room to my wife and we were already old, we had already buried children and grandchildren that we prayed waited for us in that village square at the foot of the strange mountain, but when I came near the bed, she lifted her silk gown and threw it aside and I pressed close to her and our own sweat smelled sweet on that night. I want to be with her in that square and with the rest of those we'd buried, the tiny limbs and the sullen eyes and the gray faces of the puzzled children and the surprised adults and the weary old people who have gone before us, who know the secrets now. And the sweet smell of the glaze on Hồ's hands reminds me of others that I would want in the square, the people from the ship, too, the Vietnamese boy from a village near my own who died of a fever in the Indian Ocean and the natives in Dakar who were forced by colonial officials to swim out to our ship in shark-infested waters to secure the moorings and two were killed before our eyes without a French regret. Hồ was very moved by this, and I want those men in our square and I want the Frenchman, too, who called Hồ "monsieur" for the first time. A man on the dock in Marseilles. Hồ spoke of him twice more during our years together and I want that Frenchman there. And, of course, Hồ. Was he in the village square even now, waiting? Heating his glaze fondant? My daughter was smoothing my covers around me and the smell of lavender on her was still strong.

"He was in this room," I said to her to explain the sticky doorknob.

"Who was?"

But I was very sleepy and I could say no more, though perhaps she would not have understood anyway, in spite of being the smart girl that she is.

The next night I left my light on to watch for Hồ's arrival, but I dozed off and he had to wake me. He was sitting in a chair that he'd brought from across the room. He said to me, "Đạo. Wake up, my old friend."

I must have awakened when he pulled the chair near to me, for I heard each of these words. "I am awake," I said. "I was thinking of the poor men who had to swim out to our ship."

"They are already among those I have served," Hồ said. "Before I forgot." And he raised his hands and they were still covered with sugar.

I said, "Wasn't it a marble slab?" I had a memory, strangely clear after these many years, as strange as my memory of Hồ's Paris business card.

"A marble slab," Hồ repeated, puzzled.

"That you poured the heated sugar on."

"Yes." Hồ's sweet-smelling hands came forward but they did not quite touch me. I thought to reach out from beneath the covers and take them in my own hands, but Hồ leaped up and paced about the room. "The marble slab, moderately oiled. Of course. I am to let the sugar half cool and then use the spatula to move it about in all directions, every bit of it, so that it doesn't harden and form lumps."

I asked, "Have you seen my wife?"

Hồ had wandered to the far side of the room, but he turned and crossed back to me at this. "I'm sorry, my friend. I never knew her."

I must have shown some disappointment in my face, for Hồ sat down and brought his own face near mine. "I'm sorry" he said. "There are many other people that I must find here."

"Are you very disappointed in me?" I asked. "For not having traveled the road with you?"

"It's very complicated," Hồ said softly. "You felt that you'd taken action. I am no longer in a position to question another soul's choice."

"Are you at peace, where you are?" I asked this knowing of his worry over the recipe for the glaze, but I hoped that this was only a minor difficulty in the afterlife, like the natural anticipation of the good cook expecting guests when everything always turns out fine in the end.

But Hồ said, "I am not at peace."

"Is Monsieur Escoffier over there?"

"I have not seen him. This has nothing to do with him, directly."

"What is it about?"

"I don't know."

"You won the country. You know that, don't you?"

Hồ shrugged. "There are no countries here."

I should have remembered Hồ's shrug when I began to see things in the faces of my son-in-law and grandson this morning. But something quickened in me, a suspicion. I kept my eyes shut and laid my head to the side, as if I was fast asleep, encouraging them to talk more.

My daughter said, "This is not the place to speak."

But the men did not regard her. "How?" Lợi asked his father, referring to the missing murder weapon.

"It's best not to know too much," Thắng said.

Then there was a silence. For all the quickness I'd felt at the first suspicion, I was very slow now. In fact, I did think of Hồ from that second night. Not his shrug. He had fallen silent for a long time and I had closed my eyes, for the light seemed very bright. I listened to his silence just as I listened to the silence of these two conspirators before me.

And then Hồ said, "They were fools, but I can't bring myself to grow angry anymore."

I opened my eyes in the bedroom and the light was off. Hồ had turned it off, knowing that it was bothering me. "Who were fools?" I asked.

"We had fought together to throw out the Japanese. I had very good friends among them. I smoked their lovely Salem cigarettes. They had been repressed by colonialists themselves. Did they not know their own history?"

"Do you mean the Americans?"

"There are a million souls here with me, the young men of our country, and they are all dressed in black suits and bowler hats. In the mirrors they are made ten million, a hundred million."

"I chose my path, my dear friend Quốc, so that there might be harmony."

And even with that yearning for harmony I could not overlook what my mind made of what my ears had heard this morning. Thắng was telling Lợi that the murder weapon had been disposed of. Thắng and Lợi both knew the killers, were in sympathy with them, perhaps were part of the killing. The father and son had been airborne rangers and I had several times heard them talk bitterly of the exile of our people. We were fools for trusting the Americans all along, they said. We should have taken matters forward and disposed of the infinitely corrupt Thiệu and done what needed to be done. Whenever they spoke like this in front of me, there was soon a quick exchange of sideways glances at me and then a turn and an apology. "We're sorry, Grandfather. Old times often bring old anger. We are happy our family is living a new life."

I would wave my hand at this, glad to have the peace of the family restored. Glad to turn my face and smell the dogwood tree or even smell the coffee plant across the highway. These things had come to be the new smells of our family. But then a weakness often came upon me. The others would drift away, the men, and perhaps one of my daughters would come to me and stroke my head and not say a word and none of them ever would ask why I was weeping. I would smell the rich blood smells of the afterbirth and I would hold our first son, still slippery in my arms, and there was the smell of dust from the square and the smell of the South China Sea just over the rise of the hill and there was the smell of the blood and of the inner flesh from my wife as my son's own private sea flowed from this woman that I loved, flowed and carried him into the life that would disappear from him so soon. In the afterlife would he stand before me on unsteady child's legs? Would I have to bend low to greet him or would he be a man now?

My grandson said, after the silence had nearly carried me into real sleep, troubled sleep, my grandson Lợi said to his father, "I would be a coward not to know."

Thắng laughed and said, "You have proved yourself no coward."

And I wished then to sleep, I wished to fall asleep and let go of life somewhere in my dreams and seek my village square. I have lived too long, I thought. My daughter was saying, "Are you both mad?" And then she changed her voice, making the words very precise. "Let Grandfather sleep."

So when Hồ came tonight for the third time, I wanted to ask his advice. His hands were still covered with sugar and his mind was, as it had been for the past two nights, very much distracted. "There's something still wrong with the glaze," he said to me in the dark, and I pulled back the covers and swung my legs around to get up. He did not try to stop me, but he did draw back quietly into the shadows.

"I want to pace the room with you," I said. "As we did in Paris, those tiny rooms of ours. We would talk about Marx and about Buddha and I must pace with you now."

"Very well," he said. "Perhaps it will help me remember."

I slipped on my sandals and I stood up and Hồ's shadow moved past me, through the spill of streetlight and into the dark near the door. I followed him, smelling the sugar on his hands, first before me and then moving past me as I went on into the darkness he'd just left. I stopped as I turned and I could see Hồ outlined before the window and I said, "I believe my son-in-law and grandson are involved in the killing of a man. A political killing."

Hồ stayed where he was, a dark shape against the light, and he said nothing and I could not smell his hands from across the room and I smelled only the sourness of Lợi as he laid his head on my shoulder. He was a baby and my daughter Lâm retreated to our balcony window after handing him to me and the boy turned his head and I turned mine to him and I could smell his mother's milk, sour on his breath, he had a sour smell and there was incense burning in the room, jasmine, the smoke of souls, and the boy sighed on my shoulder, and I turned my face away from the smell of him. Thắng was across the room and his eyes were quick to find his wife and he was waiting for her to take the child from me.

"You have never done the political thing," Hồ said.

"Is this true?"

"Of course."

I asked, "Are there politics where you are now, my friend?"

I did not see him moving toward me, but the smell of the sugar on his hands grew stronger, very strong, and I felt Hồ Chí Minh very close to me, though I could not see him. He was very close and the smell was strong and sweet and it was filling my lungs as if from the inside, as if Hồ was passing through my very body, and I heard the door open behind me and then close softly shut.

I moved across the room to the bed. I turned to sit down but I was facing the window, the scattering of a streetlamp on the window like a nova in some far part of the universe. I stepped to the window and touched the reflected light there, wondering if there was a great smell when a star explodes, a great burning smell of gas and dust. Then I closed the shade and slipped into bed, quite gracefully, I felt, I was quite wonderfully graceful, and I lie here now waiting for sleep. Hồ is right, of course. I will never say a word about my grandson. And perhaps I will be as restless as Hồ when I join him. But that will be all right. He and I will be together again and perhaps we can help each other. I know now what it is that he has forgotten. He has used confectioners' sugar for his glaze fondant and he should be using granulated sugar. I was only a washer of dishes but I did listen carefully when Monsieur Escoffier spoke. I wanted to understand everything. His kitchen was full of such smells that you knew you had to understand everything or you would be incomplete forever.

ROBERT OLEN BUTLER

Jealous Husband Returns in Form of Parrot

I never can quite say as much as I know. I look at other parrots and I wonder if it's the same for them, if somebody is trapped in each of them, paying some kind of price for living their life in a certain way. For instance, "Hello," I say, and I'm sitting on a perch in a pet store in Houston and what I'm really thinking is, Holy shit. It's you. And what's happened is I'm looking at my wife.

"Hello," she says, and she comes over to me, and I can't believe how beautiful she is. Those great brown eyes, almost as dark as the center of mine. And her nose—I don't remember her for her nose, but its beauty is clear to me now. Her nose is a little too long, but it's redeemed by the faint hook to it.

She scratches the back of my neck.

Her touch makes my tail flare. I feel the stretch and rustle of me back there. I bend my head to her and she whispers, "Pretty bird."

For a moment, I think she knows it's me. But she doesn't, of course. I say "Hello" again, and I will eventually pick up "pretty bird." I can tell that as soon as she says it, but for now I can only give her another "Hello." Her fingertips move through my feathers, and she seems to know about birds. She knows that to pet a bird you don't smooth his feathers down, you ruffle them.

But of course she did that in my human life as well. It's all the same for her. Not that I was complaining, even to myself, at that moment in the pet shop when she found me like I presume she was supposed to. She said it again—"Pretty bird"—and this brain that works the way it does now could feel that tiny little voice of mine ready to shape itself around these sounds. But before I could get them out of my beak, there was this guy at my wife's shoulder, and all my feathers went slick-flat to make me small enough not to be seen, and I backed away. The pupils of my eyes pinned and dilated and pinned again.

He circled around her. A guy that looked like a meat-packer, big in the chest and thick with hair, the kind of guy that I always sensed her eyes moving to when I was alive. I had a bare chest, and I'd look for little black hairs on the sheets when I'd come home on a day with the whiff of somebody else in the air. She was still in the same goddamn rut.

A "hello" wouldn't do, and I'd recently learned "good night," but it was the wrong suggestion altogether, so I said nothing and the guy circled her, and he was looking at me with a smug little smile, and I fluffed up all my feathers, made myself about twice as big, so big he'd see he couldn't mess with me. I waited for him to draw close enough for me to take off the tip of his finger.

But she intervened. Those nut-brown eyes were before me, and she said, "I want him."

And that's how I ended up in my own house once again. She bought me a large black wrought-iron cage, very large, convinced by some young guy who clerked in the bird department and who took her aside and made his voice go much too soft when he was doing the selling job. The meat-packer didn't like it. I didn't either. I'd missed a lot of chances to take a bite out of this clerk in my stay at the shop, and I regretted that suddenly.

But I got my giant cage, and I guess I'm happy enough about that. I can pace as much as I want. I can hang upside down. It's full of bird toys. That dangling thing over there with knots and strips of rawhide and a bell at the bottom needs a good thrashing a couple of times a day, and I'm the bird to do it. I look at the very dangle of it, and the thing is rough, the rawhide and the knotted rope, and I get this restlessness back in my tail, a burning, thrashing feeling, and it's like all the times when I was sure there was a man naked with my wife. Then I go to this thing that feels so familiar and I bite and bite, and it's very good.

I could have used the thing the last day I went out of this house as a man. I'd found the address of the new guy at my wife's office. He'd been there a month, in the shipping department, and three times she'd mentioned him. She didn't even have to work with him, and three times I heard about him, just dropped into the conversation. "Oh," she'd say when a car commercial came on the television, "that car there is like the one the new man in shipping owns. Just like it." Hey, I'm not stupid. She said another thing about him and then another, and right after the third one I locked myself in the bathroom, because I couldn't rage about this anymore. I felt like a damn fool whenever I actually said anything about this kind of feeling and she looked at me as though she could start hating me real easy, and so I was working on saying nothing, even if it meant locking myself up. My goal was to hold my tongue about half the time. That would be a good start.

But this guy from shipping. I found out his name and his address, and it was one of her typical Saturday afternoons of vague shopping. So I went to his house, and his car that was just like the commercial was outside. Nobody was around in the neighborhood, and there was this big tree in back of the house going up to a second-floor window that was making funny little sounds. I went up. The shade was drawn but not quite all the way. I was holding on to a limb with my arms and legs wrapped around it like it was her in those times when I could forget the others for a little while. But the crack in the shade was just out of view, and I crawled on till there was no limb left, and I fell on my head. When I think about that now, my wings flap and I feel myself lift up, and it all seems so avoidable. Though I know I'm different now. I'm a bird.

Except I'm not. That's what's confusing. It's like those times when she would tell me she loved me and I actually believed her and maybe it was true and we clung to each other in bed and at times like that I was different. I was the man in her life. I was whole with her. Except even at that moment, as I held her sweetly, there was this other creature inside me who knew a lot more about it and couldn't quite put all the evidence together to speak.

My cage sits in the den. My pool table is gone, and the cage is sitting in that space, and if I come all the way down to one end of my perch I can see through the door and down the back hallway to the master bedroom. When she keeps the bedroom door open, I can see the space at the foot of the bed but not the bed itself. I can sense it to the left, just out of sight. I watch the men go in and I hear the sounds, but I can't quite see. And they drive me crazy.

I flap my wings and I squawk and I fluff up and I slick down and I throw seed and I attack that dangly toy as if it were the guy's balls, but it does no good. It never did any good in the other life either, the thrashing around I did by myself. In that other life I'd have given anything to be standing in this den with her doing this thing with some other guy just down the hall, and all I had to do was walk down there and turn the corner and she couldn't deny it anymore.

But now all I can do is try to let it go. I sidestep down to the opposite end of the cage and I look out the big sliding glass doors to the back yard. It's a pretty yard. There are great, placid live oaks with good places to roost. There's a blue sky that plucks at the feathers on my chest. There are clouds. Other birds. Fly away. I could just fly away.

I tried once, and I learned a lesson. She forgot and left the door to my cage open, and I climbed beak and foot, beak and foot, along the bars and curled around to stretch sideways out the door, and the vast scene of peace was there, at the other end of the room. I flew.

And a pain flared through my head, and I fell straight down, and the room whirled around, and the only good thing was that she held me. She put her hands under my wings and lifted me and clutched me to her breast, and I wish there hadn't been bees in my head at the time so I could have enjoyed that, but she put me back in the cage and wept a while. That touched me, her tears. And I looked back to the wall of sky and trees. There was something invisible there between me and that dream of peace. I remembered, eventually, about glass, and I knew I'd been lucky; I knew that for the little, fragile-boned skull I was doing all this thinking in, it meant death.

She wept that day, but by the night she had another man. A guy with a thick Georgia-truck-stop accent and pale white skin and an Adam's apple big as my seed ball. This guy has been around for a few weeks, and he makes a whooping sound down the hallway, just out of my sight. At times like that, I want to fly against the bars of the cage, but I don't. I have to remember how the world has changed.

She's single now, of course. Her husband, the man that I was, is dead to her. She does not understand all that is behind my "Hello." I know many words, for a parrot. I am a yellow-nape Amazon, a handsome bird, I think, green with a splash of yellow at the back of my neck. I talk pretty well, but none of my words are adequate. I can't make her understand.

And what would I say if I could? I was jealous in life. I admit it. I would admit it to her. But it was because of my connection to her. I would explain that. When we held each other, I had no past at all, no present but her body, no future but to lie there and not let her go. I was an egg hatched beneath her crouching body, I entered as a chick into her wet sky of a body, and all that I wished was to sit on her shoulder and fluff my feathers and lay my head against her cheek, with my neck exposed to her hand. And so the glances that I could see in her troubled me deeply: the movement of her eyes in public to other men, the laughs sent across a room, the tracking of her mind behind her blank eyes, pursuing images of others, her distraction even in our bed, the ghosts that were there of men who'd touched her, perhaps even that very day. I was not part of all those other men who were part of her. I didn't want to connect to all that. It was only her that I would fluff for, but these others were there also, and I couldn't put them aside. I sensed them inside her, and so they were inside me. If I had the words, these are the things I would say.

But half an hour ago, there was a moment that thrilled me. A word, a word we all knew in the pet shop, was just the right word after all. This guy with his cowboy belt buckle and rattlesnake boots and his pasty face and his twanging words of love trailed after my wife through the den, past my cage, and I said, "Cracker." He even flipped his head back a little at this in surprise. He'd been called that before to his face, I realized. I said it again, "Cracker." But to him I was a bird, and he let it pass. "Cracker," I said. "Hello, cracker." That was even better. They were out of sight through the hall doorway, and I hustled along the perch and I caught a glimpse of them before they made the turn to the bed and I said, "Hello, cracker," and he shot me one last glance.

It made me hopeful. I eased away from that end of the cage, moved toward the scene of peace beyond the far wall. The sky is chalky blue today, blue like the brow of the blue-front Amazon who was on the perch next to me for about a week at the store. She was very sweet, but I watched her carefully for a day or two when she first came in. And it wasn't long before she nuzzled up to a cockatoo named Willy, and I knew she'd break my heart. But her color now, in the sky, is sweet, really. I left all those feelings behind me when my wife showed up. I am a faithful man, for all my suspicions. Too faithful, maybe. I am ready to give too much, and maybe that's the problem.

The whooping began down the hall, and I focused on a tree out there. A crow flapped down, his mouth open, his throat throbbing, though I could not hear his sound. I was feeling very odd. At least I'd made my point to the guy in the other room. "Pretty bird," I said, referring to myself. She called me "pretty bird," and I believed her and I told myself again, "Pretty bird."

But then something new happened, something very difficult for me. She appeared in the den naked. I have not seen her naked since I fell from the tree and had no wings to fly. She always had a certain tidiness in things. She was naked in the bedroom, clothed in the den. But now she appears from the hallway, and I look at her, and she is still slim and she is beautiful, I think—at least I clearly remember that as her husband I found her beautiful in this state. Now, though, she seems too naked. Plucked. I find that a sad thing. I am sorry for her, and she goes by me and she disappears into the kitchen. I want to pluck some of my own feathers, the feathers from my chest, and give them to her. I love her more in that moment, seeing her terrible nakedness, than I ever have before.

And since I've had success in the last few minutes with words, when she comes back I am moved to speak. "Hello," I say, meaning, You are still connected to me, I still want only you. "Hello," I say again. Please listen to this tiny heart that beats fast at all times for you.

And she does indeed stop, and she comes to me and bends to me. "Pretty bird," I say, and I am saying, You are beautiful, my wife, and your beauty cries out for protection. "Pretty." I want to cover you with my own nakedness. "Bad bird," I say. If there are others in your life, even in your mind, then there is nothing I can do. "Bad." Your nakedness is touched from inside by the others. "Open," I say. How can we be whole together if you are not empty in the place that I am to fill?

She smiles at this, and she opens the door to my cage. "Up," I say, meaning, Is there no place for me in this world where I can be free of this terrible sense of others?

She reaches in now and offers her hand, and I climb onto it and I tremble and she says, "Poor baby."

"Poor baby," I say. You have yearned for wholeness too, and somehow I failed you. I was not enough. "Bad bird," I say. I'm sorry.

And then the cracker comes around the corner. He wears only his rattlesnake boots. I take one look at his miserable, featherless body and shake my head. We keep our sexual parts hidden, we parrots, and this man is a pitiful sight. "Peanut," I say. I presume that my wife simply has not noticed. But that's foolish, of course. This is, in fact, what she wants. Not me. And she scrapes me off her hand onto the open cage door and she turns her naked back to me and embraces this man, and they laugh and stagger in their embrace around the corner.

For a moment, I still think I've been eloquent. What I've said only needs repeating for it to have its transforming effect. "Hello," I say. "Hello. Pretty bird. Pretty. Bad bird. Bad. Open. Up. Poor baby. Bad bird." And I am beginning to hear myself as I really sound to her. "Peanut." I can never say what is in my heart to her. Never.

I stand on my cage door now, and my wings stir. I look at the corner to the hallway, and down at the end the whooping has begun again. I can fly there and think of things to do about all this.

But I do not. I turn instead, and I look at the trees moving just beyond the other end of the room. I look at the sky the color of the brow of a blue-front Amazon. A shadow of birds spanks across the lawn. And I spread my wings. I will fly now. Even though I know there is something between me and that place where I can be free of all these feelings, I will fly. I will throw myself there again and again. Pretty bird. Bad bird. Good night.

ROBERT OLEN BUTLER

This Is Earl Sandt

"This is Earl Sandt of Erie Pa in his Aeroplane just before it fell"

—INSCRIPTION ON A 1913 PHOTO POSTCARD OF A BIPLANE IN FLIGHT WITH A TORN WING

I've seen a man die, but not like this. There was silence suddenly around us when he disappeared beyond the trees, silence after terrible sounds, that hammering of his engine, the engine of his aeroplane, and the other sound, after.

He had climbed miraculously up and he had circled the field and we all took off our hats as one, the men among us. Mine as well. Hooray, we cried. My son cried out, too. Hooray. This was why we'd come to this meadow. We would peek into the future and cheer it on.

And Earl Sandt hammered overhead and down to the far edge of the pasture, defying the trees, defying the earth. The propeller of his engine spun behind him and he sat in a rattan chair, as if he was on his front porch smoking a cigar. Then he came back from the tree line, heading our way.

I reached down and touched my son on the shoulder. I had never seen an aeroplane and something was changing in me as it approached. I suppose it scared me some. I had no premonition, but I needed to touch my son at that moment. The plane came toward us and there was a stiff wind blowing—the plane bucked a little, like a nervous horse, but Earl Sandt kept him steady, kept him coming forward, and I felt us all ready to cheer again.

Then there was a movement on the wing. With no particular sound. Still the engine. But there was a tearing away. If I had been Earl Sandt, if I had been sitting in that rattan chair and flying above these bared heads, I might have heard the sound and been afraid.

I lifted my camera. This had nothing to do with the thing happening on the wing. I was only vaguely aware of it in that moment. I lifted my camera and I tripped the shutter, and here was another amazing thing, it seemed to me. One man was flying above the earth, and with a tiny movement of a hand, another man had captured him.

Earl Sandt was about to die, but he was forever caught there in that box in my hand. I lowered my Kodak and for a moment the plane was before me against the sky and all I felt was a thing that I sometimes had felt as a younger man, riding up into the Alleghenys alone and there would be a turning in the path and suddenly the trees broke apart and there was a great falling away of the land.

A falling. He fell, Earl Sandt. The aeroplane suddenly lifted up from its left side and for a moment it seemed to flatten itself against the sky, but the engine hammered on and then it skidded to the right and pitched forward and it fell, disappearing behind a stand of pine.

There was a heavy thump beyond the trees, and I have nothing in my head to compare it to. Not a barn collapsing, not a horse going down, not the dead sugar maple, forty foot high, I had felled only yesterday in our yard. This sound was new.

And our silence followed. We all of us could not take this in. He had flown, this Earl Sandt, he had raised his goggles to his eyes and stepped into his machine and he had run along the meadow and had lifted into the air, and now I looked into the empty place where he had been, only a moment before. In my head I could see once again the two great wings and the spinning of the propeller and then he was gone.

"Papa?" It was my son's voice drifting up to me from the silence.

I looked into his face.

"It's all right," I said, though I knew it was not. I could feel Matthew's bones beneath my hand, which still lay on his shoulder.

"He's gone," my son said.

I looked to the others. There was a stirring. Some of the women began to cry.

"Mother of God," one man said and he moved in the direction of the pines. He was right. We had to do something now.

I let go of my son and put the camera in his hand. I turned to the place where Earl Sandt had vanished. "Stay here," I said.

We ran, perhaps a dozen of us, across the meadow grass and into the pines and I could smell burning and there was smoke up ahead and I could smell a newly familiar thing, a smell of the automobiles that had come to our town, their fuel. Then we broke into a clearing and the aeroplane was crumpled up ahead and beginning to burn.

I was behind several of the men and we were in our Sunday clothes, we had left our churches this morning and had come to see the exhibition of this wonderful thing, and now we were stripping off our coats and winding them around our hands and arms to allow us to reach into the flames, to bring Earl Sandt out. Two men were ahead of me, already bending to the tangle of canvas and wood and metal and smoke. I felt myself slow and stop.

I did not know this man. I had seen him only from afar, only briefly. He had raised his goggles and hidden his eyes and he'd had some intent in his head—to fly, of course, and he did. But he was a man, flesh and blood, and he was lying broken now, ahead of me. There were others to help him. The ones ahead, and still others now, rushing past me. I continued to hesitate, and then I turned away.

Matthew had followed me. He was standing a few yards behind, in the trees. I lifted my hand to acknowledge him, and I found it swathed in my suit coat, expecting the fire.

I moved to my son, unwrapping my arm.

"The others are helping," I said to him, so he would understand why I had turned away.

"I want to see," he said.

"No."

"Pa."

"No," I said, firm. I turned him around and we stepped out of the trees. I looked once more into the sky where Earl Sandt had been.

Matthew and I walked from the meadow and through the center of town, passing the Merchants Bank, where I had an office, where I was vice-president, and we moved beneath the maples of our street, old trees, dense above us, and we were quiet, my son and I. The meadow, the open sky, all of that, was left behind. Then we reached the place along the road where I could see my house ahead.

The maple was gone from the front edge of my property, dead from blight and felled by my own hand. I looked away, not wanting to, but I felt suddenly bereft of this tree. I was sorry for its passing, this tree. Matthew broke away from me now, began to run. I looked.

His mother was coming down the porch steps. My son ran hard to her, not calling out. She turned her face toward us, saw him approaching, sensing, I think, that something had happened.

I stopped, still separate from them. My daughter, a tall gangly girl, my sweet Naomi, emerged from the house, and for a moment they all three were before me, and the house itself, a fine house, a house we'd lived in for four years now, a solid house with its hipped roof and double-windowed dormer and its clapboard siding the color of sunlight in the brightness of noon.

My wife went down on one knee, and Matthew reached her and he threw his arms around her neck. I knew I should move forward, to explain. But what would I say? Naomi came to the two of them, put her hand on her crouching mother's shoulder. There was a seizing in my chest. I wanted to take them all three up into my arms, but instead, I stood dumbly there, watching.

Finally, Rachel's face lifted to look at me over Matthew's shoulder. I felt heavy now, rooted to this earth, as if I'd decided to take the place of the dead maple. But I made myself move. I took a step and another and there was a loosening inside me as I moved toward my family. My wife tilted her head slightly, a questioning gesture, I think. Naomi looked at me too, came around her mother, and I was glad she was drawing near, and she put her arms about me, I felt the bones in her arms pressing at my back. I held her tight.

"What was it, Daddy?"

"An accident," I said. "It was just an accident."

"Matty said he was dead, the man."

"We don't know that for sure."

"He fell?"

"Yes."

She said no more, but she needed me to hold her closer and I did. "It's all right," I said. "We're all right."

Matthew could not sleep. The house was dark and my wife and I had just extinguished the lamp, alone and undistracted at last. Then we heard his cry, wordless, and Rachel rose. I knew what it was about. As she disappeared, I looked toward the dark gape of the bedroom doorway and I gripped the sheet as if to put it aside and to rise. But I hesitated. I should not have hesitated to go to my son, but I did. For one moment and then another.

I forced myself to throw back the sheet and put my feet on the floor. I stood. I made my way across the room and down the hall, and my son's tears were fading as I approached. I stood in his doorway and his mother said to him, "It's okay, Matty. God decided he wanted an aeroplane pilot in heaven."

"Like he wanted Henry for an angel," my son said.

I turned away. I moved back down the hall and then stopped, neither here nor there. Matthew's first cousin Henry, my brother's son, had died of smallpox. My son had already encountered death. Of course he had, we had all encountered death, it was a part of our daily lives. Always, we waited for the first sneeze, the first cough, the first spot on our skin, we waited to be carried away, if not from smallpox then from influenza or from scarlet fever or from diphtheria or from pneumonia or from tuberculosis. It was the way of the world. I believed in God, that he managed our lives, that he would call us when he chose to. And I was glad my son could picture his blood kin, a child of his own age, as an angel and not as a corpse in the ground.

But I stood in the middle of the hallway and I dragged my forearm across my brow and I was having trouble drawing a breath.

I waited in bed, sitting propped up in the dark, sweating still.

Finally Rachel appeared in the door, quietly, pausing there in the dim light, her white nightgown glowing faintly, as if she were a ghost. I spoke to her at once, to drive that image from my mind. "Is he all right?"

"I don't know," she said, and she floated this way.

"Rachel," I said.

"Yes?"

She was beside the bed now. I had spoken her name without anything more to say. I just needed to say her name.

"Nothing," I said.

"What happened out there?"

"The plane crashed," I said. "These machines aren't safe."

Rachel drew back the sheet and sat beside me. "Paul."

I looked toward her.

Her face was there, turned to me, featureless in the dark. She touched my hand and repeated, almost in a whisper, "What happened?"

"I don't know."

I was Earl Sandt. Sitting in my rattan chair. I looked down and the faces all turned upward and the mouths all opened to cry out but the only sound I could hear was the rush of air about me as I flew, I flew and the lift was not in my wings it was in my chest my very chest I was buoyed up and moving quickly and there was nothing around me now, not the aeroplane, not the rattan chair, only the wide bright air. I looked down again and there was only one face below and it was my own.

Mine. I woke. I sat up quickly, expecting to rise from the bed and up through the ceiling and out into the night sky. But I was awake. I was sitting on my bed. Nevertheless, I lifted my eyes, and I saw the aeroplane, its broad wings, the fragile bones holding them in place, the bones stretching behind to the smaller back wings, the tail. And then suddenly the beast veered and showed me its dark underside and it dashed down.

And then the sound.

I jumped up from the bed, knocking into the bedstand.

"What is it?" Rachel cried.

"I'm all right," I said.
"Was it Matty?"
"It was a dream," I said.

I do not require silence at the breakfast table. We eat together each day, my wife and my son and my daughter and I. Even when my children have one leg skewed out from under the table, ready to run into the summer morning. They have their duties in this house, but the mornings are theirs. It is best to let a child feel his freedom in the morning. And they are free to speak, as well. I like to listen to the movement of my chidren's minds.

But this morning there was silence. A long period of silence. And their legs were under the table, in spite of it being early summer. And without urging, Matthew was eating his eggs, studiously sopping up the last bits of yolk with a piece of bread.

I had not picked up the newspaper that lay folded beside my plate. I could see, in large bold type, in the upturned quarter, the words Aviator Killed. It was not uncommon for me to read the newspaper at the breakfast table, but only after we'd all had a chance to speak of the day to come.

I looked at Rachel. She was lifting her coffee cup to her lips and I could see that her eyes were on Matthew. He was intent on the bread, running it around and around the plate. Naomi was looking out the kitchen door. I followed her gaze. The sun was bright. The trees quaked. A scrap of paper blew across the yard—lifting briefly into the air—and then it fell and tumbled along.

I placed my hand on the newspaper but I did not open it. I looked at my hand. It covered the words in the headline.

Finally I said, "It looks like a fine day."

Matthew lifted his face at this. "May I be excused?" he said.

"Yes."

He pushed back his chair and he rose and only now was I hearing the flatness of his voice. He was a boy. This was the moment of the day that should have been relished above all others.

"Matty," my wife said. "Are you all right?"

My son had moved toward the door. He stopped now and turned to us. His two shoulders lifted slightly and fell. It was a very small gesture, really, this shrug, but it made my eyes close so as not to see it, this gesture in my son that was not the gesture of a child at all. Too late.

I opened my eyes. He was pushing through the screen door, not having spoken a word.

A Monday morning in the year of our Lord 1913. A desk in a bank. A newspaper tucked under my arm and then put away in a drawer. I sat and my hands were flat and unmoving on the top of my desk, my mahogany desk, and above me was a high window, and I have always liked the column of sky looking over me and I have liked the hush of the bank. It is not blasphemy to say that the hush was like that of a church. We protected the money of the people of this town, and their money was a measure of their hard work, and their hard work rightly gave them the things of this world, the things of a world changing rapidly now. The hush of the bank, and there were low voices murmuring, and I knew their words, I could hear terrible and I could hear aeroplane and I could hear fire and I could hear dead. I wanted to stand up and cry out to my tellers and my customers, Go about your business, all of you. Just go about your business.

But I did not stand. I swiveled in my chair and raised my eyes to the window, to the empty morning sky. I had myself gone up into that sky. Higher even than Earl Sandt. I had stood in the air.

I had stood and looked out on a great city, on a world of business and banking, a world of making goods and buying and selling and building houses and factories and I looked out on steamships and trains and bridges and, far off, a vast sea, and I was standing within a thing as great as all of that. The Singer Building. The highest building in the world at that moment in the summer of 1909 when my host, a fellow banker, lifted his office window on the thirty-eighth floor, and I trembled like a horse before a fire. I crept forward and I felt my chest swell, I grew large with fear and happiness to look at this city, vast and multiform in its stone and marble and terracotta, the work of human hands.

I stepped closer still. I grew bold. The air moved on my face. An air only the clouds knew. But I was part of a race of creatures of the earth who were remaking themselves into something new. I took the last step a man could take and not fall. I pressed against the sill and I bent forward at the waist and looked across the rooftops below—rooftops that themselves were higher than any tree on earth, but far below me now—and I looked beyond the docks and masts and smokestacks, I followed the bright thread of the Hudson River to Ellis Island and the statue of Madame Liberty, her arm lifted high.

Earl Sandt, I lift my arm to you. I stand in the meadow beside my son, a blazing torch in my hand. Come here to me, guide your plane this way, fly down to this flame and land safely beside me. I look from where I sit in the rattan chair, my hands on the steering handle, I see the flame below, and my wing has not yet torn. I nudge my aeroplane gently downward, down toward the man and the boy. I will be safe.

But I am not Earl Sandt. He is dead.

I have seen men die before. My father, long ago, his lungs bricked up solid with pneumonia. A man in the Alleghenys, broken beneath a felled tree, when I was young and working in timber. And another in New York City on that day in 1909 when I went out of the Singer Building and into the streets that were dim even near noon, streets narrow and full of rushing men and the hammering of metal and the whine of wheels and the mutter of automobile engines and the clatter of a distant Elevated Train, and I turned to look up at the place where I'd stood, in the middle of the air, and my eyes went up and up, impossibly high, up the great bluestone and red-brick column, up to its great mansard roof and cupola and the bright sky beyond. "Step lively," a voice said, and I looked and I could not pick the speaker out of a hundred bowlered men moving all about me.

I stepped away, up the street, which was cloaked in the shadows of skyscrapers as far as I could see. I moved, and suddenly before me there was a gathering of men and some bowlers were coming off and I came up.

He was in a greatcoat in spite of the heat. He was sprawled face down, his arms outstretched, his legs spread wide. The men about him were quiet. I thought to look up. A gray stone building loomed over us, perhaps two hundred feet high. I looked back down to the dead man. A policeman pushed past me and bent to the body.

I found myself standing beside my desk in the bank on the morning after Earl Sandt died. I could not recall the act of rising from this chair. I extended my arm, touched my hand to the corner of my desk, stiffened my fingertips, held myself up. I had to go out, I realized.

I moved to the coat rack and took my hat and I put it on my head and I stepped from my office and my secretary looked up and I said to her, "I'll be back shortly." She lifted her eyebrows ever so slightly. This was unlike me, of course. But I did not pause to explain. There was no explanation.

I stepped into the sunlight before the bank and turned toward the woods where he had gone down.

A wagon was moving toward me from the tree line as I approached. I stopped. The horse had its head lowered as if the load were heavy, but the wagon moved easily, quickly. I stepped away from it. The driver turned his face to me. A man I knew, a collector of scrap goods. He nodded, but I could not return the nod. I was leaden now in my limbs. The wagon slipped past and I glanced into the bed of it: twisted metal, charred wood, a panel of canvas. I looked sharply to the side. This whole thing was a mistake, to come here again. I thought to back away, to face toward the town, the square, the bank, the maple trees, face toward my house where I would surely live the rest of my life.

I could not. I had to press on, into the stand of pine. But I had to catch my breath first. I felt as if I'd been running a long way. I bent forward and put my hands on my knees.

Above me was the sky where Earl Sandt had spent his last moments of life. I did not look. I leaned hard onto my knees. I closed my eyes. I held tight to the steering handle and there was something terribly wrong. These wings that felt like my own limbs—I sensed them stretching out from me and lifting me up—these wings went weak and so did my limbs of flesh, I was instantly aware of the very surface of my skin, the beating of my heart. And I felt a question rise like a gasp into my throat: what was it I believed? Did I sense a God all about me in the sky? Was it he who lifted me and would take me now into his arms?

Forgive me, no.

This thing I had expected to be familiar—my own death—was all new. I fell. I fell from him. His hands receded and the trees reached up and I fell.

I could not breathe at all. I rose up from where I'd been bending and I stood straight and dragged the air into my lungs and I opened my eyes, and before me was the tree line, the pines, and beyond them was the clearing where he fell and burned, Earl Sandt. And he knew something now. Right this moment. Something that I desperately wished to know. He had been alive above me, in the sunlit air, just yesterday, and now he knew the great truth of it all.

I stepped forward, moved toward the trees. My breath had returned. Fragile. Easily taken away. But I breathed deep once, and again, and I walked into the darkness of the trees and I was filled with the smell of pine all about me and the smell of the duff beneath my feet and with other smells, not of the forest, faintly still of smoke in the air and the fuel of the aeroplane.

I pressed on, my face lowered, feeling the trees on the back of my neck, in my shoulders, in a faint wrenching upward in my chest. I've been around trees often in my life, I made a life from the forests before I became who I am, a man with a desk in a bank and a Georgian revival home and a wife and a son and a daughter and a special pew in a church where the deacons sit, and I know nothing about anything, I know only that I must press past these last few trees and into this clearing, which I do.

It is empty. It is empty. Earl Sandt's aeroplane was here and now it is gone. I move out to the center, I am surrounded by high pine, and there is something. A shapeless patch of burnt earth. I slow and stop before it. He burned here. He vanished from this life here.

I take another step. I stand precisely where he fell. For a moment I stretch out my arms, as if to fly, and they are contained within this black bareness. I hold fast to the steering column and my wings are still whole and I am racing toward those distant pines, and a thought occurs to me. I sit on the back of a horse. I am high up, above the tree line, on a slender thread of a path. Not even the smell of the pines has risen this high. I pause and I look below me. Faces turn up, their hats raised high in the air. Tree tops point up to me and I have nothing inside but an enormous quiet. I find myself separated from all that I've known, from every touch every word every face, I have lifted up into the air, high on this mountain with nothing around me but the empty sky, high in the air above this meadow. And I think: This is how it feels. To be free. To be utterly alone. And my hands clench on the reins. There is only one more thing to feel, to know. My hands clench harder, wanting to slip hard to the right, to leap into that empty sky beneath me. Earl and I.

"Papa."

For a moment I do not recognize the voice.

"Papa."

It has drawn near. I look.

It is Matthew.

He stands before me. His face is smudged. His hair is tousled. His eyes are fixed hard on mine.

I want him to go away from this place, quickly. I lift my hand to him, a vague gesture, and I cannot find words. "Matty," I say, just that. I am within the circle of Earl's fire and my son is outside. I try to step to him, but I am rooted here. I look up at the trees all around. And then back to my son. His face is turned up to me, waiting.

I know too much. I want him to run away now, not just from this place but from me.

"Go on home," I say.

His brow furrows very slightly.

I step from the circle, I reach out, my hand goes to him, my thumb lands gently on his brow, tries to smooth the furrow away.

He backs off.

I didn't mean to frighten him. I carry too much in these fingertips now.

But suddenly he smiles.

"Papa," he says. "Look."

His hand comes from behind his back. I don't recognize the object at first, hanging limply over his fingers.

"It's his," Matthew says.

And now I can see. Earl Sandt's goggles.

"I found it," he says.

I struggle once again to draw a breath. The moments I have yearned to share with Earl Sandt: he entered them looking through this thing in my son's hand.

But before I can think of what to do, Matthew grasps the goggles at each end and he lifts them high and the strap goes quickly over his head and the goggles slide down and are on his face and I can see his eyes for a moment, his child's eyes, the eyes of my boy, faint there and distant, and his face angles and his eyes vanish, the panes of glass go blank from the light.

And my son lifts his arms. He lifts them like wings, and he turns to his left and he begins to run, he runs swooping and lifting and falling. "Look, Papa," he cries. "Look. I'm Earl Sandt."

Raymond Carver *(1938–1988)*

was born in the logging town of Clatskanie, Oregon, the son of a sometimes-waitress and a sawmill worker. Before the age of twenty, he was married and the father of two. He worked at a series of odd jobs—picking tulips, pumping gas, managing an apartment building, selling condensed books door-to-door—before returning to school, where, at Chico State College in Paradise, California, he studied with the novelist (and legendary teacher) John Gardner. Carver wrote most of his early stories and poems in his car, the only place he could find any quiet. He attended the Iowa Writers' Workshop but dropped out because of financial struggles and took a job as a janitor. He later got a job as a textbook editor and began to publish his poems and short stories. His first story collection, Will You Please Be Quiet, Please? *(a National Book Award nominee in 1977), led to several teaching jobs, including one at Iowa, where he became friends with his colleague John Cheever, and they "did nothing but drink." After being hospitalized several times for his drinking, Carver quit and soon thereafter began living with the poet Tess Gallagher. During the 1980s, his collections* What We Talk About When We Talk About Love *and* Cathedral *cemented his status as one of the most influential short story writers in the history of the form. His career-spanning collection* Where I'm Calling From *was published in 1988. That same year, he married Gallagher (at the Heart of Reno Chapel in Nevada), was inducted into the American Academy of Arts and Letters, and, in August, died of lung cancer.*

Introduction by **Dan Chaon**

When Raymond Carver became an iconic figure in the late twentieth century, critics attempted to find a category to affix him to. They would use the term "Carveresque" to describe what they saw as a literary movement that Carver had spearheaded. For example, there was "Carveresque minimalism," which referred to a certain kind of clipped, understated, affectless prose style. Or there was "Carveresque Dirty Realism," which referred to sociology—that down-and-out, benumbed, often working-class milieu. Or there was "Carveresque Nihilism," a particular, bleak world view that seemed to posit that 1980s bumper sticker philosophy: "Life sucks, and then you die."

These buzz words—minimalism, dirty realism, and so on—are shorthand ways of trying to define Carver's enormously influential work, but ultimately, such terms are not particularly accurate. Raymond Carver's stories are brilliant because they somehow manage to contradict themselves, to defy easy summary. They are heartbreakingly earnest and darkly hilarious at the same time. He manages to show deep compassion for his characters while remaining clear-eyed about their often comically hapless flaws. His stories are full of fairy-tale archetypes—the Heart Doctor, the Blind Man, the Husband, the Neighbor—yet they are utterly based in a naturalistic and insightful psychology. The prose seems to emulate plain, unadorned speech, but the stripped-down style is also radical, poetic, *odd.* Carver can seem to be, on the one hand, a simple working-class joe and, on the other, an avant-garde experimentalist. Every word counts in a Carver story—but more important, every un-word counts too. Carver is a master of the unspoken, and like a sculptor, he uses the empty spaces between sentences and paragraphs and scenes to devastating effect.

The use of that empty space is perhaps the most emulated aspect of Carver's art, but it is also the most difficult for his imitators to pull off. Carver's work walks the delicate, almost impossible line between the ordinary and the uncanny. According to the critic Michael Koepf, "There's a Chekhovian clarity to Ray Carver's stories but a Kafkaesque sense that something is terribly wrong behind the scenes." At first, this seems a strange combination, yet it's apt. Like Chekhov and Kafka, Carver is fascinated by the mysteries that lie behind daily life, by the unexplained and unspoken secrets that lie just beyond our perception. The novelist Peter Straub once remarked that *The Red Badge of Courage* is a ghost story in which the ghost fails to appear. The same might be said of many of Carver's stories, which tap into a kind of ambient dread and menace. We see this perhaps most clearly here in the story "Are These Actual Miles?" as the husband's uncertain anxieties build to a feverish pitch, but there's also an edge of the sinister at the end of "What We Talk About When We Talk About Love":

> "Gin's gone," Mel said.
> Terri said, "Now what?"
> I could hear my heart beating. I could hear everyone's heart. I could hear the human noise we sat there making, not one of us moving, not even when the room went dark.

One can almost imagine that there is a subtle echo of Poe here—"tear up the planks!—here, here!—it is the beating of his hideous heart!" Yet in Carver, the horror and the pathos is that the "hideous heart" belongs to all of us, and the specters are the fears that plague daily life—we may always be lonely; our luck may never change; there's something wrong that we can't name.

In the end, one of the things that makes Carver's stories so beloved is both simple and intangible. He is a splendidly trustworthy writer, and readers can sense that. He seems to write out of the depths; his bleakness is not some cloak he's putting on, his moments of awe are not faked, his humor is not coy or condescending. In short, he's not a phony.

The stories presented here draw from each of Carver's three major works of fiction, and taken together, they give a sense of some of his obsessions (romantic love, alcohol, failure, loneliness) as well as revealing the range of his skills. "Are These Actual Miles?," from his first collection *Will You Please Be Quiet, Please?,* shows off his amazing ear for dialogue and is particularly notable for the way in which it balances humor and melancholy with an unnerving ominousness—a seemingly simple story that is a masterpiece of tonal complexity.

"What We Talk About When We Talk About Love," from the collection of the same name, manages one of the most difficult types of short stories: the Conversation Story. Echoing some of Chekhov's own Conversation Stories, such as "Gooseberries," Carver creates not only a complex exploration of love's many guises, but also creates acute portraits of the main characters and their lives. The events of the story don't represent a particular turning point for these people, yet by the end of the story, we are aware of having subtly, indelibly glimpsed their futures.

"Cathedral," from the collection *Cathedral,* represents Carver at his most lighthearted. The comically boorish narrator is in many ways a parody of the down-and-out lugs of Carver's earlier work. Yet, little by little, Carver's empathetic portrayal broadens our understanding of this man, leading us toward a deeper sense of his humanity, toward a brief moment when this person, so trapped in his small world, "didn't feel like [he] was inside anything." This is not a life-changing incident, necessarily, but Carver brings such tenderness to it that even this brief moment of grace feels weighty and important.

Perhaps this is Carver's great achievement: that he was able to give significance to unheroic lives, that he was able to find what was unexplainable in the ordinary, that he was able to give voice to a part of the American experience that is frequently ignored and forgotten. Though he died tragically young, at the age of fifty, his work remains among the most important and influential contributions to the American short story form.

Dan Chaon is the author of two collections of short stories, including Among the Missing, *which was a finalist for the 2001 National Book Award. His latest book is a novel,* You Remind Me of Me. *He lives in Cleveland and teaches at Oberlin College.*

RAYMOND CARVER

Are These Actual Miles?

Fact is the car needs to be sold in a hurry, and Leo sends Toni out to do it. Toni is smart and has personality. She used to sell children's encyclopedias door to door. She signed him up, even though he didn't have kids. Afterward, Leo asked her for a date, and the date led to this. This deal has to be cash, and it has to be done tonight. Tomorrow somebody they owe might slap a lien on the car. Monday they'll be in court, home free—but word on them went out yesterday, when their lawyer mailed the letters of intention. The hearing on Monday is nothing to worry about, the lawyer has said. They'll be asked some questions, and they'll sign some papers, and that's it. But sell the convertible, he said—today, *tonight.* They can hold onto the little car, Leo's car, no problem. But they go into court with that big convertible, the court will take it, and that's that.

Toni dresses up. It's four o'clock in the afternoon. Leo worries the lots will close. But Toni takes her time dressing. She puts on a new white blouse, wide lacy cuffs, the new two-piece suit, new heels. She transfers the stuff from her straw purse into the new patent-leather handbag. She studies the lizard makeup pouch and puts that in too. Toni has been two hours on her hair and face. Leo stands in the bedroom doorway and taps his lips with his knuckles, watching.

"You're making me nervous," she says. "I wish you wouldn't just stand," she says. "So tell me how I look."

"You look fine," he says. "You look great. I'd buy a car from you anytime."

"But you don't have money," she says, peering into the mirror. She pats her hair, frowns. "And your credit's lousy. You're nothing," she says. "Teasing," she says and looks at him in the mirror. "Don't be serious," she says. "It has to be done, so I'll do it. You take it out, you'll be lucky to get three, four hundred and we both know it. Honey, you'd be lucky if you didn't have to pay *them.*" She gives her hair a final pat, gums her lips, blots the lipstick with a tissue. She turns away from the mirror and picks up her purse. "I'll have to have dinner or something, I told you that already, that's the way they work, I know them. But don't worry, I'll get out of it," she says. "I can handle it."

"Jesus," Leo says, "did you have to say that?" She looks at him steadily. "Wish me luck," she says.

"Luck," he says. "You have the pink slip?" he says.

She nods. He follows her through the house, a tall woman with a small high bust, broad hips and thighs. He scratches a pimple on his neck. "You're sure?" he says. "Make sure. You have to have the pink slip."

"I have the pink slip," she says.

"Make sure."

She starts to say something, instead looks at herself in the front window and then shakes her head.

"At least call," he says. "Let me know what's going on."

"I'll call," she says. "Kiss, kiss. Here," she says and points to the corner of her mouth. "Careful," she says.

He holds the door for her. "Where are you going to try first?" he says. She moves past him and onto the porch.

Ernest Williams looks from across the street. In his Bermuda shorts, stomach hanging, he looks at Leo and Toni as he directs a spray onto his begonias. Once, last winter, during the holidays, when Toni and the kids were visiting his mother's, Leo brought a woman home. Nine o'clock the next morning, a cold foggy Saturday, Leo walked the woman to the car, surprised Ernest Williams on the sidewalk with a newspaper in his hand. Fog drifted, Ernest Williams stared, then slapped the paper against his leg, hard.

Leo recalls that slap, hunches his shoulders, says, "You have someplace in mind first?"

"I'll just go down the line," she says. "The first lot, then I'll just go down the line."

"Open at nine hundred," he says. "Then come down. Nine hundred is low bluebook, even on a cash deal."

"I know where to start," she says.

Ernest Williams turns the hose in their direction. He stares at them through the spray of water. Leo has an urge to cry out a confession.

"Just making sure," he says.

"Okay, okay," she says. "I'm off."

It's her car, they call it her car, and that makes it all the worse. They bought it new that summer three years ago. She wanted something to do after the kids started school, so she went back selling. He was working six days a week in the fiber-glass plant. For a while they didn't know how to spend the money. Then they put a thousand on the convertible and doubled and tripled the payments until in a year they had it paid. Earlier, while she was dressing, he took the jack and spare from the trunk and emptied the glove compartment of pencils, matchbooks, Blue Chip stamps. Then he washed it and vacuumed inside. The red hood and fenders shine.

"Good luck," he says and touches her elbow.

She nods. He sees she is already gone, already negotiating.

"Things are going to be different!" he calls to her as she reaches the driveway. "We start over Monday. I mean it."

Ernest Williams looks at them and turns his head and spits. She gets into the car and lights a cigarette.

"This time next week!" Leo calls again. "Ancient history!"

He waves as she backs into the street. She changes gear and starts ahead. She accelerates and the tires give a little scream.

In the kitchen Leo pours Scotch and carries the drink to the backyard. The kids are at his mother's. There was a letter three days ago, his name penciled on the outside of the dirty envelope, the only letter all summer not demanding payment in full. We are having fun, the letter said. We like Grandma. We have a new dog called Mr. Six. He is nice. We love him. Good-bye.

He goes for another drink. He adds ice and sees that his hand trembles. He holds the hand over the sink. He looks at the hand for a while, sets down the glass, and holds out the other hand. Then he picks up the glass and goes back outside to sit on the steps. He recalls when he was a kid his dad pointing at a fine house, a tall white house surrounded by apple trees and a high white rail fence. "That's Finch," his dad said admiringly. "He's been in bankruptcy at least twice. Look at that house." But bankruptcy is a company collapsing utterly, executives cutting their wrists and throwing themselves from windows, thousands of men on the street.

Leo and Toni still had furniture. Leo and Toni had furniture and Toni and the kids had clothes. Those things were exempt. What else? Bicycles for the kids, but these he had sent to his mother's for safekeeping. The portable air-conditioner and the appliances, new washer and dryer, trucks came for those things weeks ago. What else did they have? This and that, nothing mainly, stuff that wore out or fell to pieces long ago. But there were some big parties back there, some fine travel. To Reno and Tahoe, at eighty with the top down and the radio playing. Food, that was one of the big items. They gorged on food. He figures thousands on luxury items alone. Toni would go to the grocery and put in everything she saw. "I had to do without when I was a kid," she says. "These kids are not going to do without," as if he'd been insisting they should. She joins all the book clubs. "We never had books around when I was a kid," she says as she tears open the heavy packages. They enroll in the record clubs for something to play on the new stereo. They sign up for it all. Even a pedigreed terrier named Ginger. He paid two hundred and found her run over in the street a week later. They buy what they want. If they can't pay, they charge. They sign up.

His undershirt is wet; he can feel the sweat rolling from his underarms. He sits on the step with the empty glass in his hand and watches the shadows fill up the yard. He stretches, wipes his face. He listens to the traffic on the highway and considers whether he should go to the basement, stand on the utility sink, and hang himself with his belt. He understands he is willing to be dead.

Inside he makes a large drink and he turns the TV on and he fixes something to eat. He sits at the table with chili and crackers and watches something about a blind detective. He clears the table. He washes the pan and the bowl, dries these things and puts them away, then allows himself a look at the clock.

It's after nine. She's been gone nearly five hours.

He pours Scotch, adds water, carries the drink to the living room. He sits on the couch but finds his shoulders so stiff they won't let him lean back. He stares at the screen and sips, and soon he goes for another drink. He sits again. A news program begins—it's ten o'clock—and he says, "God, what in God's name has gone wrong?" and goes to the kitchen to return with more Scotch. He sits, he closes his eyes, and opens them when he hears the telephone ringing.

"I wanted to call," she says.

"Where are you?" he says. He hears piano music, and his heart moves.

"I don't know," she says. "Someplace. We're having a drink, then we're going someplace else for dinner. I'm with the sales manager. He's crude, but he's all right. He bought the car. I have to go now. I was on my way to the ladies and saw the phone."

"Did somebody buy the car?" Leo says. He looks out the kitchen window to the place in the drive where she always parks.

"I told you," she says. "I have to go now."

"Wait, wait a minute, for Christ's sake," he says. "Did somebody buy the car or not?"

"He had his checkbook out when I left," she says. "I have to go now. I have to go to the bathroom."

"Wait!" he yells. The line goes dead. He listens to the dial tone. "Jesus Christ," he says as he stands with the receiver in his hand.

He circles the kitchen and goes back to the living room. He sits. He gets up. In the bathroom he brushes his teeth very carefully. Then he uses dental floss. He washes his face and goes back to the kitchen. He looks at the clock and takes a clean glass from a set that has a hand of playing cards painted on each glass. He fills the glass with ice. He stares for a while at the glass he left in the sink.

He sits against one end of the couch and puts his legs up at the other end. He looks at the screen, realizes he can't make out what the people are saying. He turns the empty glass in his hand and considers biting off the rim. He shivers for a time and thinks of going to bed, though he knows he will dream of a large woman with gray hair. In the dream he is always leaning over tying his shoelaces. When he straightens up, she looks at him, and he bends to tie again. He looks at his hand. It makes a fist as he watches. The telephone is ringing.

"Where are you, honey?" he says slowly, gently.

"We're at this restaurant," she says, her voice strong, bright.

"Honey, which restaurant?" he says. He puts the heel of his hand against his eye and pushes.

"Downtown someplace," she says. "I think it's New Jimmy's. Excuse me," she says to someone off the line, "is this place New Jimmy's? This is New Jimmy's, Leo," she says to him. "Everything is all right, we're almost finished, then he's going to bring me home."

"Honey?" he says. He holds the receiver against his ear and rocks back and forth, eyes closed. "Honey?"

"I have to go," she says. "I wanted to call. Anyway, guess how much?"

"Honey," he says.

"Six and a quarter," she says. "I have it in my purse. He said there's no market for convertibles. I guess we're born lucky," she says and laughs. "I told him everything. I think I had to."

"Honey," Leo says.

"What?" she says.

"Please, honey," Leo says.

"He said he sympathizes," she says. "But he would have said anything." She laughs again. "He said personally he'd rather be classified a robber or a rapist than a bankrupt. He's nice enough, though," she says.

"Come home," Leo says. "Take a cab and come home."

"I can't," she says. "I told you, we're halfway through dinner."

"I'll come for you," he says.

"No," she says. "I said we're just finishing. I told you, it's part of the deal. They're out for all they can get. But don't worry, we're about to leave. I'll be home in a little while." She hangs up.

In a few minutes he calls New Jimmy's. A man answers. "New Jimmy's has closed for the evening," the man says.

"I'd like to talk to my wife," Leo says.

"Does she work here?" the man asks. "Who is she?"

"She's a customer," Leo says. "She's with someone. A business person."

"Would I know her?" the man says. "What is her name?"

"I don't think you know her," Leo says.

"That's all right," Leo says. "That's all right. I see her now."

"Thank you for calling New Jimmy's," the man says.

Leo hurries to the window. A car he doesn't recognize slows in front of the house, then picks up speed. He waits. Two, three hours later, the telephone rings again. There is no one at the other end when he picks up the receiver. There is only a dial tone.

"I'm right here!" Leo screams into the receiver.

Near dawn he hears footsteps on the porch. He gets up from the couch. The set hums, the screen glows. He opens the door. She bumps the wall coming in. She grins. Her face is puffy, as if she's been sleeping under sedation. She works her lips, ducks heavily and sways as he cocks his fist.

"Go ahead," she says thickly. She stands there swaying. Then she makes a noise and lunges, catches his shirt, tears it down the front. "Bankrupt!" she screams. She twists loose, grabs and tears his undershirt at the neck. "You son of a bitch," she says, clawing.

He squeezes her wrists, then lets go, steps back, looking for something heavy. She stumbles as she heads for the bedroom. "Bankrupt," she mutters. He hears her fall on the bed and groan.

He waits awhile, then splashes water on his face and goes to the bedroom. He turns the lights on, looks at her, and begins to take her clothes off. He pulls and pushes her from side to side undressing her. She says something in her sleep and moves her hand. He takes off her underpants, looks at them closely under the light, and throws them into a corner. He turns back the covers and rolls her in, naked. Then he opens her purse. He is reading the check when he hears the car come into the drive.

He looks through the front curtain and sees the convertible in the drive, its motor running smoothly, the headlamps burning, and he closes and opens his eyes. He sees a tall man come around in front of the car and up to the front porch. The man lays something on the porch and starts back to the car. He wears a white linen suit.

Leo turns on the porch light and opens the door cautiously. Her makeup pouch lies on the top step. The man looks at Leo across the front of the car, and then gets back inside and releases the handbrake.

"Wait!" Leo calls and starts down the steps. The man brakes the car as Leo walks in front of the lights. The car creaks against the brake. Leo tries to pull the two pieces of his shirt together, tries to bunch it all into his trousers.

"What is it you want?" the man says. "Look," the man says, "I have to go. No offense. I buy and sell cars, right? The lady left her makeup. She's a fine lady, very refined. What is it?"

Leo leans against the door and looks at the man. The man takes his hands off the wheel and puts them back. He drops the gear into reverse and the car moves backward a little.

"I want to tell you," Leo says and wets his lips.

The light in Ernest Williams' bedroom goes on. The shade rolls up.

Leo shakes his head, tucks in his shirt again. He steps back from the car. "Monday," he says.

"Monday," the man says and watches for sudden movement.

Leo nods slowly.

"Well, goodnight," the man says and coughs. "Take it easy, hear? Monday, that's right. Okay, then." He takes his foot off the brake, puts it on again after he has rolled back two or three feet. "Hey, one question. Between friends, are these actual miles?" The man waits, then clears his throat. "Okay, look, it doesn't matter either way," the man says. "I have to go. Take it easy." He backs into the street, pulls away quickly, and turns the corner without stopping.

Leo tucks at his shirt and goes back in the house. He locks the front door and checks it. Then he goes to the bedroom and locks that door and turns back the covers. He looks at her before he flicks the light. He takes off his clothes, folds them carefully on the floor, and gets in beside her. He lies on his back for a time and pulls the hair on his stomach, considering. He looks at the bedroom door, outlined now in the faint outside light. Presently he reaches out his hand and touches her hip. She does not move. He turns on his side and puts his hand on her hip. He runs his fingers over her hip and feels the stretch marks there. They are like roads, and he traces them in her flesh. He runs his fingers back and forth, first one, then another. They run everywhere in her flesh, dozens, perhaps hundreds of them. He remembers waking up the morning after they bought the car, seeing it, there in the drive, in the sun, gleaming.

RAYMOND CARVER

What We Talk About When We Talk About Love

My friend Mel McGinnis was talking. Mel McGinnis is a cardiologist, and sometimes that gives him the right.

The four of us were sitting around his kitchen table drinking gin. Sunlight filled the kitchen from the big window behind the sink. There were Mel and me and his second wife, Teresa—Terri, we called her—and my wife, Laura. We lived in Albuquerque then. But we were all from somewhere else.

There was an ice bucket on the table. The gin and the tonic water kept going around, and we somehow got on the subject of love. Mel thought real love was nothing less than spiritual love. He said he'd spent five years in a seminary before quitting to go to medical school. He said he still looked back on those years in the seminary as the most important years in his life.

Terri said the man she lived with before she lived with Mel loved her so much he tried to kill her. Then Terri said, "He beat me up one night. He dragged me around the living room by my ankles. He kept saying, 'I love you, I love you, you bitch.' He went on dragging me around the living room. My head kept knocking on things." Terri looked around the table. "What do you do with love like that?"

She was a bone-thin woman with a pretty face, dark eyes, and brown hair that hung down her back. She liked necklaces made of turquoise, and long pendant earrings.

"My God, don't be silly. That's not love, and you know it," Mel said. "I don't know what you'd call it, but I sure know you wouldn't call it love."

"Say what you want to, but I know it was," Terri said. "It may sound crazy to you, but it's true just the same. People are different, Mel. Sure, sometimes he may have acted crazy. Okay. But he loved me. In his own way maybe, but he loved me. There was love there, Mel. Don't say there wasn't."

Mel let out his breath. He held his glass and turned to Laura and me. "The man threatened to kill me," Mel said. He finished his drink and reached for the gin bottle. "Terri's a romantic. Terri's of the kick-me-so-I'll-know-you-love-me school. Terri, hon, don't look that way." Mel reached across the table and touched Terri's cheek with his fingers. He grinned at her.

"Now he wants to make up," Terri said.

"Make up what?" Mel said. "What is there to make up? I know what I know. That's all."

"How'd we get started on this subject, anyway?" Terri said. She raised her glass and drank from it. "Mel always has love on his mind," she said. "Don't you, honey?" She smiled, and I thought that was the last of it.

"I just wouldn't call Ed's behavior love. That's all I'm saying, honey," Mel said. "What about you guys?" Mel said to Laura and me. "Does that sound like love to you?"

"I'm the wrong person to ask," I said. "I didn't even know the man. I've only heard his name mentioned in passing. I wouldn't know. You'd have to know the particulars. But I think what you're saying is that love is an absolute."

Mel said, "The kind of love I'm talking about is. The kind of love I'm talking about, you don't try to kill people."

Laura said, "I don't know anything about Ed, or anything about the situation. But who can judge anyone else's situation?"

I touched the back of Laura's hand. She gave me a quick smile. I picked up Laura's hand. It was warm, the nails polished, perfectly manicured. I encircled the broad wrist with my fingers, and I held her.

"When I left, he drank rat poison," Terri said. She clasped her arms with her hands. "They took him to the hospital in Sante Fe. That's where we lived then, about ten miles out. They saved his life. But his gums went crazy from it. I mean they pulled away from his teeth. After that, his teeth stood out like fangs. My God," Terri said. She waited a minute, then let go of her arms and picked up her glass.

"What people won't do!" Laura said.

"He's out of the action now," Mel said. "He's dead."

Mel handed me the saucer of limes. I took a section, squeezed it over my drink, and stirred the ice cubes with my finger.

"It gets worse," Terri said. "He shot himself in the mouth. But he bungled that too. Poor Ed," she said. Terri shook her head.

"Poor Ed nothing," Mel said. "He was dangerous."

Mel was forty-five years old. He was tall and rangy with curly soft hair. His face and arms were brown from the tennis he played. When he was sober, his gestures, all his movements, were precise, very careful.

"He did love me though, Mel. Grant me that," Terri said. "That's all I'm asking. He didn't love me the way you love me. I'm not saying that. But he loved me. You can grant me that, can't you?"

"What do you mean, he bungled it?" I said.

Laura leaned forward with her glass. She put her elbows on the table and held her glass in both hands. She glanced from Mel to Terri and waited with a look of bewilderment on her open face, as if amazed that such things happened to people you were friendly with.

"How'd he bungle it when he killed himself?" I said.

"I'll tell you what happened," Mel said. "He took this twenty-two pistol he'd bought to threaten Terri and me with. Oh, I'm serious, the man was always threatening. You should have seen the way we lived in those days. Like fugitives. I even bought a gun myself. Can you believe it? A guy like me? But I did. I bought one for self-defense and carried it in the glove compartment. Sometimes I'd have to leave the apartment in the middle of the night. To go to the hospital, you know? Terri and I weren't married then, and my first wife had the house and kids, the dog, everything, and Terri and I were living in this apartment here. Sometimes, as I say, I'd get a call in the middle of the night and have to go in to the hospital at two or three in the morning. It'd be dark out there in the parking lot, and I'd break into a sweat before I could even get to my car. I never knew if he was going to come up out of the shrubbery or from behind a car and start shooting. I mean, the man was crazy. He was capable of wiring a bomb, anything. He used to call my service at all hours and say he needed to talk to the doctor, and when I'd return the call, he'd say, 'Son of a bitch, your days are numbered.' Little things like that. It was scary, I'm telling you."

"I still feel sorry for him," Terri said.

"It sounds like a nightmare," Laura said. "But what exactly happened after he shot himself?"

Laura is a legal secretary. We'd met in a professional capacity. Before we knew it, it was a courtship. She's thirty-five, three years younger than I am. In addition to being in love, we like each other and enjoy one another's company. She's easy to be with.

"What happened?" Laura said.

Mel said, "He shot himself in the mouth in his room. Someone heard the shot and told the manager. They came in with a passkey, saw what had happened, and called an ambulance. I happened to be there when they brought him in, alive but past recall. The man lived for three days. His head swelled up to twice the size of a normal head. I'd never seen anything like it, and I hope I never do again. Terri wanted to go in and sit with him when she found out about it. We had a fight over it. I didn't think she should see him like that. I didn't think she should see him, and I still don't."

"Who won the fight?" Laura said.

"I was in the room with him when he died," Terri said. "He never came up out of it. But I sat with him. He didn't have anyone else."

"He was dangerous," Mel said. "If you call that love, you can have it."

"It was love," Terri said. "Sure, it's abnormal in most people's eyes. But he was willing to die for it. He did die for it."

"I sure as hell wouldn't call it love," Mel said. "I mean, no one knows what he did it for. I've seen a lot of suicides, and I couldn't say anyone ever knew what they did it for."

Mel put his hands behind his neck and tilted his chair back. "I'm not interested in that kind of love," he said. "If that's love, you can have it."

Terri said, "We were afraid. Mel even made a will out and wrote to his brother in California who used to be a Green Beret. Mel told him who to look for if something happened to him."

Terri drank from her glass. She said, "But Mel's right—we lived like fugitives. We were afraid. Mel was, weren't you, honey? I even called the police at one point, but they were no help. They said they couldn't do anything until Ed actually did something. Isn't that a laugh?" Terri said.

She poured the last of the gin into her glass and waggled the bottle. Mel got up from the table and went to the cupboard. He took down another bottle.

"Well, Nick and I know what love is," Laura said. "For us, I mean," Laura said. She bumped my knee with her knee. "You're supposed to say something now," Laura said, and turned her smile on me.

For an answer, I took Laura's hand and raised it to my lips. I made a big production out of kissing her hand. Everyone was amused.

"We're lucky," I said.

"You guys," Terri said. "Stop that now. You're making me sick. You're still on the honeymoon, for God's sake. You're still gaga, for crying out loud. Just wait. How long have you been together now? How long has it been? A year? Longer than a year?"

"Going on a year and a half," Laura said, flushed and smiling.

"Oh, now," Terri said. "Wait awhile."

She held her drink and gazed at Laura.

"I'm only kidding," Terri said.

Mel opened the gin and went around the table with the bottle.

"Here, you guys," he said. "Let's have a toast. I want to propose a toast. A toast to love. To true love," Mel said.

We touched glasses.

"To love," we said.

Outside in the backyard, one of the dogs began to bark. The leaves of the aspen that leaned past the window ticked against the glass. The afternoon sun was like a presence in this room, the spacious light of ease and generosity. We could have been anywhere, somewhere enchanted. We raised our glasses again and grinned at each other like children who had agreed on something forbidden.

"I'll tell you what real love is," Mel said. "I mean, I'll give you a good example. And then you can draw your own conclusions." He poured more gin into his glass. He added an ice cube and a sliver of lime. We waited and sipped our drinks. Laura and I touched knees again. I put a hand on her warm thigh and left it there.

"What do any of us really know about love?" Mel said. "It seems to me we're just beginners at love. We say we love each other and we do, I don't doubt it. I love Terri and Terri loves me, and you guys love each other too. You know the kind of love I'm talking about now. Physical love, that impulse that drives you to someone special, as well as love of the other person's being, his or her essence, as it were. Carnal love and, well, call it sentimental love, the day-to-day caring about the other person. But sometimes I have a hard time accounting for the fact that I must have loved my first wife too. But I did, I know I did. So I suppose I am like Terri in that regard. Terri and Ed." He thought about it and then he went on. "There was a time when I thought I loved my first wife more than life itself. But now I hate her guts. I do. How do you explain that? What happened to that love? What happened to it, is what I'd like to know. I wish someone could tell me. Then there's Ed. Okay, we're back to Ed. He loves Terri so much he tries to kill her and he winds up killing himself." Mel stopped talking and swallowed from his glass. "You guys have been together eighteen months and you love each other. It shows all over you. You glow with it. But you both loved other people before you met each other. You've both been married before, just like us. And you probably loved other people before that too, even. Terri and I have been together five years, been married for four. And the terrible thing, the terrible thing is, but the good thing too, the saving grace, you might say, is that if something happened to one of us—excuse me for saying this—but if something happened to one of us tomorrow I think the other one, the other person, would grieve for a while, you know, but then the surviving party would go out and love again, have someone else soon enough. All this, all of this love we're talking about, it would just be a memory. Maybe not even a memory. Am I wrong? Am I way off base? Because I want you to set me straight if you think I'm wrong. I want to know. I mean, I don't know anything, and I'm the first one to admit it."

"Mel, for God's sake," Terri said. She reached out and took hold of his wrist. "Are you getting drunk? Honey? Are you drunk?"

"Honey, I'm just talking," Mel said. "All right? I don't have to be drunk to say what I think. I mean, we're all just talking, right?" Mel said. He fixed his eyes on her.

"Sweetie, I'm not criticizing," Terri said.

She picked up her glass.

"I'm not on call today," Mel said. "Let me remind you of that. I am not on call," he said.

"Mel, we love you," Laura said.

Mel looked at Laura. He looked at her as if he could not place her, as if she was not the woman she was.

"Love you too, Laura," Mel said. "And you, Nick, love you too. You know something?" Mel said. "You guys are our pals," Mel said.

He picked up his glass.

Mel said, "I was going to tell you about something. I mean, I was going to prove a point. You see, this happened a few months ago, but it's still going on right now, and it ought to make us feel ashamed when we talk like we know what we're talking about when we talk about love."

"Come on now," Terri said. "Don't talk like you're drunk if you're not drunk."

"Just shut up for once in your life," Mel said very quietly. "Will you do me a favor and do that for a minute? So as I was saying, there's this old couple who had this car wreck out on the interstate. A kid hit them and they were all torn to shit and nobody was giving them much chance to pull through."

Terri looked at us and then back at Mel. She seemed anxious, or maybe that's too strong a word.

Mel was handing the bottle around the table.

"I was on call that night," Mel said. "It was May or maybe it was June. Terri and I had just sat down to dinner when the hospital called. There'd been this thing out on the interstate. Drunk kid, teenager, plowed his dad's pickup into this camper with this old couple in it. They were up in their mid-seventies, that couple. The kid—eighteen, nineteen, something—he was DOA. Taken the steering wheel through his sternum. The old couple, they were alive, you understand. I mean, just barely. But they had everything. Multiple fractures, internal injuries, hemorrhaging, contusions, lacerations, the works, and they each of them had themselves concussions. They were in a bad way, believe me. And, of course, their age was two strikes against them. I'd say she was worse off than he was. Ruptured spleen along with everything else. Both kneecaps broken. But they'd been wearing their seatbelts and, God knows, that's what saved them for the time being."

"Folks, this is an advertisement for the National Safety Council," Terri said. "This is your spokesman, Dr. Melvin R. McGinnis, talking." Terri laughed. "Mel," she said, "sometimes you're just too much. But I love you, hon," she said.

"Honey, I love you," Mel said.

He leaned across the table. Terri met him halfway. They kissed.

"Terri's right," Mel said as he settled himself again. "Get those seatbelts on. But seriously, they were in some shape, those oldsters. By the time I got down there, the kid was dead, as I said. He was off in a corner, laid out on a gurney. I took one look at the old couple and told the ER nurse to get me a neurologist and an orthopedic man and a couple of surgeons down there right away."

He drank from his glass. "I'll try to keep this short," he said. "So we took the two of them up to the OR and worked like fuck on them most of the night. They had these incredible reserves, those two. You see that once in a while. So we did everything that could be done, and toward morning we're giving them a fifty-fifty chance, maybe less than that for her. So here they are, still alive the next morning. So, okay, we move them into the ICU, which is where they both kept plugging away at it for two weeks, hitting it better and better on all the scopes. So we transfer them out to their own room."

Mel stopped talking. "Here," he said, "let's drink this cheapo gin the hell up. Then we're going to dinner, right? Terri and I know a new place. That's where we'll go, to this new place we know about. But we're not going until we finish up this cut-rate, lousy gin."

Terri said, "We haven't actually eaten there yet. But it looks good. From the outside, you know."

"I like food," Mel said. "If I had it to do all over again, I'd be a chef, you know? Right, Terri?" Mel said.

He laughed. He fingered the ice in his glass.

"Terri knows," he said. "Terri can tell you. But let me say this. If I could come back again in a different life, a different time and all, you know what? I'd like to come back as a knight. You were pretty safe wearing all that armor. It was all right being a knight until gunpowder and muskets and pistols came along."

"Mel would like to ride a horse and carry a lance," Terri said.

"Carry a woman's scarf with you everywhere," Laura said.

"Or just a woman," Mel said.

"Shame on you," Laura said.

Terri said, "Suppose you came back as a serf. The serfs didn't have it so good in those days," Terri said.

"The serfs never had it good," Mel said. "But I guess even the knights were vessels to someone. Isn't that the way it worked? But then everyone is always a vessel to someone. Isn't that right? Terri? But what I liked about knights, besides their ladies, was that they had that suit of armor, you know, and they couldn't get hurt very easy. No cars in those days, you know? No drunk teenagers to tear into your ass."

"Vassals," Terri said.

"What?" Mel said.

"Vassals," Terri said. "They were called vassals, not vessels."

"Vassals, vessels," Mel said, "what the fuck's the difference? You knew what I meant anyway. All right," Mel said. "So I'm not educated. I learned my stuff. I'm a heart surgeon, sure, but I'm just a mechanic. I go in and I fuck around and I fix things. Shit," Mel said.

"Modesty doesn't become you," Terri said.

"He's just a humble sawbones," I said. "But sometimes they suffocated in all that armor, Mel. They'd even have heart attacks if it got too hot and they were too tired and worn out. I read somewhere that they'd fall off their horses and not be able to get up because they were too tired to stand with all that armor on them. They got trampled by their own horses sometimes."

"That's terrible," Mel said. "That's a terrible thing, Nicky. I guess they'd just lay there and wait until somebody came along and made a shish kebab out of them."

"Some other vessel," Terri said.

"That's right," Mel said. "Some vassal would come along and spear the bastard in the name of love. Or whatever the fuck it was they fought over in those days."

"Same things we fight over these days," Terri said.

Laura said, "Nothing's changed."

The color was still high in Laura's cheeks. Her eyes were bright. She brought her glass to her lips.

Mel poured himself another drink. He looked at the label closely as if studying a long row of numbers. Then he slowly put the bottle down on the table and slowly reached for the tonic water.

"What about the old couple?" Laura said, "You didn't finish that story you started."

Laura was having a hard time lighting her cigarette. Her matches kept going out.

The sunshine inside the room was different now, changing, getting thinner. But the leaves outside the window were still shimmering, and I stared at the pattern they made on the panes and on the Formica counter. They weren't the same patterns, of course.

"What about the old couple?" I said.

"Older but wiser," Terri said.

Mel stared at her.

Terri said, "Go on with your story, hon. I was only kidding. Then what happened?"

"Terri, sometimes," Mel said.

"Please, Mel," Terri said. "Don't always be so serious, sweetie. Can't you take a joke?"

"Where's the joke?" Mel said.

He held his glass and gazed steadily at his wife.

"What happened?" Laura said.

Mel fastened his eyes on Laura. He said, "Laura, if I didn't have Terri and if I didn't love her so much, and if Nick wasn't my best friend, I'd fall in love with you, I'd carry you off, honey," he said.

"Tell your story," Terri said. "Then we'll go to that new place, okay?"

"Okay," Mel said. "Where was I?" he said. He stared at the table and then he began again.

"I dropped in to see each of them every day, sometimes twice a day if I was up doing other calls anyway. Casts and bandages, head to foot, the both of them. You know, you've seen it in the movies. That's just the way they looked, just like in the movies. Little eye-holes and nose-holes and mouth-holes. And she had to have her legs slung up on top of it. Well, the husband was very depressed for the longest while. Even after he found out that his wife was going to pull through, he was still very depressed. Not about the accident, though. I mean, the accident was one thing, but it wasn't everything. I'd get up to his mouth-hole, you know, and he'd say no, it wasn't the accident exactly but it was because he couldn't see her through his eye-holes. He said that was what was making him feel so bad. Can you imagine? I'm telling you, the man's heart was breaking because he couldn't turn his goddamn head and *see* his goddamn wife."

Mel looked around the table and shook his head at what he was going to say.

"I mean, it was killing the old fart just because he couldn't *look* at the fucking woman."

We all looked at Mel.

"Do you see what I'm saying?" he said.

Maybe we were a little drunk by then. I know it was hard keeping things in focus. The light was draining out of the room, going back through the window where it had come from. Yet nobody made a move to get up from the table to turn on the overhead light.

"Listen," Mel said. "Let's finish this fucking gin. There's about enough left here for one shooter all around. Then let's go eat. Let's go to the new place."

"He's depressed," Terri said. "Mel, why don't you take a pill?"

Mel shook his head. "I've taken everything there is."

"We all need a pill now and then," I said.

"Some people are born needing them," Terri said.

She was using her finger to rub at something on the table. Then she stopped rubbing.

"I think I want to call my kids," Mel said. "Is that all right with everybody? I'll call my kids," he said.

Terri said, "What if Marjorie answers the phone? You guys, you've heard us on the subject of Marjorie? Honey, you know you don't want to talk to Marjorie. It'll make you feel even worse."

"I don't want to talk to Marjorie," Mel said. "But I want to talk to my kids."

"There isn't a day goes by that Mel doesn't say he wishes she'd get married again. Or else die," Terri said. "For one thing," Terri said, "she's bankrupting us. Mel says it's just to spite him that she won't get married again. She has a boyfriend who lives with her and the kids, so Mel is supporting the boyfriend too."

"She's allergic to bees," Mel said. "If I'm not praying she'll get married again, I'm praying she'll get herself stung to death by a swarm of fucking bees."

"Shame on you," Laura said.

"Bzzzzzzz," Mel said, turning his fingers into bees and buzzing them at Terri's throat. Then he let his hands drop all the way to his sides.

"She's vicious," Mel said. "Sometimes I think I'll go up there dressed like a beekeeper. You know, that hat that's like a helmet with the plate that comes down over your face, the big gloves, and the padded coat? I'll knock on the door and let loose a hive of bees in the house. But first I'd make sure the kids were out, of course."

He crossed one leg over the other. It seemed to take him a lot of time to do it. Then he put both feet on the floor and leaned forward, elbows on the table, his chin cupped in his hands.

"Maybe I won't call the kids, after all. Maybe it isn't such a hot idea. Maybe we'll just go eat. How does that sound?"

"Sounds fine to me," I said. "Eat or not eat. Or keep drinking. I could head right on out into the sunset."

"What does that mean, honey?" Laura said.

"It just means what I said," I said. "It means I could just keep going. That's all it means."

"I could eat something myself," Laura said. "I don't think I've ever been so hungry in my life. Is there something to nibble on?"

"I'll put out some cheese and crackers," Terri said.

But Terri just sat there. She did not get up to get anything.

Mel turned his glass over. He spilled it out on the table.

"Gin's gone," Mel said.

Terri said, "Now what?"

I could hear my heart beating. I could hear everyone's heart. I could hear the human noise we sat there making, not one of us moving, not even when the room went dark.

RAYMOND CARVER

Cathedral

This blind man, an old friend of my wife's, he was on his way to spend the night. His wife had died. So he was visiting the dead wife's relatives in Connecticut. He called my wife from his in-laws'. Arrangements were made. He would come by train, a five-hour trip, and my wife would meet him at the station. She hadn't seen him since she worked for him one summer in Seattle ten years ago. But she and the blind man had kept in touch. They made tapes and mailed them back and forth. I wasn't enthusiastic about his visit. He was no one I knew. And his being blind bothered me. My idea of blindness came from the movies. In the movies, the blind moved slowly and never laughed. Sometimes they were led by seeing-eye dogs. A blind man in my house was not something I looked forward to.

That summer in Seattle she had needed a job. She didn't have any money. The man she was going to marry at the end of the summer was in officers' training school. He didn't have any money, either. But she was in love with the guy, and he was in love with her, etc. She'd seen something in the paper: HELP WANTED—*Reading to Blind Man,* and a telephone number. She phoned and went over, was hired on the spot. She'd worked with this blind man all summer. She read stuff to him, case studies, reports, that sort of thing. She helped him organize his little office in the county social-service department. They'd become good friends, my wife and the blind man. How do I know these things? She told me. And she told me something else. On her last day in the office, the blind man asked if he could touch her face. She agreed to this. She told me he touched his fingers to every part of her face, her nose—even her neck! She never forgot it. She even tried to write a poem about it. She was always trying to write a poem. She wrote a poem or two every year, usually after something really important had happened to her.

When we first started going out together, she showed me the poem. In the poem, she recalled his fingers and the way they had moved around over her face. In the poem, she talked about what she had felt at the time, about what went through her mind when the blind man touched her nose and lips. I can remember I didn't think much of the poem. Of course, I didn't tell her that. Maybe I just don't understand poetry. I admit it's not the first thing I reach for when I pick up something to read.

Anyway, this man who'd first enjoyed her favors, the officer-to-be, he'd been her childhood sweetheart. So okay. I'm saying that at the end of the summer she let the blind man run his hands over her face, said good-bye to him, married her childhood etc., who was now a commissioned officer, and she moved away from Seattle. But they'd kept in touch, she and the blind man. She made the first contact after a year or so. She called him up one night from an Air Force base in Alabama. She wanted to talk. They talked. He asked her to send a tape and tell him about her life. She did this. She sent the tape. On the tape, she told the blind man about her husband and about their life together in the military. She told the blind man she loved her husband but she didn't like it where they lived and she didn't like it that he was part of the military-industrial thing. She told the blind man she'd written a poem and he was in it. She told him that she was writing a poem about what it was like to be an Air Force officer's wife. The poem wasn't finished yet. She was still writing it. The blind man made a tape. He sent her the tape. She made a tape. This went on for years. My wife's officer was posted to one base and then another. She sent tapes from Moody AFB, McGuire, McConnell, and finally Travis, near Sacramento, where one night she got to feeling lonely and cut off from people she kept losing in that moving-around life. She got to feeling she couldn't go it another step. She went in and swallowed all the pills and capsules in the medicine chest and washed them down with a bottle of gin. Then she got into a hot bath and passed out.

But instead of dying, she got sick. She threw up. Her officer—why should he have a name? he was the childhood sweetheart, and what more does he want?—came home from somewhere, found her, and called the ambulance. In time, she put it all on a tape and sent the tape to the blind man. Over the years, she put all kinds of stuff on tapes and sent the tapes off lickety-split. Next to writing a poem every year, I think it was her chief means of recreation. On one tape, she told the blind man she'd decided to live away from her officer for a time. On another tape, she told him about her divorce. She and I began going out, and of course she told her blind man about it. She told him everything, or so it seemed to me. Once she asked me if I'd like to hear the latest tape from the blind man. This was a year ago. I was on the tape, she said. So I said okay, I'd listen to it. I got us drinks and we settled down in the living room. We made ready to listen. First she inserted the tape into the player and adjusted a couple of dials. Then she pushed a lever. The tape squeaked and someone began to talk in this loud voice. She lowered the volume. After a few minutes of harmless chitchat, I heard my own name in the mouth of this stranger, this blind man I didn't even know! And then this: "From all you've said about him, I can only conclude—" But we were interrupted, a knock at the door, something, and we didn't ever get back to the tape. Maybe it was just as well. I'd heard all I wanted to.

Now this same blind man was coming to sleep in my house.

"Maybe I could take him bowling," I said to my wife. She was at the draining board doing scalloped potatoes. She put down the knife she was using and turned around.

"If you love me," she said, "you can do this for me. If you don't love me, okay. But if you had a friend, any friend, and the friend came to visit, I'd make him feel comfortable." She wiped her hands with the dish towel.

"I don't have any blind friends," I said.

"You don't have *any* friends," she said. "Period. Besides," she said, "goddamn it, his wife's just died! Don't you understand that? The man's lost his wife!"

I didn't answer. She'd told me a little about the blind man's wife. Her name was Beulah. Beulah! That's a name for a colored woman.

"Was his wife a Negro?" I asked.

"Are you crazy?" my wife said. "Have you just flipped or something?" She picked up a potato. I saw it hit the floor, then roll under the stove. "What's wrong with you?" she said. "Are you drunk?"

"I'm just asking," I said.

Right then my wife filled me in with more detail than I cared to know. I made a drink and sat at the kitchen table to listen. Pieces of the story began to fall into place.

Beulah had gone to work for the blind man the summer after my wife had stopped working for him. Pretty soon Beulah and the blind man had themselves a church wedding. It was a little wedding—who'd want to go to such a wedding in the first place?—just the two of them, plus the minister and the minister's wife. But it was a church wedding just the same. It was what Beulah had wanted, he'd said. But even then Beulah must have been carrying the cancer in her glands. After they had been inseparable for eight years—my wife's word, *inseparable*—Beulah's health went into a rapid decline. She died in a Seattle hospital room, the blind man sitting beside the bed and holding on to her hand. They'd married, lived and worked together, slept together—had sex, sure—and then the blind man had to bury her. All this without his having ever seen what the goddamned woman looked like. It was beyond my understanding. Hearing this, I felt sorry for the blind man for a little bit. And then I found myself thinking what a pitiful life this woman must have led. Imagine a woman who could never see herself as she was seen in the eyes of her loved one. A woman who could go on day after day and never receive the smallest compliment from her beloved. A woman whose husband could never read the expression on her face, be it misery or something better. Someone who could wear makeup or not—what difference to him? She could, if she wanted, wear green eye-shadow around one eye, a straight pin in her nostril, yellow slacks, and purple shoes, no matter. And then to slip off into death, the blind man's hand on her hand, his blind eyes streaming tears—I'm imagining now—her last thought maybe this: that he never even knew what she looked like, and she on an express to the grave. Robert was left with a small insurance policy and a half of a twenty-peso Mexican coin. The other half of the coin went into the box with her. Pathetic.

So when the time rolled around, my wife went to the depot to pick him up. With nothing to do but wait—sure, I blamed him for that—I was having a drink and watching the TV when I heard the car pull into the drive. I got up from the sofa with my drink and went to the window to have a look.

I saw my wife laughing as she parked the car. I saw her get out of the car and shut the door. She was still wearing a smile. Just amazing. She went around to the other side of the car to where the blind man was already starting to get out. This blind man, feature this, he was wearing a full beard! A beard on a blind man! Too much, I say. The blind man reached into the backseat and dragged out a suitcase. My wife took his arm, shut the car door, and, talking all the way, moved him down the drive and then up the steps to the front porch. I turned off the TV. I finished my drink, rinsed the glass, dried my hands. Then I went to the door.

My wife said, "I want you to meet Robert. Robert, this is my husband. I've told you all about him." She was beaming. She had this blind man by his coat sleeve.

The blind man let go of his suitcase and up came his hand.

I took it. He squeezed hard, held my hand, and then he let it go.

"I feel like we've already met," he boomed.

"Likewise," I said. I didn't know what else to say. Then I said, "Welcome. I've heard a lot about you." We began to move then, a little group, from the porch into the living room, my wife guiding him by the arm. The blind man was carrying his suitcase in his other hand. My wife said things like, "To your left here, Robert. That's right. Now watch it, there's a chair. That's it. Sit down right here. This is the sofa. We just bought this sofa two weeks ago."

I started to say something about the old sofa. I'd liked that old sofa. But I didn't say anything. Then I wanted to say something else, small-talk, about the scenic ride along the Hudson. How going *to* New York, you should sit on the right-hand side of the train, and coming *from* New York, the left-hand side.

"Did you have a good train ride?" I said. "Which side of the train did you sit on, by the way?"

"What a question, which side!" my wife said. "What's it matter which side?" she said.

"I just asked," I said.

"Right side," the blind man said. "I hadn't been on a train in nearly forty years. Not since I was a kid. With my folks. That's been a long time. I'd nearly forgotten the sensation. I have winter in my beard now," he said. "So I've been told, anyway. Do I look distinguished, my dear?" the blind man said to my wife.

"You look distinguished, Robert," she said. "Robert," she said. "Robert, it's just so good to see you."

My wife finally took her eyes off the blind man and looked at me. I had the feeling she didn't like what she saw. I shrugged.

I've never met, or personally known, anyone who was blind. This blind man was late forties, a heavy-set, balding man with stooped shoulders, as if he carried a great weight there. He wore brown slacks, brown shoes, a light-brown shirt, a tie, a sports coat. Spiffy. He also had this full beard. But he didn't use a cane and he didn't wear dark glasses. I'd always thought dark glasses were a must for the blind. Fact was, I wished he had a pair. At first glance, his eyes looked like anyone else's eyes. But if you looked close, there was something different about them. Too much white in the iris, for one thing, and the pupils seemed to move around in the sockets without his knowing it or being able to stop it. Creepy. As I stared at his face, I saw the left pupil turn in toward his nose while the other made an effort to keep in one place. But it was only an effort, for that eye was on the roam without his knowing it or wanting it to be.

I said, "Let me get you a drink. What's your pleasure? We have a little of everything. It's one of our pastimes."

"Bub, I'm a Scotch man myself," he said fast enough in this big voice.

"Right," I said. Bub! "Sure you are. I knew it."

He let his fingers touch his suitcase, which was sitting alongside the sofa. He was taking his bearings. I didn't blame him for that.

"I'll move that up to your room," my wife said.

"No, that's fine," the blind man said loudly. "It can go up when I go up."

"A little water with the Scotch?" I said.

"Very little," he said.

"I knew it," I said.

He said, "Just a tad. The Irish actor, Barry Fitzgerald? I'm like that fellow. When I drink water, Fitzgerald said, I drink water. When I drink whiskey, I drink whiskey." My wife laughed. The blind man brought his hand up under his beard. He lifted his beard slowly and let it drop.

I did the drinks, three big glasses of Scotch with a splash of water in each. Then we made ourselves comfortable and talked about Robert's travels. First the long flight from the West Coast to Connecticut, we covered that. Then from Connecticut up here by train. We had another drink concerning that leg of the trip.

I remembered having read somewhere that the blind didn't smoke because, as speculation had it, they couldn't see the smoke they exhaled. I thought I knew that much and that much only about blind people. But this blind man smoked his cigarette down to the nubbin and then lit another one. This blind man filled his ashtray and my wife emptied it.

When we sat down at the table for dinner, we had another drink. My wife heaped Robert's plate with cube steak, scalloped potatoes, green beans. I buttered him up two slices of bread. I said, "Here's bread and butter for you." I swallowed some of my drink. "Now let us pray," I said, and the blind man lowered his head. My wife looked at me, her mouth agape. "Pray the phone won't ring and the food doesn't get cold," I said.

We dug in. We ate everything there was to eat on the table. We ate like there was no tomorrow. We didn't talk. We ate. We scarfed. We grazed that table. We were into serious eating. The blind man had right away located his foods, he knew just where everything was on his plate. I watched with admiration as he used his knife and fork on the meat. He'd cut two pieces of meat, fork the meat into his mouth, and then go all out for the scalloped potatoes, the beans next, and then he'd tear off a hunk of buttered bread and eat that. He'd follow this up with a big drink of milk. It didn't seem to bother him to use his fingers once in a while, either.

We finished everything, including half a strawberry pie. For a few moments, we sat as if stunned. Sweat beaded on our faces. Finally, we got up from the table and left the dirty plates. We didn't look back. We took ourselves into the living room and sank into our places again. Robert and my wife sat on the sofa. I took the big chair. We had us two or three more drinks while they talked about the major things that had come to pass for them in the past ten years. For the most part, I just listened. Now and then I joined in. I didn't want him to think I'd left the room, and I didn't want her to think I was feeling left out. They talked of things that had happened to them—to them!—these past ten years. I waited in vain to hear my name on my wife's sweet lips: "And then my dear husband came into my life"—something like that. But I heard nothing of the sort. More talk of Robert. Robert had done a little of everything, it seemed, a regular blind jack-of-all-trades. But most recently he and his wife had had an Amway distributorship, from which, I gathered, they'd earned their living, such as it was. The blind man was also a ham radio operator. He talked in his loud voice about conversations he'd had with fellow operators in Guam, in the Philippines, in Alaska, and even in Tahiti. He said he'd have a lot of friends there if he ever wanted to go visit those places. From time to time, he'd turn his blind face toward me, put his hand under his beard, ask me something. How long had I been in my present position? (Three years.) Did I like my work? (I didn't.) Was I going to stay with it? (What were the options?) Finally, when I thought he was beginning to run down, I got up and turned on the TV.

My wife looked at me with irritation. She was heading toward a boil. Then she looked at the blind man and said, "Robert, do you have a TV?"

The blind man said, "My dear, I have two TVs. I have a color set and a black-and-white thing, an old relic. It's funny, but if I turn the TV on, and I'm always turning it on, I turn on the color set. It's funny, don't you think?"

I didn't know what to say to that. I had absolutely nothing to say to that. No opinion. So I watched the news program and tried to listen to what the announcer was saying.

"This is a color TV," the blind man said. "Don't ask me how, but I can tell."

"We traded up a while ago," I said.

The blind man had another taste of his drink. He lifted his beard, sniffed it, and let it fall. He leaned forward on the sofa. He positioned his ashtray on the coffee table, then put the lighter to his cigarette. He leaned back on the sofa and crossed his legs at the ankles.

My wife covered her mouth, and then she yawned. She stretched. She said, "I think I'll go upstairs and put on my robe. I think I'll change into something else. Robert, you make yourself comfortable," she said.

"I'm comfortable," the blind man said.

"I want you to feel comfortable in this house," she said.

"I am comfortable," the blind man said.

After she'd left the room, he and I listened to the weather report and then to the sports roundup. By that time, she'd been gone so long I didn't know if she was going to come back. I thought she might have gone to bed. I wished she'd come back downstairs. I didn't want to be left alone with a blind man. I asked him if he wanted another drink, and he said sure. Then I asked if he wanted to smoke some dope with me. I said I'd just rolled a number. I hadn't, but I planned to do so in about two shakes.

"I'll try some with you," he said.

"Damn right," I said. "That's the stuff."

I got our drinks and sat down on the sofa with him. Then I rolled us two fat numbers. I lit one and passed it. I brought it to his fingers. He took it and inhaled.

"Hold it as long as you can," I said. I could tell he didn't know the first thing.

My wife came back downstairs wearing her pink robe and her pink slippers.

"What do I smell?" she said.

"We thought we'd have us some cannabis," I said.

My wife gave me a savage look. Then she looked at the blind man and said, "Robert, I didn't know you smoked."

He said, "I do now, my dear. There's a first time for everything. But I don't feel anything yet."

"This stuff is pretty mellow," I said. "This stuff is mild. It's dope you can reason with," I said. "It doesn't mess you up."

"Not much it doesn't, bub," he said, and laughed.

My wife sat on the sofa between the blind man and me. I passed her the number. She took it and toked and then passed it back to me. "Which way is this going?" she said. Then she said, "I shouldn't be smoking this. I can hardly keep my eyes open as it is. That dinner did me in. I shouldn't have eaten so much."

"It was the strawberry pie," the blind man said. "That's what did it," he said, and he laughed his big laugh. Then he shook his head.

"There's more strawberry pie," I said.

"Do you want some more, Robert?" my wife said.

"Maybe in a little while," he said.

We gave our attention to the TV. My wife yawned again. She said, "Your bed is made up when you feel like going to bed, Robert. I know you must have had a long day. When you're ready to go to bed, say so." She pulled his arm. "Robert?"

He came to and said, "I've had a real nice time. This beats tapes, doesn't it?"

I said, "Coming at you," and I put the number between his fingers. He inhaled, held the smoke, and then let it go. It was like he'd been doing it since he was nine years old.

"Thanks, bub," he said. "But I think this is all for me. I think I'm beginning to feel it," he said. He held the burning roach out for my wife.

"Same here," she said. "Ditto. Me, too." She took the roach and passed it to me. "I may just sit here for a while between you two guys with my eyes closed. But don't let me bother you, okay? Either one of you. If it bothers you, say so. Otherwise, I may just sit here with my eyes closed until you're ready to go to bed," she said. "Your bed's made up, Robert, when you're ready. It's right next to our room at the top of the stairs. We'll show you up when you're ready. You wake me up now, you guys, if I fall asleep." She said that and then she closed her eyes and went to sleep.

The news program ended. I got up and changed the channel. I sat back down on the sofa. I wished my wife hadn't pooped out. Her head lay across the back of the sofa, her mouth open. She'd turned so that her robe slipped away from her legs, exposing a juicy thigh. I reached to draw her robe back over her, and it was then that I glanced at the blind man. What the hell! I flipped the robe open again.

"You say when you want some strawberry pie," I said.

"I will," he said.

I said, "Are you tired? Do you want me to take you up to your bed? Are you ready to hit the hay?"

"Not yet," he said. "No, I'll stay up with you, bub. If that's all right. I'll stay up until you're ready to turn in. We haven't had a chance to talk. Know what I mean? I feel like me and her monopolized the evening." He lifted his beard and he let it fall. He picked up his cigarettes and his lighter.

"That's all right," I said. Then I said, "I'm glad for the company."

And I guess I was. Every night I smoked dope and stayed up as long as I could before I fell asleep. My wife and I hardly ever went to bed at the same time. When I did go to sleep, I had these dreams. Sometimes I'd wake up from one of them, my heart going crazy.

Something about the church and the Middle Ages was on the TV. Not your run-of-the-mill TV fare. I wanted to watch something else. I turned to the other channels. But there was nothing on them, either. So I turned back to the first channel and apologized.

"Bub, it's all right," the blind man said. "It's fine with me. Whatever you want to watch is okay. I'm always learning something. Learning never ends. It won't hurt me to learn something tonight. I got ears," he said.

We didn't say anything for a time. He was leaning forward with his head turned at me, his right ear aimed in the direction of the set. Very disconcerting. Now and then his eyelids drooped and then they snapped open again. Now and then he put his fingers into his beard and tugged, like he was thinking about something he was hearing on the television.

On the screen, a group of men wearing cowls was being set upon and tormented by men dressed in skeleton costumes and men dressed as devils. The men dressed as devils wore devil masks, horns, and long tails. This pageant was part of a procession.

The Englishman who was narrating the thing said it took place in Spain once a year. I tried to explain to the blind man what was happening.

"Skeletons," he said. "I know about skeletons," he said, and he nodded.

The TV showed this one cathedral. Then there was a long, slow look at another one. Finally, the picture switched to the famous one in Paris, with its flying buttresses and its spires reaching up to the clouds. The camera pulled away to show the whole of the cathedral rising above the skyline.

There were times when the Englishman who was telling the thing would shut up, would simply let the camera move around the cathedrals. Or else the camera would tour the countryside, men in fields walking behind oxen. I waited as long as I could. Then I felt I had to say something. I said, "They're showing the outside of this cathedral now. Gargoyles. Little statues carved to look like monsters. Now I guess they're in Italy. Yeah, they're in Italy. There's paintings on the walls of this one church."

"Are those fresco paintings, bub?" he asked, and he sipped from his drink.

I reached for my glass. But it was empty. I tried to remember what I could remember. "You're asking me are those frescoes?" I said. "That's a good question. I don't know."

The camera moved to a cathedral outside Lisbon. The differences in the Portuguese cathedral compared with the French and Italian were not that great. But they were there. Mostly the interior stuff. Then something occurred to me, and I said, "Something has occurred to me. Do you have any idea what a cathedral is? What they look like, that is? Do you follow me? If somebody says cathedral to you, do you have any notion what they're talking about? Do you know the difference between that and a Baptist church, say?"

He let the smoke dribble from his mouth. "I know they took hundreds of workers fifty or a hundred years to build," he said. "I just heard the man say that, of course. I know generations of the same families worked on a cathedral. I heard him say that, too. The men who began their life's work on them, they never lived to see the completion of their work. In that wise, bub, they're no different from the rest of us, right?" He laughed. Then his eyelids drooped again. His head nodded. He seemed to be snoozing. Maybe he was imagining himself in Portugal. The TV was showing another cathedral now. This one was in Germany. The Englishman's voice droned on. "Cathedrals," the blind man said. He sat up and rolled his head back and forth. "If you want the truth, bub, that's about all I know. What I just said. What I heard him say. But maybe you could describe one to me? I wish you'd do it. I'd like that. If you want to know, I really don't have a good idea."

I stared hard at the shot of the cathedral on the TV. How could I even begin to describe it? But say my life depended on it. Say my life was being threatened by an insane guy who said I had to do it or else.

I stared some more at the cathedral before the picture flipped off into the countryside. There was no use. I turned to the blind man and said, "To begin with, they're very tall." I was looking around the room for clues. "They reach way up. Up and up. Toward the sky. They're so big, some of them, they have to have these supports. To help hold them up, so to speak. These supports are called buttresses. They remind me of viaducts, for some reason. But maybe you don't know viaducts, either? Sometimes the cathedrals have devils and such carved into the front. Sometimes lords and ladies. Don't ask me why this is," I said.

He was nodding. The whole upper part of his body seemed to be moving back and forth.

"I'm not doing so good, am I?" I said.

He stopped nodding and leaned forward on the edge of the sofa. As he listened to me, he was running his fingers through his beard. I wasn't getting through to him, I could see that. But he waited for me to go on just the same. He nodded, like he was trying to encourage me. I tried to think what else to say. "They're really big," I said. "They're massive. They're built of stone. Marble, too, sometimes. In those olden days, when they built cathedrals, men wanted to be close to God. In those olden days, God was an important part of everyone's life. You could tell this from their cathedral-building. I'm sorry," I said, "but it looks like that's the best I can do for you. I'm just no good at it."

"That's all right, bub," the blind man said. "Hey, listen. I hope you don't mind my asking you. Can I ask you something? Let me ask you a simple question, yes or no. I'm just curious and there's no offense. You're my host. But let me ask if you are in any way religious? You don't mind my asking?"

I shook my head. He couldn't see that, though. A wink is the same as a nod to a blind man. "I guess I don't believe in it. In anything. Sometimes it's hard. You know what I'm saying?"

"Sure, I do," he said.

"Right," I said.

The Englishman was still holding forth. My wife sighed in her sleep. She drew a long breath and went on with her sleeping.

"You'll have to forgive me," I said. "But I can't tell you what a cathedral looks like. It just isn't in me to do it. I can't do any more than I've done."

The blind man sat very still, his head down, as he listened to me.

I said, "The truth is, cathedrals don't mean anything special to me. Nothing. Cathedrals. They're something to look at on late-night TV. That's all they are."

It was then that the blind man cleared his throat. He brought something up. He took a handkerchief from his back pocket. Then he said, "I get it, bub. It's okay. It happens. Don't worry about it," he said. "Hey, listen to me. Will you do me a favor? I got an idea. Why don't you find us some heavy paper? And a pen. We'll do something. We'll draw one together. Get us a pen and some heavy paper. Go on, bub, get the stuff," he said.

So I went upstairs. My legs felt like they didn't have any strength in them. They felt like they did after I'd done some running. In my wife's room, I looked around. I found some ballpoints in a little basket on her table. And then I tried to think where to look for the kind of paper he was talking about.

Downstairs, in the kitchen, I found a shopping bag with onion skins in the bottom of the bag. I emptied the bag and shook it. I brought it into the living room and sat down with it near his legs. I moved some things, smoothed the wrinkles from the bag, spread it out on the coffee table.

The blind man got down from the sofa and sat next to me on the carpet.

He ran his fingers over the paper. He went up and down the sides of the paper. The edges, even the edges. He fingered the corners.

"All right," he said. "All right, let's do her."

He found my hand, the hand with the pen. He closed his hand over my hand. "Go ahead, bub, draw," he said. "Draw. You'll see. I'll follow along with you. It'll be okay. Just begin now like I'm telling you. You'll see. Draw," the blind man said.

So I began. First I drew a box that looked like a house. It could have been the house I lived in. Then I put a roof on it. At either end of the roof, I drew spires. Crazy.

"Swell," he said. "Terrific. You're doing fine," he said. "Never thought anything like this could happen in your lifetime, did you, bub? Well, it's a strange life, we all know that. Go on now. Keep it up."

I put in windows with arches. I drew flying buttresses. I hung great doors. I couldn't stop. The TV station went off the air. I put down the pen and closed and opened my fingers. The blind man felt around over the paper. He moved the tips of his fingers over the paper, all over what I had drawn, and he nodded.

"Doing fine," the blind man said.

I took up the pen again, and he found my hand. I kept at it. I'm no artist. But I kept drawing just the same.

My wife opened up her eyes and gazed at us. She sat up on the sofa, her robe hanging open. She said, "What are you doing? Tell me, I want to know."

I didn't answer her.

The blind man said, "We're drawing a cathedral. Me and him are working on it. Press hard," he said to me. "That's right. That's good," he said. "Sure. You got it, bub, I can tell. You didn't think you could. But you can, can't you? You're cooking with gas now. You know what I'm saying? We're going to really have us something here in a minute. How's the old arm?" he said. "Put some people in there now. What's a cathedral without people?"

My wife said, "What's going on? Robert, what are you doing? What's going on?"

"It's all right," he said to her. "Close your eyes now," the blind man said to me.

I did it. I closed them just like he said.

"Are they closed?" he said. "Don't fudge."

"They're closed," I said.

"Keep them that way," he said. He said, "Don't stop now. Draw."

So we kept on with it. His fingers rode my fingers as my hand went over the paper. It was like nothing else in my life up to now.

Then he said, "I think that's it. I think you got it," he said. "Take a look. What do you think?"

But I had my eyes closed. I thought I'd keep them that way for a little longer. I thought it was something I ought to do.

"Well?" he said. "Are you looking?"

My eyes were still closed. I was in my house. I knew that. But I didn't feel like I was inside anything.

"It's really something," I said.

John Cheever *(1912–1982)*

was born in Quincy, Massachusetts. In 1929, the stock market crash drove his father's shoe factory to bankruptcy. That same year, Cheever—already accepted to Harvard—was expelled from Thayer Academy for smoking. He never finished high school, but he did use the incident as the basis of his first published story, "Expelled," which appeared the next year in The New Republic. *Soon thereafter, he began to appear regularly in the pages of* The New Yorker *and in the guest rooms at Yaddo, the artists' colony in Saratoga Springs, New York; he was a mainstay in both places for fifty years (119 stories in* The New Yorker; *twenty-four stays, some as long as a year, at Yaddo). He married and served in World War II as an infantry gunner. After the war, he published his first book of stories—*The Way Some People Live*—and began making a living writing television scripts (including several for the series "Life with Father") and teaching, including stints at Barnard College, the Iowa Writers' Workshop, and Sing Sing prison (the latter, along with his late-in-life acceptance of his own bisexuality, helped to serve as the basis for his 1977 novel* Falconer*). In the 1950s, he began writing novels, and* The Wapshot Chronicle *won the 1958 National Book Award. For years, he struggled with alcoholism, though, after his family had him sent to the Smithers Center for rehab, he spent the last seven years of his life sober. The career-spanning* The Stories of John Cheever *won the 1979 Pulitzer Prize and is widely credited (along with the 1980 publication of* The Collected Stories of Eudora Welty*) with triggering a broader readership for the American short story.*

INTRODUCTION BY **Richard Russo**

Most apprentice writers are beset by self-doubts, which is probably as it should be. After all, such doubts can be useful when they're rational and personal. An apprentice writer who enjoys movies more than books, or who likes to draft but grows bored with revision, or whose self-confidence is eroded by constructive criticism should be assailed by misgivings. More generic doubts, however, can be harmful. Would-be writers who suspect that they haven't had enough life experience to write stories or who believe that they've been unlucky enough to possess the wrong kind of experiences may be effectively paralyzed by such fears and thus prevented from discovering what their real shortcomings may be. "I grew up in the suburbs," a troubled student once confessed to me over an empty beer pitcher, his face red with shame. What business did he have imagining he could ever be a writer with only pallid suburban experiences to draw from? "Let's talk about it next week," I suggested, glad that he had summoned the necessary courage to spill his guts and that there was such a safe, effective, and inexpensive remedy. "That'll give you time to read John Cheever's stories."

Indeed, the three Cheever stories included here—one early, one mid-career, one late—offer the apprentice writer valuable lessons in just about every aspect of storytelling. In addition to their vivid settings (only two of which are suburban), what I admire most about them is the linkage Cheever always makes between character and conflict; the way one deftly reveals, deepens, and resolves the other; and the way, by the end of each story, the reader, often against his or her better judgment, is in deep complicity with its flawed protagonist. "We are a family that has always been very close in spirit," the unnamed narrator tells us in the first sentence of "Goodbye, My Brother," and already we sense trouble, for he might have simply said, "We have always been a close family," but chose not to. That he can't make this straightforward claim, that he has to resort to an awkward locution—"very close in spirit"—puts us on our guard, especially when a damaging admission immediately follows: "I don't think about the family much, but when I remember its members . . . I am happy to recall that I'm a Pommeroy." The main thing the Pommeroys have in common, it turns out, is a conviction that they are somehow special people, an illusion that can be sustained for only a few weeks each summer when they are all together at their island summer home. That they could not be more ordinary is made manifest in the story's relentless details, even before Lawrence ("Tifty"), the youngest of the siblings, arrives on the scene, determined to share with his family what he calls "the realities": that the house is poised to fall into the sea, that their mother is a drunk, their brother Chaddy dishonest, their sister Diana a loose woman, and the narrator himself a fool. The beauty of the story lies in its gradually escalating conflict, which takes place on two levels, first dramatically, between bitter Lawrence and the rest of the Pommeroys, and second thematically, between Truth and Illusion. It's rather a shock to realize that we prefer the other Pommeroys' counterfeit cheer to Tifty's defeatist realities. At least they are in the game, whereas Tifty remains a contemptuous observer. The narrator might well be a fool, as his brother claims, but it's impossible not to sympathize with his final lament—"Oh, what can you do with a man like that?" Are we wrong to sympathize with a character who would rather focus on life's illusory beauty than contemplate its too real ugliness? Perhaps. In some ways, Neddy Merrill, in "The Swimmer," might be the unnamed narrator of "Goodbye, My Brother," a decade or two later. Neddy too is determined to be "lighthearted" (in Cheever, this word often suggests the ability of superficial people to make light of serious things) and similarly "disciplined . . . in the repression of unpleasant facts." That the youth and beauty he so prizes are another illusion, that he's not the mythic character he imagines himself to be, that he's lived a life that's both shallow and disloyal—little more than a string of swimming pools and cocktail parties—is the falsehood that propels him forward. Like the Pommeroys, Neddy is both deceived and sustained by his own unwarranted sense of specialness. That everyone at the Westerhazys' is saying the same thing—we drank too much—suggests how little there is to choose between them. Here, though, the easygoing, unreliable first-person narrator of the earlier story is replaced by a merciless omniscience that somehow (and what a neat trick it is) allows us to see Neddy for the fool he is without ever losing sympathy for him. In his place, would we have done things so differently? There is something heroic in Neddy's journey, in his recognizing a pattern in these swimming pools and christening them "the Lucinda River," in his determination to swim its length, his refusal to see "the realities" of his life until he nearly drowns in them.

In "The Country Husband," it's not the ordinariness of story's protagonist that's in question so much as the world he inhabits. The plane crash that nearly kills Francis Weed awakens him to the possibility of a life that's very different from the one he has carefully constructed for himself in Shady Hill, the inhabitants of which are "united in their tacit claim that there had been no past, no war—that there was no danger or trouble in the world." Determined to remain awake and alive, Francis revels in the newly vivid world, "the miraculous physicalness of everything." Newly brave and suddenly feeling out of place in Shady Hill, he undermines his life there by insulting a woman on whom his family's social well-being depends and by allowing himself to fall in love with a neighborhood babysitter. "Like every other man," he concludes at the height of his madness, "he was made to father thousands." Poor Francis. In all of Shady Hill, the only other being who shares his world view is Jupiter, the neighborhood dog, who will be poisoned one day soon, the story's narrator informs us, when the neighbors grow weary of his rambunctious high spirits. And in all of this, we are complicitous. Too late, we understand that what has bound and limited Francis Weed's imagination has also constrained our own. We spend much of the story worrying that Francis will lose everything—his wife, his children, his home, his pleasant Shady Hill existence—as if this were possible. As if his dream of a future different from his present were any more substantial than his fleeting glimpse of the naked woman, endlessly combing her hair, on the train that blows through Shady Hill without stopping.

Richard Russo lives in coastal Maine with his wife and their two daughters. He has written five novels: Mohawk, The Risk Pool, Nobody's Fool, Straight Man, *and* Empire Falls *(which won the Pulitzer Prize for Fiction), and a collection of short stories,* The Whore's Child.

JOHN CHEEVER

Goodbye, My Brother

We are a family that has always been very close in spirit. Our father was drowned in a sailing accident when we were young, and our mother has always stressed the fact that our familial relationships have a kind of permanence that we will never meet with again. I don't think about the family much, but when I remember its members and the coast where they lived and the sea salt that I think is in our blood, I am happy to recall that I am a Pommeroy—that I have the nose, the coloring, and the promise of longevity—and that while we are not a distinguished family, we enjoy the illusion, when we are together, that the Pommeroys are unique. I don't say any of this because I'm interested in family history or because this sense of uniqueness is deep or important to me but in order to advance the point that we are loyal to one another in spite of our differences, and that any rupture in this loyalty is a source of confusion and pain.

We are four children; there is my sister Diana and the three men—Chaddy, Lawrence, and myself. Like most families in which the children are out of their twenties, we have been separated by business, marriage, and war. Helen and I live on Long Island now, with our four children. I teach in a secondary school, and I am past the age where I expect to be made headmaster—or principal, as we say—but I respect the work. Chaddy, who has done better than the rest of us, lives in Manhattan, with Odette and their children. Mother lives in Philadelphia, and Diana, since her divorce, has been living in France, but she comes back to the States in the summer to spend a month at Laud's Head. Laud's Head is a summer place on the shore of one of the Massachusetts islands. We used to have a cottage there, and in the twenties our father built the big house. It stands on a cliff above the sea and, excepting St. Tropez and some of the Apennine villages, it is my favorite place in the world. We each have an equity in the place and we contribute some money to help keep it going.

Our youngest brother, Lawrence, who is a lawyer, got a job with a Cleveland firm after the war, and none of us saw him for four years. When he decided to leave Cleveland and go to work for a firm in Albany, he wrote Mother that he would, between jobs, spend ten days at Laud's Head, with his wife and their two children. This was when I had planned to take my vacation—I had been teaching summer school—and Helen and Chaddy and Odette and Diana were all going to be there, so the family would be together. Lawrence is the member of the family with whom the rest of us have least in common. We have never seen a great deal of him, and I suppose that's why we still call him Tifty—a nickname he was given when he was a child, because when he came down the hall toward the dining room for breakfast, his slippers made a noise that sounded like "Tifty, tifty, tifty." That's what Father called him, and so did everyone else. When he grew older, Diana sometimes used to call him Little Jesus, and Mother often called him the Croaker. We had disliked Lawrence, but we looked forward to his return with a mixture of apprehension and loyalty, and with some of the joy and delight of reclaiming a brother.

★ ★ ★

Lawrence crossed over from the mainland on the four-o'clock boat one afternoon late in the summer, and Chaddy and I went down to meet him. The arrivals and departures of the summer ferry have all the outward signs that suggest a voyage—whistles, bells, hand trucks, reunions, and the smell of brine—but it is a voyage of no import, and when I watched the boat come into the blue harbor that afternoon and thought that it was completing a voyage of no import, I realized that I had hit on exactly the kind of observation that Lawrence would have made. We looked for his face behind the windshields as the cars drove off the boat, and we had no trouble in recognizing him. And we ran over and shook his hand and clumsily kissed his wife and the children. "Tifty!" Chaddy shouted. "Tifty!" It is difficult to judge changes in the appearance of a brother, but both Chaddy and I agreed, as we drove back to Laud's Head, that Lawrence still looked very young. He got to the house first, and we took the suitcases out of his car. When I came in, he was standing in the living room, talking with Mother and Diana. They were in their best clothes and all their jewelry, and they were welcoming him extravagantly, but even then, when everyone was endeavoring to seem most affectionate and at a time when these endeavors come easiest, I was aware of a faint tension in the room. Thinking about this as I carried Lawrence's heavy suitcases up the stairs, I realized that our dislikes are as deeply ingrained as our better passions, and I remembered that once, twenty-five years ago, when I had hit Lawrence on the head with a rock, he had picked himself up and gone directly to our father to complain.

I carried the suitcases up to the third floor, where Ruth, Lawrence's wife, had begun to settle her family. She is a thin girl, and she seemed very tired from the journey, but when I asked her if she didn't want me to bring a drink upstairs to her, she said she didn't think she did.

When I got downstairs, Lawrence wasn't around, but the others were all ready for cocktails, and we decided to go ahead. Lawrence is the only member of the family who has never enjoyed drinking. We took our cocktails onto the terrace, so that we could see the bluffs and the sea and the islands in the east, and the return of Lawrence and his wife, their presence in the house, seemed to refresh our responses to the familiar view; it was as if the pleasure they would take in the sweep and the color of that coast, after such a long absence, had been imparted to us. While we were there, Lawrence came up the path from the beach.

"Isn't the beach fabulous, Tifty?" Mother asked. "Isn't it fabulous to be back? Will you have a Martini?"

"I don't care," Lawrence said. "Whiskey, gin—I don't care what I drink. Give me a little rum."

"We don't have any *rum,*" Mother said. It was the first note of asperity. She had taught us never to be indecisive, never to reply as Lawrence had. Beyond this, she is deeply concerned with the propriety of her house, and anything irregular by her standards, like drinking straight rum or bringing a beer can to the dinner table, excites in her a conflict that she cannot, even with her capacious sense of humor, surmount. She sensed the asperity and worked to repair it. "Would you like some Irish, Tifty dear?" she said. "Isn't Irish what you've always liked? There's some Irish on the sideboard. Why don't you get yourself some Irish?" Lawrence said that he didn't care. He poured himself a Martini, and then Ruth came down and we went in to dinner.

In spite of the fact that we had, through waiting for Lawrence, drunk too much before dinner, we were all anxious to put our best foot forward and to enjoy a peaceful time. Mother is a small woman whose face is still a striking reminder of how pretty she must have been, and whose conversation is unusually light, but she talked that evening about a soil-reclamation project that is going on up-island. Diana is as pretty as Mother must have been; she is an animated and lovely woman who likes to talk about the dissolute friends that she has made in France, but she talked that night about the school in Switzerland where she had left her two children. I could see that the dinner had been planned to please Lawrence. It was not too rich, and there was nothing to make him worry about extravagance.

After supper, when we went back onto the terrace, the clouds held that kind of light that looks like blood, and I was glad that Lawrence had such a lurid sunset for his homecoming. When we had been out there a few minutes, a man named Edward Chester came to get Diana. She had met him in France, or on the boat home, and he was staying for ten days at the inn in the village. He was introduced to Lawrence and Ruth, and then he and Diana left.

"Is that the one she's sleeping with now?" Lawrence asked.

"What a horrid thing to say!" Helen said.

"You ought to apologize for that, Tifty," Chaddy said.

"I don't know," Mother said tiredly. "I don't know, Tifty. Diana is in a position to do whatever she wants, and I don't ask sordid questions. She's my only daughter. I don't see her often."

"Is she going back to France?"

"She's going back the week after next."

Lawrence and Ruth were sitting at the edge of the terrace, not in the chairs, not in the circle of chairs. With his mouth set, my brother looked to me then like a Puritan cleric. Sometimes, when I try to understand his frame of mind, I think of the beginnings of our family in this country, and his disapproval of Diana and her lover reminded me of this. The branch of the Pommeroys to which we belong was founded by a minister who was eulogized by Cotton Mather for his untiring abjuration of the Devil. The Pommeroys were ministers until the middle of the nineteenth century, and the harshness of their thought—man is full of misery, and all earthly beauty is lustful and corrupt—has been preserved in books and sermons. The temper of our family changed somewhat and became more lighthearted, but when I was of school age, I can remember a cousinage of old men and women who seemed to hark back to the dark days of the ministry and to be animated by perpetual guilt and the deification of the scourge. If you are raised in this atmosphere—and in a sense we were—I think it is a trial of the spirit to reject its habits of guilt, self-denial, taciturnity, and penitence, and it seemed to me to have been a trial of the spirit in which Lawrence had succumbed.

"Is that Cassiopeia?" Odette asked.

"No, dear," Chaddy said. "That isn't Cassiopeia."

"Who was Cassiopeia?" Odette said.

"She was the wife of Cepheus and the mother of Andromeda," I said.

"The cook is a Giants fan," Chaddy said. "She'll give you even money that they win the pennant."

It had grown so dark that we could see the passage of light through the sky from the lighthouse at Cape Heron. In the dark below the cliff, the continual detonations of the surf sounded. And then, as she often does when it is getting dark and she has drunk too much before dinner, Mother began to talk about the improvements and additions that would someday be made on the house, the wings and bathrooms and gardens.

"This house will be in the sea in five years," Lawrence said.

"Tifty the Croaker," Chaddy said.

"Don't call me Tifty," Lawrence said.

"Little Jesus," Chaddy said.

"The sea wall is badly cracked," Lawrence said. "I looked at it this afternoon. You had it repaired four years ago, and it cost eight thousand dollars. You can't do that every four years."

"Please, Tifty," Mother said.

"Facts are facts," Lawrence said, "and it's a damned-fool idea to build a house at the edge of the cliff on a sinking coastline. In my lifetime, half the garden has washed away and there's four feet of water where we used to have a bathhouse."

"Let's have a very *general* conversation," Mother said bitterly. "Let's talk about politics or the boat-club dance."

"As a matter of fact," Lawrence said, "the house is probably in some danger now. If you had an unusually high sea, a hurricane sea, the wall would crumble and the house would go. We could all be drowned."

"I can't *bear* it," Mother said. She went into the pantry and came back with a full glass of gin.

I have grown too old now to think that I can judge the sentiments of others, but I was conscious of the tension between Lawrence and Mother, and I knew some of the history of it. Lawrence couldn't have been more than sixteen years old when he decided that Mother was frivolous, mischievous, destructive, and overly strong. When he had determined this, he decided to separate himself from her. He was at boarding school then, and I remember that he did not come home for Christmas. He spent Christmas with a friend. He came home very seldom after he had made his unfavorable judgment on Mother, and when he did come home, he always tried, in his conversation, to remind her of his estrangement. When he married Ruth, he did not tell Mother. He did not tell her when his children were born. But in spite of these principled and lengthy exertions he seemed, unlike the rest of us, never to have enjoyed any separation, and when they are together, you feel at once a tension, an unclearness.

And it was unfortunate, in a way, that Mother should have picked that night to get drunk. It's her privilege, and she doesn't get drunk often, and fortunately she wasn't bellicose, but we were all conscious of what was happening. As she quietly drank her gin, she seemed sadly to be parting from us; she seemed to be in the throes of travel. Then her mood changed from travel to injury, and the few remarks she made were petulant and irrelevant. When her glass was nearly empty, she stared angrily at the dark air in front of her nose, moving her head a little, like a fighter. I knew that there was not room in her mind then for all the injuries that were crowding into it. Her children were stupid, her husband was drowned, her servants were thieves, and the chair she sat in was uncomfortable. Suddenly she put down her empty glass and interrupted Chaddy, who was talking about baseball. "I know one *thing,*" she said hoarsely. "I know that if there is an afterlife, I'm going to have a very different kind of family. I'm going to have nothing but fabulously rich, witty, and enchanting children." She got up and, starting for the door, nearly fell. Chaddy caught her and helped her up the stairs. I could hear their tender good-nights, and then Chaddy came back. I thought that Lawrence by now would be tired from his journey and his return, but he remained on the terrace, as if he were waiting to see the final malfeasance, and the rest of us left him there and went swimming in the dark.

When I woke the next morning, or half woke, I could hear the sound of someone rolling the tennis court. It is a fainter and a deeper sound than the iron buoy bells off the point—an unrhythmic iron chiming—that belongs in my mind to the beginnings of a summer day, a good portent. When I went downstairs, Lawrence's two kids were in the living room, dressed in ornate cowboy suits. They are frightened and skinny children. They told me their father was rolling the tennis court but that they did not want to go out because they had seen a snake under the doorstep. I explained to them that their cousins—all the other children—ate breakfast in the kitchen and that they'd better run along in there. At this announcement, the boy began to cry. Then his sister joined him. They cried as if to go in the kitchen and eat would destroy their most precious rights. I told them to sit down with me. Lawrence came in, and I asked him if he wanted to play some tennis. He said no, thanks, although he thought he might play some singles with Chaddy. He was in the right here, because both he and Chaddy play better tennis than I, and he did play some singles with Chaddy after breakfast, but later on, when the others came down to play family doubles, Lawrence disappeared. This made me cross—unreasonably so, I suppose—but we play darned interesting family doubles and he could have played in a set for the sake of courtesy.

Late in the morning, when I came up from the court alone, I saw Tifty on the terrace, prying up a shingle from the wall with his jackknife. "What's the matter, Lawrence?" I said. "Termites?" There are termites in the wood and they've given us a lot of trouble.

He pointed out to me, at the base of each row of shingles, a faint blue line of carpenter's chalk. "This house is about twenty-two years old," he said. "These shingles are about two hundred years old. Dad must have bought shingles from all the farms around here when he built the place, to make it look venerable. You can still see the carpenter's chalk put down where these antiques were nailed into place."

It was true about the shingles, although I had forgotten it. When the house was built, our father, or his architect, had ordered it covered with lichened and weather-beaten shingles. I didn't follow Lawrence's reasons for thinking that this was scandalous.

"And look at these doors," Lawrence said. "Look at these doors and window frames." I followed him over to a big Dutch door that opens onto the terrace and looked at it. It was a relatively new door, but someone had worked hard to conceal its newness. The surface had been deeply scored with some metal implement, and white paint had been rubbed into the incisions to imitate brine, lichen, and weather rot. "Imagine spending thousands of dollars to make a sound house look like a wreck," Lawrence said. "Imagine the frame of mind this implies. Imagine wanting to live so much in the past that you'll pay men carpenters' wages to disfigure your front door." Then I remembered Lawrence's sensitivity to time and his sentiments and opinions about our feelings for the past. I had heard him say, years ago, that we and our friends and our part of the nation, finding ourselves unable to cope with the problems of the present, had, like a wretched adult, turned back to what we supposed was a happier and a simpler time, and that our taste for reconstruction and candlelight was a measure of this irremediable failure. The faint blue line of chalk had reminded him of these ideas, the scarified door had reinforced them, and now clue after clue presented itself to him—the stern light at the door, the bulk of the chimney, the width of the floorboards and the pieces set into them to resemble pegs. While Lawrence was lecturing me on these frail ties, the others came up from the court. As soon as Mother saw Lawrence, she responded, and I saw that there was little hope of any rapport between the matriarch and the changeling. She took Chaddy's arm. "Let's go swimming and have Martinis on the beach," she said. "Let's have a *fabulous* morning."

The sea that morning was a solid color, like verd stone. Everyone went to the beach but Tifty and Ruth. "I don't mind *him,*" Mother said. She was excited, and she tipped her glass and spilled some gin into the sand. "I don't mind *him.* It doesn't matter to me how *rude* and *horrid* and *gloomy* he is, but what I can't bear are the faces of his wretched little children, those fabulously unhappy little children." With the height of the cliff between us, everyone talked wrathfully about Lawrence; about how he had grown worse instead of better, how unlike the rest of us he was, how he endeavored to spoil every pleasure. We drank our gin; the abuse seemed to reach a crescendo, and then, one by one, we went swimming in the solid green water. But when we came out no one mentioned Lawrence unkindly; the line of abusive conversation had been cut, as if swimming had the cleansing force claimed for baptism. We dried our hands and lighted cigarettes, and if Lawrence was mentioned, it was only to suggest, kindly, something that might please him. Wouldn't he like to sail to Barin's cove, or go fishing?

And now I remember that while Lawrence was visiting us, we went swimming oftener than we usually do, and I think there was a reason for this. When the irritability that accumulated as a result of his company began to lessen our patience, not only with Lawrence but with one another, we would all go swimming and shed our animus in the cold water. I can see the family now, smarting from Lawrence's rebukes as they sat on the sand, and I can see them wading and diving and surface-diving and hear in their voices the restoration of patience and the rediscovery of inexhaustible good will. If Lawrence noticed this change—this illusion of purification—I suppose that he would have found in the vocabulary of psychiatry, or the mythology of the Atlantic, some circumspect name for it, but I don't think he noticed the change. He neglected to name the curative powers of the open sea, but it was one of the few chances for diminution that he missed.

The cook we had that year was a Polish woman named Anna Ostrovick, a summer cook. She was first-rate—a big, fat, hearty, industrious woman who took her work seriously. She liked to cook and to have the food she cooked appreciated and eaten, and whenever we saw her, she always urged us to eat. She cooked hot bread—crescents and brioches—for breakfast two or three times a week, and she would bring these into the dining room herself and say, "Eat, eat, eat!" When the maid took the serving dishes back into the pantry, we could sometimes hear Anna, who was standing there, say, "Good! They eat." She fed the garbage man, the milkman, and the gardener. "Eat!" she told them. "Eat, eat!" On Thursday afternoons, she went to the movies with the maid, but she didn't enjoy the movies, because the actors were all so thin. She would sit in the dark theatre for an hour and a half watching the screen anxiously for the appearance of someone who had enjoyed his food. Bette Davis merely left with Anna the impression of a woman who has not eaten well. "They are all so skinny," she would say when she left the movies. In the evenings, after she had gorged all of us, and washed the pots and pans, she would collect the table scraps and go out to feed the creation. We had a few chickens that year, and although they would have roosted by then, she would dump food into their troughs and urge the sleeping fowl to eat. She fed the songbirds in the orchard and the chipmunks in the yard. Her appearance at the edge of the garden and her urgent voice—we could hear her calling "Eat, eat, eat"—had become, like the sunset gun at the boat club and the passage of light from Cape Heron, attached to that hour. "Eat, eat, eat," we could hear Anna say. "Eat, eat . . ." Then it would be dark.

When Lawrence had been there three days, Anna called me into the kitchen. "You tell your mother," she said, "that *he* doesn't come into my kitchen. If *he* comes into my kitchen all the time, I go. *He* is always coming into my kitchen to tell me what a sad woman I am. He is always telling me that I work too hard and that I don't get paid enough and that I should belong to a union with vacations. Ha! He is so skinny but he is always coming into my kitchen when I am busy to pity me, but I am as good as him, I am as good as *anybody,* and I do not have to have people like that getting into my way all the time and feeling sorry for me. I am a famous and a wonderful cook and I have jobs everywhere and the only reason I come here to work this summer is because I was never before on an island, but I can have other jobs tomorrow, and if he is always coming into my kitchen to pity me, you tell your mother I am going. I am as good as *anybody* and I do not have to have that skinny all the time telling how poor I am."

I was pleased to find that the cook was on our side, but I felt that the situation was delicate. If Mother asked Lawrence to stay out of the kitchen, he would make a grievance out of the request. He could make a grievance out of anything, and it sometimes seemed that as he sat darkly at the dinner table, every word of disparagement, wherever it was aimed, came home to him. I didn't mention the cook's complaint to anyone, but somehow there wasn't any more trouble from that quarter.

The next cause for contention that I had from Lawrence came over our backgammon games.

When we are at Laud's Head, we play a lot of backgammon. At eight o'clock, after we have drunk our coffee, we usually get out the board. In a way, it is one of our pleasantest hours. The lamps in the room are still unlighted, Anna can be seen in the dark garden, and in the sky above her head there are continents of shadow and fire. Mother turns on the light and rattles the dice as a signal. We usually play three games apiece, each with the others. We play for money, and you can win or lose a hundred dollars on a game, but the stakes are usually much lower. I think that Lawrence used to play—I can't remember—but he doesn't play any more. He doesn't gamble. This is not because he is poor or because he has any principles about gambling but because he thinks the game is foolish and a waste of time. He was ready enough, however, to waste his time watching the rest of us play. Night after night, when the game began, he pulled a chair up beside the board, and watched the checkers and the dice. His expression was scornful, and yet he watched carefully. I wondered why he watched us night after night, and, through watching his face, I think that I may have found out.

Lawrence doesn't gamble, so he can't understand the excitement of winning and losing money. He has forgotten how to play the game, I think, so that its complex odds can't interest him. His observations were bound to include the facts that backgammon is an idle game and a game of chance, and that the board, marked with points, was a symbol of our worthlessness. And since he doesn't understand gambling or the odds of the game, I thought that what interested him must be the members of his family. One night when I was playing with Odette—I had won thirty-seven dollars from Mother and Chaddy—I think I saw what was going on in his mind.

Odette has black hair and black eyes. She is careful never to expose her white skin to the sun for long, so the striking contrast of blackness and pallor is not changed in the summer. She needs and deserves admiration—it is the element that contents her—and she will flirt, unseriously, with any man. Her shoulders were bare that night, her dress was cut to show the division of her breasts and to show her breasts when she leaned over the board to play. She kept losing and flirting and making her losses seem like a part of the flirtation. Chaddy was in the other room. She lost three games, and when the third game ended, she fell back on the sofa and, looking at me squarely, said something about going out on the dunes to settle the score. Lawrence heard her. I looked at Lawrence. He seemed shocked and gratified at the same time, as if he had suspected all along that we were not playing for anything so insubstantial as money. I may be wrong, of course, but I think that Lawrence felt that in watching our backgammon he was observing the progress of a mordant tragedy in which the money we won and lost served as a symbol for more vital forfeits. It is like Lawrence to try to read significance and finality into every gesture that we make, and it is certain of Lawrence that when he finds the inner logic to our conduct, it will be sordid.

Chaddy came in to play with me. Chaddy and I have never liked to lose to each other. When we were younger, we used to be forbidden to play games together, because they always ended in a fight. We think we know each other's mettle intimately. I think he is prudent; he thinks I am foolish. There is always bad blood when we play anything—tennis or backgammon or softball or bridge—and it does seem at times as if we were playing for the possession of each other's liberties. When I lose to Chaddy, I can't sleep. All this is only half the truth of our competitive relationship, but it was the half-truth that would be discernible to Lawrence, and his presence at the table made me so self-conscious that I lost two games. I tried not to seem angry when I got up from the board. Lawrence was watching me. I went out onto the terrace to suffer there in the dark the anger I always feel when I lose to Chaddy.

When I came back into the room, Chaddy and Mother were playing. Lawrence was still watching. By his lights, Odette had lost her virtue to me, I had lost my self-esteem to Chaddy, and now I wondered what he saw in the present match. He watched raptly, as if the opaque checkers and the marked board served for an exchange of critical power. How dramatic the board, in its ring of light, and the quiet players and the crash of the sea outside must have seemed to him! Here was spiritual cannibalism made visible; here, under his nose, were the symbols of the rapacious use human beings make of one another.

Mother plays a shrewd, an ardent, and an interfering game. She always has her hands in her opponent's board. When she plays with Chaddy, who is her favorite, she plays intently. Lawrence would have noticed this. Mother is a sentimental woman. Her heart is good and easily moved by tears and frailty, a characteristic that, like her handsome nose, has not been changed at all by age. Grief in another provokes her deeply, and she seems at times to be trying to divine in Chaddy some grief, some loss, that she can succor and redress, and so re-establish the relationship that she enjoyed with him when he was sickly and young. She loves defending the weak and the childlike, and now that we are old, she misses it. The world of debts and business, men and war, hunting and fishing has on her an exacerbating effect. (When Father drowned, she threw away his fly rods and his guns.) She has lectured us all endlessly on self-reliance, but when we come back to her for comfort and for help—particularly Chaddy—she seems to feel most like herself. I suppose Lawrence thought that the old woman and her son were playing for each other's soul.

She lost. "Oh *dear,*" she said. She looked stricken and bereaved, as she always does when she loses. "Get me my glasses, get me my checkbook, get me something to drink." Lawrence got up at last and stretched his legs. He looked at us all bleakly. The wind and the sea had risen, and I thought that if he heard the waves, he must hear them only as a dark answer to all his dark questions; that he would think that the tide had expunged the embers of our picnic fires. The company of a lie is unbearable, and he seemed like the embodiment of a lie. I couldn't explain to him the simple and intense pleasures of playing for money, and it seemed to me hideously wrong that he should have sat at the edge of the board and concluded that we were playing for one another's soul. He walked restlessly around the room two or three times and then, as usual, gave us a parting shot. "I should think you'd go crazy," he said, "cooped up with one another like this, night after night. Come on, Ruth. I'm going to bed."

That night, I dreamed about Lawrence. I saw his plain face magnified into ugliness, and when I woke in the morning, I felt sick, as if I had suffered a great spiritual loss while I slept, like the loss of courage and heart. It was foolish to let myself be troubled by my brother. I needed a vacation. I needed to relax. At school, we live in one of the dormitories, we eat at the house table, and we never get away. I not only teach English winter and summer but I work in the principal's office and fire the pistol at track meets. I needed to get away from this and from every other form of anxiety, and I decided to avoid my brother. Early that day, I took Helen and the children sailing, and we stayed out until suppertime. The next day, we went on a picnic. Then I had to go to New York for a day, and when I got back, there was the costume dance at the boat club. Lawrence wasn't going to this, and it's a party where I always have a wonderful time.

The invitations that year said to come as you wish you were. After several conversations, Helen and I had decided what to wear. The thing she most wanted to be again, she said, was a bride, and so she decided to wear her wedding dress. I thought this was a good choice—sincere, lighthearted, and inexpensive. Her choice influenced mine, and I decided to wear an old football uniform. Mother decided to go as Jenny Lind, because there was an old Jenny Lind costume in the attic. The others decided to rent costumes, and when I went to New York, I got the clothes. Lawrence and Ruth didn't enter into any of this.

Helen was on the dance committee, and she spent most of Friday decorating the club. Diana and Chaddy and I went sailing. Most of the sailing that I do these days is in Manhasset, and I am used to setting a homeward course by the gasoline barge and the tin roofs of the boat shed, and it was a pleasure that afternoon, as we returned, to keep the bow on a white church spire in the village and to find even the inshore water green and clear. At the end of our sail, we stopped at the club to get Helen. The committee had been trying to give a submarine appearance to the ballroom, and the fact that they had nearly succeeded in accomplishing this illusion made Helen very happy. We drove back to Laud's Head. It had been a brilliant afternoon, but on the way home we could smell the east wind—the dark wind, as Lawrence would have said—coming in from the sea.

My wife, Helen, is thirty-eight, and her hair would be gray, I guess, if it were not dyed, but it is dyed an unobtrusive yellow—a faded color—and I think it becomes her. I mixed cocktails that night while she was dressing, and when I took a glass upstairs to her, I saw her for the first time since our marriage in her wedding dress. There would be no point in saying that she looked to me more beautiful than she did on our wedding day, but because I have grown older and have, I think, a greater depth of feeling, and because I could see in her face that night both youth and age, both her devotion to the young woman that she had been and the positions that she had yielded graciously to time, I think I have never been so deeply moved. I had already put on the football uniform, and the weight of it, the heaviness of the pants and the shoulder guards, had worked a change in me, as if in putting on these old clothes I had put off the reasonable anxieties and troubles of my life. It felt as if we had both returned to the years before our marriage, the years before the war.

The Collards had a big dinner party before the dance, and our family—excepting Lawrence and Ruth—went to this. We drove over to the club, through the fog, at about half past nine. The orchestra was playing a waltz. While I was checking my raincoat, someone hit me on the back. It was Chucky Ewing, and the funny thing was that Chucky had on a football uniform. This seemed comical as hell to both of us. We were laughing when we went down the hall to the dance floor. I stopped at the door to look at the party, and it was beautiful. The committee had hung fish nets around the sides and over the high ceiling. The nets on the ceiling were filled with colored balloons. The light was soft and uneven, and the people—our friends and neighbors—dancing in the soft light to "Three O'Clock in the Morning" made a pretty picture. Then I noticed the number of women dressed in white, and I realized that they, like Helen, were wearing wedding dresses. Patsy Hewitt and Mrs. Gear and the Lackland girl waltzed by, dressed as brides. Then Pep Talcott came over to where Chucky and I were standing. He was dressed to be Henry VIII, but he told us that the Auerbach twins and Henry Barrett and Dwight MacGregor were all wearing football uniforms, and that by the last count there were ten brides on the floor.

This coincidence, this funny coincidence, kept everybody laughing, and made this one of the most lighthearted parties we've ever had at the club. At first I thought that the women had planned with one another to wear wedding dresses, but the ones that I danced with said it was a coincidence and I'm sure that Helen had made her decision alone. Everything went smoothly for me until a little before midnight. I saw Ruth standing at the edge of the floor. She was wearing a long red dress. It was all wrong. It wasn't the spirit of the party at all. I danced with her, but no one cut in, and I was darned if I'd spend the rest of the night dancing with her and I asked her where Lawrence was. She said he was out on the dock, and I took her over to the bar and left her and went out to get Lawrence.

The east fog was thick and wet, and he was alone on the dock. He was not in costume. He had not even bothered to get himself up as a fisherman or a sailor. He looked particularly saturnine. The fog blew around us like a cold smoke. I wished that it had been a clear night, because the easterly fog seemed to play into my misanthropic brother's hands. And I knew that the buoys—the groaners and bells that we could hear then—would sound to him like half-human, half-drowned cries, although every sailor knows that buoys are necessary and reliable fixtures, and I knew that the foghorn at the lighthouse would mean wanderings and losses to him and that he could misconstrue the vivacity of the dance music. "Come on in, Tifty," I said, "and dance with your wife or get her some partners."

"Why should I?" he said. "Why should I?" And he walked to the window and looked in at the party. "Look at it," he said. "Look at that . . ."

Chucky Ewing had got hold of a balloon and was trying to organize a scrimmage line in the middle of the floor. The others were dancing a samba. And I knew that Lawrence was looking bleakly at the party as he had looked at the weather-beaten shingles on our house, as if he saw here an abuse and a distortion of time; as if in wanting to be brides and football players we exposed the fact that, the lights of youth having been put out in us, we had been unable to find other lights to go by and, destitute of faith and principle, had become foolish and sad. And that he was thinking this about so many kind and happy and generous people made me angry, made me feel for him such an unnatural abhorrence that I was ashamed, for he is my brother and a Pommeroy. I put my arm around his shoulders and tried to force him to come in, but he wouldn't.

I got back in time for the Grand March, and after the prizes had been given out for the best costumes, they let the balloons down. The room was hot, and someone opened the big doors onto the dock, and the easterly wind circled the room and went out, carrying across the dock and out onto the water most of the balloons. Chucky Ewing went running out after the balloons, and when he saw them pass the dock and settle on the water, he took off his football uniform and dove in. Then Eric Auerbach dove in and Lew Phillips dove in and I dove in, and you know how it is at a party after midnight when people start jumping into the water. We recovered most of the balloons and dried off and went on dancing, and we didn't get home until morning.

The next day was the day of the flower show. Mother and Helen and Odette all had entries. We had a pickup lunch, and Chaddy drove the women and children over to the show. I took a nap, and in the middle of the afternoon I got some trunks and a towel and, on leaving the house, passed Ruth in the laundry. She was washing clothes. I don't know why she should seem to have so much more work to do than anyone else, but she is always washing or ironing or mending clothes. She may have been taught, when she was young, to spend her time like this, or she may be at the mercy of an expiatory passion. She seems to scrub and iron with a penitential fervor, although I can't imagine what it is that she thinks she's done wrong. Her children were with her in the laundry. I offered to take them to the beach, but they didn't want to go.

It was late in August, and the wild grapes that grow profusely all over the island made the land wind smell of wine. There is a little grove of holly at the end of the path, and then you climb the dunes, where nothing grows but that coarse grass. I could hear the sea, and I remember thinking how Chaddy and I used to talk mystically about the sea. When we were young, we had decided that we could never live in the West because we would miss the sea. "It is very nice here," we used to say politely when we visited people in the mountains, "but we miss the Atlantic." We used to look down our noses at people from Iowa and Colorado who had been denied this revelation, and we scorned the Pacific. Now I could hear the waves, whose heaviness sounded like a reverberation, like a tumult, and it pleased me as it had pleased me when I was young, and it seemed to have a purgative force, as if it had cleared my memory of, among other things, the penitential image of Ruth in the laundry.

But Lawrence was on the beach. There he sat. I went in without speaking. The water was cold, and when I came out, I put on a shirt. I told him that I was going to walk up to Tanners Point, and he said that he would come with me. I tried to walk beside him. His legs are no longer than mine, but he always likes to stay a little ahead of his companion. Walking along behind him, looking at his bent head and his shoulders, I wondered what he could make of that landscape.

There were the dunes and cliffs, and then, where they declined, there were some fields that had begun to turn from green to brown and yellow. The fields were used for pasturing sheep, and I guess Lawrence would have noticed that the soil was eroded and that the sheep would accelerate this decay. Beyond the fields there are a few coastal farms, with square and pleasant buildings, but Lawrence could have pointed out the hard lot of an island farmer. The sea, at our other side, was the open sea. We always tell guests that there, to the east, lies the coast of Portugal, and for Lawrence it would be an easy step from the coast of Portugal to the tyranny in Spain. The waves broke with a noise like a "hurrah, hurrah, hurrah," but to Lawrence they would say *"Vale, vale."* I suppose it would have occurred to his baleful and incisive mind that the coast was terminal moraine, the edge of the prehistoric world, and it must have occurred to him that we walked along the edge of the known world in spirit as much as in fact. If he should otherwise have overlooked this, there were some Navy planes bombing an uninhabited island to remind him.

That beach is a vast and preternaturally clean and simple landscape. It is like a piece of the moon. The surf had pounded the floor solid, so it was easy walking, and everything left on the sand had been twice changed by the waves. There was the spine of a shell, a broomstick, part of a bottle and part of a brick, both of them milled and broken until they were nearly unrecognizable, and I suppose Lawrence's sad frame of mind—for he kept his head down—went from one broken thing to another. The company of his pessimism began to infuriate me, and I caught up with him and put a hand on his shoulder. "It's only a summer day, Tifty," I said. "It's only a summer day. What's the matter? Don't you like it here?"

"I don't like it here," he said blandly, without raising his eyes. "I'm going to sell my equity in the house to Chaddy. I didn't expect to have a good time. The only reason I came back was to say goodbye."

I let him get ahead again and I walked behind him, looking at his shoulders and thinking of all the goodbyes he had made. When Father drowned, he went to church and said goodbye to Father. It was only three years later that he concluded that Mother was frivolous and said goodbye to her. In his freshman year at college, he had been very good friends with his roommate, but the man drank too much, and at the beginning of the spring term Lawrence changed roommates and said goodbye to his friend. When he had been in college for two years, he concluded that the atmosphere was too sequestered and he said goodbye to Yale. He enrolled at Columbia and got his law degree there, but he found his first employer dishonest, and at the end of six months he said goodbye to a good job. He married Ruth in City Hall and said goodbye to the Protestant Episcopal Church; they went to live on a back street in Tuckahoe and said goodbye to the middle class. In 1938, he went to Washington to work as a government lawyer, saying goodbye to private enterprise, but after eight months in Washington he concluded that the Roosevelt administration was sentimental and he said goodbye to it. They left Washington for a suburb of Chicago, where he said goodbye to his neighbors, one by one, on counts of drunkenness, boorishness, and stupidity. He said goodbye to Chicago and went to Kansas; he said goodbye to Kansas and went to Cleveland. Now he had said goodbye to Cleveland and come East again, stopping at Laud's Head long enough to say goodbye to the sea.

It was elegiac and it was bigoted and narrow, it mistook circumspection for character, and I wanted to help him. "Come out of it," I said. "Come out of it, Tifty."

"Come out of what?"

"Come out of this gloominess. Come out of it. It's only a summer day. You're spoiling your own good time and you're spoiling everyone else's. We need a vacation, Tifty. I need one. I need to rest. We all do. And you've made everything tense and unpleasant. I only have two weeks in the year. Two weeks. I need to have a good time and so do all the others. We need to rest. You think that your pessimism is an advantage, but it's nothing but an unwillingness to grasp realities."

"What are the realities?" he said. "Diana is a foolish and a promiscuous woman. So is Odette. Mother is an alcoholic. If she doesn't discipline herself, she'll be in a hospital in a year or two. Chaddy is dishonest. He always has been. The house is going to fall into the sea." He looked at me and added, as an afterthought, "You're a fool."

"You're a gloomy son of a bitch," I said. "You're a gloomy son of a bitch."

"Get your fat face out of mine," he said. He walked along.

Then I picked up a root and, coming at his back—although I have never hit a man from the back before—I swung the root, heavy with sea water, behind me, and the momentum sped my arm and I gave him, my brother, a blow on the head that forced him to his knees on the sand, and I saw the blood come out and begin to darken his hair. Then I wished that he was dead, dead and about to be buried, not buried but about to be buried, because I did not want to be denied ceremony and decorum in putting him away, in putting him out of my consciousness, and I saw the rest of us—Chaddy and Mother and Diana and Helen—in mourning in the house on Belvedere Street that was torn down twenty years ago, greeting our guests and our relatives at the door and answering their mannerly condolences with mannerly grief. Nothing decorous was lacking so that even if he had been murdered on a beach, one would feel before the tiresome ceremony ended that he had come into the winter of his life and that it was a law of nature, and a beautiful one, that Tifty should be buried in the cold, cold ground.

He was still on his knees. I looked up and down. No one had seen us. The naked beach, like a piece of the moon, reached to invisibility. The spill of a wave, in a glancing run, shot up to where he knelt. I would still have liked to end him, but now I had begun to act like two men, the murderer and the Samaritan. With a swift roar, like hollowness made sound, a white wave reached him and encircled him, boiling over his shoulders, and I held him against the undertow. Then I led him to a higher place. The blood had spread all through his hair, so that it looked black. I took off my shirt and tore it to bind up his head. He was conscious, and I didn't think he was badly hurt. He didn't speak. Neither did I. Then I left him there.

I walked a little way down the beach and turned to watch him, and I was thinking of my own skin then. He had got to his feet and he seemed steady. The daylight was still clear, but on the sea wind fumes of brine were blowing in like a light fog, and when I had walked a little way from him, I could hardly see his dark figure in this obscurity. All down the beach I could see the heavy salt air blowing in. Then I turned my back on him, and as I got near to the house, I went swimming again, as I seem to have done after every encounter with Lawrence that summer.

When I got back to the house, I lay down on the terrace. The others came back. I could hear Mother defaming the flower arrangements that had won prizes. None of ours had won anything. Then the house quieted, as it always does at that hour. The children went into the kitchen to get supper and the others went upstairs to bathe. Then I heard Chaddy making cocktails, and the conversation about the flower show judges was resumed. Then Mother cried, "Tifty! Tifty! Oh, Tifty!"

He stood in the door, looking half dead. He had taken off the bloody bandage and he held it in his hand. "My brother did this," he said. "My brother did it. He hit me with a stone—something—on the beach." His voice broke with self-pity. I thought he was going to cry. No one else spoke. "Where's Ruth?" he cried. "Where's Ruth? Where in hell is Ruth? I want her to start packing. I don't have any more time to waste here. I have important things to do. I have *important* things to do." And he went up the stairs.

They left for the mainland the next morning, taking the six-o'clock boat. Mother got up to say goodbye, but she was the only one, and it is a harsh and an easy scene to imagine—the matriarch and the changeling, looking at each other with a dismay that would seem like the powers of love reversed. I heard the children's voices and the car go down the drive, and I got up and went to the window, and what a morning that was! Jesus, what a morning! The wind was northerly. The air was clear. In the early heat, the roses in the garden smelled like strawberry jam. While I was dressing, I heard the boat whistle, first the warning signal and then the double blast, and I could see the good people on the top deck drinking coffee out of fragile paper cups, and Lawrence at the bow, saying to the sea, *"Thalassa, thalassa,"* while his timid and unhappy children watched the creation from the encirclement of their mother's arms. The buoys would toll mournfully for Lawrence, and while the grace of the light would make it an exertion not to throw out your arms and swear exultantly, Lawrence's eyes would trace the black sea as it fell astern; he would think of the bottom, dark and strange, where full fathom five our father lies.

Oh, what can you do with a man like that? What can you do? How can you dissuade his eye in a crowd from seeking out the cheek with acne, the infirm hand; how can you teach him to respond to the inestimable greatness of the race, the harsh surface beauty of life; how can you put his finger for him on the obdurate truths before which fear and horror are powerless? The sea that morning was iridescent and dark. My wife and my sister were swimming—Diana and Helen—and I saw their uncovered heads, black and gold in the dark water. I saw them come out and I saw that they were naked, unshy, beautiful, and full of grace, and I watched the naked women walk out of the sea.

John Cheever

The Country Husband

To begin at the beginning, the airplane from Minneapolis in which Francis Weed was traveling East ran into heavy weather. The sky had been a hazy blue, with the clouds below the plane lying so close together that nothing could be seen of the earth. Then mist began to form outside the windows, and they flew into a white cloud of such density that it reflected the exhaust fires. The color of the cloud darkened to gray, and the plane began to rock. Francis had been in heavy weather before, but he had never been shaken up so much. The man in the seat beside him pulled a flask out of his pocket and took a drink. Francis smiled at his neighbor, but the man looked away; he wasn't sharing his painkiller with anyone. The plane had begun to drop and flounder wildly. A child was crying. The air in the cabin was overheated and stale, and Francis' left foot went to sleep. He read a little from a paper book that he had bought at the airport, but the violence of the storm divided his attention. It was black outside the ports. The exhaust fires blazed and shed sparks in the dark, and, inside, the shaded lights, the stuffiness, and the window curtains gave the cabin an atmosphere of intense and misplaced domesticity. Then the lights flickered and went out. "You know what I've always wanted to do?" the man beside Francis said suddenly. "I've always wanted to buy a farm in New Hampshire and raise beef cattle." The stewardess announced that they were going to make an emergency landing. All but the child saw in their minds the spreading wings of the Angel of Death. The pilot could be heard singing faintly, "I've got sixpence, jolly, jolly sixpence. I've got sixpence to last me all my life . . ." There was no other sound.

The loud groaning of the hydraulic valves swallowed up the pilot's song, and there was a shrieking high in the air, like automobile brakes, and the plane hit flat on its belly in a cornfield and shook them so violently that an old man up forward howled, "Me kidneys! Me kidneys!" The stewardess flung open the door, and someone opened an emergency door at the back, letting in the sweet noise of their continuing mortality—the idle splash and smell of heavy rain. Anxious for their lives, they filed out of the doors and scattered over the cornfield in all directions, praying that the thread would hold. It did. Nothing happened. When it was clear that the plane would not burn or explode, the crew and stewardess gathered the passengers together and led them to the shelter of a barn. They were not far from Philadelphia, and in a little while a string of taxis took them into the city. "It's just like the Marne," someone said, but there was surprisingly little relaxation of that suspiciousness with which many Americans regard their fellow-travelers.

In Philadelphia, Francis Weed got a train to New York. At the end of that journey, he crossed the city and caught, just as it was about to pull out, the commuting train that he took five nights a week to his home in Shady Hill.

He sat with Trace Bearden. "You know, I was in that plane that just crashed outside Philadelphia," he said. "We came down in a field . . ." He had traveled faster than the newspapers or the rain, and the weather in New York was sunny and mild. It was a day in late September, as fragrant and shapely as an apple. Trace listened to the story, but how could he get excited? Francis had no powers that would let him recreate a brush with death—particularly in the atmosphere of a commuting train, journeying through a sunny countryside where already, in the slum gardens, there were signs of harvest. Trace picked up his newspaper, and Francis was left alone with his thoughts. He said good night to Trace on the platform at Shady Hill and drove in his second-hand Volkswagen up to the Blenhollow neighborhood, where he lived.

The Weeds' Dutch Colonial house was larger than it appeared to be from the driveway. The living room was spacious and divided like Gaul into three parts. Around an ell to the left as one entered from the vestibule was the long table, laid for six, with candles and a bowl of fruit in the center. The sounds and smells that came from the open kitchen door were appetizing, for Julia Weed was a good cook. The largest part of the living room centered around a fireplace. On the right were some bookshelves and a piano. The room was polished and tranquil, and from the windows that opened to the west there was some late summer sunlight, brilliant and as clear as water. Nothing here was neglected; nothing had not been burnished. It was not the kind of household where, after prying open a stuck cigarette box, you would find an old shirt button and a tarnished nickel. The hearth was swept, the roses on the piano were reflected in the polish of the broad top, and there was an album of Schubert waltzes on the rack. Louisa Weed, a pretty girl of nine, was looking out the western windows. Her younger brother Henry was standing beside her. Her still younger brother, Toby, was studying the figures of some tonsured monks drinking beer on the polished brass of the wood box. Francis, taking off his hat and putting down his paper, was not consciously pleased with the scene; he was not that reflective. It was his element, his creation, and he returned to it with that sense of lightness and strength with which any creature returns to its home. "Hi, everybody," he said. "The plane from Minneapolis . . ."

Nine times out of ten, Francis would be greeted with affection, but tonight the children are absorbed in their own antagonisms. Francis has not finished his sentence about the plane crash before Henry plants a kick in Louisa's behind. Louisa swings around, saying, "*Damn* you!" Francis makes the mistake of scolding Louisa for bad language before he punishes Henry. Now Louisa turns on her father and accuses him of favoritism. Henry is always right; she is persecuted and lonely; her lot is hopeless. Francis turns to his son, but the boy has justification for the kick—she hit him first; she hit him on the ear, which is dangerous. Louisa agrees with this passionately. She hit him on the ear, and she *meant* to hit him on the ear, because he messed up her china collection. Henry says that this is a lie. Little Toby turns away from the wood box to throw in some evidence for Louisa. Henry claps his hand over little Toby's mouth. Francis separates the two boys but accidentally pushes Toby into the wood box. Toby begins to cry. Louisa is already crying. Just then, Julia Weed comes into that part of the room where the table is laid. She is a pretty, intelligent woman, and the white in her hair is premature. She does not seem to notice the fracas. "Hello, darling," she says serenely to Francis. "Wash your hands, everyone. Dinner is ready." She strikes a match and lights the six candles in this vale of tears.

This simple announcement, like the war cries of the Scottish chieftains, only refreshes the ferocity of the combatants. Louisa gives Henry a blow on the shoulder.

Henry, although he seldom cries, has pitched nine innings and is tired. He bursts into tears. Little Toby discovers a splinter in his hand and begins to howl. Francis says loudly that he has been in a plane crash and that he is tired. Julia appears again, from the kitchen, and, still ignoring the chaos, asks Francis to go upstairs and tell Helen that everything is ready. Francis is happy to go; it is like getting back to headquarters company. He is planning to tell his oldest daughter about the airplane crash, but Helen is lying on her bed reading a *True Romance* magazine, and the first thing Francis does is to take the magazine from her hand and remind Helen that he has forbidden her to buy it. She did not buy it, Helen replies. It was given to her by her best friend, Bessie Black. Everybody reads *True Romance.* Bessie Black's father reads *True Romance.* There isn't a girl in Helen's class who doesn't read *True Romance.* Francis expresses his detestation of the magazine and then tells her that dinner is ready—although from the sounds downstairs it doesn't seem so. Helen follows him down the stairs. Julia has seated herself in the candlelight and spread a napkin over her lap. Neither Louisa nor Henry has come to the table. Little Toby is still howling, lying face down on the floor. Francis speaks to him gently. "Daddy was in a plane crash this afternoon, Toby. Don't you want to hear about it?" Toby goes on crying. "If you don't come to the table now, Toby," Francis says, "I'll have to send you to bed without any supper." The little boy rises, gives him a cutting look, flies up the stairs to his bedroom, and slams the door. "Oh dear," Julia says, and starts to go after him. Francis says that she will spoil him. Julia says that Toby is ten pounds underweight and has to be encouraged to eat. Winter is coming, and he will spend the cold months in bed unless he has his dinner. Julia goes upstairs. Francis sits down at the table with Helen. Helen is suffering from the dismal feeling of having read too intently on a fine day, and she gives her father and the room a jaded look. She doesn't understand about the plane crash, because there wasn't a drop of rain in Shady Hill.

Julia returns with Toby, and they all sit down and are served. "Do I have to look at that big, fat slob?" Henry says, of Louisa. Everybody but Toby enters into this skirmish, and it rages up and down the table for five minutes. Toward the end, Henry puts his napkin over his head and, trying to eat that way, spills spinach all over his shirt. Francis asks Julia if the children couldn't have their dinner earlier. Julia's guns are loaded for this. She can't cook two dinners and lay two tables. She paints with lightning strokes that panorama of drudgery in which her youth, her beauty, and her wit have been lost. Francis says that he must be understood; he was nearly killed in an airplane crash, and he doesn't like to come home every night to a battlefield. Now Julia is deeply committed. Her voice trembles. He doesn't come home every night to a battlefield. The accusation is stupid and mean. Everything was tranquil until he arrived. She stops speaking, puts down her knife and fork, and looks into her plate as if it is a gulf. She begins to cry. "Poor Mummy!" Toby says, and when Julia gets up from the table, drying her tears with a napkin, Toby goes to her side. "Poor Mummy," he says. "Poor Mummy!" And they climb the stairs together. The other children drift away from the battlefield, and Francis goes into the back garden for a cigarette and some air.

It was a pleasant garden, with walks and flower beds and places to sit. The sunset had nearly burned out, but there was still plenty of light. Put into a thoughtful mood by the crash and the battle, Francis listened to the evening sounds of Shady Hill.

"Varmints! Rascals!" old Mr. Nixon shouted to the squirrels in his bird-feeding station. "Avaunt and quit my sight!" A door slammed. Someone was playing tennis on the Babcocks' court; someone was cutting grass. Then Donald Goslin, who lived at the comer, began to play the "Moonlight Sonata." He did this nearly every night. He threw the tempo out the window and played it *rubato* from beginning to end, like an outpouring of tearful petulance, lonesomeness, and self-pity—of everything it was Beethoven's greatness not to know. The music rang up and down the street beneath the trees like an appeal for love, for tenderness, aimed at some lonely housemaid—some fresh-faced, homesick girl from Galway, looking at old snapshots in her third-floor room. "Here, Jupiter, here, Jupiter," Francis called to the Mercers' retriever. Jupiter crashed through the tomato vines with the remains of a felt hat in his mouth.

Jupiter was an anomaly. His retrieving instincts and his high spirits were out of place in Shady Hill. He was as black as coal, with a long, alert, intelligent, rake-hell face. His eyes gleamed with mischief, and he held his head high. It was the fierce, heavily collared dog's head that appears in heraldry, in tapestry, and that used to appear on umbrella handles and walking sticks. Jupiter went where he pleased, ransacking wastebaskets, clotheslines, garbage pails, and shoe bags. He broke up garden parties and tennis matches, and got mixed up in the processional at Christ Church on Sunday, barking at the men in red dresses. He crashed through old Mr. Nixon's rose garden two or three times a day, cutting a wide swath through the Condesa de Sastagos, and as soon as Donald Goslin lighted his barbecue fire on Thursday nights, Jupiter would get the scent. Nothing the Goslins did could drive him away. Sticks and stones and rude commands only moved him to the edge of the terrace, where he remained, with his gallant and heraldic muzzle, waiting for Donald Goslin to turn his back and reach for the salt. Then he would spring onto the terrace, lift the steak lightly off the fire, and run away with the Goslins' dinner. Jupiter's days were numbered. The Wrightsons' German gardener or the Farquarsons' cook would soon poison him. Even old Mr. Nixon might put some arsenic in the garbage that Jupiter loved. "Here, Jupiter, Jupiter!" Francis called, but the dog pranced off, shaking the hat in his white teeth. Looking in at the windows of his house, Francis saw that Julia had come down and was blowing out the candles.

Julia and Francis Weed went out a great deal. Julia was well liked and gregarious, and her love of parties sprang from a most natural dread of chaos and loneliness. She went through her morning mail with real anxiety, looking for invitations, and she usually found some, but she was insatiable, and if she had gone out seven nights a week, it would not have cured her of a reflective look—the look of someone who hears distant music—for she would always suppose that there was a more brilliant party somewhere else. Francis limited her to two week-night parties, putting a flexible interpretation on Friday, and rode through the weekend like a dory in a gale. The day after the airplane crash, the Weeds were to have dinner with the Farquarsons.

Francis got home late from town, and Julia got the sitter while he dressed, and then hurried him out of the house. The party was small and pleasant, and Francis settled down to enjoy himself. A new maid passed the drinks. Her hair was dark, and her face was round and pale and seemed familiar to Francis. He had not developed his memory as a sentimental faculty. Wood smoke, lilac, and other such perfumes did not stir him, and his memory was something like his appendix—a vestigial repository. It was not his limitation at all to be unable to escape the past; it was perhaps his limitation that he had escaped it so successfully. He might have seen the maid at other parties, he might have seen her taking a walk on Sunday afternoons, but in either case he would not be searching his memory now. Her face was, in a wonderful way, a moon face—Norman or Irish—but it was not beautiful enough to account for his feeling that he had seen her before, in circumstances that he ought to be able to remember. He asked Nellie Farquarson who she was. Nellie said that the maid had come through an agency, and that her home was Trénon, in Normandy—a small place with a church and a restaurant that Nellie had once visited. While Nellie talked on about her travels abroad, Francis realized where he had seen the woman before. It had been at the end of the war. He had left a replacement depot with some other men and taken a three-day pass in Trénon. On their second day, they had walked out to a crossroads to see the public chastisement of a young woman who had lived with the German commandant during the Occupation.

It was a cool morning in the fall. The sky was overcast, and poured down onto the dirt crossroads a very discouraging light. They were on high land and could see how like one another the shapes of the clouds and the hills were as they stretched off toward the sea. The prisoner arrived sitting on a three-legged stool in a farm cart. She stood by the cart while the mayor read the accusation and the sentence. Her head was bent and her face was set in that empty half smile behind which the whipped soul is suspended. When the mayor was finished, she undid her hair and let it fall across her back. A little man with a gray mustache cut off her hair with shears and dropped it on the ground. Then, with a bowl of soapy water and a straight razor, he shaved her skull clean. A woman approached and began to undo the fastening of her clothes, but the prisoner pushed her aside and undressed herself. When she pulled her chemise over her head and threw it on the ground, she was naked. The women jeered; the men were still. There was no change in the falseness or the plaintiveness of the prisoner's smile. The cold wind made her white skin rough and hardened the nipples of her breasts. The jeering ended gradually, put down by the recognition of their common humanity. One woman spat on her, but some inviolable grandeur in her nakedness lasted through the ordeal. When the crowd was quiet, she turned—she had begun to cry—and, with nothing on but a pair of worn black shoes and stockings, walked down the dirt road alone away from the village. The round white face had aged a little, but there was no question but that the maid who passed his cocktails and later served Francis his dinner was the woman who had been punished at the crossroads.

The war seemed now so distant and that world where the cost of partisanship had been death or torture so long ago, Francis had lost track of the men who had been with him in Vésey. He could not count on Julia's discretion. He could not tell anyone. And if he had told the story now, at the dinner table, it would have been a social as well as a human error. The people in the Farquarsons' living room seemed united in their tacit claim that there had been no past, no war—that there was no danger or trouble in the world. In the recorded history of human arrangements, this extraordinary meeting would have fallen into place, but the atmosphere of Shady Hill made the memory unseemly and impolite. The prisoner withdrew after passing the coffee, but the encounter left Francis feeling languid; it had opened his memory and his senses, and left them dilated. He and Julia drove home when the party ended, and Julia went into the house. Francis stayed in the car to take the sitter home.

Expecting to see Mrs. Henlein, the old lady who usually stayed with the children, he was surprised when a young girl opened the door and came out onto the lighted stoop. She stayed in the light to count her textbooks. She was frowning and beautiful. Now, the world is full of beautiful young girls, but Francis saw here the difference between beauty and perfection. All those endearing flaws, moles, birthmarks, and healed wounds were missing, and he experienced in his consciousness that moment when music breaks glass, and felt a pang of recognition as strange, deep, and wonderful as anything in his life. It hung from her frown, from an impalpable darkness in her face—a look that impressed him as a direct appeal for love. When she had counted her books, she came down the steps and opened the car door. In the light, he saw that her cheeks were wet. She got in and shut the door.

"You're new," Francis said.

"Yes. Mrs. Henlein is sick: I'm Anne Murchison."

"Did the children give you any trouble?"

"Oh, no, no." She turned and smiled at him unhappily in the dim dashboard light. Her light hair caught on the collar of her jacket, and she shook her head to set it loose.

"You've been crying."

"Yes."

"I hope it was nothing that happened in our house."

"No, no, it was nothing that happened in your house." Her voice was bleak. "It's no secret. Everybody in the village knows. Daddy's an alcoholic, and he just called me from some saloon and gave me a piece of his mind. He thinks I'm immoral. He called just before Mrs. Weed came back."

"I'm sorry."

"Oh, *Lord!*" She gasped and began to cry. She turned toward Francis, and he took her in his arms and let her cry on his shoulder. She shook in his embrace, and this movement accentuated his sense of the fineness of her flesh and bone. The layers of their clothing felt thin, and when her shuddering began to diminish, it was so much like a paroxysm of love that Francis lost his head and pulled her roughly against him. She drew away. "I live on Belleview Avenue," she said. "You go down Lansing Street to the railroad bridge."

"All right." He started the car.

"You turn left at that traffic light. . . . Now you turn right here and go straight on toward the tracks."

The road Francis took brought him out of his own neighborhood, across the tracks, and toward the river, to a street where the near-poor lived, in houses whose peaked gables and trimmings of wooden lace conveyed the purest feelings of pride and romance, although the houses themselves could not have offered much privacy or comfort, they were all so small. The street was dark, and, stirred by the grace and beauty of the troubled girl, he seemed, in turning in to it, to have come into the deepest part of some submerged memory. In the distance, he saw a porch light burning. It was the only one, and she said that the house with the light was where she lived. When he stopped the car, he could see beyond the porch light into a dimly lighted hallway with an old-fashioned clothes tree. "Well, here we are," he said, conscious that a young man would have said something different.

She did not move her hands from the books, where they were folded, and she turned and faced him. There were tears of lust in his eyes. Determinedly—not sadly—he opened the door on his side and walked around to open hers. He took her free hand, letting his fingers in between hers, climbed at her side the two concrete steps, and went up a narrow walk through a front garden where dahlias, marigolds, and roses—things that had withstood the light frosts—still bloomed, and then she turned and kissed him swiftly. Then she crossed the porch and shut the door. The porch light went out, then the light in the hall. A second later, a light went on upstairs at the side of the house, shining into a tree that was still covered with leaves. It took her only a few minutes to undress and get into bed, and then the house was dark.

Julia was asleep when Francis got home. He opened a second window and got into bed to shut his eyes on that night, but as soon as they were shut—as soon as he had dropped off to sleep—the girl entered his mind, moving with perfect freedom through its shut doors and filling chamber after chamber with her light, her perfume, and the music of her voice. He was crossing the Atlantic with her on the old *Mauretania* and, later, living with her in Paris. When he woke from his dream, he got up and smoked a cigarette at the open window. Getting back into bed, he cast around in his mind for something he desired to do that would injure no one, and he thought of skiing. Up through the dimness in his mind rose the image of a mountain deep in snow. It was late in the day. Wherever his eyes looked, he saw broad and heartening things. Over his shoulder, there was a snow-filled valley, rising into wooded hills where the trees dimmed the whiteness like a sparse coat of hair. The cold deadened all sound but the loud, iron clanking of the lift machinery. The light on the trails was blue, and it was harder than it had been a minute or two earlier to pick the turns, harder to judge—now that the snow was all deep blue—the crust, the ice, the bare spots, and the deep piles of dry powder. Down the mountain he swung, matching his speed against the contours of a slope that had been formed in the first ice age, seeking with ardor some simplicity of feeling and circumstance. Night fell then, and he drank a Martini with some old friend in a dirty country bar.

In the morning, Francis' snow-covered mountain was gone, and he was left with his vivid memories of Paris and the *Mauretania.* He had been bitten gravely. He washed his body, shaved his jaws, drank his coffee, and missed the seven-thirty-one. The train pulled out just as he brought his car to the station, and the longing he felt for the coaches as they drew stubbornly away from him reminded him of the humors of love. He waited for the eight-two, on what was now an empty platform. It was a clear morning; the morning seemed thrown like a gleaming bridge of light over his mixed affairs. His spirits were feverish and high. The image of the girl seemed to put him into a relationship to the world that was mysterious and enthralling. Cars were beginning to fill up the parking lot, and he noticed that those that had driven down from the high land above Shady Hill were white with hoarfrost. The first clear sign of autumn thrilled him. An express train—a night train from Buffalo or Albany—came down the tracks between the platforms, and he saw that the roofs of the foremost cars were covered with a skin of ice. Struck by the miraculous physicalness of everything, he smiled at the passengers in the dining car, who could be seen eating eggs and wiping their mouths with napkins as they traveled. The sleeping car compartments, with their soiled bed linen, trailed through the fresh morning like a string of rooming-house windows. Then he saw an extraordinary thing: at one of the bedroom windows sat an unclothed woman of exceptional beauty, combing her golden hair. She passed like an apparition through Shady Hill, combing and combing her hair, and Francis followed her with his eyes until she was out of sight. Then old Mrs. Wrightson joined him on the platform and began to talk.

"Well, I guess you must be surprised to see me here the third morning in a row," she said, "but because of my window curtains I'm becoming a regular commuter. The curtains I bought on Monday, I returned Tuesday, and the curtains I bought on Tuesday I'm returning today. On Monday, I got exactly what I wanted—it's a wool tapestry with roses and birds—but when I got them home, I found they were the wrong length. Well, I exchanged them yesterday, and when I got them home, I found they were still the wrong length. Now I'm praying to high Heaven that the decorator will have them in the right length, because you know my house, you *know* my living room windows, and you can imagine what a problem they present. I don't know what to do with them."

"I know what to do with them," Francis said.

"What?"

"Paint them black on the inside, and shut up."

There was a gasp from Mrs. Wrightson, and Francis looked down at her to be sure that she knew he meant to be rude. She turned and walked away from him, so damaged in spirit that she limped. A wonderful feeling enveloped him, as if light were being shaken about him, and he thought again of Venus combing and combing her hair as she drifted through the Bronx. The realization of how many years had passed since he had enjoyed being deliberately impolite sobered him. Among his friends and neighbors, there were brilliant and gifted people—he saw that—but many of them, also, were bores and fools, and he had made the mistake of listening to them all with equal attention. He had confused a lack of discrimination with Christian love, and the confusion seemed general and destructive. He was grateful to the girl for this bracing sensation of independence. Birds were singing—cardinals and the last of the robins. The sky shone like enamel. Even the smell of ink from his morning paper honed his appetite for life, and the world that was spread out around him was plainly a paradise.

If Francis had believed in some hierarchy of love—in spirits armed with hunting bows, in the capriciousness of Venus and Eros—or even in magical potions, philtres, and stews, in scapulae and quarters of the moon, it might have explained his susceptibility and his feverish high spirits. The autumnal loves of middle age are well publicized, and he guessed that he was face to face with one of these, but there was not a trace of autumn in what he felt. He wanted to sport in the green woods, scratch where he itched, and drink from the same cup.

His secretary, Miss Rainey, was late that morning—she went to a psychiatrist three mornings a week—and when she came in, Francis wondered what advice a psychiatrist would have for him. But the girl promised to bring back into his life something like the sound of music. The realization that this music might lead him straight to a trial for statutory rape at the county courthouse collapsed his happiness. The photograph of his four children laughing into the camera on the beach at Gay Head reproached him. On the letterhead of his firm there was a drawing of the Laocoön and the figure of the priest and his sons in the coils of the snakes appeared to him to have the deepest meaning.

He had lunch with Pinky Trabert, who told him a couple of dirty stories. At a conversational level, the mores of his friends were robust and elastic, but he knew that the moral card house would come down on them all—on Julia and the children as well—if he got caught taking advantage of a baby-sitter. Looking back over the recent history of Shady Hill for some precedent, he found there was none. There was no turpitude; there had not been a divorce since he lived there; there had not even been a breath of scandal. Things seemed arranged with more propriety even than in the Kingdom of Heaven. After leaving Pinky, Francis went to a jeweler's and bought the girl a bracelet. How happy this clandestine purchase made him, how stuffy and comical the jeweler's clerks seemed, how sweet the woman who passed at his back smelled. On Fifth Avenue, passing Atlas with his shoulders bent under the weight of the world, Francis thought of the strenuousness of containing his physicalness within the patterns he had chosen.

He did not know when he would see the girl next. He had the bracelet in his inside pocket when he got home. Opening the door of his house, he found her in the hall. Her back was to him, and she turned when she heard the door close. Her smile was open and loving. Her perfection stunned him like a fine day—a day after a thunderstorm. He seized her and covered her lips with his, and she struggled but she did not have to struggle for long, because just then little Gertrude Flannery appeared from somewhere and said, "Oh, Mr. Weed. . ."

Gertrude was a stray. She had been born with a taste for exploration, and she did not have it in her to center her life with her affectionate parents. People who did not know the Flannerys concluded from Gertrude's behavior that she was the child of a bitterly divided family, where drunken quarrels were the rule. This was not true. The fact that little Gertrude's clothing was ragged and thin was her own triumph over her mother's struggle to dress her warmly and neatly. Garrulous, skinny, and unwashed, she drifted from house to house around the Blenhollow neighborhood, forming and breaking alliances based on an attachment to babies, animals, children her own age, adolescents, and sometimes adults. Opening your front door in the morning, you would find Gertrude sitting on your stoop. Going into the bathroom to shave, you would find Gertrude using the toilet. Looking into your son's crib, you would find it empty, and, looking further, you would find that Gertrude had pushed him in his baby carriage into the next village. She was helpful, pervasive, honest, hungry, and loyal. She never went home of her own choice. When the time to go arrived, she was indifferent to all its signs. "Go home, Gertrude," people could be heard saying in one house or another, night after night. "Go home, Gertrude. It's time for you to go home now, Gertrude." "You had better go home and get your supper, Gertrude." "I told you to go home twenty minutes ago, Gertrude." "Your mother will be worrying about you, Gertrude." "Go home, Gertrude, go home."

There are times when the lines around the human eye seem like shelves of eroded stone and when the staring eye itself strikes us with such a wilderness of animal feeling that we are at a loss. The look Francis gave the little girl was ugly and queer, and it frightened her. He reached into his pocket—his hands were shaking and took out a quarter. "Go home, Gertrude, go home, and don't tell anyone, Gertrude. Don't—" He choked and ran into the living room as Julia called down to him from upstairs to hurry and dress.

The thought that he would drive Anne Murchison home later that night ran like a golden thread through the events of the party that Francis and Julia went to, and he laughed uproariously at dull jokes, dried a tear when Mabel Mercer told him about the death of her kitten, and stretched, yawned, sighed, and grunted like any other man with a rendezvous at the back of his mind. The bracelet was in his pocket. As he sat talking, the smell of grass was in his nose, and he was wondering where he would park the car. Nobody lived in the old Parker mansion, and the driveway was used as a lovers' lane. Townsend Street was a dead end, and he could park there, beyond the last house. The old lane that used to connect Elm Street to the riverbanks was overgrown, but he had walked there with his children, and he could drive his car deep enough into the brushwoods to be concealed.

The Weeds were the last to leave the party, and their host and hostess spoke of their own married happiness while they all four stood in the hallway saying good night. "She's my girl," their host said, squeezing his wife. "She's my blue sky. After sixteen years, I still bite her shoulders. She makes me feel like Hannibal crossing the Alps."

The Weeds drove home in silence. Francis brought the car up the driveway and sat still, with the motor running. "You can put the car in the garage," Julia said as she got out. "I told the Murchison girl she could leave at eleven. Someone drove her home." She shut the door, and Francis sat in the dark. He would be spared nothing then, it seemed, that a fool was not spared: ravening lewdness, jealousy, this hurt to his feelings that put tears in his eyes, even scorn—for he could see clearly the image he now presented, his arms spread over the steering wheel and his head buried in them for love.

Francis had been a dedicated Boy Scout when he was young, and, remembering the precepts of his youth, he left his office early the next afternoon and played some round robin squash, but, with his body toned up by exercise and a shower, he realized that he might better have stayed at his desk. It was a frosty night when he got home. The air smelled sharply of change. When he stepped into the house, he sensed an unusual stir. The children were in their best clothes, and when Julia came down, she was wearing a lavender dress and her diamond sunburst. She explained the stir. Mr. Hubber was coming at seven to take their photograph for the Christmas card. She had put out Francis' blue suit and a tie with some color in it, because the picture was going to be in color this year. Julia was lighthearted at the thought of being photographed for Christmas. It was the kind of ceremony she enjoyed.

Francis went upstairs to change his clothes. He was tired from the day's work and tired with longing, and sitting on the edge of the bed had the effect of deepening his weariness. He thought of Anne Murchison, and the physical need to express himself instead of being restrained by the pink lamps on Julia's dressing table, engulfed him. He went to Julia's desk, took a piece of writing paper, and began to write on it. "Dear Anne, I love you, I love you, I love you . . ." No one would see the letter, and he used no restraint. He used phrases like "heavenly bliss," and "love nest." He salivated, sighed, and trembled. When Julia called him to come down, the abyss between his fantasy and the practical world opened so wide that he felt it affect the muscles of his heart.

Julia and the children were on the stoop, and the photographer and his assistant had set up a double battery of floodlights to show the family and the architectural beauty of the entrance to their house. People who had come home on a late train slowed their cars to see the Weeds being photographed for their Christmas card. A few waved and called to the family. It took half an hour of smiling and wetting their lips before Mr. Hubber was satisfied. The heat of the lights made an unfresh smell in the frosty air, and when they were turned off, they lingered on the retina of Francis' eyes.

Later that night, while Francis and Julia were drinking their coffee in the living room, the doorbell rang. Julia answered the door and let in Clayton Thomas. He had come to pay her for some theater tickets that she had given his mother some time ago, and that Helen Thomas had scrupulously insisted on paying for, though Julia had asked her not to. Julia invited him in to have a cup of coffee. "I won't have any coffee," Clayton said, "but I will come in for a minute." He followed her into the living room, said good evening to Francis, and sat awkwardly in a chair.

Clayton's father had been killed in the war, and the young man's fatherlessness surrounded him like an element. This may have been conspicuous in Shady Hill because the Thomases were the only family that lacked a piece; all the other marriages were intact and productive. Clayton was in his second or third year of college, and he and his mother lived alone in a large house, which she hoped to sell. Clayton had once made some trouble. Years ago, he had stolen some money and run away; he had got to California before they caught up with him. He was tall and homely, wore horn-rimmed glasses, and spoke in a deep voice.

"When do you go back to college, Clayton?" Francis asked.

"I'm not going back," Clayton said. "Mother doesn't have the money, and there's no sense in all this pretense. I'm going to get a job, and if we sell the house, we'll take an apartment in New York."

"Won't you miss Shady Hill?" Julia asked.

"No," Clayton said. "I don't like it."

"Why not?" Francis asked.

"Well, there's a lot here I don't approve of," Clayton said gravely. "Things like the club dances. Last Saturday night, I looked in toward the end and saw Mr. Granner trying to put Mrs. Minot into the trophy case. They were both drunk. I disapprove of so much drinking."

"It was Saturday night," Francis said.

"And all the dovecotes are phony," Clayton said. "And the way people clutter up their lives. I've thought about it a lot, and what seems to me to be really wrong with Shady Hill is that it doesn't have any future. So much energy is spent in perpetuating the place—in keeping out undesirables, and so forth—that the only idea of the future anyone has is just more and more commuting trains and more parties. I don't think that's healthy. I think people ought to be able to dream big dreams about the future. I think people ought to be able to dream great dreams."

"It's too bad you couldn't continue with college," Julia said.

"I wanted to go to divinity school," Clayton said.

"What's your church?" Francis asked.

"Unitarian, Theosophist, Transcendentalist, Humanist," Clayton said.

"Wasn't Emerson a transcendentalist?" Julia asked.

"I mean the English transcendentalists," Clayton said. "All the American transcendentalists were goops."

"What kind of job do you expect to get?" Francis asked.

"Well, I'd like to work for a publisher," Clayton said, "but everyone tells me there's nothing doing. But it's the kind of thing I'm interested in. I'm writing a long verse play about good and evil. Uncle Charlie might get me into a bank, and that would be good for me. I need the discipline. I have a long way to go in forming my character. I have some terrible habits. I talk too much. I think I ought to take vows of silence. I ought to try not to speak for a week, and discipline myself. I've thought of making a retreat at one of the Episcopalian monasteries, but I don't like Trinitarianism."

"Do you have any girl friends?" Francis asked.

"I'm engaged to be married," Clayton said. "Of course, I'm not old enough or rich enough to have my engagement observed or respected or anything, but I bought a simulated emerald for Anne Murchison with the money I made cutting lawns this summer. We're going to be married as soon as she finishes school."

Francis recoiled at the mention of the girl's name. Then a dingy light seemed to emanate from his spirit, showing everything—Julia, the boy, the chairs—in their true colorlessness. It was like a bitter turn of the weather.

"We're going to have a large family," Clayton said. "Her father's a terrible rummy, and I've had my hard times, and we want to have lots of children. Oh, she's wonderful, Mr. and Mrs. Weed, and we have so much in common. We like all the same things. We sent out the same Christmas card last year without planning it, and we both have an allergy to tomatoes, and our eyebrows grow together in the middle. Well, good night."

Julia went to the door with him. When she returned, Francis said that Clayton was lazy, irresponsible, affected, and smelly. Julia said that Francis seemed to be getting intolerant; the Thomas boy was young and should be given a chance. Julia had noticed other cases where Francis had been short-tempered. "Mrs. Wrightson has asked everyone in Shady Hill to her anniversary party but us," she said.

"I'm sorry, Julia."

"Do you know why they didn't ask us?"

"Why?"

"Because you insulted Mrs. Wrightson."

"Then you know about it?"

"June Masterson told me. She was standing behind you."

Julia walked in front of the sofa with a small step that expressed, Francis knew, a feeling of anger.

"I did insult Mrs. Wrightson, Julia, and I meant to. I've never liked her parties, and I'm glad she's dropped us."

"What about Helen?"

"How does Helen come into this?"

"Mrs. Wrightson's the one who decides who goes to the assemblies."

"You mean she can keep Helen from going to the dances?"

"Yes."

"I hadn't thought of that."

"Oh, I know you hadn't thought of it," Julia cried, thrusting hilt-deep into this chink of his armor. "And it makes me furious to see this kind of stupid thoughtlessness wreck everyone's happiness."

"I don't think I've wrecked anyone's happiness."

"Mrs. Wrightson runs Shady Hill and has run it for the last forty years. I don't know what makes you think that in a community like this you can indulge every impulse you have to be insulting, vulgar, and offensive."

"I have very good manners," Francis said, trying to give the evening a turn toward the light.

"Damn you, Francis Weed!" Julia cried, and the spit of her words struck him in the face. "I've worked hard for the social position we enjoy in this place, and I won't stand by and see you wreck it. You must have understood when you settled here that you couldn't expect to live like a bear in a cave."

"I've got to express my likes and dislikes."

"You can conceal your dislikes. You don't have to meet everything head on, like a child. Unless you're anxious to be a social leper. It's no accident that we get asked out a great deal. It's no accident that Helen has so many friends. How would you like to spend your Saturday nights at the movies? How would you like to spend your Sundays raking up dead leaves? How would you like it if your daughter spent the assembly nights sitting at her window, listening to the music from the club? How would you like it—" He did something then that was, after all, not so unaccountable, since her words seemed to raise up between them a wall so deadening that he gagged: He struck her full in the face. She staggered and then, a moment later, seemed composed. She went up the stairs to their room. She didn't slam the door. When Francis followed, a few minutes later, he found her packing a suitcase.

"Julia, I'm very sorry."

"It doesn't matter," she said. She was crying.

"Where do you think you're going?"

"I don't know. I just looked at a timetable. There's an eleven-sixteen into New York. I'll take that."

"You can't go, Julia."

"I can't stay. I know that."

"I'm sorry about Mrs. Wrightson, Julia, and I'm—"

"It doesn't matter about Mrs. Wrightson. That isn't the trouble."

"What is the trouble?"

"You don't love me."

"I do love you, Julia."

"No, you don't."

"Julia, I do love you, and I would like to be as we were—sweet and bawdy and dark—but now there are so many people."

"You hate me."

"I don't hate you, Julia."

"You have no idea of how much you hate me. I think it's subconscious. You don't realize the cruel things you've done."

"What cruel things, Julia?"

"The cruel acts your subconscious drives you to in order to express your hatred of me."

"What, Julia?"

"I've never complained."

"Tell me."

"You don't know what you're doing."

"Tell me."

"Your clothes."

"What do you mean?"

"I mean the way you leave your dirty clothes around in order to express your subconscious hatred of me."

"I don't understand."

"I mean your dirty socks and your dirty pajamas and your dirty underwear and your dirty shirts!" She rose from kneeling by the suitcase and faced him, her eves blazing and her voice ringing with emotion. "I'm talking about the fact that you've never learned to hang up anything. You just leave your clothes all over the floor where they drop, in order to humiliate me. You do it on purpose!" She fell on the bed, sobbing.

"Julia, darling!" he said, but when she felt his hand on her shoulder she got up.

"Leave me alone," she said. "I have to go." She brushed past him to the closet and came back with a dress. "I'm not taking any of the things you've given me," she said. "I'm leaving my pearls and the fur jacket."

"Oh, Julia!" Her figure, so helpless in its self-deceptions, bent over the suitcase made him nearly sick with pity. She did not understand how desolate her life would be without him. She didn't understand the hours that working women have to keep. She didn't understand that most of her friendships existed within the framework of their marriage, and that without this she would find herself alone. She didn't understand about travel, about hotels, about money. "Julia, I can't let you go! What you don't understand, Julia, is that you've come to be dependent on me."

She tossed her head back and covered her face with her hands. "Did you say that *I* was dependent on *you?*" she asked. "Is that what you said? And who is it that tells you what time to get up in the morning and when to go to bed at night? Who is it that prepares your meals and picks up your dirty clothes and invites your friends to dinner? If it weren't for me, your neckties would be greasy and your clothing would be full of moth holes. You were alone when I met you, Francis Weed, and you'll be alone when I leave. When Mother asked you for a list to send out invitations to our wedding, how many names did you have to give her? Fourteen!"

"Cleveland wasn't my home, Julia."

"And how many of your friends came to the church? Two!"

"Cleveland wasn't my home, Julia."

"Since I'm not taking the fur jacket," she said quietly, "you'd better put it back into storage. There's an insurance policy on the pearls that comes due in January. The name of the laundry and the maid's telephone number—all those things are in my desk. I hope you won't drink too much, Francis. I hope that nothing bad will happen to you. If you do get into serious trouble, you can call me."

"Oh, my darling, I can't let you go!" Francis said. "I can't let you go, Julia!" He took her in his arms.

"I guess I'd better stay and take care of you for a little while longer," she said.

Riding to work in the morning, Francis saw the girl walk down the aisle of the coach. He was surprised; he hadn't realized that the school she went to was in the city, but she was carrying books, she seemed to be going to school. His surprise delayed his reaction, but then he got up clumsily and stepped into the aisle. Several people had come between them, but he could see her ahead of him, waiting for someone to open the car door, and then, as the train swerved, putting out her hand to support herself as she crossed the platform into the next car. He followed her through that car and halfway through another before calling her name—"Anne! Anne!"—but she didn't turn. He followed her into still another car, and she sat down in an aisle seat. Coming up to her, all his feelings warm and bent in her direction, he put his hand on the back of her seat—even this touch warmed him—and, leaning down to speak to her, he saw that it was not Anne. It was an older woman wearing glasses. He went on deliberately into another car, his face red with embarrassment and the much deeper feeling of having his good sense challenged; for if he couldn't tell one person from another, what evidence was there that his life with Julia and the children had as much reality as his dreams of iniquity in Paris or the litter, the grass smell, and the cave-shaped trees in Lovers' Lane.

Late that afternoon, Julia called to remind Francis that they were going out for dinner. A few minutes later, Trace Bearden called. "Look, fellar," Trace said, "I'm calling for Mrs. Thomas. You know? Clayton, that boy of hers, doesn't seem able to get a job, and I wondered if you could help. If you'd call Charlie Bell—I know he's indebted to you—and say a good word for the kid, I think Charlie would—"

"Trace, I hate to say this," Francis said, "but I don't feel that I can do anything for that boy. The kid's worthless. I know it's a harsh thing to say, but it's a fact. Any kindness done for him would backfire in everybody's face. He's just a worthless kid, Trace, and there's nothing to be done about it. Even if we got him a job, he wouldn't be able to keep it for a week. I know that to be a fact. It's an awful thing, Trace, and I know it is, but instead of recommending that kid, I'd feel obliged to warn people against him—people who knew his father and would naturally want to step in and do something. I'd feel obliged to warn them. He's a thief . . ."

The moment this conversation was finished, Miss Rainey came in and stood by his desk. "I'm not going to be able to work for you any more, Mr. Weed," she said. "I can stay until the seventeenth if you need me, but I've been offered a whirlwind of a job, and I'd like to leave as soon as possible."

She went out leaving him to face alone the wickedness of what he had done to the Thomas boy. His children in their photograph laughed and laughed, glazed with all the bright colors of summer, and he remembered that they had met a bag-piper on the beach that day and he had paid the piper a dollar to play them a battle song of the Black Watch. The girl would be at the house when he got home. He would spend another evening among his kind neighbors, picking and choosing dead-end streets, cart tracks, and the driveways of abandoned houses. There was nothing to mitigate his feeling—nothing that laughter or a game of softball with the children would change—and, thinking back over the plane crash, the Farquarsons' new maid, and Anne Murchison's difficulties with her drunken father, he wondered how he could have avoided arriving at just where he was. He was in trouble. He had been lost once in his life, coming back from a trout stream in the north woods, and he had now the same bleak realization that no amount of cheerfulness or hopefulness or valor or perseverance could help him find, in the gathering dark, the path that he'd lost. He smelled the forest. The feeling of bleakness was intolerable, and he saw clearly that he had reached the point where he would have to make a choice.

He could go to a psychiatrist, like Miss Rainey; he could go to church and confess his lusts; he could go to a Danish massage parlor in the West Seventies that had been recommended by a salesman; he could rape the girl or trust that he would somehow be prevented from doing this; or he could get drunk. It was his life, his boat, and, like every other man, he was made to be the father of thousands, and what harm could there be in a tryst that would make them both feel more kindly toward the world? This was the wrong train of thought, and he came back to the first, the psychiatrist. He had the telephone number of Miss Rainey's doctor, and he called and asked for an immediate appointment. He was insistent with the doctor's secretary—it was his manner in business—and when she said that the doctor's schedule was full for the next few weeks, Francis demanded an appointment that day and was told to come at five.

The psychiatrist's office was in a building that was used mostly by doctors and dentists, and the hallways were filled with the candy smell of mouthwash and memories of pain. Francis' character had been formed upon a series of private resolves—resolves about cleanliness, about going off the high diving board or repeating any other feat that challenged his courage, about punctuality, honesty, and virtue. To abdicate the perfect loneliness in which he had made his most vital decisions shattered his concept of character and left him now in a condition that felt like shock. He was stupefied. The scene for his *miserere mei Deus* was, like the waiting room of so many doctors' offices, a crude token gesture toward the sweets of domestic bliss: a place arranged with antiques, coffee tables, potted plants, and etchings of snow covered bridges and geese in flight, although there were no children, no marriage bed, no stove, even, in this travesty of a house, where no one had ever spent the night and where the curtained windows looked straight onto a dark air shaft. Francis gave his name and address to a secretary and then saw, at the side of the room, a policeman moving toward him. "Hold it, hold it," the policeman said. "Don't move. Keep your hands where they are."

"I think it's all right, officer," the secretary began. "I think it will be—"

"Let's make sure," the policeman said, and he began to slap Francis' clothes, looking for what—pistols, knives, an ice-pick? Finding nothing, he went off, and the secretary began a nervous apology: "When you called on the telephone, Mr. Weed, you seemed very excited, and one of the doctor's patients has been threatening his life, and we have to be careful. If you want to go in now?" Francis pushed open a door connected to an electrical chime, and in the doctor's lair sat down heavily, blew his nose into a handkerchief, searched in his pockets for cigarettes, for matches, for something, and said hoarsely, with tears in his eyes, "I'm in love, Dr. Herzog."

It is a week or ten days later in Shady Hill. The seven-fourteen has come and gone, and here and there dinner is finished and the dishes are in the dishwashing machine. The village hangs, morally and economically, from a thread; but it hangs by its thread in the evening light. Donald Goslin has begun to worry the "Moonlight Sonata" again. *Marcato ma sempre pianissimo!* He seems to be wringing out a wet bath towel, but the housemaid does not heed him. She is writing a letter to Arthur Godfrey. In the cellar of his house, Francis Weed is building a coffee table. Dr. Herzog recommended woodwork as a therapy, and Francis finds some true consolation in the simple arithmetic involved and in the holy smell of new wood. Francis is happy. Upstairs, little Toby is crying, because he is tired. He puts off his cowboy hat, gloves, and fringed jacket, unbuckles the belt studded with gold and rubies, the silver bullets and holsters, slips off his suspenders, his checked shirt, and Levis, and sits on the edge of his bed to pull off his high boots. Leaving this equipment in a heap, he goes to the closet and takes his space suit off a nail. It is a struggle for him to get into the long tights, but he succeeds. He loops the magic cape over his shoulders and, climbing onto the footboard of his bed, he spreads his arms and flies the short distance to the floor, landing with a thump that is audible to everyone in the house but himself.

"Go home, Gertrude, go home," Mrs. Masterson says. "I told you to go home an hour ago, Gertrude. It's way past your suppertime, and your mother will be worried. Go home!" A door on the Babcocks' terrace flies open, and out comes Mrs. Babcock without any clothes on, pursued by her naked husband. (Their children are away at boarding school, and their terrace is screened by a hedge.) Over the terrace they go and in at the kitchen door, as passionate and handsome a nymph and satyr, as you will find on any wall in Venice. Cutting the last of the roses in her garden, Julia hears old Mr. Nixon shouting at the squirrels in his bird-feeding station. "Rapscallions! Varmints! Avaunt and quit my sight!" A miserable cat wanders into the garden, sunk in spiritual and physical discomfort. Tied to its head is a small straw hat—a doll's hat—and it is securely buttoned into a doll's dress, from the skirts of which protrudes its long, hairy tail. As it walks, it shakes its feet, as if it had fallen into water.

"Here, pussy, pussy, pussy!" Julia calls.

"Here, pussy, here, poor pussy!" But the cat gives her a skeptical look and stumbles away in its skirts. The last to come is Jupiter. He prances through the tomato vines, holding in his generous mouth the remains of an evening slipper. Then it is dark; it is a night where kings in golden suits ride elephants over the mountains.

JOHN CHEEVER

The Swimmer

It was one of those midsummer Sundays when everyone sits around saying, "I *drank* too much last night." You might have heard it whispered by the parishioners leaving the church, heard it from the lips of the priest himself, struggling with his cassock in the *vestiarium,* heard it from the golf links and the tennis courts, heard it from the wildlife preserve where the leader of the Audubon group was suffering from a terrible hangover. "I *drank* too much," said Donald Westerhazy. "We all *drank* too much," said Lucinda Merrill. "It must have been the wine," said Helen Westerhazy. "I *drank* too much of that claret."

This was at the edge of the Westerhazys' pool. The pool, fed by an artesian well with a high iron content, was a pale shade of green. It was a fine day. In the west there was a massive stand of cumulus cloud so like a city seen from a distance—from the bow of an approaching ship—that it might have had a name. Lisbon. Hackensack. The sun was hot. Neddy Merrill sat by the green water, one hand in it, one around a glass of gin. He was a slender man—he seemed to have the especial slenderness of youth—and while he was far from young he had slid down his banister that morning and given the bronze backside of Aphrodite on the hall table a smack, as he jogged down toward the smell of coffee in his dining room. He might have been compared to a summer's day, particularly the last hours of one, and while he lacked a tennis racket or a sail bag the impression was definitely one of youth, sport, and clement weather. He had been swimming and now he was breathing deeply, stertorously as if he could gulp into his lungs the components of that moment, the heat of the sun, the intenseness of his pleasure. It all seemed to flow into his chest. His own house stood in Bullet Park, eight miles to the south, where his four beautiful daughters would have had their lunch and might be playing tennis. Then it occurred to him that by taking a dogleg to the southwest he could reach his home by water.

His life was not confining and the delight he took in this observation could not be explained by its suggestion of escape. He seemed to see, with a cartographer's eye, that string of swimming pools, that quasi-subterranean stream that curved across the county. He had made a discovery, a contribution to modern geography; he would name the stream Lucinda after his wife. He was not a practical joker nor was he a fool but he was determinedly original and had a vague and modest idea of himself as a legendary figure. The day was beautiful and it seemed to him that a long swim might enlarge and celebrate its beauty.

He took off a sweater that was hung over his shoulders and dove in. He had an inexplicable contempt for men who did not hurl themselves into pools. He swam a choppy crawl, breathing either with every stroke or every fourth stroke and counting somewhere well in the back of his mind the one-two one-two of a flutter kick. It was not a serviceable stroke for long distances but the domestication of swimming had saddled the sport with some customs and in his part of the world a crawl was customary.

To be embraced and sustained by the light green water was less a pleasure, it seemed, than the resumption of a natural condition, and he would have liked to swim without trunks, but this was not possible, considering his project. He hoisted himself up on the far curb—he never used the ladder—and started across the lawn. When Lucinda asked where he was going he said he was going to swim home.

The only maps and charts he had to go by were remembered or imaginary but these were clear enough. First there were the Grahams, the Hammers, the Lears, the Howlands, and the Crosscups. He would cross Ditmar Street to the Bunkers and come, after a short portage, to the Levys, the Welchers, and the public pool in Lancaster. Then there were the Hallorans, the Sachses, the Biswangers, Shirley Adams, the Gilmartins, and the Clydes. The day was lovely, and that he lived in a world so generously supplied with water seemed like a clemency, a beneficence. His heart was high and he ran across the grass. Making his way home by an uncommon route gave him the feeling that he was a pilgrim, an explorer, a man with a destiny, and he knew that he would find friends all along the way; friends would line the banks of the Lucinda River.

He went through a hedge that separated the Westerhazys' land from the Grahams', walked under some flowering apple trees, passed the shed that housed their pump and filter, and came out at the Grahams' pool. "Why, Neddy," Mrs. Graham said, "what a marvelous surprise. I've been trying to get you on the phone all morning. Here, let me get you a drink." He saw then, like any explorer, that the hospitable customs and traditions of the natives would have to be handled with diplomacy if he was ever going to reach his destination. He did not want to mystify or seem rude to the Grahams nor did he have the time to linger there. He swam the length of their pool and joined them in the sun and was rescued, a few minutes later, by the arrival of two carloads of friends from Connecticut. During the uproarious reunions he was able to slip away. He went down by the front of the Grahams' house, stepped over a thorny hedge, and crossed a vacant lot to the Hammers'. Mrs. Hammer, looking up from her roses, saw him swim by although she wasn't quite sure who it was. The Lears heard him splashing past the open windows of their living room. The Howlands and the Crosscups were away. After leaving the Howlands' he crossed Ditmar Street and started for the Bunkers', where he could hear, even at that distance, the noise of a party.

The water refracted the sound of voices and laughter and seemed to suspend it in midair. The Bunkers' pool was on a rise and he climbed some stairs to a terrace where twenty-five or thirty men and women were drinking. The only person in the water was Rusty Towers, who floated there on a rubber raft. Oh, how bonny and lush were the banks of the Lucinda River! Prosperous men and women gathered by the sapphire-colored waters while caterer's men in white coats passed them cold gin. Overhead a red de Haviland trainer was circling around and around and around in the sky with something like the glee of a child in a swing. Ned felt a passing affection for the scene, a tenderness for the gathering, as if it was something he might touch. In the distance he heard thunder. As soon as Enid Bunker saw him she began to scream: "Oh, look who's here! What a marvelous surprise! When Lucinda said that you wouldn't come I thought I'd *die.*" She made her way to him through the crowd, and when they had finished kissing she led him to the bar, a progress that was slowed by the fact that he stopped to kiss eight or ten other women and shake the hands of as many men. A smiling bartender he had seen at a hundred parties gave him a gin and tonic and he stood by the bar for a moment, anxious not to get stuck in any conversation that would delay his voyage. When he seemed about to be surrounded he dove in and swam close to the side to avoid colliding with Rusty's raft. At the far end of the pool he bypassed the Tomlinsons with a broad smile and jogged up the garden path. The gravel cut his feet but this was the only unpleasantness. The party was confined to the pool, and as he went toward the house he heard the brilliant, watery sound of voices fade, heard the noise of a radio from the Bunkers' kitchen, where someone was listening to a ballgame. Sunday afternoon. He made his way through the parked cars and down the grassy border of their driveway to Alewives Lane. He did not want to be seen on the road in his bathing trunks but there was no traffic and he made the short distance to the Levys' driveway, marked with a PRIVATE PROPERTY sign and a green tube for *The New York Times.* All the doors and windows of the big house were open but there were no signs of life; not even a dog barked. He went around the side of the house to the pool and saw that the Levys had only recently left. Glasses and bottles and dishes of nuts were on a table at the deep end, where there was a bathhouse or gazebo, hung with Japanese lanterns. After swimming the pool he got himself a glass and poured a drink. It was his fourth or fifth drink and he had swum nearly half the length of the Lucinda River. He felt tired, clean, and pleased at that moment to be alone; pleased with everything.

It would storm. The stand of cumulus cloud—that city—had risen and darkened, and while he sat there he heard the percussiveness of thunder again. The de Haviland trainer was still circling overhead and it seemed to Ned that he could almost hear the pilot laugh with pleasure in the afternoon; but when there was another peal of thunder he took off for home. A train whistle blew and he wondered what time it had gotten to be. Four? Five? He thought of the provincial station at that hour, where a waiter, his tuxedo concealed by a raincoat, a dwarf with some flowers wrapped in newspaper, and a woman who had been crying would be waiting for the local. It was suddenly growing dark; it was that moment when the pinheaded birds seem to organize their song into some acute and knowledgeable recognition of the storm's approach. Then there was a fine noise of rushing water from the crown of an oak at his back, as if a spigot there had been turned. Then the noise of fountains came from the crowns of all the tall trees. Why did he love storms, what was the meaning of his excitement when the door sprang open and the rain wind fled rudely up the stairs, why had the simple task of shutting the windows of an old house seemed fitting and urgent, why did the first watery notes of a storm wind have for him the unmistakable sound of good news, cheer, glad tidings? Then there was an explosion, a smell of cordite, and rain lashed the Japanese lanterns that Mrs. Levy had bought in Kyoto the year before last, or was it the year before that?

He stayed in the Levys' gazebo until the storm had passed. The rain had cooled the air and he shivered. The force of the wind had stripped a maple of its red and yellow leaves and scattered them over the grass and the water. Since it was midsummer the tree must be blighted, and yet he felt a peculiar sadness at this sign of autumn. He braced his shoulders, emptied his glass, and started for the Welchers' pool. This meant crossing the Lindleys' riding ring and he was surprised to find it overgrown with grass and all the jumps dismantled. He wondered if the Lindleys had sold their horses or gone away for the summer and put them out to board. He seemed to remember having heard something about the Lindleys and their horses but the memory was unclear. On he went, barefoot through the wet grass, to the Welchers', where he found their pool was dry.

This breach in his chain of water disappointed him absurdly, and he felt like some explorer who seeks a torrential headwater and finds a dead stream. He was disappointed and mystified. It was common enough to go away for the summer but no one ever drained his pool. The Welchers had definitely gone away. The pool furniture was folded, stacked, and covered with a tarpaulin. The bathhouse was locked. All the windows of the house were shut, and when he went around to the driveway in front he saw a FOR SALE sign nailed to a tree. When had he last heard from the Welchers—when, that is, had he and Lucinda last regretted an invitation to dine with them? It seemed only a week or so ago. Was his memory failing or had he so disciplined it in the repression of unpleasant facts that he had damaged his sense of the truth? Then in the distance he heard the sound of a tennis game. This cheered him, cleared away all his apprehensions and let him regard the overcast sky and the cold air with indifference. This was the day that Neddy Merrill swam across the county. That was the day! He started off then for his most difficult portage.

Had you gone for a Sunday afternoon ride that day you might have seen him, close to naked, standing on the shoulders of Route 424, waiting for a chance to cross. You might have wondered if he was the victim of foul play, had his car broken down, or was he merely a fool. Standing barefoot in the deposits of the highway—beer cans, rags, and blowout patches—exposed to all kinds of ridicule, he seemed pitiful. He had known when he started that this was a part of his journey—it had been on his maps—but confronted with the lines of traffic, worming through the summery light, he found himself unprepared. He was laughed at, jeered at, a beer can was thrown at him, and he had no dignity or humor to bring to the situation. He could have gone back, back to the Westerhazys', where Lucinda would still be sitting in the sun. He had signed nothing, vowed nothing, pledged nothing, not even to himself. Why, believing as he did, that all human obduracy was susceptible to common sense, was he unable to turn back? Why was he determined to complete his journey even if it meant putting his life in danger? At what point had this prank, this joke, this piece of horseplay become serious? He could not go back, he could not even recall with any clearness the green water at the Westerhazys', the sense of inhaling the day's components, the friendly and relaxed voices saying that they had *drunk* too much. In the space of an hour, more or less, he had covered a distance that made his return impossible.

An old man, tooling down the highway at fifteen miles an hour, let him get to the middle of the road, where there was a grass divider. Here he was exposed to the ridicule of the northbound traffic, but after ten or fifteen minutes he was able to cross. From here he had only a short walk to the Recreation Center at the edge of the Village of Lancaster, where there were some handball courts and a public pool.

The effect of the water on voices, the illusion of brilliance and suspense, was the same here as it had been at the Bunkers' but the sounds here were louder, harsher, and more shrill, and as soon as he entered the crowded enclosure he was confronted with regimentation. "ALL SWIMMERS MUST TAKE A SHOWER BEFORE USING THE POOL. ALL SWIMMERS MUST USE THE FOOTBATH. ALL SWIMMERS MUST WEAR THEIR IDENTIFICATION DISKS." He took a shower, washed his feet in a cloudy and bitter solution, and made his way to the edge of the water. It stank of chlorine and looked to him like a sink. A pair of lifeguards in a pair of towers blew police whistles at what seemed to be regular intervals and abused the swimmers through a public address system. Neddy remembered the sapphire water at the Bunkers' with longing and thought that he might contaminate himself—damage his own prosperousness and charm—by swimming in this murk, but he reminded himself that he was an explorer, a pilgrim, and that this was merely a stagnant bend in the Lucinda River. He dove, scowling with distaste, into the chlorine and had to swim with his head above water to avoid collisions, but even so he was bumped into, splashed, and jostled. When he got to the shallow end both lifeguards were shouting at him: "Hey, you, you without the identification disk, get outa the water." He did, but they had no way of pursuing him and he went through the reek of suntan oil and chlorine out through the hurricane fence and passed the handball courts. By crossing the road he entered the wooded part of the Halloran estate. The woods were not cleared and the footing was treacherous and difficult until he reached the lawn and the clipped beech hedge that encircled their pool.

The Hallorans were friends, an elderly couple of enormous wealth who seemed to bask in the suspicion that they might be Communists. They were zealous reformers but they were not Communists, and yet when they were accused, as they sometimes were, of subversion, it seemed to gratify and excite them. Their beech hedge was yellow and he guessed this had been blighted like the Levys' maple. He called hullo, hullo, to warn the Hallorans of his approach, to palliate his invasion of their privacy. The Hallorans, for reasons that had never been explained to him, did not wear bathing suits. No explanations were in order, really. Their nakedness was a detail in their uncompromising zeal for reform and he stepped politely out of his trunks before he went through the opening in the hedge.

Mrs. Halloran, a stout woman with white hair and a serene face, was reading the *Times.* Mr. Halloran was taking beech leaves out of the water with a scoop. They seemed not surprised or displeased to see him. Their pool was perhaps the oldest in the county, a fieldstone rectangle, fed by a brook. It had no filter or pump and its waters were the opaque gold of the stream.

"I'm swimming across the county," Ned said.

"Why, I didn't know one could," exclaimed Mrs. Halloran.

"Well, I've made it from the Westerhazys'," Ned said. "That must be about four miles."

He left his trunks at the deep end, walked to the shallow end, and swam this stretch. As he was pulling himself out of the water he heard Mrs. Halloran say, "We've been *terribly* sorry to hear about all your misfortunes, Neddy."

"My misfortunes?" Ned asked. "I don't know what you mean."

"Why, we heard that you'd sold the house and that your poor children . . ."

"I don't recall having sold the house," Ned said, "and the girls are at home."

"Yes," Mrs. Halloran sighed. "Yes . . ." Her voice filled the air with an unseasonable melancholy and Ned spoke briskly. "Thank you for the swim."

"Well, have a nice trip," said Mrs. Halloran.

Beyond the hedge he pulled on his trunks and fastened them. They were loose and he wondered if, during the space of an afternoon, he could have lost some weight. He was cold and he was tired and the naked Hallorans and their dark water had depressed him. The swim was too much for his strength but how could he have guessed this, sliding down the banister that morning and sitting in the Westerhazys' sun? His arms were lame. His legs felt rubbery and ached at the joints. The worst of it was the cold in his bones and the feeling that he might never be warm again. Leaves were falling down around him and he smelled woodsmoke on the wind. Who would be burning wood at this time of year?

He needed a drink. Whiskey would warm him, pick him up, carry him through the last of his journey, refresh his feeling that it was original and valorous to swim across the county. Channel swimmers took brandy. He needed a stimulant. He crossed the lawn in front of the Hallorans' house and went down a little path to where they had built a house for their only daughter, Helen, and her husband, Eric Sachs. The Sachses' pool was small and he found Helen and her husband there.

"Oh, *Neddy,*" Helen said. "Did you lunch at Mother's?"

"Not *really,*" Ned said. "I *did* stop to see your parents." This seemed to be explanation enough. "I'm terribly sorry to break in on you like this but I've taken a chill and I wonder if you'd give me a drink."

"Why, I'd *love* to," Helen said, "but there hasn't been anything in this house to drink since Eric's operation. That was three years ago."

Was he losing his memory, had his gift for concealing painful facts let him forget that he had sold his house, that his children were in trouble, and that his friend had been ill? His eyes slipped from Eric's face to his abdomen, where he saw three pale sutured scars, two of them at least a foot long. Gone was his navel, and what, Neddy thought, would the roving hand, bed-checking one's gifts at 3 a.m. make of a belly with no navel, no link to birth, this breach in the succession?

"I'm sure you can get a drink at the Biswangers'," Helen said. "They're having an enormous do. You can hear it from here. Listen!"

She raised her head and from across the road, the lawns, the gardens, the woods, the fields, he heard again the brilliant noise of voices over water. "Well, I'll get wet," he said, still feeling that he had no freedom of choice about his means of travel. He dove into the Sachses' cold water and, gasping, close to drowning, made his way from one end of the pool to the other. "Lucinda and I want *terribly* to see you," he said over his shoulder, his face set toward the Biswangers'. "We're sorry it's been so long and we'll call you *very* soon."

He crossed some fields to the Biswangers' and the sounds of revelry there. They would be honored to give him a drink, they would be happy to give him a drink. The Biswangers invited him and Lucinda for dinner four times a year, six weeks in advance. They were always rebuffed and yet they continued to send out their invitations, unwilling to comprehend the rigid and undemocratic realities of their society. They were the sort of people who discussed the price of things at cocktails, exchanged market tips during dinner, and after dinner told dirty stories to mixed company. They did not belong to Neddy's set—they were not even on Lucinda's Christmas card list. He went toward their pool with feelings of indifference, charity, and some unease, since it seemed to be getting dark and these were the longest days of the year. The party when he joined it was noisy and large. Grace Biswanger was the kind of hostess who asked the optometrist, the veterinarian, the real-estate dealer, and the dentist. No one was swimming and the twilight, reflected on the water of the pool, had a wintry gleam. There was a bar and he started for this. When Grace Biswanger saw him she came toward him, not affectionately as he had every right to expect, but bellicosely.

"Why, this party has everything," she said loudly, "including a gate crasher."

She could not deal him a social blow—there was no question about this and he did not flinch. "As a gate crasher," he asked politely, "do I rate a drink?"

"Suit yourself," she said. "You don't seem to pay much attention to invitations."

She turned her back on him and joined some guests, and he went to the bar and ordered a whiskey. The bartender served him but he served him rudely. His was a world in which the caterer's men kept the social score, and to be rebuffed by a part-time barkeep meant that he had suffered some loss of social esteem. Or perhaps the man was new and uninformed. Then he heard Grace at his back say: "They went for broke overnight—nothing but income—and he showed up drunk one Sunday and asked us to loan him five thousand dollars. . . ." She was always talking about money. It was worse than eating your peas off a knife. He dove into the pool, swam its length and went away.

The next pool on his list, the last but two, belonged to his old mistress, Shirley Adams. If he had suffered any injuries at the Biswangers' they would be cured here. Love—sexual roughhouse in fact—was the supreme elixir, the pain killer, the brightly colored pill that would put the spring back into his step, the joy of life in his heart. They had had an affair last week, last month, last year. He couldn't remember. It was he who had broken it off, his was the upper hand, and he stepped through the gate of the wall that surrounded her pool with nothing so considered as self-confidence. It seemed in a way to be his pool, as the lover, particularly the illicit lover, enjoys the possessions of his mistress with an authority unknown to holy matrimony. She was there, her hair the color of brass, but her figure, at the edge of the lighted, cerulean water, excited in him no profound memories. It had been, he thought, a lighthearted affair, although she had wept when he broke it off. She seemed confused to see him and he wondered if she was still wounded. Would she, God forbid, weep again?

"What do you want?" she asked.

"I'm swimming across the county."

"Good Christ. Will you ever grow up?"

"What's the matter?"

"If you've come here for money," she said, "I won't give you another cent."

"You could give me a drink."

"I could but I won't. I'm not alone."

"Well, I'm on my way."

He dove in and swam the pool, but when he tried to haul himself up onto the curb he found that the strength in his arms and shoulders had gone, and he paddled to the ladder and climbed out. Looking over his shoulder he saw, in the lighted bathhouse, a young man. Going out onto the dark lawn he smelled chrysanthemums or marigolds—some stubborn autumnal fragrance—on the night air, strong as gas. Looking overhead he saw that the stars had come out, but why should he seem to see Andromeda, Cepheus, and Cassiopeia? What had become of the constellations of midsummer? He began to cry.

It was probably the first time in his adult life that he had ever cried, certainly the first time in his life that he had ever felt so miserable, cold, tired, and bewildered. He could not understand the rudeness of the caterer's barkeep or the rudeness of a mistress who had come to him on her knees and showered his trousers with tears. He had swum too long, he had been immersed too long, and his nose and his throat were sore from the water. What he needed then was a drink, some company, and some clean, dry clothes, and while he could have cut directly across the road to his home he went on to the Gilmartins' pool. Here, for the first time in his life, he did not dive but went down the steps into the icy water and swam a hobbled sidestroke that he might have learned as a youth. He staggered with fatigue on his way to the Clydes' and paddled the length of their pool, stopping again and again with his hand on the curb to rest. He climbed up the ladder and wondered if he had the strength to get home. He had done what he wanted, he had swum the county, but he was so stupefied with exhaustion that his triumph seemed vague. Stooped, holding on to the gateposts for support, he turned up the driveway of his own house.

The place was dark. Was it so late that they had all gone to bed? Had Lucinda stayed at the Westerhazys' for supper? Had the girls joined her there or gone someplace else? Hadn't they agreed, as they usually did on Sunday, to regret all their invitations and stay at home? He tried the garage doors to see what cars were in but the doors were locked and rust came off the handles onto his hands. Going toward the house, he saw that the force of the thunderstorm had knocked one of the rain gutters loose. It hung down over the front door like an umbrella rib, but it could be fixed in the morning. The house was locked, and he thought that the stupid cook or the stupid maid must have locked the place up until he remembered that it had been some time since they had employed a maid or a cook. He shouted, pounded on the door, tried to force it with his shoulder, and then, looking in at the windows, saw that the place was empty.

Junot Diaz (1968–)

was born in Santo Domingo, in the Dominican Republic, and moved to Parlin, New Jersey, with his family when he was seven years old; much of his fiction so far has involved growing up poor in these places. "There was an Army recruitment center on my block. In a predominantly black and Latino neighborhood, you had these Army guys riding around, trying to recruit you. My sense of the world at the time was once high school was finished, I could either get a job or join the army." But when he fell in love with a neighbor who then left to go to Rutgers, Diaz followed. He worked as a dishwasher, a pool table deliverer, a steelworker, and an editorial assistant before getting an MFA in creative writing from Cornell University. His stories have been included four times in The Best American Short Stories*—more often than any other African-American writer. Diaz is the winner of a Guggenheim Fellowship and was one of twenty writers included by* The New Yorker *on its list "Fiction Under 40: The Future of American Fiction." He has taught at Syracuse University and now lives in Boston, where he teaches in the Massachusetts Institute of Technology's Program in Writing and Humanistic Studies.*

INTRODUCTION BY **Susan Straight**

When I first read Junot Diaz, I couldn't get the narrative voice or the landscapes out of my mind. I kept seeing the recurring character, Yunior, his face as it changed with the move from sun and youth to snow and adulthood, and somehow the stories were laid out for me in photographs, like a strange and unsettling combination of Brassai, Gordon Parks, and Mary Ellen Mark. The boys, their eyes, their knees, their feet when they ran down paths through Dominican vegetation, then their shoulders in the winter coats of New Jersey.

The life laid out here in these three Junot Diaz stories is so fully realized, so casually and yet intimately detailed, that I couldn't wait to read the next story. I read "Ysrael" in *Story* magazine and looked everywhere for Diaz's next work. I found "Fiesta, 1980" in *Story* as well and then began to teach Diaz stories to my students, who found them as compelling as I had.

We begin, in "Ysrael," with Yunior as a nine-year-old in the campo, following his older brother Rafa passively, watchfully, through the rural countryside of the Dominican Republic. They have been sent to their uncles by their mother, who is on her own, as their father is in the United States, a presence only by the clothes he sends. Yunior listens, uncomprehending at the time, to Rafa's sexual exploits and opinions; Rafa constantly pushes him away, beats him up, and tortures him in the way that twelve-year-olds do. Rafa is a man already, in his own mind, and when he leaves on his various journeys, Yunior sees him "walk away until what was left of him was the color of his shirt filling in the spaces between the leaves." So Rafa is out to conquer, Yunior to merely survive, it seems. Then Rafa allows Yunior to accompany him on their most epic quest: to see the mangled face of Ysrael, a mysterious boy.

Next we see Yunior as a nervous, too-observant adolescent in "Fiesta, 1980," charting the movement of his family from the dirt paths, latrines, and colmados of the Dominican

Republic to the choked freeways, cramped apartments, and parking lot baseball of New York and New Jersey. His father has brought them to America and has taken the place of Rafa as Yunior's tormentor and mentor, all in one. Continually cheating on his wife and lashing out at Yunior, Papi is a focused man, and both Rafa and Yunior learn from him in their own ways. "I'd once told him I considered him a low-down chickenshit for moving out of the way every time Papi was going to smack me," Yunior says of his brother. "Collateral damage, Rafa had said. Ever heard of it?" Diaz is a natural at dialogue as it is meant to be written. Everything about Yunior's life turns out to be collateral damage.

Finally, in "The Sun, the Moon, the Stars," also published in *The New Yorker,* Yunior is a man, with his family completely absent from the story. Yunior is messing up now, too, having casually cheated on his girlfriend, who then consents to a vacation with him but keeps aloof in a well-rehearsed punishment. This story is the bridge to both worlds: The couple leaves New Jersey and their particular urban existence for the Dominican Republic. But Magdalena rejects Yunior's childhood, refusing to stay in the campo, choosing instead a sterile resort, where she works Yunior, just as his father and Rafa used to in the past. He isn't good enough. He has sinned, as his father and Rafa did, but he never conquers. He says, "I know what she's doing. Making me aware of my precarious position in her life. Like I'm not aware." He always knows, and he always cares, and remains helpless. Yunior gets hurt again and again, and looking around the countryside of his youth, Diaz finds perfect scenes and metaphors to deepen the pain.

Diaz has his own Faulknerian landscape; his evocations, by turns lyrical and then savage, claim a particular place that exists only in his fiction, not just the campo and towns of the Dominican Republic, but even the airspace between that country and the United States and the sterile apartment complexes and bleak projects and asphalt lots and dumps where Yunior will make his home now.

But I couldn't help being haunted by Yunior for other reasons. In the first story, he says, "I had never been sad for more than a few hours, and the thought of that sensation lasting a lifetime scared the hell out of me." In the second, we can already hear the wistfulness, the displaced boy watching his father and mother drift apart, watching his brother drift away. By the third, when he is suspended in a truly frightening jungle landscape of his ancestors and can only think desperately, painfully, of his lost love, envisioning his past and present life, we know that in Diaz's hands, Yunior is someone we'll always want to return to in fiction.

Susan Straight is the author of five novels, most recently Highwire Moon, *which was a finalist for the National Book Award in 2001, as well as essays and short stories in* The New York Times, Harper's, Zoetrope: All-Story, Salon, *and other journals.*

JUNOT DIAZ

Ysrael

I

We were on our way to the colmado for an errand, a beer for my tío, when Rafa stood still and tilted his head, as if listening to a message I couldn't hear, something beamed in from afar. We were close to the colmado; you could hear the music and the gentle clop of the drunken voices. I was nine that summer, but my brother was twelve, and he was the one who wanted to see Ysrael. Rafa looked out toward the mountains and said, We should pay that kid a visit.

II

Mami shipped me and Rafa to the campo every summer. She worked long hours at the chocolate factory and didn't have the time or the energy to look after us during the months school was out. Rafa and I stayed with our tíos in a small wooden house on the edge of Ocoa; rosebushes blazed around the yard like compass points, and the mango trees spread out deep blankets of shade where we could rest and play dominos, but the campo was nothing like our barrio in Santo Domingo. In the campo there was nothing to do, no one to see. You didn't get television or electricity and Rafa, who was older, woke up every morning pissy and dissatisfied. He stood on the patio in his shorts and looked out over the mountains, at the mists that gathered like water, at the brucal trees that blazed like fires on the hogbacks. This, he said, is shit.

Worse than shit, I said.

Yes, he said, and when I get home, I'm going to go crazy—chinga all my girls and then chinga everyone else's. I won't stop dancing, either. I'm going to be like those guys in the record books who dance four or five days straight.

Tío Miguel had chores for us (mostly we chopped wood for the smokehouse and brought water up from the river), but we finished these as easy as we threw off our shirts and had the rest of the day punching us in the face. We caught jaivas in the streams and spent hours walking across the valley to see girls who were never there; we set traps for rats we never caught and toughened up our roosters with pails of cold water. Back home in the capital, Rafa had his own friends, a bunch of tigres who liked to knock down our neighbors and who scrawled *chocha* and *toto* on walls. Back in the capital, he rarely said anything to me except Shut up.

If I was stupid enough to mouth off to him—about the hair that was growing on his back or the time the tip of his pinga had swollen to the size of a lemon—he pounded the hell out of me and then I would run as far as I could. Rafa and I fought so much that our neighbors took to smashing broomsticks over us to break it up, but in the campo it wasn't like that; in the campo we were friends.

The summer I was nine, Rafa shot whole afternoons talking about whatever chica he was getting with—not that the campo girls gave up ass like the girls back in the capital, but he told me that kissing them was pretty much the same. He'd take the campo girls down to the dams to swim and if he was lucky they let him put it in their mouths or in their asses. He'd done Yessica that way for almost a month before her parents heard about it and barred her from leaving the house.

He wore the same outfit when he went to see these girls, a shirt and pants that my father had sent him from the States the Christmas before. I always followed Rafa, trying to convince him to let me tag along.

Go home, he'd say. I'll be back in a few hours.

I'll walk you.

I don't need you to walk me anywhere. Just wait for me.

If I kept on he'd punch me in the shoulder and walk away until what was left of him was the color of his shirt filling in the spaces between the leaves. Something inside of me would sag like a sail. I would yell his name and he'd hurry on, the ferns and branches and flower pods trembling in his wake.

Later, while we were in bed listening to the rats on the zinc roof, he might tell me what he'd done. I'd hear about tetas and chochas and leche and he'd talk without looking over at me. There was a girl he'd gone to see, half Haitian, but he ended up with her mother. Another who believed she wouldn't get pregnant if she drank a Coke afterward. And one who was pregnant and didn't give a damn about anything. His hands were behind his head and his feet were crossed at the ankles. He was handsome and spoke out of the corner of his mouth. I was too young to appreciate his advice, but I listened to him like these things might be useful in the future.

III

Ysrael was a different story. Even on this side of Ocoa people had heard of him, how when he'd been a baby a pig had eaten his face off, skinned it like an orange. He was something to talk about, a name that set the kids to screaming.

I'd seen Ysrael my first time the year before, right after the dams had been finished. I was in town, farting around, when a single-prop plane swept in across the sky. A door opened on the fuselage and a man began to kick out tall bundles that exploded into thousands of leaflets as soon as the wind got to them. At first I thought maybe the paper would expand out behind the plane like smoke and then disappear, but the leaflets came down as slow as butterfly blossoms and the posters were of wrestlers, not politicians, and that was when the children began shouting. Usually the planes only covered Ocoa, but if extras had been printed the nearby towns would also get leaflets, especially if the match or the election was a big one.

I spotted Ysrael in an alley, stooping over a stack of leaflets that had not come undone from its thin cord. He was wearing his mask.

What are you doing? I said, and he answered, What do you think I'm doing?

He picked up the bundle and ran down the alley, away from me. Some of the other boys saw him and wheeled around howling, but he could run.

That's Ysrael! I was told. He's *ugly* and he's got a cousin around here but we don't like him either. And that face of his would make you *sick!*

I told my brother later, when I went home, and he sat up from his bed. Could you see under the mask?

Not really.

That's something we got to check out. I hear it's bad.

The night before we went to look for Ysrael, Rafa couldn't sleep. He kicked at the mosquito netting, and I could hear the mesh tearing just a little. My tío was yukking it up with his buddies in the yard. One of Tío's roosters had won big the day before, and Tío was thinking of taking it to the capital. People around here don't bet worth a damn, he was saying. Your average farmer only bets big when he feels lucky, and how many of them feel lucky?

You're feeling lucky.

You're damn right about that. And that's why I have to find myself some big spenders.

I wonder how much of Ysrael's face is gone, Rafa said.

He has his eyes.

That's a lot, he assured me. You'd think eyes would be the first thing a pig would go for. Eyes are soft. And salty.

How do you know that?

I licked one, he said.

Maybe his ears, I answered.

And his nose. Anything that sticks out.

Everyone had a different opinion on the damage. Tío said it wasn't bad but the father was very sensitive about anyone taunting his oldest son, which explained the mask. Tía said if we were to look on his face we would be sad for the rest of our lives. That's why the poor boy's mother spends her day in church. I had never been sad more than a few hours, and the thought of that sensation lasting a lifetime scared the hell out of me. My brother kept pinching my face during the night, like I was a mango. The cheeks, he said. And the chin. But the forehead would be a lot harder. The skin's tight.

All right, I said.

The next morning the roosters were screaming. Me and Rafa collected our shoes from the patio, careful not to step on piles of cacao pods Tía had set out to dry. He went into the smokehouse and emerged with his knife and two oranges. He peeled them and handed me mine. When we heard Tía coughing in the house, we started on our way. I kept expecting Rafa to send me home, and the longer he went without speaking, the more excited I became. I put my hands over my mouth to keep from laughing. We went slow, grabbing saplings and fence posts to stop from tumbling down the rough brambly slope. Smoke was rising from the fields that had been burned the night before, and the trees that had not exploded or collapsed stood in the black ash like spears. At the bottom of the hill we followed the road that would take us to Ocoa. I was carrying the Coca-Cola empties Tío had hidden in the chicken coop.

We joined two women, our neighbors, who were waiting by the colmado on their way to mass.

I put the bottles on the counter. Chicho folded up yesterday's *El Nacional.* When he put fresh Cokes next to the empties, I said, We want the refund.

Chicho put his elbows on the counter and looked me over. Are you supposed to be doing that?

Yes, I said.

You better be giving this money back to your tío, he said. I stared at the pastelitos and chicharrón he kept under a fly-specked glass. He slapped the coins onto the counter. I'm going to stay out of this, he said. What you do with this money is your own concern. I'm just a businessman.

How much of this do we need? I asked Rafa.

All of it.

Can't we buy something to eat?

Save it for a drink. You'll be real thirsty later.

Maybe we should eat.

Don't be stupid.

How about if I just bought us some gum?

Give me that money, he said.

Okay, I said. I was just asking.

Then stop. Rafa was looking up the road, distracted; I knew that expression better than anyone. He was scheming. Every now and then he glanced over at the two women, who were conversing loudly, their arms crossed over their big chests. When the first autobus trundled to a stop and the women got on, Rafa watched their asses bucking under their dresses. The cobrador leaned out from the passenger door and said, Well? And Rafa said, Beat it, baldy.

What are we waiting for? I said. That one had air conditioning.

I want a younger cobrador, Rafa said, still looking down the road. I went to the counter and tapped my finger on the glass case. Chicho handed me a pastelito, and after putting it in my pocket, I slid him a coin. Business is business, Chicho announced, but my brother didn't bother to look. He was flagging down the next autobus.

Get to the back, Rafa said. He framed himself in the main door, his toes out in the air, his hands curled up on the top lip of the door. He stood next to the cobrador, who was a year or two younger than he was. This boy tried to get Rafa to sit down but Rafa shook his head with that not-a-chance grin of his, and before there could be an argument the driver shifted into gear, blasting the radio. "La Chica de mi Escuela" was still on the charts. Can you believe that? the man next to me said.

They play that vaina a hundred times a day. I lowered myself stiffly into my seat but the pastelito had already put a grease stain on my pants. Fuck me, I said, and took out the pastelito and finished it in four bites. Rafa wasn't watching. Each time the autobus stopped he was hopping down and helping people bring on their packages. When a row filled he lowered the swing-down center seat for whoever was next. The cobrador, a thin big-eyed boy, was trying to keep up with him and the driver was too busy with his radio to notice what was happening. Two people paid Rafa—all of which Rafa gave to the cobrador, who was busy making change himself.

You have to watch out for stains like that, the man next to me said. He had big teeth and wore a clean fedora. His arms were ropy with muscles.

These things are too greasy, I said.

Let me help. He spit on his fingers and started to rub at the stain but then he was pinching at the tip of my pinga through the fabric of my shorts. He was smiling. I shoved him against his seat. He looked to see if anybody had seen.

You pato, I said.

The man kept smiling.

You low-down, pinga-sucking pato, I said. The man squeezed my biceps, quietly, hard, the way my friends would sneak me in church. I whimpered.

You should watch your mouth, he said.

I got up and went over to the door. Rafa slapped the roof, and as the driver slowed the cobrador said, You two haven't paid.

Sure we did, Rafa said, pushing me down into the dusty street. I gave you the money for those two people there and I gave you our fare too. His voice was tired, as if he got into these discussions all the time.

No, you didn't.

Fuck you, I did. You got the fares. Why don't you count and see?

Don't even try it. The cobrador put his hand on Rafa but Rafa wasn't having it. He yelled up to the driver. Tell your boy to learn how to count.

We crossed the road and went down into a field of guineo; the cobrador was shouting after us and we stayed in the field until we heard the driver say, Forget them.

Rafa took off his shirt and fanned himself and that's when I started to cry.

He watched for a moment. You, he said, are a pussy.

I'm sorry.

What the hell's the matter with you? We didn't do anything wrong.

I'll be okay in a second. I sawed my forearm across my nose.

He took a look around, drawing in the lay of the land. If you can't stop crying, I'll leave you. He headed toward a shack that was rusting in the sun.

I watched him disappear. From the shack you could hear voices, as bright as chrome. Columns of ants had found a pile of meatless chicken bones at my feet and were industriously carting away the crumbling marrow. I could have gone home, which was what I usually did when Rafa acted up, but we were far—eight, nine miles away.

I caught up with him beyond the shack. We walked about a mile; my head felt cold and hollow.

Are you done?

Yes, I said.

Are you always going to be a pussy?

I wouldn't have raised my head if God himself had appeared in the sky and pissed down on us.

Rafa spit. You have to get tougher. Crying all the time. Do you think our papi's crying? Do you think that's what he's been doing the last six years? He turned from me. His left foot was crackling through the weeds, breaking stems.

Rafa stopped a schoolboy in his blue-and-tan uniform, who then pointed us down a road. Rafa spoke to a young mother, whose baby was hacking like a miner. A little farther, she said, and when he smiled she looked the other way. We went too far and a farmer with a machete showed us the easiest loop back. Rafa stopped when he saw Ysrael standing in the center of a field; he was flying a kite and despite the string he seemed almost unconnected to the distant wedge of black that finned back and forth in the sky. Here we go, Rafa said. I was embarrassed. What the hell were we supposed to do?

Stay close, he said. And get ready to run. He passed me his knife, then trotted down toward the field.

IV

The summer before, I pegged Ysrael with a rock, and the way it bounced off his back, I knew I'd clocked a shoulder blade.

You did it! You fucking did it! the other boys yelled.

He'd been running from us and he arched in pain and one of the other boys nearly caught him but he recovered and took off. He's faster than a mongoose, someone said, but in truth he was faster even than that. We laughed and went back to our baseball game and forgot him until he came to town again and then we dropped what we were doing and chased him, howling. Show us your face. Let's see it just once.

V

He was about a foot taller than either of us and looked like he'd been fattened on that supergrain the farmers around Ocoa were giving their stock. Ysrael's sandals were of stiff leather and his clothes were North American. I looked over at Rafa but my brother seemed unperturbed.

Listen up, Rafa said. My hermanito's not feeling too well. Can you show us where a colmado is? I want to get him a drink.

There's a faucet up the road, Ysrael said. His voice was odd and full of spit. His mask was hand-sewn from thin blue cotton fabric and you couldn't help but see the scar tissue that circled his left eye, a red waxy crescent, and the saliva that trickled down his neck.

We're not from around here. We can't drink the water.

Ysrael spooled in his string. The kite wheeled but he righted it with a yank.

Not bad, I said.

We can't drink the water around here. It would kill us. And he's already sick.

I smiled and tried to act sick, which wasn't too difficult. I was covered with dust and I saw Ysrael looking us over.

The water here is probably better than up in the mountains, he said.

Help us out, Rafa said in a low voice.

Ysrael pointed down a path. Just go that way, you'll find it.

Are you sure?

I've lived here all my life.

I could hear the plastic kite flapping in the wind; the string was coming in fast. Rafa huffed and started on his way. We made a long circle and by then Ysrael had his kite in hand—it was no handmade local job.

We couldn't find it, Rafa said.

How stupid are you?

Where did you get that? I said.

Nueva York, he said. From my father.

No shit! Our father's there too! I shouted.

I looked at Rafa, who, for an instant, frowned. Our father only sent us letters and an occasional shirt or pair of jeans at Christmas.

What the hell are you wearing that mask for, anyway? Rafa asked.

I'm sick, Ysrael said.

It must be real hot.

Not for me.

Don't you take it off?

Not until I get better. I'm going to have an operation soon.

You better watch out for that, Rafa said. Those doctors will kill you faster than the Guardia.

These are American doctors.

Rafa sniggered. You're lying.

I saw them last spring. They want me to go next year.

They're lying to you. They probably just felt sorry.

Do you want me to show you where the colmado is or not?

Sure.

Follow me, he said, wiping the spit on his neck. At the colmado he stood off while Rafa bought me the cola. The owner was playing dominoes with the beer delivery man and didn't bother to look up, though he put a hand in the air for Ysrael. He had that lean look of every colmado owner I'd ever met.

On the way back to the road I left the bottle with Rafa to finish and caught up with Ysrael, who was ahead of us. Are you still into wrestling? I asked.

He turned to me and something rippled under the mask. How did you know that?

I heard, I said. Do they have wrestling in the States?

I hope so.

Are you a wrestler?

I'm a great wrestler. I almost went to fight in the capital.

My brother laughed, swigging on the bottle.

You want to try it, pendejo?

Not right now.

I didn't think so.

I tapped his arm. The planes haven't dropped anything this year.

It's still too early. The first Sunday of August is when it starts.

How do you know?

I'm from around here, he said. The mask twitched. I realized he was smiling, and then my brother brought his arm around and smashed the bottle on top of his head. It exploded, the thick bottom spinning away like a crazed eyeglass, and I said, Holy fucking shit. Ysrael stumbled once and slammed into a fence post that had been sunk into the side of the road. Glass crumbled off his mask. He spun toward me, then fell on his stomach. Rafa kicked him in the side. Ysrael seemed not to notice. He had his hands flat in the dirt and was concentrating on pushing himself up. Roll him on his back, my brother said, and we did, pushing like crazy. Rafa took off his mask and threw it spinning into the grass.

His left ear was a nub and you could see the thick-veined slab of his tongue through a hole in his cheek. He had no lips. His head was tipped back and his eyes had gone white and the cords stood out on his neck. He'd been an infant when the pig had come into the house. I jumped back and said, Please, Rafa, let's go! Rafa crouched and using only two of his fingers, turned Ysrael's head from side to side.

VI

We went back to the colmado, where the owner and the delivery man were now arguing, the dominoes chattering under their hands. We kept walking and after one hour, maybe two, we saw an autobus. We boarded and went right to the back. Rafa crossed his arms and watched the fields and roadside shacks scroll past, the dust and smoke and people almost frozen by our speed.

Ysrael will be okay, I said.

Don't bet on it.

They're going to fix him.

A muscle fluttered between his jawbone and his ear. Yunior, he said tiredly. They aren't going to do shit to him.

How do you know?

I know, he said.

I put my feet on the back of the chair in front of me, pushing on an old lady, who turned and glared at me. She was wearing a baseball cap and one of her eyes was milky. The autobus was heading for Ocoa, not for home.

Rafa signaled for a stop. Get ready to run, he whispered.

Okay, I said.

JUNOT DIAZ

Fiesta, 1980

Mami's youngest sister—my tía Yrma—finally made it to the United States that year. She and tío Miguel got themselves an apartment in the Bronx, off the Grand Concourse and everybody decided that we should have a party. Actually, my pops decided, but everybody—meaning Mami, tía Yrma, tío Miguel and their neighbors—thought it a dope idea. On the afternoon of the party Papi came back from work around six. Right on time. We were all dressed by then, which was a smart move on our part. If Papi had walked in and caught us lounging around in our underwear, he would have kicked our asses something serious.

He didn't say nothing to nobody, not even my moms. He just pushed past her, held up his hand when she tried to talk to him and headed right into the shower. Rafa gave me the look and I gave it back to him; we both knew Papi had been with that Puerto Rican woman he was seeing and wanted to wash off the evidence quick.

Mami looked really nice that day. The United States had finally put some meat on her; she was no longer the same flaca who had arrived here three years before. She had cut her hair short and was wearing tons of cheap-ass jewelry which on her didn't look too lousy. She smelled like herself, like the wind through a tree. She always waited until the last possible minute to put on her perfume because she said it was a waste to spray it on early and then have to spray it on again once you got to the party.

We—meaning me, my brother, my little sister and Mami—waited for Papi to finish his shower. Mami seemed anxious, in her usual dispassionate way. Her hands adjusted the buckle of her belt over and over again. That morning, when she had gotten us up for school, Mami told us that she wanted to have a good time at the party. I want to dance, she said, but now, with the sun sliding out of the sky like spit off a wall, she seemed ready just to get this over with.

Rafa didn't much want to go to no party either, and me, I never wanted to go anywhere with my family. There was a baseball game in the parking lot outside and we could hear our friends, yelling, Hey, and, Cabrón, to one another. We heard the pop of a ball as it sailed over the cars, the clatter of an aluminum bat dropping to the concrete. Not that me or Rafa loved baseball; we just liked playing with the local kids, thrashing them at anything they were doing. By the sounds of the shouting, we both knew the game was close, either of us could have made a difference. Rafa frowned and when I frowned back, he put up his fist. Don't you mirror me, he said.

Don't you mirror me, I said.

He punched me—I would have hit him back but Papi marched into the living room with his towel around his waist, looking a lot smaller than he did when he was dressed. He had a few strands of hair around his nipples and a surly closed-mouth expression, like maybe he'd scalded his tongue or something.

Have they eaten? he asked Mami.

She nodded. I made you something.

You didn't let him eat, did you?

Ay, Dios mío, she said, letting her arms fall to her side.

Ay, Dios mío is right, Papi said.

I was never supposed to eat before our car trips, but earlier, when she had put out our dinner of rice, beans and sweet platanos, guess who had been the first one to clean his plate? You couldn't blame Mami really, she had been busy—cooking, getting ready, dressing my sister Madai. I should have reminded her not to feed me but I wasn't that sort of son.

Papi turned to me. Coño, muchacho, why did you eat?

Rafa had already started inching away from me. I'd once told him I considered him a low-down chickenshit for moving out of the way every time Papi was going to smack me.

Collateral damage, Rafa had said. Ever heard of it?

No.

Look it up.

Chickenshit or not, I didn't dare glance at him. Papi was old-fashioned; he expected your undivided attention when you were getting your ass whupped. You couldn't look him in the eye either—that wasn't allowed. Better to stare at his belly button, which was perfectly round and immaculate. Papi pulled me to my feet by my ear.

If you throw up—

I won't, I cried, tears in my eyes, more out of reflex than pain.

Ya, Ramón, ya. It's not his fault, Mami said.

They've known about this party forever. How did they think we were going to get there? Fly?

He finally let go of my ear and I sat back down. Madai was too scared to open her eyes. Being around Papi all her life had turned her into a major-league wuss. Anytime Papi raised his voice her lip would start trembling, like some specialized tuning fork. Rafa pretended that he had knuckles to crack and when I shoved him, he gave me a *Don't start* look. But even that little bit of recognition made me feel better.

I was the one who was always in trouble with my dad. It was like my God-given duty to piss him off, to do everything the way he hated. Our fights didn't bother me too much. I still wanted him to love me, something that never seemed strange or contradictory until years later, when he was out of our lives.

By the time my ear stopped stinging Papi was dressed and Mami was crossing each one of us, solemnly, like we were heading off to war. We said, in turn, Bendición, Mami, and she poked us in our five cardinal spots while saying, Que Dios te bendiga.

This was how all our trips began, the words that followed me every time I left the house.

None of us spoke until we were inside Papi's Volkswagen van. Brand-new, lime-green and bought to impress. Oh, we were impressed, but me, every time I was in that VW and Papi went above twenty miles an hour, I vomited. I'd never had trouble with cars before—that van was like my curse. Mami suspected it was the upholstery. In her mind, American things—appliances, mouthwash, funny-looking upholstery—all seemed to have an intrinsic badness about them. Papi was careful about taking me anywhere in the VW, but when he had to, I rode up front in Mami's usual seat so I could throw up out a window.

¿Cómo te sientes? Mami asked over my shoulder when Papi pulled onto the turnpike. She had her hand on the base of my neck. One thing about Mami, her palms never sweated.

I'm OK, I said, keeping my eyes straight ahead. I definitely didn't want to trade glances with Papi. He had this one look, furious and sharp, that always left me feeling bruised.

Toma. Mami handed me four Mentas. She had thrown three out her window at the beginning of our trip, an offering to Eshú; the rest were for me.

I took one and sucked it slowly, my tongue knocking it up against my teeth. We passed Newark Airport without any incident. If Madai had been awake she would have cried because the planes flew so close to the cars.

How's he feeling? Papi asked.

Fine, I said. I glanced back at Rafa and he pretended like he didn't see me. That was the way he was, at school and at home. When I was in trouble, he didn't know me. Madai was solidly asleep, but even with her face all wrinkled up and drooling she looked cute, her hair all separated into twists.

I turned around and concentrated on the candy. Papi even started to joke that we might not have to scrub the van out tonight. He was beginning to loosen up, not checking his watch too much. Maybe he was thinking about that Puerto Rican woman or maybe he was just happy that we were all together. I could never tell. At the toll, he was feeling positive enough to actually get out of the van and search around under the basket for dropped coins. It was something he had once done to amuse Madai, but now it was habit. Cars behind us honked their horns and I slid down in my seat. Rafa didn't care; he grinned back at the other cars and waved. His actual job was to make sure no cops were coming. Mami shook Madai awake and as soon as she saw Papi stooping for a couple of quarters she let out this screech of delight that almost took off the top of my head.

That was the end of the good times. Just outside the Washington Bridge, I started feeling woozy. The smell of the upholstery got all up inside my head and I found myself with a mouthful of saliva. Mami's hand tensed on my shoulder and when I caught Papi's eye, he was like, No way. Don't do it.

The first time I got sick in the van Papi was taking me to the library. Rafa was with us and he couldn't believe I threw up. I was famous for my steel-lined stomach. A third-world childhood could give you that. Papi was worried enough that just as quick as Rafa could drop off the books we were on our way home. Mami fixed me one of her honey-and-onion concoctions and that made my stomach feel better. A week later we tried the library again and on this go-around I couldn't get the window open in time. When Papi got me home, he went and cleaned out the van himself, an expression of asco on his face. This was a big deal, since Papi almost never cleaned anything himself. He came back inside and found me sitting on the couch feeling like hell.

It's the car, he said to Mami. It's making him sick.

This time the damage was pretty minimal, nothing Papi couldn't wash off the door with a blast of the hose. He was pissed, though; he jammed his finger into my cheek, a nice solid thrust. That was the way he was with his punishments: imaginative. Earlier that year I'd written an essay in school called "My Father the Torturer," but the teacher made me write a new one. She thought I was kidding.

We drove the rest of the way to the Bronx in silence. We only stopped once, so I could brush my teeth. Mami had brought along my toothbrush and a tube of toothpaste and while every car known to man sped by us she stood outside with me so I wouldn't feel alone.

Tío Miguel was about seven feet tall and had his hair combed up and out, into a demi-fro. He gave me and Rafa big spleen-crushing hugs and then kissed Mami and finally ended up with Madai on his shoulder. The last time I'd seen Tío was at the airport, his first day in the United States. I remembered how he hadn't seemed all that troubled to be in another country.

He looked down at me. Carajo, Yunior, you look horrible!

He threw up, my brother explained.

I pushed Rafa. Thanks a lot, ass-face.

Hey, he said. Tío asked.

Tío clapped a bricklayer's hand on my shoulder. Everybody gets sick sometimes, he said. You should have seen me on the plane over here. Dios mio! He rolled his Asian-looking eyes for emphasis. I thought we were all going to die.

Everybody could tell he was lying. I smiled like he was making me feel better.

Do you want me to get you a drink? Tío asked. We got beer and rum.

Miguel, Mami said. He's young.

Young? Back in Santo Domingo, he'd be getting laid by now.

Mami thinned her lips, which took some doing.

Well, it's true, Tío said.

So, Mami, I said. When do I get to go visit the D.R.?

That's enough, Yunior.

It's the only pussy you'll ever get, Rafa said to me in English.

Not counting your girlfriend, of course.

Rafa smiled. He had to give me that one.

Papi came in from parking the van. He and Miguel gave each other the sort of handshakes that would have turned my fingers into Wonder bread.

Coño, compa'i, ¿cómo va todo? they said to each other.

Tía came out then, with an apron on and maybe the longest Lee Press-On Nails I've ever seen in my life. There was this one guru motherfucker in the *Guinness Book of World Records* who had longer nails, but I tell you, it was close. She gave everybody kisses, told me and Rafa how guapo we were—Rafa, of course, believed her—told Madai how bella she was, but when she got to Papi, she froze a little, like maybe she'd seen a wasp on the tip of his nose, but then kissed him all the same.

Mami told us to join the other kids in the living room. Tío said, Wait a minute, I want to show you the apartment. I was glad Tía said, Hold on, because from what I'd seen so far, the place had been furnished in Contemporary Dominican Tacky. The less I saw, the better. I mean, I liked plastic sofa covers but damn, Tío and Tía had taken it to another level. They had a disco ball hanging in the living room and the type of stucco ceilings that looked like stalactite heaven. The sofas all had golden tassels dangling from their edges. Tía came out of the kitchen with some people I didn't know and by the time she got done introducing everybody, only Papi and Mami were given the guided tour of the four-room third-floor apartment. Me and Rafa joined the kids in the living room. They'd already started eating. We were hungry, one of the girls explained, a pastelito in hand. The boy was about three years younger than me but the girl who'd spoken, Leti, was my age. She and another girl were on the sofa together and they were cute as hell.

Leti introduced them: the boy was her brother Wilquins and the other girl was her neighbor Mari. Leti had some serious tetas and I could tell that my brother was going to gun for her. His taste in girls was predictable. He sat down right between Leti and Mari and by the way they were smiling at him I knew he'd do fine. Neither of the girls gave me more than a cursory one-two, which didn't bother me. Sure, I liked girls but I was always too terrified to speak to them unless we were arguing or I was calling them stupidos, which was one of my favorite words that year. I turned to Wilquins and asked him what there was to do around here. Mari, who had the lowest voice I'd ever heard, said, He can't speak.

What does that mean?

He's mute.

I looked at Wilquins incredulously. He smiled and nodded, as if he'd won a prize or something.

Does he understand? I asked.

Of course he understands, Rafa said. He's not dumb.

I could tell Rafa had said that just to score points with the girls. Both of them nodded. Low-voice Mari said, He's the best student in his grade.

I thought, Not bad for a mute. I sat next to Wilquins. After about two seconds of TV Wilquins whipped out a bag of dominos and motioned to me. Did I want to play? Sure. Me and him played Rafa and Leti and we whupped their collective asses twice, which put Rafa in a real bad mood. He looked at me like maybe he wanted to take a swing, just one to make him feel better. Leti kept whispering into Rafa's ear, telling him it was OK.

In the kitchen I could hear my parents slipping into their usual modes. Papi's voice was loud and argumentative; you didn't have to be anywhere near him to catch his drift. And Mami, you had to put cups to your ears to hear hers. I went into the kitchen a few times—once so the tíos could show off how much bullshit I'd been able to cram in my head the last few years; another time for a bucket-sized cup of soda. Mami and Tía were frying tostones and the last of the pastelitos. She appeared happier now and the way her hands worked on our dinner you would think she had a life somewhere else making rare and precious things. She nudged Tía every now and then, shit they must have been doing all their lives. As soon as Mami saw me though, she gave me the eye. Don't stay long, that eye said. Don't piss your old man off.

Papi was too busy arguing about Elvis to notice me. Then somebody mentioned María Montez and Papi barked, María Montez? Let me tell *you* about María Montez, compa'i.

Maybe I was used to him. His voice—louder than most adults'—didn't bother me none, though the other kids shifted uneasily in their seats. Wilquins was about to raise the volume on the TV, but Rafa said, I wouldn't do that. Muteboy had balls, though. He did it anyway and then sat down. Wilquins's pop came into the living room a second later, a bottle of Presidente in hand. That dude must have had Spider-senses or something. Did you raise that? he asked Wilquins and Wilquins nodded.

Is this your house? his pops asked. He looked ready to beat Wilquins silly but he lowered the volume instead.

See, Rafa said. You nearly got your ass *kicked.*

I met the Puerto Rican woman right after Papi had gotten the van. He was taking me on short trips, trying to cure me of my vomiting. It wasn't really working but I looked forward to our trips, even though at the end of each one I'd be sick. These were the only times me and Papi did anything together. When we were alone he treated me much better, like maybe I was his son or something.

Before each drive Mami would cross me.

Bendición, Mami, I'd say.

She'd kiss my forehead. Que Dios te bendiga. And then she would give me a handful of Mentas because she wanted me to be OK. Mami didn't think these excursions would cure anything, but the one time she had brought it up to Papi he had told her to shut up, what did she know about anything anyway?

Me and Papi didn't talk much. We just drove around our neighborhood. Occasionally he'd ask, How is it?

And I'd nod, no matter how I felt.

One day I was sick outside of Perth Amboy. Instead of taking me home he went the other way on Industrial Avenue, stopping a few minutes later in front of a light blue house I didn't recognize. It reminded me of the Easter eggs we colored at school, the ones we threw out the bus windows at other cars.

The Puerto Rican woman was there and she helped me clean up. She had dry papery hands and when she rubbed the towel on my chest, she did it hard, like I was a bumper she was waxing. She was very thin and had a cloud of brown hair rising above her narrow face and the sharpest blackest eyes you've ever seen.

He's cute, she said to Papi.

Not when he's throwing up, Papi said.

What's your name? she asked me. Are you Rafa?

I shook my head.

Then it's Yunior, right?

I nodded.

You're the smart one, she said, suddenly happy with herself. Maybe you want to see my books?

They weren't hers. I recognized them as ones my father must have left in her house. Papi was a voracious reader, couldn't even go cheating without a paperback in his pocket.

Why don't you go watch TV? Papi suggested. He was looking at her like she was the last piece of chicken on earth.

We got plenty of channels, she said. Use the remote if you want.

The two of them went upstairs and I was too scared of what was happening to poke around. I just sat there, ashamed, expecting something big and fiery to crash down on our heads. I watched a whole hour of the news before Papi came downstairs and said, Let's go.

About two hours later the women laid out the food and like always nobody but the kids thanked them. It must be some Dominican tradition or something. There was everything I liked—chicharrones, fried chicken, tostones, sancocho, rice, fried cheese, yucca, avocado, potato salad, a meteor-sized hunk of pernil, even a tossed salad which I could do without—but when I joined the other kids around the serving table, Papi said, Oh no you don't, and took the paper plate out of my hand. His fingers weren't gentle.

What's wrong now? Tía asked, handing me another plate.

He ain't eating, Papi said. Mami pretended to help Rafa with the pernil.

Why can't he eat?

Because I said so.

The adults who didn't know us made like they hadn't heard a thing and Tío just smiled sheepishly and told everybody to go ahead and eat. All the kids—about ten of them now—trooped back into the living room with their plates a-heaping and all the adults ducked into the kitchen and the dining room, where the radio was playing loud-ass bachatas. I was the only one without a plate. Papi stopped me before I could get away from him. He kept his voice nice and low so nobody else could hear him.

If you eat anything, I'm going to beat you. ¿Entiendes?

I nodded.

And if your brother gives you any food, I'll beat him too. Right here in front of everybody. ¿Entiendes?

I nodded again. I wanted to kill him and he must have sensed it because he gave my head a little shove.

All the kids watched me come in and sit down in front of the TV.

What's wrong with your dad? Led asked.

He's a dick, I said.

Rafa shook his head. Don't say that shit in front of people.

Easy for you to be nice when you're eating, I said.

Hey, if I was a pukey little baby, I wouldn't get no food either.

I almost said something back but I concentrated on the TV. I wasn't going to start it. No fucking way. So I watched Bruce Lee beat Chuck Norris into the floor of the Colosseum and tried to pretend that there was no food anywhere in the house. It was Tía who finally saved me. She came into the living room and said, Since you ain't eating, Yunior, you can at least help me get some ice.

I didn't want to, but she mistook my reluctance for something else.

I already asked your father.

She held my hand while we walked; Tía didn't have any kids but I could tell she wanted them. She was the sort of relative who always remembered your birthday but who you only went to visit because you had to. We didn't get past the first-floor landing before she opened her pocketbook and handed me the first of three pastelitos she had smuggled out of the apartment.

Go ahead, she said. And as soon as you get inside make sure you brush your teeth.

Thanks a lot, Tía, I said.

Those pastelitos didn't stand a chance.

She sat next to me on the stairs and smoked her cigarette. All the way down on the first floor and we could still hear the music and the adults and the television. Tía looked a ton like Mami; the two of them were both short and light-skinned. Tía smiled a lot and that was what set them apart the most.

How is it at home, Yunior?

What do you mean?

How's it going in the apartment? Are you kids OK?

I knew an interrogation when I heard one, no matter how sugar-coated it was. I didn't say anything. Don't get me wrong, I loved my tía, but something told me to keep my mouth shut. Maybe it was family loyalty, maybe I just wanted to protect Mami or I was afraid that Papi would find out—it could have been anything really.

Is your mom all right?

I shrugged.

Have there been lots of fights?

None, I said. Too many shrugs would have been just as bad as an answer. Papi's at work too much.

Work, Tía said, like it was somebody's name she didn't like.

Me and Rafa, we didn't talk much about the Puerto Rican woman. When we ate dinner at her house, the few times Papi had taken us over there, we still acted like nothing was out of the ordinary. Pass the ketchup, man. No sweat, bro. The affair was like a hole in our living room floor, one we'd gotten so used to circumnavigating that we sometimes forgot it was there.

By midnight all the adults were crazy dancing. I was sitting outside Tía's bedroom—where Madai was sleeping—trying not to attract attention. Rafa had me guarding the door; he and Leti were in there too, with some of the other kids, getting busy no doubt. Wilquins had gone across the hall to bed so I had me and the roaches to mess around with.

Whenever I peered into the main room I saw about twenty moms and dads dancing and drinking beers. Every now and then somebody yelled, ¡Quisqueya! And then everybody else would yell and stomp their feet. From what I could see my parents seemed to be enjoying themselves.

Mami and Tía spent a lot of time side by side, whispering, and I kept expecting something to come of this, a brawl maybe. I'd never once been out with my family when it hadn't turned to shit. We weren't even theatrical or straight crazy like other families. We fought like sixth-graders, without any real dignity. I guess the whole night I'd been waiting for a blowup, something between Papi and Mami. This was how I always figured Papi would be exposed, out in public, where everybody would know.

You're a cheater!

But everything was calmer than usual. And Mami didn't look like she was about to say anything to Papi. The two of them danced every now and then but they never lasted more than a song before Mami joined Tía again in whatever conversation they were having.

I tried to imagine Mami before Papi. Maybe I was tired, or just sad, thinking about the way my family was. Maybe I already knew how it would all end up in a few years, Mami without Papi, and that was why I did it. Picturing her alone wasn't easy. It seemed like Papi had always been with her, even when we were waiting in Santo Domingo for him to send for us.

The only photograph our family had of Mami as a young woman, before she married Papi, was the one that somebody took of her at an election party that I found one day while rummaging for money to go to the arcade. Mami had it tucked into her immigration papers. In the photo, she's surrounded by laughing cousins I will never meet, who are all shiny from dancing, whose clothes are rumpled and loose. You can tell it's night and hot and that the mosquitos have been biting. She sits straight and even in a crowd she stands out, smiling quietly like maybe she's the one everybody's celebrating. You can't see her hands but I imagined they're knotting a straw or a bit of thread. This was the woman my father met a year later on the Malecón, the woman Mami thought she'd always be.

Mami must have caught me studying her because she stopped what she was doing and gave me a smile, maybe her first one of the night. Suddenly I wanted to go over and hug her, for no other reason than I loved her, but there were about eleven fat jiggling bodies between us. So I sat down on the tiled floor and waited.

I must have fallen asleep because the next thing I knew Rafa was kicking me and saying, Let's go. He looked like he'd been hitting those girls off; he was all smiles. I got to my feet in time to kiss Tía and Tío good-bye. Mami was holding the serving dish she had brought with her.

Where's Papi? I asked.

He's downstairs, bringing the van around. Mami leaned down to kiss me.

You were good today, she said.

And then Papi burst in and told us to get the hell downstairs before some pendejo cop gave him a ticket. More kisses, more handshakes and then we were gone.

I don't remember being out of sorts after I met the Puerto Rican woman, but I must have been because Mami only asked me questions when she thought something was wrong in my life. It took her about ten passes but finally she cornered me one afternoon when we were alone in the apartment. Our upstairs neighbors were beating the crap out of their kids, and me and her had been listening to it all afternoon. She put her hand on mine and said, Is everything OK, Yunior? Have you been fighting with your brother?

Me and Rafa had already talked. We'd been in the basement, where our parents couldn't hear us. He told me that yeah, he knew about her.

Papi's taken me there twice now, he said.

Why didn't you tell me? I asked.

What the hell was I going to say? *Hey, Yunior, guess what happened yesterday? I met Papi's sucia!*

I didn't say anything to Mami either. She watched me, very very closely. Later I would think, maybe if I had told her, she would have confronted him, would have done something, but who can know these things? I said I'd been having trouble in school and like that everything was back to normal between us. She put her hand on my shoulder and squeezed and that was that.

We were on the turnpike, just past Exit 11, when I started feeling it again. I sat up from leaning against Rafa. His fingers smelled and he'd gone to sleep almost as soon as he got into the van. Madai was out too but at least she wasn't snoring.

In the darkness, I saw that Papi had a hand on Mami's knee and that the two of them were quiet and still. They weren't slumped back or anything; they were both wide awake, bolted into their seats. I couldn't see either of their faces and no matter how hard I tried I could not imagine their expressions. Neither of them moved. Every now and then the van was filled with the bright rush of somebody else's headlights. Finally I said, Mami, and they both looked back, already knowing what was happening.

JUNOT DIAZ

The Sun, the Moon, the Stars

I'm not a bad guy. I know how that sounds—defensive, unscrupulous—but it's true. I'm like everybody else: weak, full of mistakes, but basically good. Magdalena disagrees. She considers me a typical Dominican man: a *sucio,* an asshole. See, many months ago, when Magda was still my girl, when I didn't have to be careful about almost everything, I cheated on her with this chick who had tons of eighties freestyle hair. Didn't tell Magda about it, either. You know how it is. A smelly bone like that, better off buried in the back yard of your life. Magda only found out because homegirl wrote her a fucking *letter.* And the letter had *details.* Shit you wouldn't even tell your boys drunk.

The thing is, that particular bit of stupidity had been over for months. Me and Magda were on an upswing. We weren't as distant as we'd been the winter I was cheating. The freeze was over. She was coming over to my place and instead of us hanging with my knucklehead boys—me smoking, her bored out of her skull—we were seeing movies. Driving out to different places to eat. Even caught a play at the Crossroads and I took her picture with some bigwig black playwrights, pictures where she's smiling so much you'd think her wide-ass mouth was going to unhinge. We were a couple again. Visiting each other's family on the weekends. Eating breakfast at diners hours before anybody else was up, rummaging through the New Brunswick library together, the one Carnegie built with his guilt money. A nice rhythm we had going. But then the Letter hits like a *Star Trek* grenade and detonates everything, past, present, future. Suddenly her folks want to kill me. It don't matter that I helped them with their taxes two years running or that I mow their lawn. Her father, who used to treat me like his *hijo,* calls me an asshole on the phone, sounds like he's strangling himself with the cord. "You no deserve I speak to you in Spanish," he says. I see one of Magda's girlfriends at the Woodbridge Mall—Claribel, the *ecuatoriana* with the biology degree and the *chinita* eyes—and she treats me like I ate somebody's kid.

You don't even want to hear how it went down with Magda. Like a five-train collision. She threw Cassandra's letter at me—it missed and landed under a Volvo—and then she sat down on the curb and started hyperventilating. "Oh, God," she wailed. "Oh, my God."

This is when my boys claim they would have pulled a Total Fucking Denial. Cassandra who? I was too sick to my stomach even to try. I sat down next to her, grabbed her flailing arms, and said some dumb shit like "You have to listen to me, Magda. Or you won't understand."

Let me tell you something about Magda. She's a Bergenline original: short with big eyes and big hips and dark curly hair you could lose a hand in. Her father's a baker, her mother sells kids' clothes door to door. She's a forgiving soul. A Catholic.

Dragged me into church every Sunday for Spanish mass, and when one of her relatives is sick, especially the ones in Cuba, she writes letters to some nuns in Pennsylvania, asks the sisters to pray for her family. She's the nerd every librarian in town knows, a teacher whose students fall in love with her. Always cutting shit out for me from the newspapers, Dominican shit. I see her like, what, every week, and she still sends me corny little notes in the mail: "So you won't forget me." You couldn't think of anybody worse to screw than Magda.

I won't bore you with the details. The begging, the crawling over glass, the crying. Let's just say that after two weeks of this, of my driving out to her house, sending her letters, and calling her at all hours of the night, we put it back together. Didn't mean I ever ate with her family again or that her girlfriends were celebrating. Those *cabronas,* they were like, *No, jamás,* never. Even Magda wasn't too hot on the rapprochement at first, but I had the momentum of the past on my side. When she asked me, "Why don't you leave me alone?" I told her the truth: "It's because I love you, *mami.*" I know this sounds like a load of doo-doo, but it's true: Magda's my heart. I didn't want her to leave me; I wasn't about to start looking for a girlfriend because I'd fucked up one lousy time.

Don't think it was a cakewalk, because it wasn't. Magda's stubborn; back when we first started dating, she said she wouldn't sleep with me until we'd been together at least a month, and homegirl stuck to it, no matter how hard I tried to get into her knickknacks. She's sensitive too. Takes to hurt the way water takes to paper. You can't imagine how many times she asked (especially after we finished fucking), "Were you ever going to tell me?" This and "Why?" were her favorite questions. My favorite answers were "Yes" and "It was a stupid mistake."

We even had some conversation about Cassandra—usually in the dark, when we couldn't see each other. Magda asked me if I'd loved Cassandra and I told her no, I didn't. "Do you still think about her?" "Nope." "Did you like fucking her?" "To be honest, baby, it was lousy." And for a while after we got back together everything was as fine as it could be.

But what was strange was that instead of shit improving between us, things got worse and worse. My Magda was turning into another Magda. Who didn't want to sleep over as much or scratch my back when I asked her to. Amazing how you notice the little things. Like how she never used to ask me to call back when she was on the line with somebody else. I always had priority. Not anymore. So of course I blamed all that shit on her girls, who I knew for a fact were still feeding her a bad line about me.

She wasn't the only one with counsel. My boys were like, "Fuck her, don't sweat that bitch," but every time I tried I couldn't pull it off. I was into Magda for real. I started working overtime on her, but nothing seemed to pan out. Every movie we went to, every night drive we took, every time she did sleep over seemed to confirm something negative about me. I felt like I was dying by degrees, but when I brought it up she told me that I was being paranoid.

About a month later, she started making the sort of changes that would have alarmed a paranoid nigger. Cuts her hair, buys better makeup, rocks new clothes, goes out dancing on Friday nights with her friends. When I ask her if we can chill, I'm no longer sure it's a done deal. A lot of the time she Bartlebys me, says, "No, I'd rather not." I ask her what the hell she thinks this is and she says, "That's what I'm trying to figure out."

I know what she's doing. Making me aware of my precarious position in her life. Like I'm not aware.

Then it was June. Hot white clouds stranded in the sky, cars being washed down with hoses, music allowed outside. Everybody getting ready for summer, even us. We'd planned a trip to Santo Domingo early in the year, an anniversary present, and had to decide whether we were still going or not. It had been on the horizon awhile, but I figured it was something that would resolve itself. When it didn't, I brought the tickets out and asked her, "How do you feel about it?"

"Like it's too much of a commitment."

"Could be worse. It's a vacation, for Christ's sake."

"I see it as pressure."

"Doesn't have to be pressure."

I don't know why I get stuck on it the way I do. Bringing it up every day, trying to get her to commit. Maybe I was getting tired of the situation we were in. Wanted to flex, wanted something to change. Or maybe I'd gotten this idea in my head that if she said, "Yes, we're going," then shit would be fine between us. If she said, "No, it's not for me," then at least I'd know that it was over.

Her girls, the sorest losers on the planet, advised her to take the trip and then never speak to me again. She, of course, told me this shit, because she couldn't stop herself from telling me everything she's thinking. "How do you feel about that suggestion?" I asked her.

She shrugged. "It's an idea."

Even my boys were like, "Nigger, sounds like you're wasting a whole lot of loot on some bullshit," but I really thought it would be good for us. Deep down, where my boys don't know me, I'm an optimist. I thought, Me and her on the Island. What couldn't this cure?

Let me confess: I love Santo Domingo. I love coming home to the guys in blazers trying to push little cups of Brugal into my hands. Love the plane landing, everybody clapping when the wheels kiss the runway. Love the fact that I'm the only nigger on board without a Cuban link or a flapjack of makeup on my face. Love the redhead woman on her way to meet the daughter she hasn't seen in eleven years. The gifts she holds on her lap, like the bones of a saint. "*M'ija* has *tetas* now," the woman whispers to her neighbor. "Last time I saw her, she could barely speak in sentences. Now she's a woman. *Imagínate.*" I love the bags my mother packs, shit for relatives and something for Magda, a gift. "You give this to her no matter what happens."

If this was another kind of story, I'd tell you about the sea. What it looks like after it's been forced into the sky through a blowhole. How when I'm driving in from the airport and see it like this, like shredded silver, I know I'm back for real. I'd tell you how many poor motherfuckers there are. More albinos, more cross-eyed niggers, more *tígueres* than you'll ever see. And the *mujeres—olvídate.* How you can't go five feet without running into one you wouldn't mind kicking it with. I'd tell you about the traffic: the entire history of late-twentieth-century automobiles swarming across every flat stretch of ground, a cosmology of battered cars, battered motorcycles, battered trucks, and battered buses, and an equal number of repair shops, run by any fool with a wrench. I'd tell you about the shanties and our no-running-water faucets and the sambos on the billboards and the fact that my family house comes equipped with an ever-reliable latrine. I'd tell you about my *abuelo* and his *campo* hands, how unhappy he is that I'm not sticking around, and I'd tell you about the street where I was born, Calle XXI, how it hasn't decided yet if it wants to be a slum or not and how it's been in this state of indecision for years.

But that would make it another kind of story, and I'm having enough trouble as it is with this one. You'll have to take my word for it. Santo Domingo is Santo Domingo. Let's pretend we all know what goes on there.

I must have been smoking dust, because I thought we were fine those first couple of days. Sure, staying locked up at my *abuelo*'s house bored Magda to tears, she even said so—"I'm bored, Yunior"—but I'd warned her about the obligatory Visit with Abuelo. I thought she wouldn't mind; she's normally mad cool with the *viejitos.* But she didn't say much to him. Just fidgeted in the heat and drank fifteen bottles of water. Point is, we were out of the capital and on a *guagua* to the interior before the second day had even begun. The landscapes were superfly—even though there was a drought on and the whole *campo,* even the houses, was covered in that red dust. There I was. Pointing out all the shit that had changed since the year before. The new Pizza Huts and Dunkin' Donuts and the little plastic bags of water the *tigueritos* were selling. Even kicked the historicals. This is where Trujillo and his Marine pals slaughtered the *gavilleros,* here's where the Jefe used to take his girls, here's where Balaguer sold his soul to the Devil. And Magda seemed to be enjoying herself. Nodded her head. Talked back a little. What can I tell you? I thought we were on a positive vibe.

I guess when I look back there were signs. First off, Magda's not quiet. She's a talker, a fucking *boca,* and we used to have this thing where I would lift my hand and say, "Time out," and she would have to be quiet for at least two minutes, just so I could process some of the information she'd been spouting. She'd be embarrassed and chastened, but not so embarrassed and chastened that when I said, "Okay, time's up," she didn't launch right into it again.

Maybe it was my good mood. It was like the first time in weeks that I felt relaxed, that I wasn't acting like something was about to give at any moment. It bothered me that she insisted on reporting to her girls every night—like they were expecting me to kill her or something—but, fuck it, I still thought we were doing better than anytime before.

We were in this crazy budget hotel near the university. I was standing outside staring out at the Septentrionales and the blacked-out city when I heard her crying. I thought it was something serious, found the flashlight, and fanned the light over her heat-swollen face. "Are you okay, *mami?*"

She shook her head. "I don't want to be here."

"What do you mean?"

"What don't you understand? I. Don't. Want. To. Be. Here."

This was not the Magda I knew. The Magda I knew was super-courteous. Knocked on a door before she opened it.

I almost shouted, "What is your fucking problem!" But I didn't. I ended up hugging and babying her and asking her what was wrong. She cried for a long time and then after a silence started talking. By then the lights had flickered back on. Turned out she didn't want to travel around like a hobo. "I thought we'd be on a beach," she said.

"We're going to be on a beach. The day after tomorrow."

"Can't we go now?"

What could I do? She was in her underwear, waiting for me to say something. So what jumped out of my mouth? "Baby, we'll do whatever you want." I called the hotel in La Romana, asked if we could come early, and the next morning I put us on an express *guagua* to the capital and then a second one to La Romana. I didn't say a fucking word to her and she didn't say nothing to me. She seemed tired and watched the world outside like maybe she was expecting it to speak to her.

By the middle of Day 3 of our All-Quisqueya Redemption Tour we were in an air-conditioned bungalow watching HBO. Exactly where I want to be when I'm in Santo Domingo. In a fucking resort. Magda was reading a book by a Trappist, in a better mood, I guess, and I was sitting on the edge of the bed, fingering my useless map.

I was thinking, For this I deserve something nice. Something physical. Me and Magda were pretty damn casual about sex, but since the breakup shit has gotten weird. First of all, it ain't regular like before. I'm lucky to score some once a week. I have to nudge her, start things up, or we won't fuck at all. And she plays like she doesn't want it, and sometimes she doesn't and then I have to cool it, but other times she does want it and I have to touch her pussy, which is my way of initiating things, of saying, "So, how about we kick it, *mami?*" And she'll turn her head, which is her way of saying, "I'm too proud to acquiesce openly to your animal desires, but if you continue to put your finger in me I won't stop you."

Today we started no problem, but then halfway through she said, "Wait, we shouldn't."

I wanted to know why.

She closed her eyes like she was embarrassed at herself. "Forget about it," she said, moving her hips under me. "Just forget about it."

I don't even want to tell you where we're at. We're in Casa de Campo. The Resort That Shame Forgot. The average asshole would love this place. It's the largest, wealthiest resort on the Island, which means it's a goddamn fortress, walled away from everybody else. *Guachimanes* and peacocks and ambitious topiaries everywhere. Advertises itself in the States as its own country, and it might as well be. Has its own airport, thirty-six holes of golf, beaches so white they ache to be trampled, and the only Island Dominicans you're guaranteed to see are either caked up or changing your sheets. Let's just say my *abuelo* has never been here, and neither has yours. This is where the Garcías and the Colóns come to relax after a long month of oppressing the masses, where the *tutumpotes* can trade tips with their colleagues from abroad. Chill here too long and you'll be sure to have your ghetto pass revoked, no questions asked.

We wake up bright and early for the buffet, get served by cheerful women in Aunt Jemima costumes. I shit you not: these sisters even have to wear hankies on their heads. Magda is scratching out a couple of cards to her family. I want to talk about the day before, but when I bring it up she puts down her pen. Jams on her shades.

"I feel like you're pressuring me."

"How am I pressuring you?" I ask.

We get into one of those no-fun twenty-minute arguments, which the waiters keep interrupting by bringing over more orange juice and *café,* the two things this island has plenty of.

"I just want some space to myself every now and then. Every time I'm with you I have this sense that you want something from me."

"Time to yourself," I say. "What does that mean?"

"Like maybe once a day, you do one thing, I do another."

"Like when? Now?"

"It doesn't have to be now." She looks exasperated. "Why don't we just go down to the beach?"

As we walk over to the courtesy golf cart, I say, "I feel like you rejected my whole country, Magda."

"Don't be ridiculous." She drops one hand in my lap. "I just wanted to relax. What's wrong with that?"

The sun is blazing and the blue of the ocean is an overload on the brain. Casa de Campo has got beaches the way the rest of the Island has got problems. These, though, have no merengue, no little kids, nobody trying to sell you *chicharrones,* and there's a massive melanin deficit in evidence. Every fifty feet there's at least one Eurofuck beached out on a towel like some scary pale monster that the sea's vomited up. They look like philosophy professors, like budget Foucaults, and too many of them are in the company of a dark-assed Dominican girl. I mean it, these girls can't be no more than sixteen, look *puro ingenio* to me. You can tell by their inability to communicate that these two didn't meet back in their Left Bank days.

Magda's rocking a dope Ochun-colored bikini that her girls helped her pick out so she could torture me, and I'm in these old ruined trunks that say "Sandy Hook Forever!" I'll admit it, with Magda half naked in public I'm feeling vulnerable and uneasy. I put my hand on her knee. "I just wish you'd say you love me."

"Yunior, please."

"Can you say you like me a lot?"

"Can you leave me alone? You're such a pestilence."

I let the sun stake me out to the sand. It's disheartening, me and Magda together. We don't look like a couple. When she smiles niggers ask her for her hand in marriage; when I smile folks check their wallets. Magda's been a star the whole time we've been here. You know how it is when you're on the Island and your girl's an octoroon. Brothers go apeshit. On buses, the machos were like, *"Tu sí eres bella, muchacha."* Every time I dip into the water for a swim, some Mediterranean Messenger of Love starts rapping to her. Of course, I'm not polite. "Why don't you beat it, *pancho?* We're on our honeymoon here." There's this one squid who's mad persistent, even sits down near us so he can impress her with the hair around his nipples, and instead of ignoring him she starts a conversation and it turns out he's Dominican too, from Quisqueya Heights, an assistant D.A. who loves his people. "Better I'm their prosecutor," he says. "At least I understand them." I'm thinking he sounds like the sort of nigger who in the old days used to lead bwana to the rest of us. After three minutes of him, I can't take it no more and say, "Magda, stop talking to that asshole."

The assistant D.A. startles. "I know you ain't talking to me," he says.

"Actually," I say, "I am."

"This is unbelievable." Magda gets to her feet and walks stiff-legged toward the water. She's got a half-moon of sand stuck to her butt. A total fucking heartbreak.

Homeboy's saying something else to me, but I'm not listening. I already know what she'll say when she sits back down. "Time for you to do your thing and me to do mine."

★ ★ ★

That night I loiter around the pool and the local bar, Club Cacique, Magda nowhere to be found. I meet a Dominicana from West New York. Fly, of course. *Trigueña,* with the most outrageous perm this side of Dyckman. Lucy is her name. She's hanging out with three of her teenage girl cousins. When she removes her robe to dive into the pool, I see a spiderweb of scars across her stomach. Tells me in Spanish, "I have family in La Romana, but I refuse to stay with them. No way. My uncle won't let any of us out of the house after dark. So I'd rather go broke and stay here than be locked in the prison."

I meet these two rich older dudes drinking cognac at the bar. Introduce themselves as the Vice President and Bárbaro, his bodyguard. I must have the footprint of fresh disaster on my face. They listen to my troubles like they're a couple of capos and I'm talking murder. They commiserate. It's a thousand degrees out and the mosquitoes hum like they're about to inherit the earth, but both these cats are wearing expensive suits, and Bárbaro is even sporting a purple ascot. Once a soldier tried to saw open his neck and now he covers the scar. "I'm a modest man," he says.

I go off to phone the room. No Magda. I check with reception. No messages. I return to the bar and smile.

The Vice President is a young brother, in his late thirties, and pretty cool for a *chupabarrio.* He advises me to find another woman. Make her *bella* and *negra.* I think, Cassandra.

The Vice President waves his hand and shots of Barcélo appear so fast you'd think it's science fiction.

"Jealousy is the best way to jump-start a relationship," the Vice President says. "I learned that when I was a student at Syracuse. Dance with another woman, dance merengue with her, and see if your *jeva*'s not roused to action."

"You mean roused to violence."

"She hit you?"

"When I first told her. She smacked me right across the chops."

"*Pero, hermano,* why'd you tell her?" Bárbaro wants to know. "Why didn't you just deny it?"

"*Compadre,* she received a letter. It had evidence."

The Vice President smiles fantastically and I can see why he's a vice president. Later, when I get home, I'll tell my mother about this whole mess, and she'll tell me what this brother was the vice president of.

"They only hit you," he says, "when they care."

"Amen," Bárbaro murmurs. "Amen."

All of Magda's friends say I cheated because I was Dominican, that all us Dominican men are dogs and can't be trusted. But it wasn't genetics; there were reasons. Causalities.

The truth is there ain't no relationship in the world that doesn't hit turbulence. Ours certainly did.

I was living in Brooklyn and she was with her folks in Jersey. We talked every day on the phone and on weekends we saw each other. Usually I went in. We were real Jersey, too: malls, the parents, movies, a lot of TV. After a year of us together, this was where we were at. Our relationship wasn't the sun, the moon, and the stars, but it wasn't bullshit, either. Especially not on Saturday mornings, over at my apartment, when she made us coffee *campo* style, straining it through the sock thing. Told her parents the night before she was staying over at Claribel's; they must have known where she was, but they never said shit. I'd sleep late and she'd read, scratching my back in slow arcs, and when I was ready to get up I would start kissing her until she would say, "God, Yunior, you're making me wet."

I wasn't unhappy and wasn't actively pursuing ass like some niggers. Sure, I checked out other females, even danced with them when I went out, but I wasn't keeping numbers or nothing.

Still, it's not like seeing somebody once a week doesn't cool shit out, because it does. Nothing you'd really notice until some new chick arrives at your job with a big chest and a smart mouth and she's like on you almost immediately, touching your pectorals, moaning about some *moreno* she's dating who's always treating her like shit, saying, "Black guys don't understand Spanish girls."

Cassandra. She organized the football pool and did crossword puzzles while she talked on the phone, and had a thing for denim skirts. We got into a habit of going to lunch and having the same conversation. I advised her to drop the *moreno,* she advised me to find a girlfriend who could fuck. First week of knowing her, I made the mistake of telling her that sex with Magda had never been topnotch.

"God, I feel sorry for you." Cassandra laughed. "At least Rupert gives me some Grade A dick."

The first night we did it—and it was good, too, she wasn't false advertising—I felt so lousy that I couldn't sleep, even though she was one of those sisters whose body fits next to you perfect. I was like, She knows, so I called Magda right from the bed and asked her if she was okay.

"You sound strange," she said.

I remember Cassandra pressing the hot cleft of her pussy against my leg and me saying, "I just miss you."

Another day, and the only thing Magda has said is "Give me the lotion." Tonight the resort is throwing a party. All guests are invited. Attire's formal, but I don't have the clothes or the energy to dress up. Magda, though, has both. She pulls on these supertight gold lame pants and a matching halter that shows off her belly ring. Her hair is shiny and as dark as night and I can remember the first time I kissed those curls, asking her, "Where are the stars?" And she said, "They're a little lower, *papi.*"

We both end up in front of the mirror. I'm in slacks and a wrinkled guayabera. She's applying her lipstick; I've always believed that the universe invented the color red solely for Latinas.

"We look good," she says.

It's true. My optimism is starting to come back. I'm thinking, This is the night for reconciliation. I put my arms around her, but she drops her bomb without blinking a fucking eye: tonight, she says, she needs space.

My arms drop.

"I knew you'd be pissed," she says.

"You're a real bitch, you know that."

"I didn't want to come here. You made me."

"If you didn't want to come, why didn't you have the fucking guts to say so?"

And on and on and on, until finally I just say, "Fuck this," and head out. I feel unmoored and don't have a clue of what comes next. This is the endgame, and instead of pulling out all the stops, instead of *pongándome más chino que un chivo,* I'm feeling sorry for myself, *como un parigüayo sin suerte.* I'm thinking, I'm not a bad guy.

Club Cacique is jammed. I'm looking for Lucy. I find the Vice President and Bárbaro instead. At the quiet end of the bar, they're drinking cognac and arguing about whether there are fifty-six Dominicans in the major leagues or fifty-seven. They clear out a space for me and clap me on the shoulder.

"This place is killing me," I say.

"How dramatic." The Vice President reaches into his suit for his keys. He's wearing those Italian leather shoes that look like braided slippers. "Are you inclined to ride with us?"

"Sure," I say. "Why the fuck not?"

"I wish to show you the birthplace of our nation."

Before we leave I check out the crowd. Lucy has arrived. She's alone at the edge of the bar in a fly black dress. Smiles excitedly, lifts her arm, and I can see the dark stubbled spot in her armpit. She's got sweat patches over her outfit, and mosquito bites on her beautiful arms. I think, I should stay, but my legs carry me right out of the club.

We pile in a diplomat's black BMW. I'm in the back seat with Bárbaro; the Vice President's up front driving. We leave Casa de Campo behind and the frenzy of La Romana, and soon everything starts smelling of processed cane. The roads are dark—I'm talking no fucking lights—and in our beams the bugs swarm like a biblical plague. We're passing the cognac around. I'm with a vice president, I figure what the fuck.

He's talking—about his time in upstate New York—but so is Bárbaro. The bodyguard's suit's rumpled and his hand shakes as he smokes his cigarettes. Some fucking bodyguard. He's telling me about his childhood in San Juan, near the border of Haiti. Liborio's country. "I wanted to be an engineer," he tells me. "I wanted to build schools and hospitals for the pueblo." I'm not really listening to him; I'm thinking about Magda, how I'll probably never taste her *chocha* again.

And then we're out of the car, stumbling up a slope, through bushes and *guineo* and bamboo, and the mosquitoes are chewing us up like we're the special of the day. Bárbaro's got a huge flashlight, a darkness obliterator. The Vice President's cursing, trampling through the underbrush, saying, "It's around here somewhere. This is what I get for being in office so long." It's only then I notice that Bárbaro's holding a huge fucking machine gun and his hand ain't shaking no more. He isn't watching me or the Vice President—he's listening. I'm not scared, but this is getting a little too freaky for me.

"What kind of gun is that?" I ask, by way of conversation.

"A P-90."

"What the fuck is that?"

"Something old made new."

Great, I'm thinking, a philosopher.

"It's here," the Vice President says.

I creep over and see that he's standing over a hole in the ground. The earth is red. Bauxite. And the hole is blacker than any of us.

"This is the Cave of the Jagua," the Vice President announces in a deep, respectful voice. "The birthplace of the Tainos."

I raise my eyebrow. "I thought they were in South America."

"We're speaking mythically here."

Bárbaro points the light down the hole, but that doesn't improve anything.

"Would you like to see inside?" the Vice President asks me.

I must have said yes, because Bárbaro gives me the flashlight and the two of them grab me by my ankles and lower me into the hole. All my coins fly out of my pockets. *Bendiciones.* I don't see much, just some odd colors on the eroded walls, and the Vice President's calling down, "Isn't it beautiful?"

This is the perfect place for insight, for a person to become somebody better. The Vice President probably saw his future self hanging in this darkness, bulldozing the poor out of their shanties, and Bárbaro too—buying a concrete house for his mother, showing her how to work the air conditioner—but me, all I can manage is a memory of the first time me and Magda talked. Back at Rutgers. We were waiting for an E bus together on George Street and she was wearing purple. All sorts of purple.

And that's when I know it's over. As soon as you start thinking about the beginning, it's the end.

I cry, and when they pull me up the Vice President says, indignantly, "God, you don't have to be a pussy about it."

That must have been some serious Island voodoo: the ending I saw in the cave came true. The next day we went back to the United States. Five months later I got a letter from my ex-baby. I was dating someone new, but Magda's handwriting still blasted every molecule of air out of my lungs.

It turned out she was also going out with somebody else. A very nice guy she'd met. Dominican, like me.

But I'm getting ahead of myself. I need to finish by showing you what kind of fool I am.

When I returned to the bungalow that night, Magda was waiting up for me. Was packed, looked like she'd been bawling.

"I'm going home tomorrow," she said.

I sat down next to her. Took her hand. "This can work," I said. "All we have to do is try."

Chitra Banerjee Divakaruni (1957–)

a devout Hindu, attended a convent school run by Irish nuns in Calcutta, India, before she came to the United States when she was nineteen. She has called immigrating "the most transformative experience of my life. It . . . made me see my own Indian culture in a different way. It made me both appreciate my culture and question some aspects of my culture." Divakaruni did not write fiction until she finished her doctoral studies in English at the University of California at Berkeley. In speaking of her path to fiction writing, she notes that academic writing didn't "touch my heart. It had nothing to do with my real life as an immigrant woman in America." To earn money for her education, she held many odd jobs, including babysitting, selling merchandise in an Indian boutique, slicing bread in a bakery, and washing instruments in a science lab. At Berkeley, she lived in the International House and worked in the dining hall. She has published four collections of poetry, five novels, and two collections of short stories: The Unknown Errors of Our Lives *and* Arranged Marriage, *which won the American Book Award. She teaches in the creative writing program at the University of Houston, serves on the board of Asians Against Domestic Abuse in Houston, and founded and helps run an organization called Maitri ("friend"), which provides counseling and referrals to South Asian women suffering from domestic violence, depression, and cultural alienation.*

INTRODUCTION BY **Elizabeth Stuckey-French**

Teachers of fiction writing pass on "rules" of fiction writing to our students because we want to save them from the common traps beginning writers often fall into. It is important to learn what the rules are and how to follow them, but all great writers, like Divakaruni, also know when to break them.

Readers of Divakaruni's fiction will delight in her use of language—the perfect metaphors, stunning images, and sensory details. But I would like to talk about some of the less obvious strengths of her work, the rules she chooses to break, and why we, as readers, let her get away with it.

"Mrs. Dutta Writes a Letter":

Fiction Writing Rule #1: Don't begin a story with an alarm clock going off.

In this story, the rattling alarm is not a signal that the writer is merely doing warm-ups before the real story begins—if it ever does. This alarm clock is doing more than that. In fact, it's doing lots of things.

First of all, the habit of rising early evokes Mrs. Dutta's past as a young wife in India, when she had to get up early each morning to start the fire before the rest of the household got up. Mrs. Dutta felt useful then, as opposed to now, in California, when nobody cares when she gets up.

She sets her alarm clock because rising early is one of a number of old habits she can't break, even though she knows these habits will get her in trouble. Mrs. Dutta has done something wrong by setting her alarm—she's done it even though she knows it will annoy her son and daughter-in-law, even though her son has asked her not to do it. We keep reading, hoping she won't get into trouble. But we know she will. Trouble is what stories are all about.

"The Lives of Strangers":

Rule #2: No surprise endings!

Most memorable in this story are two surprising moments: First, when Leela, an American who is in the midst of a religious pilgrimage to Shiva's holy shrine, suddenly decides to leave the group with Mrs. Das, the group outcast, even though she knows that her aunt and the other travelers will be horrified. The second and even bigger surprise comes at the end, when Leela publicly turns on Mrs. Das and humiliates her.

These surprises work for a few reasons. Leela herself thinks that her actions come out of the blue, which actually helps to make them more believable. Divakaruni lets her character ask herself the question we're thinking—why on earth has she done these things?

The surprises also work because Leela is in a vulnerable emotional state. We learn that she has recently tried to kill herself because of loneliness, and in Mrs. Das, she finds a person who is even more lonely and desperate than she is. She leaps to help Mrs. Das, perhaps wanting to prove that she can selflessly love another (which her former lover said she could never do). Then, even though she and Mrs. Das have made a real connection, Leela soundly rejects Mrs. Das as soon as she has another accident, when it's obvious she hasn't been able to save Mrs. Das or herself after all.

"The Blooming Season for Cacti":

Rule #3: Don't have too many characters, settings, or story lines in a short story. They're too hard to keep track of.

This story has an expansive, episodic feel. There are many major characters: Mira; her mother; her brother; her sister-in-law; her boss Malik; and her friends Priya, Radhika, and Ajit—all vivid, well-defined, and deftly drawn. And vital to the story.

There are three stories unfolding in three different settings: Bombay, Dallas, and Sacramento. These stories are told in alternating sections, and some of them aren't in linear order. But on close examination, we see that they come in the right order, because they gradually give us the answers to our questions, not giving away too much too soon. What happened to Mira's mother in Bombay? Why did Mira flee Dallas? Why is she going to Sacramento, and what will happen to her there, broke and all alone as she is?

Divakaruni brings the past and present together in another effective way: She uses Mira's memories and thoughts of the water tank in the present-time sections to remind us how Mira is still stuck in the past; for instance, when she decides to go out with Ajit, she thinks, "Perhaps, this, at last, will be how I climb out of my water tank."

Elizabeth Stuckey-French's novel Mermaids on the Moon *was published by Doubleday in June 2002, and her collection of short stories,* The First Paper Girl in Red Oak, Iowa, *in 2000. Her stories have appeared in* The Atlantic Monthly, Gettysburg Review, Southern Review, Five Points, *and other literary magazines. She teaches fiction writing at Florida State University in Tallahassee.*

Chitra Banerjee Divakaruni

Mrs. Dutta Writes a Letter

When the alarm goes off at 5:00 A.M., buzzing like a trapped wasp, Mrs. Dutta has been lying awake for quite a while. Though it has now been two months, she still has difficulty sleeping on the Perma Rest mattress Sagar and Shyamoli, her son and daughter-in-law, have bought specially for her. It is too American-soft, unlike the reassuringly solid copra ticking she used at home. *Except this is home now,* she reminds herself. She reaches hurriedly to turn off the alarm, but in the dark her fingers get confused among the knobs, and the electric clock falls with a thud to the floor. Its insistent metallic call vibrates out through the walls of her room until she is sure it will wake everyone. She yanks frantically at the wire until she feels it give, and in the abrupt silence that follows she hears herself breathing, a sound harsh and uneven and full of guilt.

Mrs. Dutta knows, of course, that this turmoil is her own fault. She should just not set the alarm. There is no need for her to get up early here in Sunnyvale, in her son's house. But the habit, taught to her by her mother-in-law when she was a bride of seventeen, *a good wife wakes before the rest of the household,* is one she finds impossible to break. How hard it was then to pull her unwilling body away from her husband's sleep-warm clasp, Sagar's father, whom she had just learned to love. To stumble to the kitchen that smelled of stale garam masala and light the coal unoon so that she could make morning tea for them all—her parents-in-law, her husband, his two younger brothers, the widowed aunt who lived with them.

After dinner, when the family sits in front of the TV, she attempts to tell her grandchildren about those days. "I was never good at starting that unoon—the smoke stung my eyes, making me cough and cough. Breakfast was never ready on time, and my mother-in-law—oh, how she scolded me until I was in tears. Every night I would pray to Goddess Durga, please let me sleep late, just one morning!"

"Mmmm," Pradeep says, bent over a model plane.

"Oooh, how awful," Mrinalini says, wrinkling her nose politely before she turns back to a show filled with jokes that Mrs. Dutta does not understand.

"That's why you should sleep in now, Mother," says Shyamoli, smiling from the recliner where she sits looking through the *Wall Street Journal.* With her legs crossed so elegantly under the shimmery blue skirt she has changed into after work, and her unusually fair skin, she could pass for an American, thinks Mrs. Dutta, whose own skin is as brown as roasted cumin. The thought fills her with an uneasy pride.

From the floor where he leans against Shyamoli's knee, Sagar adds, "We want you to be comfortable, Ma. To rest. That's why we brought you to America."

In spite of his thinning hair and the gold-rimmed glasses that he has recently taken to wearing, Sagar's face seems to Mrs. Dutta still that of the boy she used to send off to primary school with his metal tiffin box. She remembers how he crawled into her bed on stormy monsoon nights, how when he was ill no one else could make him drink his barley water. Her heart balloons in sudden gladness because she is really here, with him and his children in America. "Oh, Sagar"—she smiles—"now you're talking like this! But did you give me a moment's rest while you were growing up?" And she launches into a description of childhood pranks that has him shaking his head indulgently while disembodied TV laughter echoes through the room.

But later he comes into her bedroom and says, a little shamefaced, "Mother, please, don't get up so early in the morning. All that noise in the bathroom, it wakes us up, and Molli has such a long day at work . . ."

And she, turning a little so that he won't see her foolish eyes filling with tears as though she were a teenage bride again and not a woman well over sixty, nods her head, *yes, yes.*

Waiting for the sounds of the stirring household to release her from the embrace of her Perma Rest mattress, Mrs. Dutta repeats the 108 holy names of God. *Om Keshavaya Namah, Om Narayanaya Namah, Om Madhavaya Namah.* But underneath she is thinking of the bleached-blue aerogram from Mrs. Basu that has been waiting unanswered on her bedside table all week, filled with news from home. There was a robbery at the Sandhya Jewelry Store, the bandits had guns but luckily no one was hurt. Mr. Joshi's daughter, that sweet-faced child, has run away with her singing teacher, who would've thought it. Mrs. Barucha's daughter-in-law had one more baby girl, yes, their fourth, you'd think they'd know better than to keep trying for a boy. Last Tuesday was Bangla Bandh, another labor strike, everything closed down, even the buses not running, but you can't really blame them, can you, after all factory workers have to eat, too. Mrs. Basu's tenants, whom she'd been trying to evict forever, had finally moved out, good riddance, but you should see the state of the flat.

At the very bottom Mrs. Basu wrote, *Are you happy in America?*

Mrs. Dutta knows that Mrs. Basu, who has been her closest friend since they both came to Ghoshpara Lane as young brides, cannot be fobbed off with descriptions of Fisherman's Wharf and the Golden Gate Bridge, or even with anecdotes involving grandchildren. And so she has been putting off her reply while in her heart family loyalty battles with insidious feelings of—but she turns from them quickly and will not name them even to herself.

Now Sagar is knocking on the children's doors—a curious custom this, children being allowed to close their doors against their parents—and with relief Mrs. Dutta gathers up her bathroom things. She has plenty of time. It will take a second rapping from their mother before Pradeep and Mrinalini open their doors and stumble out. Still, she is not one to waste the precious morning. She splashes cold water on her face and neck (she does not believe in pampering herself), scrapes the night's gumminess from her tongue with her metal tongue cleaner, and brushes vigorously, though the minty toothpaste does not leave her mouth feeling as clean as did the bittersweet neem stick she'd been using all her life. She combs the knots out of her hair. Even at her age it is thicker and silkier than her daughter-in-law's permed curls. Such vanity, she scolds her reflection, and you a grandmother and a widow besides. Still, as she deftly fashions her hair into a neat coil, she remembers how her husband would always compare it to night rain.

She hears a commotion outside.

"Pat! Minnie! What d'you mean you still haven't washed up? I'm late every morning to work nowadays because of you kids."

"But, Mom, *she's* in there. She's been there forever . . ." says Mrinalini.

Pause. Then, "So go to the downstairs bathroom."

"But all our stuff is here," says Pradeep, and Mrinalini adds, "It's not fair. Why can't *she* go downstairs?"

A longer pause. Inside the bathroom Mrs. Dutta hopes Shyamoli will not be too harsh on the girl. But a child who refers to elders in that disrespectful way ought to be punished. How many times had she slapped Sagar for something far less, though he was her only one, the jewel of her eye, come to her after she had been married for seven years and everyone had given up hope already? Whenever she lifted her hand to him it was as though her heart was being put through a masala grinder. Such is a mother's duty.

But Shyamoli only says, in a tired voice, "That's enough! Go put on your clothes, hurry!"

The grumblings recede. Footsteps clatter down the stairs. Inside the bathroom Mrs. Dutta bends over the sink, gripping the folds of her sari. Hard to think through the pounding in her head to what it is she feels most—anger at the children for their rudeness, or at Shyamoli for letting them go unrebuked. Or is it shame that clogs her throat, stinging, sulfuric, indigestible?

It is 9:00 A.M., and the house, after the flurry of departures, of frantic "I can't find my socks," and "Mom, he took my lunch money," and "I swear I'll leave you kids behind if you're not in the car in exactly one minute," has settled into its placid daytime rhythms.

Busy in the kitchen, Mrs. Dutta has recovered her spirits. It is too exhausting to hold on to grudges, and besides, the kitchen—sunlight spilling across its countertops while the refrigerator hums reassuringly—is her favorite place.

Mrs. Dutta hums too as she fries potatoes for alu dum. Her voice is rusty and slightly off-key. In India she would never have ventured to sing, but with everyone gone, the house is too quiet, all that silence pressing down on her like the heel of a giant hand, and the TV voices, with their unreal accents, are no help at all. As the potatoes turn golden-brown, she permits herself a moment of nostalgia for her Calcutta kitchen—the new gas stove bought with the birthday money Sagar sent, the scoured brass pots stacked by the meat safe, the window with the lotus-pattern grille through which she could look down on children playing cricket after school. The mouth-watering smell of ginger and chili paste, ground fresh by Reba the maid, and, in the evening, strong black Assam cha brewing in the kettle when Mrs. Basu came by to visit. In her mind she writes to Mrs. Basu, *Oh, Roma, I miss it all so much, sometimes I feel that someone has reached in and torn out a handful of my chest.*

But only fools indulge in nostalgia, so Mrs. Dutta shakes her head clear of images and straightens up the kitchen. She pours the half-drunk glasses of milk down the sink, though Shyamoli has told her to save them in the refrigerator. But surely Shyamoli, a girl from a good Hindu family, doesn't expect her to put contaminated jutha things in with the rest of the food? She washes the breakfast dishes by hand instead of letting them wait inside the dishwater till night, breeding germs. With practiced fingers she throws an assortment of spices into the blender: coriander, cumin, cloves, black pepper, a few red chilies for vigor. No stale bottled curry powder for *her!*

At least the family's eating well since I arrived, she writes in her mind, *proper Indian food, rutis that puff up the way they should, fish curry in mustard sauce, and real pulao with raisins and cashews and ghee—the way you taught me, Roma—instead of Rice-a-roni.* She would like to add, *They love it,* but thinking of Shyamoli she hesitates.

At first Shyamoli had been happy enough to have someone take over the cooking. It's wonderful to come home to a hot dinner, she'd say, or, Mother, what crispy papads, and your fish gravy is out of this world. But recently she's taken to picking at her food, and once or twice from the kitchen Mrs. Dutta has caught wisps of words, intensely whispered: *cholesterol, all putting on weight, she's spoiling you.* And though Shyamoli always refuses when the children ask if they can have burritos from the freezer instead, Mrs. Dutta suspects that she would really like to say yes.

The children. A heaviness pulls at Mrs. Dutta's entire body when she thinks of them. Like so much in this country they have turned out to be—yes, she might as well admit it—a disappointment.

For this she blames, in part, the Olan Mills portrait. Perhaps it had been impractical of her to set so much store on a photograph, especially one taken years ago. But it was such a charming scene—Mrinalini in a ruffled white dress with her arm around her brother, Pradeep chubby and dimpled in a suit and bow tie, a glorious autumn forest blazing red and yellow behind them. (Later Mrs. Dutta would learn, with a sense of having been betrayed, that the forest was merely a backdrop in a studio in California, where real trees did not turn such colors.)

The picture had arrived, silver-framed and wrapped in a plastic sheet filled with bubbles, with a note from Shyamoli explaining that it was a Mother's Day gift. (A strange concept, a day set aside to honor mothers. Did the sahebs not honor their mothers the rest of the year, then?) For a week Mrs. Dutta could not decide where it should be hung. If she put it in the drawing room, visitors would be able to admire her grandchildren, but if she put it on the bedroom wall, she would be able to see the photo, last thing, before she fell asleep. She had finally opted for the bedroom, and later, when she was too ill with pneumonia to leave her bed for a month, she'd been glad of it.

Mrs. Dutta was not unused to living on her own. She had done it for the last three years, since Sagar's father died, politely but stubbornly declining the offers of various relatives, well-meaning and otherwise, to come and stay with her. In this she had surprised herself as well as others, who thought of her as a shy, sheltered woman, one who would surely fall apart without her husband to handle things for her. But she managed quite well. She missed Sagar's father, of course, especially in the evenings, when it had been his habit to read to her the more amusing parts of the newspaper while she rolled out rutis. But once the grief receded, she found it rather pleasant to be mistress of her own life, as she confided to Mrs. Basu. She liked being able, for the first time ever, to lie in bed all evening and read a new novel of Shankar's straight through if she wanted, or to send out for hot brinjal pakoras on a rainy day without feeling guilty that she wasn't serving up a balanced meal.

When the pneumonia hit, everything changed.

Mrs. Dutta had been ill before, but those illnesses had been different. Even in bed she'd been at the center of the household, with Reba coming to find out what should be cooked, Sagar's father bringing her shirts with missing buttons, her mother-in-law, now old and tamed, complaining that the cook didn't brew her tea strong enough, and Sagar running in crying because he'd had a fight with the neighbor boy. But now there was no one to ask her, querulously, *Just how long do you plan to remain sick,* no one waiting in impatient exasperation for her to take on her duties again, no one whose life was inconvenienced the least bit by her illness.

There was, therefore, no reason for her to get well.

When this thought occurred to Mrs. Dutta, she was so frightened that her body grew numb. The walls of the room spun into blackness, the bed on which she lay, a vast four-poster she had shared with Sagar's father since her marriage, rocked like a mastless dinghy caught in a storm, and a great, muted roar reverberated in the cavities of her skull. For a moment, unable to move or see, she thought, *I'm dead.* Then her vision, desperate and blurry, caught on the portrait. *My grandchildren.* She focused, with some difficulty, on the bright, oblivious sheen of their child faces, the eyes so like Sagar's that for a moment she could feel heartsickness cramping her joints like arthritis. She drew in a shuddering breath; the roaring seemed to recede. When the afternoon post brought another letter from Sagar, *Mother, you really should come and live with us, we worry about you all alone in India, especially when you're sick like this,* she wrote back the same day, with fingers that still shook a little, *You're right, my place is with you, with my grandchildren.*

But now that she is here on the other side of the world, she is wrenched by doubt. She knows the grandchildren love her—how can it be otherwise among family? And she loves them, she reminds herself, though they have put away, somewhere in the back of a closet, the vellum-bound *Ramayana for Young Readers* that she carried all the way from India in her hand luggage. Though their bodies twitch with impatience when she tries to tell them stories of her girlhood. Though they offer the most transparent excuses when she asks them to sit with her while she chants the evening arati. *They're flesh of my flesh, blood of my blood,* she reminds herself. But sometimes when she listens, from the other room, to them speaking on the phone, their American voices rising in excitement as they discuss a glittering alien world of Power Rangers, Spice Girls, and Spirit Week at school, she almost cannot believe it.

Stepping into the backyard with a bucket of newly washed clothes, Mrs. Dutta views the sky with some anxiety. The butter-gold sunlight is gone, black-bellied clouds have taken over the horizon, and the air feels still and heavy on her face, as before a Bengal storm. What if her clothes don't dry by the time the others return home?

Washing clothes has been a problem for Mrs. Dutta ever since she arrived in California.

"We can't, Mother," Shyamoli had said with a sigh when Mrs. Dutta asked Sagar to put up a clothesline for her in the backyard. (Shyamoli sighed often nowadays. Perhaps it was an American habit? Mrs. Dutta did not remember the Indian Shyamoli, the docile bride she'd mothered for a month before putting her on a Pan Am flight to join her husband, pursing her lips in quite this way to let out a breath at once patient and vexed.) "It's just not *done,* not in a nice neighborhood like this one. And being the only Indian family on the street, we have to be extra careful. People here, sometimes—." She'd broken off with a shake of her head. "Why don't you just keep your dirty clothes in the hamper I've put in your room, and I'll wash them on Sunday along with everyone else's."

Afraid of causing another sigh, Mrs. Dutta had agreed reluctantly. But she knew she should not store unclean clothes in the same room where she kept the pictures of her gods. That brought bad luck. And the odor. Lying in bed at night she could smell it distinctly, even though Shyamoli claimed the hamper was airtight. The sour, starchy old-woman smell embarrassed her.

What embarrassed her more was when, Sunday afternoons, Shyamoli brought the laundry into the family room to fold. Mrs. Dutta would bend intensely over her knitting, face tingling with shame, as her daughter-in-law nonchalantly shook out the wisps of lace, magenta and sea-green and black, that were her panties, laying them next to a stack of Sagar's briefs. And when, right in front of everyone, Shyamoli pulled out Mrs. Dutta's own crumpled, baggy bras from the clothes heap, she wished the ground would open up and swallow her, like the Sita of mythology.

Then one day Shyamoli set the clothes basket down in front of Sagar.

"Can you do them today, Sagar?" (Mrs. Dutta, who had never, through the forty-two years of her marriage, addressed Sagar's father by name, tried not to wince.) "I've got to get that sales report into the computer by tonight."

Before Sagar could respond, Mrs. Dutta was out of her chair, knitting needles dropping to the floor.

"No no no, clothes and all is no work for the man of the house. I'll do it." The thought of her son's hands searching through the basket and lifting up his wife's— and her own—underclothes filled her with horror.

"Mother!" Shyamoli said. "This is why Indian men are so useless around the house. Here in America we don't believe in men's work and women's work. Don't I work outside all day, just like Sagar? How'll I manage if he doesn't help me at home?"

"I'll help you instead," Mrs. Dutta ventured.

"You don't understand, do you, Mother?" Shyamoli said with a shaky smile. Then she went into the study.

Mrs. Dutta sat down in her chair and tried to understand. But after a while she gave up and whispered to Sagar that she wanted him to teach her how to run the washer and dryer.

"Why, Mother? Molli's quite happy to . . ."

"I've got to learn it. . . ." Her voice warped with distress as she rummaged through the tangled heap for her clothes.

Her son began to object, then shrugged. "Oh very well. If that's what you really want."

But later, when she faced them alone, the machines with their cryptic symbols and rows of gleaming knobs terrified her. What if she pressed the wrong button and flooded the entire floor with soapsuds? What if she couldn't turn the machines off and they kept going, whirring maniacally, until they exploded? (This had happened to a woman on a TV show just the other day, and she had jumped up and down, screaming. Everyone else found it hilarious, but Mrs. Dutta sat stiff-spined, gripping the armrest of her chair.) So she took to washing her clothes in the bathtub when she was alone. She had never done such a chore before, but she remembered how the village washerwomen of her childhood would beat their saris clean against river rocks. And a curious satisfaction filled her as her clothes hit the porcelain with the same solid wet *thunk*.

My small victory, my secret.

This is why everything must be dried and put safely away before Shyamoli returns. Ignorance, as Mrs. Dutta knows well from years of managing a household, is a great promoter of harmony. So she keeps an eye on the menacing advance of the clouds as she hangs up her blouse and underwear. As she drapes her sari along the redwood fence that separates her son's property from the neighbor's, first wiping it clean with a dish towel she has secretly taken from the bottom drawer of the kitchen. But she isn't too worried. Hasn't she managed every time, even after that freak hailstorm last month when she had to use the iron from the laundry closet to press everything dry? The memory pleases her. In her mind she writes to Mrs. Basu, *I'm fitting in so well here, you'd never guess I came only two months back. I've found new ways of doing things, of solving problems creatively. You would be most proud if you saw me.*

When Mrs. Dutta decided to give up her home of forty-five years, her relatives showed far less surprise than she had expected.

"Oh, we all knew you'd end up in America sooner or later," they said. "It was a foolishness to stay on alone so long after Sagar's father, may he find eternal peace, passed away. Good thing that boy of yours came to his senses and called you to join him. Everyone knows a wife's place is with her husband, and a widow's with her son."

Mrs. Dutta had nodded meek agreement, ashamed to let anyone know that the night before she had awakened weeping.

"Well, now that you're going, what'll happen to all your things?"

Mrs. Dutta, still troubled over those treacherous tears, had offered up her household effects in propitiation. "Here, Didi, you take this cutwork bedspread. Mashima, for a long time I meant for you to have these Corning Ware dishes, I know how much you admire them. And, Boudi, this tape recorder that Sagar sent a year back is for you. Yes yes, I'm quite sure. I can always tell Sagar to buy me another one when I get there."

Mrs. Basu, coming in just as a cousin made off triumphantly with a bone china tea set, had protested. "Prameela, have you gone crazy? That tea set used to belong to your mother-in-law."

"But what'll I do with it in America? Shyamoli has her own set—"

A look that Mrs. Dutta couldn't read flitted across Mrs. Basu's face. "But do you want to drink from it for the rest of your life?"

"What do you mean?"

Mrs. Basu hesitated. Then she said, "What if you don't like it there?"

"How can I not like it, Roma?" Mrs. Dutta's voice was strident, even to her own ears. With an effort she controlled it and continued, "I'll miss my friends, I know—and you most of all. The things we do together—evening tea, our walk around Rabindra Sarobar Lake, Thursday night Bhagavat Geeta class. But Sagar—they're my only family. And blood is blood after all."

"I wonder," Mrs. Basu said dryly, and Mrs. Dutta recalled that though both of Mrs. Basu's children lived just a day's journey away, they came to see her only on occasions when common decency demanded their presence. Perhaps they were tightfisted in money matters too. Perhaps that was why Mrs. Basu had started renting out her downstairs a few years ago, even though, as anyone in Calcutta knew, tenants were more trouble than they were worth. Such filial neglect must be hard to take, though Mrs. Basu, loyal to her children as indeed a mother should be, never complained. In a way Mrs. Dutta had been better off, with Sagar too far away for her to put his love to the test.

"At least don't give up the house," Mrs. Basu was saying. "It'll be impossible to find another place in case—"

"In case what?" Mrs. Dutta asked, her words like stone chips. She was surprised to find that she was angrier with Mrs. Basu than she'd ever been. Or was it fear? *My son isn't like yours,* she'd been on the verge of spitting out. She took a deep breath and made herself smile, made herself remember that she might never see her friend again.

"Ah, Roma," she said, putting her arm around Mrs. Basu, "you think I'm such an old witch that my Sagar and my Shyamoli will be unable to live with me?"

Mrs. Dutta hums a popular Rabindra Sangeet as she pulls her sari from the fence. It's been a good day, as good as it can be in a country where you might stare out the window for hours and not see one living soul. No vegetable vendors with wicker baskets balanced on their heads, no knife sharpeners calling *scissors-knives-choppers, scissors-knives-choppers* to bring the children running. No dehati women with tattoos on their arms to sell you cookware in exchange for your old silk saris. Why, even the animals that frequented Ghoshpara Lane had personality. Stray dogs that knew to line up outside the kitchen door just when leftovers were likely to be thrown out, the goat who maneuvered its head through the garden grille hoping to get at her dahlias, cows who planted themselves majestically in the center of the road, ignoring honking drivers. And right across the street was Mrs. Basu's two-story house, which Mrs. Dutta knew as well as her own. How many times had she walked up the stairs to that airy room painted sea-green and filled with plants where her friend would be waiting for her.

What took you so long today, Prameela? Your tea is cold already.

Wait till you hear what happened, Roma. Then you won't scold me for being late . . .

Stop it, you silly woman, Mrs. Dutta tells herself severely. Every single one of your relatives would give an arm and a leg to be in your place, you know that. After lunch you're going to write a nice, long letter to Roma, telling her exactly how delighted you are to be here.

From where Mrs. Dutta stands, gathering up petticoats and blouses, she can look into the next yard. Not that there's much to see, just tidy grass and a few pale-blue flowers whose name she doesn't know. There are two wooden chairs under a tree, but Mrs. Dutta has never seen anyone using them. What's the point of having such a big yard if you're not even going to sit in it? she thinks. Calcutta pushes itself into her mind again, Calcutta with its narrow, blackened flats where families of six and eight and ten squeeze themselves into two tiny rooms, and her heart fills with a sense of loss she knows to be illogical.

When she first arrived in Sagar's home, Mrs. Dutta wanted to go over and meet her next-door neighbors, maybe take them some of her special rose-water rasogollahs, as she'd often done with Mrs. Basu. But Shyamoli said she shouldn't. Such things were not the custom in California, she explained earnestly. You didn't just drop in on people without calling ahead. Here everyone was busy, they didn't sit around chatting, drinking endless cups of sugar tea. Why, they might even say something unpleasant to her.

"For what?" Mrs. Dutta had asked disbelievingly, and Shyamoli had said, "Because Americans don't like neighbors to"—here she used an English phrase—"invade their privacy." Mrs. Dutta, who didn't fully understand the word *privacy* because there was no such term in Bengali, had gazed at her daughter-in-law in some bewilderment. But she understood enough to not ask again. In the following months, though, she often looked over the fence, hoping to make contact. People were people, whether in India or America, and everyone appreciated a friendly face. When Shyamoli was as old as Mrs. Dutta, she would know that, too.

Today, just as she is about to turn away, out of the corner of her eye Mrs. Dutta notices a movement. At one of the windows a woman is standing, her hair a sleek gold like that of the TV heroines whose exploits baffle Mrs. Dutta when sometimes she tunes in to an afternoon serial. She is smoking a cigarette, and a curl of gray rises lazily, elegantly from her fingers. Mrs. Dutta is so happy to see another human being in the middle of her solitary day that she forgets how much she disapproves of smoking, especially in women. She lifts her hand in the gesture she has seen her grandchildren use to wave an eager hello.

The woman stares back at Mrs. Dutta. Her lips are a perfect-painted red, and when she raises her cigarette to her mouth, its tip glows like an animal's eye. She does not wave back or smile. Perhaps she is not well? Mrs. Dutta feels sorry for her, alone in her illness in a silent house with only cigarettes for solace, and she wishes the etiquette of America had not prevented her from walking over with a word of cheer and a bowl of her fresh-cooked alu dum.

Mrs. Dutta rarely gets a chance to be alone with her son. In the morning he is in too much of a hurry even to drink the fragrant cardamom tea which she (remembering how as a child he would always beg for a sip from her cup) offers to make him. He doesn't return until dinnertime, and afterward he must help the children with their homework, read the paper, hear the details of Shyamoli's day, watch his favorite TV crime show in order to unwind, and take out the garbage. In between, for he is a solicitous son, he converses with Mrs. Dutta. In response to his questions she assures him that her arthritis is much better now; no, no, she's not growing bored being at home all the time; she has everything she needs—Shyamoli has been so kind—but perhaps he could pick up a few aerograms on his way back tomorrow? She recites obediently for him an edited list of her day's activities and smiles when he praises her cooking. But when he says, "Oh, well, time to turn in, another working day tomorrow," she is racked by a vague pain, like hunger, in the region of her heart.

So it is with the delighted air of a child who has been offered an unexpected gift that she leaves her half-written letter to greet Sagar at the door today, a good hour before Shyamoli is due back. The children are busy in the family room doing homework and watching cartoons (mostly the latter, Mrs. Dutta suspects). But for once she doesn't mind because they race in to give their father hurried hugs and then race back again. And she has him, her son, all to herself in a kitchen filled with the familiar, pungent odors of tamarind sauce and chopped coriander leaves.

"Khoka," she says, calling him by the childhood name she hasn't used in years, "I could fry you two-three hot-hot luchis, if you like." As she waits for his reply she can feel, in the hollow of her throat, the rapid beat of her blood. And when he says yes, that would be very nice, she shuts her eyes and takes a deep breath, and it is as though merciful time has given her back her youth, that sweet, aching urgency of being needed again.

★ ★ ★

Mrs. Dutta is telling Sagar a story.

"When you were a child, how scared you were of injections! One time, when the government doctor came to give us compulsory typhoid shots, you locked yourself in the bathroom and refused to come out. Do you remember what your father finally did? He went into the garden and caught a lizard and threw it in the bathroom window, because you were even more scared of lizards than of shots. And in exactly one second you ran out screaming—right into the waiting doctor's arms."

Sagar laughs so hard that he almost upsets his tea (made with real sugar, because Mrs. Dutta knows it is better for her son than that chemical powder Shyamoli likes to use). There are tears in his eyes, and Mrs. Dutta, who had not dared to hope he would find her story so amusing, feels gratified. When he takes off his glasses to wipe them, his face is oddly young, not like a father's at all, or even a husband's, and she has to suppress an impulse to put out her hand and rub away the indentations the glasses have left on his nose.

"I'd totally forgotten," says Sagar. "How can you keep track of those old, old things?"

Because it is the lot of mothers to remember what no one else cares to, Mrs. Dutta thinks. To tell them over and over until they are lodged, perforce, in family lore. We are the keepers of the heart's dusty corners.

But as she starts to say this, the front door creaks open, and she hears the faint click of Shyamoli's high heels. Mrs. Dutta rises, collecting the dirty dishes.

"Call me fifteen minutes before you're ready to eat so I can fry fresh luchis for everyone," she tells Sagar.

"You don't have to leave, Mother," he says.

Mrs. Dutta smiles her pleasure but doesn't stop. She knows Shyamoli likes to be alone with her husband at this time, and today in her happiness she does not grudge her this.

"You think I've nothing to do, only sit and gossip with you?" she mock-scolds. "I want you to know I have a very important letter to finish."

Somewhere behind her she hears a thud, a briefcase falling over. This surprises her. Shyamoli is always so careful with her case because it was a gift from Sagar when she was finally made a manager in her company.

"Hi!" Sagar calls, and when there's no answer, "Hey, Molli, you okay?"

Shyamoli comes into the room slowly, her hair disheveled as though she's been running her fingers through it. A hectic color blotches her cheeks.

"What's the matter, Molli?" Sagar walks over to give her a kiss. "Bad day at work?" Mrs. Dutta, embarrassed as always by this display of marital affection, turns toward the window, but not before she sees Shyamoli move her face away.

"Leave me alone." Her voice is wobbly. "Just leave me alone."

"But what is it?" Sagar says in concern.

"I don't want to talk about it right now." Shyamoli lowers herself into a kitchen chair and puts her face in her hands. Sagar stands in the middle of the room, looking helpless. He raises his hand and lets it fall, as though he wants to comfort his wife but is afraid of what she might do.

A protective anger for her son surges inside Mrs. Dutta, but she leaves the room silently. In her mind-letter she writes, *Women need to be strong, not react to every little thing like this. You and I, Roma, we had far worse to cry about, but we shed our tears invisibly.*

We were good wives and daughters-in-law, good mothers. Dutiful, uncomplaining. Never putting ourselves first.

A sudden memory comes to her, one she hasn't thought of in years, a day when she scorched a special kheer dessert. Her mother-in-law had shouted at her, "Didn't your mother teach you anything, you useless girl?" As punishment she refused to let Mrs. Dutta go with Mrs. Basu to the cinema, even though *Sahib, Bibi aur Ghulam,* which all Calcutta was crazy about, was playing, and their tickets were bought already. Mrs. Dutta had wept the entire afternoon, but before Sagar's father came home she washed her face carefully with cold water and applied kajal to her eyes so he wouldn't know.

But everything is getting mixed up, and her own young, trying-not-to-cry face blurs into another—why, it's Shyamoli's—and a thought hits her so sharply in the chest she has to hold on to the bedroom wall. *And what good did it do? The more we bent, the more people pushed us, until one day we'd forgotten that we could stand up straight. Maybe Shyamoli's doing the right thing, after all . . .*

Mrs. Dutta lowers herself heavily on to her bed, trying to erase such an insidious idea from her mind. Oh, this new country where all the rules are upside down, it's confusing her. Her mind feels muddy, like a pond in which too many water buffaloes have been wading. Maybe things will settle down if she can focus on the letter to Roma.

Then she remembers that she has left the half-written aerogram on the kitchen table. She knows she should wait until after dinner, after her son and his wife have sorted things out. But a restlessness—or is it defiance?—has taken hold of her. She's sorry Shyamoli's upset, but why should she have to waste her evening because of that? She'll go get her letter—it's no crime, is it? She'll march right in and pick it up, and even if Shyamoli stops in midsentence with another one of those sighs, she'll refuse to feel apologetic. Besides, by now they're probably in the family room, watching TV.

Really, Roma, she writes in her head as she feels her way along the unlighted corridor, *the amount of TV they watch here is quite scandalous. The children too, sitting for hours in front of that box like they've been turned into painted Kesto Nagar dolls, and then talking back when I tell them to turn it off.* Of course, she will never put such blasphemy into a real letter. Still, it makes her feel better to say it, if only to herself.

In the family room the TV is on, but for once no one is paying it any attention. Shyamoli and Sagar sit on the sofa, conversing. From where she stands in the corridor, Mrs. Dutta cannot see them, but their shadows—enormous against the wall where the table lamp has cast them—seem to flicker and leap at her.

She is about to slip unseen into the kitchen when Shyamoli's rising voice arrests her. In its raw, shaking unhappiness it is so unlike her daughter-in-law's assured tones that Mrs. Dutta is no more able to move away from it than if she had heard the call of the nishi, the lost souls of the dead on whose tales she grew up.

"It's easy for you to say 'Calm down.' I'd like to see how calm *you'd* be if she came up to you and said, 'Kindly tell the old lady not to hang her clothes over the fence into my yard.' She said it twice, like I didn't understand English, like I was an idiot. All these years I've been so careful not to give these Americans a chance to say something like this, and now—"

"Shhh, Shyamoli, I *said* I'd talk to Mother about it."

"You always say that, but you never *do* anything. You're too busy being the perfect son, tiptoeing around her feelings. But how about mine?"

"Hush, Molli, the children . . ."

"Let them hear. I don't care anymore. They're not stupid. They already know what a hard time I've been having with her. You're the only one who refuses to see it."

In the passage Mrs. Dutta shrinks against the wall. She wants to move away, to not hear anything else, but her feet are formed of cement, impossible to lift, and Shyamoli's words pour into her ears like smoking oil.

"I've explained over and over, and she still keeps on doing what I've asked her not to—throwing away perfectly good food, leaving dishes to drip all over the countertops. Ordering my children to stop doing things I've given them permission for. She's taken over the entire kitchen, cooking whatever she likes. You come in the door and the smell of grease is everywhere, in all our clothes. I feel like this isn't my house anymore."

"Be patient, Molli, she's an old woman, after all."

"I know. That's why I tried so hard. I know having her here is important to you. But I can't do it any longer. I just can't. Some days I feel like taking the kids and leaving." Shyamoli's voice disappears into a sob.

A shadow stumbles across the wall to her, and then another. Behind the weatherman's nasal tones announcing a week of sunny days, Mrs. Dutta can hear a high, frightened weeping. The children, she thinks. It's probably the first time they've seen their mother cry.

"Don't talk like that, sweetheart." Sagar leans forward, his voice, too, miserable. All the shadows on the wall shiver and merge into a single dark silhouette.

Mrs. Dutta stares at that silhouette, the solidarity of it. Sagar and Shyamoli's murmurs are lost beneath a noise—is it in her veins, this dry humming, the way the taps in Calcutta used to hum when the municipality turned the water off? After a while she discovers that she has reached her room. In darkness she lowers herself on to her bed very gently, as though her body is made of the thinnest glass. Or perhaps ice, she is so cold. She sits for a long time with her eyes closed, while inside her head thoughts whirl faster and faster until they disappear in a gray dust storm.

When Pradeep finally comes to call her for dinner, Mrs. Dutta follows him to the kitchen where she fries luchis for everyone, the perfect circles of dough puffing up crisp and golden as always. Sagar and Shyamoli have reached a truce of some kind: she gives him a small smile, and he puts out a casual hand to massage the back of her neck. Mrs. Dutta demonstrates no embarrassment at this. She eats her dinner. She answers questions put to her. She smiles when someone makes a joke. If her face is stiff, as though she has been given a shot of Novocain, no one notices. When the table is cleared, she excuses herself, saying she has to finish her letter.

Now Mrs. Dutta sits on her bed, reading over what she wrote in the innocent afternoon.

Dear Roma,

Although I miss you, I know you will be pleased to hear how happy I am in America. There is much here that needs getting used to, but we are no strangers to adjusting, we old women. After all, haven't we been doing it all our lives?

Today I'm cooking one of Sagar's favorite dishes, alu-um. . . . It gives me such pleasure to see my family gathered around the table, eating my food. The children are still a little shy of me, but I am hopeful that we'll soon be friends. And Shyamoli, so confident and successful—you should see her when she's all dressed for work. I can't believe she's the same timid bride I sent off to America just a few years ago. But Sagar, most of all, is the joy of my old age . . .

With the edge of her sari Mrs. Dutta carefully wipes a tear that has fallen on the aerogram. She blows on the damp spot until it is completely dry, so the pen will not leave an incriminating smudge. Even though Roma would not tell a soul, she cannot risk it. She can already hear them, the avid relatives in India who have been waiting for something just like this to happen. *That Dutta-ginni so set in her ways, we knew she'd never get along with her daughter-in-law.* Or worse, *Did you hear about poor Prameela, how her family treated her, yes, even her son, can you imagine?*

This much surely she owes to Sagar.

And what does she owe herself, Mrs. Dutta, falling through black night with all the certainties she trusted in collapsed upon themselves like imploded stars, and only an image inside her eyelids for company? A silhouette—man, wife, children—joined on a wall, showing her how alone she is in this land of young people. And how unnecessary.

She is not sure how long she sits under the glare of the overhead light, how long her hands clench themselves in her lap. When she opens them, nail marks line the soft flesh of her palms, red hieroglyphs—her body's language, telling her what to do.

Dear Roma, Mrs. Dutta writes,

I cannot answer your question about whether I am happy, for I am no longer sure I know what happiness is. All I know is that it isn't what I thought it to be. It isn't about being needed. It isn't about being with family either. It has something to do with love, I still think that, but in a different way than I believed earlier, a way I don't have the words to explain. Perhaps we can figure it out together, two old women drinking cha in your downstairs flat (for I do hope you will rent it to me on my return), while around us gossip falls—but lightly, like summer rain, for that is all we will allow it to be. If I'm lucky—and perhaps, in spite of all that has happened, I am—the happiness will be in the figuring out.

Pausing to read over what she has written, Mrs. Dutta is surprised to discover this: Now that she no longer cares whether tears blotch her letter, she feels no need to weep.

CHITRA BANERJEE DIVAKARUNI

The Lives of Strangers

The seepage of rainwater has formed a tapestry against the peeling walls of the Nataraj Yatri House dining hall, but no one except Leela notices this. The other members of the pilgrimage party jostle around the fire that sputters in a corner and shout at the pahari boy to hurry with the tea. Aunt Seema sits at one of the scratched wooden tables with a group of women, all of them swaddled in the bright shawls they bought for this trip. From time to time they look down at their laps with a startled expression, like sparrows who have awakened to find themselves plumaged in cockatoo feathers.

Aunt beckons to Leela to come sit by her. "Baap re," she says, "I can't believe how cold it is here in Kashmir. It's quite delightful, actually. Just think, in Calcutta right now people are bathing in sweat, even with the fans on full speed!"

The women smile, pleased at having had the foresight to leave sweaty Calcutta behind at the height of summer for a journey which is going to earn them comfort on earth and goodwill in heaven. They hold their chins high and elongate their necks as classical dancers might. Plump, middle-aged women who sleepily read love stories in *Desh* magazine through the interminable train journey from Howrah Station, already they are metamorphosed into handmaidens of Shiva, adventure-bound toward his holy shrine in Amarnath. Their eyes sparkle with zeal as they discuss how remote the shrine is. How they will have to walk across treacherous glaciers for three whole days to reach it. Contemplating them, Leela wonders if this is the true lure of travel, this hope of a transformed self. Will her own journey, begun when she left America a month ago, bring her this coveted change?

Tea arrives, sweet and steaming in huge aluminum kettles, along with dinner: buttery wheat parathas, fatly stuffed with spicy potatoes. When they have eaten, the guide advises them to get their rest. This is no touristy excursion, he reminds them sternly. It is a serious and sacred yatra, and dangerous, too. He talks awhile of the laws to be observed while on pilgrimage: no non-vegetarian food, no sex. Any menstruating women should not proceed beyond this point. There is a lot more, but his Bengali is full of long, formal words that Leela does not know, and her attention wanders. He ends by saying something about sin and expiation, which seems to her terribly complex and thus very Indian.

Later in bed, Leela will think of Mrs. Das. At dinner Mrs. Das sat by herself at a table that was more rickety than the others. In a room filled with nervous laughter (for the headman had frightened them all a bit, though no one would admit it) she held herself with an absorbed stillness, her elbows pulled close as though early in life she had been taught not to take up too much space in the world. She did not speak to anyone. Under her frizzy pepper-colored hair, her face was angular and ascetic.

Leela has not met Mrs. Das, but she knows a great deal about her because Aunt Seema's friends discuss her frequently. Mostly they marvel at her bad luck.

"Can you imagine!" the doctor's wife says. "Her husband died just two years after her marriage, and right away her in-laws, who hated her because it had been a love match, claimed that the marriage wasn't legal. They were filthy rich—the Dases of Tollygunge, you understand—they hired the shrewdest lawyers. She lost everything—the money, the house, even the wedding jewelry."

"No justice in this world," Aunt says, clicking her tongue sympathetically.

"She had to go to work in an office," someone else adds. "Think of it, a woman of good family, forced to work with low-caste peons and clerks! That's how she put her son through college and got him married."

"And now the daughter-in-law refuses to live with her," Aunt says. "So she's had to move into a women's hostel. A women's hostel! At her age!"

The doctor's wife shakes her head mournfully. "Some people are like that, born under an unlucky star. They bring bad luck to themselves and everyone close to them."

Leela studies the kaleidoscope of emotions flitting across the women's faces. Excitement, pity, cheerful outrage. Can it be true, that part about an unlucky star? In America she would have dealt with such superstition with fluent, dismissive ease, but India is complicated. Like entering a murky, primal lake, in India she has to watch her step.

Leela's happiest childhood memories were of aloneness: reading in her room with the door closed, playing chess on the computer, embarking on long bike rides through the city, going to the movies by herself. You saw more that way, she explained to her parents. You didn't miss crucial bits of dialogue because your companion was busy making inane remarks. Her parents, themselves solitary individuals, didn't object. People—except for a selected handful—were noisy and messy. They knew that. Which was why, early in their lives, they had escaped India to take up research positions in America. Ever since Leela could remember, they had encouraged her taste for privacy. When Leela became a computer programmer, they applauded the fact that she could do most of her work from home. When she became involved with Dexter, another programmer whom she had met at one of the rare conferences she attended, they applauded that too, though more cautiously.

Her relationship with Dexter was a brief affair, perhaps inevitably so. Looking back in search of incidents to remember it by, Leela would only be able to recall a general feeling, something like being wound tightly in a blanket on a cold day, comforting yet restrictive. Even when things were at their best, they never moved in together. Leela preferred it that way. She preferred, too, to sleep alone, and often moved after lovemaking to the spare bed in her apartment. When you slept, you were too vulnerable. Another person's essence could invade you. She had explained it once to Dexter. He had stroked her hair with fingers she thought of as sensitive and artistic, and had seemed to understand. But apparently he hadn't. It was one of the facts he dwelt on at some bitter length before he left.

"You're like one of those spiny creatures that live at the bottom of the ocean," he said. "Everything just slides off of that watertight shell of yours. You don't need me—you don't need *anyone.*"

He wasn't totally right about that. A week after he left, Leela ended up in the emergency ward, having swallowed a bottle of sleeping pills.

An encounter with death—even an aborted one (Leela had called 911 as soon as she finished taking the pills)—alters one in unaccountable ways. After having to deal with the hospital, the police, and the mandatory counselor assigned to her, Leela should have heaved a sigh of relief when she returned to her quiet, tidy apartment. Instead, for the first time, she found her own company inadequate. Alone, there seemed no point in opening the drapes or cleaning up the TV dinner containers stacked up on the coffee table. The place took on a green, underwater dimness. Her computer gathered dust as she wandered from room to room, sometimes with her eyes closed, trailing her fingers as though they were fins across the furniture, testing the truth of Dexter's accusation.

She didn't know when it was that she started thinking about India, which she had never visited. The idea attached itself to the underneath of her mind and grew like a barnacle. In her imagination the country was vast and vague. Talismanic. For some reason she associated it with rain, scavenger crows, the clanging of orange trams, and the purplish-green of elephant-ears. Were these items from some story her parents had told in her childhood? No. Though her parents' stories had spanned many topics—from the lives of famous scientists to the legends of Greece and Rome—they never discussed their homeland, a country they seemed to have shed as easily and completely as a lizard drops its tail.

When she called her parents to inform them she was going, she did not tell them why. Perhaps she herself did not know. Nor did she speak of the suicide attempt, which filled her with a rush of mortification whenever it intruded on her thoughts. As always with her decisions, they did not venture advice, though she thought she heard her mother suppress a sigh. They waited to see if she had more to say, and when she didn't, they told her how to contact Aunt Seema, who was her mother's cousin.

"Try to stay away from the crowds," her father said.

"That's impossible," said her mother. "Just be sure to take your shots before you go, drink boiled water at all times, and don't get involved in the lives of strangers."

What did Leela expect from India? The banalities of heat and dust, poverty and squalor, yes. The elated confusion of city streets where the beetle-black Ambassador cars of the rich inched their way, honking, between sweating rickshaw-pullers and cows who stood unmoving, as dignified as dowagers. But she had not thought Calcutta would vanquish her so easily with its melancholy poetry of old cotton saris hung out to dry on rooftops. With low-ceilinged groceries filled with odors she did not recognize but knew to be indispensable. In the evenings, the shopkeeper waved a lamp in front of a vividly colored calendar depicting Rama's coronation. His waiting customers did not seem to mind. Sometimes at dawn she stood at her bedroom window and heard, cutting through the roar of buses, the cool, astonishing voice of a young man in a neighboring house practicing a morning raag.

At the airport, Aunt Seema had been large, untidy, and moist—the exact opposite of Leela's mother. She launched herself at Leela with a delighted cry, kissing her on both checks, pulling her into her ample, talcum-powder-scented bosom, exclaiming how overjoyed she was to meet her. In America Leela would have been repelled by such effusion, especially from a woman she had never seen in her life. Here it seemed as right—and as welcome—as the too-sweet glass of orange squash that the maid brought her as soon as she reached the house.

Aunt dressed Leela in her starched cotton saris, put matching bindis on her forehead, and lined her eyes with kajal. She forced her to increase her rudimentary Bengali vocabulary by refusing to speak to her in English. She cooked her rui fish sautéed with black jeera, and moglai parathas stuffed with eggs and onions, which had to be flipped over deftly at a crucial moment—food Leela loved, though it gave her heartburn. She took her to the Kalighat temple for a blessing, to night-long music concerts, and to the homes of her friends, all of whom wanted to arrange a marriage for her. Leela went unprotestingly. Like a child acting in her first play, she was thrilled by the vibrant unreality of the life she was living. At night she lay in the big bed beside Aunt (Uncle having been banished to a cot downstairs) and watched the soft white swaying of the mosquito net in the breeze from the ceiling fan. She pondered the unexpected pleasure she took in every disorganized aspect of the day. India was a Mardi Gras that never ended. Who would have thought she'd feel so at home here?

So when Aunt Seema said, "You want to see the real India, the spiritual India? Let's go on a pilgrimage," she agreed without hesitation.

The talk starts at the end of the first day's trek. In one of the women's tents, where Leela lies among pilgrims who huddle in blankets and nurse aching muscles, a voice rises from the dark.

"Do you know, Mrs. Das's bedroll didn't get to the camp. They can't figure out what happened—the guides swear they tied it onto a mule this morning. . . ."

"That's right," responds another voice. "I heard them complaining because they had to scrounge around in their own packs to find her some blankets."

In the anonymous darkness, the voices take on cruel, choric tones. They release suspicion into the close air like bacteria, ready to multiply wherever they touch down.

"It's like that time on the train, remember, when she was the only one who got food poisoning. . . ."

"Yes, yes . . ."

"I wonder what will happen next. . . ."

"As long as it doesn't affect us. . . ."

"How can you be sure? Maybe next time it will. . . ."

"I hate to be selfish, but I wish she wasn't here with us at all. . . ."

"Me, too . . ."

Leela wonders about the tent in which Mrs. Das is spending her night. She wonders what people are saying in there. What they are thinking. An image comes to her with a brief, harsh clarity: the older woman's body curled into a lean comma under her borrowed blankets. In the whispery dark, her thin, veined lids squeezed shut in a semblance of sleep.

Struggling up the trail through the morning mist, the line of pilgrims in gay woolen clothes looks like a bright garland. Soon the light will grow brutal and blinding, but at this hour it is sleepy, diffuse. A woman pauses to chant. *Om Namah Shivaya, Salutations to the Auspicious One.* The notes tremble in the air, Leela thinks, like silver bubbles. The pilgrims are quiet—there's something about the snowy crags that discourages gossip. The head guide has suggested that walking time be utilized for reflection and repentance. Leela finds herself thinking, instead, of accidents.

She remembers the first one most clearly. It must have been a special occasion, maybe a birthday or an out-of-town visitor, because her mother was cooking. She rarely made Indian food from scratch, and Leela remembers that she was snappish and distracted. Wanting to help, the four-year-old Leela had pulled at a pot and seen the steaming dal come at her in a yellow rush. It struck her arm with a slapping sound. She screamed and raced around the kitchen—as though agony could be outrun. Long after her mother immersed her arm in ice water and gave her Tylenol to reduce the pain, she continued to sob—tears of rage at being tricked, Leela realizes now. She'd had no intimations, until then, that good intentions were no match for the forces of the physical world.

More accidents followed, in spite of the fact that she was not a particularly physical child. They blur together in Leela's memory like the landscape outside a speeding car's windows. She fell from her bike in front of a moving car—luckily the driver had good reflexes, and she only needed a few stitches on her chin. She sat in the passenger seat of her mother's van, and a stone—from who knows where—shattered the windshield, filling Leela's lap with jagged silver. A defective electrical wire caught fire at night in her bedroom while she slept. Her mother, up for a drink of water, smelled the smoke and ran to the bedroom to discover the carpet smoldering around the sleeping Leela's bed. Do all these close escapes mean that Leela is lucky? Or is her unlucky star, thwarted all this time by some imbalance in the stratosphere, waiting for its opportunity?

She thinks finally of the suicide attempt which, since she arrived in India, she has quarantined in a part of her mind she seldom visits. Can it be classified as an accident, an accident she did to herself? She remembers the magnetic red gleam of the round pills in the hollow of her palm, how unexpectedly solid they had felt, like metal pellets. The shriek of the ambulance outside her window. The old man who lived across the hall peering from a crack in his door, grim and unsurprised. The acidic ache in her throat when they pumped her stomach. Leela had kept her eyes on the wall of the emergency room afterward, too ashamed to look at the paramedic who was telling her something. Something cautionary and crucial which might help her now, as she steps warily along this beautiful glacial trail, watching for crevasses. But for her life she cannot recall what it was.

Each night the pilgrims are assigned to different tents by the head guide, according to some complicated logic Leela has failed to decipher. But tonight, when she finds herself in Mrs. Das's tent, her bedroll set down next to the older woman's makeshift one, she wonders if it is destiny that has brought her here.

All her life, like her parents, Leela has been a believer in individual responsibility. But lately she finds herself wondering. When she asked Aunt Seema yesterday, she touched Leela's cheek in a gesture of amused affection. "Ah, my dear—to believe that you control everything in your life! How absurdly American!"

Destiny is a seductive concept. Ruminating on it, Leela feels the events of her life turn weightless and pass through her like clouds. The simplistic, sublunary words she assigned to them—*pride, shame, guilt, folly*—no longer seem to apply.

"Please," Mrs. Das whispers in Bengali, startling Leela from thought. She sits on the tarpaulin floor of the tent, propped against her bedroll, her legs splayed out crookedly from under her sari. "Could you ask one of the attendants to bring some warm water? My feet hurt a lot."

"Of course," Leela says, jumping up. An odd gladness fills her as she performs this small service. Aunt, who was less than happy about Leela's tent assignment tonight, had whispered to her to be sure to stay away from Mrs. Das. But Aunt is at the other end of the camp, while destiny has placed Leela here.

When the water comes in a bucket, Mrs. Das surreptitiously removes her shoes. They are made of rough leather, cheap and unlovely. They make Leela feel guilty about her fleece-lined American boots, even though the fleece is fake. Then she sucks in a horrified breath.

Freed of shoes and socks, Mrs. Das's feet are in bad shape, swollen all the way to the calves. The toes are blistered and bluish with frostbite. The heels weep yellowish pus. Mrs. Das looks concerned but not surprised—this has obviously been going on for a couple of days. She grits her teeth, lurches to her feet, and tries to lift the bucket. Leela takes it from her and follows her to the opening of the tent, and when Mrs. Das has difficulty bending over to wash her feet, she kneels and does it for her. She feels no disgust as she cleans off the odorous pus. This intrigues her. Usually she doesn't like touching people. Even with her parents, she seldom went beyond the light press of lips to cheek, the hurried pat on the shoulder. In her Dexter days, if he put his arm around her, she'd find an excuse to move away after a few minutes. Yet here she is, tearing strips from an old sari and bandaging Mrs. Das's feet, her fingers moving with a deft intelligence she did not suspect they possessed, brown against the matching brown of Mrs. Das's skin. This is the first time, she thinks, that she has known such intimacy. How amazing that it should be a stranger who has opened her like a dictionary and brought to light this word whose definition had escaped her until now.

Someone in the tent must have talked, for here through the night comes the party's doctor, his flashlight making a ragged circle of brightness on the tent floor as he enters. "Now what's the problem?" he asks Mrs. Das, who attempts a look of innocence. What problem could he be referring to? The doctor sighs, hands Leela his torch, moves the sari strips, and clicks his tongue gravely as he examines Mrs. Das's feet. There's evidence of infection, he says. She needs a tetanus shot immediately, and even then the blisters might get septic. How could she have been so foolish as to keep this a secret from him? He pulls a thick syringe from his bag and administers an injection. "But you still have to get down to the hospital at Pahelgaon as soon as possible," he ends. "I'll ask the guide to find some way of sending you back tomorrow."

Mrs. Das clutches the doctor's arm. In the flashlight's erratic beam, her eyes, magnified behind thick glasses, glint desperately. She doesn't care about her feet, she says. It's more important for her to complete the pilgrimage—she's waited so long to do it. They're only a day or so away from Shiva's shrine. If she had to turn back now, it would kill her much more surely than a septic blister.

The doctor's walrus mustache droops unhappily. He takes a deep breath and says that two extra days of hard walking could cause gangrene to set in, though a brief certainty flits over his face as he speaks. He repeats that Mrs. Das must go back tomorrow, then hurries off before she can plead further.

The darkness left behind is streaked with faint cobwebs of moonlight. Leela glances at the body prone on the bedding next to her. Mrs. Das is completely quiet, and this frightens Leela more than any fit of hysterics. She hears shufflings from the other end of the tent, whispered comments sibilant with relief. Angrily, she thinks that had the patient been anyone else, the doctor would not have been so adamant about sending her back. The moon goes behind a cloud; around her, darkness packs itself tightly, like black wool. She pushes her hand through it to where she thinks Mrs. Das's arm might be. Against her fingers Mrs. Das's skin feels brittle and stiff, like cheap waterproof fabric. Leela holds Mrs. Das's wrist awkwardly, not knowing what to do. In the context of Indian etiquette, would patting be considered a condescending gesture? She regrets her impetuosity.

Then Mrs. Das turns her wrist—it is the swift movement of a night animal who knows its survival depends on mastering such economies of action—and clasps Leela's fingers tightly in her own.

Late that night, Mrs. Das tries to continue up the trail on her own, is spotted by the lookout guide, apprehended and brought back. It happens quickly and quietly, and Leela sleeps through it all.

By the time she wakes, the tent is washed in calm mountain light and abuzz with women and gossip.

"There she was, in the dark on her own, without any supplies, not even an electric torch, can you imagine?"

"Luckily the guide saw her before she went beyond the bend in the mountain. Otherwise she'd be in a ravine by now. . . ."

"Or frozen to death . . ."

"Crazy woman! They say when they caught her, she fought them tooth and nail—I'm telling you, she actually drew blood! Like someone possessed by an evil spirit."

Leela stares at Mrs. Das's bedroll, two dark, hairy blankets topped by a sheet. It looks like the peeled skin of an animal turned inside out. The women's excitement crackles through the air, sends little shocks up her arms. Are people in India harder to understand because they've had so many extra centuries to formulate their beliefs? She recalls the expression on Dexter's face before he slammed the door, the simple incandescence of his anger. In some way, she had expected it all along. But Mrs. Das . . . ? She curls her fingers, remembering the way the older woman had clasped them in her dry, birdlike grip.

"Did she really think she could get to the shrine all by herself!" someone exclaims.

Leela spots Aunt Seema and tugs at her sari. "Where is Mrs. Das now?"

"The guides have put her in a separate tent where they can keep an eye an her until they can send her back," Aunt says, shaking her head sadly. "Poor thing—I really feel sorry for her. Still, I must confess I'm glad she's leaving." Then a suspicious frown takes over her face. "Why do you want to know? Did you talk to her last night? Leela, stop, where are you going?"

Mrs. Das, whom Leela finds in a small tent outside which a guide keeps watch, does not look like a woman who has recently battled several men tooth and nail. Cowled in a faded green shawl, she dozes peacefully against the tent pole, though this could be due to the Calmpose tablets the doctor has made her take. Or perhaps there's not much outside her head that she's interested in at this point. She has lost her glasses in her night's adventuring, and when Leela touches her shoulder, she looks up, blinking with dignity.

Leela opens her mouth to say she is sorry about how Mrs. Das has been treated. But she hears herself saying, "I'm going back with you." The dazed expression on Mrs. Das's face mirrors her own inner state. When after a moment Mrs. Das warily asks her why, all she can do is shrug her shoulders. She is uncertain of her motives. Is it her desire to prove (but to whom?) that she is somehow superior to the others? Is it *pity,* an emotion she has always distrusted? Is it some inchoate affinity she feels toward this stranger? But if you believe in destiny, no one can be a stranger, can they? There's always a connection, a reason because of which people enter your orbit, bristling with dark energy like a meteor intent on collision.

Traveling down a mountain trail fringed by fat, seeded grasses the same gray as the sky, Leela wants to ask Mrs. Das about destiny. Whether she believes in it, what she understands it to encompass. But Mrs. Das grips the saddle of the mule she is sitting on, her body rigid with the single-minded terror of a person who has never ridden an animal. Ahead, the guide's young, scraggly-bearded son whistles a movie tune Leela remembers having heard in another world, during an excursion with Aunt Seema to some Calcutta market.

Aunt Seema was terribly upset with Leela's decision to accompany Mrs. Das—no, even with that intense adverb, *upset* is too simple a word to describe the change in her urbane aunt, who had taken such gay control of Leela's life in the city. The new Aunt Seema wrung her hands and lamented, "But what would your mother say if she knew that I let you go off alone with some stranger?" (Did she really believe Leela's mother would hold her responsible? The thought made Leela smile.) Aunt's face was full of awful conviction as she begged Leela to reconsider. Breaking off a pilgrimage like this, for no good reason, would rouse the wrath of Shiva. When Leela said that the occurrences of her life were surely of no interest to a deity, Aunt gripped her shoulders with trembling hands.

"Stop!" she cried, her nostrils flaring. "You don't know what you're saying! That bad-luck woman, she's bewitched you!"

How many unguessed layers there were to people, skins that came loose at an unexpected tug, revealing raw, fearful flesh. Amazing, that folks could love one another in the face of such unreliability! It made Leela at once sad and hopeful.

Walking downhill, Leela has drifted into a fantasy. In it, she lives in a small rooftop flat on the outskirts of Calcutta. Mrs. Das, whom she has rescued from the women's hostel, lives with her. They have a maid who shops and runs their errands, so the women rarely need to leave the flat. Each evening they sit on the terrace beside the potted roses and chrysanthemums (Mrs. Das has turned out to be a skillful gardener) and listen to music—a tape of Bengali folk songs (Mrs. Das looks like a person who would enjoy that), or maybe one of Leela's jazz CDs to which Mrs. Das listens with bemused attention. When they wish each other good night, she touches Leela's arm. "Thank you," she says, her eyes deep as a forest.

They have come to a riverbed. There isn't much water, but the boulders on which they step are slippery with moss. It's starting to rain, and the guide eyes the sky nervously. He pulls at the balking mule, which stumbles. Mrs. Das gives a harsh, crow-like cry and flings out her hand. Leela grasps it and holds on until they reach the other side.

"Thank you," says Mrs. Das. It is the first time she has smiled, and Leela sees that her eyes are, indeed, deep as a forest.

"But, madam!" The proprietor at the Nataraja inn cries to Leela in an English made shaky by distress. "You people are not to be coming back for two more days! Already I am giving your rooms to other pilgrim party. Whole hotel is full. This is middle of pilgrim season—other hotels are also being full." He gives Leela and Mrs. Das, who are shivering in their wet clothes, an accusing look. "How is it you two are returned so soon?"

The guide, who has brought in the bedrolls, says something in a rapid Pahari dialect that Leela cannot follow. The clerk pulls back his head in a swift, turtlelike motion and gives Mrs. Das a glance full of misgiving.

"Please," Leela says. "We're very tired, and it's raining. Can't you find us something?"

"Sorry, madams. Maybe Mughal Gardens in marketplace is having space. . . ."

Leela can feel Mrs. Das's placid eyes on her. It is obvious that she trusts the younger woman to handle the situation. Leela sighs. Being a savior in real life has drawbacks she never imagined in her rooftop fantasy. Recalling something Aunt Seema said earlier, she digs in the waistband of her sari and comes up with a handful of rupee notes which she lays on the counter.

The clerk rocks back on his heels, torn between avarice and superstition. Then his hand darts out and covers the notes. "We are having a small-small storeroom on top of hotel. Big enough for one person only." He parts his lips in an ingenuous smile. "Maybe older madam can try Mughal Gardens?" Leela gives him a reprimanding look. "We'll manage," she says.

The clerk has not exaggerated. The room, filled with discarded furniture, is about as big as Leela's queen-size bed in America. Even after the sweeper carries all the junk out into the corridor, there isn't enough space to open the two bedrolls without their edges overlapping. Leela tries to hide her dismay. It strikes her that since she arrived in India, she has not been alone even once. With sudden homesickness, she longs for her wide, flat bedroom, its uncomplicated vanilla walls, its window from which she had looked out on to nothing more demanding than a clump of geraniums.

"I've caused you a lot of inconvenience?"

Mrs. Das's voice is small but not apologetic. (Leela rather likes this.) "You shouldn't have come back with me," she adds matter-of-factly. "What if I *am* bad luck, like people believe?"

"Do you believe that?" Leela asks. She strains to hear Mrs. Das answer above the crash of thunder.

"Belief, disbelief." Mrs. Das shrugs. "So many things I believed to be one way turned out otherwise. I believed my son's marriage wouldn't change things between us. I believed I would get to Shiva's shrine, and all my problems would disappear. Last night on the mountain I believed the best thing for me would be to fall into a crevasse and die." She smiles with unexpected sweetness as she says this. "But now—here we are together."

Together. When Mrs. Das says it in Bengali, *eksangay,* the word opens inside Leela with a faint, ringing sound, like a distant temple bell.

"I have something I want to give you," Mrs. Das says.

"No, no," says Leela, embarrassed. "Please, I'd rather you didn't."

"He who gives," says Mrs. Das, "must be prepared to receive." Is this an ancient Indian saying, or one that she has made up herself? And what exactly does it mean? Is giving then a privilege, in return for which you must allow others the opportunity to do the same? Mrs. Das unclasps a thin gold chain she is wearing. She leans forward and Leela feels her fingers fumbling for a moment on the nape of her neck. She wants to protest, to explain to Mrs. Das that she has always hated jewelry, all that metal clamped around you. But she is caught in a web of unfamiliar ideas. Is giving the touchstone by which the lives of strangers become your own? The expression on Mrs. Das's face is secretive, prayerful. And then the skin-warm, almost weightless chain is around Leela's throat.

Mrs. Das switches off the naked bulb that hangs on a bit of wire from the ceiling. The two of them lie down, each on her blanket, and listen to the wind, which moans and rattles the shutters like a madwoman wanting to be let in. Leela hopes Aunt Seema is safe, that the storm has not hit the mountain the way it has Pahelgaon. But the world outside this square, contained room has receded so far that she is unable to feel anxiety. Rain falls all around her, insulating as a lullaby. If she were to stretch out her arm, she would touch Mrs. Das's face.

She says, softly, "Once I tried to kill myself."

Mrs. Das says nothing. Perhaps she is asleep.

Leela finds herself speaking of the pills, the ambulance, the scraped-out space inside her afterward. Perhaps it had always been there, and she had not known? She talks about her father and mother, their unbearable courtesy, which she sees only this moment as having been unbearable. She asks questions about togetherness, about being alone. What the value of each might be. She sends her words into the night, and does not need a reply.

She has never spoken so much in her life. In the middle of a sentence, she falls asleep.

Leela is dreaming. In the dream, the glacial trails have been washed away by rain. She takes a false step, sinks into slush. Ice presses against her chest. She opens her mouth to cry for help, and it, too, fills with ice. With a thunderous crack, blackness opens above her, a brilliant and brutal absence of light. She knows it has found her finally, her unlucky star.

Leela wakes, her heart clenched painfully like an arthritic fist. How real the dream was. Even now she feels the freezing weight on her chest, hears the ricochet of the cracked-open sky. But, no, it is not just a dream. Her blanket is soaked through, and the floor is awash with water. She scrabbles for the light switch and sees, in the dim glare, a corner of the roof hanging down, swinging drunkenly. In the midst of all this, Mrs. Das sleeps on, covers pulled over her head. Leela is visited by a crazy wish to lie down beside her.

"Quick, quick!" she cries, shaking her. "We have to get out of here before that roof comes down."

Mrs. Das doesn't seem to understand what Leela wants from her. Another gust of wind hits the roof, which gives an ominous creak. Her eyes widen, but she makes no move to sit up.

"Come on," shouts Leela. She starts to drag her to the door. Mrs. Das offers neither resistance nor help. A long time back Leela had taken a CPR course, she has forgotten why. Mrs. Das's body, slack and rubbery, reminds her of the dummy on whose chest she had pounded with earnest energy. The thought depresses her, and this depression is the last emotion she registers before something hits her head.

Leela lies on a lumpy mattress. Even with her eyes closed, she knows that the clothes she is wearing—a baggy blouse, a limp cotton sari which swathes her loosely—are not hers. Her head feels stuffed with steel shavings. Is she in heaven, having died a heroic death? But surely celestial bedding would be more comfortable, celestial clothing more elegant—even in India? She is ashamed of having thought that last phrase. She moves her head a little. The jab of pain is like disappointed lightning.

"Doctor, doctor, she's waking up," Aunt Seema says from somewhere, her voice damp and wobbly like a cracker that's been dunked in tea. But why is Leela thinking like this? She knows she should appreciate her aunt's loving concern and say something to reassure her. But it is so private, so comfortable, behind her closed eyes.

"Finally," says the doctor's voice. "I was getting worried." Leela can smell his breath—it's cigarettes, a brand she does not know. It smells of cloves. When she has forgotten everything else, she thinks, she will remember the odors of this journey.

"Can you hear me, Leela?" the doctor asks. "Can you open your eyes?" He taps on her cheek with maddening persistence until she gives up and glares at him.

"You're lucky, young lady," he says as he changes the bandage around her head. "You should be thankful you were hit by a piece of wood. Now if that had been a sheet of rusted metal—"

Lucky. Thankful. Leela doesn't trust such words. They change their meaning as they swoop, sharp-clawed, about her head. The room is full of women; they wring their hands in gestures that echo her aunt's. She closes her eyes again. There's a question she must ask, an important one—but when she tries to catch it in a net of words, it dissolves into red fog.

"It's all my fault," Aunt Seema says in a broken voice that baffles Leela. Why should Aunt feel so much distress at problems which are, after all, hers alone? "Leela doesn't understand these things—how can she?—but I should have made her stay away from that accursed woman. . . ."

"Do try to be quiet." The doctor's voice is testy, as though he has heard this lament many times already. "Give her the medicine and let her rest."

Someone holds Leela's head, brings a cup to her lips. The medicine is thick and vile. She forces it down her throat with harsh satisfaction. Aunt sobs softly, in deference to the doctor's orders. Her friends murmur consolations. From time to time, phrases rise like a refrain from their crooning: *The poor girl, Shiva have mercy, that bad-luck woman, oh, what will I tell your mother.*

A commotion at the door.

"I've got to see her, just for a minute, just to make sure she's all right—"

There's a heaving inside Leela.

"No," says one of the women. "Daktar-babu said, no excitement."

"Please, I won't talk to her—I'll just take a look."

"Haven't you done her enough harm already? Go away. Leela, you tell her yourself . . ."

Leela doesn't want to tell anyone anything. She wants only to sleep. Is that too much to ask for? A line comes to her from a poem, *Death's second self which seals up all in rest.* She imagines snow, great fluffy quilts of it, packed around her. But the voices scrape at her, *Leela, Leela, Leela.*

The room is full of evening. Leela sees Mrs. Das at the door, trying to push her way past the determined bulk of the doctor's wife. Her disheveled hair radiates from her head like crinkly white wires, giving her, for a moment, the look of an alien in a *Star Trek* movie. When she sees that Leela's eyes are open, she stops struggling and reaches out toward her.

Why does Leela do what she does next? Is it the medication, which makes her light-headed? The pain, which won't let her think? Or is it some dark, genetic strain which, unknown to her, has pierced her pragmatic American upbringing with its sharp, knotted root? At times, later, she will tell herself, *I didn't know what I was doing.* At other times, she'll say, *Liar.* For doesn't her response to Mrs. Das come from the intrinsic and fearful depths of who she is? The part of her that knows she is no savior?

Leela sits up in bed. "Aunt's right," she says. Her teeth chatter as though she is fevered. "All of them are right. You *are* cursed. Go away. Leave me alone."

"No," says Mrs. Das. But it is a pale sound, without conviction.

"Yes!" says Leela. "Yes!" She grasps the chain Mrs. Das has given her and yanks at it. The worn gold gives easily. Falling, it makes a small, skittery sound on the wood floor.

Darkness is bursting open around Leela like black chrysanthemums.

Mrs. Das stares at the chain, then turns and stumbles from the room. Her shadow, long and misshapen, touches Leela once. Then it, too, is gone.

The pilgrimage party makes much of Leela as she lies recovering. The women bring her little gifts from their forays into town—an embroidered purse, a bunch of Kashmiri grapes, a lacquered jewelry box. When they hold out the presents, Leela burrows her hands into her blanket. But the women merely nod to each other. They whisper words like *shock* and *been through so much.* They hand the gifts to Aunt, who promises to keep them safely until Leela is better. When they leave, she feels like a petulant child.

From the doorway, the men ask Aunt Seema how Leela is coming along. Their voices are gruff and hushed, their eyes furtive with awe—as though she were a martyr-saint who took upon herself the bad luck that would have otherwise fallen on them. Is it cynical to think this? There is no one any more whom Leela can ask.

On the way back to Srinagar, where the party will catch the train to Calcutta, by unspoken consent Leela is given the best seat on the bus, up front near the big double windows.

"It's a fine view, and it won't joggle you so much," says one of the women, plumping up a pillow for her. Another places a foot rest near her legs. Aunt Seema unscrews a Thermos and pours her a glass of pomegranate juice—to replace all the blood Leela lost, she says. The juice is the color of blood. Its thin tartness makes Leela's mouth pucker up, and Aunt says, in a disappointed voice, "Oh, dear, is it not so sweet then? Why, that Bahadur at the hotel swore to me . . ."

Leela feels ungracious, boorish. She feels angry for feeling this way. "I have a headache," she says and turns to the window where, hidden behind her sunglasses, she watches the rest of the party get on the bus. Amid shouts and laughter, the bus begins to move.

She waits until the bus has lurched its way around three hairpin bends. Then she says, "Aunt . . . ?" She tries to make her voice casual, but the words come out in a croak.

"Yes, dear? A little more juice?" Aunt asks hopefully.

"Where is Mrs. Das? Why didn't she get on the bus?"

Aunt fiddles with the catch of her purse. Her face indicates her discomfort at the baldness of Leela's questions. A real Indian woman would have known to approach the matter delicately, sideways.

But the doctor's wife, who is sitting behind them, leans forward to say, "Oh, her! She went off somewhere on her own, when was it, three, no, four nights ago, right after she created that ruckus in your sickroom. She didn't take her bedroll with her, or even her suitcase. Strange, no? Personally, I think she's a little bit touched up here." She taps her head emphatically.

Misery swirls, acidic, through Leela's insides. She raises her hand with great effort to cover her mouth, so it will not spill out.

"Are you okay, dear?" Aunt asks.

"She looks terribly pale," the doctor's wife says. "It's all these winding roads—enough to make anyone vomity."

"I might have some lemon drops," says Aunt, rummaging in her handbag.

Leela accepts the sour candy and turns again to the window. Behind her she hears the doctor's wife's carrying whisper: "If I were you, I'd get a puja done for your niece once you get to Calcutta. You know, to avert the evil eye . . ."

Outside the bus, mountains and waterfalls are speeding past Leela. Sunlight slides like opportunity from the narrow green leaves of debdaru trees and is lost in the underbrush. What had the guide said, at the start of the trip, about expiation? Leela cannot remember. And even if she did, would she be capable of executing those gestures, delicate and filled with power, like the movements of a Bharatnatyam dancer, which connect humans to the gods and to each other? Back in America, her life waits to claim her, unchanged, impervious, smelling like floor polish. In the dusty window, her reflection is a blank oval. She takes off her dark glasses to see better, but the features which peer back at her are unfamiliar, as though they belong to someone she has never met.

CHITRA BANERJEE DIVAKARUNI

The Blooming Season for Cacti

To get to California I had to travel through desert. But no, the desert was part of California, too. Perhaps the best part, I would think later. Brown land, brown sky, hills like brown breasts. The Greyhound bus fishtailed in the wind, or maybe the driver was sleepy. I slid across the worn-slick vinyl seat with a slash in its center, like someone had had to hide something fast. Or maybe he'd been searching. Or merely bored and needed it, the hard, defined sound of the rip as the knife bit in, its controlled movement across the drab olive flatness. I slid all the way across and hit my head against the dusty window, but it didn't hurt because I'd seen it coming and braced myself. Oh, I was quick. Because only the quick survive. Or the fortunate—but already my life had proved I wasn't that.

We were passing the dunes now, the sand rippled into a thousand lines of cursive, a dangerous alphabet. Everywhere, mica glittered like eyes. Above, vultures waited to swoop down on the helpless skitter of smaller creatures. I loved it—how could I resist? I wanted to climb to the top of the highest dune. I wanted to be transformed to the bone.

Some of the scared hardness at my core was melting in the desert's heat. For the first time since I got to America.

I felt myself growing into all the words my sister-in-law had shouted as I packed my things in her Dallas home two days ago. Selfish, yes. Ungrateful, yes. Following only my own pleasure. I would be all that.

I was a burning wind. I was a lit fuse.

And I was coming to California.

But first there was the lush, sweaty jostle of Bombay, the torrential monsoons that swept into the city where I was born, the greedy, flooded streets that sucked at your calves. On each corner the looming billboards promised romance, a dark, air-conditioned theater and Amir Khan in your arms—or Madhuri Dixit, depending on your preference. All the passion you could want and none of the consequences. The white ocean at night, necklaced with lights from Marine Drive, rocked just for you.

Everything I had loved, and then hated.

People thought I came to Texas because my older brother was the only relative I had left. The real reason: I needed something as different as possible from Bombay. How else could I begin to bear the memories, the city smoldering in the aftermath of riot? Hindus and Muslims, hate and slaughter, smoke that rose solid in a hundred pillars. On the street, the screams of women whose accents you could not have distinguished from mine. The smell of the water tank on our terrace where my mother made me hide.

What did I imagine? Open country, dust rising from hooves as herds headed home. Fountains of iridescent oil. Cougars. Cowboys with creased smiles and eyes blue as sapphire stone. Their kisses would be hard and innocent. Behind us in the night, rockets would take off for the moon, searing a path brighter than any meteor.

I found myself in a two-bedroom semidetached exactly like a hundred others, a pocket-sized square of lawn, browning in patches because water cost too much. "We'll put in rocks, once we're sure your brother won't get laid off," said my sister-in-law, who was kind in the beginning. "Come on, Mira, let's take you to the mall."

I knew it was my fault, my desperate mythologizing of America. But I blamed her for my disappointment. And my brother. I blamed him for his patience, his second-rate career, his crumpled, apologetic shoulders. His letter which had asked me to come stay with him. *It's not safe in India, how many times have I told you and Mother this. More so now that you're unmarried and alone.*

The bus jerks to a halt. How many hours? It is a gray afternoon, a gray wind blowing Burger King wrappers across a scraggly city park. Gulls circle overhead, screaming, though there is no sign of water. I see graffiti on peeling walls, metal bars in a shop window.

"Sacramento," shouts the driver, and I climb down.

It is dusk by the time I find Malik's restaurant. The light has seeped away, leaving ink pools under the eyes of strangers in the street, in the secretive hollows of their throats.

In Bombay, before the riots, darkness had fallen decisively, dramatically, in one gay swoop.

Comparisons are futile, I know that. Now is all I have. But my feet hurt, the backpack straps bite into my shoulders, and the *frr-frr* of pigeons flying home is the rustle of my mother's sari.

"Malik-ji?" says the manager, who is at the cash register, picking his teeth. "Yes, he's in. You're lucky. He hardly ever comes into the restaurant anymore." He peers at the note that my brother had insisted on giving me. "I don't know if he'll talk to you. So many people come through here, claiming to be relatives of relatives."

The air is cumin and coriander, a roasted brown smell. They must be frying samosas inside. My mother used to make the best samosas, fat and crisp. "Stuff carefully, Mira," she'd say. "Wet the dough ends and pinch the tips together so no air bubbles remain." But I never had the patience.

"Did I say I was a relative?" I let my voice hit the shadowed ceiling. My head feels like a bubble, enormous with hot air, ready to burst. "I'm looking for a job. If you don't have one, I'll be happy to look elsewhere."

A few early diners turn to stare.

"Arre bas, what temper," says the manager, not unkindly. "Just left home, didn't you? A week on the streets and you'd be singing a different song. Sit there, on the empty side, I'll go ask if he'll see you. Ei Priya, bring this bahinji a cup of chai."

I sit in the banquet section of the restaurant, decorated with maroon velvet and mirrors, curtains with thick gold pull-ropes, wall-to-wall plush carpeting. I want to feel disdain. In our drawing room in Bombay there had been a hundred-year-old rug from Srinagar that belonged to my grandfather, its faded design a glimmering of jewels through fog. But this American carpet is so soft around my ankles, so innocent of history—like young grass—that I can't stop myself from slipping off my shoes.

The tea comes, brought by a young woman in a purple sari and neat braids. Her blackbird eyes take in my wrinkled jeans, my less-than-clean shirt, my hair bundled into a knot, even—I am sure—the giant blister taking angry shape on my left heel. She is about to speak, but someone shouts, "Pri-ya," and with a flash of a smile she is gone. The kitchen door swings open to her touch, closes on a burst of female laughter, a question that could be *Who is she,* or maybe *What does she want,* the old, known smells and the boundaries they once promised. Sputtering mustard seed, the bright green glaze of chilies cooking in my mother's karhai. I no longer feel desert-dangerous, only tired and, again, afraid.

The water tank in our Bombay house smelled of river bottoms, of rust, of sun-heated metal, and still water. Inside, it was colder than I had expected, shiver-cold, and the smallest sounds echoed and boomed against my ear.

We were lucky to have a water tank at all. It had been put in a long time ago by my grandfather, when such things were still allowed. Having grown up in the lake-filled villages of Bengal, he had liked long baths. Now it meant that when the municipal supply was cut off twice a day, we had water to cook and drink.

But our real luck lay in the fact that none of the surrounding houses had tanks. This meant the rioters would not think to look on the terrace, my mother said. From her voice I knew she was only hoping.

The tank was not large. Still, it could have held us both. When I said that, my mother shook her head. "I must padlock the house from outside," she said. "That way they might believe it's empty."

"Where will you go?" I asked.

"I've let half the tank water out," she said, "but you might need the rest. It's a good thing this old lid doesn't close too well. There'll be enough air. Don't come out, no matter what you hear. Here's some fruit, it's the only thing that'll keep in there. Eat it sparingly. Who knows when—"

There were shouts in the distance, a rumbling sound like heavy machinery. Perhaps there were guns. I thought I smelled burning oil.

My mother pushed me down into the tank, handed me a banana and two oranges. She let her hand linger for a moment on my hair. "God bless you," she said.

I thought of saying, *Who? The god that's letting this happen to us, to this city?* And, *What if they set the house on fire?* Of saying, *None of this would have happened if we'd moved to America after Baba died, like my brother invited us to.*

If there's one thing I'm glad of now, it's that I stayed silent.

I ate the banana that night. Next evening I ate the oranges. The screams had stopped by then, mostly. I let the peels fall from my hand and watched them float, slow motion, to the tank bottom. I crushed the seeds in my teeth as though the bitterness could bring me relief. For a long time, the moist, weighted air of the tank smelled of oranges and tears.

"You won't be happy working for me, not for long," says Malik in his resigned, matter-of-fact voice. "You're too educated, too smart, I can see it in your face. . . ."

What had I expected him to look like? When my brother told me of his empire of restaurants and groceries and apartment buildings, I'd pictured someone like Seth Ramchand back home, corpulent in an overstarched Nehru jacket, smoking a cheroot, flashing a diamond on every finger. Or, given the American context, maybe a suave Armani-clad villain. (Who but a villain could so easily rake in the millions that steadily eluded my brother?) Bodyguards would hover in the background as he stepped out, dark-glassed, from his limousine. But here he is, a trim man, not too tall, with a bland blue department-store shirt and a cautious haircut. (He does own a limousine, but I will not learn this fact until much later.) His mustache is neat and nondescript. I've seen a thousand mustaches like that on the streets of Bombay.

"Too pretty also," says Malik, and suddenly the look in his eyes is neither bland nor cautious.

When I announced my plans for leaving Dallas, my brother had tried his best to stop me. He explained how dangerous it was, a girl traveling America alone. *Dangerous* was a word my brother liked to use. In this he was like all men who have never experienced its reality firsthand. He cajoled and pleaded, said he'd pay for me to take classes at the local community college. He tried damage containment. "Why does it have to be California? Go to the East Coast instead, if it's excitement you want. I have friends in New Jersey, solid family men, they'll take you in, treat you like a sister."

At last he gave me Malik's address in Sacramento. He and my brother had gone to college together briefly, before Malik dropped out to start his first restaurant. Now they stayed desultorily in touch, sending each other Diwali cards, informing each other of the births of children or changes of address.

My brother kept at me until I said, Very well, I would go to Sacramento rather than Los Angeles, like I wanted. Even then he wasn't happy.

"Leaving us like this to live by yourself," he said at the bus station, handing me my backpack with a sigh. "Ma would have been most upset! Oh, well, at least Malik will be there in case you run into trouble. But you'd better . . ."

I'd shoved past him without answering. My skin felt like someone had rubbed ground glass into it. What right did he have to speak of my mother? He wasn't the one who'd searched for her through the streets filled with the stench of kerosene and burned flesh, calling her name. He wasn't the one who had gone to one police station after another with her photo, to be told by exhausted officials that there were too many missing people for them to keep track.

"Maybe it's better if you don't find her," one inspector had told me finally.

I kept my face turned away from the tinted bus window, from my brother's waving arm, the crease of worry between his brows, simple as a Crayola line drawn by a child. Still, I heard him through the engine's backfiring: ". . . watch out for Malik—he has a reputation."

I sit on one end of the sagging sofa that takes up most of our living room and watch Priya trying on makeup. She outlines her lips in sultry red and pouts into the mirror she is holding. She flutters her mascara-thickened lashes. She is practicing, because she is to be a wife soon. Her hair, unbraided now, falls in a sleek torrent over her left breast.

Malik has given me a job at the restaurant—I am to be a cashier, morning shift until I'm ready to handle the heavier evening crowds—and a room in an apartment building he owns down the street. The rent, to be deducted from my pay, is reasonable. I can eat in the restaurant kitchen for free, if I wish.

"He's a fair man, you have to admit," Priya says as she shifts her hips, trying to find a comfortable spot on the sofa. She wears a demure nightgown, high necked and long sleeved. Malik had called her into his office and told her that he was putting me in her apartment, since it had a second bedroom. I would have resented the intrusion, but she doesn't seem to mind. "Kind, even. Looking at him, you'd never believe the stories."

She pauses, lips parted expectantly, until I ask what the stories are.

I listen absently as she talks of under-the-table deals with warehouses, a partner who died too conveniently, huge bribes paid to Immigration so they won't look too closely at his employees' green cards. A manager who crossed him, and now he's gone, disappeared, even his family doesn't know where. And then there's the matter of his second wife.

Priya's sleeves are pulled up above her elbow; her arms are smooth and dimpled as she raises them in a languorous stretch. She undoes the two top buttons of her gown—it is a warm night—and fans herself with an old copy of *Good Housekeeping.* The damp gleam of her skin disturbs me. But why? Where I come from, it isn't unusual for women to undress in front of each other. Growing up, I saw naked women many times, in the jenana changing rooms by the sea, and paid them no more attention than the rickety clothes racks on which we threw our saris.

"He saw her on a trip back to India—by chance, just like in the movies. He'd gone to his cousin's village for a wedding—and saw her in the crowd of guests. He liked her so much he married her that same week, didn't even ask for a dowry. Her parents were delighted, they knew how rich he was. But when she got here she found he was married already, even had kids and all. So she tried to kill herself. Slit her wrists, right here in this building—he'd put her on the top floor, in the best apartment. What a mess it was, ambulances, police, scared us all to death."

A lot of women killed themselves after the Bombay riots. People were shocked, but not surprised. *For centuries of Indian women,* the editor of a Hindu newspaper wrote, *it has been the honorable way. Remember Queen Padmini of olden times, who, along with her attendant women, threw herself into the fire rather than become her Muslim captor's concubine?*

In modern Bombay, death by hanging, a noose made from a sari, was the most common. Those who had connections and money bought sleeping pills. A few women swam out into the ocean.

"She didn't die," Priya says, "luckily." Her voice wavers over the word, unsure if it's the right one. "Malik-ji must have felt terribly guilty, because he transferred the building to her name, yes, the whole thing, she owns it all, they say it's worth a million and a half, maybe more. I think he really loves her, but of course he can't divorce his first wife because of the children. Every Friday night he sends his limousine for her—oh, you must see it, I've heard it even has a TV and a fridge inside. And she'll come down the steps in a silk sari and diamonds, with tuberoses in her hair, beautiful, but in a sad kind of way, like Jaya Bhaduri in *Silsila,* you remember? When she finds out that Amitabh has been having an affair with Rekha. You'll see when you meet her. . . ."

My mother used to wear tuberoses. After my father died, she gave up the habit as a vanity. But she would place bowls of the slim, fragrant flowers on tables and windowsills, so that a visitor, coming in from the bustle of the Bombay streets, would be faced with cool whiteness. When I allow myself to think of it, I like to believe that she was one of the women who swam out to sea.

"Just two more months left," Priya says as she begins to wipe off her makeup, "for my wedding. He's in India. My parents have set everything up. I've been saving all my money for the trousseau."

My mother would have swum through the warm salt—we had done it many times together—her sari growing heavy with it. Maybe she would have loosened the cloth and let it drift from her so she could move more freely. The waves were silver, like flying fish. They bore her up, they sang in her ear. Behind her the charred mass of the city drifted away, terror and loss. Did she look back in the direction of our house?

"How about you?" asks Priya. "What are you saving for?"

I don't reply.

"Never mind," says Priya kindly, patting my shoulder. Her lips glisten like wet plums. "Things will work out. You're so pretty, you're sure to find a husband soon."

The trouble started about a month after I arrived in Dallas, in my sister-in-law's house. But there were signs earlier. Hushed consultations in the corners of parties, telephone conversations that turned innocuous when I entered the room. Appraising glances. Little questions here and there, sharp as ant bites.

"Mira dear, what did you think of Mr. Advani, the man in the maroon Adidas T-shirt who brought us drinks—most attentive, wasn't he?"

"Don't you just love Ashok's jokes, Mira? The one about the sardarji today—oh, I laughed so much I thought I would burst."

"He was most attentive," I would say. "That joke was hilarious." Then I would go to my room.

On this day, just as we started dinner, my sister-in-law said, "Mira, you'll never guess what happened this afternoon. Arpan Basu called your brother at work. He wants to marry you!"

She waited for excitement, delight, coy confusion at the very least—Arpan was eminently eligible; he owned his own company, something to do with bathroom cleaners.

"I don't want to get married," I said.

"Why not?" asked my sister-in-law. "So he has a slight receding-hairline problem. What does that matter when he's so enthusiastic about the match?"

I didn't reply.

"What, you think you're too good for him, for all our friends?"

"Please—" said my brother.

"Ask your sister," said my sister-in-law to my brother, "if she doesn't want to get married, what *does* she want? Now if she had a brilliant career, instead of a job selling pots and pans at Sears—"

"Please," said my brother, putting his hand on her arm. "Don't you remember how it was for you when you first came here? Mira's been through a lot. She needs time."

My sister-in-law bit her lip and was silent. When she spoke again, her voice was different. For just a moment it made me see that all our lives have depths which strangers can never chart. And that's what we were to each other, strangers.

"Unfortunately," she said, "time doesn't wait for women to recover. Today the men are buzzing around Mira. Tomorrow, who knows?"

I watched them sitting across the table from me, a graying man, a woman tending toward plumpness. They meant well. How could I tell them that when I thought of a man touching me, I smelled the water tank: smoke and corroding metal. Below, the streets were filled with weeping, struggling women, their blouses ripped open, their bodies pinned down right there, on the pavement's dirt. The mob yelling encouragement.

"A marriage might help her get over what happened," my sister-in-law said.

That night in my room in my brother's house I took down the atlas of the United States, opened it to the word that gleamed at the edge of the continent: *California.*

My mother and I had discussed California after my father's death, when we received the first of my brother's letters asking us to come stay with him. He included postcards from a trip they'd taken to Los Angeles: Hollywood, Universal Studios, a boardwalk somewhere with Ferris wheels against an unnaturally brilliant ocean. One particular card, titled *Mojave,* was all glinting rock and cactus.

"If I were a traveling kind of woman," my mother had said, "I'd go one time, just to see California. They say there's still gold in the deserts there. They say the beaches are more beautiful than ours in Bombay."

We'd caught each other's eye and laughed disbelievingly. Gold in desert sand? Beaches more beautiful than Bombay's?

Now I closed the atlas and sank back against my pillow, its small comfort. Small comforts were all I had: a softness beneath my head, a place to go next.

All night as I slept for the last time in my brother's house, California was the brightness that pulsed through the contracting chambers of my heart.

The morning after Priya has told me her story, I see Malik's second wife. I am about to go for a walk. She is emptying an apartment someone has moved out of, trying to pull a broken armchair through the doorway.

The sun is not yet up. The breeze is still cool. A hint of cloud floats like lace in the sky. Dressed in old sweats, a smudge of dust on her cheek, she is older than I am. By how much I can't tell. Is she beautiful? I can't tell that either. Already I've lost the distance you need in order to judge someone.

When she sees me she smiles crookedly, one side of her mouth quirking up a little, the way (is this memory or merely longing?) my mother once smiled.

I ask if she needs help, and she says, please. I hold the front door open so she can push the armchair out to the curb, only I miscalculate and let go too soon, and the door catches her wrist.

"It's okay, no, really," she says, over my apologies. "It doesn't hurt."

Later I'll see the bruise, swelled purple over the wrist-bone. Even later, I'll think of omens.

She takes me up to her apartment and makes me chai, boiled thick and red-brown and fragrant with cloves. To welcome me, she says. Pouring, she turns her wrist, and there it is, delicate and deadly as a bracelet sewn into her skin, the scar.

"My name is Radhika," says Malik's second wife, handing me a thin, gold-edged cup.

"Mine is Mira."

Over soft tea steam we smile at our shared ironic legacy, both of us named after women of myth, women whose lives men had tried to ruin.

This Friday afternoon I sit on a chair in Radhika's kitchen and feel the sun seep into my bones like the jabakusum oil she is rubbing into my hair. The room is filled with a sweet, sleepy smell out of my childhood. Her fingers make little circles on my scalp. They trace the small dip behind each earlobe.

I moved in here a week ago. Priya had gone back to India to get married, and a new family needed her apartment. Radhika had been asked to find me a room with someone else, but instead she said, "Why don't you stay with me? I have more space than I need." It had felt so right that I hadn't even needed to ask if she were sure.

"Next page," she says.

I'm holding a book in my lap, a big library book with a blue-and-gold cover, titled *The Great Deserts of the American West.* I read, "The blooming season for cacti is very short, a few weeks at most in the spring. But during this time the barren and sere landscape is transformed by the vibrant coronets of hedgehog cactus, candy cactus and prickly pear that push out through the plants' spiny armament."

We do this a lot, look at books together. Radhika is hesitant in English, so usually I am the reader. But she is the decipherer of details I would have passed over.

"Look," she says, pointing at a picture, and I see how, after their brief flowering, only thorns are left on the plants. I don't know much about cacti; I have always imagined their thorns to be stinging, poisonous. But in this photograph the evening light has caught their fineness so that they shine, exalted, like the hair of infants.

I want to say something to Radhika about the unexpected, redemptive beauty of the world, but the phone rings.

"Yes?" she says.

I can hear the voice inside the receiver, tinnily obsequious. "Malik-ji will be sending the car eight P.M. sharp this evening, as usual, madam. Please to be ready downstairs."

Radhika's fingers tighten on the receiver. But no. I am mistaken. Her tone is as calm as always when she says, "Tell him sorry, I'm not well today." When the voice, sounding unhappy, protests that Malik-ji will be bahut-bahut upset, she repeats the sentence patiently, as though to a child. Then she hangs up.

The silence bristles between us like a live wire. In the months we've known each other, she has talked of many things—but not Malik, or the Fridays when his limousine glides up silent as some submarine creature to the curb and opens its hinged jaw.

I know what I should ask now. *Why did you?* A question which ebbs like a wave back to that day at a village wedding when she grew aware of a man's desirous eyes. A question which gathers itself to sweep forward to the hour when she opened a tap, mixed the warm and cold right, so it wouldn't hurt, held the wrist just so under the gush of it. *Why did you?* A question that breaks over this moment now, the cool danger of her voice saying *no,* what it might mean.

But I'm afraid to ask. I've lost so much already. Besides, what would I say if someone knew to ask *me* why? As in, *Why didn't you insist that your mother remain with you that day on the terrace?*

Radhika's fingers are back in my hair, their circling unhurried, as though there had been no interruption. She nudges me with her hip. "Go on," she says, saving me, and thankfully I turn the page.

★ ★ ★

Ajit is a regular at our restaurant. He used to come once in a while, but recently it's every week, sometimes two or even three times. Which surprises me, because he's not the kind of Indian man the place attracts. Our men are usually middle-aged, balding, a little down at the heel. H-1 visa holders whose shoulders slump under the hopes of wives and children waiting back in the home country. Who want a down-home meal that doesn't cost too much and like to order the specials. (The younger Indians, the ones who want to impress their American girlfriends, go to Khyber Palace down the street, where they have Indian karaoke and disco bhangra on Saturday nights.) Ajit's shoes are laced and eagerly polished, his shirts are the button-down kind with all the buttons firmly sewed on. And though he doesn't have on a jacket or a tie, I get the feeling he's just taken them off and placed them, carefully folded, on the passenger seat of his car. There's a certain trustfulness about him that makes it clear he has never lived anywhere except America.

What I like about Ajit is the way he seems to be at home in a room full of people who are nothing like him. Perhaps he isn't aware of how different he is from us. He jokes with the waiters—he's wildly popular with them, and not just for the substantial tips he leaves behind—watches the other customers with unabashed curiosity, eats with gusto. Even Malik, the one time he dropped by, patted his shoulder and said, "Ah Ajit, just the person I wanted to see!" He brought him up to the register and introduced us. "This is our Mira, a college graduate, just like you. Sharp as a needle. Hang around her and you'll learn everything you want to know about India."

I gave him a sharp-as-a-needle glance. Was he being sarcastic? If he was, it escaped Ajit. But perhaps he was the kind of person sarcasm couldn't touch. He shook my hand with a wide-open smile and said, "Delighted," like he meant it.

Since then Ajit has taken to stopping at the register to chat before he leaves. I am a little astonished at his frankness. Are all second-generation Indians like this? Already I know that he's in finance, that he's been out here for two years working for a small start-up company. His mother is a schoolteacher and his father an engineer back in the little midwestern town where he grew up. He gets lonely for them sometimes, but thinks California is wildly exciting, mostly because of all the different kinds of South Asians he has been meeting. He doesn't have a girlfriend yet, but is hopeful. When he leaves with a cheery "Take care!" I stare after him in envy.

In his letters my brother asks if I like it here, if people are kind to me. My sister-in-law adds, Is the weather better than Texas? Have you been down to San Francisco yet? Now that you've settled down, what are your future plans?

I consider replying that I've found someone with whom to read books, who is more than kind. I think of different words to describe Radhika: friend, sister, mother. (But none of them are right.) The weather is humid and exasperatingly un-Californian. (But to admit this would be a defeat.) As for San Francisco and my future, I have left them both alone. I am happy with what I have: a brief reprieve in which I can float without thought, as in a warm bath. (Then I'm ashamed: I should have been more industrious and taken a day-trip on the Golden State Bus Line; I should have enrolled for a course at the University of California Extension.)

And so I don't write back.

★ ★ ★

That day, after the phone call from Malik's henchman, Radhika and I looked at one last photograph in the desert book. It was the picture of a woman holding out a handful of sand. WOMAN MINER PANS FOR GOLD, INYO COUNTY, read the caption. The woman wore jeans with frayed knees, a vest of some sort, a broad-brimmed hat which pulled her face into its oval of darkness. She didn't look at the camera, but at something (someone?) whose shadow fell across the edge of the photograph—coyote, perhaps, or a horse. Her lips were parted in a small, secret smile.

On Friday evening, Ajit taps his fingers on the register, slides a card shyly at me, and clears his throat to ask if I'd go out with him. Next Friday, maybe? My head is full of a dim vibration. I open my mouth to say no. But when I look, he has the eyes of an antelope. And here's another surprise: the way my heart thuds inside my chest, like runner's feet, light and rapid, *why not, why not.*

Perhaps this, at last, will be how I climb out of my water tank.

When I go to the back office to ask the manager if I can have next Friday night off, he throws up his hands. "Absolutely not possible," he says. "We don't have anyone to take your place."

"How about Ramesh? I could do his lunchtime shift, and he—"

"You must be joking. That banana-fingered bumbler? Every day after lunch we are spending one hour correcting all the things he rung up wrong."

"Come on," I say. I've gained a certain weight around here since I started sharing Radhika's apartment, and I attempt to use it. "It's just for one day!"

"What so-important thing is happening next Friday?"

I tell him about Ajit, and he throws up his hands again. "Dating with a boy who's no better than an Amreekan! Nothing except trouble in it! Chee chee, what would your mother say!"

A hardness twists its way along my shoulder bones. "None of your business," I say through rigid lips.

Then I hear the soft voice at the door: "What's all this hallah about?"

It's Malik, who seems to have a knack for appearing magically. Perhaps that is the key to his success? He is dressed with far more care than usual, in a beautiful dark suit—the way I'd originally imagined him. With his glossy new haircut, he is almost dashing. His tie looks like silk, looks like he's on his way to someplace important, a party perhaps, in some glittery penthouse, uniformed servers carrying silver trays.

Then a thought comes to me. It's Friday—could it be for Radhika that he has dressed?

When the manager has poured out his complaints, he says, "A date, hanh? Our Mira wants to go on a date?" His eyes move over me, appraising but absent, as though he is thinking of something else. In the corridor's shadows, his expression is hooded, satyrlike. Finally, he says, "Perhaps *that's* what she needs."

My cheeks burn. What does he mean?

But already he's turned a suave smile on the manager. "Oh, don't be such an old fogey. Let the girl go. And give her an advance so she can get something fancy to wear."

Still smiling, he stands back courteously to let me pass. The cologne he is wearing—understated as only the most expensive ones are—follows me down the dark corridor like a suspicion I can't quite put into words.

★ ★ ★

The evening light is rich and gold this Friday, the day of my date with Ajit, and when I enter our apartment, the tiny mirrors on the sofa cushions Radhika finished embroidering last week dance and wink. The room is filled with a smell I know well—there they are, a platter of samosas, sitting on the kitchen counter, ready for frying.

"Is that you, Mira?" Radhika calls from her room. "Good timing! I just finished filling the samosas. Let me fry you a couple."

I set down the packages I'm carrying and collapse on the sofa. My feet hurt, and my head. Already I'm regretting my extravagance, wondering if what I've bought is all wrong.

I've never been a good shopper. Even in India, where you sit on a large white sheet spread under a cool ceiling fan and drink Jusla and point while the storekeeper takes out one sari after another and tells you the name of each and where it came from, I would ask my mother to do my shopping. She always knew what was suitable for a particular occasion, what would look good on me.

Radhika comes out of her room wearing a thin batik robe that molds itself to her body as she walks. She moves, like many Indian women, with delicate, careful steps that hardly disturb the air around her. Her hips ripple under the silky robe. It's a new one, and beautiful, but not something you would go out in. My heart beats out of rhythm. Did she refuse Malik again?

"I bet you're wondering how I knew you weren't working this evening!" From the kitchen Radhika throws me a mischievous smile. "One of the girls downstairs mentioned that Ramesh would be doing his first evening shift—the entire restaurant is nervous about it! So I thought this would be the perfect time to make you some samosas—I know how much you like them—and chat a little." The oil sputters as she turns the stuffed triangles that must have taken her hours to prepare. "There's something I've been wanting to tell you."

She brings me a plate of golden-crisp samosas and a bowl of deep brown tamarind chutney, and sits across from me. Her face is flushed and lovely. I give the clock a hasty, guilty glance. In a few minutes I'm going to have to tell her about my evening plans.

"When I met Malik," says Radhika, "I was so young, just a village girl. I thought being the wife of a rich man was the best thing that could happen to a woman." Her lashes tremble darkly against her cheek as she looks down. "When he told the matchmaker he was mad for me, that he'd do anything to marry me, I couldn't believe it. I was so proud to be desired by such a successful man, I didn't stop to think of anything else. My parents didn't want to send me so far away, with a man they knew so little about, but I persuaded them. I insisted I'd be happy with him. And then I got to America and found out about his—" Her voice splinters apart.

"Radhika—" I reach for her hand—"maybe it's better if you don't talk about such—"

"No." She is crying, openly, unashamedly. Her hand closes on mine the way, in the Bombay ocean, a woman's might have closed upon sea froth at the last minute—as though it could hold her up. "I've had enough of silences. But it's not Malik I want to talk about. I learned to live with him years ago—like I learned to live with this." She turns her wrist to gaze at her scar. Then she looks at me, her lashes spiky with tears. "No. It's something quite different I want to tell you. Something sudden, like a summer rainstorm. Something that's given me more happiness than I hoped to have in this life."

I hate myself for what I'm going to say next. But it isn't merely selfishness that drives me, it is also a fear I cannot articulate.

"I'm terribly sorry, Radhika. Can we talk about this later tonight? I have to go out. I promised"—I stumble over the next word—"a friend."

She lets go of my hand right away. Wipes her eyes. "Then of course you must." Her voice is polite, but I hear the hurt in it.

"We'll talk as soon as I come back—it's just a couple of hours. . . ."

"Yes," she says distantly, then goes into her room. When, dressed in my new clothes, I knock to say that I'm leaving, she doesn't answer. I stand in front of the shut bedroom door, guilty as a teenager. I know I should turn the knob, go inside. But I don't. Right now I need to feel confident. And I know Radhika would disapprove of the lacy white dress which stops at my thighs, the stiletto heels in which I stumble a little, the glittery crimson outlining my mouth. My flyaway hair from which I've shampooed all traces of the jabakusum oil she rubbed in with such care.

When Ajit sees me, he lets out a long whistle. "I'd planned a quiet dinner," he laughs. "But now I see we've got to go dancing."

So that's what we do. And even though I've never danced in my life, in the dimly lit nightclub where music ricochets off every glistening surface, and swaying bodies brush against us unselfconsciously, I find that I can do it. I shimmy my shoulders and throw back my head, dancing my way into the new life I'd begun to dream—it seems so long ago—on the Greyhound bus. When Ajit spins me so I end up against his chest, I don't shove away as an earlier Mira would have done, the Mira on whose hair rust flecks from a water tank once settled like dried blood. I lean there a moment, savoring the wholesome, lemony smell of his skin. When after a walk along the riverfront with its glimmering waters, he kisses me, I find it pleasant, and not the disgusting, spit-and-groping occurrence I'd feared. And when, somewhat timidly, he asks if I would come to his apartment, I am not outraged or even embarrassed. I lay my fingers lightly on his lips, as a woman in a movie might do, a dangerous woman, and say, with a smile, "Not yet."

It's a little after midnight when I open the door of our apartment. Inside, all is silent. Dark. I slip off my heels, tiptoe toward my room.

"Mira, do you know how late it is! I was so worried!" Radhika's voice is a whip, lashing out of blackness. When she flicks on the light, it blinds me.

She's still wearing the batik robe. It's wrinkled now, and her hair, come undone, is mussed as though she's been running her hands through it.

"I'm sorry—"

Now she notices my dress, the high heels I'm holding. "Where did you go?" she asks hoarsely. "With whom?"

My cheeks are hot, but I lift my chin. "I went dancing—with my friend Ajit."

"Dancing! With your *friend* Ajit!" Her voice is thick. She takes a step toward me. "Look at you—out all night with some man, half-naked in that dress—" Her eyes take in my hair, my makeup, stop on my mouth, kissed bare of lipstick and a little swollen. "Like . . . like a common—"

"Like what?" I'm angry too, now. What gives her the right to talk to me this way? "Like you?"

Her eyes widen in shock. For a moment she's silent. Then she says, very quietly, "Not like me, Mira. I'd never want you to be like me. To make my mistakes. To end up tied to the man who tricked you in the worst way, because what else is possible in your life—"

There's something heavy in her voice, about to break open. To forestall it, I shout, "Stop trying to be my mother!"

"Your mother!" Radhika makes a small sound in her throat that could be a laugh. "I don't want to be your mother. I only want to save you from the suffering I see you rushing toward." She puts her hands on my shoulders. "If I could take all the pain from your life into mine, I'd do it right now. Mira, my dear." She pushes away a wisp of hair from my face, kisses my cheek. "My love," she says. Then her lips are on mine.

For a moment or a lifetime, I stand there stunned, surprised and yet not so, trying to make sense of what's happening. Trying to make sense of my body, the shivering that rises up from the soles of my feet. Do my lips want to kiss her back? Do my treacherous arms want to crush her softness against mine? Then I thrust her away.

"No," I whisper. "No." My voice shakes with horror. But who am I horrified by? My shoes have clattered to the floor. As I stumble to the apartment door, I hear Radhika cry, "Mira, don't go—" Then I slam it shut.

I stand on the curb outside our building, shivering. When numbness has seeped into all the bones of my bare feet, I call Ajit from the pay phone. I am not sure what I will do if Radhika comes looking for me. When she doesn't, I'm not sure if it's thankfulness I feel.

The choices in our lives, what impels us to them?

A few late-night folks pass by. I cringe back against the wall, but they don't seem to notice me. Perhaps an Indian girl, barefoot in a gauzy white mini, is a common sight to them. Perhaps they have worse problems of their own.

Ajit's car takes the corner too sharply, screeches to a stop.

"Mira, what happened?"

Dressed in sweats and sleep-tousled, he seems startled and young. Too young, I think tiredly.

"God, you're freezing," he says as he shepherds me into the car. He pulls off his windbreaker and guides my arms through its sleeves. In his apartment, while I sit on the couch and stare at the wall, he brings me a pair of woolen socks. When I begin to cry, he puts an awkward arm around me, not sure of what to do.

Inside I am split in two. One Mira watches the other crying, tries to figure out why. Is it Ajit's kindness? Or the loss of the only friendship in my life? Are they for a mother who believed she must keep her daughter safe at any cost, these belated tears? Or for myself, being sucked into a vortex from which whispered words rise like ancestral ghosts: *disgusting, perverted, unnatural.*

I turn to Ajit, pull his face to mine, press my lips on his. When he says he doesn't think it's a good idea, I'm too upset right now, I hold him tighter. I will the pounding in my head to grow louder, to drown my thoughts. I rake my nails across Ajit's back and hear him gasp. I tug off his sweatshirt and kiss whatever I come across—earlobe, throat, the curved line of his collarbone. He no longer protests. Against my mouth, his skin is salt and smoke. My head is exploding. Briefly, before the pounding pulls me under, I wonder if a woman's skin would have tasted different.

There is, in empty apartments, a certain shifting of energy, an absence of breathed air. I feel this as soon as I open the door to Radhika's place. But I am too exhausted to wonder where she is at 3 A.M. Or where I will go when I leave this place, as I know I must.

I stumble to the bathroom and start the water. I kick off the too-large men's sandals that Ajit had insisted on giving me, shrug off his jacket. I'll leave them for him at the restaurant. My own clothes—the lace dress ripped carelessly under the arm, the panties stained with blood—I throw into the wastebasket. My aim is shaky. The basket tips over, spilling crumpled wads of paper over the bathroom floor.

Sex had been a disappointment. I hadn't expected pleasure, but I had hoped for ecstasy—in the way the Greeks had meant the word. Something that took you out of yourself, made you forget who you were.

In Ajit's bed, no matter what I attempted, I remained myself, caught in my unresponsive flesh like the seed inside a hard, green mango. When finally he took my face in his hands and said, trying to mask his disappointment, "It's okay, Mira, stop now. We'll try again another day," I closed my eyes, shamed by his generosity. I knew there wouldn't be another day.

The water sends a welcome shock of heat through me as I climb in. I should be soaping myself clean, but I'm too tired. I lie there and watch the ripples of reflected light on white porcelain, on wet brown skin. In the stillness, it is easy to drift into other waters. Orange peels floating down, humid air that clogs the throat. When the knocking begins I have to put a hand over my mouth to stifle my scream.

But it is only one of the downstairs girls. "Sorry to disturb you so early," she says. "But I heard the water running, so I knew you were up. Do you know Radhika's in the hospital?" She nods to confirm the question in my eyes. "Yes, another suicide attempt. Late last night, in Malik-ji's apartment. She took his sleeping pills this time. Luckily they found her before it was too late. Listen, you better sit down, you don't look so good. . . ."

The waiting room of the hospital is unbearably cheery, with pastel printed sofas and posters of baby animals peering from behind unlikely objects. I sit on a bench out in the corridor, taking comfort in its plain hardness, in the way my back begins to ache after a while. Sooner or later they must allow visitors to see Radhika.

"Are you family?" the nurse had asked. I tried to say yes. But I'm only good at lying to myself.

"Sorry," said the nurse.

Radhika must have called Malik late that night, saying she felt better. She asked him to send the limo, to meet her at his apartment, as they always did. After it was over and he left for his other home—his real home, the mansion up on the hills where his wife and sons slept—she must have done it then. She reached under the bathroom sink where he kept the pills, and smiled a bitter smile. She knew all his secrets now. She looked out the window at his Porsche, its ruby lights receding into fog—but she was the one who was leaving, who was gone already. Out of my life, taking the honorable way, enduring this final night with Malik so I wouldn't have to be the one to find her body. She had planned it all—except that when she said to the limo driver, "Please take me back to my apartment tomorrow, I'm too tired right now," he had called Malik to check if that was all right.

After the girl from downstairs had left, I went back into the bathroom. I let the water out of the tub and watched its downward spinning, at once lazy and urgent. I wiped my wet footprints and righted the wastebasket, picking the wadded sheets off the floor. On an impulse I smoothed them out.

There were three of them. One said, *Mira* . . . One said, *I never expected* . . . The last was a poem of sorts.

In the desert of my heart,
you, cactus flower,
blooming without thorn.

When she wrote those words, I was dancing. I twirled on tiptoe, making myself tall. My hair wild with abandonment, I let Ajit pull me into his chest, into the possibilities of my new American life.

I think nothing of the footsteps, muffled on hospital carpeting, until they stop in front of me. Then I look up and it is Malik. His eyes are swollen and I see, with wonder, that he's been weeping. When he speaks to me, the words glow with hate.

"We were happy until you got here, until you put your sick ideas into her head. I should have gotten rid of you right at the first, when she started acting different. But I didn't—wouldn't—believe that she could . . ." A spasm shakes him and he looks away. When he turns back, his voice is cool and serrated. "I'm giving you twenty-four hours to leave."

I watch him as he walks down the hallway, his right leg dragging a little in a limp I had never noticed. It comes to me that the stories about him are true. But I am too full of other emotions to feel fear. How ironic that of the three of us, he was the one to first smell the change in the air. He brought Ajit over to the cash register, he made the manager give me the evening off for my date. *Maybe that's what she needs.* I had thought, naively, that he was talking about me. But he was talking about the woman he loved in spite of himself, the one person who had shown him how, while you tighten your fist around a life, the heart can slip away.

It takes me only an hour to pack my belongings. I should leave for the bank now, get out what little money I have. Then the Greyhound station, where I need to check the schedule, decide on my destination. Instead I wander through the apartment, touching a table mat Radhika had painted, the roses—now dying—that she arranged in a brass vase. I think how I've turned out to be all that I dreamed of on the bus—burning wind, bramble bush, things that scorch and scrape. But none of them are what I imagined. It had not struck me that a lit fuse must burn itself first, before setting the world on fire.

Finally, because I must, I go into Radhika's bedroom.

Radhika's room reflects her neatness. The bedspread is creaseless, the photos of her parents hang straight and level with each other. Even last night, after getting ready, when there was no longer any need, she had put everything back in its place. Face powder, deodorant, perfume, hair oil. They stand lined up on her dresser, precise, giving nothing away. Comb, brush, filigreed hand mirror. Kumkum powder in a silver box. I pick each one up, try to think what she had thought. Then I see the book.

Splayed at the far end of the dresser, it is the only thing that is out of place. *The Great Deserts of the American West,* turned to the picture where the miner squinches her eyes against the glare of sun on sand.

I carry the book to Radhika's bed. When I lay my head on her pillow, I think I smell her hair.

Down at the Greyhound station, the drivers are starting the engines, lifting their feet off the brakes. The buses begin to roll down the highway, each taking you to a different destiny.

Did the woman in the photo take a bus the day she moved to the hills? How many people had spoken to her in my sister-in-law's voice, saying that what she was doing, it just wasn't right, wasn't natural?

She would have shrugged her shoulders, turned her face a little. Maybe she smiled that small, secret smile.

Who is to say? If a woman finds joy in the spare, pared flesh of the desert, if she finds joy in another woman's sand-brown body, who is to say?

There are so many words I'm searching for, I who had stopped believing in their possibility. In the hospital, as I slip past the nurse's station, as I look in each room for Radhika, I hope some of them will come to me. She will turn her head away; her earring will glint like an evaporation of dew. But this time around, I've learned insistence. On the long bus ride south, and later, in sand and rock, among the fierce momentary blooming of cacti, I'll lean my head into her shoulder. I'll run my fingers over her scar the way one reads Braille. Perhaps I'll find them there, the words for my night with Ajit. The water tank. The women swimming out into the Bombay ocean. For my mother, who also believed that to save the one you love, you have to give up your own life.

On the way out, I glance at the book, the miner holding out her cupped palm, daring us to decipher what in it is sand, and what gold. I decide I know whom she is smiling at. It is her lover, the woman whose shadow has entered the photograph, and in doing so shifted the balance of light.

Louise Erdrich *(1954–)*

once described her writing style as "a mixture of the Ojibwe storyteller and the German system-maker. I find that everything that I write has to be connected into this grand scheme." The oldest of seven children, Erdrich was born in Little Falls, Minnesota, and grew up mostly in Wahpeton, North Dakota, where her German-American father and French-Ojibwe mother taught at Bureau of Indian Affairs schools. She entered Dartmouth in 1972, part of the college's first coeducational class. After graduation, she returned to North Dakota to teach writing in public schools through the State Arts Council. She returned to college, getting a degree from the creative writing program at Johns Hopkins University, then returned to Dartmouth as a writer-in-residence; there, she married one of her former professors, Michael Dorris. At age thirty, Erdrich published her first two books: Jacklight, *a collection of poems, and* Love Medicine, *a novel-in-stories that went on to win the National Book Critics Circle Award. Erdrich and Dorris raised several children together and collaborated on several books, starting with romance fiction under the pseudonym Milou North and continuing into more ambitious work, though only one novel—*The Crown of Columbus*—was published under both their names. Erdrich's other novels (many of which are made up of short story–shaped sections) include* Tracks, The Bingo Palace, *and* Tales of Burning Love. *She has also written several books of poetry and nonfiction. When Dorris and Erdrich separated, Erdrich moved six blocks down the street in order to share custody of their children, but two years later, Dorris committed suicide. Erdrich now lives in Minneapolis with her three youngest children.*

Introduction by **Brady Udall**

There's no nice way to say this: For much of my life, I've had a low opinion of women's literature. A bad experience with *Little Women* is where it began. I was in the fourth grade, and my teacher, Mr. Ebeltoft, read the novel to us for an hour every day after recess. Mr. Ebelhoft was a tough guy, a former Marine with a broken nose and a tattoo of the Virgin Mary on his arm, but when he read from *Little Women,* an odd, girlish tone would creep into his voice. Holding the book in what seemed to me a dainty way, he would purse his lips and read a line such as "'Oh dear me,' Jo said. 'The violet silk would be ever so nice indeed!'" For a boy who was trying to understand what it meant to be a man in the world, this was deeply disturbing.

In junior high, I did like everyone else and read the Judy Blume books, which gave me the heebie-jeebies. In tenth grade, I worked my way through *Pride and Prejudice,* which gave me flashbacks of Mr. Ebeltoft and *Little Women.* And then, in my senior year, the clincher: An overenthusiastic Honors English teacher assigned me to read *Middlemarch* for my final project, and after nine hundred and forty pages of what I considered to be acute and unnecessary suffering, I put the book aside and made the kind of vow only a shallow-minded dipshit teenager can make: I was never going to read a work of women's literature again.

You can imagine my lack of enthusiasm, then, when later that summer a friend gave me a copy of Louise Erdrich's *Love Medicine* and urged me to read it. "This is the best thing you'll ever read," she told me. "Oh, I doubt it," I said, smug in the way that only the ignorant can be smug. The cover of the paperback edition she handed me featured a misty watercolor painting of a young girl gazing at two geese winging in tandem toward a purple sunset. *"Love Medicine,"* I thought. "Give me a break."

I don't know why I ever opened the book and started to read. It was a moment of either weakness or severe boredom, but once I started, I couldn't put it down. Against all my best judgment, I flat loved it. What struck me most strongly was the astounding multitude of voices it contained, each one particular and compelling. One of those voices belongs to Marie Lazare, a mixed-blood teenager who engages in an epic spiritual battle with a terrifying old nun named Sister Leopolda in "Saint Marie." Plotwise, the story is elegantly simple: Marie and the nun do battle for the girl's soul. But what makes the story so uncommonly satisfying is the language Marie uses to relate the tale, a mixture of high diction and low colloquialisms that fits perfectly with the story's run-down convent setting and baroque religious themes. One moment Marie is asking the most casual of questions, "You ever seen a walleye struck so bad the lure is practically out its back end before you reel it in?" The next, in a burst of poetry, she's describing what it's like to be the object of veneration: "My name was buzzing up and down the room, like a fat autumn fly lighting on the tips of their tongues between Latin, humming up the heavy blood-dark curtains, circling their little cosseted heads." This blending of the prosaic and poetic is no easy trick, yet Erdrich pulls it off with an almost casual ease. She balances these two modes of language so expertly that she's able to create, with nothing more than words on a page, a complex and fully human voice.

Lyman Lamartine, who provides another of the voices in *Love Medicine,* is more restrained, more convential; no bursts of poetry do we get from Lyman. In "The Red Convertible," he tells his sad story in measured tones, humbly, almost reluctantly. The story takes its time and, at first, seems to be about nothing more than the relationship between two brothers and their shared ownership of a red Oldsmobile. But we learn that Henry, who is back from Vietnam, is in a state of emotional disrepair, and in Lyman's matter-of-fact voice, we begin to hear the whisperings of grief:

> My only sister, Bonita, who was just eleven years old, came out and made us stand together for a picture. Henry leaned his elbow on the red car's windshield, and he took the other arm and put it over my shoulder, very carefully, as though it was heavy for him to lift and he didn't want to bring the weight down all at once.

For me, these lines are so heartbreaking exactly because they are so unassuming, so simply told. Even when the story reaches its tragic climax, Erdrich never exaggerates or resorts to melodrama. The words that Henry calls out as he drowns—"My boots are filling"—are so anticlimactic they're almost comical. Erdrich lets the unfolding events of the story, as described by Lyman's diffident voice, provide the emotional power. She understands that it is the story itself that must dictate the language, the tone—and even the voice—with which it's told. It sounds like a fortune-cookie proverb, but it has always worked for me: Let the story be your guide.

Since reading *Love Medicine,* I have made it a point to read everything Erdrich has published. I think she just might have done her best bit of voice work with Stan Anderson's sermon in "Satan: Hijacker of a Planet." The audacity of it, the lovely, compelling weirdness of that passage. Can you tell me, after reading it, after reading lines like "The stars are the eyes of God, and they have been watching us from the beginning of the world" that you don't feel a little blasted and unsure, that maybe you ought to take account of your sins, that maybe you should pull out your wallet and present your credit card so that it can be scissored into halves by a servant of the Lord? When I read that sermon or passages like the gut-wrenching final paragraphs of this story, I have no insights, no penetrating critiques. I can only express my wonder (while offering my gratitude to Ms. Erdrich for opening my muddled teenager's mind) and say to you, the reader: Behold what a master can do.

Brady Udall is the author of the story collection Letting Loose the Hounds *and the novel* The Miracle Life of Edgar Mint. *He teaches fiction writing at Southern Illinois University.*

LOUISE ERDRICH

The Red Convertible

I was the first one to drive a convertible on my reservation. And of course it was red, a red Olds. I owned that car along with my brother Henry Junior. We owned it together until his boots filled with water on a windy night and he bought out my share. Now Henry owns the whole car, and his youngest brother Lyman (that's myself), Lyman walks everywhere he goes.

How did I earn enough money to buy my share in the first place? My own talent was I could always make money. I had a touch for it, unusual in a Chippewa. From the first I was different that way, and everyone recognized it. I was the only kid they let in the American Legion Hall to shine shoes, for example, and one Christmas I sold spiritual bouquets for the mission door to door. The nuns let me keep a percentage. Once I started, it seemed the more money I made the easier the money came. Everyone encouraged it. When I was fifteen I got a job washing dishes at the Joliet Café, and that was where my first big break happened.

It wasn't long before I was promoted to bussing tables, and then the short-order cook quit and I was hired to take her place. No sooner than you know it I was managing the Joliet. The rest is history. I went on managing. I soon became part owner, and of course there was no stopping me then. It wasn't long before the whole thing was mine.

After I'd owned the Joliet for one year, it blew over in the worst tornado ever seen around here. The whole operation was smashed to bits. A total loss. The fryalator was up in a tree, the grill torn in half like it was paper. I was only sixteen. I had it all in my mother's name, and I lost it quick, but before I lost it I had every one of my relatives, and their relatives, to dinner, and I also bought that red Olds I mentioned, along with Henry.

The first time we saw it! I'll tell you when we first saw it. We had gotten a ride up to Winnipeg, and both of us had money. Don't ask me why, because we never mentioned a car or anything, we just had all our money. Mine was cash, a big bankroll from the Joliet's insurance. Henry had two checks—a week's extra pay for being laid off, and his regular check from the Jewel Bearing Plant.

We were walking down Portage anyway, seeing the sights, when we saw it. There it was, parked, large as life. Really as *if* it was alive. I thought of the word *repose,* because the car wasn't simply stopped, parked, or whatever. That car reposed, calm and gleaming, a FOR SALE sign in its left front window. Then, before we had thought it over at all, the car belonged to us and our pockets were empty. We had just enough money for gas back home.

We went places in that car, me and Henry. We took off driving all one whole summer. We started off toward the Little Knife River and Mandaree in Fort Berthold and then we found ourselves down in Wakpala somehow, and then suddenly we were over in Montana on the Rocky Boys, and yet the summer was not even half over. Some people hang on to details when they travel, but we didn't let them bother us and just lived our everyday lives here to there.

I do remember this one place with willows. I remember I laid under those trees and it was comfortable. So comfortable. The branches bent down all around me like a tent or a stable. And quiet, it was quiet, even though there was a powwow close enough so I could see it going on. The air was not too still, not too windy either. When the dust rises up and hangs in the air around the dancers like that, I feel good. Henry was asleep with his arms thrown wide. Later on, he woke up and we started driving again. We were somewhere in Montana, or maybe on the Blood Reserve—it could have been anywhere. Anyway it was where we met the girl.

All her hair was in buns around her ears, that's the first thing I noticed about her. She was posed alongside the road with her arm out, so we stopped. That girl was short, so short her lumber shirt looked comical on her, like a nightgown. She had jeans on and fancy moccasins and she carried a little suitcase.

"Hop on in," says Henry. So she climbs in between us.

"We'll take you home," I says. "Where do you live?"

"Chicken," she says.

"Where the hell's that?" I ask her.

"Alaska."

"Okay," says Henry, and we drive.

We got up there and never wanted to leave. The sun doesn't truly set there in summer, and the night is more a soft dusk. You might doze off, sometimes, but before you know it you're up again, like an animal in nature. You never feel like you have to sleep hard or put away the world. And things would grow up there. One day just dirt or moss, the next day flowers and long grass. The girl's name was Susy. Her family really took to us. They fed us and put us up. We had our own tent to live in by their house, and the kids would be in and out of there all day and night. They couldn't get over me and Henry being brothers, we looked so different. We told them we knew we had the same mother, anyway.

One night Susy came in to visit us. We sat around in the tent talking of this thing and that. The season was changing. It was getting darker by that time, and the cold was even getting just a little mean. I told her it was time for us to go. She stood up on a chair.

"You never seen my hair," Susy said.

That was true. She was standing on a chair, but still, when she unclipped her buns the hair reached all the way to the ground. Our eyes opened. You couldn't tell how much hair she had when it was rolled up so neatly. Then my brother Henry did something funny. He went up to the chair and said, "Jump on my shoulders." So she did that, and her hair reached down past his waist, and he started twirling, this way and that, so her hair was flung out from side to side.

"I always wondered what it was like to have long pretty hair," Henry says. Well we laughed. It was a funny sight, the way he did it. The next morning we got up and took leave of those people.

On to greener pastures, as they say. It was down through Spokane and across Idaho then Montana and very soon we were racing the weather right along under the

Canadian border through Columbus, Des Lacs, and then we were in Bottineau County and soon home. We'd made most of the trip, that summer, without putting up the car hood at all. We got home just in time, it turned out, for the army to remember Henry had signed up to join it.

I don't wonder that the army was so glad to get my brother that they turned him into a Marine. He was built like a brick outhouse anyway: We liked to tease him that they really wanted him for his Indian nose. He had a nose big and sharp as a hatchet, like the nose on Red Tomahawk, the Indian who killed Sitting Bull, whose profile is on signs all along the North Dakota highways. Henry went off to training camp, came home once during Christmas, then the next thing you know we got an overseas letter from him. It was 1970, and he said he was stationed up in the northern hill country. Whereabouts I did not know. He wasn't such a hot letter writer, and only got off two before the enemy caught him. I could never keep it straight, which direction those good Vietnam soldiers were from.

I wrote him back several times, even though I didn't know if those letters would get through. I kept him informed all about the car. Most of the time I had it up on blocks in the yard or half taken apart, because that long trip did a hard job on it under the hood.

I always had good luck with numbers, and never worried about the draft myself. I never even had to think about what my number was. But Henry was never lucky in the same way as me. It was at least three years before Henry came home. By then I guess the whole war was solved in the government's mind, but for him it would keep on going. In those years I'd put his car into almost perfect shape. I always thought of it as his car while he was gone, even though when he left he said, "Now it's yours," and threw me his key.

"Thanks for the extra key," I'd said. "I'll put it up in your drawer just in case I need it." He laughed.

When he came home, though, Henry was very different, and I'll say this: the change was no good. You could hardly expect him to change for the better, I know. But he was quiet, so quiet, and never comfortable sitting still anywhere but always up and moving around. I thought back to times we'd sat still for whole afternoons, never moving a muscle, just shifting our weight along the ground, talking to whoever sat with us, watching things. He'd always had a joke, then, too, and now you couldn't get him to laugh, or when he did it was more the sound of a man choking, a sound that stopped up the throats of other people around him. They got to leaving him alone most of the time, and I didn't blame them. It was a fact: Henry was jumpy and mean.

I'd bought a color TV set for my mom and the rest of us while Henry was away. Money still came very easy. I was sorry I'd ever bought it though, because of Henry: I was also sorry I'd bought color, because with black-and-white the pictures seem older and farther away. But what are you going to do? He sat in front of it, watching it, and that was the only time he was completely still. But it was the kind of stillness that you see in a rabbit when it freezes and before it will bolt. He was not easy. He sat in his chair gripping the armrests with all his might, as if the chair itself was moving at a high speed and if he let go at all he would rocket forward and maybe crash right through the set.

Once I was in the room watching TV with Henry and I heard his teeth click at something. I looked over, and he'd bitten through his lip. Blood was going down his chin. I tell you right then I wanted to smash that tube to pieces. I went over to it but Henry must have known what I was up to. He rushed from his chair and shoved me out of the way, against the wall. I told myself he didn't know what he was doing.

My mom came in, turned the set off real quiet, and told us she had made something for supper. So we went and sat down. There was still blood going down Henry's chin, but he didn't notice it and no one said anything, even though every time he took a bit of his bread his blood fell onto it until he was eating his own blood mixed in with the food.

While Henry was not around we talked about what was going to happen to him. There were no Indian doctors on the reservation, and my mom was afraid of trusting Old Man Pillager because he courted her long ago and was jealous of her husbands. He might take revenge through her son. We were afraid that if we brought Henry to a regular hospital they would keep him.

"They don't fix them in those places," Mom said; "they just give them drugs."

"We wouldn't get him there in the first place," I agreed, "so let's just forget about it."

Then I thought about the car.

Henry had not even looked at the car since he'd gotten home, though like I said, it was in tip-top condition and ready to drive. I thought the car might bring the old Henry back somehow. So I bided my time and waited for my chance to interest him in the vehicle.

One night Henry was off somewhere. I took myself a hammer. I went out to that car and I did a number on its underside. Whacked it up. Bent the tail pipe double. Ripped the muffler loose. By the time I was done with the car it looked worse than any typical Indian car that has been driven all its life on reservation roads, which they always say are like government promises—full of holes. It just about hurt me, I'll tell you that! I threw dirt in the carburetor and I ripped all the electric tape off the seats. I made it look just as beat up as I could. Then I sat back and waited for Henry to find it.

Still, it took him over a month. That was all right, because it was just getting warm enough, not melting, but warm enough to work outside.

"Lyman," he says, walking in one day, "that red car looks like shit."

"Well it's old," I says. "You got to expect that."

"No way!" says Henry. "That car's a classic! But you went and ran the piss right out of it, Lyman, and you know it don't deserve that. I kept that car in A-one shape. You don't remember. You're too young. But when I left, that car was running like a watch. Now I don't even know if I can get it to start again, let alone get it anywhere near its old condition."

"Well you try," I said, like I was getting mad, "but I say it's a piece of junk."

Then I walked out before he could realize I knew he'd strung together more than six words at once.

After that I thought he'd freeze himself to death working on that car. He was out there all day, and at night he rigged up a little lamp, ran a cord out the window, and had himself some light to see by while he worked. He was better than he had been before, but that's still not saying much. It was easier for him to do the things the rest of us did. He ate more slowly and didn't jump up and down during the meal to get this or that or look out the window. I put my hand in the back of the TV set, I admit, and fiddled around with it good, so that it was almost impossible now to get a clear picture. He didn't look at it very often anyway. He was always out with that car or going off to get parts for it. By the time it was really melting outside, he had it fixed.

I had been feeling down in the dumps about Henry around this time. We had always been together before. Henry and Lyman. But he was such a loner now that I didn't know how to take it. So I jumped at the chance one day when Henry seemed friendly. It's not that he smiled or anything. He just said, "Let's take that old shitbox for a spin." Just the way he said it made me think he could be coming around.

We went out to the car. It was spring. The sun was shining very bright. My only sister, Bonita, who was just eleven years old, came out and made us stand together for a picture. Henry leaned his elbow on the red car's windshield, and he took his other arm and put it over my shoulder, very carefully, as though it was heavy for him to lift and he didn't want to bring the weight down all at once.

"Smile," Bonita said, and he did.

That picture. I never look at it anymore. A few months ago, I don't know why, I got his picture out and tacked it on the wall. I felt good about Henry at the time, close to him. I felt good having his picture on the wall, until one night when I was looking at television. I was a little drunk and stoned. I looked up at the wall and Henry was staring at me. I don't know what it was, but his smile had changed, or maybe it was gone. All I know is I couldn't stay in the same room with that picture. I was shaking. I got up, closed the door, and went into the kitchen. A little later my friend Ray came over and we both went back into that room. We put the picture in a brown bag, folded the bag over and over tightly, then put it way back in a closet.

I still see that picture now, as if it tugs at me, whenever I pass that closet door. The picture is very clear in my mind. It was so sunny that day Henry had to squint against the glare. Or maybe the camera Bonita held flashed like a mirror, blinding him, before she snapped the picture. My face is right out in the sun, big and round. But he might have drawn back, because the shadows on his face are deep as holes. There are two shadows curved like little hooks around the ends of his smile, as if to frame it and try to keep it there—that one, first smile that looked like it might have hurt his face. He has his field jacket on and the worn-in clothes he'd come back in and kept wearing ever since. After Bonita took the picture, she went into the house and we got into the car. There was a full cooler in the trunk. We started off, east, toward Pembina and the Red River because Henry said he wanted to see the high water.

The trip over there was beautiful. When everything starts changing, drying up, clearing off, you feel like your whole life is starting. Henry felt it, too. The top was down and the car hummed like a top. He'd really put it back in shape, even the tape on the seats was very carefully put down and glued back in layers. It's not that he smiled again or even joked, but his face looked to me as if it was clear, more peaceful. It looked as though he wasn't thinking of anything in particular except the bare fields and windbreaks and houses we were passing.

The river was high and full of winter trash when we got there. The sun was still out, but it was colder by the river. There were still little clumps of dirty snow here and there on the banks. The water hadn't gone over the banks yet, but it would, you could tell. It was just at its limit, hard swollen glossy like an old gray scar. We made ourselves a fire, and we sat down and watched the current go. As I watched it I felt something squeezing inside me and tightening and trying to let go all at the same time. I knew I was not just feeling it myself; I knew I was feeling what Henry was going through at that moment. Except that I couldn't stand it, the closing and opening. I jumped to my feet. I took Henry by the shoulders and I started shaking him. "Wake up," I says, "wake up, wake up, wake up!" I didn't know what had come over me. I sat down beside him again.

His face was totally white and hard. Then it broke, like stones break all of a sudden when water boils up inside them.

"I know it," he says. "I know it. I can't help it. It's no use."

We start talking. He said he knew what I'd done with the car. It was obvious it had been whacked out of shape and not just neglected. He said he wanted to give the car to me for good now, it was no use. He said he'd fixed it just to give it back and I should take it.

"No way," I says, "I don't want it."

"That's okay," he says, "you take it."

"I don't want it, though," I says back to him, and then to emphasize, just to emphasize, you understand, I touch his shoulder. He slaps my hand off.

"Take that car," he says.

"No," I say, "make me," I say, and then he grabs my jacket and rips the arm loose. That jacket is a class act, suede with tags and zippers. I push Henry backwards, off the log. He jumps up and bowls me over. We go down in a clinch and come up swinging hard, for all we're worth, with our fists. He socks my jaw so hard I feel like it swings loose. Then I'm at his ribcage and land a good one under his chin so his head snaps back. He's dazzled. He looks at me and I look at him and then his eyes are full of tears and blood and at first I think he's crying. But no, he's laughing. "Ha! Ha!" he says. "Ha! Ha! Take good care of it."

"Okay," I says, "okay, no problem. Ha! Ha!"

I can't help it, and I start laughing, too. My face feels fat and strange, and after a while I get a beer from the cooler in the trunk, and when I hand it to Henry he takes his shirt and wipes my germs off. "Hoof-and-mouth disease," he says. For some reason this cracks me up, and so we're really laughing for a while, and then we drink all the rest of the beers one by one and throw them in the river and see how far, how fast, the current takes them before they fill up and sink.

"You want to go on back?" I ask after a while. "Maybe we could snag a couple nice Kashpaw girls."

He says nothing. But I can tell his mood is turning again.

"They're all crazy, the girls up here, every damn one of them."

"You're crazy too," I say, to jolly him up. "Crazy Lamartine boys!"

He looks as though he will take this wrong at first. His face twists, then clears, and he jumps up on his feet. "That's right!" he says. "Crazier 'n hell. Crazy Indians!"

I think it's the old Henry again. He throws off his jacket and starts swinging his legs out from the knees like a fancy dancer. He's down doing something between a grouse dance and a bunny hop, no kind of dance I ever saw before, but neither has anyone else on all this green growing earth. He's wild. He wants to pitch whoopee! He's up and at me and all over. All this time I'm laughing so hard, so hard my belly is getting tied up in a knot.

"Got to cool me off!" he shouts all of a sudden. Then he runs over to the river and jumps in.

There's boards and other things in the current. It's so high. No sound comes from the river after the splash he makes, so I run right over. I look around. It's getting dark. I see he's halfway across the water already, and I know he didn't swim there but the current took him. It's far. I hear his voice, though, very clearly across it.

"My boots are filling," he says.

He says this in a normal voice, like he just noticed and he doesn't know what to think of it. Then he's gone. A branch comes by. Another branch. And I go in.

By the time I get out of the river, off the snag I pulled myself onto, the sun is down. I walk back to the car, turn on the high beams, and drive it up the bank. I put it in first gear and then I take my foot off the clutch. I get out, close the door, and watch it plow softly into the water. The headlights reach in as they go down, searching, still lighted even after the water swirls over the back end. I wait. The wires short out. It is all finally dark. And then there is only the water, the sound of it going and running and going and running and running.

LOUISE ERDRICH

Saint Marie

So when I went there, I knew the dark fish must rise. Plumes of radiance had soldered on me. No reservation girl had ever prayed so hard. There was no use in trying to ignore me any longer. I was going up there on the hill with the black robe women. They were not any lighter than me. I was going up there to pray as good as they could. Because I don't have that much Indian blood. And they never thought they'd have a girl from this reservation as a saint they'd have to kneel to. But they'd have me. And I'd be carved in pure gold. With ruby lips. And my toenails would be little pink ocean shells, which they would have to stoop down off their high horse to kiss.

I was ignorant. I was near age fourteen. The length of sky is just about the size of my ignorance. Pure and wide. And it was just that—the pure and wideness of my ignorance—that got me up the hill to Sacred Heart Convent and brought me back down alive. For maybe Jesus did not take my bait, but them Sisters tried to cram me right down whole.

You ever see a walleye strike so bad the lure is practically out its back end before you reel it in? That is what they done with me. I don't like to make that low comparison, but I have seen a walleye do that once. And it's the same attempt as Sister Leopolda made to get me in her clutch.

I had the mail-order Catholic soul you get in a girl raised out in the bush, whose only thought is getting into town. For Sunday Mass is the only time my father brought his children in except for school, when we were harnessed. Our soul went cheap. We were so anxious to get there we would have walked in on our hands and knees. We just craved going to the store, slinging bottle caps in the dust, making fool eyes at each other. And of course we went to church.

Where they have the convent is on top of the highest hill, so that from its windows the Sisters can be looking into the marrow of the town. Recently a windbreak was planted before the bar "for the purposes of tornado insurance." Don't tell me that. That poplar stand was put up to hide the drinkers as they get the transformation. As they are served into the beast of their burden. While they're drinking, that body comes upon them, and then they stagger or crawl out the bar door, pulling a weight they can't move past the poplars. They don't want no holy witness to their fall.

Anyway, I climbed. That was a long-ago day. There was a road then for wagons that wound in ruts to the top of the hill where they had their buildings of painted brick. Gleaming white. So white the sun glanced off in dazzling display to set forms whirling behind your eyelids. The face of God you could hardly look at. But that day it drizzled, so I could look all I wanted. I saw the homelier side. The cracked whitewash and swallows nesting in the busted ends of eaves. I saw the boards sawed the size of broken windowpanes and the fruit trees, stripped. Only the tough wild rhubarb flourished. Goldenrod rubbed up their walls. It was a poor convent. I didn't see that then but I know that now. Compared to others it was humble, ragtag, out in the middle of no place. It was the end of the world to some. Where the maps stopped. Where God had only half a hand in the creation. Where the Dark One had put in thick bush, liquor, wild dogs, and Indians.

I heard later that the Sacred Heart Convent was a catchall place for nuns that don't get along elsewhere. Nuns that complain too much or lose their mind. I'll always wonder now, after hearing that, where they picked up Sister Leopolda. Perhaps she had scarred someone else, the way she left a mark on me. Perhaps she was just sent around to test her Sisters' faith, here and there, like the spot-checker in a factory. For she was the definite most-hard trial to anyone's endurance, even when they started out with veils of wretched love upon their eyes.

I was that girl who thought the black hem of her garment would help me rise. Veils of love which was only hate petrified by longing—that was me. I was like those bush Indians who stole the holy black hat of a Jesuit and swallowed little scraps of it to cure their fevers. But the hat itself carried smallpox and was killing them with belief. Veils of faith! I had this confidence in Leopolda. She was different. The other Sisters had long ago gone blank and given up on Satan. He slept for them. They never noticed his comings and goings. But Leopolda kept track of him and knew his habits, minds he burrowed in, deep spaces where he hid. She knew as much about him as my grandma, who called him by other names and was not afraid.

In her class, Sister Leopolda carried a long oak pole for opening high windows. It had a hook made of iron on one end that could jerk a patch of your hair out or throttle you by the collar—all from a distance. She used this deadly hook-pole for catching Satan by surprise. He could have entered without your knowing it—through your lips or your nose or any one of your seven openings—and gained your mind. But she would see him. That pole would brain you from behind. And he would gasp, dazzled, and take the first thing she offered, which was pain.

She had a stringer of children who could only breathe if she said the word. I was the worst of them. She always said the Dark One wanted me most of all, and I believed this. I stood out. Evil was a common thing I trusted. Before sleep sometimes he came and whispered conversation in the old language of the bush. I listened. He told me things he never told anyone but Indians. I was privy to both worlds of his knowledge. I listened to him, but I had confidence in Leopolda. She was the only one of the bunch he even noticed.

There came a day, though, when Leopolda turned the tide with her hook-pole.

It was a quiet day with everyone working at their desks, when I heard him. He had sneaked into the closets in the back of the room. He was scratching around, tasting crumbs in our pockets, stealing buttons, squirting his dark juice in the linings and the boots. I was the only one who heard him, and I got bold. I smiled. I glanced back and smiled and looked up at her sly to see if she had noticed. My heart jumped. For she was looking straight at me. And she sniffed. She had a big stark bony nose stuck to the front of her face for smelling out brimstone and evil thoughts. She had smelled him on me. She stood up. Tall, pale, a blackness leading into the deeper blackness of the slate wall behind her. Her oak pole had flown into her grip. She had seen me glance at the closet. Oh, she knew. She knew just where he was. I watched her watch him in her mind's eye. The whole class was watching now. She was staring, sizing, following his scuffle. And all of a sudden she tensed down, posed on her bent kneesprings, cocked her arm back. She threw the oak pole singing over my head, through my braincloud. It cracked through the thin wood door of the back closet, and the heavy pointed hook drove through his heart. I turned. She'd speared her own black rubber overboot where he'd taken refuge in the tip of her darkest toe.

Something howled in my mind. Loss and darkness. I understood. I was to suffer for my smile.

He rose up hard in my heart. I didn't blink when the pole cracked. My skull was tough. I didn't flinch when she shrieked in my ear. I only shrugged at the flowers of hell. He wanted me. More than anything he craved me. But then she did the worst. She did what broke my mind to her. She grabbed me by the collar and dragged me, feet flying, through the room and threw me in the closet with her dead black overboot. And I was there. The only light was a crack beneath the door. I asked the Dark One to enter into me and boost my mind. I asked him to restrain my tears, for they was pushing behind my eyes. But he was afraid to come back there. He was afraid of her sharp pole. And I was afraid of Leopolda's pole for the first time, too. I felt the cold hook in my heart. How it could crack through the door at any minute and drag me out, like a dead fish on a gaff, drop me on the floor like a gutshot squirrel.

I was nothing. I edged back to the wall as far as I could. I breathed the chalk dust. The hem of her full black cloak cut against my cheek. He had left me. Her spear could find me any time. Her keen ears would aim the hook into the beat of my heart.

What was that sound?

It filled the closet, filled it up until it spilled over, but I did not recognize the crying wailing voice as mine until the door cracked open, brightness, and she hoisted me to her camphor-smelling lips.

"He *wants* you," she said. "That's the difference. I give you love."

Love. The black hook. The spear singing through the mind. I saw that she had tracked the Dark One to my heart and flushed him out into the open. So now my heart was an empty nest where she could lurk.

Well, I was weak. I was weak when I let her in, but she got a foothold there. Hard to dislodge as the year passed. Sometimes I felt him—the brush of dim wings—but only rarely did his voice compel. It was between Marie and Leopolda now, and the struggle changed. I began to realize I had been on the wrong track with the fruits of hell. The real way to overcome Leopolda was this: I'd get to heaven first. And then, when I saw her coming, I'd shut the gate. She'd be out! That is why, besides the bowing and the scraping I'd be dealt, I wanted to sit on the altar as a saint.

To this end, I went up on the hill. Sister Leopolda was the consecrated nun who had sponsored me to come there.

"You're not vain," she said. "You're too honest, looking into the mirror, for that. You're not smart. You don't have the ambition to get clear. You have two choices. One, you can marry a no-good Indian, bear his brats, die like a dog. Or two, you can give yourself to God."

"I'll come up there," I said, "but not because of what you think."

I could have had any damn man on the reservation at the time. And I could have made him treat me like his own life. I looked good. And I looked white. But I wanted Sister Leopolda's heart. And here was the thing: sometimes I wanted her heart in love and admiration. Sometimes. And sometimes I wanted her heart to roast on a black stick.

★ ★ ★

She answered the back door where they had instructed me to call. I stood there with my bundle. She looked me up and down.

"All right," she said finally. "Come in."

She took my hand. Her fingers were like a bundle of broom straws, so thin and dry, but the strength of them was unnatural. I couldn't have tugged loose if she was leading me into rooms of white-hot coal. Her strength was a kind of perverse miracle, for she got it from fasting herself thin. Because of this hunger practice her lips were a wounded brown and her skin deadly pale. Her eye sockets were two deep lashless hollows in a taut skull. I told you about the nose already. It stuck out far and made the place her eyes moved even deeper, as if she stared out the wrong end of a gun barrel. She took the bundle from my hands and threw it in the corner.

"You'll be sleeping behind the stove, child."

It was immense, like a great furnace. There was a small cot close behind it.

"Looks like it could get warm there," I said.

"Hot. It does."

"Do I get a habit?"

I wanted something like the thing she wore. Flowing black cotton. Her face was strapped in white bandages, and a sharp crest of starched white cardboard hung over her forehead like a glaring beak. If possible, I wanted a bigger, longer, whiter beak than hers.

"No," she said, grinning her great skull grin. "You don't get one yet. Who knows, you might not like us. Or we might not like you."

But she had loved me, or offered me love. And she had tried to hunt the Dark One down. So I had this confidence.

"I'll inherit your keys from you," I said.

She looked at me sharply, and her grin turned strange. She hissed, taking in her breath. Then she turned to the door and took a key from her belt. It was a giant key, and it unlocked the larder where the food was stored.

Inside there was all kinds of good stuff. Things I'd tasted only once or twice in my life. I saw sticks of dried fruit, jars of orange peel, spice like cinnamon. I saw tins of crackers with ships painted on the side. I saw pickles. Jars of herring and the rind of pigs. There was cheese, a big brown block of it from the thick milk of goats. And besides that there was the everyday stuff, in great quantities, the flour and the coffee.

It was the cheese that got to me. When I saw it my stomach hollowed. My tongue dripped. I loved that goat-milk cheese better than anything I'd ever ate. I stared at it. The rich curve in the buttery cloth.

"When you inherit my keys," she said sourly, slamming the door in my face, "you can eat all you want of the priest's cheese."

Then she seemed to consider what she'd done. She looked at me. She took the key from her belt and went back, sliced a hunk off, and put it in my hand.

"If you're good you'll taste this cheese again. When I'm dead and gone," she said.

Then she dragged out the big sack of flour. When I finished that heavenly stuff she told me to roll my sleeves up and begin doing God's labor. For a while we worked in silence, mixing up the dough and pounding it out on stone slabs.

"God's work," I said after a while. "If this is God's work, I've done it all my life."

"Well, you've done it with the Devil in your heart then," she said. "Not God."

"How do you know?" I asked. But I knew she did. And wished I had not brought up the subject.

"I see right into you like a clear glass," she said. "I always did."

"You don't know it," she continued after a while, "but he's come around here sulking. He's come around here brooding. You brought him in. He knows the smell of me, and he's going to make a last ditch try to get you back. Don't let him." She glared over at me. Her eyes were cold and lighted. "Don't let him touch you. We'll be a long time getting rid of him."

So I was careful. I was careful not to give him an inch. I said a rosary, two rosaries, three, underneath my breath. I said the Creed. I said every scrap of Latin I knew while we punched the dough with our fists. And still, I dropped the cup. It rolled under that monstrous iron stove, which was getting fired up for baking.

And she was on me. She saw he'd entered my distraction.

"Our good cup," she said. "Get it out of there, Marie."

I reached for the poker to snag it out from beneath the stove. But I had a sinking feel in my stomach as I did this. Sure enough, her long arm darted past me like a whip. The poker lighted in her hand.

"Reach," she said. "Reach with your arm for that cup. And when your flesh is hot, remember that the flames you feel are only one fraction of the heat you will feel in his hellish embrace."

She always did things this way, to teach you lessons. So I wasn't surprised. It was playacting, anyway, because a stove isn't very hot underneath right along the floor. They aren't made that way. Otherwise a wood floor would burn. So I said yes and got down on my stomach and reached under. I meant to grab it quick and jump up again, before she could think up another lesson, but here it happened. Although I groped for the cup, my hand closed on nothing. That cup was nowhere to be found. I heard her step toward me, a slow step. I heard the creak of thick shoe leather, the little *plat* as the folds of her heavy skirts met, a trickle of fine sand sifting, somewhere, perhaps in the bowels of her, and I was afraid. I tried to scramble up, but her foot came down lightly behind my ear, and I was lowered. The foot came down more firmly at the base of my neck, and I was held.

"You're like I was," she said. "He wants you very much."

"He doesn't want me no more," I said. "He had his fill. I got the cup!"

I heard the valve opening, the hissed intake of breath, and knew that I should not have spoke.

"You lie," she said. "You're cold. There is a wicked ice forming in your blood. You don't have a shred of devotion for God. Only wild cold dark lust. I know it. I know how you feel. I see the beast . . . the beast watches me out of your eyes sometimes. Cold."

The urgent scrape of metal. It took a moment to know from where. Top of the stove. Kettle. Lessons. She was steadying herself with the iron poker. I could feel it like pure certainty, driving into the wood floor. I would not remind her of pokers. I heard the water as it came, tipped from the spout, cooling as it fell but still scalding as it struck. I must have twitched beneath her foot, because she steadied me, and then the poker nudged up beside my arm as if to guide. "To warm your cold ash heart," she said. I felt how patient she would be. The water came. My mind went dead blank. Again. I could only think the kettle would be cooling slowly in her hand. I could not stand it. I bit my lip so as not to satisfy her with a sound. She gave me more reason to keep still.

"I will boil him from your mind if you make a peep," she said, "by filling up your ear."

Any sensible fool would have run back down the hill the minute Leopolda let them up from under her heel. But I was snared in her black intelligence by then. I could not think straight. I had prayed so hard I think I broke a cog in my mind. I prayed while her foot squeezed my throat. While my skin burst. I prayed even when I heard the wind come through, shrieking in the busted bird nests. I didn't stop when pure light fell, turning slowly behind my eyelids. God's face. Even that did not disrupt my continued praise. Words came. Words came from nowhere and flooded my mind.

Now I could pray much better than any one of them. Than all of them full force. This was proved. I turned to her in a daze when she let me up. My thoughts were gone, and yet I remember how surprised I was. Tears glittered in her eyes, deep down, like the sinking reflection in a well.

"It was so hard, Marie," she gasped. Her hands were shaking. The kettle clattered against the stove. "But I have used all the water up now. I think he is gone."

"I prayed," I said foolishly. "I prayed very hard."

"Yes," she said. "My dear one, I know."

We sat together quietly because we had no more words. We let the dough rise and punched it down once. She gave me a bowl of mush, unlocked the sausage from a special cupboard, and took that in to the Sisters. They sat down the hall, chewing their sausage, and I could hear them. I could hear their teeth bite through their bread and meat. I couldn't move. My shirt was dry but the cloth stuck to my back, and I couldn't think straight. I was losing the sense to understand how her mind worked. She'd gotten past me with her poker and I would never be a saint. I despaired. I felt I had no inside voice, nothing to direct me, no darkness, no Marie. I was about to throw that cornmeal mush out to the birds and make a run for it, when the vision rose up blazing in my mind.

I was rippling gold. My breasts were bare and my nipples flashed and winked. Diamonds tipped them. I could walk through panes of glass. I could walk through windows. She was at my feet, swallowing the glass after each step I took. I broke through another and another. The glass she swallowed ground and cut until her starved insides were only a subtle dust. She coughed. She coughed a cloud of dust. And then she was only a black rag that flapped off, snagged in bob wire, hung there for an age, and finally rotted into the breeze.

I saw this, mouth hanging open, gazing off into the flagged boughs of trees.

"Get up!" she cried. "Stop dreaming. It is time to bake."

Two other Sisters had come in with her, wide women with hands like paddles. They were evening and smoothing out the firebox beneath the great jaws of the oven.

"Who is this one?" they asked Leopolda. "Is she yours?"

"She is mine," said Leopolda. "A very good girl."

"What is your name?" one asked me.

"Marie."

"Marie. Star of the Sea."

"She will shine," said Leopolda, "when we have burned off the dark corrosion."

The others laughed, but uncertainly. They were mild and sturdy French, who did not understand Leopolda's twisted jokes, although they muttered respectfully at things she said. I knew they wouldn't believe what she had done with the kettle. There was no question. So I kept quiet.

"Elle est docile," they said approvingly as they left to starch the linens.

"Does it pain?" Leopolda asked me as soon as they were out the door.

I did not answer. I felt sick with the hurt.

"Come along," she said.

The building was wholly quiet now. I followed her up the narrow staircase into a hall of little rooms, many doors. Her cell was the quietest, at the very end. Inside, the air smelled stale, as if the door had not been opened for years. There was a crude straw mattress, a tiny bookcase with a picture of Saint Francis hanging over it, a ragged palm, a stool for sitting on, a crucifix. She told me to remove my blouse and sit on the stool. I did so. She took a pot of salve from the bookcase and began to smooth it upon my burns. Her hands made slow, wide circles, stopping the pain. I closed my eyes. I expected to see blackness. Peace. But instead the vision reared up again. My chest was still tipped with diamonds. I was walking through windows. She was chewing up the broken litter I left behind.

"I am going," I said. "Let me go."

But she held me down.

"Don't go," she said quickly. "Don't. We have just begun."

I was weakening. My thoughts were whirling pitifully. The pain had kept me strong, and as it left me I began to forget it; I couldn't hold on. I began to wonder if she'd really scalded me with the kettle. I could not remember. To remember this seemed the most important thing in the world. But I was losing the memory. The scalding. The pouring. It began to vanish. I felt like my mind was coming off its hinge, flapping in the breeze, hanging by the hair of my own pain. I wrenched out of her grip.

"He was always in you," I said. "Even more than in me. He wanted you even more. And now he's got you. Get thee behind me!"

I shouted that, grabbed my shirt, and ran through the door throwing it on my body. I got down the stairs and into the kitchen, even, but no matter what I told myself, I couldn't get out the door. It wasn't finished. And she knew I would not leave. Her quiet step was immediately behind me.

"We must take the bread from the oven now," she said.

She was pretending nothing happened. But for the first time I had gotten through some chink she'd left in her darkness. Touched some doubt. Her voice was so low and brittle it cracked off at the end of her sentence.

"Help me, Marie," she said slowly.

But I was not going to help her, even though she had calmly buttoned the back of my shirt up and put the big cloth mittens in my hands for taking out the loaves. I could have bolted for it then. But I didn't. I knew that something was nearing completion. Something was about to happen. My back was a wall of singing flame. I was turning. I watched her take the long fork in one hand, to tap the loaves. In the other hand she gripped the black poker to hook the pans.

"Help me," she said again, and I thought, Yes, this is part of it. I put the mittens on my hands and swung the door open on its hinges. The oven gaped. She stood back a moment, letting the first blast of heat rush by. I moved behind her. I could feel the heat at my front and at my back. Before, behind. My skin was turning to beaten gold. It was coming quicker than I thought. The oven was like the gate of a personal hell. Just big enough and hot enough for one person, and that was her. One kick and Leopolda would fly in headfirst. And that would be one-millionth of the heat she would feel when she finally collapsed in his hellish embrace.

Saints know these numbers.

She bent forward with her fork held out. I kicked her with all my might. She flew in. But the outstretched poker hit the back wall first, so she rebounded. The oven was not so deep as I had thought.

There was a moment when I felt a sort of thin, hot disappointment, as when a fish slips off the line. Only I was the one going to be lost. She was fearfully silent. She whirled. Her veil had cutting edges. She had the poker in one hand. In the other she held that long sharp fork she used to tap the delicate crusts of loaves. Her face turned upside down on her shoulders. Her face turned blue. But saints are used to miracles. I felt no trace of fear.

If I was going to be lost, let the diamonds cut! Let her eat ground glass!

"Bitch of Jesus Christ!" I shouted. "Kneel and beg! Lick the floor!"

That was when she stabbed me through the hand with the fork, then took the poker up alongside my head, and knocked me out.

It must have been a half an hour later when I came around. Things were so strange. So strange I can hardly tell it for delight at the remembrance. For when I came around this was actually taking place. I was being worshiped. I had somehow gained the altar of a saint.

I was laying back on the stiff couch in the Mother Superior's office. I looked around me. It was as though my deepest dream had come to life. The Sisters of the convent were kneeling to me. Sister Bonaventure. Sister Dympna. Sister Cecilia Saint-Claire. The two French with hands like paddles. They were down on their knees. Black capes were slung over some of their heads. My name was buzzing up and down the room, like a fat autumn fly lighting on the tips of their tongues between Latin, humming up the heavy blood-dark curtains, circling their little cosseted heads. Marie! Marie! A girl thrown in a closet. Who was afraid of a rubber overboot. Who was half overcome. A girl who came in the back door where they threw their garbage. Marie! Who never found the cup. Who had to eat their cold mush. Marie! Leopolda had her face buried in her knuckles. Saint Marie of the Holy Slops! Saint Marie of the Bread Fork! Saint Marie of the Burnt Back and Scalded Butt!

I broke out and laughed.

They looked up. All holy hell burst loose when they saw I'd woke. I still did not understand what was happening. They were watching, talking, but not to me.

"The marks. . ."

"She has her hand closed."

"Je ne peux pas voir."

I was not stupid enough to ask what they were talking about. I couldn't tell why I was laying in white sheets. I couldn't tell why they were praying to me. But I'll tell you this: it seemed entirely natural. It was me. I lifted up my hand as in my dream. It was completely limp with sacredness.

"Peace be with you."

My arm was dried blood from the wrist down to the elbow. And it hurt. Their faces turned like flat flowers of adoration to follow that hand's movements. I let it swing through the air, imparting a saint's blessing. I had practiced. I knew exactly how to act.

They murmured. I heaved a sigh, and a golden beam of light suddenly broke through the clouded window and flooded down directly on my face. A stroke of perfect luck! They had to be convinced.

Leopolda still knelt in the back of the room. Her knuckles were crammed halfway down her throat. Let me tell you, a saint has senses honed keen as a wolf. I knew that she was over my barrel now. How it happened did not matter. The last thing I remembered was how she flew from the oven and stabbed me. That one thing was most certainly true.

"Come forward, Sister Leopolda." I gestured with my heavenly wound. Oh, it hurt. It bled when I reopened the slight heal: "Kneel beside me," I said.

She kneeled, but her voice box evidently did not work, for her mouth opened, shut, opened, but no sound came out. My throat clenched in noble delight I had read of as befitting a saint. She could not speak. But she was beaten. It was in her eyes. She stared at me now with all the deep hate of the wheel of devilish dust that rolled wild within her emptiness.

"What is it you want to tell me?" I asked. And at last she spoke.

"I have told my Sisters of your passion," she managed to choke out. "How the stigmata . . . the marks of the nails . . . appeared in your palm and you swooned at the holy vision . . . ."

"Yes," I said curiously.

And then, after a moment, I understood.

Leopolda had saved herself with her quick brain. She had witnessed a miracle. She had hid the fork and told this to the others. And of course they believed her, because they never knew how Satan came and went or where he took refuge.

"I saw it from the first," said the large one who put the bread in the oven. "Humility of the spirit. So rare in these girls."

"I saw it too," said the other one with great satisfaction. She sighed quietly. "If only it was me."

Leopolda was kneeling bolt upright, face blazing and twitching, a barely held fountain of blasting poison.

"Christ has marked me," I agreed.

I smiled the saint's smirk into her face. And then I looked at her. That was my mistake.

For I saw her kneeling there. Leopolda with her soul like a rubber overboot. With her face of a starved rat. With the desperate eyes drowning in the deep wells of her wrongness. There would be no one else after me. And I would leave. I saw Leopolda kneeling within the shambles of her love.

My, heart had been about to surge from my chest with the blackness of my joyous heat. Now it dropped. I pitied her. I pitied her. Pity twisted in my stomach like that hook-pole was driven through me. I was caught. It was a feeling more terrible than any amount of boiling water and worse than being forked. Still, still, I could not help what I did. I had already smiled in a saint's mealy forgiveness. I heard myself speaking gently.

"Receive the dispensation of my sacred blood," I whispered.

But there was no heart in it. No joy when she bent to touch the floor. No dark leaping. I fell back into the white pillows. Blank dust was whirling through the light shafts. My skin was dust. Dust my lips. Dust the dirty spoons on the ends of my feet.

Rise up! I thought. Rise up and walk! There is no limit to this dust!

LOUISE ERDRICH

Satan: Highjacker of a Planet

On the outskirts of a small town in the West, on an afternoon when rain was promised, we sat upon the deck of our new subdivision ranchette and watched the sky pitch over Hungry Horse. It was a drought-dry summer, and in the suspension of rain everything seemed to flex. The trees stretched to their full length, each leaf open. I could almost feel the ground shake the timbers under my feet, as if the great searching taproots of the lodgepole pines all around trembled. Lust. Lust. Still, the rain held off. I left my mother sitting in her chair and went to the old field behind the house, up a hill. There the storm seemed even likelier. The wind came off the eastern mountains, smelling like a lake, and the grass reached for it, butter-yellow, its life concentrated in its fiber mat, the stalks so dry they gave off puffs of smoke when snapped. Grasshoppers sprang from each step I took, tripped off my arms, legs, glasses. I saw a small pile of stones halfway up the hill, which someone had cleared once, when this was orchard land. I sat down and continued to watch the sky as, out of nowhere, great solid-looking clouds built hot stacks and cotton cones. The trend was upward, upward, until you couldn't feel it anymore. I was sixteen years old.

I was looking down the hill, waiting for the rain to start, when his white car pulled into our yard. The driver was a big man, built long and square just like the Oldsmobile. He was wearing a tie and a shirt that was not yet sweaty. I noticed this as I was walking back down the hill. I was starting to notice these things about men—the way their hips moved when they hauled feed or checked fence lines. The way their forearms looked so tanned and hard when they rolled up their white sleeves after church. I was looking at men not with intentions, because I didn't know yet what I would have done with one if I got him, but with a studious mind.

I was looking at them just to figure, for pure survival, the way a girl does. The way a farmer, which my dad was before he failed, gets to know the lay of the land. He loves his land, so he has to figure how to cultivate it—what it needs in each season, how much abuse it will sustain, what in the end it will yield.

And I, too, in order to increase my yield and use myself right, was taking my lessons. I never tried out my information, though, until the man arrived, pulled with a slow crackle into our lake-pebble driveway. He got out and looked at me where I stood in the shade of my mother's butterfly bush. I'm not saying that I flirted right off. I didn't know how to. I walked into the sunlight and looked him in the eye.

"What are you selling?" I smiled, and told him that my mother would probably buy it, since she had all sorts of things—a pruning saw you could use from the ground, a cherry pitter, a mechanical apple peeler that also removed the seeds and core, a sewing machine that remembered all the stitches it had sewed. He smiled back at me and walked with me to the steps of the house.

"You're a bright young lady," he said, though he was young himself. "Stand close. You'll see what I'm selling by looking into the middle of my eyes."

He pointed a finger between his eyebrows.

"I don't see a thing," I told him, as my mother came around the corner, off the deck out back, holding a glass of iced tea in her hand.

While they were talking, I didn't look at Stan Anderson. I felt challenged, as if I were supposed to make sense of what he did. At sixteen I didn't have perspective on the things men did. I'd never gotten a whiff of that odor that rolls off them like an acid. Later only a certain look was required, a tone of voice, a word, no more than a variation in the way he drew breath. A dog gets tuned that way, sensitized to an exquisite degree, but it wasn't like that in the beginning. I took orders from Stan as if I were doing him a favor—the way, since I'd hit my growth, I'd taken orders from my dad.

My dad, who was at the antiques store, gave orders only when he was tired. All other times he did the things he wanted done himself. My dad was not, in the end, the man I should have studied if I wanted to learn cold survival. He was too ineffective. All my life my parents had been splitting up. I lived in a no-man's-land between them, and the ground was pitted, scarred with ruts, useless. And yet no matter how hard they fought each other, they stuck together. He could not get away from my mother, somehow, nor she from him. So I couldn't look to my father for information on what a man was—nor could I look to my grandfather. Gramp was too nice a man. You should have seen him when he planted a tree.

"A ten-dollar hole for a two-bit seedling," he'd say. That was the way he dug, so as not to crowd the roots. He kept the little tree in water while he pried out any rocks that might be there, though our land was just as good as Creston soil, dirt that went ten feet down in that part of Montana, black as coal, rich as tar, fine as face powder. Gramp put the bare-root tree in and carefully, considerately even, sifted the soil around the roots, rubbing it to fine crumbs between his fingers. He packed the dirt in; he watered until the water pooled. Looking into my grandfather's eyes I would see the knowledge, tender and offhand, of the way roots took hold in the earth.

I saw no such knowledge in Stan's eyes. I watched him from behind my mother. I discovered what he had to sell.

"It's Bibles, isn't it?" I said.

"No fair." He put his hand across his heart and grinned at the two of us. He had seen my eyes flicker to the little gold cross in his lapel. "Something even better."

"What?" my mother asked.

"Spirit."

My mother turned and walked away. She had no time for conversion attempts. I was only intermittently religious, but I suppose I felt that I had to make up for her rudeness, and so I stayed a moment longer. I was wearing very short cutoff jeans and a little brown T-shirt, tight—old clothes for dirty work. I was supposed to help my mom clean out her hobby brooder house that afternoon, to set in new straw and wash down the galvanized feeders, to destroy the thick whorls of ground-spider cobwebs and shine the windows with vinegar and newspapers. All my stuff, rags and buckets, was scattered behind me on the steps. And, as I said, I was never all that religious.

"We'll be having a meeting tonight," he said. "I'm going to tell you where."

He always told in advance what he was going to say; that was the preaching habit in him. It made you wait and wonder in spite of yourself.

"Where?" I said finally.

As he told me the directions, how to get where the tent was pitched, as he spoke to me, looking full on with the whole intensity of his blue gaze, I was deciding that I would go, without anyone else in my family, to the fairground that evening. Just to study. Just to see.

I drove a small sledge and a tractor at the age of eleven, and a car back and forth into town, with my mother in the passenger seat, when I was fourteen. So I often went where I wanted to go. The storm had veered off. Disappointed, we watched rain drop across the valley. We got no more than a slash of moisture in the air, which dried before it fell. In town the streets were just on the edge of damp, but the air was still thin and dry. White moths fluttered in and out under the rolled flaps of the revival tent, but since the month of August was half spent, the mosquitoes were mainly gone. Too dry for them, too. Even though the tent was open-sided, the air within seemed close, compressed, and faintly salty with evaporated sweat. The space was three-quarters full of singing people, and I slipped into one of the rear rows. I sat on a gray metal folding chair, just sat there, keeping my eyes open and my mouth shut.

He was not the main speaker, I discovered, and I didn't see him until the one whom the others had come to hear finished a prayer. He called Stan to the front with a little preface. Stan was newly saved, endowed with a message from the Lord, and could play several musical instruments. We were to listen to what the Lord would reveal to us through Stan's lips. He took the stage. A white vest finished off his white suit, and a red-silk shirt with a pointed collar. He started talking. I can tell you what he said just about word for word, because after that night and long away into the next few years, sometimes four or five times in one day, I'd hear it over and over. You don't know preaching until you've heard Stan Anderson. You don't suffer with Christ, or fear loss of faith, a barbed wire ripped from your grasp, until you've heard it from Stan Anderson. You don't know subjection, the thorough happiness of letting go. You don't know how light and comforted you feel, how cherished.

I was too young to stand against it.

The stars are the eyes of God, and they have been watching us from the beginning of the world. Do you think there isn't an eye for each of us? Go on and count. Go on and look in The Book and add up all the nouns and adverbs, as if somehow you'd grasp the meaning of what you held if you did. You can't. The understanding is in you or it isn't. You can hide from the stars by daylight, but at night, under all of them, so many, you are pierced by the sight and by the vision.

Get under the bed!

Get under the sheet!

I say to you, Stand up, and if you fall, fall forward!

I'm going to go out blazing. I'm going to go out like a light. I'm going to burn in glory. I say to you, Stand up!

And so there's one among them. You have heard Luce, Light, Lucifer, the Fallen Angel. You have seen it with your own eyes, and you didn't know he came upon you. In the night, and in his own disguises, like the hijacker of a planet, he fell out of the air, he fell out of the dark leaves, he fell out of the fragrance of a woman's body, he fell out of you and entered you as though he'd reached through the earth.

Reached his hand up and pulled you down.

Fell into you with a jerk.

Like a hangman's noose.

Like nobody.

Like the slave of night.

Like you were coming home and all the lights were blazing and the ambulance sat out front in the driveway and you said, *Lord, which one?*

And the Lord said, *All of them.*

You, too, follow, follow, I'm pointing you down. In the sight of the stars and in the sight of the Son of Man. The grace is on me. Stand up, I say. *Stand.* Yes, and yes, I'm gonna scream, because I like it that way. Let yourself into the gate. Take it with you. In four years the earth will shake in its teeth.

Revelations. Face of the beast. In all fairness, in all fairness, let us quiet down and let us think.

Stan Anderson looked intently, quietly, evenly, at each person in the crowd and spoke to each one, proving things about the future that seemed complicated, like the way the Mideast had shaped up as such a trouble zone. How the Chinese armies were predicted in Tibet and that came true, and how they'll keep marching, moving, until they reach the Fertile Crescent. Stan Anderson told about the number. He slammed his forehead with his open hand and left a red mark. *There,* he yelled, gutshot, *there it will be scorched.* He was talking about the number of the beast, and said that they would take it from your Visa card, your Mastercard, your household insurance. That already, through these numbers, you are under the control of last things and you don't know it.

The Antichrist is among us.

He is the plastic in our wallets.

You want credit? Credit?

Then you'll burn for it, and you will starve. You'll eat sticks, you'll eat black bits of paper, your bills, and all the while you'll be screaming from the dark place, *Why the hell didn't I just pay cash?*

Because the number of the beast is a computerized number, and the computer is the bones, it is the guts, of the Antichrist, who is Lucifer, who is pure brain.

Pure brain got us to the moon, got us past the moon.

The voice of lonely humanity is in a space probe calling, *Anybody home? Anybody home out there?* The Antichrist will answer. The Antichrist is here, all around us in the tunnels and webs of radiance, in the microchips; the great mind of the Antichrist is fusing in a pattern, in a destiny, waking up nerve by nerve.

Serves us right. Don't it serve us right not to be saved?

It won't come easy. Not by waving a magic wand. You've got to close your eyes and hold out those little plastic cards.

Look at this!

He held a scissors high and turned it to every side so that the light gleamed off the blades.

The sword of Michael! Now I'm coming. I'm coming down the aisle. I'm coming with the sword that sets you free.

Stan Anderson started a hymn and walked down the rows of chairs, singing. Every person who held out a credit card he embraced, and then he plucked that card out of their fingers. He cut once, crosswise. Dedicated to the Lord! He cut again. He kept the song flowing, walked up and down the rows cutting, until the tough, trampled grass beneath the tent was littered with pieces of plastic. He came to me last of all, and noticed me, and smiled.

"You're too young to have established a line of credit," he said, "but I'm glad to see you here."

Then he stared at me, his eyes the blue of winter ice, cold in the warmth of his tanned blondness, so chilling I just melted.

"Stay," he said. "Stay afterward and join us in the trailer. We're going to pray over Ed's mother."

So I did stay. It didn't sound like a courting invitation, but that was the way I thought of it at the time, and I was right. Ed was the advertised preacher, and his mother was a sick, sick woman. She lay flat and still on a couch at the front of the house trailer, where she just fit end to end. The air around her was dim, close with the smell of sweat-out medicine and what the others had cooked and eaten—hamburger, burnt onions, coffee. The table was pushed to one side, and chairs were wedged around the couch. Ed's mother, poor old dying woman, was covered with a white sheet that her breathing hardly moved. Her face was caved in, sunken around the mouth and cheeks. She looked to me like a bird fallen out of its nest before it feathered, her shut eyelids bulging blue, wrinkled, beating with tiny nerves. Her head was covered with white wisps of hair. Her hands, just at her chest, curled like little pale claws. Her nose was a large and waxen bone.

I drew up a chair, the farthest to the back of the eight or so people who had gathered. One by one they opened their mouths, rolled their eyes or closed them tight, and let the words fly out until they began to garble and the sounds from their mouths resembled some ancient, dizzying speech. At first I was so uncomfortable with all the strangeness, and even a little faint from the airlessness and smells, that I breathed in with shallow gulps and shut the language out. Gradually, slowly, it worked its way in anyway, and I began to *feel* its effect—not hear, not understand, not listen.

The words are inside and outside of me, hanging in the air like small pottery triangles, broken and curved. But they are forming and crumbling so fast that I'm breathing dust, the sharp antibiotic bitterness, medicine, death, sweat. My eyes sting, and I'm starting to choke. All the blood goes out of my head and down along my arms into the ends of my fingers, and my hands feel swollen, twice as big as normal, like big puffed gloves. I get out of the chair and turn to leave, but he is there.

"Go on," he says. "Go on and touch her."

The others have their hands on Ed's mother. They are touching her with one hand and praying, the other palm held high, blind, feeling for the spirit like an antenna. Stan pushes me, not by making any contact, just by inching up behind me so I feel the forcefulness and move. Two people make room, and then I am standing over Ed's mother. She is absolutely motionless, as though she were a corpse, except that her pinched mouth has turned down at the edges so that she frowns into her own dark unconsciousness.

I put my hands out, still huge, prickling. I am curious to see what will happen when I do touch her—if she'll respond. But when I place my hands on her stomach, low and soft, she makes no motion at all. Nothing flows from me, no healing powers.

Instead I am filled with the rushing dark of what she suffers. It fills me suddenly, as water from a faucet brims a jug, and spills over.

This is when it happens.

I'm not stupid; I have never been stupid. I have pictures. I can get a picture in my head at any moment, focus it so brilliant and detailed that it seems real. That's what I do, what I started when my mom and dad first went for each other. When I heard them downstairs, I always knew a moment would come. One of them would scream, tearing through the stillness. It would rise up, that howl, and fill the house, and then one would come running. One would come and get me and hold me. It would be my mother, smelling of smoked chicken, rice, and coffee grounds. It would be my father, sweat-soured, scorched with cigarette smoke from the garage, bitter with the dust of his fields. Then I would be somewhere in no-man's-land, between them, and that was the unsafest place in the world. So I would leave it. I would go limp and enter my pictures.

I have a picture. I go into it right off when I touch Ed's mother, veering off her thin pain. Here's a grainy mountain, a range of deep-blue Missions hovering off the valley in the west. Their foothills are blue, strips of dark-blue flannel, and their tops are cloudy walls. The sun strikes through once, twice, a pink radiance that dazzles patterns into their faces so that they gleam back, moon-pocked. Watch them, watch close, Ed's mother, and they start to walk. I keep talking until I know she is watching too. She is dimming her lights, she is turning as thin as tissue under my hands. She is dying until she goes into my picture with me, goes in strong, goes in willingly. And once she is in the picture, she gains peace from it, gains the rock strength, the power.

I was young. I was younger than I had a right to be. I was drawn the way a deer is drawn into the halogen lamplight, curious and calm. Heart about to explode. I wasn't helpless, though, not me. I had pictures.

"Show me what you did," Stan said that night, once Ed's mother was resting calmly.

We went into the room at the Red Lion that was Stan's, all carpet and deodorizer. All flocked paper on the walls. Black-red. Gold. Hilarious. Stan lay down on the king-size bed and patted the broad space beside him in a curious, not sexual, way. I lay down there and closed my eyes.

"Show me Milwaukee," Stan whispered. I breathed deep and let out the hems of my thoughts. After a while, then, I got the heft of it, the green medians in June, the way you felt entering your favorite restaurant with a dinner reservation, hungry, knowing that within fifteen minutes German food would start to fill you, German bread, German beer, German schnitzel. I got the neighborhood where Stan had lived, the powdery stucco, the old-board rotting infrastructure and the back yard, all shattered sun and shade, leaves; got Stan's mother lying on the ground full-length in a red suit, asleep; got the back porch, full of suppressed heat; and got the june bugs razzing indomitable against the night screens. Got the smell of Stan's river, got the first-day-of-school smell, the chalk and wax, the cleaned-and-stored, paper-towel scent of Milwaukee schools in the beginning of September. Got the milk cartons, got the straws. Got Stan's brother, thin and wiry arms holding Stan down. Got Stan a hot-dog stand, a nickel bag of peanuts, thirst.

"No," Stan said. "No more."

He could feel it coming, though I avoided it. I steered away from the burning welts, the scissors, pinched nerves, the dead eye, the strap, the belt, the spike-heeled shoe, the razor, the boiling-hot spilled tapioca, the shards of glass, the knives, the chinked armor, the small sister, the small sister, the basement, anything underground.

"Enough." Stan turned to me.

He didn't know what he wanted to see, and I don't mean to imply that he would see the whole of my picture anyway. I would walk the edge of his picture, and he'd walk the edge of mine, get the crumbs, the drops of water that flew off when a bird shook its feathers. That's how much I got across, but that was all it took. When you share like that, the rest of the earth shuts. You are locked in, twisted close, braided, born.

He smoothed his hands across my hair and closed me against him, and then we shut the door to everything and everyone but us. He stood me next to the bed, took off my clothing piece by piece, and made me climax just by brushing me, slowly, here, there, just by barely touching me until he forced apart my legs and put his mouth on me hard. Stood up. He came into me without a sound. I cried out. He pushed harder and then withdrew. It took more than an hour, by the bedside clock. It took a long time. He held my wrists behind my back and forced me down onto the carpet. Then he bent over me and gently, fast and slow, helplessly, without end or beginning, he went in and out until I grew bored, until I wanted to sleep, until I moaned, until I cried out, until I wanted nothing else, until I wanted him the way I always would from then on, since that first dry summer.

Richard Ford (1944–)

was born in Jackson, Mississippi, in 1944, the only child of a traveling salesman for a starch company. He has said that his work's frequent preoccupation with family strife came about as a direct result of his "fine and wholesome childhood," explaining that "when you come from a close family, it's not hard to imagine a family breakup because it seems such a dramatic and important thing." He went to college at Michigan State University, then attended law school very briefly before entering the University of California at Irvine, where he received his MFA in writing in 1970. After publishing two novels, A Piece of My Heart *and* The Ultimate Good Luck, *Ford took a job writing for* Inside Sports *magazine. When the magazine was sold, he decided to write a book about a sportswriter; the resulting novel,* The Sportswriter, *published in 1986, received widespread acclaim. It was followed by* Rock Springs, *a highly praised book of short stories. In 1996, his novel* Independence Day*—a sequel to* The Sportswriter*—won the Pulitzer Prize and the PEN/Faulkner Award for fiction, the first novel ever to win both awards. He has also won the PEN/Malamud Award for excellence in short fiction, and his most recent book,* A Multitude of Sins, *is a collection of stories. Ford lives in New Orleans, Louisiana, where his wife was the head of the city planning commission, and also has homes in Mississippi and Maine. He is the literary executor for Eudora Welty, whom Ford first saw at the age of seven when his mother pointed out the fellow Jackson resident in the grocery store.*

Introduction by **Sheila Kohler**

Richard Ford, interestingly enough, in his introduction to the *Granta* volume of American short stories, says that he doesn't see much difference between American stories and the stories of other nationalities. "A few Giuseppes and Nigels where ours turn out to be Lukes and Cindys." He appears to feel that the European idea of America and therefore of American literature is false. Ford quotes Frank O'Connor (who is Irish) and Stephen Spender (a Brit) who describe America as a brutal place, a place full of dislocated and lonely people and particularly brooding male figures, situated in a vast, windy continent, which makes it in an ideal place for the short story to flourish.

Yet it seems to me that this description aptly fits Richard Ford's own stories and is perhaps the origin of his unusual gift for this form. He appears to me to be a particularly American author, and his roots lie deep in the great American short story tradition. In the strong, sonorous ring of his prose, the almost biblical cadences, and even in his themes, we can hear clear echoes of the great American short story writers such as Faulkner, Hemingway, and Raymond Carver.

Richard Ford, particularly in the three stories that represent him here but also in many of his novels and certainly *A Piece of My Heart,* places his characters in bleak, dangerous, and very American landscapes that echo the loneliness and rage in his characters' hearts. In the solitude of his landscapes, his stories make us think of that quintessentially American painter Edward Hopper or, perhaps more exactly, the American photographers Gary Winograd and Robert Frank or even Richard Avedon's portraits of people from the West. In all three of these stories, the characters are literally on the road, a lonely road, that most favorite of American places. They are all driving somewhere, and they are all getting nowhere.

They drive in dangerous conditions of one kind or another. Ford, an ace storyteller with a perfect sense of timing, places his characters immediately into perilous situations and in this way creates tension from the start. In "Rock Springs," the narrator, his girl, Edna, and his child, Cheryl, plus dog set off for Florida in a stolen cranberry Mercedes, which breaks down in a desolate part of the country. (One thinks immediately of Flannery O'Connor's "A Good Man Is Hard to Find.") "Where the car went bad there wasn't a town in sight or even a house, just some low mountains maybe fifty miles away or maybe a hundred, a barbed-wire fence in both directions. . . ."

In "Communist," Glen Baxter, who is the sixteen-year-old narrator's mother's lover, drives them in his Nash to go hunting geese in Montana. They drive out through this barren landscape "onto the high flat prairie" along a dirt road fenced on both sides. "'All right,' he said, looking in the rear-view mirror at my mother. 'You wouldn't think there was anything here, would you?'" Here, the desolate landscape echoes the tension that lies between the couple and the aggression of the act of hunting itself, the harm they set out to do to the great number of geese. (Here we think immediately of Raymond Carver's "Distance.")

In "Under the Radar," Stephen and Marjorie Reeves are driving out to dinner when she announces that she had an affair, a year ago, with their host. The landscape here, though apparently a manicured one (we are in Connecticut), is still spooky, dimly lit, mysterious in its sounds and silences, and, we sense from the start, murderously dangerous—which, indeed, it turns out to be.

Ford writes about people who are capable of brutality, of criminal and often murderous acts. By using succinct and well-placed flashbacks, he both anchors the characters in reality, telling us about their past, their work, and their weaknesses, and carries his story forward inexorably to its conclusion. He skillfully lets us know what actions his characters might commit, because they have committed them in the past.

In "Rock Springs," we know that not only has the narrator had several scrapes with the law, but also his girl friend, Edna, has accidentally strangled a monkey. We immediately fear for the child, little Cheryl, and particularly for the dog, who is left with Edna in the car, in the dark, when the narrator goes off to find a telephone. "'They shouldn't be left in the dark by themselves,' the woman said and frowned. 'There's too much unsavoriness out there.'"

In "Communist," Glen Baxter, who is the Communist, has fought in Vietnam, where he too has killed animals: "monkeys and beautiful parrots—using military guns for sport." Indeed, he turns out to be capable of aggression.

In "Under the Radar," Stephen Reeves has been a hockey player and has hit and been hit before, and Marjorie has told Stephen of countless misdemeanors, including holdups and heroin addiction. The people who drive by in the beat-up Ford pickup are capable of taking a perverse delight in running over a raccoon.

There are a lot of dead animals in these stories, which heightens the tension considerably and echoes what happens in the lives of the characters. For all these characters are brought ineluctably and with great grace to a moment of change, a luminous moment, when their emptiness becomes apparent to them, when they grasp their rage and loneliness, their inability to know one another, to reach one another, which makes us grasp our own isolation. I won't give away the endings of these three wonderful stories but only welcome you to this entire fictive world—a very American world, which Ford creates here with all his rage and his rage for order, which these stories entirely satisfy.

Sheila Kohler's most recent collection is Stories from Another World. *Her previous books include* Cracks, Children of Pithiviers, The Perfect Place, *and* The House on R. Street. *Born in South Africa, she now lives in New York City and teaches at Bennington College.*

RICHARD FORD

Rock Springs

Edna and I had started down from Kalispell, heading for Tampa-St. Pete where I still had some friends from the old glory days who wouldn't turn me in to the police. I had managed to scrape with the law in Kalispell over several bad checks—which is a prison crime in Montana. And I knew Edna was already looking at her cards and thinking about a move, since it wasn't the first time I'd been in law scrapes in my life. She herself had already had her own troubles, losing her kids and keeping her ex-husband, Danny, from breaking in her house and stealing her things while she was at work, which was really why I had moved in in the first place, that and needing to give my little daughter, Cheryl, a better shake in things.

I don't know what was between Edna and me, just beached by the same tides when you got down to it. Though love has been built on frailer ground than that, as I well know. And when I came in the house that afternoon, I just asked her if she wanted to go to Florida with me, leave things where they sat, and she said, "Why not? My datebook's not that full."

Edna and I had been a pair eight months, more or less man and wife, some of which time I had been out of work, and some when I'd worked at the dog track as a lead-out and could help with the rent and talk sense to Danny when he came around. Danny was afraid of me because Edna had told him I'd been in prison in Florida for killing a man, though that wasn't true. I had once been in jail in Tallahassee for stealing tires and had gotten into a fight on the country farm where a man had lost his eye. But I hadn't done the hurting, and Edna just wanted the story worse than it was so Danny wouldn't act crazy and make her have to take her kids back, since she had made a good adjustment to not having them, and I already had Cheryl with me. I'm not a violent person and would never put a man's eye out, much less kill someone. My former wife, Helen, would come all the way from Waikiki Beach to testify to that. We never had violence and I believe in crossing the street to stay out of trouble's way. Though Danny didn't know that.

But we were half down through Wyoming, going toward I-80 and feeling good about things, when the oil light flashed on in the car I'd stolen, a sign I knew to be a bad one.

I'd gotten us a good car, a cranberry Mercedes I'd stolen out of an ophthalmologist's lot in Whitefish, Montana. I stole it because I thought it would be comfortable over a long haul, because I thought it got good mileage, which it didn't, and because I'd never had a good car in my life, just old Chevy junkers and used trucks back from when I was a kid swamping citrus with Cubans.

The car made us all high that day. I ran the windows up and down, and Edna told us some jokes and made faces. She could be lively. Her features would light up like a beacon and you could see her beauty, which wasn't ordinary. It all made me giddy, and I drove clear down to Bozeman, then straight on through the park to Jackson Hole. I rented us the bridal suite in the Quality Court in Jackson and left Cheryl and her little dog, Duke, sleeping while Edna and I drove to a rib barn and drank beer and laughed till after midnight.

It felt like a whole new beginning for us, bad memories left behind and a new horizon to build on. I got so worked up, I had a tattoo done on my arm that said FAMOUS TIMES, and Edna bought a Bailey hat with an Indian feather band and a little turquoise-and-silver bracelet for Cheryl, and we made love on the seat of the car in the Quality Court parking lot just as the sun was burning up on the Snake River, and everything seemed then like the end of the rainbow.

It was that very enthusiasm, in fact, that made me keep the car one day longer instead of driving it into the river and stealing another one, like I should've done and *had* done before.

Where the car went bad there wasn't a town in sight or even a house, just some low mountains maybe fifty miles away or maybe a hundred, a barbed-wire fence in both directions, hardpan prairie, and some hawks riding the evening air seizing insects.

I got out to look at the motor, and Edna got out with Cheryl and the dog to let them have a pee by the car. I checked the water and checked the oil stick, and both of them said perfect.

"What's that light mean, Earl?" Edna said. She had come and stood by the car with her hat on. She was just sizing things up for herself.

"We shouldn't run it," I said. "Something's not right in the oil."

She looked around at Cheryl and Little Duke, who were peeing on the hardtop side by side like two little dolls, then out at the mountains, which were becoming black and lost in the distance. "What're we doing?" she said. She wasn't worried yet, but she wanted to know what I was thinking about.

"Let me try it again."

"That's a good idea," she said, and we all got back in the car.

When I turned the motor over, it started right away and the red light stayed off and there weren't any noises to make you think something was wrong. I let it idle a minute, then pushed the accelerator down and watched the red bulb. But there wasn't any light on, and I started wondering if maybe I hadn't dreamed I saw it, or that it had been the sun catching an angle off the window chrome, or maybe I was scared of something and didn't know it.

"What's the matter with it, Daddy?" Cheryl said from the backseat. I looked back at her and she had on her turquoise bracelet and Edna's hat set back on the back of her head and that little black-and-white Heinz dog on her lap. She looked like a little cowgirl in the movies.

"Nothing, honey, everything's fine now," I said.

"Little Duke tinkled where I tinkled," Cheryl said, and laughed.

"You're two of a kind," Edna said, not looking back. Edna was usually good with Cheryl, but I knew she was tired now. We hadn't had much sleep, and she had a tendency to get cranky when she didn't sleep. "We oughta ditch this damn car first chance we get," she said.

"What's the first chance we got?" I asked, because I knew she'd been at the map.

"Rock Springs, Wyoming," Edna said with conviction. "Thirty miles down this road." She pointed out ahead.

I had wanted all along to drive the car into Florida like a big success story. But I knew Edna was right about it, that we shouldn't take crazy chances. I had kept thinking of it as my car and not the ophthalmologist's, and that was how you got caught in these things.

"Then my belief is we ought to go to Rock Springs and negotiate ourselves a new car," I said. I wanted to stay upbeat, like everything was panning out right.

"That's a great idea," Edna said, and she leaned over and kissed me hard on the mouth.

"That's a great idea," Cheryl said. "Let's pull on out of here right now."

The sunset that day I remember as being the prettiest I'd ever seen. Just as it touched the rim of the horizon, it all at once fired the air into jewels and red sequins the precise likes of which I had never seen before and haven't seen since. The West has it all over everywhere for sunsets, even Florida, where it's supposedly flat but where half the time trees block your view.

"It's cocktail hour," Edna said after we'd driven awhile. "We ought to have a drink and celebrate something." She felt better thinking we were going to get rid of the car. It certainly had dark troubles and was something you'd want to put behind you.

Edna had out a whiskey bottle and some plastic cups and was measuring levels on the glove box lid. She liked drinking, and she liked drinking in the car, which was something you got used to in Montana, where it wasn't against the law, but where, strangely enough, a bad check would land you in Deer Lodge Prison for a year.

"Did I ever tell you I once had a monkey?" Edna said, setting my drink on the dashboard where I would reach it when I was ready. Her spirits were already picked up. She was like that, up one minute and down the next.

"I don't think you ever did tell me that," I said. "Where were you then?"

"Missoula," she said. She put her bare feet on the dash and rested the cup on her breasts. "I was waitressing at the Am Vets. This was before I met you. Some guy came in one day with a monkey. A spider monkey. And I said, just to be joking, 'I'll roll you for that monkey.' And the guy said, 'Just one roll?' And I said, 'Sure.' He put the monkey down on the bar, picked up the cup, and rolled out boxcars. I picked it up and rolled out three fives. And I just stood there looking at the guy. He was just some guy passing through, I guess a vet. He got a strange look on his face—I'm sure not as strange as the one I had—but he looked kind of sad and surprised and satisfied all at once. I said, 'We can roll again,' But he said, 'No, I never roll twice for anything.' And he sat and drank a beer and talked about one thing and another for a while, about nuclear war and building a stronghold somewhere up in the Bitterroot, whatever it was, while I just watched the monkey, wondering what I was going to do with it when the guy left. And pretty soon he got up and said, 'Well, good-bye, Chipper'—that was his monkey's name, of course. And then he left before I could say anything. And the monkey just sat on the bar all that night. I don't know what made me think of that, Earl. Just something weird. I'm letting my mind wander."

"That's perfectly fine," I said. I took a drink of my drink. "I'd never own a monkey," I said after a minute. "They're too nasty. I'm sure Cheryl would like a monkey, though, wouldn't you, honey?" Cheryl was down on the seat playing with Little Duke. She used to talk about monkeys all the time then. "What'd you ever do with that monkey?" I said, watching the speedometer. We were having to go slower now because the red light kept fluttering on. And all I could do to keep it off was go slower. We were going maybe thirty-five and it was an hour before dark, and I was hoping Rock Springs wasn't far away.

"You really want to know?" Edna said. She gave me a quick glance, then looked back at the empty desert as if she was brooding over it.

"Sure," I said. I was still upbeat. I figured *I* could worry about breaking down and let other people be happy for a change.

"I kept it a week." And she seemed gloomy all of a sudden, as if she saw some aspect of the story she had never seen before. "I took it home and back and forth to the Am Vets on my shifts. And it didn't cause any trouble. I fixed a chair up for it to sit on, back of the bar, and people liked it. It made a nice little clicking noise. We changed its name to Mary because the bartender figured out it was a girl. Though I was never really comfortable with it at home. I felt like it watched me too much. Then one day a guy came in, some guy who'd been in Vietnam, still wore a fatigue coat. And he said to me, 'Don't you know that a monkey'll kill you? It's got more strength in its fingers than you got in your whole body.' He said people had been killed in Vietnam by monkeys, bunches of them marauding while you were asleep, killing you and covering you with leaves. I didn't believe a word of it, except that when I got home and got undressed I started looking over across the room at Mary on her chair in the dark watching me. And I got the creeps. And after a while I got up and went out to the car, got a length of clothesline wire, and came back in and wired her to the doorknob through her little silver collar, then went back and tried to sleep. And I guess I must've slept the sleep of the dead—though I don't remember it—because when I got up I found Mary had tipped off her chair-back and hanged herself on the wire line. I'd made it too short."

Edna seemed badly affected by that story and slid low in the seat so she couldn't see out over the dash. "Isn't that a shameful story, Earl, what happened to that poor little monkey?"

"I see a town! I see a town!" Cheryl started yelling from the back seat, and right up Little Duke started yapping and the whole car fell into a racket. And sure enough she had seen something I hadn't, which was Rock Springs, Wyoming, at the bottom of a long hill, a little glowing jewel in the desert with I-80 running on the north side and the black desert spread out behind.

"That's it, honey," I said. "That's where we're going. You saw it first."

"We're hungry," Cheryl said. "Little Duke wants some fish, and I want spaghetti." She put her arms around my neck and hugged me.

"Then you'll just get it," I said. "You can have anything you want. And so can Edna and so can Little Duke." I looked over at Edna, smiling, but she was staring at me with eyes that were fierce with anger. "What's wrong?" I said.

"Don't you care anything about that awful thing that happened to me?" Her mouth was drawn tight, and her eyes kept cutting back at Cheryl and Little Duke, as if they had been tormenting her.

"Of course I do," I said. "I thought that was an awful thing." I didn't want her to be unhappy. We were almost there, and pretty soon we could sit down and have a real meal without thinking somebody might be hunting us.

"You want to know what I did with that monkey?" Edna said.

"Sure I do," I said.

"I put her in a green garbage bag, put it in the trunk of my car, drove to the dump, and threw her in the trash." She was staring at me darkly, as if the story meant something to her that was real important but that only she could see and that the rest of the world was a fool for.

"Well, that's horrible," I said. "But I don't see what else you could do. You didn't mean to kill it. You'd have done it differently if you had. And then you had to get rid of it, and I don't know what else you could have done. Throwing it away might seem unsympathetic to somebody, probably, but not to me. Sometimes that's all you can do, and you can't worry about what somebody else thinks." I tried to smile at her, but the red light was staying on if I pushed the accelerator at all, and I was trying to gauge if we could coast to Rock Springs before the car gave out completely. I looked at Edna again. "What else can I say?" I said.

"Nothing," she said, and stared back at the dark highway. "I should've known that's what you'd think. You've got a character that leaves something out, Earl. I've known that a long time."

"And yet here you are," I said. "And you're not doing so bad. Things could be a lot worse. At least we're all together here."

"Things could always be worse," Edna said. "You could go to the electric chair tomorrow."

"That's right," I said. "And somewhere somebody probably will. Only it won't be you."

"I'm hungry," said Cheryl. "When're we gonna eat? Let's find a motel. I'm tired of this. Little Duke's tired of it too."

Where the car stopped rolling was some distance from the town, though you could see the clear outline of the interstate in the dark with Rock Springs lighting up the sky behind. You could hear the big tractors hitting the spacers in the overpass, revving up for the climb to the mountains.

I shut off the lights.

"What're we going to do now?" Edna said irritably, giving me a bitter look.

"I'm figuring it," I said. "It won't be hard, whatever it is. You won't have to do anything."

"I'd hope not," she said and looked the other way.

Across the road and across a dry wash a hundred yards was what looked like a huge mobile-home town, with a factory or a refinery of some kind lit up behind it and in full swing. There were lights on in a lot of the mobile homes, and there were cars moving along an access road that ended near the freeway overpass a mile the other way. The lights in the mobile homes seemed friendly to me, and I knew right then what I should do.

"Get out," I said, opening my door.

"Are we walking?" Edna said.

"We're pushing."

"I'm not pushing." Edna reached up and locked her door.

"All right," I said. "Then you just steer."

"You're pushing us to Rock Springs, are you, Earl? It doesn't look like it's more than about three miles."

"I'll push," Cheryl said from the back.

"No, hon. Daddy'll push. You just get out with Little Duke and move out of the way."

Edna gave me a threatening look, just as if I'd tried to hit her. But when I got out she slid into my seat and took the wheel, staring angrily ahead straight into the cottonwood scrub.

"Edna can't drive that car," Cheryl said from out in the dark. "She'll run it in the ditch."

"Yes, she can, hon. Edna can drive it as good as I can. Probably better."

"No she can't," Cheryl said. "No she can't either." And I thought she was about to cry, but she didn't.

I told Edna to keep the ignition on so it wouldn't lock up and to steer into the cottonwoods with the parking lights on so she could see. And when I started, she steered it straight off into the trees, and I kept pushing until we were twenty yards into the cover and the tires sank in the soft sand and nothing at all could be seen from the road.

"Now where are we?" she said, sitting at the wheel. Her voice was tired and hard, and I knew she could have put a good meal to use. She had a sweet nature, and I recognized that this wasn't her fault but mine. Only I wished she could be more hopeful.

"You stay right here, and I'll go over to that trailer park and call us a cab," I said.

"What cab?" Edna said, her mouth wrinkled as if she'd never heard anything like that in her life.

"There'll be cabs," I said, and tried to smile at her. "There's cabs everywhere."

"What're you going to tell him when he gets here? Our stolen car broke down and we need a ride to where we can steal another one? That'll be a big hit, Earl."

"I'll talk," I said. "You just listen to the radio for ten minutes and then walk on out to the shoulder like nothing was suspicious. And you and Cheryl act nice. She doesn't need to know about this car."

"Like we're not suspicious enough already, right?" Edna looked up at me out of the lighted car. "You don't think right, did you know that, Earl? You think the world's stupid and you're smart. But that's not how it is. I feel sorry for you. You might've *been* something, but things just went crazy someplace."

I had a thought about poor Danny. He was a vet and crazy as a shit-house mouse, and I was glad he wasn't in for all this. "Just get the baby in the car," I said, trying to be patient. "I'm hungry like you are."

"I'm tired of this," Edna said. "I wish I'd stayed in Montana."

"Then you can go back in the morning," I said. "I'll buy the ticket and put you on the bus. But not till then."

"Just get on with it, Earl." She slumped down in the seat, turning off the parking lights with one foot and the radio on with the other.

The mobile home community was as big as any I'd ever seen. It was attached in some way to the plant that was lighted up behind it, because I could see a car once in a while leave one of the trailer streets, turn in the direction of the plant, then go slowly into it. Everything in the plant was white, and you could see that all the trailers were painted white and looked exactly alike. A deep hum came out of the plant, and I thought as I got closer that it wouldn't be a location I'd ever want to work in.

I went right to the first trailer where there was a light, and knocked on the metal door. Kids' toys were lying in the gravel around the little wood steps, and I could hear talking on TV that suddenly went off. I heard a woman's voice talking, and then the door opened wide.

A large Negro woman with a wide, friendly face stood in the doorway. She smiled at me and moved forward as if she was going to come out, but she stopped at the top step. There was a little Negro boy behind her peeping out from behind her legs, watching me with his eyes half closed. The trailer had that feeling that no one else was inside, which was a feeling I knew something about.

"I'm sorry to intrude," I said. "But I've run up on a little bad luck tonight. My name's Earl Middleton."

The woman looked at me, then out into the night toward the freeway as if what I had said was something she was going to be able to see. "What kind of bad luck?" she said, looking down at me again.

"My car broke down out on the highway," I said. "I can't fix it myself, and I wondered if I could use your phone to call for help."

The woman smiled at me knowingly. "We can't live without cars, can we?"

"That's the honest truth," I said.

"They're like our hearts," she said, her face shining in the little bulb light that burned beside the door. "Where's your car situated?"

I turned and looked over into the dark, but I couldn't see anything because of where we'd put it. "It's over there," I said. "You can't see it in the dark."

"Who all's with you now?" the woman said. "Have you got your wife with you?"

"She's with my little girl and our dog in the car," I said. "My daughter's asleep or I would have brought them."

"They shouldn't be left in the dark by themselves," the woman said and frowned. "There's too much unsavoriness out there."

"The best I can do is hurry back." I tried to look sincere, since everything except Cheryl being asleep and Edna being my wife was the truth. The truth is meant to serve you if you'll let it, and I wanted it to serve me. "I'll pay for the phone call," I said. "If you'll bring the phone to the door I'll call from right here."

The woman looked at me again as if she was searching for a truth of her own, then back out into the night. She was maybe in her sixties, but I couldn't say for sure. "You're not going to rob me, are you, Mr. Middleton?" She smiled like it was a joke between us.

"Not tonight," I said, and smiled a genuine smile. "I'm not up to it tonight. Maybe another time."

"Then I guess Terrel and I can let you use our phone with Daddy not here, can't we, Terrel? This is my grandson, Terrel Junior, Mr. Middleton." She put her hand on the boy's head and looked down at him. "Terrel won't talk. Though if he did he'd tell you to use our phone. He's a sweet boy." She opened the screen for me to come in.

The trailer was a big one with a new rug and a new couch and a living room that expanded to give the space of a real house. Something good and sweet was cooking in the kitchen, and the trailer felt like it was somebody's comfortable new home instead of just temporary. I've lived in trailers, but they were just snailbacks with one room and no toilet, and they always felt cramped and unhappy—though I've thought maybe it might've been me that was unhappy in them.

There was a big Sony TV and a lot of kids' toys scattered on the floor. I recognized a Greyhound bus I'd gotten for Cheryl. The phone was beside a new leather recliner, and the Negro woman pointed for me to sit down and call and gave me the phone book. Terrel began fingering his toys and the woman sat on the couch while I called, watching me and smiling.

There were three listings for cab companies, all with one number different. I called the numbers in order and didn't get an answer until the last one, which answered with the name of the second company. I said I was on the highway beyond the interstate and that my wife and family needed to be taken to town and I would arrange for a tow later. While I was giving the location, I looked up the name of a tow service to tell the driver in case he asked.

When I hung up, the Negro woman was sitting looking at me with the same look she had been staring with into the dark, a look that seemed to want truth. She was smiling, though. Something pleased her and I reminded her of it.

"This is a very nice home," I said, resting in the recliner, which felt like the driver's seat of the Mercedes, and where I'd have been happy to stay.

"This isn't *our* house, Mr. Middleton," the Negro woman said. "The company owns these. They give them to us for nothing. We have our own home in Rockford, Illinois."

"That's wonderful," I said.

"It's never wonderful when you have to be away from home, Mr. Middleton, though we're only here three months, and it'll be easier when Terrel Junior begins his special school. You see, our son was killed in the war, and his wife ran off without Terrel Junior. Though you shouldn't worry. He can't understand us. His little feelings can't be hurt." The woman folded her hands in her lap and smiled in a satisfied way. She was an attractive woman, and had on a blue-and-pink floral dress that made her seem bigger than she could've been, just the right woman to sit on the couch she was sitting on. She was good nature's picture, and I was glad she could be, with her little brain-damaged boy, living in a place where no one in his right mind would want to live a minute. "Where do *you* live, Mr. Middleton?" she said politely, smiling in the same sympathetic way.

"My family and I are in transit," I said. "I'm an ophthalmologist, and we're moving back to Florida, where I'm from. I'm setting up practice in some little town where it's warm year-round. I haven't decided where."

"Florida's a wonderful place," the woman said. "I think Terrel would like it there."

"Could I ask you something?" I said.

"You certainly may," the woman said. Terrel had begun pushing his Greyhound across the front of the TV screen, making a scratch that no one watching the set could miss. "Stop that, Terrel Junior," the woman said quietly. But Terrel kept pushing his bus on the glass, and she smiled at me again as if we both understood something sad. Except I knew Cheryl would never damage a television set. She had respect for nice things, and I was sorry for the lady that Terrel didn't. "What did you want to ask?" the woman said.

"What goes on in that plant or whatever it is back there beyond these trailers, where all the lights are on?"

"Gold," the woman said and smiled.

"It's what?" I said.

"Gold," the Negro woman said, smiling as she had for almost all the time I'd been there. "It's a gold mine."

"They're mining gold back there?" I said, pointing.

"Every night and every day." She smiled in a pleased way.

"Does your husband work there?" I said.

"He's the assayer," she said. "He controls the quality. He works three months a year, and we live the rest of the time at home in Rockford. We've waited a long time for this. We've been happy to have our grandson, but I won't say I'll be sorry to have him go. We're ready to start our lives over." She smiled broadly at me and then at Terrel, who was giving her a spiteful look from the floor. "You said you had a daughter," the Negro woman said. "And what's her name?"

"Irma Cheryl," I said. "She's named for my mother."

"That's nice. And she's healthy, too. I can see it in your face." She looked at Terrel Junior with pity.

"I guess I'm lucky," I said.

"So far you are. But children bring you grief, the same way they bring you joy. We were unhappy for a long time before my husband got his job in the gold mine. Now, when Terrel starts to school, we'll be kids again." She stood up. "You might miss your cab, Mr. Middleton," she said, walking toward the door, though not to be forcing me out. She was too polite. "If *we* can't see your car, the cab surely won't be able to."

"That's true." I got up off the recliner, where I'd been so comfortable. "None of us have eaten yet, and your food makes me know how hungry we probably all are."

"There are fine restaurants in town, and you'll find them," the Negro woman said. "I'm sorry you didn't meet my husband. He's a wonderful man. He's everything to me."

"Tell him I appreciate the phone," I said. "You saved me."

"You weren't hard to save," the woman said. "Saving people is what we were all put on earth to do. I just passed you on to whatever's coming to you."

"Let's hope it's good," I said, stepping back into the dark.

"I'll be hoping, Mr. Middleton. Terrel and I will both be hoping."

I waved to her as I walked out into the darkness toward the car where it was hidden in the night.

The cab had already arrived when I got there. I could see its little red-and-green roof lights all the way across the dry wash, and it made me worry that Edna was already saying something to get us in trouble, something about the car or where we'd come from, something that would cast suspicion on us. I thought, then, how I never planned things well enough. There was always a gap between my plan and what happened, and I only responded to things as they came along and hoped I wouldn't get in trouble. I was an offender in the law's eyes. But I always *thought* differently, as if I weren't an offender and had no intention of being one, which was the truth. But as I read on a napkin once, between the idea and the act a whole kingdom lies. And I had a hard time with my acts, which were oftentimes offender's acts, and my ideas, which were as good as the gold they mined there where the bright lights were blazing.

"We're waiting for you, Daddy," Cheryl said when I crossed the road. "The taxicab's already here."

"I see, hon," I said, and gave Cheryl a big hug. The cab driver was sitting in the driver's seat having a smoke with the lights on inside. Edna was leaning against the back of the cab between the taillights, wearing her Bailey hat. "What'd you tell him?" I said when I got close.

"Nothing," she said. "What's there to tell?"

"Did he see the car?"

She glanced over in the direction of the trees where we had hid the Mercedes. Nothing was visible in the darkness, though I could hear Little Duke combing around in the underbrush tracking something, his little collar tinkling. "Where're we going?" she said. "I'm so hungry I could pass out."

"Edna's in a terrible mood," Cheryl said. "She already snapped at me."

"We're tired, honey," I said. "So try to be nicer."

"She's never nice," Cheryl said.

"Run go get Little Duke," I said. "And hurry back."

"I guess *my* questions come last here, right?" Edna said.

I put my arm around her. "That's not true."

"Did you find somebody over there in the trailers you'd rather stay with? You were gone long enough."

"That's not a thing to say," I said. "I was just trying to make things look right, so we don't get put in jail."

"So *you* don't, you mean." Edna laughed a little laugh I didn't like hearing.

"That's right. So I don't," I said. "I'd be the one in Dutch." I stared out at the big, lighted assemblage of white buildings and white lights beyond the trailer community, plumes of white smoke escaping up into the heartless Wyoming sky, the whole company of buildings looking like some unbelievable castle, humming away in a distorted dream. "You know what all those buildings are there?" I said to Edna, who hadn't moved and who didn't really seem to care if she ever moved anymore ever.

"No. But I can't say it matters, because it isn't a motel and it isn't a restaurant."

"It's a gold mine," I said, staring at the gold mine, which, I knew now, was a greater distance from us than it seemed, though it seemed huge and near, up against the cold sky. I thought there should've been a wall around it with guards instead of just the lights and no fence. It seemed as if anyone could go in and take what they wanted, just the way I had gone up to that woman's trailer and used the telephone, though that obviously wasn't true.

Edna began to laugh then. Not the mean laugh I didn't like, but a laugh that had something caring behind it, a full laugh that enjoyed a joke, a laugh she was laughing the first time I laid eyes on her, in Missoula in the East Gate Bar in 1979, a laugh we used to laugh together when Cheryl was still with her mother and I was working steady at the track and not stealing cars or passing bogus checks to merchants. A better time all around. And for some reason it made me laugh just hearing her, and we both stood there behind the cab in the dark, laughing at the gold mine in the desert, me with my arm around her and Cheryl out rustling up Little Duke and the cab driver smoking in the cab and our stolen Mercedes-Benz, which I'd had such hopes for in Florida, stuck up to its axle in sand, where I'd never get to see it again.

"I always wondered what a gold mine would look like when I saw it," Edna said, still laughing, wiping a tear from her eye.

"Me too," I said. "I was always curious about it."

"We're a couple of fools, aren't we, Earl?" she said, unable to quit laughing completely. "We're two of a kind."

"It might be a good sign, though," I said.

"How could it be? It's not our gold mine. There aren't any drive-up windows." She was still laughing.

"We've seen it," I said, pointing. "That's it right there. It may mean we're getting closer. Some people never see it at all."

"In a pig's eye, Earl," she said. "You and me see it in a pig's eye."

And she turned and got in the cab to go.

The cab driver didn't ask anything about our car or where it was, to mean he'd noticed something queer. All of which made me feel like we had made a clean break from the car and couldn't be connected with it until it was too late, if ever. The driver told us a lot about Rock Springs while he drove, that because of the gold mine a lot of people had moved there in just six months, people from all over, including New York, and that most of them lived out in the trailers. Prostitutes from New York City, who he called "B-girls," had come into town, he said, on the prosperity tide, and Cadillacs with New York plates cruised the little streets every night, full of Negroes with big hats who ran the women. He told us that everybody who got in his cab now wanted to know where the women were, and when he got our call he almost didn't come because some of the trailers were brothels operated by the mine for engineers and computer people away from home. He said he got tired of running back and forth out there just for vile business. He said that *60 Minutes* had even done a program about Rock Springs and that a blow-up had resulted in Cheyenne, though nothing could be done unless the boom left town. "It's prosperity's fruit," the driver said. "I'd rather be poor, which is lucky for me."

He said all the motels were sky-high, but since we were a family he could show us a nice one that was affordable. But I told him we wanted a first-rate place where they took animals, and the money didn't matter because we had had a hard day and wanted to finish on a high note. I also knew that it was in the little nowhere places that the police look for you and find you. People I'd known were always being arrested in cheap hotels and tourist courts with names you'd never heard of before. Never in Holiday Inns or Travelodges.

I asked him to drive us to the middle of town and back out again so Cheryl could see the train station, and while we were there I saw a pink Cadillac with New York plates and a TV aerial being driven slowly by a Negro in a big hat down a narrow street where there were just bars and a Chinese restaurant. It was an odd sight, nothing you could ever expect.

"There's your pure criminal element," the cabdriver said and seemed sad. "I'm sorry for people like you to see a thing like that. We've got a nice town here, but there're some that want to ruin it for everybody. There used to be a way to deal with trash and criminals, but those days are gone forever."

"You said it," Edna said.

"You shouldn't let it get you down," I said to him. "There's more of you than them. And there always will be. You're the best advertisement this town has. I know

Cheryl will remember you and not *that* man, won't you, honey?" But Cheryl was asleep by then, holding Little Duke in her arms on the taxi seat.

The driver took us to the Ramada Inn on the interstate, not far from where we'd broken down. I had a small pain of regret as we drove under the Ramada awning that we hadn't driven up in a cranberry-colored Mercedes but instead in a beat-up old Chrysler taxi driven by an old man full of complaints. Though I knew it was for the best. We were better off without that car; better, really, in any other car but that one, where the signs had turned bad.

I registered under another name and paid for the room in cash so there wouldn't be any questions. On the line where it said "representing" I wrote "Ophthalmologist" and put "M.D." after the name. It had a nice look to it, even though it wasn't my name.

When we got to the room, which was in the back where I'd asked for it, I put Cheryl on one of the beds and Little Duke beside her so they'd sleep. She'd missed dinner, but it only meant she'd be hungry in the morning, when she could have anything she wanted. A few missed meals don't make a kid bad. I'd missed a lot of them myself and haven't turned out completely bad.

"Let's have some fried chicken," I said to Edna when she came out of the bathroom. "They have good fried chicken at Ramadas, and I noticed the buffet was still up. Cheryl can stay right here, where it's safe, till we're back."

"I guess I'm not hungry anymore," Edna said. She stood at the window staring out into the dark. I could see out the window past her some yellowish foggy glow in the sky. For a moment I thought it was the gold mine out in the distance lighting the night, though it was only the interstate.

"We could order up," I said. "Whatever you want. There's a menu on the phone book. You could just have a salad."

"You go ahead," she said. "I've lost my hungry spirit." She sat on the bed beside Cheryl and Little Duke and looked at them in a sweet way and put her hand on Cheryl's cheek just as if she'd had a fever. "Sweet little girl," she said. "Everybody loves you."

"What do you want to do?" I said. "I'd like to eat. Maybe *I'll* order up some chicken."

"Why don't you do that?" she said. "It's your favorite." And she smiled at me from the bed.

I sat on the other bed and dialed room service. I asked for chicken, garden salad, potato and a roll, plus a piece of hot apple pie and iced tea. I realized I hadn't eaten all day. When I put down the phone I saw that Edna was watching me, not in a hateful way or a loving way, just in a way that seemed to say she didn't understand something and was going to ask me about it.

"When did watching me get so entertaining?" I said and smiled at her. I was trying to be friendly. I knew how tired she must be. It was after nine o'clock.

"I was just thinking how much I hated being in a motel without a car that was mine to drive. Isn't that funny? I started feeling like that last night when that purple car wasn't mine. That purple car just gave me the willies, I guess, Earl."

"One of those cars *outside* is yours," I said. "Just stand right there and pick it out."

"I know," she said. "But that's different, isn't it?" She reached and got her blue Bailey hat, put it on her head, and set it way back like Dale Evans. She looked sweet.

"I used to like to go to motels, you know," she said. "There's something secret about them and free—I was never paying, of course. But you felt safe from everything and free to do what you wanted because you'd made the decision to be there and paid that price, and all the rest was the good part. Fucking and everything, you know." She smiled at me in a good-natured way.

"Isn't that the way this is?" I was sitting on the bed, watching her, not knowing what to expect her to say next.

"I don't guess it is, Earl," she said and stared out the window. "I'm thirty-two and I'm going to have to give up on motels. I can't keep that fantasy going anymore."

"Don't you like this place?" I said and looked around at the room. I appreciated the modern paintings and the lowboy bureau and the big TV. It seemed like a plenty nice enough place to me, considering where we'd been.

"No, I don't," Edna said with real conviction. "There's no use in my getting mad at you about it. It isn't your fault. You do the best you can for everybody. But every trip teaches you something. And I've learned I need to give up on motels before some bad thing happens to me. I'm sorry."

"What does that mean?" I said, because I really didn't know what she had in mind to do, though I should've guessed.

"I guess I'll take that ticket you mentioned," she said, and got up and faced the window. "Tomorrow's soon enough. We haven't got a car to take me anyhow."

"Well, that's a fine thing," I said, sitting on the bed, feeling like I was in shock. I wanted to say something to her, to argue with her, but I couldn't think what to say that seemed right. I didn't want to be mad at her, but it made me mad.

"You've got a right to be mad at me, Earl," she said, "but I don't think you can really blame me." She turned around and faced me and sat on the windowsill, her hands on her knees. Someone knocked on the door, and I just yelled for them to set the tray down and put it on the bill.

"I guess I *do* blame you," I said, and I was angry. I thought about how I could've disappeared into that trailer community and hadn't, had come back to keep things going, had tried to take control of things for everybody when they looked bad.

"Don't. I wish you wouldn't," Edna said and smiled at me like she wanted me to hug her. "Anybody ought to have their choice in things if they can. Don't you believe that, Earl? Here I am out here in the desert where I don't know anything, in a stolen car, in a motel room under an assumed name, with no money of my own, a kid that's not mine, and the law after me. And I have a choice to get out of all of it by getting on a bus. What would you do? I know exactly what you'd do."

"You think you do," I said. But I didn't want to get into an argument about it and tell her all I could've done and didn't do. Because it wouldn't have done any good. When you get to the point of arguing, you're past the point of changing anybody's mind, even though it's supposed to be the other way, and maybe for some classes of people it is, just never mine.

Edna smiled at me and came across the room and put her arms around me where I was sitting on the bed. Cheryl rolled over and looked at us and smiled, then closed her eyes, and the room was quiet. I was beginning to think of Rock Springs in a way I knew I would always think of it, a low-down city full of crimes and whores and disappointments, a place where a woman left me, instead of a place where I got things on the straight track once and for all, a place I saw a gold mine.

"Eat your chicken, Earl," Edna said. "Then we can go to bed. I'm tired, but I'd like to make love to you anyway. None of this is a matter of not loving you, you know that."

Sometime late in the night, after Edna was asleep, I got up and walked outside into the parking lot. It could've been anytime because there was still the light from the interstate frosting the low sky and the big red Ramada sign humming motionlessly in the night and no light at all in the east to indicate it might be morning. The lot was full of cars all nosed in, a couple of them with suitcases strapped to their roofs and their trunks weighed down with belongings the people were taking someplace, to a new home or a vacation resort in the mountains. I had laid in bed a long time after Edna was asleep, watching the Atlanta Braves on television, trying to get my mind off how I'd feel when I saw that bus pull away the next day, and how I'd feel when I turned around and there stood Cheryl and Little Duke and no one to see about them but me alone, and that the first thing I had to do was get hold of some automobile and get the plates switched, then get them some breakfast and get us all on the road to Florida, all in the space of probably two hours, since that Mercedes would certainly look less hid in the daytime than the night, and word travels fast. I've always taken care of Cheryl myself as long as I've had her with me. None of the women ever did. Most of them didn't even seem to like her, though they took care of me in a way so that I could take care of her. And I knew that once Edna left, all that was going to get harder. Though what I wanted most to do was not think about it just for a little while, try to let my mind go limp so it could be strong for the rest of what there was. I thought that the difference between a successful life and an unsuccessful one, between me at that moment and all the people who owned the cars that were nosed into their proper places in the lot, maybe between me and that woman out in the trailers by the gold mine, was how well you were able to put things like this out of your mind and not be bothered by them, and maybe, too, by how many troubles like this one you had to face in a lifetime. Through luck or design they had all faced fewer troubles, and by their own characters, they forgot them faster. And that's what I wanted for me. Fewer troubles, fewer memories of trouble.

I walked over to a car, a Pontiac with Ohio tags, one of the ones with bundles and suitcases strapped to the top and a lot more in the trunk, by the way it was riding. I looked inside the driver's window. There were maps and paperback books and sunglasses and the little plastic holders for cans that hang on the window wells. And in the back there were kids' toys and some pillows and a cat box with a cat sitting in it staring up at me like I was the face of the moon. It all looked familiar to me, the very same things I would have in my car if I had a car. Nothing seemed surprising, nothing different. Though I had a funny sensation at that moment and turned and looked up at the windows along the back of the motel. All were dark except two. Mine and another one. And I wondered, because it seemed funny, what would you think a man was doing if you saw him in the middle of the night looking in the windows of cars in the parking lot of the Ramada Inn? Would you think he was trying to get his head cleared? Would you think he was trying to get ready for a day when trouble would come down on him? Would you think his girlfriend was leaving him? Would you think he had a daughter? Would you think he was anybody like you?

RICHARD FORD

Communist

My mother once had a boyfriend named Glen Baxter. This was in 1961. We—my mother and I—were living in the little house my father had left her up the Sun River, near Victory, Montana, west of Great Falls. My mother was thirty-two at the time. I was sixteen. Glen Baxter was somewhere in the middle, between us, though I cannot be exact about it.

We were living then off the proceeds of my father's life insurance policies, with my mother doing some part-time waitressing work up in Great Falls and going to the bars in the evenings, which I know is where she met Glen Baxter. Sometimes he would come back with her and stay in her room at night, or she would call up from town and explain that she was staying with him in his little place on Lewis Street by the GN yards. She gave me his number every time, but I never called it. I think she probably thought that what she was doing was terrible, but simply couldn't help herself. I thought it was all right, though. Regular life it seemed, and still does. She was young, and I knew that even then.

Glen Baxter was a Communist and liked hunting, which he talked about a lot. Pheasants. Ducks. Deer. He killed all of them, he said. He had been to Vietnam as far back as then, and when he was in our house he often talked about shooting the animals over there—monkeys and beautiful parrots—using military guns just for sport. We did not know what Vietnam was then, and Glen, when he talked about that, referred to it only as "the Far East." I think now he must've been in the CIA and been disillusioned by something he saw or found out about and been thrown out, but that kind of thing did not matter to us. He was a tall, dark-eyed man with short black hair, and was usually in a good humor. He had gone halfway through college in Peoria, Illinois, he said, where he grew up. But when he was around our life he worked wheat farms as a ditcher, and stayed out of work winters and in the bars drinking with women like my mother, who had work and some money. It is not an uncommon life to lead in Montana.

What I want to explain happened in November. We had not been seeing Glen Baxter for some time. Two months had gone by. My mother knew other men, but she came home most days from work and stayed inside watching television in her bedroom and drinking beers. I asked about Glen once, and she said only that she didn't know where he was, and I assumed they had had a fight and that he was gone off on a flyer back to Illinois or Massachusetts, where he said he had relatives. I'll admit that I liked him. He had something on his mind always. He was a labor man as well as a Communist, and liked to say that the country was poisoned by the rich, and strong men would need to bring it to life again, and I liked that because my father had been a labor man, which was why we had a house to live in and money coming through. It was also true that I'd had a few boxing bouts by then—just with town boys and one with an Indian from Choteau—and there were some girlfriends I knew from that. I did not like my mother being around the house so much at night, and I wished Glen Baxter would come back, or that another man would come along and entertain her somewhere else.

At two o'clock on a Saturday, Glen drove up into our yard in a car. He had had a big brown Harley-Davidson that he rode most of the year, in his black-and-red irrigators and a baseball cap turned backwards. But this time he had a car, a blue Nash Ambassador. My mother and I went out on the porch when he stopped inside the olive trees my father had planted as a shelter belt, and my mother had a look on her face of not much pleasure. It was starting to be cold in earnest by then. Snow was down already onto the Fairfield Bench, though on this day a chinook was blowing, and it could as easily have been spring, though the sky above the Divide was turning over in silver and blue clouds of winter.

"We haven't seen you in a long time, I guess," my mother said coldly.

"My little retarded sister died," Glen said, standing at the door of his old car. He was wearing his orange VFW jacket and canvas shoes we called wino shoes, something I had never seen him wear before. He seemed to be in a good humor. "We buried her in Florida near the home."

"That's a good place," my mother said in a voice that meant she was a wronged party in something.

"I want to take this boy hunting today, Aileen," Glen said. "There're snow geese down now. But we have to go right away, or they'll be gone to Idaho by tomorrow."

"He doesn't care to go," my mother said.

"Yes I do," I said, and looked at her.

My mother frowned at me. "Why do you?"

"Why does he need a reason?" Glen Baxter said and grinned.

"I want him to have one, that's why." She looked at me oddly. "I think Glen's drunk, Les."

"No, I'm not drinking," Glen said, which was hardly ever true. He looked at both of us, and my mother bit down on the side of her lower lip and stared at me in a way to make you think she thought something was being put over on her and she didn't like you for it. She was very pretty, though when she was mad her features were sharpened and less pretty by a long way. "All right, then I don't care," she said to no one in particular. "Hunt, kill, maim. Your father did that too." She turned to go back inside.

"Why don't you come with us, Aileen?" Glen was smiling still, pleased.

"To do what?" my mother said. She stopped and pulled a package of cigarettes out of her dress pocket and put one in her mouth.

"It's worth seeing."

"See dead animals?" my mother said.

"These geese are from Siberia, Aileen," Glen said. "They're not like a lot of geese. Maybe I'll buy us dinner later. What do you say?"

"Buy what with?" my mother said. To tell the truth, I didn't know why she was so mad at him. I would've thought she'd be glad to see him. But she just suddenly seemed to hate everything about him.

"I've got some money," Glen said. "Let me spend it on a pretty girl tonight."

"Find one of those and you're lucky," my mother said, turning away toward the front door.

"I already found one," Glen Baxter said. But the door slammed behind her, and he looked at me then with a look I think now was helplessness, though I could not see a way to change anything.

My mother sat in the backseat of Glen's Nash and looked out the window while we drove. My double gun was in the seat between us beside Glen's Belgian pump, which he kept loaded with five shells in case, he said, he saw something beside the road he wanted to shoot. I had hunted rabbits before, and had ground-sluiced pheasants and other birds, but I had never been on an actual hunt before, one where you drove out to some special place and did it formally. And I was excited. I had a feeling that something important was about to happen to me, and that this would be a day I would always remember.

My mother did not say anything for a long time, and neither did I. We drove up through Great Falls and out the other side toward Fort Benton, which was on the benchland where wheat was grown.

"Geese mate for life," my mother said, just out of the blue, as we were driving. "I hope you know that. They're special birds."

"I know that," Glen said in the front seat. "I have every respect for them."

"So where were you for three months?" she said. "I'm only curious."

"I was in the Big Hole for a while," Glen said, "and after that I went over to Douglas, Wyoming."

"What were you planning to do there?" my mother asked.

"I wanted to find a job, but it didn't work out."

"I'm going to college," she said suddenly, and this was something I had never heard about before. I turned to look at her, but she was staring out her window and wouldn't see me.

"I knew French once," Glen said. "*Rosé*'s pink. *Rouge*'s red." He glanced at me and smiled. "I think that's a wise idea, Aileen. When are you going to start?"

"I don't want Les to think he was raised by crazy people all his life," my mother said.

"Les ought to go himself," Glen said.

"After I go, he will."

"What do you say about that, Les?" Glen said, grinning.

"He says it's just fine," my mother said.

"It's just fine," I said.

Where Glen Baxter took us was out onto the high flat prairie that was disked for wheat and had high, high mountains out to the east, with lower heartbreak hills in between. It was, I remember, a day for blues in the sky, and down in the distance we could see the small town of Floweree, and the state highway running past it toward Fort Benton and the Hi-line. We drove out on top of the prairie on a muddy dirt road fenced on both sides, until we had gone about three miles, which is where Glen stopped.

"All right," he said, looking up in the rearview mirror at my mother. "You wouldn't think there was anything here, would you?"

"*We're* here," my mother said. "You brought us here."

"You'll be glad though," Glen said, and seemed confident to me. I had looked around myself but could not see anything. No water or trees, nothing that seemed like a good place to hunt anything. Just wasted land. "There's a big lake out there, Les," Glen said. "You can't see it now from here because it's low. But the geese are there. You'll see."

"It's like the moon out here, I recognize that," my mother said, "only it's worse." She was staring out at the flat wheatland as if she could actually see something in particular, and wanted to know more about it. "How'd you find this place?"

"I came once on the wheat push," Glen said.

"And I'm sure the owner told you just to come back and hunt anytime you like and bring anybody you wanted. Come one, come all. Is that it?"

"People shouldn't own land anyway," Glen said. "Anybody should be able to use it."

"Les, Glen's going to poach here," my mother said. "I just want you to know that, because that's a crime and the law will get you for it. If you're a man now, you're going to have to face the consequences."

"That's not true," Glen Baxter said, and looked gloomily out over the steering wheel down the muddy road toward the mountains. Though for myself I believed it was true, and didn't care. I didn't care about anything at that moment except seeing geese fly over me and shooting them down.

"Well, I'm certainly not going out there," my mother said. "I like towns better, and I already have enough trouble."

"That's okay," Glen said. "When the geese lift up you'll get to see them. That's all I wanted. Les and me'll go shoot them, won't we, Les?"

"Yes," I said, and I put my hand on my shotgun, which had been my father's and was heavy as rocks.

"Then we should go on," Glen said, "or we'll waste our light."

We got out of the car with our guns. Glen took off his canvas shoes and put on his pair of black irrigators out of the trunk. Then we crossed the barbed wire fence, and walked out into the high, tilled field toward nothing. I looked back at my mother when we were still not so far away, but I could only see the small, dark top of her head, low in the backseat of the Nash, staring out and thinking what I could not then begin to say.

On the walk toward the lake, Glen began talking to me. I had never been alone with him, and knew little about him except what my mother said—that he drank too much, or other times that he was the nicest man she had ever known in the world and that someday a woman would marry him, though she didn't think it would be her. Glen told me as we walked that he wished he had finished college, but that it was too late now, that his mind was too old. He said he had liked the Far East very much, and that people there knew how to treat each other, and that he would go back some day but couldn't go now. He said also that he would like to live in Russia for a while and mentioned the names of people who had gone there, names I didn't know. He said it would be hard at first, because it was so different, but that pretty soon anyone would learn to like it and wouldn't want to live anywhere else, and that Russians treated Americans who came to live there like kings. There were Communists everywhere now, he said. You didn't know them, but they were there. Montana had a large number, and he was in touch with all of them. He said that Communists were always in danger and that he had to protect himself all the time. And when he said that he pulled back his VFW jacket and showed me the butt of a pistol he had stuck under his shirt against his bare skin. "There are people who want to kill me right now," he said, "and I would kill a man myself if I thought I had to." And we kept walking. Though in a while he said, "I don't think I know much about you, Les. But I'd like to. What do you like to do?"

"I like to box," I said. "My father did it. It's a good thing to know."

"I suppose you have to protect yourself too," Glen said.

"I know how to," I said.

"Do you like to watch TV," Glen asked, and smiled.

"Not much."

"I love to," Glen said. "I could watch it instead of eating if I had one."

I looked out straight ahead over the green tops of sage that grew to the edge of the disked field, hoping to see the lake Glen said was there. There was an airishness and a sweet smell that I thought might be the place we were going, but I couldn't see it. "How will we hunt these geese?" I said.

"It won't be hard," Glen said. "Most hunting isn't even hunting. It's only shooting. And that's what this will be. In Illinois you would dig holes in the ground and hide and set out your decoys. Then the geese come to you, over and over again. But we don't have time for that here." He glanced at me. "You have to be sure the first time here."

"How do you know they're here now," I asked. And I looked toward the Highwood Mountains twenty miles away, half in snow and half dark blue at the bottom. I could see the little town of Floweree then, looking shabby and dimly lighted in the distance. A red bar sign shone. A car moved slowly away from the scattered buildings.

"They always come November first," Glen said.

"Are we going to poach them?"

"Does it make any difference to you," Glen asked.

"No, it doesn't."

"Well then, we aren't," he said.

We walked then for a while without talking. I looked back once to see the Nash far and small in the flat distance. I couldn't see my mother, and I thought that she must've turned on the radio and gone to sleep, which she always did, letting it play all night in her bedroom. Behind the car the sun was nearing the rounded mountains southwest of us, and I knew that when the sun was gone it would be cold. I wished my mother had decided to come along with us, and I thought for a moment of how little I really knew her at all.

Glen walked with me another quarter-mile, crossed another barbed wire fence where sage was growing, then went a hundred yards through wheatgrass and spurge until the ground went up and formed a kind of long hillock bunker built by a farmer against the wind. And I realized the lake was just beyond us. I could hear the sound of a car horn blowing and a dog barking all the way down in the town, then the wind seemed to move and all I could hear then and after then were geese. So many geese, from the sound of them, though I still could not see even one. I stood and listened to the high-pitched shouting sound, a sound I had never heard so close, a sound with size to it—though it was not loud. A sound that meant great numbers and that made your chest rise and your shoulders tighten with expectancy. It was a sound to make you feel separate from it and everything else, as if you were of no importance in the grand scheme of things.

"Do you hear them singing," Glen asked. He held his hand up to make me stand still. And we both listened. "How many do you think, Les, just hearing?"

"A hundred," I said. "More than a hundred."

"Five thousand," Glen said. "More than you can believe when you see them. Go see."

I put down my gun and on my hands and knees crawled up the earthwork through the wheatgrass and thistle, until I could see down to the lake and see the geese. And they were there, like a white bandage laid on the water, wide and long and continuous, a white expanse of snow geese, seventy yards from me, on the bank, but stretching far onto the lake, which was large itself—a half-mile across, with thick tules on the far side and wild plums farther and the blue mountain behind them.

"Do you see the big raft?" Glen said from below me, in a whisper.

"I see it," I said, still looking. It was such a thing to see, a view I had never seen and have not since.

"Are any on the land?" he said.

"Some are in the wheatgrass," I said, "but most are swimming."

"Good," Glen said. "They'll have to fly. But we can't wait for that now."

And I crawled backwards down the heel of land to where Glen was, and my gun. We were losing our light, and the air was purplish and cooling. I looked toward the car but couldn't see it, and I was no longer sure where it was below the lighted sky.

"Where do they fly to?" I said in a whisper, since I did not want anything to be ruined because of what I did or said. It was important to Glen to shoot the geese, and it was important to me.

"To the wheat," he said. "Or else they leave for good. I wish your mother had come, Les. Now she'll be sorry."

I could hear the geese quarreling and shouting on the lake surface. And I wondered if they knew we were here now. "She might be," I said with my heart pounding, but I didn't think she would be much.

It was a simple plan he had. I would stay behind the bunker, and he would crawl on his belly with his gun through the wheatgrass as near to the geese as he could. Then he would simply stand up and shoot all the ones he could close up, both in the air and on the ground. And when all the others flew up, with luck some would turn toward me as they came into the wind, and then I could shoot them and turn them back to him, and he would shoot them again. He could kill ten, he said, if he was lucky, and I might kill four. It didn't seem hard.

"Don't show them your face," Glen said. "Wait till you think you can touch them, then stand up and shoot. To hesitate is lost in this."

"All right," I said. "I'll try it."

"Shoot one in the head, and then shoot another one," Glen said. "It won't be hard." He patted me on the arm and smiled. Then he took off his VFW jacket and put it on the ground, climbed up the side of the bunker, cradling his shotgun in his arms, and slid on his belly into the dry stalks of yellow grass out of my sight.

Then, for the first time in that entire day, I was alone. And I didn't mind it. I sat squat down in the grass, loaded my double gun and took my other two shells out of my pocket to hold. I pushed the safety off and on to see that it was right. The wind rose a little, scuffed the grass and made me shiver. It was not the warm chinook now, but a wind out of the north, the one geese flew away from if they could.

Then I thought about my mother, in the car alone, and how much longer I would stay with her, and what it might mean to her for me to leave. And I wondered when Glen Baxter would die and if someone would kill him, or whether my mother would marry him and how I would feel about it. And though I didn't know why, it occurred to me that Glen Baxter and I would not be friends when all was said and done, since I didn't care if he ever married my mother or didn't.

Then I thought about boxing and what my father had taught me about it. To tighten your fists hard. To strike out straight from the shoulder and never punch backing up. How to cut a punch by snapping your fist inwards, how to carry your chin low, and to step toward a man when he is falling so you can hit him again. And most important, to keep your eyes open when you are hitting in the face and causing damage, because you need to see what you're doing to encourage yourself, and because it is when you close your eyes that you stop hitting and get hurt badly. "Fly all over your man, Les," my father said. "When you see your chance, fly on him and hit him till he falls." That, I thought, would always be my attitude in things.

And then I heard the geese again, their voices in unison, louder and shouting, as if the wind had changed again and put all new sounds in the cold air. And then a *boom.* And I knew Glen was in among them and had stood up to shoot. The noise of geese rose and grew worse, and my fingers burned where I held my gun too tight to the metal, and I put it down and opened my fist to make the burning stop so I could feel the trigger when the moment came. *Boom,* Glen shot again, and I heard him shuck a shell, and all the sounds out beyond the bunker seemed to be rising—the geese, the shots, the air itself going up. *Boom,* Glen shot another time, and I knew he was taking his careful time to make his shots good. And I held my gun and started to crawl up the bunker so as not to be surprised when the geese came over me and I could shoot.

From the top I saw Glen Baxter alone in the wheatgrass field, shooting at a white goose with black tips of wings that was on the ground not far from him, but trying to run and pull into the air. He shot it once more, and it fell over dead with its wings flapping.

Glen looked back at me and his face was distorted and strange. The air around him was full of white rising geese and he seemed to want them all. "Behind you, Les," he yelled at me and pointed. "They're all behind you now." I looked behind me, and there were geese in the air as far as I could see, more than I knew how many, moving so slowly, their wings wide out and working calmly and filling the air with noise, though their voices were not as loud or as shrill as I had thought they would be. And they were so close! Forty feet, some of them. The air around me vibrated and I could feel the wind from their wings and it seemed to me I could kill as many as the times I could shoot—a hundred or a thousand—and I raised my gun, put the muzzle on the head of a white goose, and fired. It shuddered in the air, its wide feet sank below its belly, its wings cradled out to hold back air, and it fell straight down and landed with an awful sound, a noise a human would make, a thick, soft, *hump* noise. I looked up again and shot another goose, could hear the pellets hit its chest, but it didn't fall or even break its pattern for flying. *Boom,* Glen shot again. And then again. "Hey," I heard him shout, "Hey, hey." And there were geese flying over me, flying in line after line. I broke my gun and reloaded, and thought to myself as I did: I need confidence here, I need to be sure with this. I pointed at another goose and shot it in the head, and it fell the way the first one had, wings out, its belly down, and with the same thick noise of hitting. Then I sat down in the grass on the bunker and let geese fly over me.

By now the whole raft was in the air, all of it moving in a slow swirl above me and the lake and everywhere, finding the wind and heading out south in long wavering lines that caught the last sun and turned to silver as they gained a distance. It was a thing to see, I will tell you now. Five thousand white geese all in the air around you, making a noise like you have never heard before. And I thought to myself then: this is something I will never see again. I will never forget this. And I was right.

Glen Baxter shot twice more. One he missed, but with the other he hit a goose flying away from him, and knocked it half falling and flying into the empty lake not far from shore, where it began to swim as though it was fine and make its noise.

Glen stood in the stubby grass, looking out at the goose, his gun lowered. "I didn't need to shoot that one, did I, Les?"

"I don't know," I said, sitting on the little knoll of land, looking at the goose swimming in the water.

"I don't know why I shoot 'em. They're so beautiful." He looked at me.

"I don't know either," I said.

"Maybe there's nothing else to do with them." Glen stared at the goose again and shook his head. "Maybe this is exactly what they're put on earth for."

I did not know what to say because I did not know what he could mean by that, though what I felt was embarrassment at the great numbers of geese there were, and a dulled feeling like a hunger because the shooting had stopped and it was over for me now.

Glen began to pick up his geese, and I walked down to my two that had fallen close together and were dead. One had hit with such an impact that its stomach had split and some of its inward parts were knocked out. Though the other looked unhurt, its soft white belly turned up like a pillow, its head and jagged bill-teeth, its tiny black eyes looking as they would if they were alive.

"What's happened to the hunters out here?" I heard a voice speak. It was my mother, standing in her pink dress on the knoll above us, hugging her arms. She was smiling, though she was cold. And I realized that I had lost all thought of her in the shooting. "Who did all this shooting? Is this your work, Les?"

"No," I said.

"Les is a hunter, though, Aileen," Glen said. "He takes his time." He was holding two white geese by their necks, one in each hand, and he was smiling. He and my mother seemed pleased.

"I see you didn't miss too many," my mother said and smiled. I could tell she admired Glen for his geese, and that she had done some thinking in the car alone. "It *was* wonderful, Glen," she said. "I've never seen anything like that. They were like snow."

"It's worth seeing once, isn't it?" Glen said. "I should've killed more, but I got excited."

My mother looked at me then. "Where's yours, Les?"

"Here," I said and pointed to my two geese on the ground beside me.

My mother nodded in a nice way, and I think she liked everything then and wanted the day to turn out right and for all of us to be happy. "Six, then. You've got six in all."

"One's still out there," I said, and motioned where the one goose was swimming in circles on the water.

"Okay," my mother said and put her hand over her eyes to look. "Where is it?"

Glen Baxter looked at me then with a strange smile, a smile that said he wished I had never mentioned anything about the other goose. And I wished I hadn't either. I looked up in the sky and could see the lines of geese by the thousands shining silver in the light, and I wished we could just leave and go home.

"That one's my mistake there," Glen Baxter said and grinned. "I shouldn't have shot that one, Aileen. I got too excited."

My mother looked out on the lake for a minute, then looked at Glen and back again. "Poor goose." She shook her head. "How will you get it, Glen?"

"I can't get that one now," Glen said.

My mother looked at him. "What do you mean?"

"I'm going to leave that one," Glen said.

"Well, no. You can't leave one," my mother said. "You shot it. You have to get it. Isn't that a rule?"

"No," Glen said.

And my mother looked from Glen to me. "Wade out and get it, Glen," she said in a sweet way, and my mother looked young then, like a young girl, in her flimsy short-sleeved waitress dress and her skinny, bare legs in the wheatgrass.

"No." Glen Baxter looked down at his gun and shook his head. And I didn't know why he wouldn't go, because it would've been easy. The lake was shallow. And you could tell that anyone could've walked out a long way before it got deep, and Glen had on his boots.

My mother looked at the white goose, which was not more than thirty yards from the shore, its head up, moving in slow circles, its wings settled and relaxed so you could see the black tips. "Wade out and get it, Glenny, won't you, please?" she said. "They're special things."

"You don't understand the world, Aileen," Glen said. "This can happen. It doesn't matter."

"But that's so cruel, Glen," she said, and a sweet smile came on her lips.

"Raise up your own arms, 'Leeny," Glen said. "I can't see any angel's wings, can you, Les?" He looked at me, but I looked away.

"Then you go on and get it, Les," my mother said. "You weren't raised by crazy people." I started to go, but Glen Baxter suddenly grabbed me by my shoulder and pulled me back hard, so hard his fingers made bruises in my skin that I saw later.

"Nobody's going," he said. "This is over with now."

And my mother gave Glen a cold look then. "You don't have a heart, Glen," she said. "There's nothing to love in you. You're just a son of a bitch, that's all."

And Glen Baxter nodded at my mother, then, as if he understood something he had not understood before, but something that he was willing to know. "Fine," he said, "that's fine." And he took his big pistol out from against his belly, the big blue revolver I had only seen part of before and that he said protected him, and he pointed it out at the goose on the water, his arm straight away from him, and shot and missed. And then he shot and missed again. The goose made its noise once. And then he hit it dead, because there was no splash. And then he shot it three times more until the gun was empty and the goose's head was down and it was floating toward the middle of the lake where it was empty and dark blue. "Now who has a heart?" Glen said. But my mother was not there when he turned around. She had already started back to the car and was almost lost from sight in the darkness. And Glen smiled at me then and his face had a wild look on it. "Okay, Les?" he said.

"Okay," I said.

"There're limits to everything, right?"

"I guess so," I said.

"Your mother's a beautiful woman, but she's not the only beautiful woman in Montana." And I did not say anything. And Glen Baxter suddenly said, "Here," and he held the pistol out at me. "Don't you want this? Don't you want to shoot me? Nobody thinks they'll die. But I'm ready for it right now." And I did not know what to do then. Though it is true that what I wanted to do was to hit him, hit him as hard in the face as I could, and see him on the ground bleeding and crying and pleading for me to stop. Only at that moment he looked scared to me, and I had never seen a grown man scared before—though I have seen one since—and I felt sorry for him, as though he was already a dead man. And I did not end up hitting him at all.

A light can go out in the heart. All of this happened years ago, but I still can feel now how sad and remote the world was to me. Glen Baxter, I think now, was not a bad man, only a man scared of something he'd never seen before—something soft in himself—his life going a way he didn't like. A woman with a son. Who could blame him there? I don't know what makes people do what they do, or call themselves what they call themselves, only that you have to live someone's life to be the expert.

My mother had tried to see the good side of things, tried to be hopeful in the situation she was handed, tried to look out for us both, and it hadn't worked. It was a strange time in her life then and after that, a time when she had to adjust to being an adult just when she was on the thin edge of things. Too much awareness too early in life was her problem, I think.

And what I felt was only that I had somehow been pushed out into the world, into the real life then, the one I hadn't lived yet. In a year I was gone to hard-rock mining and no-paycheck jobs and not to college. And I have thought more than once about my mother saying that I had not been raised by crazy people, and I don't know what that could mean or what difference it could make, unless it means that love is a reliable commodity, and even that is not always true, as I have found out.

Late on the night that all this took place I was in bed when I heard my mother say, "Come outside, Les. Come and hear this." And I went out onto the front porch barefoot and in my underwear, where it was warm like spring, and there was a spring mist in the air. I could see the lights of the Fairfield Coach in the distance, on its way up to Great Falls.

And I could hear geese, white birds in the sky, flying. They made their high-pitched sound like angry yells, and though I couldn't see them high up, it seemed to me they were everywhere. And my mother looked up and said, "Hear them?" I could smell her hair wet from the shower. "They leave with the moon," she said. "It's still half wild out here."

And I said, "I hear them," and I felt a chill come over my bare chest, and the hair stood up on my arms the way it does before a storm. And for a while we listened.

"When I first married your father, you know, we lived on a street called Bluebird Canyon, in California. And I thought that was the prettiest street and the prettiest name. I suppose no one brings you up like your first love. You don't mind if I say that, do you?" She looked at me hopefully.

"No," I said.

"We have to keep civilization alive somehow." And she pulled her little housecoat together because there was a cold vein in the air, a part of the cold that would be on us the next day. "I don't feel part of things tonight, I guess."

"It's all right," I said.

"Do you know where I'd like to go?"

"No," I said. And I suppose I knew she was angry then, angry with life, but did not want to show me that.

"To the Straits of Juan de Fuca. Wouldn't that be something? Would you like that?"

"I'd like it," I said. And my mother looked off for a minute, as if she could see the Straits of Juan de Fuca out against the line of mountains, see the lights of things alive and a whole new world.

"I know you liked him," she said after a moment. "You and I both suffer fools too well."

"I didn't like him too much," I said. "I didn't really care."

"He'll fall on his face. I'm sure of that," she said. And I didn't say anything because I didn't care about Glen Baxter anymore, and was happy not to talk about him. "Would you tell me something if I asked you? Would you tell me the truth?"

"Yes," I said.

And my mother did not look at me. "Just tell the truth," she said.

"All right," I said.

"Do you think I'm still very feminine? I'm thirty-two years old now. You don't know what that means. But do you think I am?"

And I stood at the edge of the porch, with the olive trees before me, looking straight up into the mist where I could not see geese but could still hear them flying, could almost feel the air move below their white wings. And I felt the way you feel when you are on a trestle all alone and the train is coming, and you know you have to decide. And I said, "Yes, I do." Because that was the truth. And I tried to think of something else then and did not hear what my mother said after that.

And how old was I then? Sixteen. Sixteen is young, but it can also be a grown man. I am forty-one years old now, and I think about that time without regret, though my mother and I never talked in that way again, and I have not heard her voice now in a long, long time.

RICHARD FORD

Under the Radar

On the drive over to the Nicholsons' for dinner—their first in some time—Marjorie Reeves told her husband, Steven Reeves, that she had had an affair with George Nicholson (their host) a year ago, but that it was all over with now and she hoped he—Steven—would not be mad about it and could go on with life.

At this point they were driving along Quaker Bridge Road where it leaves the Perkins Great Woods Road and begins to border the Shenipsit Reservoir, dark and shadowy and calmly mirrored in the late spring twilight. On the right was dense young timber, beech and alder saplings in pale leaf, the ground damp and cakey. Peepers were calling out from the watery lows. Their turn onto Apple Orchard Lane was still a mile on.

Steven, on hearing this news, began gradually and very carefully to steer their car—a tan Mercedes wagon with hooded yellow headlights—off of Quaker Bridge Road and onto the damp grassy shoulder so he could organize this information properly before going on.

They were extremely young. Steven Reeves was twenty-eight. Marjorie Reeves a year younger. They weren't rich, but they'd been lucky. Steven's job at Packard-Wells was to stay on top of a small segment of a larger segment of a rather small prefabrication intersection that serviced the automobile industry, and where any sudden alteration, or even the rumor of an alteration in certain polymer-bonding formulas could tip crucial down-the-line demand patterns, and in that way affect the betting lines and comfort zones of a good many meaningful client positions. His job meant poring over dense and esoteric petrochemical-industry journals, attending technical seminars, flying to vendor conventions, then writing up detailed status reports and all the while keeping an eye on the market for the benefit of his higher-ups. He'd been a scholarship boy at Bates, studied chemistry, was the only son of a hard-put but upright lobstering family in Pemaquid, Maine, and had done well. His bosses at Packard-Wells liked him, saw themselves in him, and also in him saw character qualities they'd never quite owned—blond and slender callowness tending to gullibility, but backed by caution, ingenuity and a thoroughgoing, compact toughness. He was sharp. It was his seventh year with the company—his first job. He and Marjorie had been married two years. They had no children. The car had been his bonus two Christmases ago.

When the station wagon eased to a stop, Steven sat for a minute with the motor running, the salmon-colored dash lights illuminating his face. The radio had been playing softly—the last of the news, then an interlude for French horns. Responding to no particular signal, he pressed off the radio and in the same movement switched off the ignition, which left the headlights shining on the empty, countrified road. The windows were down to attract the fresh spring air, and when the engine noise ceased the evening's ambient sounds were waiting. The peepers. A sound of thrush wings fluttering in the brush only a few yards away. The noise of something falling from a small distance and hitting an invisible water surface. Beyond the stand of saplings was the west, and through the darkened trunks, the sky was still pale yellow with the day's light, though here on Quaker Bridge Road it was nearly dark.

When Marjorie said what she had just said, she'd been looking straight ahead to where the headlights made a bright path in the dark. Perhaps she'd looked at Steven once, but having said what she'd said, she kept her hands in her lap and continued looking ahead. She was a pretty, blond, convictionless girl with small demure features—small nose, small ears, small chin, though with a surprisingly full-lipped smile which she practiced on everyone. She was fond of getting a little tipsy at parties and lowering her voice and sitting on a flowered ottoman or a burl table top with a glass of something and showing too much of her legs or inappropriate amounts of her small breasts. She had grown up in Indiana, studied art at Purdue. Steven had met her in New York at a party while she was working for a firm that did child-focused advertising for a large toymaker. He'd liked her bobbed hair, her fragile, wispy features, translucent skin and the slightly husky voice that made her seem more sophisticated than she was, but somehow convinced her she was, too. In their community, east of Hartford, the women who knew Marjorie Reeves thought of her as a bimbo who would not stay married to sweet Steven Reeves for very long. His second wife would be the right wife for him. Marjorie was just a starter.

Marjorie, however, did not think of herself that way, only that she liked men and felt happy and confident around them and assumed Steven thought this was fine and that in the long run it would help his career to have a pretty, spirited wife no one could pigeonhole. To set herself apart and to take an interest in the community she'd gone to work as a volunteer at a grieving-children's center in Hartford, which meant all black. And it was in Hartford that she'd had the chance to encounter George Nicholson and fuck him at a Red Roof Inn until they'd both gotten tired of it. It would never happen again, was her view, since in a year it hadn't happened again.

For the two or possibly five minutes now that they had sat on the side of Quaker Bridge Road in the still airish evening, with the noises of spring floating in and out of the open window, Marjorie had said nothing and Steven had also said nothing, though he realized that he was saying nothing because he was at a loss for words. A loss for words, he realized, meant that nothing that comes to mind seems very interesting to say as a next thing to what has just been said. He knew he was a callow man—a boy in some ways, still—but he was not stupid. At Bates, he had taken Dr. Sudofsky's class on Ulysses, and come away with a sense of irony and humor and the assurance that true knowledge was a spiritual process, a quest, not a storage of dry facts—a thing like freedom, which you only fully experienced in practice. He'd also played hockey, and knew that knowledge and aggressiveness were a subtle and surprising and uncommon combination. He had sought to practice both at Packard-Wells.

But for a brief and terrifying instant in the cool padded semi-darkness, just when he began experiencing his loss for words, he entered or at least nearly slipped into a softened fuguelike state in which he began to fear that he perhaps could not say another word; that something (work fatigue, shock, disappointment over what Marjorie had admitted) was at that moment causing him to detach from reality and to slide away from the present, and in fact to begin to lose his mind and go crazy to the extent that he was in jeopardy of beginning to gibber like a chimp, or just to slowly slump sideways against the upholstered door and not speak for a long, long time—months—and then only with the aid of drugs be able merely to speak in simple utterances that would seem cryptic, so that eventually he would have to be looked after by his mother's family in Damariscotta. A terrible thought.

And so to avoid that—to save his life and sanity—he abruptly just said a word, any word that he could say into the perfumed twilight inhabiting the car, where his wife was obviously anticipating his reply to her unhappy confession.

And for some reason the word—phrase, really—that he uttered was "ground clutter." Something he'd heard on the TV weather report as they were dressing for dinner.

"Hm?" Marjorie said. "What was it?" She turned her pretty, small-featured face toward him so that her pearl earrings caught light from some unknown source. She was wearing a tiny green cocktail dress and green satin shoes that showed off her incredibly thin ankles and slender, bare brown calves. She had two tiny matching green bows in her hair. She smelled sweet. "I know this wasn't what you wanted to hear, Steven," she said, "but I felt I should tell you before we got to George's. The Nicholsons', I mean. It's all over. It'll never happen again. I promise you. No one will ever mention it. I just lost my bearings last year with the move. I'm sorry." She had made a little steeple of her fingertips, as if she'd been concentrating very hard as she spoke these words. But now she put her hands again calmly in her minty green lap. She had bought her dress especially for this night at the Nicholsons'. She'd thought George would like it and Steven, too. She turned her face away and exhaled a small but detectable sigh in the car. It was then that the headlights went off automatically.

George Nicholson was a big squash-playing, thick-chested, hairy-armed Yale lawyer who sailed his own Hinckley 61 out of Essex and had started backing off from his high-priced Hartford plaintiffs' practice at fifty to devote more time to competitive racket sports and senior skiing. George was a college roommate of one of Steven's firm's senior partners and had "adopted" the Reeveses when they moved into the community following their wedding. Marjorie had volunteered Saturdays with George's wife, Patsy, at the Episcopal Thrift Shop during their first six months in Connecticut. To Steven, George Nicholson had recounted a memorable, seasoning summer spent hauling deep-water lobster traps with some tough old sea dogs out of Matinicus, Maine. Later, he'd been a Marine, and sported a faded anchor, ball and chain tattooed on his forearm. Later yet he'd fucked Steven's wife.

Having said something, even something that made no sense, Steven felt a sense of glum and deflated relief as he sat in the silent car beside Marjorie, who was still facing forward. Two thoughts had begun to compete in his reviving awareness. One was clearly occasioned by his conception of George Nicholson. He thought of George Nicholson as a gasbag, but also a forceful man who'd made his pile by letting very little stand in his way. When he thought about George he always remembered the story about Matinicus, which then put into his mind a mental picture of his own father and himself hauling traps somewhere out toward Monhegan. The reek of the bait, the toss of the ocean in late spring, the consoling monotony of the solid, tree-lined shore barely visible through the mists. Thinking through that circuitry always made him vaguely admire George Nicholson and, oddly, made him think he liked George even now, in spite of everything.

The other competing thought was that part of Marjorie's character had always been to confess upsetting things that turned out, he believed, not to be true: being a hooker for a summer up in Saugatuck; topless dancing while she was an undergraduate; heroin experimentation; taking part in armed robberies with her high-school boyfriend in Goshen, Indiana, where she was from. When she told these far-fetched stories she would grow distracted and shake her head, as though they were true. And now, while he didn't particularly think any of these stories was a bit truer, he did realize that he didn't really know his wife at all; and that in fact the entire conception of knowing another person—of trust, of closeness, of marriage itself—while not exactly a lie since it existed someplace if only as an idea (in his parents' life, at least marginally) was still completely out-of-date, defunct, was something typifying another era, now unfortunately gone. Meeting a girl, falling in love, marrying her, moving to Connecticut, buying a fucking house, starting a life with her and thinking you really knew anything about her—the last part was a complete fiction, which made all the rest a joke. Marjorie might as well have been a hooker or held up 7-Elevens and shot people, for all he really knew about her. And what was more, if he'd said any of this to her, sitting next to him thinking he would never know what, she either would not have understood a word of it or simply would've said, "Well, okay, that's fine." When people talked about the bottom line, Steven Reeves thought, they weren't talking about money, they were talking about what this meant, this kind of fatal ignorance. Money—losing it, gaining it, spending it, hoarding it—all that was only an emblem, though a good one, of what was happening here right now.

At this moment a pair of car lights rounded a curve somewhere out ahead of where the two of them sat in their station wagon. The lights found both their white faces staring forward in silence. The lights also found a raccoon just crossing the road from the reservoir shore, headed for the woods that were beside them. The car was going faster than might've been evident. The raccoon paused to peer up into the approaching beams, then continued on into the safe, opposite lane. But only then did it look up and notice Steven and Marjorie's car stopped on the verge of the road, silent in the murky evening. And because of that notice it must've decided that where it had been was much better than where it was going, and so turned to scamper back across Quaker Bridge Road toward the cool waters of the reservoir, which was what caused the car—actually it was a beat-up Ford pickup—to rumble over it, pitching and spinning it off to the side and then motionlessness near the opposite shoulder. "Yaaaa-haaaa-yipeeee!" a man's shrill voice shouted from inside the dark cab of the pickup, followed by another man's laughter.

And then it became very silent again. The raccoon lay on the road twenty yards in front of the Reeveses' car. It didn't struggle. It was merely there.

"Gross," Marjorie said.

Steven said nothing, though he felt less at a loss for words now. His eyes, indeed, felt relieved to fix on the still corpse of the raccoon.

"Do we do something?" Marjorie said. She had leaned forward a few inches as if to study the raccoon through the windshield. Light was dying away behind the slender young beech trees to the west of them.

"No," Steven said. These were his first words—except for the words he took no responsibility for—since Marjorie had said what she'd importantly said and their car was still moving toward dinner.

It was then that he hit her. He hit her before he knew he'd hit her, but not before he knew he wanted to. He hit her with the back of his open hand without even looking at her, hit her straight in the front of her face, straight in the nose. And hard. In a way, it was more a gesture than a blow, though it was, he understood, a blow. He felt the soft tip of her nose, and then the knuckly cartilage against the hard bones of the backs of his fingers. He had never hit a woman before, and he had never even thought of hitting Marjorie, always imagining he couldn't hit her when he'd read newspaper accounts of such things happening in the sad lives of others. He'd hit other people, been hit by other people, plenty of times—tough Maine boys on the ice rinks. Girls were out, though. His father always made that clear. His mother, too.

"Oh, my goodness" was all that Marjorie said when she received the blow. She put her hand over her nose immediately, but then sat silently in the car while neither of them said anything. His heart was not beating hard. The back of his hand hurt a little. This was all new ground. Steven had a small rosy birthmark just where his left sideburn ended and his shaved face began. It resembled the shape of the state of West Virginia. He thought he could feel this birthmark now. His skin tingled there.

And the truth was he felt even more relieved, and didn't feel at all sorry for Marjorie, sitting there stoically, making a little tent of her hand to cover her nose and staring ahead as if nothing had happened. He thought she would cry, certainly. She was a girl who cried—when she was unhappy, when he said something insensitive, when she was approaching her period. Crying was natural. Clearly, though, it was a new experience for her to be hit. And so it called upon something new, and if not new then some strength, resilience, self-mastery normally reserved for other experiences.

"I can't go to the Nicholsons' now," Marjorie said almost patiently. She removed her hand and viewed her palm as if her palm had her nose in it. Of course it was blood she was thinking about. He heard her breathe in through what sounded like a congested nose, then the breath was completed out through her mouth. She was not crying yet. And for that moment he felt not even sure he had smacked her—if it hadn't just been a thought he'd entertained, a gesture somehow uncommissioned.

What he wanted to do, however, was skip to the most important things now, not get mired down in wrong, extraneous details. Because he didn't give a shit about George Nicholson or the particulars of what they'd done in some shitty motel. Marjorie would never leave him for George Nicholson or anyone like George Nicholson, and George Nicholson and men like him—high rollers with Hinckleys—didn't throw it all away for unimportant little women like Marjorie. He thought of her nose, red, swollen, smeared with sticky blood dripping onto her green dress. He didn't suppose it could be broken. Noses held up. And, of course, there was a phone in the car. He could simply make a call to the party. He pictured the Nicholsons' great rambling white-shingled house brightly lit beyond the curving drive, the original elms exorbitantly preserved, the footlights, the low-lit clay court where they'd all played, the heated pool, the Henry Moore out on the darkened lawn where you just stumbled onto it. He imagined saying to someone—not George Nicholson—that Marjorie was ill, had thrown up on the side of the road.

The right details, though. The right details to ascertain from her were: Are you sorry? (he'd forgotten Marjorie had already said she was sorry) and What does this mean for the future? These were the details that mattered.

Surprisingly, the raccoon that had been cartwheeled by the pickup and then lain motionless, a blob in the near darkness, had come back to life and was now trying to drag itself and its useless hinder parts off of Quaker Bridge Road and onto the grassy verge and into the underbrush that bordered the reservoir.

"Oh, for God's sake," Marjorie said, and put her hand over her damaged nose again. She could see the raccoon's struggle and turned her head away.

"Aren't you even sorry?" Steven said.

"Yes," Marjorie said, her nose still covered as if she wasn't thinking about the fact that she was covering it. Probably, he thought, the pain had gone away some. It hadn't been so bad. "I mean no," she said.

He wanted to hit her again then—this time in the ear—but he didn't. He wasn't sure why not. No one would ever know. "Well, which is it?" he said, and felt for the first time completely furious. The thing that made him furious—all his life, the very maddest—was to be put into a situation in which everything he did was wrong, when right was no longer an option. Now felt like one of those situations. "Which is it?" he said again angrily. "Really." He should just take her to the Nicholsons', he thought, swollen nose, bloody lips, all stoppered up, and let her deal with it. Or let her sit out in the car, or else start walking the 11.6 miles home. Maybe George could come out and drive her in his Rover. These were only thoughts, of course. "Which is it?" he said for the third time. He was stuck on these words, on this bit of barren curiosity.

"I was sorry when I told you," Marjorie said, very composed. She lowered her hand from her nose to her lap. One of the little green bows that had been in her hair was now resting on her bare shoulder. "Though not very sorry," she said. "Only sorry because I had to tell you. And now that I've told you and you've hit me in my face and probably broken my nose, I'm not sorry about anything—except that. Though I'm sorry about being married to you, which I'll remedy as soon as I can." She was still not crying. "So now, will you as a gesture of whatever good there is in you, get out and go over and do something to help that poor injured creature that those motherfucking rednecks maimed with their motherfucking pickup truck and then because they're pieces of shit and low forms of degraded humanity, laughed about? Can you do that, Steven? Is that in your range?" She sniffed back hard through her nose, then expelled a short, deep and defeated moan. Her voice seemed more nasal, more midwestern even, now that her nose was congested.

"I'm sorry I hit you," Steven Reeves said, and opened the car door onto the silent road.

"I know," Marjorie said in an emotionless voice. "And you'll be sorrier."

When he had walked down the empty macadam road in his tan suit to where the raccoon had been struck then bounced over onto the road's edge, there was nothing now there. Only a small circle of dark blood he could just make out on the nubbly road surface and that might've been an oil smudge. No raccoon. The raccoon with its last reserves of savage, unthinking will had found the strength to pull itself off into the bushes to die. Steven peered down into the dark, stalky confinement of scrubs and bramble that separated the road from the reservoir. It was very still there. He thought he heard a rustling in the low brush where a creature might be, getting itself settled into the soft grass and damp earth to go to sleep forever. Someplace out on the lake he heard a young girl's voice, very distinctly laughing. Then a car door closed farther away. Then another sort of door, a screen door, slapped shut. And then a man's voice saying "Oh no, oh-ho-ho-ho-ho, no." A small white light came on farther back in the trees beyond the reservoir, where he hadn't imagined there was a house. He wondered about how long it would be before his angry feelings stopped mattering to him. He considered briefly why Marjorie would admit this to him now. It seemed so odd.

Then he heard his own car start. The muffled-metal diesel racket of the Mercedes. The headlights came smartly on and disclosed him. Music was instantly loud inside. He turned just in time to see Marjorie's pretty face illuminated, as his own had been, by the salmon dashboard light. He saw the tips of her fingers atop the arc of the steering wheel, heard the surge of the engine. In the woods he noticed a strange glow coming through the trees, something yellow, something out of the low wet earth, a mist, a vapor, something that might be magical. The air smelled sweet now. The peepers stopped peeping. And then that was all.

Barry Hannah (1942–)

was born in Clinton, Mississippi, and grew up wanting to be "the white Miles Davis, which God did not allow," he told an interviewer. "I had only adequate talent and that hurt more than having no talent. I was in the Jackson Symphony and a decent jazz player, but there are thousands of those." He started Mississippi College as a premed major but finished it wanting to be a writer and went on to get an MFA from the University of Arkansas. Hannah's first novel, Geronimo Rex, *won the William Faulkner Prize and was nominated for the National Book Award. His first collection of short stories,* Airships, *won the Arnold Gingrich Short Fiction Award, and in 2003, he won the PEN/Malamud Award for excellence in short fiction. His other novels include* Ray, Never Die, *and, most recently,* Yonder Stands Your Orphan. *His collections of short fiction include* Captain Maximus, Bats Out of Hell, *and* High Lonesome. *He has written screenplays for the director Robert Altman and taught creative writing at Clemson University, Middlebury College, the University of Iowa, and the University of Montana. He is currently writer-in-residence at the University of Mississippi. Called "the best fiction writer to appear in the South since Flannery O'Connor" by Larry McMurtry, Hannah describes his writing with characteristic humility: "You read a bunch of books, you go to church, play jazz, and it all comes together in a way that you hope is fresh."*

INTRODUCTION BY **Tom Franklin**

When I first read Barry Hannah's writing, it was too strong for me. I'd been into a lot of Stephen King in those days. The science fiction writer Harlan Ellison, too. Myself, I was twenty-three years old and writing stories about assassins out to kill Santa Claus. Cops that enforced the law of averages. Then an editor at a magazine said "Barry" and "Hannah" to me in the same sentence. Said, "Get *Airships.*"

I got it.

I read "Water Liars."

I put down the book. What had I just read?

I picked it back up and read the next story, "Love Too Long." There were two sentences in that one, referring to the narrator's ex-wife, that said, "I want to rip her arm off. I want to sleep in her uterus with my foot hanging out."

There. That was it. Those two sentences (a) seemed too raw, too outrageous, and (b) were juxtaposed against one another in such a strange, new way that it made me uncomfortable. Or something. It was a sensation I couldn't define then, so I put the book away for a while. Stephen King would never do that. Ellison either. I returned to them.

Sometime later, I read an interview with King in which he said that his novels and stories were the literary equivalent of a Big Mac and fries, which got me to thinking I needed a better reading diet. So I tried the old stuff they thrust on you in college: Defoe and Melville, Twain, Jane Austen, Faulkner and Hemingway. Though I didn't always understand it—or felt like I might be missing something—this grand old Lit was okay. Then I updated. Updike, Heller, Vonnegut, Alice Walker. All good. At some point, I arrived at Raymond Carver. What short, simple sentences. How easy, it seemed, to imitate. I read all the

Carver I could find, including an interview in which he named who he was reading. There were the words "Barry" and "Hannah" again. So I found *Airships,* dusty on my shelf. I read it again. This time I *got* it.

Barry Hannah, I realized, isn't interested in anything I'd seen or heard in fiction before. In a world full of beginning-middle-end stories, stories that go by the rules, Hannah serves up something else. No generic epiphanies here. If there's a narrative arc in a Hannah story, it's a shape you've never seen before. What he does is nail down character and experience by using words in ways that revitalize them. Nobody can un-rug you the way he can. Nobody can stab you so precisely in the heart with a noun. "I want to rip her arm off. I want to sleep in her uterus with my foot hanging out." That first sentence is like a perfect set in a volleyball game, clear and precise. But the next sentence is the spike, a line only Hannah could invent. "I want to sleep in her uterus" is pretty damn good in itself. The word "uterus" there is odd and unexpected; plenty of other (far less interesting) synonyms would work, but Hannah is the master of finding the perfect word, the odd choice only his view of the world can reveal. After "uterus" he slams it home: ". . . with my foot hanging out." Which closes off the idea with a startling image. Those two lines get right at the heart of busted, corrupt love, the point in life that this narrator and many of Hannah's characters find themselves.

The first thing to notice about the trio of stories in this anthology is that they're all told from the first person point of view. The writer William Harrison (Barry Hannah's teacher—and mine—at the University of Arkansas) says that a writer should use first person only as a last resort, when that "I" demands to be heard, when you can't write the story any other way. Why? Because there are inherent complications with this point of view. For one thing, the narrator may be unreliable. He or she may not have all the facts, may be naive, mentally unbalanced, on drugs, and so on. In other words, a reader now has to consider the possibility of irony. Unlike third person, in which the reader can generally accept the narration as straightforward, first person gives the writer a whole new range of possibilities; in addition to the tale being told, there's now the way it's told, the voice that delivers it.

"Water Liars" is so short that it's almost all voice; the plot is simple: A man fleeing his problems and jealousies goes on vacation and finds a kindred spirit. But you don't read Hannah for plot. Note how he doesn't spend the time or space to flesh out every detail. Instead, he chooses the one perfect, painterly image that lets the reader fill in the blanks (the old liars with "coats full of bran cookies"; the man you'd know was on vacation only because he'd "removed his tie"). What replaces fastidiously built scene and typical character development is an in-your-face narrator dripping with attitude, working on his own terms ("My vacation . . . wasn't like that easy little bit you get as a rich New Yorker"). "Testimony of Pilot" rebels against convention, too, and gives the narrator's entire history with the strange Quadberry. That the pilot dies, with little fanfare, in the story's final four lines leaves you ringing and as deaf-feeling as the story's narrator.

"Water Liars" and "Testimony of Pilot" are from Hannah's first collection, *Airships* (1978). "Nicodemus Bluff" is a later story, from *Bats Out of Hell* (1993). It is jammed with strangeness: an almost biblical rainstorm; several bizarre, philosophical male characters you don't really even worry about telling apart; an epic chess match during which the narrator's father becomes "inhabited" by the spirit of a "crafty, clever" woman—all bookended by the narrator's confession that the event he's telling about caused his father's suicide and his, the narrator's, decline into years of drug abuse. This story is, like many of Hannah's other later ones, much more dense and layered than "Water Liars" and "Testimony of Pilot." But like them, it seems to invent itself as it goes, its voice urging itself on with its own fierce telling, flying in the face of convention, surging with a raw, hard beauty.

Each of Barry Hannah's voices demands to be heard. His stories are like no other stories, his world like no other world.

Tom Franklin, recipient of a 2001 Guggenheim Fellowship, is the author of Poachers, *a book of stories, and* Hell at the Breech, *a novel, both published by William Morrow. He teaches at the University of Mississippi.*

Barry Hannah

Testimony of Pilot

When I was ten, eleven and twelve, I did a good bit of my play in the backyard of a three-story wooden house my father had bought and rented out, his first venture into real estate. We lived right across the street from it, but over here was the place to do your real play. Here there was a harrowed but overgrown garden, a vine-swallowed fence at the back end, and beyond the fence a cornfield which belonged to someone else. This was not the country. This was the town, Clinton, Mississippi, between Jackson on the east and Vicksburg on the west. On this lot stood a few water oaks, a few plum bushes, and much overgrowth of honeysuckle vine. At the very back end, at the fence, stood three strong nude chinaberry trees.

In Mississippi it is difficult to achieve a vista. But my friends and I had one here at the back corner of the garden. We could see across the cornfield, see the one lone tin-roofed house this side of the railroad tracks, then on across the tracks many other bleaker houses with rustier tin roofs, smoke coming out of the chimneys in the late fall. This was niggertown. We had binoculars and could see the colored children hustling about and perhaps a hopeless sow or two with her brood enclosed in a tiny boarded-up area. Through the binoculars one afternoon in October we watched some men corner and beat a large hog on the brain. They used an ax and the thing kept running around, head leaning toward the ground, for several minutes before it lay down. I thought I saw the men laughing when it finally did. One of them was staggering, plainly drunk to my sight from three hundred yards away. He had the long knife. Because of that scene I considered Negroes savage cowards for a good five more years of my life. Our maid brought some sausage to my mother and when it was put in the pan to fry, I made a point of running out of the house.

I went directly across the street and to the back end of the garden behind the apartment house we owned, without my breakfast. That was Saturday. Eventually, Radcleve saw me. His parents had him mowing the yard that ran alongside my dad's property. He clicked off the power mower and I went over to his fence, which was storm wire. His mother maintained handsome flowery grounds at all costs; she had a leaf-mold bin and St Augustine grass as solid as a rug.

Radcleve himself was a violent experimental chemist. When Radcleve was eight, he threw a whole package of .22 shells against the sidewalk in front of his house until one of them went off, driving lead fragments into his calf, most of them still deep in there where the surgeons never dared tamper. Radcleve knew about the sulfur, potassium nitrate and charcoal mixture for gunpowder when he was ten. He bought things through the mail when he ran out of ingredients in his chemistry sets. When he was an infant, his father, a quiet man who owned the Chevrolet agency in town, bought an entire bankrupt sporting-goods store, and in the middle of their backyard he built a house, plain-painted and neat, one room and a heater, where Radcleve's redundant toys forevermore were kept—all the possible toys he would need for boyhood. There were things in there that Radcleve and I were not mature enough for and did not know the real use of. When we were eleven, we uncrated the new Dunlop golf balls and went on up a shelf for the tennis rackets, went out in the middle of his yard, and served new golf ball after new golf ball with blasts of the rackets over into the cornfield, out of sight. When the strings busted we just went in and got another racket. We were absorbed by how a good smack would set the heavy little pills on an endless flight. Then Radcleve's father came down. He simply dismissed me. He took Radcleve into the house and covered his whole body with a belt. But within the week Radcleve had invented the mortar. It was a steel pipe into which a flashlight battery fit perfectly, like a bullet into a muzzle. He had drilled a hole for the fuse of an M-80 firecracker at the base, for the charge. It was a grand cannon, set up on a stack of bricks at the back of my dad's property, which was the free place to play. When it shot, it would back up violently with thick smoke and you could hear the flashlight battery whistling off. So that morning when I ran out of the house protesting the hog sausage, I told Radcleve to bring over the mortar. His ma and dad were in Jackson for the day, and he came right over with the pipe, the batteries and the M-80 explosives. He had two gross of them.

Before, we'd shot off toward the woods to the right of niggertown. I turned the bricks to the left; I made us a very fine cannon carriage pointing toward niggertown. When Radcleve appeared, he had two pairs of binoculars around his neck, one pair a newly plundered German unit as big as a brace of whiskey bottles. I told him I wanted to shoot for that house where we saw them killing the pig. Radcleve loved the idea. We singled out the house with heavy use of the binoculars.

There were children in the yard. Then they all went in. Two men came out of the back door. I thought I recognized the drunkard from the other afternoon. I helped Radcleve fix the direction of the cannon. We estimated the altitude we needed to get down there. Radcleve put the M-80 in the breech with its fuse standing out of the hole. I dropped the flashlight battery in. I lit the fuse. We backed off. The M-80 blasted off deafeningly, smoke rose, but my concentration was on that particular house over there. I brought the binoculars up. We waited six or seven seconds. I heard a great joyful wallop on tin. "We've hit him on the first try, the first try!" I yelled. Radcleve was ecstatic. "Right on his roof!" We bolstered up the brick carriage. Radcleve remembered the correct height of the cannon exactly. So we fixed it, loaded it, lit it and backed off. The battery landed on the roof, blat, again, louder. I looked to see if there wasn't a great dent or hole in the roof. I could not understand why niggers weren't pouring out distraught from that house: We shot the mortar again and again and always our battery hit the tin roof. Sometimes there was only a dull thud, but, other times there was a wild distress of tin. I was still looking through the binoculars, amazed that the niggers wouldn't even come out of their house to see what was hitting their roof. Radcleve was on to it better than me. I looked over at him and he had the huge German binocs much lower than I did. He was looking straight through the cornfield, which was all bare and open, with nothing left but rotten stalks. "What we've been hitting is the roof of that house just this side of the tracks. White people live in there," he said.

I took up my binoculars again. I looked around the yard of that white wooden house on this side of the tracks, almost next to the railroad. When I found the tin roof, I saw four significant dents in it. I saw one of our batteries lying in the middle of a sort of crater. I took the binoculars down into the yard and saw a blond middle-aged woman looking our way.

"Somebody's coming up toward us. He's from that house and he's got, I think, some sort of fancy gun with him. It might be an automatic weapon."

I ran my binoculars all over the cornfield. Then, in a line with the house, I saw him. He was coming our way but having some trouble with the rows and dead stalks of the cornfield.

"That is just a boy like us. All he's got is a saxophone with him," I told Radcleve. I had recently got in the school band, playing drums, and had seen all the weird horns that made up a band.

I watched this boy with the saxophone through the binoculars until he was ten feet from us. This was Quadberry. His name was Ard, short for Arden. His shoes were foot-square wads of mud from the cornfield. When he saw us across the fence and above him, he stuck out his arm in my direction.

"My dad says stop it!"

"We weren't doing anything," says Radcleve.

"Mother saw the smoke puff up from here. Dad has a hangover."

"A what?"

"It's a headache from indiscretion. You're lucky he does. He's picked up the poker to rap on you, but he can't move further the way his head is."

"What's your name? You're not in the band," I said, focusing on the saxophone.

"It's Ard Quadberry. Why do you keep looking at me through the binoculars?"

It was because he was odd, with his hair and its white ends, and his Arab nose, and now his name. Add to that the saxophone.

"My dad's a doctor at the college. Mother's a musician. You better quit what you're doing . . . I was out practicing in the garage. I saw one of those flashlight batteries roll off the roof. Could I see what you shoot 'em with?"

"No," said Radcleve. Then he said: "If you'll play that horn."

Quadberry stood out there ten feet below us in the field, skinny, feet and pants booted with black mud, and at his chest the slung-on, very complex, radiant horn.

Quadberry began sucking and licking the reed. I didn't care much for this act, and there was too much desperate oralness in his face when he began playing. That was why I chose the drums. One had to engage himself like suck's revenge with a horn. But what Quadberry was playing was pleasant and intricate. I was sure it was advanced, and there was no squawking, as from the other eleven-year-olds on sax in the band room. He made the end with a clean upward riff, holding the final note high, pure and unwavering.

"Good!" I called to him.

Quadberry was trying to move out of the sunken row toward us, but his heavy shoes were impeding him.

"Sounded like a duck. Sounded like a girl duck," said Radcleve, who was kneeling down and packing a mudball around one of the M-80s. I saw and I was an accomplice, because I did nothing. Radcleve lit the fuse and heaved the mudball over the fence. An M-80 is a very serious firecracker; it is like the charge they use to shoot up those sprays six hundred feet on July Fourth at country clubs. It went off, this one, even bigger than most M-80s.

When we looked over the fence, we saw Quadberry all muck specks and fragments of stalks. He was covering the mouthpiece of his horn with both hands. Then I saw there was blood pouring out of, it seemed, his right eye. I thought he was bleeding directly out of his eye.

"Quadberry?" I called.

He turned around and never said a word to me until I was eighteen. He walked back holding his eye and staggering through the cornstalks. Radcleve had him in the binoculars. Radcleve was trembling . . . but intrigued.

"His mother just screamed. She's running out in the field to get him."

I thought we'd blinded him, but we hadn't. I thought the Quadberrys would get the police or call my father, but they didn't. The upshot of this is that Quadberry had a permanent white space next to his right eye, a spot that looked like a tiny upset crown.

I went from sixth through half of twelfth grade ignoring him and that wound. I was coming on as a drummer and a lover, but if Quadberry happened to appear within fifty feet of me and my most tender, intimate sweetheart, I would duck out. Quadberry grew up just like the rest of us. His father was still a doctor—professor of history—at the town college; his mother was still blond, and a musician. She was organist at an Episcopalian church in Jackson, the big capital city ten miles east of us.

As for Radcleve, he still had no ear for music but he was there, my buddy. He was repentant about Quadberry, although not so much as I. He'd thrown the mud grenade over the fence only to see what would happen. He had not really wanted to maim. Quadberry had played his tune on the sax, Radcleve had played his tune on the mud grenade. It was just a shame they happened to cross talents.

Radcleve went into a long period of nearly nothing after he gave up violent explosives. Then he trained himself to copy the comic strips, *Steve Canyon to Major Hoople,* until he became quite a versatile cartoonist with some very provocative new faces and bodies that were gesturing intriguingly. He could never fill in the speech balloons with the smart words they needed. Sometimes he would pencil in 'Err' or 'What?' in the empty speech places. I saw him a great deal. Radcleve was not spooked by Quadberry. He even once asked Quadberry what his opinion was of his future as a cartoonist. Quadberry told Radcleve that if he took all his cartoons and stuffed himself with them, he would make an interesting dead man. After that, Radcleve was shy of him too.

When I was a senior we had an extraordinary band. Word was we had outplayed all the big A.A.A. division bands last April in the state contest. Then came news that a new blazing saxophone player was coming into the band as first chair. This person had spent summers in Vermont in music camps, and he was coming in with us for the concert season. Our director, a lovable aesthete named Richard Prender, announced to us in a proud silent moment that the boy was joining us tomorrow night. The effect was that everybody should push over a seat or two and make room for this boy and his talent. I was annoyed. Here I'd been with the band and had kept hold of the taste among the whole percussion section. I could play rock and jazz drum and didn't even really need to be here. I could be in Vermont too, give me a piano and a bass. I looked at the kid on first sax, who was going to be supplanted tomorrow. For two years he had thought he was the star, then suddenly enters this boy who's three times better.

The new boy was Quadberry. He came in, but he was meek, and when he tuned up he put his head almost on the floor, bending over trying to be inconspicuous. The girls in the band had wanted him to be handsome, but Quadberry refused and kept himself in such hiding among the sax section that he was neither handsome, ugly, cute or anything. What he was was pretty near invisible, except for the bell of his horn, the all-but-closed eyes, the Arabian nose, the brown hair with its halo of white ends, the desperate oralness, the giant reed punched into his face, and hazy Quadberry, loving the wound in a private dignified ecstasy.

I say dignified because of what came out of the end of his horn. He was more than what Prender had told us he would be. Because of Quadberry, we could take the band arrangement of Ravel's *Bolero* with us to the state contest. Quadberry would do the saxophone solo. He would switch to alto sax, he would do the sly Moorish ride. When he played, I heard the sweetness, I heard the horn which finally brought human talk into the realm of music. It could sound like the mutterings of a field nigger, and then it could get up into inhumanly careless beauty, it could get among mutinous helium bursts around Saturn. I already loved *Bolero* for the constant drum part. The percussion was always there, driving along with the subtly increasing triplets, insistent, insistent, at last outraged and trying to steal the whole show from the horns and the others. I knew a large boy with dirty blond hair, name of Wyatt, who played viola in the Jackson Symphony and sousaphone in our band—one of the rare closet transmutations of my time—who was forever claiming to have discovered the central *Bolero* one Sunday afternoon over FM radio as he had seven distinct sexual moments with a certain B., girl flutist with black bangs and skin like mayonnaise, while the drums of Ravel carried them on and on in a ceremony of Spanish sex. It was agreed by all the canny in the band that *Bolero* was exactly the piece to make the band soar—now especially as we had Quadberry, who made his walk into the piece like an actual lean Spanish bandit. This boy could blow his horn. He was, as I had suspected, a genius. His solo was not quite the same as the New York Phil's saxophonist's, but it was better. It came in and was with us. It entered my spine and, I am sure, went up the skirts of the girls. I had almost deafened myself playing drums in the most famous rock and jazz band in the state, but I could hear the voice that went through and out that horn. It sounded like a very troubled forty-year-old man, a man who had had his brow in his hands a long time.

The next time I saw Quadberry up close, in fact the first time I had seen him up close since we were eleven and he was bleeding in the cornfield, was in late February. I had only three classes this last semester, and went up to the band room often, to loaf and complain and keep up my touch on the drums. Prender let me keep my set in one of the instrument rooms, with a tarpaulin thrown over it, and I would drag it out to the practice room and whale away. Sometimes a group of sophomores would come up and I would make them marvel, whaling away as if not only deaf but blind to them, although I wasn't at all. If I saw a sophomore girl with exceptional bod or face, I would do miracles of technique I never knew were in me. I would amaze myself. I would be threatening Buddy Rich and Sam Morello. But this time when I went into the instrument room, there was Quadberry on one side, and, back in a dark corner, a small ninth-grade euphonium player whose face was all red. The little boy was weeping and grinning at the same time.

"Queerberry," the boy said softly.

Quadberry flew upon him like a demon. He grabbed the boy's collar, slapped his face, and yanked his arm behind him in a merciless wrestler's grip, the one that made them bawl on TV. Then the boy broke it and slugged Quadberry in the lips and ran across to my side of the room. He said 'Queerberry' softly again and jumped for the door. Quadberry plunged across the room and tackled him on the threshold. Now that the boy was under him, Quadberry pounded the top of his head with his fist made like a mallet. The boy kept calling him 'Queerberry' throughout this. He had not learned his lesson. The boy seemed to be going into concussion, so I stepped over and touched Quadberry, telling him to quit. Quadberry obeyed and stood up off the boy, who crawled on out into the band room. But once more the boy looked back with a bruised grin, saying 'Queerberry.' Quadberry made a move toward him, but I blocked it.

"Why are you beating up on this little guy?" I said. Quadberry was sweating and his eyes were wild with hate; he was a big fellow now, though lean. He was, at six feet tall, bigger than me.

"He kept calling me Queerberry."

"What do you care?" I asked.

"I care," Quadberry said, and left me standing there.

We were to play at Millsaps College Auditorium for the concert. It was April. We got on the buses, a few took their cars, and were a big tense crowd getting over there. To Jackson was only a twenty-minute trip. The director, Prender, followed the bus in his Volkswagen. There was a thick fog. A flashing ambulance, snaking the lanes, piled into him head on. Prender, who I would imagine was thinking of *Bolero* and hearing the young horn voices in his band—perhaps he was dwelling on Quadberry's spectacular gypsy entrance, or perhaps he was meditating on the percussion section, of which I was the king—passed into the airs of band-director heaven. We were told by the student director as we set up on the stage. The student director was a senior from the town college, very much afflicted, almost to the point of drooling, by a love and respect for Dick Prender, and now afflicted by a heartbreaking esteem for his ghost. As were we all.

I loved the tough and tender director awesomely and never knew it until I found myself bawling along with all the rest of the boys of the percussion. I told them to keep setting up, keep tuning, keep screwing the stands together, keep hauling in the kettledrums. To just quit and bawl seemed a betrayal to Prender. I caught some girl clarinetists trying to flee the stage and go have their cry. I told them to get the hell back to their section. They obeyed me. Then I found the student director. I had to have my say.

"Look. I say we just play *Bolero* and junk the rest. That's our horse. We can't play *Brighton Beach* and *Neptune's Daughter.* We'll never make it through them. And they're too happy."

"We aren't going to play anything," he said. "Man, to play is filthy. Did you ever hear Prender play piano? Do you know what a cool man he was in all things?"

"We play. He got us ready, and we play."

"Man, you can't play any more than I can direct. You're bawling your face off. Look out there at the rest of them. Man, it's a herd, it's a weeping herd."

"What's wrong? Why aren't you pulling this crowd together?" This was Quadberry, who had come up urgently. "I got those little brats in my section sitting down, but we've got people abandoning the stage, tearful little finks throwing their horns on the floor."

"I'm not directing," said the mustached college man.

"Then get out of here. You're weak, weak!"

"Man, we've got teenagers in ruin here, we got sorrowville. Nobody can—"

"Go ahead. Do your number. Weak out on us."

"Man, I—"

Quadberry was already up on the podium, shaking his arms.

"We're right here! The band is right here! Tell your friends to get back in their seats. We're doing *Bolero.* Just put *Bolero* up and start tuning. *I'm* directing. I'll be right here in front of you. You look at *me!* Don't you dare quit on Prender. Don't you dare quit on me. You've got to be heard. *I've* got to be heard. Prender wanted me to be heard. I am the star, and I say we sit down and blow."

And so we did. We all tuned and were burning low for the advent into *Bolero,* though we couldn't believe that Quadberry was going to remain with his saxophone strapped to him and conduct us as well as play his solo. The judges, who apparently hadn't heard about Prender's death, walked down to their balcony desks.

One of them called out "Ready" and Quadberry's hand was instantly up in the air, his fingers hard as if around the stem of something like a torch. This was not Prender's way, but it had to do. We went into the number cleanly and Quadberry one-armed it in the conducting. He kept his face, this look of hostility, at the reeds and the trumpets. I was glad he did not look toward me and the percussion boys like that. But he must have known we would be constant and tasteful because I was the king there. As for the others, the soloists especially, he was scaring them into excellence. Prender had never got quite this from them. Boys became men and girls became women as Quadberry directed us through Bolero. I even became a bit better of a man myself; though Quadberry did not look my way. When he turned around toward the people in the auditorium to enter on his solo, I knew it was my baby. I and the drums were the metronome. That was no trouble. It was talent to keep the metronome ticking amidst any given chaos of sound.

But this keeps one's mind occupied and I have no idea what Quadberry sounded like on his sax ride. All I know is that he looked grief-stricken and pale, and small. Sweat had popped out on his forehead. He bent over extremely. He was wearing the red brass-button jacket and black pants, black bow tie at the throat, just like the rest of us. In this outfit he bent over his horn almost out of sight. For a moment, before I caught the glint of his horn through the music stands, I thought he had pitched forward off the stage. He went down so far to do his deep oral thing, his conducting arm had disappeared so quickly, I didn't know but what he was having a seizure.

When *Bolero* was over, the audience stood up and made meat out of their hands applauding. The judges themselves applauded. The band stood up, bawling again, for Prender and because we had done so well. The student director rushed out crying to embrace Quadberry, who eluded him with his dipping shoulders. The crowd was still clapping insanely. I wanted to see Quadberry myself. I waded through the red backs, through the bow ties, over the white bucks. Here was the first-chair clarinetist; who had done his bit like an angel; he sat close to the podium and could hear Quadberry.

"Was Quadberry good?" I asked him.

"Are you kidding? These tears in my eyes, they're for how good he was. He was too good. I'll never touch my clarinet again." The clarinetist slung the pieces of his horn into their case like underwear and a toothbrush.

I found Quadberry fitting the sections of his alto in the velvet holds of his case.

"Hooray," I said. "Hip damn hooray for you."

Arden was smiling too, showing a lot of teeth I had never seen. His smile was sly. He knew he had pulled off a monster unlikelihood.

"Hip hip hooray for me," he said. "Look at her. I had the bell of the horn almost smack in her face."

There was a woman of about thirty sitting in the front row of the auditorium. She wore a sundress with a drastic cleavage-up front; looked like something that hung around New Orleans and kneaded your heart to death with her feet. She was still mesmerized by Quadberry. She bore on him with a stare and there was moisture in her cleavage.

"You played well."

"Well? Play well? Yes."

He was trying not to look at her directly. Look at *me,* I beckoned to her with full face: I was the *drums.* She arose and left.

"I was walking downhill in a valley, is all I was doing," said Quadberry. "Another man, a wizard, was playing my horn." He locked his sax case. "I feel nasty for not being able to cry like the rest of them. Look at them. Look at them crying."

True, the children of the band were still weeping, standing around the stage. Several moms and dads had come up among them, and they were misty-eyed too. The mixture of grief and superb music had been unbearable.

A girl in tears appeared next to Quadberry. She was a majorette in football season and played third-chair sax during the concert season. Not even her violent sorrow could take the beauty out of the face of this girl. I had watched her for a number of years—her alertness to her own beauty, the pride of her legs in the majorette outfit—and had taken out her younger sister, a second-rate version of her and a wayward overcompensating nymphomaniac whom several of us made a hobby out of pitying. Well, here was Lilian herself crying in Quadberry's face. She told him that she'd run off the stage when she heard about Prender, dropped her horn and everything, and had thrown herself into a tavern across the street and drunk two beers quickly for some kind of relief. But she had come back through the front doors of the auditorium and sat down, dizzy with beer, and seen Quadberry, the miraculous way he had gone on with Bolero. And now she was eaten up by feelings of guilt, weakness, cowardice.

"We didn't miss you," said Quadberry.

"Please forgive me. Tell me to do something to make up for it."

"Don't breathe my way, then. You've got beer all over your breath."

"I want to talk to you."

"Take my horn case and go out, get in my car, and wait for me. It's the ugly Plymouth in front of the school bus."

"I know," she said.

Lilian Field, this lovely teary thing, with the rather pious grace of her carriage, with the voice full of imminent swoon, picked up Quadberry's horn case and her own and walked off the stage.

I told the percussion boys to wrap up the packing. Into my suitcase I put my own gear and also managed to steal drum keys, two pairs of brushes, a twenty-inch Turkish cymbal, a Gretsch snare drum that I desired for my collection, a wood block, kettledrum mallets, a tuning harp and a score sheet of *Bolero* full of marginal notes I'd written down straight from the mouth of Dick Prender, thinking I might want to look at the score sheet sometime in the future when I was having a fit of nostalgia such as I am having right now as I write this. I had never done any serious stealing before, and I was stealing for my art. Prender was dead, the band had done its last thing of the year, I was a senior. Things were finished at the high school. I was just looting a sinking ship. I could hardly lift the suitcase. As I was pushing it across the stage, Quadberry was there again.

"You can ride back with me if you want to."

"But you've got Lilian."

"Please ride back with me . . . us. Please."

"Why?"

"To help me get rid of her. Her breath is full of beer. My father always had that breath. Every time he was friendly, he had that breath. And she looks a great deal like my mother." We were interrupted by the Tupelo band director. He put his baton against Quadberry's arm.

"You were big with *Bolero,* son, but that doesn't mean you own the stage."

Quadberry caught the end of the suitcase and helped me with it out to the steps behind the auditorium. The buses were gone. There sat his ugly ocher Plymouth; it was a failed, gay, experimental shade from the Chrysler people. Lilian was sitting in the front wearing her shirt and bow tie, her coat off.

"Are you going to ride back with me?" Quadberry said to me.

"I think I would spoil something. You never saw her when she was a majorette. She's not stupid, either. She likes to show off a little, but she's not stupid. She's in the History Club."

"My father has a doctorate in history. She smells of beer."

I said, "She drank two cans of beer when she heard about Prender."

"There are a lot of other things to do when you hear about death. What I did, for example. She ran away. She fell to pieces."

"She's waiting for us," I said.

"One damned thing I am never going to do is drink."

"I've never seen your mother up close, but Lilian doesn't look like your mother. She doesn't look like anybody's mother."

I rode with them silently to Clinton. Lilian made no bones about being disappointed I was in the car, though she said nothing. I knew it would be like this and I hated it. Other girls in town would not be so unhappy that I was in the car with them. I looked for flaws in Lilian's face and neck and hair, but there weren't any. Couldn't there be a mole, an enlarged pore, too much gum on a tooth, a single awkward hair around the ear? No. Memory, the whole lying opera of it, is killing me now. Lilian was faultless beauty, even sweating, even and especially in the white man's shirt and the bow tie clamping together her collar, when one knew her uncomfortable bosoms, her poor nipples. . . .

"Don't take me back to the band room. Turn off here and let me off at my house," I said to Quadberry. He didn't turn off.

"Don't tell Arden what to do. He can do what he wants to," said Lilian, ignoring me and speaking to me at the same time. I couldn't bear her hatred. I asked Quadberry to please just stop the car and let me out here, wherever he was: this front yard of the mobile home would do. I was so earnest that he stopped the car. He handed back the keys and I dragged my suitcase out of the trunk, then flung the keys back at him and kicked the car to get it going again.

★ ★ ★

My band came together in the summer. We were the Bop Fiends . . . that was our name. Two of them were from Ole Miss, our bass player was from Memphis State, but when we got together this time, I didn't call the tenor sax, who went to Mississippi Southern, because Quadberry wanted to play with us. During the school year the college boys and I fell into minor groups to pick up twenty dollars on a weekend, playing dances for the Moose Lodge, medical-student fraternities in Jackson, teenage recreation centers in Greenwood, and such as that: But come summer we were the Bop Fiends again, and the price for us went up to $1,200 a gig. Where they wanted the best rock and bop and they had some bread, we were called. The summer after I was a senior, we played in Alabama, Louisiana and Arkansas. Our fame was getting out there on the interstate route.

This was the summer that I made myself deaf.

Years ago Prender had invited down an old friend from a high school in Michigan. He asked me over to meet the friend, who had been a drummer with Stan Kenton at one time and was now a band director just like Prender. This fellow was almost totally deaf and he warned me very sincerely about deafing myself. He said there would come a point when you had to lean over and concentrate all your hearing on what the band was doing and that was the time to quit for a while, because if you didn't you would be irrevocably deaf like him in a month or two. I listened to him but could not take him seriously. Here was an oldish man who had his problems. My ears had ages of hearing left. Not so. I played the drums so loud the summer after I graduated from high school that I made myself, eventually, stone deaf.

We were at, say, the National Guard Armory in Lake Village, Arkansas, Quadberry out in front of us on the stage they'd built: Down on the floor were hundreds of sweaty teenagers. Four girls in sundresses, showing what they could, were leaning on the stage with broad ignorant lust on their minds. I'd play so loud for one particular chick, I'd get absolutely out of control. The guitar boys would have to turn the volume up full blast to compensate. Thus I went deaf. Anyhow, the dramatic idea was to release Quadberry on a very soft sweet ballad right in the middle of a long ear-piercing run of rock-and-roll tunes. I'd get out the brushes and we would astonish the crowd with our tenderness. By August, I was so deaf I had to watch Quadberry's fingers clanging notes on the saxophone, had to use my eyes to keep time. The other members of the Bop Fiends told me I was hitting out of time. I pretended I was trying to do experimental things with rhythm when the truth was I simply could no longer hear. I was no longer a tasteful drummer, either. I had become deaf through lack of taste.

Which was—taste—exactly the quality that made Quadberry wicked on the saxophone. During the howling, during the churning, Quadberry had taste. The noise did not affect his personality; he was solid as a brick. He could blend. Oh, he could hoot through his horn when the right time came, but he could do supporting roles for an hour. Then, when we brought him out front for his solo on something like "Take Five," he would play with such light blissful technique that he even eclipsed Paul Desmond. The girls around the stage did not cause him to enter into excessive loudness or vibrato.

Quadberry had his own girl friend now, Lilian back at Clinton, who put all the sundressed things around the stage in the shade. In my mind I had congratulated him for getting up next to this beauty, but in June and July, when I was still hearing things a little, he never said a word about her. It was one night in August, when I could hear nothing and was driving him to his house, that he asked me to turn on the inside light and spoke in a retarded deliberate way. He knew I was deaf and counted on my being able to read lips.

"Don't . . . make . . . fun . . . of her . . . or me . . . We . . . think . . . she . . . is . . . in trouble."

I wagged my head. Never would I make fun of him or her. She detested me because I had taken out her helpless little sister for a few weeks, but I would never think there was anything funny about Lilian, for all her haughtiness. I only thought of this event as monumentally curious.

"No one except you knows," he said.

"Why did you tell me?"

"Because I'm going away and you have to take care of her. I wouldn't trust her with anybody but you."

"She hates the sight of my face. Where are you going?"

"Annapolis."

"You aren't going to any damned Annapolis."

"That was the only school that wanted me."

"You're going to play your saxophone on a boat?"

"I don't know what I'm going to do."

"How . . . how can you just leave her?"

"She wants me to. She's very excited about me at Annapolis. William [this is my name], there is no girl I could imagine who has more inner sweetness than Lilian."

I entered the town college, as did Lilian. She was in the same chemistry class I was. But she was rows away. It was difficult to learn anything, being deaf. The professor wasn't a pantomimer—but finally he went to the blackboard with the formulas and the algebra of problems, to my happiness. I hung in and made a B. At the end of the semester I was swaggering around the grade sheet he'd posted. I happened to see Lilian's grade. She'd only made a C. Beautiful Lilian got only a C while I, with my handicap, had made a B.

It had been a very difficult chemistry class. I had watched Lilian's stomach the whole way through. It was not growing. I wanted to see her look like a watermelon, make herself an amazing mother shape.

When I made the B and Lilian made the C, I got up my courage and finally went by to see her. She answered the door. Her parents weren't home. I'd never wanted this office of watching over her as Quadberry wanted me to, and this is what I told her. She asked me into the house. The rooms smelled of nail polish and pipe smoke. I was hoping her little sister wasn't in the house, and my wish came true. We were alone.

"You can quit watching over me."

"Are you pregnant?"

"No." Then she started crying. "I wanted to be. But I'm not."

"What do you hear from Quadberry?"

She said something but she had her back to me. She looked to me for an answer, but I had nothing to say. I knew she'd said something, but I hadn't heard it.

"He doesn't play the saxophone anymore," she said.

This made me angry.

"Why not?"

"Too much math and science and navigation. He wants to fly. That's what his dream is now. He wants to get into an F-something jet."

I asked her to say this over and she did. Lilian really was full of inner sweetness, as Quadberry had said. She understood that I was deaf. Perhaps Quadberry had told her.

The rest of the time in her house I simply witnessed her beauty and her mouth moving.

I went through college. To me it is interesting that I kept a B average and did it all deaf, though I know this isn't interesting to people who aren't deaf. I loved music, and never heard it. I loved poetry, and never heard a word that came out of the mouths of the visiting poets who read at the campus. I loved my mother and dad, but never heard a sound they made. One Christmas Eve, Radcleve was back from Ole Miss and threw an M-80 out in the street for old times' sake. I saw it explode, but there was only a pressure in my ears. I was at parties when lusts were raging and I went home with two girls (I am medium handsome) who lived in apartments of the old two-story 1920 vintage, and I took my shirt off and made love to them. But I have no real idea what their reaction was. They were stunned and all smiles when I got up, but I have no idea whether I gave them the last pleasure or not. I hope I did. I've always been partial to women and have always wanted to see them satisfied till their eyes popped out.

Through Lilian I got the word that Quadberry was out of Annapolis and now flying jets off the *Bonhomme Richard,* an aircraft carrier headed for Vietnam. He telegrammed her that he would set down at the Jackson airport at ten o'clock one night. So Lilian and I were out there waiting. It was a familiar place to her. She was a stewardess and her loops were mainly in the South. She wore a beige raincoat, had red sandals on her feet; I was in a black turtleneck and corduroy jacket, feeling significant, so significant I could barely stand it. I'd already made myself the lead writer at Gordon-Marx Advertising in Jackson. I hadn't seen Lilian in a year. Her eyes were strained, no longer the bright blue things they were when she was a pious beauty. We drank coffee together. I loved her. As far as I knew, she'd been faithful to Quadberry.

He came down in an F-something Navy jet right on the dot of ten. She ran out on the airport pavement to meet him. I saw her crawl up the ladder. Quadberry never got out of the plane. I could see him in his blue helmet. Lilian backed down the ladder. Then Quadberry had the cockpit cover him again. He turned the plane around so its flaming red end was at us. He took it down the runway. We saw him leap out into the night at the middle of the runway going west, toward San Diego and the *Bonhomme Richard.* Lilian was crying.

"What did he say?" I asked.

"He said, 'I am a dragon. America the beautiful, like you will never know.' He wanted to give you a message. He was glad you were here."

"What was the message?"

"The same thing. 'I am a dragon. America the beautiful, like you will never know.'"

"Did he say anything else?"

"Not a thing."

"Did he express any love toward you?"

"He wasn't Ard. He was somebody with a sneer in a helmet."

"He's going to war, Lilian."

"I asked him to kiss me and he told me to get off the plane, he was firing up and it was dangerous."

"Arden is going to war. He's just on his way to Vietnam and he wanted us to know that. It wasn't just him he wanted us to see. It was him in the jet he wanted us to see. He is that black jet. You can't kiss an airplane."

"And what are we supposed to do?" cried sweet Lilian.

"We've just got to hang around. He didn't have to lift off and disappear straight up like that. That was to tell us how he isn't with us anymore."

Lilian asked me what she was supposed to do now. I told her she was supposed to come with me to my apartment in the old 1920 Clinton place where I was. I was supposed to take care of her. Quadberry had said so. His six-year-old directive was still working.

She slept on the fold-out bed of the sofa for a while. This was the only bed in my place. I stood in the dark in the kitchen and drank a quarter bottle of gin on ice. I would not turn on the light and spoil her sleep. The prospect of Lilian asleep in my apartment made me feel like a chaplain on a visit to the Holy Land; I stood there getting drunk, biting my tongue when dreams of lust burst on me. That black jet Quadberry wanted us to see him in, its flaming rear end, his blasting straight up into the night at mid-runway—what precisely was he wanting to say in this stunt? Was he saying remember him forever or forget him forever? But I had my own life and was neither going to mother-hen it over his memory nor his old sweetheart. What did he mean, *America the beautiful, like you will never know?* I, William Howly, knew a goddamn good bit about America the beautiful, even as a deaf man. Being deaf had brought me up closer to people. There were only about five I knew, but I knew their mouth movements, the perspiration under their noses, their tongues moving over the crowns of their teeth, their fingers on their lips. Quadberry, I said, you don't have to get up next to the stars in your black jet to see America the beautiful.

I was deciding to lie down on the kitchen floor and sleep the night, when Lilian turned on the light and appeared in her panties and bra. Her body was perfect except for a tiny bit of fat on her upper thighs. She'd sunbathed herself so her limbs were brown, and her stomach, and the instinct was to rip off the white underwear and lick, suck, say something terrific into the flesh that you discovered.

She was moving her mouth.

"Say it again slowly."

"I'm lonely. When he took off in his jet, I think it meant he wasn't ever going to see me again. I think it meant he was laughing at both of us. He's an astronaut and he spits on us."

"You want me on the bed with you?"

"I know you're an intellectual. We could keep on the lights so you'd know what I said."

"You want to say things? This isn't going to be just sex?"

"It could never be just sex."

"I agree. Go to sleep. Let me make up my mind whether to come in there. Turn out the lights."

Again the dark, and I thought I would cheat not only Quadberry but the entire Quadberry family if I did what was natural.

I fell asleep.

Quadberry escorted B-52s on bombing missions into North Vietnam. He was catapulted off the *Bonhomme Richard* in his suit at 100 degrees temperature, often at night, and put the F-8 on all it could get—the tiny cockpit, the immense long two-million-dollar fuselage, wings, tail and jet engine, Quadberry, the genius master of his dragon, going up to twenty thousand feet to be cool. He'd meet with the big B-52 turtle of the air and get in a position, his cockpit glowing with green and orange lights, and turn on his transistor radio: There was only one really good band, never mind the old American rock-and-roll from Cambodia, and that was Red Chinese opera. Quadberry loved it. He loved the nasal horde in the finale, when the peasants won over the old fat dilettante mayor. Then he'd turn the jet around when he saw the squatty abrupt little fires way down there after the B-52s had dropped their diet. It was a seven-hour trip. Sometimes he slept, but his body knew when to wake up. Another thirty minutes and there was his ship waiting for him out in the waves.

All his trips weren't this easy. He'd have to blast it out in daytime and get with the B-52s, and a SAM missile would come up among them. Two of his mates were taken down by these missiles. But Quadberry, as on saxophone, had endless learned technique. He'd put his jet perpendicular in the air and make the SAMs look silly. He even shot down two of them. Then, one day in daylight, an MIG came floating up level with him and his squadron. Quadberry couldn't believe it. Others in the squadron were shy, but Quadberry knew where and how the MIG could shoot. He flew below the cannons and then came in behind it. He knew the MIG wanted one of the B-52s and not mainly him. The MIG was so concentrated on the fat B-52 that he forgot about Quadberry. It was really an amateur suicide pilot in the MIG. Quadberry got on top of him and let down a missile, rising out of the way of it. The missile blew off the tail of the MIG. But then Quadberry wanted to see if the man got safely out of the cockpit. He thought it would be pleasant if the fellow got out with his parachute working. Then Quadberry saw that the fellow wanted to collide his wreckage with the B-52, so Quadberry turned himself over and cannoned, evaporated the pilot and cockpit. It was the first man he'd killed.

The next trip out, Quadberry was hit by a ground missile. But his jet kept flying. He flew it a hundred miles and got to the sea. There was the *Bonhomme Richard,* so he ejected. His back was snapped but, by God, he landed right on the deck. His mates caught him in their arms and cut the parachute off him. His back hurt for weeks, but he was all right. He rested and recuperated in Hawaii for a month.

Then he went off the front of the ship. Just like that, his F-6 plopped and sank like a rock. Quadberry saw the ship go over him. He knew he shouldn't eject just yet. If he ejected now he'd knock his head on the bottom and get chewed up in the motor blades. So Quadberry waited. His plane was sinking in the green and he could see the hull of the aircraft getting smaller, but he had oxygen through his mask and it didn't seem that urgent a decision. Just let the big ship get over. Down what later proved to be sixty feet, he pushed the ejection button. It fired him away, bless it, and he woke up ten feet under the surface swimming against an almost overwhelming body of underwater parachute. But two of his mates were in a helicopter, one of them on the ladder to lift him out.

Now Quadberry's back was really hurt. He was out of this war and all wars for good.

Lilian, the stewardess, was killed in a crash. Her jet exploded with a hijacker's bomb, an inept bomb which wasn't supposed to go off, fifteen miles out of Havana; the poor pilot, the poor passengers, the poor stewardesses were all splattered like flesh sparklers over the water just out of Cuba. A fisherman found one seat of the airplane. Castro expressed regrets.

Quadberry came back to Clinton two weeks after Lilian and the others bound for Tampa were dead. He hadn't heard about her. So I told him Lilian was dead when I met him at the airport. Quadberry was thin and rather meek in his civvies—a gray suit and an out-of-style tie. The white ends of his hair were not there—the halo had disappeared—because his hair was cut short. The Arab nose seemed a pitiable defect in an ash-whiskered face that was beyond anemic now. He looked shorter, stooped. The truth was he was sick, his back was killing him. His breath was heavy-laden with airplane martinis and in his limp right hand he held a wet cigar. I told him about Lilian. He mumbled something sideways that I could not possibly make out.

"You've got to speak right at me, remember? Remember me, Quadberry?"

"Mom and Dad of course aren't here."

"No. Why aren't they?"

"He wrote me a letter after we bombed Hué. Said he hadn't sent me to Annapolis to bomb the architecture of Hué. He had been there once and had some important experience—French-kissed the queen of Hué or the like. Anyway, he said I'd have to do a hell of a lot of repentance for that. But he and Mom are separate people. Why isn't *she* here?"

"I don't know."

"I'm not asking you the question. The question is to God."

He shook his head. Then he sat down on the floor of the terminal. People had to walk around. I asked him to get up.

"No. How is old Clinton?"

"Horrible. Aluminum subdivisions, cigar boxes with four thin columns in front, thick as a hive. We got a turquoise water tank; got a shopping center, a monster Jitney Jungle, fifth-rate teenyboppers covering the place like ants." Why was I being so frank just now, as Quadberry sat on the floor downcast, drooped over like a long weak candle? "It's not our town anymore, Ard. It's going to hurt to drive back into it. Hurts me every day. Please get up."

"And Lilian's not even over there now."

"No. She's a cloud over the Gulf of Mexico. You flew out of Pensacola once. You know what beauty those pink and blue clouds are. That's how I think of her."

"Was there a funeral?"

"Oh, yes. Her Methodist preacher and a big crowd over at Wright Ferguson funeral home. Your mother and father were there. Your father shouldn't have come. He could barely walk. Please get up."

"Why? What am I going to do, where am I going?"

"You've got your saxophone."

"Was there a coffin? Did you all go by and see the pink or blue cloud in it?" He was sneering now as he had done when he was eleven and fourteen and seventeen.

"Yes, they had a very ornate coffin."

"Lilian was the Unknown Stewardess. I'm not getting up."

"I said you still have your saxophone."

"No, I don't. I tried to play it on the ship after the last time I hurt my back. No go. I can't bend my neck or spine to play it. The pain kills me."

"Well, *don't* get up, then. Why am I asking you to get up? I'm just a deaf drummer, too vain to buy a hearing aid. Can't stand to write the ad copy I do. Wasn't I a good drummer?"

"Superb."

"But we can't be in this condition forever. The police are going to come and make you get up if we do it much longer."

The police didn't come. It was Quadberry's mother who came. She looked me in the face and grabbed my shoulders before she saw Ard on the floor. When she saw him she yanked him off the floor, hugging him passionately. She was shaking with sobs. Quadberry was gathered to her as if he were a rope she was trying to wrap around herself. Her mouth was all over him. Quadberry's mother was a good-looking woman of fifty. I simply held her purse. He cried out that his back was hurting. At last she let him go.

"So now we walk," I said.

"Dad's in the car trying to quit crying," said his mother.

"This is nice," Quadberry said. "I thought everything and everybody was dead around here." He put his arms around his mother. "Let's all go off and kill some time together." His mother's hair was on his lips. "You?" he asked me.

"Murder the devil out of it," I said.

I pretended to follow their car back to their house in Clinton. But when we were going through Jackson, I took the North 55 exit and disappeared from them, exhibiting a great amount of taste, I thought. I would get in their way in this reunion. I had an unimprovable apartment on Old Canton Road in a huge plaster house, Spanish style, with a terrace and ferns and yucca plant, and a green door where I went in. When I woke up I didn't have to make my coffee or fry my egg. The girl who slept in my bed did that. She was Lilian's little sister, Esther Field. Esther was pretty in a minor way and I was proud how I had tamed her to clean and cook around the place. The Field family would appreciate how I lived with her. I showed her the broom and the skillet, and she loved them. She also learned to speak very slowly when she had to say something.

Esther answered the phone when Quadberry called me seven months later. She gave me his message. He wanted to know my opinion on a decision he had to make. There was this Dr. Gordon, a surgeon at Emory Hospital in Atlanta, who said he could cure Quadberry's back problem. Quadberry's back was killing him. He was in torture even holding the phone to say this. The surgeon said there was a seventy-five/twenty-five chance. Seventy-five that it would be successful, twenty-five that it would be fatal. Esther waited for my opinion. I told her to tell Quadberry to go over to Emory. He'd got through with luck in Vietnam, and now he should ride it out in this petty back operation.

Esther delivered the message and hung up.

"He said the surgeon's just his age; he's some genius from Johns Hopkins Hospital. He said this Gordon guy has published a lot of articles on spinal operations," said Esther.

"Fine and good. All is happy. Come to bed."

I felt her mouth and her voice on my ears, but I could hear only a sort of loud pulse from the girl. All I could do was move toward moisture and nipples and hair.

Quadberry lost his gamble at Emory Hospital in Atlanta. The brilliant surgeon his age lost him. Quadberry died. He died with his Arabian nose up in the air.

That is why I told this story and will never tell another.

Barry Hannah

Water Liars

When I am run down and flocked around by the world, I go down to Farte Cove off the Yazoo River and take my beer to the end of the pier where the old liars are still snapping and wheezing at one another. The line-up is always different, because they're always dying out or succumbing to constipation, etc., whereupon they go back to the cabins and wait for a good day when they can come out and lie again, leaning on the rail with coats full of bran cookies. The son of the man the cove was named for is often out there. He pronounces his name Far*tay,* with a great French stress on the last syllable. Otherwise you might laugh at his history or ignore it in favor of the name as it's spelled on the sign.

I'm glad it's not my name.

This poor dignified man has had to explain his nobility to the semiliterate of half of America before he could even begin a decent conversation with them. On the other hand, Farte, Jr., is a great liar himself. He tells about seeing ghost people around the lake and tells big loose ones about the size of the fish those ghosts took out of Farte Cove in years past.

Last year I turned thirty-three years old and, raised a Baptist, I had a sense of being Jesus and coming to something decided in my life—because we all know Jesus was crucified at thirty-three. It had all seemed especially important, what you do in this year, and holy with meaning.

On the morning after my birthday party, during which I and my wife almost drowned in vodka cocktails, we both woke up to the making of a truth session about the lovers we'd had before we met each other. I had a mildly exciting and usual history, and she had about the same, which surprised me. For ten years she'd sworn I was the first. I could not believe her history was exactly equal with mine. It hurt me to think that in the era when there were supposed to be virgins she had allowed anyone but *me,* and so on.

I was dazed and exhilarated by this information for several weeks. Finally, it drove me crazy, and I came out to Farte Cove to rest, under the pretense of a fishing week with my chum Wyatt.

I'm still figuring out why I couldn't handle it.

My sense of the past is vivid and slow. I hear every sign and see every shadow. The movement of every limb in every passionate event occupies my mind. I have a prurience on the grand scale. It makes no sense that I should be angry about happenings before she and I ever saw each other. Yet I feel an impotent homicidal urge in the matter of her lovers. She has excused my episodes as the course of things, though she has a vivid memory too. But there is a blurred nostalgia women have that men don't.

You could not believe how handsome and delicate my wife is naked.

I was driven wild by the bodies that had trespassed her twelve and thirteen years ago.

My vacation at Farte Cove wasn't like that easy little bit you get as a rich New Yorker. My finances weren't in great shape; to be true, they were about in ruin, and I left the house knowing my wife would have to answer the phone to hold off, for instance, the phone company itself. Everybody wanted money and I didn't have any.

I was going to take the next week in the house while she went away, watch our three kids and all the rest. When you both teach part-time in the high schools, the income can be slow in summer.

No poor-mouthing here. I don't want anybody's pity. I just want to explain. I've got good hopes of a job over at Alabama next year. Then I'll get myself among higher-paid liars, that's all.

Sidney Farte was out there prevaricating away at the end of the pier when Wyatt and I got there Friday evening. The old faces I recognized; a few new harkening idlers I didn't.

"Now, Doctor Mooney, he not only saw the ghost of Lily, he says he had intercourse with her. Said it was involuntary. Before he knew what he was doing, he was on her making cadence and all their clothes blown away off in the trees around the shore. She turned into a wax candle right under him."

"Intercourse," said an old-timer, breathing heavy. He sat up on the rail. It was a word of high danger to his old mind. He said it with a long disgust, glad, I guess, he was not involved.

"MacIntire, a Presbyterian preacher, I seen him come out here with his son-and-law, anchor near the bridge, and pull up fifty or more white perch big as small pumpkins. You know what they was using for bait?"

"What?" asked another geezer.

"*Nuthin.* Caught on the bare hook. It was Gawd made them fish bite," said Sidney Farte, going at it good.

"Naw. There be a season they bite a bare hook. Gawd didn't have to've done that," said another old guy, with a fringe of red hair and a racy Florida shirt.

"Nother night," said Sidney Farte, "I saw the ghost of Yazoo hisself with my pa, who's dead. A Indian king with four deer around him."

The old boys seemed to be used to this one. Nobody said anything. They ignored Sidney.

"Tell you what," said a well-built small old boy. "That was somethin when we come down here and had to chase that whole high-school party off the end of this pier, them drunken children. They was smokin dope and two-thirds a them nekid swimmin in the water. Good hunnerd of em. From your so-called *good* high school. What you think's happnin at the bad ones?"

I dropped my beer and grew suddenly sick. Wyatt asked me what was wrong. I could see my wife in 1960 in the group of high-schoolers she must have had. My jealousy went out into the stars of the night above me. I could not bear the roving carelessness of teen-agers, their judgeless tangling of wanting and bodies. But I was the worst back then. In the mad days back then, I dragged the panties off girls I hated and talked badly about them once the sun came up.

"Worst time in my life," said a new, younger man, maybe sixty but with the face of a man who had surrendered, "me and Woody was fishing. Had a lantern. It was about eleven. We was catching a few fish but rowed on into that little cove over there near town. We heard all these sounds, like they was ghosts. We was scared. We thought it might be the Yazoo hisself. We known of some fellows the Yazoo had killed to death just from fright. It was over the sounds of what was normal human sighin and amoanin. It was big unhuman sounds. We just stood still in the boat. Ain't nuthin else us to do. For thirty minutes."

"An what was it?" said the old geezer, letting himself off the rail.

"We had a big flashlight. There came up this rustlin in the brush and I beamed it over there. The two of em makin the sounds get up with half they clothes on. It was my own daughter Charlotte and an older guy I didn't even know with a mustache. My *own* daughter, and them sounds over the water scarin us like ghosts."

"My Gawd, that's awful," said the old geezer by the rail. "Is that the truth? I wouldn't've told that. That's terrible."

Sidney Farte was really upset.

"This ain't the place!" he said. "Tell your kind of story somewhere else."

The old man who'd told his story was calm and fixed to his place. He'd told the truth. The crowd on the pier was outraged and discomfited. He wasn't one of them. But he stood his place. He had a distressed pride. You could see he had never recovered from the thing he'd told about.

I told Wyatt to bring the old man back to the cabin. He was out here away from his wife the same as me and Wyatt. Just an older guy with a big hurting bosom. He wore a suit and the only way you'd know he was on vacation was he'd removed his tie. He didn't know where the bait house was. He didn't know what to do on vacation at all. But he got drunk with us and I can tell you he and I went out the next morning with our poles, Wyatt driving the motorboat, fishing for white perch in the cove near the town. And we were kindred.

We were both crucified by the truth.

BARRY HANNAH

Nicodemus Bluff

That old woman has money, we know. The old withered dugs used to teach high school. They say she even taught me thirty years ago, but I'm not sure as I was mostly away on drugs. One thing about my body or blood flow or whatall, I'm twice as put away as anybody else on a drug, always have been. I declare that I stayed away from the world thirty years and more. So when I saw the old woman on her porch chair as we ran by—running out the drugs of three decades—I just saw a new crone, not somebody I'd ever known. She was sitting there taking up space and money, the green leaves of the tree limbs reaching over her head looking like money itself. Say she used to teach me. I wonder what.

They stood me up and walked me when I was on those 'ludes and reds. No man ever liked a 'lude or red better than this man. They walked me around the high school halls and set me on the benches and showed me food, I guess, in the cafeteria. It is amazing what I never knew, amazing. I accompanied people. I was a devoted accomplice, accompanier, associate, minion, stooge. The term *et al.* was made for me. But I can't remember how. We would be in church or jail. I would just look around and take stock of the ten-foot-or-so box around me and see what was in it, my "space," yes really. Couldn't tell you further what was out there. It could be bars or a stained glass picture of Saint John baptizing Jesus Christ in the Jordan River, boulders and olive trees hanging over the water.

What I wanted to be away from I believe was the memory of my father and his friends years ago at the deer camp in Arkansas. Something happened when I was out there. My father died that next week, but even so he still seemed to hang at the border of my space—the bars, the church window, that ten-foot cube—bloody and broken up and flattened in the nose, a black bruise on his cheekbone because of what happened to him with those others years ago down in the swamps.

We used to be better folks even though my father's people had nothing. There was hope then of rising in the community. My mother was a secretary to a wealthy lawyer in town. It's vague how you get to be "somebody" here, but mainly it has to do with marrying the right woman. Acts of kindness or neighborliness do not really count. I have seen people do acts of kindness over and over and although they get smiled at and thanked with a "Much obliged"—this doing for folks and making them "much obliged" is funny, don't you think? What really made esteem was not acts of kindness but money, clothes, car, house, posture, lawn. We knew, though, that we belonged on the edge of being respected "gentlefolk" (not my term but Dr. Debord's, the preacher friend and chairman of the Sociology Department at the Methodist college in town who helped me for a while). My mother had an easy gracious manner and dressed well naturally although she was not of moneyed people. She was a person of "modest understated grace," Mr. Kervochian told me once, wanting me not to forget what a valuable woman she was, so I'd have something to get up in the morning for. I run around the block again and again, gasping "success, success."

It was hard for Dr. Debord to get me to admit the story of my father Gomar. It was tough and deep, but in talking it up Dr. Debord believed I would get better and be about my work at the animal shelter. My father that week was among those new acquaintances he hoped would be his new and lasting crowd—up from the failed farmers, the beer-for-breakfast mechanics, loiterers and petty-thieving personnel who were his people. Yay for him, some people said, as my father tried to bring himself up into genteel society. I think most people approved of his rise. In the old days the whole county knew each other, don't doubt it, and you might have thought there was some god placed in an office with account books where he let out the word on the social worth of all citizens hereabouts, keeping tab on these as they rose, fell, or simply trod down the rut left by prior generations; the word went around and was known.

But at ten years old what did I know when my father and the rest of them were out at that lodge? I did not know my father had borrowed heavily from Mr. Pool and that was why we had a nice house, lawn, two cars, even a yard man who rode a riding mower, a Negro named Whit who was nice to me. Whit cut himself chopping down trees for us and I recall thinking that his blood might be bluer and was surprised. Why do people live here at all, I ask. They must know this is a filthy, wrong, haunted place. Even the trees that are left look wrong or wronged, beat up. The red dirt is hopeless. The squirrels are thin and there is much—you can't get around it—suicide on the part of possums, coons, armadillos, and deer who tried to exist in the puny scratch but could not, deciding then to leap out on the highway. There are no stories of any merit to come out of this place. The only good woods are near the base of the little mountain. (Let me tell you something about all the drug pushers around here. They are no mystery to me. They aren't a new wave of punk. They are just country sorry, like my father's people.) Someone had a house and land and saved the woods at the west base of the little mountain (805 feet). This person would shoot trespassers, hunters and fishermen (there was a deep black pond in the middle). Nobody went in. The woods were saved. They were thick and dark with very high great oaks and ashes and wild magnolias, even bamboo, like nothing else around. Thicker, much, even than the woods over at the deer camp near the Mississippi River in Arkansas, with sloughs and irrigation ditches where the ducks come down too. You also could catch winter crappie in the oxbow lakes if you could sit still in the cold. (Allow me to express myself about those woods near the mountain here. They were owned by a doctor who was an enormous dealer in drugs. Well I know.) The only thing better I would ever see was the marijuana plantation at the state university where they grew it legally for government experimentation. I saw that plantation once driving by with somebody when I was seventeen and almost came out of my cube of space to get them to stop the car. (No, I could never drive; didn't learn to drive until I was twenty and that was when I finished high school too. All of this delay, I believe, is because of what they did to my father.)

My father then had these acquaintances: a banker, an insurance man, a clothing store owner, a lawyer (employer of my mother), an owner of a small company that made oil pumps for aircraft engines, a medical doctor. Then there was Mr. Kervochian, a druggist, who turned out to be the kindest, and the one who told me the whole story years later when he was dying of pancreatic cancer. My father—we had the lawn, the porch, the two cars, the nice fishing boat, the membership in the country club—I say again was lent heavily some money by three of these men. They told him it was a new kind of loan they were practicing with, a way to help really deserving men from the county who wanted to better themselves. It was agricultural rates interest, very low. It was "special" money on collateral of his personality and promise; and it entailed his being close by to aid these men at some business schemes; close by like at beck and call, said Mr. Kervochian. My father would get nice things immediately and pay it off so that he could enjoy the good life and pay along for it, not waiting until he was old like many men did, left only a few years to enjoy their station and bounty after a lifetime of work. They liked my mother and they thought my father was admirable the way he tried to sell real estate out in the country where the dead farms were. He knew them when they were dying and could be had.

He managed to get Mr. Pool and Mr. Hester a piece of land from a crazy man for almost nothing. The man went down to Whitfield, the asylum at Jackson. The land they used for turkey houses. That's where I came in: at age ten I went out there twice a day on my bicycle to feed and water the turkeys. I had a job, I was a little man. I was worthy of an invitation to the deer hunt. Everything was fitting together. My father had some prestige. He was arriving and I was well on the way to becoming a man of parts myself.

I can't remember why I was the only boy out at the deer camp in Arkansas. But I went along with my father, Gomar, and had my own gun, a little .410 single shot, for the delta squirrels, very fat, if I saw them, which I did but could not hit them much, at age ten. Something would happen when a live squirrel showed up in the bead at the end of the barrel. The squirrel would blur out and I'd snap the gun to the side, missing all of it. I think I embarrassed my father. A boy around here should be able to shoot at ten. The rest of them weren't hunting yet. They were in the lodge drinking and playing cards. I could hear the laughter getting louder and how it changed—louder and meaner, I guess—while I was out in those short stumps and wood chips on the edge of the forest. I remember seeing that cold oily-looking water in a pool in one stump and felt odd because of the rotten smell. They didn't know why I was frowning and missing squirrels out there and had gone back in to laugh harder, drinking. I could smell the whiskey from where I was and liked it. It smelled like a hospital, where I was once to have a hernia repaired.

The large thing I didn't know was that my father owed all this money to the three men, and he was not repaying it on time. I thought they were just his new friends, having them in this sort of club at the lodge, which was as good as a house inside or better with polished knotty pine walls and deer heads and an entire bobcat on a ledge. Also a joke stuffed squirrel with its head blown off, as I couldn't do out there smelling that rotten water, standing in the wet leaves in rubber boots made for a man, not my own, which I was saving for dry big hunting. I remember in December everything was wet and black.

They said flash floods were around, water over the highway, and we were trapped in until the water went down. Then it began to get very cold. I went inside, without much to do. I came back outside with a box of white-head kitchen matches and started licking them on the head, striking them and sailing them out so they made a trail like rockets, then hit and flamed up before the wet took care of them. I thought the future belonged to rockets—this had been said around—and I was very excited to get into the future. My father was providing a proud place for me to grow and play on our esteemed yard. One night I was watching television, an old movie with June

Allyson. Her moist voice reached into me and I began crying I was so happy—she favored my mother some. But my father owed all this money, many years of money. It seemed that two of them, Mr. Hester and Colonel Wren, weren't that anxious about it. But the banker, Garrand Pool, who owned the lodge, was a different kind.

The trouble was, Mr. Kervochian told me, as he was dying, that my father thought he had considerably reduced the debt by getting that piece of land from that insane man for almost nothing. This provided grounds for a prosperous turkey farm for the men. Twenty or more houses of turkeys it would be. My father supposed that he had done them a real turn, a very handy favor, and he felt easy about his lateness of payment. He assumed they had taken off several thousand dollars from it and were easy themselves. He thought things had been indicated more than "much obliged." It was riling somebody, though. Just the money—considerable—wasn't all of it. Something else very terrible was mixed in.

I didn't catch on to much except their voices grew louder and here and there a bad word came out. My father asked me to go back to my bunk in another room. There wasn't anything to do back there but read an R encyclopedia. I could read well. Almost nothing stopped me. My father could read but it was like he learned the wrong way. He took forever and the words seemed to fly off on him like spooked game. He held his finger on the page and ran it along like fastening down the sounds. My mother taught me and I could not see the trouble. I was always ahead of the teacher. I felt for my dad when I saw him reading. I knew this feeling wasn't right, but I wanted to hold his hand and read for him. It almost made me cry. Because it made me afraid, is what it did. He wasn't us.

The terrible thing mixed in it was that my dad was good at the game of chess and vain about it. He had no degree at all—I don't believe he had finished high school, really, unlike such as Mr. Pool, who had college and a law degree. He had never played Mr. Pool but he had whipped some other college men and he was apt to brag about it. He would even call himself "country trash," winking, when he boasted around the house, until Mother asked him to quit, please—gloating was not character. But Mother did not know that my father, when he played chess, became the personality of a woman, a lady of the court born in the eighteenth century (said Mr. Kervochian). The woman would "invest" Dad and he would win at chess with her character, not his own man's person at all. Mr. Kervochian took a long time explaining this. The chess game, as it went on, changed him more and more into a woman, a crafty woman. He began sitting there like a plain man, but at the end of the game he couldn't help it, the signs came out, his voice went up, and his arms and hands were set out in a sissy way. He was all female as the climax of his victory neared. He would rock back and forth nervously and sputter in little giggles, always pursing his lips. It wasn't something you wanted to look at and those he defeated didn't want to remember it. It unnerved them and made them feel eerie and nervous to have been privy to it, not to be talked about. I didn't know what was going on, with the noise out there in the great "den" of the lodge. Mr. Hester and Colonel Wren, the doctor (Dr. Harvard) and the oil pump company owner (Ralph Lovett), with Mr. Kervochian just leaning near them, drinking, were playing poker that night. Only two of them had gone out to hunt a little in the rain and vicious cold but come back. My father and Mr. Pool were at the other end playing chess very seriously. My father's feet became light, tapping on the floor as with princess slippers. All through the other quiet I heard them.

Mr. Kervochian, dying of cancer, told me it was not clear how my father's change came about or even where he learned to play chess, which was a surprise—his chessmanship—unto itself. He was not from chessly people. They were uneducated, sorry trash; even my grandmother Meemaw—a loud hypochondriac, a screamer—had failed on the farm and in town both and lived between them, looking both ways and hating both of what she saw. But Gomar, my dad, knew chess, maybe from one month in the army at the time of the Korean conflict, after which he came back unacceptable because of something in his shoulders (as he said when I asked him once). My mother looked at the floor. She hated war and was glad he'd never been in one. But I wanted him to have been in the war. Mr. Kervochian believed somebody in the service taught him, but where he came in contact with the "woman" he does not precisely know.

But early on he was playing chess with the circuit-church-riding minister at the church near Meemaw's home. Sometime somewhere the woman in him appeared. It was a crafty, clever, "treacherous" woman; a "scheming, snooty, snarling" woman, rougher than a man somehow in spitefulness. She knew the court and its movements and chess was a breeze for her. She'd take him over about mid-game or when things got tough. It would lurch into him, this creature, and nobody could beat him. He beat a college professor; a hippie who was a lifetime chess bum who lived at a bohemian cafe; a brilliant Negro from New Orleans; two other town men who thought they were really good. Something was wrong, terrible about it. He wasn't supposed to be that good.

He might have picked up the woman who inhabited him from somebody in the army, or from that preacher, whose religion had its strange parts, its "dark enthusiasms," Mr. Kervochian said, weakly speaking from his cancer. We don't know, but it led to that long rain of four days at the deer camp, the matter of the owed money, and Mr. Pool, the banker, who professed himself a superior, very superior chess player.

Voices were short but loud and I heard cursing from the "den" where the men were. They were some drunk and angry about the rain. When I peeped out I saw the banker looking angrily into my father's face. My father's face was red, too. He saw me at the door and told me to go back in the other room.

I said, "Daddy there's nothing to do." He brought our guns over to me and said, "Clean them," without looking at me. Then he shut the door. It was only me, the R volume of the encyclopedia and the guns with their oil kit. I went on reading at something, I think Rhode Island, which was known for potatoes. I could hear Dr. Harvard complaining and very concerned about the rain cutting us off, although we had plenty of food. I recall he wasn't drinking and was chubby with spectacles, like an owl, looking frightened, which wasn't right. I didn't like a doctor acting frightened about the weather. My father and Mr. Pool were in a trance over the board of pieces. Mr. Kervochian was drinking a lot, but he wasn't acting odd or loud. This I saw when I cracked the door and peeked again. Mr. Kervochian had a long darkish foreign face with heavy cheek whiskers. He stared out the window at the white cold rain like a philosopher, sad. He liked big-band music—there was some he had brought on his tape machine—and I learned later that he wrote some poetry and might be a drug addict. He seemed to be a kind man, soft, and would talk with you—or me, a kid—straight ahead. He never made jokes or bragged about killing game like the others, my father too. I remembered he had given me a box of polished hickory nuts. They were under the bed and I got them out and started playing with them.

The thing was, Mr. Pool did not believe any of my father's chess victories. Something was wrong, or fluked, he thought. It couldn't be that a man from my father's circumstances could come forth with much of a chess game, to Mr. Pool, who, with his law degree and bankership, hunting, golf and chess, thought of himself as a "peer of the realm," Mr. Kervochian said later. "A Renaissance man, a Leonardo of the backwater." There was a creature in Mr. Pool, too, Mr. Kervochian said, hoarse and small because of his cancer. Mr. Pool owned the lodge and midway ("in *medias res,*" said Mr. Kervochian) in his affairs he began thinking to own people too. He had a "dormant serfdom" in his head. His eyes would grow big, his tongue would move around on his teeth, and he would start demanding things, "like an old czar." Thing was, there was nobody to "quell" him when he had these fits. He did pretty much "own" several people, and this was his delight. People were "much obliged" to him left and right. Then he would have a riot of remembering this. He would leer "like Rasputin leching on a maid-in-waiting." Mr. Kervochian knew history. Pool was "beside himself" as the term had it: "himself outside the confines of his own psyche." Like he was calling in all his money and the soul attached to it. I could hear they had been talking about money and Mr. Pool was taking over all the conversation. My father's point was that the purchase transfer from the old loony man was worth a great deal as a piece of work and should make some favorable patience about the loan on Mr. Pool's part. But I didn't know all that, what their voices were saying. I knew hardly anything except for the strange loudness of their voices with the whiskey in them, which was an awful thing I'd never heard.

I knew my father wasn't used to drinking and did not do it well. Once the last summer when he was coming up in the world, he had bought a bag and some clubs, some bright maroon-over-white saddle golf shoes, a cart, and took me with him to try out the country club. I remember he had an all-green outfit on. This was the club where those men who were his new group played; but this weekday, a workday, and he wanted to come out alone (only with me) because he'd never played. So he rolled his cart into the clubhouse and we sat in a place with a bar. He began ordering glasses of whiskey almost one after the other. I went around here and there in the chairs and came back and sat, with him looking straight at me, his ears getting red and his eyes narrowing. I didn't know what was happening but the man behind the bar made me think everything was all right, saying "sure" and "certainly" when Daddy wanted another glass of whiskey. But then he, my father, wouldn't answer me at all when I asked wasn't it time to play golf. I wanted to chase the balls and had several on the floor, playing.

"You know, really. You're not supposed to bring your bag in here," said the barman, kindly.

My father looked like he didn't know what the man was talking about. I pointed at the golf bag and said, "He means your club bag, Daddy."

"What?" He looked at me, whining-like at me.

Then he drank another whole glass and something happened. I watched my father fall to the side off the chair, knock over the golf cart and bag, and hit the floor, with his golf hat falling off. I got up and saw he was really down, asleep, at the other end of his saddle shoes, maroon and white. He had passed out.

My mother came from the office of the lawyer to pick him up after the barman called. I sat in the chair and waited for him to wake up while other people came in, not helping, just shutting their eyes and looking away. I was awfully scared, crying some. It wasn't until a long time later I learned (from Mother) that he was afraid to start playing golf and embarrass himself, although there were just a few people at the course. He wasn't sure about the sticks or the count. My mother whispered this to me but I never understood why he'd go out there at all. My father, I say, had no whiskey problem, he just couldn't drink it very well and hardly ever did. My mother I don't think had any problems at all and she had high literacy and beauty.

At the deer camp the weather would not quit. I can't recall that kind of cold with that much rain. One or the other usually stops but on top of the roof the roar of water kept up and my window outside was laid on by a curtain of white, like frost alive. They were quiet in the "den" for a long, long time. I imagined they were all asleep from drinking the whiskey. I liked imagining that because what was out there was not nice. I'd seen it, even if they were only playing chess, a game I knew nothing about, but it looked expensive and serious, those pieces out there, made of marble, a mysterious thing I knew my father was very good at.

Mr. Kervochian knew the game and had watched Mr. Pool defeat many good players around the town and in big cities. Mr. Pool wore a gray mustache and looked something like an old hefty soldier "of a Prussian sort," said Mr. Kervochian. You could picture him ordering people around. You could feel him staring at you, bossing. He'd hardly looked at me, though. I was not sure, again, why I was the only child out there.

It got late at night but the lights were still on out there. I had gone to sleep for a while, dreaming about those polished hickory nuts and squirrels up to your hips. When I peeped out I saw all the others asleep, but Garrand Pool and my father, Gomar, were staring at the board without a sound. They had quit drinking but were angry in the eyes and resolved on some mean victory, seemed to me. It was fearsome. The others in the chairs snoring, the rain outside. Nothing seemed right in the human world I knew. Then Mr. Pool began whispering something, more hissing maybe, as grown men I knew of never did. Pool was saying "Stop it. Stop that. Stop that, damn you!" This made my father's body rise up and he put his hand down and moved a piece. He stiffened to a proper upright posture with shoulders spread back, and then this light queer voice came from him. I didn't know, but it was the woman overcoming him. Even in his wrist—thinking back—you could see a womanly draped thing. His fingers seemed to have become longer. Now this was another evil: Mr. Pool knew nothing about the woman and thought my father was mimicking him. He seemed to be getting even angrier and I shut the door. Let me tell you, it was odd but *not* like a nightmare. Another kind of dream, maybe even more wicked and curious, a quality of dream where the world was changed and there was a haze to it, and you couldn't get out by opening your eyes. It made you weird and excited, my father's voice and posture and hands.

"Now hunt, old toad," he had actually said to Mr. Pool, jangling high-voiced like a woman in a church choir.

So I had to open the door a crack again.

Mr. Pool stood up and cursed him and told him something about "deadbeat white trash." But my father said something back shrilly and Mr. Pool I thought was coming out of his skin.

"Don't you mock me with that white-trash homo voice! I won't stand for it!"

The other men woke up and wanted to know what was happening. Nobody had had any supper. They ate some crackers and cheese, commented on the steady rain, then went back to their rooms to sleep. My father and Mr. Pool had never halted the chess and paid no attention to anybody else. I was very sleepy and lost-feeling (in this big lodge, like something in a state park made for tourists). I lay there in the bunk for hours and heard the female voice very faintly and was sick in my stomach through the early morning hours. Ice was on the inside of the window. I could feel the cold gripping the wall and a gloomy voice started talking in the rain, waving back and forth. It wasn't any nightmare and it was very long, the cold wet dark woods talking to me, the woman's voice curling to the room under the doorjamb. Another whole person was out there playing chess, somebody I never knew. A woman and, I thought, somehow sin were in the lodge. Without a dream I was out of the regular world and had prickly sparking feelings like they had put you in a tub of ice and then run you through a wind tunnel.

At daybreak they were still at the game. Garrand Pool had started drinking again. He was up looking out a kitchen window and my father was leaning over studying the board, cooing and chirping. Mr. Pool was going to say something, turning around, but then he saw me in the doorway and stopped, coughing. When my father turned in the chair, I didn't recognize his face. It was longer and his mouth was bigger. His eyes were lost behind his nose. I was very glad he didn't say anything to me. He hurled himself back then as if my eyes hurt him. I shut the door again. I felt cold and withered.

Soon there was a knock on the door. It was Mr. Kervochian. He told me to dress up, that it was cold out, it had quit raining, and he was going to take me out, bring my gun. In a few minutes the two of us walked by Mr. Pool and Daddy, frozen at the board, not looking up. Mr. Kervochian brought me some breakfast out on the porch—some coffee (my first), a banana and some jerky. It was hurtfully cold while we sat there on the step. I could smell whiskey on Mr. Kervochian, but he had showered and combed his hair and had on fresh clothes. My boots were new and I liked them, bright brown with brass eyelets. I felt manly. I think Mr. Kervochian was having whiskey in his coffee.

"Let's go about our way and see what we can see, little Harris," he said.

"Don't you want your gun?" I asked him.

"No. Your big shooter's all we need."

I picked up the .410 single, which was heavy. He told me how to carry it safely. We walked a long time into the muddy woods, down truck tracks and then into deep slimy leaves with brown vines eye-high. I tripped once, went down gun and all with shells scattered out of my coat pocket. Mr. Kervochian didn't say anything but "That happens." We went on very deep in there, toward the river, I guess. How could cobwebs have lived through that rain? They were in my face. Mr. Kervochian, high up there with his thermos, could float on the leaves and go along with no danger, but I was all webby. He began talking, just a slight muddiness in his voice because of the drink.

"He used to have a colored man out here with us, like successful Southern white men have at a deer camp. A happy coon, laughing and grinning, step and fetch it. Named Nicodemus, you know. Factotum luxury-maker. Owing so much to Pool Abe Lincoln's proclamation didn't even touch him. Measureless debt of generations. Even his pa owed Pool when he died."

"Mr. Kervochian, what's happening with my daddy and Mr. Pool back in the lodge?"

"Old Pool's calling in his debts. He always does, especially with some whiskey in him. He's that kind, perfect for a banker, gives so gladly and freely, then when you don't know when, angry about the deal and set on revenge. Gives and then hates it. One of those kind that despises the borrower come any legal time to collect."

"Are they playing for money? Is that why they're so mad?"

"They could be, a lot of money if I heard right, whatall through their whispering. I don't know for sure. It's a private thing and you can be sure Pool's not going to let it go."

"It's like nobody else's in the lodge."

"Let's hunt. Tell you what: there's got to be big game down by the river."

We walked on and on. Cold and tired, stitch in the side, sleepy, was I.

We were on a little bluff and then there was just air. He caught me before I walked out into the Mississippi River. It was like a sea and I'd almost sleepwalked into it, that deep muddy running water. "Watch ho, son!" he said. Then I was pulled back, looking at our home state across the big water.

"You've got to watch it around here. Something's in that bluff under us. It's haunted here. This would be a very bad place to fall off."

The river was huge like a sea and angry, waves of water running. "Why is it haunted?"

"Nicodemus is under the bluff, son."

"That colored man? Why?"

"Old Pool and Colonel Wren."

"Are you drunk now, Mr. Kervochian?"

"Yes, son, I am."

"Please don't scare me."

"I'm sorry. Pay no attention to me. I can get sober in just three minutes, though, boy."

We walked back toward the lodge very slowly, the Nicodemus place behind me and the chess game going on, I guessed, ahead. We saw two squirrels, but again, I missed them. I didn't care. Mr. Kervochian said I was all right, he wasn't much of a hunter either.

"You know, all under our feet are frozen snakes, moccasins and rattlers, sleeping. All these holes in the ground around us. Snakes are cold-blooded and they freeze up asleep in the cold winter."

I didn't like to think of that at all.

Then it began raining all of a sudden, very hard, as if it had just yawned awhile to come back where it was. We were already stepping around ditches full of running water.

"Little Harris, there is a certain kind of woman," he all at once said, for what? "A woman with her blond hair pulled back straight from her forehead, a high and winsome forehead, that has forever been in fashion and lovely, through the ages. And that is your mother. Like basic black. Always in fashion. Blond against basic black and the exquisite forehead, for centuries."

I said nothing. We stopped and saw through the forest where Mr. Hester and Colonel Wren went across a cut with their guns, out trying to hunt but now caught by the rain, heading back to the lodge. We didn't say anything to them, like we were animals watching them.

"She used to come in the drugstore for her headaches. A woman like that in this town, I predicted, would always have some kind of trouble. That nice natural carriage, big trusting gray eyes."

"It's raining hard, Mr. Kervochian."

When we at last returned to the lodge my eyes were hanging down out of their holes I was so tired. There were empty plates on the bar of the kitchen and nobody in the chess seats, just empty glasses and cups on the table. Dr. Harvard said they had left off the game and finally gone to bed, thank God. He peered at the rain past us beyond the doorway and commenced fretting, almost whining about the weather and the thunder and when were we ever going to get out of here, the way the roads were flooded over. There was no telephone, and so on. To see a grown medical doctor going on like this, well, it was amiss, ugly. It changed me. I went right on to bed and was out a long time.

When I woke it was late into the day and going out I saw Mr. Pool and my father were sitting there again, at it after their nap. They looked neither left nor right. My father suddenly gave a yelp, shrill, and I thought Garrand Pool had done something to him. But he was only making a move with a chess piece that must have been a good and mean one, because Mr. Pool cursed and drank half a glass of whiskey.

Mr. Kervochian took his place at the window with a new glass. He looked out into the weather as if he could see a number of people, all making him melancholy. Colonel Wren and Mr. Hester were all wet. They threw more logs on the fire and got it really blazing. They talked about more poker. Nobody knew quite what to do with all their big grown-up bodies and eyes and ears trapped in by the rain these days. Dr. Harvard nagged himself asleep again. The insurance man, Mr. Ott, came tumbling in the door holding his hand. He had cut it on an ax out there chopping wood. The blood was all over it and when he put his hand in the sink it dripped down in splotches around the drain. They woke up Dr. Harvard and he was in the kitchen with Mr. Ott a long time. Then he went out in the rain to get his bag. Mr. Ott needed stitches. I was fascinated by this, sewing up a man. Dr. Harvard worked over Mr. Ott for a long time. Every now and then Mr. Ott would cry out, but in a man's way, just a deep *uff!* I looked over at my father and Mr. Pool. They had never even looked up during the whole hour.

Then Colonel Wren said he was going to have something, damn it all, and went outside with his gun, where in late evening it was just sprinkling rain. Everybody had read all the magazines. I found an old *Reader's Digest* Condensed Book and went back to read something by Somerset Maugham.

It put me to sleep although I liked the story. I guess it was after midnight when I heard them making more sound than usual. I went out in my pajamas. The men at the poker table were high on beer, maybe, but they were very concerned about Colonel Wren. It was raining, thundering and lightning, and he hadn't returned. One of them called him a crazy Davy Crockett kind of fool. Mr. Kervochian, sipping at the fireplace, put in, "Closer to it, Kaiser Wilhelm the Second. Shot ten thousand stags, most of them near tame. Had a feeble arm he was trying to make up for."

Then who comes in all bloody and drenched, with a knife in one hand and a spotlight in the other, but Colonel Wren. He was tracking mud in and shouting.

"There's breakfast out on the hook, by God!"

We went to the door past Mr. Pool and my father, frozen there, and saw a cleaned deer carcass hanging on a board between two trees. In all the rain it showed up sparkling in the spotlight beam.

"That's just a little doe, isn't it?" said Mr. Kervochian.

"That's all the woods gave up, help of this spotlight," said Colonel Wren, very loudly. "It'll eat fine. Come that liver and eggs in the morning, partners, we'll have an attitude change here!"

I won't say again that my father and Mr. Pool paid no attention to any of this, and didn't do anything but play and take little naps for the next two days straight.

After breakfast around eleven that day, I drove out with Mr. Kervochian and Dr. Harvard to check the roads. We looked out of the truck cab and saw wide water much bigger than it used to be, the current of the creek rushing along limbs and bushes. It was frightening, not a hint of the road. Dr. Harvard was white when I looked at him. Later Mr. Kervochian explained that every man has a deathly fear and that Harvard's just happened to be water.

There was more poker and big-band music on Mr. Kervochian's tape player, with now and then a piece of radio music or weather announcement. But the next two days they argued mainly about Killarney Island. Colonel Wren said he knew the deer were all gathered there from all the flooding. And that there was an old boat, they could go out in the Mississippi and shoot all the deer they wanted. The rain shouldn't stop them. This wasn't a goddamned retirement lodge, they were all hung over and bitchy from cabin fever. He wanted to start the expedition.

"Our old boat should be right under Nicodemus Bluff," he said. There would be nothing to rowing out there.

I looked over at Mr. Kervochian. The others were arguing about whether that old boat was any good anymore, the river would be raging, it was stupid and dangerous. Mr. Kervochian, looking with meaning at me, said that was hardly any hunting at all. The deer on that island, which was only fifty yards square, would just be standing around and it would be nothing but a slaughter.

"You couldn't shoot your own foot anyway, Kervochian," said Colonel Wren meanly. "You're an old thought-fucked man." Then Wren looked down at me. "Sorry," he said.

But early the next morning we were all ready to get out of the place. Except for you know who, at it, in another world. Mr. Pool suddenly won a game, but he just got tight-lipped and red in the face to celebrate. I didn't want to look at my father's face. When Mr. Pool said "Checkmate, Gomar!" it sounded like a foreign name in the house.

I went along with them, taking my gun. Mr. Kervochian took a gun and his thermos. The rain was very light now in the early morning. The plan was, when they got to the island, Colonel Wren was going to scare a deer off the island just for me. It couldn't swim anywhere but almost right to me on the shore, and I could blow it down. I wanted to do this. A deer was larger than the squirrels and I wasn't likely to miss. So there I was at ten all bloody in my thoughts, almost crazy from staying in that lodge around that chess tournament that who knows when it would end, both of them looking sick when I could stand to look at them.

We tracked that long way out to the bluff. They went down and found the boat and set out with the paddles, three of them. Mr. Kervochian stayed with me. He seemed to either care for me or wanted a level place to drink. With all these people the bluff didn't seem that fearsome, so I asked him what about Nicodemus, what happened?

"You can't tell this around, little Harris."

"I wouldn't."

We watched them flapping and plowing the water, heading left and north to the island, just a hump out there a half mile away.

"Looking at it several ways, it's still a wretched thing. The man was full of cancer. Owed Pool a lifetime's money. Couldn't afford a hospital. He asked Pool to shoot him and so they did. I don't know which one."

"He'd been with them—"

"His whole life. You could blame Pool for the cancer too. The way he gave, then hounded. Nicodemus, that man, still wanted 'to keep it in the family.'"

They were hollering now out in the tan water, paddles up in the air. Something was wrong with the boat. They turned it around and headed back in. You could see the boat was getting lower in the water. The going was very slow and there was a great deal of grief shouted out. They must've been up to their knees. I heard Mr. Kervochian laughing, but my sense of humor must not have been attuned correctly. The river to me looked like the worst, fiercest place to drown. They came back under the bluff, their guns underwater and their throats stuffed with rage.

Then of course the rain came on, half-strong but mocking, and you could feel the sleet in it. The wet men said almost nothing, flapping back through the woods. It took forever.

There was a shout ahead, a cackling. Down the cut I could see some motion in those stumps in the edge of the lodge clearing. The cackling and now a yipping called at us through the last yards, a stand of walnuts where on the ground you crunched the ball husks of the nuts with your boots.

Mr. Pool was beating my father on the neck with a hard pepperoni sausage. It was a long pepperoni. He kept whacking it down. But my father, holding his hands over his head and trying to dodge, kept cackling and yipping. Thing was, he was laughing, down on his knees, fingers on the top of his head, knee-walking and sloshing through the pools. It was there where the water lay rotten-smelling in the tops of the stumps, putrid and deep back in your nostrils.

"It's all mine, free and clear. I won it, I won it!" my father was shrieking, in that woman's voice.

He couldn't know we were standing all around him. He was shrieking at the ground. Mr. Pool didn't know we were there either. He hit my father again. The pepperoni stick made an awful fleshy thunk on him.

"You trash scoundrel. Stop it, stop it!"

Then Mr. Pool drew around and saw us all, me especially. He hauled my father around facing me, on his knees. Garrand Pool was a big man and my father had gone all limp. His face was cut, his nose was smashed down. He looked horrible, the rain all over his face, and his face long, his mouth hanging down agape, as if frozen in a holler.

"Show him. Talk for your son. Let him see who you are."

I went up close to stop Mr. Pool. I was right in front of my father. He came up with his face, and you could tell he didn't want to, but couldn't help it. He spilled out in that cracking, cackling female voice, "I won! I won!"

Then Mr. Pool just thrust him off and he fell on his face out there in that stinking water.

What Garrand Pool had done seemed awful, but my father almost canceled it out. Nobody could make a direction toward either one. I know how they felt.

The next morning we left. Dr. Harvard was terrified, but the water had receded some and the tall trucks whipped right out through it and to the highway.

He couldn't even look at me for days when we got home. He was all bandaged up and sore. I never saw my father full in the face again. His face would start to turn my way, then he'd shake it back forward.

Nobody, I heard from Mother, ever bothered us about payments of any sort ever again while she was a widow. We had the house, the nice lawn, the two cars, a standing membership in the country club, which I only used to get loaded at and fall in the pool over and over again, swimming underwater long distances full of narcotics until my wrung-out lungs drove me to the surface.

My father never got it right at the country club either, you see. The next week after the deer lodge he was walking at twilight down the road next to the golf course. The driver of the car says he swerved out suddenly right into the nose of his car. They didn't find any alcohol in his blood, and none of it made much sense unless you had seen his eyes trying to call back that terrible woman's voice, pleading right at me.

The extra money my mother had, her legal secretary's salary free and clear, was in a way my downfall. She did not know how not to spoil me, and I always had plenty of money, more money than anybody. And Mr. Kervochian felt for me deeply, truly. I will never blame him. He was of that certain druggist's habit of thought that drugs are made to help people through hurtful times. You wouldn't call him a pusher because he meant only the kindly thing. He saw I was numbed, shocked and injured, so he provided plenty of medicine for me. He gave some to my mother too. She wouldn't take hers, so I got it and took it. I went back and he was always a cheerful giver. Later, he even came down to the jail and brought me out after I'd been taken there, accompanying somebody, some group, somehow an accomplice, just lugging there and nearly keeling over in that racing little sleep I loved. Never did I fight or even complain much.

My mother never remarried. Her looks, her high brightness and carriage, you would have thought she could have a number of prominent handsome men, but she was the kind of woman, I found out—maybe there are a few of them—who don't want but just the one marriage. They are quite all right going along alone. I was shocked, I believe when I was eighteen or thereabouts, only slightly nembied in the kitchen, when she told me she actually had loved my father very much. Then I was confused even a bit more when she said, "Your father was a good man, Harris."

"He *was?*" This confused me, as I say. I'd hated him for being on his knees with that voice at the lodge, I'd hated him for being killed, and I was angry at him through his brother, his own country-trash brother, when I saw him at Dad's funeral in a long-sleeved black silky shirt with a gold chain on his chest. His own brother in not even a suit.

Soon I needed some more drugs and went by Kervochian's.

"My mother said my father was a good man. Is that how you saw him, Gomar Greeves?"

"Gomar?. . . Well, Harris. Frankly, I just don't know. I hadn't known him that well. But he was probably a good man."

Later, but before he got sick, Mr. Kervochian, sharing a 'lude with me, began trying to have a theory, like so: "This state is very proud of its men's men. Its football-playing, tough rough whiskey-drinking men. But I tell you, you calculate those boys at the Methodist college who come by the store here. At least *half* of them are what you call epicene—leaning toward the womanly. The new Southern man is about half girl in many cases, Harris. Now that means their mothers raised them. Their fathers didn't get into it at all. So these men, maybe Gomar was a country version, the woman came—"

"I don't want to hear that, any of that." I was thinking of that awful Meemaw.

"But it was—I watched and heard closely, closely—a brilliant courtly woman who invested him, a spirit—"

I just walked off.

Of course I returned for drugs. He told me two things about Mr. Pool and one about Colonel Wren, but I hate to repeat them because here my testimony gets pushy toward life's revenge, but I'll say the real fact is, Kervochian didn't have to tell me, I saw Pool plain enough around town. The man began losing his face. It just fell down and he got gruesomer and gruesomer and at last just almost unbearably ugly. He went and had galvanized electric facial therapy—five hundred dollars at the beautician's, but nothing would save him. The last time I saw him in a car windshield he was driving with naught but two deep eyeholes hanging on to a slab of red wrinkled tissue. He had got strange, too. He had women out to the deer lodge. His wife found out about it and went over and burned it down. Then Colonel Wren, whom I never saw again, did a thing that got him "roundly mocked," said Mr. Kervochian. Wren was a veteran of Wake Island, where the U.S. soldiers had bravely held off a horde of Japanese before they were beaten down, the survivors going to a prison in China until the end of the war. Wren wrote a long article for an American history magazine, telling the true story, in which he figured modestly and with "much self-deprecation." Then in the next issue in the letters section there was a long letter from a man who was a private at Wake with the others. He went on to say how modest the then Captain Wren was, too modest. He had exposed himself to danger over and over, carrying wounded in one arm and firing his .45 with the other, etc. The letter was signed Pvt. Martin Lewis, Portland, Oregon. All was fine until somebody found out Wren had written the letter himself.

"In his seventies, old Wren. Pathetic," smacked Mr. Kervochian.

None of these happenings raised my spirits and I am putting them in only in memory of Mr. Kervochian, who died such a long painful death, but had explained nearly the whole town to me before he passed on.

When we lap that old woman's house and see her sitting there, on her porch, grand car to the side, safe and nestled in, blasted dry with age, I still say over and over, "Success, success," to my running buddy. Forever on—maybe I'll get over it—I hate a good house, a lawn, the right trees, I despise that smart gloating Mercedes in the drive, all of it. Early on, I moved out of our house, way back there, thirteen or fifteen or something like that. I believe I moved into a shack, maybe I even lived once in a chicken shack. I have missed a great deal, but as the drugs run out with each kick and step, I am beginning to see the crone, once my teacher, go back in time. My legs are pushing her back to a smoother face, a standing position, an elegant stride, a happy smile, instructing the young cheerfully and with great love.

Now there is something for tomorrow. What are women like? What is time like? Most people, you might notice, walk around as if they are needed somewhere, like the animals out at the shelter need me. I want to look into this.

Gish Jen (1956–)

was born Lillian Jen in Queens, New York, to immigrant parents from Shanghai, China. She adopted the name "Gish"—after the actress Lillian Gish—while in high school. "It was part of becoming a writer," she told The New York Times, *". . . not becoming the person I was supposed to be." Jen went to Harvard University as both a literature and premed major. During her junior year, she took her first writing class, a course on prosody taught by the eminent translator Robert Fitzgerald. The first assignment was to write something in Catullan hendecasyllables; after she turned it in, Fitzgerald pulled her aside and asked whether she had ever considered becoming a writer. She hadn't. But she soon abandoned her plans to become a doctor, graduated, and got a job in publishing. Soon thereafter, she went to Stanford University's Graduate School of Business, but she dropped out after a year. She spent a year in China, teaching English to coal-mining engineers who planned to study in the United States. When she returned to the United States, Jen went to the Iowa Writers' Workshop. She began publishing her short stories in* The New Yorker *and* The Atlantic Monthly *and published her first novel,* Typical American, *in 1991. Her second novel,* Mona in the Promised Land, *came out in 1996, followed by a collection of stories,* Who's Irish?, *in 1999, the same year she won the $75,000 Lannan Literary Award. In 2002, a jury composed of John Updike, Don DeLillo, Cynthia Ozick, and Joyce Carol Oates awarded Jen the $250,000 Mildred and Harold Strauss Living Award from the American Academy of Arts and Letters.*

INTRODUCTION BY **Millicent Dillon**

When you first read these three stories by Gish Jen, you will probably laugh and think she is a writer of comic stories. But then, if you read them again, you will wonder whether you should be laughing.

In fact, Gish Jen has said of her own work that when she first started writing, she thought she was supposed to "resolve" her work so that it would be either funny or sad. But then there came a point when she finally decided she was "somebody who simultaneously sees things as happy *and* sad. I *am* the kind of person who would make a joke on someone's deathbed, tacky as it may seem." She came to see that this doubleness in her vision was "an Asian part of my sensibility, in the sense that it's a very Asian thing to imagine that opposites go together. Ying-yang, sweet and sour."

Gish Jen's parents were born in China, but she was born in the United States and lived as a child in Scarsdale, New York. That doubled viewpoint, what she received from the culture of her heritage and what she received from the culture she grew up in, permeates her work. You feel the tension, but you also feel reconciliation. You feel the comedy; you also feel the sadness.

Take, for example, "Who's Irish?," in which the grandmother tells of her difficulty with her grandchild, Sophie. In a language that carries the inflection of her earlier language, she speaks of her own fierceness but then proceeds to tell of her struggle taking care of this "wild" child, half-Chinese, half-Irish, who keeps doing things that, the narrator says, a Chinese child would not do. It is a battle of wills of sorts, which the grandmother ultimately loses. We cannot help but feel for the grandmother, but we also cannot help but feel for the child. At the same time, we laugh. But what is involved is not a mockery of the grandmother or of the child. Each is somehow given her due.

In "The Water Faucet Vision," the grown woman tells a story of her childhood, of how she tried as a girl to counter loss through attempting "miracles." Her parents are native Chinese, who, whenever they argue, speak in a Shanghai dialect that is incomprehensible to her. Then, suddenly, in the course of a fight between the mother and the father, the mother "somehow" falls out of the bedroom window. Now the girl, who attends a Catholic school, attempts a miracle, not only to have her mother survive and have no serious injuries, which she did, but to arrange it so that the fall never happened. In the process of seeking this miracle, she experiences a vision so ludicrous in the eyes of others that she ends by giving up all saintly ambitions. Again the story is told with great humor. Yet only on rereading do we see that there is another story behind this story. In the midst of a paragraph about how she wanted to be a martyr as a girl, there is inserted a sentence having to do with the present. Her mother, she says, died four months ago, but "there are still nights when sleep stands away from me, stiff as a well-paid sentry. But that is another story." And that other story, the death of the mother in present time, lurks behind the comic story of the girl who tried to work miracles.

"Birthmates" is also, ostensibly, a comedy. Here is a Chinese-American man, Art Woo, making his way in the contemporary business world, covering over disappointment, longing, and need, escaping feeling, but finally forced into feeling. The whole tone of the story is comical; detail after detail makes us laugh—for example, "Art had come to few conclusions about life in his thirty-eight years, but this was one of them—that men turned surly when their clothes didn't fit them." Yet at the end, all that has been pushed aside as he pursued his career suddenly surfaces in a realization of the actuality—an actuality he has previously denied—of the baby he and his wife lost.

In reading—and rereading—you might also notice how in the telling of her stories, Gish Jen uses sudden shifts and doubling back in her narrative. She slips from past to present and back again. Her language also has sudden shifts, sudden surprises, shifting from one way of thinking to another and then doubling back again.

One could say, then, that everything in her work is characterized by doubleness, yet everything is all of a piece.

Millicent Dillon's latest novel, A Version of Love, *was published in 2003. The novel before that,* Harry Gold *(2000), was a finalist for the PEN/Faulkner Award for Fiction. She has received five O. Henry Awards for the short story. She has also published biographies of Paul and Jane Bowles and of Isadora Duncan and Mary Cassatt.*

GISH JEN

The Water Faucet Vision

To protect my sister, Mona, and me from the pains—or, as they pronounced it, the *pens*—of life, my parents did their fighting in Shanghai dialect, which we didn't understand; and when my father one day pitched a brass vase through the kitchen window, my mother told us he had done it by accident. "By accident?" said Mona.

My mother chopped the foot off a mushroom.

"By accident?" said Mona. "By *accident?*"

Later, I tried to explain to her that she shouldn't have persisted like that, but it was hopeless.

"What's the matter with throwing things?" she shrugged. "He was *mad.*"

That was the difference between Mona and me: fighting was just fighting to her. If she worried about anything, it was only that she might turn out too short to become a ballerina, in which case she was going to be a piano player.

I, on the other hand, was going to be a martyr. I was in fifth grade then, and the hyperimaginative sort—the kind of girl who grows morbid in Catholic school, who longs to be chopped or frozen to death but then has nightmares about it from which she wakes up screaming and clutching a stuffed bear. It was not a bear that I clutched, though, but a string of three malachite beads that I had found in the marsh by the old aqueduct one day. Apparently once part of a necklace, they were each wonderfully striated and swirled, and slightly humped toward the center, like a jellyfish; so that if I squeezed one, it would slip smoothly away, with a grace that altogether enthralled and—on those dream-harrowed nights—soothed me, soothed me as nothing had before or has since. Not that I've lacked occasion for soothing: Though it's been four months since my mother died, there are still nights when sleep stands away from me, stiff as a well-paid sentry. But that is another story. Back then, I had my malachite beads, and if I worried them long and patiently enough, I was sure to start feeling better, more awake, even a little special—imagining, as I liked to, that my nightmares were communications from the Almighty Himself, preparation for my painful destiny. Discussing them with Patty Creamer, who had also promised her life to God, I called them "almost visions"; and Patty, her mouth wadded with the three or four sticks of Doublemint she always seemed to have going at once, said, "I bet you'll be doin' miracleth by seventh grade."

Miracles. Today Patty laughs to think she ever spent good time stewing on such matters, her attention having long turned to rugs, and artwork, and antique Japanese bureaus—things she believes in.

"A good bureau's more than just a bureau," she explained last time we had lunch. "It's a hedge against life. I tell you, if there's one thing I believe, it's that cheap stuff's just money out the window. Nice stuff, on the other hand—now *that* you can always cash out, if life gets rough. *That* you can count on." In fifth grade, though, she counted on different things.

"You'll be doing miracles, too," I told her, but she shook her shaggy head and looked doleful.

"Na' me," she chomped. "Buzzit's okay. The kin' things I like, prayers work okay on."

"Like?"

"Like you 'member that dreth I liked?"

She meant the yellow one, with the crisscross straps.

"Well gueth what."

"Your mom got it for you."

She smiled. "And I only jutht prayed for it for a week," she said.

As for myself, though, I definitely wanted to be able to perform a wonder or two. Miracle working! It was the carrot of carrots. It kept me doing my homework, taking the sacraments; it kept me mournfully on key in music hour, while my classmates hiccupped and squealed their carefree hearts away. Yet I couldn't have said what I wanted such powers for, exactly. That is, I thought of them the way one might think of, say, an ornamental sword—as a kind of collectible, which also happened to be a means of defense.

But then Patty's father walked out on her mother, and for the first time, there was a miracle I wanted to do. I wanted it so much, I could see it: Mr. Creamer made into a spitball. Mr. Creamer shot through a straw into the sky. Mr. Creamer unrolled and replumped, plop back on Patty's doorstep. I would've cleaned out his mind and given him a shave en route. I would've given him a box of peanut fudge, tied up with a ribbon, to present to Patty with a kiss.

But instead, all I could do was try to tell her he'd come back.

"He will not, he will not!" she sobbed. "He went on a boat to Rio Deniro. To Rio Deniro!"

I tried to offer her a stick of gum, but she wouldn't take it.

"He said he would rather look at water than at my mom's fat face. He said he would rather look at water than at me." Now she was really wailing, and holding her ribs so tightly that she almost seemed to be hurting herself—so tightly that just looking at her arms wound around her like snakes made my heart feel squeezed.

I patted her on the arm. A one-winged pigeon waddled by.

"He said I wasn't even his kid, he said I came from Uncle Johnny. He said I was garbage, just like my mom and Uncle Johnny. He said I wasn't even his kid, he said I wasn't his Patty, he said I came from Uncle Johnny!"

"From your Uncle Johnny?" I said stupidly.

"From Uncle Johnny," she cried. "From Uncle Johnny!"

"He said that?"

She kept crying.

I tried again. "Oh Patty, don't cry," I said. Then I said, "Your dad was a jerk anyway."

The pigeon produced a large runny dropping.

It was a good twenty minutes before Patty was calm enough for me to run to the girls' room to get her some toilet paper; and by the time I came back she was sobbing again, saying "to Rio Deniro, to Rio Deniro" over and over, as though the words had stuck in her and couldn't be gotten out. Seeing as how we had missed the regular bus home and the late bus, too, I had to leave her a second time to go call my mother, who was only mad until she heard what had happened. Then she came and picked us up, and bought us each a Fudgsicle.

★ ★ ★

Some days later, Patty and I started a program to work on getting her father home. It was a serious business. We said extra prayers, and lit votive candles. I tied my malachite beads to my uniform belt, fondling them as though they were a rosary, and I a nun. We even took to walking about the school halls with our hands folded—a sight so ludicrous that our wheeze of a principal personally took us aside one day.

"I must tell you," she said, using her nose as a speaking tube, "that there is really no need for such peee-ity."

But we persisted, promising to marry God and praying to every saint we could think of. We gave up gum, then gum and Slim Jims both, then gum and Slim Jims and ice cream; and when even that didn't work, we started on more innovative things. The first was looking at flowers. We held our hands beside our eyes like blinders as we hurried past the violets by the flagpole. Next it was looking at boys: Patty gave up angel-eyed Jamie Halloran, and I, gymnastic Anthony Rossi. It was hard, but in the end our efforts paid off. Mr. Creamer came back a month later, and though he brought with him nothing but dysentery, he was at least too sick to have all that much to say.

Then, in the course of a fight with my father, my mother somehow fell out of their bedroom window.

Recently—thinking a mountain vacation might cheer me—I sublet my apartment to a handsome but somber newlywed couple, who turned out to be every bit as responsible as I'd hoped. They cleaned out even the eggshell chips I'd sprinkled around the base of my plants as fertilizer, leaving behind only a shiny silver-plate cake server and a list of their hopes and goals for the summer. The list, tacked precariously to the back of the kitchen door, began with a fervent appeal to God to help them get their wedding thank-yous written in three weeks or less. (You could see they had originally written "two weeks" but scratched it out—no miracles being demanded here.) It went on:

> *Please help us, Almighty Father in Heaven Above, to get Ann a teaching job within a half-hour drive of here in a nice neighborhood.*
>
> *Please help us, Almighty Father in Heaven Above, to get John a job doing anything where he won't strain his back and that is within a half-hour drive of here.*
>
> *Please help us, Almighty Father in Heaven Above, to get us a car.*
>
> *Please help us, A. F. in H. A., to learn French.*
>
> *Please help us, A. F. in H. A., to find seven dinner recipes that cost less than 60 cents a serving and can be made in a half hour. And that don't have tomatoes, since You in Your Heavenly Wisdom made John allergic.*
>
> *Please help us, A. F. in H. A., to avoid books in this apartment such as You in Your Heavenly Wisdom allowed John, for Your Heavenly Reasons, to find three nights ago (June 2nd).*

Et cetera. In the left-hand margin they had kept score of how they had fared with their requests, and it was heartening to see that nearly all of them were marked "Yes! Praise the Lord" (sometimes shortened to "PTL"), with the sole exception of learning French, which was mysteriously marked "No! PTL to the Highest."

That note touched me. Strange and familiar both, it seemed as though it had been written by some cousin of mine—some cousin who had stayed home to grow up, say, while I went abroad and learned painful things. This, of course, is just a manner of speaking. In fact, I did my growing up at home, like anybody else.

But the learning was painful. I never knew exactly how it happened that my mother went hurtling through the air that night years ago, only that the wind had been chopping at the house, and that the argument had started about the state of the roof. Someone had been up to fix it the year before, but it wasn't a roofer, only a man my father had insisted could do just as good a job for a quarter of the price. And maybe he could have, had he not somehow managed to step through a knot in the wood under the shingles and break his uninsured ankle. Now the shingles were coming loose again, and the attic insulation was mildewing besides, and my father was wanting to sell the house altogether, which he said my mother had wanted to buy so she could send pictures of it home to her family in China.

"The Americans have a saying," he said. "They saying, 'You have to keep up with Jones family.' I'm saying if Jones family in Shanghai, you can send any picture you want, *an-y* picture. Go take picture of those rich guys' house. You want to act like rich guys, right? Go take picture of those rich guys' house."

At that point, my mother sent Mona and me to wash up, and started speaking Shanghainese. They argued for some time in the kitchen, while we listened from the top of the stairs, our faces wedged between the bumpy Spanish scrolls of the wrought-iron railing. First my mother ranted, then my father, and then they both ranted at once, until finally there was a thump, followed by a long quiet.

"Do you think they're kissing now?" said Mona. "I bet they're kissing, like this." She pursed her lips like a fish, and was about to put them to the railing when we heard my mother locking the back door. We hightailed it into bed; my parents creaked up the stairs. Everything at that point seemed fine. Once in their bedroom, though, they started up again, first softly, then more and more loudly, until my mother turned on a radio to try to disguise the noise. A door slammed; they began shouting at each other; another door slammed; a shoe or something banged the wall behind Mona's bed.

"How're we supposed to *sleep?*" said Mona, sitting up.

There was another thud; more yelling in Shanghainese; and then my mother's voice pierced the wall, in English. "So what you want I should do? Go to work like Theresa Lee?"

My father rumbled something back.

"You think you are big shot, but you never get promotion, you never get raise. All I do is spend money, right? So what do you do, you tell me. So what do you do!"

Something hit the floor so hard, our room shook.

"So kill me," screamed my mother. "You know what you are? You are failure. Failure! You are failure!"

Then there was a sudden, terrific, bursting crash—and after it, as if on a bungled cue, the serene blare of an a capella soprano picking her way down a scale.

By the time Mona and I knew to look out the window, a neighbor's pet beagle was already on the scene, sniffing and barking at my mother's body, his tail crazy with excitement. Then he was barking at my stunned and trembling father, at the shrieking ambulance, at the police, at crying Mona in her bunny-footed pajamas, and at me, barefoot in the cold grass, squeezing my sister's shoulder with one hand and clutching my malachite beads with the other.

My mother wasn't dead, only unconscious—the paramedics figured that out right away—but there was blood everywhere, and though they were reassuring about her head wounds as they strapped her to the stretcher—commenting also on how small she was, how delicate, how light—my father kept saying, *I killed her, I killed her* as the ambulance screeched and screeched headlong, forever, to the hospital. I was afraid to touch her, and glad of the metal rail between us, even though its sturdiness made her seem even frailer than she was. I wished she were bigger, somehow, and noticed, with a pang, that the new red slippers we had given her for Mother's Day had been lost somewhere along the way. How much she seemed to be leaving behind, as we careened along—still not there, still not there—Mona and Dad and the medic and I taking up the whole ambulance, all the room, so that there was no room for anything else; no room even for my mother's real self, the one who should have been pinching the color back to my father's gray face, the one who should have been calming Mona's cowlick—the one who should have been bending over us, to help us be strong, to help us get through, even as we bent over her.

Then suddenly we were there, the glowing square of the emergency room entrance opening like the gates of heaven; and immediately the talk of miracles began. Alive, a miracle. No bones broken, a miracle. A miracle that the hemlocks had cushioned her fall, a miracle that they hadn't been trimmed in a year and a half. It was a miracle that all that blood, the blood that had seemed that night to be everywhere, was from one shard of glass, a single shard, can you imagine, and as for the gash in her head, the scar would be covered by hair. The next day, my mother cheerfully described just how she would part it so that nothing would show at all.

"You're a lucky duck-duck," agreed Mona, helping herself, with a little pirouette, to the cherry atop my mother's chocolate pudding.

That wasn't enough for me, though. I was relieved, yes, but what I wanted by then was a real miracle. Not for my mother simply to have survived, but for the whole thing never to have happened—for my mother's head never to have been shaved and bandaged like that, for her high, proud forehead never to have been swollen down over her eyes, for her face and neck and hands never to have been painted so many shades of blue-black, and violet, and chartreuse. I still want those things—for my parents not to have had to live with this affair like a prickle bush between them, for my father to have been able to look my mother in her swollen eyes and curse the madman, the monster who had dared do this to the woman he loved. I wanted to be able to touch my mother without shuddering, to be able to console my father, to be able to get that crash out of my head, the sound of that soprano—so many things that I didn't know how to pray for them, that I wouldn't have known where to start even if I had had the power to work miracles, right there, right then.

A week later, when my mother's head was beginning to bristle with new hairs, I lost my malachite beads. I had been carrying them in a white cloth pouch that Patty had given me, and was swinging the pouch on my pinkie on my way home from school, when I swung just a bit too hard; the pouch went sailing in a long arc through the air, *whooshing* like a perfectly thrown basketball through one of the holes of a nearby sewer. There was no chance of fishing it out. I looked and looked, crouching on the sticky pavement until the asphalt had crazed the skin of my hands and knees, but all I could discern was an evil-smelling murk, glassy and smug and impenetrable.

My loss didn't quite hit me until I was home, but then it produced an agony all out of proportion to my string of pretty beads. I hadn't cried at all during my mother's accident, but now I was crying all afternoon, all through dinner, and then after dinner, too—crying past the point where I knew what I was crying for, wishing dimly that I had my beads to hold, wishing dimly that I could pray, but refusing, refusing, I didn't know why, until I finally fell into an exhausted sleep on the couch. There my parents left me for the night—glad, no doubt, that one of the more tedious of my childhood crises seemed to be winding off the reel of life, onto the reel of memory. They covered me, and somehow grew a pillow under my head, and, with uncharacteristic disregard for the living room rug, left some milk and Pecan Sandies on the coffee table, in case I woke up hungry. Their thoughtfulness was prescient. I did wake up in the early part of the night; and it was then, amid the unfamiliar sounds and shadows of the living room, that I had what I was sure was a true vision.

Even now, what I saw retains an odd clarity: the requisite strange light flooding the room, first orange, and then a bright yellow-green. A crackling bright burst like a Roman candle going off near the piano. There was a distinct smell of coffee, and a long silence. The room seemed to be getting colder. Nothing. A creak; the light starting to wane, then waxing again, brilliant pink now. Still nothing. Then, as the pink started to go a little purple, a perfectly normal, middle-aged man's voice, speaking something very like pig latin, told me not to despair, not to despair, my beads would be returned to me.

That was all. I sat a moment in the dark, then turned on the light, gobbled down the cookies—and in a happy flash understood that I was so good, really, so near to being a saint that my malachite beads would come back through the town water system. All I had to do was turn on all the faucets in the house. This I did, stealing quietly into the bathroom and kitchen and basement. The old spigot by the washing machine was too gunked up to be coaxed very far open, but that didn't matter. The water didn't have to be full blast, I understood that. Then I gathered together my pillow and blanket and trundled up to my bed to sleep.

By the time I woke in the morning, I knew that my beads hadn't shown up; but when I knew it for certain, I was still disappointed. And as if that weren't enough, I had to face my parents and sister, who were all abuzz with the mystery of the faucets. Not knowing what else to do, I, like a puddlebrain, told them the truth. The results were predictably painful.

"Callie had a *vision,*" Mona told everyone at the bus stop. "A vision with lights, and sinks in it!"

Sinks, visions. I got it all day, from my parents, from my classmates, even from some sixth and seventh graders. Someone drew a cartoon of me with a halo over my head in one of the girls' room stalls; Anthony Rossi made gurgling noises as he walked on his hands at recess. Only Patty tried not to laugh, though even she was something less than unalloyed understanding.

"I don' think miracles are thupposed to happen in *thewers,*" she said.

Such was the end of my saintly ambitions. It wasn't the end of all holiness. The ideas of purity and goodness still tippled my brain, and over the years I came slowly to grasp of what grit true faith is made. Last night, though, when my father called to say that he couldn't go on living in our old house, that he was going to move to a smaller place, another place, maybe a condo—he didn't know how, or where—I found myself still wistful for the time religion seemed all I wanted it to be. Back then, the world was a place that could be set right. One had only to direct the hand of the Almighty and say, just here, Lord, we hurt here—and here, and here, and here.

GISH JEN

Birthmates

This was what responsibility meant in a dinosaur industry, toward the end of yet another quarter of bad-to-worse news: You called the travel agent back, and even though there was indeed an economy room in the hotel where the conference was being held, a room overlooking the cooling towers, you asked if there wasn't something still cheaper. And when Marie the new girl came back with something amazingly cheap, you took it—only to discover, as Art Woo was discovering now, that the doors were locked after nine o'clock. The neighborhood had looked not great but not bad, and the building itself, regular enough. Brick, four stories, a rolled-up awning. A bright-lit hotel logo, with a raised-plastic, smiling sun. But there was a kind of crossbar rigged across the inside of the glass door, and that was not at all regular. A two-by-four, it appeared, wrapped in rust-colored carpet. Above this, inside the glass, hung a small gray sign. If the taxi had not left, Art might not have rung the buzzer, as per the instructions.

But the taxi had indeed left, and the longer Art huddled on the stoop in the clumpy December snow, the emptier and more poorly lit the street appeared. His buzz was answered by an enormous black man wearing a neck brace. The shoulder seams of the man's blue waffle-weave jacket were visibly straining; around the brace was tied a necktie, which reached only a third of the way down his chest. All the same, it was neatly fastened together with a hotel-logo tie tack about two inches from the bottom. The tie tack was smiling; the man was not. He held his smooth, round face perfectly expressionless, and he lowered his gaze at every opportunity—not so that it was rude, but so that it was clear he wasn't selling anything to anybody. Regulation tie, thought Art, regulation jacket. He wondered if the man would turn surly soon enough.

For Art had come to few conclusions about life in his thirty-eight years, but this was one of them—that men turned surly when their clothes didn't fit them. This man, though, belied the rule. He was courteous, almost formal in demeanor; and if the lobby seemed not only too small for him, like his jacket, but also too much like a bus station, what with its smoked mirror wall, and its linoleum, and its fake wood, and its vending machines, what did that matter to Art? The sitting area looked as though it was in the process of being cleaned—the sixties Scandinavian chairs and couch and coffee table were pulled every which way, as if by someone hell-bent on the dust balls. Still, Art proceeded with his check-in. He was going with his gut here. Here, as in any business situation, he was looking foremost at the personnel; and the man with the neck brace had put him at some ease. It wasn't until after Art had taken his credit card back that he noticed, above the check-out desk, a wooden plaque from a neighborhood association. He squinted at its brass face plate: FEWEST CUSTOMER INJURIES, 1972-73.

What about the years since '73? Had the hotel gotten more dangerous since then or had other hotels gotten safer? Maybe neither. For all he knew, the neighborhood association had dissolved and was no longer distributing plaques. Art reminded himself that in life, some signs were no signs. It's what he used to tell his ex-wife, Lisa—Lisa who loved to read everything into everything; Lisa who was attuned. She left him on a day when she saw a tree get split by lightning. Of course, that was an extraordinary thing to see. An event of a lifetime. Lisa said the tree had sizzled. He wished he had seen it, too. But what did it mean, except that the tree had been the tallest in the neighborhood, and was no longer? It meant nothing; ditto with the plaque. Art made his decision, which perhaps was not the right decision. Perhaps he should have looked for another hotel.

But it was late—on the way out, his plane had sat on the runway, just sat and sat, as if it were never going to take off—and God only knew what he would have ended up paying if he had relied on a cabbie to simply bring him somewhere else. Forget twice—it could have been three, four times what he would have paid for that room with the view of the cooling towers, easy. At this hour, after all, and that was a conference rate.

So he double-locked his door instead. He checked behind the hollow-core doors of the closet, and under the steel-frame bed, and also in the swirly-green shower-stall unit. He checked behind the seascapes, to be sure there weren't any peepholes. That *Psycho*—how he wished he'd never seen that movie. Why hadn't anyone ever told him that movies could come back to haunt you? No one had warned him. The window opened onto a fire escape; not much he could do about that except check the window locks, big help that those were—a sure deterrent for the subset of all burglars that was burglars too skittish to break glass. Which was what percent of intruders, probably? Ten percent? Fifteen? He closed the drapes, then decided he would be more comfortable with the drapes open. He wanted to be able to see what approached, if anything did. He unplugged the handset of his phone from the rest, a calculated risk. On the one hand, he wouldn't be able to call the police if there was an intruder. On the other, he would be armed. He had read somewhere a story about a woman who threw the handset of her phone at an attacker, and killed him. Needless to say, there had been some luck involved in that eventuality. Still, Art thought (a) surely he could throw as hard as that woman, and (b) even without the luck, his throw would most likely be hard enough to at least slow up an intruder. Especially since this was an old handset, the hefty kind that made you feel the seriousness of human communication. In a newer hotel, he probably would have had a new phone, with lots of buttons he would never use but which would make him feel he had many resources at his disposal. In the hotel where the conference was, there were probably buttons for the health club, and for the concierge, and for the three restaurants, and for room service. He tried not to think about this as he went to sleep, clutching the handset.

He did not sleep well.

In the morning he debated whether to take the handset with him into the elevator. Again he wished he hadn't seen so many movies. It was movies that made him think, that made him imagine things like, *What if in the elevator?* Of course, a handset was an awkward thing to hide. It wasn't like a knife, say, that could be whipped out of nowhere. Even a pistol at least fit in a guy's pocket. Whereas a telephone handset did not. All the same, he brought it with him. He tried to carry it casually, as if he were going out for a run and using it for a hand weight, or as if he were in the telephone business.

He strode down the hall. Victims shuffled; that's what everybody said. A lot of mugging had to do with nonverbal cues, which is why Lisa used to walk tall after dark, sending vibes. For this he used to tease her. If she was so worried, she should lift weights and run, the way he did; that, he maintained, was the substantive way of helping oneself. She had agreed. For a while they had met after work at the gym. That was before she dropped a weight on her toe and decided she preferred to sip piña coladas and watch. Naturally, he grunted on. But to what avail. Who could appreciate his pectorals through his suit and overcoat? Pectorals had no deterrent value, that was what he was thinking now. And he was, though not short, not tall. He continued striding. Sending vibes. He was definitely going to eat in the dining room of the hotel where the conference was being held, he decided. What's more, he was going to have a full American breakfast, with bacon and eggs, none of this Continental breakfast bullshit.

In truth, he had always considered the sight of men eating croissants slightly ridiculous, especially at the beginning, when for the first bite they had to maneuver the point of the crescent into their mouths. No matter what a person did, he ended up with an asymmetrical mouthful of pastry, which he then had to relocate with his tongue to a more central location, and this made him look less purposive than he might. Also, croissants were more apt than other breakfast foods to spray little flakes all over one's clean dark suit. Art himself had accordingly never ordered a croissant in any working situation, and he believed that attention to this sort of detail was how it was that he had not lost his job like so many of his colleagues.

This was, in other words, how it was that he was still working in his fitfully dying industry, and was now carrying a telephone handset with him into the elevator. Art braced himself as the elevator doors opened slowly, jerkily, in the low-gear manner of elevator doors in the Third World. He strode in, and was surrounded by, of all things, children. Down in the lobby, too, there were children, and here and there, women he knew to be mothers by their looks of dogged exasperation. A welfare hotel! He laughed out loud. Almost everyone was black, the white children stood out like little missed opportunities of the type that made Art's boss throw his tennis racket across the room. Of course, the racket was always in its padded protective cover and not in much danger of getting injured, though the person in whose vicinity it was aimed sometimes was. Art once suffered what he rather hoped would turn out to be a broken nose, but was only a bone bruise with so little skin discoloration that people had a hard time believing the incident had actually taken place. Yet it had. *Don't talk to me about fault, bottom line it's you Japs who are responsible for this whole fucking mess,* his boss had said—this though what was the matter with minicomputers, really, was personal computers. A wholly American phenomenon. And of course, Art could have sued over this incident if he could have proved that it had happened. Some people, most notably Lisa, thought he certainly ought to have at least quit.

But he didn't sue and he didn't quit. He took his tennis racket on the nose, so to speak, and when the next day his boss apologized for losing control, Art said he understood. And when his boss said that Art shouldn't take what he said personally—that he knew Art was not a Jap, but a Chink, plus he had called someone else a lazy wop just that morning, it was just his style—Art said again that he understood. And then Art said that he hoped his boss would remember Art's great understanding come promotion time. Which his boss did, to Art's satisfaction. In Art's view, this was a victory. In Art's view, he had perceived leverage where others would only perceive affront. He had maintained a certain perspective.

But this certain perspective was, in addition to the tree, why Lisa left him. He thought of that now, the children underfoot, his handset in hand. So many children. It was as if he were seeing before him all the children he would never have. He stood a moment, paralyzed; his heart lost its muscle. A child in a red running suit ran by, almost grabbed the handset out of Art's grasp; then another, in a brown jacket with a hood. He looked up to see a group of grade-school boys arrayed about the seating area, watching. Already he had become the object of a dare, apparently—there was so little else in the way of diversion in the lobby—and realizing this, he felt renewed enough to want to laugh again. When a particularly small child swung by in his turn—a child of maybe five or six, small enough to be wearing snowpants—Art almost tossed the handset to him, but thought better of the idea. Who wanted to be charged for a missing phone?

As it was, Art wondered if he shouldn't put the handset back in his room rather than carry it around all day: For what was he going to do at the hotel where the conference was, check it? He imagined himself running into Billy Shore—that was his counterpart at Info-Edge, his competitor in the insurance market. A man with no management ability, and no technical background either. But he could offer customers a personal computer option, which Art could not; and what's more, Billy had been a quarterback in college. This meant he strutted around as though it still mattered that he had connected with his tight end in the final minutes of what Art could not help but think of as the Wilde-Beastie game. And it meant that Billy was sure to ask him, *What are you doing with a phone in your hand? Talking to yourself again?* Making everyone around them laugh.

Billy was that kind of guy. He had come up through sales, and was always cracking a certain type of joke—about drinking, or sex, or how much the wife shopped. Of course, he never used those words. He never called things by their plain names. He always talked in terms of knocking back some brewskis, or running the triple option, or doing some damage. He made assumptions as though it were a basic bodily function: of course his knowledge was the common knowledge. Of course people understood what it was that he was referring to so delicately. *Listen, champ,* he said, putting his arm around you. If he was smug, it was in an affable kind of way. *So what do you think the poor people are doing tonight?* Billy not only spoke what Art called Mainstreamese, he spoke such a pure dialect of it that Art once asked him if he realized that he was a pollster's delight. He spoke the thoughts of thousands, Art told him, he breathed their very words. Naturally, Billy did not respond, except to say, *What's that?* and turn away. He rubbed his torso as he turned, as if ruffling his chest hairs through the long-staple cotton. Primate behavior, Lisa used to call this. It was her belief that neckties evolved in order to check this very motion, uncivilized as it was. She also believed that this was the sort of thing you never saw Asian men do—at least not if they were brought up properly.

Was that true? Art wasn't so sure. Lisa had grown up on the West Coast, she was full of Asian consciousness; whereas all he knew was that no one had so much as smiled politely at his pollster remark. On the other hand, the first time Art was introduced to Billy, and Billy said, *Art Woo, how's that for a nice Pole-ack name,* everyone broke right up in great rolling guffaws. Of course, they laughed the way people laughed at conferences, which was not because something was really funny, but because it was part of being a good guy, and because they didn't want to appear to have missed their cue.

The phone, the phone. If only Art could fit it in his briefcase! But his briefcase was overstuffed; it was always overstuffed; really, it was too bad he had the slim silhouette type, and hard-side besides. Italian. That was Lisa's doing, she thought the fatter kind made him look like a salesman. Not that there was really anything the matter with that, in his view. Billy Shore notwithstanding, sales were important. But she was the liberal arts type, Lisa was, the type who did not like to think about money, but only about her feelings. Money was not money to her, but support, and then a means of support much inferior to hand-holding or other forms of finger play. She did not believe in a modern-day economy, in which everyone played a part in a large and complex whole that introduced efficiencies that at least theoretically raised everyone's standard of living. She believed in expressing herself. Also in taking classes, and in knitting. There was nothing, she believed, like taking a walk in the autumn woods wearing a hand-knit sweater. Of course, she did look beautiful in them, especially the violet ones. That was her color—Asians are winters, she always said—and sometimes she liked to wear the smallest smidgeon of matching violet eyeliner, even though it was, as she put it, less than organic to wear eyeliner on a hike.

Little Snowpants ran at Art again, going for the knees—a *tackle,* thought Art, as he went down; Red Running Suit snatched away the handset and went sprinting off, triumphant. Teamwork! The children chortled together; how could Art not smile a little, even if they had gotten his overcoat dirty? He brushed himself off, ambled over.

"Hey, guys," he said. "That was some move back there."

"Chin chang polly wolly wing wong," said Little Snowpants.

"Now, now, that's no way to talk," said Art.

"Go to hell!" Brown Jacket pulled at the corners of his eyes to make them slanty.

"Listen up," said Art. "I'll make you a deal." Really he only meant to get the handset back, so as to avoid getting charged for it.

But the next thing he knew, something had hit his head with a crack, and he was out.

Lisa had left in a more or less amicable way. She had not called a lawyer, or a mover; she had simply pressed his hands with both of hers and, in her most California voice, said, *Let's be nice.* And then she had asked him if he wouldn't help her move her boxes, at least the heavy ones that really were too much for her. He had helped. He had carried the heavy boxes, and also the less heavy ones. Being a weight lifter, after all. He had sorted books and rolled glasses into pieces of newspaper, feeling all the while like a statistic. A member of the modern age, a story for their friends to rake over, and all because he had not gone with Lisa to her grieving group. Or at least that was the official beginning of the trouble; probably the real beginning had been when Lisa—no, *they*—had trouble getting pregnant. When they decided to, as the saying went, do infertility. Or had he done the deciding, as Lisa later maintained? He had thought it was a joint decision, though it was true that he had done the analysis that led to the joint decision. He had been the one to figure the odds, to do the projections. He had drawn the decision tree, according to whose branches they had nothing to lose by going ahead.

Neither one of them had realized then how much would be involved—the tests, the procedures, the drugs, the ultrasounds. Lisa's arms were black and blue from having her blood drawn every day, and before long he was giving practice shots to an orange, that he might prick her some more. He was telling her to take a breath so that on the exhale he could poke her in the buttocks. This was no longer practice, and neither was it like poking an orange. The first time, he broke out in such a sweat that his vision blurred and he had to blink, with the result that he pulled the needle out slowly and crookedly, occasioning a most unorangelike cry. The second time, he wore a sweatband. Later he jabbed her like nothing; her ovaries swelled to the point where he could feel them through her jeans.

Art still had the used syringes—snapped in half and stored, as per their doctor's recommendation, in plastic soda bottles. She had left him those. Bottles of medical waste, to be disposed of responsibly, meaning that he was probably stuck with them, ha-ha, for the rest of his life. A little souvenir of this stage of their marriage, his equivalent of the pile of knit goods she had to show for the ordeal; for through it all, she had knit, as if to gently demonstrate an alternative use of needles. Sweaters, sweaters, but also baby blankets, most to give away, only one or two to keep. She couldn't help herself. There was anesthesia, and egg harvesting, and anesthesia and implanting, until she finally did get pregnant, twice, and then a third time she went to four and a half months before they found a problem. On the amnio, it showed up, brittle bone disease—a genetic abnormality such as could happen to anyone.

He steeled himself for another attempt; she grieved. And this was the difference between them, that he saw hope still, some feeble, skeletal hope, where she saw loss. She called the fetus her baby, though it was not a baby, just a baby-to-be, as he tried to say; as even the grieving-group facilitator tried to say. She said he didn't understand, couldn't possibly understand, it was something you understood with your body, and it was not his body but hers that knew the baby, loved the baby, lost the baby. In the grieving class the women agreed. They commiserated. They bonded, subtly affirming their common biology by doing 85 percent of the talking. The room was painted mauve—a feminine color that seemed to support them in their process. At times it seemed that the potted palms were female, too; nodding, nodding, though really their sympathy was just rising air from the heating vents. Other husbands started missing sessions—they never talked, anyway, you hardly noticed their absence—and finally he missed some also. One, maybe two, for real reasons, nothing cooked up. But the truth was, as Lisa sensed, that he thought she had lost perspective. They could try again, after all. What did it help to despair? Look, they knew they could get pregnant and, what's more, sustain the pregnancy. That was progress. But she was like an island in her grief, a retreating island, if there was such a thing, receding to the horizon of their marriage, and then to its vanishing point.

Of course, he had missed her terribly at first; now he missed her still, but more sporadically. At odd moments, for example now, waking up in a strange room with ice on his head. He was lying on an unmade bed just like the bed in his room, except that everywhere around it were heaps of what looked to be blankets and clothes. The only clothes on a hanger were his jacket and overcoat; these hung neatly, side by side, in the otherwise empty closet. There was also an extra table in this room, with a two-burner hot plate, a pan on top of that, and a pile of dishes. A brown cube refrigerator.

The drapes were closed; a chair had been pulled up close to him; the bedside light was on. A woman was leaning into its circle, mopping his brow.

"Don't you move, now," she said.

She was the shade of black Lisa used to call mochaccino, and she was wearing a blue flowered apron. Kind eyes; a long face—the kind of face where you could see the muscles of the jaw working alongside the cheekbone. An upper lip like an archery bow; and a graying Afro, shortish. She smelled of smoke. Nothing unusual except that she was so very thin, about the thinnest person he had ever seen, and yet she was cooking something—burning something, it smelled like, though maybe it was just a hair fallen onto the heating element. She stood up to tend the pan. The acrid smell faded. He saw powder on the table. It was white, a plastic bagful. His eyes widened. He sank back, trying to figure out what to do. His head pulsed. Tylenol, he needed, two. Lisa always took one because she was convinced the dosages recommended were based on large male specimens; and though she had never said that she thought he ought to keep it to one also, not being so tall, he was adamant about taking two. Two, two, two. He wanted his drugs, he wanted them now. And his own drugs, that was, not somebody else's.

"Those kids kind of rough," said the woman. "They getting to that age. I told them one of these days somebody gonna get hurt, and sure enough, they knocked you right out. You might as well been hit with a bowling ball. I never saw anything like it. We called the man, but they got other things on their mind besides to come see about trouble here. Nobody shot, so they went on down to the Dunkin' Donuts. They know they can count on a ruckus there." She winked. "How you feeling? That egg hurt?"

He felt his head. A lump sat right on top of it, incongruous as something left by a glacier. What were those called, those stray boulders you saw perched in hair-raising positions? On cliffs?

"I feel like I died and came back to life head-first," he said.

"I'm going to make you something nice. Make you feel a whole lot better."

"Uh," said Art. "If you don't mind, I'd rather just have a Tylenol. You got any Tylenol? I had some in my briefcase. If I still have my briefcase."

"Your what?"

"My briefcase," said Art again, with a panicky feeling. "Do you know what happened to my briefcase?"

"Oh, it's right by the door. I'll get it, don't move."

And then there it was, his briefcase, its familiar hard-sided, Italian slenderness resting right on his stomach. He clutched it. "Thank you," he whispered.

"You need help with that thing?"

"No," said Art, but when he opened the case, it slid, and everything spilled out—his notes, his files, his papers. All that figuring—how strange his concerns looked here, on this brown shag carpet.

"Here," said the woman, and again—"I'll get it, don't move"—as gently, beautifully, she gathered up all the folders and put them in the case. There was an odd, almost practiced finesse to her movements; the files could have been cards in a card dealer's hands. "I used to be a nurse," she explained, as if reading his mind. "I picked up a few folders in my time. Here's the Tylenol."

"I'll have two."

"Course you will," she said. "Two Tylenol and some hot milk with honey. Hope you don't mind the powdered, we just got moved here, we don't have no supplies. I used to be a nurse, but I don't got no milk and I don't got no Tylenol, my guests got to bring their own. How you like that."

Art laughed as much as he could. "You got honey, though, how's that?"

"I don't know, it got left here by somebody," said the nurse. "Hope there's nothing growing in it."

Art laughed again, then let her help him sit up to take his pills. The nurse—her name was Cindy—plumped his pillows. She administered his milk. Then she sat—very close to him, it seemed—and chatted amiably about this and that. How she wasn't going to be staying at the hotel for too long, how her kids had had to switch schools, how she wasn't afraid to take in a strange, injured man. After all, she grew up in the projects, she could take care of herself. She showed him her switchblade, which had somebody's initials carved on it, she didn't know whose. She had never used it, she said, somebody gave it to her. And that somebody didn't know whose initials those were, either, she said, at least so far as she knew. Then she lit a cigarette and smoked while he told her first about his conference and then about how he had ended up at the hotel by mistake. He told her the latter with some hesitation, hoping he wasn't offending her. But she wasn't offended. She laughed with a cough, emitting a series of smoke puffs.

"Sure must've been a shock," she said. "Land up in a place like this. This no place for a nice boy like you."

That stung a little. *Boy!* But more than the stinging, he felt something else. "What about you? It's no place for you, either, you and your kids."

"Maybe so," she said. "But that's how the Almighty planned it, right? You folk rise up while we set and watch." She said this with so little rancor, with something so like intimacy, that it almost seemed an invitation of sorts.

But maybe he was kidding himself. Maybe he was assuming things, just like Billy Shore, just like men throughout the ages. Projecting desire where there was none, assigning and imagining, and in juicy detail. Being Asian didn't exempt him from that. *You folk.*

Art was late, but it didn't much matter. This conference was being held in conjunction with a much larger conference, the real draw; the idea being that maybe between workshops and on breaks, the conferees would drift down and see what minicomputers could do for them. That mostly meant lunch. In the meantime, things were totally dead, allowing Art to appreciate just how much the trade show floor had shrunk—down to a fraction of what it had been in previous years, and the booths were not what they had been, either. It used to be that the floor was crammed with the fanciest booths on the market; Art's used to be twenty by twenty. It took days to put together. Now you saw blank spots on the floor where exhibitors didn't even bother to show up, and those weren't even as demoralizing as some of the makeshift jobbies—exhibit booths that looked like high school science fair projects. They might as well have been made out of cardboard and Magic Marker. Art himself had a booth you could buy from an airplane catalog, the kind that rolled up into Cordura bags. And people were stingy with brochures now, too. Gone were the twelve-page, four-color affairs; now the pamphlets were four-page, two-color, with extra bold graphics for attempted pizzazz, and not everybody got one, only people who were serious.

Art set up. Then, even though he should have been manning his spot, he drifted from booth to booth, saying hello to people he should have seen at breakfast. They were happy to see him, to talk shop, to pop some grapes off the old grapevine. Really, if he weren't staying in a welfare hotel, he would have felt downright respected. *You folk.* What folk did Cindy mean? Maybe she was just being matter-of-fact, keeping her perspective. Although how could anyone be so matter-of-fact about something so bitter? He wondered this even as he took his imaginative liberties with her. These began with a knock on her door and coursed through some hot times but ended (what a good boy he was) with him rescuing her and her children (he wondered how many there were) from their dead-end life. What was the matter with him, that he could not imagine mating without legal sanction? His libido was not what it should be, clearly, or at least it was not what Billy Shore's was. Art tried to think *game plan,* but in truth he could not even identify what a triple option would be in this case. All he knew was that, assuming, to begin with, that she was willing, he couldn't sleep with a woman like Cindy and then leave her flat. She could *you folk* him, he could never *us folk* her.

He played with some software at a neighboring booth; it appeared interesting enough but kept crashing so he couldn't tell too much. Then he dutifully returned to his own booth, where he was visited by a number of people he knew, people with whom he was friendly enough. The sort of people to whom he might have shown pictures of his children. He considered telling one or two of them about the events of the morning. Not about the invitation that might not have been an invitation, but about finding himself in a welfare hotel and being beaned with his own telephone. Phrases drifted through his head. *Not so bad as you'd think. You'd be surprised how friendly the people are. Unpretentious. Though, of course, no health club.* But in the end the subject simply did not come up and did not come up until he realized that he was keeping it to himself, and that he was committing more resources to this task than he had readily available. He felt invaded—as if he had been infected by a self-replicating bug. Something that was iterating and iterating, growing and growing, crowding out everything else in the CPU. The secret was intolerable; it was bound to spill out of him sooner or later. He just hoped it wouldn't be sooner.

He just hoped it wouldn't be to Billy Shore, for whom he began to search, so as to be certain to avoid him.

Art had asked about Billy at the various booths, but no one had seen him; his absence was weird. It spooked Art. When finally some real live conferees stopped by to see his wares, he had trouble concentrating; everywhere in the conversation he was missing opportunities, he knew it. And all because his CPU was full of iterating nonsense. Not too long ago, in looking over some database software in which was loaded certain fun facts about people in the industry, Art had looked up Billy, and discovered that he had been born the same day Art was, only four years later. It just figured that Billy would be younger. That was irritating. But Art was happy for the information, too. He had made a note of it, so that when he ran into Billy at this conference, he would remember to kid him about their birthdays. Now, he rehearsed. *Have I got a surprise for you. I always knew you were a Leo. I believe this makes us birthmates.* Anything not to mention the welfare hotel and all that had happened to him there.

In the end, he did not run into Billy at all. In the end, he wondered about Billy all day, only to finally learn that Billy had moved on to a new job in the Valley, with a startup. In personal computers, naturally. A good move, no matter what kind of beating he took on his house.

"Life is about the long term," said Ernie Ford, the informant. "And let's face it, there is no long term here."

Art agreed as warmly as he could. In one way, he was delighted that his competitor had left—if nothing else, that would mean a certain amount of disarray at InfoEdge. The insurance market was, unfortunately, some 40 percent of his business, and he could use any advantage he could get. Another bonus was that Art was never going to have to see Billy again. Billy his birthmate, with his jokes and his Mainstreamese. Still, Art felt depressed.

"We should all have gotten out way before this," he said.

"Truer words were never spoke," said Ernie. Ernie had never been a particular friend of Art's, but somehow, talking about Billy was making him chummier. It was as if Billy were a force even in his absence. "I'd have packed my bags by now if it weren't for the wife, the kids—they don't want to leave their friends, you know? Plus the oldest is a junior in high school, we can't afford for him to move now, he's got to stay put and make those nice grades so he can make a nice college. Meaning I've got to stay, if it means pushing McMuffins for Ronald McDonald. But now you . . ."

"Maybe I should go," said Art.

"Definitely, you should go," said Ernie. "What's keeping you?"

"Nothing," said Art. "I'm divorced now. And that's that, right? Sometimes people get undivorced, but you can't exactly count on it."

"Go," said Ernie. "Take my advice. If I hear of anything, I'll send it your way."

"Thanks," said Art.

But of course, he did not expect that Ernie would really turn anything up. It had been a long time since anyone had called him or anybody else he knew of; too many people had gotten stranded, and they were too desperate. Everybody knew it. Also, the survivors were looked upon with suspicion. Anybody who was any good had jumped ship early, that was the conventional wisdom. There was Art, struggling to hold on to his job, only to discover that there were times you didn't want to hold on to your job, times to maneuver for the golden parachute and jump. That was another thing no one had told him, that sometimes it spoke well of you to be fired. Who would have figured that? Sometimes it seemed to Art that he knew nothing at all, that he had dug his own grave and didn't even know to lie down in it, he was still trying to stand up.

A few more warm-blooded conferees at the end of the day—at least they were polite. Then, as he was packing up to go back to the hotel, a mega-surprise. A headhunter approached him, a friend of Ernest's, he said.

"Ernest?" said Art. "Oh, Ernie! Ford! Of course!"

The headhunter was a round, ruddy man with a ring of hair like St. Francis of Assisi, and sure enough, a handful of bread crumbs: A great opportunity, he said. Right now he had to run, but he knew just the guy Art had to meet, a guy who was coming in that evening. For something else, it happened, but he also needed someone like Art. Needed him yesterday, really. Should've been a priority, the guy realized that now, had said so the other day. It might just be a match. Maybe a quick breakfast in the A.M.? Could he call in an hour or so? Art said, Of course. And when St. Francis asked his room number, Art hesitated, but then gave the name of the welfare hotel.

How would St. Francis know what kind of hotel it was? Art gave the name out confidently, making his manner count. He almost didn't make it to the conference at all, he said. Being so busy. It was only at the last minute that he realized he could do it—things moved around, he found an opening and figured what the hell. But it was too late to book the conference hotel, he explained. That was why he was staying elsewhere.

Success. All day Art's mind had been churning; suddenly it seemed to empty. He might as well have been Billy, born on the same day as Art was, but in another year, under different stars. How much simpler things seemed. He did not labor on two, three, six tasks at once, multiprocessing. He knew one thing at a time, and that thing just now was that the day was a victory. And all because he had kept his mouth shut. He had said nothing; he had kept his cool. He walked briskly back to the hotel. He crossed the lobby in a no-nonsense manner. An impervious man. He did not knock on Cindy's door. He was moving on, moving west. There would be a good job there, and a new life. Perhaps he would take up tennis. Perhaps he would own a Jacuzzi. Perhaps he would learn to like all those peculiar foods they ate out there, like jicama, and seaweed. Perhaps he would go macrobiotic.

It wasn't until he got to his room that he remembered that his telephone had no handset.

He sat on his bed. There was a noise at his window, followed, sure enough, by someone's shadow. He wasn't even surprised. Anyway, the fellow wasn't stopping at his room, at least not on this trip. That was luck. *You folk,* Cindy had said, taking back the ice bag. Art could see her perspective; she was right. He was luckier than she, by far. But just now, as the shadow crossed his window again, he thought mostly about how unarmed he was. If he had a telephone, he would probably call Lisa—that was how big a pool seemed to be forming around him, all of a sudden; an ocean, it seemed. Also, he would call the police. But first he would call Lisa, and see how she felt about his possibly moving west. *Quite possibly,* he would say, not wanting to make it sound as though he was calling her for nothing, not wanting to make it sound as though he was awash, at sea, perhaps drowning. He would not want to sound like a haunted man; he would not want to sound as though he was calling from a welfare hotel, years too late, to say, *Yes, that was a baby we had together, it would have been a baby.* For he could not help now but recall the doctor explaining about that child, a boy, who had appeared so mysteriously perfect in the ultrasound. Transparent, he had looked, and gelatinous, all soft head and quick heart; but he would have, in being born, broken every bone in his body.

Gish Jen

Who's Irish?

In China, people say mixed children are supposed to be smart, and definitely my granddaughter Sophie is smart. But Sophie is wild, Sophie is not like my daughter Natalie, or like me. I am work hard my whole life, and fierce besides. My husband always used to say he is afraid of me, and in our restaurant, busboys and cooks all afraid of me too. Even the gang members come for protection money, they try to talk to my husband. When I am there, they stay away. If they come by mistake, they pretend they are come to eat. They hide behind the menu, they order a lot of food. They talk about their mothers. Oh, my mother have some arthritis, need to take herbal medicine, they say. Oh, my mother getting old, her hair all white now.

I say, Your mother's hair used to be white, but since she dye it, it become black again. Why don't you go home once in a while and take a look? I tell them, Confucius say a filial son knows what color his mother's hair is.

My daughter is fierce too, she is vice president in the bank now. Her new house is big enough for everybody to have their own room, including me. But Sophie take after Natalie's husband's family, their name is Shea. Irish. I always thought Irish people are like Chinese people, work so hard on the railroad, but now I know why the Chinese beat the Irish. Of course, not all Irish are like the Shea family, of course not. My daughter tell me I should not say Irish this, Irish that.

How do you like it when people say the Chinese this, the Chinese that, she say.

You know, the British call the Irish heathen, just like they call the Chinese, she say.

You think the Opium War was bad, how would you like to live right next door to the British, she say.

And that is that. My daughter have a funny habit when she win an argument, she take a sip of something and look away, so the other person is not embarrassed. So I am not embarrassed. I do not call anybody anything either. I just happen to mention about the Shea family, an interesting fact: four brothers in the family, and not one of them work. The mother, Bess, have a job before she got sick, she was executive secretary in a big company. She is handle everything for a big shot, you would be surprised how complicated her job is, not just type this, type that. Now she is a nice woman with a clean house. But her boys, every one of them is on welfare, or so-called severance pay, or so-called disability pay. Something. They say they cannot find work, this is not the economy of the fifties, but I say, Even the black people doing better these days, some of them live so fancy, you'd be surprised. Why the Shea family have so much trouble? They are white people, they speak English. When I come to this country, I have no money and do not speak English. But my husband and I own our restaurant before he die. Free and clear, no mortgage. Of course, I understand I am just lucky, come from a country where the food is popular all over the world. I understand it is not the Shea family's fault they come from a country where everything is boiled. Still, I say.

She's right, we should broaden our horizons, say one brother, Jim, at Thanksgiving. Forget about the car business. Think about egg rolls.

Pad thai, say another brother, Mike. I'm going to make my fortune in pad thai. It's going to be the new pizza.

I say, You people too picky about what you sell. Selling egg rolls not good enough for you, but at least my husband and I can say, We made it. What can you say? Tell me. What can you say?

Everybody chew their tough turkey.

I especially cannot understand my daughter's husband John, who has no job but cannot take care of Sophie either. Because he is a man, he say, and that's the end of the sentence.

Plain boiled food, plain boiled thinking. Even his name is plain boiled: John. Maybe because I grew up with black bean sauce and hoisin sauce and garlic sauce, I always feel something is missing when my son-in-law talk.

But, okay: so my son-in-law can be man, I am baby-sitter. Six hours a day, same as the old sitter, crazy Amy, who quit. This is not so easy, now that I am sixty-eight, Chinese age almost seventy. Still, I try. In China, daughter take care of mother. Here it is the other way around. Mother help daughter, mother ask, Anything else I can do? Otherwise daughter complain mother is not supportive. I tell daughter, We do not have this word in Chinese, *supportive.* But my daughter too busy to listen, she has to go to meeting, she has to write memo while her husband go to the gym to be a man. My daughter say otherwise he will be depressed. Seems like all his life he has this trouble, depression.

No one wants to hire someone who is depressed, she say. It is important for him to keep his spirits up.

Beautiful wife, beautiful daughter, beautiful house, oven can clean itself automatically. No money left over, because only one income, but lucky enough, got the babysitter for free. If John lived in China, he would be very happy. But he is not happy. Even at the gym things go wrong. One day, he pull a muscle. Another day, weight room too crowded. Always something.

Until finally, hooray, he has a job. Then he feel pressure.

I need to concentrate, he say. I need to focus.

He is going to work for insurance company. Salesman job. A paycheck, he say, and at least he will wear clothes instead of gym shorts. My daughter buy him some special candy bars from the health-food store. They say THINK! on them, and are supposed to help John think.

John is a good-looking boy, you have to say that, especially now that he shave so you can see his face.

I am an old man in a young man's game, say John.

I will need a new suit, say John.

This time I am not going to shoot myself in the foot, say John.

Good, I say.

She means to be supportive, my daughter say. Don't start the send her back to China thing, because we can't.

Sophie is three years old American age, but already I see her nice Chinese side swallowed up by her wild Shea side. She looks like mostly Chinese. Beautiful black hair, beautiful black eyes. Nose perfect size, not so flat looks like something fell down, not so large looks like some big deal got stuck in wrong face. Everything just right, only her skin is a brown surprise to John's family. So brown, they say. Even John say it. She never goes in the sun, still she is that color, he say. Brown. They say, Nothing the matter with brown. They are just surprised. So brown. Nattie is not that brown, they say. They say, It seems like Sophie should be a color in between Nattie and John. Seems funny, a girl named Sophie Shea be brown. But she is brown, maybe her name should be Sophie Brown. She never go in the sun, still she is that color, they say. Nothing the matter with brown. They are just surprised.

The Shea family talk is like this sometimes, going around and around like a Christmas-tree train.

Maybe John is not her father, I say one day, to stop the train. And sure enough, train wreck. None of the brothers ever say the word *brown* to me again.

Instead, John's mother, Bess, say, I hope you are not offended.

She say, I did my best on those boys. But raising four boys with no father is no picnic.

You have a beautiful family, I say.

I'm getting old, she say.

You deserve a rest, I say. Too many boys make you old.

I never had a daughter, she say. You have a daughter.

I have a daughter, I say. Chinese people don't think a daughter is so great, but you're right. I have a daughter.

I was never against the marriage, you know, she say. I never thought John was marrying down. I always thought Nattie was just as good as white.

I was never against the marriage either, I say. I just wonder if they look at the whole problem.

Of course you pointed out the problem, you are a mother, she say. And now we both have a granddaughter. A little brown granddaughter, she is so precious to me.

I laugh. A little brown granddaughter, I say. To tell you the truth, I don't know how she came out so brown.

We laugh some more. These days Bess need a walker to walk. She take so many pills, she need two glasses of water to get them all down. Her favorite TV show is about bloopers, and she love her bird feeder. All day long, she can watch that bird feeder, like a cat.

I can't wait for her to grow up, Bess say. I could use some female company.

Too many boys, I say.

Boys are fine, she say. But they do surround you after a while.

You should take a break, come live with us, I say. Lots of girls at our house.

Be careful what you offer, say Bess with a wink. Where I come from, people mean for you to move in when they say a thing like that.

Nothing the matter with Sophie's outside, that's the truth. It is inside that she is like not any Chinese girl I ever see. We go to the park, and this is what she does. She stand up in the stroller. She take off all her clothes and throw them in the fountain.

Sophie! I say. Stop!

But she just laugh like a crazy person. Before I take over as baby-sitter, Sophie has that crazy-person sitter, Amy the guitar player. My daughter thought this Amy very creative—another word we do not talk about in China. In China, we talk about whether we have difficulty or no difficulty. We talk about whether life is bitter or not bitter. In America, all day long, people talk about creative. Never mind that I cannot even look at this Amy, with her shirt so short that her belly button showing. This Amy think Sophie should love her body. So when Sophie take off her diaper, Amy laugh. When Sophie run around naked, Amy say she wouldn't want to wear a diaper either. When Sophie go *shu-shu* in her lap, Amy laugh and say there are no germs in pee. When Sophie take off her shoes, Amy say bare feet is best, even the pediatrician say so. That is why Sophie now walk around with no shoes like a beggar child. Also why Sophie love to take off her clothes.

Turn around! say the boys in the park. Let's see that ass!

Of course, Sophie does not understand. Sophie clap her hands, I am the only one to say, No! This is not a game.

It has nothing to do with John's family, my daughter say. Amy was too permissive, that's all.

But I think if Sophie was not wild inside, she would not take off her shoes and clothes to begin with.

You never take off your clothes when you were little, I say. All my Chinese friends had babies, I never saw one of them act wild like that.

Look, my daughter say. I have a big presentation tomorrow.

John and my daughter agree Sophie is a problem, but they don't know what to do.

You spank her, she'll stop, I say another day.

But they say, Oh no.

In America, parents not supposed to spank the child.

It gives them low self-esteem, my daughter say. And that leads to problems later, as I happen to know.

My daughter never have big presentation the next day when the subject of spanking come up.

I don't want you to touch Sophie, she say. No spanking, period.

Don't tell me what to do, I say.

I'm not telling you what to do, say my daughter. I'm telling you how I feel.

I am not your servant, I say. Don't you dare talk to me like that.

My daughter have another funny habit when she lose an argument. She spread out all her fingers and look at them, as if she like to make sure they are still there.

My daughter is fierce like me, but she and John think it is better to explain to Sophie that clothes are a good idea. This is not so hard in the cold weather. In the warm weather, it is very hard.

Use your words, my daughter say. That's what we tell Sophie. How about if you set a good example.

As if good example mean anything to Sophie. I am so fierce, the gang members who used to come to the restaurant all afraid of me, but Sophie is not afraid.

I say, Sophie, if you take off your clothes, no snack.

I say, Sophie, if you take off your clothes, no lunch.

I say, Sophie, if you take off your clothes, no park.

Pretty soon we are stay home all day, and by the end of six hours she still did not have one thing to eat. You never saw a child stubborn like that.

I'm hungry! she cry when my daughter come home.

What's the matter, doesn't your grandmother feed you? My daughter laugh.

No! Sophie say. She doesn't feed me anything!

My daughter laugh again. Here you go, she say.

She say to John, Sophie must be growing.

Growing like a weed, I say.

Still Sophie take off her clothes, until one day I spank her. Not too hard, but she cry and cry, and when I tell her if she doesn't put her clothes back on I'll spank her again, she put her clothes back on. Then I tell her she is good girl, and give her some food to eat. The next day we go to the park and, like a nice Chinese girl, she does not take off her clothes.

She stop taking off her clothes, I report. Finally!

How did you do it? my daughter ask.

After twenty-eight years experience with you, I guess I learn something, I say.

It must have been a phase, John say, and his voice is suddenly like an expert.

His voice is like an expert about everything these days, now that he carry a leather briefcase, and wear shiny shoes, and can go shopping for a new car. On the company, he say. The company will pay for it, but he will be able to drive it whenever he want.

A free car, he say. How do you like that.

It's good to see you in the saddle again, my daughter say. Some of your family patterns are scary.

At least I don't drink, he say. He say, And I'm not the only one with scary family patterns.

That's for sure, say my daughter.

Everyone is happy. Even I am happy, because there is more trouble with Sophie, but now I think I can help her Chinese side fight against her wild side. I teach her to eat food with fork or spoon or chopsticks, she cannot just grab into the middle of a bowl of noodles. I teach her not to play with garbage cans. Sometimes I spank her, but not too often, and not too hard.

Still, there are problems. Sophie like to climb everything. If there is a railing, she is never next to it. Always she is on top of it. Also, Sophie like to hit the mommies of her friends. She learn this from her playground best friend, Sinbad, who is four. Sinbad wear army clothes every day and like to ambush his mommy. He is the one who dug a big hole under the play structure, a foxhole he call it, all by himself. Very hard-working. Now he wait in the foxhole with a shovel full of wet sand. When his mommy come, he throw it right at her.

Oh, it's all right, his mommy say. You can't get rid of war games, it's part of their imaginative play. All the boys go through it.

Also, he like to kick his mommy, and one day he tell Sophie to kick his mommy too.

I wish this story is not true.

Kick her, kick her! Sinbad say.

Sophie kick her. A little kick, as if she just so happened was swinging her little leg and didn't realize that big mommy leg was in the way. Still I spank Sophie and make Sophie say sorry, and what does the mommy say?

Really, it's all right, she say. It didn't hurt.

After that, Sophie learn she can attack mommies in the playground, and some will say, Stop, but others will say, Oh, she didn't mean it, especially if they realize Sophie will be punished.

This is how, one day, bigger trouble come. The bigger trouble start when Sophie hide in the foxhole with that shovel full of sand. She wait, and when I come look for her, she throw it at me. All over my nice clean clothes.

Did you ever see a Chinese girl act this way?

Sophie! I say. Come out of there, say you're sorry.

But she does not come out. Instead, she laugh. Naaah, naahna, naaa-naaa, she say.

I am not exaggerate: millions of children in China, not one act like this.

Sophie! I say. Now! Come out now!

But she know she is in big trouble. She know if she come out, what will happen next. So she does not come out. I am sixty-eight, Chinese age almost seventy, how can I crawl under there to catch her? Impossible. So I yell, yell, yell, and what happen? Nothing. A Chinese mother would help, but American mothers, they look at you, they shake their head, they go home. And, of course, a Chinese child would give up, but not Sophie.

I hate you! she yell. I hate you, Meanie!

Meanie is my new name these days.

Long time this goes on, long long time. The foxhole is deep, you cannot see too much, you don't know where is the bottom. You cannot hear too much either. If she does not yell, you cannot even know she is still there or not. After a while, getting cold out, getting dark out. No one left in the playground, only us.

Sophie, I say. How did you become stubborn like this? I am go home without you now.

I try to use a stick, chase her out of there, and once or twice I hit her, but still she does not come out. So finally I leave. I go outside the gate.

Bye-bye! I say. I'm go home now.

But still she does not come out and does not come out. Now it is dinnertime, the sky is black. I think I should maybe go get help, but how can I leave a little girl by herself in the playground? A bad man could come. A rat could come. I go back in to see what is happen to Sophie. What if she have a shovel and is making a tunnel to escape?

Sophie! I say.

No answer.

Sophie!

I don't know if she is alive. I don't know if she is fall asleep down there. If she is crying, I cannot hear her.

So I take the stick and poke.

Sophie! I say. I promise I no hit you. If you come out, I give you a lollipop.

No answer. By now I worried. What to do, what to do, what to do? I poke some more, even harder, so that I am poking and poking when my daughter and John suddenly appear.

What are you doing? What is going on? say my daughter.

Put down that stick! say my daughter.

You are crazy! say my daughter.

John wiggle under the structure, into the foxhole, to rescue Sophie.

She fell asleep, say John the expert. She's okay. That is one big hole.

Now Sophie is crying and crying.

Sophia, my daughter say, hugging her. Are you okay, peanut? Are you okay?

She's just scared, say John.

Are you okay? I say too. I don't know what happen, I say.

She's okay, say John. He is not like my daughter, full of questions. He is full of answers until we get home and can see by the lamplight.

Will you look at her? he yell then. What the hell happened?

Bruises all over her brown skin, and a swollen-up eye.

You are crazy! say my daughter. Look at what you did! You are crazy!

I try very hard, I say.

How could you use a stick? I told you to use your words!

She is hard to handle, I say.

She's three years old! You cannot use a stick! say my daughter.

She is not like any Chinese girl I ever saw, I say.

I brush some sand off my clothes. Sophie's clothes are dirty too, but at least she has her clothes on.

Has she done this before? ask my daughter. Has she hit you before?

She hits me all the time, Sophie say, eating ice cream.

Your family, say John.

Believe me, say my daughter.

A daughter I have, a beautiful daughter. I took care of her when she could not hold her head up. I took care of her before she could argue with me, when she was a little girl with two pigtails, one of them always crooked. I took care of her when we have to escape from China, I took care of her when suddenly we live in a country with cars everywhere, if you are not careful your little girl get run over. When my husband die, I promise him I will keep the family together, even though it was just two of us, hardly a family at all.

But now my daughter take me around to look at apartments. After all, I can cook, I can clean, there's no reason I cannot live by myself, all I need is a telephone. Of course, she is sorry. Sometimes she cry, I am the one to say everything will be okay. She say she have no choice, she doesn't want to end up divorced. I say divorce is terrible, I don't know who invented this terrible idea. Instead of live with a telephone, though, surprise, I come to live with Bess. Imagine that. Bess make an offer and, sure enough, where she come from, people mean for you to move in when they say things like that. A crazy idea, go to live with someone else's family, but she like to have some female company, not like my daughter, who does not believe in company. These days when my daughter visit, she does not bring Sophie. Bess say we should give Nattie time, we will see Sophie again soon. But seems like my daughter have more presentation than ever before, every time she come she have to leave.

I have a family to support, she say, and her voice is heavy, as if soaking wet. I have a young daughter and a depressed husband and no one to turn to.

When she say no one to turn to, she mean me.

These days my beautiful daughter is so tired she can just sit there in a chair and fall asleep. John lost his job again, already, but still they rather hire a baby-sitter than ask me to help, even they can't afford it. Of course, the new baby-sitter is much younger, can run around. I don't know if Sophie these days is wild or not wild. She call me Meanie, but she like to kiss me too, sometimes. I remember that every time I see a child on TV Sophie like to grab my hair, a fistful in each hand, and then kiss me smack on the nose. I never see any other child kiss that way.

The satellite TV has so many channels, more channels than I can count, including a Chinese channel from the Mainland and a Chinese channel from Taiwan, but most of the time I watch bloopers with Bess. Also, I watch the bird feeder—so many, many kinds of birds come. The Shea sons hang around all the time, asking when will I go home, but Bess tell them, Get lost.

She's a permanent resident, say Bess. She isn't going anywhere.

Then she wink at me, and switch the channel with the remote control.

Of course, I shouldn't say Irish this, Irish that, especially now I am become honorary Irish myself, according to Bess. Me! Who's Irish? I say, and she laugh. All the same, if I could mention one thing about some of the Irish, not all of them of course, I like to mention this: Their talk just stick. I don't know how Bess Shea learn to use her words, but sometimes I hear what she say a long time later. *Permanent resident. Not going anywhere.* Over and over I hear it, the voice of Bess.

Jamaica Kincaid (1949–)

was born Elaine Potter Richardson in St. Johns, Antigua. Her mother taught her to read by the age of three and, for her seventh birthday, gave her an Oxford dictionary and apprenticed her to a seamstress, training that went on for almost ten years. Only boys of her background had the chance to go to college, and so when she was seventeen, she went to New York to work as an au pair. For the next several years, she worked at various jobs and took classes at Westchester Community College, the New School for Social Research, and Franconia College. In 1973, Richardson started to publish nonfiction in magazines and changed her name to Jamaica Kincaid, in part because she wanted the anonymity to write freely. She chose Jamaica because she liked its distant evocation of the Caribbean, Kincaid because it seemed to go well with Jamaica. In 1976, Kincaid became a staff writer for The New Yorker; *for many years, she wrote "Talk of the Town" columns, using that form to teach herself to write the short stories that made up her first collection,* At the Bottom of the River. *Her novels include* Annie John, Lucy, *and* The Autobiography of My Mother. *She married the son of* The New Yorker *editor who hired her, and they live in Vermont, where he is a composer at Bennington College.*

Introduction by **Victor LaValle**

Haven't you noticed how many ugly people you pass on the street every day? Whether it's how they look, how they dress, or even how they smell, aren't there just a whole bunch of unattractive people today? Yes is the answer. Yes yes yes. And yet have you noticed that when you read a novel or short story everyone is suddenly fine? Attractive enough and, deep down, really pretty nice.

Luckily for us, there's Jamaica Kincaid, a writer who refuses to believe in the simple truths that so much contemporary writing holds dear. That people are basically decent, that all you really need in this world is love. Don't be mistaken, it's not that Kincaid is just a pessimist, that's too simple, but she demands that her writing reflect the whole world, not simply the sweet parts.

In "Girl," Kincaid writes one long, breathless paragraph in which a mother passes lessons on to her little girl. The messages are sinister, even painful to read, and this is definitely Kincaid's intent, but as you read the mother's lessons, take notice of the world being described. A land of blackbirds, hot sun, and Sunday school; fresh bread at the bakery and bread pudding.

"Figures in the Distance" features a girl again, this time portraying a perverse, naïve obsession with death. Her greatest hope is that someone she knows will die so that she, like Kincaid, can examine it up close. When a humpbacked girl dies, she writes, "On hearing that she was dead, I wished I had tapped the hump to see if it was hollow. . . . At last, though, someone I knew was dead."

The final piece, "Xuela," comes from Kincaid's novel *The Autobiography of My Mother.* It's the story of Xuela, whose mother died giving birth to her, and the way in which this loss affected Xuela for the rest of her days. The language is spare, smart, and full of misery, but as with "Girl," you've got to read for the beauty as much as the pain. The life shown in these pieces is indeed a wretched one, and most writers would fill every line with self-pity, but notice how Kincaid refuses to do this.

Terrible things happen to Xuela, but she never asks for sympathy. In fact, sometimes she is absolutely unlikeable. Xuela states the facts in lovely language and lets you try to decide who is right and who is wrong. Is it Xuela? Her father? Madame Labatte? You begin to understand that people are essentially both.

While she savages colonialism (she's from Antigua), Kincaid also takes the blacks of Antigua to task for failing to achieve much more than their freedom. Men are portrayed as vain and stupid; women are violent and cruel. There is gender equality in her fiction: Everyone can be terrible. Still, more worthwhile than all this is her honesty about the bond between mother and daughter. For her, it can be a safety net or, just as easily, a noose.

Jamaica Kincaid has been criticized for being cruel; whether to mothers or men or women or blacks or Europeans and a few others I can't think of. And it's true. I'm a black American, and whenever she turns her critical eye on us, I boil over, wishing she wouldn't say something bad about my group—but why am I not just as appalled when she savages other people? Oh, yes, right, because I often worry about my comfort but maybe less so about yours. I'm not proud of that, but it's true.

Luckily, Kincaid writes in a staightforward style that makes the work easy to understand. Instead of spending time deciphering sentences, she wants you to expend your energy on her ideas. You might breeze through each of the stories you find here; if so, go back and read them again. You've missed so much. Jamaica Kincaid's work is a spyglass; use it to catch sight of the humanity floating just offshore.

I wrote earlier of ugly people, but I didn't make it clear that I meant you too. Don't be offended; I'll say the same about myself. Our job in life isn't to attain perfection, but to try to understand existence in this chaotic, often baffling place. Human beings have devised lots of ways to gain perspective. Literature is one of them. Literature helps.

Victor LaValle is the author of the short story collection Slapboxing with Jesus, *winner of the PEN Open Book Award. He has also been awarded the key to Southeastern Queens. He lives in California, where he is the Distinguished Visiting Writer at Mills College.*

Jamaica Kincaid

Girl

Wash the white clothes on Monday and put them on the stone heap; wash the color clothes on Tuesday and put them on the clothes-line to dry; don't walk barehead in the hot sun; cook pumpkin fritters in very hot sweet oil; soak your little cloths right after you take them off; when buying cotton to make yourself a nice blouse, be sure that it doesn't have gum on it, because that way it won't hold up well after a wash; soak salt fish overnight before you cook it; is it true that you sing benna in Sunday school?; always eat your food in such a way that it won't turn someone else's stomach; on Sundays try to walk like a lady and not like the slut you are so bent on becoming; don't sing benna in Sunday school; you mustn't speak to wharf-rat boys, not even to give directions; don't eat fruits on the street—flies will follow you; *but I don't sing benna on Sundays at all and never in Sunday school;* this is how to sew on a button; this is how to make a buttonhole for the button you have just sewed on; this is how to hem a dress when you see the hem coming down and so to prevent yourself from looking like the slut I know you are so bent on becoming; this is how you iron your father's khaki shirt so that it doesn't have a crease; this is how you iron your father's khaki pants so that they don't have a crease; this is how you grow okra—far from the house, because okra tree harbors red ants; when you are growing dasheen, make sure it gets plenty of water or else it makes your throat itch when you are eating it; this is how you sweep a corner; this is how you sweep a whole house; this is how you sweep a yard; this is how you smile to someone you don't like too much; this is how you smile to someone you don't like at all; this is how you smile to someone you like completely; this is how you set a table for tea; this is how you set a table for dinner; this is how you set a table for dinner with an important guest; this is how you set a table for lunch; this is how you set a table for breakfast; this is how to behave in the presence of men who don't know you very well, and this way they won't recognize immediately the slut I have warned you against becoming; be sure to wash every day, even if it is with your own spit; don't squat down to play marbles—you are not a boy, you know; don't pick people's flowers—you might catch something; don't throw stones at blackbirds, because it might not be a blackbird at all; this is how to make a bread pudding; this is how to make doukona; this is how to make pepper pot; this is how to make a good medicine for a cold; this is how to make a good medicine to throw away a child before it even becomes a child; this is how to catch a fish; this is how to throw back a fish you don't like, and that way something bad won't fall on you; this is how to bully a man; this is how a man bullies you; this is how to love a man, and if this doesn't work there are other ways, and if they don't work don't feel too bad about giving up; this is how to spit up in the air if you feel like it, and this is how to move quick so that it doesn't fall on you; this is how to make ends meet; always squeeze bread to make sure it's fresh; *but what if the baker won't let me feel the bread?;* you mean to say that after all you are really going to be the kind of woman who the baker won't let near the bread?

JAMAICA KINCAID

Figures in the Distance

For a short while during the year I was ten, I thought only people I did not know died. At the time I thought this I was on my summer holidays and we were living far out on Fort Road. Usually, we lived in our house on Dickenson Bay Street, a house my father built with his own hands, but just now it needed a new roof and so we were living in a house out on Fort Road. We had only two neighbors, Mistress Maynard and her husband. That summer, we had a pig that had just had piglets; some guinea fowl; and some ducks that laid enormous eggs that my mother said were big even for ducks. I hated to eat any food except for the enormous duck eggs, hardboiled. I had nothing to do every day except to feed the birds and the pig in the morning and in the evening. I spoke to no one other than my parents, and sometimes to Mistress Maynard, if I saw her when I went to pick up the peelings of vegetables which my mother had asked her to save for the pig, which was just the thing the pig really liked. From our yard, I could see the cemetery. I did not know it was the cemetery until one day when I said to my mother that sometimes in the evening, while feeding the pig, I could see various small, sticklike figures, some dressed in black, some dressed in white, bobbing up and down in the distance. I noticed, too, that sometimes the black and white sticklike figures appeared in the morning. My mother said that it was probably a child being buried, since children were always buried in the morning. Until then, I had not known that children died.

I was afraid of the dead, as was everyone I knew. We were afraid of the dead because we never could tell when they might show up again. Sometimes they showed up in a dream, but that wasn't so bad, because they usually only brought a warning, and in any case you wake up from a dream. But sometimes they would show up standing under a tree just as you were passing by. Then they might follow you home, and even though they might not be able to come into your house, they might wait for you and follow you wherever you went; in that case, they would never give up until you joined them. My mother knew of many people who had died in such a way. My mother knew of many people who had died, including her own brother.

After I found out about the cemetery, I would stand in my yard and wait for a funeral to come. Some days, there were no funerals. "No one died," I would say to my mother. Some days, just as I was about to give up and go inside, I would see the small specks appear. "What made them so late?" I would ask my mother. Probably someone couldn't bear to see the coffin lid put in place, and so as a favor the undertaker might let things go on too long, she said. The undertaker! On our way into town, we would pass the undertaker's workshop. Outside, a little sign read "STRAFFEE & SONS, UNDERTAKERS & CABINETMAKERS." I could always tell we were approaching this place, because of the smell of pitch pine and varnish in the air.

Later, we moved back to our house in town, and I no longer had a view of the cemetery. Still no one I knew had died. One day, a girl smaller than I, a girl whose mother was a friend of my mother's, died in my mother's arms. I did not know this girl at all, though I may have got a glimpse of her once or twice as I passed her and her mother coming out of our yard, and I tried to remember everything I had heard about her. Her name was Nalda; she had red hair; she was very bony; she did not like to eat any food. In fact, she liked to eat mud, and her mother always had to keep a strict eye on her to prevent her from doing that. Her father made bricks, and her mother dressed in a way that my father found unbecoming. I heard my mother describe to my father just how Nalda had died: She had a fever, they noticed a change in her breathing, so they called a car and were rushing her off to Dr. Bailey when, just as they were crossing over a bridge, she let out a long sigh and went limp. Dr. Bailey pronounced her dead, and when I heard that I was so glad he wasn't my doctor. My mother asked my father to make the coffin for Nalda, and he did, carving bunches of tiny flowers on the sides. Nalda's mother wept so much that my mother had to take care of everything, and since children were never prepared by undertakers, my mother had to prepare the little girl to be buried. I then began to look at my mother's hands differently. They had stroked the dead girl's forehead; they had bathed and dressed her and laid her in the coffin my father had made. My mother would come back from the dead girl's house smelling of bay rum—a scent that for a long time afterward would make me feel ill. For a while, though not for very long, I could not bear to have my mother caress me or touch my food or help me with my bath. I especially couldn't bear the sight of her hands lying still in her lap.

At school, I told all my friends about this death. I would take them aside individually, so I could repeat the details over and over again. They would listen to me with their mouths open. In turn, they would tell me of someone they had known or heard of who had died. I would listen with my mouth open. One person had known very well a neighbor who had gone swimming after eating a big lunch at a picnic and drowned. Someone had a cousin who in the middle of something one day just fell down dead. Someone knew a boy who had died after eating some poisonous berries. "Fancy that," we said to each other.

I loved very much—and so used to torment until she cried—a girl named Sonia. She was smaller than I, even though she was almost two years older, and she was a dunce—the first real dunce I had ever met. She was such a dunce that sometimes she could not remember the spelling of her own name. I would try to get to school early and give her my homework, so that she could copy it, and in class I would pass her the answers to sums. My friends ignored her, and whenever I mentioned her name in a favorable way they would twist up their lips and make a sound to show their disdain. I thought her beautiful and I would say so. She had long, thick black hair that lay down flat on her arms and legs; and then running down the nape of her neck, down the middle of her back for as far as could be seen before it was swallowed up by her school uniform, was a line of the same long, thick black hair, only here it flared out as if a small breeze had come and parted it. At recess, I would buy her a sweet—something called a frozen joy—with money I had stolen from my mother's purse, and then we would go and sit under a tree in our schoolyard. I would then stare and stare at her, narrowing and opening wide my eyes until she began to fidget under my gaze. Then I would pull at the hair on her arms and legs gently at first, and then awfully hard, holding it up taut with the tips of my fingers until she cried out. For a few weeks, she didn't appear in school, and we were told that her mother, who had been with child, had died suddenly. I couldn't ever again bring myself to speak to her, even though we spent two more years as classmates. She seemed such a shameful thing, a girl whose mother had died and left her alone in the world.

Not long after the little girl died in my mother's arms on the way to the doctor, Miss Charlotte, our neighbor across the street, collapsed and died while having a conversation with my mother. If my mother hadn't caught her, she would have fallen to the ground. When I came home from school that day, my mother said, "Miss Charlotte is dead." I had known Miss Charlotte very well, and I tried to imagine her dead. I couldn't. I did not know what someone looked like dead. I knew what Miss Charlotte looked like coming from market. I knew what she looked like going to church. I knew what she looked like when she told her dog not to frighten me by chasing me up and down the street. Once, when Miss Charlotte was sick, my mother asked me to take her a bowl with some food, so I saw her lying in her bed in her nightgown. Miss Charlotte was buried in a coffin my father did not make, and I was not allowed to go to the funeral.

At school, almost everyone I knew had seen a dead person, and not a spirit of a dead person but a real dead person. The girl who sat at the desk next to mine suddenly stopped sucking her thumb because her mother had washed it in water in which a dead person had been given a bath. I told her that her mother must have been playing a trick on her, that I was sure the water was plain water, since it was just the sort of trick my mother would play on me. But she had met my mother and she said she could see that my mother and her mother weren't alike at all.

I began to go to funerals. I didn't actually go to the funerals as an official mourner, since I didn't know any of the people who had died and I was going without my parents' permission. I visited the funeral parlors or the drawing rooms where the dead were laid out for viewing by the mourners. When I heard the church bell toll in the way it tolled when someone had died, I would try to find out who had died and where the funeral was to be—home or funeral parlor. The funeral parlor was in much the same direction as my route home, but sometimes to get to someone's house I would have to go in the opposite direction of my way home. At first, I didn't go in; I would just stand outside and watch the people come and go, hear the close relatives and friends let out incredible loud wails and moans, and then watch the procession march off to church. But then I began to go in and take a look. The first time I actually saw a dead person, I didn't know what to think. Since it wasn't someone I knew, I couldn't make a comparison. I had never seen the person laugh or smile or frown or shoo a chicken out of a garden. So I looked and looked for as long as I could without letting anyone know I was just there out of curiosity.

One day, a girl my own age died. I did not know her name or anything personal about her except that she was my own age and that she had a humpback. She attended another school, and on the day of her funeral her whole school got the day off. At my school, it was all we could talk about: "Did you know the humpbacked girl?" I remembered once standing behind her in a line to take out books at the library; then I saw a fly land on the collar of her uniform and walk up and down as the collar lay flat on her hump. On hearing that she was dead, I wished I had tapped the hump to see if it was hollow. I also remembered that her hair was parted into four plaits and that the parts were crooked. "She must have combed her hair herself," I said. At last, though, someone I knew was dead. The day of her funeral, I bolted from school as soon as we finished the last amen of our evening prayers, and I made my way to the funeral home. When I got there, the whole street was full of girls from her school, all in their white dress uniforms. It was a big crowd of them, and they were milling around, talking to each other quietly and looking very important. I didn't have time to stop and really envy them; I made my way to the door and entered the funeral parlor. There she was. She was lying in the regular pitch-pine, varnished coffin, on a bed of mauve-and-white lilacs. She wore a white dress, and it may have come all the way down to her ankles, but I didn't have time to look carefully. It was her face that I wanted to see. I remembered how she had looked the day in the library. Her face was just a plain face. She had black eyes, flat nostrils, broad lips. Lying there dead, she looked the same, except her eyes were closed and she was so still. I once had heard someone say about another dead person that it was as if the dead person were asleep. But I had seen a person asleep, and this girl did not look asleep. My parents had just bought me a View-Master. The View-Master came with pictures of the pyramids, the Taj Mahal, Mt. Everest, and scenes of the Amazon River. When the View-Master worked properly, all the scenes looked as if they were alive, as if we could just step into the View-Master and sail down the Amazon River or stand at the foot of the pyramids. When the View-Master didn't work properly, it was as if we were looking at an ordinary, colorful picture. When I looked at this girl, it was as if the View-Master wasn't working properly. I stared at her a long time—long enough so that I caused the line of people waiting to stop by the coffin to grow long and on the verge of impatience. Of course, as I stared I kept my fingers curled up tight against my palms, because I didn't want to make a mistake and point and then have them rot and drop off right there. I then went and sat among the mourners. Her family smiled at me, thinking, I am sure, that I was a school friend, even though I wore the uniform of another school. We sang a hymn—"All Things Bright and Beautiful"—and her mother said it was the first hymn the humpbacked girl had learned to sing by heart.

I walked home. By then, I was very late getting home from school, but I was too excited to worry about it. I wondered if one day while going somewhere alone I would see the humpbacked girl standing under a tree, and if she would try to get me to go for a swim or eat a piece of fruit, and the next thing my mother would know, she would be asking my father to make a coffin for me. Of course, he would be so overcome with grief he wouldn't be able to make my coffin and would have to ask Mr. Oatie to do it, and he just hated to ask Mr. Oatie to do him a favor, because, as I heard him tell my mother, Mr. Oatie was such a leech he tried to suck you dry by making you pay for everything twice.

When I got home, my mother asked me for the fish I was to have picked up from Mr. Earl, one of our fishermen, on the way home from school. But in my excitement I had completely forgotten. Trying to think quickly, I said that when I got to the market Mr. Earl told me that they hadn't gone to sea that day because the sea was too rough. "Oh?" said my mother, and uncovered a pan in which were lying, flat on their sides and covered with lemon juice and butter and onions, three fish: an angelfish for my father, a kanya fish for my mother, and a lady doctorfish for me—the special kind of fish each of us liked. While I was at the funeral parlor, Mr. Earl had got tired of waiting for me and had brought the fish to our house himself. That night, as a punishment, I ate my supper outside, alone, under the breadfruit tree, and my mother said that she would not be kissing me good night later, but when I climbed into bed she came and kissed me anyway.

Jamaica Kincaid

Xuela

My mother died at the moment I was born, and so for my whole life there was nothing standing between me and eternity; at my back was always a bleak, black wind. I could not have known at the beginning of my life that this would be so; I only came to know this in the middle of my life, just at the time when I was no longer young and realized that I had less of some of the things I used to have in abundance and more of some of the things I had scarcely had at all. And this realization of loss and gain made me look backward and forward: at my beginning was this woman whose face I had never seen, but at my end was nothing, no one; there was nothing between me and the black room of the world. I came to feel that for my whole life I had been standing on a precipice, that my loss had made me vulnerable, that it had made me hard and helpless; on knowing this, I became overwhelmed with sadness and shame and pity for myself.

When my mother died, leaving me a small child vulnerable to all the world, my father took me and placed me in the care of the same woman he paid to wash his clothes. It is possible that he emphasized to her the difference between the two bundles; one was his child, perhaps not the only child of his in the world but the only child he had had with the only woman he had married so far, the other was his soiled clothes. He would have handled one more gently than the other, he would have given more careful instructions for the care of one than for the other, he would have expected better care for one than the other—but which one I do not know, because he was a vain man, his appearance was very important to him. That I was a burden to him then, I know; that his soiled clothes were a burden to him then, I know; that he did not know how to take care of me by himself, that he did not know how to clean his own clothes himself then, I know.

He had lived in a very small house with my mother. He was poor, but it was not because he was good; he had simply not done enough bad things yet to get rich. The house was on a hill, and he had walked down the hill balancing in one hand his child, in the other his clothes, and he gave them, bundle and child, to this woman. She was not a relative of his or of my mother's; her name was Eunice Paul, and she had six children already, the last one still a baby. That was why she still had some milk to give me, but in my mouth it tasted sour, and I would not drink it. She lived in a house that was far from other houses, and from it there was a broad view of the sea and the mountains, and when I was irritable and unable to console myself she would prop me up on a pile of old clothes and place me under a tree, and at the sight of that sea and those mountains, so unpitying, I would exhaust myself in tears.

Ma Eunice was not unkind: she treated me just the way she treated her own children—but that is not to say that she was kind to her own children. In a place like this, brutality is the only real inheritance and cruelty is sometimes the only thing freely given. I did not like her, and I missed the face I had never seen; I looked over my shoulder to see if someone was coming, as if I were expecting someone to come, and Ma Eunice would ask me what I was looking for, at first as a joke, but when, after a time, I did not stop doing it, she thought that it meant I could see spirits. I could not see spirits at all, I was just looking for that face, that face I would never see, even if I lived forever.

I never grew to love this woman my father left me with, this woman who was not unkind to me but who could not be kind because she did not know how—and perhaps I could not love her because I, too, did not know how. She fed me food forced through a sieve when I would not drink her milk and did not yet have teeth; when I grew teeth, the first thing I did was to sink them into her hand as she fed me. A small sound escaped her mouth then, more from surprise than from pain, and she knew this for what it was—my first act of ingratitude—and it put her on her guard against me for the rest of the time we knew each other.

Until I was four I did not speak. This did not cause anyone to lose a minute of happiness; there was no one who would have worried about it in any case. I knew I could speak, but I did not want to. I saw my father every fortnight, when he came to get his clean clothes. I never thought of him as coming to visit me; I thought of him as coming to pick up his clean clothes. When he came, I was brought to him, and he would ask me how I was, but it was a formality; he would never touch me or look into my eyes. What was there to see in my eyes then? Eunice washed, ironed, and folded his clothes; they were wrapped up like a gift in two pieces of clean nankeen cloth and placed on a table, the only table in the house, waiting for him to come and pick them up. His visits were quite steady, and so when one time he did not appear as he usually did I noticed it. I said, "Where is my father?"

I said it in English—not patois French or English but plain English—and that should have been the surprise; not that I spoke but that I spoke English, a language I had never heard anyone speak. Ma Eunice and her children spoke the language Dominica, which is French patois, and my father, when he spoke to me, spoke that language also. But no one noticed; they only marvelled at the fact that I had finally spoken. That the first words I said were in the language of a people I would never like or love is now a mystery to me; almost everything in my life to which I am inextricably bound is a source of pain.

I was then four years old and saw the world as a series of sketches, soft strokes in charcoal; and so when my father would come and take his clothes away I saw only that he suddenly appeared on the small path that led from the main road to the door of the house in which I lived and then, after completing his mission, disappeared as he turned onto the road, where it met the path. I did not know what lay beyond the path; I did not know if after he passed from my sight he remained my father or dissolved into something altogether different and I would never see him again in the form of my father. I would have accepted it.

I did not talk and I would not talk.

One day, without meaning to, I broke a plate, the only bone-china plate that Eunice had ever owned, and the words "I am sorry" would not pass my lips. The sadness she expressed over this loss fascinated me; it was so intense, so overwhelming, so deep: she grabbed the thick pouch that was her stomach, she pulled at her hair, she pounded her bosom, large tears rolled out of her eyes and down her cheeks, and they came in such profusion that if they had become a new source of water, as in a myth or a fairy tale, my small self would not have been surprised. I had been warned repeatedly by her not to touch this plate, for she had seen me look at it with an obsessive curiosity. I would look at it and wonder about the picture painted on its surface, a picture of a wide-open field filled with grass and flowers in the most tender shades of yellow, pink, blue, and green; the sky had a sun in it that shone but did not burn bright; the clouds were thin and scattered about like a decoration, not thick and banked up, not harbingers of doom; it was nothing but a field full of grass and flowers on a sunny day, but it had an atmosphere of secret abundance, happiness, and tranquillity; underneath this picture, written in gold letters, was the word "Heaven." Of course it was not a picture of Heaven at all. It was a picture of the English countryside idealized, but I did not know that, I did not know that such a thing as the English countryside existed. And neither did Eunice; she thought that this picture was a picture of Heaven, offering as it did a promise of a life without worry or care or want.

When I broke the china plate on which this picture was painted, and caused Ma Eunice to cry so, I did not immediately feel sorry, I did not feel sorry shortly after; I only felt sorry long afterward, and by then it was too late to tell her so, she had died by then; perhaps she went to Heaven and it fulfilled what was promised on that plate. When I broke the plate, she cursed my dead mother, she cursed my father, she cursed me. The words she used were without meaning; I understood them, but they did not hurt me, for I did not love her. And she did not love me; she made me kneel down on her stone heap—which was situated in a spot that got direct sun all day long—with my hands raised high above my head and with a large stone in each hand. She meant to keep me in this position until I said the words "I am sorry," but I would not say them, I could not say them. It was beyond my own will; those words could not pass my lips then. I stayed like that until she exhausted herself cursing me and all whom I came from.

And should this punishment, redolent as it was in every way of the relationship between captor and captive, master and slave, with its motif of the big and the small, the powerful and the powerless, the strong and the weak, and against a background of earth, sea and sky, and Eunice standing over me, metamorphosing into a succession of things furious and not human with each syllable that passed her lips; with her dress of a thin, badly woven cotton, the bodice of a contrary color and pattern that clashed with the skirt; her hair uncombed, unwashed for many months, wrapped in a piece of old cloth that had been unwashed for longer than her hair; the dress had once been new and clean, and dirt had made it old but dirt had made it new again by giving it shadings it did not have before, and dirt would finally cause it to disintegrate altogether, but she was not a dirty woman, she washed her feet every night; the day was clear, it was not the rainy time, some men were on the sea casting nets for fish, but they would not catch too many because it was a clear day; and three of her children were eating bread and they rolled up the inside of the bread into small pebblelike shapes and threw it at me as I knelt there and they laughed at me; and the sky was without a cloud and there was not a breeze, a fly flew back and forth across my face, sometimes landing on a corner of my mouth; an overripe breadfruit fell off its tree, and that sound was like a fist meeting the soft, fleshy part of a body . . . All this, all this I can remember—should it have made a lasting impression on me?

But as I was kneeling there I saw three land turtles crawling in and out of the small space under the house, and I fell in love with them, I wanted to have them near me, I wanted to speak only to them each day for the rest of my life. Long after my ordeal was over—resolved in a way that did not please Ma Eunice, for I did not say I was sorry—I took all three turtles and placed them in an enclosed area where they could not come and go as they pleased and where they were completely dependent on me for food. I would bring to them the leaves of vegetables, and water in seashells. I thought them beautiful, with their shells dark-gray with faint yellow circles, their long necks, their unjudging eyes, the slow deliberateness of their crawl. But they would withdraw into their shells when I did not want them to, and when I called them they would not come out; to teach them a lesson, I took some mud from the riverbed and covered up the small hole from which each neck would emerge, and I allowed it to dry; I covered over the place where they lived with stones, and for days afterward I forgot about them. When they came into my mind again, I went to take a look at them in the place where I had left them. They were by then all dead.

It was my father's wish that I be sent to school. It was an unusual request; girls did not attend school. I shall never know what made him do such a thing. I can only imagine that he desired such a thing for me without giving it too much thought, because in the end what could an education do for someone like me? I can only say what I did not have; I can only measure it against what I did have and find misery in the difference. And yet, and yet—it was for that reason that I came to see for the first time what lay beyond the path that led away from my house.

I can so well remember the feel of the cloth of my skirt and blouse—coarse because it was new—a green skirt and beige blouse, a uniform, its colors and style mimicking the colors and style of a school somewhere else, somewhere far away; and I had on a pair of brown canvas shoes and brown cotton socks which my father had got for me, I did not know from where. And to mention that I did not know where these things came from, to say that I wondered about them is really to say that this was the first time I had worn such things as shoes and socks, and they caused my feet to ache and swell and the skin to blister and break, but I was made to wear them until my feet got used to it. That morning was a morning like any other, so ordinary it was profound: it was sunny in some places and not in others, and the two (sunny, cloudy) occupied different parts of the sky quite comfortably; the green of the trees, the red burst of the flowers from the flamboyant trees, the sickly yellow fruit of the cashew, the smell of lime, the smell of almonds, the coffee on my breath, Eunice's skirt blowing in my face, and the stirring up of the smells that came from between her legs, which I shall never forget, and whenever I smell myself I am reminded of her; the river was low, so I did not hear the sound of the water rushing over stones; the breeze was soft, so the leaves did not rustle in the trees.

And I had these sensations of seeing, smelling, and hearing during my journey down the path that began at Eunice's door and ended where it met the road; and when I reached the road and placed my newly shod foot on it, that was the first time I had done so; I was aware of this. It was a road of small stones and dirt tightly packed together, and each step I took was awkward; the ground shifted, my feet slipped backward. The road stretched out ahead of me and then it vanished in a bend; we kept walking toward this bend and then we came to the bend and the bend gave way to more of the same road and then another bend. We came to my school long before the end of the last bend: it was a small building with one door and four windows; it had a wooden floor; there was a lizard crawling along a beam in the roof; there were three long desks lined up one behind the other; there was a large wooden table and a chair facing the three long desks; on the wall behind the wooden table and chair was a map; at the top of the map were the words "The British Empire." Those were the first words I learned to read.

In that room there were always boys; I did not sit in a schoolroom with other girls until I was older. I was not afraid in that new situation: I did not know how to be that then and do not know how to be that now. I was not afraid then, because my mother had already died, and that is the only thing a child is really afraid of; when I was born my mother was dead, and I had already lived all those years with Eunice, a woman who was not my mother and who could not love me, and I had lived without my father, never knowing when I would see him again, so I was not afraid for myself in this situation. (And if it is not really true that I was not afraid then, it was not the only time that I did not admit to myself my own vulnerability.)

At the time, each thing as it took place stood out in my mind with a sharpness that I now take for granted; it did not then have a meaning, it did not have a context, I did not yet know the history of events, I did not know their antecedents. My teacher was a woman who had been trained by Methodist missionaries; she was of the African people, that I could see, and she found in this a source of humiliation and self-loathing, and she wore despair like an article of clothing, like a mantle, or a staff on which she leaned constantly, a birthright which she would pass on to us without effort. She did not love us; we did not love her; we did not love one another, not then, not ever. There were seven boys and myself. The boys, too, were all of the African people. My teacher and these boys looked at me and looked at me: I had thick eyebrows; my hair was coarse, thick, and wavy; my eyes were set far apart from each other and they had the shape of almonds; my lips were wide and narrow in an unexpected way. I was of the African people, but not exclusively. My mother was a Carib woman, and when they looked at me this is what they saw; and it was my teacher who, at the end of the day, in bidding me good evening, called me Miss Boiled Fish—she thought me pale and weak.

I started to speak quite openly then—to myself frequently, to others only when it was absolutely necessary. We spoke English in school—proper English, not patois—and among ourselves we spoke French patois, a language that was not considered proper at all, a language that a person from France could not speak and could only with difficulty understand. I spoke to myself because I grew to like the sound of my own voice. It had a sweetness to me, it made my loneliness less, for I was lonely and wished to see people in whose faces I could see something of myself. Because who was I? My mother was dead; when I saw my father I could not tell what I meant to him.

I learned to read and write very quickly. My memory, my ability to retain information, to remember the tiniest detail, to recall who said what and when, was regarded as unusual, so unusual that my teacher, who was trained to think only of good and evil and whose judgment of such things was always mistaken, said I was evil, I was possessed—and to establish that there could be no doubt of this she pointed to the fact that my mother was a Carib woman.

My world, then—silent, soft, and vegetablelike in its vulnerability, subject to the powerful whims of others, diurnal, beginning with the pale opening of light on the horizon each morning and ending with a sudden onset of dark at the beginning of each night—was both a mystery to me and the source of much pleasure. I loved the face of a gray sky, porous, grainy, wet, following me to school for mornings on end, shooting down soft arrows of water on me; the face of that same sky when it was a hard, unsheltering blue, a backdrop for a cruel sun; the harsh heat that eventually became a part of me, like my blood; the massive trees, the stems of some of them the size of small trunks, that grew without restraint, as if beauty were only size, and which I could tell apart by closing my eyes and listening to the sound the leaves made when they rubbed together; and I loved that moment when the white flowers from the cedar tree started to fall to the ground with a silence that I could hear, their petals at first still fresh, a soft kiss of pink and white, then a day later crushed, wilted, and brown, a nuisance to the eye; and the river that had become a small lagoon when one day on its own it changed its course, on whose bank I would sit and watch families of birds, and frogs laying their eggs, and the sky turning from black to blue and blue to black, and rain falling on the sea beyond the lagoon but not on the mountain that was beyond the sea.

It was while sitting in this place that I first began to dream about my mother; I had fallen asleep on the stones that covered the ground around me, my small body sinking into this surface as if it were a bed of feathers. I saw my mother come down a ladder. She wore a long white gown, the hem of it falling just above her heels, and that was all of her that was exposed, just her heels; she came down and down, but no more of her was ever revealed. Only her heels, only the hem of the gown. At first I longed to see more, and then I became satisfied just to see her heels coming down toward me. When I awoke, I was not the same child I had been before I fell asleep. I longed to see my father and to be in his presence constantly.

On a day that began in no special way that I can remember, I was taught the principles involved in writing an ordinary letter. A letter has six parts: the address of the sender, the date, the address of the recipient, the salutation or greeting, the body of the letter, the closing of the letter. It was well known that a person in the position I was expected to occupy—the position of a woman, and a poor one—would have no need whatsoever to write a letter, but the sense of satisfaction it gave everyone connected with teaching me this, writing a letter, must have been immense. I was beaten and harsh words were said to me when I made a mistake. The exercise of copying the letters of someone whose complaints or perceptions or joys were of no interest to me did not make me angry then; it only made me want to write my own letters, letters in which I would express my own feelings about my own life, as it appeared to me at seven years old. I started to write to my father. "My Dear Papa," I wrote, in a lovely, decorative penmanship, a penmanship born of beatings and harsh words. I would say to him that I was mistreated by Eunice in word and deed and that I missed him and loved him very much. I wrote the same thing over and over again. It was without detail; it was without color. It was nothing but the plaintive cry of a small, wounded animal: "My Dear Papa, you are the only person I have left in the world, no one loves me, only you can, I am beaten with words, I am beaten with sticks, I am beaten with stones, I love you more than anything, only you can save me." These words were not meant for my father at all, but the person for whom they were meant—I could see only her heels. Night after night I saw her heels, only her heels coming down to meet me.

I wrote these letters without any intention of sending them to my father; I did not know how to do that, to send them. I folded them up in such a way that if they were torn along the folds they would make eight small squares. There was no mysterious significance to this; I did it to make them fit more neatly under a large stone just outside the gate to my school. Each day, as I left, I would place a letter I had written to my father under it. I had, of course, written these letters in secret, during the small amount of time allotted to us as recess, or during some time when I was supposed to be doing other work but had finished before I was noticed. Pretending to be deeply involved in what I was supposed to be doing, I would write my father a letter.

This small cry for help did not bring me instant relief. I recognized my own misery, but that it could be alleviated—that my life could change, that my circumstances could change—did not occur to me.

My letters did not remain a secret. A boy named Roman had seen me putting them in their secret storage place and, behind my back, he removed them. He had no empathy or pity; any instinct to protect the weak had been destroyed in him. He took my letters to our teacher. In my letters to my father I had said, "Everyone hates me, only you love me," but I had not truly meant these letters to be sent to my father, and they were not really addressed to my father; if I had been asked then if I really felt that everyone hated me, that only my father loved me, I would not have known how to answer. But my teacher's reaction to my letters, those small scribblings, was fascinating to me—a tonic. She believed the "everybody" I referred to was herself, and only herself. She said that my words were calumny, a lie, libellous, that she was ashamed of me, that she was not afraid of me. My teacher said all this to me in front of the other pupils at my school. They thought I was humiliated, and they felt joy to see me brought so low. I did not feel humiliated at all. Her teeth were crooked and yellow, and I wondered then how they had got that way. Large half-moons of perspiration stained the under-arms of her dress, and I wondered if when I became a woman I, too, would perspire so profusely and how it would smell. Behind her shoulder on the wall was a large female spider carrying its sac of eggs, and I wanted to reach out and crush it with the bare palm of my hand, because I wondered if it was the same kind of spider or a relative of the spider that had sucked saliva from the corner of my mouth the night before as I lay sleeping, leaving three small, painful bites. There was a drizzle of rain outside; I could hear the sound of it on the galvanized roof.

She sent my letters to my father, apparently to show me that she had a clear conscience. She said that I had mistaken her scoldings, which were administered out of love for me, as an expression of hatred and that this showed that I was guilty of the sin called pride. And she said that she hoped I would learn to tell the difference between the two, love and hate. And when she said this I did look in her face to see if I could tell whether it was true that she loved me and to see if her words, which so often seemed to be a series of harsh blows, were really an expression of love. Her face to me then did not appear loving, and perhaps I was mistaken—perhaps I was too young to judge, too young to know.

I did not immediately recognize what had happened, what I had done: however unconsciously, however without direction, I had, through the use of some words, changed my situation, I had perhaps even saved my life. To speak of my own situation, to myself or to others, is something I would always do thereafter. It is in that way that I came to be so extremely conscious of myself, so interested in my own needs, so interested in fulfilling them, aware of my grievances, aware of my pleasures. From this unfocussed, childish expression of pain, my life was changed, and I took note of it.

My father came to fetch me wearing the uniform of a jailer. To him this had no meaning, it was without significance. He was returning to Roseau from the village of St. Joseph, where he had been carrying out his duties as a policeman. I was not told that he would arrive on that day, I had not expected him. I returned from school and saw him standing at the final bend in the road that led to the house in which I lived. I was surprised to see him, but I would only admit this to myself; I did not let anyone know.

The reason I had missed my father so—the reason he no longer came to the house in which I lived, bringing his dirty clothes and taking away clean ones—was that he had married again. I had been told about this, but it was a mystery to me what it might mean; it was not unlike when I had been told that the world was round and it was the first time I had heard such a thing. I thought, What could it mean, why should it be? My father had married again. He took my hand, he said something, he spoke in English, his mouth had begun to curl around the words he spoke, and it made him appear benign, attractive, even kind. I understood what he said: He had a home for me now, a good home; I would love his wife, my new mother; he loved me as much as he loved himself, perhaps even more, because I reminded him of someone he knew with certainty he had loved even more than he had loved himself. I would love my new home; I would love the sky above me and the earth below.

The word "love" was spoken with such frequency that it became a clue to my seven-year-old mind, a clue that the love being spoken of did not exist. My father's eyes grew small and then they grew big; he believed what he said, and that was a good thing, because I did not. But I would not have wanted to stop this progression, this going away from here; and though I did not believe him I did not have any reason not to, and I was not yet cynical, I did not yet think that behind everything I heard lay another story altogether.

I thanked Eunice for taking care of me. I did not mean it, I could not mean it, but I would mean it if I said it now. I did not say goodbye. All my belongings were in a muslin knapsack, and my father placed it in a bag that was strapped on the donkey he had been riding. He placed me on the donkey, and then he sat behind me. And this was how we looked as my back was turned on the small house in which I spent the first seven years of my life: a man and his small daughter on the back of a donkey at the end of an ordinary day, a day that had no meaning if you were less than a smudge on a page covered with print. I could hear my father's breath, it was not the breath of my life; the back of my head touched his chest from time to time; I could hear the sound of his heart beating through the shirt of his uniform, a uniform that made people afraid when they saw him coming toward them. His presence in my life then was a good thing, and it was too bad that he had not thought of changing his clothes. It was too bad that I noticed he had not done so; it was too bad that such a thing would matter to me.

This new experience of leaving the past behind—of going from one place to another and knowing that whatever had been would remain just as it had been—was something I immediately accepted, a gift. This simple movement, the turning of your back to leave something behind, is among the most difficult to make, but once it has been made you cannot imagine that it was at all hard to accomplish. I had not been able to do it all by myself, but I could see that I had set in motion the events that would make it possible. If I were ever to find myself sitting in that schoolroom again, or sitting in Eunice's yard again, sleeping in her bed, eating with her children, none of it would have the same power it had once had over me—the power to make me feel helpless and ashamed of my own helplessness.

I could not see the look on my father's face as we rode, I did not know what he was thinking, I did not know him well enough to guess. He set off down the road in the opposite direction from the schoolhouse. This stretch of road was new to me, and yet it had a familiarity that made me sad. Around each bend was the familiar dark green of the trees that grew with a ferociousness that no hand had yet attempted to restrain, green unrelenting and complete; nothing could be added to it and nothing could be taken away from it. Each precipice along the road was steep and dangerous, and a fall down one of them would result in death or a lasting injury. And each climb up was followed by a slope down, at the bottom of which clustered, along the road, a choke of flowering plants, each plant with a purpose not yet known to me. And each curve that ran left would soon give way to a curve that ran right.

The day then began to have the colors of an ending, the colors of a funeral, gray and mauve, and my sadness became manifest to me. I was a part of a procession of sadness, which was moving away from my old life, a life I had lived then for only seven years. I did not become overwhelmed, though. The dark of night came on with its usual suddenness. My father placed an arm around me then, as if to ward off something—a danger I could not see in the cool air, an evil spirit, a fall. His clasp was at first gentle; then it grew tighter; it had the strength of an iron band. I did not become overwhelmed.

We entered the village in the dark. There were no lights anywhere, no dog barked, we did not pass anyone. We entered the house in which my father lived, and there was a light coming from a beautiful glass lamp, something I had never seen before; the light was fuelled by a clear liquid that I could see through the base of the lamp, which was embossed with the heads of animals unfamiliar to me. The lamp was on a shelf, and the shelf was made of mahogany, its brackets curling in the shape of two tightly closed paws. The room was crowded, containing a chair on which two people could sit at once, two other chairs on which only one person could sit, and a small, low table draped with a piece of white linen. The walls of the house and the partition that separated this first room from the other rooms of the house were covered with a kind of paper, and the paper was decorated with small pink roses. I had never seen anything like this before, except once, while looking through a book at my school—but the picture I had seen then was a drawing, illustrating a story about the domestic life of a small mammal who lived in a field with his family. In their burrow, the walls had been covered with similar paper. I had understood that story about the small mammal to be a pretense, something to amuse a child, but this was my father's very real house, a house with a bright lamp in a room, and a room that seemed to exist only for an occasional purpose.

At that moment I realized that there were so many things I did not know, not including the very big thing I did not know—my mother. I did not know my father; I did not know where he was from or whom and what he liked; I did not know the land whose surface I had just crossed on an animal's back; I did not know who I was or why I was standing there in that room of occasional purpose with the lamp. A great sea of what I did not know opened up before me, and its treacherous currents pulsed over my head repeatedly until I was sure I was dead. I had only fainted. I opened my eyes soon after that to see the face of my father's wife not too far above mine. She had the face of evil. I had no other face to compare it with; I only knew that this was the face of evil as far as I could tell. She did not like me. I could see that. She did not love me. I could see that. I could not see the rest of her right away—only her face. She was of the African people and the French people. It was nighttime and she was in her own house, so her hair was exposed; it was smooth and yet tightly curled, and she wore it parted in the middle and plaited in two braids that were pinned up in the back. Her lips were shaped like those of people from a cold climate: thin and ungenerous. Her eyes were black, and not with beauty but with deceit. Her nose was long and sharp, like an arrow; her cheekbones were also sharp.

She did not like me. She did not love me. I could see it in her face. My spirit rose to meet this obstacle. No love. I could live in a place like this. I knew this atmosphere all too well. Love would have defeated me. Love would always defeat me. In an atmosphere of no love I could live well; in this atmosphere of no love I could make a life for myself. She held a cup to my mouth; one of her hands brushed against my face, and it felt cold; she was feeding me a tea, something to revive me, but it tasted bitter, like a bad potion. My small tongue allowed no more than a drop of it to come into my mouth, but the bad and bitter taste of it warmed my young heart. I sat up. Our eyes did not meet and lock; I was too young to throw out such a challenge. I could then act only on instinct.

I was led down a short hallway to a room. It was to be my own room. My father lived in a house in which there were so many rooms that I could occupy my own. This small event immediately became central to my life: I adjusted to this evidence of privacy without question. My room was lit by a small lamp, the size of my fist, and I could see my bed: small, of wood, a white sheet on its copra-filled mattress, a square, flat pillow. I had a washstand, on which stood a basin and an urn that had water in it. I did not see a towel. (I did not then know how to wash myself properly in any case, and the lesson I eventually got came with many words of abuse.) There was not a picture on the wall. The walls were not covered with paper; the bare wood—pine—was not painted. It was the plainest of plain rooms, but it had in it more luxury than I had ever imagined; it offered me something I did not even know I needed; it offered me solitude.

All of my little being, physical and spiritual, could find peace here, in this little place where I could sit and take stock.

I sat down on the bed. My heart was breaking; I wanted to cry, I felt so alone. I felt in danger, I felt threatened; I felt as each minute passed that someone wished me dead. My father's wife came to say goodnight, and she turned out the lamp. She spoke to me then in French patois; in his presence she had spoken to me in English. She would do this to me through all the time we knew each other, but that first time, in the sanctuary of my room, at seven years old, I recognized this as an attempt on her part to make an illegitimate of me, to associate me with the made-up language of people regarded as not real—the shadow people, the forever humiliated, the forever low. Then she went to the part of the house where she and my father slept; it was far away; I could hear the sound of her footsteps fade; I could hear their voices as they spoke, the sounds swirling upward to the empty space beneath the ceiling; they had a conversation; I could not make out the words; the emotions seemed neutral, neither hot nor cold; there was some silence; there were short gasps and sighs; there was the sound of people sleeping, breath escaping through their mouths.

I lay down to sleep, to dream of my mother—for I knew I would do that, I knew I would make myself do that. She came down the ladder again and again, over and over, just her heels and the hem of her white dress visible; down, down, I watched her all night in my dream. I did not see her face. I was not disappointed. I would have loved to see her face, but I didn't long for it anymore. She sang a song, but it had no words; it was not a lullaby, it was not sentimental, not meant to calm me when my soul roiled at the harshness of life; it was only a song, but the sound of her voice was like treasure found in an abandoned chest, a treasure that inspires not astonishment but contentment and eternal pleasure.

All night I slept and in my sleep saw her feet come down the ladder, step after step, and I heard her voice singing that song, sometimes humming, sometimes through an open mouth. To this day she will appear in my dreams from time to time, but never again to sing or utter a sound of any kind—only as before, coming down a ladder, her heels visible and the white hem of her garment above them.

I came to my father's house in the blanket of voluptuous blackness that was the night; a morning naturally followed. I awoke to the same landscape that I had always known, each aspect of it beyond reproach, at once beautiful, ugly; humble, and proud; full of life, full of death, able to sustain the one, inevitably to claim the other.

My father's wife showed me how to wash myself. It was not done with kindness. My human form and odor were an opportunity to heap scorn on me. I responded in a fashion by now characteristic of me: whatever I was told to hate I loved. I loved the smell of the thin dirt behind my ears, the smell that comes from between my legs, the smell in the pits of my arms, the smell of my unwashed feet. Whatever about me caused offense, whatever was native to me, whatever I could not help and was not a moral failing—those things about me I loved with the fervor of the devoted. Her hands as they touched me were cold and caused me pain. In her was a despair rooted in a desire long thwarted; she had not yet been able to bear my father a child. She was afraid of me; she was afraid that because of me my father would think of my mother more often than he thought of her. On that first morning, she gave me some food, and it was old, moldy, as if she had saved it especially for me in order to make me sick. I did not eat what she offered after that; I learned then how to prepare my own food and made this a trait by which others would know me: I was a girl who prepared her own food.

Parts of my life then, incidents in my life then, seem, when I remember them now, as if they were taking place in a very small, dark place, a place the size of a doll's house, and the doll's house is at the bottom of a cellar, and I am way up at the top of the stairs peering down into this little house trying to make out exactly what is happening down there. And sometimes when I look down at this scene certain things are not in the same place they were in last time I looked; different things are in the shadows, different things are in the light.

Who was my father? Not just who was he to me, his child—but who was he? He was a policeman, but not an ordinary policeman; he inspired more than the expected amount of fear for someone in his position. He made appointments to see people, men, at his house, the place where he lived with his family—this entity of which I was now a sort of member—and he would make these people wait for hours or he wouldn't show up at all. They waited for him, sometimes sitting on a stone that was just inside the gate of the yard, sometimes pacing back and forth from inside the yard to outside the yard, causing the gate to creak, and this always made his wife cross, and she would complain to these people speaking rudely to them, the rudeness way out of proportion to the annoyance of the creaky gate. They waited for him without complaint, sometimes falling asleep standing up, sometimes falling asleep as they sat on the ground. They waited, and when he did not show up they left and returned the next day, hoping to see him; sometimes they did, sometimes they did not. He suffered no consequences for his behavior; he just treated people in this way. He did not care, or so I thought at first—but of course he did care; it was well thought out, this way he had of causing suffering; he was part of a whole way of life on the island which perpetuated pain.

At the time I came to live with him, he had just mastered the mask that he wore for the remainder of his life: the skin taut, the eyes small and drawn back as though deep inside his head, so that it wasn't possible to get a clue to him from them, the lips parted in a smile. He seemed trustworthy. His clothes were always ironed, clean, spotless. He did not like people to know him very well; he tried never to eat food in the presence of strangers or in the presence of people who were afraid of him.

Who was he? I ask myself this all the time, to this day. Who was he? He was a tall man; his hair was red; his eyes were gray. He must have loved me then, he had told me so. I never heard him say words of love to anyone. He wanted me to continue going to school, but I did not know why. It was a great sacrifice that I should go to school, because, as his wife often pointed out, I would have been more useful at home. He gave me books to read. He gave me a life of John Wesley, and as I read it I wondered what the life of a man so full of spiritual tumult and piety had to do with me. My father had become a Methodist and attended church every Sunday; he taught Sunday school. The more money he had, the more he went to church. And the richer he became, the more fixed the mask of his face grew, so that now I no longer remember what he really looked like when I first knew him long ago, before I came to live with him. And so my mother and father then were a mystery to me: one through death, the other through the maze of living; one I had never seen, the other I saw constantly.

The world I came to know was full of treachery, but I did not remain afraid, I did not become cautious. I was not indifferent to the danger my father's wife posed to me, and I was not indifferent to the danger she thought my presence posed to her. So in my father's house, which was her home, I tried to cloak myself in an atmosphere of apology. I did not in fact feel sorry for anything at all, and I had not done anything, either deliberately or by accident, that warranted my begging for forgiveness, but my gait was a weapon—a way of deflecting her attention from me, of persuading her to think of me as someone who was pitiable, an ignorant child. I did not like her, I did not wish her dead, I only wanted her to leave me alone.

I would lie in my bed at night and turn my ear to the sounds that were inside and outside the house, identifying each noise, separating the real from the unreal: whether the screeches that criss-crossed the night, leaving the blackness to fall to the earth like so many ribbons, were the screeches of bats or of someone who had taken the shape of a bat; whether the sound of wings beating in that space so empty of light was a bird or someone who had taken the shape of a bird. The sound of the gate being opened was my father coming home long after the stillness of sleep had overtaken most of his household, his footsteps stealthy but sure, coming into the yard, up the steps, his hand opening the door to his house, closing the door behind him, turning the bar that made the door secure, walking to another part of the house; he never ate meals when he returned home late at night. The sound of the sea then, at night, could be heard clearly, sometimes as a soft swish, a lapping of waves against the shore of black stones, sometimes with the anger of water boiling in a cauldron resting unsteadily on a large fire. And sometimes, when the night was completely still and completely black, I could hear, outside, the long sigh of someone on the way to eternity; and this, of all things, would disturb the troubled peace of all that was real: the dogs asleep under houses, the chickens in the trees, the trees themselves moving about, not in a way that suggested an uprooting, just a moving about, as if they wished they could run away. And if I listened again I could hear the sound of those who crawled on their bellies, of those who carried poisonous lances, and those who carried a deadly poison in their saliva; I could hear the ones who were hunting, the ones who were hunted, the pitiful cry of the small ones who were about to be devoured, followed by the temporary satisfaction of the ones doing the devouring: all this I heard night after night. And it ended only after my hands had travelled up and down all over my own body in a loving caress, finally coming to the soft, moist spot between my legs, and a gasp of pleasure had escaped my lips which I would allow no one to hear.

Bernard Malamud (1914–1986)

the elder son of an immigrant grocer, Max Malamud, and his theatrically talented wife, Bertha Fidelman, grew up in the Gravesend section of Brooklyn. His first stories and sketches appeared in the Erasmus Hall High School literary magazine. He got a bachelor's degree from the City College of New York, then worked for the U.S. Census Bureau and at a series of sales jobs before returning to school and getting a master's degree from Columbia University, where he wrote his thesis on the poetry of Thomas Hardy. He also studied short story writers, particularly Anton Chekhov, as well as Yiddish folktales, and his own writing reflected this dual interest in both the realism of his immediate predecessors and the fantastic realm of myths, tales, and legends. His stories began appearing in The Partisan Review, Harper's Bazaar, *and* Commentary; *his first collection,* The Magic Barrel, *won the 1959 National Book Award. His novels include* The Natural, The Fixer *(which in 1967 won both the National Book Award and the Pulitzer Prize), and* Pictures of Fidelman. *His several books of short stories are collected in 1983's career-spanning* The Stories of Bernard Malamud. *He taught for many years at Oregon State University and Bennington College. Soon after his death, the PEN/Malamud Award for excellence in short fiction was established in his honor.*

Introduction by **Debra Spark**

List your all-time favorite books for your dinner companions, and there it is: Chekov's *Collected Stories* and Crockett Johnson's *Harold and the Purple Crayon* on the same list. Why not include what caught your imagination as a child with what concerns you as an adult? Why not, if fairy tale, myth, and magic don't distract you from reality but lead you to it in the most profound way? And that, of course, is exactly what Bernard Malamud's work does.

Bernard Malamud tells stories of human suffering and striving, tales that are leavened (though never truly buoyed up; his fiction can be desperate) by humor and fantasy. His forebearers are the best writers of the Western tradition but also Charlie Chaplin and the Yiddish folklorists. Within a largely naturalistic piece—one that might look at the cramped quarters and impossible poverty of a Jewish urban slum, or the poor fortune of a grocer, or the unsuccessful efforts of an artist—comes something unusual: A talking bird. An elfin beggar—starving, a noodge, yet with the apparent ability to appear and disappear at will. A marriage broker—an archetype from the folktales—with his magic barrel.

"If you live, you suffer," Malamud writes in his novel *The Assistant,* and the short story writer Malamud agrees with his novelist self. Suffering is a given. Sympathy is a possibility. As a result, charity (the giving of it, the taking of it) is often an issue in Malamud's work. So, too, is the past. Many of Malamud's characters are refugees, and the horrors of the Holocaust serve as subtext to his stories. The Jew who forgets his Jewishness—which means the Jew who forgets his past—is as undignified as the crass frozen food salesman in "The Jewbird." ("Why would a non-Jew want to read these stories?" my mother once asked me. Malamud might answer with his famous line, "All men are Jews." We all suffer. The Jews' story is a universal one. None of us get to forget.)

We don't lose our need for magic as we age, and Malamud's stories charm partially by their sheer inventiveness. Malamud got the idea for the Jewbird from a Howard Nemerov story, "Digressions on a Crow." The writer Steve Stern suggests that the bird itself might be an allusion to the golden peacock, the emblem of Yiddish poetry. But reading the story, one is most aware of the cleverness of putting what would otherwise be an unbearably brutal story of family violence in fanciful terms. The Jewbird is clearly a stand-in for an aging Jewish relative. Like Cohen's ill mother in the Bronx, the Jewbird is an inconvenience. What's more, he eats the old-fashioned Jewish foods. Not the packaged food of Cohen's trade but herring. He smells bad, he dovens (how outré!), but he does have the virtues of wisdom and patience. He's willing to help Cohen's modest son with his schoolwork, and Cohen—the assimilated, new Jew—doesn't value that learning for itself but for what it might do for his son. ("'If he keeps up like this,' Cohen said, 'I'll get him in an Ivy League college for sure.'")

Fidelman, the protagonist of "The Last Mohican," is a far more sympathetic character than Cohen is, but he too has forgotten his past. The first thing we learn about him is that he's a Jew who has arrived in Rome with a pigskin (!) leather briefcase, ready to study that most talented of Christian artists, Giotto. And why would a Jew (even an entirely secularized Jew like Fidelman) choose to study a Christian painter? Why, indeed. Fidelman is a critic because he failed as a painter. And why did he fail as a painter? "The Last Mohican" is the first of a series of stories Malamud wrote about Fidelman, and the answer to that question is elsewhere (as is the fun fact that Fidelman is Malamud's mother's maiden name). But even here, we can see that there is something Fidelman doesn't quite get about art, scholar though he is. Fidelman can find delight and wonder in Rome—"Imagine. Imagine all that history."—but of his own, far more recent history, he is dismissive. "Ah, that's so long ago," he says when the beggar Susskind makes it clear that Fidelman has escaped not one but three of the century's most recent pogroms. In Italy, the one time Fidelman feels completely out of his element is when he enters Rome's old Jewish synagogue.

Like Philip Roth's "Defender of the Faith," "The Last Mohican" asks what a Jew owes his fellow Jew, but in Malamud's story, the exchange is (presumably) not all one-sided. "I don't wish to take only, professor," the schnorrer Susskind insists. "If I had something to give you, I would gladly give it to you." And what he has to give is an understanding of art. At the story's close, the beggar asks—in a dream—whether Fidelman has read Tolstoy. He asks, in essence, whether Fidelman understands the purpose of art, which is (in Tolstoy's mind) to convey feeling from one man's heart to another. It is only when this question is posed to Fidelman (though technically Fidelman poses it to himself) that Fidelman "gets" the very Giotto image that he has been studying for so long. A triumphant insight indeed.

There's a visionary dimension to Malamud (Flannery O'Connor recognized him as a kindred spirit), and one sees this strongly in the strange end of "The Magic Barrel," which takes the miserable, lonely rabbi—a creature of the Old World—and the "fallen" marriage broker's daughter (we don't know her crime, but it is surely a crime of the New World) and gives them an archetypal stature, making them emblems of eternal love and freezing them (as Malamud intended) in something like a Chagall painting at story's end.

In an essay also titled "The Magic Barrel," Malamud talks about the origin of his story and some of its sources. Along the way, he reveals that his stories are all thought out before he writes them. "The Magic Barrel" grew from a series of notebook entries, none of which clinched the story for Malamud until his wife made this chance remark: "You talk a good deal about love, but you don't always love." True enough, Malamud had to admit; the problem of loving and of not being able to love struck him as "one of the central problems of our existence." At the same time, he recalled a recent book review in which a reviewer wondered whether the author truly loved God, given that his book showed no evidence of love for man. Malamud decided to make his protagonist—formerly just a young man—a rabbinical student who struggles to love, and his story took its final shape.

As for the marriage broker, Malamud happened to be translating a Yiddish story with six marriage anecdotes, and they served as inspiration for his story. He says, "From the first anecdote I got the basic idea for the story. From the second and one or two of the others, enough of the personality of the marriage broker to develop him with comparative ease. In other words, I recognized and understood him; I was able to recognize him in my past, though I had never met a marriage broker." Part of Malamud's genius is contained in this final sentence. He recognizes elements of his past that he has never experienced and is able to combine these elements with the world he has experienced for his reader. Which isn't to say that a reader experiences these two worlds as split. The world that Malamud recognizes—certainly when it is the world of the past and even when it is the world of his fantastic imagination—is a seamless part of the world in which we all live.

Debra Spark is the author of the novels Coconuts for the Saint *and* The Ghost of Bridgetown.

BERNARD MALAMUD

The Magic Barrel

Not long ago there lived in uptown New York, in a small, almost meager room, though crowded with books, Leo Finkle, a rabbinical student in the Yeshivah University. Finkle, after six years of study, was to be ordained in June and had been advised by an acquaintance that he might find it easier to win himself a congregation if he were married. Since he had no present prospects of marriage, after two tormented days of turning it over in his mind, he called in Pinye Salzman, a marriage broker whose two-line advertisement he had read in the *Forward.*

The matchmaker appeared one night out of the dark, fourth-floor hallway of the graystone rooming house where Finkle lived, grasping a black, strapped portfolio that had been worn thin with use. Salzman, who had been long in the business, was of slight but dignified build, wearing an old hat, and an overcoat too short and tight for him. He smelled frankly of fish, which he loved to eat, and although he was missing a few teeth, his presence was not displeasing, because of an amiable manner curiously contrasted with mournful eyes. His voice, his lips, his wisp of beard, his bony fingers were animated, but give him a moment of repose and his mild blue eyes revealed a depth of sadness, a characteristic that put Leo a little at ease although the situation, for him, was inherently tense.

He at once informed Salzman why he had asked him to come, explaining that his home was in Cleveland, and that but for his parents, who had married comparatively late in life, he was alone in the world. He had for six years devoted himself almost entirely to his studies, as a result of which, understandably, he had found himself without time for a social life and the company of young women. Therefore he thought it the better part of trial and error—of embarrassing fumbling—to call in an experienced person to advise him on these matters. He remarked in passing that the function of the marriage broker was ancient and honorable, highly approved in the Jewish community, because it made practical the necessary without hindering joy. Moreover, his own parents had been brought together by a matchmaker. They had made, if not a financially profitable marriage—since neither had possessed any worldly goods to speak of—at least a successful one in the sense of their everlasting devotion to each other. Salzman listened in embarrassed surprise, sensing a sort of apology. Later, however, he experienced a glow of pride in his work, an emotion that had left him years ago, and he heartily approved of Finkle.

The two went to their business. Leo had led Salzman to the only clear place in the room, a table near a window that overlooked the lamp-lit city. He seated himself at the matchmaker's side but facing him, attempting by an act of will to suppress the unpleasant tickle in his throat. Salzman eagerly unstrapped his portfolio and removed a loose rubber band from a thin packet of much-handled cards. As he flipped through them, a gesture and sound that physically hurt Leo, the student pretended not to see and gazed steadfastly out the window. Although it was still February, winter was on its last legs, signs of which he had for the first time in years begun to notice. He now observed the round white moon, moving high in the sky through a cloud menagerie, and watched with half-open mouth as it penetrated a huge hen, and dropped out of her like an egg laying itself. Salzman, though pretending through eyeglasses he had just slipped on to be engaged in scanning the writing on the cards, stole occasional glances at the young man's distinguished face, noting with pleasure the long, severe scholar's nose, brown eyes heavy with learning, sensitive yet ascetic lips, and a certain, almost hollow quality of the dark cheeks. He gazed around at shelves upon shelves of books and let out a soft, contented sigh.

When Leo's eyes fell upon the cards, he counted six spread out in Salzman's hand.

"So few?" he asked in disappointment.

"You wouldn't believe me how much cards I got in my office," Salzman replied. "The drawers are already filled to the top, so I keep them now in a barrel, but is every girl good for a new rabbi?"

Leo blushed at this, regretting all he had revealed of himself in a curriculum vitae he had sent to Salzman. He had thought it best to acquaint him with his strict standards and specifications, but in having done so, felt he had told the marriage broker more than was absolutely necessary.

He hesitantly inquired, "Do you keep photographs of your clients on file?"

"First comes family, amount of dowry, also what kind promises," Salzman replied, unbuttoning his tight coat and settling himself in the chair. "After comes pictures, rabbi."

"Call me Mr. Finkle, I'm not yet a rabbi."

Salzman said he would, but instead called him doctor, which he changed to rabbi when Leo was not listening too attentively.

Salzman adjusted his horn-rimmed spectacles, gently cleared his throat and read in an eager voice the contents of the top card:

"Sophie P. Twenty-four years. Widow one year. No children. Educated high school and two years college. Father promises eight thousand dollars. Has wonderful wholesale business. Also real estate. On the mother's side comes teachers, also one actor. Well known on Second Avenue."

Leo gazed up in surprise. "Did you say a widow?"

"A widow don't mean spoiled, rabbi. She lived with her husband maybe four months. He was a sick boy she made a mistake to marry him."

"Marrying a widow has never entered my mind."

"This is because you have no experience. A widow, especially if she is young and healthy like this girl, is a wonderful person to marry. She will be thankful to you the rest of her life. Believe me, if I was looking now for a bride, I would marry a widow."

Leo reflected, then shook his head.

Salzman hunched his shoulders in an almost imperceptible gesture of disappointment. He placed the card down on the wooden table and began to read another:

"Lily H. High school teacher. Regular. Not a substitute. Has savings and new Dodge car. Lived in Paris one year. Father is successful dentist thirty-five years. Interested in professional man. Well Americanized family. Wonderful opportunity.

"I know her personally," said Salzman. "I wish you could see this girl. She is a doll. Also very intelligent. All day you could talk to her about books and theater and what not. She also knows current events."

"I don't believe you mentioned her age?"

"Her age?" Salzman said, raising his brows. "Her age is thirty-two years."

Leo said after awhile, "I'm afraid that seems a little too old."

Salzman let out a laugh. "So how old are you, rabbi?"

"Twenty-seven."

"So what is the difference, tell me, between twenty-seven and thirty-two? My own wife is seven years older than me. So what did I suffer?—Nothing. If Rothschild's daughter wants to marry you, would you say on account her age, no?"

"Yes," Leo said dryly.

Salzman shook off the no in the yes. "Five years don't mean a thing. I give you my word that when you will live with her for one week you will forget her age. What does it mean five years—that she lived more and knows more than somebody who is younger? On this girl, God bless her, years are not wasted. Each one that it comes makes better the bargain."

"What subject does she teach in high school?"

"Languages. If you heard the way she speaks French, you will think it is music. I am in the business twenty-five years, and I recommend her with my whole heart. Believe me, I know what I'm talking, rabbi."

"What's on the next card?" Leo said abruptly.

Salzman reluctantly turned up the third card:

"Ruth K. Nineteen years. Honor student. Father offers thirteen thousand cash to the right bridegroom. He is a medical doctor. Stomach specialist with marvelous practice. Brother-in-law owns own garment business. Particular people."

Salzman looked as if he had read his trump card.

"Did you say nineteen?" Leo asked with interest.

"On the dot."

"Is she attractive?" He blushed. "Pretty?"

Salzman kissed his finger tips. "A little doll. On this I give you my word. Let me call the father tonight and you will see what means pretty."

But Leo was troubled. "You're sure she's that young?"

"This I am positive. The father will show you the birth certificate."

"Are you positive there isn't something wrong with her?" Leo insisted.

"Who says there is wrong?"

"I don't understand why an American girl her age should go to a marriage broker."

A smile spread over Salzman's face.

"So for the same reason you went, she comes."

Leo flushed. "I am pressed for time."

Salzman, realizing he had been tactless, quickly explained. "The father came, not her. He wants she should have the best, so he looks around himself. When we will locate the right boy he will introduce him and encourage. This makes a better marriage than if a young girl without experience takes for herself. I don't have to tell you this."

"But don't you think this young girl believes in love?" Leo spoke uneasily.

Salzman was about to guffaw but caught himself and said soberly, "Love comes with the right person, not before."

Leo parted dry lips but did not speak. Noticing that Salzman had snatched a glance at the next card, he cleverly asked, "How is her health?"

"Perfect," Salzman said, breathing with difficulty. "Of course, she is a little lame on her right foot from an auto accident that it happened to her when she was twelve years, but nobody notices on account she is so brilliant and also beautiful."

Leo got up heavily and went to the window. He felt curiously bitter and upbraided himself for having called in the marriage broker. Finally, he shook his head.

"Why not?" Salzman persisted, the pitch of his voice rising.

"Because I detest stomach specialists."

"So what do you care what is his business? After you marry her do you need him? Who says he must come every Friday night in your house?"

Ashamed of the way the talk was going, Leo dismissed Salzman, who went home with heavy, melancholy eyes.

Though he had felt only relief at the marriage broker's departure, Leo was in low spirits the next day. He explained it as arising from Salzman's failure to produce a suitable bride for him. He did not care for his type of clientele. But when Leo found himself hesitating whether to seek out another matchmaker, one more polished than Pinye, he wondered if it could be—his protestations to the contrary, and although he honored his father and mother—that he did not, in essence, care for the matchmaking institution? This thought he quickly put out of mind yet found himself still upset. All day he ran around in the woods—missed an important appointment, forgot to give out his laundry, walked out of a Broadway cafeteria without paying and had to run back with the ticket in his hand; had even not recognized his landlady in the street when she passed with a friend and courteously called out, "A good evening to you, Doctor Finkle." By nightfall, however, he had regained sufficient calm to sink his nose into a book and there found peace from his thoughts.

Almost at once there came a knock on his door. Before Leo could say enter, Salzman, commercial cupid, was standing in the room. His face was gray and meager, his expression hungry, and he looked as if he would expire on his feet. Yet the marriage broker managed, by some trick of the muscles, to display a broad smile.

"So good evening. I am invited?"

Leo nodded, disturbed to see him again, yet unwilling to ask the man to leave. Beaming still, Salzman laid his portfolio on the table. "Rabbi, I got for you tonight good news."

"I've asked you not to call me rabbi. I'm still a student."

"Your worries are finished. I have for you a first-class bride."

"Leave me in peace concerning this subject." Leo pretended lack of interest.

"The world will dance at your wedding."

"Please, Mr. Salzman, no more."

"But first must come back my strength," Salzman said weakly. He fumbled with the portfolio straps and took out of the leather case an oily paper bag, from which he extracted a hard, seeded roll and a small, smoked white fish. With a quick motion of his hand he stripped the fish out of its skin and began ravenously to chew. "All day in a rush," he muttered.

Leo watched him eat.

"A sliced tomato you have maybe?" Salzman hesitantly inquired.

"No."

The marriage broker shut his eyes and ate. When he had finished he carefully cleaned up the crumbs and rolled up the remains of the fish, in the paper bag. His spectacled eyes roamed the room until he discovered, amid some piles of books, a one-burner gas stove. Lifting his hat he humbly asked. "A glass tea you got, rabbi?"

Conscience-stricken, Leo rose and brewed the tea. He served it with a chunk of lemon and two cubes of lump sugar, delighting Salzman.

After he had drunk his tea, Salzman's strength and good spirits were restored.

"So tell me, rabbi," he said amiably, "you considered some more the three clients I mentioned yesterday?"

"There was no need to consider."

"Why not?"

"None of them suits me."

"What then suits you?"

Leo let it pass because he could give only a confused answer.

Without waiting for a reply, Salzman asked, "You remember this girl I talked to you—the high school teacher?"

"Age thirty-two?"

But, surprisingly, Salzman's face lit in a smile. "Age twenty-nine."

Leo shot him a look. "Reduced from thirty-two?"

"A mistake," Salzman avowed. "I talked today with the dentist. He took me to his safety deposit box and showed me the birth certificate. She was twenty-nine years last August. They made her a party in the mountains where she went for her vacation. When her father spoke to me the first time I forgot to write the age and I told you thirty-two, and now I remember this was a different client, a widow."

"The same one you told me about? I thought she was twenty-four?"

"A different. Am I responsible that the world is filled with widows?"

"No, but I'm not interested in them, nor for that matter, in school teachers."

Salzman pulled his clasped hands to his breast. Looking at the ceiling he devoutly exclaimed, "Yiddishe kinder, what can I say to somebody that he is not interested in high school teachers? So what then you are interested?"

Leo flushed but controlled himself.

"In what else will you be interested," Salzman went on, "if you not interested in this fine girl that she speaks four languages and has personally in the bank ten thousand dollars? Also her father guarantees further twelve thousand. Also she has a new car, wonderful clothes, talks on all subjects, and she will give you a first-class home and children. How near do we come in our life to paradise?"

"If she's so wonderful, why wasn't she married ten years ago?"

"Why?" said Salzman with a heavy laugh. "—Why? Because she is *partikiler.* This is why. She wants the *best.*"

Leo was silent, amused at how he had entangled himself. But Salzman had aroused his interest in Lily H., and he began seriously to consider calling on her. When the marriage broker observed how intently Leo's mind was at work on the facts he had supplied, he felt certain they would soon come to an agreement.

Late Saturday afternoon, conscious of Salzman, Leo Finkle walked with Lily Hirschorn along Riverside Drive. He walked briskly and erectly, wearing with distinction the black fedora he had that morning taken with trepidation out of the dusty hat box on his closet shelf, and the heavy black Saturday coat he had thoroughly whisked clean. Leo also owned a walking stick, a present from a distant relative, but quickly put temptation aside and did not use it. Lily, petite and not unpretty, had on something signifying the approach of spring. She was au courant, animatedly, with all sorts of subjects, and he weighed her words and found her surprisingly sound—score another for Salzman, whom he uneasily sensed to be somewhere around, hiding perhaps high in a tree along the street, flashing the lady signals with a pocket mirror; or perhaps a cloven-hoofed Pan, piping nuptial ditties as he danced his invisible way before them, strewing wild buds on the walk and purple grapes in their paths, symbolizing fruit of a union, though there was of course still none.

Lily startled Leo by remarking, "I was thinking of Mr. Salzman, a curious figure, wouldn't you say?"

Not certain what to answer, he nodded.

She bravely went on, blushing, "I for one am grateful for his introducing us. Aren't you?"

He courteously replied, "I am."

"I mean," she said with a little laugh—and it was all in good taste, or at least gave the effect of being not in bad—"do you mind that we came together so?"

He was not displeased with her honesty, recognizing that she meant to set the relationship aright, and understanding that it took a certain amount of experience in life, and courage, to want to do it quite that way. One had to have some sort of past to make that kind of beginning.

He said that he did not mind. Salzman's function was traditional and honorable—valuable for what it might achieve, which, he pointed out, was frequently nothing.

Lily agreed with a sigh. They walked on for a while and she said after a long silence, again with a nervous laugh, "Would you mind if I asked you something a little bit personal? Frankly, I find the subject fascinating." Although Leo shrugged, she went on half embarrassedly, "How was it that you came to your calling? I mean was it a sudden passionate inspiration?"

Leo, after a time, slowly replied, "I was always interested in the Law."

"You saw revealed in it the presence of the Highest?"

He nodded and changed the subject. "I understand that you spent a little time in Paris, Miss Hirschorn?"

"Oh, did Mr. Salzman tell you, Rabbi Finkle?" Leo winced but she went on, "It was ages ago and almost forgotten. I remember I had to return for my sister's wedding."

And Lily would not be put off. "When," she asked in a trembly voice, "did you become enamored of God?"

He stared at her. Then it came to him that she was talking not about Leo Finkle, but of a total stranger, some mystical figure, perhaps even a passionate prophet that Salzman had dreamed up for her—no relation to the living or dead. Leo trembled with rage and weakness. The trickster had obviously sold her a bill of goods, just as he had him, who'd expected to become acquainted with a young lady of twenty-nine, only to behold, the moment he laid eyes upon her strained and anxious face, a woman past thirty-five and aging rapidly. Only his self-control had kept him this long in her presence.

"I am not," he said gravely, "a talented religious person," and in seeking words to go on found himself possessed by shame and fear. "I think," he said in a strained manner, "that I came to God not because I loved Him but because I did not."

This confession he spoke harshly because its unexpectedness shook him.

Lily wilted. Leo saw a profusion of loaves of bread go flying like ducks high over his head, not unlike the winged loaves by which he had counted himself to sleep last night. Mercifully, then, it snowed, which he would not put past Salzman's machinations.

He was infuriated with the marriage broker and swore he would throw him out of the room the minute he reappeared. But Salzman did not come that night, and when Leo's anger had subsided, an unaccountable despair grew in its place. At first he thought this was caused by his disappointment in Lily, but before long it became evident that he had involved himself with Salzman without a true knowledge of his own intent. He gradually realized—with an emptiness that seized him with six hands—that he had called in the broker to find him a bride because he was incapable of doing it himself. This terrifying insight he had derived as a result of his meeting and conversation with Lily Hirschorn. Her probing questions had somehow irritated him into revealing—to himself more than her—the true nature of his relationship to God, and from that it had come upon him, with shocking force, that apart from his parents, he had never loved anyone. Or perhaps it went the other way, that he did not love God so well as he might, because he had not loved man. It seemed to Leo that his whole life stood starkly revealed and he saw himself for the first time as he truly was—unloved and loveless. This bitter but somehow not fully unexpected revelation brought him to a point of panic, controlled only by extraordinary effort. He covered his face with his hands and cried.

The week that followed was the worst of his life. He did not eat and lost weight. His beard darkened and grew ragged. He stopped attending seminars and almost never opened a book. He seriously considered leaving the Yeshivah, although he was deeply troubled at the thought of the loss of all his years of study—saw them like pages torn from a book, strewn over the city—and at the devastating effect of this decision upon his parents. But he had lived without knowledge of himself, and never in the Five Books and all the Commentaries—mea culpa—had the truth been revealed to him. He did not know where to turn, and in all this desolating loneliness there was no *to whom,* although he often thought of Lily but not once could bring himself to go downstairs and make the call. He became touchy and irritable, especially with his landlady, who asked him all manner of personal questions; on the other hand, sensing his own disagreeableness, he waylaid her on the stairs and apologized abjectly, until mortified, she ran from him. Out of this, however, he drew the consolation that he was a Jew and that a Jew suffered. But gradually, as the long and terrible week drew to a close, he regained his composure and some idea of purpose in life: to go on as planned. Although he was imperfect, the ideal was not. As for his quest of a bride, the thought of continuing afflicted him with anxiety and heartburn, yet perhaps with this new knowledge of himself he would be more successful than in the past. Perhaps love would now come to him and a bride to that love. And for this sanctified seeking who needed a Salzman?

The marriage broker, a skeleton with haunted eyes, returned that very night. He looked, withal, the picture of frustrated expectancy—as if he had steadfastly waited the week at Miss Lily Hirschorn's side for a telephone call that never came.

Casually coughing, Salzman came immediately to the point: "So how did you like her?"

Leo's anger rose and he could not refrain from chiding the matchmaker: "Why did you lie to me, Salzman?"

Salzman's pale face went dead white, the world had snowed on him.

"Did you not state that she was twenty-nine?" Leo insisted.

"I give you my word—"

"She was thirty-five, if a day. *At least* thirty-five."

"Of this don't be too sure. Her father told me—"

"Never mind. The worst of it was that you lied to her."

"How did I lie to her, tell me?"

"You told her things about me that weren't true. You made me out to be more, consequently less than I am. She had in mind a totally different person, a sort of semi-mystical Wonder Rabbi."

"All I said, you was a religious man."

"I can imagine."

Salzman sighed. "This is my weakness that I have," he confessed. "My wife says to me I shouldn't be a salesman, but when I have two fine people that they would be wonderful to be married, I am so happy that I talk too much." He smiled wanly. "This is why Salzman is a poor man."

Leo's anger left him. "Well, Salzman, I'm afraid that's all."

The marriage broker fastened hungry eyes on him.

"You don't want any more a bride?"

"I do," said Leo, "but I have decided to seek her in a different way. I am no longer interested in an arranged marriage. To be frank, I now admit the necessity of premarital love. That is, I want to be in love with the one I marry."

"Love?" said Salzman, astounded. After a moment he remarked, "For us, our love is our life, not for the ladies. In the ghetto they—"

"I know, I know," said Leo. "I've thought of it often. Love, I have said to myself, should be a by-product of living and worship rather than its own end. Yet for myself I find it necessary to establish the level of my need and fulfill it."

Salzman shrugged but answered, "Listen, rabbi, if you want love, this I can find for you also. I have such beautiful clients that you will love them the minute your eyes will see them."

Leo smiled unhappily, "I'm afraid you don't understand."

But Salzman hastily unstrapped his portfolio and withdrew a manila packet from it.

"Pictures," he said, quickly laying the envelope on the table.

Leo called after him to take the pictures away, but as if on the wings of the wind, Salzman had disappeared.

March came. Leo had returned to his regular routine. Although he felt not quite himself yet—lacked energy—he was making plans for a more active social life. Of course it would cost something, but he was an expert in cutting corners; and when there were no corners left he would make circles rounder. All the while Salzman's pictures had lain on the table, gathering dust. Occasionally as Leo sat studying, or enjoying a cup of tea, his eyes fell on the manila envelope, but he never opened it.

The days went by and no social life to speak of developed with a member of the opposite sex—it was difficult, given the circumstances of his situation. One morning Leo toiled up the stairs to his room and stared out the window at the city. Although the day was bright his view of it was dark. For some time he watched the people in the street below hurrying along and then turned with a heavy heart to his little room. On the table was the packet. With a sudden relentless gesture he tore it open. For a half-hour he stood by the table in a state of excitement, examining the photographs of the ladies Salzman had included. Finally, with a deep sigh he put them down. There were six, of varying degrees of attractiveness, but look at them long enough and they all became Lily Hirschorn: all past their prime, all starved behind bright smiles, not a true personality in the lot: Life, despite their frantic yoohooings, had passed them by; they were pictures in a briefcase that stank of fish. After a while, however, as Leo attempted to return the photographs into the envelope, he found in it another, a snapshot of the type taken by a machine for a quarter. He gazed at it a moment and let out a cry.

Her face deeply moved him. Why, he could at first not say. It gave him the impression of youth—spring flowers, yet age—a sense of having been used to the bone, wasted; this came from the eyes, which were hauntingly familiar, yet absolutely strange. He had a vivid impression that he had met her before, but try as he might he could not place her although he could almost recall her name, as if he had read it in her own handwriting. No, this couldn't be; he would have remembered her. It was not, he affirmed, that she had an extraordinary beauty—no, though her face was attractive enough; it was that *something* about her moved him. Feature for feature, even some of the ladies of the photographs could do better; but she leaped forth to his heart—had *lived,* or wanted to—more than just wanted, perhaps regretted how she had lived—had somehow deeply suffered: it could be seen in the depths of those reluctant eyes, and from the way the light enclosed and shone from her, and within her, opening realms of possibility: this was her own. Her he desired. His head ached and eyes narrowed with the intensity of his gazing, then as if an obscure fog had blown up in the mind, he experienced fear of her and was aware that he had received an impression, somehow, of evil. He shuddered, saying softly, it is thus with us all. Leo brewed some tea in a small pot and sat sipping it without sugar, to calm himself. But before he had finished drinking, again with excitement he examined the face and found it good: good for Leo Finkle. Only such a one could understand him and help him seek whatever he was seeking. She might, perhaps, love him. How she had happened to be among the discards in Salzman's barrel he could never guess, but he knew he must urgently go find her.

Leo rushed downstairs, grabbed up the Bronx telephone book, and searched for Salzman's home address. He was not listed, nor was his office. Neither was he in the Manhattan book. But Leo remembered having written down the address on a slip of paper after he had read Salzman's advertisement in the "personals" column of the *Forward.* He ran up to his room and tore through his papers, without luck. It was exasperating. Just when he needed the matchmaker he was nowhere to be found. Fortunately Leo remembered to look in his wallet. There on a card he found his name written and a Bronx address. No phone number was listed, the reason—Leo now recalled—he had originally communicated with Salzman by letter. He got on his coat, put a hat over his skull cap and hurried to the subway station. All the way to the far end of the Bronx he sat on the edge of his seat. He was more than once tempted to take out the picture and see if the girl's face was as he remembered it, but he refrained, allowing the snapshot to remain in his inside coat pocket, content to have her so close. When the train pulled into the station he was waiting at the door and bolted out. He quickly located the street Salzman had advertised.

The building he sought was less than a block from the subway, but it was not an office building, nor even a loft, nor a store in which one could rent office space. It was a very old tenement house. Leo found Salzman's name in pencil on a soiled tag under the bell and climbed three dark flights to his apartment. When he knocked, the door was opened by a thin, asthmatic, gray-haired woman, in felt slippers.

"Yes?" she said, expecting nothing. She listened without listening. He could have sworn he had seen her, too, before but knew it was an illusion.

"Salzman—does he live here? Pinye Salzman," he said, "the matchmaker?"

She stared at him a long minute. "Of course."

He felt embarrassed. "Is he in?"

"No." Her mouth, though left open, offered nothing more.

"The matter is urgent. Can you tell me where his office is?"

"In the air." She pointed upward.

"You mean he has no office?" Leo asked.

"In his socks."

He peered into the apartment. It was sunless and dingy, one large room divided by a half-open curtain, beyond which he could see a sagging metal bed. The near side of the room was crowded with rickety chairs, old bureaus, a three-legged table, racks of cooking utensils, and all the apparatus of a kitchen. But there was no sign of Salzman or his magic barrel, probably also a figment of the imagination. An odor of frying fish made Leo weak to the knees.

"Where is he?" he insisted. "I've got to see your husband."

At length she answered, "So who knows where he is? Every time he thinks a new thought he runs to a different place. Go home, he will find you."

"Tell him Leo Finkle."

She gave no sign she had heard.

He walked downstairs, depressed.

But Salzman, breathless, stood waiting at his door.

Leo was astounded and overjoyed. "How did you get here before me?"

"I rushed."

"Come inside."

They entered. Leo fixed tea, and a sardine sandwich for Salzman. As they were drinking he reached behind him for the packet of pictures and handed them to the marriage broker.

Salzman put down his glass and said expectantly, "You found somebody you like?"

"Not among these."

The marriage broker turned away.

"Here is the one I want." Leo held forth the snapshot.

Salzman slipped on his glasses and took the picture into his trembling hand. He turned ghastly and let out a groan.

"What's the matter?" cried Leo.

"Excuse me. Was an accident this picture. She isn't for you."

Salzman frantically shoved the manila packet into his portfolio. He thrust the snapshot into his pocket and fled down the stairs.

Leo, after momentary paralysis, gave chase and cornered the marriage broker in the vestibule. The landlady made hysterical outcries but neither of them listened.

"Give me back the picture, Salzman."

"No." The pain in his eyes was terrible.

"Tell me who she is then."

"This I can't tell you. Excuse me."

He made to depart, but Leo, forgetting himself, seized the matchmaker by his tight coat and shook him frenziedly.

"Please," sighed Salzman. "*Please.*"

Leo ashamedly let him go. "Tell me who she is," he begged. "It's very important for me to know."

"She is not for you. She is a wild one—wild, without shame. This is not a bride for a rabbi."

"What do you mean wild?"

"Like an animal. Like a dog. For her to be poor was a sin. This is why to me she is dead now."

"In God's name, what do you mean?"

"Her I can't introduce to you," Salzman cried.

"Why are you so excited?"

"Why, he asks," Salzman said, bursting into tears. "This is my baby, my Stella, she should burn in hell."

Leo hurried up to bed and hid under the covers. Under the covers he thought his life through. Although he soon fell asleep he could not sleep her out of his mind. He woke, beating his breast. Though he prayed to be rid of her, his prayers went unanswered. Through days of torment he endlessly struggled not to love her; fearing success, he escaped it. He then concluded to convert her to goodness, himself to God. The idea alternately nauseated and exalted him.

He perhaps did not know that he had come to a final decision until he encountered Salzman in a Broadway cafeteria. He was sitting alone at a rear table, sucking the bony remains of a fish. The marriage broker appeared haggard, and transparent to the point of vanishing.

Salzman looked up at first without recognizing him. Leo had grown a pointed beard and his eyes were weighted with wisdom.

"Salzman," he said, "love has at last come to my heart."

"Who can love from a picture?" mocked the marriage broker.

"It is not impossible."

"If you can love her, then you can love anybody. Let me show you some new clients that they just sent me their photographs. One is a little doll."

"Just her I want," Leo murmured.

"Don't be a fool, doctor. Don't bother with her."

"Put me in touch with her, Salzman," Leo said humbly. "Perhaps I can be of service."

Salzman had stopped eating and Leo understood with emotion that it was now arranged.

Leaving the cafeteria, he was, however, afflicted by a tormenting suspicion that Salzman had planned it all to happen this way.

★ ★ ★

Leo was informed by letter that she would meet him on a certain corner, and she was there one spring night, waiting under a street lamp. He appeared, carrying a small bouquet of violets and rosebuds. Stella stood by the lamp post, smoking. She wore white with red shoes, which fitted his expectations, although in a troubled moment he had imagined the dress red, and only the shoes white. She waited uneasily and shyly. From afar he saw that her eyes—clearly her father's—were filled with desperate innocence. He pictured, in her, his own redemption. Violins and lit candles revolved in the sky. Leo ran forward with flowers outthrust.

Around the corner, Salzman, leaning against a wall, chanted prayers for the dead.

BERNARD MALAMUD

The Last Mohican

Fidelman, a self-confessed failure as a painter, came to Italy to prepare a critical study of Giotto, the opening chapter of which he had carried across the ocean in a new pigskin, leather briefcase, now gripped in his perspiring hand. Also new were his gum-soled oxblood shoes, a tweed suit he had on despite the late-September sun slanting hot in the Roman sky, although there was a lighter one in his bag; and a Dacron shirt and set of cotton-Dacron underwear, good for quick and easy washing for the traveler. His suitcase, a bulky, two-strapped affair which embarrassed him slightly, he had borrowed from his sister Bessie. He planned, if he had any money left at the end of the year, to buy a new one in Florence. Although he had been in not much of a mood when he had left the U.S.A., Fidelman picked up in Naples, and at the moment, as he stood in front of the Rome railroad station, after twenty minutes still absorbed in his first sight of the Eternal City, he was conscious of a certain exaltation that devolved on him after he had discovered that directly across the many-vehicled piazza stood the remains of the Baths of Diocletian. Fidelman remembered having read that Michelangelo had had a hand in converting the baths into a church and convent, the latter ultimately changed into the museum that presently was there. "Imagine," he muttered. "Imagine all that history."

In the midst of his imagining, Fidelman experienced the sensation of suddenly seeing himself as he was, to the pinpoint, outside and in, not without bittersweet pleasure; and as the well-known image of his face rose before him he was taken by the depth of pure feeling in his eyes, slightly magnified by glasses, and the sensitivity of his elongated nostrils and often tremulous lips, nose divided from lips by a mustache of recent vintage that looked, Fidelman thought, as if it had been sculptured there, adding to his dignified appearance although he was a little on the short side. But almost at the same moment, this unexpectedly intense sense of his being—it was more than appearance—faded, exaltation having gone where exaltation goes, and Fidelman became aware that there was an exterior source to the strange, almost tri-dimensional reflection of himself he had felt as well as seen. Behind him, a short distance to the right, he had noticed a stranger—give a skeleton a couple of pounds—loitering near a bronze statue on a stone pedestal of the heavy-dugged Etruscan wolf suckling the infant Romulus and Remus, the man contemplating Fidelman already acquisitively so as to suggest to the traveler that he had been mirrored (lock, stock, barrel) in the other's gaze for some time, perhaps since he had stepped off the train. Casually studying him, though pretending no, Fidelman beheld a person of about his own height, oddly dressed in brown knickers and black, knee-length woolen socks drawn up over slightly bowed, broomstick legs, these grounded in small, porous, pointed shoes. His yellowed shirt was open at the gaunt throat, both sleeves rolled up over skinny, hairy arms. The stranger's high forehead was bronzed, his black hair thick behind small ears, the dark, close-shaven beard tight on the face; his experienced nose was weighted at the tip, and the soft brown eyes, above all, *wanted.* Though his expression suggested humility, he all but licked his lips as he approached the ex-painter.

"Shalom," he greeted Fidelman.

"Shalom," the other hesitantly replied, uttering the word—so far as he recalled—for the first time in his life. My God, he thought, a handout for sure. My first hello in Rome and it has to be a schnorrer.

The stranger extended a smiling hand. "Susskind," he said, "Shimon Susskind."

"Arthur Fidelman." Transferring his briefcase to under his left arm while standing astride the big suitcase, he shook hands with Susskind. A blue-smocked porter came by, glanced at Fidelman's bag, looked at him, then walked away.

Whether he knew it or not Susskind was rubbing his palms contemplatively together.

"Parla italiano?"

"Not with ease, although I read it fluently. You might say I need the practice."

"Yiddish?"

"I express myself best in English."

"Let it be English then." Susskind spoke with a slight British intonation. "I knew you were Jewish," he said, "the minute my eyes saw you."

Fidelman chose to ignore the remark. "Where did you pick up your knowledge of English?"

"In Israel."

Israel interested Fidelman. "You live there?"

"Once, not now," Susskind answered vaguely. He seemed suddenly bored.

"How so?"

Susskind twitched a shoulder. "Too much heavy labor for a man of my modest health. Also I couldn't stand the suspense."

Fidelman nodded.

"Furthermore, the desert air makes me constipated. In Rome I am lighthearted."

"A Jewish refugee from Israel, no less," Fidelman said good-humoredly.

"I'm always running," Susskind answered mirthlessly. If he was lighthearted, he had yet to show it.

"Where else from, if I may ask?"

"Where else but Germany, Hungary, Poland? Where not?"

"Ah, that's so long ago." Fidelman then noticed the gray in the man's hair. "Well, I'd better be going," he said. He picked up his bag as two porters hovered uncertainly nearby.

But Susskind offered certain services. "You got a hotel?"

"All picked and reserved."

"How long are you staying?"

What business is it of his? However, Fidelman courteously replied, "Two weeks in Rome, the rest of the year in Florence, with a few side trips to Siena, Assisi, Padua and maybe also Venice."

"You wish a guide in Rome?"

"Are you a guide?"

"Why not?"

"No," said Fidelman. "I'll look as I go along to museums, libraries, et cetera."

This caught Susskind's attention. "What are you, a professor?"

Fidelman couldn't help blushing. "Not exactly, really just a student."

"From which institution?"

He coughed a little. "By that I mean a professional student, you might say. Call me Trofimov, from Chekhov. If there's something to learn I want to learn it."

"You have some kind of a project?" the other persisted. "A grant?"

"No grant. My money is hard earned. I worked and saved a long time to take a year in Italy. I made certain sacrifices. As for a project, I'm writing on the painter Giotto. He was one of the most important—"

"You don't have to tell me about Giotto," Susskind interrupted with a little smile.

"You've studied his work?"

"Who doesn't know Giotto?"

"That's interesting to me," said Fidelman, secretly irritated. "How do you happen to know him?"

"How do you?"

"I've given a good deal of time and study to his work."

"So I know him too."

I'd better get this over with before it begins to amount up to something, Fidelman thought. He set down his bag and fished with a finger in his leather coin purse. The two porters watched with interest, one taking a sandwich out of his pocket, unwrapping the newspaper and beginning to eat.

"This is for yourself," Fidelman said.

Susskind hardly glanced at the coin as he let it drop into his pants pocket. The porters then left.

The refugee had an odd way of standing motionless, like a cigar store Indian about to burst into flight. "In your luggage," he said vaguely, "would you maybe have a suit you can't use? I could use a suit."

At last he comes to the point. Fidelman, though annoyed, controlled himself. "All I have is a change from the one you now see me wearing. Don't get the wrong idea about me, Mr. Susskind. I'm not rich. In fact, I'm poor. Don't let a few new clothes deceive you. I owe my sister money for them."

Susskind glanced down at his shabby, baggy knickers.

"I haven't had a suit for years. The one I was wearing when I ran away from Germany fell apart. One day I was walking around naked."

"Isn't there a welfare organization that could help you out—some group in the Jewish community, interested in refugees?"

"The Jewish organizations wish to give me what they wish, not what I wish," Susskind replied bitterly. "The only thing they offer me is a ticket back to Israel."

"Why don't you take it?"

"I told you already, here I feel free."

"Freedom is a relative term."

"Don't tell me about freedom."

He knows all about that, too, Fidelman thought. "So you feel free," he said, "but how do you live?"

Susskind coughed, a brutal cough.

Fidelman was about to say something more on the subject of freedom but left it unsaid. Jesus, I'll be saddled with him all day if I don't watch out.

"I'd better be getting off to the hotel." He bent again for his bag.

Susskind touched him on the shoulder and when Fidelman exasperatedly straightened up, the half dollar he had given the man was staring him in the eye.

"On this we both lose money."

"How do you mean?"

"Today the lira sells six twenty-three on the dollar, but for specie they only give you five hundred."

"In that case, give it here and I'll let you have a dollar." From his billfold Fidelman quickly extracted a crisp bill and handed it to the refugee.

"Not more?" Susskind sighed.

"Not more," the student answered emphatically.

"Maybe you would like to see Diocletian's bath? There are some enjoyable Roman coffins inside. I will guide you for another dollar."

"No, thanks." Fidelman said goodbye and, lifting the suitcase, lugged it to the curb. A porter appeared and the student, after some hesitation, let him carry it toward the line of small dark-green taxis in the piazza. The porter offered to carry the briefcase too, but Fidelman wouldn't part with it. He gave the cab driver the address of the hotel, and the taxi took off with a lurch. Fidelman at last relaxed. Susskind, he noticed, had disappeared. Gone with his breeze, he thought. But on the way to the hotel he had an uneasy feeling that the refugee, crouched low, might be clinging to the little tire on the back of the cab; he didn't look out to see.

Fidelman had reserved a room in an inexpensive hotel not far from the station, with its very convenient bus terminal. Then, as was his habit, he got himself quickly and tightly organized. He was always concerned with not wasting time, as if it were his only wealth—not true, of course, though Fidelman admitted he was ambitious—and he soon arranged a schedule that made the most of his working hours. Mornings he usually visited the Italian libraries, searching their catalogues and archives, read in poor light, and made profuse notes. He napped for an hour after lunch, then at four, when the churches and museums were re-opening, hurried off to them with lists of frescoes and paintings he must see. He was anxious to get to Florence, at the same time a little unhappy at all he would not have time to take in in Rome. Fidelman promised himself to return again if he could afford it, perhaps in the spring, and look at anything he pleased.

After dark he managed to unwind himself and relax. He ate as the Romans did, late, enjoyed a half liter of white wine and smoked a cigarette. Afterwards he liked to wander—especially in the old sections near the Tiber. He had read that here, under his feet, were the ruins of ancient Rome. It was an inspiring business, he, Arthur Fidelman, after all born a Bronx boy, walking around in all this history. History was mysterious, the remembrance of things unknown, in a way burdensome, in a way a sensuous experience. It uplifted and depressed, why he did not know, except that it excited his thoughts more than he thought good for him. This kind of excitement was all right up to a point, perfect maybe for a creative artist, but less so for a critic. A critic, he thought, should live on beans. He walked for miles along the winding river, gazing at the star-strewn skies. Once, after a couple of days in the Vatican Museum, he saw flights of angels—gold, blue, white—intermingled in the sky. "My God, I got to stop using my eyes so much," Fidelman said to himself. But back in his room he sometimes wrote till morning.

Late one night, about a week after his arrival in Rome, as Fidelman was writing notes on the Byzantine-style mosaics he had seen during the day, there was a knock on the door, and though the student, immersed in his work, was not conscious he had said "Avanti," he must have, for the door opened, and instead of an angel, in came Susskind in his shirt and baggy knickers.

Fidelman, who had all but forgotten the refugee, certainly never thought of him, half rose in astonishment. "Susskind," he exclaimed, "how did you get in here?"

Susskind for a moment stood motionless, then answered with a weary smile, "I'll tell you the truth, I know the desk clerk."

"But how did you know where I live?"

"I saw you walking in the street so I followed you."

"You mean you saw me accidentally?"

"How else? Did you leave me your address?"

Fidelman resumed his seat. "What can I do for you, Susskind?" He spoke grimly.

The refugee cleared his throat. "Professor, the days are warm but the nights are cold. You see how I go around naked." He held forth bluish arms, goosefleshed. "I came to ask you to reconsider about giving away your old suit."

"And who says it's an old suit?" Despite himself, Fidelman's voice thickened.

"One suit is new, so the other is old."

"Not precisely. I am afraid I have no suit for you, Susskind. The one I presently have hanging in the closet is a little more than a year old and I can't afford to give it away. Besides, it's gabardine, more like a summer suit."

"On me it will be for all seasons."

After a moment's reflection, Fidelman drew out his billfold and counted four single dollars. These he handed to Susskind.

"Buy yourself a warm sweater."

Susskind also counted the money. "If four," he said, "why not five?"

Fidelman flushed. The man's warped nerve. "Because I happen to have four available," he answered. "That's twenty-five hundred lire. You should be able to buy a warm sweater and have something left over besides."

"I need a suit," Susskind said. "The days are warm but the nights are cold." He rubbed his arms. "What else I need I won't say."

"At least roll down your sleeves if you're so cold."

"That won't help me."

"Listen, Susskind," Fidelman said gently, "I would gladly give you the suit if I could afford to, but I can't. I have barely enough money to squeeze out a year for myself here. I've already told you I am indebted to my sister. Why don't you try to get yourself a job somewhere, no matter how menial? I'm sure that in a short while you'll work yourself up into a decent position."

"A job, he says," Susskind muttered gloomily. "Do you know what it means to get a job in Italy? Who will give me a job?"

"Who gives anybody a job? They have to go out and look for it."

"You don't understand, professor. I am an Israeli citizen and this means I can only work for an Israeli company. How many Israeli companies are there here?—maybe two, El Al and Zim, and even if they had a job, they wouldn't give it to me because I have lost my passport. I would be better off now if I were stateless. A stateless person shows his laissez-passer and sometimes he can find a small job."

"But if you lost your passport why didn't you put in for a duplicate?"

"I did, but did they give it to me?"

"Why not?"

"Why not? They say I sold it."

"Had they reason to think that?"

"I swear to you somebody stole it from me."

"Under such circumstances," Fidelman asked, "how do you live?"

"How do I live?" He chomped with his teeth. "I eat air."

"Seriously?"

"Seriously, on air. I also peddle," he confessed, "but to peddle you need a license, and that the Italians won't give me. When they caught me peddling I was interned for six months in a work camp."

"Didn't they attempt to deport you?"

"They did, but I sold my mother's old wedding ring that I kept in my pocket so many years. The Italians are a humane people. They took the money and let me go but they told me not to peddle anymore."

"So what do you do now?"

"I peddle. What should I do, beg?—I peddle. But last spring I got sick and gave my little money away to the doctors. I still have a bad cough." He coughed fruitily. "Now I have no capital to buy stock with. Listen, professor, maybe we can go in partnership together? Lend me twenty thousand lire and I will buy ladies' nylon stockings. After I sell them I will return you your money."

"I have no funds to invest, Susskind."

"You will get it back, with interest."

"I honestly am sorry for you," Fidelman said, "but why don't you at least do something practical? Why don't you go to the Joint Distribution Committee, for instance, and ask them to assist you? That's their business."

"I already told you why. They wish me to go back, but I wish to stay here."

"I still think going back would be the best thing for you."

"No," cried Susskind angrily.

"If that's your decision, freely made, then why pick on me? Am I responsible for you then, Susskind?"

"Who else?" Susskind loudly replied.

"Lower your voice, please, people are sleeping around here," said Fidelman, beginning to perspire. "Why should I be?"

"You know what responsibility means?"

"I think so."

"Then you are responsible. Because you are a man. Because you are a Jew, aren't you?"

"Yes, goddamn it, but I'm not the only one in the whole wide world. Without prejudice, I refuse the obligation. I am a single individual and can't take on everybody's personal burden. I have the weight of my own to contend with."

He reached for his billfold and plucked out another dollar.

"This makes five. It's more than I can afford, but take it and after this please leave me alone. I have made my contribution."

Susskind stood there, oddly motionless, an impassioned statue, and for a moment Fidelman wondered if he would stay all night, but at last the refugee thrust forth a stiff arm, took the fifth dollar and departed.

Early the next morning Fidelman moved out of the hotel into another, less convenient for him, but far away from Shimon Susskind and his endless demands.

This was Tuesday. On Wednesday, after a busy morning in the library, Fidelman entered a nearby trattoria and ordered a plate of spaghetti with tomato sauce. He was reading his *Messaggero,* anticipating the coming of the food, for he was unusually hungry, when he sensed a presence at the table. He looked up, expecting the waiter, but beheld instead Susskind standing there, alas, unchanged.

Is there no escape from him? thought Fidelman, severely vexed. Is this why I came to Rome?

"Shalom, professor," Susskind said, keeping his eyes off the table. "I was passing and saw you sitting here alone, so I came in to say shalom."

"Susskind," Fidelman said in anger, "have you been following me again?"

"How could I follow you?" asked the astonished Susskind. "Do I know where you live now?"

Though Fidelman blushed a little, he told himself he owed nobody an explanation. So he had found out he had moved—good.

"My feet are tired. Can I sit five minutes?"

"Sit."

Susskind drew out a chair. The spaghetti arrived, steaming hot. Fidelman sprinkled it with cheese and wound his fork into several tender strands. One of the strings of spaghetti seemed to stretch for miles, so he stopped at a certain point and swallowed the forkful. Having foolishly neglected to cut the long spaghetti string he was left sucking it, seemingly endlessly. This embarrassed him.

Susskind watched with rapt attention.

Fidelman at last reached the end of the long spaghetti, patted his mouth with a napkin, and paused in his eating.

"Would you care for a plateful?"

Susskind, eyes hungry, hesitated. "Thanks," he said.

"Thanks yes or thanks no?"

"Thanks no." The eyes looked away.

Fidelman resumed eating, carefully winding his fork; he had had not too much practice with this sort of thing and was soon involved in the same dilemma with the spaghetti. Seeing Susskind still watching him, he soon became tense.

"We are not Italians, professor," the refugee said. "Cut it in small pieces with your knife. Then you will swallow it easier."

"I'll handle it as I please," Fidelman responded testily. "This is my business. You attend to yours."

"My business," Susskind sighed, "don't exist. This morning I had to let a wonderful chance get away from me. I had a chance to buy ladies' stockings at three hundred lire if I had money to buy half a gross. I could easily sell them for five hundred a pair. We would have made a nice profit."

"The news doesn't interest me."

"So if not ladies' stockings, I can also get sweaters, scarves, men's socks, also cheap leather goods, ceramics—whatever would interest you."

"What interests me is what you did with the money I gave you for a sweater."

"It's getting cold, professor," Susskind said worriedly. "Soon comes the November rains, and in winter the tramontana. I thought I ought to save your money to buy a couple of kilos of chestnuts and a bag of charcoal for my burner. If you sit all day on a busy street corner you can sometimes make a thousand lire. Italians like hot chestnuts. But if I do this I will need some warm clothes, maybe a suit."

"A suit," Fidelman remarked sarcastically, "why not an overcoat?"

"I have a coat, poor that it is, but now I need a suit. How can anybody come in company without a suit?"

Fidelman's hand trembled as he laid down his fork. "To my mind you are utterly irresponsible and I won't be saddled with you. I have the right to choose my own problems and the right to my privacy."

"Don't get excited, professor, it's bad for your digestion. Eat in peace." Susskind got up and left the trattoria.

Fidelman hadn't the appetite to finish his spaghetti. He paid the bill, waited ten minutes, then departed, glancing around from time to time to see if he were being followed. He headed down the sloping street to a small piazza where he saw a couple of cabs. Not that he could afford one, but he wanted to make sure Susskind didn't tail him back to his new hotel. He would warn the clerk at the desk never to allow anybody of the refugee's name or description even to make inquiries about him.

Susskind, however, stepped out from behind a plashing fountain at the center of the little piazza. Modestly addressing the speechless Fidelman, he said, "I don't wish to take only, professor. If I had something to give you, I would gladly give it to you."

"Thanks," snapped Fidelman, "just give me some peace of mind."

"That you have to find yourself," Susskind answered.

In the taxi Fidelman decided to leave for Florence the next day, rather than at the end of the week, and once and for all be done with the pest.

That night, after returning to his room from an unpleasurable walk in the Trastevere—he had a headache from too much wine at supper—Fidelman found his door ajar and at once recalled that he had forgotten to lock it, although he had as usual left the key with the desk clerk. He was at first frightened, but when he tried the armadio in which he kept his clothes and suitcase, it was shut tight. Hastily unlocking it, he was relieved to see his blue gabardine suit—a one-button jacket affair, the trousers a little frayed on the cuffs, but all in good shape and usable for years to come—hanging amid some shirts the maid had pressed for him; and when he examined the contents of the suitcase he found nothing missing, including, thank God, his passport and travelers' checks. Gazing around the room, Fidelman saw all in place. Satisfied, he picked up a book and read ten pages before he thought of his briefcase. He jumped to his feet and began to search everywhere, remembering distinctly that it had been on the night table as he had lain on the bed that afternoon, rereading his chapter. He searched under the bed and behind the night table, then again throughout the room, even on top of and behind the armadio. Fidelman hopelessly opened every drawer, no matter how small, but found neither the briefcase, nor, what was worse, the chapter in it.

With a groan he sank down on the bed, insulting himself for not having made a copy of the manuscript, for he had more than once warned himself that something like this might happen to it. But he hadn't because there were some revisions he had contemplated making, and he had planned to retype the entire chapter before beginning the next. He thought now of complaining to the owner of the hotel, who lived on the floor below, but it was already past midnight and he realized nothing could be done until morning. Who could have taken it? The maid or hall porter? It seemed unlikely they would risk their jobs to steal a piece of leather goods that would bring them only a few thousand lire in a pawn shop. Possibly a sneak thief? He would ask tomorrow if other persons on the floor were missing something. He somehow doubted it. If a thief, he would then and there have ditched the chapter and stuffed the briefcase with Fidelman's oxblood shoes, left by the bed, and the fifteen-dollar R. H. Macy sweater that lay in full view of the desk. But if not the maid or porter or a sneak thief, then who? Though Fidelman had not the slightest shred of evidence to support his suspicions he could think of only one person—Susskind. This thought stung him. But if Susskind, why? Out of pique, perhaps, that he had not been given the suit he had coveted, nor was able to pry it out of the armadio? Try as he would, Fidelman could think of no one else and no other reason. Somehow the peddler had followed him home (he suspected their meeting at the fountain) and had got into his room while he was out to supper.

Fidelman's sleep that night was wretched. He dreamed of pursuing the refugee in the Jewish catacombs under the ancient Appian Way, threatening him a blow on the presumptuous head with a seven-flamed candelabrum he clutched in his hand; while Susskind, clever ghost, who knew the ins and outs of all the crypts and alleys, eluded him at every turn. Then Fidelman's candles all blew out, leaving him sightless and alone in the cemeterial dark; but when the student arose in the morning and wearily drew up the blinds, the yellow Italian sun winked him cheerfully in both bleary eyes.

Fidelman postponed going to Florence. He reported his loss to the Questura, and though the police were polite and eager to help, they could do nothing for him. On the form on which the inspector noted the complaint, he listed the brief case as worth ten thousand lire, and for "valore del manuscritto" he drew a line. Fidelman, after giving the matter a good deal of thought, did not report Susskind, first, because he had absolutely no proof, for the desk clerk swore he had seen no stranger around in knickers; second, because he was afraid of the consequences for the refugee if he were written down "suspected thief" as well as "unlicensed peddler" and inveterate refugee. He tried instead to rewrite the chapter, which he felt sure he knew by heart, but when he sat down at the desk, there were important thoughts, whole paragraphs, even pages, that went blank in the mind. He considered sending to America for his notes for the chapter but they were in a barrel in his sister's attic in Levittown, among many notes for other projects. The thought of Bessie, a mother of five, poking around in his things, and the work entailed in sorting the cards, then getting them packaged and mailed to him across the ocean, wearied Fidelman unspeakably; he was certain she would send the wrong ones. He laid down his pen and went into the street, seeking Susskind. He searched for him in neighborhoods where he had seen him before, and though Fidelman spent hours looking, literally days, Susskind never appeared; or if he perhaps did, the sight of Fidelman caused him to vanish. And when the student inquired about him at the Israeli consulate, the clerk, a new man on the job, said he had no record of such a person or his lost passport; on the other hand, he was known at the

Joint Distribution Committee, but by name and address only, an impossibility, Fidelman thought. They gave him a number to go to but the place had long since been torn down to make way for an apartment house.

Time went without work, without accomplishment. To put an end to this appalling waste Fidelman tried to force himself back into his routine of research and picture viewing. He moved out of the hotel, which he now could not stand for the harm it had done him (leaving a telephone number and urging he be called if the slightest clue turned up), and he took a room in a small pensione near the Stazione and here had breakfast and supper rather than go out. He was much concerned with expenditures and carefully recorded them in a notebook he had acquired for the purpose. Nights, instead of wandering in the city, feasting himself upon its beauty and mystery, he kept his eyes glued to paper, sitting steadfastly at his desk in an attempt to recreate his initial chapter, because he was lost without a beginning. He had tried writing the second chapter from notes in his possession but it had come to nothing. Always Fidelman needed something solid behind him before he could advance, some worthwhile accomplishment upon which to build another. He worked late, but his mood, or inspiration, or whatever it was, had deserted him, leaving him with growing anxiety, almost disorientation; of not knowing—it seemed to him for the first time in months—what he must do next, a feeling that was torture. Therefore he again took up his search for the refugee. He thought now that once he had settled it; knew that the man had or hadn't stolen his chapter—whether he recovered it or not seemed at the moment immaterial—just the knowing of it would ease his mind and again he would *feel* like working, the crucial element.

Daily he combed the crowded streets, searching for Susskind wherever people peddled. On successive Sunday mornings he took the long ride to the Porta Portese market and hunted for hours among the piles of second-hand goods and junk lining the back streets, hoping his briefcase would magically appear, though it never did. He visited the open market at Piazza Fontanella Borghese, and observed the ambulant vendors at Piazza Dante. He looked among fruit and vegetable stalls set up in the streets, whenever he chanced upon them, and dawdled on busy street corners after dark, among beggars and fly-by-night peddlers. After the first cold snap at the end of October, when the chestnut sellers appeared throughout the city, huddled over pails of glowing coals, he sought in their faces the missing Susskind. Where in all of modern and ancient Rome was he? The man lived in the open air—he had to appear somewhere. Sometimes when riding in a bus or tram, Fidelman thought he had glimpsed somebody in a crowd, dressed in the refugee's clothes, and he invariably got off to run after whoever it was—once a man standing in front of the Banco di Santo Spirito, gone when Fidelman breathlessly arrived; and another time he overtook a person in knickers, but this one wore a monocle. Sir Ian Susskind?

In November it rained. Fidelman wore a blue beret with his trench coat and a pair of black Italian shoes, smaller, despite their pointed toes, than his burly oxbloods which overheated his feet and whose color he detested. But instead of visiting museums he frequented movie houses, sitting in the cheapest seats and regretting the cost. He was, at odd hours in certain streets, several times accosted by prostitutes, some heartbreakingly pretty, one a slender, unhappy-looking girl with bags under her eyes whom he desired mightily, but Fidelman feared for his health. He had got to know the face of Rome and spoke Italian fairly fluently, but his heart was burdened, and in his blood raged a murderous hatred of the bandy-legged refugee—although there were times when he bethought himself he might be wrong—so Fidelman more than once cursed him to perdition.

One Friday night, as the first star glowed over the Tiber, Fidelman, walking aimlessly along the left riverbank, came upon a synagogue and wandered in among a crowd of Sephardim with Italianate faces. One by one they paused before a sink in an antechamber to dip their hands under a flowing faucet, then in the house of worship touched with loose fingers their brows, mouths, and breasts as they bowed to the Ark, Fidelman doing likewise. Where in the world am I? Three rabbis rose from a bench and the service began, a long prayer, sometimes chanted, sometimes accompanied by invisible organ music, but no Susskind anywhere. Fidelman sat at a desk-like pew in the last row, where he could inspect the congregants yet keep an eye on the door. The synagogue was unheated and the cold rose like an exudation from the marble floor. The student's freezing nose burned like a lit candle. He got up to go, but the beadle, a stout man in a high hat and short caftan, wearing a long thick silver chain around his neck, fixed the student with his powerful left eye.

"From New York?" he inquired, slowly approaching.

Half the congregation turned to see who.

"State, not city," answered Fidelman, nursing an active guilt for the attention he was attracting. Then, taking advantage of a pause, he whispered, "Do you happen to know a man named Susskind? He wears knickers."

"A relative?" The beadle gazed at him sadly.

"Not exactly."

"My own son—killed in the Ardeatine Caves." Tears stood forth in his eyes.

"Ah, for that I'm sorry."

But the beadle had exhausted the subject. He wiped his wet lids with pudgy fingers and the curious Sephardim turned back to their prayer books.

"Which Susskind?" the beadle wanted to know.

"Shimon."

He scratched his ear. "Look in the ghetto."

"I looked."

"Look again."

The beadle walked slowly away and Fidelman sneaked out.

The ghetto lay behind the synagogue for several crooked, well-packed blocks, encompassing aristocratic palazzi ruined by age and unbearable numbers, their discolored facades strung with lines of withered wet wash, the fountains in the piazzas, dirt-laden, dry. And dark stone tenements, built partly on centuries-old ghetto walls, inclined towards one another across narrow, cobblestoned streets. In and among the impoverished houses were the wholesale establishments of wealthy Jews, dark holes ending in jeweled interiors, silks and silver of all colors. In the mazed streets wandered the present-day poor, Fidelman among them, oppressed by history, although, he joked to himself, it added years to his life.

A white moon shone upon the ghetto, lighting it like dark day. Once he thought he saw a ghost he knew by sight, and hastily followed him through a thick stone passage to a blank wall where shone in white letters under a tiny electric bulb: VIETATO URINARE. Here was a smell but no Susskind.

For thirty lire the student bought a dwarfed, blackened banana from a street vendor (not S) on a bicycle, and stopped to eat. A crowd of ragazzi gathered to watch.

"Anybody here know Susskind, a refugee wearing knickers?" Fidelman announced, stooping to point with the banana where the pants went beneath the knees. He also made his legs a trifle bowed but nobody noticed.

There was no response until he had finished his fruit, then a thin-faced boy with brown liquescent eyes out of Murillo, piped: "He sometimes works in the Cimitero Verano, the Jewish section."

There too? thought Fidelman. "Works in the cemetery?" he inquired. "With a shovel?"

"He prays for the dead," the boy answered, "for a small fee."

Fidelman bought him a quick banana and the others dispersed.

In the cemetery, deserted on the Sabbath—he should have come Sunday—Fidelman went among the graves, reading legends carved on tombstones, many topped with small brass candelabra, whilst withered yellow chrysanthemums lay on the stone tablets of other graves, dropped stealthily, Fidelman imagined, on All Souls' Day—a festival in another part of the cemetery—by renegade sons and daughters unable to bear the sight of their dead bereft of flowers, while the crypts of the goyim were lit and in bloom. Many were burial places, he read on the stained stones, of those who, for one reason or another, had died in the late large war, including an empty place, it said under a six-pointed star engraved upon a marble slab that lay on the ground, for "My beloved father / Betrayed by the damned Fascists / Murdered at Auschwitz by the barbarous Nazis / *O Crime Orribile.*" But no Susskind.

Three months had gone by since Fidelman's arrival in Rome. Should he, he many times asked himself, leave the city and this foolish search? Why not off to Florence, and there, amid the art splendors of the world, be inspired to resume his work? But the loss of his first chapter was like a spell cast over him. There were times he scorned it as a man-made thing, like all such, replaceable; other times he feared it was not the chapter per se, but that his volatile curiosity had become somehow entangled with Susskind's strange personality—Had he repaid generosity by stealing a man's life work? Was he so distorted? To satisfy himself, to know man, Fidelman had to know, though at what a cost in precious time and effort. Sometimes he smiled wryly at all this; ridiculous, the chapter grieved him for itself only—the precious thing he had created then lost—especially when he got to thinking of the long diligent labor, how painstakingly he had built each idea, how cleverly mastered problems of order, form, how impressive the finished product, Giotto reborn! It broke the heart. What else, if after months he was here, still seeking?

And Fidelman was unchangingly convinced that Susskind had taken it, or why would he still be hiding? He sighed much and gained weight. Mulling over his frustrated career, on the backs of envelopes containing unanswered letters from his sister Bessie he aimlessly sketched little angels flying. Once, studying his minuscule drawings, it occurred to him that he might someday return to painting, but the thought was more painful than Fidelman could bear.

One bright morning in mid-December, after a good night's sleep, his first in weeks, he vowed he would have another look at the Navicella and then be off to Florence. Shortly before noon he visited the porch of St. Peter's, trying, from his remembrance of

Giotto's sketch, to see the mosaic as it had been before its many restorations. He hazarded a note or two in shaky handwriting, then left the church and was walking down the sweeping flight of stairs, when he beheld at the bottom—his heart misgave him, was he still seeing pictures, a sneaky apostle added to the overloaded boatful?—ecco, Susskind! The refugee, in beret and long green G.I. raincoat, from under whose skirts showed his black-stockinged, rooster's ankles—indicating knickers going on above though hidden—was selling black and white rosaries to all who would buy. He held several strands of beads in one hand, while in the palm of the other a few gilded medallions glinted in the winter sun. Despite his outer clothing, Susskind looked, it must be said, unchanged, not a pound more of meat or muscle, the face, though aged, ageless. Gazing at him, the student ground his teeth in remembrance. He was tempted quickly to hide, and unobserved observe the thief; but his impatience, after the long unhappy search, was too much for him. With controlled trepidation he approached Susskind on his left as the refugee was busily engaged on the right, urging a sale of beads upon a woman drenched in black.

"Beads, rosaries, say your prayers with holy beads."

"Greetings, Susskind," Fidelman said, coming shakily down the stairs, dissembling the Unified Man, all peace and contentment. "One looks for you everywhere and finds you here. Wie gehts?"

Susskind, though his eyes flickered, showed no surprise to speak of. For a moment his expression seemed to say he had no idea who was this, had forgotten Fidelman's existence, but then at last remembered—somebody long ago from another country, whom you smiled on, then forgot.

"Still here?" he perhaps ironically joked.

"Still." Fidelman was embarrassed at his voice slipping.

"Rome holds you?"

"Rome," faltered Fidelman, "—the air." He breathed deep and exhaled with emotion.

Noticing the refugee was not truly attentive, his eyes roving upon potential customers, Fidelman, girding himself, remarked, "By the way, Susskind, you didn't happen to notice—did you?—the briefcase I was carrying with me around the time we met in September?"

"Briefcase—what kind?" This he said absently, his eyes on the church doors.

"Pigskin. I had in it—" Here Fidelman's voice could be heard cracking, "—a chapter of a critical work on Giotto I was writing. You know, I'm sure, the Trecento painter?"

"Who doesn't know Giotto?"

"Do you happen to recall whether you saw, if, that is—" He stopped, at a loss for words other than accusatory.

"Excuse me—business." Susskind broke away and bounced up the steps two at a time. A man he approached shied away. He had beads, didn't need others.

Fidelman had followed the refugee. "Reward," he muttered up close to his ear. "Fifteen thousand for the chapter, and who has it can keep the brand new briefcase. That's his business, no questions asked. Fair enough?"

Susskind spied a lady tourist, including camera and guide book. "Beads—holy beads." He held up both hands, but she was just a Lutheran, passing through.

"Slow today," Susskind complained as they walked down the stairs, "but maybe it's the items. Everybody has the same. If I had some big ceramics of the Holy Mother, they go like hot cakes—a good investment for somebody with a little cash."

"Use the reward for that," Fidelman cagily whispered, "buy Holy Mothers."

If he heard, Susskind gave no sign. At the sight of a family of nine emerging from the main portal above, the refugee, calling addio over his shoulder, fairly flew up the steps. But Fidelman uttered no response. I'll get the rat yet. He went off to hide behind a high fountain in the square. But the flying spume raised by the wind wet him, so he retreated behind a massive column and peeked out at short intervals to keep the peddler in sight.

At two o'clock, when St. Peter's closed to visitors, Susskind dumped his goods into his raincoat pockets and locked up shop. Fidelman followed him all the way home, indeed the ghetto, although along a street he had not consciously been on before, which led into an alley where the refugee pulled open a left-handed door, and without transition, was "home." Fidelman, sneaking up close, caught a dim glimpse of an overgrown closet containing bed and table. He found no address on wall or door, nor, to his surprise, any door lock. This for a moment depressed him. It meant Susskind had nothing worth stealing. Of his own, that is. The student promised himself to return tomorrow, when the occupant was elsewhere.

Return he did, in the morning, while the entrepreneur was out selling religious articles, glanced around once and was quickly inside. He shivered—a pitch black freezing cave. Fidelman scratched up a thick match and confirmed bed and table, also a rickety chair, but no heat or light except a drippy candle stub in a saucer on the table. He lit the yellow candle and searched all over the place. In the table drawer a few eating implements plus safety razor, though where he shaved was a mystery, probably a public toilet. On a shelf above the thin-blanketed bed stood half a flask of red wine, part of a package of spaghetti, and a hard panino. Also an unexpected little fish bowl with a bony goldfish swimming around in Arctic seas. The fish, reflecting the candle flame, gulped repeatedly, threshing its frigid tail as Fidelman watched. He loves pets, thought the student. Under the bed he found a chamber pot, but nowhere a briefcase with a fine critical chapter in it. The place was not more than an ice-box someone probably had lent the refugee to come in out of the rain. Alas, Fidelman sighed. Back in the pensione, it took a hot water bottle two hours to thaw him out; but from the visit he never fully recovered.

In this latest dream of Fidelman's he was spending the day in a cemetery all crowded with tombstones, when up out of an empty grave rose this long-nosed brown shade, Virgilio Susskind, beckoning.

Fidelman hurried over.

"Have you read Tolstoy?"

"Sparingly."

"Why is art?" asked the shade, drifting off.

Fidelman, willy-nilly, followed, and the ghost, as it vanished, led him up steps going through the ghetto and into a marble synagogue.

The student, left alone, for no reason he could think of lay down upon the stone floor, his shoulders keeping strangely warm as he stared at the sunlit vault above. The fresco therein revealed this saint in fading blue, the sky flowing from his head, handing an old knight in a thin red robe his gold cloak. Nearby stood a humble horse and two stone hills.

Giotto. San Francesco dona le vesti al cavaliere povero.

Fidelman awoke running. He stuffed his blue gabardine into a paper bag, caught a bus, and knocked early on Susskind's heavy portal.

"Avanti." The refugee, already garbed in beret and raincoat (probably his pajamas), was standing at the table, lighting the candle with a flaming sheet of paper. To Fidelman the paper looked the underside of a typewritten page. Despite himself, the student recalled in letters of fire his entire chapter.

"Here, Susskind," he said in a trembling voice, offering the bundle, "I bring you my suit. Wear it in good health."

The refugee glanced at it without expression. "What do you wish for it?"

"Nothing at all." Fidelman laid the bag on the table, called goodbye and left.

He soon heard footsteps clattering after him across the cobblestones.

"Excuse me, I kept this under my mattress for you." Susskind thrust at him the pigskin briefcase.

Fidelman savagely opened it, searching frenziedly in each compartment, but the bag was empty. The refugee was already in flight. With a bellow the student started after him. "You bastard, you burned my chapter!"

"Have mercy," cried Susskind, "I did you a favor."

"I'll do you one and cut your throat."

"The words were there but the spirit was missing."

In a towering rage, Fidelman forced a burst of speed, but the refugee, light as the wind in his marvelous knickers, his green coattails flying, rapidly gained ground.

The ghetto Jews, framed in amazement in their medieval windows, stared at the wild pursuit. But in the middle of it, Fidelman, stout and short of breath, moved by all he had lately learned, had a triumphant insight.

"Susskind, come back," he shouted, half sobbing. "The suit is yours. All is forgiven."

He came to a dead halt but the refugee ran on. When last seen he was still running.

BERNARD MALAMUD

The Jewbird

The window was open so the skinny bird flew in. Flappity-flap with its frazzled black wings. That's how it goes. It's open, you're in. Closed, you're out and that's your fate. The bird wearily flapped through the open kitchen window of Harry Cohen's top-floor apartment on First Avenue near the lower East River. On a rod on the wall hung an escaped canary cage, its door wide open, but this black-type long-beaked bird—its ruffled head and small dull eyes, crossed a little, making it look like a dissipated crow—landed if not smack on Cohen's thick lamb chop, at least on the table, close by. The frozen foods salesman was sitting at supper with his wife and young son on a hot August evening a year ago. Cohen, a heavy man with hairy chest and beefy shorts; Edie, in skinny yellow shorts and red halter; and their ten-year-old Morris (after his father)—Maurie, they called him, a nice kid though not overly bright—were all in the city after two weeks out, because Cohen's mother was dying. They had been enjoying Kingston, New York, but drove back when Mama got sick in her flat in the Bronx.

"Right on the table," said Cohen, putting down his beer glass and swatting at the bird. "Son of a bitch."

"Harry, take care with your language," Edie said, looking at Maurie, who watched every move.

The bird cawed hoarsely and with a flap of its bedraggled wings—feathers tufted this way and that—rose heavily to the top of the open kitchen door, where it perched staring down.

"Gevalt, a pogrom!"

"It's a talking bird," said Edie in astonishment.

"In Jewish," said Maurie.

"Wise guy," muttered Cohen. He gnawed on his chop, then put down the bone. "So if you can talk, say what's your business. What do you want here?"

"If you can't spare a lamb chop," said the bird, "I'll settle for a piece of herring with a crust of bread. You can't live on your nerve forever."

"This ain't a restaurant," Cohen replied. "All I'm asking is what brings you to this address?"

"The window was open," the bird sighed; adding after a moment, "I'm running. I'm flying but I'm also running."

"From whom?" asked Edie with interest.

"Anti-Semeets."

"Anti-Semites?" they all said.

"That's from who."

"What kind of anti-Semites bother a bird?" Edie asked.

"Any kind," said the bird, "also including eagles, vultures, and hawks. And once in a while some crows will take your eyes out."

"But aren't you a crow?"

"Me? I'm a Jewbird."

Cohen laughed heartily. "What do you mean by that?"

The bird began dovening. He prayed without Book or tallith, but with passion. Edie bowed her head though not Cohen. And Maurie rocked back and forth with the prayer, looking up with one wide-open eye.

When the prayer was done Cohen remarked, "No hat, no phylacteries?"

"I'm an old radical."

"You're sure you're not some kind of a ghost of dybbuk?"

"Not a dybbuk," answered the bird, "though one of my relatives had such an experience once. It's all over now, thank God. They freed her from a former lover, a crazy jealous man. She's now the mother of two wonderful children."

"Birds?" Cohen asked slyly.

"Why not?"

"What kind of birds?"

"Like me. Jewbirds."

Cohen tipped back in his chair and guffawed. "That's a big laugh. I heard of a Jewfish but not a Jewbird."

"We're once removed." The bird rested on one skinny leg, then on the other. "Please, could you spare maybe a piece of herring with a small crust of bread?"

Edie got up from the table.

"What are you doing?" Cohen asked her.

"I'll clear the dishes."

Cohen turned to the bird. "So what's your name, if you don't mind saying?"

"Call me Schwartz."

"He might be an old Jew changed into a bird by somebody," said Edie, removing a plate.

"Are you?" asked Harry, lighting a cigar.

"Who knows?" answered Schwartz. "Does God tell us everything?"

Maurie got up on his chair. "What kind of herring?" he asked the bird in excitement.

"Get down, Maurie, or you'll fall," ordered Cohen.

"If you haven't got matjes, I'll take schmaltz," said Schwartz.

"All we have is marinated, with slices of onion—in a jar," said Edie.

"If you'll open for me the jar I'll eat marinated. Do you have also, if you don't mind, a piece of rye bread—the spitz?"

Edie thought she had.

"Feed him out on the balcony," Cohen said. He spoke to the bird. "After that take off."

Schwartz closed both bird eyes. "I'm tired and it's a long way."

"Which direction are you headed, north or south?"

Schwartz, barely lifting his wings, shrugged.

"You don't know where you're going?"

"Where there's charity I'll go."

"Let him stay, papa," said Maurie. "He's only a bird."

"So stay the night," Cohen said, "but no longer."

In the morning Cohen ordered the bird out of the house but Maurie cried, so Schwartz stayed for a while. Maurie was still on vacation from school and his friends were away He was lonely and Edie enjoyed the fun he had, playing with the bird.

"He's no trouble at all," she told Cohen, "and besides his appetite is very small."

"What'll you do when he makes dirty?"

"He flies across the street in a tree when he makes dirty, and if nobody passes below, who notices?"

"So all right," said Cohen, "but I'm dead set against it. I warn you he ain't gonna stay here long."

"What have you got against the poor bird?"

"Poor bird, my ass. He's a foxy bastard. He thinks he's a Jew."

"What difference does it make what he thinks?"

"A Jewbird, what a chutzpah. One false move and he's out on his drumsticks."

At Cohen's insistence Schwartz lived out on the balcony in a new wooden birdhouse Edie had bought him.

"With many thanks," said Schwartz, "though I would rather have a human roof over my head. You know how it is at my age. I like the warm, the windows, the smell of cooking. I would also be glad to see once in a while the *Jewish Morning Journal* and have now and then a schnapps because it helps my breathing, thanks God. But whatever you give me, you won't hear complaints."

However, when Cohen brought home a bird feeder full of dried corn, Schwartz said, "Impossible."

Cohen was annoyed. "What's the matter, crosseyes, is your life getting too good for you? Are you forgetting what it means to be migratory? I'll bet a helluva lot of crows you happen to be acquainted with, Jews or otherwise, would give their eyeteeth to eat this corn."

Schwartz did not answer. What can you say to a grubber yung?

"Not for my digestion," he later explained to Edie. "Cramps. Herring is better even if it makes you thirsty. At least rainwater don't cost anything." He laughed sadly in breathy caws.

And herring, thanks to Edie, who knew where to shop, was what Schwartz got, with an occasional piece of potato pancake, and even a bit of soupmeat when Cohen wasn't looking.

When school began in September, before Cohen would once again suggest giving the bird the boot, Edie prevailed on him to wait a little while until Maurie adjusted.

"To deprive him right now might hurt his school work, and you know what trouble we had last year."

"So okay, but sooner or later the bird goes. That I promise you."

Schwartz, though nobody had asked him, took on full responsibility for Maurie's performance in school. In return for favors granted, when he was let in for an hour or two at night, he spent most of his time overseeing the boy's lessons. He sat on top of the dresser near Maurie's desk as he laboriously wrote out his homework. Maurie was a restless type and Schwartz gently kept him to his studies. He also listened to him practice his screechy violin, taking a few minutes off now and then to rest his ears in the bathroom. And they afterwards played dominoes. The boy was an indifferent checker player and it was impossible to teach him chess. When he was sick, Schwartz read him comic books though he personally disliked them. But Maurie's work improved in school and even his violin teacher admitted his playing was better.

Edie gave Schwartz credit for these improvements though the bird pooh-poohed them.

Yet he was proud there was nothing lower than C minuses on Maurie's report card, and on Edie's insistence celebrated with a little schnapps.

"If he keeps up like this," Cohen said, "I'll get him in any Ivy League college for sure."

"Oh, I hope so," sighed Edie.

But Schwartz shook his head. "He's a good boy—you don't have to worry. He won't be a shicker or a wife beater, God forbid, but a scholar he'll never be, if you know what I mean, although maybe a good mechanic. It's no disgrace in these times."

"If I were you," Cohen said, angered, "I'd keep my big snoot out of other people's private business."

"Harry, please," said Edie.

"My goddamn patience is wearing out. That crosseyes butts into everything."

Though he wasn't exactly a welcome guest in the house, Schwartz gained a few ounces although he did not improve in appearance. He looked bedraggled as ever, his feathers unkempt, as though he had just flown out of a snowstorm. He spent, he admitted, little time taking care of himself. Too much to think about. "Also outside plumbing," he told Edie. Still there was more glow to his eyes so that though Cohen went on calling him crosseyes he said it less emphatically.

Liking his situation, Schwartz tried tactfully to stay out of Cohen's way, but one night when Edie was at the movies and Maurie was taking a hot shower, the frozen foods salesman began a quarrel with the bird.

"For Christ sake, why don't you wash yourself sometimes? Why must you always stink like a dead fish?"

"Mr. Cohen, if you'll pardon me, if somebody eats garlic he will smell from garlic. I eat herring three times a day. Feed me flowers and I will smell like flowers.

"Who's obligated to feed you anything at all? You're lucky to get herring."

"Excuse me, I'm not complaining," said the bird. "You're complaining."

"What's more," said Cohen, "Even from out on the balcony I can hear you snoring away like a pig. It keeps me awake at night."

"Snoring," said Schwartz, "isn't a crime, thanks God."

"All in all you are a goddamn pest and free loader. Next thing you'll want to sleep in bed next to my wife."

"Mr. Cohen," said Schwartz, "on this rest assured. A bird is a bird."

"So you say, but how do I know you're a bird and not some kind of a goddamn devil?"

"If I was a devil you would know already. And I don't mean because of your son's good marks."

"Shut up, you bastard bird," shouted Cohen.

"Grubber yung," cawed Schwartz, rising to the tips of his talons, his long wings outstretched.

Cohen was about to lunge for the bird's scrawny neck but Maurie came out of the bathroom, and for the rest of the evening until Schwartz's bedtime on the balcony, there was pretend peace.

But the quarrel had deeply disturbed Schwartz and he slept badly. His snoring woke him, and awake, he was fearful of what would become of him. Wanting to stay out of Cohen's way, he kept to the birdhouse as much as possible. Cramped by it, he paced back and forth on the balcony ledge, or sat on the birdhouse roof, staring into space. In evenings, while overseeing Maurie's lessons, he often fell asleep. Awakening, he nervously hopped around exploring the four corners of the room. He spent much time in Maurie's closet, and carefully examined his bureau drawers when they were left open. And once when he found a large paper bag on the floor, Schwartz poked his way into it to investigate what possibilities were. The boy was amused to see the bird in the paper bag.

"He wants to build a nest," he said to his mother.

Edie, sensing Schwartz's unhappiness, spoke to him quietly.

"Maybe if you did some of the things my husband wants you, you would get along better with him."

"Give me a for instance," Schwartz said.

"Like take a bath, for instance."

"I'm too old for baths," said the bird. "My feathers fall out without baths."

"He says you have a bad smell."

"Everybody smells. Some people smell because of their thoughts or because who they are. My bad smell comes from the food I eat. What does his come from?"

"I better not ask him or it might make him mad," said Edie.

In late November Schwartz froze on the balcony in the fog and cold, and especially on rainy days he woke with stiff joints and could barely move his wings. Already he felt twinges of rheumatism. He would have liked to spend more time in the warm house, particularly when Maurie was in school and Cohen at work. But though Edie was good-hearted and might have sneaked him in in the morning just to thaw out, he was afraid to ask her. In the meantime Cohen, who had been reading articles about the migration of birds, came out on the balcony one night after work when Edie was in the kitchen preparing pot roast, and peeking into the birdhouse, warned Schwartz to be on his way soon if he knew what was good for him. "Time to hit the flyways."

"Mr. Cohen, why do you hate me so much?" asked the bird. "What did I do to you?"

"Because you're an A-number-one trouble maker, that's why. What's more, whoever heard of a Jewbird! Now scat or it's open war."

But Schwartz stubbornly refused to depart so Cohen embarked on a campaign of harassing him, meanwhile hiding it from Edie and Maurie. Maurie hated violence and Cohen didn't want to leave a bad impression. He thought maybe if he played dirty tricks on the bird he would fly off without being physically kicked out. The vacation was over, let him make his easy living off the fat of somebody else's land. Cohen worried about the effect of the bird's departure on Maurie's schooling but decided to take the chance, first, because the boy now seemed to have the knack of studying—give the black bird-bastard credit—and second, because Schwartz was driving him bats by being there always, even in his dreams.

The frozen-foods salesman began his campaign against the bird by mixing watery cat food with the herring slices in Schwartz's dish. He also blew up and popped numerous paper bags outside the birdhouse as the bird slept, and when he got Schwartz good and nervous, though not enough to leave, he brought a full-grown cat into the house, supposedly a gift for little Maurie, who had always wanted a pussy. The cat never stopped springing up at Schwartz whenever he saw him, one day managing to claw out several of his tail feathers. And even at lesson time, when the cat was usually excluded from Maurie's room, though somehow or other he quickly found his way in at the end of the lesson, Schwartz was desperately fearful of his life and flew from pinnacle to pinnacle—light fixture to clothestree to door-top—in order to elude the beast's wet jaws.

Once when the bird complained to Edie how hazardous his existence was, she said, "Be patient, Mr. Schwartz. When the cat gets to know you better he won't try to catch you any more."

"When he stops trying we will both be in Paradise," Schwartz answered. "Do me a favor and get rid of him. He makes my whole life worry. I'm losing feathers like a tree loses leaves."

"I'm awfully sorry but Maurie likes the pussy and sleeps with it."

What could Schwartz do? He worried but came to no decision, being afraid to leave. So he ate the herring garnished with cat food, tried hard not to hear the paper bags bursting like fire crackers outside the birdhouse at night, and lived terror-stricken closer to the ceiling than the floor, as the cat, his tail flicking, endlessly watched him.

Weeks went by. Then on the day after Cohen's mother had died in her flat in the Bronx, when Maurie came home with a zero on an arithmetic test, Cohen, enraged, waited until Edie had taken the boy to his violin lesson, then openly attacked the bird. He chased him with a broom on the balcony and Schwartz frantically flew back and forth, finally escaping into his birdhouse. Cohen triumphantly reached in, and grabbing both skinny legs, dragged the bird out, cawing loudly, his wings wildly beating. He whirled the bird around and around his head. But Schwartz, as he moved in circles, managed to swoop down and catch Cohen's nose in his beak, and hung on for dear life. Cohen cried out in great pain, punched the bird with his fist, and tugging at its legs with all his might, pulled his nose free. Again he swung the yawking Schwartz around until the bird grew dizzy, then with a furious heave, flung him into the night. Schwartz sank like a stone into the street. Cohen then tossed the birdhouse and feeder after him, listening at the ledge until they crashed on the sidewalk below. For a full hour, broom in hand, his heart palpitating and nose throbbing with pain, Cohen waited for Schwartz to return but the broken-hearted bird didn't.

That's the end of that dirty bastard, the salesman thought and went in. Edie and Maurie had come home.

"Look," said Cohen, pointing to his bloody nose swollen three times its normal size, "what that sonofabitchy bird did. It's a permanent scar."

"Where is he now?" Edie asked, frightened.

"I threw him out and he flew away. Good riddance."

Nobody said no, though Edie touched a handkerchief to her eyes and Maurie rapidly tried the nine-times table and found he knew approximately half.

In the spring when the winter's snow had melted, the boy, moved by a memory, wandered in the neighborhood, looking for Schwartz. He found a dead black bird in a small lot near the river, his two wings broken, neck twisted, and both bird-eyes plucked clean.

"Who did it to you, Mr. Schwartz?" Maurie wept.

"Anti-Semeets," Edie said later.

Rick Moody (1961–)

was born Hiram Frederick Moody III into an old New England family (a distant relative was the basis for Nathaniel Hawthorne's story "The Minister's Black Veil") and grew up in Fairfield County, Connecticut. He grew up surrounded by books—his father, a financier, used to read passages from Moby-Dick *aloud before each Thanksgiving dinner—and has said that "the only singular thing about [my childhood] was that I read like a maniac": comic books, science fiction, American literary giants such as Hemingway, Fitzgerald, and Salinger. Moody studied creative writing at Brown University with novelists John Hawkes and Angela Carter and went on to get an MFA at Columbia University. He worked in publishing for several years and was beginning to publish his short stories when a bout with depression and alcoholism landed him in a psychiatric hospital. He quit drinking and became a devout Christian. His first novel,* Garden State, *was rejected by dozens of publishers before it was published by the Pushcart Press. In short order thereafter, Moody published two more novels—*The Ice Storm *and* Purple America*—and two collections of stories,* The Ring of Brightest Angels Around Heaven *and* Demonology, *the title story of which, based on the death of his photographer sister Meredith, won an O. Henry Award. He lives on Fishers Island, New York, and teaches in the creative writing program at Bennington College in Vermont.*

INTRODUCTION BY **Ken Foster**

"If you need to assume anything, assume that all silences from now on have grief in them."

This is a line from a Rick Moody story, "The Albertine Notes." At the same time, it could easily be instructions for reading any of his work. From his first novel, *Garden State,* through his more accomplished works—*The Ice Storm, Purple America, The Ring of Brightest Angels Around Heaven,* and the three pieces included here—Moody has staked a persuasive claim to the malaise of a certain group of people (baby boomers generally), of a certain class (middle to upper), and a certain geographic location (the chilly Northeast). With that territory has come a lot of praise, certainly, but also a surprising heap of resentment from people who have misread his work and its intent—a common problem among writers who do their work so effectively that people can't make out the messy seams of their construction. What Moody is brilliant at—and what some people willfully refuse to see—is examining the chilly intellectual sensibility that his characters use to cover up their emotions. It isn't his writing that is cold; it is his people and the world they live in.

There has been a school of literature in recent years—the practitioners nearly always men—in which the intellect of the author is of primary importance, above character, action, or even theme. All that matters to these smart-alecky writers is the opportunity to put themselves on display, though what they manage to express isn't a self so much as it is an intellect devoid of any context. But in Moody's work, these same voids are capable of breaking the reader's heart. Like a French film, his stories are about what isn't said sometimes as much as what is.

"The Apocalypse Commentary of Bob Paisner" might *seem* to belong to this particular school of poseurs, but rest assured, it only seems this way, because Moody is capable of doing what others don't even attempt: suggesting that the narrative we receive is just the tip of the story and trusting that given the proper clues, we, the readers, are smart enough to know what he's doing. The primary thing that drives writers is a desire to give form and meaning to life, to make sense of things where in reality none might exist. This is what the fictional Bob Paisner is doing here, with biblical references, footnotes, and parentheticals, culminating in a hilariously manic term paper with all those italics and parentheses, totally appropriate here though frequently misused elsewhere.

There might not be another story, anywhere, as deceptively simple, serene, romantic, and heartbreakingly lonely as "The Grid." (Again, I am reminded of a French film, *Amelie,* though Moody's story came first.) Like a summer pop song, "The Grid" makes your heart ache even while you try to deny it. It might be the starkest example of Moody's sensibility: surface intellect and cynicism masking vulnerability and yearning. But not quite.

There is a remarkable simplicity here, though one doesn't see it at first with all the swooping cinematic choreography of the prose. Cut down the *details* that make it a story, and the premise is remarkably spare: a first kiss. Yet look at how, through the detail and the active *telling* of it, we are transformed. Reading this story for the first time, I was inspired to invert my storytelling to see how simple a story I could tell, stripping things down to their essence and then building them up again in service to the story. Too often, we do the reverse, tossing in as many ideas as possible and hoping that something sticks.

After reading "Demonology," one of my students said, "You could put that last paragraph at the end of *anything* and it would still be, like, *boom!*" That last paragraph—which likely wouldn't work at all without what comes before it—manages to convey every question and doubt that we writers have about our work and the futility of trying to capture life in the form of letters on the page. But Moody does capture a life in this story/essay (it has been anthologized as both). It is told in a series of still-lifes, and only careful readers will catch what it is that makes dread well up early in the story: the use of the past tense when describing a single character while the others apparently still exist in the present. That the life in question is gloriously ordinary is what makes Meredith Moody's passing so devastating even to those of us who met her only in these brief pages. Here's another lesson: We care about her because we see her faults and her simplicity. That she takes pictures but isn't really a photographer, sings in the choir but doesn't keep track of church holidays, these are the things that make her real, that give her death an unspoken *what if.* We see Moody struggle in his writing about her, just as she struggled in her own mundane choices, just as we, in our own work, struggle with our demons too.

Ken Foster is the author of a collection of stories, The Kind I'm Likely to Get, *and the editor of two anthologies,* The KGB Bar Reader *and* Dog Culture. *His work has appeared in* McSweeney's, The Believer, Salon, The New York Times Book Review, The San Francisco Chronicle, *and elsewhere.*

Rick Moody

The Grid

Inside, in the warm light of contemporary domesticity, her roommate is talking long-distance to the first boy she ever kissed. She's talking while vengefully chasing their cats, the cordless phone cradled like a papoose at an interstice of ear and hand and shoulder. We can just make out the melody of her joy. We are standing outside under the window, on the front step. There's not much more to the tableau than this. The screen in the window above us is frayed; the paint on the sill is peeling. Crumbling masonry. A taxi eases by, prowling. There's a profusion of couples and dog walkers on the block—dog walkers with those little rodents that pass here for *canis familiaris.* A siren passes—Doppler-style—down Seventh Avenue.

And it's late and we have to work tomorrow and we are in our twenties and *we too* are about to kiss. We are going to kiss one another for the first time. The arrangement of our faces and noses, whether there is a complete mutuality to our kiss, whether particles are trapped between our teeth, whether she will action-paint me with lipstick—these are some of the variables of the instant. Do I let my palm rest lightly on her shoulder, on the right angle of her black pullover sweater? Do I pull her to me, gently? Do I let her pull me closer? It seems easy enough to do, to kiss her, as I have kissed others, but even so, the implications of the practice expand around us, like the spirits of our baptized ancestors, like airborne pollutants. There are legislative issues surrounding us, there are sociological and aesthetic issues, there are issues of fashion. And then there's this awkward personal stuff.

Later, for example, she will believe that her lips yielded too easily during this kiss, that she didn't react with an equal and opposite *frontal lip force coefficient.* A kiss, she thinks, has to be entirely balanced—it has to have a little conflict, a little dialectic, a little revolution. And since in her view this particular kiss didn't have these things she will worry that she doesn't know how to kiss a boy, really, or anyone else, that her mouth is unaccustomed to the proximity of other mouths, and this worry will trouble her on the afternoons when she should be working on her dissertation. During a period in which we are again briefly dating she will ask me to teach her how to kiss. I will spend a number of evenings with my mouth open trying to instruct and be kissed at the same time, my lips painfully chapped as a result. *No, it's better if you move really slowly at first. Slower, even. Right, good.* Initially, during these lessons, her tongue will just swab at my lips, as if she's taking a tissue sample from me, but then she will learn to dart with it, to dart lustfully. It will be late on a Saturday night when the meaning of lust will come to her and at the same time the couple in the next apartment will be fucking. Through the wall: *yes, oh, faster, oh yes, oh God, oh, yes, yes, deeper, oh yes.* She will learn to kiss and she will take these lessons in kissing and put them to good use with someone else.

The frayed screen in the window above where we are standing will be the weak link later when her apartment, this very apartment, is robbed. By then, however, this woman I am about to kiss will have moved elsewhere with her new girlfriend, her girl lover. A different tenant will have undergone the ritual initiation of looking at the space and signing the lease and repainting. This new inhabitant will be different in every way, blond and completely heterosexual, or so she will say, and successful, at least in the accumulation of things. A professional woman, a financial analyst downtown. Her specialty: the energy industry. At work she will have an aged bumper sticker on her Quotron machine that says *More people died in Ted Kennedy's car than at Three Mile Island.* One night while this analyst, Nina, is in a bar on the Upper East Side with a guy wearing a Jerry Garcia tie, a guy who mousses his hair and drives a Jeep Wrangler, her apartment—frayed screen and open window serving as the method of ingress—will be robbed.

In the bar, in fact, she will be having a first kiss with this trader, and the lighting will be low, and she will be playing with the wax on the table candle, and then they will reach for one another—their hands crawling across the table, fingers meshing; their faces falling together; their lips colliding—and she will feel a ripple of contentment for a second that will spike through her like 220 volts of household current. This electromagnetic pulse will come to rest in her spine, and it will feel great, even if she's had too many margaritas. At the same moment her CD player (but not her Joan Armatrading and Shawn Colvin albums) and her personal computer (but not her Quicken software and Microsoft Works) and her jewelry (but not her Vermont teddy bear) will all be carried out the front door of her apartment and sold on the street. Other people, with their own indelibly memorable tales of first kisses, will then enjoy these fine personal effects.

The perpetrator of this felony will be Joe, who no longer makes love with his girlfriend, no longer disrobes in bed with her, no longer becomes aroused, no longer feels this high-pressure system of consolation, no longer recognizes that there is an equation in him that is balanced only by the presence of a certain kind of companionship, but who can, in the recesses of his semiconsciousness, *recall a first kiss on a really dark night in the Bronx when he was a little bit drunk and she was too and this kiss was so easy like slotting a diamond stylus into the grooves of an old LP.* This is the guy who will manhandle the dangerous cross-hatching of screen in the window of Nina's apartment. His first kiss with Joanne—who still lives with him—is always distant, always lost, always something from which he has lapsed or fallen. It is a hollow in him. To fill this abscess, he steals and then he cops and then, temporarily, the hollow is plugged—with an amber oblivion. Or at least this is the pattern until he gets clean and goes to *Narcotics Anonymous* and *Drugs Anonymous* and *Assholes Anonymous* as he calls it and relapses and relapses and relapses and causes the woman he loves a lot of heartache, so much that she eventually leaves, after which he goes to a halfway house and finds religion. But that's much later. On the night in question, the window in the apartment will be open and the early autumn breeze will be blowing through it and then Joe will empty out the premises.

One of the couples passing on the street that night—it's almost one in the morning and Joe is standing on Sixteenth Street prying up the frayed and unwinding grid of the screen, crowbarring the window grating—will be Eleanor and Max. They will be walking home from a dinner parry arguing vehemently about whether to have children now or later. At the party Eleanor will have loudly remarked to a friend that children were no more than *bloodthirsty dwarves* and this glib lie will have set Max off.

As their arguments usually take place *sotto voce,* restrained to the point of whispering, Joe (looking for a good handhold just inside the windowsill) won't notice Max and Eleanor coming up the block. And anyway they will have become impenetrably quiet and regretful. Max would prefer to have children *now,* because his job is going badly. Eleanor totally disagrees. She will be holding his arm. They will proceed very slowly, both through the narrative of their argument and up the street, as if one of the burdens of disagreement were sluggishness.

And neither of them will know that they are each recollecting their first kiss, which took place in Baltimore seven years ago. They were students at Hopkins. At a pitcher party. All you can drink for five dollars. A number of the carousers there became sick. One woman, Nina, visiting a frat boy for the weekend, had to have her stomach pumped. Eleanor and Max didn't get sick, however. They just kissed. It was a sloppy kiss—it tasted of beer and pizza and cigarettes and there was a platoon of wasted school chums egging them on—but when they were through with it, when Max let go of the back of her head, let go of that handful of her blond hair, when their lips parted, when the music on the sound system unaccountably lapsed, they *laughed.* It was the most incredible laugh—for both of them—it contained all the tonal shades of laughter, the sputtering of wonder, the chuckle of discovery, the guffaw at the idea of not being a kid and not being alone, of being part of some larger migratory pattern, some history of lovers. They decided to go home with one another on the spot. They dropped everything. Left behind their cronies. And they stayed together after that.

On the night of the robbery, Max will look up from the wow and flutter of this recollection—and from the cyclical and endless heart-to-heart about whether or not to have a baby—to see a pair of legs disappear into a ground-floor window up the block. *Holy shit,* he will say. *Did you see that?*

Eleanor will reply flatly: *See what?*

I think that apartment is being robbed. Look at that! Really!

Other first kisses will be taking place at this very moment. At a phenomenal rate. All across the city. If there were a light-up map showing the pattern of the dispersal of these kisses it would put to shame any of the other light-up maps used to oversimplify the scale and range of our decaying metropolis. Ginny and Steve. Mark and Dan. Ramon and Samantha. Miles and Kay. Lola and Kim and Pete. Bernard and Elisheva. Eliza and Katie. Innumerable others. The first kisses of this day alone, if harnessed, could realize a city-wide savings on the power grid; solar cells or a Mars shot could be developed with the money that would result as savings. These first kisses could wipe away the tendency in the five boroughs toward spontaneous street violence, except in the cases of first kisses that would actually cause street violence (adulterous or unfaithful first kisses). These first kisses could cushion financial hardships and class differences. They could bring the ethnicities closer together—except when they would drive them farther apart (unfaithful multiracial kisses). These kisses would result in millions of dollars in lost productivity due to excessive happiness and on-the-job ennui. And it's this way because first kisses preceded the discovery of atoms by tens of thousands of years and preceded the wheel and preceded the lever and the screw and the arrowhead and the papoose and the paving of, say, Sixteenth Street, where according to archives kept by the Church of Latter Day Saints, 14,131 first kisses have taken place since the first humanoid amphibian crawled from the East River and gasped a breath before beginning its desperate search for a mate.

I will be crossing Sixteenth Street myself that night. The night of the robbery. While Joe is liberating the apartment of Nina's CD player and ugly Tiffany jewelry, etc., I will be coming from the East Side. While Max and Eleanor are coming from Chelsea. I will be looking at my feet, dragging my heels disconsolately as I occasionally do on this block because it is a gauntlet of memories, but I will look up for a second because I cannot pass that window without thinking about this woman (the woman whom, at the beginning of this account, I was about to kiss) and I will see these black jeans and Converse All Stars slipping in through the half-opened window, the screen wrenched out of its frame. This will stop me, draw me up short, and I will simply stare.

I'll realize then that I will pass this window even in years in which she is a part of my life and she lives elsewhere, in SoHo, and I will be sad on these occasions just as I am sad in the years when I am not involved with her. On a variety of missions, both aimless and purposeful, I will pass this spot—131 West Sixteenth—and when I pass I will remember and be sad and the only thing worse than that, the only thing sadder, will be when I forget, and am sad for forgetting. Sadness will mark the period with her and the period after and the time in between and it will even mark—a little bit—my next first kiss—which will perhaps be with Eleanor, who is soon to be divorced.

Meanwhile, the drama of the robbery will begin. I will meet Eleanor's eyes as we pass. Joe will fall into Nina's apartment through the open window. Banging his knee. Seizing the stereo. And right then the Allstate representative who sold Nina her renter's policy will be kissing his wife, and his daughter will be kissing her boyfriend (in a Mustang in the parking lot at the Roosevelt Mall), and her best friend Alene will be kissing a boy Nick whose cousin Tony will be benevolently kissing his dog, the father of which dog (a husky) is owned by the First Councilman of Roslyn, Long Island, a radical Republican and sexual asphyxiatist, who will be kissing a seventeen-year-old boy in a motel in the next town, the father of which boy will be kissing his mistress, Cairo, whose boyfriend is back in her apartment in Bay Ridge actually kissing Cairo's sister, whose boyfriend has gone off on scholarship to the state school in New Paltz, where he is kissing his academic adviser (consensually but even so inadvisably), Katherine Miller, Ph.D., who has kissed several of her students as she herself was kissed by Leonard Blandings, the novelist, who was fired from one appointment for kissing a female student who was herself just discovering that she was a lesbian, who was discovering that nothing was fixed in her life, that all was drift and erosion and that the road to her identity would be littered with broken hearts and unfulfilled crushes until at last she found this girl at the Clit Club and they went back to this girl's place on Sixteenth Street in the middle of a blizzard and kissed.

But before all that, before all these things happen in this order and this way, before I go on to kiss others and you do too (and perhaps in this way you and I have something close to a kiss), *I have to kiss Susan.* The woman to whom I have pledged myself for this brief instant. And so I do. Her face is small and round, but she has enormous blue eyes that seem to say that *all the stuff you are thinking is true,* melancholy eyes, eyes with a sorrowful determination, and she has lips made for kissing, made for the sympathetic gesture, made for declarations of affection. I am close to her face now, and lacing my fingers around her back, the better to make the instant irrevocable, and then I am grazing her lips with mine, measuring their pitch and arc and force, and then we are falling into the lassitude of kisses where I am going to dwell.

We are together. Everything, even the busted lamp above us on the step, and the job I'm going to lose, and her brother who is going to die, and the way she will leave me later, and the apartment that will be robbed, and the people spinning out around us, all this doesn't matter for the moment and that's the way I prefer to remember it, before our lips part, with her roommate cackling in the background on the phone with the boy who first made her dance. Her roommate dancing in that low wattage as she talks to him, that first boy, pressing the light-up buttons on the sentimental jukebox of human affiliations, singing, knowing, remembering.

Rick Moody

The Apocalypse Commentary of Bob Paisner

INTRODUCTION: John, Composing on Patmos

I use the K.J., or Authorized Version, where the *thees* are *thees* and the *thous* are *thous.* Ever since I was a kid I used it, ever since the sixties, ever since St. Luke's Parish in Manchester, N.H. You don't get the same kind of line in the Revised Standard Version. You don't find "I am Alpha and Omega, the beginning and the ending, saith the Lord, which is, and which was, and which is to come, the Almighty" (i:8), with its Elizabethan implications of damnation and immortality. Which is pretty much how Revelation begins.

Okay, so it was the first century after Christ's martyrdom at Calvary. His followers were suffering. They were spurned, they were flogged, they were flayed, crucified upside down, torn apart by horses, left out to be fed upon by vultures. You name it. Every conceivable torture was visited upon them. Meanwhile, in the midst of this persecution, St. John the Divine goes off to Patmos,[1] an island off the coast of Greece, and begins—in this intense rage—to write a screed on which his reputation rests among fundamentalists. It's about the future of the church, about the coming housecleaning among the *chosen.* This is the screed called Revelation. It's his prophecy. A prophecy that contains things "which must shortly come to pass" (I:I). "He which testifieth these things saith, Surely I come quickly" (22:20).

Here's what I imagine: John living a life of complete poverty, confined to a monastic cell with only charcoal and parchment to divert him, unfed, unattended, in a building as scorched as the sands of the Middle East. Or maybe he was even one of those cave-dwelling monks. Unwashed, solitary, in retirement from light. In constant fear of the authorities. Panicked at the thought of his own martyrdom. In cycles, John wept, shouted oaths, prayed joyously. He had visions. Because of migraines. I'd say John had a migrainous personality. That's my guess. Anyhow, in the midst of John's rage, in the midst of his abandonment, an angel came to him and said to take up his pen.

MYSELF, Bob Paisner, in Chapin House

John saw a future marked by persecutors, false gods, Antichrists, Gog and Magog, plagues, floods, earthquakes. He saw it this way because this was how he felt about the church in the first century. Saw it this way because this was the *moral environment* in which he lived. And of course he's not the only guy that ever had these feelings. Jerome probably felt this way in the wilderness. Nostradamus probably felt this way

[1] For this stuff about John on Patmos and other information on the book of Revelation and all its commentators, I'm really indebted to David Burr, *Olivi's Peaceable Kingdom: A Reading of the Apocalypse Commentary* (Philadelphia: Univ. of Pennsylvania Press, 1974).

when he was predicting John F. Kennedy's assassination, the rise of Idi Amin, Ayatollah Khomeini, the invasion of Afghanistan, and the Third World War. Barry Goldwater may also have felt the bruising solitude of moral superiority and maybe he still does. Or take the case of James Earl Carter. And I feel that way too. I feel it now, here in Chapin House at Temple University, Phila., P.A. I suffer with rectitude. I have tunnel vision sometimes. I get these compulsions to drop everything and run, to go in search of a girl with whom I worked bagging groceries in Nashua, N.H. Her hair fell in amber ringlets. She took me into her confidence.

Therefore and thus, I am up at 3:00 A.M. on the night before this religious studies term paper is due. I have taken two Vivarin caffeine tablets. I'm seated inside a large spherical chair—early seventies-type design—packed with cushions, which I, along with Anthony Edward Nicholas (hereafter, Tony) stole from the Graduate Housing Lounge. We had to roll it down College Street. There's no other furniture in my dorm room, now, except for a mattress and a portable cassette player. I'm wearing only worn boxer shorts. I have stockpiled Quaaludes and generic beer.

I'll just briefly expatiate on how I ended up living alone. The room is a double. Tony moved in. It was a week after school began (Sept. 1980). His shit was everywhere. He had a plug-in pink flamingo. He had congas. Bowling shoes. Hawaiian shirts. He left his records on the floor, out of their sleeves. He didn't bathe. And then, just as suddenly as he moved in, he moved out. Maybe a month later.

I *thought* we got along pretty well. He agreed to dine with me in the refectory each night. We chain-smoked. True: I gave him a number of polite but direct suggestions about that lingering hacking cough of his and about his frequent nosebleeds; I offered to separate the whites from the colored items that lay strewn all over our little room. Maybe I wasn't too politic sometimes—one time when he came back from a frat party with some floozy I barricaded the door. I couldn't stand to *overhear that groping.* One night—it's true—I even threw some of his shit out the window at him when I saw him passing below. These things come over you sometimes. I offered apologies. After Tony left, the housing office moved in a rugby player *actually named Scooter.* He didn't last long either.

So here I am.

This solitude I've described counts among the similarities between myself and St. John the Divine. There are additional concordances[2] between my life and the prophecy written down in the book of Revelation, to which I would now like to draw your attention. My comments on them will form the major work of this paper. Blessed is he that readeth.

The Angel Appears to John

"What thou seest, write in a book, and send it unto the seven churches," the angel commands John in the first chapter of the final book of the Bible (I:II), and later, "Write the things which thou hast seen, and the things which are, and the things

[2] Joachim of Fiore in his *Expositio in apocalypsim* (manuscript in the Vatican someplace) believed that there was an exact concordance between the events of the O.T. and the N.T. To him I owe this concordance idea. And I'm aware, if my life is mapped onto Revelation, that there must also be a concordance between my life and the O.T., and between your life and mine, and between the Bible and the Koran, etc.

which shall be hereafter" (1:19). The appearance of the angel bearing the word of Christ is intended to foster in John the act of writing scripture.[3] But the way I see it, the testamentary approach, this emphasis on *writing things down,* is important not only to Revelation but to the Bible as a whole. The Bible is about writing, about persuasion and the dissemination of belief and practice, and its subject is *praise,* pure and simple, praise for God's stuff. The stuff he made.

Moreover, the Holy Bible, of course, was the first book ever printed with a printing press—the Gutenberg Bible. The revolution of dissemination brought about by the printing press came first to sacred ground, get it? and that's not just coincidence. All books, as a result, refer back to the Bible and to the truth contained in it, just as all writing refers back to divine creation, and, by extension, all critical papers ought to be contained in this concordance too. Between all covers, joined by all bindings, sewn, glued, or Velo-bound, is the word of God, like the movement of radiation out from Ground Zero.

And that, you see, is what John's *writing* is about in the Apocalypse. Christ is the "Alpha and Omega, the beginning and the ending" of all alphabets (and all words) and all books and all society and all of society's works.[4]

Now, let's examine me for a minute. Ever since I was a little boy, I have felt the significance of the printed word. I read a *lot* of science fiction. But as for writing, I avoided this shit like the plague. From the age of twelve, when I went away to boarding school, I was exposed to classes in rhetoric and composition. I didn't enjoy these classes. I think I might have a learning disability. Really. When I have to write something, I get really bored. I never wrote my parents or my uncle, and they never wrote me. (My father[5] lived in a tent—heated, with electricity, outhouse in back—at the furthermost corner of our property. Early mornings he would stride across fallow acreage with a shotgun and his dog, Claw. As the sun teased through the remote woods of New Hampshire, my father would fire off round after round at the crows on his property. He took shots he could never make. This was his kind of dissemination. The dissemination of buckshot. His oaths of rage crackled across the White Mountains.)

In the weeks leading to the deadline for my religious studies term paper, I know I am compelled to write in order to proceed to my junior year or at least in order to pass this class, and yet I can't do it. I want to write, but I can't. I'll do anything to avoid it. I'm wandering around dangerous parts of South Philly in a torn overcoat throwing rocks at stray dogs. I'm sleeping in public places. And then—all at once—a paper on Revelation comes to me, *all at once,* in a convulsion of inspiration, *in a revelation you*

---

[3] Likewise, Jacques Derrida, when writing of Jean Genet's method of composition, found traces of the Apocalypse: "Why not search there for the remains of John (Jean)? The Gospel and the Apocalypse, violently selected, fragmented, redistributed, with blanks, shifts of accent, lines skipped or moved out of place." *Glas.* Paris: Editions Galilée, 1974. Trans. by Robert P. Paisner.

[4] Note also that there are *books within the book* called Revelation. There's the book with the seven seals "next to the one who sits on the throne" (5:6), and there's the book "which is open in the hand of the angel which standeth upon the sea and upon the earth" (10:8).

[5] Some more information on my dad appears in my Deviant Personality final, December 6, 1980. I received a C-minus—partly because I had stayed up till 4:00 A.M. buying drinks for Annie Parsons. Later she used her hand on me, in the hall of her dorm, as revelers stumbled by. The exam was a few hours after that.

might say, just as the angel comes to John. It's not that I set out to write down the story of my life this semester, I'm just trying to think up a good paper topic, like, say, *Christ as literary character in the three Synoptic Gospels.* But instead the words just tumble out, as if it's a fit or a seizure. As though I'm taking dictation. My dorm room is a grotto and I totter around in it like an autistic until that moment when suddenly I can't stop myself from writing.

Without too much of a stretch, therefore, we can see that the angel's injunction to compose (in I:I) can actually refer *to this very religious studies paper,* and to problems in its composition and in my life generally.

The Letters to the Seven Churches

The seven churches to which John is enjoined to write by the angel are in Asia.[6] Here are their names: Ephesus, Smyrna, Pergamos, Thyatira, Sardis, Laodicea, and *Philadelphia.* The point here is pretty obvious, right? John's letters to these churches are intended to reward and punish the various successes and failures of these institutions. The language of each letter is dictated by the angel of I:I. My paper—this very paper—is being written in *the city of Philadelphia, Pa.* Here's an excerpt from John's letter to the church of this very name (3:12): "Him that overcometh will I make a pillar in the temple of my God, and he shall go no more out: and I will write upon him the name of my God, and the name of the city of my God, *which is* new Jerusalem" (italics in original). Therefore, all that I'm telling you is true, *it fulfills prophecy,* and plus, it all happened in the one-time capital of the United States of America.

I came to Temple in the fall of 1979 after being rejected at Brown, Yale, Hampshire, Haverford, Union, and U.N.H. My first year was uneventful, although I did meet a guy, Malcolm, who eventually became my pharmacist. In the spring of that year, I began the frequent use of Quaaludes. My first bona fide blackout—loss of memory from the combination of drugs and alcohol—followed not long after. I was getting ready to go to a bar at the Tyler School of Art (it's all the way across town). Then, however, a gap in the narrative of these events ensues until the moment when I found myself suddenly, inexplicably, in a men's lavatory wearing a gray suitcoat with both sleeves torn off. I was shirtless underneath this garment, and I was also—I noticed in the smudgy mirror before me—wearing lipstick and eyeliner. I reviewed the facts. I had been drinking on top of downs, I guessed, and was luckily at the very bar to which I had set out. To a guy urinating in the stall behind me I gleefully shouted the following:

—I don't want to seem like I'm giving you a pop quiz or anything, friend, but do you happen to know anything about what time it is or what day it is or what presidential administration is currently tangling things up or whether there's selective service registration yet? Is there anything you might know about these things?

I cackled good-naturedly, but my new acquaintance left me (in haste) to my confusion. I decided, because of my condition, to make my way back to my dorm, a journey

---

[6] My close friend Shusaku C. Sunami (who is Asian) dropped out of school just about the time this story takes place, just before exams last fall. After a long, expensive cocaine binge, he skipped his exams and took the first train home to NYC.

of forty-five minutes, where, along with Shusaku Sunami (see note 6), I got into the systematic destruction of my college-issue furniture. The desk and desk chair, the chest of drawers, etc.[7]

The Throne of God in Heaven

What can I tell you about the Tap Room, as Tyler's bar was called? When I was there, when I was immersed in its liquid dankness, its crimson lighting, its unlistenable music, I felt like I was *breathing properly,* I felt that people weren't whispering invidiously about my wardrobe and comportment. I loved and revered bars in freshman year and I still do. I seemed, in spite of my faith in the community and fellowship of Christ, in spite of my belief in an eternal life as promised by him, to need to degrade myself with drink (and compulsive masturbation). Again and again I found myself scamming, pretending to be a Tyler student in order to find a way into the Tap Room. It was a tiny, rundown space, with no more than six or seven booths, maybe twenty-four seats in all. (And twenty-four, just by coincidence, is my very age as I write this paper—because I took two years off bagging groceries and receiving psychotherapy.) An enfeebled citronella candle dwindled on each table; a mild adhesive varnished all surfaces. You had to yell into the ear of the person next to you. The men sometimes wore skirts; everyone wore black.

I fell on my knees in places like that. I succumbed to a joy in my heart. I heard God whisper the good news. Even if they could tell there that I was a liberal arts guy. We were interlopers, those of us from Temple and Penn, in tweed suits from the fifties and skinny ties and peg-legged pants. They could tell us apart.

Compare this bar and its charms with the fourth chapter of the Apocalypse: "Round about the throne *were* four and twenty seats: and upon the seats I saw four and twenty elders sitting, clothed in white raiment" (4:4), and, later, "*There were* seven lamps burning before the throne, which are the Seven Spirits of God" (4:5).

The Seven Ages of Church History

Seven lamps, the seven letters to the seven churches, the seven seals of the Great Book—there are even seven visions in the book of Revelation as a whole. With these sevens in mind, I will now briefly discuss the work of Petrus Olivi, the Franciscan biblical commentator.

Olivi, before being condemned posthumously in the early fourteenth century, was notable for insisting on a sevenfold division in church history to accord with the system of sevens in Revelation. He also insisted on a threefold division—borrowed from a Franciscan predecessor—to go with the Holy Trinity. The three ages went roughly like this: God the father went with the age of the Old Testament, Christ went with the age of the New Testament up to about 1300 A.D. (the time at which Olivi composed his *Lectura Supra Apocalypsim*), and the age of the Holy Ghost was, according to Olivi, to last from the time of his composition (1300) for about 666 years—the num-

[7] I've considered the possibility that John suffered with some kind of alcoholic or drug-inspired vision, maybe toxic withdrawal. This would account for the "four beasts full of eyes before and behind" (4:6) and like imagery.

ber of the beast—until circa 1966 A.D. Or roughly ten years after my own difficult childbirth at Mass General in 1956. This third period would accord more or less with the sixth age of church history, in which, according to Olivi, we would find the war between the Holy Ghost and Antichrist.

If we consider that Olivi's first defense of his views before the Franciscans occurred in about 1292, not 1300, we can see that the Apocalypse and with it the end of the reign of Antichrist may well occur on or close to the year of my own birth. All baby boomers, therefore, the countless offspring of the late sixth age—of that great period of darkness, the fifties—will be around to see the Apocalypse. In recognizing this concordance, I'm also alluding to another trinitarian construct—the three writers and prophets: St. John the Divine, Petrus Olivi, and Bob Paisner.

And here's one last interesting equation! The first Olivians, the followers who made pilgrimages to his grave, were burned at the stake for heresy somewhere between 1314 and 1318. If we take these dates (instead of 1300) as indicative of the onset of the sixth age (the beginning of the reign of Antichrist before final Judgment), and add to them the 666 years signifying the beast, then we can see, of course, that the Apocalypse arrives between 1980 and 1984.[8]

The Book, Its Seven Seals, and an Angel

What happens next in Revelation is that John, in the throne room of heaven, is given a chance to view the great book of prophecy spread wide on an ample table there. "No man in heaven, nor in earth, neither under the earth, was able to open the book, neither to look thereon" (5:3).

I've told you about my own reading habits—mostly s.f. and light psychology books, although I am also a big fan of the writings of Ayn Rand. And there is this little "book" I'm writing here, this book of my own life, which I hope will top out around the required twenty-five pages and be done about three hours from now. But none of these books seems to resonate with the book described above in Revelation.

In fact, I would submit to you that a real book is not intended here. Sometimes you have to admit that Revelation has both a literal and symbolic level. The truth of Revelation floats between the two registers like a mostly submerged iceberg. In the case of the book referred to here, I think we can confidently speak of the symbolic. The book John intends to anoint as the highest book of prophecy and the book of Judgment is not a regular *book,* a product of the printing press. It's the ancient and all-powerful book of the affections. The book of life, as described in 20:12, is *the book of love.*

I know a little bit about it, about love. For example, my roommate Tony Nicholas and I had had a few drinks one night. At the Tap Room. End of fall semester 1980. After Tony had moved out. And we had smoked some pot, which was always bad for me, since in its clutches I imagined not only that people but tables and chairs, all the objects in the cosmos, were secretly passing messages about my mood and complexion, my family, or my sickly childhood. That night I had smoked this marijuana and

[8] On the other hand, Olivi's posthumous condemnation by the Pope wasn't completed until 1328, which would slide the whole thing back to the early 1990s.

was suffering with the predictable *referential mania.* A malefic world spun out around me. I was powerless over it. I drank to cut the edge of this bad noise. Tony was telling me in some litanical and repetitive way about a stylish mystery film he wanted to direct. The eternal globe-trotting semiotics of mystery. The hermeneutics of murder and power pop. It all sounded the same. I was drinking faster. I had aphasia. I was nuts.

The music in the bar, some fusion of punk and funk that was going around then, obliterated all the ambient noise. I couldn't hear anything. I couldn't see anything. But I could tell, suddenly, that Tony wasn't talking to me anymore. It dawned on me. Through some sixth-sense heartache. He *hated* me. He was five or ten minutes into a conversation with a woman in the next booth. Five or ten minutes? Or longer? He had actually slid into the next booth and was chatting her up and I hadn't even noticed.

That was Judith. That was the first time I laid eyes on Judith. What did she look like? In the dark? Greater forces than my brute desire directed me at the moment, so her beauty wasn't uppermost in my mind. I can't tell you what she looked like, therefore, and her face was mostly turned away. She was chatting amiably with my former roommate. Still, I knew her immediately for who she was.

She was the angel of the seventh seal. She was Mary and Mary Magdalene, she was my mom before my mom got sick, but that's not all, she was like Christ, she was Francis or Gandhi or Thomas Merton, she was the grinch after his heart got bigger, she was Patti Smith after the broken neck, she was the transcendental signified, she was the thing that rid me of Tony Nicholas, she was the thing that was going to thaw my ache, and I *knew.* I'm aware that it sounds pretty sudden. But consider the evidence: "And there appeared a great wonder in heaven; a woman clothed with the sun, and the moon upon her feet, and upon her head a crown of twelve stars" (12:1). Judith's address at the time was 1212 Rodman St., Philadelphia.

My head cleared when she turned—from where Tony was yelling something in her ear. They were in the next booth. Backs to me. And she turned. As if according to some higher purpose. She turned and looked at me. My head cleared. Something tricky was going on in my life. There was contempt in the air, Tony's contempt, but contempt couldn't last in that furnace. I felt the absolute and irrefutable faith in an instantaneous bond. Love at first sight. My feelings would be boundless and exact and I would grow fat and bald cherishing memories of Judith. I would comfort her even when she was really wrinkled. I knew all of this by the time she was leaning over the booth:

—Hey . . . Hey, what's your name? You're a friend of Tony's, right?

She screwed up her face. Her smile was dimpled, uneven, overpowering. She evidently thought she was really having some fun. I nodded.

—Tony here says you were raised by wild animals.

She started to laugh. Couldn't stop laughing. And I could see Tony looking away, too, shaking from the effort to control himself.

Look, I know when I am the object of fun. Often I can laugh right along. But the little romantic skirmishes of the past, the meager recon missions of my heart in which I risked nothing and lost less, they didn't prepare me for this. This was a comment like a blow dart. I had to respond. I got right up in her face, leaned toward her and took hold of her bangled wrists. Tightly.

—Listen, you don't go in for this bait-the-misfit stuff, do you? Because you don't look like the kind of person that would, right?

Then I bowed my head in a prayerful way. I was wobbling and bowing.

—I dare you to treat me like a human being, I said. That's my dare for you and Tony . . . I dare you. And I'm sorry you're both so hard up for fun. I'm sorry about your *empty lives,* okay?

I knew how it would turn out, you know. I knew she would overcome my barb. She thought she didn't care about me, but when she turned nervously back to her conversation with Tony there was no conversation. Tony and she sat there, backs to me, like they'd never met at all. The space between them had widened. My chatter, meanwhile, was with the stars.

Believe it or not, this is how the book of the affections gets opened. It's right there in the Bible. Deep calls unto deep, across expanses of loss. In the course of my stupid life, I've tried to crack the seals of this great book, the way a kid might, six times I have, with six girls I guess you'd say, each with her different lances and charms and sadnesses, a woman with balances, a woman with hell behind, a woman who carried the souls of the dead with her, and a woman who felt earthquakes when we made love.[9] The seventh was Judith.

Now I'll tell you the number of those lost to heartbreak in all of history because this number is worth remembering: *a hundred and forty-four thousand of all the tribes of the children of Israel.*

The Half-Hour of Silence

On the way back home from the Tap Room I had another blackout. Or this is my guess. They were getting worse. I was slipping into bad situations the way others in my family had. The next morning, I showed up for Semiotics Twelve coming in and out of consciousness. I was still tanked. I napped facedown on my desk. Migrainous auras, flares, and lights burst from the margins of the passage we were reading (in Saussure). And the worst thing was that I regretted what I'd said to Judith. Not only that, I knew I was going to be troubling her again in the future.

St. John: "And when he had opened the seventh seal [of the book of love] there was a silence in heaven about the space of half an hour."

The Seven Trumpets

We're down to only a couple of hours remaining, so I'm going to have to summarize the five months that followed. In December 1980, in a sudden display of collegiality and mirth, Chapin House, where I live, anointed me dorm president. I was elected by acclamation. Unopposed. In my new post, I would be making a number of important decisions, such as what parties we would be giving, how to deal with communal problems like loud stereos, whether to have special study hours, and so forth. I called meetings on these subjects, which we held in our ample, unfurnished common room,

---

[9] Their names were as follows: Susan Ward (in fourth grade); Lisa Burns; Debby Madden (in eighth grade), who replied to my request to go steady, "Lisa Burns says you are a fag and I agree"; Liz Overton; Laura Drummond; Liza Benedict, whose dad caught us trying to do *it* (my first time) in the basement.

but I could never get a complete set of officers to show up. No one would come to the dorm meetings either. In the absence of consensus, therefore, I went ahead to make a few decisions myself.

My first act was to propose a house party entitled Inquisition Night. It was to take place in January, after Xmas break.[10] The party would feature period costume. We could burn effigies on the lawn in front of the dorm. Crucifixes everywhere. Drinks dyed red to simulate the running blood of heretics. We'd haul up people on false charges.

Not surprisingly, the other dorm officers wouldn't agree to the party, especially when it became clear I was serious. They would, they said, have to *run it by the deans, health services, security.* And then they told me that my election had been a big joke in the first place; they told me that I had misunderstood a simple prank. My powers as president were thereby completely revoked. But I simply proceeded without my housemates. I printed up fliers. The design, if I do say so myself, was lovely, featuring a photocopied woodcut (from an art history text) of Francis bleeding from his stigmata. I stapled these fliers to locations far and wide, including 1212 Rodman Street, which I had learned was Judith's address—from Tony Nicholas, in one of our last conversations. I plastered her street with handbills. Inquisition night! Rodman Street, a barren lane of overturned grocery carts, blind cars, and leafless trees, provided ample surfaces for my literature.

And though I had been forbidden to hold the party, the night on which it was scheduled to take place eventually arrived. I purchased, for the occasion, some luminous food colorings and in my empty dorm room I mixed up a shaker full of red vodka and tonic and crushed valium. While no one joined me for my advertised party, I managed to have a good time—

That is, until I found myself, in a bathrobe dyed black and worn backwards—apparently to simulate priestly garments—at a party miles from my dorm at which a venerated local band, The Egyptians, was playing. (They turned out these angular dance tunes, really loud—one of which, "Ancient Times," can still move me powerfully: "Oh, I wanna get a boat and go to ancient times; / Go any farther gonna lose my miiiiiinnnnnd."[11]) Luckily, however, Judith was at the party. Wearing black paint-stained jeans and a white thrift-store dress shirt. She also had on a white leather jacket. Her hair was a long hennaed tangle, madwoman-in-the-attic style. She looked like a go-go girl ten years into a devastating nervous illness. I reminded her that Tony had introduced us a month or so earlier and she was obviously happy to see me again. I gallantly volunteered to walk her home (though, in my bathrobe, I was a little underdressed), but she said she wasn't going home. She was catching a train that night to Trenton or Pittsburgh or something.

—What's with the bathrobe? she asked.

—I'll take you to the station.

—I'm taking a cab.

---

[10] My mother, who has been pretty sick for a long time, was, over the holidays, readmitted to a private psychiatric hospital in Concord. We spent Xmas morning with her in the visiting room. She was disoriented. I brought her gourmet cheeses. I held her in my arms while she slept.

[11] Another song I liked by The Egyptians was based on a painting by Hieronymus Bosch: *Cure of Folly.*

—I'll join you.

She smiled.

—Look, I slurred. I'm not going to hold you down behind a bush and assault you or anything. I just want to have a conversation.

There must have been some credible or deeply heartfelt catch in my voice, because she suddenly changed her mind and admitted she was going home. I won't try to excuse my behavior. I remember, unfortunately, every garbled sentence of this encounter. I know, for example, that at one point I quoted Revelation to Judith: "And I will give power unto my two witnesses, and they shall prophesy a thousand two hundred and threescore days, clothes in sackcloth" (II:3). I told her that our association, therefore, was circumscribed by Scripture. This line was supposed to be romantic.

She said:

—Even if you weren't completely nuts I would still say you are expecting too much, you know? I've talked to you, what, two times?

Okay, this was probably true. But I must not have cared then, because soon we were in the laundry room of the apartment house on Rodman that Judith shared with three other Tyler students. We were sitting on the cement floor—it was really cold—and I was trying to persuade her, in a language that was awkward and desperate, that she shouldn't go upstairs to her apartment. In fact, I told her she couldn't leave until she agreed to let me hug her. I asked for this hug many times. Seven times.

—Forget it, Judith said. Look, I don't want to be rude or anything, but if you think this is the way to get through to me, if you think this'll win me over . . . you're completely wrong, okay? Do I have to be clearer?

—Just a hug, I said. A hug, not anything . . . more than that. Just a hug.

—Come on, she said. This is embarrassing. It's stupid.

Mine was a sad story, but it didn't move her. I remember when she moved up onto the coin-operated dryer—still warm from a recent load—she fell into banging the backs of her heels against the front-loading door.

—It's cold, she said. How long do we have to sit down here?

And then she said the worst possible thing, a sentence of death and confusion. These dismal, lacerating words banged around in that reverberant space:

—And anyway, you know, I'm seeing someone else.

I brushed it off at first.

—One hug? I mumbled. One little hug . . .

You want to know why it was so important, that hug? May I answer a question with another? Why does the wilted house plant need its weekly flooding with the Philadelphia Phillies plastic pitcher? Why did St. John look for the resurrection to come? Why was Judith still in the basement with me? She had her reasons. I had mine.

She slid off the dryer and the tail of her untucked shirt fluttered behind her.

—What the fuck.

See how easily the weather changes? She had to reach up a little bit. I was that much taller. My constitution improved immediately. I saw the generations of causation, from the great first cause, lined up behind me. On the other hand, maybe I was just a lonely guy. I wish I had been more awake for it, my cheek flush against hers, her hands around my waist, a strange supernatural pounding inside the ineffectual radiator on the wall. Footsteps in one of the apartments above.

I said:

—Lemme come upstairs with you.

—Forget it.

—Then promise me you'll . . .

—Forget it. Out. Now. Out. *Go.*

—Then let me come see you at your . . . at your studio . . . tomorrow . . .

—Not until you promise to leave. And even then I'm not promising anything.

I hung my head. And in that lapse of vigilance she skittered upstairs. In the moment of my shame. I idled in the basement. Then, in my priestly robes, I weaved up and down deserted streets blessing the night and the inhabitants of night.

The Number of the Beast

According to most scholarship, it's *not a number at all,* but a sequence of letters. It's likely, therefore, that 666 probably represented initials of some kind.[12] A lowercase beta, e.g., from the Greek alphabet. In English we would use the letter *b*; So for my name, Robert (or Bob, if you prefer) Benson Paisner, you have two *b's* and a *p*, which is really an upside-down and backwards *b*. I'm leaving the conclusion here to the reader. I didn't feel too happy with myself the morning after the laundry incident.

The Seven Plagues

At 12:3 in the Apocalypse a giant red dragon appears with seven heads and ten horns, to threaten the chosen, "That old serpent called the Devil, and Satan, which deceiveth the whole world" (12:9). The nature of his leadership is discussed by John in the next chapter, "He that leadeth into captivity shall go into captivity: he that killeth with the sword must be killed with the sword" (13: 10).

You get a pretty good idea about sin, about life in the sixth age, from this description. Sin is like a vigorous movement away from the freedom of everlasting life (as described, e.g., in the Synoptic Gospels). In contrast to *affection,* especially as it has played itself out in my life, sin (and its agents, Satan and Antichrist) represents a contrary movement toward . . . well, toward separation, apartness. In the place where Satan's followers dwell, the smoke of those in torment "ascendeth [from Hell] for ever and ever: and they have no rest day nor night, who worship the beast and his image, and whosoever receiveth the mark of his name."

Sounds like a college environment, right? And which of us students is numbered with Satan's legions? I'll give you one example. Steve Dodgson, the bisexual sculptor/performance terrorist from Tyler School of Art.

Judith's boyfriend.

First, his gums were really bad. (I can find a couple of oblique references to bad skin or gums in Revelation, of which the best is 16:2, which speaks of the first plague of final judgment as consisting of a "grievous sore upon the men.") Dodgson always buttoned his shirts all the way up to the neck and greased his hair in the rockabilly style. His face was round and cherubic but also with a deeply angry cast. It was the

---

[12] Some of my thinking about the number of the beast derives from a fine Gregory Peck vehicle entitled *The Omen.*

face of a murderous shoe salesman. He had, as far as I could tell, no human compassion of any kind. In his effort to assure himself that he was not really attracted to men, Dodgson exercised a vigorous control over Judith. In his presence, she was to wear her hair tightly bound into a bun. She was not to wear slacks of any kind. He abhorred, at the same time, any situation in which he had to watch her eat. (I learned all this later.) When she was at his house, she ate in a room off the kitchen, at least until he realized that he hated *hearing* her eat. He asked that she *suck* her potato chips. Similarly, he asked that she avoid him during the worst part of her menstrual period. She was to keep any razor that she used to shave her body hidden from him at all times. She was not permitted to wear any shade of violet or purple, because, he told her, it was the color of the anus. And, above all, she was not to speak to other men, whether attractive or threatening, whether gay or straight, whether jock or artiste or academic, whether tall, short, fat, lean, desperate, androgynous, or anything else.

No men. Judith hovered in the periphery of his vision at all times and her brilliant smile became infrequent under his control. Dodgson said once, in public, at a party, *See this girl here? See my girl? The mother of all abominations!*

The Lamb

The hug in the basement (in the deep of night, in the trance of love) wasn't the only thing that stuck with me in this academic year, but it was right up there. As demonstrated above (mspp. 15–16), my experiences with women weren't all that broad. And though I knew about Dodgson, though I knew he was calling Judith and seeing her and dropping by Store 24, where she worked as a cashier, I tried to pretend it wasn't happening. I too began to stake my claim upon her attentions, standing in the back of the all-night convenience store, with the guys thumbing copies of *Motor Trend* and *Juggs.* I found a way to visit her each day.

She was seeing Dodgson, theoretically, but he was frequently distracted, it seemed, or out of town, or simply breaking into houses on the Main Line or shooting speed or whatever it was he did. And Judith and I were having some laughs. She tolerated my visits to her on the job and to her studio and my telephone calls all hours of the day and night. I was twenty-four years old and I didn't see how I was going to get along with people—it was a skill I didn't have; I had imagined that, after capitulating to the decline of my family, I would be hospitalized or would move into the deep woods, into a shotgun shack with no electricity or running water; but here I was *exploring intimacy* with one person, with Judith, and I didn't care if she was a little preoccupied, or peculiar looking, or anything else, because she had forgiven me for that hug.

But when I got back from spring break I called and she broke me the bad news. She'd told Dodgson about me. He had returned from his breaking-and-entering spree, and she'd told him. She'd told him *she was friends with this guy.* She'd confessed a fealty, a devotion. I didn't know whether to take or lose heart. Dodgson made it clear immediately that she was never to see me again. She was to expunge our conversations from the record of her life. She was to deny me.

—No no no, I mumbled into the phone. No. Let me see you just one more time. *Just one more time.*

—Can't, she said, can't do it.

But two weeks later, after a lengthy negotiation with her criminal boyfriend, she agreed to meet me in a public place, Airport Lounge at Temple University, for exactly fifteen minutes. She had arranged with Dodgson that she would call him at the beginning and the end of this conversation, she would *bookend* it, in order to demonstrate its precise duration. They had covered, Judith and Dodgson, every aspect of this event. They had thought it out. Our meeting was to be bounded by the ordinary, by Temple students dragging their knapsacks and buying packs of Marlboros, by kids sprawled on modular sofas, by security guys and snack bar employees (work-study slaves) coming on and off break. I arrived twenty minutes early. A trebly radio at the snack bar played the college station. The carpets were trampled down. Paths of grime led to and from that lounge of dreams.

The Fall of Babylon

"Therefore shall her plagues come in one day, death and mourning, and famine; and she shall be utterly burned with fire" (18:8).

So much of our lives take place in the *spiritus mundi,* in the ether of the numinous, under the pressures of Antichrist and his servants, with the music of Heaven drifting toward us distantly as if overheard in an agreeable daydream. We're little puppets playing out the drama of the sublime. It's no wonder therefore that my conversation with Judith was difficult. The entire spiritual chemistry of the age hung in the balance. We were whispering. Judith looked all wrong. Her hair was pulled back tightly; she was wearing some cheap polka-dotted dress she'd bought at a thrift shop. Our meeting was all full of false starts. What's going on at school? How is your painting? What did you do over spring break? What music are you listening to? Then it got into harder stuff. I took her hands. I grabbed at them greedily and held them in my lap. *Why wasn't I good enough?* I asked. Why couldn't I be closer to her than I was? What was I doing wrong? Why was I so bad at human commerce when it was the thing I wanted more than anything?

Then I asked:

—Why do you let him do this to you? I wouldn't do this to you. I wouldn't treat you like this, pen you in.

Her expression didn't change.

—Because I'm in love with him, she said. I'm in love with him and I'm *not* in love with you. Simple as that. You're always making things bigger than they are, or harder than they have to be, so you don't even know what I'm talking about. Besides how could you know what's going on with me? You couldn't. You have no idea—

Of course, this is just how college kids talk. Their language is crude and simple, like the language of ancient practitioners of physick, medieval guys, when considered by the scientists at Lawrence Livermore Laboratory. College students can't talk about their own feelings. They blunder around or cut themselves off. I bet they don't know anything for a good ten years after those *best years of their lives.* I don't hold it against them. Their feelings might as well be in Aramaic. But I can tell you what college students *mean;* they mean that grief follows grief like the tides running in and out; they mean that feelings are just a code for the intentions of God; they mean that numbers or letters or decimals can be attributed to feelings; they mean that the words of love and loss are just labials, dentals, or gutturals[13]; they mean that these words are pronounced with the hard palate or aspirated and that the revelations fashioned from them will outlive this sitcom of today. That's what I have to say about feelings.

CONCLUSION: The New Jerusalem

Then Judith and I backpedaled, talking about movies, about painters, about the Egyptians. In the middle of this, the fifteen minutes was suddenly past, though we'd said nothing, really. Our meeting was over. Abruptly, Judith took her hands from mine and moved off to cloister herself in the phone booth outside the lounge. I could see her shoulders and the back of her hair.

That was eleven days ago.

After that, after I skirted around the phone booth where she was huddled—protesting and denying to Dodgson—I was on my way back to the dorm when a sudden rain, a freak sun-storm, fell glistening on my face and hands. The cursed pansies pushed up their perditious heads all along the margins of my path. I said, *Alleluia!* I said, *All salvation and glory and honor and power unto the Lord our God!* Well, at any rate, I *thought* this stuff. The completeness of my solitude prevented me, that afternoon, from making a scene.

So: youth is apocalypse.

When the great whore, Babylon, is finally fallen, St. John the Divine enters into the New Jerusalem, into the seventh age, where God and Christ will reign eternal over the faithful. Heaven and earth pass away. God wipes away the tears from the eyes of his flock, announcing that there will be no more death and no more term papers. The foundations of the new city are garnished with gems and the nations that are saved walk in the light of the Lamb. A pure river of water of life, clear as crystal, proceeds out of the throne of God and of the Lamb. There are no more curses and no more night. We're all innocents. Then the Lord says to John, "Blessed is he that keepeth the sayings of the prophecy of this book. If any man shall take away from the words of this prophecy, God shall take away his part out of the book of life, and out of the holy city, and from the things which are written in this book. Surely I come quickly."

This is how the Bible ends. This is its terminus. It's a big ending, a crowd scene. John knows this too. He knows there is a powerful prophetic dimension to endings. And I know that I have come to the end of my education. And to the end of childish longing. This draft will have to do the trick, because the sun has risen over the burned-out frats on the quadrangle, Professor Soren, and I have to get this over to you, to the department office, in less than an hour. Sorry there's no bibliography. That's the least of my concerns. In this afterlife.

---

[13] See, e.g., Ferdinand de Saussure's *Course in General Linguistics.* In his later years, Saussure became obsessed with anagrams, word games, with systems, with codes, with the worlds that he felt were hidden behind our words, with all the life that was beyond his reach.

RICK MOODY

Demonology

They came in twos and threes, dressed in the fashionable Disney costumes of the year, Lion King, Pocahontas, Beauty and the Beast, or in the costumes of televised superheroes, protean, shape-shifting, thus arrayed, in twos and threes, complaining it was too hot with the mask on, *Hey, I'm really hot!,* lugging those orange plastic buckets, bartering, haggling with one another, *Gimme your Smarties, please?* as their parents tarried behind, grownups following after, grownups bantering about the schools, or about movies, about local sports, about their marriages, about the difficulties of long marriages, kids sprinting up the next driveway, kids decked out as demons or superheroes or dinosaurs or as advertisements for our multinational entertainment-providers, beating back the restless souls of the dead, in search of sweets.

They came in bursts of fertility, my sister's kids, when the bar drinking, or home-grown dope-smoking, or bed-hopping had lost its luster; they came with shrill cries and demands—little gavels, she said, instead of fists—*Feed me! Change me! Pay attention to me!* Now it was Halloween and the mothers in town, my sister among them, trailed after their kids, warned them away from items not fully wrapped, *Just give me that, you don't even like apples,* laughing at the kids hobbling in their bulky costumes—my nephew dressed as a shark, dragging a mildewed gray tail behind him. But what kind of shark? A great white? A blue? A tiger shark? A hammerhead? A nurse shark?

She took pictures of costumed urchins, my sister, as she always took pictures, e.g., my nephew on his first birthday (six years prior), blackfaced with cake and ice cream, a dozen relatives attempting in turn to read to him—about a tugboat—from a brand-new rubberized book. *Toot toot!* His desperate, needy expression, in the photo, all out of phase with our excitement. The first nephew! The first grandchild! He was trying to get the cake in his mouth. Or: a later photo of my niece (his younger sister) attempting to push my nephew out of the shot—against a backdrop of autumn foliage; or a photo of my brother wearing my dad's yellow double-knit paisley trousers (with a bit of flare in the cuffs), twenty-five years after the heyday of such stylings; or my father and stepmother on their powerboat, peaceful and happy, the riotous wake behind them; or my sister's virtuosic photos of *dogs*—Mom's irrepressible golden retriever chasing a tennis ball across an overgrown lawn, or my dad's setter on the beach with a perspiring Löwenbräu leaning against his snout. Fifteen or twenty photo albums on the shelves in my sister's living room, a whole range of leathers and faux-leathers, no particular order, and just as many more photos loose, floating around the basement, castoffs, and files of negatives in their plastic wrappers.

She drank the *demon rum,* and she taught me how to do it, too, when we were kids; she taught me how to drink. We stole drinks, or we got people to steal them for us; we got reprobates of age to venture into the pristine suburban liquor stores. Later,

I drank bourbon. My brother drank beer. My father drank single malt scotches. My grandmother drank half-gallons and then fell ill. My grandfather drank the finest collectibles. My sister's ex-husband drank more reasonably priced facsimiles. My brother drank until a woman lured him out of my mother's house. I drank until I was afraid to go outside. My uncle drank until the last year of his life. And I carried my sister in a blackout from a bar once—she was mumbling to herself, humming melodies, mostly unconscious. I took her arms; Peter Hunter took her legs. She slept the whole next day. On Halloween, my sister had a single gin and tonic before going out with the kids, before ambling around the condos of Kensington Court, circling from multifamily unit to multifamily unit, until my nephew's shark tail was grass-stained from the freshly mown lawns of the common areas. Then she drove her children across town to her ex-husband's house, released them into his supervision, and there they walked along empty lots, beside a brook, under the stars.

When they arrived home, these monsters, disgorged from their dad's Jeep, there was a fracas between girl and boy about which was superior (in the Aristotelian hierarchies), Milky Way, Whoppers, Slim Jim, Mike 'n Ikes, Sweet Tarts, or Pez—this bounty counted, weighed, and inventoried (on my niece's bed). Which was the Pez dispenser of greatest value? A Hanna-Barbera Pez dispenser? Or, say, a demonic *totem pole Pez dispenser?* And after this fracas, which my sister refereed wearily *(Look, if he wants to save the Smarties, you can't make him trade!),* they all slept, and this part is routine, my sister was tired as hell; she slept the sleep of the besieged, of the overworked, she fell precipitously into whorls of unconsciousness, of which no snapshot can be taken.

In one photograph, my sister is wearing a Superman outfit. This, from a prior Halloween. I think it was a *Supermom* outfit, actually, because she always liked these bad jokes, degraded jokes, things other people would find ridiculous. (She'd take a joke and repeat it until it was leaden, until it was funny only in its awfulness.) Jokes with the fillip of sentimentality. Anyway, in this picture her blond hair—brightened a couple of shades with the current technologies—cascades around her shoulders, disordered and impulsive. *Supermom.* And her expression is skeptical, as if she assumes the mantle of Supermom—raising the kids, accepting wage-slavery, growing old and contented—and thinks it's dopey at the same time.

Never any good without coffee. Never any good in the morning. Never any good until the second cup. Never any good without freshly ground Joe, because of my dad's insistence, despite advantages of class and style, on *instant coffee.* No way. Not for my sister. At my dad's house, where she stayed in summer, she used to grumble derisively, while staring out the kitchen windows, out the expanse of windows that gave onto the meadow there, *Instant coffee!* There would be horses in the meadow and the ocean just over the trees, the sound of the surf and *instant coffee!* Thus the morning after Halloween, with my nephew the shark (who took this opportunity to remind her, in fact, that last year he saved his Halloween candy *all the way till Easter, Mommy*) and my niece, the Little Mermaid, orbiting around her like a fine dream. My sister was making this coffee with the automatic grinder and the automatic drip device, and the dishes were piled in the sink behind her, and the wall calendar was staring her in the face, with its hundred urgent appointments, e.g., *jury duty* (the following Monday) and *R & A to pediatrician;* the kids whirled around the kitchen, demanding to know who got the last of the Lucky Charms, who had to settle for the Kix. My sister's eyes barely open.

Now this portrait of her cat, Pointdexter, twelve years old—he slept on my face when I stayed at her place in 1984—Pointdexter with the brain tumor, Pointdexter with the phenobarbital habit. That morning—All Saints' Day—he stood entirely motionless before his empty dish. His need was clear. His dignity was immense. Well, except for the seizures. Pointdexter had these seizures. He was possessed. He was a demon. He would bounce off the walls, he would get up *a head of steam,* mouth frothing, and run straight at the wall, smack into it, shake off the ghosts, and start again. His screeches were unearthly. Phenobarbital was prescribed. My sister medicated him preemptively, before any other chore, before diplomatic initiatives on matters of cereal allocation. *Hold on you guys, I'll be with you in a second.* Drugging the cat, slipping him the Mickey Finn in the Science Diet, feeding the kids, then getting out the door, pecking her boyfriend on the cheek (he was stumbling sleepily down the stairs).

She printed snapshots. At this photo lab. She'd sold cameras (mnemonic devices) for years, and then she'd been kicked upstairs to the lab. Once she sold a camera to Pete Townshend, the musician. She told him—in her way both casual and rebellious—that she didn't really like The Who. Later, from her job at the lab, she used to bring home *other people's pictures,* e.g., an envelope of photographs of the Pope. Had she been out to Giants Stadium to use her telephoto lens to photograph John Paul II? No, she'd just printed up an extra batch of, say, Agnes Venditi's or Joey Mueller's photos. *Caveat emptor.* Who knew what else she'd swiped? Those Jerry Garcia pix from the show right before he died? Garcia's eyes squeezed tightly shut, as he sang in that heartbroken, exhausted voice of his? Or: somebody's trip to the Caribbean or to the Liberty Bell in Philly? Or: her neighbor's private documentations of love? Who knew? She'd get on the phone at work and gab, call up her friends, call up my family, printing pictures while gabbing, sheet after sheet of negatives, of memories. Oh, and circa Halloween, she was working in the lab with some new, exotic chemicals. She had a wicked headache.

My sister didn't pay much attention to the church calendar. Too busy. Too busy to concentrate on theologies, too busy to go to the doctor, too busy to deal with her finances, her credit-card debt, etc. Too busy. (And maybe afraid, too.) She was unclear on this day set aside for God's awesome tabernacle, unclear on the feast for the departed faithful, didn't know about the church of the Middle Ages, didn't know about the particulars of the Druidic ritual of Halloween—it was a Hallmark thing, a marketing event—or how All Saints' Day emerged as an alternative to Halloween. She was not much preoccupied with nor attendant to articulations of loss, nor interested in how this feast in the church calendar was hewn into two separate holy days, one for the saints, *that great cloud of witnesses,* one for the dearly departed, the regular old believers. She didn't know of any attachments that bound together these constituencies, didn't know, e.g., that God would *wipe away all tears from our eyes and there would be no more death,* according to the evening's reading from the book of Revelation. All this academic stuff was lost on her, though she sang in the church choir, and though on All Saints' Day, a guy from the church choir happened to come into the camera store, just to say hi, a sort of an angel (let's say), and she said, *Hey Bob, you know, I never asked you what you do.*

To which Bob replied, *I'm a designer.*

My sister: *What do you design?*

Bob: *Steel wool.*

She believed him.

She was really small. She barely held down her clothes. Five feet tall. Tiny hands and feet. Here's a photo from my brother's wedding (two weeks before Halloween); we were dancing on the dance floor, she and I. She liked to *pogo* sometimes. It was the dance we preferred when dancing together. We created mayhem on the dance floor. Scared people off. We were demons for dance, for noise and excitement. So at my brother's wedding reception I hoisted her up onto my shoulder, and she was so light, just as I remembered from years before, twenty years of dances, still tiny, and I wanted to crowd-surf her across the reception, pass her across upraised hands, I wanted to impose her on older couples, gentlemen in their cummerbunds, old guys with tennis elbow or arthritis, with red faces and gin blossoms; they would smile, passing my sister hither, to the microphone, where the wedding band was playing, where she would suddenly burst into song, into some sort of reconciliatory song, backed by the wedding band, and there would be stills of this moment, flashbulbs popping, a spotlight on her face, a tiny bit of reverb on her microphone, she would smile and concentrate and sing. Unfortunately, the situation around us, on the dance floor, was more complicated than this. Her boyfriend was about to have back surgery. He wasn't going to do any heavy lifting. And my nephew was too little to hold her up. And my brother was preoccupied with his duties as groom. So instead I twirled her once and put her down. We were laughing, out of breath.

On All Saints' Day she had lunch with Bob the angelic designer of steel wool (maybe he had a crush on her) or with the younger guys from the lab (because she was a middle-aged free spirit), and then she printed more photos of Columbus Day parades across Jersey, or photos of other people's kids dressed as Pocahontas or as the Lion King, and then at 5:30 she started home, a commute of forty-five minutes, Morristown to Hackettstown, on two-laners. She knew every turn. Here's the local news photo that never was: my sister slumped over the wheel of her Plymouth Saturn after having run smack into a local deer. All along those roads the deer were upended, disemboweled, set upon by crows and hawks, and my sister on the way back from work, or on the way home from a bar, must have grazed an entire herd of them at one time or another, missed them narrowly, frozen in the headlights of her car, on the shoulders of the meandering back roads, pulverized.

Her boy lives on air. Disdains food. My niece, meanwhile, will eat only candy. By dinnertime, they had probably made a dent in the orange plastic bucket with the Three Musketeers, the Cadbury's, Hot Tamales, Kit Kats, Jujyfruits, Baby Ruths, Bubble Yum—at least my niece had. They had insisted on bringing a sampling of this booty to school and from there to their afterschool play group. Neither of them wanted to eat anything; they complained about the whole idea of supper, and thus my sister offered, instead, to take them to the *McDonaldLand play area* on the main drag in Hackettstown, where she would buy them a Happy Meal, or equivalent, a hamburger topped with *American processed cheese food,* and, as an afterthought, she would insist on their each trying a little bit of a salad from the brand-new McDonald's salad bar. She had to make a deal to get the kids to accept the salad. She suggested six mouthfuls of lettuce each and drew a hard line there, but then she allowed herself to be talked down to two mouthfuls each. They ate indoors at first, the three of them, and then went out to the playground, where there were slides and jungle gyms in the reds and yellows of Ray Kroc's empire. My sister made the usual conversation, *How did the other kids make out on Halloween? What happened at school?* and she thought of her boyfriend, fresh from spinal surgery, who had limped downstairs in the morning to give her a kiss, and then she thought about *bills, bills, bills,* as she caught my niece at the foot of a slide. It was time to go sing. Home by nine.

My sister as she played the guitar in the late sixties with her hair in braids; she played it before anyone else in my family, wandering around the chords, "House of the Rising Sun" or "Blackbird," on classical guitar, sticking to the open chords of guitar tablature. It never occurred to me to wonder about which instruments were used on those AM songs of the period (the Beatles with their sitars and comets, Brian Wilson with his theremin), not until my sister started to play the guitar. (All of us sang—we used to sing and dance in the living room when my parents were married, especially to *Abbey Road* and *Bridge Over Troubled Water.*) And when she got divorced she started hanging around this bar where they had live music, this Jersey bar, and then she started hanging around at a local record label, an indy operation, and then she started *managing a band* (on top of everything else), and then she started to sing again. She joined the choir at St. James Church of Hackettstown and she started to sing, and after singing she started to pray—prayer and song being, I guess, styles of the same beseechment.

I don't know what songs they rehearsed at choir rehearsal, but Bob was there, as were others, Donna, Frank, Eileen, and Tim (I'm making the names up), and I know that the choir was warm and friendly, though perhaps a little bit out of tune. It was one of those Charles Ives small-town choruses that slip in and out of pitch, that misses exits and entrances. But they had a good time rehearsing, with the kids monkeying around in the pews, the kids climbing sacrilegiously over that furniture, dashing up the aisle to the altar and back, as somebody kept half an eye on them (five of the whelps in all) and after the last notes ricocheted around the choir loft, my sister offered her summation of the proceedings, *Totally cool! Totally cool!,* and now the intolerable part of this story begins—with joy and excitement and a church interior. My sister and her kids drove from St. James to her house, her condo, this picturesque drive home, Hackettstown as if lifted from picture postcards of autumn, the park with its streams and ponds and lighted walkways, leaves in the streetlamps, in the headlights, leaves three or four days past their peak, the sound of leaves in the breeze, the construction crane by her place (they were digging up the road), the crane swaying above a fork in the road, a left turn after the fast-food depots, and then into her parking spot in front of the condo. The porch by the front door with the Halloween pumpkins: a cat's face complete with whiskers, a clown, a jack-o'lantern. My sister closed the front door of her house behind her. Bolted it. Her daughter reminded her to light the pumpkins. Just inside the front door, Pointdexter, on the top step, waiting.

Her keys on the kitchen table. Her coat in the closet. She sent the kids upstairs to get into their pajamas. She called up to her boyfriend, who was in bed reading a textbook, *What are you doing in bed, you total slug!* and then, after checking the messages on the answering machine, looking at the mail, she trudged up to my niece's room to kiss her good night. Endearments passed between them. My sister loved her kids, above all, and in spite of all the work and the hardships, in spite of my niece's reputation as a firecracker, in spite of my nephew's sometimes diabolical smarts. She loved them. There were endearments, therefore, lengthy and repetitive, as there would have been with my nephew, too. And my sister kissed her daughter multiply, because my niece is a little impish redhead, and it's hard *not* to kiss her. *Look, it's late, so I can't read to you tonight, okay?* My niece protested temporarily, and then my sister arranged the stuffed animals around her daughter (for the sake of arranging), and plumped a feather pillow, and switched off the bedside lamp on the bedside table, and she made sure the night-light underneath the table (a plug-in shaped like a ghost) was illumined, and then on the way out the door she stopped for a second. And looked back. The tableau of domesticity was what she last contemplated. Or maybe she was composing endearments for my nephew. Or maybe she wasn't looking back at my niece at all. Maybe she was lost in this next tempest.

Out of nowhere. All of a sudden. All at once. In an instant. Without warning. In no time. Helter-skelter. *In the twinkling of an eye.* Figurative language isn't up to the task. My sister's legs gave out, and she fell over toward my niece's desk, by the door, dislodging a pile of toys and dolls (a Barbie in evening wear, a posable Tinkerbell doll), colliding with the desk, sweeping its contents off with her, toppling onto the floor, falling heavily, her head by the door. My niece, startled, rose up from under covers.

More photos: my sister, my brother and I, *back in our single digits,* dressed in matching, or nearly matching outfits (there was a naval flavor to our look), playing with my aunt's basset hound—my sister grinning mischievously; or: my sister, my father, my brother and I, in my dad's Karmann-Ghia, just before she totaled it on the straightaway on Fishers Island (she skidded, she said, *on antifreeze or something slippery*); or: my sister, with her newborn daughter in her lap, sitting on the floor of her living room—mother and daughter with the same bemused impatience.

My sister started to seize.

The report of her fall was, of course, loud enough to stir her boyfriend from the next room. He was out of bed fast. (Despite physical pain associated with his recent surgery.) I imagine there was a second in which other possibilities occurred to him—hoax, argument, accident, anything—but quickly the worst of these seemed most likely. You know these things somewhere. You know immediately the content of all middle-of-the-night telephone calls. He was out of bed. And my niece called out to her brother, to my nephew, next door. She called my nephew's name, plaintively, like it was a question.

★ ★ ★

My sister's hands balled up. Her heels drumming on the carpeting. Her muscles all like nautical lines, pulling tight against cleats. Her jaw clenched. Her heart rattling desperately. Fibrillating. If it was a conventional seizure, she was unconscious for this part—maybe even unconscious throughout—because of reduced blood flow to the brain, because of the fibrillation, because of her heart condition; which is to say that my sister's *mitral valve prolapse*—technical feature of her *broken heart*—was here engendering an arrhythmia, and now, if not already, she began to hemorrhage internally. Her son stood in the doorway, in his pajamas, shifting from one foot to the other (there was a draft in the hall). Her daughter knelt at the foot of the bed, staring, and my sister's boyfriend watched, as my poor sister shook, and he held her head, and then changed his mind and bolted for the phone.

After the seizure, she went slack. (Meredith's heart stopped. And her breathing. She was still.) For a second, she was alone in the room, with her children, silent. After he dialed 911, Jimmy appeared again, to try to restart her breathing. Here's how: he pressed his lips against hers. He didn't think to say, *Come on, breathe, dammit,* or to make similar imprecations, although he did manage to shout at the kids, *Get the hell out of here, please! Go downstairs!* (It was advice they followed only for a minute.) At last, my sister took a breath. Took a deep breath, a sigh, and there were two more of these. Deep resigned sighs. Five or ten seconds between each. For a few moments more, instants, she looked at Jimmy, as he pounded on her chest with his fists, thoughtless about anything but results, stopping occasionally to press his ear between her breasts. Her eyes were sad and frightened, even in the company of the people she most loved. So it seemed. More likely she was unconscious. The kids sat cross-legged on the floor in the hall, by the top of the stairs, watching. Lots of stuff was left to be accomplished in these last seconds, even if it wasn't anything unusual, people and relationships and small kindnesses, the best way to fry pumpkin seeds, what to pack for Thanksgiving, whether to make turnips or not, snapshots to be culled and arranged, photos to be taken—these possibilities spun out of my sister's grasp, torrential futures, my beloved sister, solitary with pictures taken and untaken, gone.

EMS technicians arrived and carried her body down to the living room, where they tried to start her pulse with expensive engines and devices. Her body jumped while they shocked her—she was a revenant in some corridor of simultaneities—but her heart wouldn't start. Then they put her body on the stretcher. To carry her away. Now the moment arrives when they bear her out the front door of her house and she leaves it to us, leaves to us the house and her things and her friends and her memories and the involuntary assemblage of these into language. Grief. The sound of the ambulance. The road is mostly clear on the way to the hospital; my sister's route is clear.

I should fictionalize it more, I should conceal myself. I should consider the responsibilities of characterization, I should conflate her two children into one, or reverse their genders, or otherwise alter them, I should make her boyfriend a husband, I should explicate all the tributaries of my extended family (its remarriages, its internecine politics), I should novelize the whole thing, I should make it multigenerational, I should work in my forefathers (stonemasons and newspapermen), I should let artifice create an elegant surface, I should make the events orderly, I should wait and write about it later, I should wait until I'm not angry, I shouldn't clutter a narrative with fragments, with mere recollections of good times, or with regrets, I should make Meredith's death shapely and persuasive, not blunt and disjunctive, I shouldn't have to think the unthinkable, I shouldn't have to suffer, I should address her here directly (these are the ways I miss you), I should write only of affection, I should make our travels in this earthly landscape safe and secure, I should have a better ending, I shouldn't say her life was short and often sad, I shouldn't say she had her demons, as I do too.

Lorrie Moore *(1958–)*

was born in Glens Falls, New York, a small town in the Adirondack Mountains, and attended St. Lawrence University. While still a student there, she won Seventeen *magazine's short story contest—the first story she'd ever sent out. "I proceeded to send* Seventeen *magazine everything I ever wrote," she later told Salon.com. "They couldn't get rid of me. I was like a stalker. I sent them everything, and of course they didn't want anything more from me. I accumulated some rejections, then I got to some normal place where I thought I should think of something else to do for a living. So there was a big high and then kind of an adjustment—a 'correction,' as stock market people say." She worked in New York as a paralegal before receiving her MFA at Cornell, where she studied with novelist Allison Lurie. Her master's thesis there was also her first book, the story collection* Self-Help. *The book appropriates the "second-person, mock imperative" voice from pop psychology articles and books and applies it in stories such as "How to Be an Other Woman," "The Kid's Guide to Divorce," and "How to Become a Writer." Her second collection,* Like Life, *provoked* The New York Times *to call Moore "the most astute and lasting" writer of her generation; John Updike chose one of the stories from that book, "You're Ugly, Too," for* The Best American Short Stories of the Century. *Moore's stories have appeared regularly in* The New Yorker, The Best American Short Stories, *and* Prize Stories: The O. Henry Awards. *She is the Delmore Schwartz Professor in the Humanities at the University of Wisconsin.*

INTRODUCTION BY **Elissa Schappell**

Lorrie Moore is an American master of the tragicomic form. In her three story collections and two novels, she is, by turns, laceratingly funny and heart-breakingly honest about how one solves the problem of being alive in the modern world.

Every writer should commit to memory her short story, "How to Become a Writer," which appears in Moore's first short story collection, *Self-Help*. Like all the stories in that book, it is a satirical send-up of the self-help form and perhaps the best example of how to write from the second-person point of view. "How to Become a Writer" details the alienation writer-types feel from the rest of the world and the ways in which the ego is assailed every day. She describes the condition as: ". . . you have a calling, an urge, a delusion, an unfortunate habit. You have, as your mother would say, fallen in with a bad crowd."

Moore's second collection of stories, *Like Life*, is composed of more traditional short story forms. In "You're Ugly Too," we see the ways in which dialogue and banter can be used to create tension as well as to advance the plot. Through dialogue, Moore authentically captures the inarticulateness and awkwardness of people who have just met. She shows how people, when they are feeling vulnerable, talk around difficult subjects, and that often what isn't said by a character is as important as what is said.

Zoë is the prototypical Moore character—she is a painfully self-knowing oddball whose life has not unfolded the way she imagined it. Unlike her sister, who lives in Manhattan in a gorgeous apartment with a rich boyfriend, Zoë is stuck in a small Midwestern town, teaching American History to a boorish lot of college students and suffering through a string of unfulfilling relationships. In typical Moore fashion, Zoë makes jokes and engages in wordplay (spoken or in her mind), when she is nervous or defensive or bored—or as is often the case with Moore's characters, all three. Language functions as a shield in Moore's world.

In "People Like That Are the Only People Here," arguably one of the finest short stories of the last twenty years and a classic example of what sets Moore apart from other writers, Moore uses irony and an artful premise to create a story depicting the horror of a child's illness in a way that is fresh, original, and unforgettable.

The narrator of the story is a writer alternately enraged and baffled by the grim reality of finding out her baby has a malignant tumor. The frame of the story is the idea that the narrator, at the urging of her husband, is going to take notes throughout this ordeal so she can write an article about the experience in order to pay the enormous medical bills they are going to incur. Perhaps only through writing can this narrator make sense—if there is sense to be made—of this tragedy, and only through writing can she vent her rage.

Moore chooses not give her characters names but instead refers to everyone in the story by archetypes; there is the Baby, the Husband, the Mother, the Surgeon, the Oncologist. This gives the story the sense of being universal—this story happens all the time, this story could happen to you. It also sets the narrator apart from her story, it gives her distance, the idea being that this story is too close to her, too terrible for her to put in the first person and report as actually having happened to her. The fact that it seems the only way she'd write about it is for money heightens the drama.

There is nothing funny in the sickness of a child, but we all know that even the most terrible and tragic experiences are punctuated with shotgun blasts of hilarity. Grief is messy and uncontainable—humor happens. We laugh out of anxiety, we laugh in defense, we laugh as we whistle past the graveyard, thinking there, but for the grace of God, go I.

So while Moore is creating tension through her humor, the jokes also relieve tension, making what could be an unbearable tale one of catharsis. Moore gets readers to laugh and then cry in "People Like That Are the Only People Here," providing readers with the full spectrum of human experience.

Elissa Schappell is the author of the novel Use Me, *which was runner-up for the PEN/Hemingway Award, a New York Times Notable Book, a Los Angeles Times Best Book of the Year, and a Borders Original Voices selection. She is a cofounder of the literary magazine* Tin House *and a contributing editor at* Vanity Fair, *where she writes the "Hot Type" column.*

LORRIE MOORE

How to Become a Writer

First, try to be something, anything, else. A movie star/astronaut. A movie star/missionary. A movie star/kindergarten teacher. President of the World. Fail miserably. It is best if you fail at an early age—say, fourteen. Early, critical disillusionment is necessary so that at fifteen you can write long haiku sequences about thwarted desire. It is a pond, a cherry blossom, a wind brushing against sparrow wing leaving for mountain. Count the syllables. Show it to your mom. She is tough and practical. She has a son in Vietnam and a husband who may be having an affair. She believes in wearing brown because it hides spots. She'll look briefly at your writing, then back at you with a face blank as a donut. She'll say: "How about emptying the dishwasher?" Look away. Shove the forks in the fork drawer. Accidentally break one of the freebie gas station glasses. This is the required pain and suffering. This is only for starters.

In your high school English class look only at Mr. Killian's face. Decide faces are important. Write a villanelle about pores. Struggle. Write a sonnet. Count the syllables: nine, ten, eleven, thirteen. Decide to experiment with fiction. Here you don't have to count syllables. Write a short story about an elderly man and woman who accidentally shoot each other in the head, the result of an inexplicable malfunction of a shotgun which appears mysteriously in their living room one night. Give it to Mr. Killian as your final project. When you get it back, he has written on it: "Some of your images are quite nice, but you have no sense of plot." When you are home, in the privacy of your own room, faintly scrawl in pencil beneath his black-inked comments: "Plots are for dead people, pore-face."

Take all the babysitting jobs you can get. You are great with kids. They love you. You tell them stories about old people who die idiot deaths. You sing them songs like "Blue Bells of Scotland," which is their favorite. And when they are in their pajamas and have finally stopped pinching each other, when they are fast asleep, you read every sex manual in the house, and wonder how on earth anyone could ever do those things with someone they truly loved. Fall asleep in a chair reading Mr. McMurphy's *Playboy.* When the McMurphys come home, they will tap you on the shoulder, look at the magazine on your lap, and grin. You will want to die. They will ask you if Tracey took her medicine all right. Explain, yes, she did, that you promised her a story if she would take it like a big girl and that seemed to work out just fine. "Oh, marvelous," they will exclaim.

Try to smile proudly.

Apply to college as a child psychology major.

As a child psychology major, you have some electives. You've always liked birds. Sign up for something called "The Ornithological Field Trip." It meets Tuesdays and

Thursdays at two. When you arrive at Room 134 on the first day of class, everyone is sitting around a seminar table talking about metaphors. You've heard of these. After a short, excruciating while, raise your hand and say diffidently, "Excuse me, isn't this Birdwatching One-oh-one?" The class stops and turns to look at you. They seem to all have one face—giant and blank as a vandalized clock. Someone with a beard booms out, "No, this is Creative Writing." Say: "Oh—right," as if perhaps you knew all along. Look down at your schedule. Wonder how the hell you ended up here. The computer, apparently, has made an error. You start to get up to leave and then don't. The lines at the registrar this week are huge. Perhaps you should stick with this mistake. Perhaps your creative writing isn't all that bad. Perhaps it is fate. Perhaps this is what your dad meant when he said, "It's the age of computers, Francie, it's the age of computers."

Decide that you like college life. In your dorm you meet many nice people. Some are smarter than you. And some, you notice, are dumber than you. You will continue, unfortunately, to view the world in exactly these terms for the rest of your life.

The assignment this week in creative writing is to narrate a violent happening. Turn in a story about driving with your Uncle Gordon and another one about two old people who are accidentally electrocuted when they go to turn on a badly wired desk lamp. The teacher will hand them back to you with comments: "Much of your writing is smooth and energetic. You have, however, a ludicrous notion of plot." Write another story about a man and a woman who, in the very first paragraph, have their lower torsos accidentally blitzed away by dynamite. In the second paragraph, with the insurance money, they buy a frozen yogurt stand together. There are six more paragraphs. You read the whole thing out loud in class. No one likes it. They say your sense of plot is outrageous and incompetent. After class someone asks you if you are crazy.

Decide that perhaps you should stick to comedies. Start dating someone who is funny, someone who has what in high school you called a "really great sense of humor" and what now your creative writing class calls "self-contempt giving rise to comic form." Write down all of his jokes, but don't tell him you are doing this. Make up anagrams of his old girlfriend's name and name all of your socially handicapped characters with them. Tell him his old girlfriend is in all your stories and then watch how funny he can be, see what a really great sense of humor he can have.

Your child psychology advisor tells you you are neglecting courses in your major. What you spend the most time on should be what you're majoring in. Say yes, you understand.

In creative writing seminars over the next two years, everyone continues to smoke cigarettes and ask the same things: "But does it work?" "Why should we care about this character?" "Have you earned this cliché?" These seem like important questions.

On days when it is your turn, you look at the class hopefully as they scour your mimeographs for a plot. They look back up at you, drag deeply, and then smile in a sweet sort of way.

★ ★ ★

You spend too much time slouched and demoralized. Your boyfriend suggests bicycling. You roommate suggests a new boyfriend. You are said to be self-mutilating and losing weight, but you continue writing. The only happiness you have is writing something new, in the middle of the night, armpits damp, heart pounding, something no one has yet seen. You have only those brief, fragile, untested moments of exhilaration when you know: you are a genius. Understand what you must do. Switch majors. The kids in your nursery project will be disappointed, but you have a calling, an urge, a delusion, an unfortunate habit. You have, as your mother would say, fallen in with a bad crowd.

Why write? Where does writing come from? These are questions to ask yourself. They are like: Where does dust come from? Or: Why is there war? Or: If there's a God, then why is my brother now a cripple?

These are questions that you keep in your wallet, like calling cards. These are questions, your creative writing teacher says, that are good to address in your journals but rarely in your fiction.

The writing professor this fall is stressing the Power of the Imagination. Which means he doesn't want long descriptive stories about your camping trip last July. He wants you to start in a realistic context but then to alter it. Like recombinant DNA. He wants you to let your imagination sail, to let it grow big-bellied in the wind. This is a quote from Shakespeare.

Tell your roommate your great idea, your great exercise of imaginative power: a transformation of Melville to contemporary life. It will be about monomania and the fish-eat-fish world of life insurance in Rochester, New York. The first line will be "Call me Fishmeal," and it will feature a menopausal suburban husband named Richard, who because he is so depressed all the time is called "Mopey Dick" by his witty wife Elaine. Say to your roommate: "Mopey Dick, get it?" Your roommate looks at you, her face blank as a large Kleenex. She comes up to you, like a buddy, and puts an arm around your burdened shoulders. "Listen, Francie," she says, slow as speech therapy: "Let's go out and get a big beer."

The seminar doesn't like this one either. You suspect they are beginning to feel sorry for you. They say: "You have to think about what is happening. Where is the story here?"

The next semester the writing professor is obsessed with writing from personal experience. You must write from what you know, from what has happened to you. He wants death, he wants camping trips. Think about what has happened to you. In three years there have been three things: you lost your virginity; your parents got divorced; and your brother came home from a forest ten miles from the Cambodian border with only half a thigh, a permanent smirk nestled into one corner of his mouth.

About the first you write: "It created a new space, which hurt and cried in a voice that wasn't mine, 'I'm not the same anymore, but I'll be okay.'"

About the second you write an elaborate story of an old married couple who stumble upon an unknown land mine in their kitchen and accidentally blow themselves up. You call it: "For Better or for Liverwurst."

About the last thing you write nothing. There are no words for this. Your typewriter hums. You can find no words.

At undergraduate cocktail parties, people say, "Oh, you write? What do you write about?" Your roommate, who has consumed too much wine, too little cheese, and no crackers at all, blurts: "Oh, my god, she always writes about her dumb boyfriend."

Later on in life you will learn that writers are merely open, helpless texts with no real understanding of what they have written and therefore must half-believe anything and everything that is said of them. You, however, have not yet reached this stage of literary criticism. You stiffen and say, "I do not," the same way you said it when someone in the fourth grade accused you of really liking oboe lessons and your parents really weren't just making you take them.

Insist you are not very interested in any one subject at all, that you are interested in the music of language, that you are interested in—in—syllables, because they are the atoms of poetry, the cells of the mind, the breath of the soul. Begin to feel woozy. Stare into your plastic wine cup.

"Syllables?" you will hear someone ask, voice trailing off, as they glide slowly toward the reassuring white of the dip.

Begin to wonder what you do write about. Or if you have anything to say. Or if there even is such a thing as a thing to say. Limit these thoughts to no more than ten minutes a day; like sit-ups, they can make you thin.

You will read somewhere that all writing has to do with one's genitals. Don't dwell on this. It will make you nervous.

Your mother will come visit you. She will look at the circles under your eyes and hand you a brown book with a brown briefcase on the cover. It is entitled: *How to Become a Business Executive.* She has also brought the *Names for Baby* encyclopedia you asked for; one of your characters, the aging clown-schoolteacher, needs a new name. Your mother will shake her head and say: "Francie, Francie, remember when you were going to be a child psychology major?"

Say: "Mom, I like to write."

She'll say: "Sure you like to write. Of course. Sure you like to write."

Write a story about a confused music student and title it: "Schubert Was the One with the Glasses, Right?" It's not a big hit, although your roommate likes the part where the two violinists accidentally blow themselves up in a recital room. "I went out with a violinist once," she says, snapping her gum.

Thank god you are taking other courses. You can find sanctuary in nineteenth-century ontological snags and invertebrate courting rituals. Certain globular mollusks have what is called "Sex by the Arm." The male octopus, for instance, loses the end of one arm when placing it inside the female body during intercourse. Marine biologists call it "Seven Heaven." Be glad you know these things. Be glad you are not just a writer. Apply to law school.

From here on in, many things can happen. But the main one will be this: you decide not to go to law school after all, and, instead, you spend a good, big chunk of your adult life telling people how you decided not to go to law school after all. Somehow you end up writing again. Perhaps you go to graduate school. Perhaps you work odd jobs and take writing courses at night. Perhaps you are working on a novel and writing down all the clever remarks and intimate personal confessions you hear during the day. Perhaps you are losing your pals, your acquaintances, your balance.

You have broken up with your boyfriend. You now go out with men who, instead of whispering "I love you," shout: "Do it to me, baby." This is good for your writing.

Sooner or later you have a finished manuscript more or less. People look at it in a vaguely troubled sort of way and say, "I'll bet becoming a writer was always a fantasy of yours, wasn't it?" Your lips dry to salt. Say that of all the fantasies possible in the world, you can't imagine being a writer even making the top twenty. Tell them you were going to be a child psychology major. "I bet," they always sigh, "you'd be great with kids." Scowl fiercely. Tell them you're a walking blade.

Quit classes. Quit jobs. Cash in old savings bonds. Now you have time like warts on your hands. Slowly copy all of your friends' addresses into a new address book.

Vacuum. Chew cough drops. Keep a folder full of fragments.

An eyelid darkening sideways.

World as conspiracy.

Possible plot? A woman gets on a bus.

Suppose you threw a love affair and nobody came.

At home drink a lot of coffee. At Howard Johnson's order the cole slaw. Consider how it looks like the soggy confetti of a map: where you've been, where you're going—"You Are Here," says the red star on the back of the menu.

Occasionally a date with a face blank as a sheet of paper asks you whether writers often become discouraged. Say that sometimes they do and sometimes they do. Say it's a lot like having polio.

"Interesting," smiles your date, and then he looks down at his arm hairs and starts to smooth them, all, always, in the same direction.

LORRIE MOORE

You're Ugly, Too

You had to get out of them occasionally, those Illinois towns with the funny names: Paris, Oblong, Normal. Once, when the Dow-Jones dipped two hundred points, the Paris paper boasted a banner headline: NORMAL MAN MARRIES OBLONG WOMAN. They knew what was important. They did! But you had to get out once in a while, even if it was just across the border to Terre Haute, for a movie.

Outside of Paris, in the middle of a large field, was a scatter of brick buildings, a small liberal arts college with the improbable name of Hilldale-Versailles. Zoë Hendricks had been teaching American History there for three years. She taught "The Revolution and Beyond" to freshmen and sophomores, and every third semester she had the Senior Seminar for Majors, and although her student evaluations had been slipping in the last year and a half—*Professor Hendricks is often late for class and usually arrives with a cup of hot chocolate, which she offers the class sips of*—generally, the department of nine men was pleased to have her. They felt she added some needed feminine touch to the corridors—that faint trace of Obsession and sweat, the light, fast clicking of heels. Plus they had had a sex-discrimination suit, and the dean had said, well, it was time.

The situation was not easy for her, they knew. Once, at the start of last semester, she had skipped into her lecture hall singing "Getting to Know You"—both verses. At the request of the dean, the chairman had called her into his office, but did not ask her for an explanation, not really. He asked her how she was and then smiled in an avuncular way. She said, "Fine," and he studied the way she said it, her front teeth catching on the inside of her lower lip. She was almost pretty, but her face showed the strain and ambition of always having been close but not quite. There was too much effort with the eyeliner, and her earrings, worn no doubt for the drama her features lacked, were a little frightening, jutting out from the side of her head like antennae.

"I'm going out of my mind," said Zoë to her younger sister, Evan, in Manhattan. *Professor Hendricks seems to know the entire sound track to* The King and I. *Is this history?* Zoë phoned her every Tuesday.

"You always say that," said Evan, "but then you go on your trips and vacations and then you settle back into things and then you're quiet for a while and then you say you're fine, you're busy, and then after a while you say you're going crazy again, and you start all over." Evan was a part-time food designer for photo shoots. She cooked vegetables in green dye. She propped up beef stew with a bed of marbles and shopped for new kinds of silicone sprays and plastic ice cubes. She thought her life was "OK." She was living with her boyfriend of many years, who was independently wealthy and had an amusing little job in book publishing. They were five years out of college, and they lived in a luxury midtown high-rise with a balcony and access to a pool. "It's not the same as having your own pool," Evan was always sighing, as if to let Zoë know that, as with Zoë, there were still things she, Evan, had to do without.

"Illinois. It makes me sarcastic to be here," said Zoë on the phone. She used to insist it was irony, something gently layered and sophisticated, something alien to the Midwest, but her students kept calling it sarcasm, something they felt qualified to recognize, and now she had to agree. It wasn't irony. *What is your perfume?* a student once asked her. *Room freshener,* she said. She smiled, but he looked at her, unnerved.

Her students were by and large good Midwesterners, spacey with estrogen from large quantities of meat and cheese. They shared their parents' suburban values; their parents had given them things, things, things. They were complacent. They had been purchased. They were armed with a healthy vagueness about anything historical or geographic. They seemed actually to know very little about anything, but they were extremely good-natured about it. "All those states in the East are so tiny and jagged and bunched up," complained one of her undergraduates the week she was lecturing on "The Turning Point of Independence: The Battle at Saratoga." "Professor Hendricks, you're from Delaware originally, right?" the student asked her.

"Maryland," corrected Zoë.

"Aw," he said, waving his hand dismissively "New England."

Her articles—chapters toward a book called *Hearing the One About:—Uses of Humor in the American Presidency*—were generally well received, though they came slowly for her. She liked her pieces to have something from every time of day in them—she didn't trust things written in the morning only—so she reread and rewrote painstakingly. No part of a day, its moods, its light, was allowed to dominate. She hung on to a piece for over a year sometimes, revising at all hours, until the entirety of a day had registered there.

The job she'd had before the one at Hilldale-Versailles had been at a small college in New Geneva, Minnesota, Land of the Dying Shopping Mall. Everyone was so blond there that brunettes were often presumed to be from foreign countries. *Just because Professor Hendricks is from Spain doesn't give her the right to be so negative about our country.* There was a general emphasis on cheerfulness. In New Geneva you weren't supposed to be critical or complain. You weren't supposed to notice that the town had overextended and that its shopping malls were raggedy and going under. You were never to say you weren't fine thank you and yourself. You were supposed to be Heidi. You were supposed to lug goat milk up the hills and not think twice. Heidi did not complain. Heidi did not do things like stand in front of the new IBM photocopier, saying, "If this fucking Xerox machine breaks on me one more time, I'm going to slit my wrists."

But now, in her second job, in her fourth year of teaching in the Midwest, Zoë was discovering something she never suspected she had: a crusty edge, brittle and pointed. Once she had pampered her students, singing them songs, letting them call her at home, even, and ask personal questions. Now she was losing sympathy. They were beginning to seem different. They were beginning to seem demanding and spoiled.

"You act," said one of her Senior Seminar students at a scheduled conference, "like your opinion is worth more than everybody else's in the class."

Zoë's eyes widened. "I *am* the teacher," she said. "I *do* get paid to act like that." She narrowed her gaze at the student, who was wearing a big leather bow in her hair, like a cowgirl in a TV ranch show. "I mean, otherwise *everybody* in the class would have little offices and office hours." *Sometimes Professor Hendricks will take up the class's time just talking about movies she's seen.* She stared at the student some more, then added, "I bet you'd like that."

"Maybe I sound whiny to you," said the girl, "but I simply want my history major to mean something."

"Well, there's your problem," said Zoë, and with a smile, she showed the student to the door. "I like your bow," she added.

Zoë lived for the mail, for the postman, that handsome blue jay, and when she got a real letter, with a real full-price stamp, from someplace else, she took it to bed with her and read it over and over. She also watched television until all hours and had her set in the bedroom, a bad sign. *Professor Hendricks has said critical things about Fawn Hall, the Catholic religion, and the whole state of Illinois. It is unbelievable.* At Christmastime she gave twenty-dollar tips to the mailman and to Jerry, the only cabbie in town, whom she had gotten to know from all her rides to and from the Terre Haute airport, and who, since he realized such rides were an extravagance, often gave her cut rates.

"I'm flying in to visit you this weekend," announced Zoë.

"I was hoping you would," said Evan. "Charlie and I are having a party for Halloween. It'll be fun."

"I have a costume already. It's a bonehead. It's this thing that looks like a giant bone going through your head."

"Great," said Evan.

"It is, it's great."

"Alls I have is my moon mask from last year and the year before. I'll probably end up getting married in it."

"Are you and Charlie getting *married?*" Foreboding filled her voice.

"Hmmmmmmnnno, not immediately."

"Don't get married."

"Why?"

"Just not yet. You're too young."

"You're only saying that because you're five years older than I am and *you're* not married."

"*I'm* not married? Oh, my God," said Zoë. "I forgot to get married."

Zoë had been out with three men since she'd come to Hilldale-Versailles. One of them was a man in the Paris municipal bureaucracy who had fixed a parking ticket she'd brought in to protest and who then asked her to coffee. At first she thought he was amazing—at last, someone who did not want Heidi! But soon she came to realize that all men, deep down, wanted Heidi. Heidi with cleavage. Heidi with outfits. The parking ticket bureaucrat soon became tired and intermittent. One cool fall day, in his snazzy, impractical convertible, when she asked him what was wrong, he said, "You would not be ill-served by new clothes, you know." She wore a lot of gray-green corduroy. She had been under the impression that it brought out her eyes, those shy stars. She flicked an ant from her sleeve.

"Did you have to brush that off in the car?" he said, driving. He glanced down at his own pectorals, giving first the left, then the right, a quick survey. He was wearing a tight shirt.

"Excuse me?"

He slowed down at a yellow light and frowned. "Couldn't you have picked it up and thrown it outside?"

"The ant? It might have bitten me. I mean, what difference does it make?"

"It might have bitten you! Ha! How ridiculous! Now it's going to lay eggs in my car!"

The second guy was sweeter, lunkier, though not insensitive to certain paintings and songs, but too often, too, things he'd do or say would startle her. Once, in a restaurant, he stole the garnishes off her dinner plate and waited for her to notice. When she didn't, he finally thrust his fist across the table and said, "Look," and when he opened it, there was her parsley sprig and her orange slice, crumpled to a wad. Another time he described to her his recent trip to the Louvre. "And there I was in front of Géricault's *Raft of the Medusa,* and everyone else had wandered off, so I had my own private audience with it, all those painted, drowning bodies splayed in every direction, and there's this motion in that painting that starts at the bottom left, swirling and building, and building, and building, and going up to the right-hand corner, where there's this guy waving a flag, and on the horizon in the distance you could see this teeny tiny boat . . . ." He was breathless in the telling. She found this touching and smiled in encouragement. "A painting like that," he said, shaking his head. "It just makes you shit."

"I have to ask you something," said Evan. "I know every woman complains about not meeting men, but really, on my shoots, I meet a lot of men. And they're not all gay, either." She paused. "Not anymore."

"What are you asking?"

The third guy was a political science professor named Murray Peterson, who liked to go out on double dates with colleagues whose wives he was attracted to. Usually the wives would consent to flirt with him. Under the table sometimes there was footsie, and once there was even kneesie. Zoë and the husband would be left to their food, staring into their water glasses, chewing like goats. "Oh, Murray," said one wife, who had never finished her master's in physical therapy and wore great clothes. "You know, I know everything about you: your birthday, your license plate number. I have everything memorized. But then that's the kind of mind I have. Once at a dinner party I amazed the host by getting up and saying good-bye to every single person there, first *and* last names."

"I knew a dog who could do that," said Zoë, with her mouth full. Murray and the wife looked at her with vexed and rebuking expressions, but the husband seemed suddenly twinkling and amused. Zoë swallowed. "It was a Talking Lab, and after about ten minutes of listening to the dinner conversation this dog knew everyone's name. You could say, 'Bring this knife to Murray Peterson,' and it would."

"Really," said the wife, frowning, and Murray Peterson never called again.

"Are you seeing anyone?" said Evan. "I'm asking for a particular reason, I'm not just being like mom."

"I'm seeing my house. I'm tending to it when it wets, when it cries, when it throws up." Zoë had bought a mint-green ranch house near campus, though now she was thinking that maybe she shouldn't have. It was hard to live in a house. She kept wandering in and out of the rooms, wondering where she had put things. She went downstairs into the basement for no reason at all except that it amused her to own a basement. It also amused her to own a tree. The day she moved in, she had tacked to her tree a small paper sign that said *Zoë's Tree.*

Her parents, in Maryland, had been very pleased that one of their children had at last been able to afford real estate, and when she closed on the house they sent her flowers with a Congratulations card. Her mother had even UPS'd a box of old decorating magazines saved over the years, photographs of beautiful rooms her mother used to moon over, since there never had been any money to redecorate. It was like getting her mother's pornography, that box, inheriting her drooled-upon fantasies, the endless wish and tease that had been her life. But to her mother it was a rite of passage that pleased her. "Maybe you will get some ideas from these," she had written. And when Zoë looked at the photographs, at the bold and beautiful living rooms, she was filled with longing. Ideas and ideas of longing.

Right now Zoë's house was rather empty. The previous owner had wallpapered around the furniture, leaving strange gaps and silhouettes on the walls, and Zoë hadn't done much about that yet. She had bought furniture, then taken it back, furnishing and unfurnishing, preparing and shedding, like a womb. She had bought several plain pine chests to use as love seats or boot boxes, but they came to look to her more and more like children's coffins, so she returned them. And she had recently bought an Oriental rug for the living room, with Chinese symbols on it she didn't understand. The salesgirl had kept saying she was sure they meant *Peace* and *Eternal Life,* but when Zoë got the rug home, she worried. What if they didn't mean *Peace* and *Eternal Life?* What if they meant, say, *Bruce Springsteen.* And the more she thought about it, the more she became convinced she had a rug that said *Bruce Springsteen,* and so she returned that, too.

She had also bought a little baroque mirror for the front entryway, which she had been told, by Murray Peterson, would keep away evil spirits. The mirror, however, tended to frighten her, startling her with an image of a woman she never recognized. Sometimes she looked puffier and plainer than she remembered. Sometimes shifty and dark. Most times she just looked vague. *You look like someone I know,* she had been told twice in the last year by strangers in restaurants in Terre Haute. In fact, sometimes she seemed not to have a look of her own, or any look whatsoever, and it began to amaze her that her students and colleagues were able to recognize her at all. How did they know? When she walked into a room, how did she look so that they knew it was her? Like this? Did she look like this? And so she returned the mirror.

"The reason I'm asking is that I know a man I think you should meet," said Evan. "He's fun. He's straight. He's single. That's all I'm going to say"

"I think I'm too old for fun," said Zoë. She had a dark bristly hair in her chin, and she could feel it now with her finger. Perhaps when you had been without the opposite sex for too long, you began to resemble them. In an act of desperate invention, you began to grow your own. "I just want to come, wear my bonehead, visit with Charlie's tropical fish, ask you about your food shoots."

She thought about all the papers on "Our Constitution: How It Affects Us" she was going to have to correct. She thought about how she was going in for ultrasound tests on Friday, because, according to her doctor and her doctor's assistant, she had a large, mysterious growth in her abdomen. Gallbladder, they kept saying. Or ovaries or colon. "You guys practice medicine?" asked Zoë, aloud, after they had left the room. Once, as a girl, she brought her dog to a vet, who had told her, "Well, either your dog has worms or cancer or else it was hit by a car."

She was looking forward to New York.

"Well, whatever: We'll just play it cool. I can't wait to see you, hon. Don't forget your bonehead," said Evan.

"A bonehead you don't forget," said Zoë.

"I suppose," said Evan.

The ultrasound Zoë was keeping a secret, even from Evan. "I feel like I'm dying," Zoë had hinted just once on the phone.

"You're not dying," said Evan. "You're just annoyed."

"Ultrasound," Zoë now said jokingly to the technician who put the cold jelly on her bare stomach. "Does that sound like a really great stereo system, or what?" She had not had anyone make this much fuss over her bare stomach since her boyfriend in graduate school, who had hovered over her whenever she felt ill, waved his arms, pressed his hands upon her navel, and drawled evangelically, "Heal! Heal for thy Baby Jesus' sake!" Zoë would laugh and they would make love, both secretly hoping she would get pregnant. Later they would worry together, and he would sink a cheek to her belly and ask whether she was late, was she late, was she sure, she might be late, and when after two years she had not gotten pregnant, they took to quarreling and drifted apart.

"OK," said the technician absently.

The monitor was in place, and Zoë's insides came on the screen in all their gray and ribbony hollowness. They were marbled in the finest gradations of black and white, like stone in an old church or a picture of the moon. "Do you suppose," she babbled at the technician, "that the rise in infertility among so many couples in this country is due to completely different species trying to reproduce?" The technician moved the scanner around and took more pictures. On one view in particular, on Zoë's right side, the technician became suddenly alert, the machine he was operating clicking away.

Zoë stared at the screen. "That must be the growth you found there," suggested Zoë.

"I can't tell you anything," said the technician rigidly. "Your doctor will get the radiologist's report this afternoon and will phone you then."

"I'll be out of town," said Zoë.

"I'm sorry," said the technician.

Driving home, Zoë looked in the rearview mirror and decided she looked—well, how would one describe it? A little wan. She thought of the joke about the guy who visits his doctor and the doctor says, "Well, I'm sorry to say you've got six weeks to live."

"I want a second opinion," says the guy. *You act like your opinion is worth more than everyone else's in the class.*

"You want a second opinion? OK," says the doctor. "You're ugly, too." She liked that joke. She thought it was terribly, terribly funny.

She took a cab to the airport, Jerry the cabbie happy to see her.

"Have fun in New York," he said, getting her bag out of the trunk. He liked her, or at least he always acted as if he did. She called him "Jare."

"Thanks, Jare."

"You know, I'll tell you a secret: I've never been to New York. I'll tell you two secrets: I've never been on a plane." And he waved at her sadly as she pushed her way in through the terminal door. "Or an escalator!" he shouted.

The trick to flying safe, Zoë always said, was never to buy a discount ticket and to tell yourself you had nothing to live for anyway, so that when the plane crashed it was no big deal. Then, when it didn't crash, when you had succeeded in keeping it aloft with your own worthlessness, all you had to do was stagger off, locate your luggage, and, by the time a cab arrived, come up with a persuasive reason to go on living.

"You're here!" shrieked Evan over the doorbell, before she even opened the door. Then she opened it wide. Zoë set her bags on the hall floor and hugged Evan hard. When she was little, Evan had always been affectionate and devoted. Zoë had always taken care of her, advising, reassuring, until recently, when it seemed Evan had started advising and reassuring *her.* It startled Zoë. She suspected it had something to do with Zoë's being alone. It made people uncomfortable. "How *are* you?"

"I threw up on the plane. Besides that, I'm OK."

"Can I get you something? Here, let me take your suitcase. Sick on the plane. Eeeyew."

"It was into one of those sickness bags," said Zoë, just in case Evan thought she'd lost it in the aisle. "I was very quiet."

The apartment was spacious and bright, with a view all the way downtown along the East Side. There was a balcony and sliding glass doors. "I keep forgetting how nice this apartment is. Twentieth floor, doorman . . ." Zoë could work her whole life and never have an apartment like this. So could Evan. It was Charlie's apartment. He and Evan lived in it like two kids in a dorm, beer cans and clothes strewn around. Evan put Zoë's bag away from the mess, over by the fish tank. "I'm so glad you're here," she said. "Now what can I get you?"

Evan made them a snack—soup from a can, and saltines.

"I don't know about Charlie," she said, after they had finished. "I feel like we've gone all sexless and middle-aged already."

"Hmmm," said Zoë. She leaned back into Evan's sofa and stared out the window at the dark tops of the buildings. It seemed a little unnatural to live up in the sky like this, like birds that out of some wrongheaded derring-do had nested too high. She nodded toward the lighted fish tanks and giggled. "I feel like a bird," she said, "with my own personal supply of fish."

Evan sighed. "He comes home and just sacks out on the sofa, watching fuzzy football. He's wearing the psychic cold cream and curlers, if you know what I mean."

Zoë sat up, readjusted the sofa cushions. "What's fuzzy football?"

"We haven't gotten cable yet. Everything comes in fuzzy. Charlie just watches it that way."

"Hmmm, yeah, that's a little depressing," Zoë said. She looked at her hands. "Especially the part about not having cable."

"This is how he gets into bed at night." Evan stood up to demonstrate. "He whips all his clothes off, and when he gets to his underwear, he lets it drop to one ankle. Then he kicks up his leg and flips the underwear in the air and catches it. I, of course, watch from the bed. There's nothing else. There's just that."

"Maybe you should just get it over with and get married."

"Really?"

"Yeah. I mean, you guys probably think living together like this is the best of both worlds, but . . ." Zoë tried to sound like an older sister; an older sister was supposed to be the parent you could never have, the hip, cool mom. ". . . I've always found that as soon as you think you've got the best of both worlds"—she thought now of herself, alone in her house; of the toad-faced cicadas that flew around like little caped men at night, landing on her screens, staring; of the size fourteen shoes she placed at the doorstep, to scare off intruders; of the ridiculous inflatable blow-up doll someone had told her to keep propped up at the breakfast table—"it can suddenly twist and become the worst of both worlds."

"Really?" Evan was beaming. "Oh, Zoë. I have something to tell you. Charlie and I *are* getting married."

"Really." Zoë felt confused.

"I didn't know how to tell you."

"Yes, well, I guess the part about fuzzy football misled me a little."

"I was hoping you'd be my maid of honor," said Evan, waiting. "Aren't you happy for me?"

"Yes," said Zoë, and she began to tell Evan a story about an award-winning violinist at Hilldale-Versailles, how the violinist had come home from a competition in Europe and taken up with a local man, who made her go to all his summer softball games, made her cheer for him from the stands, with the wives, until she later killed herself. But when she got halfway through, to the part about cheering at the softball games, Zoë stopped.

"What?" said Evan. "So what happened?"

"Actually, nothing," said Zoë lightly. "She just really got into softball. I mean, really. You should have seen her."

Zoë decided to go to a late-afternoon movie, leaving Evan to chores she needed to do before the party—*I have to do them alone,* she'd said, a little tense after the violinist story. Zoë thought about going to an art museum, but women alone in art museums had to look good. They always did. Chic and serious, moving languidly, with a great handbag. Instead, she walked over and down through Kips Bay, past an earring boutique called Stick It in Your Ear, past a beauty salon called Dorian Gray's. That was the funny thing about *beauty,* thought Zoë. Look it up in the yellow pages, and you found a hundred entries, hostile with wit, cutesy with warning. But look up *truth*—ha! There was nothing at all.

Zoë thought about Evan getting married. Would Evan turn into Peter Pumpkin Eater's wife? Mrs. Eater? At the wedding would she make Zoë wear some flouncy lavender dress, identical with the other maids'? Zoë hated uniforms, had even, in the first grade, refused to join Elf Girls, because she didn't want to wear the same dress as everyone else. Now she might have to. But maybe she could distinguish it. Hitch it up on one side with a clothespin. Wear surgical gauze at the waist. Clip to her bodice one of those pins that said in loud letters, SHIT HAPPENS.

At the movie—*Death by Number*—she bought strands of red licorice to tug and chew. She took a seat off to one side in the theater. She felt strangely self-conscious sitting alone and hoped for the place to darken fast. When it did, and the coming attractions came on, she reached inside her purse for her glasses. They were in a Baggie. Her Kleenex was also in a Baggie. So were her pen and her aspirin and her mints. Everything was in Baggies. This was what she'd become: *a woman alone at the movies with everything in a Baggie.*

At the Halloween party, there were about two dozen people. There were people with ape heads and large hairy hands. There was someone dressed as a leprechaun.

There was someone dressed as a frozen dinner. Some man had brought his two small daughters: a ballerina and a ballerina's sister, also dressed as a ballerina. There was a gaggle of sexy witches—women dressed entirely in black, beautifully made up and jeweled. "I hate those sexy witches. It's not in the spirit of Halloween," said Evan. Evan had abandoned the moon mask and dolled herself up as a hausfrau, in curlers and an apron, a decision she now regretted. Charlie, because he liked fish, because he owned fish, collected fish, had decided to go as a fish. He had fins and eyes on the side of his head. "Zoë! How are you! I'm sorry I wasn't here when you first arrived!" He spent the rest of his time chatting up the sexy witches.

"Isn't there something I can help you with here?" Zoë asked her sister. "You've been running yourself ragged." She rubbed her sister's arm, gently, as if she wished they were alone.

"Oh, God, not at all," said Evan, arranging stuffed mushrooms on a plate. The timer went off, and she pulled another sheetful out of the oven. "Actually, you know what you can do?"

"What?" Zoë put on her bonehead.

"Meet Earl. He's the guy I had in mind for you. When he gets here, just talk to him a little. He's nice. He's fun. He's going through a divorce."

"I'll try." Zoë groaned. "OK? I'll try." She looked at her watch.

When Earl arrived, he was dressed as a naked woman, steel wool glued strategically to a body stocking, and large rubber breasts protruding like hams.

"Zoë, this is Earl," said Evan.

"Good to meet you," said Earl, circling Evan to shake Zoë's hand. He stared at the top of Zoë's head. "Great bone."

Zoë nodded. "Great tits," she said. She looked past him, out the window at the city thrown glitteringly up against the sky; people were saying the usual things: how it looked like jewels, like bracelets and necklaces unstrung. You could see Grand Central station, the clock of the Con Ed building, the red-and-gold-capped Empire State, the Chrysler like a rocket ship dreamed up in a depression. Far west you could glimpse the Astor Plaza, its flying white roof like a nun's habit. "There's beer out on the balcony, Earl—can I get you one?" Zoë asked.

"Sure, uh, I'll come along. Hey, Charlie, how's it going?"

Charlie grinned and whistled. People turned to look. "Hey, Earl," someone called, from across the room. "Va-va-va-voom."

They squeezed their way past the other guests, past the apes and the sexy witches. The suction of the sliding door gave way in a whoosh, and Zoë and Earl stepped out onto the balcony, a bonehead and a naked woman, the night air roaring and smoky cool. Another couple was out here, too, murmuring privately. They were not wearing costumes. They smiled at Zoë and Earl. "Hi," said Zoë. She found the plastic-foam cooler, dug into it, and retrieved two beers.

"Thanks," said Earl. His rubber breasts folded inward, dimpled and dented, as he twisted open the bottle.

"Well," sighed Zoë anxiously. She had to learn not to be afraid of a man, the way, in your childhood, you learned not to be afraid of an earthworm or a bug. Often, when she spoke to men at parties, she rushed things in her mind. As the man politely blathered on, she would fall in love, marry, then find herself in a bitter custody battle with him for the kids and hoping for a reconciliation, so that despite all his betrayals she might no longer despise him, and in the few minutes remaining, learn, perhaps, what his last name was and what he did for a living, though probably there was already too much history between them. She would nod, blush, turn away.

"Evan tells me you're a professor. Where do you teach?"

"Just over the Indiana border into Illinois."

He looked a little shocked. "I guess Evan didn't tell me that part."

"She didn't?"

"No."

"Well, that's Evan for you. When we were kids we both had speech impediments."

"That can be tough," said Earl. One of his breasts was hidden behind his drinking arm, but the other shone low and pink, full as a strawberry moon.

"Yes, well, it wasn't a total loss. We used to go to what we called peach pear-apy. For about ten years of my life I had to map out every sentence in my mind, way ahead, before I said it. That was the only way I could get a coherent sentence out."

Earl drank from his beer. "How did you do that? I mean, how did you get through?"

"I told a lot of jokes. Jokes you know the lines to already—you can just say them. I love jokes. Jokes and songs."

Earl smiled. He had on lipstick, a deep shade of red, but it was wearing off from the beer. "What's your favorite joke?"

"Uh, my favorite joke is probably . . . OK, all right. This guy goes into a doctor's office and—"

"I think I know this one," interrupted Earl, eagerly. He wanted to tell it himself. "A guy goes into a doctor's office, and the doctor tells him he's got some good news and some bad news—that one, right?"

"I'm not sure," said Zoë. "This might be a different version."

"So the guy says, 'Give me the bad news first,' and the doctor says, 'OK. You've got three weeks to live.' And the guy cries, 'Three weeks to live! Doctor, what is the good news?' And the doctor says, 'Did you see that secretary out front? I finally fucked her.'"

Zoë frowned.

"That's not the one you were thinking of?"

"No." There was accusation in her voice. "Mine was different."

"Oh," said Earl. He looked away and then back again. "You teach history, right? What kind of history do you teach?"

"I teach American, mostly—eighteenth and nineteenth century." In graduate school, at bars, the pickup line was always: "So what's your century?"

"Occasionally I teach a special theme course," she added, "say, 'Humor and Personality in the White House.' That's what my book's on." She thought of something someone once told her about bowerbirds, how they build elaborate structures before mating.

"Your book's on *humor?*"

"Yeah, and, well, when I teach a theme course like that, I do all the centuries." *So what's your century?*

"All three of them."

"Pardon?" The breeze glistened her eyes. Traffic revved beneath them. She felt high and puny, like someone lifted into heaven by mistake and then spurned.

"Three. There's only three."

"Well, four, really." She was thinking of Jamestown, and of the Pilgrims coming here with buckles and witch hats to say their prayers.

"I'm a photographer," said Earl. His face was starting to gleam, his rouge smearing in a sunset beneath his eyes.

"Do you like that?"

"Well, actually I'm starting to feel it's a little dangerous."

"Really?"

"Spending all your time in a darkroom with that red light and all those chemicals. There's links with Parkinson's, you know."

"No, I didn't."

"I suppose I should wear rubber gloves, but I don't like to. Unless I'm touching it directly, I don't think of it as real."

"Hmmm," said Zoë. Alarm buzzed through her, mildly, like a tea.

"Sometimes, when I have a cut or something, I feel the sting and think, *Shit.* I wash constantly and just hope. I don't like rubber over the skin like that."

"Really."

"I mean, the physical contact. That's what you want, or why bother?"

"I guess," said Zoë. She wished she could think of a joke, something slow and deliberate, with the end in sight. She thought of gorillas, how when they had been kept too long alone in cages, they would smack each other in the head instead of mating.

"Are you . . . in a relationship?" Earl suddenly blurted.

"Now? As we speak?"

"Well, I mean, I'm sure you have a relationship to your *work.*" A smile, a weird one, nestled in his mouth like an egg. She thought of zoos in parks, how when cities were under siege, during world wars, people are the animals. "But I mean, with a *man.*"

"No, I'm not in a relationship with a *man.*" She rubbed her chin with her hand and could feel the one bristly hair there. "But my last relationship was with a very sweet man," she said. She made something up. "From Switzerland. He was a botanist—a weed expert. His name was Jerry. I called him 'Jare.' He was so funny. You'd go to the movies with him and all he would notice were the plants. He would never pay attention to the plot. Once, in a jungle movie, he started rattling off all these Latin names, out loud. It was very exciting for him." She paused, caught her breath. "Eventually he went back to Europe to, uh, study the edelweiss." She looked at Earl. "Are you involved in a relationship? With a *woman?*"

Earl shifted his weight, and the creases in his body stocking changed, splintering outward like something broken. His pubic hair slid over to one hip, like a corsage on a saloon girl. "No," he said, clearing his throat. The steel wool in his underarms was inching toward his biceps. "I've just gotten out of a marriage that was full of bad dialogue, like 'You want more *space?* I'll give you more space!' *Clonk.* Your basic Three Stooges."

Zoë looked at him sympathetically. "I suppose it's hard for love to recover after that."

His eyes lit up. He wanted to talk about love. "But *I* keep thinking love should be like a tree. You look at trees and they've got bumps and scars from tumors, infestations, what have you, but they're still growing. Despite the bumps and bruises, they're . . . straight."

"Yeah, well," said Zoë, "where I'm from, they're all married or gay. Did you see that movie *Death by Number?*"

Earl looked at her, a little lost. She was getting away from him. "No," he said.

One of his breasts had slipped under his arm, tucked there like a baguette. She kept thinking of trees, of gorillas and parks, of people in wartime eating the zebras. She felt a stabbing pain in her abdomen.

"Want some hors d'oeuvres?" Evan came pushing through the sliding door. She was smiling, though her curlers were coming out, hanging bedraggled at the ends of her hair like Christmas decorations, like food put out for the birds. She thrust forward a plate of stuffed mushrooms.

"Are you asking for donations or giving them away," said Earl, wittily. He liked Evan, and he put his arm around her.

"You know, I'll be right back," said Zoë.

"Oh," said Evan, looking concerned.

"Right back. I promise."

Zoë hurried inside, across the living room, into the bedroom, to the adjoining bath. It was empty; most of the guests were using the half bath near the kitchen. She flicked on the light and closed the door. The pain had stopped and she didn't really have to go to the bathroom, but she stayed there anyway, resting. In the mirror above the sink she looked haggard beneath her bonehead, violet grays showing under the skin like a plucked and pocky bird. She leaned closer, raising her chin a little to find the bristly hair. It was there, at the end of the jaw, sharp and dark as a wire. She opened the medicine cabinet, pawed through it until she found some tweezers. She lifted her head again and poked at her face with the metal tips, grasping and pinching and missing. Outside the door she could hear two people talking low. They had come into the bedroom and were discussing something. They were sitting on the bed. One of them giggled in a false way. She stabbed again at her chin, and it started to bleed a little. She pulled the skin tight along the jawbone, gripped the tweezers hard around what she hoped was the hair, and tugged. A tiny square of skin came away with it, but the hair remained, blood bright at the root of it. Zoë clenched her teeth. "Come on," she whispered. The couple outside in the bedroom were now telling stories, softly, and laughing. There was a bounce and squeak of mattress, and the sound of a chair being moved out of the way. Zoë aimed the tweezers carefully, pinched, then pulled gently away, and this time the hair came, too, with a slight twinge of pain and then a great flood of relief. "Yeah!" breathed Zoë. She grabbed some toilet paper and dabbed at her chin. It came away spotted with blood, and so she tore off some more and pressed hard until it stopped. Then she turned off the light and opened the door, to return to the party. "Excuse me," she said to the couple in the bedroom. They were the couple from the balcony, and they looked at her, a bit surprised. They had their arms around each other, and they were eating candy bars.

Earl was still out on the balcony, alone, and Zoë rejoined him there.

"Hi," she said. He turned around and smiled. He had straightened his costume out a bit, though all the secondary sex characteristics seemed slightly doomed, destined to shift and flip and zip around again any moment.

"Are you OK?" he asked. He had opened another beer and was chugging.

"Oh, yeah. I just had to go to the bathroom." She paused. "Actually I have been going to a lot of doctors recently."

"What's wrong?" asked Earl.

"Oh, probably nothing. But they're putting me through tests." She sighed. "I've had sonograms. I've had mammograms. Next week I'm going in for a candygram." He looked at her worriedly. "I've had too many gram words," she said.

"Here, I saved you these." He held out a napkin with two stuffed mushroom caps. They were cold and leaving oil marks on the napkin.

"Thanks," said Zoë, and pushed them both in her mouth. "Watch," she said, with her mouth full. "With my luck, it'll be a gallbladder operation."

Earl made a face. "So your sister's getting married," he said, changing the subject. "Tell me, really, what you think about love."

"*Love?*" Hadn't they done this already? "I don't know." She chewed thoughtfully and swallowed. "All right. I'll tell you what I think about love. Here is a love story. This friend of mine—"

"You've got something on your chin," said Earl, and he reached over to touch it.

"*What?*" said Zoë, stepping back. She turned her face away and grabbed at her chin. A piece of toilet paper peeled off it, like tape. "It's nothing," she said. "It's just—it's nothing."

Earl stared at her.

"At any rate," she continued, "this friend of mine was this award-winning violinist. She traveled all over Europe and won competitions; she made records, she gave concerts, she got famous. But she had no social life. So one day she threw herself at the feet of this conductor she had a terrible crush on. He picked her up, scolded her gently, and sent her back to her hotel room. After that she came home from Europe. She went back to her old hometown, stopped playing the violin, and took up with a local boy. This was in Illinois. He took her to some Big Ten bar every night to drink with his buddies from the team. He used to say things like 'Katrina here likes to play the violin,' and then he'd pinch her cheek. When she once suggested that they go home, he said, 'What, you think you're too famous for a place like this? Well, let me tell you something. You may think you're famous, but you're not *famous* famous.' Two famouses. 'No one here's ever heard of you.' Then he went and bought a round of drinks for everyone but her. She got her coat, went home and shot a gun through her head."

Earl was silent.

"That's the end of my love story," said Zoë.

"You're not at all like your sister," said Earl.

"Ho, really," said Zoë. The air had gotten colder, the wind singing minor and thick as a dirge.

"No." He didn't want to talk about love anymore. "You know, you should wear a lot of blue—blue and white—around your face. It would bring out your coloring." He reached an arm out to show her how the blue bracelet he was wearing might look against her skin, but she swatted it away.

"Tell me, Earl. Does the word *fag* mean anything to you?"

He stepped back, away from her. He shook his head in disbelief. "You know, I just shouldn't try to go out with career women. You're all stricken. A guy can really tell what life has done to you. I do better with women who have part-time jobs."

"Oh, yes?" said Zoë. She had once read an article entitled "Professional Women and the Demographics of Grief." Or no, it was a poem: *If there were a lake, the moonlight would dance across it in conniptions.* She remembered that line. But perhaps the title was

"The Empty House: Aesthetics of Barrenness." Or maybe "Space Gypsies: Girls in Academe." She had forgotten.

Earl turned and leaned on the railing of the balcony. It was getting late. Inside, the party guests were beginning to leave. The sexy witches were already gone. "Live and learn," Earl murmured.

"Live and get dumb," replied Zoë. Beneath them on Lexington there were no cars, just the gold rush of an occasional cab. He leaned hard on his elbows, brooding.

"Look at those few people down there," he said. "They look like bugs. You know how bugs are kept under control? They're sprayed with bug hormones, female bug hormones. The male bugs get so crazy in the presence of this hormone, they're screwing everything in sight: trees, rocks—everything but female bugs. Population control. That's what's happening in this country," he said drunkenly. "Hormones sprayed around, and now men are screwing rocks. Rocks!"

In the back the Magic Marker line of his buttocks spread wide, a sketchy black on pink like a funnies page. Zoë came up, slow, from behind and gave him a shove. His arms slipped forward, off the railing, out over the street. Beer spilled out of his bottle, raining twenty stories down to the street.

"Hey, what are you doing?!" he said, whipping around. He stood straight and readied and moved away from the railing, sidestepping Zoë. "What the *hell* are you doing?"

"Just kidding," she said. "I was just kidding." But he gazed at her, appalled and frightened, his Magic Marker buttocks turned away now toward all of downtown, a naked pseudowoman with a blue bracelet at the wrist, trapped out on a balcony with—with *what? "Really, I was just kidding!"* Zoë shouted. The wind lifted the hair up off her head, skyward in spines behind the bone. If there were a lake, the moonlight would dance across it in conniptions. She smiled at him, and wondered how she looked.

LORRIE MOORE

People Like That Are the Only People Here

A beginning, an end: there seems to be neither. The whole thing is like a cloud that just lands and everywhere inside it is full of rain. A start: the Mother finds a blood clot in the Baby's diaper. What is the story? Who put this here? It is big and bright, with a broken khaki-colored vein in it. Over the weekend, the Baby had looked listless and spacey, clayey and grim. But today he looks fine—so what is this thing, startling against the white diaper, like a tiny mouse heart packed in snow? Perhaps it belongs to someone else. Perhaps it is something menstrual, something belonging to the Mother or to the Babysitter, something the Baby has found in a wastebasket and for his own demented baby reasons stowed away here. (Babies: they're crazy! What can you do?) In her mind, the Mother takes this away from his body and attaches it to someone else's. There. Doesn't that make more sense?

Still, she phones the clinic at the children's hospital. "Blood in the diaper," she says, and, sounding alarmed and perplexed, the woman on the other end says, "Come in now."

Such pleasingly instant service! Just say "blood." Just say "diaper." Look what you get!

In the examination room, pediatrician, nurse, head resident—all seem less alarmed and perplexed than simply perplexed. At first, stupidly, the Mother is calmed by this. But soon, besides peering and saying "Hmmmm," the pediatrician, nurse, and head resident are all drawing their mouths in, bluish and tight—morning glories sensing noon. They fold their arms across their white-coated chests, unfold them again and jot things down. They order an ultrasound. Bladder and kidneys. "Here's the card. Go downstairs; turn left."

In Radiology, the Baby stands anxiously on the table, naked against the Mother as she holds him still against her legs and waist, the Radiologist's cold scanning disc moving about the Baby's back. The Baby whimpers, looks up at the Mother. *Let's get out of here,* his eyes beg. *Pick me up!* The Radiologist stops, freezes one of the many swirls of oceanic gray, and clicks repeatedly, a single moment within the long, cavernous weather map that is the Baby's insides.

"Are you finding something?" asks the Mother. Last year, her uncle Larry had had a kidney removed for something that turned out to be benign. These imaging machines! They are like dogs, or metal detectors: they find everything, but don't know what they've found. That's where the surgeons come in. They're like the owners of the dogs. "Give me that," they say to the dog. "What the heck is that?"

"The surgeon will speak to you," says the Radiologist.

"Are you finding something?"

"The surgeon will speak to you," the Radiologist says again. "There seems to be something there, but the surgeon will talk to you about it."

"My uncle once had something on his kidney," says the Mother. "So they removed the kidney and it turned out the something was benign."

The Radiologist smiles a broad, ominous smile. "That's always the way it is," he says. "You don't know exactly what it is until it's in the bucket."

"'In the bucket,'" the Mother repeats.

The Radiologist's grin grows scarily wider—is that even possible? "That's doctor talk," he says.

"It's very appealing," says the Mother. "It's a very appealing way to talk." Swirls of bile and blood, mustard and maroon in a pail, the colors of an African flag or some exuberant salad bar: *in the bucket*—she imagines it all.

"The Surgeon will see you soon," he says again. He tousles the Baby's ringletty hair. "Cute kid," he says.

"Let's see now," says the Surgeon in one of his examining rooms. He has stepped in, then stepped out, then come back in again. He has crisp, frowning features, sharp bones, and a tennis-in-Bermuda tan. He crosses his blue-cottoned legs. He is wearing clogs.

The Mother knows her own face is a big white dumpling of worry. She is still wearing her long, dark parka, holding the Baby, who has pulled the hood up over her head because he always thinks it's funny to do that. Though on certain windy mornings she would like to think she could look vaguely romantic like this, like some French Lieutenant's Woman of the Prairie, in all of her saner moments she knows she doesn't. Ever. She knows she looks ridiculous—like one of those animals made out of twisted party balloons. She lowers the hood and slips one arm out of the sleeve. The Baby wants to get up and play with the light switch. He fidgets, fusses, and points.

"He's big on lights these days," explains the Mother.

"That's okay," says the Surgeon, nodding toward the light switch. "Let him play with it." The Mother goes and stands by it, and the Baby begins turning the lights off and on, off and on.

"What we have here is a Wilms' tumor," says the Surgeon, suddenly plunged into darkness. He says "tumor" as if it were the most normal thing in the world.

"Wilms'?" repeats the Mother. The room is quickly on fire again with light, then wiped dark again. Among the three of them here, there is a long silence, as if it were suddenly the middle of the night. "Is that apostrophe *s* or *s* apostrophe?" the Mother says finally. She is a writer and a teacher. Spelling can be important—perhaps even at a time like this, though she has never before been at a time like this, so there are barbarisms she could easily commit and not know.

The lights come on: the world is doused and exposed.

"*S* apostrophe," says the Surgeon. "I think." The lights go back out, but the Surgeon continues speaking in the dark. "A malignant tumor on the left kidney."

Wait a minute. Hold on here. The Baby is only a baby, fed on organic applesauce and soy milk—a little prince!—and he was standing so close to her during the ultrasound. How could he have this terrible thing? It must have been *her* kidney. A fifties kidney. A DDT kidney. The Mother clears her throat. "Is it possible it was my kidney on the scan? I mean, I've never heard of a baby with a tumor, and, frankly, I was standing very close." She would make the blood hers, the tumor hers; it would all be some treacherous, farcical mistake.

"No, that's not possible," says the Surgeon. The light goes back on.

"It's not?" says the Mother. Wait until it's *in the bucket,* she thinks. Don't be so sure. *Do we have to wait until it's in the bucket to find out a mistake has been made?*

"We will start with a radical nephrectomy," says the Surgeon, instantly thrown into darkness again. His voice comes from nowhere and everywhere at once. "And then we'll begin with chemotherapy after that. These tumors usually respond very well to chemo."

"I've never heard of a baby having chemo," the Mother says. *Baby* and *Chemo,* she thinks: they should never even appear in the same sentence together, let alone the same life. In her other life, her life before this day, she had been a believer in alternative medicine. Chemotherapy? Unthinkable. Now, suddenly, alternative medicine seems the wacko maiden aunt to the Nice Big Daddy of Conventional Treatment. How quickly the old girl faints and gives way, leaves one just standing there. Chemo? Of course: chemo! Why by all means: chemo. Absolutely! Chemo!

The Baby flicks the switch back on, and the walls reappear, big wedges of light checkered with small framed watercolors of the local lake. The Mother has begun to cry: all of life has led her here, to this moment. After this, there is no more life. There is something else, something stumbling and unlivable, something mechanical, something for robots, but not life. Life has been taken and broken, quickly, like a stick. The room goes dark again, so that the Mother can cry more freely. How can a baby's body be stolen so fast? How much can one heaven-sent and unsuspecting child endure? Why has he not been spared this inconceivable fate?

Perhaps, she thinks, she is being punished: too many babysitters too early on. ("Come to Mommy! Come to Mommy-Baby-sitter!" she used to say. But it was a joke!) Her life, perhaps, bore too openly the marks and wigs of deepest drag. Her unmotherly thoughts had all been noted: the panicky hope that his nap would last longer than it did; her occasional desire to kiss him passionately on the mouth (to make out with her baby!); her ongoing complaints about the very vocabulary of motherhood, how it degraded the speaker ("Is this a poopie onesie! Yes, it's a very poopie onesie!"). She had, moreover, on three occasions used the formula bottles as flower vases. She twice let the Baby's ears get fudgy with wax. A few afternoons last month, at snacktime, she placed a bowl of Cheerios on the floor for him to eat, like a dog. She let him play with the Dustbuster. Just once, before he was born, she said, "Healthy? I just want the kid to be rich." A joke, for God's sake! After he was born she announced that her life had become a daily sequence of mind-wrecking chores, the same ones over and over again, like a novel by Mrs. Camus. Another joke! These jokes will kill you! She had told too often, and with too much enjoyment, the story of how the Baby had said "Hi" to his high chair, waved at the lake waves, shouted "Goody-goody-goody" in what seemed to be a Russian accent, pointed at his eyes and said "Ice." And all that nonsensical baby talk: wasn't it a stitch? "Canonical babbling," the language experts called it. He recounted whole stories in it—totally made up, she could tell. He embroidered; he fished; he exaggerated. What a card! To friends, she spoke of his eating habits (carrots yes, tuna no). She mentioned, too much, his sidesplitting giggle. Did she have to be so boring? Did she have no consideration for others, for the intellectual demands and courtesies of human society? Would she not even attempt to be more interesting? It was a crime against the human mind not even to try.

Now her baby, for all these reasons—lack of motherly gratitude, motherly judgment, motherly proportion—will be taken away.

The room is fluorescently ablaze again. The Mother digs around in her parka pocket and comes up with a Kleenex. It is old and thin, like a mashed flower saved from a dance; she dabs it at her eyes and nose.

"The Baby won't suffer as much as you," says the Surgeon.

And who can contradict? Not the Baby, who in his Slavic Betty Boop voice can say only *mama, dada, cheese, ice, bye-bye, outside, boogie-boogie, goody-goody, eddy-eddy,* and *car.* (Who is Eddy? They have no idea.) This will not suffice to express his mortal suffering. Who can say what babies do with their agony and shock? Not they themselves. (Baby talk: isn't it a stitch?) They put it all no place anyone can really see. They are like a different race, a different species: they seem not to experience pain the way we do. Yeah, that's it: their nervous systems are not as fully formed, and *they just don't experience pain the way we do.* A tune to keep one humming through the war. "You'll get through it," the Surgeon says.

"How?" asks the Mother. "How does one get through it?"

"You just put your head down and go," says the Surgeon. He picks up his file folder. He is a skilled manual laborer. The tricky emotional stuff is not to his liking. The babies. The babies! What can be said to console the parents about the babies? "I'll go phone the oncologist on duty to let him know," he says, and leaves the room.

"Come here, sweetie," the Mother says to the Baby, who has toddled off toward a gum wrapper on the floor. "We've got to put your jacket on." She picks him up and he reaches for the light switch again. Light, dark. Peekaboo: where's baby? Where did baby go?

At home, she leaves a message—"Urgent! Call me!"—for the Husband on his voice mail. Then she takes the Baby upstairs for his nap, rocks him in the rocker. The Baby waves good-bye to his little bears, then looks toward the window and says, "Bye-bye, outside." He has, lately, the habit of waving goodbye to everything, and now it seems as if he senses an imminent departure, and it breaks her heart to hear him. *Bye-bye!* She sings low and monotonously, like a small appliance, which is how he likes it. He is drowsy, dozy, drifting off. He has grown so much in the last year, he hardly fits in her lap anymore; his limbs dangle off like a pietà. His head rolls slightly inside the crook of her arm. She can feel him falling backward into sleep, his mouth round and open like the sweetest of poppies. All the lullabies in the world, all the melodies threaded through with maternal melancholy now become for her—abandoned as a mother can be by working men and napping babies—the songs of hard, hard grief. Sitting there, bowed and bobbing, the Mother feels the entirety of her love as worry and heartbreak. A quick and irrevocable alchemy: there is no longer one unworried scrap left for happiness. "If you go," she keens low into his soapy neck, into the ranunculus coil of his ear, "we are going with you. We are nothing without you. Without you, we are a heap of rocks. We are gravel and mold. Without you, we are two stumps, with nothing any longer in our hearts. Wherever this takes you, we are following. We will be there. Don't be scared. We are going, too. That is that."

"Take Notes," says the Husband, after coming straight home from work, midafternoon, hearing the news, and saying all the words out loud—*surgery, metasta-*

sis, dialysis, transplant—then collapsing in a chair in tears. "Take notes. We are going to need the money."

"Good God," cries the Mother. Everything inside her suddenly begins to cower and shrink, a thinning of bones. Perhaps this is a soldier's readiness, but it has the whiff of death and defeat. It feels like a heart attack, a failure of will and courage, a power failure: a failure of everything. Her face, when she glimpses it in a mirror, is cold and bloated with shock, her eyes scarlet and shrunk. She has already started to wear sunglasses indoors, like a celebrity widow. From where will her own strength come? From some philosophy? From some frigid little philosophy? She is neither stalwart nor realistic and has trouble with basic concepts, such as the one that says events move in one direction only and do not jump up, turn around, and take themselves back.

The Husband begins too many of his sentences with "What if." He is trying to piece everything together like a train wreck. He is trying to get the train to town.

"We'll just take all the steps, move through all the stages. We'll go where we have to go. We'll hunt; we'll find; we'll pay what we have to pay. What if we can't pay?"

"Sounds like shopping."

"I cannot believe this is happening to our little boy," he says, and starts to sob again. "Why didn't it happen to one of us? It's so unfair. Just last week, my doctor declared me in perfect health: the prostate of a twenty-year-old, the heart of a ten-year-old, the brain of an insect—or whatever it was he said. What a nightmare this is."

What words can be uttered? You turn just slightly and there it is: the death of your child. It is part symbol, part devil, and in your blind spot all along, until, if you are unlucky, it is completely upon you. Then it is a fierce little country abducting you; it holds you squarely inside itself like a cellar room—the best boundaries of you are the boundaries of it. Are there windows? Sometimes aren't there windows?

The Mother is not a shopper. She hates to shop, is generally bad at it, though she does like a good sale. She cannot stroll meaningfully through anger, denial, grief, and acceptance. She goes straight to bargaining and stays there. How much? she calls out to the ceiling, to some makeshift construction of holiness she has desperately, though not uncreatively, assembled in her mind and prayed to; a doubter, never before given to prayer, she must now reap what she has not sown; she must assemble from scratch an entire altar of worship and begging. She tries for noble abstractions, nothing too anthropomorphic, just some Higher Morality, though if this particular Highness looks something like the manager at Marshall Field's, sucking a Frango mint, so be it. Amen. Just tell me what you want, requests the Mother. And how do you want it? More charitable acts? A billion starting now. Charitable thoughts? Harder, but of course! Of course! I'll do the cooking, honey; I'll pay the rent. Just tell me. *Excuse me?* Well, if not to you, to whom do I speak? Hello? To whom do I have to speak around here? A higher-up? A superior? Wait? I can wait. I've got all day. I've got the whole damn day.

The Husband now lies next to her in bed, sighing. "Poor little guy could survive all this, only to be killed in a car crash at the age of sixteen," he says.

The wife, bargaining, considers this. "We'll take the car crash," she says.

"What?"

"Let's Make a Deal! Sixteen Is a Full Life! We'll take the car crash. We'll take the car crash, in front of which Carol Merrill is now standing."

Now the Manager of Marshall Field's reappears. "To take the surprises out is to take the life out of life," he says.

The phone rings. The Husband gets up and leaves the room.

"But I don't want these surprises," says the Mother. "Here! You take these surprises!"

"To know the narrative in advance is to turn yourself into a machine," the Manager continues. "What makes humans human is precisely that they do not know the future. That is why they do the fateful and amusing things they do: who can say how anything will turn out? Therein lies the only hope for redemption, discovery, and—let's be frank—fun, fun, fun! There might be things people will get away with. And not just motel towels. There might be great illicit loves, enduring joy, faith-shaking accidents with farm machinery. But you have to not know in order to see what stories your life's efforts bring you. The mystery is all."

The Mother, though shy, has grown confrontational. "Is this the kind of bogus, random crap they teach at merchandising school? We would like fewer surprises, fewer efforts and mysteries, thank you. K through eight; can we just get K through eight?" It now seems like the luckiest, most beautiful, most musical phrase she's ever heard: K through eight. The very lilt. The very thought.

The Manager continues, trying things out. "I mean, the whole conception of 'the story,' of cause and effect, the whole idea that people have a clue as to how the world works is just a piece of laughable metaphysical colonialism perpetrated upon the wild country of time."

Did they own a gun? The Mother begins looking through drawers.

The Husband comes back into the room and observes her. "Ha! The Great Havoc that is the Puzzle of all Life!" he says of the Marshall Field's management policy. He has just gotten off a conference call with the insurance company and the hospital. The surgery will be Friday. "It's all just some dirty capitalist's idea of a philosophy."

"Maybe it's just a fact of narrative and you really can't politicize it," says the Mother. It is now only the two of them.

"Whose side are you on?"

"I'm on the Baby's side."

"Are you taking notes for this?"

"No."

"You're not?"

"No. I can't. Not this! I write fiction. This isn't fiction."

"Then write nonfiction. Do a piece of journalism. Get two dollars a word."

"Then it has to be true and full of information. I'm not trained. I'm not that skilled. Plus, I have a convenient personal principle about artists not abandoning art. One should never turn one's back on a vivid imagination. Even the whole memoir thing annoys me."

"Well, make things up, but pretend they're real."

"I'm not that insured."

"You're making me nervous."

"Sweetie, darling, I'm not that good. I can't *do this.* I can do—what can I do? I can do quasi-amusing phone dialogue. I can do succinct descriptions of weather. I can do screwball outings with the family pet. Sometimes I can do those. Honey, I only do what I can. I do *the careful ironies of daydream.* I do *the marshy ideas upon which intimate life is built.* But this? Our baby with cancer? I'm sorry. My stop was two stations back. This is irony at its most gaudy and careless. This is a Hieronymus Bosch of facts and figures and blood and graphs. This is a nightmare of narrative slop. This cannot be designed. This cannot even be noted in preparation for a design—"

"We're going to need the money."

"To say nothing of the moral boundaries of pecuniary recompense in a situation such as this—"

"What if the other kidney goes? What if he needs a transplant? Where are the moral boundaries there? What are we going to do, have bake sales?"

"We can sell the house. I hate this house. It makes me crazy."

"And we'll live—where again?"

"The Ronald McDonald place. I hear it's nice. It's the least McDonald's can do."

"You have a keen sense of justice."

"I try. What can I say?" She pauses. "Is all this really happening? I keep thinking that soon it will be over—the life expectancy of a cloud is supposed to be only twelve hours—and then I realize something has occurred that can never ever be over."

The Husband buries his face in his hands: "Our poor baby. How did this happen to him?" He looks over and stares at the bookcase that serves as the nightstand. "And do you think even one of these baby books is any help?" He picks up the Leach, the Spock, the *What to Expect.* "Where in the pages or index of any of these does it say 'chemotherapy' or 'Hickman catheter' or 'renal sarcoma'? Where does it say 'carcinogenesis'? You know what these books are obsessed with? *Holding a fucking spoon.*" He begins hurling the books off the night table and against the far wall.

"Hey," says the Mother, trying to soothe. "Hey, hey, hey." But compared to his stormy roar, her words are those of a backup singer—a Shondell, a Pip—a doo-wop ditty. Books, and now more books, continue to fly.

Take Notes.

Is *fainthearted* one word or two? Student prose has wrecked her spelling.

It's one word. Two words—*Faint Hearted*—what would that be? The name of a drag queen.

Take Notes. In the end, you suffer alone. But at the beginning you suffer with a whole lot of others. When your child has cancer, you are instantly whisked away to another planet: one of bald-headed little boys. Pediatric Oncology. Peed Onk. You wash your hands for thirty seconds in antibacterial soap before you are allowed to enter through the swinging doors. You put paper slippers on your shoes. You keep your voice down. A whole place has been designed and decorated for your nightmare. Here is where your nightmare will occur. We've got a room all ready for you. We have cots. We have refrigerators. "The children are almost entirely boys," says one of the nurses. "No one knows why. It's been documented, but a lot of people out there still don't realize it." The little boys are all from sweet-sounding places—Janesville and Appleton—little heartland towns with giant landfills, agricultural runoff, paper factories, Joe McCarthy's grave (Alone, a site of great toxicity, thinks the Mother. The soil should be tested).

All the bald little boys look like brothers. They wheel their IVs up and down the single corridor of Peed Onk. Some of the lively ones, feeling good for a day, ride the lower bars of the IV while their large, cheerful mothers whiz them along the halls. *Wheee!*

The Mother does not feel large and cheerful. In her mind, she is scathing, acid-tongued, wraith-thin, and chain-smoking out on a fire escape somewhere. Beneath her lie the gentle undulations of the Midwest, with all its aspirations to be—to be what? To be Long Island. How it has succeeded! Strip mall upon strip mall. Lurid water, poisoned potatoes. The Mother drags deeply, blowing clouds of smoke out over the disfigured cornfields. When a baby gets cancer, it seems stupid ever to have given up smoking. When a baby gets cancer, you think, Whom are we kidding? Let's all light up. When a baby gets cancer, you think, Who came up with *this* idea? What celestial abandon gave rise to *this*? Pour me a drink, so I can refuse to toast.

The Mother does not know how to be one of these other mothers, with their blond hair and sweatpants and sneakers and determined pleasantness. She does not think that she can be anything similar. She does not feel remotely like them. She knows, for instance, too many people in Greenwich Village. She mail-orders oysters and tiramisu from a shop in SoHo. She is close friends with four actual homosexuals. Her husband is asking her to Take Notes.

Where do these women get their sweatpants? She will find out.

She will start, perhaps, with the costume and work from there.

She will live according to the bromides. Take one day at a time. Take a positive attitude. *Take a hike!* She wishes that there were more interesting things that were useful and true, but it seems now that it's only the boring things that are useful and true. *One day at a time.* And *at least we have our health.* How ordinary. How obvious. One day at a time. You need a brain for that?

While the Surgeon is fine-boned, regal, and laconic—they have correctly guessed his game to be doubles—there is a bit of the mad, overcaffeinated scientist to the Oncologist. He speaks quickly. He knows a lot of studies and numbers. He can do the math. Good! Someone should be able to do the math! "It's a fast but wimpy tumor," he explains. "It typically metastasizes to the lung." He rattles off some numbers, time frames, risk statistics. Fast but wimpy: the Mother tries to imagine this combination of traits, tries to think and think, and can only come up with Claudia Osk from the fourth grade, who blushed and almost wept when called on in class, but in gym could outrun everyone in the quarter-mile fire-door-to-fence dash. The Mother thinks now of this tumor as Claudia Osk. They are going to get Claudia Osk, make her sorry. All right! Claudia Osk must die. Though it has never been mentioned before, it now seems clear that Claudia Osk should have died long ago. Who was she anyway? So conceited: not letting anyone beat her in a race. Well, hey, hey, hey: don't look now, Claudia!

The Husband nudges her. "Are you listening?"

"The chances of this happening even just to one kidney are one in fifteen thousand. Now given all these other factors, the chances on the second kidney are about one in eight."

"One in eight," says the Husband. "Not bad. As long as it's not one in fifteen thousand."

The Mother studies the trees and fish along the ceiling's edge in the Save the Planet wallpaper border. Save the Planet. Yes! But the windows in this very building don't open and diesel fumes are leaking into the ventilating system, near which, outside, a delivery truck is parked. The air is nauseous and stale.

"Really," the Oncologist is saying, "of all the cancers he could get, this is probably the best."

"We win," says the Mother.

"*Best,* I know, hardly seems the right word. Look, you two probably need to get some rest. We'll see how the surgery and histology go. Then we'll start with chemo the week following. A little light chemo: vincristine and—"

"Vincristine?" interrupts the Mother. "Wine of Christ?"

"The names are strange, I know. The other one we use is actinomycin-D. Sometimes called 'dactinomycin.' People move the *D* around to the front."

"They move the *D* around to the front," repeats the Mother.

"Yup!" the Oncologist says. "I don't know why—they just do!"

"Christ didn't survive his wine," says the Husband.

"But of course he did," says the Oncologist, and nods toward the Baby, who has now found a cupboard full of hospital linens and bandages and is yanking them all out onto the floor. "I'll see you guys tomorrow, after the surgery." And with that, the Oncologist leaves.

"Or, rather, Christ *was* his wine," mumbles the Husband. Everything he knows about the New Testament, he has gleaned from the sound track of *Godspell.* "His blood was the wine. What a great beverage idea."

"A little light chemo. Don't you like that one?" says the Mother. "*Eine kleine* dactinomycin. I'd like to see Mozart write that one up for a big wad o' cash."

"Come here, honey," the Husband says to the Baby, who has now pulled off both his shoes.

"It's bad enough when they refer to medical science as 'an inexact science,'" says the Mother. "But when they start referring to it as 'an art,' I get extremely nervous."

"Yeah. If we wanted art, Doc, we'd go to an art museum." The Husband picks up the Baby. "You're an artist," he says to the Mother, with the taint of accusation in his voice. "They probably think you find creativity reassuring."

The Mother sighs. "I just find it inevitable. Let's go get something to eat." And so they take the elevator to the cafeteria, where there is a high chair, and where, not noticing, they all eat a lot of apples with the price tags still on them.

Because his surgery is not until tomorrow, the Baby likes the hospital. He likes the long corridors, down which he can run. He likes everything on wheels. The flower carts in the lobby! ("Please keep your boy away from the flowers," says the vendor. "We'll buy the whole display," snaps the Mother, adding, "Actual children in a children's hospital—unbelievable, isn't it?") The Baby likes the other little boys. Places to go! People to see! Rooms to wander into! There is Intensive Care. There is the Trauma Unit. The Baby smiles and waves. What a little Cancer Personality! Bandaged citizens smile and wave back. In Peed Onk, there are the bald little boys to play with. Joey, Eric, Tim, Mort, and Tod (Mort! Tod!). There is the four-year-old, Ned, holding his little deflated rubber ball, the one with the intriguing curling hose. The Baby wants to play with it. "It's mine. Leave it alone," says Ned. "Tell the Baby to leave it alone."

"Baby, you've got to share," says the Mother from a chair some feet away.

Suddenly, from down near the Tiny Tim Lounge, comes Ned's mother, large and blond and sweatpanted. "Stop that! Stop it!" she cries out, dashing toward the Baby and Ned and pushing the Baby away. "Don't touch that!" she barks at the Baby, who is only a Baby and bursts into tears because he has never been yelled at like this before.

Ned's mom glares at everyone. "This is drawing fluid from Neddy's liver!" She pats at the rubber thing and starts to cry a little.

"Oh my God," says the Mother. She comforts the Baby, who is also crying. She and Ned, the only dry-eyed people, look at each other. "I'm so sorry," she says to Ned and then to his mother. "I'm so stupid. I thought they were squabbling over a toy."

"It does look like a toy," agrees Ned. He smiles. He is an angel. All the little boys are angels. Total, sweet, bald little angels, and now God is trying to get them back for himself. Who are they, mere mortal women, in the face of this, this powerful and overwhelming and inscrutable thing, God's will? They are the mothers, that's who. You can't have him! they shout every day. You dirty old man! *Get out of here! Hands off!*

"I'm so sorry," says the Mother again. "I didn't know."

Ned's mother smiles vaguely. "Of course you didn't know," she says, and walks back to the Tiny Tim Lounge.

The Tiny Tim Lounge is a little sitting area at the end of the Peed Onk corridor. There are two small sofas, a table, a rocking chair, a television and a VCR. There are various videos: *Speed, Dune,* and *Star Wars.* On one of the lounge walls there is a gold plaque with the singer Tiny Tim's name on it: his son was treated once at this hospital and so, five years ago, he donated money for this lounge. It is a cramped little lounge, which, one suspects, would be larger if Tiny Tim's son had actually lived. Instead, he died here, at this hospital and now there is this tiny room which is part gratitude, part generosity, part *fuck-you.*

Sifting through the videocassettes, the Mother wonders what science fiction could begin to compete with the science fiction of cancer itself—a tumor with its differentiated muscle and bone cells, a clump of wild nothing and its mad, ambitious desire to be something: something inside you, instead of you, another organism, but with a monster's architecture, a demon's sabotage and chaos. Think of leukemia, a tumor diabolically taking liquid form, better to swim about incognito in the blood. George Lucas, direct that!

Sitting with the other parents in the Tiny Tim Lounge, the night before the surgery, having put the Baby to bed in his high steel crib two rooms down, the Mother begins to hear the stories: leukemia in kindergarten, sarcomas in Little League, neuroblastomas discovered at summer camp. "Eric slid into third base, but then the scrape didn't heal." The parents pat one another's forearms and speak of other children's hospitals as if they were resorts. "You were at St. Jude's last winter? So were we. What did you think of it? We loved the staff." Jobs have been quit, marriages hacked up, bank accounts ravaged; the parents have seemingly endured the unendurable. They speak not of the *possibility* of comas brought on by the chemo, but of the *number* of them. "He was in his first coma last July," says Ned's mother. "It was a scary time, but we pulled through."

Pulling through is what people do around here. There is a kind of bravery in their lives that isn't bravery at all. It is automatic, unflinching, a mix of man and machine, consuming and unquestionable obligation meeting illness move for move in a giant even-steven game of chess—an unending round of something that looks like shadow-boxing, though between love and death, which is the shadow? "Everyone admires us for our courage," says one man. "They have no idea what they're talking about."

I could get out of here, thinks the Mother. I could just get on a bus and go, never come back. Change my name. A kind of witness relocation thing.

"Courage requires options," the man adds.

The Baby might be better off.

"There are options," says a woman with a thick suede headband. "You could give up. You could fall apart."

"No, you can't. Nobody does. I've never seen it," says the man. "Well, not *really* fall apart." Then the lounge falls quiet. Over the VCR someone has taped the fortune from a fortune cookie. "Optimism," it says, "is what allows a teakettle to sing though up to its neck in hot water." Underneath, someone else has taped a clipping from a summer horoscope. "Cancer rules!" it says. Who would tape this up? Somebody's twelve-year-old brother. One of the fathers—Joey's father—gets up and tears them both off, makes a small wad in his fist.

There is some rustling of magazine pages.

The Mother clears her throat. "Tiny Tim forgot the wet bar," she says.

Ned, who is still up, comes out of his room and down the corridor, whose lights dim at nine. Standing next to her chair, he says to the Mother, "Where are you from? What is wrong with your baby?"

In the tiny room that is theirs, she sleeps fitfully in her sweatpants, occasionally leaping up to check on the Baby. This is what the sweatpants are for: leaping. In case of fire. In case of anything. In case the difference between day and night starts to dissolve, and there is no difference at all, so why pretend? In the cot beside her, the Husband, who has taken a sleeping pill, is snoring loudly, his arms folded about his head in a kind of origami. How could either of them have stayed back at the house, with its empty high chair and empty crib? Occasionally the Baby wakes and cries out, and she bolts up, goes to him, rubs his back, rearranges the linens. The clock on the metal dresser shows that it is five after three. Then twenty to five. And then it is really morning, the beginning of this day, nephrectomy day. Will she be glad when it's over, or barely alive, or both? Each day this week has arrived huge, empty, and unknown, like a spaceship, and this one especially is lit a bright gray.

"He'll need to put this on," says John, one of the nurses, bright and early, handing the Mother a thin greenish garment with roses and teddy bears printed on it. A wave of nausea hits her; this smock, she thinks, will soon be splattered with—with what?

The Baby is awake but drowsy. She lifts off his pajamas. "Don't forget, *bubeleh,*" she whispers, undressing and dressing him. "We will be with you every moment, every step. When you think you are asleep and floating off far away from everybody, Mommy will still be there." If she hasn't fled on a bus. "Mommy will take care of you. And Daddy, too." She hopes the Baby does not detect her own fear and uncertainty, which she must hide from him, like a limp. He is hungry, not having been allowed to eat, and he is no longer amused by this new place, but worried about its hardships. Oh, my baby, she thinks. And the room starts to swim a little. The Husband comes in to take over. "Take a break," he says to her. "I'll walk him around for five minutes."

She leaves but doesn't know where to go. In the hallway, she is approached by a kind of social worker, a customer-relations person, who had given them a video to watch about the anesthesia: how the parent accompanies the child into the operating room, and how gently, nicely the drugs are administered.

"Did you watch the video?"

"Yes," says the Mother.

"Wasn't it helpful?"

"I don't know," says the Mother.

"Do you have any questions?" asks the video woman. "Do you have any questions?" asked of someone who has recently landed in this fearful, alien place seems to the Mother an absurd and amazing little courtesy. The very specificity of a question would give a lie to the overwhelming strangeness of everything around her.

"Not right now," says the Mother. "Right now, I think I'm just going to go to the bathroom."

When she returns to the Baby's room, everyone is there: the surgeon, the anesthesiologist, all the nurses, the social worker. In their blue caps and scrubs, they look like a clutch of forget-me-nots, and forget them, who could? The Baby, in his little teddy-bear smock, seems cold and scared. He reaches out and the Mother lifts him from the Husband's arms, rubs his back to warm him.

"Well, it's time!" says the Surgeon, forcing a smile.

"Shall we go?" says the Anesthesiologist.

What follows is a blur of obedience and bright lights. They take an elevator down to a big concrete room, the anteroom, the greenroom, the backstage of the operating room. Lining the walls are long shelves full of blue surgical outfits. "Children often become afraid of the color blue," says one of the nurses. But of course. Of course! "Now, which one of you would like to come into the operating room for the anesthesia?"

"I will," says the Mother.

"Are you sure?" asks the Husband.

"Yup." She kisses the Baby's hair. "Mr. Curlyhead," people keep calling him here, and it seems both rude and nice. Women look admiringly at his long lashes and exclaim, "Always the boys! Always the boys!"

Two surgical nurses put a blue smock and a blue cotton cap on the Mother. The Baby finds this funny and keeps pulling at the cap. "This way," says another nurse, and the Mother follows. "Just put the Baby down on the table."

In the video, the mother holds the baby and fumes are gently waved under the baby's nose until he falls asleep. Now, out of view of camera or social worker, the Anesthesiologist is anxious to get this under way and not let too much gas leak out into the room generally. The occupational hazard of this, his chosen profession, is gas exposure and nerve damage, and it has started to worry him. No doubt he frets about it to his wife every night. Now he turns the gas on and quickly clamps the plastic mouthpiece over the baby's cheeks and lips.

The Baby is startled. The Mother is startled. The Baby starts to scream and redden behind the plastic, but he cannot be heard. He thrashes. "Tell him it's okay," says the nurse to the Mother.

Okay? "It's okay," repeats the Mother, holding his hand, but she knows he can tell it's not okay, because he can see not only that she is still wearing that stupid paper cap but that her words are mechanical and swallowed, and she is biting her lips to keep them from trembling. Panicked, he attempts to sit. He cannot breathe; his arms reach up. *Bye-bye, outside.* And then, quite quickly, his eyes shut; he untenses and has fallen not *into* sleep but aside to sleep, an odd, kidnapping kind of sleep, his terror now hidden someplace deep inside him.

"How did it go?" asks the social worker, waiting in the concrete outer room. The Mother is hysterical. A nurse has ushered her out.

"It wasn't at all like the filmstrip!" she cries. "It wasn't like the filmstrip at all!"

"The filmstrip? You mean the video?" asks the social worker.

"It wasn't like that at all! It was brutal and unforgivable."

"Why that's terrible," she says, her role now no longer misinformational but janitorial, and she touches the Mother's arm, though the Mother shakes it off and goes to find the Husband.

She finds him in the large mulberry Surgery Lounge, where he has been taken and where there is free hot chocolate in small Styrofoam cups. Red cellophane garlands festoon the doorways. She has totally forgotten it is as close to Christmas as this. A pianist in the corner is playing "Carol of the Bells," and it sounds not only unfestive but scary, like the theme from *The Exorcist.*

There is a giant clock on the far wall. It is a kind of porthole into the operating room, a way of assessing the Baby's ordeal: forty-five minutes for the Hickman implant; two and a half hours for the nephrectomy. And then, after that, three months of chemotherapy. The magazine on her lap stays open at a ruby-hued perfume ad.

"Still not taking notes," says the Husband.

"Nope."

"You know, in a way, this is the kind of thing you've *always* written about."

"You are really something, you know that? This is life. This isn't a 'kind of thing.'"

"But this is the kind of thing that fiction is: it's the unlivable life, the strange room tacked onto the house, the extra moon that is circling the earth unbeknownst to science."

"I told you that."

"I'm quoting you."

She looks at her watch, thinking of the Baby. "How long has it been?"

"Not long. Too long. In the end, maybe those're the same things."

"What do you suppose is happening to him right this second?"

Infection? Slipping knives? "I don't know. But you know what? I've gotta go. I've gotta just walk a bit." The Husband gets up, walks around the lounge, then comes back and sits down.

The synapses between the minutes are unswimmable. An hour is thick as fudge. The Mother feels depleted; she is a string of empty tin cans attached by wire, something a goat would sniff and chew, something now and then enlivened by a jolt of electricity.

She hears their names being called over the intercom. "Yes? Yes?" She stands up quickly. Her words have flown out before her, an exhalation of birds. The piano music has stopped. The pianist is gone. She and the Husband approach the main desk, where a man looks up at them and smiles. Before him is a xeroxed list of patients' names. "That's our little boy right there," says the Mother, seeing the Baby's name on the list and pointing at it. "Is there some word? Is everything okay?"

"Yes," says the man. "Your boy is doing fine. They've just finished with the catheter, and they are moving on to the kidney."

"But it's been two hours already! Oh my God, did something go wrong? What happened? What went wrong?"

"Did something go wrong?" The Husband tugs at his collar.

"Not really. It just took longer than they expected. I'm told everything is fine. They wanted you to know."

"Thank you," says the Husband. They turn and walk back toward where they were sitting.

"I'm not going to make it." The Mother sighs, sinking into a fake leather chair shaped somewhat like a baseball mitt. "But before I go, I'm taking half this hospital out with me."

"Do you want some coffee?" asks the Husband.

"I don't know," says the Mother. "No, I guess not. No. Do you?"

"Nah, I don't, either, I guess," he says.

"Would you like part of an orange?"

"Oh, maybe, I guess, if you're having one." She takes an orange from her purse and just sits there peeling its difficult skin, the flesh rupturing beneath her fingers, the juice trickling down her hands, stinging the hangnails. She and the Husband chew and swallow, discreetly spit the seeds into Kleenex, and read from photocopies of the latest medical research, which they begged from the intern. They read, and underline, and sigh and close their eyes, and after some time, the surgery is over. A nurse from Peed Onk comes down to tell them.

"Your little boy's in recovery right now. He's doing well. You can see him in about fifteen minutes."

How can it be described? How can any of it be described? The trip and the story of the trip are always two different things. The narrator is the one who has stayed home, but then, afterward, presses her mouth upon the traveler's mouth, in order to make the mouth work, to make the mouth say, say, say. One cannot go to a place and speak of it; one cannot both see and say, not really. One can go, and upon returning make a lot of hand motions and indications with the arms. The mouth itself, working at the speed of light, at the eye's instructions, is necessarily struck still; so fast, so much to report, it hangs open and dumb as a gutted bell. All that unsayable life! That's where the narrator comes in. The narrator comes with her kisses and mimicry and tidying up. The narrator comes and makes a slow, fake song of the mouth's eager devastation.

It is a horror and a miracle to see him. He is lying in his crib in his room, tubed up, splayed like a boy on a cross, his arms stiffened into cardboard "no-no's" so that he cannot yank out the tubes. There is the bladder catheter, the nasal-gastric tube, and the Hickman, which, beneath the skin, is plugged into his jugular, then popped out his chest wall and capped with a long plastic cap. There is a large bandage taped over his abdomen. Groggy, on a morphine drip, still he is able to look at her when, maneuvering through all the vinyl wiring, she leans to hold him, and when she does, he begins to cry, but cry silently, without motion or noise. She has never seen a baby cry without motion or noise. It is the crying of an old person: silent, beyond opinion, shattered. In someone so tiny, it is frightening and unnatural. She wants to pick up the Baby and run—out of there, out of there. She wants to whip out a gun: *No-no's, eh? This whole thing is what I call a no-no.* Don't you touch him! she wants to shout at the surgeons and the needle nurses. Not anymore! No more! No more! She would crawl up and lie beside him in the crib if she could. But instead, because of all his intricate wiring, she must lean and cuddle, sing to him, songs of peril and flight: "We gotta get out of this place, if it's the last thing we ever do. We gotta get out of this place . . . there's a better life for me and you."

Very 1967. She was eleven then and impressionable.

The Baby looks at her, pleadingly, his arms splayed out in surrender. To where? Where is there to go? Take me! Take me!

That night, postop night, the Mother and Husband lie afloat in the cot together. A fluorescent lamp near the crib is kept on in the dark. The Baby breathes evenly but thinly in his drugged sleep. The morphine in its first flooding doses apparently makes him feel as if he were falling backward—or so the Mother has been told—and it causes the Baby to jerk, to catch himself over and over, as if he were being dropped from a tree. "Is this right? Isn't there something that should be done?" The nurses come in hourly, different ones—the night shifts seem strangely short and frequent. If the Baby stirs or frets, the nurses give him more morphine through the Hickman catheter, then leave to tend to other patients. The Mother rises to check on him in the low light. There is gurgling from the clear plastic suction tube coming out of his mouth. Brownish clumps have collected in the tube. What is going on? The Mother rings for the nurse. Is it Renée or Sarah or Darcy? She's forgotten.

"What, what is it?" murmurs the Husband, waking up.

"Something is wrong," says the Mother. "It looks like blood in his N-G tube."

"What?" The Husband gets out of bed. He, too, is wearing sweatpants.

The nurse—Valerie—pushes open the heavy door to the room and enters quietly. "Everything okay?"

"There's something wrong here. The tube is sucking blood out of his stomach. It looks like it may have perforated his stomach and that now he's bleeding internally. Look!"

Valerie is a saint, but her voice is the standard hospital saint voice: an infuriating, pharmaceutical calm. It says, Everything is normal here. Death is normal. Pain is normal. Nothing is abnormal. So there is nothing to get excited about. "Well now, let's see." She holds up the plastic tube and tries to see inside it. "Hmmm," she says. "I'll call the attending physician."

Because this is a research and teaching hospital, all the regular doctors are at home sleeping in their Mission-style beds. Tonight, as is apparently the case every weekend night, the attending physician is a medical student. He looks fifteen. The authority he attempts to convey, he cannot remotely inhabit. He is not even in the same building with it. He shakes everyone's hands, then strokes his chin, a gesture no doubt gleaned from some piece of dinner theater his parents took him to once. As if there were an actual beard on that chin! As if beard growth on that chin were even possible! *Our Town! Kiss Me Kate! Barefoot in the Park!* He is attempting to convince, if not to impress.

"We're in trouble," the Mother whispers to the Husband. She is tired, tired of young people grubbing for grades. "We've got Dr. 'Kiss Me Kate,' here."

The Husband looks at her blankly, a mix of disorientation and divorce.

The medical student holds the tubing in his hands. "I don't really see anything," he says.

He flunks! "You don't?" The Mother shoves her way in, holds the clear tubing in both hands. "That," she says. "Right here and here." Just this past semester, she said to one of her own students, "If you don't see how this essay is better than that one, then I want you just to go out into the hallway and stand there until you do." Is it important to keep one's voice down? The Baby stays asleep. He is drugged and dreaming, far away.

"Hmmm," says the medical student. "Perhaps there's a little irritation in the stomach."

"A little irritation?" The Mother grows furious. "This is blood. These are clumps and clots. This stupid thing is sucking the life right out of him!" Life! She is starting to cry.

They turn off the suction and bring in antacids, which they feed into the Baby through the tube. Then they turn the suction on again. This time on low.

"What was it on before?" asks the Husband.

"High," says Valerie. "Doctor's orders, though I don't know why. I don't know why these doctors do a lot of the things they do."

"Maybe they're . . . not all that bright?" suggests the Mother. She is feeling relief and rage simultaneously: there is a feeling of prayer and litigation in the air. Yet essentially, she is grateful. Isn't she? She thinks she is. And still, and still: look at all the things you have to do to protect a child, a hospital merely an intensification of life's cruel obstacle course.

The Surgeon comes to visit on Saturday morning. He steps in and nods at the Baby, who is awake but glazed from the morphine, his eyes two dark unseeing grapes. "The boy looks fine," the Surgeon announces. He peeks under the Baby's bandage. "The stitches look good," he says. The Baby's abdomen is stitched all the way across like a baseball. "And the other kidney, when we looked at it yesterday face-to-face, looked fine. We'll try to wean him off the morphine a little, and see how he's doing on Monday." He clears his throat. "And now," he says, looking about the room at the nurses and medical students, "I would like to speak with the Mother, alone."

The Mother's heart gives a jolt. "Me?"

"Yes," he says, motioning, then turning.

She gets up and steps out into the empty hallway with him, closing the door behind her. What can this be about? She hears the Baby fretting a little in his crib. Her brain fills with pain and alarm. Her voice comes out as a hoarse whisper. "Is there something—"

"There is a particular thing I need from you," says the Surgeon, turning and standing there very seriously.

"Yes?" Her heart is pounding. She does not feel resilient enough for any more bad news.

"I need to ask a favor."

"Certainly," she says, attempting very hard to summon the strength and courage for this occasion, whatever it is; her throat has tightened to a fist.

From inside his white coat, the surgeon removes a thin paperback book and thrusts it toward her. "Will you sign my copy of your novel?"

The Mother looks down and sees that it is indeed a copy of a novel she has written, one about teenaged girls.

She looks up. A big, spirited grin is cutting across his face. "I read this last summer," he says, "and I still remember parts of it! Those girls got into such trouble!"

Of all the surreal moments of the last few days, this, she thinks, might be the most so.

"Okay," she says, and the Surgeon merrily hands her a pen.

"You can just write 'To Dr.—' Oh, I don't need to tell you what to write."

The Mother sits down on a bench and shakes ink into the pen A sigh of relief washes over and out of her. Oh, the pleasure of a sigh of relief, like the finest moments of love; has anyone properly sung the praises of sighs of relief? She opens the book to the title page. She breathes deeply. What is he doing reading novels about teenaged girls, anyway? And why didn't he buy the hardcover? She inscribes something grateful and true, then hands the book back to him.

"Is he going to be okay?"

"The boy? The boy is going to be fine," he says, then taps her stiffly on the shoulder. "Now you take care. It's Saturday. Drink a little wine."

Over the weekend, while the Baby sleeps, the Mother and Husband sit together in the Tiny Tim Lounge. The Husband is restless and makes cafeteria and sundry runs, running errands for everyone. In his absence, the other parents regale her further with their sagas. Pediatric cancer and chemo stories: the children's amputations, blood poisoning, teeth flaking like shale, the learning delays and disabilities caused by chemo frying the young, budding brain. But strangely optimistic codas are tacked on—endings as stiff and loopy as carpenter's lace, crisp and empty as lettuce, reticulate as a net—ah, words. "After all that business with the tutor, he's better now, and fitted with new incisors by my wife's cousin's husband, who did dental school in two and a half years, if you can believe that. We hope for the best. We take things as they come. Life is hard."

"Life's a big problem," agrees the Mother. Part of her welcomes and invites all their tales. In the few long days since this nightmare began, part of her has become addicted to disaster and war stories. She wants only to hear about the sadness and emergencies of others. They are the only situations that can join hands with her own; everything else bounces off her shiny shield of resentment and unsympathy. Nothing else can even stay in her brain. From this, no doubt, the philistine world is made, or should one say recruited? Together, the parents huddle all day in the Tiny Tim Lounge—no need to watch *Oprah.* They leave Oprah in the dust. Oprah has nothing on them. They chat matter-of-factly, then fall silent and watch *Dune* or *Star Wars,* in which there are bright and shiny robots, whom the Mother now sees not as robots at all but as human beings who have had terrible things happen to them.

Some of their friends visit with stuffed animals and soft greetings of "Looking good" for the dozing baby, though the room is way past the stuffed-animal limit. The

Mother arranges, once more, a plateful of Mint Milano cookies and cups of take-out coffee for guests. All her nutso pals stop by—the two on Prozac, the one obsessed with the word *penis* in the word *happiness,* the one who recently had her hair foiled green. "Your friends put the *de* in *fin de siècle,*" says the husband. Overheard, or recorded, all marital conversation sounds as if someone must be joking, though usually no one is.

She loves her friends, especially loves them for coming, since there are times they all fight and don't speak for weeks. Is this friendship? For now and here, it must do and is, and is, she swears it is. For one, they never offer impromptu spiritual lectures about death, how it is part of life, its natural ebb and flow, how we all must accept that, or other such utterances that make her want to scratch out some eyes. Like true friends, they take no hardy or elegant stance loosely choreographed from some broad perspective. They get right in there and mutter "Jesus Christ!" and shake their heads. Plus, they are the only people who not only will laugh at her stupid jokes but offer up stupid ones of their own. *What do you get when you cross Tiny Tim with a pit bull?* A child's illness is a strain on the mind. They know how to laugh in a fluty, desperate way—unlike the people who are more her husband's friends and who seem just to deepen their sorrowful gazes, nodding their heads with Sympathy. How exiling and estranging are everybody's Sympathetic Expressions! When anyone laughs, she thinks, Okay! Hooray: a buddy. In disaster as in show business.

Nurses come and go; their chirpy voices both startle and soothe. Some of the other Peed Onk parents stick their heads in to see how the Baby is and offer encouragement.

Green Hair scratches her head. "Everyone's so friendly here. Is there someone in this place who isn't doing all this airy, scripted optimism—or are people like that the only people here?"

"It's Modern Middle Medicine meets the Modern Middle Family," says the Husband. "In the Modern Middle West."

Someone has brought in take-out lo mein, and they all eat it out in the hall by the elevators.

Parents are allowed use of the Courtesy Line.

"You've got to have a second child," says a different friend on the phone, a friend from out of town. "An heir and a spare. That's what we did. We had another child to ensure we wouldn't off ourselves if we lost our first."

"Really?"

"I'm serious."

"A formal suicide? Wouldn't you just drink yourself into a lifelong stupor and let it go at that?"

"Nope. I knew how I would do it even. For a while, until our second came along, I had it all planned."

"What did you plan?"

"I can't go into too much detail, because—Hi, honey!—the kids are here now in the room. But I'll spell out the general idea: R-O-P-E."

Sunday evening, she goes and sinks down on the sofa in the Tiny Tim Lounge next to Frank, Joey's father. He is a short, stocky man with the currentless, flatlined look behind the eyes that all the parents eventually get here. He has shaved his head bald in solidarity with his son. His little boy has been battling cancer for five years. It is now in the liver, and the rumor around the corridor is that Joey has three weeks to live. She knows that Joey's mother, Heather, left Frank years ago, two years into the cancer, and has remarried and had another child, a girl named Brittany. The Mother sees Heather here sometimes with her new life—the cute little girl and the new, young, full-haired husband who will never be so maniacally and debilitatingly obsessed with Joey's illness the way Frank, her first husband, was. Heather comes to visit Joey, to say hello and now good-bye, but she is not Joey's main man. Frank is.

Frank is full of stories—about the doctors, about the food, about the nurses, about Joey. Joey, affectless from his meds, sometimes leaves his room and comes out to watch TV in his bathrobe. He is jaundiced and bald, and though he is nine, he looks no older than six. Frank has devoted the last four and a half years to saving Joey's life. When the cancer was first diagnosed, the doctors gave Joey a 20 percent chance of living six more months. Now here it is, almost five years later, and Joey's still here. It is all due to Frank, who, early on, quit his job as vice president of a consulting firm in order to commit himself totally to his son. He is proud of everything he's given up and done, but he is tired. Part of him now really believes things are coming to a close, that this is the end. He says this without tears. There are no more tears.

"You have probably been through more than anyone else on this corridor," says the Mother.

"I could tell you stories," he says. There is a sour odor between them, and she realizes that neither of them has bathed for days.

"Tell me one. Tell me the worst one." She knows he hates his ex-wife and hates her new husband even more.

"The worst? They're all the worst. Here's one: one morning, I went out for breakfast with my buddy—it was the only time I'd left Joey alone ever; left him for two hours is all—and when I came back, his N-G tube was full of blood. They had the suction on too high, and it was sucking the guts right out of him."

"Oh my God. That just happened to us," said the Mother.

"It did?"

"Friday night."

"You're kidding. They let that happen again? I gave them such a chewing-out about that!"

"I guess our luck is not so good. We get your very worst story on the second night we're here."

"It's not a bad place, though."

"It's not?"

"Naw. I've seen worse. I've taken Joey everywhere."

"He seems very strong." Truth is, at this point, Joey seems like a zombie and frightens her.

"Joey's a fucking genius. A biological genius. They'd given him six months, remember."

The Mother nods.

"Six months is not very long," says Frank. "Six months is nothing. He was four and a half years old."

All the words are like blows. She feels flooded with affection and mourning for this man. She looks away, out the window, out past the hospital parking lot, up toward the black marbled sky and the electric eyelash of the moon. "And now he's nine," she says. "You're his hero."

"And he's mine," says Frank, though the fatigue in his voice seems to overwhelm him. "He'll be that forever. Excuse me," he says, "I've got to go check. His breathing hasn't been good. Excuse me."

"Good news and bad," says the Oncologist on Monday. He has knocked, entered the room, and now stands there. Their cots are unmade. One wastebasket is overflowing with coffee cups. "We've got the pathologist's report. The bad news is that the kidney they removed had certain lesions, called 'rests,' which are associated with a higher risk for disease in the other kidney. The good news is that the tumor is stage one, regular cell structure, and under five hundred grams, which qualifies you for a national experiment in which chemotherapy isn't done but your boy is monitored with ultrasound instead. It's not all that risky, given that the patient's watched closely, but here is the literature on it. There are forms to sign, if you decide to do that. Read all this and we can discuss it further. You have to decide within four days."

Lesions? Rests? They dry up and scatter like M&M's on the floor. All she hears is the part about no chemo. Another sigh of relief rises up in her and spills out. In a life where there is only the bearable and the unbearable, a sigh of relief is an ecstasy.

"No chemo?" says the Husband. "Do you recommend that?"

The Oncologist shrugs. What casual gestures these doctors are permitted! "I know chemo. I like chemo," says the Oncologist. "But this is for you to decide. It depends how you feel."

The Husband leans forward. "But don't you think that now that we have the upper hand with this thing, we should keep going? Shouldn't we stomp on it, beat it, smash it to death with the chemo?"

The Mother swats him angrily and hard. "Honey, you're delirious!" She whispers, but it comes out as a hiss. "This is our lucky break!" Then she adds gently, "We don't want the Baby to have chemo."

The Husband turns back to the Oncologist. "What do *you* think?"

"It could be," he says, shrugging. "It could be that this is your lucky break. But you won't know for sure for five years."

The Husband turns back to the Mother. "Okay," he says. "Okay."

The Baby grows happier and strong. He begins to move and sit and eat. Wednesday morning, they are allowed to leave, and leave without chemo. The Oncologist looks a little nervous. "Are you nervous about this?" asks the Mother.

"Of course I'm nervous." But he shrugs and doesn't look that nervous. "See you in six weeks for the ultrasound," he says, waves and then leaves, looking at his big black shoes as he does.

The Baby smiles, even toddles around a little, the sun bursting through the clouds, an angel chorus crescendoing. Nurses arrive. The Hickman is taken out of the Baby's neck and chest; antibiotic lotion is dispensed. The Mother packs up their bags. The Baby sucks on a bottle of juice and does not cry.

"No chemo?" says one of the nurses. "Not even a *little* chemo?"

"We're doing watch and wait," says the Mother.

The other parents look envious but concerned. They have never seen any child get out of there with his hair and white blood cells intact.

"Will you be okay?" asks Ned's mother.

"The worry's going to kill us," says the Husband.

"But if all we have to do is worry" chides the Mother, "every day for a hundred years, it'll be easy. It'll be nothing. I'll take all the worry in the world, if it wards off the thing itself."

"That's right," says Ned's mother. "Compared to everything else, compared to all the actual events, the worry is nothing."

The Husband shakes his head. "I'm such an amateur," he moans.

"You're both doing admirably," says the other mother. "Your baby's lucky, and I wish you all the best."

The Husband shakes her hand warmly. "Thank you," he says. "You've been wonderful."

Another mother, the mother of Eric, comes up to them. "It's all very hard," she says, her head cocked to one side. "But there's a lot of collateral beauty along the way."

Collateral beauty? Who is entitled to such a thing? A child is ill. No one is entitled to any collateral beauty!

"Thank you," says the Husband.

Joey's father, Frank, comes up and embraces them both.

"It's a journey," he says. He chucks the Baby on the chin. "Good luck, little man."

"Yes, thank you so much," says the Mother. "We hope things go well with Joey." She knows that Joey had a hard, terrible night.

Frank shrugs and steps back. "Gotta go," he says. "Goodbye!"

"Bye," she says, and then he is gone. She bites the inside of her lip, a bit tearily, then bends down to pick up the diaper bag, which is now stuffed with little animals; helium balloons are tied to its zipper. Shouldering the thing, the Mother feels she has just won a prize. All the parents have now vanished down the hall in the opposite direction. The Husband moves close. With one arm, he takes the Baby from her; with the other, he rubs her back. He can see she is starting to get weepy.

"Aren't these people nice? Don't you feel better hearing about their lives?" he asks.

Why does he do this, form clubs all the time; why does even this society of suffering soothe him? When it comes to death and dying, perhaps someone in this family ought to be more of a snob.

"All these nice people with their brave stories," he continues as they make their way toward the elevator bank, waving good-bye to the nursing staff as they go, even the Baby waving shyly. *Bye-bye! Bye-bye!* "Don't you feel consoled, knowing we're all in the same boat, that we're all in this together?"

But who on earth would want to be in this boat? the Mother thinks. This boat is a nightmare boat. Look where it goes: to a silver-and-white room, where, just before your eyesight and hearing and your ability to touch or be touched disappear entirely, you must watch your child die.

Rope! Bring on the rope.

"Let's make our own way," says the Mother, "and not in this boat."

Woman Overboard! She takes the Baby back from the Husband, cups the Baby's cheek in her hand, kisses his brow and then, quickly, his flowery mouth. The Baby's heart—she can hear it—drums with life. "For as long as I live," says the Mother, pressing the elevator button—up or down, everyone in the end has to leave this way—"I never want to see any of these people again."

There are the notes.
Now where is the money?

Alice Munro (1931–)

was born in Wingham, Ontario, in the western part of the province. This is the landscape for most of her fiction, as she returns again and again to the farms and villages of the Huron County of her youth and the constraints this provincial life places on the lives of girls and women. Her stories frequently achieve the breadth and complexity of novels, and critics have often compared Munro's mastery of short fiction to Chekhov's (a strong influence on her work, as were the stories of Eudora Welty). Many have called her the greatest living short story writer and even (this from The Atlantic Monthly*) "the living writer most likely to be read in a hundred years." She published her first story in 1950 while a student at Western Ontario University, but she left school to marry and moved to British Columbia, where she had three children and helped her husband establish a bookstore. This marriage broke up in 1972 when she returned to Ontario, and she remarried in 1976. Her first collection of stories,* Dance of the Happy Shades *(1968), won the Governor General's Award, Canada's most prestigious literary prize (an honor two of her subsequent collections also won). She has published nine other collections of stories, is a fixture in* The New Yorker, *and appears nearly every year in* The Best American Short Stories *and* Prize Stories: The O. Henry Awards.

INTRODUCTION BY **Lorrie Moore**

The observant child's witnessing of adult sexuality—recalled with physical immediacy and hinted-at meaning—is a great narrative element on which the writer Alice Munro has focused unblinkingly (though also with subtlety and respect for mystery) throughout her career. Her narrators puzzle as well as tell the story. They take time to ponder the dramatic implications in the lives of others, even positing eventful substitutions. The old-fashioned storyness of people's lives never loses its place to cool stasis or drift, and the often ridiculous fatefulness of erotic choice is everywhere made clear. Most of her stories, Munro has said, began in her head as novels, and within any single narrative, one can see a novelist's symphonic strategies, as stories blend and segue into other stories and create within a single one the dramatic and emotional richness of a novel. Her themes include love, sin, and the stunningly indifferent and transforming passage of time—a novelist's great subjects. The young narrator of "Walker Brothers Cowboy," a story set in the Great Depression, comes to realize that there are strands of her father's life that are crooked and unknowable, though the brother with whom she has witnessed this seems not to notice at all. "He does not notice enough," she says. Their down-and-out salesman father has a bedpan emptied on his head and drinks whiskey with a strange dancing woman—this in front of his children. It remains up to the perceptive and watchful daughter to figure out what it all implies.

In "Friend of My Youth," it is up to a daughter character too, another one of Munro's thoughtful unravelers, to shape and ponder her glimpse of a parent's world. In this story, the object of contemplation is not just a mother but two sisters who were once the mother's friends, all of them living out the aftermath of their marital choices. Here, Munro considers the landscape of possible happiness for women, finding the paths traversing it few, rocky, rutted, full of heat and self-death. Lightness and pleasure—what the narrator, out of temperament and belief, so wants to embrace for herself and remember in her mother—are juxtaposed with deadly rigidity (quite literally in the case of her mother's later Parkinson's disease, or the character of Nurse Atkinson, or the frigid if religious flight from life that both mutes and preserves the mother's youthful friend, Flora). This story's arguments and speculations are part of its narrative examination of duty and guilt and contribute to its eccentric structure and multilayered sadness.

Mothers and daughters in a world of "flyby fathers" are also the focal point of "Save the Reaper," Munro's final story here. Punctuated with mythical allusions (to Demeter, Greek goddess of the corn, and her daughter Persephone, figures of harvest, capture, and loss), the story begins in the midst of a grandchild's game involving space aliens. But the game "What did you hate most about your mother?" is the one the protagonist-grandmother recalls most significantly from her own past. "Her corns" is the punning reply Munro has given her. "Save the Reaper" is an example of what Munro's fellow Canadian Margaret Atwood has called "Southern Ontario Gothic," and it contains deliberate reference to that other Southern Gothic writer, Flannery O'Connor, whom Munro has claimed as an influence. As in Flannery O'Connor's "A Good Man Is Hard to Find," the dramatic elements of "Save the Reaper" start with a grandmother on a road trip, leading her grandchildren down a hidden and remote dirt road. Both women are in ostensible search of a house they recall, perhaps faultily, from their girlhoods; both have memories of beautiful glass at its entryway. And though in each story, the car ominously gets stuck and dangerous men suddenly appear, Munro, who shares O'Connor's wicked eye but not her theological certitude, quickly parts company with O'Connor in favor of her own concerns. Grace, Munro suggests, might be not a divine nod but an accident of the human heart, a random pardon, say, from loneliness. Life's susceptible shape is determined (or not) by a half-mocking trick of the loins (in this case, the sexual touch of a stranger or, in the parlance of the grandson's game, "the signals offered by plausible-looking people in other cars or from somebody standing by a mailbox or even riding a tractor in a field"). At the story's end, as in "Walker Brothers Cowboy," the child who has witnessed an adult adventure begins conspiratorially "the private work of storing and secreting"—a writer, perhaps, in the making. He would decide "on his own what should be preserved and how, and what these things were going to mean to him, in his unknown future." That, no doubt, is how Munro began her own brilliant literary ascent.

For Lorrie Moore's bio, see page 694.

ALICE MUNRO

Walker Brothers Cowboy

After supper my father says, "Want to go down and see if the Lake's still there?" We leave my mother sewing under the dining-room light, making clothes for me against the opening of school. She has ripped up for this purpose an old suit and an old plaid wool dress of hers, and she has to cut and match very cleverly and also make me stand and turn for endless fittings, sweaty, itching from the hot wool, ungrateful. We leave my brother in bed in the little screened porch at the end of the front verandah, and sometimes he kneels on his bed and presses his face against the screen and calls mournfully, "Bring me an ice cream cone!" but I call back, "You will be asleep," and do not even turn my head.

Then my father and I walk gradually down a long, shabby sort of street, with Silverwoods Ice Cream signs standing on the sidewalk, outside tiny, lighted stores. This is in Tuppertown, an old town on Lake Huron, an old grain port. The street is shaded, in some places, by maple trees whose roots have cracked and heaved the sidewalk and spread out like crocodiles into the bare yards. People are sitting out, men in shirtsleeves and undershirts and women in aprons—not people we know but if anybody looks ready to nod and say, "Warm night," my father will nod too and say something the same. Children are still playing. I don't know them either because my mother keeps my brother and me in our own yard, saying he is too young to leave it and I have to mind him. I am not so sad to watch their evening games because the games themselves are ragged, dissolving. Children, of their own will, draw apart, separate into islands of two or one under the heavy trees, occupying themselves in such solitary ways as I do all day, planting pebbles in the dirt or writing in it with a stick.

Presently we leave these yards and houses behind, we pass a factory with boarded-up windows, a lumberyard whose high wooden gates are locked for the night. Then the town falls away in a defeated jumble of sheds and small junkyards, the sidewalk gives up and we are walking on a sandy path with burdocks, plantains, humble nameless weeds all around. We enter a vacant lot, a kind of park really, for it is kept clear of junk and there is one bench with a slat missing on the back, a place to sit and look at the water. Which is generally grey in the evening, under a lightly overcast sky, no sunsets, the horizon dim. A very quiet, washing noise on the stones of the beach. Further along, towards the main part of town, there is a stretch of sand, a water slide, floats bobbing around the safe swimming area, a life guard's rickety throne. Also a long dark green building, like a roofed verandah, called the Pavilion, full of farmers and their wives, in stiff good clothes, on Sundays. That is the part of the town we used to know when we lived at Dungannon and came here three or four times a summer, to the Lake. That, and the docks where we would go and look at the grain boats, ancient, rusty, wallowing, making us wonder how they got past the breakwater let alone to Fort William.

Tramps hang around the docks and occasionally on these evenings wander up the dwindling beach and climb the shifting, precarious path boys have made, hanging onto dry bushes, and say something to my father which, being frightened of tramps, I am too alarmed to catch. My father says he is a bit hard up himself. "I'll roll you a cigarette if it's any use to you," he says, and he shakes tobacco out carefully on one of the thin butterfly papers, flicks it with his tongue, seals it and hands it to the tramp who takes it and walks away. My father also rolls and lights and smokes one cigarette of his own.

He tells me how the Great Lakes came to be. All where Lake Huron is now, he says, used to be flat land, a wide flat plain. Then came the ice, creeping down from the north, pushing deep into the low places. Like *that*—and he shows me his hand with his spread fingers pressing the rock-hard ground where we are sitting. His fingers make hardly any impression at all and he says, "Well, the old ice cap had a lot more power behind it than this hand has." And then the ice went back, shrank back towards the North Pole where it came from, and left its fingers of ice in the deep places it had gouged, and ice turned to lakes and there they were today. They were *new,* as time went. I try to see that plain before me, dinosaurs walking on it, but I am not able even to imagine the shore of the Lake when the Indians were there, before Tuppertown. The tiny share we have of time appalls me, though my father seems to regard it with tranquillity. Even my father, who sometimes seems to me to have been at home in the world as long as it has lasted, has really lived on this earth only a little longer than I have, in terms of all the time there has been to live in. He has not known a time, any more than I, when automobiles and electric lights did not at least exist. He was not alive when this century started. I will be barely alive—old, old—when it ends. I do not like to think of it. I wish the Lake to be always just a lake, with the safe-swimming floats marking it, and the breakwater and the lights of Tuppertown.

My father has a job, selling for Walker Brothers. This is a firm that sells almost entirely in the country, the back country. Sunshine, Boylesbridge, Turnaround—that is all his territory. Not Dungannon where we used to live, Dungannon is too near town and my mother is grateful for that. He sells cough medicine, iron tonic, corn plasters, laxatives, pills for female disorders, mouth wash, shampoo, liniment, salves, lemon and orange and raspberry concentrate for making refreshing drinks, vanilla, food colouring, black and green tea, ginger, cloves and other spices, rat poison. He has a song about it, with these two lines:

And have all liniments and oils,
For everything from corns to boils. . . .

Not a very funny song, in my mother's opinion. A pedlar's song, and that is what he is, a pedlar knocking at backwoods kitchens. Up until last winter we had our own business, a fox farm. My father raised silver foxes and sold their pelts to the people who make them into capes and coats and muffs. Prices fell, my father hung on hoping they would get better next year, and they fell again, and he hung on one more year and one more and finally it was not possible to hang on any more, we owed everything to the feed company. I have heard my mother explain this, several times, to Mrs. Oliphant who is the only neighbour she talks to. (Mrs. Oliphant also has come down in the world, being a schoolteacher who married the janitor.) We poured all we had into it, my mother says, and we came out with nothing. Many people could say the same thing, these days, but my mother has no time for the national calamity, only ours. Fate has flung us onto a street of poor people (it does not matter that we were poor before, that was a different sort of poverty), and the only way to take this, as she sees it, is with dignity, with bitterness, with no reconciliation. No bathroom with a claw-footed tub and a flush toilet is going to comfort her, nor water on tap and sidewalks past the house and milk in bottles, not even the two movie theatres and the Venus Restaurant and Woolworths so marvellous it has live birds singing in its fan-cooled corners and fish as tiny as fingernails, as bright as moons, swimming in its green tanks. My mother does not care.

In the afternoons she often walks to Simon's Grocery and takes me with her to help carry things. She wears a good dress, navy blue with little flowers, sheer, worn over a navy-blue slip. Also a summer hat of white straw, pushed down on the side of the head, and white shoes I have just whitened on a newspaper on the back steps. I have my hair freshly done in long damp curls which the dry air will fortunately soon loosen, a stiff large hair-ribbon on top of my head. This is entirely different from going out after supper with my father. We have not walked past two houses before I feel we have become objects of universal ridicule. Even the dirty words chalked on the sidewalk are laughing at us. My mother does not seem to notice. She walks serenely like a lady shopping, like a *lady* shopping, past the housewives in loose beltless dresses torn under the arms. With me her creation, wretched curls and flaunting hair bow, scrubbed knees and white socks—all I do not want to be. I loathe even my name when she says it in public, in a voice so high, proud and ringing, deliberately different from the voice of any other mother on the street.

My mother will sometimes carry home, for a treat, a brick of ice cream—pale Neapolitan; and because we have no refrigerator in our house we wake my brother and eat it at once in the dining room, always darkened by the wall of the house next door. I spoon it up tenderly, leaving the chocolate till last, hoping to have some still to eat when my brother's dish is empty. My mother tries then to imitate the conversations we used to have at Dungannon, going back to our earliest, most leisurely days before my brother was born, when she would give me a little tea and a lot of milk in a cup like hers and we would sit out on the step facing the pump, the lilac tree, the fox pens beyond. She is not able to keep from mentioning those days. "Do you remember when we put you in your sled and Major pulled you?" (Major our dog, that we had to leave with neighbours when we moved.) "Do you remember your sandbox outside the kitchen window?" I pretend to remember far less than I do, wary of being trapped into sympathy or any unwanted emotion.

My mother has headaches. She often has to lie down. She lies on my brother's narrow bed in the little screened porch, shaded by heavy branches. "I look up at that tree and I think I am at home," she says.

"What you need," my father tells her, "is some fresh air and a drive in the country." He means for her to go with him, on his Walker Brothers route.

That is not my mother's idea of a drive in the country.

"Can I come?"

"Your mother might want you for trying on clothes."

"I'm beyond sewing this afternoon," my mother says.

"I'll take her then. Take both of them, give you a rest."

What is there about us that people need to be given a rest from? Never mind. I am glad enough to find my brother and make him go to the toilet and get us both into the car, our knees unscrubbed, my hair unringleted. My father brings from the house his two heavy brown suitcases, full of bottles, and sets them on the back seat. He wears a white shirt, brilliant in the sunlight, a tie, light trousers belonging to his summer suit (his other suit is black, for funerals, and belonged to my uncle before he died) and a creamy straw hat. His salesman's outfit, with pencils clipped in the shirt pocket. He goes back once again, probably to say goodbye to my mother, to ask her if she is sure she doesn't want to come, and hear her say, "No. No thanks, I'm better just to lie here with my eyes closed." Then we are backing out of the driveway with the rising hope of adventure, just the little hope that takes you over the bump into the street, the hot air starting to move, turning into a breeze, the houses growing less and less familiar as we follow the short cut my father knows, the quick way out of town. Yet what is there waiting for us all afternoon but hot hours in stricken farmyards, perhaps a stop at a country store and three ice cream cones or bottles of pop, and my father singing? The one he made up about himself has a title—"The Walker Brothers Cowboy"—and it starts out like this:

Old Ned Fields, he now is dead,
So I am ridin' the route instead. . . .

Who is Ned Fields? The man he has replaced, surely, and if so he really is dead; yet my father's voice is mournful-jolly, making his death some kind of nonsense, a comic calamity. "Wisht I was back on the Rio Grande, plungin' through the dusky sand." My father sings most of the time while driving the car. Even now, heading out of town, crossing the bridge and taking the sharp turn onto the highway, he is humming something, mumbling a bit of a song to himself, just tuning up, really, getting ready to improvise, for out along the highway we pass the Baptist Camp, the Vacation Bible Camp, and he lets loose:

"Where are the Baptists, where are the Baptists,
where are all the Baptists today?
They're down in the water, in Lake Huron water,
with their sins all a-gittin' washed away."

My brother takes this for straight truth and gets up on his knees trying to see down to the Lake. "I don't see any Baptists," he says accusingly. "Neither do I, son," says my father. "I told you, they're down in the Lake."

No roads paved when we left the highway. We have to roll up the windows because of dust. The land is flat, scorched, empty. Bush lots at the back of the farms hold shade, black pine-shade like pools nobody can ever get to. We bump up a long lane and at the end of it what could look more unwelcoming, more deserted than the tall unpainted farmhouse with grass growing uncut right up to the front door, green blinds down and a door upstairs opening on nothing but air? Many houses have this door, and I have never yet been able to find out why. I ask my father and he says they are for walking in your sleep. *What?* Well if you happen to be walking in your sleep and you want to step outside. I am offended, seeing too late that he is joking, as usual, but my brother says sturdily, "If they did that they would break their necks."

The nineteen-thirties. How much this kind of farmhouse, this kind of afternoon, seem to me to belong to that one decade in time, just as my father's hat does, his bright flared tie, our car with its wide running board (an Essex, and long past its prime). Cars somewhat like it, many older, none dustier, sit in the farmyards. Some are past running and have their doors pulled off, their seats removed for use on porches. No living things to be seen, chickens or cattle. Except dogs. There are dogs, lying in any kind of shade they can find, dreaming, their lean sides rising and sinking rapidly. They get up when my father opens the car door, he has to speak to them. "Nice boy, there's a boy, nice old boy." They quiet down, go back to their shade. He should know how to quiet animals, he has held desperate foxes with tongs around their necks. One gentling voice for the dogs and another, rousing, cheerful, for calling at doors. "Hello there, Missus, it's the Walker Brothers man and what are you out of today?" A door opens, he disappears. Forbidden to follow, forbidden even to leave the car, we can just wait and wonder what he says. Sometimes trying to make my mother laugh he pretends to be himself in a farm kitchen, spreading out his sample case. "Now then, Missus, are you troubled with parasitic life? Your children's scalps, I mean. All those crawly little things we're too polite to mention that show up on the heads of the best of families? Soap alone is useless, kerosene is not too nice a perfume, but I have here—" Or else, "Believe me, sitting and driving all day the way I do I *know* the value of these fine pills. Natural relief. A problem common to old folks, too, once their days of activity are over—How about you, Grandma?" He would wave the imaginary box of pills under my mother's nose and she would laugh finally, unwillingly. "He doesn't say that really, does he?" I said, and she said no of course not, he was too much of a gentleman.

One yard after another, then, the old cars, the pumps, dogs, views of grey barns and falling-down sheds and unturning windmills. The men, if they are working in the fields, are not in any fields that we can see. The children are far away, following dry creek beds or looking for blackberries, or else they are hidden in the house, spying at us through cracks in the blinds. The car seat has grown slick with our sweat. I dare my brother to sound the horn, wanting to do it myself but not wanting to get the blame. He knows better. We play *I Spy,* but it is hard to find many colours. Grey for the barns and sheds and toilets and houses, brown for the yard and fields, black or brown for the dogs. The rusting cars show rainbow patches, in which I strain to pick out purple or green; likewise I peer at doors for shreds of old peeling paint, maroon or yellow. We can't play with letters, which would be better, because my brother is too young to spell. The game disintegrates anyway. He claims my colours are not fair, and wants extra turns.

In one house no door opens, though the car is in the yard. My father knocks and whistles, calls, "Hullo there! Walker Brothers man!" but there is not a stir of reply anywhere. This house has no porch, just a bare, slanting slab of cement on which my father stands. He turns around, searching the barnyard, the barn whose mow must be empty because you can see the sky through it, and finally he bends to pick up his suitcases. Just then a window is opened upstairs, a white pot appears on the sill, is tilted over and its contents splash down the outside wall. The window is not directly above my father's head, so only a stray splash would catch him. He picks up his suitcases with no particular hurry and walks, no longer whistling, to the car. "Do you know what that was?" I say to my brother. *"Pee."* He laughs and laughs.

My father rolls and lights a cigarette before he starts the car.

The window has been slammed down, the blind drawn, we never did see a hand or face. "Pee, pee," sings my brother ecstatically. "Somebody dumped down pee!" "Just don't tell your mother that," my father says. "She isn't liable to see the joke." "Is it in your song?" my brother wants to know. My father says no but he will see what he can do to work it in.

I notice in a little while that we are not turning in any more lanes, though it does not seem to me that we are headed home. "Is this the way to Sunshine?" I ask my father, and he answers, "No ma'am it's not." "Are we still in your territory?" He shakes his head. "We're going *fast,*" my brother says approvingly, and in fact we are bouncing along through dry puddle-holes so that all the bottles in the suitcases clink together and gurgle promisingly.

Another lane, a house, also unpainted, dried to silver in the sun.

"I thought we were out of your territory."

"We are."

"Then what are we going in here for?"

"You'll see."

In front of the house a short, sturdy woman is picking up washing, which had been spread on the grass to bleach and dry. When the car stops she stares at it hard for a moment, bends to pick up a couple more towels to add to the bundle under her arm, comes across to us and says in a flat voice, neither welcoming nor unfriendly, "Have you lost your way?"

My father takes his time getting out of the car. "I don't think so," he says. "I'm the Walker Brothers man."

"George Golley is our Walker Brothers man," the woman says, "and he was out here no more than a week ago. Oh, my Lord God," she says harshly, "it's you."

"It was, the last time I looked in the mirror," my father says. The woman gathers all the towels in front of her and holds on to them tightly, pushing them against her stomach as if it hurt.

"Of all the people I never thought to see. And telling me you were the Walker Brothers man."

"I'm sorry if you were looking forward to George Golley," my father says humbly.

"And look at me, I was prepared to clean the hen-house. You'll think that's just an excuse but it's true. I don't go round looking like this every day." She is wearing a farmer's straw hat, through which pricks of sunlight penetrate and float on her face, a loose, dirty print smock and running shoes. "Who are those in the car, Ben? They're not yours?"

"Well I hope and believe they are," my father says, and tells our names and ages. "Come on, you can get out. This is Nora, Miss Cronin. Nora, you better tell me, is it still Miss, or have you got a husband hiding in the woodshed?"

"If I had a husband that's not where I'd keep him, Ben," she says, and they both laugh, her laugh abrupt and somewhat angry. "You'll think I got no manners, as well as being dressed like a tramp," she says. "Come on in out of the sun. It's cool in the house."

We go across the yard ("Excuse me taking you in this way but I don't think the front door has been opened since Papa's funeral, I'm afraid the hinges might drop off"), up the porch steps, into the kitchen, which really is cool, high-ceilinged, the blinds of course down, a simple, clean, threadbare room with waxed worn linoleum, potted geraniums, drinking-pail and dipper, a round table with scrubbed oilcloth. In spite of the cleanness, the wiped and swept surfaces, there is a faint sour smell—maybe of the dishrag or the tin dipper or the oilcloth, or the old lady, because there is one, sitting in an easy chair under the clock shelf. She turns her head slightly in our direction and says, "Nora? Is that company?"

"Blind," says Nora in a quick explaining voice to my father. Then, "You won't guess who it is, Momma. Hear his voice."

My father goes to the front of her chair and bends and says hopefully, "Afternoon, Mrs. Cronin."

"Ben Jordan," says the old lady with no surprise. "You haven't been to see us in the longest time. Have you been out of the country?"

My father and Nora look at each other.

"He's married, Momma," says Nora cheerfully and aggressively. "Married and got two children and here they are." She pulls us forward, makes each of us touch the old lady's dry, cool hand while she says our names in turn. Blind! This is the first blind person I have ever seen close up. Her eyes are closed, the eyelids sunk away down, showing no shape of the eyeball, just hollows. From one hollow comes a drop of silver liquid, a medicine, or a miraculous tear.

"Let me get into a decent dress," Nora says. "Talk to Momma. It's a treat for her. We hardly ever see company, do we Momma?"

"Not many makes it out this road," says the old lady placidly. "And the ones that used to be around here, our old neighbours, some of them have pulled out."

"True everywhere," my father says.

"Where's your wife then?"

"Home. She's not too fond of the hot weather, makes her feel poorly."

"Well." This is a habit of country people, old people, to say "well," meaning, "is that so?" with a little extra politeness and concern.

Nora's dress, when she appears again—stepping heavily on Cuban heels down the stairs in the hall—is flowered more lavishly than anything my mother owns, green and yellow on brown, some sort of floating sheer crepe, leaving her arms bare. Her arms are heavy, and every bit of her skin you can see is covered with little dark freckles like measles. Her hair is short, black, coarse and curly, her teeth very white and strong. "It's the first time I knew there was such a thing as green poppies," my father says, looking at her dress.

"You would be surprised all the things you never knew," says Nora, sending a smell of cologne far and wide when she moves and displaying a change of voice to go with the dress, something more sociable and youthful. "They're not poppies anyway, they're just flowers. You go and pump me some good cold water and I'll make these children a drink." She gets down from the cupboard a bottle of Walker Brothers Orange syrup.

"You telling me you were the Walker Brothers man!"

"It's the truth, Nora. You go and look at my sample cases in the car if you don't believe me. I got the territory directly south of here."

"Walker Brothers? Is that a fact? You selling for Walker Brothers?"

"Yes ma'am."

"We always heard you were raising foxes over Dungannon way."

"That's what I was doing, but I kind of run out of luck in that business."

"So where're you living? How long've you been out selling?"

"We moved into Tuppertown. I been at it, oh, two, three months. It keeps the wolf from the door. Keeps him as far away as the back fence."

Nora laughs. "Well I guess you count yourself lucky to have the work. Isabel's husband in Brantford, he was out of work the longest time. I thought if he didn't find something soon I was going to have them all land in here to feed, and I tell you I was hardly looking forward to it. It's all I can manage with me and Momma."

"Isabel married," my father says. "Muriel married too?"

"No, she's teaching school out west. She hasn't been home for five years. I guess she finds something better to do with her holidays. I would if I was her." She gets some snapshots out of the table drawer and starts showing him. "That's Isabel's oldest boy, starting school. That's the baby sitting in her carriage. Isabel and her husband. Muriel. That's her roommate with her. That's a fellow she used to go around with, and his car. He was working in a bank out there. That's her school, it has eight rooms. She teaches Grade Five." My father shakes his head. "I can't think of her any way but when she was going to school, so shy I used to pick her up on the road—I'd be on my way to see you—and she would not say one word, not even to agree it was a nice day."

"She's got over that."

"Who are you talking about?" says the old lady.

"Muriel. I said she's got over being shy."

"She was here last summer."

"No Momma that was Isabel. Isabel and her family were here last summer. Muriel's out west."

"I meant Isabel."

Shortly after this the old lady falls asleep, her head on the side, her mouth open. "Excuse her manners," Nora says. "It's old age." She fixes an afghan over her mother and says we can all go into the front room where our talking won't disturb her.

"You two," my father says. "Do you want to go outside and amuse yourselves?"

Amuse ourselves how? Anyway I want to stay. The front room is more interesting than the kitchen, though barer. There is a gramophone and a pump organ and a picture on the wall of Mary, Jesus' mother—I know that much—in shades of bright blue and pink with a spiked band of light around her head. I know that such pictures are found only in the homes of Roman Catholics and so Nora must be one. We have never known any Roman Catholics at all well, never well enough to visit in their houses. I think of what my grandmother and my Aunt Tena, over in Dungannon, used to always say to indicate that somebody was a Catholic. *So-and-so digs with the wrong foot,* they would say. *She digs with the wrong foot.* That was what they would say about Nora.

Nora takes a bottle, half full, out of the top of the organ and pours some of what is in it into the two glasses that she and my father have emptied of the orange drink.

"Keep it in case of sickness?" my father says.

"Not on your life," says Nora. "I'm never sick. I just keep it because I keep it. One bottle does me a fair time, though, because I don't care for drinking alone. Here's luck!" She and my father drink and I know what it is. Whisky. One of the things my mother has told me in our talks together is that my father never drinks whisky. But I see he does. He drinks whisky and he talks of people whose names I have never heard before. But after a while he turns to a familiar incident. He tells about the chamberpot that was emptied out the window. "Picture me there," he says, "hollering my heartiest. *Oh, lady, it's your Walker Brothers man, anybody home?*" He does himself hollering, grinning absurdly, waiting, looking up in pleased expectation and then—oh, ducking, covering his head with his arms, looking as if he begged for mercy (when he never did anything like that, I was watching), and Nora laughs, almost as hard as my brother did at the time.

"That isn't true! That's not a word true!"

"Oh, indeed it is ma'am. We have our heroes in the ranks of Walker Brothers. I'm glad you think it's funny," he says sombrely.

I ask him shyly, "Sing the song."

"What song? Have you turned into a singer on top of everything else?"

Embarrassed, my father says, "Oh, just this song I made up while I was driving around, it gives me something to do, making up rhymes."

But after some urging he does sing it, looking at Nora with a droll, apologetic expression, and she laughs so much that in places he has to stop and wait for her to get over laughing so he can go on, because she makes him laugh too. Then he does various parts of his salesman's spiel. Nora when she laughs squeezes her large bosom under her folded arms. "You're crazy," she says. "That's all you are." She sees my brother peering into the gramophone and she jumps up and goes over to him. "Here's us sitting enjoying ourselves and not giving you a thought, isn't it terrible?" she says. "You want me to put a record on, don't you? You want to hear a nice record? Can you dance? I bet your sister can, can't she?"

I say no. "A big girl like you and so good-looking and can't dance!" says Nora. "It's high time you learned. I bet you'd make a lovely dancer. Here, I'm going to put on a piece I used to dance to and even your daddy did, in his dancing days. You didn't know your daddy was a dancer, did you? Well, he is a talented man, your daddy!"

She puts down the lid and takes hold of me unexpectedly around the waist, picks up my other hand and starts making me go backwards. "This is the way, now, this is how they dance. Follow me. This foot, see. One and one-two. One and one-two. That's fine, that's lovely, don't look at your feet! Follow me, that's right, see how easy? You're going to be a lovely dancer! One and one-two. One and one-two. Ben, see your daughter dancing!" *Whispering while you cuddle near me, Whispering where no one can hear me. . . .*

Round and round the linoleum, me proud, intent, Nora laughing and moving with great buoyancy, wrapping me in her strange gaiety, her smell of whisky, cologne, and sweat. Under the arms her dress is damp, and little drops form along her upper lip, hang in the soft black hairs at the corners of her mouth. She whirls me around in front of my father—causing me to stumble, for I am by no means so swift a pupil as she pretends—and lets me go, breathless.

"Dance with me, Ben."

"I'm the world's worst dancer, Nora, and you know it."

"I certainly never thought so."

"You would now."

She stands in front of him, arms hanging loose and hopeful, her breasts, which a moment ago embarrassed me with their warmth and bulk, rising and falling under her loose flowered dress, her face shining with the exercise, and delight.

"Ben."

My father drops his head and says quietly, "Not me, Nora."

So she can only go and take the record off. "I can drink alone but I can't dance alone," she says. "Unless I am a whole lot crazier than I think I am."

"Nora," says my father smiling. "You're not crazy."

"Stay for supper."

"Oh, no. We couldn't put you to the trouble."

"It's no trouble. I'd be glad of it."

"And their mother would worry. She'd think I'd turned us over in a ditch."

"Oh, well. Yes."

"We've taken a lot of your time now."

"Time," says Nora bitterly. "Will you come by ever again?"

"I will if I can," says my father.

"Bring the children. Bring your wife."

"Yes I will," says my father. "I will if I can."

When she follows us to the car he says, "You come to see us too, Nora. We're right on Grove Street, left-hand side going in, that's north, and two doors this side—east—of Baker Street."

Nora does not repeat these directions. She stands close to the car in her soft, brilliant dress. She touches the fender, making an unintelligible mark in the dust there.

On the way home my father does not buy any ice cream or pop, but he does go into a country store and get a package of licorice, which he shares with us. *She digs with the wrong foot,* I think, and the words seem sad to me as never before, dark, perverse. My father does not say anything to me about not mentioning things at home, but I know, just from the thoughtfulness, the pause when he passes the licorice, that there are things not to be mentioned. The whisky, maybe the dancing. No worry about my brother, he does not notice enough. At most he might remember the blind lady, the picture of Mary.

"Sing," my brother commands my father, but my father says gravely, "I don't know, I seem to be fresh out of songs. You watch the road and let me know if you see any rabbits."

So my father drives and my brother watches the road for rabbits and I feel my father's life flowing back from our car in the last of the afternoon, darkening and turning strange, like a landscape that has an enchantment on it, making it kindly, ordinary and familiar while you are looking at it, but changing it, once your back is turned, into something you will never know, with all kinds of weathers, and distances you cannot imagine.

When we get closer to Tuppertown the sky becomes gently overcast, as always, nearly always, on summer evenings by the Lake.

ALICE MUNRO

Friend of My Youth

I used to dream about my mother, and though the details in the dream varied, the surprise in it was always the same. The dream stopped, I suppose because it was too transparent in its hopefulness, easy in its forgiveness.

In the dream I would be the age I really was, living the life I was really living, and I would discover that my mother was still alive. (The fact is, she died when I was in my early twenties and she in her early fifties.) Sometimes I would find myself in our old kitchen, where my mother would be rolling out piecrust on the table, or washing the dishes in the battered cream-colored dishpan with the red rim. But other times I would run into her on the street, in places where I would never have expected to see her. She might be walking through a handsome hotel lobby, or lining up in an airport. She would be looking quite well—not exactly youthful, not entirely untouched by the paralyzing disease that held her in its grip for a decade or more before her death, but so much better than I remembered that I would be astonished. Oh, I just have this little tremor in my arm, she would say, and a little stiffness up this side of my face. It is a nuisance but I get around.

I recovered then what in waking life I had lost—my mother's liveliness of face and voice before her throat muscles stiffened and a woeful, impersonal mask fastened itself over her features How could I have forgotten this, I would think in the dream—the casual humor she had, not ironic but merry, the lightness and impatience and confidence? I would say that I was sorry I hadn't been to see her in such a long time—meaning not that I felt guilty but that I was sorry I had kept a bugbear in my mind, instead of this reality—and the strangest, kindest thing of all to me was her matter-of-fact reply.

Oh, well, she said, better late than never. I was sure I'd see you someday.

When my mother was a young woman with a soft, mischievous face and shiny, opaque silk stockings on her plump legs (I have seen a photograph of her, with her pupils), she went to teach at a one-room school, called Grieves School, in the Ottawa Valley. The school was on a corner of the farm that belonged to the Grieves family—a very good farm for that country. Well-drained fields with none of the Precambrian rock shouldering through the soil, a little willow-edged river running alongside, a sugar bush, log barns, and a large, unornamented house whose wooden walls had never been painted but had been left to weather. And when wood weathers in the Ottawa Valley, my mother said, I do not know why this is, but it never turns gray, it turns black. There must be something in the air, she said. She often spoke of the Ottawa Valley, which was her home—she had grown up about twenty miles away from Grieves School—in a dogmatic, mystified way, emphasizing things about it that distinguished it from any other place on earth. Houses turn black, maple syrup has a taste no maple syrup produced elsewhere can equal, bear amble within sight of farmhouses. Of course I was disappointed when I finally got to see this place. It was not a valley at all, if by that you mean a cleft between hills; it was a mixture of flat fields and low rocks and heavy bush and little lakes—a scrambled, disarranged sort of country with no easy harmony about it, not yielding readily to any description.

The log barns and unpainted house, common enough on poor farms, were not in the Grieveses' case a sign of poverty but of policy. They had the money but they did not spend it. That was what people told my mother. The Grieveses worked hard and they were far from ignorant, but they were very backward. They didn't have a car or electricity or a telephone or a tractor.

Some people thought this was because they were Cameronians—they were the only people in the school district who were of that religion—but in fact their church (which they themselves always called the Reformed Presbyterian) did not forbid engines or electricity or any inventions of that sort, just card playing, dancing, movies, and, on Sundays, any activity at all that was not religious or unavoidable.

My mother could not say who the Cameronians were or why they were called that. Some freak religion from Scotland, she said from the perch of her obedient and lighthearted Anglicanism. The teacher always boarded with the Grieveses, and my mother was a little daunted at the thought of going to live in that black board house with its paralytic Sundays and coal-oil lamps and primitive notions. But she was engaged by that time, she wanted to work on her trousseau instead of running around the country having a good time, and she figured she could get home one Sunday out of three. (On Sundays at the Grieveses' house, you could light a fire for heat but not for cooking, you could not even boil the kettle to make tea, and you were not supposed to write a letter or swat a fly. But it turned out that my mother was exempt from these rules. "No, no," said Flora Grieves, laughing at her. "That doesn't mean you. You must just go on as you're used to doing." And after a while my mother had made friends with Flora to such an extent that she wasn't even going home on the Sundays when she'd planned to.)

Flora and Ellie Grieves were the two sisters left of the family. Ellie was married—to a man called Robert Deal, who lived there and worked the farm but had not changed its name to Deal's in anyone's mind. By the way people spoke, my mother expected the Grieves sisters and Robert Deal to be middle-aged at least, but Ellie, the younger sister, was only about thirty, and Flora seven or eight years older. Robert Deal might be in between.

The house was divided in an unexpected way. The married couple didn't live with Flora. At the time of their marriage, she had given them the parlor and the dining room, the front bedrooms and staircase, the winter kitchen. There was no need to decide about the bathroom, because there wasn't one. Flora had the summer kitchen, with its open rafters and uncovered brick walls, the old pantry made into a narrow dining room and sitting room, and the two back bedrooms, one of which was my mother's. The teacher was housed with Flora, in the poorer part of the house. But my mother didn't mind. She immediately preferred Flora, and Flora's cheerfulness, to the silence and sickroom atmosphere of the front rooms. In Flora's domain it was not even true that all amusements were forbidden. She had a crokinole board—she taught my mother how to play.

The division had been made, of course, in the expectation that Robert and Ellie would have a family, and that they would need the room. This hadn't happened. They had been married for more than a dozen years and there had not been a live child. Time and again Ellie had been pregnant, but two babies had been stillborn, and the rest she had miscarried. During my mother's first year, Ellie seemed to be staying in bed more and more of the time, and my mother thought that she must be pregnant again; but there was no mention of it. Such people would not mention it. You could not tell from the look of Ellie, when she got up and walked around, because she showed a stretched and ruined though slack-chested shape. She carried a sickbed odor and she fretted in a childish way about everything. Flora took care of her and did all the work. She washed the clothes and tidied up the rooms and cooked the meals served in both sides of the house, as well as helping Robert with the milking and separating. She was up before daylight and never seemed to tire. During the first spring my mother was there, a great housecleaning was embarked upon, during which Flora climbed the ladders herself and carried down the storm windows, washed and stacked them away, carried all the furniture out of one room after another so that she could scrub the woodwork and varnish the floors. She washed every dish and glass that was sitting in the cupboards supposedly clean already. She scalded every pot and spoon. Such need and energy possessed her that she could hardly sleep—my mother would wake up to the sound of stovepipes being taken down, or the broom, draped in a dish towel, whacking at the smoky cobwebs. Through the washed uncurtained windows came a torrent of unmerciful light. The cleanliness was devastating. My mother slept now on sheets that had been bleached and starched and that gave her a rash. Sick Ellie complained daily of the smell of varnish and cleansing powders. Flora's hands were raw. But her disposition remained topnotch. Her kerchief and apron and Robert's baggy overalls that she donned for the climbing jobs gave her the air of a comedian—sportive, unpredictable. My mother called her a whirling dervish.

"You're a regular whirling dervish, Flora," she said, and Flora halted. She wanted to know what was meant. My mother went ahead and explained, though she was a little afraid lest piety should be offended. (Not piety exactly—you could not call it that. Religious strictness.) Of course it wasn't. There was not a trace of nastiness or smug vigilance in Flora's observance of her religion. She had no fear of heathens—she had always lived in the midst of them. She liked the idea of being a dervish, and went to tell her sister.

"Do you know what the teacher says I am?"

Flora and Ellie were both dark-haired, dark-eyed women, tall and narrow-shouldered and long-legged. Ellie was a wreck, of course, but Flora was still superbly straight and graceful. She could look like a queen, my mother said—even riding into town in that cart they had. For church they used a buggy or a cutter, but when they went to town they often had to transport sacks of wool—they kept a few sheep—or of produce, to sell, and they had to bring provisions home. The trip of a few miles was not made often. Robert rode in front, to drive the horse—Flora could drive a horse perfectly well, but it must always be the man who drove. Flora would be standing behind holding on to the sacks. She rode to town and back standing up, keeping an easy balance, wearing her black hat. Almost ridiculous but not quite. A gypsy queen, my mother thought she looked like, with her black hair and her skin that always looked slightly tanned, and her lithe and bold serenity. Of course she lacked the gold bangles and the bright clothes. My mother envied her her slenderness, and her cheekbones.

★ ★ ★

Returning in the fall for her second year, my mother learned what was the matter with Ellie.

"My sister has a growth," Flora said. Nobody then spoke of cancer.

My mother had heard that before. People suspected it. My mother knew many people in the district by that time. She had made particular friends with a young woman who worked in the post office; this woman was going to be one of my mother's bridesmaids. The story of Flora and Ellie and Robert had been told—or all that people knew of it—in various versions. My mother did not feel that she was listening to gossip, because she was always on the alert for any disparaging remarks about Flora—she would not put up with that. But indeed nobody offered any. Everybody said that Flora had behaved like a saint. Even when she went to extremes, as in dividing up the house—that was like a saint.

Robert came to work at Grieveses' some months before the girls' father died. They knew him already, from church. (Oh, that church, my mother said, having attended it once, out of curiosity—that dreary building miles on the other side of town, no organ or piano and plain glass in the windows and a doddery old minister with his hours-long sermon, a man hitting a tuning fork for the singing.) Robert had come out from Scotland and was on his way west. He had stopped with relatives or people he knew, members of the scanty congregation. To earn some money, probably, he came to Grieveses'. Soon he and Flora were engaged. They could not go to dances or to card parties like other couples, but they went for long walks. The chaperone—unofficially—was Ellie. Ellie was then a wild tease, a long-haired, impudent, childish girl full of lolloping energy. She would run up hills and smite the mullein stalks with a stick, shouting and prancing and pretending to be a warrior on horseback. That, or the horse itself. This when she was fifteen, sixteen years old. Nobody but Flora could control her, and generally Flora just laughed at her, being too used to her to wonder if she was quite right in the head. They were wonderfully fond of each other. Ellie, with her long skinny body, her long pale face, was like a copy of Flora—the kind of copy you often see in families, in which because of some carelessness or exaggeration of features or coloring, the handsomeness of one person passes into the plainness—or almost plainness—of the other. But Ellie had no jealousy about this. She loved to comb out Flora's hair and pin it up. They had great times, washing each other's hair. Ellie would press her face into Flora's throat, like a colt nuzzling its mother. So when Robert laid claim to Flora, or Flora to him—nobody knew how it was—Ellie had to be included. She didn't show any spite toward Robert, but she pursued and waylaid them on their walks; she sprung on them out of the bushes or sneaked up behind them so softly that she could blow on their necks. People saw her do it. And they heard of her jokes. She had always been terrible for jokes and sometimes it had got her into trouble with her father, but Flora had protected her. Now she put thistles in Robert's bed. She set his place at the table with the knife and fork the wrong way around. She switched the milk pails to give him the old one with the hole in it. For Flora's sake, maybe, Robert humored her.

The father had made Flora and Robert set the wedding day a year ahead, and after he died they did not move it any closer. Robert went on living in the house. Nobody knew how to speak to Flora about this being scandalous, or looking scandalous. Flora would just ask why. Instead of putting the wedding ahead, she put it back—from next spring to early fall, so that there should be a full year between it and her father's death. A year from wedding to funeral—that seemed proper to her. She trusted fully in Robert's patience and in her own purity.

So she might. But in the winter a commotion started. There was Ellie, vomiting, weeping, running off and hiding in the haymow, howling when they found her and pulled her out, jumping to the barn floor, running around in circles, rolling in the snow. Ellie was deranged. Flora had to call the doctor. She told him that her sister's periods had stopped—could the backup blood be driving her wild? Robert had had to catch her and tie her up, and together he and Flora had put her to bed. She would not take food, just whipped her head from side to side, howling. It looked as if she would die speechless. But somehow the truth came out. Not from the doctor, who could not get close enough to examine her, with all her thrashing about. Probably, Robert confessed. Flora finally got wind of the truth, through all her high-mindedness. Now there had to be a wedding, though not the one that had been planned.

No cake, no new clothes, no wedding trip, no congratulations. Just a shameful hurry-up visit to the manse. Some people, seeing the names in the paper, thought the editor must have got the sisters mixed up. They thought it must be Flora. A hurry-up wedding for Flora! But no—it was Flora who pressed Robert's suit—it must have been—and got Ellie out of bed and washed her and made her presentable. It would have been Flora who picked one geranium from the window plant and pinned it to her sister's dress. And Ellie hadn't torn it out. Ellie was meek now, no longer flailing or crying. She let Flora fix her up, she let herself be married, she was never wild from that day on.

Flora had the house divided. She herself helped Robert build the necessary partitions. The baby was carried full term—nobody even pretended that it was early—but it was born dead, after a long, tearing labor. Perhaps Ellie had damaged it when she jumped from the barn beam and rolled in the snow and beat on herself. Even if she hadn't done that, people would have expected something to go wrong, with that child or maybe one that came later. God dealt out punishment for hurry-up marriages—not just Presbyterians but almost everybody else believed that. God rewarded lust with dead babies, idiots, harelips and withered limbs and clubfeet.

In this case the punishment continued. Ellie had one miscarriage after another, then another stillbirth and more miscarriages. She was constantly pregnant, and the pregnancies were full of vomiting fits that lasted for days, headaches, cramps, dizzy spells. The miscarriages were as agonizing as full-term births. Ellie could not do her own work. She walked around holding on to chairs. Her numb silence passed off, and she became a complainer. If anybody came to visit, she would talk about the peculiarities of her headaches or describe her latest fainting fit, or even—in front of men, in front of unmarried girls or children—go into bloody detail about what Flora called her "disappointments." When people changed the subject or dragged the children away, she turned sullen. She demanded new medicine, reviled the doctor, nagged Flora. She accused Flora of washing the dishes with a great clang and clatter, out of spite, of pulling her—Ellie's—hair when she combed it out, of stingily substituting water-and-molasses for her real medicine. No matter what she said, Flora soothed her. Everybody who came into the house had some story of that kind to tell. Flora said, "Where's my little girl, then? Where's my Ellie? This isn't my Ellie, this is some crosspatch got in here in place of her!"

In the winter evenings after she came in from helping Robert with the barn chores, Flora would wash and change her clothes and go next door to read Ellie to sleep. My mother might invite herself along, taking whatever sewing she was doing, on some item of her trousseau. Ellie's bed was set up in the big dining room, where there was a gas lamp over the table. My mother sat on one side of the table, sewing; and Flora sat on the other side, reading aloud. Sometimes Ellie said, "I can't hear you." Or if Flora paused for a little rest Ellie said, "I'm not asleep yet."

What did Flora read? Stories about Scottish life—not classics. Stories about urchins and comic grandmothers. The only title my mother could remember was *Wee Macgregor.* She could not follow the stories very well, or laugh when Flora laughed and Ellie gave a whimper, because so much was in Scots dialect or read with that thick accent. She was surprised that Flora could do it—it wasn't the way Flora ordinarily talked, at all.

(But wouldn't it be the way Robert talked? Perhaps that is why my mother never reports anything that Robert said, never has him contributing to the scene. He must have been there, he must have been sitting there in the room. They would only heat the main room of the house. I see him black-haired, heavy-shouldered, with the strength of a plow horse, and the same kind of sombre, shackled beauty.)

Then Flora would say, "That's all of that for tonight." She would pick up another book, an old book written by some preacher of their faith. There was in it such stuff as my mother had never heard. What stuff? She couldn't say. All the stuff that was in their monstrous old religion. That put Ellie to sleep, or made her pretend she was asleep, after a couple of pages.

All that configuration of the elect and the damned, my mother must have meant—all the arguments about the illusion and necessity of free will. Doom and slippery redemption. The torturing, defeating, but for some minds irresistible pileup of interlocking and contradictory notions. My mother could resist it. Her faith was easy, her spirits at that time robust. Ideas were not what she was curious about, ever.

But what sort of thing was that, she asked (silently), to read to a dying woman? This was the nearest she got to criticizing Flora.

The answer—that it was the only thing, if you believed it—never seemed to have occurred to her.

By spring a nurse had arrived. That was the way things were done then. People died at home, and a nurse came in to manage it.

The nurse's name was Audrey Atkinson. She was a stout woman with corsets as stiff as barrel hoops, marcelled hair the color of brass candlesticks, a mouth shaped by lipstick beyond its own stingy outlines. She drove a car into the yard—her own car, a dark-green coup, shiny and smart. News of Audrey Atkinson and her car spread quickly. Questions were asked. Where did she get the money? Had some rich fool altered his will on her behalf? Had she exercised influence? Or simply helped herself to a stash of bills under the mattress? How was she to be trusted?

Hers was the first car ever to sit in the Grieveses' yard overnight.

Audrey Atkinson said that she had never been called out to tend a case in so primitive a house. It was beyond her, she said, how people could live in such a way.

"It's not that they're poor, even," she said to my mother. "It isn't, is it? That I could understand. Or it's not even their religion. So what is it? They do not care!"

She tried at first to cozy up to my mother, as if they would be natural allies in this benighted place. She spoke as if they were around the same age—both stylish, intelligent women who liked a good time and had modern ideas. She offered to teach my mother to drive the car. She offered her cigarettes. My mother was more tempted by the idea of learning to drive than she was by the cigarettes. But she said no, she would wait for her husband to teach her. Audrey Atkinson raised her pinkish-orange eyebrows at my mother behind Flora's back, and my mother was furious. She disliked the nurse far more than Flora did.

"I knew what she was like and Flora didn't," my mother said. She meant that she caught a whiff of a cheap life, maybe even—of drinking establishments and unsavory men, of hard bargains, which Flora was too unworldly to notice.

Flora started into the great housecleaning again. She had the curtains spread out on stretchers, she beat the rugs on the line, she leapt up on the stepladder to attack the dust on the molding. But she was impeded all the time by Nurse Atkinson's complaining.

"I wondered if we could have a little less of the running and clattering?" said Nurse Atkinson with offensive politeness. "I only ask for my patient's sake." She always spoke of Ellie as "my patient" and pretended that she was the only one to protect her and compel respect. But she was not so respectful of Ellie herself. "Allee-oop," she would say, dragging the poor creature up on her pillows. And she told Ellie she was not going to stand for fretting and whimpering. "You don't do yourself any good that way," she said. "And you certainly don't make me come any quicker. What you just as well might do is learn to control yourself." She exclaimed at Ellie's bedsores in a scolding way, as if they were a further disgrace of the house. She demanded lotions, ointments, expensive soap—most of them, no doubt, to protect her own skin, which she claimed suffered from the hard water. (How could it be hard, my mother asked her—sticking up for the household when nobody else would—how could it be hard when it came straight from the rain barrel?)

Nurse Atkinson wanted cream, too—she said that they should hold some back, not sell it all to the creamery. She wanted to make nourishing soups and puddings for her patient. She did make puddings, and jellies, from packed mixes such as had never before entered this house. My mother was convinced that she ate them all herself.

Flora still read to Ellie, but now it was only short bits from the Bible. When she finished and stood up, Ellie tried to cling to her. Ellie wept, sometimes she made ridiculous complaints. She said there was a horned cow outside, trying to get into the room and kill her.

"They often get some kind of idea like that," Nurse Atkinson said. "You mustn't give in to her or she won't let you go day or night. That's what they're like, they only think about themselves. Now, when I'm here alone with her, she behaves herself quite nice. I don't have any trouble at all. But after you been in here I have trouble all over again because she sees you and she gets upset. You don't want to make my job harder for me, do you? I mean, you brought me here to take charge, didn't you?"

"Ellie, now, Ellie dear, I must go," said Flora, and to the nurse she said, "I understand. I do understand that you have to be in charge and I admire you, I admire you for your work. In your work you have to have so much patience and kindness."

My mother wondered at this—was Flora really so blinded, or did she hope by this undeserved praise to exhort Nurse Atkinson to the patience and kindness that she didn't have? Nurse Atkinson was too thick-skinned and self-approving for any trick like that to work.

"It is a hard job, all right, and not many can do it," she said. "It's not like those nurses in the hospital, where they got everything laid out for them." She had no time for more conversation—she was trying to bring in "Make-Believe Ballroom" on her battery radio.

My mother was busy with the final exams and the June exercises at the school. She was getting ready for her wedding in July. Friends came in cars and whisked her off to the dressmaker's, to parties, to choose the invitations and order the cake. The lilacs came out, the evenings lengthened, the birds were back and nesting, my mother bloomed in everybody's attention, about to set out on the deliciously solemn adventure of marriage. Her dress was to be appliquéd with silk roses, her veil held by a cap of seed pearls. She belonged to the first generation of young women who saved their money and paid for their own weddings—far fancier than their parents could have afforded.

On her last evening, the friend from the post office came to drive her away, with her clothes and her books and the things she had made for her trousseau and the gifts her pupils and others had given her. There was great fuss and laughter about getting everything loaded into the car. Flora came out and helped. "This getting married is even more of a nuisance than I thought," said Flora, laughing. She gave my mother a dresser scarf, which she had crocheted in secret. Nurse Atkinson could not be shut out of an important occasion—she presented a spray bottle of cologne. Flora stood on the slope at the side of the house to wave goodbye. She had been invited to the wedding, but of course she had said she could not come, she could not "go out" at such a time. The last my mother ever saw of her was this solitary, energetically waving figure in her housecleaning apron and bandanna, on the green slope by the black-walled house, in the evening light.

"Well, maybe now she'll get what she should've got the first time round," the friend from the post office said. "Maybe now they'll be able to get married. Is she too old to start a family? How old is she, anyway?"

My mother thought that this was a crude way of talking about Flora and replied that she didn't know. But she had to admit to herself that she had been thinking the very same thing.

When she was married and settled in her own home, three hundred miles away, my mother got a letter from Flora. Ellie was dead. She had died firm in her faith, Flora said, and grateful for her release. Nurse Atkinson was staying on for a little while, until it was time for her to go off to her next case. This was late in the summer.

News of what happened next did not come from Flora. When she wrote at Christmas, she seemed to take for granted that information would have gone ahead of her.

"You have in all probability heard," wrote Flora, "that Robert and Nurse Atkinson have been married. They are living on here, in Robert's part of the house. They are fixing it up to suit themselves. It is very impolite of me to call her Nurse Atkinson, as I see I have done. I ought to have called her Audrey."

Of course the post-office friend had written, and so had others. It was a great shock and scandal and a matter that excited the district—the wedding as secret and surprising as Robert's first one had been (though surely not for the same reason), Nurse Atkinson permanently installed in the community, Flora losing out for the second time. Nobody had been aware of any courtship, and they asked how the woman could have enticed him. Did she promise children, lying about her age?

The surprises were not to stop with the wedding. The bride got down to business immediately with the "fixing up" that Flora mentioned. In came the electricity and then the telephone. Now Nurse Atkinson—she would always be called Nurse Atkinson—was heard on the party line lambasting painters and paperhangers and delivery services. She was having everything done over. She was buying an electric stove and putting in a bathroom, and who knew where the money was coming from? Was it all hers, got in her deathbed dealings, in shady bequests? Was it Robert's, was he claiming his share? Ellie's share, left to him and Nurse Atkinson to enjoy themselves with, the shameless pair?

All these improvements took place on one side of the house only. Flora's side remained just as it was. No electric lights there, no fresh wallpaper or new venetian blinds. When the house was painted on the outside—cream with dark-green trim—Flora's side was left bare. This strange open statement was greeted at first with pity and disapproval, then with less sympathy, as a sign of Flora's stubbornness and eccentricity (she could have bought her own paint and made it look decent), and finally as a joke. People drove out of their way to see it.

There was always a dance given in the schoolhouse for a newly married couple. A cash collection—called "a purse of money"—was presented to them. Nurse Atkinson sent out word that she would not mind seeing this custom followed, even though it happened that the family she had married into was opposed to dancing. Some people thought it would be a disgrace to gratify her, a slap in the face to Flora. Others were too curious to hold back. They wanted to see how the newlyweds would behave. Would Robert dance? What sort of outfit would the bride show up in? They delayed a while, but finally the dance was held, and my mother got her report.

The bride wore the dress she had worn at her wedding, or so she said. But who would wear such a dress for a wedding at the manse? More than likely it was bought specially for her appearance at the dance. Pure-white satin with a sweetheart neckline, idiotically youthful. The groom was got up in a new dark-blue suit, and she had stuck a flower in his buttonhole. They were a sight. Her hair was freshly done to blind the eye with brassy reflections, and her face looked as if it would come off on a man's jacket, should she lay it against his shoulder in the dancing. Of course she did dance. She danced with every man present except the groom, who sat scrunched into one of the school desks along the wall. She danced with every man present—they all claimed they had to do it, it was the custom—and then she dragged Robert out to receive the money and to thank everybody for their best wishes. To the ladies in the cloakroom she even hinted that she was feeling unwell, for the usual newlywed reason. Nobody believed her, and indeed nothing ever came of this hope, if she really had it. Some of the women thought that she was lying to them out of malice, insulting them, making them out to be so credulous. But nobody challenged her, nobody was rude to her—maybe because it was plain that she could summon a rudeness of her own to knock anybody flat.

Flora was not present at the dance.

"My sister-in-law is not a dancer," said Nurse Atkinson. "She is stuck in the olden times." She invited them to laugh at Flora, whom she always called her sister-in-law, though she had no right to do so.

My mother wrote a letter to Flora after hearing about all these things. Being removed from the scene, and perhaps in a flurry of importance due to her own newly married state, she may have lost sight of the kind of person she was writing to. She offered sympathy and showed outrage, and said blunt disparaging things about the woman who had—as my mother saw it—dealt Flora such a blow. Back came a letter from Flora saying that she did not know where my mother had been getting her information, but that it seemed she had misunderstood, or listened to malicious people, or jumped to unjustified conclusions. What happened in Flora's family was nobody else's business, and certainly nobody needed to feel sorry for her or angry on her behalf. Flora said that she was happy and satisfied in her life, as she always had been, and she did not interfere with what others did or wanted, because such things did not concern her. She wished my mother all happiness in her marriage and hoped that she would soon be too busy with her own responsibilities to worry about the lives of people that she used to know.

This well-written letter cut my mother, as she said, to the quick. She and Flora stopped corresponding. My mother did become busy with her own life and finally a prisoner in it.

But she thought about Flora. In later years, when she sometimes talked about the things she might have been, or done, she would say, "If I could have been a writer—I do think I could have been; I could have been a writer—then I would have written the story of Flora's life. And do you know what I would have called it? 'The Maiden Lady.'"

The Maiden Lady. She said these words in a solemn and sentimental tone of voice that I had no use for. I knew, or thought I knew, exactly the value she found in them. The stateliness and mystery. The hint of derision turning to reverence. I was fifteen or sixteen years old by that time, and I believed that I could see into my mother's mind. I could see what she would do with Flora, what she had already done. She would make her into a noble figure, one who accepts defection, treachery, who forgives and stands aside, not once but twice. Never a moment of complaint. Flora goes about her cheerful labors, she cleans the house and shovels out the cow byre, she removes some bloody mess from her sister's bed, and when at last the future seems to open up for her—Ellie will die and Robert will beg forgiveness and Flora will silence him with the proud gift of herself—it is time for Audrey Atkinson to drive into the yard and shut Flora out again, more inexplicably and thoroughly the second time than the first. She must endure the painting of the house, the electric lights, all the prosperous activity next door. "Make-Believe Ballroom," "Amos 'n' Andy." No more Scottish comedies or ancient sermons. She must see them drive off to the dance—her old lover and that coldhearted, stupid, by no means beautiful woman in the white satin wedding dress. She is mocked. (And of course she has made over the farm to Ellie and Robert, of course he has inherited it, and now everything belongs to Audrey Atkinson.) The wicked flourish. But it is all right. It is all right—the elect are veiled in patience and humility and lighted by a certainty that events cannot disturb.

That was what I believed my mother would make of things. In her own plight her notions had turned mystical, and there was sometimes a hush, a solemn thrill in her voice that grated on me, alerted me to what seemed a personal danger. I felt a great fog of platitudes and pieties lurking, an incontestable crippled-mother power, which could capture and choke me. There would be no end to it. I had to keep myself sharp-tongued and cynical, arguing and deflating. Eventually I gave up even that recognition and opposed her in silence.

This is a fancy way of saying that I was no comfort and poor company to her when she had almost nowhere else to turn.

I had my own ideas about Flora's story. I didn't think that I could have written a novel but that I would write one. I would take a different tack. I saw through my mother's story and put in what she left out. My Flora would be as black as hers was white. Rejoicing in the bad turns done to her and in her own forgiveness, spying on the shambles of her sister's life. A Presbyterian witch, reading out of her poisonous book. It takes a rival ruthlessness, the comparatively innocent brutality of the thick-skinned nurse, to drive her back, to flourish in her shade. But she is driven back; the power of sex and ordinary greed drive her back and shut her up in her own part of the house with the coal-oil lamps. She shrinks, she caves in, her bones harden and her joints thicken, and—oh, this is it, this is it, I see the bare beauty of the ending I will contrive!—she becomes crippled herself, with arthritis, hardly able to move. Now Audrey Atkinson comes into her full power—she demands the whole house. She wants those partitions knocked out that Robert put up with Flora's help when he married Ellie. She will provide Flora with a room, she will take care of her. (Audrey Atkinson does not wish to be seen as a monster, and perhaps she really isn't one.) So one day Robert carries Flora—for the first and last time he carries her in his arms—to the room that his wife Audrey has prepared for her. And once Flora is settled in her well-lit, well-heated corner Audrey Atkinson undertakes to clean out the newly vacated rooms, Flora's rooms. She carries a heap of old books out into the yard. It's spring again, housecleaning time, the season when Flora herself performed such feats, and now the pale face of Flora appears behind the new net curtains. She has dragged herself from her corner, she sees the light-blue sky with its high skidding clouds over the watery fields, the contending crows, the flooded creeks, the reddening tree branches. She sees the smoke rise out of the incinerator in the yard, where her books are burning. Those smelly old books, as Audrey has called them. Words and pages, the ominous dark spines. The elect, the damned, the slim hopes, the mighty torments—up in smoke. There was the ending.

To me the really mysterious person in the story, as my mother told it, was Robert. He never has a word to say. He gets engaged to Flora. He is walking beside her along the river when Ellie leaps out at them. He finds Ellie's thistles in his bed. He does the carpentry made necessary by his and Ellie's marriage. He listens or does not listen while Flora reads. Finally he sits scrunched up in the school desk while his flashy bride dances by with all the men.

So much for his public acts and appearances. But he was the one who started everything, in secret. He *did it to* Ellie. He did it to that skinny wild girl at a time when he was engaged to her sister, and he did it to her again and again when she was nothing but a poor botched body, a failed childbearer, lying in bed.

He must have done it to Audrey Atkinson, too, but with less disastrous results.

Those words, did it to—the words my mother, no more than Flora, would never bring herself to speak—were simply exciting to me. I didn't feel any decent revulsion or reasonable indignation. I refused the warning. Not even the fate of Ellie could put me off. Not when I thought of that first encounter—the desperation of it, the ripping and striving. I used to sneak longing looks at men in those days. I admired their wrists and their necks and any bit of their chests a loose button let show, and even their ears and their feet in shoes. I expected nothing reasonable of them, only to be engulfed by their passion. I had similar thoughts about Robert.

What made Flora evil in my story was just what made her admirable in my mother's—her turning away from sex. I fought against everything my mother wanted to tell me on this subject; I despised even the drop in her voice, the gloomy caution, with which she approached it. My mother had grown up in a time and in a place where sex was a dark undertaking for women. She knew that you could die of it. So she honored the decency, the prudery, the frigidity, that might protect you. And I grew up in horror of that very protection, the dainty tyranny that seemed to me to extend to all areas of life, to enforce tea parties and white gloves and all other sorts of tinkling inanities. I favored bad words and a breakthrough, I teased myself with the thought of a man's recklessness and domination. The odd thing is that my mother's ideas were in line with some progressive notions of her times, and mine echoed the notions that were favored in my time. This in spite of the fact that we both believed ourselves independent, and lived in backwaters that did not register such changes. It's as if tendencies that seem most deeply rooted in our minds, most private and singular, have come in as spores on the prevailing wind, looking for any likely place to land, any welcome.

Not long before she died, but when I was still at home, my mother got a letter from the real Flora. It came from that town near the farm, the town that Flora used to ride to, with Robert, in the cart, holding on to the sacks of wool or potatoes.

Flora wrote that she was no longer living on the farm.

"Robert and Audrey are still there," she wrote. "Robert has some trouble with his back but otherwise he is very well. Audrey has poor circulation and is often short of breath. The doctor says she must lose weight but none of the diets seem to work. The farm has been doing very well. They are out of sheep entirely and into dairy cattle. As you may have heard, the chief thing nowadays is to get your milk quota from the government and then you are set. The old stable is all fixed up with milking machines and the latest modem equipment, it is quite a marvel. When I go out there to visit I hardly know where I am."

She went on to say that she had been living in town for some years now, and that she had a job clerking in a store. She must have said what kind of a store this was, but I cannot now remember. She said nothing, of course, about what had led her to this decision—whether she had in fact been put off her own farm, or had sold out her share, apparently not to much advantage. She stressed the fact of her friendliness with Robert and Audrey. She said her health was good.

"I hear that you have not been so lucky in that way," she wrote. "I ran into Cleta Barnes who used to be Cleta Stapleton at the post office out at home, and she told me that there is some problem with your muscles and she said your speech is affected too. This is sad to hear but they can do such wonderful things nowadays so I am hoping that the doctors may be able to help you."

An unsettling letter, leaving so many things out. Nothing in it about God's will or His role in our afflictions. No mention of whether Flora still went to that church. I don't think my mother ever answered. Her fine legible handwriting, her schoolteacher's writing, had deteriorated, and she had difficulty holding a pen. She was always beginning letters and not finishing them. I would find them lying around the house. *My dearest Mary,* they began. *My darling Ruth, My dear little Joanne (though I realize you are not little anymore), My dear old friend Cleta, My lovely Margaret.* These women were friends from her teaching days, her Normal School days, and from high school. A few were former pupils. I have friends all over the country, she would say defiantly. I have dear, dear friends.

I remember seeing one letter that started out: *Friend of my Youth.* I don't know whom it was to. They were all friends of her youth. I don't recall one that began with *My dear and most admired Flora.* I would always look at them, try to read the salutation and the few sentences she had written, and because I could not bear to feel sadness I would feel an impatience with the flowery language, the direct appeal for love and pity. She would get more of that, I thought (more from myself, I meant), if she could manage to withdraw with dignity, instead of reaching out all the time to cast her stricken shadow.

I had lost interest in Flora by then. I was always thinking of stories, and by this time I probably had a new one on my mind.

But I have thought of her since. I have wondered what kind of a store. A hardware store or a five-and-ten, where she has to wear a coverall, or a drugstore, where she is uniformed like a nurse, or a Ladies' Wear, where she is expected to be genteelly fashionable? She might have had to learn about food blenders or chain saws, negligees, cosmetics, even condoms. She would have to work all day under electric lights, and operate a cash register.

Would she get a permanent, paint her nails, put on lipstick? She must have found a place to live—a little apartment with a kitchenette, overlooking the main street, or a room in a boarding house. How could she go on being a Cameronian? How could she get to that out-of-the-way church unless she managed to buy a car and learned to drive it? And if she did that she might drive not only to church but to other places. She might go on holidays. She might rent a cottage on a lake for a week, learn to swim, visit a city. She might eat meals in a restaurant, possibly in a restaurant where drinks were served. She might make friends with women who were divorced.

She might meet a man. A friend's widowed brother, perhaps. A man who did not know that she was a Cameronian or what Cameronians were. Who knew nothing of her story. A man who had never heard about the partial painting of the house or the two betrayals, or that it took all her dignity and innocence to keep her from being a joke. He might want to take her dancing, and she would have to explain that she could not go. He would be surprised but not put off—all that Cameronian business might seem quaint to him, almost charming. So it would to everybody. She was brought up in some weird religion, people would say. She lived a long time out on some godforsaken farm. She is a little bit strange but really quite nice. Nice-looking, too. Especially since she went and got her hair done.

I might go into a store and find her.

No, no. She would be dead a long time now.

But suppose I had gone into a store—perhaps a department store. I see a place with the brisk atmosphere, the straightforward displays, the old-fashioned modern look of the fifties. Suppose a tall, handsome woman, nicely turned out, had come to wait on me, and I had known, somehow, in spite of the sprayed and puffed hair and the pink or coral lips and fingernails—I had known that this was Flora. I would have wanted to tell her that I knew, I knew her story, though we had never met. I imagine myself trying to tell her. (This is a dream now, I understand it as a dream.) I imagine her listening, with a pleasant composure. But she shakes her head. She smiles at me, and in her smile there is a degree of mockery, a faint, self-assured malice. Weariness, as well. She is not surprised that I am telling her this, but she is weary of it, of me and my idea of her, my information, my notion that I can know anything about her.

Of course it's my mother I'm thinking of, my mother as she was in those dreams, saying, It's nothing, just this little tremor; saying with such astonishing lighthearted forgiveness, Oh, I knew you'd come someday. My mother surprising me, and doing it almost indifferently. Her mask, her fate, and most of her affliction taken away. How relieved I was, and happy. But I now recall that I was disconcerted as well. I would have to say that I felt slightly cheated. Yes. Offended, tricked, cheated, by this welcome turnaround, this reprieve. My mother moving rather carelessly out of her old prison, showing options and powers I never dreamed she had, changes more than herself. She changes the bitter lump of love I have carried all this time into a phantom—something useless and uncalled for, like a phantom pregnancy.

The Cameronians, I have discovered, are or were an uncompromising remnant of the Covenanters—those Scots who in the seventeenth century bound themselves, with God, to resist prayer books, bishops, any taint of popery or interference by the King. Their name comes from Richard Cameron, an outlawed, or "field," preacher, soon cut down. The Cameronians—for a long time they have preferred to be called the Reformed Presbyterians—went into battle singing the seventy-fourth and the seventy-eighth Psalms. They hacked the haughty Bishop of St. Andrews to death on the highway and rode their horses over his body. One of their ministers, in a mood of firm rejoicing at his own hanging, excommunicated all the other preachers in the world.

Alice Munro

Save the Reaper

The game they played was almost the same one that Eve had played with Sophie, on long dull car trips when Sophie was a little girl. Then it was spies—now it was aliens. Sophie's children, Philip and Daisy, were sitting in the backseat. Daisy was barely three and could not understand what was going on. Philip was seven, and in control. He was the one who picked the car they were to follow, in which there were newly arrived space travellers on their way to the secret headquarters, the invaders' lair. They got their directions from the signals offered by plausible-looking people in other cars or from somebody standing by a mailbox or even riding a tractor in a field. Many aliens had already arrived on earth and been translated—this was Philip's word—so that anybody might be one. Gas station attendants or women pushing baby carriages or even the babies riding in the carriages. They could be giving signals.

Usually Eve and Sophie had played this game on a busy highway where there was enough traffic that they wouldn't be detected. (Though once they had got carried away and ended up in a suburban drive.) On the country roads that Eve was taking today that wasn't so easy. She tried to solve the problem by saying that they might have to switch from following one vehicle to another because some were only decoys, not heading for the hideaway at all, but leading you astray.

"No, that isn't it," said Philip. "What they do, they suck the people out of one car into another car, just in case anybody is following. They can be like inside one body and then they go *schlup* through the air into another body in another car. They go into different people all the time and the people never know what was in them."

"Really?" Eve said. "So how do we know which car?"

"The code's on the license plate," said Philip. "It's changed by the electrical field they create in the car. So their trackers in space can follow them. It's just one simple little thing, but I can't tell you."

"Well no," said Eve. "I suppose very few people know it."

Philip said, "I am the only one right now in Ontario."

He sat as far forward as he could with his seat belt on, tapping his teeth sometimes in urgent concentration and making light whistling noises as he cautioned her.

"Unh-unh, watch out here," he said. "I think you're going to have to turn around. Yeah. Yeah. I think this may be it."

They had been following a white Mazda, and were now, apparently, to follow an old green pickup truck, a Ford. Eve said, "Are you sure?"

"Sure."

"You felt them sucked through the air?"

"They're translated simultaneously," Philip said. "I might have said 'sucked,' but that's just to help people understand it."

What Eve had originally planned was to have the headquarters turn out to be in the village store that sold ice cream, or in the playground. It could be revealed that all the aliens were congregated there in the form of children, seduced by the pleasures of ice cream or slides and swings, their powers temporarily in abeyance. No fear they could abduct you—or get into you—unless you chose the one wrong flavor of ice cream or swung the exact wrong number of times on the designated swing. (There would have to be some remaining danger, or else Philip would feel let down, humiliated.) But Philip had taken charge so thoroughly that now it was hard to manage the outcome. The pickup truck was turning from the paved country road onto a graveled side road. It was a decrepit truck with no topper, its body eaten by rust—it would not be going far. Home to some farm, most likely. They might not meet another vehicle to switch to before the destination was reached.

"You're positive this is it?" said Eva "It's only one man by himself you know. I thought they never travelled alone."

"The dog," said Philip.

For there was a dog riding in the open back of the truck, running back and forth from one side to the other as if there were events to be kept track of everywhere.

"The dog's one too," Philip said.

That morning, when Sophie was leaving to meet Ian at the Toronto airport, Philip had kept Daisy occupied in the children's bedroom. Daisy had settled down pretty well in the strange house—except for wetting her bed every night of the holiday—but this was the first time that her mother had gone off and left her behind. So Sophie had asked Philip to distract her, and he did so with enthusiasm (happy at the new turn events had taken?). He shot the toy cars across the floor with angry engine noises to cover up the sound of Sophie's starting the real rented car and driving away. Shortly after that he shouted to Eve, "Has the B.M. gone?"

Eve was in the kitchen, clearing up the remains of breakfast and disciplining herself. She walked into the living room. There was the boxed tape of the movie that she and Sophie had been watching last night.

The Bridges of Madison County.

"What does mean 'B.M.'?" said Daisy.

The children's room opened off the living room. This was a cramped little house, fixed up on the cheap for summer rental. Eve's idea had been to get a lakeside cottage for the holiday—Sophie's and Philip's first visit with her in nearly five years and Daisy's first. She had picked this stretch of the Lake Huron shore because her parents used to bring her here with her brother when they were children. Things had changed—the cottages were all as substantial as suburban houses, and the rents were out of sight. This house half a mile inland from the rocky, unfavored north end of the usable beach had been the best she could manage. It stood in the middle of a cornfield. She had told the children what her father had once told her—that at night you could hear the corn growing.

Every day when Sophie took Daisy's hand-washed sheets off the line, she had to shake out the corn bugs.

"It means 'bowel' movement," said Philip with a look of sly challenge at Eve.

Eve halted in the doorway. Last night she and Sophie had watched Meryl Streep sitting in the husband's truck, in the rain, pressing down on the door handle, choking with longing, as her lover drove away. Then they had turned and had seen each other's eyes full of tears and shook their heads and started laughing.

"Also it means 'Big Mama,'" Philip said in a more conciliatory tone. "Sometimes that's what Dad calls her."

"Well then," said Eve. "If that's your question, the answer to your question is yes."

She wondered if he thought of Ian as his real father. She hadn't asked Sophie what they'd told him. She wouldn't, of course. His real father had been an Irish boy who was travelling around North America trying to decide what to do now that he had decided not to be a priest. Eve had thought of him as a casual friend of Sophie's, and it seemed that Sophie had thought of him that way too, until she seduced him. ("He was so shy I never dreamed it would take," she said.) It wasn't until Eve saw Philip that Eve could really picture what the boy had looked like. Then she saw him faithfully reproduced—the bright-eyed, pedantic, sensitive, scornful, fault-finding, blushing, shrinking, arguing young Irishman. Something like Samuel Beckett, she said, even to the wrinkles. Of course as the baby got older, the wrinkles tended to disappear.

Sophie was a full-time archaeology student then. Eve took care of Philip while she was off at her classes. Eve was an actress—she still was, when she could get work. Even in those days there were times when she wasn't working, or if she had daytime rehearsals she could take Philip along. For a couple of years they all lived together—Eve and Sophie and Philip—in Eve's apartment in Toronto. It was Eve who wheeled Philip in his baby carriage—and, later on, in his stroller—along all the streets between Queen and College and Spadina and Ossington, and during these walks she would sometimes discover a perfect, though neglected, little house for sale in a previously unknown to her two-block-long, tree-shaded, dead-end street. She would send Sophie to look at it; they would go round with the real-estate agent, talk about a mortgage, discuss what renovations they would have to pay for, and which they could do themselves. Dithering and fantasizing until the house was sold to somebody else, or until Eve had one of her periodic but intense fits of financial prudence, or until somebody persuaded them that these charming little side streets were not half so safe for women and children as the bright, ugly, brash, and noisy street that they continued to live on.

Ian was a person Eve took even less note of than she had of the Irish boy. He was a friend; he never came to the apartment except with others. Then he went to a job in California—he was an urban geographer—and Sophie ran up a phone bill which Eve had to speak to her about, and there was a change altogether in the atmosphere of the apartment. (Should Eve not have mentioned the bill?) Soon a visit was planned, and Sophie took Philip along, because Eve was doing a summer play in a regional theater.

Not long afterwards came the news from California. Sophie and Ian were going to get married.

"Wouldn't it be smarter to try living together for a while?" said Eve on the phone from her boarding house, and Sophie said, "Oh, no. He's weird. He doesn't believe in that."

But I can't get off for a wedding," Eve said. "We run till the middle of September."

"That's okay," said Sophie. "It won't be a *wedding* wedding."

And until this summer, Eve had not seen her again. There was the lack of money at both ends, in the beginning. When Eve *was* working she had a steady commitment, and when she wasn't working she couldn't afford anything extra. Soon Sophie had a job, too—she was a receptionist in a doctor's office. Once Eve was just about to book a flight, when Sophie phoned to say that Ian's father had died and that he was flying to England for the funeral and bringing his mother back with him.

"And we only have the one room," she said.

"Perish the thought," said Eve. "Two mothers-in-law in one house, let alone in one room."

"Maybe after she's gone?" said Sophie.

But that mother stayed till after Daisy was born, stayed till they moved into the new house, stayed eight months in all. By then Ian was starting to write his book, and it was difficult for him if there were visitors in the house. It was difficult enough anyway. The time passed during which Eve felt confident enough to invite herself. Sophie sent pictures of Daisy, the garden, all the rooms of the house.

Then she announced that they could come, she and Philip and Daisy could come back to Ontario this summer. They would spend three weeks with Eve while Ian worked alone in California. At the end of that time he would join them and they would fly from Toronto to England to spend a month with his mother.

"I'll get a cottage on the lake," said Eve. "Oh, it will be lovely."

"It will," said Sophie. "It's crazy that it's been so long."

And so it had been. Reasonably lovely, Eve had thought. Sophie hadn't seemed much bothered or surprised by Daisy's wetting the bed. Philip had been finicky and standoffish for a couple of days, responding coolly to Eve's report that she had known him as a baby, and whining about the mosquitoes that descended on them as they hurried through the shoreline woods to get to the beach. He wanted to be taken to Toronto to see the Science Centre. But then he settled down, swam in the lake without complaining that it was cold, and busied himself with solitary projects—such as boiling and scraping the meat off a dead turtle he'd lugged home, so he could keep its shell. The turtle's stomach contained an undigested crayfish, and its shell came off in strips, but none of this dismayed him.

Eve and Sophie, meanwhile, developed a pleasant, puttering routine of morning chores, afternoons on the beach, wine with supper, and late-evening movies. They were drawn into half-serious speculations about the house. What could be done about it? First strip off the living-room wallpaper, an imitation of imitation-wood panelling. Pull up the linoleum with its silly pattern of gold fleurs-de-lis turned brown by ground-in sand and dirty scrub water. Sophie was so carried away that she loosened a bit of it that had rotted in front of the sink and discovered pine floorboards that surely could be sanded. They talked about the cost of renting a sander (supposing, that is, that the house was theirs) and what colors they would choose for the paint on the doors and woodwork, shutters on the windows, open shelves in the kitchen instead of the dingy plywood cupboards. What about a gas fireplace?

And who was going to live here? Eve. The snowmobilers who used the house for a winter clubhouse were building a place of their own, and the landlord might be happy to rent it year-round. Or maybe sell it very cheaply, considering its condition. It could be a retreat, if Eve got the job she was hoping for, next winter. And if she didn't, why not sublet the apartment and live here? There'd be the difference in the rents, and the old-age pension she started getting in October, and the money that still came in from a commercial she had made for a diet supplement. She could manage.

"And then if we came in the summers we could help with the rent," said Sophie.

Philip heard them. He said, "Every summer?"

"Well you like the lake now," Sophie said. "You like it here now."

"And the mosquitoes, you know they're not as bad every year," Eve said. "Usually they're just bad in the early summer. June, before you'd even get here. In the spring there are all these boggy places full of water, and they breed there, and then the boggy places dry up, and they don't breed again. But this year there was so much rain earlier, those places didn't dry up, so the mosquitoes got a second chance, and there's a whole new generation."

She had found out how much he respected information and preferred it to her opinions and reminiscences.

Sophie was not keen on reminiscence either. Whenever the past that she and Eve had shared was mentioned—even those months after Philip's birth that Eve thought of as some of the happiest, the hardest, the most purposeful and harmonious, in her life—Sophie's face took on a look of gravity and concealment, of patiently withheld judgments. The earlier time, Sophie's own childhood, was a positive minefield, as Eve discovered, when they were talking about Philip's school. Sophie thought it a little too rigorous, and Ian thought it just fine.

"What a switch from Blackbird," Eve said, and Sophie said at once, almost viciously, "Oh, Blackbird. What a farce. When I think that you paid for that. You *paid.*"

Blackbird was an ungraded alternative school that Sophie had gone to (the name came from "Morning Has Broken"). It had cost Eve more than she could afford, but she thought it was better for a child whose mother was an actress and whose father was not in evidence. When Sophie was nine or ten, it had broken up because of disagreements among the parents.

"I learned Greek myths and I didn't know where Greece was," said Sophie. "I didn't know *what* it was. We had to spend art period making antinuke signs."

Eve said, "Oh, no, surely."

"We did. And they literally badgered us—they badgered us—to talk about sex. It was verbal molestation. You *paid.*"

"I didn't know it was as bad as all that."

"Oh well," said Sophie. "I survived."

"That's the main thing," Eve said shakily. "Survival."

Sophie's father was from Kerala, in the southern part of India. Eve had met him, and spent her whole time with him, on a train going from Vancouver to Toronto. He was a young doctor studying in Canada on a fellowship. He had a wife already, and a baby daughter, at home in India.

The train trip took three days. There was a half-hour stop in Calgary. Eve and the doctor ran around looking for a drugstore where they could buy condoms. They didn't find one. By the time they got to Winnipeg, where the train stopped for a full hour, it was too late. In fact—said Eve, when she told their story—by the time they got to the Calgary city limits, it was probably too late.

He was travelling in the day coach—the fellowship was not generous. But Eve had splurged and got herself a roomette. It was this extravagance—a last-minute decision—it was the convenience and privacy of the roomette that were responsible, Eve said, for the existence of Sophie and the greatest change in her, Eve's, life. That, and the fact that you couldn't get condoms anywhere around the Calgary station, not for love or money.

In Toronto she waved goodbye to her lover from Kerala, as you would wave to any train acquaintance, because she was met there by the man who was at that time the serious interest and main trouble in her life. The whole three days had been underscored by the swaying and rocking of the train—the lovers' motions were never just what they contrived themselves, and perhaps for that reason seemed guiltless, irresistible. Their feelings and conversations must have been affected, too. Eve remembered these as sweet and generous, never solemn or desperate. It would have been hard to be solemn when you were dealing with the dimensions and the projections of the roomette.

She told Sophie his Christian name—Thomas, after the saint. Until she met him, Eve had never heard about the ancient Christians in southern India. For a while when she was in her teens Sophie had taken an interest in Kerala. She brought home books from the library and took to going to parties in a sari. She talked about looking her father up, when she got older. The fact that she knew his first name and his special study—diseases of the blood—seemed to her possibly enough. Eve stressed to her the size of the population of India and the chance that he had not even stayed there. What she could not bring herself to explain was how incidental, how nearly unimaginable, the existence of Sophie would be, necessarily, in her father's life. Fortunately the idea faded, and Sophie gave up wearing the sari when all those dramatic, ethnic costumes became too commonplace. The only time she mentioned her father, later on, was when she was carrying Philip, and making jokes about keeping up the family tradition of flyby fathers.

No jokes like that now. Sophie had grown stately, womanly, graceful, and reserved. There had been a moment—they were getting through the woods to the beach, and Sophie had bent to scoop up Daisy, so that they might move more quickly out of range of the mosquitoes—when Eve had been amazed at the new, late manifestation of her daughter's beauty. A full-bodied, tranquil, classic beauty, achieved not by care and vanity but by self-forgetfulness and duty. She looked more Indian now, her creamed-coffee skin had darkened in the California sun, and she bore under her eyes the lilac crescents of a permanent mild fatigue.

But she was still a strong swimmer. Swimming was the only sport she had ever cared for, and she swam as well as ever, heading it seemed for the middle of the lake. The first day she had done it she said "That was wonderful. I felt so free." She didn't say that it was because Eve was watching the children that she had felt that way, but Eve understood that it didn't need to be said. "I'm glad," she said—though in fact she had been frightened. Several times she had thought, Turn around now, and Sophie had swum right on, disregarding this urgent telepathic message. Her dark head became a spot, then a speck, then an illusion tossed among the steady waves. What Eve feared, and could not think about, was not a failure of strength but of the desire to return. As if this new Sophie, this grown woman so tethered to life, could be actually more indifferent to it than the girl Eve used to know, the young Sophie with her plentiful risks and loves and dramas.

★ ★ ★

"We have to get that movie back to the store," Eve said to Philip. "Maybe we should do it before we go to the beach."

Philip said, "I'm sick of the beach."

Eve didn't feel like arguing. With Sophie gone, with all plans altered, so that they were leaving, all of them leaving later in the day, she was sick of the beach, too. And sick of the house—all she could see now was the way this room would look tomorrow. The crayons, the toy cars, the large pieces of Daisy's simple jigsaw puzzle, all swept up and taken away. The storybooks gone that she knew by heart. No sheets drying outside the window. Eighteen more days to last, by herself, in this place.

"How about we go somewhere else today?" she said. Philip said, "Where is there?"

"Let it be a surprise."

Eve had come home from the village the day before, laden with provisions. Fresh shrimp for Sophie—the village store was actually a classy supermarket these days, you could find almost anything—coffee, wine, rye bread without caraway seeds because Philip hated caraway, a ripe melon, the dark cherries they all loved, though Daisy had to be watched with the stones, a tub of mocha-fudge ice cream, and all the regular things to keep them going for another week.

Sophie was clearing up the children's lunch. "Oh," she cried. "Oh, what'll we do with all that stuff?"

Ian had phoned, she said. Ian had phoned and said he was flying into Toronto tomorrow. Work on his book had progressed more quickly than he had expected; he had changed his plans. Instead of waiting for the three weeks to be up, he was coming tomorrow to collect Sophie and the children and take them on a little trip. He wanted to go to Quebec City. He had never been there, and he thought the children should see the part of Canada where people spoke French.

"He got lonesome," Philip said.

Sophie laughed. She said, "Yes. He got lonesome for us."

Twelve days, Eve thought. Twelve days had passed of the three weeks. She had had to take the house for a month. She was letting her friend Dev use the apartment. He was another out-of-work actor, and was in such real or imagined financial peril that he answered the phone in various stage voices. She was fond of Dev, but she couldn't go back and share the apartment with him.

Sophie said that they would drive to Quebec in the rented car, then drive straight back to the Toronto airport, where the car was to be turned in. No mention of Eve's going along. There wasn't room in the rented car. But couldn't she have taken her own car? Philip riding with her, perhaps, for company. Or Sophie. Ian could take the children, if he was so lonesome for them, and give Sophie a rest. Eve and Sophie could ride together as they used to in the summer, travelling to some town they had never seen before, where Eve had got a job.

That was ridiculous. Eve's car was nine years old and in no condition to make a long trip. And it was Sophie Ian had got lonesome for—you could tell that by her warm averted face. Also, Eve hadn't been asked.

"Well that's wonderful," said Eve. "That he's got along so well with his book."

"It is," said Sophie. She always had an air of careful detachment when she spoke of Ian's book, and when Eve had asked what it was about she had said merely, "Urban geography." Perhaps this was the correct behavior for academic wives—Eve had never known any.

"Anyway you'll get some time by yourself," Sophie said. "After all this circus. You'll find out if you really would like to have a place in the country. A retreat."

Eve had to start talking about something else, anything else so that she wouldn't bleat out a question about whether Sophie still thought of coming next summer.

"I had a friend who went on one of those real retreats," she said. "He's a Buddhist. No, maybe a Hindu. Not a real Indian." (At this mention of Indians Sophie smiled in a way that said this was another subject that need not be gone into.) "Anyway, you could not speak on this retreat for three months. There were other people around all the time, but you could not speak to them. And he said that one of the things that often happened and that they were warned about was that you fell in love with one of these people you'd never spoken to. You felt you were communicating in a special way with them when you couldn't talk. Of course it was a kind of spiritual love, and you couldn't do anything about it. They were strict about that kind of thing. Or so he said."

Sophie said, "So? When you were finally allowed to speak what happened?"

"It was a big letdown. Usually the person you thought you'd been communicating with hadn't been communicating with you at all. Maybe they thought they'd been communicating that way with somebody else, and they thought—"

Sophie laughed with relief. She said, "So it goes." Glad that there was to be no show of disappointment, no hurt feelings.

Maybe they had a tiff, thought Eve. This whole visit might have been tactical. Sophie might have taken the children off to show him something. Spent time with her mother, just to show him something. Planning future holidays without him, to prove to herself that she could do it. A diversion.

And the burning question was, Who did the phoning?

"Why don't you leave the children here?" she said. "Just while you drive to the airport? Then just drive back and pick them up and take off. You'd have a little time to yourself and a little time alone with Ian. It'll be hell with them in the airport."

Sophie said, "I'm tempted."

So in the end that was what she did.

Now Eve had to wonder if she herself had engineered that little change just so she could get to talk to Philip.

(Wasn't it a big surprise when your Dad phoned from California?

He didn't phone. My mom phoned him.

Did she? Oh I didn't know. What did she say?

She said, I can't stand it here, I'm sick of it, let's figure out some plan to get me away.")

Eve dropped her voice to a matter-of-fact level, to indicate an interruption of the game. She said, "Philip. Philip, listen. I think we've got to stop this. That truck just belongs to some farmer and it's going to turn in someplace and we can't go on following."

"Yes we can," Philip said.

"No we can't. They'd want to know what we were doing. They might be very mad."

"We'll call up our helicopters to come and shoot them."

"Don't be silly. You know this is just a game."

"They'll shoot them."

"I don't think they have any weapons," said Eve, trying another tack. "They haven't developed any weapons to destroy aliens."

Philip said, "You're wrong," and began a description of some kind of rockets, which she did not listen to.

When she was a child staying in the village with her brother and her parents, Eve had sometimes gone for drives in the country with her mother. They didn't have a car—it was wartime, they had come here on the train. The woman who ran the hotel was friends with Eve's mother, and they would be invited along when she drove to the country to buy corn or raspberries or tomatoes. Sometimes they would stop to have tea and look at the old dishes and bits of furniture for sale in some enterprising farm woman's front parlor. Eve's father preferred to stay behind and play checkers with some other men on the beach. There was a big cement square with a checkerboard painted on it, a roof protecting it but no walls, and there, even in the rain, the men moved oversized checkers around in a deliberate way, with long poles. Eve's brother watched them or went swimming unsupervised—he was older. That was all gone now—the cement, even, was gone, or something had been built right on top of it. The hotel with its verandas extending over the sand was gone, and the railway station with its flower beds spelling out the name of the village. The railway tracks too. Instead there was a fake-old-fashioned mall with the satisfactory new supermarket and wineshop and boutiques for leisure wear and country crafts.

When she was quite small and wore a great hair bow on top of her head, Eve was fond of these country expeditions. She ate tiny jam tarts and cakes whose frosting was stiff on top and soft underneath, topped with a bleeding maraschino cherry. She was not allowed to touch the dishes or the lace-and-satin pincushions or the sallow-looking old dolls, and the women's conversations passed over her head with a temporary and mildly depressing effect, like the inevitable clouds. But she enjoyed riding in the backseat imagining herself on horseback or in a royal coach. Later on she refused to go. She began to hate trailing along with her mother and being identified as her mother's daughter. My daughter, Eve. How richly condescending, how mistakenly possessive, that voice sounded in her ears. (She was to use it, or some version of it, for years as a staple in some of her broadest, least accomplished acting.) She detested also her mother's habit of dressing up, wearing large hats and gloves in the country, and sheer dresses on which there were raised flowers, like warts. The oxford shoes, on the other hand—they were worn to favor her mother's corns—appeared embarrassingly stout and shabby.

"What did you hate most about your mother?" was a game that Eve would play with her friends in her first years free of home.

"Corsets," one girl would say, and another would say, "Wet aprons."

Hair nets. Fat arms. Bible quotations. "Danny Boy."

Eve always said. "Her corns."

She had forgotten all about this game until recently. The thought of it now was like touching a bad tooth.

Ahead of them the truck slowed and without signalling turned into a long tree-lined lane. Eve said, "I can't follow them any farther, Philip," and drove on. But as she passed the lane she noticed the gateposts. They were unusual, being shaped something like crude minarets and decorated with whitewashed pebbles and bits of colored glass. Neither one of them was straight, and they were half hidden by goldenrod and wild carrot, so that they had lost all reality as gateposts and looked instead like lost stage props from some gaudy operetta. The minute she saw them Eve remembered something else—a whitewashed outdoor wall in which there were pictures set. The pictures were stiff, fantastic, childish scenes. Churches with spires, castles with towers, square houses with square, lopsided, yellow windows. Triangular Christmas trees and tropical-colored birds half as big as the trees, a fat horse with dinky legs and burning red eyes, curly blue rivers, like lengths of ribbon, a moon and drunken stars and fat sunflowers nodding over the roofs of houses. All of this made of pieces of colored glass set into cement or plaster. She had seen it, and it wasn't in any public place. It was out in the country, and she had been with her mother. The shape of her mother loomed in front of the wall—she was talking to an old farmer. He might only have been her mother's age, of course, and looked old to Eve.

Her mother and the hotel woman did go to look at odd things on those trips; they didn't just look at antiques. They had gone to see a shrub cut to resemble a bear, and an orchard of dwarf apple trees.

Eve didn't remember the gateposts at all, but it seemed to her that they could not have belonged to any other place. She backed the car and swung around into the narrow track beneath the trees. The trees were heavy old Scotch pines, probably dangerous—you could see dangling half-dead branches, and branches that had already blown down or fallen down were lying in the grass and weeds on either side of the track. The car rocked back and forth in the ruts, and it seemed that Daisy approved of this motion. She began to make an accompanying noise. *Whoppy. Whoppy. Whoppy.*

This was something Daisy might remember—all she might remember—of this day. The arched trees, the sudden shadow, the interesting motion of the car. Maybe the white faces of the wild carrot that brushed at the windows. The sense of Philip beside her—his incomprehensible serious excitement, the tingling of his childish voice brought under unnatural control. A much vaguer sense of Eve—bare, freckly, sun-wrinkled arms, gray-blond frizzy curls held back by a black hairband. Maybe a smell. Not of cigarettes anymore, or of the touted creams and cosmetics on which Eve once spent so much of her money. Old skin? Garlic? Wine? Mouthwash? Eve might be dead when Daisy remembered this. Daisy and Philip might be estranged. Eve had not spoken to her own brother for three years. Not since he said to her on the phone, "You shouldn't have become an actress if you weren't equipped to make a better go of it."

There wasn't any sign of a house ahead, but through a gap in the trees the skeleton of a barn rose up, walls gone, beams intact, roof whole but flopping to one side like a funny hat. There seemed to be pieces of machinery, old cars or trucks, scattered around it, in the sea of flowering weeds. Eve had not much leisure to look—she was busy controlling the car on this rough track. The green truck had disappeared ahead of her—how far could it have gone? Then she saw that the lane curved. It curved; they left the shade of the pines and were out in the sunlight. The same sea foam of wild carrot, the same impression of rusting junk strewed about. A high wild hedge to one side, and there was the house, finally, behind it. A big house, two stories of yellowish-gray brick, an attic story of wood, its dormer windows stuffed with dirty foam rubber. One of the lower windows shone with aluminum foil covering it on the inside.

She had come to the wrong place. She had no memory of this house. There was no wall here around mown grass. Saplings grew up at random in the weeds.

The truck was parked ahead of her. And ahead of that she could see a patch of cleared ground where gravel had been spread and where she could have turned the car around. But she couldn't get past the truck to do that. She had to stop, too. She wondered if the man in the truck had stopped where he did on purpose, so that she would have to explain herself. He was now getting out of the truck in a leisurely way. Without looking at her, he released the dog, which had been running back and forth and barking with a great deal of angry spirit. Once on the ground, it continued to bark, but didn't leave the man's side. The man wore a cap that shaded his face, so that Eve could not see his expression. He stood by the truck looking at them, not yet deciding to come any closer.

Eve unbuckled her seat belt.

"Don't get out," said Philip. "Stay in the car. Turn around. Drive away."

"I can't," said Eve. "It's all right. That dog's just a yapper, he won't hurt me."

"Don't get out."

She should never have let that game get so far out of control. A child of Philip's age could get too carried away. "This isn't part of the game," she said. "He's just a man."

"I know," said Philip. "But *don't get out.*"

"Stop that," said Eve, and got out and shut the door.

"Hi," she said. "I'm sorry. I made a mistake. I thought this was somewhere else."

The man said something like "Hey."

"I was actually looking for another place," said Eve. "It was a place where I came once when I was a little girl. There was a wall with pictures on it all made with pieces of broken glass. I think a cement wall, whitewashed. When I saw those pillars by the road, I thought this must be it. You must have thought we were following you. It sounds so silly."

She heard the car door open. Philip got out, dragging Daisy behind him. Eve thought he had come to be close to her, and she put out her arm to welcome him. But he detached himself from Daisy and circled round Eve and spoke to the man. He had brought himself out of the alarm of a moment before and now he seemed steadier than Eve was.

"Is your dog friendly?" he said in a challenging way.

"She won't hurt you," the man said. "Long as I'm here, she's okay. She gets in a tear because she's not no more than a pup. She's still not no more than a pup."

He was a small man, no taller than Eve. He was wearing jeans and one of those open vests of colorful weave, made in Peru or Guatemala. Gold chains and medallions sparkled on his hairless, tanned, and muscular chest. When he spoke he threw his head back and Eve could see that his face was older than his body. Some front teeth were missing.

"We won't bother you anymore," she said. "Philip, I was just telling this man we drove down this road looking for a place I came when I was a little girl, and there were pictures made of colored glass set in a wall. But I made a mistake, this isn't the place."

"What's its name?" said Philip.

"Trixie," the man said, and on hearing her name the dog jumped up and bumped his arm. He swatted her down. "I don't know about no pictures. I don't live here. Harold, he's the one would know."

"It's all right," said Eve, and hoisted Daisy up on her hip. "If you could just move the truck ahead, then I could turn around."

"I don't know no pictures. See, if they was in the front part the house I never would've saw them because Harold, he's got the front part of the house shut off."

"No, they were outside," said Eve. "It doesn't matter. This was years and years ago."

"Yeah. Yeah. Yeah," the man was saying, warming to the conversation. "You come in and get Harold to tell you about it. You know Harold? He's who owns it here. Mary, she owns it, but Harold he put her in the Home, so now he does. It wasn't his fault, she had to go there." He reached into the truck and took out two cases of beer. "I just had to go to town, Harold sent me into town. You go on. You go in. Harold be glad to see you.

"Here Trixie," said Philip sternly.

The dog came yelping and bounding around them. Daisy squealed with fright and pleasure and somehow they were all on the route to the house, Eve carrying Daisy, and Philip and Trixie scrambling around her up some earthen bumps that had once been steps. The man came close behind them, smelling of the beer that he must have been drinking in the truck.

"Open it up, go ahead in," he said. "Make your way through. You don't mind it's got a little untidy here? Mary's in the Home, nobody to keep it tidied up like it used to be."

Massive disorder was what they had to make their way through—the kind that takes years to accumulate. The bottom layer of it made up of chairs and tables and couches and perhaps a stove or two, with old bedclothes and newspapers and window shades and dead potted plants and ends of lumber and empty bottles and broken lighting fixtures and curtain rods piled on top of that, up to the ceiling in some places, blocking nearly all the light from outside. To make up for that, a light was burning by the inside door.

The man shifted the beer and got that door open, and shouted for Harold. It was hard to tell what sort of room they were in now—there were kitchen cupboards with the doors off the hinges, some cans on the shelves, but there were also a couple of cots with bare mattresses and rumpled blankets. The windows were so successfully covered up with furniture or hanging quilts that you could not tell where they were, and the smell was that of a junk store, a plugged sink, or maybe a plugged toilet, cooking and grease and cigarettes and human sweat and dog mess and unremoved garbage.

Nobody answered the shouts. Eve turned around—there was room to turn around here, as there hadn't been in the porch—and said, "I don't think we should—" but Trixie got in her way and the man ducked round her to bang on another door.

"Here he is," he said—still at the top of his voice, though the door had opened. "Here's Harold in here." At the same time Trixie rushed forward, and another man's voice said, "Fuck. Get that dog out of here."

"Lady here wants to see some pictures," the little man said. Trixie whined in pain—somebody had kicked her. Eve had no choice but to go on into the room.

This was a dining room. There was the heavy old dining-room table and the substantial chairs. Three men were sitting down, playing cards. The fourth man had got up to kick the dog. The temperature in the room was about ninety degrees.

"Shut the door, there's a draft," said one of the men at the table.

The little man hauled Trixie out from under the table and threw her into the outer room, then closed the door behind Eve and the children.

"Christ. Fuck," said the man who had got up. His chest and arms were so heavily tattooed that he seemed to have purple or bluish skin. He shook one foot as if it hurt. Perhaps he had also kicked a table leg when he kicked Trixie.

Sitting with his back to the door was a young man with sharp narrow shoulders and a delicate neck. At least Eve assumed he was young, because he wore his hair in dyed golden spikes and had gold rings in his ears. He didn't turn around. The man across from him was as old as Eve herself, and had a shaved head, a tidy gray beard, and bloodshot blue eyes. He looked at Eve without any friendliness but with some intelligence or comprehension, and in this he was unlike the tattooed man, who had looked at her as if she was some kind of hallucination that he had decided to ignore.

At the end of the table, in the host's or the father's chair, sat the man who had given the order to close the door, but who hadn't looked up or otherwise paid any attention to the interruption. He was a large-boned, fat, pale man with sweaty brown curls, and as far as Eve could tell he was entirely naked. The tattooed man and the blond man were wearing jeans, and the gray-bearded man was wearing jeans and a checked shirt buttoned up to the neck and a string tie. There were glasses and bottles on the table. The man in the host's chair—he must be Harold—and the gray-bearded man were drinking whiskey. The other two were drinking beer.

"I told her maybe there was pictures in the front but she couldn't go in there you got that shut up," the little man said.

Harold said, "You shut up."

Eve said, "I'm really sorry." There seemed to be nothing to do but go into her spiel, enlarging it to include staying at the village hotel as a little girl, drives with her mother, the pictures in the wall, her memory of them today, the gateposts, her obvious mistake, her apologies. She spoke directly to the graybeard, since he seemed the only one willing to listen or capable of understanding her. Her arm and shoulder ached from the weight of Daisy and from the tension which had got hold of her entire body. Yet she was thinking how she would describe this—she'd say it was like finding yourself in the middle of a Pinter play. Or like all her nightmares of a stolid, silent, hostile audience.

The graybeard spoke when she could not think of any further charming or apologetic thing to say. He said, "I don't know. You'll have to ask Harold. Hey. Hey Harold. Do you know anything about some pictures made out of broken glass?"

"Tell her when she was riding around looking at pictures I wasn't even born yet," said Harold, without looking up.

"You're out of luck, lady," said the graybeard.

The tattooed man whistled. "Hey you," he said to Philip. "Hey kid. Can you play the piano?"

There was a piano in the room behind Harold's chair. There was no stool or bench—Harold himself taking up most of the room between the piano and the table—and inappropriate things, such as plates and overcoats, were piled on top of it, as they were on every surface in the house.

"No," said Eve quickly. "No he can't."

"I'm asking him," the tattooed man said. "Can you play a tune?"

The graybeard said, "Let him alone."

"Just asking if he can play a tune, what's the matter with that?"

"Let him alone."

"You see I can't move until somebody moves the truck," Eve said.

She thought, There is a smell of semen in this room.

Philip was mute, pressed against her side.

"If you could just move—" she said turning and expecting to find the little man behind her. She stopped when she saw he wasn't there, he wasn't in the room at all, he had got out without her knowing when. What if he had locked the door?

She put her hand on the knob and it turned, the door opened with a little difficulty and a scramble on the other side of it. The little man had been crouched right there, listening.

Eve went out without speaking to him, out through the kitchen, Philip trotting along beside her like the most tractable little boy in the world. Along the narrow pathway on the porch, through the junk, and when they reached the open air she sucked it in, not having taken a real breath for a long time.

"You ought to go along down the road ask down at Harold's cousin's place," the little man's voice came after her. "They got a nice place. They got a new house, she keeps it beautiful. They'll show you pictures or anything you want, they'll make you welcome. They'll sit you down and feed you, they don't let nobody go away empty."

He couldn't have been crouched against the door all the time, because he had moved the truck. Or somebody had. It had disappeared altogether, been driven away to some shed or parking spot out of sight.

Eve ignored him. She got Daisy buckled in. Philip was buckling himself in, without having to be reminded. Trixie appeared from somewhere and walked around the car in a disconsolate way, sniffing at the tires.

Eve got in and closed the door, put her sweating hand on the key. The car started, she pulled ahead onto the gravel—a space that was surrounded by thick bushes, berry bushes she supposed, and old lilacs, as well as weeds. In places these bushes had been flattened by piles of old tires and bottles and tin cans. It was hard to think that things had been thrown out of that house, considering all that was left in it, but apparently they had, and as Eve swung the car around she saw, revealed by this flattening, some fragment of a wall, to which bits of whitewash still clung.

She thought she could see pieces of glass embedded there, glinting.

She didn't slow down to look. She hoped Philip hadn't noticed—he might want to stop. She got the car pointed towards the lane and drove past the dirt steps to the house. The little man stood there with both arms waving and Trixie was wagging her tail, roused from her scared docility sufficiently to bark farewell and chase them part-way down the lane. The chase was only a formality; she could have caught up with them if she wanted to. Eve had had to slow down at once when she hit the ruts.

She was driving so slowly that it was possible, it was easy, for a figure to rise up out of the tall weeds on the passenger side of the car and open the door—which Eve had not thought of locking—and jump in.

It was the blond man who had been sitting at the table, the one whose face she had never seen.

"Don't be scared. Don't be scared anybody. I just wondered if I could hitch a ride with you guys, okay?"

It wasn't a man or a boy; it was a girl. A girl now wearing a dirty sort of undershirt.

Eve said, "Okay." She had just managed to hold the car in the track.

"I couldn't ask you back in the house," the girl said. "I went in the bathroom and got out the window and run out here. They probably don't even know I'm gone yet. They're boiled." She took hold of a handful of the undershirt which was much too large for her and sniffed at it. "Stinks," she said. "I just grabbed this of Harold's, was in the bathroom. Stinks."

Eve left the ruts, the darkness of the lane, and turned onto the ordinary road. "Jesus I'm glad to get out of there," the girl said. "I didn't know nothing about what I was getting into. I didn't know even how I got there, it was night. It wasn't no place for me. You know what I mean?"

"They seemed pretty drunk all right," said Eve.

"Yeah. Well. I'm sorry if I scared you."

"That's okay."

"If I hadn't've jumped in I thought you wouldn't stop for me. Would you?"

"I don't know," said Eve. "I guess I would have if it got through to me you were a girl. I didn't really get a look at you before."

"Yeah. I don't look like much now. I look like shit now. I'm not saying I don't like to party. I like to party. But there's party and there's party, you know what I mean?"

She turned in the seat and looked at Eve so steadily that Eve had to take her eyes from the road for a moment and look back. And what she saw was that this girl was much more drunk than she sounded. Her dark-brown eyes were glazed but held wide open, rounded with effort, and they had the imploring yet distant expression that drunks' eyes get, a kind of last-ditch insistence on fooling you. Her skin was blotched in some places and ashy in others, her whole face crumpled with the effects of a mighty bingeing. She was a natural brunette—the gold spikes were intentionally and provocatively dark at the roots—and pretty enough, if you disregarded her present dinginess, to make you wonder how she had ever got mixed up with Harold and Harold's crew. Her way of living and the style of the times must have taken fifteen or twenty natural pounds off her—but she wasn't tall and she really wasn't boyish. Her true inclination was to be a cuddly chunky girl, a darling dumpling.

"Herb was crazy bringing you in there like that," she said. "He's got a screw loose, Herb."

Eve said, "I gathered that."

"I don't know what he does around there, I guess he works for Harold. I don't think Harold uses him too good, neither."

Eve had never believed herself to be attracted to women in a sexual way. And this girl in her soiled and crumpled state seemed unlikely to appeal to anybody. But perhaps the girl did not believe this possible—she must be so used to appealing to people. At any rate she slid her hand along Eve's bare thigh, just getting a little way beyond the hem of her shorts. It was a practiced move, drunk as she was. To spread the fingers, to grasp flesh on the first try, would have been too much. A practiced, automatically hopeful move, yet so lacking in any true, strong, squirmy, comradely lust that Eve felt that the hand might easily have fallen short and caressed the car upholstery.

"I'm okay," the girl said, and her voice, like the hand, struggled to put herself and Eve on a new level of intimacy. "You know what I mean? You understand me. Okay?"

"Of course," said Eve briskly, and the hand trailed away, its tired whore's courtesy done with. But it had not failed—not altogether. Blatant and halfhearted as it was, it had been enough to set some old wires twitching.

And the fact that it could be effective in any way at all filled Eve with misgiving, flung a shadow backwards from this moment over all the rowdy and impulsive as well as all the hopeful and serious, the more or less unrepented-of, couplings of her life. Not a real flare-up of shame, a sense of sin—just a dirty shadow. What a joke on her, if she started to hanker now after a purer past and a cleaner slate.

But it could be just that still, and always, she hankered after love.

She said, "Where is it you want to go?"

The girl jerked backwards, faced the road. She said, "Where you going? You live around here?" The blurred tone of seductiveness had changed, as no doubt it would change after sex, into a mean-sounding swagger.

"There's a bus goes through the village," Eve said. "It stops at the gas station. I've seen the sign."

"Yeah but just one thing," the girl said. "I got no money. See, I got away from there in such a hurry I never got to collect my money. So what use would it be me getting on a bus without no money?"

The thing to do was not to recognize a threat. Tell her that she could hitchhike, if she had no money. It wasn't likely that she had a gun in her jeans. She just wanted to sound as if she might have one.

But a knife?

The girl turned for the first time to look into the backseat.

"You kids okay back there?" she said.

No answer.

"They're cute," she said. "They shy with strangers?"

How stupid of Eve to think about sex, when the reality, the danger, were elsewhere.

Eve's purse was on the floor of the car in front of the girl's feet. She didn't know how much money was in it. Sixty, seventy dollars. Hardly more. If she offered money for a ticket the girl would name an expensive destination. Montreal. Or at least Toronto. If she said, "Just take what's there," the girl would see capitulation. She would sense Eve's fear and might try to push further. What was the best she could do? Steal the car? If she left Eve and the children beside the road, the police would be after her in a hurry. If she left them dead in some thicket, she might get farther. Or if she took them along while she needed them, a knife against Eve's side or a child's throat.

Such things happen. But not as regularly as on television or in the movies. Such things don't often happen.

Eve turned onto the county road, which was fairly busy. Why did that make her feel better? Safety there was an illusion. She could be driving along the highway in the midst of the day's traffic taking herself and the children to their deaths.

The girl said, "Where's this road go?"

"It goes out to the main highway."

"Let's drive out there."

"That's where I am driving," Eve said.

"Which way's the highway go?"

"It goes north to Owen Sound or up to Tobermory where you get the boat. Or south to—I don't know. But it joins another highway, you can get to Sarnia. Or London. Or Detroit or Toronto if you keep going."

Nothing more was said until they reached the highway. Eve turned onto it and said, "This is it."

"Which way you heading now?"

"I'm heading north," Eve said.

"That the way you live then?"

"I'm going to the village. I'm going to stop for gas."

"You got gas," the girl said. "You got over half a tank."

That was stupid. Eve should have said groceries.

Beside her the girl let out a long groan of decision, maybe of relinquishment.

"You know," she said, "you know. I might as well get out here if I'm going to hitch a ride. I could get a ride here as easy as anyplace."

Eve pulled over onto the gravel. Relief was turning into something like shame. It was probably true that the girl had run away without collecting any money, that she had nothing. What was it like to be drunk, wasted, with no money, at the side of the road?

"Which way you said we're going?"

"North," Eve told her again.

"Which way you said to Sarnia?"

"South. Just cross the road, the cars'll be headed south. Watch out for the traffic."

"Sure," the girl said. Her voice was already distant; she was calculating new chances. She was half out of the car as she said, "See you." And into the backseat, "See you guys. Be good."

"Wait," said Eve. She leaned over and felt in her purse for her wallet, got out a twenty-dollar bill. She got out of the car and came round to where the girl was waiting. "Here," she said. "This'll help you."

"Yeah. Thanks," the girl said, stuffing the bill in her pocket, her eyes on the road.

"Listen," said Eve. "If you're stranded I'll tell you where my house is. It's about two miles north of the village and the village is about half a mile north of here. North. This way. My family's there now, but they should be gone by evening, if that bothers you. It's got the name Ford on the mailbox. That's not my name, I don't know why it's there. It's all by itself in the middle of a field. It's got one ordinary window on one side of the front door and a funny-looking little window on the other. That's where they put in the bathroom."

"Yeah," the girl said.

"It's just that I thought, if you don't get a ride—"

"Okay," the girl said. "Sure."

When they had started driving again, Philip said, "Yuck. She smelled like vomit."

A little farther on he said, "She didn't even know you should look at the sun to tell directions. She was stupid. Wasn't she?"

"I guess so," Eve said.

"Yuck. I never ever saw anybody so stupid."

As they went through the village he asked if they could stop for ice-cream cones. Eve said no.

"There's so many people stopping for ice cream it's hard to find a place to park," she said. "We've got enough ice cream at home."

"You shouldn't say 'home,'" said Philip. "It's just where we're staying. You should say 'the house.'"

The big hay rolls in a field to the east of the highway were facing ends-on into the sun, so tightly packed they looked like shields or gongs or faces of Aztec metal. Past that was a field of pale soft gold tails or feathers.

"That's called barley, that gold stuff with the tails on it," she said to Philip.

He said, "I know."

"The tails are called beards sometimes." She began to recite, "'But the reapers, reaping early, in among the bearded barley—'"

Daisy said, "What does mean 'pearly'?"

Philip said, "Bar-ley."

"'Only reapers, reaping early,'" Eve said. She tried to remember. "'Save the reapers, reaping early—'" "Save" was what sounded best. Save the reapers.

Sophie and Ian had bought corn at a roadside stand. It was for dinner. Plans had changed—they weren't leaving till morning. And they had bought a bottle of gin and some tonic and limes. Ian made the drinks while Eve and Sophie sat husking the corn. Eve said, "Two dozen. That's crazy."

"Wait and see," said Sophie. "Ian loves corn."

Ian bowed when he presented Eve with her drink, and after she had tasted it she said, "This is most heavenly."

Ian wasn't much as she had remembered or pictured him. He was not tall, Teutonic, humorless. He was a slim fair-haired man of medium height, quick moving, companionable. Sophie was less assured, more tentative in all she said and did, than she had seemed since she'd been here. But happier, too.

Eve told her story. She began with the checkerboard on the beach, the vanished hotel, the drives into the country. It included her mother's city-lady outfits, her sheer dresses and matching slips, but not the young Eve's feelings of repugnance. Then the things they went to see—the dwarf orchard, the shelf of old dolls, the marvellous pictures made of colored glass.

"They were a little like Chagall?" Eve said.

Ian said, "Yep. Even us urban geographers know about Chagall."

Eve said, "Sor-ry." Both laughed.

Now the gateposts, the sudden memory, the dark lane and ruined barn and rusted machinery, the house a shambles.

"The owner was in there playing cards with his friends," Eve said. "He didn't know anything about it. Didn't know or didn't care. And my God, it could have been nearly sixty years ago I was there—think of that."

Sophie said, "Oh, Mom. What a shame." She was glowing with relief to see Ian and Eve getting on so well together.

"Are you sure it was even the right place?" she said.

"Maybe not," said Eve. "Maybe not."

She would not mention the fragment of wall she had seen beyond the bushes. Why bother, when there were so many things she thought best not to mention? First, the game that she had got Philip playing, overexciting him. And nearly everything about Harold and his companions. Everything, every single thing about the girl who had jumped into the car.

There are people who carry decency and optimism around with them, who seem to cleanse every atmosphere they settle in, and you can't tell such people things, it is too disruptive. Ian struck Eve as being one of those people, in spite of his present graciousness, and Sophie as being someone who thanked her lucky stars that she had found him. It used to be older people who claimed this protection from you, but now it seemed more and more to be younger people, and someone like Eve had to try not to reveal how she was stranded in between. Her whole life liable to be seen as some sort of unseemly thrashing around, a radical mistake.

She could say that the house smelled vile, and that the owner and his friends looked altogether boozy and disreputable, but not that Harold was naked and never that she herself was afraid. And never what she was afraid of.

Philip was in charge of gathering up the corn husks and carrying them outside to throw them along the edge of the field. Occasionally Daisy picked up a few on her own, and took them off to be distributed around the house. Philip had added nothing to Eve's story and had not seemed to be concerned with the telling of it. But once it was told, and Ian (interested in bringing this local anecdote into line with his professional studies) was asking Eve what she knew about the breakup of older patterns of village and rural life, about the spread of what was called agribusiness, Philip did look up from his stooping and crawling work around the adults' feet. He looked at Eve. A flat look, a moment of conspiratorial blankness, a buried smile, that passed before there could be any need for recognition of it. What did this mean? Only that he had begun the private work of storing and secreting, deciding on his own what should be preserved and how, and what these things were going to mean to him, in his unknown future.

If the girl came looking for her, they would all still be here. Then Eve's carefulness would go for nothing.

The girl wouldn't come. Much better offers would turn up before she'd stood ten minutes by the highway. More dangerous offers perhaps, but more interesting, likely to be more profitable.

The girl wouldn't come. Unless she found some homeless, heartless wastrel of her own age. *(I know where there's a place we can stay, if we can get rid of the old lady.)*

Not tonight but tomorrow night Eve would lie down in this hollowed-out house, its board walls like a paper shell around her, willing herself to grow light, relieved of consequence, with nothing in her head but the rustle of the deep tall corn which might have stopped growing now but still made its live noise after dark.

Antonya Nelson (1961–)

was born in Wichita, Kansas, daughter of two English professors at Wichita State University (her father was among the first scholars in the country to write a master's thesis on William Faulkner). "I was given a lot of freedom in terms of what I read and what I was exposed to," Nelson told The Atlantic Monthly. *"I read all the time, and because the house was so full of books—trashy books as well as literature—I was given free range of everything from pornography to Baudelaire." She attended the University of Kansas and at twenty-two won* Mademoiselle *magazine's young writers contest. She received an MFA from the University of Arizona in 1986, and the next year Raymond Carver chose her story "The Expendables" as the first-prize winner in the anthology* American Fiction 88.

*Three years later, that story was the title story of her first book. She has followed that with three other story collections—*In the Land of Men, Family Terrorists, *and* Female Trouble*—and three novels—*Talking in Bed, Nobody's Girl, *and* Living to Tell. *She lives in Houston, Texas, and Telluride, Colorado, and teaches creative writing in the Warren Wilson MFA Program as well as at the University of Houston. She is married to the writer Robert Boswell, with whom she has two children.*

INTRODUCTION BY **Charles Baxter**

What amazes me about Antonya Nelson's stories is what might be called the "sandwich effect." When we write stories, most of us follow our characters through a succession of scenes more or less in a straight line. If we have to bring up the past, we usually drop in a flashback. But in Nelson's expertly counterpointed stories, events are layered on top of one another like the contents of a sandwich, except that the contents this time are events in the present squeezed together with events in the past, as if the past is still vibrantly alive in the present and is nestled next to it. The past isn't really the past in these stories. It hasn't gone away. It's right *here, now.*

A second feature that the stories share is that a seemingly minor event is placed in front of you and therefore seems large, and a huge event is placed in the back of the story and therefore seems small, even though it isn't. This is the reverse of what we usually think of as storytellers' logic and the reverse of what's often done in the movies for melodramatic effect. In "The Control Group," for example, TV Mitchell's love for his fourth-grade teacher is in the front of the story. That's the big thing, and it seems fairly ordinary. Kids fall in love with their teachers all the time. But in the second paragraph, we find out that TV is a murderer's child: His mother killed TV's grandfather with a hammer. That's the background that never goes away. It has taken on an almost matter-of-fact quality for TV, a terrible event that he has to reduce in size as part of his life if he's going to go on living, undestroyed by what was not his own doing. That event is the key to his desperation.

But the story isn't called "The Murderer's Child" or "The Boy Who Loved His Teacher." Its title is "The Control Group," which alerts us to another story buried amidst these other stories: the story of two pet rats in the classroom given different diets—one healthy, the other full of sugary junk. One animal thrives; the other sickens. What does this have to do with TV? The story never announces its metaphoric or symbolic meaning (it is much too subtle for that), but the meaning is there, right in front of you—as are the common accidents of life, and TV's panic and forgetfulness, and the beautiful gesture that ends the story that unites both the present and the past. The story is finally about how love makes us desperate, and its central dramatic arc involves a date for lunch between a boy and his teacher. In the background are violence and craziness, but in the foreground is the most terrible and ordinary thing: a boy who has lost his money.

Notice how, this sandwich effect—a bad phrase, but it's what I mean—works in "Naked Ladies." Right in front of us is a seemingly ordinary event, the Easter Frolic party hosted by Mr. House, which the central character, Laura, must attend with her mother, who is the hired nanny (my phrase, not the story's) for the House children. But the party is rather peculiar, as the reader soon discovers, and the artwork in the House house is in effect a bizarre clue to the past and what might still exist in the present. This artwork gradually reveals the second story, one much larger than the one we've been introduced to, though it stays resolutely in the background; and it brings to the surface a desperation in the main characters we might never had guessed they would have.

Love and obsession, come to think of it, are the pivots for all three of these tales. Four almost simultaneous stories make up the story "Female Trouble," the story of McBride-and-Daisy, the story of McBride-and-Martha, and the story of McBride-and-Claire. There is also the story of Martha-and-Daisy, which McBride sees only in glimpses. Readers may be forgiven if they occasionally get the women mixed up. So does McBride, whose problem is that he regards all women as generic. In this story, the interior stories are sandwiched so closely together that they induce confusion in McBride, who can't keep them, or his women, straight. He goes from woman to woman, calmly seeding disaster and walking away when it happens. In McBride, lust is triggered by pity, a terrible combination. He is a desperately destructive man, of course, who regards women as desperately destructive themselves; here the foreground/background switching effect moves the highly charged and almost melodramatic acts of madness into the deep background (where they seem quiet and small) and the smaller events, such as the birth of a child, into the foreground, where they seem impossibly huge and unmanageable, especially to McBride.

The truth is, almost every good story consists of several stories happening at once. The trick is in seeing the correspondences and similarities among the various stories and combining them into one coherent narrative. Every one of Antonya Nelson's stories is a concatenation of events viewed almost simultaneously in place and time by someone who seems to see *through* one story to the story beneath it. The result is a set of stories so lively and passionate and mindful that you must read them slowly, savoring as you go, because even as you are going forward, you are going back.

For Charles Baxter's bio, see page 231.

Antonya Nelson

The Control Group

TV Mitchell fell in love with his fourth-grade teacher. An odd and uncomfortable prospect, his love was a secret he confessed to nobody, not that there was anybody he could have confessed to, and not that he quite understood his feelings as, in fact, ones of love. He knew simply an unbearable ache like illness, the knot in his gut Mrs. Dugas could tie and twist with such torque he thought he might, quite literally, die.

And TV, alone among his nine-year-old peers at Hamilton Elementary, *did* comprehend death. Unlike his baffling love for his fifty-two-year-old teacher, he spoke freely about that which he understood. His mother had murdered her father, TV's grandfather. TV's tale did not differ substantially from the other gruesome stories heard over lunch from the boys' corner of the playground, but his had the unbeatable edge of truth. The others might escalate their stakes, recount babysitters finding dripping blood in the bath or vampires under the bed, phone calls from hatchet-bearing mental escapees, timely electrical blackouts, hairy hands sprouting from the seeming innocence of wing chairs or garden spigots.

But they couldn't outdo TV's penetrating simplicity. "She pounded him with a hammer," he told the boys. They stood scuffing dirt, hands balled in front pockets. "She stuffed a handkerchief in his mouth," TV went on, "to keep him quiet." He carried the handkerchief with him for further drama, its pure whiteness and ancient embroidered monogram somehow proof enough. TVM, his grandfather's and his own initials, the navy threads worn nearly away under TV's worrying fingertips. A single blow to the forehead, a round blue contusion meant to resemble a bruise from an accidental fall.

Mrs. Dugas's classroom was a portable annex set off from the rest of the school. Her students studied, primarily, animals. There were tanks of fish and gerbils and mice and miniature frogs and little chicks who'd been hatched from plain eggs under a heat lamp. Those eggs that did not result in chicks were buried outside the annex, cracked open and poured into a hole deep enough to discourage roaming dogs. Embryonic beaks and feet could be identified floating in the bloody yolk. A snapping turtle had once escaped from Mrs. Dugas's room and now lived beneath the annex. When the class read, they read about the migration of loons, or about panda bears whose babies were so small they could get lost in their own mothers' fur. History was the study of those animals who were now extinct. Mrs. Dugas taught evolution, made all the children remove their shoes and contemplate their fifth, finlike, useless little toes, which would someday disappear. Her favorite subject was science. The same day TV had stepped into her classroom, Mrs. Dugas introduced two rats who would help the students understand the dangers of Coke and potato chips and candy bars.

They wrote in their experiment diaries. One rat would be given vegetables and cheese and milk; the other would eat Bugles and Froot Loops and Orange Crush. TV was grateful for the rats, as they held the attention that otherwise would surely have been directed toward him. The children named the control rat Batman and the junk-food rat Joker. On Friday afternoons the animals were packed off to different homes, each child promising to maintain the experiment.

The changes came quickly, Joker's white coat turning slightly gray, his tail losing its pink, his eyes their shine. TV had thought neither of the rats especially handsome but eventually, by comparison, Joker became ugly. Batman continued to look the way he had. Bigger, better. They sat in their two cages, next to each other, one eating an apple wedge, one a Frito. Both rats spent most of their time standing on their hind legs reaching for the screens that kept them caged. TV had noted that, though Joker *looked* worse, he didn't seem to *feel* worse. Moreover, it was Batman, the rat named as control, who ate the more exotic diet. TV couldn't remember when he himself had last eaten a raw vegetable. But, of course, that was Mrs. Dugas's point. When TV's turn came to take home a rat, he was happy to get Joker. He cheated, poking into the cage little cubes of cheddar cheese and a nutritious piece of wheat toast. Joker obliged by eating whatever was shoved his way. TV had worried Mrs. Dugas would not give him an opportunity with a rat. It seemed natural to him that she might have reservations concerning his character. But though he looked for fretfulness in her face the Friday he departed the annex with Joker in his traveling cage, she did not reveal any.

That weekend the temperature dropped into the negative. TV, believing Joker needed more space to move, turned him loose in a large cardboard box that had once held a microwave oven. He reinforced the top flaps with three volumes of the encyclopedia to make sure he wouldn't escape. In the morning he found the rat frozen, curled in what he assumed was a death position. He immediately thought of fleeing; he could not face Mrs. Dugas. Screaming his foster mother's name, he ran to her bedroom. He made note of the fact that he could see his breath.

"He can't have frozen," his foster mother told him, groggily following to the box. The rat lay where he'd been, scraggly and dead. His foster mother squatted, laying her forefinger warily on the animal's chest.

"Hibernation," she diagnosed after a moment. She carried the box to the floor heat register in the hallway and set it down. "He'll thaw," she assured TV, then giggled. "I'd like to call the landlord and tell him even the rats are freezing."

But TV found nothing about the situation comical. He watched Joker slowly come to. When he fed him, later, he made sure the food was bad, a lidful of red wine, a few chocolate chips.

In the end no gesture would have made any impression whatsoever. At the conclusion of the experiment, Week 10, a man from a lab came and took both rats away. TV was shocked. He had assumed the next step would be to rehabilitate Joker, record in their diaries the bringing back of his shiny eyes and coat. The class asked if they couldn't take the rats home to keep as pets. Mrs. Dugas explained that experimental animals had to be destroyed. Joker and Batman went together. As consolation, Joker's leftover box of Cracker Jacks was passed around the room for the kids to eat.

TV's new foster mother said, "I wonder which lesson will stick? You Are What You Eat? or, Life Sucks?"

But TV began loving Mrs. Dugas then, trusting her to judge him without sentimentality. She did not, it was clear, feel sorry for anyone.

★ ★ ★

TV had moved in with his new foster mother just three months ago. He was, actually, unsure he would stay with her. The last foster arrangement had not worked out; the committee deciding his future had tried an opposite approach this time, placing him not with a large family, as he had been last time, but with a single woman. This was intended to replicate his natural situation, though in his real life he had also lived with his grandfather. Joanne Link, his new parent, had another month left on trial time. She could turn him back, he understood that. He was trying to behave. She was preferable, mostly, by default. TV felt Joanne sometimes watching him. They had discussed his mother a few times, approaching the subject delicately, Joanne only too eager to back off. She did not ask him questions point blank, pretending she wasn't interested in the details. For instance, TV had heard his mother and her boyfriend Wade planning to kill TV's grandfather. The old man had been sick for a long time, peeing his bed and screaming at people. In more lucid moments, he would apologize, saying, "I forget myself." Wade wanted to inject him with an air bubble. Apparently, air could kill you.

TV had stood on the landing in his old house listening to his grandfather wheeze in an upstairs room, his mother and Wade talking in a downstairs one. He had no idea what to do. His stealth in returning unheard to bed gave him a headache, which he nursed through the night into genuine illness. The next day, however, he did not want to remain at home with his grandfather, afraid he would be included in the conspiracy, participant or victim.

But his grandfather lived for months following TV's eavesdropping. TV had convinced himself it was a nightmare, had been on the verge of confessing this to his mother when he came home one day from school to find his whole life turned inside out; that is, what he'd held close and fought in himself suddenly was free, open to anyone's inspection.

Though Joanne sympathized with him, he could tell he made her nervous. She embarrassed easily and, when driven to exclamation, would not say *Shit!* but *Sugar!* She was likable, that way. But alien. She provided TV with a generous allowance and, on weekends, let him loose and seemed happy not to know what he did. They shared a small apartment in a dirty neighborhood miles and miles from Hamilton Elementary, which was by reputation one of the best schools in Wichita. TV rode the bus.

Mrs. Dugas made it standard policy to invite the children to her home once during the year. She lived near a drainage canal and after the twenty-two fourth graders had consumed Dixie cups of orange juice and a sesame rice cake each, a rabbit-watching expedition embarked. Three mothers—the drivers—opted to stay in Mrs. Dugas's living room with a tag-along toddler. Mrs. Dugas herself changed shoes and tied a peach chiffon scarf over her hair so that she could join the search.

"Do we frighten rabbits?" she asked the group before opening the gate between her tidy yard and the wild canal. It was late spring in Kansas, but the sky looked as if it could still threaten snow. Houses precisely like Mrs. Dugas's lined both sides of the cement-walled canal, and TV imagined them sliding in, crumpling, all of them except Mrs. Dugas's. The dank odor of stagnant water drifted in the air. "Do we frighten rabbits?"

"No," the girls in the class answered.

"Do we jab sticks in their homes or throw rocks at their tails?"

Again, the girls chimed no.

"Do we take nature as we find it, not as we wish to manipulate it?"

A few girls, shivering, eager to get on with the hunt, having sensed the general direction of this line of questioning, answered once more in the negative. Mrs. Dugas raised her eyebrows. TV's heart lurched; he could make out the little quiver her lip made toward smiling. It was her eyebrows, still black despite her silver hair, that most intrigued him. She knew something he wished to learn.

"Yes, yes," the girls amended.

Mrs. Dugas opened her gate. She had shared with them her secret method of watching the rabbits, the way she had discovered them years ago by coming to the canal to think—about what? TV wondered desperately—sitting down among the broken pieces of concrete and holding perfectly still until she became part of the picture, the life already there soon forgetting her presence and getting on with business. "They see the world differently," she told her class. "They rely on movement, on instinct." She could wiggle her nose, a gesture that meant disapproval. She could hear, from one end of her fourth grade annex to the other, the illicit whisper of notes being passed, of secrets on the verge of leaving lips. Hostile looks, cast between enemies, reflected unerringly from the satellite of her sharp eyes. TV would watch her eyebrows, the lift that signaled unspoken intercession.

He followed her down the canal. Some days it mattered to him what the boys thought but other days he couldn't remember to care. They had been a group since kindergarten, neighbors and Cub Scouts together, summer camp initiates. TV's acceptance into their midst was based on his mother's celebrity, his own frankness concerning her crime and incarceration. Around Mrs. Dugas he felt a twinge taking advantage of his mother's notoriety, so around her he pretended the boys had not accepted him. He pretended he had higher matters on his mind, the same matters, coincidentally, that Mrs. Dugas seemed to have on hers—rabbits, today, perhaps a pheasant.

True to her anecdotes in the classroom, Mrs. Dugas soon settled on a broken piece of concrete and proceeded to stop moving. She had changed her clear lenses for sunglasses. The last motion she made was to secure the chiffon scarf's knot under her chin. TV knelt a few yards from her. While she waited for rabbits, he stared at her.

On Tuesdays, after school, TV took his regular bus home, then boarded a city line to his psychologist's office in a medical complex that resembled a strip mall. For a while, the psychologist had discussed adopting him. Then his wife had gotten pregnant and the idea had been dropped. They talked about Joanne a lot, the psychologist making sure she was better than the last family, assuaging his own guilt. They'd made jokes about General Patton, the name they gave the father at the first home. TV's own name was not short for anything less ridiculous, simply TV. It was his mother's little joke on her father, whose name had been Terrence Valley Mitchell.

TV's psychologist liked the fact that Joanne was studying to be a psychiatric nurse, though he worried openly about her weak financial setup. "It's true you can't buy happiness," he told TV, "but you *can* buy better odds."

After their sessions, TV walked across the street to a Russell Stover candy shop and bought a chocolate turtle. Waiting for his bus home, he rewarded himself for another week safely passed.

★ ★ ★

During the time TV squatted in the dried weeds growing from the upended chunks of canal concrete at Mrs. Dugas's, he devised a plan. He would invite Mrs. Dugas to lunch next Saturday. He would take his saved allowance and meet her somewhere he could reach by bus. Soon it would be summer, he would leave her classroom forever. His love for her frightened him; he did not want to kiss her or see her naked. He did not know exactly what he wanted but he felt a hunger, a physical depth of daily need for her that was going to be denied him.

On the ride back to school, in the cramped quarters of a foreign station wagon, a few kids claimed to have seen rabbits. The boys, in fear, in respect, out of anger, asked TV if he'd seen any.

He shook his head, though in truth, he had. Mrs. Dugas, without turning around, had lifted her arm slowly so as not to seem out of keeping with the rest of the animal's picture, knowing TV was behind her, knowing he would follow the point. A small brown rabbit sat terrified between the rocks.

He phoned her while Joanne was still at the hospital, hanging up on her husband the first time, feeling ashamed when she answered—as if she knew—the second.

Before inviting her he thanked her for the orange juice. She told him, formally, perhaps with irritation, he was most welcome. He would have hung up if he had not heard her turn the receiver away and cough, once, a moist sound that carried through the line and gave TV a window of vulnerability, a shot.

"Can you go to lunch with me?" he asked. "At the . . ." he blinked hard at the Yellow Pages he'd found, the penciled line he'd drawn beneath the ideal establishment now invisible. "Depot!" he cried. "The Depot, on this Saturday, at twelve noon?"

Her pause sent sweat streaming down his ribs. He imagined a most amorphous Mr. Dugas turning a newspaper, receiving his wife's curious raised eyebrows with a smile. He heard the rustle of wild rabbits in the dry grass. TV sat on the floor heat register, the only square of warmth in the whole apartment, sat there in Joanne's director's chair asking his teacher for a date. The lead of the pencil in his hand snapped, the Yellow page tore, his rubber-soled hightop shoes melted onto the metal register and lifted the cover when he raised his feet. He panicked, thinking immediately of fire, of having to roll in the frayed and undersized Oriental carpet runner in the hall. The cover banged down in place just as Mrs. Dugas spoke.

"What?" TV nearly shouted. "I—"

She repeated, "I would be pleased."

He made a dry run on Friday after school. The day had been difficult, the subject of murder having come up during a lesson on buffaloes in the Wild West. But it came up everywhere, and it always would. Later, at the tornado drill, TV had abstained from attempting to peek up Mrs. Dugas's skirt with the other children, girls as well as boys, while she canvassed the halls, checking for exposed necks or proximity to windows. In his anxiety, he had not looked her in the eye all day, not wanting to give her the opportunity to cancel.

After school, he leapt from the school bus and ran hard for the city stop, taking the first downtown bus that came. Not until it was too late did he realize he'd chosen an East-West line instead of a North-South. He wound up at the transit station, a mile from his destination, near tears. This dry run would predict tomorrow's outcome, he felt. He did not want to fail. After calming himself and then consulting the elaborate city map on the wall, he took off running once more, ducking in and out of the rush-hour traffic, taking shortcuts through alleys. TV had grown up in his grandfather's old house on the east side. Wichita's downtown, though not large by any real measure, still was daunting. TV crossed a set of railroad tracks without realizing a train, moving slowly, had been approaching, the red lights of the crossing flashing, the bells ringing. A flagman, free hand on his hip, shouted out, wanted to know if TV was trying to kill himself. He ran on.

The Depot, true to its name, was located near the tracks. But it didn't appear to have existed for very long; it had never been a real depot, the only concession to authenticity a blue-and-white sign announcing its name. TV had counted on atmosphere, a romantic setting of shoeshine stands and antiquated arrival and departure charts. Its awnings, maroon, full of water, were torn. A Christmas scene, months or possibly years out of date, had been soaped onto the front windows and never washed off. TV entered, setting an alarm buzzing which ceased when the door slid shut.

"We are not opened," a voice shouted from the kitchen. "Our door is, but we aren't." TV took stock of the restaurant where he would, tomorrow, meet Mrs. Dugas. They could sit in the farthest corner, the small table under the one clean window. TV saw that the window was clean because it had been replaced in the recent past, dried caulking still left on its edges, hundreds of white fingerprints framing the glass, suggesting a frantic coded message. Nevertheless, he and Mrs. Dugas would sit here, she facing the window, TV the restaurant. It seemed to be a totally functional establishment, not one part charming.

"We're closed," a woman said from behind an opening in the cheap paneling between the dining room and kitchen. Over her head were the words PICK UP; on the other side, over a second opening, ORDER. New problems confronted TV.

"I know," TV said. "I'm just looking."

She leaned out and made an angry swipe at the iced tea dispenser before disappearing into the back once more. TV stood in the empty fluorescent-lighted restaurant ready to cry.

He did not sleep well. Joanne came to his room more than once in the night, frumpy and sour-smelling, sitting next to him on the bed, sleepily trying to make him feel better, misunderstanding his fear. She reminded him that he would be able to see his mother soon, that she, Joanne, would never prevent his seeing his mother. Yawning, she informed him that his grandfather had lived a full life, a prosperous life, that he had loved TV very much.

TV counted while she spoke. First he simply counted, and then he counted by twos, threes, sevens. His mother had struck his grandfather just once, killed him for money. TV counted the number of strokes Joanne idly made on his back, the way her thoughtless hand fell just between his shoulder blades and ran in a perfunctory line to his waist, over and over. She was thirty-seven years old, unmarried, studying to be a psychiatric nurse. TV wanted to stay with her because he knew he could be placed in a worse situation. His first foster home resembled a halfway house, a full family of orphaned or delinquent children, an ex-Marine running the show like the military. Names were stenciled on towels and bedsheets and clothes. Joanne was not a bad sponsor; she tried to do the right thing. It just always turned out like this backrub, without any more than superficial thought of how he might feel receiving it.

Then he began counting rabbits, imagined himself standing above a field of them as they darted, barely visible, through the blowing grass.

Joanne asked him in the morning if he was part of the 69ers, a young gang in the neighborhood. Their Friday night graffiti was the apartment building's topic of conversation each Saturday morning.

"I'm not," he told her, though he had run with them just last weekend. They, too, stood in awe of TV's past. For some reason, TV could not keep the information to himself. He tried, it wasn't that he didn't try, but it spilled, always. The 69ers had become famous for drawing the sexy yin-yang symbol of their name, a linked, naked circle, man and woman.

Joanne said, blushing, "I don't object to nudity, myself, but some people, the older ones in the building, find it offensive. I would rather you didn't hang out with them, okay?"

"I won't," TV told her.

"You get enough sleep?" she asked.

"I'm fine."

"Let's do something together," Joanne said suddenly, brightly. "Want to?"

TV looked at the clock over the stove, calculating rapidly. What could she have in mind? Why today? And how long till it was satisfied?

Now Joanne scrutinized him, crossing her arms over her scrappy bathrobe. "Are you in that gang?" she demanded.

"No!" TV croaked.

She sat back and a full minute ticked by. Then she said, more confidently, "The only thing we have going for us is honesty."

"I swear to God I'm not!"

The phone rang. For a second, when Joanne didn't move, TV believed his lunch with Mrs. Dugas was not the only thing hanging in the balance. Then, after the third ring, Joanne pushed herself away from the table and scuffed to the telephone.

TV grabbed his skateboard as a prop, held it over his chest to show her his intentions, this Saturday, were wholesome. He waited for her to nod, hoping she would not note his pocketful of fives and singles, saved allowance.

She met his eyes as he threw the front door locks, then looked away, talking to one of her parents, who made her defensive. TV slipped out.

He made the same mistake he had the day before, boarding the wrong bus. He rode along hitting his thigh with his fist to prevent tears. He yanked his grandfather's handkerchief from his pocket and wiped mud off his hightops. At the transit station a cool rain began falling. He ran, his skateboard banging at his hip.

Mrs. Dugas had not arrived when he entered The Depot. He took the opportunity to claim the corner table, rolling his skateboard under it. He used the bathroom, throwing his hair over his head to dry, again and again until he was dizzy. The mirrors were not glass but aluminum, like at a roadside rest stop, as if someone might want to break them. His image was wavy and blanched, unhealthy looking. He slapped his cheeks for color.

Mrs. Dugas wore green slacks and carried an umbrella that had a map of the world on it, half a globe. She stopped at the doorway and, backing in, shook the umbrella before releasing its spring. She touched her silver hair.

"Good afternoon, TV," she said. She stood at the table until he rose, then nestled into the plastic chair across from him.

"Hello," he said. He wanted her to like him so badly he felt sure she could read it in his eyes, like a dog's. Knowing she would have other students, he other teachers, pained TV the way irreversible facts always did. "What do you want to eat?" he asked.

Mrs. Dugas squinted at the signs over the Order window. "A Monte Cristo," she told him.

TV stood and pulled his shirt down. He went to the Order window and waited, hearing the clanging of pans in the back. He cleared his throat and said, "Excuse me." He tapped the counter with his fingers. Mrs. Dugas, her back to him, appeared to be watching the rain, which gushed through a hole in the awning like a small waterfall.

"Put forth," the woman from yesterday said, motioning with her hand for him to speak.

TV ordered a Monte Cristo, french fries, two waters and ketchup. She did not write any of it down. He started to reach for his pocket to pay but she told him he paid when he picked up. He returned to the table with a playing card, the seven of hearts, which he was to insert in the napkin holder.

"But we're the only ones here," Mrs. Dugas laughed.

He laughed with her, eager to find this funny. "Did you drive?" he asked.

"My husband dropped me off. He's lunching at the Shrine Club, around the corner."

"What kind of car?"

She rolled her lips and said, "A moderate-sized blue one."

"I rode the bus."

"Did you?"

"I only got wet because the stop is a ways from here."

She nodded, raising her black eyebrows.

"I liked those rats," TV told her quickly. "That was a good experiment."

"Have you been eating better?"

TV flushed, horrified at what his lunch of french fries would reveal.

Mrs. Dugas lowered her chin and looked up at him in what was supposed to be a teacherly manner. Yet her lip twitched, and TV knew she did not really find fault. "Never mind," she said. "Someday it will register. You know, I don't believe I've ever had a lunch invitation from one of my students before. I've had hundreds of students—it's not my habit to exaggerate—and not a single lunch. I once went to a birthday party and another time I attended a funeral."

TV nodded, hoping she'd keep talking. If only she would just keep talking, he thought he might catch up, he might find his bearings in her voice.

"The birthday I enjoyed but the funeral, well, it was predictably depressing. The pallbearers were your age, so solemn in their suits. One of my students died, a few years ago. Actually, more than a few. Of all those hundreds, she's the only one dead." Then she added, "That I know of."

TV thought of the cemetery his grandfather had gone to. It did not allow vertical headstones and so resembled a golf course, marked every few feet by flat bouquets of plastic flowers. Only the American flag could be upright at Resthaven.

Mrs. Dugas said, "She wasn't wearing a seatbelt, though that is another lesson my classes generally learn. Along with food."

The woman behind the counter shouted, "Seven of hearts?"

TV jumped up. "I'll get it," he told Mrs. Dugas, though she'd made no move to help.

On the way to the Pick-Up window TV realized his money was gone. He reached for the pocket and could feel the bulk missing. His handkerchief was gone, too, probably worked loose during his dash to the restaurant. All he felt was his warm leg beneath the wet corduroy of his pants. Still, he continued to the counter, hoping something would occur to him, hoping he'd trip over a solution on the sticky linoleum floor.

"Four seventy-three, with tax," the waitress said. She was without heart, TV saw.

He took hold of the tray on which his and Mrs. Dugas's lunch rested. "I lost my money," he said quietly, looking into the woman's hard face. He could not bear what was happening to him. "Please let me pay you tomorrow."

"You lost your money," she said skeptically, loudly. TV turned to meet Mrs. Dugas's eyes. She had heard; her eyebrows perked.

TV looked back at the waitress. "I lost it on the bus. Or running. I lost my grandfather's handkerchief, too."

"Big whoop," she said, twirling her finger in the air.

He said, more softly, "He's dead."

She stared, unfazed.

"My mother killed him," he was whispering. "With a hammer. The handkerchief was stuffed in his mouth."

The woman cocked her head, finger still in the air. "You're saying you're that kid?"

He nodded.

"No way. Really? And her boyfriend helped, right?"

He nodded again, already sorry. Mrs. Dugas had turned back to the window. TV did not know whether or not she'd heard him. Then he saw her shoulders rise, a shrug accompanying a sigh. She had heard, once again.

"Please, I promise to pay you back. I'll leave my skateboard here for collateral."

"Get some money from grandma."

"What?"

She nudged her head toward Mrs. Dugas.

TV pleaded, "I came here yesterday."

She seemed to understand that he meant he would come back tomorrow and finally released her side of the tray. "You're lying," she said. TV blinked. If only he *was* lying. But maybe she meant about the money.

TV set the tray on the table. Mrs. Dugas picked up her sandwich and briefly smiled at him. But it was her bad smile, the one she used when she'd been disappointed. Last week she had smiled that way before bodily seating John Coffey and stretching masking tape to bind him to his desk.

To TV, between bites, she quoted, "'What you suffer does not defile you; what you do does.'"

TV ate his french fries without tasting them, working not to choke on their greasy mass, imagining his psychologist's office and the only *file* he knew anything about, the manila one with his name on the tab, crammed full of his bad life.

He found his handkerchief on the way home. It lay like a hamburger wrapper in a muddy puddle. TV made a strangling noise when he saw it there, wrung it out, and pushed it in his pocket. The money was gone but he didn't care. Mrs. Dugas had refused his offer to walk her over to the Shrine Club to meet her husband. She opened her purse at the end of the meal and TV had started to tell her not to pay when she pulled out an envelope and then a stamp, leaving them on the table like a tip. She'd had no intention of producing money.

"I'll see you bright and early Monday," she told TV. Forty-eight hours, he thought. He'd waited until she was gone before taking his skateboard to the waitress.

"This ain't no pawn shop," she told him. She pointed at his and Mrs. Dugas's table. "Gimme that envelope." When he had obeyed, she penciled an address on it and handed it back to him. "Don't forget," she warned, then laughed for the first time. She rolled her eyes, leaned through her Pick-Up hole, and spoke out the corner of her mouth melodramatically. "Just send me the fin, kid."

When he arrived home Joanne was sleeping, curled under a man's coat on the living room couch. Watching her breathe, it was not hard to imagine the ease with which a person could be killed. TV stood for a moment contemplating her, wondering if he would ever love her. Then he went into the kitchen and quietly shut the door. He washed his grandfather's handkerchief in the sink, using plenty of dish soap and scrubbing it between his knuckles until they stung. He rinsed it, running his fingers across the navy monogram, then dried it over the heat register, standing with his feet spread so as not to melt his shoes. His lips parched and his eyes burned. Afterward, he folded the wrinkled cloth to fit the envelope.

Antonya Nelson

Naked Ladies

Laura's family was going to Easter brunch at the Houses'. They were invited every year by Mr. House, but this was the first time Laura's mother could accept. Mr. House called the party his Easter Frolic, and Laura's father never wanted to go. "Frolic at the House house?" he always said. "We'll pass." The family was going this year because he was away showing his paintings at spring arts fairs. He had got lucky, securing more booth spaces than ever before. Already he'd been gone for a month, traveling in his old Land Cruiser, among his canvases, phoning home every few nights to report on his sales. Of the eight checks he'd sent to them, only one had proved rubber. Laura's mother mailed a letter to the woman who'd written it, chastising her for behaving badly. The letter came back from Las Vegas marked "NO LONGER AT THIS ADDRESS," and Laura intercepted it and burned it in the back yard before her mother got home.

Laura's mother raised other people's children—that was her job. She departed each weekday morning in order to arrive at the Houses' before the three school-age children left, which meant that her own family had to fend for itself. The youngest House child, four-year-old Mikey, had Down's syndrome and was her main responsibility. Mrs. House, who blamed herself for his condition, could not be counted upon; she sometimes spent the whole day lying in bed circling catalogue merchandise and punching 800 numbers.

There were four House children, two boys and two girls, just like Laura's family. Except not like them at all. The House children were neatly spaced, like elections, every two years—ten, eight, six, four—while Laura's family was helter-skelter, seventeen, thirteen, eight, and seven, testimony to their parents' ambivalent feelings about kids. In fact, the two youngest—her brothers—were the same age from October until December, which made Laura acutely embarrassed about the obvious recklessness of her parents' lovemaking. When she was younger, when her mother first began working for the Houses, Laura longed for the same tidy procession of children, longed to recite the healthy even numbers of their ages. If she could have, she would have arranged for a new sibling to arrive every two years, until there were eight or ten of them, because she loved quantity as well as orderliness. It proved stability, something aggressively substantial.

The Houses did not call Laura's mother Mrs. Laughlin but Nana, a name Laura found irritatingly intimate. Laura's father said that it made her sound like the family sheepdog. More than he hated the name, he hated the almost-uniform she wore, a large green smock with four square pockets. "Cover those breasts, Broom Hilda," he would say when she brought it home to launder. "Hide that butt."

"This gruesome thing pays the rent," she would say to him, wadding it into a ball and throwing it among the dirty clothes. Her husband would turn out his lower lip like a child. Though his paintings sold only sporadically, when they did sell the family was rich for a week or two. This seemed, to him, to make up for the other, anxious times.

Always as part of Laura's consciousness was the worry that her parents would divorce. They weren't volatile and didn't fight—not the way married people fought in books or movies—but instead picked at one another in a sly, monkeylike manner, each baiting the other until one of them might be forced to slam a door or yell at the dog. Laura both looked forward to and dreaded what her parents called *scenes.* They didn't like to make them, but after one had played itself out Laura felt a kind of humming glee, as if she had seen a vision of the future, a moment of her womanly life briefly revealed to her. From her parents Laura had learned to attach weight to the most subtle vocal inflection, the most fleeting glance. She often lay awake at night replaying the day, hearing again and again words that might have been meant, or taken, unkindly, biting her nails until she could go no farther down.

To the Easter Frolic the five Laughlins wore their good clothes. Their mother debated about a hat—hats, at Easter, seemed necessary to her—and decided upon a turquoise beret, which sat tilted like a dinner plate on her head. She wore a simple silk dress, a lighter shade of turquoise, belted at her hips with a Guatemalan scarf that Mrs. House had given her after their trip over Christmas.

"You look pretty," said Laura's younger sister, Pammy, who was thirteen. "The Houses probably never saw you in anything but your ugly green shirt. Won't they be surprised?"

"Won't they?" Laura agreed, proud that her forty-year-old mother still had a figure to show off.

Admiring herself in the mirror, lifting her chin to draw her throat taut, their mother said, "And at the front door, no less."

They were the first to arrive. The day was a perfect midwestern spring day, sunny and still. The Houses' neighborhood was incorporated, a city unto itself in the middle of Wichita. Traffic had to slow to parade speed in order to pass through; Eastborough had its own police department, whose officers drove understated, cream-colored sedans instead of the typical black-and-white ones, and whose only responsibility was to issue speeding tickets. Laura's father complained because residents here did not have to pay Wichita city taxes; Laura's friends, crawling through at twenty miles per hour, bemoaned the fact that of course the best mall would be built on the other side of Eastborough. Laura tried to pinpoint what, exactly, distinguished it from her neighborhood, Riverside, because the houses there were older and more stately. The difference seemed to have to do with the small details—the clusters of pansies and antique park benches along the street, the absence of loud city buses and delivery trucks, the long path of black mushroom lights that led to the House door. Nothing stirred this Sunday morning but the songbirds.

The Laughlins stood on the flagstone front porch while Laura's mother rang the bell. Inside the House home a long, elegant bonging sounded—the Big Ben tune, their mother told them—and then Mr. House opened the door wearing a tuxedo jacket over a sweatsuit. Laura understood that this was his outfit. His running shoes were brand-new, the kind you could pump air into.

"Nana!" he exclaimed. "Well, well, Nana, aren't you a piece of work!" He was a large-featured, sinister-looking man. His nose was long and wide, his dark hair oiled back from a vampirish widow's peak. His face had the sleek eagerness of a wet dog's. "For Godsakes, come in!" he roared.

Their mother had big breasts, which neither Laura nor her sister had inherited. Mr. House stared at them now, revealed as they were beneath the thin silk. Under his gaze, she lifted her hand to her throat, covering her chest with her forearm. Her face was flushed, and her silver-blond hair shone underneath her rakish hat. She led her children through the foyer of her employer's house.

Mr. House offered them drinks. Laura's mother allowed the three youngest children Cokes and accepted a cocktail of champagne and orange juice for herself, turning her wrist to check her delicate dress watch for the time. "So early," she laughed. When Mr. House tried to give Laura the same kind of drink, her mother shook her head, so that Laura was left with nothing, because she was too embarrassed to take a Coke in consolation.

They were gathered awkwardly in what appeared to be a modern ballroom, done in uncompromising black and white and red. An ebony grand piano gleamed in the corner like an advertisement for furniture polish. Beside it stood a brilliant white statue, a life-size naked woman whose head was coyly ducked. A marble drape fell lazily from her fingertips to pool at her ankles. The expanse of bright red tiled floor was broken only by white fur throw rugs, which floated on it like clouds. Mr. House seemed to recall that he, too, had a family, and turned his head to shout out their names.

Pammy nudged Laura, pointing above their heads to the walls. They were lined with ink drawings, also of naked women, but for one astonishing exception: a painting of their father's, a piece from his "Over the Shoulder" series. Though there could be no mistake, Laura looked for his signature in the corner just to be sure. There it was, "Luke Laughlin," in his typically impatient penmanship. The painting stood out among the women like a beggar. She wondered how it had got here. It was of a winter field, silos and shredded haystacks, wind through bare trees, all of it seen over the large foreground shoulder of a scruffy jacket. For this series her father had been using dental tools to scrape paint onto the canvas. He'd come up with a polished-steel tone by mixing molten aluminum foil with his oils. It gave the effect of frozen metal, a surface your warm finger might stick to. Laura's arms broke out in goose bumps. Around her father's painting and its sober subject, the naked women seemed to preen, silly and moneyed. To them, his painting took itself too seriously, like a street character preaching doom on a sunny day. Loosen up, the naked figures implored, their curves and arches like a languorous cat in the sun. Laura's stomach turned with tension, and she began marking time until it would be permissible for her to suggest they go home.

The House children trooped in wearing jeans and T-shirts, high-tops and spandex. Mrs. House wore peacock colors—a fashion trick Laura recognized from the discarded French magazines her mother brought home from here. The plumage was supposed to distract from her bulk, but still she looked as if she were filled with sand. Like Mr. House, she entered in high spirits, grinning in surprise at Mrs. Laughlin, eyeing the four children in such a way that the two boys stepped behind their older sisters. Laura felt ridiculous in her dress and hose. Her brothers wore neckties and dark suits from a grandfather's funeral last fall; of course their wrists stuck out, their pants were too short, their shoes were unbearably squeaky. Only Mikey House, unkempt as the retarded often seem, kept Laura from burning up in shame. He had loped over to her mother and thrown his arms around her knees. Mrs. Laughlin ran her fingers through his stiff hair and Laura saw she loved him at least as much as she did her own children. In what was obviously a ritual, he reached for her wedding band, wrestled it from her finger and slid it on his own thumb.

"He misses his Nana—don't you, Mikey?" said Mrs. House, unjealous. "And here she is, come to see you on a Sunday. What do you think?"

Mikey snuggled into Mrs. Laughlin's dress once more, this time leaving a large wet spot at her crotch. No one else seemed to notice, though Laura saw her mother's lips crimp as she brushed her palm over her lap. This, Laura realized, was the reason for the smock. Gently, Mrs. Laughlin directed Mikey's mouth away from her. Now that he had attached himself to her, she seemed more at home, and she asked the other House boy, Frank, Jr., to show her family around.

"Kitchen," he said as he led Laura and the others rapidly through the house. "Dining room." "Pantry." The doorbell began bonging again, and shrill greetings could be heard, women's voices rising in exclamation, then falling into confidences, Mr. House booming out, "Well, come on in, you old son of a such-and-such!" The tour terminated at the back of the house, in a plushly carpeted bedroom that had no windows. They had gone too quickly for Laura's taste, ten-year-old Frank gliding through each room in a bored, mature manner, reciting square footage, flipping on lights for a moment, then extinguishing them. He'd gestured toward paintings and statues, mentioning the names of artists, until he realized his guests had never heard of them and were not impressed. This bedroom with no natural light was his, and it was with true enthusiasm that he now showed Laura's brothers his *Playboys,* stacked beside his small television.

"I have my own subscription," he said, pointing out his name on the mailing label. "Dad got it for me."

"He did?" the boys asked in unison.

Frank nodded. "He was tired of me stealing his."

Laura's brothers settled happily on the rug, each with a magazine. Pammy, who often didn't know if she ought to stay with her brothers or go with her sister, finally gave in to curiosity and shyly hefted December's issue, folding herself into a cross-legged position on the floor.

Left alone, Laura returned by the route Frank had just taken, moving slowly this time through the rooms. The house was full of things, each wall hidden by furniture or art and by beautiful and unbeautiful clutter like department-store displays, pillows and decorative knickknacks, large vases sporting wheat stalks, needlepoint footrests, porcelain dolls, exotic foreign masks and figurines. Laura wondered if her mother was tempted, as she was, to pretend she lived in this modern palace. It was cavelike, and there were many rooms that seemed without function, merely pretty; rooms one retreated to for contemplation. They appealed to Laura for that reason—that, and their cleanliness. Each had a peaceful view of the vast lawn—"the grounds," she imagined it was called—where guests now clustered like floral arrangements.

In one of the rooms rested an immaculate easel, and Laura pictured Mrs. House sitting here, looking out over her estate, using a pristine set of watercolors to render a sunset. The stool before the easel was padded and spun smoothly around; in the corner stretched an old-fashioned chaise lounge, rosewood and velvet. Laura could not help comparing this to her father's studio, which was the back porch, and which stank of mineral spirits, oil paints, and cat litter. His easels, all of them, were chaotic with splattered color and were mended with duct tape. Plastic weatherproofing covered the windows, obscuring the outdoors. From the ceiling hung bare two-hundred-watt bulbs; beside his feet he kept an electric space heater turned on—a fire hazard, her mother always claimed. When her father was home, Laura often sat in his studio with him, listening to him talk about his unsavory and impoverished Oklahoman family, his dismal yet serendipitous life's journey. She was the only one of his children he allowed to stay while he painted; the others always wanted him to paint a particular thing, or, if not that, then to explain what he *was* painting, and then felt free to criticize. But Laura was too nervous to do anything more than simply watch him. She brought him his Earl Grey tea with a squirt of honey in it, and sat on a small metal stepladder until her back ached. With the heater on, the porch provided a cozy and heady atmosphere. She'd cried when the gallery in Chicago that showed him had gone under, leaving him and his work to the mercy of arts-and-crafts fairs.

Out of Mrs. House's painting room led two closed doors. The first Laura tried opened into a bathroom.

"Hey!" shouted Mrs. House, who sat inside with her jumpsuit around her knees. Laura slammed the door and stood squinting, willing the thing to unhappen. From the lawn she heard a group of men laugh together, as if at a punch line. A beach ball thwapped the window, then rolled away. Mrs. House's bare flesh, in the glimpse Laura had, was astonishing, plentiful, melting over her like vanilla ice cream. The second door—she opened it tentatively—revealed the kitchen, where the caterers were heating food. They looked at Laura with disdain, as if she must live in this house or one like it.

Laura moved briskly through the ballroom, through vaporous clouds of different strong perfumes. A glass fell from a woman's slim fingers and popped neatly into shards. "My word," the woman said to Laura, and then walked off, leaving the sparkling mess. Laura found her mother outside, away from the party, and stood in her shadow, safe haven. She and Mr. House were beneath a pink magnolia tree, peering up. Laura had the strange impression that they had been touching, though at the moment they weren't. Little Mikey sat on the ground at Mrs. Laughlin's feet, playing with a basket of toys. He had tiny Guatemalan "trouble dolls"—the Houses had brought back sets for Laura and Pammy, too—a Lego doorway, a small plastic reindeer whose legs had been gnawed off, the connector from a Hot Wheels track, a white barrette, and two metal keys, along with Mrs. Laughlin's wedding ring. He had created a game for himself, walking the keys through the doorway, slipping the connector into his mouth to make a tongue, babbling around it to the trouble dolls.

"See him?" Mr. House was saying as he pointed to the tree's branches. "Get out of there, you sneaky shit!" Laura looked up. A squirrel stared placidly down at the humans below, his head protruding from a small wooden house. The fur at his neck ruffled like a mane; the hole was not large enough to accommodate him, and Laura wondered aloud if he was stuck. "He chewed his way in," Mr. House said, swinging his arm as if opening a door. "Right into a wren house. Impertinent little shit." He went on smiling.

To Laura, Mrs. Laughlin said, "Mr. House loves birds. He builds them houses in his spare time." To him, she said, "You'll have to cultivate a taste for squirrels." She took a last sip from her glass, spinning the ice as she finished off the drink.

Mr. House went, "Ah ha ha ha," his face distorted with cracks and crevices. He seemed to laugh frequently, whether a thing was funny or not. Laura did not like him, but for some reason her mother did. At home she poked fun at him, imitating his monstrous guffaw, his incessant cursing. But here she smiled serenely at him as he sighted along his pointed finger, which he aimed at the squirrel like a gun. Mikey looked up when he heard his father laugh and now followed the motion attentively, as if real bullets might emerge from the big hand.

Mr. House said, "This the one who wants to be a model?"

"That's Pammy," her mother told him. "Pammy's been prancing around in her underwear since she was two or three. No," she said. She paused, and rolled her hip toward Laura, then recited the familiar line, "This one is the thinker."

Mr. House instantly fell into a pose, bent at the waist, resting his elbow on his raised knee, fist under his chin. He grimaced as if in pain. His tux tail touched the pale spring grass. "Get it?" he asked. "Row Dan? 'The Thinker'?"

Her mother laughed again. Laura couldn't tell if it was with him or at him. Mrs. Laughlin was sly, in her own way—unpredictable and sometimes unkind. At home she had said, "He's no Einstein but at least he's jolly. At least he knows how to have fun."

"'Jolly,'" Laura's father had repeated, tasting the word.

"Of course you two know Rodin," Mr. House said, rising and unself-consciously reaching inside his sweatpants to make an adjustment. "What with an artist in the house." This time it was *his* tone she couldn't read. "Maybe Laura will be an artist herself. You paint, Laura?"

She shook her head.

"Draw?" he persisted. "Play an instrument? Compose song lyrics?"

"She debates," Mrs. Laughlin told him. "She has trophies—don't you, sweetheart?"

He made a sour face. "Careful, you might end up a lawyer, like yours truly." He emptied his glass of ice by throwing it out over the lawn. "But probably in public defense, am I right?"

Laura shrugged. Mrs. Laughlin squatted to put Mikey's toys back in their basket, her thighs pressed together in the tight silk dress, the fabric between them tense. Mikey snuffled disconsolately until Mrs. Laughlin gave him a kiss on the nose. Mr. House turned his fat, gleaming face to Laura again and winked. "Quit this debating baloney," he advised as they approached the house and the other guests. "You're pretty—nothing wrong with that—so be pretty! Wear nice clothes, be a model. You could make a wonderful model—you just have to smile."

It was a tradition of the Easter Frolic to have an egg hunt, Mr. House told them in the ballroom. He had been playing requests at the piano, his long, wide fingers gliding over the keys while people hummed along. The sun shone without remorse through large, clean windows, reflecting blindingly off the red floor, off the crystal glasses and ice cubes. Every song had an identical choppy rhythm meant to sound jazzy and light, like one-liners. Beside Laura a woman snapped her fingers a little too slowly. A small man with a strange lump on his forehead danced with whoever would consent. He liked to spin his partners with his fingertips so their dresses flared. Mr. House tinkled a few high keys—like a bird trill—and then abruptly stopped playing.

"The hunt!" he announced. Weakly, the woman next to Laura snapped once more. Mr. House patted her rump when he stood up, as if in consolation.

"He's crude," Laura told her sister as they wandered around the swimming pool, looking halfheartedly for eggs. The first they'd found was plastic and contained a cheap necklace and pendant: turned one way, Betty Boop smiled under her long lashes; turned the other way, her mouth became an "O" and her dotted dress disappeared. Pammy put the necklace on. They found hard-boiled eggs with the beginnings of riddles on them ("How many Catholics does it take to change a light bulb?") or with the answers ("Because it was a *hung jury*"), and they found chocolates in the shape of naked women—buxom, foil-wrapped little candies nestled in the tender crocuses.

"He sure likes naked ladies," Pammy observed. She, like Laura's brothers, was enjoying the morning. To them it did not spell disaster but adventure—something they would tell all their friends about.

"I think he's having an affair with Mom," Laura told Pammy by the pool. She said it in order to feel her heart race, not entirely concerned with whether she believed it.

"Bullshit," Pammy said. After she'd thought for a moment, she added, "Dad is a lot better-looking, and younger and skinnier and everything. Mr. House is kind of"—she searched for the right word—"gross."

"Like that matters," Laura told her. The prospect of her mother's affair would give Laura a headache—it was her nature to keep peace—but a small, evolving, renegade emotion made her want something extraordinary to happen. She and Pammy sat by the pool and took their shoes and stockings off, dangling their feet in the icy water. On the other side of the lawn, guests crawled along the shrubbery, still seeking eggs, absurd in their good clothes. Laura's brothers and Frank held grocery sacks for easy collection. Her mother helped Mikey while Mr. House stood on the porch yelling, "You're getting hot, very hot, even hotter!" and laughing loudly.

"I bet anything she tells us not to tell Dad we were here," Pammy said suddenly, as if the whole party had come clear to her.

"No," Laura said, "she'll let us tell him. This is her way of getting back at him for being gone so much. While he's away we're all out here with Mr. House, like he's our other dad, the pervert one." But his compliment—telling her she could be a model—kept lightening Laura's opinion of him. Unlike most people, he seemed to have faith in something besides her intelligence, and she was not above feeling flattered.

"Isn't this place funny?" Pammy said. "So funny and weird. I never thought there could be a place like this. And Mom comes here every day—that's the weirdest part of all." She pulled her pale legs from the water and brushed off the drops that clung to them. "Do you think Dad knows one of his paintings is here?"

"No. If he knew, he'd come steal it off the wall." Laura was positive he had not given it to the Houses. Perhaps her mother had made a gift of it, but that was unlikely. For all their curious bickering, she would not have betrayed him this way, through his work. So Laura deduced that Mr. House had bought the painting, without her father knowing, possibly as a way of pleasing her mother, though Laura understood that it would not please her, and she understood that Mr. House knew it, too.

"It looks so funny with those other pictures," Pammy went on.

"So depressing and . . . brown."

"It's not depressing," Laura said. "It's just more realistic."

"Naked ladies are real," Pammy said. "They're just as real as a blizzard on a farm, only prettier."

Laura didn't want to argue with Pammy, so she repeated what they agreed upon: "His painting is all wrong here."

Pammy lifted her plastic pendant from between her new, small breasts and fingered it in the sunlight. "If I was Mom," she said, "I think I'd like to work here. It's cool."

"Girls!" Mr. House shouted out at them, waving his arms toward himself like a coach. The lawn was so wide that his voice seemed out of synch. "Come on, you bathing beauties! Come eat, drink, be merry, and limbo!"

They joined the party on the deck, passing through a croquet game. The people playing made the game seem glamorous, the disproportion of their size to their mallets not at all silly. Bright wooden balls rolled quietly through the grass and went *clok* against one another. Mrs. House sat watching the game, feeding a fat black dog on her lap. Laura averted her eyes, hoping that Mrs. House had been too stunned to recognize her when she opened the bathroom door. "Here you go," Mrs. House told the dog, handing him a Jordan almond.

Everyone was eating. Plates decorated every surface; a melting ice swan swam in a sea of ripe fruit. In a budding tree whose two largest branches reached like arms toward the sky, a young man sat with his shirt off, feet above his head, popping stuffed mushrooms into his mouth. Mr. House stood below him, tossing up more. "Handle a beer?" he asked the boy, who nodded agreeably in answer. At one barbecue a side of beef spun while at another a whole pig revolved, big and pink as a fat child. The caterers circulated with champagne and miniature quiches, studiously ignoring the goings-on.

Laura found her mother again. She had grown dreamy with drink and lay on a padded lounge chair at the far end of the deck, her beret tilted over her eyes to block the sun. Her bare legs were white as eggshell, pale blue veins beneath the mildly translucent skin like splintering cracks. Mikey lay asleep beside her, his feet tucked beneath her knees for warmth. His ordinarily strange features appeared normal in sleep—freckled and pug—and this made Laura briefly sad.

From inside, Laura heard the doorbell ring. Until it sounded, she had thought she might want something to happen; now she knew otherwise. No one else seemed to have heard the long chime, and she waited for it to begin again before she went to answer it herself.

Her father stood on the flagstone porch, investigating the House mailbox, to which an enormous, black, screaming eagle was attached at the claws.

"Dad."

"Hi, honey. How's the Frolic?"

"Awful, really."

"Got you answering the door?" He stepped gently past her, moving quietly, as he always did, as if someone might jump out and surprise him.

"I was the only one who heard the bell," she told him. "We didn't think you'd be home until tonight," she added.

"You don't say?" he said.

"How was Oregon?"

"Wet," he said. "Earthy and impoverished, though happy. They have happy industries out there—Christmas trees and vineyards, happy, happy. I preferred Nevada—you ought to see the neon."

"That's too bad," Laura said, just to say something.

He gave his shoulders and head a slight shake, as if to wake up. "I've been driving since yesterday afternoon." He looked at his paint-dirtied plastic watch. "Twenty-four hours. I was ready to be home." He ran a thumbnail behind his earlobe. "And then nobody was there."

"Want to wait here while I get Mom and everybody?"

"No." He looked around the dark foyer for the first time. He was unshaven and smelled of his vehicle and the road. "No, I certainly don't want to wait here."

Laura took his hand, which was callused and warm, like a work glove, and led him along the circuitous route she'd discovered earlier instead of through the ballroom where his painting hung. He followed, grunting in amusement every now and then, dropping her hand to study an abstract painting in one room.

"Some of it's nice," Laura said, about the clutter, "but most of it's junk." She waited for him to agree.

"That's your opinion?" He spoke without looking at her, tipping his face so close to the painting that he seemed to be smelling it. "This is a marvelous piece," he said, sighing. "Absolutely marvelous." Art he admired made him melancholy, Laura had noticed. Her father had once spent nine thousand dollars on a painting. That was before the children were born. It now hung in his and Mrs. Laughlin's bedroom at home where no one but the family ever saw it.

"I interrupted Mrs. House on the toilet," Laura told him as they left the room, trying to cheer him up.

He smiled distractedly.

"Have you been here before?" she asked when they came to a patio door.

"Never," he said, stepping onto the deck.

"But not," Mr. House boomed beside them, "for lack of an invitation."

Her mother was where Laura had last seen her, asleep on the lounge chair next to Mikey. Her turquoise dress was hiked halfway up her bare thighs and her arms were crossed—as if she were carrying on an angry conversation in her dream. She was deeply asleep and looked cold, with Mikey curled against her so trustingly that Laura forgave her—whatever the infraction, whether it was preferring this child and home to her own or loving peculiar Mr. House or something else, something private between her parents which Laura might and might not wish to understand.

"You must be the mister," Mr. House had gone on when he had so suddenly materialized beside her and her father.

Mr. Laughlin showed his teeth like a hyena, the expression he reserved for people to whom he felt superior.

"Lemme buy you a drink," Mr. House said, waving in the direction of a passing caterer.

"O.K.," Mr. Laughlin agreed. "Get your brothers and sister," he said to Laura, nodding toward the pool, where all the party's children sat eating chocolate and comparing parents.

As she hurried, fearing a fight, she felt the headache she had expected descend like a hat over her skull. "Dad's here," she hissed to Pammy.

Pammy's eyebrows jumped. "Oh, man."

They each grabbed a brother and headed back. Mr. House and their father were standing over their mother's chair looking at her as she slept.

"Hey, Dad!" the youngest Laughlin greeted his father.

"Son."

"Guess what? I won third prize in the—what's his name?"

"Bacchus," Mr. House supplied.

"Bacchus Look-Alike Contest." He held up a Polaroid photo of himself wearing a crown of rubber purple grapes and holding a plastic set of pipes. "I got a prize," he added, pulling a fluorescent-orange feather boa from his suit-jacket pocket.

Mr. Laughlin accepted the boa, studying it as it slid like water through his fingers and onto the ground.

"First prize was Royals tickets," Laura's brother went on, bending to retrieve the wrap. "But we couldn't go all the way Kansas City, anyway. Could we?" He looked up at his father, who shook his head.

On the chair Mikey jolted awake, his face becoming the familiar flattened, pink-eyed one of Down's syndrome once more.

"Nana," he snuffled, to warn her, and Mrs. Laughlin turned toward him without opening her eyes, nuzzling, attempting to close him in her arms. When he would not comply, she pushed aside her beret and squinted up.

Her husband waved his fingers down at her.

"Surprise, surprise!" said Mr. House.

When Mr. and Mrs. Laughlin agreed the family had to be going ("Oh, it's a school day tomorrow, and he's been driving all night." "I've been driving all night." "All night, honey, really?" "Really, all night."), Mr. House said he would walk them to the door. He led them toward the ballroom, and Pammy and Laura gave each other agonized looks. Now the crisis would come, the painting would be discovered.

Curiously, Laura's mother seemed unfazed by what was happening. She yawned and then shivered, crossing her arms and allowing Mr. House to put his tuxedo jacket around her shoulders as they moved toward the house, Mr. Laughlin in front walking with his nose tilted toward the ground, a pained grin lifting the left side of his mouth.

"Goodbye, goodbye!" the boys shouted to Frank, Jr., who stood with his legs spread on the other side of the lawn, waving and laughing—a perfect, reduced replica of his father.

"Thank you, Mrs. House," Pammy told the hostess, whom they met at the ballroom door. The group stopped to give her space to pass.

"You're surely welcome, baby," Mrs. House said to Pammy. "See you Monday," she said over her shoulder to Laura's mother as she joined her other guests outside.

They could have moved quickly through the room; Mr. Laughlin could have kept staring at the floor, walking on the lipstick red tile, thinking, smirking. But from the yard came a terrible wail; Mikey House had discovered that his Nana had left, and as he barreled at her, running lopsidedly, Mr. Laughlin raised his eyes to take in the pictures on the walls.

Without breathing, Laura watched him see them, the naked women, one drawing after another, their rolling, seductive ease, and then his own painting among them like a slammed door. What surprised her was that his eyes jumped over his painting—no alarm, no anger, not even, it seemed, recognition—and concentrated on the nudes. She looked up again. They were not very well rendered, obviously done by a hobbyist—or, as her father would say, "a draw-er, as in chest of." Laura tried to see what he saw—the round bottoms, the heavy breasts, the faces half hidden in ink smudge. Then her father turned to his wife, who had bent over Mikey once more, calming him. Her hat fell to the floor and her pale hair covered her eyes.

Laura blinked. It could be her, she thought. The woman in the pictures could be her mother—which would make Mr. House the artist. She saw them in a flash, together in the House studio, her mother on the chaise, Mr. House staring at her ardently, scratching away with his pens. She wanted to meet her father's eyes for confirmation, but he would not look at Laura. He waited for his wife, patiently.

In the foyer, Mr. Laughlin removed Mr. House's enormous tuxedo jacket from Mrs. Laughlin's shoulders.

"She can wear it home," Mr. House said magnanimously.

"She *can,*" Mr. Laughlin agreed, handing over the dark garment. "But she won't."

Mrs. Laughlin never went back. She began working for the phone company a few days later. They didn't divorce, and, after Laura left home—when she was in college and then law school—she found herself alternately proud of and annoyed by her parents' enduring marriage. As to the significance of what had happened at the Houses', Laura could only look to the fact that soon her father acquired a partner to share booth space with and represent him—a single man, a photographer who lived on the road anyway and didn't mind the traveling—and to her mother's fierce tears one dinnertime when Laura's youngest brother carelessly asked what in the world would happen to Mikey House.

On the drive across town that Easter, Mr. Laughlin told them the story of his trip west, of how he'd had to spend the nights in his Land Cruiser—he illustrated by curling himself spasmodically as he steered—because he'd run out of hotel money, of his stiff back and stinky clothes, the way he'd eaten at restaurants that offered two-for-one meals. He kept turning to check Mrs. Laughlin's expression, but she was still sleepy, sluggish, looking blankly out the window, shivering. Even without Mr. House's jacket, every now and then Laura caught a whiff of his cologne—so powerful it was as if he were among them for a moment. Mr. Laughlin's stories weren't pathetic tales; he managed to have Laura and Pammy and their brothers laughing at his bad luck by the time they reached their driveway on the other side of the city.

Later, he and Laura drove back to the Houses' to pick up Mrs. Laughlin's car; her old Maverick had been hopelessly trapped in the overcrowded driveway, Mercedeses and Cadillacs and BMWs packed four-deep behind and beside it. "We'll get it tonight," Laura's father had said, guiding Mrs. Laughlin to his boxy vehicle parked across the street. When he and Laura returned for the car, they didn't speak, as if they were in agreement—as if he, too, she thought, had recognized his pretty wife in the mediocre art. It would be easy to say something, and Laura nearly did: a little evidence would go a long way, would twist tight whatever was already tense.

Her father pulled up in front of the Houses' once more. The driveway was empty except for Mrs. Laughlin's car. The windows of the house were dark, as if the family had all gone to bed early. Or as if they didn't want to be seen.

"Your mother's left headlight is out," Mr. Laughlin said to Laura.

It was the first thing he'd said in thirty minutes, and Laura tried to make some symbolic sense of his words but couldn't. "What do you mean?" she asked tentatively.

"Her Mav, the left headlight. You ought to just follow me home." He stretched his arms and tapped the ceiling of the Land Cruiser with his fingers. The smell of his sweat filled the front seat. Then he laughed. "Man, have I driven enough today or what?" And Laura saw that nothing was going to happen. They were going to go home and watch television with the rest of the family. The Easter Frolic was over. "Hoppity hop," her father said, which was his way of prodding her into action.

Laura continued to intercept the mail, which one day led her to think about the woman who'd taken her mother's place at the Houses'. Because the envelope with the Eastborough return address was so light, Laura had thought it might be empty; instead, a slim gold ring slid out. Nothing more. Had her father even noticed its absence, Laura wondered. She slipped the ring on her pinkie and imagined another woman, interviewing for the position of Nana, marveling at her odd employer, and, after taking the job, playing with Mikey, loving him, wondering at his eclectic basket of toys—at the barrette and the black tongue, the swinging red door and the legless reindeer, the two keys and trouble dolls, someone's mysterious, modest wedding band.

ANTONYA NELSON

Female Trouble

McBride found himself at the Pima County Psychiatric Hospital in the middle of the day. "Don't visit me here," Daisy told him. She slid her palms over her frizzy white hair as if to keep it from flying off like dandelion fluff: "It embarrasses me, these crazy people make me ashamed."

"I thought you wanted to see me. I thought that was the point. Why else are you in Tucson?" Daisy, McBride's girlfriend of the year before, had been discovered on the highway near the Triple T truck-stop carrying a portable typewriter, trying to hitch a ride. Native New Yorker, she'd never learned to drive; maybe that was why McBride had assumed she would stay in Salt Lake City, where he'd left her. He certainly preferred to think of that chapter as a closed one, a place he had chosen against.

Daisy said, "I want to see you when I'm normal again. I just feel like you're staring at me, at my flabby skin and everything." She began jerking her shoulders in some simulation of crying but her eyes remained dry. McBride did not wish to touch her. She'd taken on an institutional smell and her sweatsuit hid any physical charm. Her eyes had lost whatever snappish wit they'd once held, glazed with depression and the medication used to treat it. McBride reached to hold her and felt she was made of something more inert than her former substance, dull as clay, and pale as an albino, as if she'd been dipped in bleach. In the past, she'd been burnished, tanned twice weekly in a salon coffin, hair dyed golden and frowsily restrained with combs and barrettes, a Victoria's Secret kind of girl, pubic hair dyed to match.

Had his leaving her brought about such thorough transformation? He felt like asking her. He was sort of flattered, sort of appalled.

When she'd fallen in love with him she'd gone to his apartment and climbed into his bed and waited for him to come home. She was a free spirit with a crush, a mission, a taste for disaster. His roommate had greeted him in the kitchen that late night, wearing boxers and socks, whispering as he stepped daintily on tiptoes, "There's a *girl* in your bed" with such admiration and awe that McBride seemed stripped of very many options. A naked girl in your bed was not a thing to take lightly.

"Drunk?" he asked, pulling off his own clothes.

His roommate had given an elaborate impatient shrug and shiver: who cared? Or: of course drunk; you had to ask?

Was she desperate? No—devoted. Spontaneous. Outrageous. A girl on fire, burning so that you wanted to stand in the radiating glow, a girl on the verge, confident in not caring. The prospect of death did not deter her. She was up for whatever.

And this had led her here, McBride supposed, later and after, immolation imminent. The Arizona desert was forgiving in February, springlike by Eastern standards. They sat in the building's courtyard. A general wooden catatonia in the human population—patients and orderlies both—made the Adirondack chairs seem full of personality, resting at jaunty angles and in conversational clusters over the evergreen grass. Other visitors carried Styrofoam cups of coffee to other patients, crossing the lawn quickly, trying to be spry in the face of lethargy. McBride felt trapped by his past, and kept sneaking covert glances at his watch. His tapping foot ached for an accelerator.

What he remembered about Daisy was sex. Even when he'd stopped loving her, he'd wanted to fuck her. They'd been strangers their first night together, Daisy waiting for him drunk on that crowded single mattress. His roommate's awe, "There's a *girl* in your bed." Like a gift, a girl between the sheets, a gift, this girl, like an animal in a gunnysack, and on fire, in heat.

Was there a word for the way you winced, recalling a former affection, that place in your ribcage that briefly collapsed, your glance that no longer lingered but skimmed over her face like a skipped stone over water?

Now Daisy said, "Look," and pointed toward the hospital entrance. "Family theater." They watched a woman wrench herself free of the guiding hands of an older couple, her parents, McBride guessed, the three of them sharing a lankiness. Their daughter was easily in her forties, long-limbed and angry, crossing her arms defiantly and refusing to enter the front doors. McBride was sympathetic to the parents, who looked harried and doomed, as if they hadn't slept in days. Daisy said, "Old farts just want to get rid of her." McBride supposed that was true but he didn't blame them.

When the woman suddenly sprinted down the walk toward the street, the parents began shouting. The woman ran like a dancer, straight into the street without looking. Her mother screamed, putting her hands to her cheeks. Cars weaved around the daughter as she stood between lanes but nobody stopped driving. Nobody in Tucson ever stopped driving. The woman stood facing traffic like the oblivious prow of a ship. McBride looked to the orderlies, who'd jumped up yet made no move toward action.

"Help her," Daisy said to him, pushing his elbow from the chair arm. He rose and started reluctantly for the street, jogging in such a way that his teeth hurt. When he reached the woman she took his arm as if she'd been waiting for him, her partner on their dance stage. She stared at him with clear, unmedicated eyes, startled like a deer, pretty and skittish.

"What am I doing?" she asked.

McBride told her what he'd seen as he escorted her up the walk. They passed her parents, who simply watched as if at a wedding.

"*You'd* never do a thing like this," she informed McBride as they entered the building's foyer. She held his arm lightly, with long shaking fingers. A group had clustered at the commotion and now drifted away, disappointed at the tame outcome.

"A thing like what?"

"Like impulsive behavior. It's a feminine trait."

McBride recalled a similar complaint Daisy had made when he refused to try sushi or inhale an illicit powder. No, he wouldn't eat raw fish, or snort alien drug. Nor would he bolt, barefooted, into traffic.

"Party pooper," Daisy called him. "Wet blanket. Coward." What was so brave about taking risks, he'd asked her. What separated it from stepping off a cliff?

"You step off holding my hand," she'd said, popping a pill, removing a garment, switching off the headlights at high speed on a dark highway. But he'd wanted a bungee, a net, a loophole.

The woman's parents had followed them inside and now stood deferentially behind McBride. The woman let loose of his arm, surrendering to her parents. "This way," she said quietly, leading them toward the admissions desk.

Daisy had her eyes closed when McBride got back to their chairs. "I'm not asleep," she told him.

McBride sat on the arm of the chair, ready to leave.

"Fix everything?" she asked acidly; this was like her, to tell him to do something, then ridicule him for doing it.

"I should go," he said.

"You should," she agreed, starting to not-cry again.

"I'll come back."

"I'll be here."

At home that evening McBride's current girlfriend, Martha, sat on newspapers painting chairs. In her spare time she decorated secondhand furniture; her house was full of it, colorful as a toy store. Yellow snakes wound up the spindles of one chair, blue tulips drawn freehand popped along the arms of another. Sad music came from a bedroom, the mournful wailing of loons. Martha's gray head was tilted and her tongue was lodged beneath her upper lip in concentration. There was the odor of hearty food beneath the paint fumes, that and the burnt herby smell of marijuana, which she'd smoked earlier. The ordinariness of the evening, the simple and somehow unbelievable normalness of it—the way McBride could accept a healthy woman in the house where he lived doing something so utterly charming as painting furniture and cooking food—should have made him happy. Instead, he was irritated by the tableau. He felt domesticated, as if it had happened against his will. Time with Daisy, however brief, had left something under his skin.

"How was she?" Martha asked.

"Drugged. Nuts. I ended up dragging some other woman out of the street in front of the hospital."

"Alive?"

"More or less." He told her about the morning while she worked her brush around in her patient, stoned method. The room grew dim and she quit, leaning back on her hands, legs splayed open lazily. She was the first woman McBride had ever known who was not at war with her body: she liked it, it liked her. She walked around in the world unselfconscious inside of it, completely casual with its shortcomings as well as its gifts. Fond, as if of a beloved pet.

"Oh, Daisy," McBride said, trying to sound as if he could dismiss his old girlfriend, laboring to evoke that useful wince that meant he was over her, ashamed of former passion. "How was *your* day?"

Martha quoted some of her accident victims' depositions to cheer him up. She worked in the police court downtown taking statements from bad drivers. This was only one of her jobs. She also interviewed rape victims for a professor at the University of Arizona, having some talent at listening. She was thirty-six, six years older than McBride, prematurely gray, and had lived with a number of men so she knew how to do it. Calmly. With a great deal of forbearance and humor. Even her name: Martha. Not Muffy, not Marti, nothing cute or hip, an old-fashioned name designating a person with both feet on the ground. She said, "'Coming home I drove into the wrong house and collided with a tree I don't have.'"

McBride smiled. Martha smiled, too, and rose to extract whatever she had cooked from the oven, which had the bloody odor of red meat and mushrooms. Wine. He suspected she made up depositions but she swore they were authentic. Her favorite went: "I had been driving for forty years when I fell asleep at the wheel and hit a telephone pole." The rape victims she and McBride had agreed not to discuss.

They ate on the front porch in the breeze of an oscillating fan. Even in February, the birds went on and on, noisy as a coffee klatch. The next door neighbor, the transvestite, came out, as he always did, as the sun fell, lips a red bow, bosom an emphatic bolster. His era was the 50s: floral, with forgiving hemlines.

"Imagine going through all of that nonsense he must go through to look like that," McBride had once mistakenly said. The shaving, the plucking, the makeup, the heels: torture. Martha had thrown her head back to laugh. She could really laugh. "Just imagine," she'd said.

They waved, as usual. The pretense seemed to be that two people shared the little house next door, a man and a woman who were never seen together yet wore the same shoe size. "Whatever," McBride muttered, also as usual. Martha liked her funky neighborhood. She liked the tree full of umbrellas as well as the lawn art on the corner, toasters and blenders and microwave ovens set out as ornaments among the plastic flowers and spinning pinwheels. She liked the car with toys glued to its chassis. She had told McBride, when he complained of the weirdness, that as he grew older he would treasure the odd, shun the ordinary, grow easy as she was with eccentricity. It would not threaten him so.

Personally, McBride thought that Martha lived among the bizarre in order not to feel so bizarre herself, normal by comparison. Plus, her neighbors' obvious dilemmas distracted her from her own, which was that she wanted a baby. Women were on timetables, cycles, deadlines. That ticking clock, bomb or alarm, irked McBride. His gender had forever, plenitude, a wealth of progeny waiting in the wings. Babies, like the rape interviews, was a topic best avoided.

Predictably, he dreamed about Daisy that night. He was in his old house, the one he'd grown up in in Oklahoma City. In the dream Daisy lived around the corner from his parents. She rented a small sunny room. McBride visited her there and she kissed him on the cheek. He woke feeling tender toward her. It had been such a sweet kiss, so innocent and discreet, like the kiss of a child, free of history or future, and it had such melancholy force that McBride woke in a state of pure desire, which impelled his waking Martha to make love with her, his fantasy life blurred by dream. Perhaps when he came, it was into the memory of his sleeping vision of Daisy. The memory—combined, Martha and Daisy, sanity and sickness—carried him through the day, their faces next to his, his sexual past shoved against his sexual present, an interesting friction.

He visited Daisy again a week later. The tenderness of his dream had faded. Her depression made him impatient. This aspect of Daisy seemed to him an enormous weakness and he did not tolerate weakness well, trying to get a handle on his own. She wore the same sweat suit, the same muzzy expression, the same drained pallor. Today it was cloudy but they sat in the same hopeful Adirondack chairs outside, staring at the front door as if the drama they'd witnessed last time might also replay itself, the middle-aged woman fleeing her parents, the need to run into traffic. McBride was annoyed to discover he had on the identical shirt he'd worn then, too.

Without apparent emotion, Daisy said, "I'm pregnant I think."

McBride looked hard at her, trying to figure where the sensible part of her went when the other part came out.

"Don't worry," she continued, "it's not yours."

"It *couldn't* be," he said.

"True." She said nothing for a while, then added, "I could have had your baby after you moved away. I could have left her in Salt Lake, given her up to the Mormons to raise. Don't men ever wonder what happens to their sperm? I'd worry, if I were a man, but men—it's all just hit and run."

What occurred to McBride was that all the nasty forces of nature had female pronouns, typhoons and tornadoes and those mythic creatures, the Furies and Sirens. They were powerful, and they sent you reeling, they trapped you.

"Daisy, what are you going to do?"

"I don't know." She shook her fluffy head. "I have to get off of these drugs if I'm pregnant, that's for sure. But what else? You got me." She picked at the chipped green paint on her chair arm for a few minutes in silence. Then added, "There were two men in Salt Lake. We all three lived together, very French-movie. Either one could be the dad, though they'd both suck at it."

McBride said, "You know, your life is kind of crisis-oriented, have you noticed that?"

She lifted her face to the brightest cloud, the one that hid the sun, and said, sullenly, "No," and then wouldn't say another word.

Two men. The image of Daisy at the fulcrum of a threesome wouldn't leave McBride. Somehow this wrinkle intrigued him, against his will. What kind of sleeping arrangements had prevailed? Was there an alpha male, stud one, stud two? Some homosexual stuff? How did the three of them behave at breakfast, sitting together over coffee in their underwear and ruffled hair?

At home Martha attempted to cheer him. "To avoid hitting the bumper of the car in front, I struck the pedestrian."

McBride told her, "I'm starting to believe these reports of yours."

Martha feigned shock, sucking on a joint. "You mean you didn't before?"

"Not before Daisy."

"Daisy," Martha said, looking bemused, annoyed in the unthreatened way a strong woman does in the face of a puny one.

"She lived with two men at once, she says."

"She's done everything, that gal, all the things I always thought I would do. It's disappointing to realize how staid I've become." But she smiled. Her complacency didn't really trouble her—look at what surrounded her, arty furniture, queer neighbors, clacking birds.

The pregnancy part went unmentioned, but the next time he visited the hospital Martha wanted to come with him. She insisted. She drove. For someone who evaluated car accidents for a living, she handled an automobile very badly, swerving arrogantly through traffic, refusing to do head checks, one palm ever ready on the horn. She had lapses but mostly Martha was reliable, grown up. Now that he'd become one, it surprised McBride how few adults were grown ups. It still seemed all seventh grade, and you had to keep on your toes.

Daisy had dressed for McBride's visit this week. Someone—some anal retentive obsessive compulsive with a lot of time on her hands—had lassoed Daisy's wild hair into tiny braids which criss-crossed her shapely skull in a flattering style. The sweat suit had been traded for black jeans and a glossy button-down shirt, under which her breasts bobbed. She'd smeared makeup over the sores around her mouth and the dark circles beneath her eyes, and she looked like a country western singer ready to make a comeback. Next to her, Martha seemed far too robust, big and indestructible, like a Hereford beside an impala. McBride saw that the visit was going to go wrong in a way he hadn't anticipated.

Women intimidated Daisy; even in the sanest of moments she didn't like them, though she pretended otherwise. Without the possibility of an encounter ending in sex, Daisy was a bit at sea. McBride sat on the grass before the willing Adirondack chairs where the women sat leaning back, faces to the sun. He thought of triangles, the two women here together only because of him; the two men in Salt Lake maybe waiting to hear from Daisy, wandering around the house wondering what they were doing together, stuck with each other and a legally binding lease. Because he could come up with nothing to say in front of Martha, McBride understood he was not innocent in his current relationship with Daisy, a fact that made him tired of himself.

Martha said, "So how are you feeling?"

Daisy took the finger she was chewing from her mouth and said, "Sad. I'm having an abortion tomorrow and that makes me *really* sad, even though I don't think I'm ready for a child."

McBride felt Martha appraising him, compiling all the data, his not telling her about the baby, his phony forgetfulness on the matter. Then she nodded at Daisy. "That's understandable. I'm just now feeling ready for a child."

"You have time. You're not old."

"I *am* old, but it's nice of you to say. I've had three abortions and every time I think, I just saved another kid from being fucked up. It's one way not to feel bad."

"Well, tomorrow I'll save my second from being fucked up."

McBride was grateful he hadn't fathered any of these fetuses. Both women looked down at him, their expressions identical: what good was he, there on the grass? He didn't want to donate his sperm to Martha's desire, and though he was in the position of footstool, they couldn't even put their feet upon him.

"Coffee," he said, hopping to. And once he'd left them together he did not want to return and so roamed the hospital halls.

The place was poorly funded, understaffed, cheaply built and maintained. It was not old enough to seem Gothically romantic nor new enough to appear at least clean and modern. In all the popular spots, the carpet was worn through; the furniture was crooked, broken plastic from the 70s, and the windows were smudged with years' worth of fingerprints, people pressing against the glass, longing to escape the big box they seemed to find themselves trapped inside. Everywhere televisions, laugh-tracks and commercials fading in and out of every open doorway as McBride passed. Was there anything more representative of illness and confinement than daytime TV, anything more definitively the killing of time? This first floor was public; the upper ones required speaking with a station manager. To avoid returning to Martha and Daisy—he could see them from the second floor window near the elevator, still talking together in the sun, Daisy tilted back with her eyes closed, Martha watching her—he gave himself the challenge of lying his way past a station manager. The fourth was Daisy's floor; the higher one went, the crazier the occupants.

But it was no challenge at all. He merely mentioned Daisy's name and was pointed in the direction of her room. The woman at the desk didn't even have him sign in. He opened her dresser drawers and looked in her closet. Nothing but the portable typewriter she'd been found with on the highway. Also some odd articles of clothing, obviously stuff that had been donated, discards. Plain white underpants, high-waisted and modest, nothing like what she'd worn before. A picture of Jesus over her headboard, eyes pitched upward, just as exasperated as anyone else who had to deal with Daisy.

"I didn't know you were a patient here."

McBride whirled, caught. At the doorway stood the woman from the street, arms crossed as if chilly. She resembled Audrey Hepburn, he thought, willowy, frail and jittery as a stray. "I'm not," he said, recovering. "I'm waiting for Daisy."

"Daisy." She said it skeptically. "Well, I'm glad you're not a patient because I would feel bad about not struggling more if you were. Couldn't have let another inmate be my undoing."

McBride smiled because she seemed to be joking but she didn't return the smile. She simply walked away, as if he'd made the wrong answer, the bones of her ribs and hips visible beneath her gray dress. From the hallway, he looked back outside. The Adirondack chairs were abandoned, big yawning laps.

Somehow Daisy wound up at McBride's house. This was because it was officially, legally, Martha's house, and Martha had invited her. She didn't believe Daisy was crazy. Confused, yes. In trouble, yes. Maybe even more trouble than craziness but not crazy. The thing on the highway, with the typewriter? McBride whispered this in their bedroom after Daisy had fallen asleep on the study couch.

"She was pregnant," Martha said. "Overwrought."

"She still is pregnant."

"True. But that's only till tomorrow. Then we work on getting her off the heavy-duty meds."

"What makes you want to do this? You don't even know her."

"She's your friend," Martha said simply. She wore a large white nightgown with ruffles and lace, matronly on her though it would have seemed sexy and Victorian on someone else, someone skinny, anorexic or strung out like a junkie, like the woman at the hospital, like Daisy.

"She might still be in love with me," McBride warned Martha in the dark.

Martha laughed and wouldn't stop. It was lusty, gutsy laughter, and McBride didn't like that.

"What's funny? She might be."

"Oh you sound so serious, like you wouldn't be able to defend yourself." She held her hands above her head as if shielding herself from an oncoming train. "Stop, stop! Don't love me." She laughed again. "Gimme a break. You're a big strong man, capable of fending off a crazy woman's love."

"You said she wasn't crazy."

"She shows all the signs of molestation."

"Naturally. She's a tabloid story, waiting to happen."

"I'm pretty sure she's been sexually abused."

"Only with permission," McBride said. "Only because she wanted to be."

"You don't believe that." In fact he did believe it, but best to keep that to himself. Best to leave that can of worms in the cupboard. On this subject they could not have an agreeable conversation. Martha had interviewed over a hundred rape victims, her specific interest in their notions of dress and how they felt about their bodies, before and after. She and McBride lay with thoughts of rape between them, a few moments of respectful silence. She believed he was better than he was; often he did not feel like dispelling this.

Then she rolled on top of him and became heavy. She loved to start sex this way, covering him like a blanket, breathing into his neck, heat, comfort. Her bed she'd made herself, headboard a pilfered road sign from high school days. Her friends had wanted DIP or PROCEED WITH CAUTION or MEN AT WORK but what had Martha stolen? SOFT SHOULDER.

"The act of rape and the act of love are the same gesture," she'd told him once, explaining the messiness, the warring, scarring horror.

"Insert tab A into slot B," McBride said, deflecting, going for the joke.

"No, I mean that something twisted and confusing like that is called a paradox."

"A pair of ducks?" He didn't want to be educated; he knew he'd fail the final exam. He'd had it with complexity.

"A pair of fucked ducks."

There was something between McBride's girlfriends and it began to grow, like a romance, as if they had secrets. Daisy had only to say a word and the two of them would be uncontrollably amused, laughing so hard they couldn't speak. McBride vaguely remembered this about her, how she pulled into her private closet, made you feel that only you and she lived there, in the heady and ticklish dark. Her bratty sense of humor was surfacing, now that she'd stepped down from her meds. As well as her readiness to lie. "My brother was sexually ambivalent," she said, when the transvestite next door walked out one evening.

"Before or after the heroin overdose?" McBride said flatly. "Or maybe that was your cousin? She's always got a relative or ex-boyfriend to one-up with," he explained to Martha, who blinked at him, unmoved as a lizard.

"You're just jealous of my radar," Daisy claimed.

"Gaydar," Martha amended. And there they were, hysterical again.

There'd been no abortion, a decision made without McBride's input. One of those roommates in Utah had sent some little seed out innocent in the world, trapped and growing now inside crazy Daisy.

Meanwhile McBride continued to visit the county hospital. He went to see Claire. Claire: tall, and faintly British.

"Why are you here?" she asked him.

He shook his head. She never smiled, never let loose of a somehow reassuring seriousness. She was very somber. You could say anything. She never evaded. "Why are *you* here?" he asked.

"I can't keep house," she said. "I forget to eat. I take walks and get lost. I leave the doors unlocked. My parents' television and video camera and every single CD they owned were stolen last time they left me alone." Her parents were on an extended vacation in Greece. When they traveled, Claire stayed at the hospital.

"You're not sick," McBride told her, "you're just forgetful. If forgetfulness were an illness, the whole city would be in a strait jacket."

"I'm pathologically forgetful," Claire said. "I forget so I can hurt my parents."

"But not consciously?"

"Of course not consciously. They're retired, so this vacation they're taking is from me. Do you understand? They are sitting on a beach, a million miles away from their troubles. Meaning me. I am their troubles."

Then it was summer and McBride began sleeping with Claire. She put on her shoes and they signed her out and drove to a motel on the highway not far from the hospital. Coincidentally, it was across the street from the Triple T truckstop where Daisy had been found. Twenty-five dollars, no questions asked. The cash exchange without receipt or bill, no evidence, no residue. What McBride liked about the Sands Motel was its air-conditioning—no swampy evaporative cooler here—which worked beautifully. Otherwise, the rooms were typically hideous and disturbing. They would not let you forget they'd accommodated hundreds of strangers before you, some sogginess in the carpet, lingering odor of cigarette, ripped sheet where someone else's toenail had pierced through. Claire in sex was the same as Claire in conversation: thoroughly confrontational, right there. "I've heard that this is the most sensitive spot on a man," she might say, pressing the pad of her thumb against his perineum.

"Yes," he would breathe, lifted as if upon a salty sea wave. "You heard right."

She had a thespian's voice, or a smoker's, and she hummed when she was up against McBride, melancholy and rousing as a distant train whistle. She alone called him by his first name, murmuring it. "Your name is like a kiss," she claimed, illustrating by placing it in the hollow of his throat. "Peter," she said, humming lungs, mouth releasing warm air. After sex she lay quietly on his chest and slept, a small smile on her lips. He nestled his palm against her scalp. She had a dainty head. Everywhere her bones were close to the surface, where her fair skin showed tiny blue veins, a network of hairline cracks, porcelain. When he pulled his hand away, her fine black hair shivered with static electricity. In sleep, she looked like what she must have looked like as a child, that smile like a dim memory, as if she were happy.

As he stroked her hair and the painfully knobby knuckles of her spinal column, he wondered why it was he had begun fucking older women. He thought he'd matured, but maybe younger women just didn't like him anymore. Was he more complicated, or more desperate? "We love each other's damage," Martha had once said, to explain their relationship. Apparently, Martha loved his, whatever it was. But only now did McBride actually follow her meaning. He couldn't have said that he loved Claire, but he felt ready to go to the mat for her. To protect this brief easy sleep. To defend her against her parents, for example, if need be, against her own self-loathing.

"You don't have to worry about suicide," she told him one day as he dropped her off after.

McBride had not, until that moment, given it a thought but from then on, of course, he thought of it frequently.

"She hates me," McBride told Martha, referring to Daisy. What he meant was that he hated her.

He and Martha had met for lunch downtown near the courthouse where McBride was laying brick. The summer had become so hot that the workday began at 5 A.M., ending by 1:00. Martha chewed her taco before answering. "She thinks you take me for granted."

"*I* take you for granted? The total stranger who's not even helping with bills, let along *house*keeping, thinks *I'm* taking you for granted?" He was outraged; then he remembered his affair with Claire and calmed down. The checks and balances of intimacy.

Martha smiled. "I have a feeling she's got a kind of crush on me, frankly. I think she thinks I saved her. She's had enough of men, for a while."

He didn't say that he didn't believe Daisy *could* capture a man, these days, so changed was her body, skin, appeal. She had an aura of illness, contagion, that only a maternal impulse could love. "How do I take you for granted?"

"I didn't say you did. Daisy said it."

"But why does she think so?"

Martha leaned forward over the paper wrappings of their lunch, looked at him with her healthy hazel eyes. "She says you used to be much more physical with her than you are with me."

"You listen to this stuff?" His voice was louder than he intended; the lawyers at the next table shifted. Daisy was right, and it made him want to go kill her.

Martha leaned back. "I'm not worried about us. I like you, I think you like me. We laugh enough, even though we don't fuck as often as we used to." She tilted her head, squinted; she could wait. "You asked me what Daisy thought and I told you, but it doesn't bother me. So don't fret."

McBride found Daisy in Martha's sewing room, asleep on the Hide-A-Bed. When he sat beside her she woke without alarm; nothing in human nature would surprise her.

She propped herself sleepily on an elbow, letting the sheet drop to reveal she wore a soiled spaghetti strap t-shirt, nipples large and brown through the sheer material, abdomen like a cantaloupe. "I was thinking you might come to me some day, Mac," she said, placing a warm hand on his thigh.

McBride stood abruptly. "I'm not seducing you," he told her. "I want you out of here, in fact. If you're well enough to think I'd sleep with you, you're well enough to get the fuck out."

"I know you're sleeping with someone else," Daisy said, her eyes leveraging the threat. She would tell. She would ruin his life. There was no correct response so he simply stared at her, hating her. Then she began crying, and it was all McBride could do to keep from throwing a tantrum himself. Her face before him—quivering chapped lips, fair eyebrows full of acne—seemed to want to be struck. What did she expect from him? It enraged him to see her sobbing; he felt like grabbing her by the shoulders and flinging her back against the couch. How dare she know his secret? She looked up from under her hair and suddenly smiled through her tears, as if she'd caught on to a trick. She was a slutty, easy girl, and McBride could not deny the appeal. He remembered her in bed: her pleasure came only in extremity, at the very moment that might mark pain. She liked to bite and be bitten, hair clutched and yanked. Now she laid a hand on his kneecap and spread her fingers slowly, as if she might insinuate herself just this way throughout his system. Infuriated, McBride lurched away, onto the floor. She followed, into his lap, and they were wrestling, Daisy sinking her teeth first into his arm and next his neck, hard enough for his nerves to trill. He put a knee between her legs and forced her arms apart. Below him, crucified, she breathed deeply, a strand of saliva across her cheek. The fact that her t-shirt and underwear did not cover her made McBride aware of her odor, which was powerful, unwashed and sexual. Rank, with a need to be hurt, and him not so far from obliging.

"Go away," he told her desperately. "Please. Go. Away." He felt his swelling erection as a betrayal—but of whom? What?

She rolled out from under him and curled toward the dark cavern beneath the bed like an animal. From the back she looked just like she always had, sinuous, nocturnal.

In the bathroom McBride tilted his head and checked the spot she'd bitten on his neck in the mirror. There were tiny broken capillaries but they looked enough like razor burn to reassure him his struggle with Daisy would go undiscovered. His heart, he noted, was beating so hard he could see it in his chest, in his reflection, pulsing there like a mouse in his pocket.

"If you want to make love with me, you can't do it with anyone else," Claire told him the next day as she ran her fingers over the bite marks on his arm. Leave it to the woman he didn't live with to sniff out his deception. "I know you live with Martha, but that doesn't necessarily mean you make love with her."

"We have sex," McBride told her, wondering why he found it necessary to convince her of this fact while obscuring others.

"Sex with someone you live with is more like masturbation," she said. "Just some warm object to rub on until you come. 'Do-it-yourself sex.' "

"I'm a do-it-yourselfer from way back," McBride said, wanting the punchline, wanting to stay out of the deep well, out of the tricky web. Women were so prone to abstraction, to pitching you into outer space. They were not afraid of the dark, the absence of gravity.

"Fucking her isn't necessarily making love," Claire said. "*We* make love." Then she fell into her post-coital nap, a little gift her body gave her, exhausted childish sleep.

He took home Claire's theory and tried it on the next time he and Martha had sex. In the living room, Daisy watched television, a habit she'd adopted at the psychiatric hospital and had not given up. She sat around the house indulging an adolescent appetite, Cheetos and Skittles, Count Chocula. "Where are you?" Martha whispered in his face, holding it in her plump fingers, peering inside him, nose to nose. She was stoned, a state that made her want orgasm and honesty. McBride thought of Claire's words and Daisy's pregnant breasts while he worked his penis inside Martha. Where was he, indeed?

"You can go," she breathed into his ear, his mature girlfriend with her solid legs around his hips, feet locked behind him, "but you have to come back."

The next time he visited the hospital, Claire had been moved to a new ward. They were doing what an aide called a suicide watch. Claire had been caught sawing at her wrists, using a plastic knife but still. "Those things have serrated edges, man," the aide said. "Ser*rated*," he repeated.

McBride found her tranquilized, staring apathetically at a *New York Review of Books* tabloid. "I can't read this," she said. "The words are floating around like boats."

Her wrists were wrapped with gauze, bright clean bracelets. "I feel poisoned," she declared, sailing the book review across the room like a Frisbee. "They're trying to kill me." Considering her behavior, McBride couldn't hold it against the hospital.

"Why?" he asked, hoping simplicity would be his strong suit.

"Why not, you big asshole? That's the real question." She drew a soppy breath, her fine features bruisey, as if she weren't getting enough oxygen. She cried in the slow, drugged way of hopeless sedation. "Asshole" was not really part of her vocabulary. That was the drugs talking.

"Baby," he said, embracing her, careful of her bandages.

"That's what I need," she said, "a term of endearment. *Muffin. Kitten.*"

"Maybe you should eat? You look kind of . . ."

"I hate fat," Claire said flatly. "I work hard to be thin. I *don't* eat, in order to be thin."

"That's kind of sick."

She simply stared at him, waiting for something she didn't know to emerge from his mouth. "Your girlfriend is fat," she added. It wasn't a good moment. McBride liked her better when she wasn't catty. Also, he was too tempted to respond in kind, to be catty with her. They could get nasty together, it turned out, eat each other's spleen. "She's a got a big *tush,* that girlfriend of yours."

"Where are mom and dad?"

"Flying home, wringing their. . ." She held out her own hands, illustrating by twisting her palms, wrists stiff in their wrapping. "They don't have a notion what to do."

"What should *I* do?" he asked.

"Save me," she said, collapsing against him. She wanted to take him with her, he thought. She was drowning, and if he did not escape this clutch, he would wind up washed ashore somewhere, bloated and blue.

"You can't save her," he told Martha that very night, referring to Daisy, hoping he was right. Daisy, seven months pregnant, had disappeared into South Tucson. The three of them had been eating Mexican food across from the greyhound track; they'd made money betting on those strange creatures, then celebrated with burritos and beer, Daisy on her best behavior, sipping a soda, consuming protein and calcium, like a good mother. But after the bathroom run, she was gone.

Their waiter gave an elaborate shrug, his mustache a wriggling caterpillar on his upper lip.

"Fucking Daisy," McBride said, vindicated. She could not be saved, see? "I guess we have to call the police." He got ahead of himself, saw himself standing around with a cop describing his lunatic ex-girlfriend, driving through dangerous South Tucson looking for a fuzzy-headed pregnant woman . . . But Martha was giving him such a glance full of disappointment and impatience that he returned to the present moment, Corona bottles, coagulated quesadilla.

"It scares me how much you hate her. You used to love her."

"Come on, Martha, she's manipulative and dishonest and so totally fucked up . . ." Wasn't the evidence capable of speaking for itself? Furthermore, he refused to believe he'd ever loved Daisy. No one could prove it.

"We have to find her," Martha said, rising from their booth. "You pay, I'll be out on 4th Ave., walking."

"You can't walk on Fourth—" But she was through the door, and the waiter was handing McBride the ticket, shrugging again, apologetic.

They fought while they searched for Daisy. McBride considered how efficient the situation was—usually a fight required so much energy, such a commitment of time, the yelling part, the pulling-the-phone-out-of-the-wall part, the walk-around-the-block part, the silent thoughtful part, the making up part, the crying and fucking, headache and hangover, raked-over-the-coals, run-through-the-wringer, launched-into-space, deep-in-the-hole part. Hours could go by; a person could lose a day. So it was good, in his opinion, to be occupied with the quest for Daisy while they had their squabble. The problem was that Martha had more experience fighting, a more logical mindset, and made points like a lawyer. Like a public defender, the type doing pro bono business, the righteous path of the do-gooder. She took the moral high-road—Daisy in trouble, loyalty, humanity—which left McBride with the inevitable role of bastard. Add to this the affair with suicidal Claire, and you had the picture of a man in a futile argument, perhaps about to be dumped by a nice woman in whose nice house he was living, driving badly in a bad neighborhood, to boot.

He found himself hoping they would see Daisy out there in the dark.

But Daisy was gone for five days, and the fight with Martha wasn't resolved even after all that time. Somehow the stages had gotten messed up; they couldn't progress past sullen silence with each other. Martha was *disappointed* in him. He couldn't make himself fix it. She had every right to be *disappointed* in him. As much as he'd once lusted after Daisy, he now reviled her; that was what troubled Martha, the degree to which love could flip to hate. "Paradox," he wanted to tell her savagely. "That old saw."

He avoided Claire. He abandoned her by telling himself he was being true to Martha.

Daisy managed to phone them up from Phoenix, where a truck driver had left her after buying her a new wardrobe and giving her a stack of *Watchtowers* to contemplate. His name was Buck, and Daisy entered the house referring to his kindness constantly.

Martha hugged her wayward stray, patting Daisy's back maternally; McBride resisted the urge to punch her in the face.

"You're not a burden," Martha insisted when Daisy tried to explain her running away. "I want you to stay with me, even after the baby. I love babies." Embracing, the two women looked decidedly freakish, in McBride's opinion. "You're just bored," Martha insisted. "You need some meaningful activity during these last weeks. Maybe I could teach you how to drive?"

They settled on shopping. Neither of them was a mall type, which made the trip that much more thrilling. Daisy came home wearing her old perfume again, an expensive scent, describable in the way of fine wine: the amber plushness of pears, velvet, oak, wealth. McBride remembered it with equal parts revulsion and nostalgia.

"*Hos*talgia," he thought: sick desire.

That night, when he couldn't get into the spirit of a fashion show featuring maternity clothes and hair clips, Martha accused him of impersonating an adult. Abruptly she threw him a curve, direct from her stoned keenness. "Are you in love with someone else?"

"What?"

She waited.

"No," he croaked, wanting to ask if Daisy had told her something, knowing that would backfire. "No," he repeated, unconvincingly. Just a week ago it would have been a lie, but how could he explain now? The timing made him want to laugh like a madman.

"I'm sleeping in the sewing room tonight," Martha said, taking her pillow.

"Maybe you should fuck Daisy!" he blurted.

"Maybe I should," she agreed, calmly, leveling an unashamed glance in his direction.

Where did women get it, that composure, that open-minded fluid sense that not only might anything happen, but that it might be amazing? McBride could all too easily envision Daisy and Martha naked together, tongue to nape of neck, breast to breast, quivering haunch to ropy one, the homecoming embrace pushed to a climax. It was pretty, candlelit, its soundtrack full of saxophone.

Men with men: who could look upon it with anything but perplexity? Erections bobbing between them like those annoying trick snakes, coiled in a peanut can, unsealed and sent sproinging in your face. Ha ha. Meanwhile in the background, soundtrack a circus organ grinder, perhaps a kazoo.

He lay awake alone beneath the SOFT SHOULDER sign thinking of Martha. Was she trying to make him her little boy? Punish him? Improve him? "You know what your problem is?" she'd once told him, laughing yet serious, "You have gag reflex."

"Meaning?"

"Meaning, you can't deal." She did not suffer from this impediment. Why had she attached herself to *him?* Only lately had he wondered—was he a project, not unlike flaky Daisy, someone shell-shocked and deemed for whatever reason worthy of Martha's concern? He didn't want to be her project. He preferred to think of himself as her willing plaything, the party boy, the one who could choose to leave the party. He paid rent, he stocked beer and toilet paper, he had volition.

"You're a coward," Martha told him in the morning. Overnight, she seemed to have chosen against him. She didn't even seem concerned enough to be hurt. Just that disappointed. "You won't commit to anything. The hard parts embarrass you. You feel like everything's a scene instead of just another opportunity to get close to someone. That's what's unforgivable. You're terrible in a crisis. You just want the easy parts, none of the work."

He could not think of Claire, but what he said was, "Is this about having a baby?"

"This is about *you,*" Martha said. "A topic with which you should be fairly familiar. This is about a woman you not only left behind like some dog on the highway, but about whom you won't say one kind word." McBride had to marvel: even angry she wouldn't leave her prepositions dangling. "Not one," said Martha. "I can't get over what a jerk you seem to be. Actually, what I can't get over is that I'm in love with a jerk. I should know better."

"I love you, too," he said quickly.

Martha sighed. "That is *so* not the point."

Meanwhile, Claire's parents sprang her from the psych hospital, which meant that McBride had to sit in their living room drinking iced tea making small talk with them before taking Claire to the motel across from the Triple T. He was conducting an experiment, testing his maturity, trying to recapture what seemed to have scurried off. Were his intentions honorable? her parents' faces asked, forlorn, unsure how to behave if the answer were no. The scars on Claire's wrists were disconcerting, raised welts with tiny suture holes on either side.

"Will those go away?" he asked at the motel, putting his lips on her scars, working at not being disgusted.

"How should I know?" Claire was naked now, but what she'd removed were sea foam green scrubs, as if qualified to dress like a doctor, having hung around them for a while.

"Why so testy?" McBride asked, checking his watch. The iced tea and chat had seriously cut into their time. When Claire smacked him, he didn't know if it was for the question or the looking-at-the-watch. She was one unpredictable girl. They made love then, and following, went through the requisite small sleep. Everyone was different after sex; McBride preferred chatting, himself. Daisy, back when she'd been his girlfriend, smoked cigarettes afterward, like people in the 1940s movies, leaving little cinder burns in the bedsheets, soulful and alone, teary. Martha got talkative and affectionate, told jokes, tickled his ribs, wanted to eat sandwiches and leave crumbs. But Claire, she went into that wee coma.

Leaving McBride to think. Who did he love? Could he ask his women to put in bids for him, sell himself to the one who turned in the most impressive vita? Was he looking for a particular kind of woman and had to have these three to provide one whole? He considered the virtues of each—Martha's good humor and stability, Claire's startling honesty and tragic openness, Daisy's wild sexuality and obsessiveness—and understood their individual appeal as well as their limitations. But perhaps it was having three of them that really excited him. His affection was maybe like a dropped watermelon, three rocking wet seedy parts. Or like a trident. He pictured his penis, three-pronged instead of one. Or maybe he needed the compounded guilt each relationship made him feel, especially as it related to the other two. High drama had its own charm, like living on a fault plane.

Claire's parents sat right where they'd been left, on plush Barca Loungers before the television. Their iced tea glasses still full of tea, diluted, sweating puddles. The strange stasis that had apparently prevailed here while McBride had been off in a rutting fever, ravishing their middle-aged daughter in a cheesy motel gave him pause. *This* gave him pause—her father looking sad, her mother looking sadder—not the preceding insanity.

He would not be back. His last look at Claire was like his first: she was with her parents, sullen, struggling.

He arrived home to find Daisy entertaining the transvestite. They sat in the chairs that McBride and Martha had used to sit in, in the breeze from the oscillating fan. The transvestite had left lipstick prints on a hand thrown coffee cup. In his large palms, the cup was dwarfed, silly. His nails, unpainted, were smooth, on the verge of being long, and his knuckles, McBride took a moment to notice, were shaved. Unbelievable. The man stayed seated as he extended one of these hands for a shake, like a lady.

"Alberta," he announced, "your neighbor."

"We've seen you around," McBride said, gripping a little too firmly, a little too masculinely.

"I love the furniture! Your wife is *amazing* with a paintbrush!"

"Not his wife," Daisy was quick to say. "How was *your* day, Mackle?" she asked coquettishly, grinning up at him, employing a long-ago pet name, reminding him of others: *Prozac,* because he'd pulled her out of a depression, way back when. *Moon Pie,* he'd called her. And meant it.

"I gotta pee," McBride said, exiting. Entering. Well, here was his house but where was his confidence about belonging in it? On the porch sat the man, the woman, the soon-to-be baby, a fundamental threesome unrelated and weird. "You're not strong enough to accept the limitations of others," insightful Martha had informed him. He wished she would quit knowing him so well, stop being so smart. Why *did* she love a jerk like him? Was that the weakness he would have to object to? He felt like a rung bell, jangling in a lonesome tower, village idiot down below yanking his chain.

"Did you know it was going to be black?" McBride asked Martha.

"I knew it was a fifty-fifty chance." Martha was flushed, wearing a set of green scrubs like the ones Claire owned. Six women had attended Daisy's labor and delivery, Daisy screaming like a tortured crow, the rest of them murmuring and assuring, a room of pigeons. The baby, a perfectly healthy girl, was purple as a Nigerian. McBride could only gawk. No one else was fazed; their role was to adore, congratulate, rally. Martha cradled the baby in such a manner that McBride finally understood he would have to leave her. Already that baby meant more to her than he did, or could. Never had a decision been clearer. It made him feel oddly selfless, to see his responsibility.

"Isn't it amazing?" Martha positively glowed, face ruddy with the effort, good work, the species' only real priority. She could have been the mother herself, with her wide hips and open heart.

"Unbelievable," McBride said. He looked at the tiny bundle in her arms, dark and constricted. Hard to believe she'd grow up to wear cheap jewelry and eat junk food. Let boys put their hands between her thighs. "Reminds me of an eggplant," he told Martha.

She looked at him as if through the retracting lens of a spyglass: goodbye. "You're so cold," she said, turning back to the room of women.

The deal is, it always goes from bad to worse. The living trajectory, birth to death, going up means coming down. Like that.

McBride told himself these things as he drove to the hospital emergency room a week after Donatella's birth. Claire had jumped from one of Tucson's few overpasses into the traffic below. Everything was broken, head to toe; she would die. She lay now unconscious while a team of experts tried to put her back together. McBride was not innocent in this, as he had not seen her for more than a month, pretending he was tired, pretending he felt guilty about deceiving Martha, pretending he had problems as profound as hers. How was it that affection turned, tiny tender gears no longer meshing, gone suddenly, overnight, eroded with pity? Sour with scorn? When her mother called, three in the morning, Martha had handed him the phone with a single scathing word, that one that had been like a kiss: *Peter.* They'd just failed to have sex, McBride pumping furiously, stiff as a stick of dynamite, unable to explode.

Now he screamed into the E.R parking lot, horrified. One more portion of his life, another member of his tribe of female troubles, gone haywire. You build complication like a house of cards, geometrical, tricky, fragile. And like a child, you then like to step aside and stamp your feet, watch as it folds up on itself, flat one-dimensional deck. Dead.

Oh, those parents. Once again, sitting unmoving, identical drinks before them, same condensation. On the television: television. His intentions hadn't been honorable, apparently, after all. Had she wanted to die for his love, or its lack? She lay in the highly technical, highly temporary ICU, wrapped, strapped, tracheotomy tube in her neck, metal bolt in her skull, suction hose in her mouth, monitors around her like a recording studio, flashing numbers, graphs. Crust of rusty blood here and there, and her beautiful eyelashes, like folded fragile spider legs, wilted on those pale cheeks. Did this sleep replicate the one she fell into after sex? McBride swooned. Fainting wasn't what he had imagined. He was aware of himself crashing, vital fluids rushing from head, hands, feet to pool and churn in his stomach. His thought was that he would vomit, and be left empty as a pocket. And there was the nurse, the woman who, like a mother, materialized beside him at just the proper moment to smooth his brow, bring him 'round.

He held Claire's letter to him, unopened, missive from the grave, given over by the parents. Her heart, in his hands. On his porch sat four females, lover, ex-girlfriend, her black infant, and the neighbor who counted himself among the girls. Where did McBride fit? He could not be what they required. Nothing to do but squeeze out, he had already been squeezed out.

And he was glad, he told himself. Glad for his simple body, its fixtures out in the open, the expression on his face projecting exactly what was behind it in his head. What was it with women and all this hidden equipment? They dressed up, made-up, faked orgasms, cried when happy, laughed when bitter, stirred up protoplasmic stews of life and then pulled rabbits from hats, wreaked havoc all the wide world over, forever refusing to come clean.

That was how he wanted to feel, driving his car with his worldly possessions: clean. Free. Were those the same as being cold? Cowardly? He'd left Salt Lake City and he could leave Tucson; the West was full of cities where his slate would be blank, his plate would be empty. There was a girl out there, he could almost see her, radiant, blond, a healthy hiker a few years younger than he, straight teeth, muscular calves, sentimental taste in music. He would find *her* . . . But how did that accident claim go, the one that had amused him not so long ago? "I saw a slow moving, sad-faced old gentleman as he bounded off the roof of my car. . ." Nothing to do but plunge on. Set the cruise control, lower the windows, raise the radio, stay between the broken yellow lines, and don't look back. No no no.

Joyce Carol Oates (*1938–*)

one of the most prolific and honored writers in history, is the author of over one hundred books, including forty-five novels and twenty-six collections of short stories. In 1962, her story "The Fine White Mist of Winter" appeared in both The Best American Short Stories *and* Prize Stories: The O. Henry Awards*—her first appearance in either annual. In most of the years since, she has been in one or both volumes: the most frequently honored writer in the history of each of those nearly century-old series (four times as often as Eudora Welty, three times as often as John Cheever, more than twice as often as John Updike or William Faulkner). She is perhaps the greatest writer ever about American violence, something that, early in her career, she was criticized for, a criticism she called "always sexist. . . . The serious male writer is allowed his vision and takes as his rightful subject a world as vast as Dostoyevsky's Russia, or Melville's oceans or Faulkner's 'postage stamp of earth' in Mississippi. One does not inquire of them, 'Why is your writing so violent?'" She is a recipient of the National Book Award (and was nominated for it five other times, including four years in a row, from 1968–1971) and the PEN/Malamud Award for Excellence in Short Fiction. She has written some of the most enduring fiction of our time, including the national bestsellers* We Were the Mulvaneys *and* Blonde*. She is the Roger S. Berlind Distinguished Professor of Humanities at Princeton University and has been a member since 1978 of the American Academy of Arts and Letters.*

Introduction by **Jennifer Egan**

It would be pointless to tally up the works of Joyce Carol Oates; by the time you read these words, the numbers will be irrelevant. The rate of her production—of novels, short stories, essays, poetry, plays, book reviews, children's books, and more—is frankly staggering. When I try to imagine what writing must feel like for Oates, I think of Hilda Pederson, the fourteen-year-old mathematical genius she portrayed in her magnificent early novel *Wonderland*. Overexcited during a competition, Hilda struggles to tame the pullulation of numbers in her head. "A fountain of numbers shoots up in the air . . . The numbers spin into a tower, fatter and fatter at the top . . . the tower floats upward, a galaxy of numbers. How can I make them into a single number? How can I still the bursting of these numbers?"

Oates has said, quite reasonably, that she should be judged not by the quantity of work she has produced, but by her best; and by any standard, her best is exceptional. Her double-jointed prose can flick from stream of consciousness to idiomatic speech to telescopic distance with so little obvious effort that one forgets the arsenal of technical skills these moves require. Her subject matter is bold to the point of presumption, as every writer's should be. Nothing is off limits to Oates, be it graphic sexuality, excruciating violence, encounters with the supernatural, or the inner lives of Teddy Kennedy, Marilyn Monroe, or a serial child molester. If I learned that her next novel took place among a colony of hamsters on Mars, I would feel only mild surprise.

But for all her freewheeling range, Oates does have a fictional roosting post: the minds and lives of young girls. Some of her best novels—*You Must Remember This*, *Because*

It Is Bitter and Because It Is My Heart, Blonde—deal in large part with the experience of female adolescence: its vanities and vulnerabilities, its uneasy mix of chaotic sexuality and relative innocence. The stories collected here are vintage Oates; two involve teenage girls, the third a girl of indeterminate age looking back on events that happened when she was five.

"Life After High School" begins in characteristic Oates fashion: with a bit of dialogue that transports the reader directly inside a climactic moment of the story, from which Oates backtracks to show us how we got there. The virtuous and goodhearted Sunny Burhman might seem too narrow a character to hang a short story on, but Oates makes it clear that Sunny's impossible innocence is transitory: "Though one day, and soon, Sunny would examine her beliefs, and question the faith into which she'd been born; she had not done so by the age of seventeen and a half. She was a virgin, and virginal in all, or most, of her thoughts." That last sentence is slyly revealing: "all" and "most" are very different things, of course, but Oates leaves the gap between them unexamined, ". . . just as Sonny herself" does. In the final movement of "Life After High School," Oates turns the story inside out; Sunny learns that the central drama of her adolescence—namely, the tale we've just read—was never the real story at all but a cover for a very different story that couldn't be told in 1959. Likewise, the real protagonist of "Life After High School" was never Sunny Burhman so much as the era she typifies.

"Ghost Girls" showcases Oates's love of colloquial language—the tics and irregularities of an individual voice. It starts like a campfire ghost story: "The story I want to tell began in upstate New York, in the Chautauqua Mountains, in August 1972." Oates luxuriates in the childish rhythms of the voice of Ingrid, the young narrator, who says of her mother, "She didn't hear, she was starting to snore, not like Daddy snored but softer and discontinuous like asking questions? each little breathy snore a question? And I smelled Momma's special smell when she was tired and hadn't washed in a while. . . ." Ingrid and her mother have embarked on a hasty and ominous journey from which Ingrid's father is mysteriously absent; it's not clear to Ingrid whether he is orchestrating their escape from afar or whether it's him they're escaping from. Into this faintly menacing environment, Oates interjects the ghosts of two young girls who were murdered by their father. It is worth looking carefully at how she handles the final interaction between the "real" girl and the ghost girls. It's a scary scene, but not because ghosts are involved—rather, because Ingrid's own future and safety seem suddenly in doubt.

"Where Are You Going, Where Have You Been?" is the masterpiece of this trio. Oates requires barely a sentence to conjure up Connie, her protagonist: "She was fifteen and she had a quick nervous giggling habit of craning her neck to glance into mirrors, or checking other people's faces to make sure her own was alright." We've all known this girl—vain, uncertain, searching for an identity, dismissive of her family, the sort of teenager whom it's hard to imagine grown up because she's still so immature.

The long scene between Connie and Arnold Friend is a tour de force of controlled revelation. At first, Connie (and, most likely, the reader) assumes that the boy coming up the driveway in the gold jalopy is a teenager from Connie's world. "Her heart began to pound and her fingers snatched at her hair, checking it, and she whispered, 'Christ. Christ,' wondering how bad she looked." But Connie comes to recognize not just that this boy isn't from her world, but that he's not even a boy, and the scene turns threatening. Even then, Oates unspools the horror very slowly. Okay, the reader thinks, so he's a man. He's a bad man. He's going to rob her, even rape her. As Oates nudges the true extent of Arnold Friend's depravity into view and as Connie perceives and reacts to her own defenselessness, she seems to mature before our eyes. In a matter of a few paragraphs, she is transformed from a sulky teen into a woman struggling heroically against great danger. And in the moment of achieving this maturity, Connie also grasps the truth of her situation: "She thought, I'm not going to see my mother again. She thought, I'm not going to sleep in my bed again. Her bright green blouse was all wet."

Oates ends the story with Connie leaving her house and walking into the future she is finally prepared for and that she probably won't live to experience. "Where Are You Going, Where Have You Been?" is as devastating a short story as I've ever read. And it's worth studying closely because the qualities that allow Oates to bring off a tragedy of this scale in the span of a few pages—power and compression—are the axes of all great short fiction.

Jennifer Egan is the author, most recently, of the novel Look at Me, *which was a finalist for the National Book Award in 2001. She also writes frequently for the* New York Times Magazine.

JOYCE CAROL OATES

Where Are You Going, Where Have You Been?

Her name was Connie. She was fifteen and she had a quick nervous giggling habit of craning her neck to glance into mirrors, or checking other people's faces to make sure her own was all right. Her mother, who noticed everything and knew everything and who hadn't much reason any longer to look at her own face, always scolded Connie about it. "Stop gawking at yourself. Who are you? You think you're so pretty?" she would say. Connie would raise her eyebrows at these familiar complaints and look right through her mother, into a shadowy vision of herself as she was right at that moment: she knew she was pretty and that was everything. Her mother had been pretty once too, if you could believe those old snapshots in the album, but now her looks were gone and that was why she was always after Connie.

"Why don't you keep your room clean like your sister? How've you got your hair fixed—what the hell stinks? Hair spray? You don't see your sister using that junk."

Her sister June was twenty-four and still lived at home. She was a secretary in the high school Connie attended, and if that wasn't bad enough—with her in the same building—she was so plain and chunky and steady that Connie had to hear her praised all the time by her mother and her mother's sisters. June did this, June did that, she saved money and helped clean the house and cooked and Connie couldn't do a thing, her mind was all filled with trashy daydreams. Their father was away at work most of the time and when he came home he wanted supper and he read the newspaper at supper and after supper he went to bed. He didn't bother talking much to them, but around his bent head Connie's mother kept picking at her until Connie wished her mother was dead and she herself was dead and it was all over. "She makes me want to throw up sometimes," she complained to her friends. She had a high, breathless, amused voice which made everything she said sound a little forced, whether it was sincere or not.

There was one good thing: June went places with girl friends of hers, girls who were just as plain and steady as she, and so when Connie wanted to do that her mother had no objections. The father of Connie's best friend drove the girls the three miles to town and left them off at a shopping plaza, so that they could walk through the stores or go to a movie, and when he came to pick them up again at eleven he never bothered to ask what they had done.

They must have been familiar sights, walking around that shopping plaza in their shorts and flat ballerina slippers that always scuffed the sidewalk, with charm bracelets jingling on their thin wrists; they would lean together to whisper and laugh secretly if someone passed by who amused or interested them. Connie had long dark blond hair that drew anyone's eye to it, and she wore part of it pulled up on her head and puffed out and the rest of it she let fall down her back. She wore a pull-over jersey blouse that looked one way when she was at home and another way when she was away from home. Everything about her had two sides to it, one for home and one for anywhere that was not home: her walk that could be childlike and bobbing, or languid enough to make anyone think she was hearing music in her head, her mouth which was pale and smirking most of the time, but bright and pink on these evenings out, her laugh which was cynical and drawling at home—"Ha, ha, very funny,"—but high-pitched and nervous anywhere else, like the jingling of the charms on her bracelet.

Sometimes they did go shopping or to a movie, but sometimes they went across the highway, ducking fast across the busy road, to a drive-in restaurant where older kids hung out. The restaurant was shaped like a big bottle, though squatter than a real bottle, and on its cap was a revolving figure of a grinning boy who held a hamburger aloft. One night in mid-summer they ran across, breathless with daring, and right away someone leaned out a car window and invited them over, but it was just a boy from high school they didn't like. It made them feel good to be able to ignore him. They went up through the maze of parked and cruising cars to the bright-lit, fly-infested restaurant, their faces pleased and expectant as if they were entering a sacred building that loomed out of the night to give them what haven and what blessing they yearned for. They sat at the counter and crossed their legs at the ankles, their thin shoulders rigid with excitement, and listened to the music that made everything so good: the music was always in the background like music at a church service; it was something to depend upon.

A boy named Eddie came in to talk with them. He sat backwards on his stool, turning himself jerkily around in semi-circles and then stopping and turning again, and after a while he asked Connie if she would like something to eat. She said she did and so she tapped her friend's arm on her way out—her friend pulled her face up into a brave droll look—and Connie said she would meet her at eleven, across the way. "I just hate to leave her like that," Connie said earnestly, but the boy said that she wouldn't be alone for long. So they went out to his car and on the way Connie couldn't help but let her eyes wander over the windshields and faces all around her, her face gleaming with a joy that had nothing to do with Eddie or even this place; it might have been the music. She drew her shoulders up and sucked in her breath with the pure pleasure of being alive, and just at that moment she happened to glance at a face just a few feet from hers. It was a boy with shaggy black hair, in a convertible jalopy painted gold. He stared at her and then his lips widened into a grin. Connie slit her eyes at him and turned away, but she couldn't help glancing back and there he was still watching her. He wagged a finger and laughed and said, "Gonna get you, baby," and Connie turned away again without Eddie noticing anything.

She spent three hours with him, at the restaurant where they ate hamburgers and drank Cokes in wax cups that were always sweating, and then down an alley a mile or so away, and when he left her off at five to eleven only the movie house was still open at the plaza. Her girl friend was there, talking with a boy. When Connie came up the two girls smiled at each other and Connie said, "How was the movie?" and the girl said, "*You* should know." They rode off with the girl's father, sleepy and pleased, and Connie couldn't help but look at the darkened shopping plaza with its big empty parking lot and its signs that were faded and ghostly now, and over at the drive-in restaurant where cars were still circling tirelessly. She couldn't hear the music at this distance.

Next morning June asked her how the movie was and Connie said, "So-so."

She and that girl and occasionally another girl went out several times a week that way, and the rest of the time Connie spent around the house—it was summer vacation—getting in her mother's way and thinking, dreaming, about the boys she met. But all the boys fell back and dissolved into a single face that was not even a face but an idea, a feeling, mixed up with the urgent insistent pounding of the music and the humid night air of July. Connie's mother kept dragging her back to the daylight by finding things for her to do or saying, suddenly, "What's this about the Pettinger girl?"

And Connie would say nervously, "Oh, her. That dope." She always drew thick clear lines between herself and such girls, and her mother was simple and kindly enough to believe her. Her mother was so simple, Connie thought, that it was maybe cruel to fool her so much. Her mother went scuffling around the house in old bedroom slippers and complained over the telephone to one sister about the other, then the other called up and the two of them complained about the third one. If June's name was mentioned her mother's tone was approving, and if Connie's name was mentioned it was disapproving. This did not really mean she disliked Connie and actually Connie thought that her mother preferred her to June because she was prettier, but the two of them kept up a pretense of exasperation, a sense that they were tugging and struggling over something of little value to either of them. Sometimes, over coffee, they were almost friends, but something would come up—some vexation that was like a fly buzzing suddenly around their heads—and their faces went hard with contempt.

One Sunday Connie got up at eleven—none of them bothered with church—and washed her hair so that it could dry all day long in the sun. Her parents and sister were going to a barbecue at an aunt's house and Connie said no, she wasn't interested, rolling her eyes to let her mother know just what she thought of it. "Stay home alone then," her mother said sharply. Connie sat out back in a lawn chair and watched them drive away, her father quiet and bald, hunched around so that he could back the car out, her mother with a look that was still angry and not at all softened through the windshield, and in the back seat poor old June all dressed up as if she didn't know what a barbecue was, with all the running yelling kids and the flies. Connie sat with her eyes closed in the sun, dreaming and dazed with the warmth about her as if this were a kind of love, the caresses of love, and her mind slipped over onto thoughts of the boy she had been with the night before and how nice he had been, how sweet it always was, not the way someone like June would suppose but sweet, gentle, the way it was in movies and promised in songs; and when she opened her eyes she hardly knew where she was, the back yard ran off into the weeds and a fence-like line of trees and behind it the sky was perfectly blue and still. The asbestos "ranch house" that was now three years old startled her—it looked small. She shook her head as if to get awake.

It was too hot. She went inside the house and turned on the radio to drown out the quiet. She sat on the edge of her bed, barefoot, and listened for an hour and a half to a program called XYZ Sunday Jamboree, record after record of hard, fast, shrieking songs she sang along with, interspersed by exclamations from "Bobby King": "An' look here you girls at Napoleons—Son and Charley want you to pay real close attention to this song coming up!"

And Connie paid close attention herself, bathed in a glow of slow-pulsed joy that seemed to rise mysteriously out of the music itself and lay languidly about the airless little room, breathed in and breathed out with each gentle rise and fall of her chest.

After a while she heard a car coming up the drive. She sat up at once, startled, because it couldn't be her father so soon. The gravel kept crunching all the way in from the road—the driveway was long—and Connie ran to the window. It was a car she didn't know. It was an open jalopy, painted a bright gold that caught the sunlight opaquely. Her heart began to pound and her fingers snatched at her hair, checking it, and she whispered "Christ. Christ," wondering how bad she looked. The car came to a stop at the side door and the horn sounded four short taps as if this were a signal Connie knew.

She went into the kitchen and approached the door slowly, then hung out the screen door, her bare toes curling down off the step. There were two boys in the car and now she recognized the driver: he had shaggy, shabby black hair that looked crazy as a wig and he was grinning at her.

"I ain't late, am I?" he said.

"Who the hell do you think you are?" Connie said.

"Toldja I'd be out, didn't I?"

"I don't even know who you are."

She spoke sullenly, careful to show no interest or pleasure, and he spoke in a fast, bright monotone. Connie looked past him to the other boy, taking her time. He had fair brown hair, with a lock that fell onto his forehead. His sideburns gave him a fierce, embarrassed look, but so far he hadn't even bothered to glance at her. Both boys wore sunglasses. The driver's glasses were metallic and mirrored everything in miniature.

"You wanta come for a ride?" he said.

Connie smirked and let her hair fall loose over one shoulder.

"Don'tcha like my car? New paint job," he said. "Hey."

"What?"

"You're cute."

She pretended to fidget, chasing flies away from the door.

"Don'tcha believe me, or what?" he said.

"Look, I don't even know who you are," Connie said in disgust.

"Hey, Ellie's got a radio, see. Mine's broke down." He lifted his friend's arm and showed her the little transistor the boy was holding, and now Connie began to hear the music. It was the same program that was playing inside the house.

"Bobby King?" she said.

"I listen to him all the time. I think he's great."

"He's kind of great," Connie said reluctantly.

"Listen, that guy's *great.* He knows where the action is."

Connie blushed a little, because the glasses made it impossible for her to see just what this boy was looking at. She couldn't decide if she liked him or if he was just a jerk, and so she dawdled in the doorway and wouldn't come down or go back inside. She said, "What's all that stuff painted on your car?"

"Can'tcha read it?" He opened the door very carefully, as if he was afraid it might fall off. He slid out just as carefully, planting his feet firmly on the ground, the tiny metallic world in his glasses slowing down like gelatin hardening and in the midst of it Connie's bright green blouse. "This here is my name, to begin with," he said. ARNOLD FRIEND was written in tarlike black letters on the side, with a drawing of a round, grinning face that reminded Connie of a pumpkin, except it wore sunglasses. "I wanta introduce myself, I'm Arnold Friend and that's my real name and I'm gonna be your friend, honey, and inside the car's Ellie Oscar, he's kinda shy." Ellie brought his transistor radio up to his shoulder and balanced it there. "Now these numbers are a secret code, honey," Arnold Friend explained. He read off the numbers 33, 19, 17 and raised his eyebrows at her to see what she thought of that, but she didn't think much of it. The left rear fender had been smashed and around it was written, on the gleaming gold background: DONE BY CRAZY WOMAN DRIVER. Connie had to laugh at that. Arnold Friend was pleased at her laughter and looked up at her. "Around the other side's a lot more—you wanta come and see them?"

"No."

"Why not?"

"Why should I?"

"Don'tcha wanta see what's on the car? Don'tcha wanta go for a ride?"

"I don't know."

"Why not?"

"I got things to do."

"Like what?"

"Things."

He laughed as if she had said something funny. He slapped his thighs. He was standing in a strange way, leaning back against the car as if he were balancing himself. He wasn't tall, only an inch or so taller than she would be if she came down to him. Connie liked the way he was dressed, which was the way all of them dressed: tight faded jeans stuffed into black, scuffed boots, a belt that pulled his waist in and showed how lean he was, and a white pull-over shirt that was a little soiled and showed the hard small muscles of his arms and shoulders. He looked as if he probably did hard work, lifting and carrying things. Even his neck looked muscular. And his face was a familiar face, somehow: the jaw and chin and cheeks slightly darkened, because he hadn't shaved for a day or two, and the nose long and hawklike, sniffing as if she were a treat he was going to gobble up and it was all a joke.

"Connie, you ain't telling the truth. This is your day set aside for a ride with me and you know it," he said, still laughing. The way he straightened and recovered from his fit of laughing showed that it had been all fake.

"How do you know what my name is?" she said suspiciously.

"It's Connie."

"Maybe and maybe not."

"I know my Connie," he said, wagging his finger. Now she remembered him even better, back at the restaurant, and her cheeks warmed at the thought of how she sucked in her breath just at the moment she passed him—how she must have looked to him. And he had remembered her. "Ellie and I come out here especially for you," he said. "Ellie can sit in back. How about it?"

"Where?"

"Where what?"

"Where're we going?"

He looked at her. He took off the sunglasses and she saw how pale the skin around his eyes was, like holes that were not in shadow but instead in light. His eyes were like chips of broken glass that catch the light in an amiable way. He smiled. It was as if the idea of going for a ride somewhere, to some place, was a new idea to him.

"Just for a ride, Connie sweetheart."

"I never said my name was Connie," she said.

"But I know what it is. I know your name and all about you, lots of things," Arnold Friend said. He had not moved yet but stood still leaning back against the side of his jalopy. "I took a special interest in you, such a pretty girl, and found out all about you—like I know your parents and sister are gone somewheres and I know where and how long they're going to be gone, and I know who you were with last night, and your best girl friend's name is Betty. Right?"

He spoke in a simple lilting voice, exactly as if he were reciting the words to a song. His smile assured her that everything was fine. In the car Ellie turned up the volume on his radio and did not bother to look around at them.

"Ellie can sit in the back seat," Arnold Friend said. He indicated his friend with a casual jerk of his chin, as if Ellie did not count and she should not bother with him.

"How'd you find out all that stuff?" Connie said.

"Listen: Betty Schultz and Tony Fitch and Jimmy Pettinger and Nancy Pettinger," he said, in a chant. "Raymond Stanley and Bob Hutter—"

"Do you know all those kids?"

"I know everybody."

"Look, you're kidding. You're not from around here."

"Sure."

"But—how come we never saw you before?"

"Sure you saw me before," he said. He looked down at his boots, as if he were a little offended. "You just don't remember."

"I guess I'd remember you," Connie said.

"Yeah?" He looked up at this, beaming. He was pleased. He began to mark time with the music from Ellie's radio, tapping his fists lightly together. Connie looked away from his smile to the car, which was painted so bright it almost hurt her eyes to look at it. She looked at that name, ARNOLD FRIEND. And up at the front fender was an expression that was familiar—MAN THE FLYING SAUCERS. It was an expression kids had used the year before, but didn't use this year. She looked at it for a while as if the words meant something to her that she did not yet know.

"What're you thinking about? Huh?" Arnold Friend demanded. "Not worried about your hair blowing around in the car, are you?"

"No."

"Think I maybe can't drive good?"

"How do I know?"

"You're a hard girl to handle. How come?" he said. "Don't you know I'm your friend? Didn't you see me put my sign in the air when you walked by?"

"What sign?"

"My sign." And he drew an X in the air, leaning out toward her. They were maybe ten feet apart. After his hand fell back to his side the X was still in the air, almost visible. Connie let the screen door close and stood perfectly still inside it, listening to the music from her radio and the boy's blend together. She stared at Arnold

Friend. He stood there so stiffly relaxed, pretending to be relaxed, with one hand idly on the door handle as if he were keeping himself up that way and had no intention of ever moving again. She recognized most things about him, the tight jeans that showed his thighs and buttocks and the greasy leather boots and the tight shirt, and even that slippery friendly smile of his, that sleepy dreamy smile that all the boys used to get across ideas they didn't want to put into words. She recognized all this and also the sing-song way he talked, slightly mocking, kidding, but serious and a little melancholy, and she recognized the way he tapped one fist against the other in homage to the perpetual music behind him. But all these things did not come together.

She said suddenly, "Hey, how old are you?"

His smile faded. She could see then that he wasn't a kid, he was much older—thirty, maybe more. At this knowledge her heart began to pound faster.

"That's a crazy thing to ask. Can'tcha see I'm your own age?"

"Like hell you are."

"Or maybe a coupla years older. I'm eighteen."

"Eighteen?" she said doubtfully.

He grinned to reassure her and lines appeared at the corners of his mouth. His teeth were big and white. He grinned so broadly his eyes became slits and she saw how thick the lashes were, thick and black as if painted with a black tarlike material. Then, abruptly, he seemed to become embarrassed and looked over his shoulder at Ellie. "*Him,* he's crazy," he said. "Ain't he a riot? He's a nut, a real character." Ellie was still listening to the music. His sunglasses told nothing about what he was thinking. He wore a bright orange shirt unbuttoned halfway to show his chest, which was a pale, bluish chest and not muscular like Arnold Friend's. His shirt collar was turned up all around and the very tips of the collar pointed out past his chin as if they were protecting him. He was pressing the transistor radio up against his ear and sat there in a kind of daze, right in the sun.

"He's kinda strange," Connie said.

"Hey, she says you're kinda strange! Kinda strange!" Arnold Friend cried. He pounded on the car to get Ellie's attention. Ellie turned for the first time and Connie saw with shock that he wasn't a kid either—he had a fair, hairless face, cheeks reddened slightly as if the veins grew too close to the surface of his skin, the face of a forty-year-old baby. Connie felt a wave of dizziness rise in her at this sight and she stared at him as if waiting for something to change the shock of the moment, make it all right again. Ellie's lip kept shaping words, mumbling along with the words blasting in his ear.

"Maybe you two better go away," Connie said faintly.

"What? How come?" Arnold Friend cried. "We come out here to take you for a ride. It's Sunday." He had the voice of the man on the radio now. It was the same voice, Connie thought. "Don'tcha know it's Sunday all day? And honey, no matter who you were with last night, today you're with Arnold Friend and don't you forget it! Maybe you better step out here," he said, and this last was in a different voice. It was a little flatter, as if the heat was finally getting to him.

"No, I got things to do."

"Hey."

"You two better leave."

"We ain't leaving until you come with us."

"Like hell I am—"

"Connie, don't fool around with me. I mean—I mean, don't fool *around,*" he said, shaking his head. He laughed incredulously. He placed his sunglasses on top of his head, carefully, as if he were indeed wearing a wig, and brought the stems down behind his ears. Connie stared at him, another wave of dizziness and fear rising in her so that for a moment he wasn't even in focus but was just a blur standing there against his gold car, and she had the idea that he had driven up the driveway all right but had come from nowhere before that and belonged nowhere and that everything about him and even about the music that was so familiar to her was only half real.

"If my father comes and sees you—"

"He ain't coming. He's at the barbecue."

"How do you know that?"

"Aunt Tillie's. Right now they're—uh—they're drinking. Sitting around," he said vaguely, squinting as if he were staring all the way to town and over to Aunt Tillie's back yard. Then the vision seemed to get clear and he nodded energetically. "Yeah. Sitting around. There's your sister in a blue dress, huh? And high heels, the poor sad bitch—nothing like you, sweetheart! And your mother's helping some fat woman with the corn, they're cleaning the corn—husking the corn—"

"What fat woman?" Connie cried.

"How do I know what fat woman, I don't know every goddamn fat woman in the world!" Arnold Friend laughed.

"Oh, that's Mrs. Hornsby . . . Who invited her?" Connie said. She felt a little light-headed. Her breath was coming quickly.

"She's too fat. I don't like them fat. I like them the way you are, honey," he said, smiling sleepily at her. They stared at each other for a while, through the screen door. He said softly, "Now what you're going to do is this: you're going to come out that door. You're going to sit up front with me and Ellie's going to sit in the back, the hell with Ellie, right? This isn't Ellie's date. You're my date. I'm your lover, honey."

"What? You're crazy—"

"Yes, I'm your lover. You don't know what that is but you will," he said. "I know that too. I know all about you. But look: it's real nice and you couldn't ask for nobody better than me, or more polite. I always keep my word. I'll tell you how it is, I'm always nice at first, the first time. I'll hold you so tight you won't think you have to try to get away or pretend anything because you'll know you can't. And I'll come inside you where it's all secret and you'll give in to me and you'll love me—"

"Shut up! You're crazy!" Connie said. She backed away from the door. She put her hands against her ears as if she'd heard something terrible, something not meant for her. "People don't talk like that, you're crazy," she muttered. Her heart was almost too big now for her chest and its pumping made sweat break out all over her. She looked out to see Arnold Friend pause and then take a step toward the porch lurching. He almost fell. But, like a clever drunken man, he managed to catch his balance. He wobbled in his high boots and grabbed hold of one of the porch posts.

"Honey?" he said. "You still listening?"

"Get the hell out of here!"

"Be nice, honey. Listen."

"I'm going to call the police—"

He wobbled again and out of the side of his mouth came a fast spat curse, an aside not meant for her to hear. But even this "Christ!" sounded forced. Then he began to smile again. She watched this smile come, awkward as if he were smiling from inside a mask. His whole face was a mask, she thought wildly, tanned down onto his throat but then running out as if he had plastered make-up on his face but had forgotten about his throat.

"Honey—? Listen, here's how it is. I always tell the truth and I promise you this: I ain't coming in that house after you."

"You better not! I'm going to call the police if you—if you don't—"

"Honey," he said, talking right through her voice, "honey, I'm not coming in there but you are coming out here. You know why?"

She was panting. The kitchen looked like a place she had never seen before, some room she had run inside but which wasn't good enough, wasn't going to help her. The kitchen window had never had a curtain, after three years, and there were dishes in the sink for her to do—probably—and if you ran your hand across the table you'd probably feel something sticky there.

"You listening, honey? Hey?"

"—going to call the police—"

"Soon as you touch the phone I don't need to keep my promise and can come inside. You won't want that."

She rushed forward and tried to lock the door. Her fingers were shaking. "But why lock it," Arnold Friend said gently, talking right into her face. "It's just a screen door. It's just nothing." One of his boots was at a strange angle, as if his foot wasn't in it. It pointed out to the left, bent at the ankle. "I mean, anybody can break through a screen door and glass and wood and iron or anything else if he needs to, anybody at all and especially Arnold Friend. If the place got lit up with a fire, honey, you'd come runnin' out into my arms, right into my arms an' safe at home—like you knew I was your lover and'd stopped fooling around. I don't mind a nice shy girl but I don't like no fooling around." Part of those words were spoken with a slight rhythmic lilt, and Connie somehow recognized them—the echo of a song from last year, about a girl rushing into her boy friend's arms and coming home again—Connie stood barefoot on the linoleum floor, staring at him. "What do you want?" she whispered.

"I want you," he said.

"What?"

"Seen you that night and thought, that's the one, yes sir. I never needed to look anymore."

"But my father's coming back. He's coming to get me. I had to wash my hair first—" She spoke in a dry, rapid voice, hardly raising it for him to hear.

"No, your daddy is not coming and yes, you had to wash your hair and you washed it for me. It's nice and shining and all for me. I thank you, sweetheart," he said with a mock bow, but again he almost lost his balance. He had to bend and adjust his boots. Evidently his feet did not go all the way down; the boots must have been stuffed with something so that he would seem taller. Connie stared out at him and behind him at Ellie in the car, who seemed to be looking off toward Connie's right, into nothing. This Ellie said, pulling the words out of the air one after another as if he were just discovering them, "You want me to pull out the phone?"

"Shut your mouth and keep it shut," Arnold Friend said, his face red from bending over or maybe from embarrassment because Connie had seen his boots. "This ain't none of your business."

"What—what are you doing? What do you want?" Connie said. "If I call the police they'll get you, they'll arrest you—"

"Promise was not to come in unless you touch that phone, and I'll keep that promise," he said. He resumed his erect position and tried to force his shoulders back. He sounded like a hero in a movie, declaring something important. He spoke too loudly and it was as if he were speaking to someone behind Connie. "I ain't made plans for coming in that house where I don't belong but just for you to come out to me, the way you should. Don't you know who I am?"

"You're crazy," she whispered. She backed away from the door but did not want to go into another part of the house, as if this would give him permission to come through the door. "What do you. . . . you're crazy, you. . . ."

"Huh? What're you saying, honey?"

Her eyes darted everywhere in the kitchen. She could not remember what it was, this room.

"This is how it is, honey: you come out and we'll drive away, have a nice ride. But if you don't come out we're gonna wait till your people come home and then they're all going to get it."

"You want that telephone pulled out?" Ellie said. He held the radio away from his ear and grimaced, as if without the radio the air was too much for him.

"I toldja shut up, Ellie," Arnold Friend said, "you're deaf, get a hearing aid, right? Fix yourself up. This little girl's no trouble and's gonna be nice to me, so Ellie keep to yourself, this ain't your date—right? Don't hem in on me, don't hog, don't crush, don't bird dog, don't trail me," he said in a rapid meaningless voice, as if he were running through all the expressions he'd learned but was no longer sure which one of them was in style, then rushing on to new ones, making them up with his eyes closed, "Don't crawl under my fence, don't squeeze in my chipmunk hole, don't sniff my glue, suck my popsicle, keep your own greasy fingers on yourself!" He shaded his eyes and peered in at Connie, who was backed against the kitchen table. "Don't mind him, honey, he's just a creep. He's a dope. Right? I'm the boy for you and like I said, you come out here nice like a lady and give me your hand, and nobody else gets hurt, I mean, your nice old bald-headed daddy and your mummy and your sister in her high heels. Because listen: why bring them in this?"

"Leave me alone," Connie whispered.

"Hey, you know that old woman down the road, the one with the chickens and stuff—you know her?"

"She's dead!"

"Dead? What? You know her?" Arnold Friend said.

"She's dead—"

"Don't you like her?"

"She's dead—she's—she isn't here any more—"

"But don't you like her, I mean, you got something against her? Some grudge or something?" Then his voice dipped as if he were conscious of rudeness. He touched the sunglasses perched on top of his head as if to make sure they were still there. "Now, you be a good girl."

"What are you going to do?"

"Just two things, or maybe three," Arnold Friend said. "But I promise it won't last long and you'll like me the way you get to like people you're close to. You will.

It's all over for you here, so come on out. You don't want your people in any trouble, do you?"

She turned and bumped against a chair or something, hurting her leg, but she ran into the back room and picked up the telephone. Something roared in her ear, a tiny roaring, and she was so sick with fear that she could do nothing but listen to it—the telephone was clammy and very heavy and her fingers groped down to the dial but were too weak to touch it. She began to scream into the phone, into the roaring. She cried out, she cried for her mother, she felt her breath start jerking back and forth in her lungs as if it were something Arnold Friend was stabbing her with again and again with no tenderness. A noisy sorrowful wailing rose all about her and she was locked inside it the way she was locked inside this house.

After a while she could hear again. She was sitting on the floor with her wet back against the wall.

Arnold Friend was saying from the door, "That's a good girl. Put the phone back."

She kicked the phone away from her.

"No, honey. Pick it up. Put it back right."

She picked it up and put it back. The dial tone stopped.

"That's a good girl. Now you come outside."

She was hollow with what had been fear, but what was now just an emptiness. All that screaming had blasted it out of her. She sat, one leg cramped under her, and deep inside her brain was something like a pinpoint of light that kept going and would not let her relax. She thought, I'm not going to see my mother again. She thought, I'm not going to sleep in my bed again. Her bright green blouse was all wet.

Arnold Friend said, in a gentle-loud voice that was like a stage voice, "The place where you came from ain't there any more, and where you had in mind to go is cancelled out. This place you are now—inside your daddy's house—is nothing but a cardboard box I can knock down any time. You know that and always did know it. You hear me?"

She thought, I have got to think. I have got to know what to do.

"We'll go out to a nice field, out in the country here where it smells so nice and it's sunny," Arnold Friend said. "I'll have my arms tight around you so you won't need to try to get away and I'll show you what love is like, what it does. The hell with this house! It looks solid all right," he said. He ran a fingernail down the screen and the noise did not make Connie shiver, as it would have the day before. "Now put your hand on your heart, honey. Feel that? That feels solid too but we know better. Be nice to me, be sweet like you can because what else is there for a girl like you but to be sweet and pretty and give in?—and get away before her people come back?"

She felt her pounding heart. Her hand seemed to enclose it. She thought for the first time in her life that it was nothing that was hers, that belonged to her, but just a pounding, living thing inside this body that wasn't really hers either.

"You don't want them to get hurt," Arnold Friend went on. "Now get up, honey. Get up all by yourself."

She stood.

"Now turn this way: That's right. Come over here to me—Ellie, put that away, didn't I tell you? You dope. You miserable creepy dope," Arnold Friend said. His words were not angry but only part of an incantation. The incantation was kindly.

"Now come out through the kitchen to me, honey, and let's see a smile, try it, you're a brave, sweet little girl and now they're eating corn and hotdogs cooked to bursting over an outdoor fire, and they don't know one thing about you and never did and honey, you're better than them because not a one of them would have done this for you."

Connie felt the linoleum under her feet; it was cool. She brushed her hair back out of her eyes. Arnold Friend let go of the post tentatively and opened his arms for her, his elbows pointing in toward each other and his wrists limp, to show that this was an embarrassed embrace and a little mocking, he didn't want to make her self-conscious.

She put out her hand against the screen. She watched herself push the door slowly open as if she were back safe somewhere in the other doorway, watching this body and this head of long hair moving out into the sunlight where Arnold Friend waited.

"My sweet little blue-eyed girl," he said, in a half-sung sigh that had nothing to do with her brown eyes but was taken up just the same by the vast sunlit reaches of the land behind him and on all sides of him—so much land that Connie had never seen before and did not recognize except to know that she was going to it.

JOYCE CAROL OATES

Life After High School

"Sunny? Sun-ny?"

On that last night of March 1959, in soiled sheepskin parka, unbuckled overshoes, but bare-headed in the lightly falling snow, Zachary Graff, eighteen years old, six feet one and a half inches tall, weight 203 pounds, IQ 160, stood beneath Sunny Burhman's second-storey bedroom window, calling her name softly, urgently, as if his very life depended upon it. It was nearly midnight: Sunny had been in bed for a half hour, and woke from a thin dissolving sleep to hear her name rising mysteriously out of the dark, low, gravelly, repetitive as the surf. "Sun-ny—?" She had not spoken with Zachary Graff since the previous week, when she'd told him, quietly, tears shining in her eyes, that she did not love him; she could not accept his engagement ring, still less marry him. This was the first time in the twelve weeks of Zachary's pursuit of her that he'd dared to come to the rear of the Burhmans' house, by day or night; the first time, as Sunny would say afterward, he'd ever appealed to her in such a way.

They would ask, In what way?

Sunny would hesitate, and say, So—emotionally. In a way that scared me.

So you sent him away?

She did. She'd sent him away.

It was much talked-of, at South Lebanon High School, how, in this spring of their senior year, Zachary Graff, who had never to anyone's recollection asked a girl out before, let alone pursued her so publicly and with such clumsy devotion, seemed to have fallen in love with Sunny Burhman.

Of all people—Sunny Burhman.

Odd too that Zachary should seem to have discovered Sunny, when the two had been classmates in the South Lebanon, New York, public schools since first grade, back in 1947.

Zachary, whose father was Homer Graff, the town's preeminent physician, had, since ninth grade, cultivated a clipped, mock-gallant manner when speaking with female classmates; his Clifton Webb style. He was unfailingly courteous, but unfailingly cool; measured; formal. He seemed impervious to the giddy rise and ebb of adolescent emotion, moving, clumsy but determined, like a grizzly bear on its hind legs, through the school corridors, rarely glancing to left or right: his gaze, its myopia corrected by lenses encased in chunky black plastic frames, was firmly fixed on the horizon. Dr. Graff's son was not unpopular so much as feared, thus disliked.

If Zachary's excellent academic record continued uninterrupted through final papers, final exams, and there was no reason to suspect it would not, Zachary would be valedictorian of the Class of 1959. Barbara ("Sunny") Burhman, later to distinguish herself at Cornell, would graduate only ninth, in a class of eighty-two.

Zachary's attentiveness to Sunny had begun, with no warning, immediately after Christmas recess, when classes resumed in January. Suddenly, a half-dozen times a day, in Sunny's vicinity, looming large, eyeglasses glittering, there Zachary was. His Clifton Webb pose had dissolved, he was shy, stammering, yet forceful, even bold, waiting for the advantageous moment (for Sunny was always surrounded by friends) to push forward and say, "Hi, Sunny!" The greeting, utterly commonplace in content, sounded, in Zachary's mouth, like a Latin phrase tortuously translated.

Sunny, so-named for her really quite astonishing smile, that dazzling white Sunny-smile that transformed a girl of conventional freckled snub-nosed prettiness to true beauty, might have been surprised, initially, but gave no sign, saying, "Hi, Zach!"

In those years, the corridors of South Lebanon High School were lyric crossfires of *Hi!* and *H'lo!* and *Good to see ya!* uttered hundreds of times daily by the golden girls, the popular, confident, good-looking girls, club officers, prom queens, cheerleaders like Sunny Burhman and her friends, tossed out indiscriminately, for that was the style.

Most of the students were in fact practicing Christians of Lutheran, Presbyterian, Methodist stock.

Like Sunny Burhman who was, or seemed, even at the time of this story, too good to be true.

That's to say—*good.*

So, though Sunny soon wondered why on earth Zachary Graff was hanging around her, why, again, at her elbow, or lying in wait for her at the foot of a stairs, why, for the nth time that week, *him,* she was too *good* to indicate impatience, or exasperation; too *good* to tell him, as her friends advised, to get lost.

He telephoned her too. Poor Zachary. Stammering over the phone, his voice lowered as if he were in terror of being overheard, "Is S-Sunny there, Mrs. B-Burhman? May I speak with her, please?" And Mrs. Burhman, who knew Dr. Graff and his wife, of course, since everyone in South Lebanon, population 3,800, knew everyone else or knew of them, including frequently their family histories and facts about them of which their children were entirely unaware, hesitated, and said, "Yes, I'll put her on, but I hope you won't talk long—Sunny has homework tonight." Or, apologetically but firmly: "No, I'm afraid she isn't here. May I take a message?"

"N-no message," Zachary would murmur, and hurriedly hang up.

Sunny, standing close by, thumbnail between her just perceptibly gap-toothed front teeth, expression crinkled in dismay, would whisper "Oh Mom. I feel so bad. I just feel so—bad."

Mrs. Burhman said briskly, "You don't have time for all of them, honey."

Still, Zachary was not discouraged, and with the swift passage of time it began to be observed that Sunny engaged in conversations with him—the two of them sitting, alone, in a corner of the cafeteria, or walking together after a meeting of the Debate Club, of which Zachary was president, and Sunny a member. They were both on the staff of the South Lebanon High Beacon, and the South Lebanon High Yearbook 1959, and the South Lebanon Torch (the literary magazine). They were both members of the National Honor Society and the Quill & Scroll Society. Though Zachary Graff in his aloofness and impatience with most of his peers would be remembered as anti-social, a "loner," in fact, as his record of activities suggested, printed beneath his photograph in the yearbook, he had time, or made time, for things that mattered to him.

He shunned sports, however. High school sports, at least.

His life's game, he informed Sunny Burhman, unaware of the solemn pomposity with which he spoke, would be *golf.* His father had been instructing him, informally, since his twelfth birthday.

Said Zachary, "I have no natural talent for it, and I find it profoundly boring, but gold will be my game." And he pushed his chunky black glasses roughly against the bridge of his nose, as he did countless times a day, as if they were in danger of sliding off.

Zachary Graff had such a physical presence, few of his contemporaries would have described him as unattractive, still less homely, ugly. His head appeared oversized, even for his massive body; his eyes were deep-set, with a look of watchfulness and secrecy; his skin was tallow-colored, and blemished, in wavering patches like topographical maps. His big teeth glinted with filaments of silver, and his breath, oddly for one whose father was a doctor, was stale, musty, cobwebby—not that Sunny Burhman ever alluded to this fact, to others.

Her friends began to ask of her, a bit jealously, reproachfully, "What do you two talk about so much?—you and *him?*" and Sunny replied, taking care not to hint, with the slightest movement of her eyebrows, or rolling of her eyes, that, yes, she found the situation peculiar too, "Oh—Zachary and I talk about all kinds of things. He talks, mainly. He's brilliant. He's—" pausing, her forehead delicately crinkling in thought, her lovely brown eyes for a moment clouded, "—well, *brilliant.*"

In fact, at first, Zachary spoke, in his intense, obsessive way, of impersonal subjects: the meaning of life, the future of Earth, whether science or art best satisfies the human hunger for self-expression. He said, laughing nervously, fixing Sunny with his shyly bold stare, "Just to pose certain questions is, I guess, to show your hope they can be answered."

Early on, Zachary seemed to have understood that, if he expressed doubt, for instance about "whether God exists" and so forth, Sunny Burhman would listen seriously; and would talk with him earnestly with the air of a nurse giving a transfusion to a patient in danger of expiring for loss of blood. She was not a religious fanatic, but she was a devout Christian—the Burhmans were members of the First Presbyterian Church of South Lebanon, and Sunny was president of her youth group, and, among other good deeds, did YWCA volunteer work on Saturday afternoons. She had not the slightest doubt that Jesus Christ, that's to say His spirit, dwelled in her heart, and that, simply by speaking the truth of what she believed, she could convince others.

Though one day, and soon, Sunny would examine her beliefs, and question the faith into which she'd been born; she had not done so by the age of seventeen and a half. She was a virgin, and virginal in all, or most, of her thoughts.

Sometimes, behind her back, even by friends, Sunny was laughed at, gently—never ridiculed, for no one would ridicule Sunny.

Once, when Sunny Burhman and her date and another couple were gazing up into the night sky, standing in the parking lot of the high school, following a prom, Sunny had said in a quavering voice, "It's so big it would be terrifying wouldn't it?—except for Jesus, who makes us feel at home."

When popular Chuck Crueller, a quarterback for the South Lebanon varsity football team, was injured during a game, and carried off by ambulance to undergo emergency surgery, Sunny mobilized the other cheerleaders, tears fierce in her eyes, "We can do it for Chuck—we can *pray.*" And so the eight girls in their short-skirted crimson jumpers and starched white cotton blouses had gripped one another's hands tight, weeping, on the verge of hysteria, had prayed, prayed, *prayed*—hidden away in the depths of the girls' locker room for hours. Sunny had led the prayers, and Chuck Crueller recovered.

So you wouldn't ridicule Sunny Burhman, somehow it wouldn't have been appropriate.

As her classmate Tobias Shanks wrote of her, as one of his duties as literary editor of the 1959 South Lebanon yearbook: *"Sunny" Burhman!—an all-American girl too good to be true who is nonetheless TRUE!*

If there was a slyly mocking tone to Tobias Shanks's praise, a hint that such goodness was predictable, and superficial, and of no genuine merit, the caption, mere print, beneath Sunny's dazzlingly beautiful photograph, conveyed nothing of this.

Surprisingly, for all his pose of skepticism and superiority, Zachary Graff too was a Christian. He'd been baptized Lutheran, and never failed to attend Sunday services with his parents at the First Lutheran Church. Amid the congregation of somber, somnambulant worshippers, Zachary Graff's frowning young face, the very set of his beefy shoulders, drew the minister's uneasy eye; it would be murmured of Dr. Graff's precocious son, in retrospect, that he'd been perhaps too *serious.*

Before falling in love with Sunny Burhman, and discussing his religious doubts with her, Zachary had often discussed them with Tobias Shanks, who'd been his friend, you might say his only friend, since seventh grade. (But only sporadically since seventh grade, since the boys, each highly intelligent, inclined to impatience and sarcasm, got on each other's nerves.) Once, Zachary confided in Tobias that he prayed every morning of his life—immediately upon waking he scrambled out of bed, knelt, hid his face in his hands, and prayed. For his sinful soul, for his sinful thoughts, deeds, desires. He lacerated his soul the way he'd been taught by his mother to tug a fine-toothed steel comb through his coarse, oily hair, never less than once a day.

Tobias Shanks, a self-professed agonistic since the age of fourteen, laughed, and asked derisively, "Yes, but what do you pray for, exactly?" and Zachary had thought a bit, and said, not ironically, but altogether seriously, "To get through the day. Doesn't everyone?"

This melancholy reply, Tobias was never to reveal.

Zachary's parents were urging him to go to Muhlenberg College, which was church-affiliated; Zachary hoped to go elsewhere. He said, humbly, to Sunny Burhman, "If you go to Cornell, Sunny, I—maybe I'll go there too?"

Sunny hesitated, then smiled. "Oh. That would be nice."

"You wouldn't mind, Sunny?"

"Why would I *mind,* Zachary?" Sunny laughed, to hide her impatience. They were headed for Zachary's car, parked just up the hill from the YM-YWCA building. It was a gusty Saturday afternoon in early March. Leaving the YWCA, Sunny had seen Zachary Graff standing at the curb, hands in the pockets of his sheepskin parka, head lowered, but eyes nervously alert. Standing there, as if accidentally.

It was impossible to avoid him, she had to allow him to drive her home. Though she was beginning to feel panic, like darting tongues of flame, at the prospect of Zachary Graff always *there.*

Tell the creep to get lost, her friends counseled. Even her nice friends were without sentiment regarding Zachary Graff.

Until sixth grade, Sunny had been plain little Barbara Burhman. Then, one day, her teacher had said, to all the class, in one of those moments of inspiration that can alter, by whim, the course of an entire life, "Tell you what, boys and girls—let's call Barbara 'Sunny' from now on—that's what she *is.*"

Ever afterward, in South Lebanon, she was "Sunny" Burhman. Plain little Barbara had been left behind, seemingly forever.

So, of course, Sunny could not tell Zachary Graff to get lost. Such words were not part of her vocabulary.

Zachary owned a plum-colored 1956 Plymouth which other boys envied—it seemed to them distinctly unfair that Zachary, of all people, had his own car, when so few of them, who loved cars, did. But Zachary was oblivious of their envy, as, in a way, he seemed oblivious of his own good fortune. He drove the car as if it were an adult duty, with middle-aged fussiness and worry. He drove the car as if he were its own chauffeur. Yet, driving Sunny home, he talked—chattered—continuously. Speaking of college, and of religious "obligations," and of his parents' expectations of him; speaking of medical school; the future; the life—"beyond South Lebanon."

He asked again, in that gravelly, irksomely humble voice, if Sunny would mind if he went to Cornell. And Sunny said, trying to sound merely reasonable, "Zachary, it's a *free world.*"

Zachary said, "Oh no it isn't, Sunny. For some of us, it isn't."

This enigmatic remark Sunny was determined not to follow up.

Braking to a careful stop in front of the Burhmans' house, Zachary said, with an almost boyish enthusiasm, "So—Cornell? In the fall? We'll both go to Cornell?"

Sunny was quickly out of the car before Zachary could put on the emergency brake and come around, ceremoniously, to open her door. Gaily, recklessly, infinitely relieved to be out of his company, she called back over her shoulder, "Why not?"

Sunny's secret vanity must have been what linked them.

For several times, gravely, Zachary had said to her, "When I'm with you, Sunny, it's possible for me to believe."

He meant, she thought, in God. In Jesus. In the life hereafter.

The next time Zachary maneuvered Sunny into his car, under the pretext of driving her home, it was to present the startled girl with an engagement ring.

He'd bought the ring at Stern's Jewelers, South Lebanon's single good jewelry store, with money secretly withdrawn from his savings account; that account to which, over a period of more than a decade, he'd deposited modest sums with a painstaking devotion. This was his "college fund," or had been—out of the $3,245 saved, only $1,090 remained. How astonished, upset, furious his parents would be when they learned—Zachary hadn't allowed himself to contemplate.

The Graffs knew nothing about Sunny Burhman. So far as they might have surmised, their son's frequent absences from home were nothing out of the ordinary—he'd always spent time at the public library, where his preferred reading was reference books. He'd begin with Volume One of an encyclopedia, and made his diligent way through each successive volume, like a horse grazing a field, rarely glancing up, uninterested in his surroundings.

"Please—will you accept it?"

Sunny was staring incredulously at the diamond ring, which was presented to her, not in Zachary's big clumsy fingers, with the dirt-edged nails, but in the plush-lined little box, as if it might be more attractive that way, more like a gift. The ring was 24-karat gold and the diamond was small but distinctive, and coldly glittering. A beautiful ring, but Sunny did not see it that way.

She whispered, "Oh. Zachary. Oh *no*—there must be some misunderstanding."

Zachary seemed prepared for her reaction, for he said, quickly, "Will you just try it on?—see if it fits?"

Sunny shook her head. No she couldn't.

"They'll take it back to adjust it, if it's too big," Zachary said. "They promised."

"Zachary, no," Sunny said gently. "I'm so sorry."

Tears flooded her eyes and spilled over onto her cheeks.

Zachary was saying, eagerly, his lips flecked with spittle, "I realize you don't l-love me, Sunny, at least not yet, but—you could wear the ring, couldn't you? Just—wear it?" He continued to hold the little box out to her, his hand visibly shaking. "On your right hand, if you don't want to wear it on your left? Please?"

"Zachary, no. That's impossible."

"Just, you know, as a, a gift—? Oh Sunny—"

They were sitting in the plum-colored Plymouth, parked, in an awkwardly public place, on Upchurch Avenue three blocks from Sunny's house. It was 4:25 P.M., March 26, a Thursday: Zachary had lingered after school in order to drive Sunny home after choir practice. Sunny would afterward recall, with an odd haltingness, as if her memory of the episode were blurred with tears, that, as usual, Zachary had done most of the talking. He had not argued with her nor exactly begged, but spoke almost formally, as if setting out the basic points of his debating strategy: If Sunny did not love him, he could love enough for both; and, if Sunny did not want to be "officially" engaged, she could wear his ring anyway, couldn't she?

It would mean so much to him, Zachary said.

Life or death, Zachary said.

Sunny closed the lid of the little box, and pushed it from her gently. She was crying, and her smooth pageboy was now disheveled. "Oh Zachary, I'm *sorry.* I *can't.*"

Sunny knelt by her bed, hid her face in her hands, prayed.

Please help Zachary not to be in love with me. Please help me not to be cruel. Have mercy on us both O God.

O God help him to realize he doesn't love me—doesn't know *me.*

Days passed, and Zachary did not call. If he was absent from school, Sunny did not seem to notice.

Sunny Burhman and Zachary Graff had two classes together, English and physics; but, in the busyness of Sunny's high school life, surrounded by friends, mesmerized by her own rapid motion as if she were lashed to the prow of a boat bearing swiftly through the water, she did not seem to notice.

She was not a girl of secrets. She was not a girl of stealth. Still, though she had confided in her mother all her life, she did not tell her mother about Zachary's desperate proposal; perhaps, so flattered, she did not acknowledge it as desperate. She reasoned that if she told either of her parents they would have telephoned Zachary's parents immediately. I can't betray him, she thought.

Nor did she tell her closest girl friends, or the boy she was seeing most frequently at the time, knowing that the account would turn comical in the telling, that she and her listeners would collapse into laughter, and this too would be a betrayal of Zachary.

She happened to see Tobias Shanks, one day, looking oddly at her. That boy who might have been twelve years old, seen from a short distance. Sunny knew that he was, or had been, a friend of Zachary Graff's; she wondered if Zachary confided in him; yet made no effort to speak with him. He didn't like her, she sensed.

No, Sunny didn't tell anyone about Zachary and the engagement ring. Of all sins, she thought, betrayal is surely the worst.

"Sunny? Sun-ny?"

She did not believe she had been sleeping but the low, persistent, gravelly sound of Zachary's voice penetrated her consciousness like a dream-voice—felt, not heard.

Quickly, she got out of bed. Crouched at her window without turning on the light. Saw, to her horror, Zachary down below, standing in the shrubbery, his large head uplifted, face round like the moon, and shadowed like the moon's face. There was a light, damp snowfall; blossomlike clumps fell on the boy's broad shoulders, in his matted hair. Sighting her, he began to wave excitedly, like an impatient child.

"Oh. Zachary. My God."

In haste, fumbling, she put on a bulky-knit ski sweater over her flannel nightgown, kicked on bedroom slippers, hurried downstairs. The house was already darkened; the Burhmans were in the habit of going to bed early. Sunny's only concern was that she could send Zachary away without her parents knowing he was there. Even in her distress she was not thinking of the trouble Zachary might make for her: she was thinking of the trouble he might make for himself.

Yet, as soon as she saw him close up, she realized that something was gravely wrong. Here was Zachary Graff—yet not Zachary.

He told her he had to talk with her, and he had to talk with her now. His car was parked in the alley, he said.

He made a gesture as if to take her hand, but Sunny drew back, he loomed over her, his breath steaming. She could not see his eyes.

She said no she couldn't go with him. She said he must go home, at once, before her parents woke up.

He said he couldn't leave without her, he had to talk with her. There was a raw urgency, a forcefulness, in him, that Sunny had never seen before, and that frightened her.

She said no. He said yes.

He reached again for her hand, this time taking hold of her wrist.

His fingers were strong.

"I told you—I can love enough for both!"

Sunny stared up at him, for an instant mute, paralyzed, seeing not Zachary Graff's eyes but the lenses of his glasses which appeared, in the semidark, opaque. Large snowflakes were falling languidly, there was no wind. Sunny saw Zachary Graff's face which was pale and clenched as a muscle, and she heard his voice which was the voice of a stranger, and she felt him tug at her so roughly her arm was strained in its very socket, and she cried, "No! no! go away! no!"—and the spell was broken, the boy gaped at her another moment, then released her, turned, and ran.

No more than two or three minutes had passed since Sunny unlocked the rear door and stepped outside, and Zachary fled.

Yet, afterward, she would recall the encounter as if it had taken a very long time, like a scene in a protracted and repetitive nightmare.

It would be the last time Sunny Burhman saw Zachary Graff alive.

Next morning, all of South Lebanon talked of the death of Dr. Graff's son Zachary: he'd committed suicide by parking his car in a garage behind an unoccupied house on Upchurch Avenue, and letting the motor run until the gas tank was emptied. Death was diagnosed as the result of carbon monoxide poisoning, the time estimated at approximately 4:30 A.M. of April 1,1959.

Was the date deliberate?—Zachary had left only a single note behind, printed in firm block letters and taped to the outside of the car windshield:

April Fool's Day 1959

To Whom It May (Or May Not) Concern:

I, Zachary A. Graff, being of sound mind & body, do hereby declare that I have taken my own life of my own free will & I hereby declare all others guiltless as they are ignorant of the death of the aforementioned & the life.

(signed)
ZACHARY A. GRAFF

Police officers, called to the scene at 7:45 A.M., reported finding Zachary, lifeless, stripped to his underwear, in the rear seat of the car; the sheepskin parka was oddly draped over the steering wheel, and the interior of the car was, again oddly, for a boy known for his fastidious habits, littered with numerous items: a Bible, several high school textbooks, a pizza carton and some uneaten crusts of pizza, several empty Pepsi bottles, an empty bag of M&M's candies, a pair of new, unlaced gym shoes (size eleven), a ten-foot length of clothesline (in the glove compartment), and the diamond ring in its plush-lined little box from Stern's Jewelers (in a pocket of the parka).

Sunny Burhman heard the news of Zachary's suicide before leaving for school that morning, when a friend telephoned. Within earshot of both her astonished parents, Sunny burst into tears, and sobbed, "Oh my God—it's my fault."

So the consensus in South Lebanon would be, following the police investigation, and much public speculation, not that it was Sunny Burhman's fault, exactly, not that the girl was to blame, exactly, but, yes, poor Zachary Graff, the doctor's son, had killed himself in despondency over her: her refusal of his engagement ring, her rejection of this love.

That was the final season of her life as "Sunny" Burhman.

She was out of school for a full week following Zachary's death, and, when she returned, conspicuously paler, more subdued, in all ways less sunnier, she did not speak, even with her closest friends, of the tragedy; nor did anyone bring up the subject with her. She withdrew her name from the balloting for the senior prom queen, she withdrew from her part in the senior play, she dropped out of the school choir, she did not participate in the annual statewide debating competition—in which, in previous years, Zachary Graff had excelled. Following her last class of the day she went home immediately, and rarely saw her friends on weekends. Was she in mourning?—or was she simply ashamed? Like the bearer of a deadly virus, herself unaffected, Sunny knew how, on all sides, her classmates and her teachers were regarding her: She was the girl for whose love a boy had thrown away his life, she was an unwitting agent of death.

Of course, her family told her that it wasn't her fault that Zachary Graff had been mentally unbalanced.

Even the Graffs did not blame her—or said they didn't.

Sunny said, "Yes. But it's my fault he's dead."

The Presbyterian minister, who counseled Sunny, and prayed with her, assured her that Jesus surely understood, and that there could be no sin in *her*—it wasn't her fault that Zachary Graff had been mentally unbalanced. And Sunny replied, not stubbornly, but matter-of-factly, sadly, as if stating a self-evident truth, "Yes. But it's my fault he's dead."

Her older sister, Helen, later that summer, meaning only well, said, in exasperation, "Sunny, when are you going to cheer *up?*" and Sunny turned on her with uncharacteristic fury, and said, "Don't call me that idiotic name ever again!—I want it *gone!*"

When in the fall she enrolled at Cornell University, she was "Barbara Burhman."

She would remain "Barbara Burhman" for the rest of her life.

Barbara Burhman excelled as an undergraduate, concentrating on academic work almost exclusively; she went on to graduate school at Harvard, in American studies; she taught at several prestigious universities, rising rapidly through administrative ranks before accepting a position, both highly paid and politically visible, with a well-known research foundation based in Manhattan. She was the author of numerous books and articles; she was married, and the mother of three children; she lectured widely, she was frequently interviewed in the popular press, she lent her name to good causes. She would not have wished to think of herself as extraordinary—in the world she now inhabited, she was surrounded by similarly active, energetic, professionally engaged men and women—except in recalling as she sometimes did, with a mild pang of nostalgia, her old, lost self, sweet "Sunny" Burhman of South Lebanon, New York.

She hadn't been queen of the senior prom. She hadn't even continued to be a Christian.

The irony had not escaped Barbara Burhman that, in casting away his young life so recklessly, Zachary Graff had freed her for hers.

With the passage of time, grief had lessened. Perhaps in fact it had disappeared. After twenty, and then twenty-five, and now thirty-one years, it was difficult for Barbara, known in her adult life as an exemplar of practical sense, to feel a kinship with the adolescent girl she'd been, or that claustrophobic high school world of the late 1950s. She'd never returned for a single reunion. If she thought of Zachary Graff—about whom, incidentally, she'd never told her husband of twenty-eight years—it was with the regret we think of remote acquaintances, lost to us by accidents of fate. Forever, Zachary Graff, the most brilliant member of the class of 1959 of South Lebanon High, would remain a high school boy, trapped, aged eighteen.

Of that class, the only other person to have acquired what might be called a national reputation was Tobias Shanks, now known as T. R. Shanks, a playwright and director of experimental drama; Barbara Burhman had followed Tobias's career with interest, and had sent him a telegram congratulating him on his most recent play, which went on to win a number of awards, dealing, as it did, with the vicissitudes of gay life in the 1980s. In the winter of 1990 Barbara and Tobias began to encounter each other socially, when Tobias was playwright-in-residence at Bard College, close by Hazelton-on-Hudson where Barbara lived. At first they were strangely shy of each other; even guarded; as if, in even this neutral setting, their South Lebanon ghost-selves exerted a powerful influence. The golden girl, the loner. The splendidly normal, the defiantly "odd." One night Tobias Shanks, shaking Barbara Burhman's hand, had smiled wryly, and said, "It *is* Sunny, isn't it?" and Barbara Burhman, laughing nervously, hoping no one had overheard, said, "No, in fact it isn't. It's Barbara."

They looked at each other, mildly dazed. For one saw a small-boned but solidly built man of youthful middle-age, sweet-faced, yet with ironic, pouched eyes, thinning gray hair, and a close-trimmed gray beard; the other saw a woman of youthful middle-age, striking in appearance, impeccably well-groomed, with fading hair of no distinctive color and faint, white, puckering lines at the edges of her eyes. Their ghost-selves were there—not aged, or not aged merely, but transformed, as the genes of a previous generation are transformed by the next.

Tobias stared at Barbara for a long moment, as if unable to speak. Finally he said, "I have something to tell you, Barbara. When can we meet?"

Tobias Shanks handed the much-folded letter across the table to Barbara Burhman, and watched as she opened it, and read it, with an expression of increasing astonishment and wonder.

"*He* wrote this? Zachary? To you?"

"He did."

"And you—? Did you—?"

Tobias shook his head.

His expression was carefully neutral, but his eyes swam suddenly with tears.

"We'd been friends, very close friends, for years. Each other's only friend, most of the time. The way kids that age can be, in certain restricted environments—kids who aren't what's called 'average' or 'normal.' We talked a good deal about religion—Zachary was afraid of hell. We both liked science fiction. We both had very strict parents. I suppose I might have been attracted to Zachary at times—I knew I was attracted to other guys—but of course I never acted upon it; I wouldn't have dared. Almost no one dared, in those days." He laughed, with a mild shudder. He passed a hand over his eyes. "I couldn't have *loved* Zachary Graff as he claimed he loved me, because—I couldn't. But I could have allowed him to know that he wasn't sick, crazy, "perverted' as he called himself in that letter." He paused. For a long painful moment Barbara thought he wasn't going to continue. Then he said, with that same mirthless shuddering laugh, "I could have made him feel less lonely. But I didn't. I failed him. My only friend."

Barbara had taken out a tissue, and was dabbing at her eyes.

She felt as if she'd been dealt a blow so hard she could not gauge how she'd been hurt—if there was hurt at all.

She said, "Then it hadn't ever been 'Sunny'—she was an illusion."

Tobias said thoughtfully, "I don't know. I suppose so. There was the sense, at least as I saw it at the time, that, yes, he'd chosen you; decided upon you."

"As a symbol."

"Not just a symbol. We all adored you—we were all a little in love with you." Tobias laughed, embarrassed. "Even me."

"I wish you'd come to me and told me, back then. After—it happened."

"I was too cowardly. I was terrified of being exposed, and, maybe, doing to myself what he'd done to himself. Suicide is so very attractive to adolescents." Tobias paused and reached over to touch Barbara's hand. His fingertips were cold. "I'm not proud of myself Barbara, and I've tried to deal with it in my writing, but—that's how I was, back then." Again he paused. He pressed a little harder against Barbara's hand. "Another thing—after Zachary went to you, that night, he came to me."

"To you?"

"To me."

"And—?"

"And I refused to go with him too. I was furious with him for coming to the house like that, risking my parents discovering us. I guess I got a little hysterical. And he fled."

"He fled."

"Then, afterward. I just couldn't bring myself to come forward. Why I saved that letter I don't know—I'd thrown away some others that were less incriminating. I suppose I figured—no one knew about me, everyone knew about you. 'Sunny' Burhman."

They were at lunch—they ordered two more drinks—they'd forgotten their surroundings—they talked.

After an hour or so Barbara Burhman leaned across the table, as at one of her professional meetings to ask, in a tone of intellectual curiosity, "What do you think Zachary planned to do with the clothesline?"

JOYCE CAROL OATES

Ghost Girls

This story I want to tell began in upstate New York, in the Chautauqua Mountains, in August 1972.

It was a time when Momma had to take us—her and me—into hiding. The first time I saw what isn't there to be seen.

Arrangements had been made for Daddy's friend Vaughn Brownlee he'd known in Vietnam to fly us from Marsena where we'd been living to Wolf's Head Lake in the Chautauqua Mountains where we'd stay at somebody's camp. How long? Momma wanted to know, and Brownlee shrugged saying, As long as required.

I was five years old and sharp for my age, Smartass they called me but I didn't know if Momma and me had to go into hiding because Daddy had enemies who wanted to hurt us or if it was Daddy himself who was the danger.

Some things you know without asking. Other things, you can't ask. And you never know.

That airstrip at Marsena!—just a single unpainted hangar outside town, rusty corrugated tin roof and rotted wind sock slapping listless in the breeze, a single dirt runway between cornfields you'd swear wouldn't be long enough for even the smallest plane to rise from. On the far side of one of the cornfields, out of sight from the airport, was the Chautauqua River, narrow as a creek above Marsena, rocky white-water rapids. There were airports Daddy used in those years at Mt. Ephraim, Tintern Falls, South Lebanon and each one of them is clear in my memory but Marsena is the most vivid because of what happened afterward. Also, the biggest plane you could rent at Marsena was an ex-Air Force trainer with a canopied open cockpit, a two-seater that flew at an altitude of twelve thousand feet, higher than any of the other planes, that was Daddy's favorite. It was a Vultee basic trainer—VULTEE in fading black letters on the fuselage—Daddy said of another era, World War II, not his war but his own father's now gone. That past spring he'd taken Momma up in the Vultee and they flew to Lake Ontario and back, gone for almost an hour and I kept having to go to the bathroom to pee in the concrete-stinking stall where the hard dry shells of beetles lay underfoot, at last returning to the airport and buzzing the hangar so Gus Speer the owner ran out shaking his fist, and the others hanging around watching and drinking beer on a Sunday afternoon and Daddy in the Vultee was circling the field, landing in a deafening blurred roar like a dream you can't wake from, Fucking-O perfect landing they said. And taxiing back to the hangar, and the sun glaring like knife blades off the wings. And the terrible wind of the twin propellers dying. And Momma emerged from the cockpit shaken and white-faced and not so pretty, dazed pulling off her helmet and goggles and trying to smile squinting at me and the others, and climbing down half-falling into Daddy's arms, groping as if she couldn't see him clearly, nor the ground which must have seemed strange to her, so solid, but still Momma was smiling, her happy smile, her mouth bright red like something shiny pressed into soft white bread dough. And there was the promise Daddy would take me up in the Vultee some Sunday afternoon, too.

One of these days, Birdie, Daddy would say. Smiling the way he did. Like there was some secret understanding between him and me, even Momma couldn't guess.

Birdie wasn't my name!—my name is Ingrid.

Momma pulled me by the hand murmuring under her breath Oh God, oh Jesus, and there was Brownlee waiting for us on the other side of the hangar, with a look of a man who isn't happy with waiting. His big sunburnt face like a red cabbage, and his mouth working—he was always chewing something, a big wad of gum, or a plug of tobacco. Brownlee was heavier than Daddy in those days, in his flying clothes a sky blue nylon zip-up jacket and oil-spotted khakis, brown helmet and goggles that made him look like a big beetle on its hind legs. Brownlee waved at us and Momma pulled me along. The plane he'd be flying was one of the small ones, a two-seater Cessna silvery yellow across the wings, with fading black trim. One propeller. Seeing it, hearing the motor, I pulled back on Momma's arm and she didn't like that. She was half carrying half-pushing me. "Honey, stop crying!" she said. "Crying never did anybody any Goddamned good."

I didn't know I'd been crying. Mommas eyes were wet, too. Shining like tarnished-coppery pennies.

I knew not to cross Momma in certain of her moods. However scared I was. Just let myself go limp, a rag doll, boneless.

Brownlee stared at Momma like it hurt him to see her, the way men stared at Momma in those days. Saying, "O.K., Chloe, let's go. We need to land up there before dark."

Brownlee and Daddy had been Navy pilots in the War, Airman First Class they called each other, saluting, sneering like kids. Like the words tasted bad in their mouths. But the War was over for them now. That's some of the trouble, Momma said.

Brownlee helped Momma into the Cessna stooping beneath the wing, then I climbed inside onto her lap. It was unlawful for Brownlee to take us like this, no belt for me, the space cramped smaller than a motorcycle sidecar. But Gus Speer who owned the airport was a friend of Daddy's and Brownlee's and no friend of the law.

Brownlee shut Momma's door. She latched it from the inside. We watched as Brownlee spat into the dirt and hitched up his khaki trousers slung low on his hips and went to start the propeller, that way of squinting that was Daddy's way, too, starting a propeller by hand. Slow at first like a ceiling fan you can follow the turning of the blade with your eyes then faster and faster until you can't make out the blade any longer only the blurred circular motion it would hurt you to set your hand inside.

"Now sit still, Ingrid," Momma said. "And be brave, OK?"

Brownlee spat out the rest of what was in his month and climbed into the cockpit behind us with a grunt. The plane creaked beneath his weight. Momma was holding me tight murmuring under her breath Oh God, oh Jesus, her quick warm breath, her beery-sour breath in my face. She'd been drinking beer in the car, her and the man who'd driven us to the airport whose name I didn't know, a six-pack she'd taken from the refrigerator on our way out the door. No time for Momma to throw together more than a few things of ours in her zebra-stripe tote bag. We'd only been living in the farmhouse off a dirt road outside Marsena for about two weeks, there were other people living there too and trouble of some kind and Daddy drove away in the night and next day men came by to ask about him, yesterday morning two Eden County sheriff's deputies. The first thing you hear when a police car turns up the drive is radio voices, ratchety and loud. Looking for Lucas Boone, they said. The German shepherd was barking like crazy straining at his leash, neck hairs bristling and ears laid back and one of the deputies had his pistol drawn ready to fire but Happy was tied to a clothesline post and Momma was screaming, Don't shoot him please!—he's no harm to you! and the deputy didn't shoot Happy.

Brownlee was asking Momma was she belted in? O.K.?

Momma said, "O.K." Hugging me tight.

Brownlee started the Cessna in motion, taxiing out the runway. Slow at first. The wheels bumping. Gus Speer in his overalls lifted a hand as we passed, a worried look on his face. We passed the row of parked planes, the Vultee at the end. The sun was beginning to set like fire melting into the sky atop the cliff above the river. Momma whispered to me gripping me tight saying it was a short flight, we'd be there before we knew it, just stay still. I understood that if there was any danger Momma would be holding me like that, Momma would never give me up. Daddy had said these little shithead civilian planes were the dangerous ones not the bomber jets he'd flown in Nam but I was thinking even if we crashed and died I would be safe in Momma's arms.

The plane was rushing along the runway and the wheels began to skip. With Brownlee behind us it was like no one was the pilot, no one in control just Momma and me staring past the plane's nose and the spinning blades. There was a sickening lurch into the air, straight into the wind. The hardpacked dirt rushing beneath like a torrent. Weeds coated with dust, and a stack of scrap lumber and corrugated tin in a field, and beyond the cornstalks in almost-uniform rows dun-colored and bleached in the heat of August looking like paper cutouts. We were in the air now, and banking right. Headed north where the sky was dense with clouds. We saw telephone poles and wires above the highway, and the asphalt highway too, and a lone pickup truck moving on it, everything falling suddenly away as if sucked down. And now the Chautauqua River was visible, the color of tin, rippling red streaks from the sunset, a long snaky stretch of it out of sight. The plane was shuddering so in the wind, the engine was so loud, you would think it would break into pieces, it would never hold.

"Here we go," Momma said, raising her voice so I could hear her over the propeller, "—we're having *fun,* aren't we?"

She knows I love her, I'm crazy about her, doesn't she? It's just a hard time right now.

Of course she knows, Luke.

And you, too?

Momma's voice dipped so I almost couldn't hear lying still not breathing my eyes shut tight so I was seeing flashes of light like fireflies against my eyelids. *That's what I've been saying, darling. Me, too.*

Because I wouldn't want any further misunderstanding. Not at this crucial time.

Luke, no! There's no misunderstanding on my part.

That's how people get hurt. They cause their own sorrow. If things get confused.

That can't happen with us, we've been together too long. You know that.

I know it, and I want you to know it, too. And her.

Ingrid's too young to understand, darling.
Well, you explain to her, then. You're her mother for Christ's sake.

North of Marsena, in the mountains, everything was changed. The wind was stronger and Brownlee seemed to be having trouble keeping on course. I'd been asleep on Momma's lap, the wind was so loud shaking the plane, voices shouting past, I couldn't stay awake. My drooling mouth against Momma's soft breast so finally it hurt her and she woke me up. Outside the sky was darkening in the direction we were headed. Clouds roiling up at the horizon thick with storms, heat lightning flashing in the distance like eyes blinking. Below were thick expanses of woods, foothills and mountains and curving streams and pockets of low-lying clouds. The sun was just a narrow funnel of rapidly diminishing pale red light and it scared and excited me seeing it from such a height like we were above the sun, we could see it sinking over. *The edge of the world that's always there whether you see it or not or know of it or not. So close you could be sucked over easy as sleep.*

Momma pointed out Wolf's Head Lake, or what she thought was the lake, below us. The valley was a deep ditch of shadow smudged with mist. A mirrorlike patch of water inside. We were starting to descend, not smoothly but in lurches, like going down steps in the dark. I wasn't afraid, with Momma holding me so tight. I stared at the light skimming the mountaintops, the pines beginning to become distinct, individual. And there was a road!—curving alongside one of the mountains, suddenly visible. And another road, crossing a strip of water. Narrow lakes like fingers, so many of them, and closer in farmland and pastures in neat rectangles, I could see cattle grazing, the tin-glaring roof of a barn, a truck moving along a highway. We were coming in to land—where? A narrow airstrip ahead. The plane's shadow wasn't visible skimming the ground below, the sun was too far gone.

Momma said worried in my ear, "Hold on, darling. It might be a little—" but already the runway was coming up fast, our little plane swerved in a gust of wind and Brownlee cursed behind us and there was a split second when he might've raised the nose and risen again to circle for another try but instead he brought us down clumsily hitting the ground so Momma and I screamed and the plane went bouncing and skipping and finally rolled dazed along the runway the right wing tilted almost skimming the ground. We came to a skidding stop at the end of the runway, a field beyond, as the first fat hissing raindrops began to fall.

Momma was half-sobbing screaming at Brownlee, "You asshole! All of you! You want to kill us don't you!"

A woman friend of Brownlee's named Maude was waiting for us at the airport and by the time we drove out to Wolf's Head Lake to the hunting camp it was dark and raining hard. The mountain road curved, the car's yellow headlights flew ahead. Where we'd all be staying wasn't a house exactly, they called it a lodge, single-story with missing shingles and a crumbling stone chimney and a rotted porch across the width of the front. Wild bushes pushing up close. Scrap lumber, an old auto chassis in the yard. Inside it smelled of kerosene. There were few pieces of furniture—a battered sofa, some chairs—and no carpet on the loose-fitting floorboards. Above the fireplace stuffed with debris was a deer's handsome mounted head and antlers. From Daddy I knew to count the points: there were ten. I stood staring at the deer on the wall seeing his fur was faded to the color of sand and mangy with time, his dark-glassy eyes were coated with dust.

Brownlee said, like he was playing Daddy, in that way Daddy would with me, "He can't see you, Birdie: he's blind."

I said, "I know that."

Brownlee said, smiling, and winking at Momma and the woman named Maude, "I mean he's blinder than blind, poor fucker. His eyes are glass."

Momma said, "Did you shoot him, Vaughn?—he's your trophy?"

"Hell, no. I'm not a hunter. I don't give a shit about hunting animals."

Brownlee said this and there was a silence and the woman named Maude laughed like she was clearing her throat, and Momma said nothing just took my hand and pulled me along into one of the back rooms where we'd be sleeping. When she switched on the light the first thing we saw was something dead on the floor beneath a window—"Jesus!" Momma said. She thought it was a bat, kept me from getting too close. I stared seeing two long columns of black ants leading to it from the wall.

Not Death only but what follows, you don't want to know.

The things I saw, in Nam, Daddy said, *oh sweet fucking Christ you don't want to know.*

Momma was breathing hard. Ran her hands through her hair in that way of hers, angry, but like she's about to cry, too. Instead lighting a cigarette from out of her tote bag. She laughed, her eyes shining so you'd swear she was happy. "What the hell, honey, right? We're alive, and we're here."

"Is Daddy going to be with us?"

Momma was stamping the ants to death. Both feet. These tinsel-looking flat sandals, and her feet delicate, narrow, bluish-pale, red polish on the toenails chipped. Momma was wearing her white rayon slacks fitted close to her body, her shiny white plastic belt that made her waist so tiny, red jersey top that pulled across her breasts. A thin gold chain with a green cross on it Daddy said was jade, bought in Saigon. Momma was so young, only twenty-three. She was just a girl, wasn't she. And so beautiful, it hurt you to look but you had to look. Silky white-blond hair, her brown eyes set deep, her mouth that seemed always pouting, even when she smiled. Momma was smoking her cigarette at the same time pushing the dead thing away with her foot, toward the door, the door was open and in the front room Brownlee and the woman named Maude were talking. Sometimes when Momma spoke up her voice was so loud and laughing-angry you'd be surprised, and it was like that now.

"Say, Vaughn—Airman First Class Brownlee—get your ass in here, will you? There's something nasty scaring my little girl I want taken care of *now.*"

I was disappointed, Wolf's Head Lake wasn't close by the damn old "lodge" at all. A mile away, at least, down a bumpy dirt lane. You couldn't hear any waves, and you couldn't smell any water. Outside everywhere you looked, no moon, no stars and nothing but pitch-black night.

Maude had brought some food in grocery bags that ripped and spilled on the counter and she and Momma made supper finally though it took a long while, always it seemed to take a long while to make meals in those days because people got interrupted, there was drinking to be done, cigarettes lit and relit, pots and pans missing or nonexistent and often there was a problem locating cutlery—what was called "silverware." And there were arguments, discussions. But finally a meal would be prepared like this late-night supper which was hamburger patties grilled in the fireplace, big doughy-soft buns the size of a man's hand, and ketchup, and relish sugary-tasting as candy, and Frito-Lay potato chips the kind that came in the cardboard box and smelled of the cardboard—we were all starving, especially Brownlee who as he ate blinked like his eyes were welling tears. And there was beer for them, just water for me that Momma wasn't too happy about—rust-streaked trickling out of the kitchen faucet.

It started then, my way of eating. If it's ground meat like hamburger pink or runny-red in the center I'll eat just the edges shutting my eyes, if it's muscle-meat like steak or cutlets where you can see the texture of the flesh I can't eat it at all unless I'm drunk or stoned and somebody can talk me out of seeing what it is.

It was around midnight when we were eating and headlights flashed up the drive and I ran to see if it was Daddy but it wasn't—two men I'd never seen before, one of them with spidery tattoos up and down his arms. They'd brought more six-packs of beer, and a bottle of Four Roses, and a little plastic Baggie of what Momma called "dope"—which she said scared her for the weird thoughts it made her think but she couldn't say no to trying it most of the time. Later on they played cards, Momma and Maude and Brownlee who got happy and loud when he drank and the man with the tattooed arms whose name was Skaggs and the other man, a little younger, with a mustache, moist yellowish-dark eyes like Happy's eyes, whose name was McCarry. McCarry's hair was greased back in quills and his skin was pimply but he was sweet-boy-looking sitting close beside Momma offering to help her with her cards but Momma laughed saying no thanks, friend, she didn't need anybody's help she'd been playing gin rummy since the age of ten.

"And winning my fair share, too."

"*That,* Miz Boone, I don't doubt."

It was one of those times that any minute Daddy would drive up and come through the door except he didn't and I started to cry and Momma said I was tired and it's time for bed and I said no I didn't want to go to bed not in that nasty bed I was scared I said and everybody was looking at me holding their cards, Momma's voice was soft and pleading and guilty-sounding and she was stroking my face she said was feverish, my skin was sunburnt, my hair all tangles and I kicked at her and she grabbed my ankles to stop me and a little table fell over with some empty beer cans on it and a Styrofoam cup used as an ash tray and Maude helped Momma and I squirmed away from them but Momma caught me harder, carried me into our room, I went limp and boneless and too tired to cry or protest, Momma shined a flashlight into the corners of the room and under the bed to see there wasn't anything waiting to hurt me, Momma pulled off my T-shirt and slacks and laid me atop the lumpy bed that creaked and pulled a spread over me, it was a thin chenille spread with a smell of damp and mildew, a familiar smell like the smell of Black Flag insecticide that was an undercurrent in the air, you could never escape. Momma said, "Things are going to be O.K., Ingrid," kissing me on the cheek, her kiss tasting of beer and cigarette smoke, "—we'll make it up to you, honey, we promise." I grabbed her hair to pull her down next to me but she slapped my hand away and then she was gone back out to the card game and I'd wake up hearing low murmurous voices like water rushing past, the noise of the water churning white and frothy below the dam at Marsena, Daddy lifting me on his shoulder to see it better, except Daddy wasn't here, I was somewhere hearing men's voices I didn't know, now and then they'd laugh loud, and women's voices too, that rising-wailing sound of women's voices late at night. *Oh you bastard! You Goddamned motherfucker-bastard!*—a woman's voice loud in teasing.

Waking then when Momma came tiptoeing into the room carrying her sandals. Trying to be quiet but colliding with a chair and cursing under her breath and climbing onto the bed and the springs creaking beneath her and she was too exhausted even to draw the cover partway over her, just fell asleep. A wet gurgling click in her throat. "Momma," I whispered. "Momma, I hate you."

She didn't hear, she was starting to snore, not like Daddy snored but softer and discontinuous like asking questions? each little breathy snore a question? and I smelled Mommas special smell when she was tired and hadn't washed in a while, I tried to nudge into her arms so she might hold me like she used to all the time when I was little, "Momma, I love you," I said. Big Mommy Cat she'd called herself and I was Baby Kitten and we'd nap together during the day sometimes, sometimes in the backseat of the car if Daddy was late getting back but Momma was deep asleep now and didn't give a damn about me. I was wide awake. Those shrill insect noises outside in the night like tiny chain saws and there were Goddamned mosquitoes in the room that'd come through the broken screen drawn by the smell of our blood. Bites on my face that swelled and itched, I scratched at them hard and mean to spite Momma, it was Momma's fault I was so bit up, in the morning she'd be sorry.

Now this happened. I'd been hearing these voices thinking it was Maude and somebody else, but after a while I decided it was not, it was girls' voices, *little girls somewhere outside.* I climbed down from the bed where Momma was sleeping so hard and I went to the window to look out and the sky surprised me, it was lighter than the trees, a hard-glaring blue like ink. The insects were singing like crazy but over on top of them were these girls' voices, "*—eena?*" one of them was saying, "*—eena?*" like it was part of a name. I couldn't make out any words, I pressed my face against the dirty screen and at first I couldn't see anybody but then I saw them, I'd been looking at them not recognizing what it was, these figures toward the front of the lodge by the porch. The girls were a little older than me I estimated, and they were sisters. I knew that. They were sisters crouched and hiding, the taller one hugging the other who was crying trying to make her hush, "*—eena?—eena?*" I wondered if they'd just crawled out from under the porch? or were they about to crawl under the porch? Was somebody after them, was that why they were so scared? Out there in the dark, in the dripping bushes. If they were Maude's children where'd they been earlier, why hadn't they eaten with us, I wanted to wake Momma to ask but didn't dare, I knew that kind of hard panting sleep of Momma's, skin clammy with sweat.

The girls made me feel sad. And scared something was going to happen that couldn't be stopped.

How long I listened to them not hearing any actual words but only their voices, I don't know. Pressing my face against the screen until finally the voices went away, the little girls were gone without my noticing and there was just the night insects like before, crazy and loud. And Mommas breathless little pants and snores in the bed behind me.

"Momma?—hey!"

It was early morning. I tried to wake Momma but she groaned and shoved me away. She was still sleeping hard, her mouth open, eyelids fluttering and twitching like she was arguing with somebody in a dream. I laughed seeing Momma's face swollen with mosquito bites, her upper lip was swollen twice its normal size. Her red jersey top was pulled off one shoulder and her bra strap, which was white, but a kind of yellow-white, was twisted. Momma'd kicked the chenille cover onto the floor, I saw her white rayon slacks were stained, she wasn't going to like that. I touched her in stealth like I'd do sometimes when she didn't know, when she was flat on her back asleep I'd touch her stomach, that's where I'd come from Momma had told me, I'd stare and stare wondering was it so, how could I be so little, wouldn't I suffocate, it scared me to think of it and so I did not think of it except at such times and even then I didn't think of it, I said, "Momma damn you!"—gave up trying to wake her and went into the front room barefoot quiet as I could hoping nobody would see me, I hoped Skaggs and McCarry were gone, the room was empty except for the buck's head above the mantel, those glassy-dusty eyes watching me.

Always, there's been somebody watching me. Holding me in His vision, so I can't escape even if I wished to escape.

This was a room like so many rooms where there'd been a party and the smells of such a room in the morning, the stale smoke, the beer spillage, potato chips—these were smells I knew. Scattered over the table they'd been using which was a wooden table with scars and burns in it were beer cans and bottles and Styrofoam cups and ashes and butts, a flattened Frito-Lay box, playing cards. I always liked playing cards, watching Daddy and Momma and their friends at their games, the cards were precious things because adults handled them with such importance, you didn't ever interrupt them at a serious moment, especially you didn't interrupt any man. There was the queen of hearts on the floor I picked up to look at, also the ace of clubs, the cards were sticky and the reverse side disappointing—no picture just a design of black and mustard-yellow stripes.

Outside in the puddled-dirt drive Maude's car was the only car, Skaggs and McCarry were gone. There'd been times when people who showed up late at night were not gone in the morning nor would be gone for days, a friend of Daddy's once only a few months ago before Marsena in a back bedroom shouting and crying and Daddy had to watch over him, try to talk to him Momma said, he'd had a shotgun with him and some grievance to make right and Daddy and Brownlee had finally talked him out of it but it was a long time before he went away.

I went outside. Barefoot onto the splintery porch. Some of the planks too were rotted, you had to be careful where you walked.

I was shivering looking to where the little girls had been hiding—but I couldn't see anything. Tall grasses gone to seed, a straggly bush speckled with aphids. Momma wouldn't like me going barefoot out here, but I crawled under the railing and jumped down to the ground and it was strange how still my mind got, and how empty like I was waiting for something to fill it. "Hey? Are you here? Where are you?—I saw you," I said, like calling out but not raising my voice much, too scared to raise my voice. I squatted down to look under the porch but couldn't see much—it was a nasty dark cobwebby place, smelling of damp. That was when I started shivering hard and jumped up and backed away.

Walked around the yard, in the high grass that was wet from the night, and some of it sharp against my feet, and cold. My eyes swung up seeing how clear the sky was this morning, no clouds, everything washed clean, a sharp whitish light so you couldn't tell where the sun was, and everywhere, excited, calling out to one another, were birds in the pine trees.

There was an old rotted doghouse or rabbit hutch I looked into behind the lodge but nobody was there, nor any sign of anybody.

When Momma was up finally and her face mottled and swollen with mosquito bites, her lip still swollen so she looked like somebody'd punched her with his fist, I told her about the little girls, I was talking fast and excited and Momma said, squinting at me like the morning light was hurtful to her eyes, "Honey, you were just dreaming, there aren't any other children here. Only you." I said, "Yes there are, Momma. I heard them, and I saw them." Momma went out into the kitchen where she tried to get the gas stove to light up so she could make coffee and I followed her repeating what I'd said, the girls were here somewhere hiding I said, but Momma didn't pay too much attention to me. She was cursing under her breath looking for something then she found a box of wooden matches and with a shaky hand tried to light one, scraping it against a stove burner but the match must've been damp, the stick broke in her hand, she let the pieces fall to the floor and went to get her silver lighter Daddy'd given her out of her tote bag and that did work, a bluish flame flaring up at one of the burners with a hissing noise. I repeated what I said about the little girls, I'd seen them right outside by the front porch and they were sisters and they were crying because somebody was after them, it wasn't any Goddamn dream I told Momma it was not. Bringing my bare heels down hard on the worn-out linoleum floor so the floorboards wobbled. Not minding how I was hurting myself till Momma slapped at me to quiet me.

I was like the gas burner flaring up, the blue flame going to orange if the gas's turned too high.

The others came in, Maude and Brownlee, and after a while we ate breakfast, some stale sweet rolls out of a package, and some mealy bananas, and the adults had coffee and smoked their cigarettes and I was telling them about the little girls I knew were somewhere at the camp, Momma kept trying to hush me but I wouldn't be shushed and there came a look into Maude's face' and her eyes moved onto me for the first time like she hadn't seen me before. "What little girls are you talking about, Ingrid?" she asked. I said I didn't know their names, how would I know their names. I'd seen them in the middle of the night when everybody was asleep, out by the front porch they'd been, hiding in the grass, and crying. They were scared of something, I said. Like somebody was after them.

"What's this?" Maude asked, looking from me to Momma, and back again. "When was this?"

Maude was older than Momma by five or six years, heavier, with streaked brown hair tied up in a kerchief, eyebrows plucked thin and arching like she was in perpetual surprise, and her bloodshot eyes too she was always widening to show surprise or interest or mockery. She was good-looking I guess but I didn't like her and for sure I knew she didn't like me. Earlier that morning I'd heard her and Brownlee curse each other because Brownlee was flying back to Marsena instead of staying with her the way she wanted. Now she was staring at me asking what did the little girls look like? and I tried to say but there weren't the right words, I was getting excited and picking at my mosquito bites and Momma took both my hands to calm me saying, "Ingrid, that's enough. Jesus, you had one of your dreams, that's all." But Maude was exhaling smoke in that slow watchful way of grown women, and she was looking at Brownlee, and Brownlee who hadn't been listening said, "What?" like he was pissed and Maude said, "Vaughn, she's talking about Earl Meltzer's little girls—that's who she's talking about. My God." Brownlee said, "She isn't talking about anything, she's just a kid making things up," and Maude said, shaking her head, her voice quick and scared, "She's talking about Earl Meltzer's little girls, there's nobody else she's talking about."

Now Momma set her coffee cup down. "Who's Earl Meltzer?—what is this?"

Brownlee was telling Maude, "She couldn't know about them, it was two-three years ago at least. So drop it. You're wasted from last night." But Maude was making these soft sighing scared-sounding noises to herself, fluttering her eyes, "Oh God, oh Jesus. She's seen them. Those poor little girls," and Momma said, "Maude? Vaughn? What the hell is this?" and Brownlee was telling Maude, "Look, somebody must've told her, that's all. She had a dream, that's all." Momma said, "Tell her what, for Christ's sake?" Momma's eyes were sore-looking and her lip so swollen she hadn't even tried to put on lipstick like she always did, her skin looked dry as ashes in the morning light. Maude said, "Meltzer's little girls Cheryl and Doreen—*I* knew them! Meltzer and Lena his wife weren't living together, Lena was living with this other guy, in Watertown, and one night Meltzer went with a gun to get the girls from Lena's mother where they were staying, and he brought them out to the camp here, and—" and Brownlee cut her off saying, "Maude, shut the fuck up, you'll scare the kid," and Maude said, "*You* shut the fuck up, God damn you—you were a buddy of Meltzer's weren't you—thank God the prick put a bullet through his own brains too—"

Brownlee brought his opened hand around and hit the side of Maude's face, she screamed spilling hot coffee, and Momma screamed, and already I was running, out of the kitchen and through the back door where the screen was rusted and torn and I forgot I was barefoot running in the high grass around the side of the lodge, I wasn't crying because it wasn't me he'd hit, but I was scared, I crawled under the porch near where the girls had been and jays were screaming at me out of the pine trees and I pushed my way head-on through a rotted lattice covered in poison ivy and cobwebs till I was inside in this dark place smelling of something sharp crawling on my hands and knees and stones were stabbing me, pieces of glass, I was panting like a dog crawling halfway under the porch hearing how back in the kitchen they were still arguing.

Then it was quiet. It was still. Under the porch where the sun came through cracks in the floorboards in cobwebbed rays and there was this smell so sharp my nostrils pinched like something had died there, and old soft decayed leaves sticking to my skin, gnats buzzing in my face. And a mosquito whining, close by my ear. I knew to make myself as small as I could hugging my knees to my chest, hunched over so nobody could see if they came looking peering through the lattice. My right knee stung where it was bleeding but I wasn't crying. My hands were bleeding, too, but I paid them no mind. Momma's footsteps came quick overhead, I knew they were Momma's, so light and fast and then she was on the porch calling, "Ingrid? Honey, where are you?"

I waited like I knew to wait. I was used to hiding and some times I'd hidden nobody had even known I was gone, that was the safest kind of hiding and a principle to take to heart all your life.

So Momma didn't know where I was and she came down the porch steps talking to herself, muttering and cursing and I could see her legs, her legs in the white slacks, not clear but like I was seeing them through greenish water. Momma calling my name in that tight-scared way of hers so I knew if I revealed myself she'd be angry so I stayed where I was not making a sound.

I saw them then. At the farthest corner where it was darkest. The sisters crouched together in each other's arms. I saw their faces that were pale but smeared with something—dirt? blood? and I saw they were crying and they saw me, for a long time we looked at each other. "I'm an alive girl," I whispered. "I'm an alive girl not like you."

Tim O'Brien (*1946–*)

was born in Worthington, Minnesota, son of an insurance agent and an elementary school teacher. Inspired by newspaper clippings of articles his father wrote about his experiences in the Navy during World War II, O'Brien considered a writing career, but after graduating magna cum laude *from Macalester College in St. Paul, he was planning to attend Harvard's Graduate School of Government when, at the height of the Vietnam War, he was drafted into the Army. He considered dodging the draft by escaping to Canada, something he has since called himself a "coward" for failing to do. Instead, he served as an infantryman from 1969 to 1970. He received a Purple Heart after suffering a shrapnel wound, returned home, and began graduate school at Harvard. While there, he wrote and published his first book,* If I Die in a Combat Zone, *a memoir of his war experience. Since then, he has written seven novels, including* Going After Cacciato, *winner of the 1979 National Book Award, and* The Things They Carried, *a finalist for both the National Book Critics Circle Award and the Pulitzer Prize. Asked by* The Atlantic Monthly *whether he considered himself a Vietnam writer, O'Brien said, "In a way I do and in a way I don't. It's like asking Toni Morrison, 'Do you view yourself as a black writer?' She's had a black experience and her characters are black people, but she'd look at you and have a little frown. And I'm sure Conrad would too if you said, 'You're a sea writer,' or Shakespeare if you called him a 'king writer.' They'd look at you funny, and the funny look would say 'yeah, on one level.' . . . Every book I've written has the shadow of Vietnam on it, sometimes directly and sometimes obliquely. But . . . stories are meant to be about the human heart under pressure. Vietnam is a way of applying that pressure."*

INTRODUCTION BY **Julianna Baggott**

I first read *The Things They Carried* in college. Imagine me back then—sweet, wide-eyed, restless to shrug off some innocence, suddenly helicopter-dropped into the wilds of Tim O'Brien, much like his character Mary Anne Bell showing up in Vietnam in her pink sweater and culottes. *The Things They Carried* was then and is still the most dangerous book ever handed to me. I was already privately desperate and keenly aware of my desire for desire and love; life's unrelenting demands to choose soft, regrettable compromises; and how we sometimes save each other and sometimes fail to. I knew that I needed to be a writer, but until reading *The Things They Carried,* I had only an inkling that stories could serve as salvation.

The Things They Carried was assigned reading. It had to be. I would never have picked up a work of fiction (O'Brien, interestingly, doesn't call it a collection of stories, though it is one, or a novel, though it's that, too) about the Vietnam War on my own; yet once I was inside of it, Tim O'Brien had me convinced that he had written the novel for me specifically. (Alas, I was the kind of kid who, when listening to Carly Simon sing, "You probably think this song is about you, don't you?," had to admit that I did.) I found O'Brien telling me how to write. In "Sweetheart of the Song Tra Bong," he lets Mitchell Sanders go off on my bad habit: "... trust your own story. Get the hell out of the way and let it tell itself." And he gave me permissions. If it was okay for Rat Kiley "to heat up the truth, to make it burn so hot that you would feel exactly what he felt," then it had to be okay for me too.

In fact, the novel permanently changed my relationship with factuality and my dedication, as a writer, to sort out the deeper truths.

I found myself most consumed by the title story, the first in the book. It wasn't a story at all. It was an attempted list of the things they carried ("P-38 can openers, pocket knives, heat tabs") that dissolved into desire and memory and then pulled itself together and began again ("maps, code books, binoculars, and a .45 caliber pistol that weighed 2.9 pounds fully loaded"), only to dissolve again into hints that repeated and reappeared as moments that repeated and swelled into scenes until the story emerged from the list and settled down on me—a weight to bear, something that I had to carry with me into the world. The novel was about the Vietnam War, yet it was talking to my private desperation.

O'Brien doesn't allow me to read only with my writer's mind—dissecting structures, looking for lessons. He digs too fiercely. On its surface, the story "Half Gone" in *July, July* bears little resemblance to the stories in *The Things They Carried;* however, the heartache is trademark. These three stories—"The Things They Carried," "Sweetheart of the Song Tra Bong," and "Half Gone"—haunt the same emotional jungle. Lieutenant Jimmy Cross with the pebble from a Jersey girl in his mouth, Rat Kiley with his heavy sighs and long pauses, and Dorothy stripped to the waist in the front yard of her suburban neighborhood—they each want to be desired, loved, understood, whether by a girl, by some buddies, or by a husband washing down his twin Volvos.

And in each story, decisions are made, and compromises are considered. Jimmy Cross shuts down on the idea of romantic love because of his guilt over the death of a soldier, Ted Lavender. Mary Anne Bell tries to compromise, promising the big wedding back in Cleveland Heights, but eventually is seduced by the jungle and the mysteries of her soul. Dorothy compromised in the past, marrying for comfort, a comfort it's too late to cast off.

In their desperation, the characters make their stabs at saving one another. Dorothy, on the edge of leaving her husband, is perhaps saved by her cunning, invasive neighbor Fred as they swim in the pool. Jimmy Cross can't save Lavender or his own dreamy love, but perhaps he can save the other men under his command. And Rat Kiley can't save Mary Anne Bell, but she didn't want to be saved anyway.

And what about Mary Anne Bell? She's still a sound metaphor.

After reading O'Brien for the first time all those years ago, some part of my old self never came back. The world rose up, lush, mysterious, fully mined all around me. Like Mary Anne Bell, I chose to move gracefully forward into dangerous territory; for me, it was the territory of language and story. Mary Anne from Cleveland Heights now wearing her necklace made of human tongues—"the tips curled upward as if caught in a final shrill syllable"—after a line like that how can *anything* remain the same? Reading O'Brien marked the beginning of my addiction—a slipping off into the wilds, into the soul. It was that mix of "unnamed terror and unnamed pleasure" that continues to save me again and again.

Julianna Baggott is the author of three novels, Girl Talk, The Miss America Family, *and* The Madam, *as well as a book of poems,* This Country of Mothers, *and a collaboration with Steve Almond,* Which Brings Me to You: A Novel in Confessions.

Tim O'Brien

The Things They Carried

First Lieutenant Jimmy Cross carried letters from a girl named Martha, a junior at Mount Sebastian College in New Jersey. They were not love letters, but Lieutenant Cross was hoping, so he kept them folded in plastic at the bottom of his rucksack. In the late afternoon, after a day's march, he would dig his foxhole, wash his hands under a canteen, unwrap the letters, hold them with the tips of his fingers, and spend the last hour of light pretending. He would imagine romantic camping trips into the White Mountains in New Hampshire. He would sometimes taste the envelope flaps, knowing her tongue had been there. More than anything, he wanted Martha to love him as he loved her, but the letters were mostly chatty, elusive on the matter of love. She was a virgin, he was almost sure. She was an English major at Mount Sebastian, and she wrote beautifully about her professors and roommates and midterm exams, about her respect for Chaucer and her great affection for Virginia Woolf. She often quoted lines of poetry; she never mentioned the war, except to say, Jimmy, take care of yourself. The letters weighed ten ounces. They were signed Love, Martha, but Lieutenant Cross understood that Love was only a way of signing and did not mean what he sometimes pretended it meant. At dusk, he would carefully return the letters to his rucksack. Slowly, a bit distracted, he would get up and move among his men, checking the perimeter, then at full dark he would return to his hole and watch the night and wonder if Martha was a virgin.

The things they carried were largely determined by necessity. Among the necessities or near-necessities were P-38 can openers, pocket knives, heat tabs, wristwatches, dog tags, mosquito repellent, chewing gum, candy, cigarettes, salt tablets, packets of Kool-Aid, lighters, matches, sewing kits, Military Payment Certificates, C rations, and two or three canteens of water. Together, these items weighed between fifteen and twenty pounds, depending upon a man's habits or rate of metabolism. Henry Dobbins, who was a big man, carried extra rations; he was especially fond of canned peaches in heavy syrup over pound cake. Dave Jensen, who practiced field hygiene, carried a toothbrush, dental floss, and several hotel-sized bars of soap he'd stolen on R&R in Sydney, Australia. Ted Lavender, who was scared, carried tranquilizers until he was shot in the head outside the village of Than Khe in mid-April. By necessity, and because it was SOP, they all carried steel helmets that weighed five pounds including the liner and camouflage cover. They carried the standard fatigue jackets and trousers. Very few carried underwear. On their feet they carried jungle boots—2.1 pounds—and Dave Jensen carried three pairs of socks and a can of Dr. Scholl's foot powder as a precaution against trench foot. Until he was shot, Ted Lavender carried six or seven ounces of premium dope, which for him was a necessity. Mitchell Sanders, the RTO, carried condoms. Norman Bowker carried a diary. Rat Kiley carried comic books. Kiowa, a devout Baptist, carried an illustrated New Testament that had been presented to him by his father, who taught Sunday school in Oklahoma City, Oklahoma. As a hedge against bad times, however, Kiowa also carried his grandmother's distrust of the white man, his grandfather's old hunting hatchet. Necessity dictated. Because the land was mined and booby-trapped, it was SOP for each man to carry a steel-centered, nylon-covered flak jacket, which weighed 6.7 pounds, but which on hot days seemed much heavier. Because you could die so quickly, each man carried at least one large compress bandage, usually in the helmet band for easy access. Because the nights were cold, and because the monsoons were wet, each carried a green plastic poncho that could be used as a raincoat or groundsheet or makeshift tent. With its quilted liner, the poncho weighed almost two pounds, but it was worth every ounce. In April, for instance, when Ted Lavender was shot, they used his poncho to wrap him up, then to carry him across the paddy, then to lift him into the chopper that took him away.

They were called legs or grunts.

To carry something was to hump it, as when Lieutenant Jimmy Cross humped his love for Martha up the hills and through the swamps. In its intransitive form, to hump meant to walk, or to march, but it implied burdens far beyond the intransitive.

Almost everyone humped photographs. In his wallet, Lieutenant Cross carried two photographs of Martha. The first was a Kodacolor snapshot signed Love, though he knew better. She stood against a brick wall. Her eyes were gray and neutral, her lips slightly open as she stared straight-on at the camera. At night, sometimes, Lieutenant Cross wondered who had taken the picture, because he knew she had boyfriends, because he loved her so much, and because he could see the shadow of the picture taker spreading out against the brick wall. The second photograph had been clipped from the 1968 Mount Sebastian yearbook. It was an action shot—women's volleyball—and Martha was bent horizontal to the floor, reaching, the palms of her hands in sharp focus, the tongue taut, the expression frank and competitive. There was no visible sweat. She wore white gym shorts. Her legs, he thought, were almost certainly the legs of a virgin, dry and without hair, the left knee cocked and carrying her entire weight, which was just over one-hundred pounds. Lieutenant Cross remembered touching that left knee. A dark theater, he remembered, and the movie was *Bonnie and Clyde,* and Martha wore a tweed skirt, and during the final scene, when he touched her knee, she turned and looked at him in a sad, sober way that made him pull his hand back, but he would always remember the feel of the tweed skirt and the knee beneath it and the sound of the gunfire that killed Bonnie and Clyde, how embarrassing it was, how slow and oppressive. He remembered kissing her goodnight at the dorm door. Right then, he thought, he should've done something brave. He should've carried her up the stairs to her room and tied her to the bed and touched that left knee all night long. He should've risked it. Whenever he looked at the photographs, he thought of new things he should've done.

What they carried was partly a function of rank, partly of field specialty.

As a first lieutenant and platoon leader, Jimmy Cross carried a compass, maps, code books, binoculars, and a .45-caliber pistol that weighed 2.9 pounds fully loaded. He carried a strobe light and the responsibility for the lives of his men.

As an RTO, Mitchell Sanders carried the PRC-25 radio, a killer, twenty-six pounds with its battery.

As a medic, Rat Kiley carried a canvas satchel filled with morphine and plasma and malaria tablets and surgical tape and comic books and all the things a medic must carry, including M&Ms for especially bad wounds, for a total weight of nearly twenty pounds.

As a big man, therefore a machine gunner, Henry Dobbins carried the M-60, which weighed twenty-three pounds unloaded, but which was almost always loaded. In addition, Dobbins carried between ten and fifteen pounds of ammunition draped in belts across his chest and shoulders.

As PFCs or Spec 4s, most of them were common grunts and carried the standard M-16 gas-operated assault rifle. The weapon weighed 7.5 pounds unloaded, 8.2 pounds with its full twenty-round magazine. Depending on numerous factors, such as topography and psychology, the riflemen carried anywhere from twelve to twenty magazines, usually in cloth bandoliers, adding on another 8.4 pounds at minimum, fourteen pounds at maximum. When it was available, they also carried M-16 maintenance gear—rods and steel brushes and swabs and tubes of LSA oil—all of which weighed about a pound. Among the grunts, some carried the M-79 grenade launcher, 5.9 pounds unloaded, a reasonably light weapon except for the ammunition, which was heavy. A single round weighed ten ounces. The typical load was twenty-five rounds. But Ted Lavender, who was scared, carried thirty-four rounds when he was shot and killed outside Than Khe, and he went down under an exceptional burden, more than twenty pounds of ammunition, plus the flak jacket and helmet and rations and water and toilet paper and tranquilizers and all the rest, plus the unweighed fear. He was dead weight. There was no twitching or flopping. Kiowa, who saw it happen, said it was like watching a rock fall, or a big sandbag or something—just boom, then down—not like the movies where the dead guy rolls around and does fancy spins and goes ass over teakettle—not like that, Kiowa said, the poor bastard just flat-fuck fell. Boom. Down. Nothing else. It was a bright morning in mid-April. Lieutenant Cross felt the pain. He blamed himself. They stripped off Lavender's canteens and ammo, all the heavy things, and Rat Kiley said the obvious, the guy's dead, and Mitchell Sanders used his radio to report one U.S. KIA and to request a chopper. Then they wrapped Lavender in his poncho. They carried him out to a dry paddy, established security, and sat smoking the dead man's dope until the chopper came. Lieutenant Cross kept to himself. He pictured Martha's smooth young face, thinking he loved her more than anything, more than his men, and now Ted Lavender was dead because he loved her so much and could not stop thinking about her. When the dust-off arrived, they carried Lavender aboard. Afterward they burned Than Khe. They marched until dusk, then dug their holes, and that night Kiowa kept explaining how you had to be there, how fast it was, how the poor guy just dropped like so much concrete. Boom-down, he said. Like cement.

In addition to the three standard weapons—the M-60, M-16, and M-79—they carried whatever presented itself, or whatever seemed appropriate as a means of killing or staying alive. They carried catch-as-catch-can. At various times, in various situations, they carried M-14s and CAR-15s and Swedish Ks and grease guns and captured AK-47s and Chi-Coms and RPGs and Simonov carbines and blackmarket

Uzis and .38 caliber Smith & Wesson handguns and 66 mm LAWS and shotguns and silencers and blackjacks and bayonets and C-4 plastic explosives. Lee Strunk carried a slingshot; a weapon of last resort, he called it. Mitchell Sanders carried brass knuckles. Kiowa carried his grandfather's feathered hatchet. Every third or fourth man carried a Claymore antipersonnel mine—3.5 pounds with its firing device. They all carried fragmentation grenades—fourteen ounces each. They all carried at least one M-18 colored smoke grenade—twenty-four ounces. Some carried CS or teargas grenades. Some carried white-phosphorus grenades. They carried all they could bear, and then some, including a silent awe for the terrible power of the things they carried.

In the first week of April, before Lavender died, Lieutenant Jimmy Cross received a good-luck charm from Martha. It was a simple pebble, an ounce at most. Smooth to the touch, it was a milky-white color with flecks of orange and violet, oval-shaped, like a miniature egg. In the accompanying letter, Martha wrote that she had found the pebble on the Jersey shoreline, precisely where the land touched water at high tide, where things came together but also separated. It was this separate-but-together quality, she wrote, that had inspired her to pick up the pebble and to carry it in her breast pocket for several days, where it seemed weightless, and then to send it through the mail, by air, as a token of her truest feelings for him. Lieutenant Cross found this romantic. But he wondered what her truest feelings were, exactly, and what she meant by separate-but-together. He wondered how the tides and waves had come into play on that afternoon along the Jersey shoreline when Martha saw the pebble and bent down to rescue it from geology. He imagined bare feet. Martha was a poet, with the poet's sensibilities, and her feet would be brown and bare, the toenails unpainted, the eyes chilly and somber like the ocean in March, and though it was painful, he wondered who had been with her that afternoon. He imagined a pair of shadows moving along the strip of sand where things came together but also separated. It was phantom jealousy, he knew, but he couldn't help himself. He loved her so much. On the march, through the hot days of early April, he carried the pebble in his mouth, turning it with his tongue, tasting sea salts and moisture. His mind wandered. He had difficulty keeping his attention on the war. On occasion he would yell at his men to spread out the column, to keep their eyes open, but then he would slip away into daydreams, just pretending, walking barefoot along the Jersey shore, with Martha, carrying nothing. He would feel himself rising. Sun and waves and gentle winds, all love and lightness.

What they carried varied by mission.

When a mission took them to the mountains, they carried mosquito netting, machetes, canvas tarps, and extra bug juice.

If a mission seemed especially hazardous, or if it involved a place they knew to be bad, they carried everything they could. In certain heavily mined AOs, where the land was dense with Toe Poppers and Bouncing Betties, they took turns humping a twenty-eight-pound mine detector. With its headphones and big sensing plate, the equipment was a stress on the lower back and shoulders, awkward to handle, often useless because of the shrapnel in the earth, but they carried it anyway, partly for safety, partly for the illusion of safety.

On ambush, or other night missions, they carried peculiar little odds and ends. Kiowa always took along his New Testament and a pair of moccasins for silence. Dave

Jensen carried night-sight vitamins high in carotene. Lee Strunk carried his slingshot; ammo, he claimed, would never be a problem. Rat Kiley carried brandy and M&Ms. Until he was shot, Ted Lavender carried the starlight scope, which weighed 6.3 pounds with its aluminum carrying case. Henry Dobbins carried his girlfriend's panty hose wrapped around his neck as a comforter. They all carried ghosts. When dark came, they would move out single file across the meadows and paddies to their ambush coordinates, where they would quietly set up the Claymores and lie down and spend the night waiting.

Other missions were more complicated and required special equipment. In mid-April, it was their mission to search out and destroy the elaborate tunnel complexes in the Than Khe area south of Chu Lai. To blow the tunnels, they carried one-pound blocks of pentrite high explosives, four blocks to a man, sixty-eight pounds in all. They carried wiring, detonators, and battery-powered clackers. Dave Jensen carried earplugs. Most often, before blowing the tunnels, they were ordered by higher command to search them, which was considered bad news, but by and large they just shrugged and carried out orders. Because he was a big man, Henry Dobbins was excused from tunnel duty. The others would draw numbers. Before Lavender died there were seventeen men in the platoon, and whoever drew the number seventeen would strip off his gear and crawl in headfirst with a flashlight and Lieutenant Cross's .45-caliber pistol. The rest of them would fan out as security. They would sit down or kneel, not facing the hole, listening to the ground beneath them, imagining cobwebs and ghosts, whatever was down there—the tunnel walls squeezing in—how the flashlight seemed impossibly heavy in the hand and how it was tunnel vision in the very strictest sense, compression in all ways, even time, and how you had to wriggle in—ass and elbows—a swallowed-up feeling—and how you found yourself worrying about odd things—will your flashlight go dead? Do rats carry rabies? If you screamed, how far would the sound carry? Would your buddies hear it? Would they have the courage to drag you out? In some respects, though not many, the waiting was worse than the tunnel itself. Imagination was a killer.

On April 16, when Lee Strunk drew the number seventeen, he laughed and muttered something and went down quickly. The morning was hot and very still. Not good, Kiowa said. He looked at the tunnel opening, then out across a dry paddy toward the village of Than Khe. Nothing moved. No clouds or birds or people. As they waited, the men smoked and drank Kool-Aid, not talking much, feeling sympathy for Lee Strunk but also feeling the luck of the draw. You win some, you lose some, said Mitchell Sanders, and sometimes you settle for a rain check. It was a tired line and no one laughed.

Henry Dobbins ate a tropical chocolate bar. Ted Lavender popped a tranquilizer and went off to pee.

After five minutes, Lieutenant Jimmy Cross moved to the tunnel, leaned down, and examined the darkness. Trouble, he thought—a cave-in maybe. And then suddenly, without willing it, he was thinking about Martha. The stresses and fractures, the quick collapse, the two of them buried alive under all that weight. Dense, crushing love. Kneeling, watching the hole, he tried to concentrate on Lee Strunk and the war, all the dangers, but his love was too much for him, he felt paralyzed, he wanted to sleep inside her lungs and breathe her blood and be smothered. He wanted her to be a virgin and not a virgin, all at once. He wanted to know her. Intimate secrets—

why poetry? Why so sad? Why that grayness in her eyes? Why so alone? Not lonely, just alone—riding her bike across campus or sitting off by herself in the cafeteria. Even dancing, she danced alone—and it was the aloneness that filled him with love. He remembered telling her that one evening. How she nodded and looked away. And how, later, when he kissed her, she received the kiss without returning it, her eyes wide open, not afraid, not a virgin's eyes, just flat and uninvolved.

Lieutenant Cross gazed at the tunnel. But he was not there. He was buried with Martha under the white sand at the Jersey shore. They were pressed together, and the pebble in his mouth was her tongue. He was smiling. Vaguely, he was aware of how quiet the day was, the sullen paddies, yet he could not bring himself to worry about matters of security. He was beyond that. He was just a kid at war, in love. He was twenty-two years old. He couldn't help it.

A few moments later Lee Strunk crawled out of the tunnel. He came up grinning, filthy but alive. Lieutenant Cross nodded and closed his eyes while the others clapped Strunk on the back and made jokes about rising from the dead.

Worms, Rat Kiley said. Right out of the grave. Fuckin' zombie.

The men laughed. They all felt great relief.

Spook City, said Mitchell Sanders.

Lee Strunk made a funny ghost sound, a kind of moaning, yet very happy, and right then, when Strunk made that high happy moaning sound, when he went *Ahhooooo,* right then Ted Lavender was shot in the head on his way back from peeing. He lay with his mouth open. The teeth were broken. There was a swollen black bruise under his left eye. The cheekbone was gone. Oh shit, Rat Kiley said, the guy's dead. The guy's dead, he kept saying, which seemed profound—the guy's dead. I mean really.

The things they carried were determined to some extent by superstition. Lieutenant Cross carried his good-luck pebble. Dave Jensen carried a rabbit's foot. Norman Bowker, otherwise a very gentle person, carried a thumb that had been presented to him as a gift by Mitchell Sanders. The thumb was dark brown, rubbery to the touch, and weighed four ounces at most. It had been cut from a VC corpse, a boy of fifteen or sixteen. They'd found him at the bottom of an irrigation ditch, badly burned, flies in his mouth and eyes. The boy wore black shorts and sandals. At the time of his death he had been carrying a pouch of rice, a rifle, and three magazines of ammunition.

You want my opinion, Mitchell Sanders said, there's a definite moral here.

He put his hand on the dead boy's wrist. He was quiet for a time, as if counting a pulse, then he patted the stomach, almost affectionately, and used Kiowa's hunting hatchet to remove the thumb.

Henry Dobbins asked what the moral was.

Moral?

You know. *Moral.*

Sanders wrapped the thumb in toilet paper and handed it across to Norman Bowker. There was no blood. Smiling, he kicked the boy's head, watched the flies scatter, and said, It's like with that old TV show—Paladin. Have gun, will travel.

Henry Dobbins thought about it.

Yeah, well, he finally said. I don't see no moral.

There it *is,* man.
Fuck off.

They carried USO stationery and pencils and pens. They carried Sterno, safety pins, trip flares, signal flares, spools of wire, razor blades, chewing tobacco, liberated joss sticks and statuettes of the smiling Buddha, candles, grease pencils, *The Stars and Stripes,* fingernail clippers, Psy Ops leaflets, bush hats, bolos, and much more. Twice a week, when the resupply choppers came in, they carried hot chow in green mermite cans and large canvas bags filled with iced beer and soda pop. They carried plastic water containers, each with a two-gallon capacity. Mitchell Sanders carried a set of starched tiger fatigues for special occasions. Henry Dobbins carried Black Flag insecticide. Dave Jensen carried empty sandbags that could be filled at night for added protection. Lee Strunk carried tanning lotion. Some things they carried in common. Taking turns, they carried the big PRC-77 scrambler radio, which weighed thirty pounds with its battery. They shared the weight of memory. They took up what others could no longer bear. Often, they carried each other, the wounded or weak. They carried infections. They carried chess sets, basketballs, Vietnamese-English dictionaries, insignia of rank, Bronze Stars and Purple Hearts, plastic cards imprinted with the Code of Conduct. They carried diseases, among them malaria and dysentery. They carried lice and ringworm and leeches and paddy algae and various rots and molds. They carried the land itself—Vietnam, the place, the soil—a powdery orange-red dust that covered their boots and fatigues and faces. They carried the sky. The whole atmosphere, they carried it, the humidity, the monsoons, the stink of fungus and decay, all of it, they carried gravity. They moved like mules. By daylight they took sniper fire, at night they were mortared, but it was not battle, it was just the endless march, village to village, without purpose, nothing won or lost. They marched for the sake of the march. They plodded along slowly, dumbly, leaning forward against the heat, unthinking, all blood and bone, simple grunts, soldiering with their legs, toiling up the hills and down into the paddies and across the rivers and up again and down, just humping, one step and then the next and then another, but no volition, no will, because it was automatic, it was anatomy, and the war was entirely a matter of posture and carriage, the hump was everything, a kind of inertia, a kind of emptiness, a dullness of desire and intellect and conscience and hope and human sensibility. Their principles were in their feet. Their calculations were biological. They had no sense of strategy or mission. They searched the villages without knowing what to look for, not caring, kicking over jars of rice, frisking children and old men, blowing tunnels, sometimes setting fires and sometimes not, then forming up and moving on to the next village, then other villages, where it would always be the same. They carried their own lives. The pressures were enormous. In the heat of early afternoon, they would remove their helmets and flak jackets, walking bare, which was dangerous but which helped ease the strain. They would often discard things along the route of march. Purely for comfort, they would throw away rations, blow their Claymores and grenades, no matter, because by nightfall the resupply choppers would arrive with more of the same, then a day or two later still more, fresh watermelons and crates of ammunition and sunglasses and woolen sweaters—the resources were stunning—sparklers for the Fourth of July, colored eggs for Easter. It was the great American war chest—the fruits of science, the smokestacks, the canneries, the arsenals at Hartford, the Minnesota forests, the machine shops, the vast fields of corn and wheat—they carried like freight trains; they carried it on their backs and shoulders—and for all the ambiguities of Vietnam, all the mysteries and unknowns, there was at least the single abiding certainty that they would never be at a loss for things to carry.

After the chopper took Lavender away, Lieutenant Jimmy Cross led his men into the village of Than Khe. They burned everything. They shot chickens and dogs, they trashed the village well, they called in artillery and watched the wreckage, they marched for several hours through the hot afternoon, and then at dusk, while Kiowa explained how Lavender died, Lieutenant Cross found himself trembling.

He tried not to cry. With his entrenching tool, which weighed five pounds, he began digging a hole in the earth.

He felt shame. He hated himself. He had loved Martha more than his men, and as a consequence Lavender was now dead, and this was something he would have to carry like a stone in his stomach for the rest of the war.

All he could do was dig. He used his entrenching tool like an ax, slashing, feeling both love and hate, and then later, when it was full dark, he sat at the bottom of his foxhole and wept. It went on for a long while. In part, he was grieving for Ted Lavender, but mostly it was for Martha, and for himself, because she belonged to another world, which was not quite real, and because she was a junior at Mount Sebastian College in New Jersey, a poet and a virgin and uninvolved, and because he realized she did not love him and never would.

Like cement, Kiowa whispered in the dark. I swear to God—boom, down. Not a word.

I've heard this, said Norman Bowker.

A pisser, you know? Still zipping himself up. Zapped while zipping.

All right, fine. That's enough.

Yeah, but you had to see it, the guy just—

I *heard,* man. Cement. So why not shut the fuck *up?*

Kiowa shook his head sadly and glanced over at the hole where Lieutenant Jimmy Cross sat watching the night. The air was thick and wet. A warm, dense fog had settled over the paddies and there was the stillness that precedes rain.

After a time, Kiowa sighed.

One thing for sure, he said. The Lieutenant's in some deep hurt. I mean that crying jag—the way he was carrying on—it wasn't fake or anything, it was real heavy-duty hurt. The man cares.

Sure, Norman Bowker said.

Say what you want, the man does care.

We all got problems.

Not Lavender.

No, I guess not, Bowker said. Do me a favor, though.

Shut up?

That's a smart Indian. Shut up.

Shrugging, Kiowa pulled off his boots. He wanted to say more, just to lighten up his sleep, but instead he opened his New Testament and arranged it beneath his head as a pillow. The fog made things seem hollow and unattached. He tried not to think about Ted Lavender, but then he was thinking how fast it was, no drama, down and dead, and how it was hard to feel anything except surprise. It seemed un-Christian. He wished he could find some great sadness, or even anger, but the emotion wasn't there and he couldn't make it happen. Mostly he felt pleased to be alive. He liked the smell of the New Testament under his cheek, the leather and ink and paper and glue, whatever the chemicals were. He liked hearing the sounds of night. Even his fatigue, it felt fine, the stiff muscles and the prickly awareness of his own body, a floating feeling. He enjoyed not being dead. Lying there, Kiowa admired Lieutenant Jimmy Cross's capacity for grief. He wanted to share the man's pain, he wanted to care as Jimmy Cross cared. And yet when he closed his eyes, all he could think was Boom-down, and all he could feel was the pleasure of having his boots off and the fog curling in around him and the damp soil and the Bible smells and the plush comfort of night.

After a moment Norman Bowker sat up in the dark.

What the hell, he said. You want to talk, *talk.* Tell it to me.

Forget it.

No, man, go on. One thing I hate, it's a silent Indian.

For the most part they carried themselves with poise, a kind of dignity. Now and then, however, there were times of panic, when they squealed or wanted to squeal but couldn't, when they twitched and made moaning sounds and covered their heads and said Dear Jesus and flopped around on the earth and fired their weapons blindly and cringed and sobbed and begged for the noise to stop and went wild and made stupid promises to themselves and to God and to their mothers and fathers, hoping not to die. In different ways, it happened to all of them. Afterward, when the firing ended, they would blink and peek up. They would touch their bodies, feeling shame, then quickly hiding it. They would force themselves to stand. As if in slow motion, frame by frame, the world would take on the old logic—absolute silence, then the wind, then sunlight, then voices. It was the burden of being alive. Awkwardly, the men would reassemble themselves, first in private, then in groups, becoming soldiers again. They would repair the leaks in their eyes. They would check for casualties, call in dust-offs, light cigarettes, try to smile, clear their throats and spit and begin cleaning their weapons. After a time someone would shake his head and say, No lie, I almost shit my pants, and someone else would laugh, which meant it was bad, yes, but the guy had obviously not shit his pants, it wasn't that bad, and in any case nobody would ever do such a thing and then go ahead and talk about it. They would squint into the dense, oppressive sunlight. For a few moments, perhaps, they would fall silent, lighting a joint and tracking its passage from man to man, inhaling, holding in the humiliation. Scary stuff, one of them might say. But then someone else would grin or flick his eyebrows and say, Rodger-dodger, almost cut me a new asshole, *almost.*

There were numerous such poses. Some carried themselves with a sort of wistful resignation, others with pride or stiff soldierly discipline or good humor or macho zeal. They were afraid of dying but they were even more afraid to show it.

They found jokes to tell.

They used a hard vocabulary to contain the terrible softness. *Greased,* they'd say. *Offed, lit up, zapped while zipping.* It wasn't cruelty, just stage presence. They were actors and the war came at them in 3-D. When someone died, it wasn't quite dying, because in a curious way it seemed scripted, and because they had their lines mostly memorized, irony mixed with tragedy, and because they called it by other names, as if to encyst and destroy the reality of death itself. They kicked corpses. They cut off thumbs. They talked grunt lingo. They told stories about Ted Lavender's supply of tranquilizers, how the poor guy didn't feel a thing, how incredibly tranquil he was.

There's a moral here, said Mitchell Sanders.

They were waiting for Lavender's chopper, smoking the dead man's dope.

The moral's pretty obvious, Sanders said, and winked. Stay away from drugs. No joke, they'll ruin your day every time.

Cute, said Henry Dobbins.

Mind-blower, get it? Talk about wiggy—nothing left, just blood and brains.

They made themselves laugh.

There it is, they'd say. Over and over—there it is, my friend, there it is—as if the repetition itself were an act of poise, a balance between crazy and almost crazy, knowing without going, there it is, which meant be cool, let it ride, because Oh yeah, man, you can't change what can't be changed, there it is, there it absolutely and positively and fucking well *is*.

They were tough.

They carried all the emotional baggage of men who might die. Grief, terror, love, longing—these were intangibles, but the intangibles had their own mass and specific gravity, they had tangible weight. They carried shameful memories. They carried the common secret of cowardice barely restrained, the instinct to run or freeze or hide, and in many respects this was the heaviest burden of all, for it could never be put down, it required perfect balance and perfect posture. They carried their reputations. They carried the soldier's greatest fear, which was the fear of blushing. Men killed, and died, because they were embarrassed not to. It was what had brought them to the war in the first place, nothing positive, no dreams of glory or honor, just to avoid the blush of dishonor. They died so as not to die of embarrassment. They crawled into tunnels and walked point and advanced under fire. Each morning, despite the unknowns, they made their legs move. They endured. They kept humping. They did not submit to the obvious alternative, which was simply to close the eyes and fall. So easy, really. Go limp and tumble to the ground and let the muscles unwind and not speak and not budge until your buddies picked you up and lifted you into the chopper that would roar and dip its nose and carry you off to the world. A mere matter of falling, yet no one ever fell. It was not courage, exactly; the object was not valor. Rather, they were too frightened to be cowards.

By and large they carried these things inside, maintaining the masks of composure. They sneered at sick call. They spoke bitterly about guys who had found release by shooting off their own toes or fingers. Pussies, they'd say. Candy-asses. It was fierce, mocking talk, with only a trace of envy or awe, but even so, the image played itself out behind their eyes.

They imagined the muzzle against flesh. So easy: squeeze the trigger and blow away a toe. They imagined it. They imagined the quick, sweet pain, then the evacuation to Japan, then a hospital with warm beds and cute geisha nurses.

They dreamed of freedom birds.

At night, on guard, staring into the dark, they were carried away by jumbo jets. They felt the rush of takeoff. *Gone!* they yelled. And then velocity, wings and engines, a smiling stewardess—but it was more than a plane, it was a real bird, a big sleek silver bird with feathers and talons and high screeching. They were flying. The weights fell off; there was nothing to bear. They laughed and held on tight, feeling the cold slap of wind and altitude, soaring, thinking *It's over, I'm gone!*—they were naked, they were light and free—it was all lightness, bright and fast and buoyant, light as light, a helium buzz in the brain, a giddy bubbling in the lungs as they were taken up over the clouds and the war, beyond duty, beyond gravity and mortification and global entanglements—*Sin loi!* they yelled, *I'm sorry, motherfuckers, but I'm out of it, I'm goofed, I'm on a space cruise, I'm gone!*—and it was a restful, unencumbered sensation, just riding the light waves, sailing that big silver freedom bird over the mountains and oceans, over America, over the farms and great sleeping cities and cemeteries and highways and the Golden Arches of McDonald's. It was flight, a kind of fleeing, a kind of falling, falling higher and higher, spinning off the edge of the earth and beyond the sun and through the vast, silent vacuum where there were no burdens and where everything weighed exactly nothing. *Gone!* they screamed, *I'm sorry but I'm gone!* And so at night, not quite dreaming, they gave themselves over to lightness, they were carried, they were purely borne.

On the morning after Ted Lavender died, First Lieutenant Jimmy Cross crouched at the bottom of his foxhole and burned Martha's letters. Then he burned the two photographs. There was a steady rain falling, which made it difficult, but he used heat tabs and Sterno to build a small fire, screening it with his body, holding the photographs over the tight blue flame with the tips of his fingers.

He realized it was only a gesture. Stupid, he thought. Sentimental, too, but mostly just stupid.

Lavender was dead. You couldn't burn the blame.

Besides, the letters were in his head. And even now, without photographs, Lieutenant Cross could see Martha playing volleyball in her white gym shorts and yellow T-shirt. He could see her moving in the rain.

When the fire died out, Lieutenant Cross pulled his poncho over his shoulders and ate breakfast from a can.

There was no great mystery, he decided.

In those burned letters Martha had never mentioned the war, except to say, Jimmy, take care of yourself. She wasn't involved. She signed the letters Love, but it wasn't love, and all the fine lines and technicalities did not matter.

The morning came up wet and blurry. Everything seemed part of everything else, the fog and Martha and the deepening rain.

It was a war, after all.

Half smiling, Lieutenant Jimmy Cross took out his maps. He shook his head hard, as if to clear it, then bent forward and began planning the day's march. In ten minutes, or maybe twenty, he would rouse the men and they would pack up and head west, where the maps showed the country to be green and inviting. They would do what they had always done. The rain might add some weight, but otherwise it would be one more day layered upon all the other days.

He was realistic about it. There was that new hardness in his stomach.

No more fantasies, he told himself.

Henceforth, when he thought about Martha, it would be only to think that she belonged elsewhere. He would shut down the daydreams. This was not Mount

Sebastian, it was another world, where there were no pretty poems or midterm exams, a place where men died because of carelessness and gross stupidity. Kiowa was right. Boom-down, and you were dead, never partly dead.

Briefly, in the rain, Lieutenant Cross saw Martha's gray eyes gazing back at him.

He understood.

It was very sad, he thought. The things men carried inside. The things men did or felt they had to do.

He almost nodded at her, but didn't.

Instead he went back to his maps. He was now determined to perform his duties firmly and without negligence. It wouldn't help Lavender, he knew that, but from this point on he would comport himself as a soldier. He would dispose of his good-luck pebble. Swallow it, maybe, or use Lee Strunk's slingshot, or just drop it along the trail. On the march he would impose strict field discipline. He would be careful to send out flank security, to prevent straggling or bunching up, to keep his troops moving at the proper pace and at the proper interval. He would insist on clean weapons. He would confiscate the remainder of Lavender's dope. Later in the day, perhaps, he would call the men together and speak to them plainly. He would accept the blame for what had happened to Ted Lavender. He would be a man about it. He would look them in the eyes, keeping his chin level, and he would issue the new SOPs in a calm, impersonal tone of voice, an officer's voice, leaving no room for argument or discussion. Commencing immediately, he'd tell them, they would no longer abandon equipment along the route of march. They would police up their acts. They would get their shit together, and keep it together, and maintain it neatly and in good working order.

He would not tolerate laxity. He would show strength, distancing himself.

Among the men there would be grumbling, of course, and maybe worse, because their days would seem longer and their loads heavier, but Lieutenant Cross reminded himself that his obligation was not to be loved but to lead. He would dispense with love; it was not now a factor. And if anyone quarreled or complained, he would simply tighten his lips and arrange his shoulders in the correct command posture. He might give a curt little nod. Or he might not. He might just shrug and say, Carry on, then they would saddle up and form into a column and move out toward the villages west of Than Khe.

TIM O'BRIEN

Sweetheart of the Song Tra Bong

Vietnam was full of strange stories, some improbable, some well beyond that, but the stories that will last forever are those that swirl back and forth across the border between trivia and bedlam, the mad and the mundane. This one keeps returning to me. I heard it from Rat Kiley, who swore up and down to its truth, although in the end, I'll admit, that doesn't amount to much of a warranty. Among the men in Alpha Company, Rat had a reputation for exaggeration and overstatement, a compulsion to rev up the facts, and for most of us it was normal procedure to discount sixty or seventy percent of anything he had to say. If Rat told you, for example, that he'd slept with four girls one night, you could figure it was about a girl and a half. It wasn't a question of deceit. Just the opposite: he wanted to heat up the truth, to make it burn so hot that you would feel exactly what he felt. For Rat Kiley, I think, facts were formed by sensation, not the other way around, and when you listened to one of his stories, you'd find yourself performing rapid calculations in your head, subtracting superlatives, figuring the square root of an absolute and then multiplying by maybe.

Still, with this particular story, Rat never backed down. He claimed to have witnessed the incident with his own eyes, and I remember how upset he became one morning when Mitchell Sanders challenged him on its basic premise.

"It can't happen," Sanders said. "Nobody ships his honey over to Nam. It don't ring true. I mean, you just can't import your own personal poontang."

Rat shook his head. "I *saw* it, man. I was right there. This guy did it."

"His girlfriend?"

"Straight on. It's a fact." Rat's voice squeaked a little. He paused and looked at his hands. "Listen, the guy sends her the money. Flies her over. This cute blonde—just a kid, just barely out of high school—she shows up with a suitcase and one of those plastic cosmetic bags. Comes right out to the boonies. I swear to God, man, she's got on culottes. White culottes and this sexy pink sweater. There she *is*."

I remember Mitchell Sanders folding his arms. He looked over at me for a second, not quite grinning, not saying a word, but I could read the amusement in his eyes.

Rat saw it, too.

"No lie," he muttered. "Culottes."

When he first arrived in-country, before joining Alpha Company, Rat had been assigned to a small medical detachment up in the mountains west of Chu Lai, near the village of Tra Bong, where along with eight other enlisted men he ran an aid station that provided basic emergency and trauma care. Casualties were flown in by helicopter, stabilized, then shipped out to hospitals in Chu Lai or Danang. It was gory work, Rat said, but predictable. Amputations, mostly—legs and feet. The area was heavily mined, thick with Bouncing Betties and homemade booby traps. For a medic, though, it was ideal duty, and Rat counted himself lucky. There was plenty of cold beer, three hot meals a day, a tin roof over his head. No humping at all. No officers, either. You could let your hair grow, he said, and you didn't have to polish your boots or snap off salutes or put up with the usual rear-echelon nonsense. The highest ranking NCO was an E-6 named Eddie Diamond, whose pleasures ran from dope to Darvon, and except for a rare field inspection there was no such thing as military discipline.

As Rat described it, the compound was situated at the top of a flat-crested hill along the northern outskirts of Tra Bong. At one end was a small dirt helipad; at the other end, in a rough semicircle, the mess hall and medical hootches overlooked a river called the Song Tra Bong. Surrounding the place were tangled rolls of concertina wire, with bunkers and reinforced firing positions at staggered intervals, and base security was provided by a mixed unit of RFs, PFs, and ARVN infantry. Which is to say virtually no security at all. As soldiers, the ARVNs were useless; the Ruff-and-Puffs were outright dangerous. And yet even with decent troops the place was clearly indefensible. To the north and west the country rose up in thick walls of wilderness, triple-canopied jungle, mountains unfolding into higher mountains, ravines and gorges and fast-moving rivers and waterfalls and exotic butterflies and steep cliffs and smoky little hamlets and great valleys of bamboo and elephant grass. Originally, in the early 1960s, the place had been set up as a Special Forces outpost, and when Rat Kiley arrived nearly a decade later, a squad of six Green Berets still used the compound as a base of operations. The Greenies were not social animals. Animals, Rat said, but far from social. They had their own hootch at the edge of the perimeter, fortified with sandbags and a metal fence, and except for the bare essentials they avoided contact with the medical detachment. Secretive and suspicious, loners by nature, the six Greenies would sometimes vanish for days at a time, or even weeks, then late in the night they would just as magically reappear, moving like shadows through the moonlight, filing in silently from the dense rain forest off to the west. Among the medics there were jokes about this, but no one asked questions.

While the outpost was isolated and vulnerable, Rat said, he always felt a curious sense of safety there. Nothing much ever happened. The place was never mortared, never taken under fire, and the war seemed to be somewhere far away. On occasion, when casualties came in, there were quick spurts of activity, but otherwise the days flowed by without incident, a smooth and peaceful time. Most mornings were spent on the volleyball court. In the heat of midday the men would head for the shade, lazing away the long afternoons, and after sundown there were movies and card games and sometimes all-night drinking sessions.

It was during one of those late nights that Eddie Diamond first brought up the tantalizing possibility. It was an offhand comment. A joke, really. What they should do, Eddie said, was pool some bucks and bring in a few mamasans from Saigon, spice things up, and after a moment one of the men laughed and said, "Our own little EM club," and somebody else said, "Hey, yeah, we pay our fuckin' dues, don't we?" It was nothing serious. Just passing time, playing with the possibilities, and so for a while they tossed the idea around, how you could actually get away with it, no officers or anything, nobody to clamp down, then they dropped the subject and moved on to cars and baseball.

Later in the night, though, a young medic named Mark Fossie kept coming back to the subject.

"Look, if you think about it," he said, "it's not that crazy. You could actually do it."

"Do what?" Rat said.

"You know. Bring in a girl. I mean, what's the problem?"

Rat shrugged. "Nothing. A war."

"Well, see, that's the thing," Mark Fossie said. "No war *here.* You could really do it. A pair of solid brass balls, that's all you'd need."

There was some laughter, and Eddie Diamond told him he'd best strap down his dick, but Fossie just frowned and looked at the ceiling for a while and then went off to write a letter.

Six weeks later his girlfriend showed up.

The way Rat told it, she came in by helicopter along with the daily resupply shipment out of Chu Lai. A tall, big-boned blonde. At best, Rat said, she was seventeen years old, fresh out of Cleveland Heights Senior High. She had long white legs and blue eyes and a complexion like strawberry ice cream. Very friendly, too.

At the helipad that morning, Mark Fossie grinned and put his arm around her and said, "Guys, this is Mary Anne."

The girl seemed tired and somewhat lost, but she smiled.

There was a heavy silence. Eddie Diamond, the ranking NCO, made a small motion with his hand, and some of the others murmured a word or two, then they watched Mark Fossie pick up her suitcase and lead her by the arm down to the hootches. For a long while the men were quiet.

"That fucker," somebody finally said.

At evening chow Mark Fossie explained how he'd set it up. It was expensive, he admitted, and the logistics were complicated, but it wasn't like going to the moon. Cleveland to Los Angeles, LA to Bangkok, Bangkok to Saigon. She'd hopped a C-130 up to Chu Lai and stayed overnight at the USO and the next morning hooked a ride west with the resupply chopper.

"A cinch," Fossie said, and gazed down at his pretty girlfriend. "Thing is, you just got to *want* it enough."

Mary Anne Bell and Mark Fossie had been sweethearts since grammar school. From the sixth grade on they had known for a fact that someday they would be married, and live in a fine gingerbread house near Lake Erie, and have three healthy yellow-haired children, and grow old together, and no doubt die in each other's arms and be buried in the same walnut casket. That was the plan. They were very much in love, full of dreams, and in the ordinary flow of their lives the whole scenario might well have come true.

On the first night they set up house in one of the bunkers along the perimeter, near the Special Forces hootch, and over the next two weeks they stuck together like a pair of high school steadies. It was almost disgusting, Rat said, the way they mooned over each other. Always holding hands, always laughing over some private joke. All they needed, he said, were a couple of matching sweaters. But among the medics there was some envy. It was Vietnam, after all, and Mary Anne Bell was an attractive girl. Too wide in the shoulders, maybe, but she had terrific legs, a bubbly personality, a happy smile. The men genuinely liked her. Out on the volleyball court she wore cutoff blue jeans and a black swimsuit top, which the guys appreciated, and in the evenings she liked to dance to music from Rat's portable tape deck. There was a novelty to it; she was good for morale. At times she gave off a kind of come-get-me energy, coy and flirtatious, but apparently it never bothered Mark Fossie. In fact he seemed to enjoy it, just grinning at her, because he was so much in love, and because it was the sort of show that a girl will sometimes put on for her boyfriend's entertainment and education.

Though she was young, Rat said, Mary Anne Bell was no timid child. She was curious about things. During her first days in-country she liked to roam around the compound asking questions: What exactly was a trip flare? How did a Claymore work? What was behind those scary green mountains to the west? Then she'd squint and listen quietly while somebody filled her in. She had a good quick mind. She paid attention. Often, especially during the hot afternoons, she would spend time with the ARVNs out along the perimeter, picking up little phrases of Vietnamese, learning how to cook rice over a can of Sterno, how to eat with her hands. The guys sometimes liked to kid her about it—our own little native, they'd say—but Mary Anne would just smile and stick out her tongue. "I'm here," she'd say, "I might as well learn something."

The war intrigued her. The land, too, and the mystery. At the beginning of her second week she began pestering Mark Fossie to take her down to the village at the foot of the hill. In a quiet voice, very patiently, he tried to tell her that it was a bad idea, way too dangerous, but Mary Anne kept after him. She wanted to get a feel for how people lived, what the smells and customs were. It did not impress her that the VC owned the place.

"Listen, it can't be that bad," she said. "They're human beings, aren't they? Like everybody else?"

Fossie nodded. He loved her.

And so in the morning Rat Kiley and two other medics tagged along as security while Mark and Mary Anne strolled through the ville like a pair of tourists. If the girl was nervous, she didn't show it. She seemed comfortable and entirely at home; the hostile atmosphere did not seem to register. All morning Mary Anne chattered away about how quaint the place was, how she loved the thatched roofs and naked children, the wonderful simplicity of village life. A strange thing to watch, Rat said. This seventeen-year-old doll in her goddamn culottes, perky and fresh-faced, like a cheerleader visiting the opposing team's locker room. Her pretty blue eyes seemed to glow. She couldn't get enough of it. On their way back up to the compound she stopped for a swim in the Song Tra Bong, stripping down to her underwear, showing off her legs while Fossie tried to explain to her about things like ambushes and snipers and the stopping power of an AK-47.

The guys, though, were impressed.

"A real tiger," said Eddie Diamond. "D-cup guts, trainer-bra brains."

"She'll learn," somebody said.

Eddie Diamond gave a solemn nod. "There's the scary part. I promise you, this girl will most definitely learn."

In parts, at least, it was a funny story, and yet to hear Rat Kiley tell it you'd almost think it was intended as straight tragedy. He never smiled. Not even at the crazy stuff. There was always a dark, far-off look in his eyes, a kind of sadness, as if he were troubled by something sliding beneath the story's surface. Whenever we laughed, I remember, he'd sigh and wait it out, but the one thing he could not tolerate was disbelief. He'd get edgy if someone questioned one of the details. "She *wasn't* dumb," he'd snap. "I never said that. Young, that's all I said. Like you and me. A *girl,* that's the only difference, and I'll tell you something: it didn't amount to jack. I mean, when we first got here—all of us—we were real young and innocent, full of romantic bullshit, but we learned pretty damn quick. And so did Mary Anne."

Rat would peer down at his hands, silent and thoughtful. After a moment his voice would flatten out.

"You don't believe it?" he'd say. "Fine with me. But you don't know human nature. You don't know Nam."

Then he'd tell us to listen up.

A good sharp mind, Rat said. True, she could be silly sometimes, but she picked up on things fast. At the end of the second week, when four casualties came in, Mary Anne wasn't afraid to get her hands bloody. At times, in fact, she seemed fascinated by it. Not the gore so much, but the adrenaline buzz that went with the job, that quick hot rush in your veins when the choppers settled down and you had to do things fast and right. No time for sorting through options, no thinking at all; you just stuck your hands in and started plugging up holes. She was quiet and steady. She didn't back off from the ugly cases. Over the next day or two, as more casualties trickled in, she learned how to clip an artery and pump up a plastic splint and shoot in morphine. In times of action her face took on a sudden new composure, almost serene, the fuzzy blue eyes narrowing into a tight, intelligent focus. Mark Fossie would grin at this. He was proud, yes, but also amazed. A different person, it seemed, and he wasn't sure what to make of it.

Other things, too. The way she quickly fell into the habits of the bush. No cosmetics, no fingernail filing. She stopped wearing jewelry, cut her hair short and wrapped it in a dark green bandanna. Hygiene became a matter of small consequence. In her second week Eddie Diamond taught her how to disassemble an M-16, how the various parts worked, and from there it was a natural progression to learning how to use the weapon. For hours at a time she plunked away at C-ration cans, a bit unsure of herself, but as it turned out she had a real knack for it. There was a new confidence in her voice, a new authority in the way she carried herself. In many ways she remained naive and immature, still a kid, but Cleveland Heights now seemed very far away.

Once or twice, gently, Mark Fossie suggested that it might be time to think about heading home, but Mary Anne laughed and told him to forget it. "Everything I want," she said, "is right here."

She stroked his arm, and then kissed him.

On one level things remained the same between them. They slept together. They held hands and made plans for after the war. But now there was a new imprecision in the way Mary Anne expressed her thoughts on certain subjects. Not necessarily three kids, she'd say. Not necessarily a house on Lake Erie. "Naturally we'll still get married," she'd tell him, "but it doesn't have to be right away. Maybe travel first. Maybe live together. Just test it out, you know?"

Mark Fossie would nod at this, even smile and agree, but it made him uncomfortable. He couldn't pin it down. Her body seemed foreign somehow—too stiff in places, too firm where the softness used to be. The bubbliness was gone. The nervous giggling, too. When she laughed now, which was rare, it was only when something struck her as truly funny. Her voice seemed to reorganize itself at a lower pitch. In the evenings, while the men played cards, she would sometimes fall into long elastic silences, her eyes fixed on the dark, her arms folded, her foot tapping out a coded message against the floor. When Fossie asked about it one evening, Mary Anne looked at him for a long moment and then shrugged. "It's nothing," she said. "Really nothing. To tell the truth, I've never been happier in my whole life. Never."

Twice, though, she came in late at night. Very late. And then finally she did not come in at all.

Rat Kiley heard about it from Fossie himself. Before dawn one morning, the kid shook him awake. He was in bad shape. His voice seemed hollow and stuffed up, nasal-sounding, as if he had a bad cold. He held a flashlight in his hand, clicking it on and off.

"Mary Anne," he whispered, "I can't *find* her."

Rat sat up and rubbed his face. Even in the dim light it was clear that the boy was in trouble. There were dark smudges under his eyes, the frayed edges of somebody who hadn't slept in a while.

"Gone," Fossie said. "Rat, listen, she's sleeping with somebody. Last night, she didn't even . . . I don't know what to *do.*"

Abruptly then, Fossie seemed to collapse. He squatted down, rocking on his heels, still clutching the flashlight. Just a boy—eighteen years old. Tall and blond. A gifted athlete. A nice kid, too, polite and good-hearted, although for the moment none of it seemed to be serving him well.

He kept clicking the flashlight on and off.

"All right, start at the start," Rat said. "Nice and slow. Sleeping with who?"

"I don't know who. Eddie Diamond."

"Eddie?"

"Has to be. The guy's always there, always hanging on her."

Rat shook his head. "Man, I don't know. Can't say it strikes a right note, not with Eddie."

"Yes, but he's—"

"Easy does it," Rat said. He reached out and tapped the boy's shoulder. "Why not just check some bunks? We got nine guys. You and me, that's two, so there's seven possibles. Do a quick body count."

Fossie hesitated. "But I can't . . . If she's there, I mean, if she's with somebody—"

"Oh, Christ."

Rat pushed himself up. He took the flashlight, muttered something, and moved down to the far end of the hootch. For privacy, the men had rigged up curtained walls around their cots, small makeshift bedrooms, and in the dark Rat went quickly from room to room, using the flashlight to pluck out the faces. Eddie Diamond slept a hard deep sleep—the others, too. To be sure, though, Rat checked once more, very carefully, then he reported back to Fossie.

"All accounted for. No extras."

"Eddie?"

"Darvon dreams." Rat switched off the flashlight and tried to think it out. "Maybe she just—I don't know—maybe she camped out tonight. Under the stars or something. You search the compound?"

"Sure I did."

"Well, come on," Rat said. "One more time."

Outside, a soft violet light was spreading out across the eastern hillsides. Two or three ARVN soldiers had built their breakfast fires, but the place was mostly quiet and unmoving. They tried the helipad first, then the mess hall and supply hootches, then they walked the entire six hundred meters of perimeter.

"Okay," Rat finally said. "We got a problem."

When he first told the story, Rat stopped there and looked at Mitchell Sanders for a time.

"So what's your vote? Where was she?"

"The Greenies," Sanders said.

"Yeah?"

Sanders smiled. "No other option. That stuff about the Special Forces—how they used the place as a base of operations, how they'd glide in and out—all that had to be there for a reason. That's how stories work, man."

Rat thought about it, then shrugged.

"All right, sure, the Greenies. But it's not what Fossie thought. She wasn't sleeping with any of them. At least not exactly. I mean, in a way she was sleeping with *all* of them, more or less, except it wasn't sex or anything. They was just lying together, so to speak, Mary Anne and these six grungy weirded-out Green Berets."

"Lying down?" Sanders said.

"You got it."

"Lying down how?"

Rat smiled. "Ambush. All night long, man, Mary Anne's out on fuckin' *ambush.*"

Just after sunrise, Rat said, she came trooping in through the wire, tired-looking but cheerful as she dropped her gear and gave Mark Fossie a brisk hug. The six Green Berets did not speak. One of them nodded at her, and the others gave Fossie a long stare, then they filed off to their hootch at the edge of the compound.

"Please," she said. "Not a word."

Fossie took a half step forward and hesitated. It was as though he had trouble recognizing her. She wore a bush hat and filthy green fatigues; she carried the standard M-16 automatic assault rifle; her face was black with charcoal.

Mary Anne handed him the weapon. "I'm exhausted," she said. "We'll talk later."

She glanced over at the Special Forces area, then turned and walked quickly across the compound toward her own bunker. Fossie stood still for a few seconds. A little dazed, it seemed. After a moment, though, he set his jaw and whispered something and went after her with a hard, fast stride.

"Not later!" he yelled. "Now!"

What happened between them, Rat said, nobody ever knew for sure. But in the mess hall that evening it was clear that an accommodation had been reached. Or more likely, he said, it was a case of setting down some new rules. Mary Anne's hair was freshly shampooed. She wore a white blouse, a navy blue skirt, a pair of plain black flats. Over dinner she kept her eyes down, poking at her food, subdued to the point of silence. Eddie Diamond and some of the others tried to nudge her into talking about the ambush—What was the feeling out there? What exactly did she see and hear?—but the questions seemed to give her trouble. Nervously, she'd look across the table at

Fossie. She'd wait a moment, as if to receive some sort of clearance, then she'd bow her head and mumble out a vague word or two. There were no real answers.

Mark Fossie, too, had little to say.

"Nobody's business," he told Rat that night. Then he offered a brief smile. "One thing for sure, though, there won't be any more ambushes. No more late nights."

"You laid down the law?"

"Compromise," Fossie said. "I'll put it this way—we're officially engaged."

Rat nodded cautiously.

"Well hey, she'll make a sweet bride," he said. "Combat ready."

Over the next several days there was a strained, tightly wound quality to the way they treated each other, a rigid correctness that was enforced by repetitive acts of willpower. To look at them from a distance, Rat said, you would think they were the happiest two people on the planet. They spent the long afternoons sunbathing together, stretched out side by side on top of their bunker, or playing backgammon in the shade of a giant palm tree, or just sitting quietly. A model of togetherness, it seemed. And yet at close range their faces showed the tension. Too polite, too thoughtful. Mark Fossie tried hard to keep up a self-assured pose, as if nothing had ever come between them, or ever could, but there was a fragility to it, something tentative and false. If Mary Anne happened to move a few steps away from him, even briefly, he'd tighten up and force himself not to watch her. But then a moment later he'd be watching.

In the presence of others, at least, they kept on their masks. Over meals they talked about plans for a huge wedding in Cleveland Heights—a two-day bash, lots of flowers. And yet even then their smiles seemed too intense. They were too quick with their banter; they held hands as if afraid to let go.

It had to end, and eventually it did.

Near the end of the third week Fossie began making arrangements to send her home. At first, Rat said, Mary Anne seemed to accept it, but then after a day or two she fell into a restless gloom, sitting off by herself at the edge of the perimeter. She would not speak. Shoulders hunched, her blue eyes opaque, she seemed to disappear inside herself. A couple of times Fossie approached her and tried to talk it out, but Mary Anne just stared out at the dark green mountains to the west. The wilderness seemed to draw her in. A haunted look, Rat said—partly terror, partly rapture. It was as if she had come up on the edge of something, as if she were caught in that no-man's-land between Cleveland Heights and deep jungle. Seventeen years old. Just a child, blond and innocent, but then weren't they all?

The next morning she was gone. The six Greenies were gone, too.

In a way, Rat said, poor Fossie expected it, or something like it, but that did not help much with the pain. The kid couldn't function. The grief took him by the throat and squeezed and would not let go.

"Lost," he kept whispering.

It was nearly three weeks before she returned. But in a sense she never returned. Not entirely, not all of her.

By chance, Rat said, he was awake to see it. A damp misty night, he couldn't sleep, so he'd gone outside for a quick smoke. He was just standing there, he said, watching the moon, and then off to the west a column of silhouettes appeared as if by magic at the edge of the jungle. At first he didn't recognize her—a small, soft shadow among six other shadows. There was no sound. No real substance either. The seven silhouettes seemed to float across the surface of the earth, like spirits, vaporous and unreal. As he watched, Rat said, it made him think of some weird opium dream. The silhouettes moved without moving. Silently, one by one, they came up the hill, passed through the wire, and drifted in a loose file across the compound. It was then, Rat said, that he picked out Mary Anne's face. Her eyes seemed to shine in the dark—not blue, though, but a bright glowing jungle green. She did not pause at Fossie's bunker. She cradled her weapon and moved swiftly to the Special Forces hootch and followed the others inside.

Briefly, a light came on, and someone laughed, then the place went dark again.

Whenever he told the story, Rat had a tendency to stop now and then, interrupting the flow, inserting little clarifications or bits of analysis and personal opinion. It was a bad habit, Mitchell Sanders said, because all that matters is the raw material, the stuff itself, and you can't clutter it up with your own half-baked commentary. That just breaks the spell. It destroys the magic. What you have to do, Sanders said, is trust your own story. Get the hell out of the way and let it tell itself.

But Rat Kiley couldn't help it. He wanted to bracket the full range of meaning.

"I know it sounds far-out," he'd tell us, "but it's not like *impossible* or anything. We all heard plenty of wackier stories. Some guy comes back from the bush, tells you he saw the Virgin Mary out there, she was riding a goddamn goose or something. Everybody buys it. Everybody smiles and asks how fast was they going, did she have spurs on. Well, it's not like that. This Mary Anne wasn't no virgin but at least she was real. I saw it. When she came in through the wire that night, I was right there, I saw those eyes of hers, I saw how she wasn't even the same person no more. What's so impossible about that? She was a girl, that's all. I mean, if it was a guy, everybody'd say, Hey, no big deal, he got caught up in the Nam shit, he got seduced by the Greenies. See what I mean? You got these blinders on about women. How gentle and peaceful they are. All that crap about how if we had a pussy for president there wouldn't be no more wars. Pure garbage. You got to get rid of that sexist attitude."

Rat would go on like that until Mitchell Sanders couldn't tolerate it any longer. It offended his inner ear.

"The story," Sanders would say. "The whole tone, man, you're wrecking it."

"Tone?"

"The *sound.* You need to get a consistent sound, like slow or fast, funny or sad. All these digressions, they just screw up your story's *sound.* Stick to what happened."

Frowning, Rat would close his eyes.

"Tone?" he'd say. "I didn't know it was all that complicated. The girl joined the zoo. One more animal—end of story."

"Yeah, fine. But tell it right."

At daybreak the next morning, when Mark Fossie heard she was back, he stationed himself outside the fenced-off Special Forces area. All morning he waited for her, and all afternoon. Around dusk Rat brought him something to eat.

"She has to come out," Fossie said. "Sooner or later, she has to."

"Or else what?" Rat said.

"I go get her. I bring her out."

Rat shook his head. "Your decision. I was you, though, no way I'd mess around with any Greenie types, not for nothing."

"It's Mary Anne in there."

"Sure, I know that. All the same, I'd knock real extra super polite."

Even with the cooling night air Fossie's face was slick with sweat. He looked sick. His eyes were bloodshot; his skin had a whitish, almost colorless cast. For a few minutes Rat waited with him, quietly watching the hootch, then he patted the kid's shoulder and left him alone.

It was after midnight when Rat and Eddie Diamond went out to check on him. The night had gone cold and steamy, a low fog sliding down from the mountains, and somewhere out in the dark they heard music playing. Not loud but not soft either. It had a chaotic, almost unmusical sound, without rhythm or form or progression, like the noise of nature. A synthesizer, it seemed, or maybe an electric organ. In the background, just audible, a woman's voice was half singing, half chanting, but the lyrics seemed to be in a foreign tongue.

They found Fossie squatting near the gate in front of the Special Forces area. Head bowed, he was swaying to the music, his face wet and shiny. As Eddie bent down beside him, the kid looked up with dull eyes, ashen and powdery, not quite in register.

"Hear that?" he whispered. "You *hear?* It's Mary Anne."

Eddie Diamond took his arm. "Let's get you inside. Somebody's radio, that's all it is. Move it now."

"Mary Anne. Just listen."

"Sure, but—"

"Listen?"

Fossie suddenly pulled away, twisting sideways, and fell back against the gate. He lay there with his eyes closed. The music—the noise, whatever it was—came from the hootch beyond the fence. The place was dark except for a small glowing window, which stood partly open, the panes dancing in bright reds and yellows as though the glass were on fire. The chanting seemed louder now. Fiercer, too, and higher pitched.

Fossie pushed himself up. He wavered for a moment then forced the gate open.

"That voice," he said. "Mary Anne."

Rat took a step forward, reaching out for him, but Fossie was already moving fast toward the hootch. He stumbled once, caught himself, and hit the door hard with both arms. There was a noise—a short screeching sound, like a cat—and the door swung in and Fossie was framed there for an instant, his arms stretched out, then he slipped inside. After a moment Rat and Eddie followed quietly. Just inside the door they found Fossie bent down on one knee. He wasn't moving.

Across the room a dozen candles were burning on the floor near the open window. The place seemed to echo with a weird deep-wilderness sound—tribal music—bamboo flutes and drums and chimes. But what hit you first, Rat said, was the smell. Two kinds of smells. There was a topmost scent of joss sticks and incense, like the fumes of some exotic smokehouse, but beneath the smoke lay a deeper and much more powerful stench. Impossible to describe, Rat said. It paralyzed your lungs. Thick and numbing, like an animal's den, a mix of blood and scorched hair and excrement and the sweet-sour odor of moldering flesh—the stink of the kill. But that wasn't all. On a post at the rear of the hootch was the decayed head of a large black leopard; strips of yellow-brown skin dangled from the overhead rafters. And bones. Stacks of bones—all kinds. To one side, propped up against a wall, stood a poster in neat black lettering: ASSEMBLE YOUR OWN GOOK! FREE SAMPLE KIT!! The images came in a swirl, Rat said, and there was no way you could process it all. Off in the gloom a few dim figures lounged in hammocks, or on cots, but none of them moved or spoke. The background music came from a tape deck near the circle of candles, but the high voice was Mary Anne's.

After a second Mark Fossie made a soft moaning sound. He started to get up but then stiffened.

"Mary Anne?" he said.

Quietly then, she stepped out of the shadows. At least for a moment she seemed to be the same pretty young girl who had arrived a few weeks earlier. She was barefoot. She wore her pink sweater and a white blouse and a simple cotton skirt.

For a long while the girl gazed down at Fossie, almost blankly, and in the candlelight her face had the composure of someone perfectly at peace with herself. It took a few seconds, Rat said, to appreciate the full change. In part it was her eyes: utterly flat and indifferent. There was no emotion in her stare, no sense of the person behind it. But the grotesque part, he said, was her jewelry. At the girl's throat was a necklace of human tongues. Elongated and narrow, like pieces of blackened leather, the tongues were threaded along a length of copper wire, one overlapping the next, the tips curled upward as if caught in a final shrill syllable.

Briefly, it seemed, the girl smiled at Mark Fossie.

"There's no sense talking," she said. "I know what you think, but it's not . . . it's not *bad.*"

"Bad?" Fossie murmured.

"It's not."

In the shadows there was laughter.

One of the Greenies sat up and lighted a cigar. The others lay silent.

"You're in a place," Mary Anne said softly, "where you don't belong."

She moved her hand in a gesture that encompassed not just the hootch but everything around it, the entire war, the mountains, the mean little villages, the trails and trees and rivers and deep misted-over valleys.

"You just don't *know,*" she said. "You hide in this little fortress, behind wire and sandbags, and you don't know what it's all about. Sometimes I want to *eat* this place. Vietnam. I want to swallow the whole country—the dirt, the death—I just want to eat it and have it there inside me. That's how I feel. It's like . . . this appetite. I get scared sometimes—lots of times—but it's not *bad.* You know? I feel close to myself. When I'm out there at night, I feel close to my own body, I can feel my blood moving, my skin and my fingernails, everything, it's like I'm full of electricity and I'm glowing in the dark—I'm on fire almost—I'm burning away into nothing—but it doesn't matter because I know exactly who I am. You can't feel like that anywhere else."

All this was said softly, as if to herself, her voice slow and impassive. She was not trying to persuade. For a few moments she looked at Mark Fossie, who seemed to shrink away, then she turned and moved back into the gloom.

There was nothing to be done.

Rat took Fossie's arm, helped him up, and led him outside. In the darkness there was that weird tribal music, which seemed to come from the earth itself, from the deep rain forest, and a woman's voice rising up in a language beyond translation.

Mark Fossie stood rigid.

"Do something," he whispered. "I can't just let her go like that."

Rat listened for a time, then shook his head.

"Man, you must be deaf. She's already gone."

Rat Kiley stopped there, almost in midsentence, which drove Mitchell Sanders crazy.

"What next?" he said.

Next?"

"The girl. What happened to her?"

Rat made a small, tired motion with his shoulders. "Hard to tell for sure. Maybe three, four days later I got orders to report here to Alpha Company. Jumped the first chopper out, that's the last I ever seen of the place. Mary Anne, too."

Mitchell Sanders stared at him.

"You can't do that."

"Do what?"

"Jesus Christ, it's against the *rules,*" Sanders said. "Against human *nature.* This elaborate story, you can't say, Hey, by the way, I don't know the *ending.* I mean, you got certain obligations."

Rat gave a quick smile. "Patience, man. Up to now, everything I told you is from personal experience, the exact truth, but there's a few other things I heard secondhand. Thirdhand, actually. From here on it gets to be . . . I don't know what the word is."

"Speculation."

"Yeah, right." Rat looked off to the west, scanning the mountains, as if expecting something to appear on one of the high ridgelines. After a second he shrugged. "Anyhow, maybe two months later I ran into Eddie Diamond over in Bangkok—I was on R&R, just this fluke thing—and he told me some stuff I can't vouch for with my own eyes. Even Eddie didn't really see it. He heard it from one of the Greenies, so you got to take this with a whole shakerful of salt."

Once more, Rat searched the mountains, then he sat back and closed his eyes.

"You know," he said abruptly, "I loved her."

"Say again?"

"A lot. We all did, I guess. The way she looked, Mary Anne made you think about those girls back home, how clean and innocent they all are, how they'll never understand any of this, not in a billion years. Try to tell them about it, they'll just stare at you with those big round candy eyes. They won't understand zip. It's like trying to tell somebody what chocolate tastes like."

Mitchell Sanders nodded. "Or shit."

"There it is, you got to taste it, and that's the thing with Mary Anne. She was *there.* She was up to her eyeballs in it. After the war, man, I promise you, you won't find nobody like her."

Suddenly, Rat pushed up to his feet, moved a few steps away from us, then stopped and stood with his back turned. He was an emotional guy.

"Got hooked, I guess," he said. "I loved her. So when I heard from Eddie about what happened, it almost made me . . . Like you say, it's pure speculation."

"Go on," Mitchell Sanders said. "Finish up."

What happened to her, Rat said, was what happened to all of them. You come over clean and you get dirty and then afterward it's never the same. A question of degree. Some make it intact, some don't make it at all. For Mary Anne Bell, it seemed, Vietnam had the effect of a powerful drug: that mix of unnamed terror and unnamed pleasure that comes as the needle slips in and you know you're risking something. The endorphins start to flow, and the adrenaline, and you hold your breath and creep quietly through the moonlit nightscapes; you become intimate with danger; you're in touch with the far side of yourself, as though it's another hemisphere, and you want to string it out and go wherever the trip takes you and be host to all the possibilities inside yourself. Not *bad,* she'd said. Vietnam made her glow in the dark. She wanted more, she wanted to penetrate deeper into the mystery of herself, and after a time the wanting became needing, which turned then to craving.

According to Eddie Diamond, who heard it from one of the Greenies, she took a greedy pleasure in night patrols. She was good at it; she had the moves. All camouflaged up, her face smooth and vacant, she seemed to flow like water through the dark, like oil, without sound or center. She went barefoot. She stopped carrying a weapon. There were times, apparently, when she took crazy, death-wish chances—things that even the Greenies balked at. It was as if she were taunting some wild creature out in the bush, or in her head, inviting it to show itself, a curious game of hide-and-go-seek that was played out in the dense terrain of a nightmare. She was lost inside herself. On occasion, when they were taken under fire, Mary Anne would stand quietly and watch the tracer rounds snap by, a little smile at her lips, intent on some private transaction with the war. Other times she would simply vanish altogether—for hours, for days.

And then one morning, all alone, Mary Anne walked off into the mountains and did not come back.

No body was ever found. No equipment, no clothing. For all he knew, Rat said, the girl was still alive. Maybe up in one of the high mountain villes, maybe with the Montagnard tribes. But that was guesswork.

There was an inquiry, of course, and a week-long air search, and for a time the Tra Bong compound went crazy with MP and CID types. In the end, however, nothing came of it. It was a war and the war went on. Mark Fossie was busted to PFC, shipped back to a hospital in the States, and two months later received a medical discharge. Mary Anne Bell joined the missing.

But the story did not end there. If you believed the Greenies, Rat said, Mary Anne was still somewhere out there in the dark. Odd movements, odd shapes. Late at night, when the Greenies were out on ambush, the whole rain forest seemed to stare in at them—a watched feeling—and a couple of times they almost saw her sliding through the shadows. Not quite, but almost. She had crossed to the other side. She was part of the land. She was wearing her culottes, her pink sweater, and a necklace of human tongues. She was dangerous. She was ready for the kill.

TIM O'BRIEN

Half Gone

On a balmy, sunlit afternoon in midsummer of 1997, a Saturday, nine and a half months after her surgery, Dorothy Stier removed her shirt, removed her bra, adjusted her wig, slipped into a pair of sandals, finished off a glass of lemonade, cursed, muttered to herself—"Enough of *this!*"—threw open the back door, marched across the patio and down a slate sidewalk that led to the driveway at the side of the house, where her husband, Ron, a senior vice-president at Cargill, had just finished washing and waxing his two prized Volvos. "The twins," he called them. Inanely, Dorothy thought. One was an aqua-blue station wagon, the other a boxy, oversized, much-gadgeted silver sedan. Since acquiring the vehicles, a few weeks back, in what he too repetitively called a "package steal," Ron had lavished upon his new automobiles a preposterous mix of time and labor and paternal love. Which struck Dorothy as perverse. The man was already father to two spiffy boys. Not twins, perhaps, but well polished and mechanically sound. And he had a wife, too. A terrific wife. A wife, for that matter, who herself had once been awfully damned sporty, a vintage Bentley amid a fleet of utilitarian SUV housewives.

Dorothy was angry. Beyond anger, in fact. She had been contemplating departure. The "where" was irrelevant: Paris or Hong Kong or Duluth, maybe even the frigid streets of Winnipeg. No matter. At that particular instant, which registered in the suburban heavens at just after 2 P.M., July 19, 1997—and which found Dorothy Stier twelve tipsy strides down the cement driveway, bare to the waist, committed, pinned to the glaring present by the bewildered gaze of her gardener Jimmy—at that radiant, savage, remotely noble moment, Dorothy feared she might vomit. Her stomach wobbled. She had been propelled down the driveway by four or five vodka lemonades. Not quite drunk, perhaps, but she'd done her best. She lifted a hand as if to steady herself against the summer air. She nodded crisply at Jimmy, who glanced down at his hedge clipper, inspected it, and then looked back at her again. The man said nothing. Nor did Ron, whose attention was fastened on a sparkling hubcap and a pad of steel wool.

But, on the adjoining lawn, behind a low, freshly painted picket fence, Dorothy's dear friend and next-door neighbor, Fred Engelmann, a retired Marine Corps colonel, had plainly taken notice. Only a moment earlier, Fred had raised his garden hose by way of greeting. He had started to say something, to wave, but, midway, his jaw had locked into a curious smile. The hose had shifted in his hands. He was now watering his collie's doghouse.

"Freddie, darling!" cried Dorothy.

She released her grip on the air and fluttered her fingers at the man—thoughtful neighbor, confidant, domestic adviser, ex-assassin. Cheerfully, in a magnified, somewhat slurry across-the-fence voice, Dorothy cried, "Gorgeous day!"

"Roger that," Fred said.

"Wet doghouse!"

"Affirmative again," he said, and redirected the hose. Crinkles formed at the man's eyes. He had decided, apparently, to treat this with humor. "Catching rays, I guess?"

"That I am!" said Dorothy.

"Good, then. Good for you."

"Goodie for me! One second, I'll pop right over."

"Do that for sure," said Fred.

All this had consumed little more than a few moments of Saturday, July 19th. Ron had not yet turned to encounter his future. He knelt alongside the aqua-blue station wagon, his forehead puckered in concern over a scarred hubcap. Dorothy was six strides away, closing fast. Two or three elongated heartbeats elapsed: Jimmy pruning, Fred watering, a buzzing lawnmower, a child squealing, a radio playing Wagner, the two waxed Volvos gleaming like precious stones under a flagrant summer sun.

Ron pivoted on one knee.

He began to rise, stopped, squinted up at Dorothy.

"What's this?" he said.

"A wife," said Dorothy. She was now two strides away, accelerating.

"Jesus Christ."

"Look at me," said Dorothy.

He glanced at her shins.

"Higher," she said. "Pretend I'm a Volvo."

She had braked directly in front of him, seven or eight inches away. Her smile was genuine, even dazzling in the July sunlight, but it was also a foolhardy, belligerent, challenging smile.

"Suck it up," she said. "One look."

"Honey," Ron said.

He rose to his feet, threw an arm around her.

"Come on," he said. "Inside."

"One look. Don't be afraid."

"What is this?" Ron said. "Lady Godiva? Some nude freak show?"

"Freak?"

"I didn't mean freak."

"You did. Very distinct. Freak."

"Dorth, you're drunk."

She spun out of his arms and stepped back to present a vista. Ron's gaze shifted into the summer distance, as though seeking a more easeful angle on the world, and then, with a hiss of dismay, more or less directly, he looked at her.

"Ghastly?" she said.

"No," he said. "It makes me want to cry."

"Touch me."

"We're in a driveway, honey. It's daylight."

"Go on. Touch."

"Don't do this," he said, almost in a whisper, as if the essential problem were one of volume. "I'm asking nice, Dorth. Let's please go inside. Fred and Jimmy, they're getting an eyeful."

"Half full," said Dorothy.

"Half full. Touché. Can we go inside?"

"You haven't looked yet."

"What the hell am I doing right now?"

"Pretending," said Dorothy.

"I'm not pretending."

"Oh, you are, you are," she said, and then she went up on her toes, extending her arms like a ballerina, and executed a twirl in the driveway. Again her stomach wobbled. It occurred to her that the radio music was coming from the aqua-blue station wagon. She hadn't realized Ron liked Wagner. She hadn't realized, in fact, that he cared much for music.

"There," Ron said. "I've looked."

"Barely. And you haven't touched."

He frowned and said, "Stop this."

"Not in four months," she said. "It's breast cancer, Ron. It's not the flu, you can't catch it."

"I realize that."

"No lookie, no nookie."

"Lay off," he said. "I know."

Dorothy felt a gust of sickness go through her. Stupidly, she giggled. She cupped her hands and called out across the picket fence, "One sec, Freddie!"

"Jesus," Ron said.

Fred waved a hand. Generously, the man kept his back to them, aiming his hose at a patch of giant sunflowers.

"Nice guy," said Dorothy.

"He sure is. Are we finished here?"

"I guess we are." She wanted to be held and loved, wanted to return these things, but she also wanted to notch up the hurt. She flicked her head at his shiny Volvos. "How're the twins?"

"They're good."

"Praise God. Huge load off my mind."

"You're jealous of cars?"

"Gosh, I don't even know," Dorothy said. "Am I jealous? Am I? Too tough to call. Hot cars, obviously."

Ron took a step toward the house. "I've had it. Gone. Out of here."

"Bye, then."

"I'm not begging," he said.

He didn't move.

Dorothy leaned back against the station wagon, tipped up her head, and let the sunlight strike her straight on. She was forty-nine years old. She was a Reagan Republican, mother of two, loser of a left breast, off kilter, terrified, stomach-sick, head-sick, co-chair with Fred Engelmann of the Highland Park Neighborhood Watch Committee.

Also, at the moment, she was a woman in need of redefinition.

She looked at her husband. The anger was mostly gone now, replaced by a powerful, much more frightening weariness. "No sweat," she said. "Go watch a ballgame. I'm fine right here."

"Dorth, this isn't fair."

"Just go. Give me a minute."

Ron made a frustrated choking sound under his breath, then swung around, stalked up the driveway, crossed the patio, and went into the house.

Sad thing, Dorothy thought.

For an instant Dorothy considered chasing after him. Put her shirt on. Blame it on the lemonade. After all, he was a miracle of a husband. Wonderful father, wonderful partner. Reliable as a Volvo. Back in 1969, three months out of college, she had married him for his looks, which were boyish and lean and almond-eyed, a beautiful man, still drop-dead delicious even in middle age. But over twenty-eight years of marriage she'd come to appreciate him, even love him, for more substantial reasons. His good nature. His corny, old-fashioned ethics. The uncomplicated pleasure he took in providing for his family: an elegant home, expensive cars, memberships in two ritzy country clubs. True, Ron came off stiff in the personality department—"Anal Andy," the boys called him—but, at heart, he was a virtuous, honorable, suitably solid man. And through the whole breast-cancer nightmare he was all courage and confidence, citing survival statistics, clipping articles, calling her attention to recent advances in drug therapy. His relentless, can-do solicitude had almost killed her. Always the cheerleader. Rah-rahing the oncologists, rooting for the cure, clapping his hands and saying, "Atta girl," as she puked out the chemo poisons.

Couldn't blame him, Dorothy thought. Funny thing about breasts: husbands expect two of them. "Freak" was the word. And Dorothy herself wasn't all that crazy about mirrors or pool parties or negligees. Still, it seemed a pity that she'd been robbed of a husband and a decent sex life along with the killer breast.

Dorothy gave the station wagon a slap, switched off the radio, and joined Fred in his sunflower patch. "Freddie, Freddie," she said, and kissed the man's leathery cheek. "I've had a drink or two, maybe seven, probably eight, so cut me some slack." She put her hands on her hips. She hid nothing. "Amazing flowers, lovely day. How's Alice? I haven't got a shirt on."

Fred chuckled and said, "Guess you don't."

"I actually don't," said Dorothy. "Apologies."

"No need," Fred said. "Case closed. Over 'n' out."

"I'll go put a shirt on."

"No need for that either."

Fred turned off his hose, took her by the elbow, and in his firm, courtly way escorted her into the shade of an ornate iron rose trellis. They sat on the lawn. For ten years, almost eleven, she and Fred Engelmann had been the closest of friends, trading gossip and Clinton jokes, co-purveyors of "Nuke the Liberals" bumper stickers. Together, they had joyfully maligned the modern age. They agreed upon certain bedrock principles—less is more in affairs of state, prayer in the schools, the indisputable un-Americanism of so-called affirmative action. With mutual good humor, mutual horror, they had grieved over what seemed a vast ice age of turpitude and moral amnesia. They laughed a good deal. They enjoyed each other. More than that, Fred seemed to understand Dorothy exactly as she most wanted to be understood. On occasion, especially after a few back-yard cocktails, it was as if the man had unlocked the code of her personal history, developed a dossier on her dreams: certain regrets and longings. Forks in the road. Missed opportunities. Years ago, as a Marine Corps colonel in Vietnam, Fred had been affiliated in some cryptic way with the Phoenix program, which, as he sketchily described it, had to do with terminal solutions. "Find 'em, fry 'em," he'd say, then his eyes would twinkle and he'd gaze at her—gaze through her—wink, and say, "Ghost work."

She'd never pressed him. But it was sometimes spooky. Nothing obvious, just that wink of his. The way he'd stare whenever she exaggerated or fibbed or put a little self-advertising spin on the world.

Now, for instance.

As she lay back on his lawn. As she kicked off her sandals and said, "No big deal, Freddie. Woman problems."

Dorothy felt the man studying her.

"The midlife follies," she said, too quickly. "My topless phase."

Fred smiled, cleared his throat, waited, kept smiling, gave her time to consider corrections and modifiers.

"I'm leaving him," she said.

"Gotcha. Ron trouble?"

Dorothy squinted at him. "Don't act like you didn't know."

"All right, I'm pinned down." His eyes were like clean, fresh water. "Maybe I noticed a couple things. One plus one. Did the math, figured out a wee bit."

"Not wee and not maybe," said Dorothy. "You notice everything. But even if I wanted to, which, for the record, I definitely do not want—and forgive me, Freddie, I'm stinko, totally lemonaded, just psycho-sicko shitfaced. Anyway, even if I actually decided to stick around, let's face it, how the heck *could* I? After this." She gestured at her chest. "God help the one-boobed nymphs. Down with the queen. The Highland Park crowd—me included, you included—they don't go in for risqué. Right now, I'll bet a couple hundred phones are ringing. Bet I'm on their naked-lady watch list."

"You're on mine," Fred said.

"Yeah, thanks. What about Alice?"

Fred grinned. "Put it this way, she had a peek out the window. Probably took to bed."

The man studied her chest, not coldly or indifferently but as if concentrating on some intricate endgame. Then he sighed and said, "Lock 'n' load. Old Fred's dyin' to hear this."

"I should really go put something on."

"Negative, let 'er rip," he said.

Dorothy could think of little to say. Words came to her—grotesque, rather be dead, how could this happen?—but it all sounded so banal and ridiculous. After a few garbled sentences, she stopped and stared up at the brilliant July sky. She couldn't withhold a short giggle. "It's not all Ron's fault. I don't much like touching me, either. Hate showers. Hate bedtime."

"Oh, yes?" Fred said.

"Very true. Hate. And I don't mean this chopped-liver mess up here. Not just the breast."

"Right," he said. "You don't mean that."

Dorothy nodded. "It's worse. Like my whole life's got cancer."

"Exactly," he said.

"And I'm not—" She exhaled. "What the heck was *that,* Fred?"

"What was what, darlin'?"

"That word. 'Exactly,' you said."

"Did I?"

"You did. It's *my* screwed-up life—how could you know?"

Fred gave her a pained, persecuted look, as though the question were unneighborly. "Not born yesterday," he said. He grunted, satisfied. "Mind if I take off my trousers? I'm an old bastard. Nothing to worry about."

"You're not old, Freddie."

"Yeah, well, older than you'd think. Ex-leatherneck, ex-widow maker. Hell, we're all old."

He peeled off his pants, tossed them aside, looked across the picket fence, then waved and saluted. Ron stood watching them from the patio. He seemed lost and angry. He did not salute back. After a few moments, he turned and went inside.

"Upset husband," Fred said mildly.

"Who isn't?"

"Good point. But if I was in your naked-lady shoes I'd probably trot back to the drawin' board and rethink my tactics. Not too late. Except, of course, this problem we've got here, it's not just Ron, right?" He winked at her. "Can I ask something?"

"You may."

"Yeah. May. Ever vote Democrat?"

Dorothy glanced up. It was not the question she'd expected. "Vote Democrat?" she said. "Maybe once."

"May I guess?"

"You may, sure," Dorothy said, "and I've got this strange feeling you can."

"Sixty-eight primary. Gene McCarthy."

"Freddie, how do you know this?"

"Sources. My ex-specialty."

"Fred!"

"Deal is, you're my best pal, my neighbor," he said, "so it's good to figure out what's what. One more question. Ever tell Ron? About—you know—the fall from grace? The pinko left-wing lapse?"

"You tell me, Freddie. Did I?"

His eyes brightened, impish. "No, sweetheart, I reckon you probably didn't. Not a bad place to start, though. Might clear the air about a whole bucketful of trouble. Second thoughts. Life cancer." Fred lay back in the grass, shading his eyes against the sun. He wore black boxer shorts, black socks, black tennis shoes. The skin on his shins and thighs looked mummified. "If it helps any . . . Me, I was a Kennedy man. RFK. End the war, save the intestines."

Dorothy hunched forward, rocking, arms across her chest. She now felt the pressure of her nakedness. "I surrender," she said. "What's the point?"

"Points," Fred said lightly, "are mucho overrated. By the way, Ron's back. Patio. Binoculars."

"I can't look."

"Up to you. Anyway, about this harebrained Clean Gene business, I'm not gonna pry. Had your reasons. Maybe that college boy you almost ran off with. The one before Ron. What's his name?"

"Billy."

"Yeah, yeah. Billy. Left him in the lurch, I'd say. Cold, cold Winnipeg. Draft dodger, sure, and I don't truck with that, but even so it's gotta be tough gettin' dumped for your best friend. Good pals, weren't they? Ron and Billy? No fun. Figure it had to eat at you, too, the way you changed horses in midstream. Missed that flight to Canada. Went for handsome. Went for conservative. No-risk marriage, so to speak. And then all these years down the road, yikes, along comes cancer, eight nodes, enough to give a gal the middle-age willies. Certain what-ifs pop up. Roads not taken. Grass-might've-been-greener poppycock."

"That was decades ago," Dorothy said.

"You bet," he said. "Yesterday, huh?"

Dorothy tightened her lips, straightened up. Recently, late at night, Dorothy had found herself reviewing history, picturing the face of Billy McMann, wondering if she'd made a terrible, cowardly, very stupid mistake three decades ago. She had chosen one man over another, one life over another, and now the cancer and the disfigurement and the shadow of a waiting grave had filled her nights with dreams of Billy, dreams of Winnipeg. She had loved Billy with her whole heart: that ponytail of his, those sharp blue eyes. But Dorothy was no flower child. She needed her comforts. She was a Goldwater babe, and proud of it, and running off to Canada with Billy McMann had never been a real option. She had made the sensible choice. Now, bare-chested and drunk and maimed, she tried to blink away Billy's face.

"I need to put something on," Dorothy said. "This instant."

"Oh, boy."

"Hand me those pants, Fred. And I don't appreciate the snooping." She covered herself with his stained chinos, tied the pant legs behind her neck. "Not funny. It's like you've been checking up on me. Had me followed or tracked or—what's the word?"

"Tailed," he said.

"That's it. And we were friends."

Fred clenched his jaw. "We are, darlin'. Can't get friendlier. Fact finding, that's probably more like it. Research, you could say."

"Whatever," Dorothy said. "Shame on you."

She began to rise, pushing hard, but it was as if her muscles had come loose from the bone. Too much lemonade, she reasoned, or too much stress, but either way she had the sensation of being fastened to the lawn by Fred Engelmann's water-clear gaze.

It was now 2:43 P.M., Saturday, July 19, 1997. Still hot, still sunny. A light breeze had come up. The two Volvos glistened in the driveway. Her boys were at camp. Her gardener had vanished. Her husband was back on the patio, pacing, a very nice man. Her left breast was gone. Dorothy Stier could not move and was not sure she wanted to.

"Yeah, shame on me," Fred Engelmann said. "Old habits."

"I'm shocked and I'm hurt," said Dorothy. Even speech was an effort. "You voted for a Kennedy?"

Fred nodded unhappily. "Don't tell Alice."

"Well, I won't, but you have to explain."

"RFK? The fella had this—"

"No," she said. "The spying. I mean, God, I tell you everything anyway."

"Not quite everything," he said. The man seemed gleeful, plainly enjoying himself, but there was also a patient, expectant quality in the way he regarded her. After a second, he motioned at his swimming pool. "What say we invite Ron over? Take a dip, pry Alice out of bed, grill up some burgers? Might file off the tension."

"I'm leaving him," said Dorothy. "Maybe you didn't stumble across that little fact in your research."

"Oh, I did, I did," Fred said.

"Then you know. He won't come near me. Hideous, repulsive, freaky wife." She paused. "Is he watching?"

"Appears so, unless he's asleep behind those binoculars." Fred pulled off his shirt and tennis shoes and socks. "Come on, now, let's you and me hop in the pool. If I got this doped out right, Ron'll be showing up pronto."

"I can't move."

"Sure you can."

The man did his winking thing and took her by the wrist and helped her stand. She seemed to glide the ten or fifteen yards over to his pool.

"My pants," he said, and removed the chinos from her chest. "Expensive fuckers, no need to ruin 'em."

"Who *are* you?"

He chuckled and said, "Name's Freddie. USMC, retired."

The water was warm and lovely. Highland Park was a new place. Fred swam a few laps, Dorothy floated, and then the man paddled up beside her and said, "Eight nodes, that's a killer. Some gals make it. Not you, I'm afraid. I'll give it five years. Five years, two months, handful of days. Can't nail it down any tighter."

"Five?" Dorothy said.

"And two months."

"You seem sure."

"I am. Awful darn sure."

"Who are you?" she asked again. "God? Some sort of angel?"

Fred grinned and said, "Not exactly." He looked at her for what seemed a long while. "A neighbor. In the vicinity, so to speak. Let it go at that."

Dorothy looked at the bright suburban sky. She was on her back in the middle of the pool, pleased to be wet, pleased to be floating. Her wig floated beside her.

"Now, the thing is, we're talkin' five real good years," Fred said. "Way I see it, you won't be heading for Hong Kong. Not Duluth. Not Winnipeg, either. Two super kids, one fairly rock-ribbed husband. What I'd recommend, though, is you take what you took. The comfy route. Nice house, nice cars. Not so terrible." The man started to swim away, but then turned and treaded water. "No need to feel guilty, either. That old boyfriend you're dreamin' about. Billy. He's fine. He made it, too."

"Secret sources?" said Dorothy.

"Roger that. Here comes Ron."

Dorothy Stier took a breath, went under, came up again. It was Saturday, July 19, 1997, but no longer seemed to be. Dorothy hit the water with the heel of her hand. "Five years, what a pile of bull," she said. "Stick around, Freddie. I'll make it. Wait and see."

"Will do," he said.

Flannery O'Connor (1925–1964)

*was born in Savannah, Georgia, the only child of Roman Catholic parents. When she was thirteen, her father was found to have disseminated lupus, an incurable disease in which antibodies in the immune system attack the body's own substances. After her father's death in 1941, O'Connor attended Georgia State College for Women in Milledgeville, where she published stories and edited the literary magazine. On the strength of these stories, she was awarded a fellowship at the Writers' Workshop at the University of Iowa, and she earned her MFA degree there. Late in 1950, she became ill with what was diagnosed as lupus, and she returned to Milledgeville to start a series of treatments that temporarily arrested the disease. Living with her mother on the family's 500-acre dairy farm, O'Connor began to work again, writing from nine to twelve in the morning and spending the rest of the day resting, reading, writing letters, and raising peacocks. In the fourteen years that followed, she published two novels (*Wise Blood *and* The Violent Bear It Away*) and two collections of stories (*A Good Man Is Hard to Find *in 1955 and* Everything That Rises Must Converge, *published a year after her death). Though she died at the age of thirty-nine, having written only thirty-one stories—collected in her* Complete Stories, *which won the National Book Award in 1972—she is nonetheless one of the most influential and admired figures in the history of the short story.*

INTRODUCTION BY **Antonya Nelson**

Flannery O'Connor is the patron saint of the contemporary American short story and its writers. She wrote short stories with wicked brilliance, relinquishing not one shred of her own quirky—provincial, religious, topical—vision and voice while answering, honoring, an enduring mythic need. That alone won't canonize; but O'Connor also wrote *about* writing. Her *Mystery and Manners* is among the finest books on the craft of writing; in it, she shed (refracted perhaps) a Joycean light on the short story form, illuminating her own work and work habits, providing both transcendent insight into meaning and crisp pull-your-socks-up guidance for others. Another of her laudatory accomplishments was her attendance in an MFA program. Whenever the vampire comes out of its lair to sink its teeth into the state of American arts and letters, blaming all bad fiction on the glut of graduate programs in the United States, the student of writing can brandish Flannery O'Connor, shining protector and talisman, and watch the creature hiss and fizzle.

O'Connor writes with a simultaneous fondness for and shrewdness about her characters; she knows their foibles, and she loves them anyway. Trapped somewhat by her own illness, she turned her fictional eye on the small region of her birth and rendered it emblematically inclusive. She resembles, to some degree, her literary ancestors Jane Austen and Emily Dickinson, whose imaginative interrogation of the homes in which they were confined provided their soaring artistic freedom. O'Connor's gentle prodding mockery of the Southern bigot, whose "weaknesses proceed from innocence," showcases a model sensibility displaying the lapses in the flawed humans it concocts. Her characters' self-delusions earn our sympathy rather than our scorn—as they must have had to do for their author first. She knew that going to college didn't make you smart, just disconsolate.

Her adult children chafe against their mothers' presence—chafe and love concurrently. The mothers live by thoughtless platitude, but they die sincerely redeemed when they die. The old ladies lament a nostalgic past, the youngsters yearn for an impossible future, and their particular poignancy is the *now,* at the intersecting present. Her characters are pushed often by violent means to reveal their hearts. "True culture is in the mind," Julian hisses at his mother in "Everything That Rises Must Converge." But she and all of O'Connor's characters staunchly disagree: "It's in the heart."

The stories contained herein hold up under repeated readings. You don't at first notice those "five *or six*" gravestones in "A Good Man Is Hard to Find"; they're the planted hope that maybe the grandmother won't have to die. On, say, the eighth time through the story, you might notice the cat winding around the Misfit's legs, the living legacy that the "prophet gone wrong" takes with him, physical evidence of "the mustard-seed" O'Connor claims the grandmother may have spilled onto his hard, hard heart to take root. It wasn't until I had taught the story for fifteen years that a student demystified the "head-doctor" moment in the Misfit's ramblings. His father did indeed die of influenza in "19 ought 19"; the psychiatrist was speaking of his Oedipal complex, which the concrete-minded Misfit can no more symbolically suss out than he can the parable of Jesus—hence his problems in the murky world of metaphor and spirituality.

O'Connor credits editor Robert Giroux for having insisted on the last lines of her story "Good Country People." Hulga/Joy watches from her stranded position in the barn loft as the bible salesman makes off with her wooden leg. Her vision is blurry, but with it, she sees the boy appear to walk on water. Naturally, the two old women on the ground do not share this vision. He isn't their Jesus, and he hasn't saved them. O'Connor's Christian lesson always depends on the thoroughly modern, enduring truth that the individual determines his or her own cosmic alliance and that it often arrives, by necessity among the stubborn, in a moment of violent upheaval. Mrs. Hopewell and Mrs. Freeman will have to find their own spiritual healing.

O'Connor asserts that in the process of crafting the story, she didn't know that the bible salesman was going to steal the leg until a few lines before he did it. This description of the happy accident, the larky way in which great art often unveils itself, provides another of her talismanic shields: Acquire "the habit of art," she says, and these plums will fall into your hands. She argues for a way of viewing the world that is, in itself, a kind of religion. This "habit" allowed her to put her characters into contact with their perfect fate, pitting the nattering Grandmother against the literalist Misfit; leading Julian and bigoted Mrs. Chestny onto the bus where they will meet themselves in the form of another mother and son, after which Julian will have to watch his mother die before he understands that he can't live without her; and, finally, forcing Hulga, the proclaimed "atheist" ("I have a number of degrees," she insists to the bible salesman; "I don't care a thing about what all you done," he forgives) to discover that her true nature is not nihilistic but *romantic.*

Revelation up-ends these characters; they are saved even as it costs a life. It doesn't cost the reader's life, but it might save it. I think the writer's mission was no less than this; she would like you to take to heart the Misfit's wisdom; you, too, would be "a good woman, if it had been somebody there to shoot [you] every minute of [your] life." The Christian template does not reduce the reading of these stories so much as they expand the reader's understanding of a pure Christian vision. The perversion of that vision was O'Connor's incessant subject.

She favored the short story; she continues to legitimize the form. She fearlessly engaged stunning violence and killing comedy; her characters are hilarious and cruel, profound and profane, silly and sublime. The reader senses a supremely forgiving intelligence behind the stories, also a faint woundedness in the writer. The friction that her ignorant, lovable, irritating protagonists and their sidekicks dramatically, frenetically, comically enact on the page is accompanied by a steady humanitarian heartbeat in the background. This moral authority is what finally elevates and distinguishes Flannery O'Connor, raising her to a state of saintly grace.

For Antonya Nelson's bio, see page 782.

Flannery O'Connor

A Good Man Is Hard to Find

The grandmother didn't want to go to Florida. She wanted to visit some of her connections in east Tennessee and she was seizing at every chance to change Bailey's mind. Bailey was the son she lived with, her only boy. He was sitting on the edge of his chair at the table, bent over the orange sports section of the *Journal*. "Now look here, Bailey," she said, "see here, read this," and she stood with one hand on her thin hip and the other rattling the newspaper at his bald head. "Here this fellow that calls himself The Misfit is aloose from the Federal Pen and headed toward Florida and you read here what it says he did to these people. Just you read it. I wouldn't take my children in any direction with a criminal like that aloose in it. I couldn't answer to my conscience if I did."

Bailey didn't look up from his reading so she wheeled around then and faced the children's mother, a young woman in slacks, whose face was as broad and innocent as a cabbage and was tied around with a green head-kerchief that had two points on the top like rabbit's ears. She was sitting on the sofa, feeding the baby his apricots out of a jar. "The children have been to Florida before," the old lady said. "You all ought to take them somewhere else for a change so they would see different parts of the world and be broad. They never have been to east Tennessee."

The children's mother didn't seem to hear her but the eight-year-old boy, John Wesley, a stocky child with glasses, said, "If you don't want to go to Florida, why dontcha stay at home?" He and the little girl, June Star, were reading the funny papers on the floor.

"She wouldn't stay at home to be queen for a day," June Star said without raising her yellow head.

"Yes and what would you do if this fellow, The Misfit, caught you?" the grandmother said.

"I'd smack his face," John Wesley said.

"She wouldn't stay at home for a million bucks," June Star said. "Afraid she'd miss something. She has to go everywhere we go."

"All right, Miss," the grandmother said. "Just remember that the next time you want me to curl your hair."

June Star said her hair was naturally curly.

The next morning the grandmother was the first one in the car, ready to go. She had her big black valise that looked like the head of a hippopotamus in one corner, and underneath it she was hiding a basket with Pitty Sing, the cat, in it. She didn't intend for the cat to be left alone in the house for three days because he would miss her too much and she was afraid he might brush against one of the gas burners and accidentally asphyxiate himself. Her son, Bailey, didn't like to arrive at a motel with a cat.

She sat in the middle of the back seat with John Wesley and June Star on either side of her. Bailey and the children's mother and the baby sat in front and they left

Atlanta at eight forty-five with the mileage on the car at 55890. The grandmother wrote this down because she thought it would be interesting to say how many miles they had been when they got back. It took them twenty minutes to reach the outskirts of the city.

The old lady settled herself comfortably, removing her white cotton gloves and putting them up with her purse on the shelf in front of the back window. The children's mother still had on slacks and still had her hair tied up in a green kerchief, but the grandmother had on a navy blue straw sailor hat with a bunch of white violets on the brim and a navy blue dress with a small white dot in the print. Her collars and cuffs were white organdy trimmed with lace and at her neckline she had pinned a purple spray of cloth violets containing a sachet. In case of an accident, anyone seeing her dead on the highway would know at once that she was a lady.

She said she thought it was going to be a good day for driving, neither too hot nor too cold, and she cautioned Bailey that the speed limit was fifty-five miles an hour and that the patrolmen hid themselves behind billboards and small clumps of trees and sped out after you before you had a chance to slow down. She pointed out interesting details of the scenery: Stone Mountain; the blue granite that in some places came up to both sides of the highway; the brilliant red clay banks slightly streaked with purple; and the various crops that made rows of green lace-work on the ground. The trees were full of silver-white sunlight and the meanest of them sparkled. The children were reading comic magazines and their mother had gone back to sleep.

"Let's go through Georgia fast so we won't have to look at it much," John Wesley said.

"If I were a little boy," said the grandmother, "I wouldn't talk about my native state that way. Tennessee has the mountains and Georgia has the hills."

"Tennessee is just a hillbilly dumping ground," John Wesley said, "and Georgia is a lousy state too."

"You said it," June Star said.

"In my time," said the grandmother, folding her thin veined fingers, "children were more respectful of their native states and their parents and everything else. People did right then. Oh look at the cute little pickaninny!" she said and pointed to a Negro child standing in the door of a shack. "Wouldn't that make a picture, now?" she asked and they all turned and looked at the little Negro out of the back window. He waved.

"He didn't have any britches on," June Star said.

"He probably didn't have any," the grandmother explained. "Little niggers in the country don't have things like we do. If I could paint, I'd paint that picture," she said.

The children exchanged comic books.

The grandmother offered to hold the baby and the children's mother passed him over the front seat to her. She set him on her knee and bounced him and told him about the things they were passing. She rolled her eyes and screwed up her mouth and stuck her leathery thin face into his smooth bland one. Occasionally he gave her a faraway smile. They passed a large cotton field with five or six graves fenced in the middle of it, like a small island. "Look at the graveyard!" the grandmother said, pointing it out. "That was the old family burying ground. That belonged to the plantation."

"Where's the plantation?" John Wesley asked.

"Gone With the Wind," said the grandmother. "Ha. Ha."

When the children finished all the comic books they had brought, they opened the lunch and ate it. The grandmother ate a peanut butter sandwich and an olive and would not let the children throw the box and the paper napkins out the window. When there was nothing else to do they played a game by choosing a cloud and making the other two guess what shape it suggested. John Wesley took one the shape of a cow and June Star guessed a cow and John Wesley said, no, an automobile, and June Star said he didn't play fair, and they began to slap each other over the grandmother.

The grandmother said she would tell them a story if they would keep quiet. When she told a story, she rolled her eyes and waved her head and was very dramatic. She said once when she was a maiden lady she had been courted by a Mr. Edgar Atkins Teagarden from Jasper, Georgia. She said he was a very good-looking man and a gentleman and that he brought her a watermelon every Saturday afternoon with his initials cut in it, E. A. T. Well, one Saturday, she said, Mr. Teagarden brought the watermelon and there was nobody at home and he left it on the front porch and returned in his buggy to Jasper, but she never got the watermelon, she said, because a nigger boy ate it when he saw the initials, E. A. T.! This story tickled John Wesley's funny bone and he giggled and giggled but June Star didn't think it was any good. She said she wouldn't marry a man that just brought her a watermelon on Saturday. The grandmother said she would have done well to marry Mr. Teagarden because he was a gentleman and had bought Coca-Cola stock when it first came out and that he had died only a few years ago, a very wealthy man.

They stopped at The Tower for barbecued sandwiches. The Tower was a part stucco and part wood filling station and dance hall set in a clearing outside of Timothy. A fat man named Red Sammy Butts ran it and there were signs stuck here and there on the building and for miles up and down the highway saying, TRY RED SAMMY'S FAMOUS BARBEQUE. NONE LIKE FAMOUS RED SAMMY'S! RED SAM! THE FAT BOY WITH THE HAPPY LAUGH! A VETERAN! RED SAMMY'S YOUR MAN!

Red Sammy was lying on the bare ground outside The Tower with his head under a truck while a gray monkey about a foot high, chained to a small chinaberry tree, chattered nearby. The monkey sprang back into the tree and got on the highest limb as soon as he saw the children jump out of the car and run toward him.

Inside, The Tower was a long dark room with a counter at one end and tables at the other and dancing space in the middle. They all sat down at a board table next to the nickelodeon and Red Sam's wife, a tall burnt-brown woman with hair and eyes lighter than her skin, came and took their order. The children's mother put a dime in the machine and played "The Tennessee Waltz," and the grandmother said that tune always made her want to dance. She asked Bailey if he would like to dance but he only glared at her. He didn't have a naturally sunny disposition like she did and trips made him nervous. The grandmother's brown eyes were very bright. She swayed her head from side to side and pretended she was dancing in her chair. June Star said play something she could tap to so the children's mother put in another dime and played a fast number and June Star stepped out onto the dance floor and did her tap routine.

"Ain't she cute?" Red Sam's wife said, leaning over the counter. "Would you like to come be my little girl?"

"No I certainly wouldn't," June Star said. "I wouldn't live in a broken-down place like this for a million bucks!" and she ran back to the table.

"Ain't she cute?" the woman repeated, stretching her mouth politely.

"Aren't you ashamed?" hissed the grandmother.

Red Sam came in and told his wife to quit lounging on the counter and hurry up with these people's order. His khaki trousers reached just to his hip bones and his stomach hung over them like a sack of meal swaying under his shirt. He came over and sat down at a table nearby and let out a combination sigh and yodel. "You can't win," he said. "You can't win," and he wiped his sweating red face off with a gray handkerchief. "These days you don't know who to trust," he said. "Ain't that the truth?"

"People are certainly not nice like they used to be," said the grandmother.

"Two fellers come in here last week," Red Sammy said, "driving a Chrysler. It was a old beat-up car but it was a good one and these boys looked all right to me. Said they worked at the mill and you know I let them fellers charge the gas they bought? Now why did I do that?"

"Because you're a good man!" the grandmother said at once.

"Yes'm, I suppose so," Red Sam said as if he were struck with this answer.

His wife brought the orders, carrying the five plates all at once without a tray, two in each hand and one balanced on her arm. "It isn't a soul in this green world of God's that you can trust," she said. "And I don't count nobody out of that, not nobody," she repeated, looking at Red Sammy.

"Did you read about that criminal, The Misfit, that's escaped?" asked the grandmother.

"I wouldn't be a bit surprised if he didn't attact this place right here," said the woman. "If he hears about it being here, I wouldn't be none surprised to see him. If he hears it's two cent in the cash register, I wouldn't be a-tall surprised if he . . ."

"That'll do," Red Sam said. "Go bring these people their Co'-Colas," and the woman went off to get the rest of the order.

"A good man is hard to find," Red Sammy said. "Everything is getting terrible. I remember the day you could go off and leave your screen door unlatched. Not no more."

He and the grandmother discussed better times. The old lady said that in her opinion Europe was entirely to blame for the way things were now. She said the way Europe acted you would think we were made of money and Red Sam said it was no use talking about it, she was exactly right. The children ran outside into the white sunlight and looked at the monkey in the lacy chinaberry tree. He was busy catching fleas on himself and biting each one carefully between his teeth as if it were a delicacy.

They drove off again into the hot afternoon. The grandmother took cat naps and woke up every five minutes with her own snoring. Outside of Toombsboro she woke up and recalled an old plantation that she had visited in this neighborhood once when she was a young lady. She said the house had six white columns across the front and that there was an avenue of oaks leading up to it and two little wooden trellis arbors on either side in front where you sat down with your suitor after a stroll in the garden. She recalled exactly which road to turn off to get to it. She knew that Bailey would not be willing to lose any time looking at an old house, but the more she talked about it, the more she wanted to see it once again and find out if the little twin arbors were still standing. "There was a secret panel in this house," she said craftily, not telling the truth but wishing that she were, "and the story went that all the family silver was hidden in it when Sherman came through but it was never found. . ."

"Hey!" John Wesley said. "Let's go see it! We'll find it! We'll poke all the woodwork and find it! Who lives there? Where do you turn off at? Hey, Pop, can't we turn off there?"

"We never have seen a house with a secret panel!" June Star shrieked. "Let's go to the house with the secret panel! Hey Pop, can't we go see the house with the secret panel!"

"It's not far from here, I know," the grandmother said. "It wouldn't take over twenty minutes."

Bailey was looking straight ahead. His jaw was as rigid as a horseshoe. "No," he said.

The children began to yell and scream that they wanted to see the house with the secret panel. John Wesley kicked the back of the front seat and June Star hung over her mother's shoulder and whined desperately into her ear that they never had any fun even on their vacation, that they could never do what THEY wanted to do. The baby began to scream and John Wesley kicked the back of the seat so hard that his father could feel the blows in his kidney.

"All right!" he shouted and drew the car to a stop at the side of the road. "Will you all shut up? Will you all just shut up for one second? If you don't shut up, we won't go anywhere."

"It would be very educational for them," the grandmother murmured.

"All right," Bailey said, "but get this: this is the only time we're going to stop for anything like this. This is the one and only time."

"The dirt road that you have to turn down is about a mile back," the grandmother directed. "I marked it when we passed."

"A dirt road," Bailey groaned.

After they had turned around and were headed toward the dirt road, the grandmother recalled other points about the house, the beautiful glass over the front doorway and the candle-lamp in the hall. John Wesley said that the secret panel was probably in the fireplace.

"You can't go inside this house," Bailey said. "You don't know who lives here."

"While you all talk to the people in front, I'll run around behind and get in a window," John Wesley suggested.

"We'll all stay in the car," his mother said.

They turned onto the dirt road and the car raced roughly along in a swirl of pink dust. The grandmother recalled the times when there were no paved roads and thirty miles was a day's journey. The dirt road was hilly and there were sudden washes in it and sharp curves on dangerous embankments. All at once they would be on a hill, looking down over the blue tops of trees for miles around, then the next minute, they would be in a red depression with the dust-coated trees looking down on them.

"This place had better turn up in a minute," Bailey said, "or I'm going to turn around."

The road looked as if no one had traveled on it for months.

"It's not much farther," the grandmother said and just as she said it, a horrible thought came to her. The thought was so embarrassing that she turned red in the face and her eyes dilated and her feet jumped up, upsetting her valise in the corner. The instant the valise moved, the newspaper top she had over the basket under it rose with a snarl and Pitty Sing, the cat, sprang onto Bailey's shoulder.

The children were thrown to the floor and their mother, clutching the baby, was thrown out the door onto the ground; the old lady was thrown into the front seat. The car turned over once and landed right-side-up in a gulch off the side of the road. Bailey remained in the driver's seat with the cat—gray-striped with a broad white face and an orange nose—clinging to his neck like a caterpillar.

As soon as the children saw they could move their arms and legs, they scrambled out of the car, shouting, "We've had an ACCIDENT!" The grandmother was curled up under the dashboard, hoping she was injured so that Bailey's wrath would not come down on her all at once. The horrible thought she had had before the accident was that the house she had remembered so vividly was not in Georgia but in Tennessee.

Bailey removed the cat from his neck with both hands and flung it out the window against the side of a pine tree. Then he got out of the car and started looking for the children's mother. She was sitting against the side of the red gutted ditch, holding the screaming baby, but she only had a cut down her face and a broken shoulder. "We've had an ACCIDENT!" the children screamed in a frenzy of delight.

"But nobody's killed," June Star said with disappointment as the grandmother limped out of the car, her hat still pinned to her head but the broken front brim standing up at a jaunty angle and the violet spray hanging off the side. They all sat down in the ditch, except the children, to recover from the shock. They were all shaking.

"Maybe a car will come along," said the children's mother hoarsely.

"I believe I have injured an organ," said the grandmother, pressing her side, but no one answered her. Bailey's teeth were clattering. He had on a yellow sport shirt with bright blue parrots designed in it and his face was as yellow as the shirt. The grandmother decided that she would not mention that the house was in Tennessee.

The road was about ten feet above and they could see only the tops of the trees on the other side of it. Behind the ditch they were sitting in there were more woods, tall and dark and deep. In a few minutes they saw a car some distance away on top of a hill, coming slowly as if the occupants were watching them. The grandmother stood up and waved both her arms dramatically to attract their attention. The car continued to come on slowly, disappeared around a bend and appeared again, moving even slower, on top of the hill they had gone over. It was a big black battered hearse-like automobile. There were three men in it.

It came to a stop just over them and for some minutes, the driver looked down with a steady expressionless gaze to where they were sitting, and didn't speak. Then he turned his head and muttered something to the other two and they got out. One was a fat boy in black trousers and a red sweat shirt with a silver stallion embossed on the front of it. He moved around on the right side of them and stood staring, his mouth partly open in a kind of loose grin. The other had on khaki pants and a blue striped coat and a gray hat pulled down very low, hiding most of his face. He came around slowly on the left side. Neither spoke.

The driver got out of the car and stood by the side of it, looking down at them. He was an older man than the other two. His hair was just beginning to gray and he wore silver-rimmed spectacles that gave him a scholarly look. He had a long creased face and didn't have on any shirt or undershirt. He had on blue jeans that were too tight for him and was holding a black hat and a gun. The two boys also had guns.

"We've had an ACCIDENT!" the children screamed.

The grandmother had the peculiar feeling that the bespectacled man was someone she knew. His face was as familiar to her as if she had known him all her life but she could not recall who he was. He moved away from the car and began to come down the embankment, placing his feet carefully so that he wouldn't slip. He had on tan and white shoes and no socks, and his ankles were red and thin. "Good afternoon," he said. "I see you all had you a little spill."

"We turned over twice!" said the grandmother.

"Oncet," he corrected. "We seen it happen. Try their car and see will it run, Hiram," he said quietly to the boy with the gray hat.

"What you got that gun for?" John Wesley asked. "Whatcha gonna do with that gun?"

"Lady," the man said to the children's mother, "would you mind calling them children to sit down by you? Children make me nervous. I want all you all to sit down right together there where you're at."

"What are you telling us what to do for?" June Star asked.

Behind them the line of woods gaped like a dark open mouth. "Come here," said their mother.

"Look here now," Bailey, began suddenly, "we're in a predicament! We're in . . ."

The grandmother shrieked. She scrambled to her feet and stood staring. "You're The Misfit!" she said. "I recognized you at once!"

"Yes'm," the man said, smiling slightly as if he were pleased in spite of himself to be known, "but it would have been better for all of you, lady, if you hadn't of reckernized me."

Bailey turned his head sharply and said something to his mother that shocked even the children. The old lady began to cry and The Misfit reddened.

"Lady," he said, "don't you get upset. Sometimes a man says things he don't mean. I don't reckon he meant to talk to you thataway."

"You wouldn't shoot a lady, would you?" the grandmother said and removed a clean handkerchief from her cuff and began to slap at her eyes with it.

The Misfit pointed the toe of his shoe into the ground and made a little hole and then covered it up again. "I would hate to have to," he said.

"Listen," the grandmother almost screamed, "I know you're a good man. You don't look a bit like you have common blood. I know you must come from nice people!"

"Yes mam," he said, "finest people in the world." When he smiled he showed a row of strong white teeth. "God never made a finer woman than my mother and my daddy's heart was pure gold," he said. The boy with the red sweat shirt had come around behind them and was standing with his gun at his hip. The Misfit squatted down on the ground. "Watch them children, Bobby Lee," he said. "You know they make me nervous." He looked at the six of them huddled together in front of him and he seemed to be embarrassed as if he couldn't think of anything to say. "Ain't a cloud in the sky," he remarked, looking up at it. "Don't see no sun but don't see no cloud neither."

"Yes, it's a beautiful day," said the grandmother. "Listen," she said, "you shouldn't call yourself The Misfit because I know you're a good man at heart. I can just look at you and tell."

"Hush!" Bailey yelled. "Hush! Everybody shut up and let me handle this!" He was squatting in the position of a runner about to sprint forward but he didn't move.

"I pre-chate that, lady," The Misfit said and drew a little circle in the ground with the butt of his gun.

"It'll take a half a hour to fix this here car," Hiram called, looking over the raised hood of it.

"Well, first you and Bobby Lee get him and that little boy to step over yonder with you," The Misfit said, pointing to Bailey and John Wesley. "The boys want to ask you something," he said to Bailey. "Would you mind stepping back in them woods there with them?"

"Listen," Bailey began, "we're in a terrible predicament! Nobody realizes what this is," and his voice cracked. His eyes were as blue and intense as the parrots in his shirt and he remained perfectly still.

The grandmother reached up to adjust her hat brim as if she were going to the woods with him but it came off in her hand. She stood staring at it and after a second she let it fall on the ground. Hiram pulled Bailey up by the arm as if he were assisting an old man. John Wesley caught hold of his father's hand and Bobby Lee followed. They went off toward the woods and just as they reached the dark edge, Bailey turned and supporting himself against a gray naked pine trunk, he shouted, "I'll be back in a minute, Mamma, wait on me!"

"Come back this instant!" his mother shrilled but they all disappeared into the woods.

"Bailey Boy!" the grandmother called in a tragic voice but she found she was looking at The Misfit squatting on the ground in front of her. "I just know you're a good man," she said desperately. "You're not a bit common!"

"Nome, I ain't a good man," The Misfit said after a second as if he had considered her statement carefully, "but I ain't the worst in the world neither. My daddy said I was a different breed of dog from my brothers and sisters. 'You know,' Daddy said, 'it's some that can live their whole life out without asking about it and it's others has to know why it is, and this boy is one of the latters. He's going to be into everything!'" He put on his black hat and looked up suddenly and then away deep into the woods as if he were embarrassed again. "I'm sorry I don't have on a shirt before you ladies," he said, hunching his shoulders slightly. "We buried our clothes that we had on when we escaped and we're just making do until we can get better. We borrowed these from some folks we met," he explained.

"That's perfectly all right," the grandmother said. "Maybe Bailey has an extra shirt in his suitcase."

"I'll look and see terrectly," The Misfit said.

"Where are they taking him?" the children's mother screamed.

"Daddy was a card himself," The Misfit said. "You couldn't put anything over on him. He never got in trouble with the Authorities though. Just had the knack of handling them."

"You could be honest too if you'd only try," said the grandmother. "Think how wonderful it would be to settle down and live a comfortable life and not have to think about somebody chasing you all the time."

The Misfit kept scratching in the ground with the butt of his gun as if he were thinking about it. "Yes'm, somebody is always after you," he murmured.

The grandmother noticed how thin his shoulder blades were just behind his hat because she was standing up looking down on him. "Do you ever pray?" she asked.

He shook his head. All she saw was the black hat wiggle between his shoulder blades. "Nome," he said.

There was a pistol shot from the woods, followed closely by another. Then silence. The old lady's head jerked around. She could hear the wind move through the tree tops like a long satisfied insuck of breath. "Bailey Boy!" she called.

"I was a gospel singer for a while," The Misfit said. "I been most everything. Been in the arm service, both land and sea, at home and abroad, been twict married, been an undertaker, been with the railroads, plowed Mother Earth, been in a tornado, seen a man burnt alive oncet," and he looked up at the children's mother and the little girl who were sitting close together, their faces white and their eyes glassy; "I even seen a woman flogged," he said.

"Pray, pray," the grandmother began, "pray, pray . . ."

"I never was a bad boy that I remember of," The Misfit said in an almost dreamy voice, "but somewheres along the line I done something wrong and got sent to the penitentiary. I was buried alive," and he looked up and held her attention to him by a steady stare.

"That's when you should have started to pray," she said. "What did you do to get sent to the penitentiary that first time?"

"Turn to the right, it was a wall," The Misfit said, looking up again at the cloudless sky. "Turn to the left, it was a wall. Look up it was a ceiling, look down it was a floor. I forget what I done, lady. I set there and set there, trying to remember what it was I done and I ain't recalled it to this day. Oncet in a while, I would think it was coming to me, but it never come."

"Maybe they put you in by mistake," the old lady said vaguely.

"Nome," he said. "It wasn't no mistake. They had the papers on me."

"You must have stolen something," she said.

The Misfit sneered slightly. "Nobody had nothing I wanted," he said. "It was a head-doctor at the penitentiary said what I had done was kill my daddy but I known that for a lie. My daddy died in nineteen ought nineteen of the epidemic flu and I never had a thing to do with it. He was buried in the Mount Hopewell Baptist churchyard and you can go there and see for yourself."

"If you would pray," the old lady said, "Jesus would help you."

"That's right," The Misfit said.

"Well then, why don't you pray?" she asked trembling with delight suddenly.

"I don't want no hep," he said. "I'm doing all right by myself."

Bobby Lee and Hiram came ambling back from the woods. Bobby Lee was dragging a yellow shirt with bright blue parrots in it.

"Thow me that shirt, Bobby Lee," The Misfit said. The shirt came flying at him and landed on his shoulder and he put it on. The grandmother couldn't name what the shirt reminded her of. "No, lady," The Misfit said while he was buttoning it up, "I found out the crime don't matter. You can do one thing or you can do another, kill a man or take a tire off his car, because sooner or later you're going to forget what it was you done and just be punished for it."

The children's mother had begun to make heaving noises as if she couldn't get her breath. "Lady," he asked, "would you and that little girl like to step off yonder with Bobby Lee and Hiram and join your husband?"

"Yes, thank you," the mother said faintly. Her left arm dangled helplessly and she was holding the baby, who had gone to sleep, in the other. "Hep that lady up, Hiram," The Misfit said as she struggled to climb out of the ditch, "and Bobby Lee, you hold onto that little girl's hand."

"I don't want to hold hands with him," June Star said. "He reminds me of a pig."

The fat boy blushed and laughed and caught her by the arm and pulled her off into the woods after Hiram and her mother.

Alone with The Misfit, the grandmother found that she had lost her voice. There was not a cloud in the sky nor any sun. There was nothing around her but woods. She wanted to tell him that he must pray. She opened and closed her mouth several times before anything came out. Finally she found herself saying, "Jesus. Jesus," meaning, Jesus will help you, but the way she was saying it, it sounded as if she might be cursing.

"Yes'm," The Misfit said as if he agreed. "Jesus thown everything off balance. It was the same case with Him as with me except He hadn't committed any crime and they could prove I had committed one because they had the papers on me. Of course," he said, "they never shown me my papers. That's why I sign myself now. I said long ago, you get you a signature and sign everything you do and keep a copy of it. Then you'll know what you done and you can hold up the crime to the punishment and see do they match and in the end you'll have something to prove you ain't been treated right. I call myself The Misfit," he said, "because I can't make what all I done wrong fit what all I gone through in punishment."

There was a piercing scream from the woods, followed closely by a pistol report. "Does it seem right to you, lady, that one is punished a heap and another ain't punished at all?"

"Jesus!" the old lady cried. "You've got good blood! I know you wouldn't shoot a lady! I know you come from nice people! Pray! Jesus, you ought not to shoot a lady. I'll give you all the money I've got!"

"Lady," The Misfit said, looking beyond her far into the woods, "there never was a body that give the undertaker a tip."

There were two more pistol reports and the grandmother raised her head like a parched old turkey hen crying for water and called, "Bailey Boy, Bailey Boy!" as if her heart would break.

"Jesus was the only One that ever raised the dead," The Misfit continued, "and He shouldn't have done it. He thrown everything off balance. If He did what He said, then it's nothing for you to do but throw away everything and follow Him, and if He didn't, then it's nothing for you to do but enjoy the few minutes you got left the best way you can—by killing somebody or burning down his house or doing some other meanness to him. No pleasure but meanness," he said and his voice had become almost a snarl.

"Maybe He didn't raise the dead," the old lady mumbled, not knowing what she was saying and feeling so dizzy that she sank down in the ditch with her legs twisted under her.

"I wasn't there so I can't say He didn't," The Misfit said. "I wisht I had of been there," he said, hitting the ground with his fist. "It ain't right I wasn't there because if I had of been there I would of known. Listen lady," he said in a high voice, "if I had of been there I would of known and I wouldn't be like I am now." His voice seemed about to crack and the grandmother's head cleared for an instant. She saw the man's face twisted close to her own as if he were going to cry and she murmured, "Why you're one of my babies. You're one of my own children!" She reached out and touched him on the shoulder. The Misfit sprang back as if a snake had bitten him and shot her three times through the chest. Then he put his gun down on the ground and took off his glasses and began to clean them.

Hiram and Bobby Lee returned from the woods and stood over the ditch, looking down at the grandmother who half sat and half lay in a puddle of blood with her legs crossed under her like a child's and her face smiling up at the cloudless sky.

Without his glasses, The Misfit's eyes were red-rimmed and pale and defenseless-looking. "Take her off and thow her where you thown the others," he said, picking up the cat that was rubbing itself against his leg.

"She was a talker, wasn't she?" Bobby Lee said, sliding down the ditch with a yodel.

"She would of been a good woman," The Misfit said, "if it had been somebody there to shoot her every minute of her life."

"Some fun!" Bobby Lee said.

"Shut up, Bobby Lee," The Misfit said. "It's no real pleasure in life."

Everything That Rises Must Converge

Her doctor had told Julian's mother that she must lose twenty pounds on account of her blood pressure, so on Wednesday nights Julian had to take her downtown on the bus for a reducing class at the Y. The reducing class was designed for working girls over fifty, who weighed from 165 to 200 pounds. His mother was one of the slimmer ones, but she said ladies did not tell their age or weight. She would not ride the buses by herself at night since they had been integrated, and because the reducing class was one of her few pleasures, necessary for her health, and *free,* she said Julian could at least put himself out to take her, considering all she did for him. Julian did not like to consider all she did for him, but every Wednesday night he braced himself and took her.

She was almost ready to go, standing before the hall mirror, putting on her hat, while he, his hands behind him, appeared pinned to the door frame, waiting like Saint Sebastian for the arrows to begin piercing him. The hat was new and had cost her seven dollars and a half. She kept saying, "Maybe I shouldn't have paid that for it. No, I shouldn't have. I'll take it off and return it tomorrow. I shouldn't have bought it."

Julian raised his eyes to heaven. "Yes, you should have bought it," he said. "Put it on and let's go." It was a hideous hat. A purple velvet flap came down on one side of it and stood up on the other; the rest of it was green and looked like a cushion with the stuffing out. He decided it was less comical than jaunty and pathetic. Everything that gave her pleasure was small and depressed him.

She lifted the hat one more time and set it down slowly on top of her head. Two wings of gray hair protruded on either side of her florid face, but her eyes, sky-blue, were as innocent and untouched by experience as they must have been when she was ten. Were it not that she was a widow who had struggled fiercely to feed and clothe and put him through school and who was supporting him still, "until he got on his feet," she might have been a little girl that he had to take to town.

"It's all right, it's all right," he said. "Let's go." He opened the door himself and started down the walk to get her going. The sky was a dying violet and the houses stood out darkly against it, bulbous liver-colored monstrosities of a uniform ugliness though no two were alike. Since this had been a fashionable neighborhood forty years ago, his mother persisted in thinking they did well to have an apartment in it. Each house had a narrow collar of dirt around it in which sat, usually, a grubby child. Julian walked with his hands in his pockets, his head down and thrust forward, and his eyes glazed with the determination to make himself completely numb during the time he would be sacrificed to her pleasure.

The door closed and he turned to find the dumpy figure, surmounted by the atrocious hat, coming toward him. "Well," she said, "you only live once and paying a little more for it, I at least won't meet myself coming and going."

"Some day I'll start making money," Julian said gloomily—he knew he never would—"and you can have one of those jokes whenever you take the fit." But first they would move. He visualized a place where the nearest neighbor would be three miles away on either side.

"I think you're doing fine," she said, drawing on her gloves. "You've only been out of school a year. Rome wasn't built in a day."

She was one of the few members of the Y reducing class who arrived in hat and gloves and who had a son who had been to college. "It takes time," she said, "and the world is in such a mess. This hat looked better on me than any of the others, though when she brought it out I said, 'Take that thing back. I wouldn't have it on my head,' and she said, 'Now wait till you see it on,' and when she put it on me, I said, 'We-ull,' and she said, 'If you ask me, that hat does something for you and you do something for the hat, and besides,' she said, 'with that hat, you won't meet yourself coming and going.'"

Julian thought he could have stood his lot better if she had been selfish, if she had been an old hag who drank and screamed at him. He walked along, saturated in depression, as if in the midst of his martyrdom he had lost his faith. Catching sight of his long, hopeless, irritated face, she stopped suddenly with a grief-stricken look, and pulled back on his arm. "Wait on me," she said. "I'm going back to the house and take this thing off and tomorrow I'm going to return it. I was out of my head. I can pay the gas bill with the seven-fifty."

He caught her arm in a vicious grip. "You are not going to take it back," he said. "I like it."

"Well," she said, "I don't think I ought . . ."

"Shut up and enjoy it," he muttered, more depressed than ever.

"With the world in the mess it's in," she said, "it's a wonder we can enjoy anything. I tell you, the bottom rail is on the top."

Julian sighed.

"Of course," she said, "if you know who you are, you can go anywhere." She said this every time he took her to the reducing class. "Most of them in it are not our kind of people," she said, "but I can be gracious to anybody. I know who I am."

"They don't give a damn for your graciousness," Julian said savagely. "Knowing who you are is good for one generation only. You haven't the foggiest idea where you stand now or who you are."

She stopped and allowed her eyes to flash at him. "I most certainly do know who I am," she said, "and if you don't know who you are, I'm ashamed of you."

"Oh hell," Julian said.

"Your great-grandfather was a former governor of this state," she said. "Your grandfather was a prosperous landowner. Your grandmother was a Godhigh."

"Will you look around you," he said tensely, "and see where you are now?" and he swept his arm jerkily out to indicate the neighborhood, which the growing darkness at least made less dingy.

"You remain what you are," she said. "Your great-grandfather had a plantation and two hundred slaves."

"There are no more slaves," he said irritably.

"They were better off when they were," she said. He groaned to see that she was off on that topic. She rolled onto it every few days like a train on an open track. He knew every stop, every junction, every swamp along the way, and knew the exact point at which her conclusion would roll majestically into the station: "It's ridiculous. It's simply not realistic. They should rise, yes, but on their own side of the fence."

"Let's skip it," Julian said.

"The ones I feel sorry for," she said, "are the ones that are half white. They're tragic."

"Will you skip it?"

"Suppose we were half white. We would certainly have mixed feelings."

"I have mixed feelings now," he groaned.

"Well let's talk about something pleasant," she said. "I remember going to Grandpa's when I was a little girl. Then the house had double stairways that went up to what was really the second floor—all the cooking was done on the first. I used to like to stay down in the kitchen on account of the way the walls smelled. I would sit with my nose pressed against the plaster and take deep breaths. Actually the place belonged to the Godhighs but your grandfather Chestny paid the mortgage and saved it for them. They were in reduced circumstances," she said, "but reduced or not, they never forgot who they were."

"Doubtless that decayed mansion reminded them," Julian muttered. He never spoke of it without contempt or thought of it without longing. He had seen it once when he was a child before it had been sold. The double stairways had rotted and had been torn down. Negroes were living in it. But it remained in his mind as his mother had known it. It appeared in his dreams regularly. He would stand on the wide porch, listening to the rustle of oak leaves, then wander through the high-ceilinged hall into the parlor that opened onto it and gaze at the worn rugs and faded draperies. It occurred to him that it was he, not she, who could have appreciated it. He preferred its threadbare elegance to anything he could name and it was because of it that all the neighborhoods they had lived in had been a torment to him—whereas she had hardly known the difference. She called her insensitivity "being adjustable."

"And I remember the old darky who was my nurse, Caroline. There was no better person in the world. I've always had a great respect for my colored friends," she said. "I'd do anything in the world for them and they'd . . ."

"Will you for God's sake get off that subject?" Julian said. When he got on a bus by himself, he made it a point to sit down beside a Negro, in reparation as it were for his mother's sins.

"You're mighty touchy tonight," she said. "Do you feel all right?"

"Yes I feel all right," he said. "Now lay off."

She pursed her lips. "Well, you certainly are in a vile humor," she observed. "I just won't speak to you at all."

They had reached the bus stop. There was no bus in sight and Julian, his hands still jammed in his pockets and his head thrust forward, scowled down the empty street. The frustration of having to wait on the bus as well as ride on it began to creep up his neck like a hot hand. The presence of his mother was borne in upon him as she gave a pained sigh. He looked at her bleakly. She was holding herself very erect under the preposterous hat, wearing it like a banner of her imaginary dignity. There was in him an evil urge to break her spirit. He suddenly unloosened his tie and pulled it off and put it in his pocket.

She stiffened. "Why must you look like *that* when you take me to town?" she said. "Why must you deliberately embarrass me?"

"If you'll never learn where you are," he said, "you can at least learn where I am."

"You look like a—thug," she said.

"Then I must be one," he murmured.

"I'll just go home," she said. "I will not bother you. If you can't do a little thing like that for me . . ."

Rolling his eyes upward, he put his tie back on. "Restored to my class," he muttered. He thrust his face toward her and hissed, "True culture is in the mind, the *mind,*" he said, and tapped his head, "the mind."

"It's in the heart," she said, "and in how you do things and how you do things is because of who you *are.*"

"Nobody in the damn bus cares who you are."

"I care who I am," she said icily.

The lighted bus appeared on top of the next hill and as it approached, they moved out into the street to meet it. He put his hand under her elbow and hoisted her up on the creaking step. She entered with a little smile, as if she were going into a drawing room where everyone had been waiting for her. While he put in the tokens, she sat down on one of the broad front seats for three which faced the aisle. A thin woman with protruding teeth and long yellow hair was sitting on the end of it. His mother moved up beside her and left room for Julian beside herself. He sat down and looked at the floor across the aisle where a pair of thin feet in red and white canvas sandals were planted.

His mother immediately began a general conversation meant to attract anyone who felt like talking. "Can it get any hotter?" she said and removed from her purse a folding fan, black with a Japanese scene on it, which she began to flutter before her.

"I reckon it might could," the woman with the protruding teeth said, "but I know for a fact my apartment couldn't get no hotter."

"It must get the afternoon sun," his mother said. She sat forward and looked up and down the bus. It was half filled. Everybody was white. "I see we have the bus to ourselves," she said. Julian cringed.

"For a change," said the woman across the aisle, the owner of the red and white canvas sandals. "I come on one the other day and they were thick as fleas—up front and all through."

"The world is in a mess everywhere," his mother said. "I don't know how we've let it get in this fix."

"What gets my goat is all those boys from good families stealing automobile tires," the woman with the protruding teeth said. "I told my boy, I said you may not be rich but you been raised right and if I ever catch you in any such mess, they can send you on to the reformatory. Be exactly where you belong."

"Training tells," his mother said. "Is your boy in high school?"

"Ninth grade," the woman said.

"My son just finished college last year. He wants to write but he's selling typewriters until he gets started," his mother said.

The woman leaned forward and peered at Julian. He threw her such a malevolent look that she subsided against the seat. On the floor across the aisle there was an abandoned newspaper. He got up and got it and opened it out in front of him. His mother discreetly continued the conversation in a Flower tone but the woman across the aisle said in a loud voice, "Well that's nice. Selling typewriters is close to writing. He can go right from one to the other."

"I tell him," his mother said, "that Rome wasn't built in a day."

Behind the newspaper Julian was withdrawing into the inner compartment of his mind where he spent most of his time. This was a kind of mental bubble in which he established himself when he could not bear to be part of what was going on around him. From it he could see out and judge but in it he was safe from any kind of penetration from without. It was the only place where he felt free of the general idiocy of his fellows. His mother had never entered it but from it he could see her with absolute clarity.

The old lady was clever enough and he thought that if she had started from any of the right premises, more might have been expected of her. She lived according to the laws of her own fantasy world, outside of which he had never seen her set foot. The law of it was to sacrifice herself for him after she had first created the necessity to do so by making a mess of things. If he had permitted her sacrifices, it was only because her lack of foresight had made them necessary. All of her life had been a struggle to act like a Chestny without the Chestny goods, and to give him everything she thought a Chestny ought to have; but since, said she, it was fun to struggle, why complain? And when you had won, as she had won, what fun to look back on the hard times! He could not forgive her that she had enjoyed the struggle and that she thought *she* had won.

What she meant when she said she had won was that she had brought him up successfully and had sent him to college and that he had turned out so well—good looking (her teeth had gone unfilled, so that his could be straightened), intelligent (he realized he was too intelligent to be a success), and with a future ahead of him (there was of course no future ahead of him). She excused his gloominess on the grounds that he was still growing up and his radical ideas on his lack of practical experience. She said he didn't yet know a thing about "life," that he hadn't even entered the real world—when already he was as disenchanted with it as a man of fifty.

The further irony of all this was that in spite of her, he had turned out so well. In spite of going to only a third-rate college, he had, on his own initiative, come out with a first-rate education; in spite of growing up dominated by a small mind, he had ended up with a large one; in spite of all her foolish views, he was free of prejudice and unafraid to face facts. Most miraculous of all, instead of being blinded by love for her as she was for him, he had cut himself emotionally free of her and could see her with complete objectivity. He was not dominated by his mother.

The bus stopped with a sudden jerk and shook him from his meditation. A woman from the back lurched forward with little steps and barely escaped falling in his newspaper as she righted herself. She got off and a large Negro got on. Julian kept his paper lowered to watch. It gave him a certain satisfaction to see injustice in daily operation. It confirmed his view that with a few exceptions there was no one worth knowing within a radius of three hundred miles. The Negro was well dressed and carried a briefcase. He looked round and then sat down on the other end of the seat where the woman with the red and white canvas sandals was sitting. He immediately unfolded a newspaper and obscured himself behind it. Julian's mother's elbow at once prodded insistently into his ribs. "Now you see why I won't ride on these buses by myself," she whispered.

The woman with the red and white canvas sandals had risen at the same time the Negro sat down and had gone further back in the bus and taken the seat of the woman who had got off. His mother leaned forward and cast her an approving look.

Julian rose, crossed the aisle, and sat down in the place of the woman with the canvas sandals. From this position, he looked serenely across at his mother. Her face had turned an angry red. He stared at her, making his eyes the eyes of a stranger. He felt his tension suddenly lift as if he had openly declared war on her.

He would have liked to get in conversation with the Negro and to talk with him about art or politics or any subject that would be above the comprehension of those around them, but the man remained entrenched behind his paper. He was either ignoring the change of seating or had never noticed it. There was no way for Julian to convey his sympathy.

His mother kept her eyes fixed reproachfully on his face. The woman with the protruding teeth was looking at him avidly as if he were a type of monster new to her.

"Do you have a light?" he asked the Negro.

Without looking away from his paper, the man reached in his pocket and handed him a packet of matches.

"Thanks," Julian said. For a moment he held the matches foolishly. A no smoking sign looked down upon him from over the door. This alone would not have deterred him; he had no cigarettes. He had quit smoking some months before because he could not afford it. "Sorry," he muttered and handed back the matches. The Negro lowered the paper and gave him an annoyed look. He took the matches and raised the paper again.

His mother continued to gaze at him but she did not take the advantage of his momentary discomfort. Her eyes retained their battered look. Her face seemed to be unnaturally red, as if her blood pressure had risen. Julian allowed no glimmer of sympathy to show on his face. Having got the advantage, he wanted desperately to keep it and carry it through. He would have liked to teach her a lesson that would last her a while, but there seemed no way to continue the point. The Negro refused to come out from behind his paper.

Julian folded his arms and looked stolidly before him, facing her but as if he did not see her, as if he had ceased to recognize her existence. He visualized a scene in which, the bus having reached their stop, he would remain in his seat and when she said, "Aren't you going to get off?" he would look at her as a stranger who had rashly addressed him. The corner they got off on was usually deserted, but it was well lighted and it would not hurt her to walk by herself the four blocks to the Y. He decided to wait until the time came and then decide whether or not he would let her get off by herself. He would have to be at the Y at ten to bring her back, but he could leave her wondering if he was going to show up. There was no reason for her to think she could always depend on him.

He retired again into the high-ceilinged room sparsely settled with large pieces of antique furniture. His soul expanded momentarily but then he became aware of his mother across from him and the vision shriveled. He studied her coldly. Her feet in little pumps dangled like a child's and did not quite reach the floor. She was training on him an exaggerated look of reproach. He felt completely detached from her. At that moment he could with pleasure have slapped her as he would have slapped a particularly obnoxious child in his charge.

He began to imagine various unlikely ways by which he could teach her a lesson. He might make friends with some distinguished Negro professor or lawyer and bring him home to spend the evening. He would be entirely justified but her blood pressure would rise to 300. He could not push her to the extent of making her have a stroke, and moreover, he had never been successful at making any Negro friends. He had tried to strike up an acquaintance on the bus with some of the better types, with ones that looked like professors or ministers or lawyers. One morning he had sat down next to a distinguished-looking dark brown man who had answered his questions with a sonorous solemnity but who had turned out to be an undertaker. Another day he had sat down beside a cigar-smoking Negro with a diamond ring on his finger, but after a few stilted pleasantries, the Negro had rung the buzzer and risen, slipping two lottery tickets into Julian's hand as he climbed over him to leave.

He imagined his mother lying desperately ill and his being able to secure only a Negro doctor for her. He toyed with that idea for a few minutes and then dropped it for a momentary vision of himself participating as a sympathizer in a sit-in demonstration. This was possible but he did not linger with it. Instead, he approached the ultimate horror. He brought home a beautiful suspiciously Negroid woman. Prepare yourself, he said. There is nothing you can do about it. This is the woman I've chosen. She's intelligent, dignified, even good, and she's suffered and she hasn't thought it *fun.* Now persecute us, go ahead and persecute us. Drive her out of here, but remember, you're driving me too. His eyes were narrowed and through the indignation he had generated, he saw his mother across the aisle, purple-faced, shrunken to the dwarf-like proportions of her moral nature, sitting like a mummy beneath the ridiculous banner of her hat.

He was tilted out of his fantasy again as the bus stopped. The door opened with a sucking hiss and out of the dark a large, gaily dressed, sullen-looking colored woman got on with a little boy. The child, who might have been four, had on a short plaid suit and a Tyrolean hat with a blue feather in it. Julian hoped that he would sit down beside him and that the woman would push in beside his mother. He could think of no better arrangement.

As she waited for her tokens, the woman was surveying the seating possibilities—he hoped with the idea of sitting where she was least wanted. There was something familiar-looking about her but Julian could not place what it was. She was a giant of a woman. Her face was set not only to meet opposition but to seek it out. The downward tilt of her large lower lip was like a warning sign: DON'T TAMPER WITH ME. Her bulging figure was encased in a green crepe dress and her feet overflowed in red shoes. She had on a hideous hat. A purple velvet flap came down on one side of it and stood up on the other; the rest of it was green and looked like a cushion with the stuffing out. She carried a mammoth red pocketbook that bulged throughout as if it were stuffed with rocks.

To Julian's disappointment, the little boy climbed up on the empty seat beside his mother. His mother lumped all children, black and white, into the common category, "cute," and she thought little Negroes were on the whole cuter than little white children. She smiled at the little boy as he climbed on the seat.

Meanwhile the woman was bearing down upon the empty seat beside Julian. To his annoyance, she squeezed herself into it. He saw his mother's face change as the woman settled herself next to him and he realized with satisfaction that this was more objectionable to her than it was to him. Her face seemed almost gray and there was a look of dull recognition in her eyes, as if suddenly she had sickened at some awful confrontation. Julian saw that it was because she and the woman had, in a sense, swapped sons. Though his mother would not realize the symbolic significance of this, she would feel it. His amusement showed plainly on his face.

The woman next to him muttered something unintelligible to herself. He was conscious of a kind of bristling next to him, muted growling like that of an angry cat. He could not see anything but the red pocketbook upright on the bulging green thighs. He visualized the woman as she had stood waiting for her tokens—the ponderous figure, rising from the red shoes upward over the solid hips, the mammoth bosom, the haughty face, to the green and purple hat.

His eyes widened.

The vision of the two hats, identical, broke upon him with the radiance of a brilliant sunrise. His face was suddenly lit with joy. He could not believe that Fate had thrust upon his mother such a lesson. He gave a loud chuckle so that she would look at him and see that he saw. She turned her eyes on him slowly. The blue in them seemed to have turned a bruised purple. For a moment he had an uncomfortable sense of her innocence, but it lasted only a second before principle rescued him. Justice entitled him to laugh. His grin hardened until it said to her as plainly as if he were saying aloud: Your punishment exactly fits your pettiness. This should teach you a permanent lesson.

Her eyes shifted to the woman. She seemed unable to bear looking at him and to find the woman preferable. He became conscious again of the bristling presence at his side. The woman was rumbling like a volcano about to become active. His mother's mouth began to twitch slightly at one corner. With a sinking heart, he saw incipient signs of recovery on her face and realized that this was going to strike her suddenly as funny and was going to be no lesson at all. She kept her eyes on the woman and an amused smile came over her face as if the woman were a monkey that had stolen her hat. The little Negro was looking up at her with large fascinated eyes. He had been trying to attract her attention for some time.

"Carver," the woman said suddenly. "Come heah!"

When he saw that the spotlight was on him at last, Carver drew his feet up and turned himself toward Julian's mother and giggled.

"Carver!" the woman said. "You heah me? Come heah!"

Carver slid down from the seat but remained squatting with his back against the base of it, his head turned slowly around toward Julian's mother, who was smiling at him. The woman reached a hand across the aisle and snatched him to her. He righted himself and hung backwards on her knees, grinning at Julian's mother. "Isn't he cute?" Julian's mother said to the woman with the protruding teeth.

"I reckon he is," the woman said without conviction.

The Negress yanked him upright but he eased out of her grip and shot across the aisle and scrambled, giggling wildly, onto the seat beside his love.

"I think he likes me," Julian's mother said, and smiled at the woman. It was the smile she used when she was being particularly gracious to an inferior. Julian saw everything lost. The lesson had rolled off her like rain on a roof.

The woman stood up and yanked the little boy off the seat as if she were snatching him from contagion. Julian could feel the rage in her at having no weapon like his mother's smile. She gave the child a sharp slap across his leg. He howled once and then thrust his head into her stomach and kicked his feet against her shins. "Behave," she said vehemently.

The bus stopped and the Negro who had been reading the newspaper got off. The woman moved over and set the little boy down with a thump between herself and Julian. She held him firmly by the knee. In a moment he put his hands in front of his face and peeped at Julian's mother through his fingers.

"I see yoooooooo!" she said and put her hand in front of her face and peeped at him.

The woman slapped his hand down. "Quit yo' foolishness," she said, "before I knock the living Jesus out of you!"

Julian was thankful that the next stop was theirs. He reached up and pulled the cord. The woman reached up and pulled it at the same time. Oh my God, he thought. He had the terrible intuition that when they got off the bus together, his mother would open her purse and give the little boy a nickel. The gesture would be as natural to her as breathing. The bus stopped and the woman got up and lunged to the front, dragging the child, who wished to stay on, after her. Julian and his mother got up and followed. As they neared the door, Julian tried to relieve her of her pocketbook.

"No," she murmured, "I want to give the little boy a nickel."

"No!" Julian hissed. "No!"

She smiled down at the child and opened her bag. The bus door opened and the woman picked him up by the arm and descended with him, hanging at her hip. Once in the street she set him down and shook him.

Julian's mother had to close her purse while she got down the bus step but as soon as her feet were on the ground, she opened it again and began to rummage inside. "I can't find but a penny," she whispered, "but it looks like a new one."

"Don't do it!" Julian said fiercely between his teeth. There was a streetlight on the corner and she hurried to get under it so that she could better see into her pocketbook. The woman was heading off rapidly down the street with the child still hanging backward on her hand.

"Oh little boy!" Julian's mother called and took a few quick steps and caught up with them just beyond the lamppost. "Here's a bright new penny for you," and she held out the coin, which shone bronze in the dim light.

The huge woman turned and for a moment stood, her shoulders lifted and her face frozen with frustrated rage, and stared at Julian's mother. Then all at once she seemed to explode like a piece of machinery that had been given one ounce of pressure too much. Julian saw the black fist swing out with the red pocketbook. He shut his eyes and cringed as he heard the woman shout, "He don't take nobody's pennies!" When he opened his eyes, the woman was disappearing down the street with the little boy staring wide-eyed over her shoulder. Julian's mother was sitting on the sidewalk.

"I told you not to do that," Julian said angrily. "I told you not to do that!"

He stood over her for a minute, gritting his teeth. Her legs were stretched out in front of her and her hat was on her lap. He squatted down and looked her in the face. It was totally expressionless. "You got exactly what you deserved," he said. "Now get up."

He picked up her pocketbook and put what had fallen out back in it. He picked the hat up off her lap. The penny caught his eye on the sidewalk and he picked that up and let it drop before her eyes into the purse. Then he stood up and leaned over and held his hands out to pull her up. She remained immobile. He sighed. Rising above them on either side were black apartment buildings, marked with irregular rectangles of light. At the end of the block a man came out of a door and walked off in the opposite direction. "All right," he said, "suppose somebody happens by and wants to know why you're sitting on the sidewalk?"

She took the hand and, breathing hard, pulled heavily up on it and then stood for a moment, swaying slightly as if the spots of light in the darkness were circling around her. Her eyes, shadowed and confused, finally settled on his face. He did not try to conceal his irritation. "I hope this teaches you a lesson," he said. She leaned forward and her eyes raked his face. She seemed trying to determine his identity. Then, as if she found nothing familiar about him, she started off with a headlong movement in the wrong direction.

"Aren't you going to the Y?" he asked.

"Home," she muttered.

"Well, are we walking?"

For answer she kept going. Julian followed along, his hands behind him. He saw no reason to let the lesson she had had go without backing it up with an explanation of its meaning. She might as well be made to understand what had happened to her. "Don't think that was just an uppity Negro woman," he said. "That was the whole colored race which will no longer take your condescending pennies. That was your black double. She can wear the same hat as you, and to be sure," he added gratuitously (because he thought it was funny), "it looked better on her than it did on you. What all this means," he said, "is that the old world is gone. The old manners are obsolete and your graciousness is not worth a damn." He thought bitterly of the house that had been lost for him. "You aren't who you think you are," he said.

She continued to plow ahead, paying no attention to him. Her hair had come undone on one side. She dropped her pocketbook and took no notice. He stopped and picked it up and handed it to her but she did not take it.

"You needn't act as if the world had come to an end," he said, "because it hasn't. From now on you've got to live in a new world and face a few realities for a change. Buck up," he said, "it won't kill you."

She was breathing fast.

"Let's wait on the bus," he said.

"Home," she said thickly.

"I hate to see you behave like this," he said. "Just like a child. I should be able to expect more of you." He decided to stop where he was and make her stop and wait for a bus. "I'm not going any farther," he said, stopping. "We're going on the bus."

She continued to go on as if she had not heard him. He took a few steps and caught her arm and stopped her. He looked into her face and caught his breath. He was looking into a face he had never seen before. "Tell Grandpa to come get me," she said.

He stared, stricken.

"Tell Caroline to come get me," she said.

Stunned, he let her go and she lurched forward again, walking as if one leg were shorter than the other. A tide of darkness seemed to be sweeping her from him.

"Mother!" he cried. "Darling, sweetheart, wait!" Crumpling, she fell to the pavement. He dashed forward and fell at her side, crying, "Mamma, Mamma!" He turned her over. Her face was fiercely distorted. One eye, large and staring, moved slightly to the left as if it had become unmoored. The other remained fixed on him, raked his face again, found nothing, and closed.

"Wait here, wait here!" he cried and jumped up and began to run for help toward a cluster of lights he saw in the distance ahead of him. "Help, help!" he shouted, but his voice was thin, scarcely a thread of sound. The lights drifted farther away the faster he ran and his feet moved numbly as if they carried him nowhere. The tide of darkness seemed to sweep him back to her, postponing from moment to moment his entry into the world of guilt and sorrow.

FLANNERY O'CONNOR

Good Country People

Besides the neutral expression that she wore when she was alone, Mrs. Freeman had two others, forward and reverse, that she used for all her human dealings. Her forward expression was steady and driving like the advance of a heavy truck. Her eyes never swerved to left or right but turned as the story turned as if they followed a yellow line down the center of it. She seldom used the other expression because it was not often necessary for her to retract a statement, but when she did, her face came to a complete stop, there was an almost imperceptible movement of her black eyes, during which they seemed to be receding, and then the observer would see that Mrs. Freeman, though she might stand there as real as several grain sacks thrown on top of each other, was no longer there in spirit. As for getting anything across to her when this was the case, Mrs. Hopewell had given it up. She might talk her head off. Mrs. Freeman could never be brought to admit herself wrong on any point. She would stand there and if she could be brought to say anything, it was something like, "Well, I wouldn't of said it was and I wouldn't of said it wasn't," or letting her gaze range over the top kitchen shelf where there was an assortment of dusty bottles, she might remark, "I see you ain't ate many of them figs you put up last summer."

They carried on their most important business in the kitchen at breakfast. Every morning Mrs. Hopewell got up at seven o'clock and lit her gas heater and Joy's. Joy was her daughter, a large blonde girl who had an artificial leg. Mrs. Hopewell thought of her as a child though she was thirty-two years old and highly educated. Joy would get up while her mother was eating and lumber into the bathroom and slam the door, and before long, Mrs. Freeman would arrive at the back door. Joy would hear her mother call, "Come on in," and then they would talk for a while in low voices that were indistinguishable in the bathroom. By the time Joy came in, they had usually finished the weather report and were on one or the other of Mrs. Freeman's daughters, Glynese or Carramae, Joy called them Glycerin and Caramel. Glynese, a redhead, was eighteen and had many admirers; Carramae, a blonde, was only fifteen but already married and pregnant. She could not keep anything on her stomach. Every morning Mrs. Freeman told Mrs. Hopewell how many times she had vomited since the last report.

Mrs. Hopewell liked to tell people that Glynese and Carramae were two of the finest girls she knew and that Mrs. Freeman was a *lady* and that she was never ashamed to take her anywhere or introduce her to anybody they might meet. Then she would tell how she had happened to hire the Freemans in the first place and how they were a godsend to her and how she had had them four years. The reason for her keeping them so long was that they were not trash. They were good country people. She had telephoned the man whose name they had given as a reference and he had told her that Mr. Freeman was a good farmer but that his wife was the nosiest woman ever to walk the earth. "She's got to be into everything," the man said. "If she don't get there before the dust settles, you can bet she's dead, that's all. She'll want to know all your business. I can stand him real good," he had said, "but me nor my wife neither could have stood that woman one more minute on this place." That had put Mrs. Hopewell off for a few days.

She had hired them in the end because there were no other applicants but she had made up her mind beforehand exactly how she would handle the woman. Since she was the type who had to be into everything, then, Mrs. Hopewell had decided, she would not only let her be into everything, she would *see to it* that she was into everything—she would give her the responsibility of everything, she would put her in charge. Mrs. Hopewell had no bad qualities of her own but she was able to use other people's in such a constructive way that she never felt the lack. She had hired the Freemans and she had kept them four years.

Nothing is perfect. This was one of Mrs. Hopewell's favorite sayings. Another was: that is life! And still another, the most important, was: well, other people have their opinions too. She would make these statements, usually at the table, in a tone of gentle insistence as if no one held them but her, and the large hulking Joy, whose constant outrage had obliterated every expression from her face, would stare just a little to the side of her, her eyes icy blue, with the look of someone who has achieved blindness by an act of will and means to keep it.

When Mrs. Hopewell said to Mrs. Freeman that life was like that, Mrs. Freeman would say, "I always said so myself." Nothing had been arrived at by anyone that had not first been arrived at by her. She was quicker than Mr. Freeman. When Mrs. Hopewell said to her after they had been on the place a while, "You know, you're the wheel behind the wheel," and winked, Mrs. Freeman had said, "I know it. I've always been quick. It's some that are quicker than others."

"Everybody is different," Mrs. Hopewell said.

"Yes, most people is," Mrs. Freeman said.

"It takes all kinds to make the world."

"I always said it did myself."

The girl was used to this kind of dialogue for breakfast and more of it for dinner; sometimes they had it for supper too. When they had no guest they ate in the kitchen because that was easier. Mrs. Freeman always managed to arrive at some point during the meal and to watch them finish it. She would stand in the doorway if it were summer but in the winter she would stand with one elbow on top of the refrigerator and look down on them, or she would stand by the gas heater, lifting the back of her skirt slightly. Occasionally she would stand against the wall and roll her head from side to side. At no time was she in any hurry to leave. All this was very trying on Mrs. Hopewell but she was a woman of great patience. She realized that nothing is perfect and that in the Freemans she had good country people and that if, in this day and age, you get good country people, you had better hang onto them.

She had had plenty of experience with trash. Before the Freemans she had averaged one tenant family a year. The wives of these farmers were not the kind you would want to be around you for very long. Mrs. Hopewell, who had divorced her husband long ago, needed someone to walk over the fields with her; and when Joy had to be impressed for these services, her remarks were usually so ugly and her face so glum that Mrs. Hopewell would say, "If you can't come pleasantly, I don't want you at all," to which the girl, standing square and rigid-shouldered with her neck thrust slightly forward, would reply, "If you want me, here I am—LIKE I AM."

Mrs. Hopewell excused this attitude because of the leg (which had been shot off in a hunting accident when Joy was ten). It was hard for Mrs. Hopewell to realize that her child was thirty-two now and that for more than twenty years she had had only one leg. She thought of her still as a child because it tore her heart to think instead of the poor stout girl in her thirties who had never danced a step or had any *normal* good times. Her name was really Joy but as soon as she was twenty-one and away from home, she had had it legally changed. Mrs. Hopewell was certain that she had thought and thought until she had hit upon the ugliest name in any language. Then she had gone and had the beautiful name, Joy, changed without telling her mother until after she had done it. Her legal name was Hulga.

When Mrs. Hopewell thought the name, Hulga, she thought of the broad blank hull of a battleship. She would not use it. She continued to call her Joy to which the girl responded but in a purely mechanical way.

Hulga had learned to tolerate Mrs. Freeman who saved her from taking walks with her mother. Even Glynese and Carramae were useful when they occupied attention that might otherwise have been directed at her. At first she had thought she could not stand Mrs. Freeman for she had found that it was not possible to be rude to her. Mrs. Freeman would take on strange resentments and for days together she would be sullen. But the source of her displeasure was always obscure; a direct attack, a positive leer, blatant ugliness to her face—these never touched her. And without warning one day, she began calling her Hulga.

She did not call her that in front of Mrs. Hopewell who would have been incensed but when she and the girl happened to be out of the house together, she would say something and add the name Hulga to the end of it, and the big spectacled Joy-Hulga would scowl and redden as if her privacy had been intruded upon. She considered the name her personal affair. She had arrived at it first purely on the basis of its ugly sound and then the full genius of its fitness had struck her. She had a vision of the name working like the ugly sweating Vulcan who stayed in the furnace and to whom, presumably, the goddess had to come when called. She saw it as the name of her highest creative act. One of her major triumphs was that her mother had not been able to turn her dust into Joy, but the greater one was that she had been able to turn it herself into Hulga. However, Mrs. Freeman's relish for using the name only irritated her. It was as if Mrs. Freeman's beady steel-pointed eyes had penetrated far enough behind her face to reach some secret fact. Something about her seemed to fascinate Mrs. Freeman and then one day Hulga realized that it was the artificial leg. Mrs. Freeman had a special fondness for the details of secret infections, hidden deformities, assaults upon children. Of diseases, she preferred the lingering or incurable. Hulga had heard Mrs. Hopewell give her the details of the hunting accident, how the leg had been literally blasted off, how she had never lost consciousness. Mrs. Freeman could listen to it any time as if it had happened an hour ago.

When Hulga stumped into the kitchen in the morning (she could walk without making the awful noise but she made it—Mrs. Hopewell was certain—because it was ugly-sounding), she glanced at them and did not speak. Mrs. Hopewell would be in her red kimono with her hair tied around her head in rags. She would be sitting at the table, finishing her breakfast and Mrs. Freeman would be hanging by her elbow outward from the refrigerator, looking down at the table. Hulga always put her eggs on the stove to boil and then stood over them with her arms folded, and Mrs. Hopewell would look at her—a kind of indirect gaze divided between her and Mrs. Freeman—and would think that if she would only keep herself up a little, she wouldn't be so bad looking. There was nothing wrong with her face that a pleasant expression wouldn't help. Mrs. Hopewell said that people who looked on the bright side of things would be beautiful even if they were not.

Whenever she looked at Joy this way, she could not help but feel that it would have been better if the child had not taken the Ph.D. It had certainly not brought her out any and now that she had it, there was no more excuse for her to go to school again. Mrs. Hopewell thought it was nice for girls to go to school to have a good time but Joy had "gone through." Anyhow, she would not have been strong enough to go again. The doctors had told Mrs. Hopewell that with the best of care, Joy might see forty-five. She had a weak heart. Joy had made it plain that if it had not been for this condition, she would be far from these red hills and good country people. She would be in a university lecturing to people who knew what she was talking about. And Mrs. Hopewell could very well picture her there, looking like a scarecrow and lecturing to more of the same. Here she went about all day in a six-year-old skirt and a yellow sweat shirt with a faded cowboy on a horse embossed on it. She thought this was funny; Mrs. Hopewell thought it was idiotic and showed simply that she was still a child. She was brilliant but she didn't have a grain of sense. It seemed to Mrs. Hopewell that every year she grew less like other people and more like herself—bloated, rude, and squint-eyed. And she said such strange things! To her own mother she had said—without warning, without excuse, standing up in the middle of a meal with her face purple and her mouth half full—"Woman! do you ever look inside? Do you ever look inside and see what you are *not?* God!" she had cried sinking down again and staring at her plate, "Malebranche was right: we are not our own light. We are not our own light!" Mrs. Hopewell had no idea to this day what brought that on. She had only made the remark, hoping Joy would take it in, that a smile never hurt anyone.

The girl had taken the Ph.D. in philosophy and this left Mrs. Hopewell at a complete loss. You could say, "My daughter is a nurse," or "My daughter is a schoolteacher," or even, "My daughter is a chemical engineer." You could not say, "My daughter is a philosopher." That was something that had ended with the Greeks and Romans. All day Joy sat on her neck in a deep chair, reading. Sometimes she went for walks but she didn't like dogs or cats or birds or flowers or nature or nice young men. She looked at nice young men as if she could smell their stupidity.

One day Mrs. Hopewell had picked up one of the books the girl had just put down and opening it at random, she read, "Science, on the other hand, has to assert its soberness and seriousness afresh and declare that it is concerned solely with what-is. Nothing—how can it be for science anything but a horror and a phantasm? If science is right, then one thing stands firm: science wishes to know nothing of nothing. Such is after all the strictly scientific approach to Nothing. We know it by wishing to know nothing of Nothing." These words had been underlined with a blue pencil and they worked on Mrs. Hopewell like some evil incantation in gibberish. She shut the book quickly and went out of the room as if she were having a chill.

This morning when the girl came in, Mrs. Freeman was on Carramae. "She thrown up four times after supper," she said, "and was up twict in the night after three o'clock. Yesterday she didn't do nothing but ramble in the bureau drawer. All she did. Stand up there and see what she could run up on."

"She's got to eat," Mrs. Hopewell muttered, sipping her coffee, while she watched Joy's back at the stove. She was wondering what the child had said to the Bible salesman. She could not imagine what kind of a conversation she could possibly have had with him.

He was a tall gaunt hatless youth who had called yesterday to sell them a Bible. He had appeared at the door, carrying a large black suitcase that weighted him so heavily on one side that he had to brace himself against the door facing. He seemed on the point of collapse but he said in a cheerful voice, "Good morning, Mrs. Cedars!" and set the suitcase down on the mat. He was not a bad-looking young man though he had on a bright blue suit and yellow socks that were not pulled up far enough. He had prominent face bones and a streak of sticky-looking brown hair falling across his forehead.

"I'm Mrs. Hopewell," she said.

"Oh!" he said, pretending to look puzzled but with his eyes sparkling, "I saw it said 'The Cedars' on the mailbox so I thought you was Mrs. Cedars!" and he burst out in a pleasant laugh. He picked up the satchel and under cover of a pant, he fell forward into her hall. It was rather as if the suitcase had moved first, jerking him after it. "Mrs. Hopewell!" he said and grabbed her hand. "I hope you are well!" and he laughed again and then all at once his face sobered completely. He paused and gave her a straight earnest look and said, "Lady, I've come to speak of serious things."

"Well, come in," she muttered, none too pleased because her dinner was almost ready. He came into the parlor and sat down on the edge of a straight chair and put the suitcase between his feet and glanced around the room as if he were sizing her up by it. Her silver gleamed on the two sideboards; she decided he had never been in a room as elegant as this.

"Mrs. Hopewell," he began, using her name in a way that sounded almost intimate, "I know you believe in Chrustian service."

"Well yes," she murmured.

"I know," he said and paused, looking very wise with his head cocked on one side, "that you're a good woman. Friends have told me."

Mrs. Hopewell never liked to be taken for a fool. "What are you selling?" she asked.

"Bibles," the young man said and his eye raced around the room before he added, "I see you have no family Bible in your parlor, I see that is the one lack you got!"

Mrs. Hopewell could not say, "My daughter is an atheist and won't let me keep the Bible in the parlor." She said, stiffening slightly, "I keep my Bible by my bedside." This was not the truth. It was in the attic somewhere.

"Lady," he said, "the word of God ought to be in the parlor."

"Well, I think that's a matter of taste," she began. "I think . . ."

"Lady," he said, "for a Chrustian, the word of God ought to be in every room in the house besides in his heart. I know you're a Chrustian because I can see it in every line of your face."

She stood up and said, "Well, young man, I don't want to buy a Bible and I smell my dinner burning."

He didn't get up. He began to twist his hands and looking down at them, he said softly, "Well lady, I'll tell you the truth—not many people want to buy one nowadays and besides, I know I'm real simple. I don't know how to say a thing but to say it. I'm just a country boy." He glanced up into her unfriendly face. "People like you don't like to fool with country people like me!"

"Why!" she cried, "good country people are the salt of the earth! Besides, we all have different ways of doing, it takes all kinds to make the world go 'round. That's life!"

"You said a mouthful," he said.

"Why, I think there aren't enough good country people in the world!" she said, stirred. "I think that's what's wrong with it!"

His face had brightened. "I didn't inraduce myself," he said. "I'm Manley Pointer from out in the country around Willohobie, not even from a place, just from near a place."

"You wait a minute," she said. "I have to see about my dinner." She went out to the kitchen and found Joy standing near the door where she had been listening.

"Get rid of the salt of the earth," she said, "and let's eat."

Mrs. Hopewell gave her a pained look and turned the heat down under the vegetables. "*I* can't be rude to anybody," she murmured and went back into the parlor.

He had opened the suitcase and was sitting with a Bible on each knee.

"You might as well put those up," she told him. "I don't want one."

"I appreciate your honesty," he said. "You don't see any more real honest people unless you go way out in the country."

"I know," she said, "real genuine folks!" Through the crack in the door she heard a groan.

"I guess a lot of boys come telling you they're working their way through college," he said, "but I'm not going to tell you that. Somehow," he said, "I don't want to go to college. I want to devote my live to Chrustian service. See," he said, lowering his voice, "I got this heart condition. I may not live long. When you know it's something wrong with you and you may not live long, well then, lady . . ." He paused, with his mouth open, and stared at her.

He and Joy had the same condition! She knew that her eyes were filling with tears but she collected herself quickly and murmured, "Won't you stay for dinner? We'd love to have you!" and was sorry the instant she heard herself say it.

"Yes mam," he said in an abashed voice, "I would sher love to do that!"

Joy had given him one look on being introduced to him and then throughout the meal had not glanced at him again. He had addressed several remarks to her, which she had pretended not to hear. Mrs. Hopewell could not understand deliberate rudeness, although she lived with it, and she felt she had always to overflow with hospitality to make up for Joy's lack of courtesy. She urged him to talk about himself and he did. He said he was the seventh child of twelve and that his father had been crushed under a tree when he himself was eight year old. He had been crushed very badly, in fact, almost cut in two and was practically not recognizable. His mother had got along the best she could by hard working and she had always seen that her children went to Sunday School and that they read the Bible every evening. He was now nineteen year old and he had been selling Bibles for four months. In that time he had sold seventy-seven Bibles and had the promise of two more sales. He wanted to become a missionary because he thought that was the way you could do most for people. "He who losest his life shall find it," he said simply and he was so sincere, so genuine and earnest that Mrs. Hopewell would not for the world have smiled. He prevented his peas from sliding onto the table by blocking them with a piece of bread which he later cleaned his plate with. She could see Joy observing sidewise how he handled his knife and fork and she saw too that every few minutes, the boy would dart a keen appraising glance at the girl as if he were trying to attract her attention.

After dinner Joy cleared the dishes off the table and disappeared and Mrs. Hopewell was left to talk with him. He told her again about his childhood and his father's accident and about various things that had happened to him. Every five minutes or so she would stifle a yawn. He sat for two hours until finally she told him she must go because she had an appointment in town. He packed his Bibles and thanked her and prepared to leave, but in the doorway he stopped and wrung her hand and said that not on any of his trips had he met a lady as nice as her and he asked if he could come again. She had said she would always be happy to see him.

Joy had been standing in the road, apparently looking at something in the distance, when he came down the steps toward her, bent to the side with his heavy valise. He stopped where she was standing and confronted her directly. Mrs. Hopewell could not hear what he said but she trembled to think what Joy would say to him. She could see that after a minute Joy said something and that then the boy began to speak, again, making an excited gesture with his free hand. After a minute Joy said something else at which the boy began to speak once more. Then to her amazement, Mrs. Hopewell saw the two of them walk off together, toward the gate. Joy had walked all the way to the gate with him and Mrs. Hopewell could not imagine what they had said to each other, and she had not yet dared to ask.

Mrs. Freeman was insisting upon her attention. She had moved from the refrigerator to the heater so that Mrs. Hopewell had to turn and face her in order to seem to be listening. "Glynese gone out with Harvey Hill again last night," she said. "She had this sty."

"Hill," Mrs. Hopewell said absently, "is that the one who works in the garage?"

"Nome, he's the one that goes to chiropracter school," Mrs. Freeman said. "She had this sty. Been had it two days. So she says when he brought her in the other night he says, 'Lemme get rid of that sty for you,' and she says, 'How?' and he says, 'You just lay yourself down acrost the seat of that car and I'll show you.' So she done it and he popped her neck. Kept on a-popping it several times until she made him quit. This morning," Mrs. Freeman said, "she ain't got no sty. She ain't got no traces of a sty."

"I never heard of that before," Mrs. Hopewell said.

"He ast her to marry him before the Ordinary," Mrs. Freeman went on, "and she told him she wasn't going to be married in no *office.*"

"Well, Glynese is a fine girl," Mrs. Hopewell said. "Glynese and Carramae are both fine girls."

"Carramae said when her and Lyman was married Lyman said it sure felt sacred to him. She said he said he wouldn't take five hundred dollars for being married by a preacher."

"How much would he take?" the girl asked from the stove.

"He said he wouldn't take five hundred dollars," Mrs. Freeman repeated.

"Well we all have work to do," Mrs. Hopewell said.

"Lyman said it just felt more sacred to him," Mrs. Freeman said. "The doctor wants Carramae to eat prunes. Says instead of medicine. Says them cramps is coming from pressure. You know where I think it is?"

"She'll be better in a few weeks," Mrs. Hopewell said.

"In the tube," Mrs. Freeman said. "Else she wouldn't be as sick as she is."

Hulga had cracked her two eggs into a saucer and was bringing them to the table along with a cup of coffee that she had filled too full. She sat down carefully and began to eat, meaning to keep Mrs. Freeman there by questions if for any reason she showed an inclination to leave. She could perceive her mother's eye on her. The first round-about question would be about the Bible salesman and she did not wish to bring it on. "How did he pop her neck?" she asked.

Mrs. Freeman went into a description of how he had popped her neck. She said he owned a '55 Mercury but that Glynese said she would rather marry a man with only a '36 Plymouth who would be married by a preacher. The girl asked what if he had a '32 Plymouth and Mrs. Freeman said what Glynese had said was a '36 Plymouth.

Mrs. Hopewell said there were not many girls with Glynese's common sense. She said what she admired in those girls was their common sense. She said that reminded her that they had had a nice visitor yesterday, a young man selling Bibles. "Lord," she said, "he bored me to death but he was so sincere and genuine I couldn't be rude to him. He was just good country people, you know," she said, "—just the salt of the earth."

"I seen him walk up," Mrs. Freeman said, "and then later—I seen him walk off," and Hulga could feel the slight shift in her voice, the slight insinuation, that he had not walked off alone, had he? Her face remained expressionless but the color rose into her neck and she seemed to swallow it down with the next spoonful of egg. Mrs. Freeman was looking at her as if they had a secret together.

"Well, it takes all kinds of people to make the world go 'round," Mrs. Hopewell said. "It's very good we aren't all alike."

"Some people are more alike than others," Mrs. Freeman said.

Hulga got up and stumped, with about twice the noise that was necessary, into her room and locked the door. She was to meet the Bible salesman at ten o'clock at the gate. She had thought about it half the night. She had started thinking of it as a great joke and then she had begun to see profound implications in it. She had lain in bed imagining dialogues for them that were insane on the surface but that reached below to depths that no Bible salesman would be aware of. Their conversation yesterday had been of this kind.

He had stopped in front of her and had simply stood there. His face was bony and sweaty and bright, with a little pointed nose in the center of it, and his look was different from what it had been at the dinner table. He was gazing at her with open curiosity, with fascination, like a child watching a new fantastic animal at the zoo, and he was breathing as if he had run a great distance to reach her. His gaze seemed somehow familiar but she could not think where she had been regarded with it before. For almost a minute he didn't say anything. Then on what seemed an insuck of breath, he whispered, "You ever ate a chicken that was two days old?"

The girl looked at him stonily. He might have just put this question up for consideration at the meeting of a philosophical association. "Yes," she presently replied as if she had considered it from all angles.

"It must have been mighty small!" he said triumphantly and shook all over with little nervous giggles, getting very red in the face, and subsiding finally into his gaze of complete admiration, while the girl's expression remained exactly the same.

"How old are you?" he asked softly.

She waited sometime before she answered. Then in a flat voice she said, "Seventeen."

His smiles came in succession like waves breaking on the surface of a little lake. "I see you got a wooden leg," he said. "I think you're brave. I think you're real sweet."

The girl stood blank and solid and silent.

"Walk to the gate with me," he said. "You're a brave sweet little thing and I liked you the minute I seen you walk in the door."

Hulga began to move forward.

"What's your name?" he asked, smiling down on the top of her head.

"Hulga," she said.

"Hulga," he murmured, "Hulga. Hulga. I never heard of anybody name Hulga before. You're shy, aren't you, Hulga?" he asked.

She nodded, watching his large red hand on the handle of the giant valise.

"I like girls that wear glasses," he said. "I think a lot. I'm not like these people that a serious thought don't ever enter their heads. It's because I may die."

"I may die too," she said suddenly and looked up at him. His eyes were very small and brown, glittering feverishly.

"Listen," he said, "don't you think some people was meant to meet on account of what all they got in common and all? Like they both think serious thoughts and all?" He shifted the valise to his other hand so that the hand nearest her was free. He caught hold of her elbow and shook it a little. "I don't work on Saturday," he said. "I like to walk in the woods and see what Mother Nature is wearing. O'er the hills and far away. Pic-nics and things. Couldn't we go on a pic-nic tomorrow? Say yes, Hulga," he said and gave her a dying look as if he felt his insides about to drop out of him. He had even seemed to sway slightly toward her.

During the night she had imagined that she seduced him. She imagined that the two of them walked on the place until they came to the storage barn beyond the two back fields and there, she imagined, that things came to such a pass that she very easily seduced him and that then, of course, she had to reckon with his remorse. True genius can get an idea across even to an inferior mind. She imagined that she took his remorse in hand and changed it into a deeper understanding of life. She took all his shame away and turned it into something useful.

She set off for the gate at exactly ten o'clock, escaping without drawing Mrs. Hopewell's attention. She didn't take anything to eat, forgetting that food is usually taken on a pic-nic. She wore a pair of slacks and a dirty white shirt, and as an afterthought, she had put some Vapex on the collar of it since she did not own any perfume. When she reached the gate no one was there.

She looked up and down the empty highway and had the furious feeling that she had been tricked, that he had only meant to make her walk to the gate after the idea of him. Then suddenly he stood up, very tall, from behind a bush on the opposite embankment. Smiling, he lifted his hat which was new and wide-brimmed. He had not worn it yesterday and she wondered if he had bought it for the occasion. It was toast-colored with a red and white band around it and was slightly too large for him. He stepped from behind the bush still carrying the black valise. He had on the same suit and the same yellow socks sucked down in his shoes from walking. He crossed the highway and said, "I knew you'd come!"

The girl wondered acidly how he had known this. She pointed to the valise and asked, "Why did you bring your Bibles?"

He took her elbow, smiling down on her as if he could not stop. "You can never tell when you'll need the word of God, Hulga," he said. She had a moment in which she doubted that this was actually happening and then they began to climb the embankment. They went down into the pasture toward the woods. The boy walked lightly by her side, bouncing on his toes. The valise did not seem to be heavy today; he even swung it. They crossed half the pasture without saying anything and then, putting his hand easily on the small of her back, he asked softly, "Where does your wooden leg join on?"

She turned an ugly red and glared at him and for an instant the boy looked abashed. "I didn't mean you no harm," he said. "I only meant you're so brave and all. I guess God takes care of you."

"No," she said, looking forward and walking fast, "I don't even believe in God."

At this he stopped and whistled. "No!" he exclaimed as if he were too astonished to say anything else.

She walked on and in a second he was bouncing at her side, fanning with his hat. "That's very unusual for a girl," he remarked, watching her out of the corner of his eye. When they reached the edge of the wood, he put his hand on her back again and drew her against him without a word and kissed her heavily.

The kiss, which had more pressure than feeling behind it, produced that extra surge of adrenaline in the girl that enables one to carry a packed trunk out of a burning house, but in her, the power went at once to the brain. Even before he released her, her mind, clear and detached and ironic anyway, was regarding him from a great distance, with amusement but with pity. She had never been kissed before and she was pleased to discover that it was an unexceptional experience and all a matter of the mind's control. Some people might enjoy drain water if they were told it was vodka. When the boy, looking expectant but uncertain, pushed her gently away, she turned and walked on, saying nothing as if such business, for her, were common enough.

He came along panting at her side, trying to help her when he saw a root that she might trip over. He caught and held back the long swaying blades of thorn vine until she had passed beyond them. She led the way and he came breathing heavily behind her. Then they came out on a sunlit hillside, sloping softly into another one a little smaller. Beyond, they could see the rusted top of the old barn where the extra hay was stored.

The hill was sprinkled with small pink weeds. "Then you ain't saved?" he asked suddenly, stopping.

The girl smiled. It was the first time she had smiled at him at all. "In my economy," she said, "I'm saved and you are damned but I told you I didn't believe in God."

Nothing seemed to destroy the boy's look of admiration. He gazed at her now as if the fantastic animal at the zoo had put its paw through the bars and given him a loving poke. She thought he looked as if he wanted to kiss her again and she walked on before he had the chance.

"Ain't there somewheres we can sit down sometime?" he murmured, his voice softening toward the end of the sentence.

"In that barn," she said.

They made for it rapidly as if it might slide away like a train. It was a large two-story barn, cool and dark inside. The boy pointed up the ladder that led into the loft and said, "It's too bad we can't go up there."

"Why can't we?" she asked.

"Yer leg," he said reverently.

The girl gave him a contemptuous look and putting both hands on the ladder, she climbed it while he stood below, apparently awestruck. She pulled herself expertly through the opening and then looked down at him and said, "Well, come on if you're coming," and he began to climb the ladder, awkwardly bringing the suitcase with him.

"We won't need the Bible," she observed.

"You never can tell," he said, panting. After he had got into the loft, he was a few seconds catching his breath. She had sat down in a pile of straw. A wide sheath of sunlight, filled with dust particles, slanted over her. She lay back against a bale, her face turned away, looking out the front opening of the barn where hay was thrown from a wagon into the loft. The two pink-speckled hillsides lay back against a dark ridge of woods. The sky was cloudless and cold blue. The boy dropped down by her side and put one arm under her and the other over her and began methodically kissing her face, making little noises like a fish. He did not remove his hat but it was pushed far enough back not to interfere. When her glasses got in his way, he took them off of her and slipped them into his pocket.

The girl at first did not return any of the kisses but presently she began to and after she had put several on his cheek, she reached his lips and remained there, kissing him again and again as if she were trying to draw all the breath out of him. His breath was clear and sweet like a child's and the kisses were sticky like a child's. He mumbled about loving her and about knowing when he first seen her that he loved her, but the mumbling was like the sleepy fretting of a child being put to sleep by his mother. Her mind, throughout this, never stopped or lost itself for a second to her feelings. "You ain't said you loved me none," he whispered finally, pulling back from her. "You got to say that."

She looked away from him off into the hollow sky and then down at a black ridge and then down farther into what appeared to be two green swelling lakes. She didn't realize he had taken her glasses but this landscape could not seem exceptional to her for she seldom paid any close attention to her surroundings.

"You got to say it," he repeated. "You got to say you love me."

She was always careful how she committed herself. "In a sense," she began, "if you use the word loosely, you might say that. But it's not a word I use. I don't have illusions. I'm one of those people who see *through* to nothing."

The boy was frowning. "You got to say it. I said it and you got to say it," he said.

The girl looked at him almost tenderly. "You poor baby," she murmured. "It's just as well you don't understand," and she pulled him by the neck, facedown, against her. "We are all damned," she said, "but some of us have taken off our blindfolds and see that there's nothing to see. It's a kind of salvation."

The boy's astonished eyes looked blankly through the ends of her hair. "Okay," he almost whined, "but do you love me or don'tcher?"

"Yes," she said and added, "in a sense. But I must tell you something. There mustn't be anything dishonest between us." She lifted his head and looked him in the eye. "I am thirty years old," she said. "I have a number of degrees."

The boy's look was irritated but dogged. "I don't care," he said. "I don't care a thing about what all you done. I just want to know if you love me or don'tcher?" and he caught her to him and wildly planted her face with kisses until she said, "Yes, yes."

"Okay then," he said, letting her go. "Prove it."

She smiled, looking dreamily out on the shifty landscape. She had seduced him without even making up her mind to try. "How?" she asked, feeling that he should be delayed a little.

He leaned over and put his lips to her ear. "Show me where your wooden leg joins on," he whispered.

The girl uttered a sharp little cry and her face instantly drained of color. The obscenity of the suggestion was not what shocked her. As a child she had sometimes been subject to feelings of shame but education had removed the last traces of that as a good surgeon scrapes for cancer; she would no more have felt it over what he was asking than she would have believed in his Bible. But she was as sensitive about the artificial leg as a peacock about his tail. No one ever touched it but her. She took care of it as someone else would his soul, in private and almost with her own eyes turned away. "No," she said.

"I known it," he muttered, sitting up. "You're just playing me for a sucker."

"Oh no no!" she cried. "It joins on at the knee. Only at the knee. Why do you want to see it?"

The boy gave her a long penetrating look. "Because," he said, "it's what makes you different. You ain't like anybody else."

She sat staring at him. There was nothing about her face or her round freezing-blue eyes to indicate that this had moved her; but she felt as if her heart had stopped and left her mind to pump her blood. She decided that for the first time in her life she was face to face with real innocence. This boy, with an instinct that came from beyond wisdom, had touched the truth about her. When after a minute, she said in a hoarse high voice, "All right," it was like surrendering to him completely. It was like losing her own life and finding it again, miraculously, in his.

Very gently he began to roll the slack leg up. The artificial limb, in a white sock and brown flat shoe, was bound in a heavy material like canvas and ended in an ugly jointure where it was attached to the stump. The boy's face and his voice were entirely reverent as he uncovered it and said, "Now show me how to take it off and on."

She took it off for him and put it back on again and then he took it off himself, handling it as tenderly as if it were a real one. "See!" he said with a delighted child's face. "Now I can do it myself!"

"Put it back on," she said. She was thinking that she would run away with him and that every night he would take the leg off and every morning put it back on again. "Put it back on," she said.

"Not yet," he murmured, setting it on its foot out of her reach. "Leave it off for a while. You got me instead."

She gave a little cry of alarm but he pushed her down and began to kiss her again. Without the leg she felt entirely dependent on him. Her brain seemed to have stopped thinking altogether and to be about some other function that it was not very good at. Different expressions raced back and forth over her face. Every now and then the boy, his eyes like two steel spikes, would glance behind him where the leg stood. Finally she pushed him off and said, "Put it back on me now."

"Wait," he said. He leaned the other way and pulled the valise toward him and opened it. It had a pale blue spotted lining and there were only two Bibles in it. He took one of these out and opened the cover of it. It was hollow and contained a pocket flask of whiskey, a pack of cards, and a small blue box with printing on it. He laid these out in front of her one at a time in an evenly-spaced row, like one presenting offerings at the shrine of a goddess. He put the blue box in her hand. THIS PRODUCT TO BE USED ONLY FOR THE PREVENTION OF DISEASE, she read, and dropped it. The boy was unscrewing the top of the flask. He stopped and pointed, with a smile, to the deck of cards. It was not an ordinary deck but one with an obscene picture on the back of each card. "Take a swig," he said, offering her the bottle first. He held it in front of her, but like one mesmerized, she did not move.

Her voice when she spoke had an almost pleading sound. "Aren't you," she murmured, "aren't you just good country people?"

The boy cocked his head. He looked as if he were just beginning to understand that she might be trying to insult him. "Yeah," he said, curling his lip slightly, "but it ain't held me back none. I'm as good as you any day in the week."

"Give me my leg," she said.

He pushed it farther away with his foot. "Come on now, let's begin to have us a good time," he said coaxingly. "We ain't got to know one another good yet."

"Give me my leg!" she screamed and tried to lunge for it but he pushed her down easily.

"What's the matter with you all of a sudden?" he asked, frowning as he screwed the top of the flask and put it quickly back inside the Bible. "You just a while ago said you didn't believe in nothing. I thought you was some girl!"

Her face was almost purple. "You're a Christian!" she hissed. "You're a fine Christian! You're just like them all—say one thing and do another. You're a perfect Christian, you're . . ."

The boy's mouth was set angrily. "I hope you don't think," he said in a lofty indignant tone, "that I believe in that crap! I may sell Bibles but I know which end is up and I wasn't born yesterday and I know where I'm going!"

"Give me my leg!" she screeched. He jumped up so quickly that she barely saw him sweep the cards and the blue box into the Bible and throw the Bible into the valise. She saw him grab the leg and then she saw it for an instant slanted forlornly across the inside of the suitcase with a Bible at either side of its opposite ends. He slammed the lid shut and snatched up the valise and swung it down the hole and then stepped through himself.

When all of him had passed but his head, he turned and regarded her with a look that no longer had any admiration in it. "I've gotten a lot of interesting things," he said. "One time I got a woman's glass eye this way. And you needn't to think you'll catch me because Pointer ain't really my name. I use a different name at every house I call at and don't stay nowhere long. And I'll tell you another thing, Hulga," he said, using the name as if he didn't think much of it, "you ain't so smart. I been believing in nothing ever since I was born!" and then the toast-colored hat disappeared down the hole and the girl was left, sitting on the straw in the dusty sunlight. When she turned her churning face toward the opening, she saw his blue figure struggling successfully over the green speckled lake.

Mrs. Hopewell and Mrs. Freeman, who were in the back pasture, digging up onions, saw him emerge a little later from the woods and head across the meadow toward the highway. "Why, that looks like that nice dull young man that tried to sell me a Bible yesterday," Mrs. Hopewell said, squinting. "He must have been selling them to the Negroes back in there. He was so simple," she said, "but I guess the world would be better off if we were all that simple."

Mrs. Freeman's gaze drove forward and just touched him before he disappeared under the hill. Then she returned her attention to the evil-smelling onion shoot she was lifting from the ground. "Some can't be that simple," she said. "I know I never could."

Grace Paley (1922–)

was born to Russian immigrant parents in 1922 in the Bronx, New York. She grew up in a neighborhood "so dense with Jews I thought we were the great imposing majority." Countless stories told by her father and aunts colored her childhood and provided material for her later writing. She grew up hearing Russian, Yiddish, and English—all contributing to her distinct writing voice. Paley briefly attended Hunter College, married at the age of nineteen, and had two children. She soon separated from her husband. Writing only poetry into her thirties, Paley published her first book of stories, The Little Disturbances of Man, *in 1959. It was followed by two more highly regarded collections,* Enormous Changes at the Last Minute *and* Later the Same Day. *All three books are combined in the career-spanning* The Collected Stories. *Long an antiwar activist and feminist, Paley was one of the founders of the Greenwich Village Peace Center in 1961; she considers herself a "somewhat combative pacifist and cooperative anarchist." Paley has received awards and grants from the Guggenheim Foundation, the National Endowment for the Arts, and the National Institute of Arts and Letters. She has taught at Columbia and Syracuse Universities and currently teaches at both Sarah Lawrence College and the City College of New York, where she is writer-in-residence.*

Introduction by **Amy Bloom**

Now prose
Find the paragraph to hold the poem steady
for six or eight pages . . .

Don't let her lose the poem
in the telling of the day by day
because the subject
is time   the place is only
paper the story is still
a puzzle   the teller
knows why

—from the poem "How to Tell a Story (My Method) (Most of the Time)"

The crowded apartments and playgrounds and broken glass of New York City claim her as their own authentic, affectionate, witty, and guileless writer laureate, in poetry and prose—and so does the verdant splendor of Vermont. She is the chronicler of women on their own and men out the door and of the joy and painful necessities of erotic love. No one loves an old man in an autumnal garden, a newborn baby with an unsure and adulterous mother, or politically active middle-aged women, "the soft-speaking tough souls of anarchy," more, embraces them more fully, or paints them more clearly. Grace Paley sings a song of the practical and the ideal, of the kitchen and the bedroom, of hope and stubbornness in such a tuneful, rueful, penetrating, and offhand manner that even the most tone-deaf reader can catch the melody.

There is poetry and character, melody and dialogue in Grace Paley's work; there's not much plot. For the chase of the big whale, the transformation from man to bug, or the dazzling wordplay of the self-consciously clever, the reader must go elsewhere.

As the poet Robert Pinsky once wrote of Paley's work, "the adult characters in these stories often have more brains than money, more passion than wisdom, more wit than understanding." And forty years ago, she was one of the very few writers telling, with care and art, the stories of the lives of women with a unique, poetic voice, lilting in English, with the roots in Russian and Yiddish and shaped by W. H. Auden, the first poet Paley studied with and the one she imitated en route to her own voice.

In "Goodbye and Good Luck," an early, essential, and much-read story, language illuminates character, and character moves the plot, such as it is, into the full, ardent, charming reality of a long and fitful love affair; we are all, Christians and Jews, actors and otherwise, first-generation Americans and children of people who speak English beautifully, given a passport to Rose Lieber's life and the Russian Art Theater of Second Avenue. It is impossible not to root for young Rose, who adores Volodya Vlashkin and gives him up ("No more. This isn't for me. I am sick from it all. I am no home breaker." "Girlie," he said, "don't be foolish." "No, no, goodbye, good luck," I said. "I am sincere."), for the older Rose, resuming with Vlashkin, "full of interest but not with our former speed," and for the old Rose, who knows how life goes and gives up nothing, approaching the world and its gifts and disappointments with what Grace Paley once called, as she described her own life, a "good, hard greed."

"An Interest in Life" describes our sense of the author herself, a person who is always listening for the stories that need to be told, the storyteller who wants us to understand and hear even the painful stories, with nothing like a happy ending. A woman with more looks than ambition, already saddled with four children before she is thirty, is the pariah of her apartment building, the barely adequate mother of the four; she longs for her missing husband and longs, almost as much, for even a brief, unsatisfactory romance. "I was happy but I am now in possession of the knowledge that this is wrong. Happiness isn't so bad for a woman . . . she could lie down, nuzzling a regiment of men and little children, she could just die of the pleasure. But men are different." What she cannot see is her life, her possibilities, any route to becoming a whole, responsible person, steering her own ship. It is the most compassionate, gentle, clear-eyed indictment of a woman's life lived for men and without any other dreams or ambition that one can imagine. It is the sensible, hopeful Paley feminism, the one that says, "Don't we want our sisters and mothers and daughters to be people too?"

"A Conversation with My Father" is Paley's meditation not only on life and death, on the shock of mortality, but also on the nature of storytelling and its meaning within families, between people who want to tell each other things. As it always does with Paley, the language—wisecracking, tender, intense, and understated—carries the story, in which, as is almost always the case with Paley, not much happens. The father wants a better, more elegant story. The daughter wants to accommodate him, but the writer in her cannot, and the story grows not simpler, but darker. It is also the story of what a parent wishes for a child, both the story-within-the-story and the dying father and his loving, recalcitrant daughter, what children wish from their parents, and what writers must do. "I had promised my family to always let him have the last word when arguing, but in this case I had a different responsibility. That woman . . . she's my knowledge and my invention."

These three stories, like the best of Paley's fifty or so, from the 1950s to the present, have the depth and breadth of novels, the music and unmistakable, lyric rhythm of poetry, and the impish, uncompromising wisdom that signifies pure Paley.

Amy Bloom is a novelist and essayist. She lives in Connecticut.

GRACE PALEY

An Interest in Life

My husband gave me a broom one Christmas. This wasn't right. No one can tell me it was meant kindly.

"I don't want you not to have anything for Christmas while I'm away in the army," he said. "Virginia, please look at it. It comes with this fancy dustpan. It hangs off a stick. Look at it, will you? Are you blind or cross-eyed?"

"Thanks, chum," I said. I had always wanted a dustpan hooked up that way. It was a good one. My husband doesn't shop in bargain basements or January sales.

Still and all, in spite of the quality, it was a mean present to give a woman you planned on never seeing again, a person you had children with and got onto all the time, drunk or sober, even when everybody had to get up early in the morning.

I asked him if he could wait and join the army in a half hour, as I had to get the groceries. I don't like to leave kids alone in a three-room apartment full of gas and electricity. Fire may break out from a nasty remark. Or the oldest decides to get even with the youngest.

"Just this once," he said. "But you better figure out how to get along without me."

"You're a handicapped person mentally," I said. "You should've been institutionalized years ago." I slammed the door. I didn't want to see him pack his underwear and ironed shirts.

I never got farther than the front stoop, though, because there was Mrs. Raftery, wringing her hands, tears in her eyes as though she had a monopoly on all the good news.

"Mrs. Raftery!" I said, putting my arm around her. "Don't cry." She leaned on me because I am such a horsey build. "Don't cry, Mrs. Raftery, please!" I said.

"That's like you, Virginia. Always looking at the ugly side of things. 'Take in the wash. It's rainin'!' That's you. You're the first one knows it when the dumbwaiter breaks."

"Oh, come on now, that's not so. It just isn't so," I said. "I'm the exact opposite."

"Did you see Mrs. Cullen yet?" she asked, paying no attention.

"Where?"

"Virginia!" she said, shocked. "She's passed away. The whole house knows it. They've got her in white like a bride and you never saw a beautiful creature like that. She must be eighty. Her husband's proud."

"She was never more than an acquaintance; she didn't have any children," I said.

"Well, I don't care about that. Now, Virginia, you do what I say now, you go downstairs and you say like this—listen to me—say, 'I hear, Mr. Cullen, your wife's passed away. I'm sorry.' Then ask him how he is. Then you ought to go around the corner and see her. She's in Witson & Wayde. Then you ought to go over to the church when they carry her over."

"It's not my church," I said.

"That's no reason, Virginia. You go up like this," she said, parting from me to do a prancy dance. "Up the big front steps, into the church you go. It's beautiful in there. You can't help kneeling only for a minute. Then round to the right. Then up the other stairway. Then you come to a great oak door that's arched above you, then," she said, seizing a deep, deep breath, for all the good it would do her, "and then turn the knob slo-owly and open the door and see for yourself: Our Blessed Mother is in charge. Beautiful. Beautiful. Beautiful."

I sighed in and I groaned out, so as to melt a certain pain around my heart. A steel ring like arthritis, at my age.

"You are a groaner," Mrs. Raftery said, gawking into my mouth.

"I am not," I said. I got a whiff of her, a terrible cheap wine lush.

My husband threw a penny at the door from the inside to take my notice from Mrs. Raftery. He rattled the glass door to make sure I looked at him. He had a fat duffel bag on each shoulder. Where did he acquire so much worldly possession? What was in them? My grandma's goose feathers from across the ocean? Or all the diaper-service diapers? To this day the truth is shrouded in mystery.

"What the hell are you doing, Virginia?" he said, dumping them at my feet. "Standing out here on your hind legs telling everybody your business? The army gives you a certain time, for godsakes, they're not kidding." Then he said, "I beg your pardon," to Mrs. Raftery. He took hold of me with his two arms as though in love and pressed his body hard against mine so that I could feel him for the last time and suffer my loss. Then he kissed me in a mean way to nearly split my lip. Then he winked and said, "That's all for now," and skipped off into the future, duffel bags full of rags.

He left me in an embarrassing situation, nearly fainting, in front of that old widow, who can't even remember the half of it. "He's a crock," said Mrs. Raftery. "Is he leaving for good or just temporarily, Virginia?"

"Oh, he's probably deserting me," I said, and sat down on the stoop, pulling my big knees up to my chin.

"If that's the case, tell the Welfare right away," she said. "He's a bum, leaving you just before Christmas. Tell the cops," she said. "They'll provide the toys for the little kids gladly. And don't forget to let the grocer in on it. He won't be so hard on you expecting payment."

She saw that sadness was stretched worldwide across my face. Mrs. Raftery isn't the worst person. She said, "Look around for comfort, dear." With a nervous finger she pointed to the truckers eating lunch on their haunches across the street, leaning on the loading platforms. She waved her hand to include in all the men marching up and down in search of a decent luncheonette. She didn't leave out the six longshoremen loafing under the fish-market marquee. "If their lungs and stomachs ain't crushed by overwork, they disappear somewhere in the world. Don't be disappointed, Virginia. I don't know a man living'd last you a lifetime."

Ten days later Girard asked, "Where's Daddy?"

"Ask me no questions, I'll tell you no lies." I didn't want the children to know the facts. Present or past, a child should have a father.

"Where *is* Daddy?" Girard asked the week after that.

"He joined the army," I said.

"He made my bunk bed," said Philip.

"The truth shall make ye free," I said.

Then I sat down with pencil and pad to get in control of my resources. The facts, when I added and subtracted them, were that my husband had left me with fourteen dollars, and the rent unpaid, in an emergency state. He'd claimed he was sorry to do this, but my opinion is, out of sight out of mind. "The city won't let you starve," he'd said. "After all, you're half the population. You're keeping up the good work. Without you the race would die out. Who'd pay the taxes? Who'd keep the streets clean? There wouldn't be no army. A man like me wouldn't have no place to go."

I sent Girard right down to Mrs. Raftery with a request about the whereabouts of Welfare. She responded R.S.V.P. with an extra comment in left-handed script: "Poor Girard . . . he's never the boy my John was!"

Who asked her?

I called on Welfare right after the new year. In no time I discovered that they're rigged up to deal with liars, and if you're truthful it's disappointing to them. They may even refuse to handle your case if you're too truthful.

They asked sensible questions at first. They asked where my husband had enlisted. I didn't know. They put some letter writers and agents after him. "He's not in the United States Army," they said. "Try the Brazilian Army," I suggested.

They have no sense of kidding around. They're not the least bit lighthearted and they tried. "Oh no," they said. "That was incorrect. He is not in the Brazilian Army."

"No?" I said. "How strange! He must be in the Mexican Navy."

By law, they had to hound his brothers. They wrote to his brother who has a first-class card in the Teamsters and owns an apartment house in California. They asked his two brothers in Jersey to help me. They have large families. Rightfully they laughed. Then they wrote to Thomas, the oldest, the smart one (the one they all worked so hard for years to keep him in college until his brains could pay off). He was the one who sent ten dollars immediately, saying, "What a bastard! I'll send something time to time, Ginny, but whatever you do, don't tell the authorities." Of course I never did. Soon they began to guess they were better people than me, that I was in trouble because I deserved it, and then they liked me better.

But they never fixed my refrigerator. Every time I called I said patiently, "The milk is sour . . ." I said, "Corn beef went bad." Sitting in that beer-stinking phone booth in Felan's for the sixth time (sixty cents) with the baby on my lap and Barbie tapping at the glass door with an American flag, I cried into the secretary's hard-hearted ear, "I bought real butter for the holiday, and it's rancid . . ." They said, "You'll have to get a better bid on the repair job."

While I waited indoors for a man to bid, Girard took to swinging back and forth on top of the bathroom door, just to soothe himself, giving me the laugh, dreamy, nibbling calcimine off the ceiling. On first sight Mrs. Raftery said, "Whack the monkey, he'd be better off on arsenic."

But Girard is my son and I'm the judge. It means a terrible thing for the future, though I don't know what to call it.

It was from constantly thinking of my foreknowledge on this and other subjects, it was from observing when I put my lipstick on daily, how my face was just curling up to die, that John Raftery came from Jersey to rescue me.

On Thursdays, anyway, John Raftery took the tubes in to visit his mother. The whole house knew it. She was cheerful even before breakfast. She sang out loud in a girlish brogue that only came to tongue for grand occasions. Hanging out the wash, she blushed to recall what a remarkable boy her John had been. "Ask the sisters around the corner," she said to the open kitchen windows. "They'll never forget John."

That particular night after supper Mrs. Raftery said to her son, "John, how come you don't say hello to your old friend Virginia? She's had hard luck and she's gloomy."

"Is that so, Mother?" he said, and immediately climbed two flights to knock at my door.

"Oh, John," I said at the sight of him, hat in hand in a white shirt and blue-striped tie, spick-and-span, a Sunday-school man. "Hello!"

"Welcome, John!" I said. "Sit down. Come right in. How are you? You look awfully good. You do. Tell me, how've you been all this time, John?"

"How've I been?" he asked thoughtfully. To answer within reason, he described his life with Margaret, marriage, work, and children up to the present day.

I had nothing good to report. Now that he had put the subject around before my very eyes, every burnt-up day of my life smoked in shame, and I couldn't even get a clear view of the good half hours.

"Of course," he said, "you do have lovely children. Noticeable-looking, Virginia. Good looks is always something to be thankful for."

"Thankful?" I said. "I don't have to thank anything but my own foolishness for four children when I'm twenty-six years old, deserted, and poverty-struck, regardless of looks. A man can't help it, but I could have behaved better."

"Don't be so cruel on yourself, Ginny," he said. "Children come from God."

"You're still great on holy subjects, aren't you? You know damn well where children come from."

He did know. His red face reddened further. John Raftery has had that color coming out on him boy and man from keeping his rages so inward.

Still he made more sense in his conversation after that, and I poured fresh tea to tell him how my husband used to like me because I was a passionate person. That was until he took a look around and saw how in the long run this life only meant more of the same thing. He tried to turn away from me once he came to this understanding, and make me hate him. His face changed. He gave up his brand of cigarettes which we had in common. He threw out the two pairs of socks I knitted by hand. "If there's anything I hate in this world, it's navy blue," he said. Oh, I could have dyed them. I would have done anything for him, if he were only not too sorry to ask me.

"You were a nice kid in those days," said John, referring to certain Saturday nights. "A wild, nice kid."

"Aaah," I said, disgusted. Whatever I was then was on the way to where I am now. "I was fresh. If I had a kid like me, I'd slap her cross-eyed."

The very next Thursday John gave me a beautiful radio with a record player. "Enjoy yourself," he said. That really made Welfare speechless. We didn't own any records, but the investigator saw my burden was lightened and he scribbled a dozen pages about it in his notebook.

On the third Thursday he brought a walking doll (twenty-four inches) for Linda and Barbie with a card inscribed, "A baby doll for a couple of dolls." He had also had a couple of drinks at his mother's, and this made him want to dance. "La-la-la," he sang, a ramrod swaying in my kitchen chair. "La-la-la, let yourself go . . ."

"You gotta give a little," he sang, "live a little . . ." He said, "Virginia, may I have this dance?"

"Sssh, we finally got them asleep. Please, turn the radio down. Quiet. Deathly silence, John Raftery."

"Let me do your dishes, Virginia."

"Don't be silly, you're a guest in my house," I said. "I still regard you as a guest."

"I want to do something for you, Virginia."

"Tell me I'm the most gorgeous thing," I said, dipping my arm to the funny bone in dish soup.

He didn't answer. "I'm having a lot of trouble at work," was all he said. Then I heard him push the chair back. He came up behind me, put his arms around my waistline, and kissed my cheek. He whirled me around and took my hands. He said, "An old friend is better than rubies." He looked me in the eye. He held my attention by trying to be honest. And he kissed me a short sweet kiss on my mouth.

"Please sit down, Virginia," he said. He kneeled before me and put his head in my lap. I was stirred by so much activity. Then he looked up at me and, as though proposing marriage for life, he offered—because he was drunk—to place his immortal soul in peril to comfort me.

First I said, "Thank you." Then I said, "No."

I was sorry for him, but he's devout, a leader of the Fathers' Club at his church, active in all the lay groups for charities, orphans, etc. I knew that if he stayed late to love with me, he would not do it lightly but would in the end pay terrible penance and ruin his long life. The responsibility would be on me.

So I said no.

And Barbie is such a light sleeper. All she has to do, I thought, is wake up and wander in and see her mother and her new friend John with his pants around his knees, wrestling on the kitchen table. A vision like that could affect a kid for life.

I said no.

Everyone in this building is so goddamn nosy. That evening I had to say no.

But John came to visit, anyway, on the fourth Thursday. This time he brought the discarded dresses of Margaret's daughters, organdy party dresses and glazed cotton for every day. He gently admired Barbara and Linda, his blue eyes rolling to back up a couple of dozen oohs and ahs.

Even Philip, who thinks God gave him just a certain number of hellos and he better save them for the final judgment, Philip leaned on John and said, "Why don't you bring your boy to play with me? I don't have nobody who to play with." (Philip's a liar. There must be at least seventy-one children in this house, pale pink to medium brown, English-talking and gibbering in Spanish, rough-and-tough boys, the Lone Ranger's bloody pals, or the exact picture of Supermouse. If a boy wanted a friend, he could pick the very one out of his neighbors.)

Also, Girard is a cold fish. He was in a lonesome despair. Sometimes he looked in the mirror and said, "How come I have such an ugly face? My nose is funny. Mostly people don't like me." He was a liar too. Girard has a face like his father's. His eyes are the color of those little blue plums in August. He looks like an advertisement in a magazine. He could be a child model and make a lot of money. He is my first child, and if he thinks he is ugly, I think I am ugly.

John said, "I can't stand to see a boy mope like that. . . . What do the Sisters say in school?"

"He doesn't pay attention is all they say. You can't get much out of them."

"My middle boy was like that," said John. "Couldn't take an interest. Aaah, I wish I didn't have all that headache on the job. I'd grab Girard by the collar and make him take notice of the world. I wish I could ask him out to Jersey to play in all that space."

"Why not?" I said.

"Why, Virginia, I'm surprised you don't know why not. You know I can't take your children out to meet my children."

I felt a lot of strong arthritis in my ribs.

"My mother's the funny one, Virginia." He felt he had to continue with the subject matter. "I don't know. I guess she likes the idea of bugging Margaret. She says, 'You goin' up, John?' 'Yes, Mother,' I say. 'Behave yourself, John,' she says. 'That husband might come home and hacksaw you into hell. You're a Catholic man, John,' she says. But I figured it out. She likes to know I'm in the building. I swear, Virginia, she wishes me the best of luck."

"I do too, John," I said. We drank a last glass of beer to make sure of a peaceful sleep. "Good night, Virginia," he said, looping his muffler neatly under his chin. "Don't worry. I'll be thinking of what to do about Girard."

I got into the big bed that I share with the girls in the little room. For once I had no trouble falling asleep. I only had to worry about Linda and Barbara and Philip. It was a great relief to me that John had taken over the thinking about Girard.

John was sincere. That's true. He paid a lot of attention to Girard, smoking out all his sneaky sorrows. He registered him into a wild pack of Cub Scouts that went up to the Bronx once a week to let off steam. He gave him a Junior Erector Set. And sometimes when his family wasn't listening he prayed at great length for him.

One Sunday, Sister Veronica said in her sweet voice from another life, "He's not worse. He might even be a little better. How are *you,* Virginia?" putting her hand on mine. Everybody around here acts like they know everything.

"Just fine," I said.

"We ought to start on Philip," John said, "if it's true Girard's improving."

"You should've been a social worker, John."

"A lot of people have noticed that about me," said John.

"Your mother was always acting so crazy about you, how come she didn't knock herself out a little to see you in college? Like we did for Thomas?"

"Now, Virginia, be fair. She's a poor old woman. My father was a weak earner. She had to have my wages, and I'll tell you, Virginia, I'm not sorry. Look at Thomas. He's still in school. Drop him in this jungle and he'd be devoured. He hasn't had a touch of real life. And here I am with a good chunk of a family, a home of my own, a name in the building trades. One thing I have to tell you, the poor old woman is sorry. I said one day (oh, in passing—years ago) that I might marry you. She stuck a knife in herself. It's a fact. Not more than an eighth of an inch. You never saw such a gory Sunday. One thing—you would have been a better daughter-in-law to her than Margaret."

"Marry me?" I said.

"Well, yes . . . Aaah—I always liked you, then . . . Why do you think I'd sit in the shade of this kitchen every Thursday night? For godsakes, the only warm thing around here is this teacup. Yes sir, I did want to marry you, Virginia."

"No kidding, John? Really?" It was nice to know. Better late than never, to learn you were desired in youth.

I didn't tell John, but the truth is, I would never have married him. Once I met my husband with his winking looks, he was my only interest. Wild as I had been with John and others, I turned all my wildness over to him and then there was no question in my mind.

Still, face facts, if my husband didn't budge on in life, it was my fault. On me, as they say, be it. I greeted the morn with a song. I had a hello for everyone but the landlord. Ask the people on the block, come or go—even the Spanish ones, with their sad dark faces—they have to smile when they see me.

But for his own comfort, he should have done better lifewise and moneywise. I was happy, but I am now in possession of knowledge that this is wrong. Happiness isn't so bad for a woman. She gets fatter, she gets older, she could lie down, nuzzling a regiment of men and little kids, she could just die of the pleasure. But men are different, they have to own money, or they have to be famous, or everybody on the block has to look up to them from the cellar stairs.

A woman counts her children and acts snotty, like she invented life but men *must* do well in the world. I know that men are not fooled by being happy.

"A funny guy," said John, guessing where my thoughts had gone. "What stopped him up? He was nobody's fool. He had a funny thing about him, Virginia, if you don't mind my saying so. He wasn't much distance up, but he was all set and ready to be looking down on us all."

"He was very smart, John. You don't realize that. His hobby was crossword puzzles, and I said to him real often, as did others around here, that he ought to go out on the '$64 Question.' Why not? But he laughed. You know what he said? He said, 'That proves how dumb you are if you think I'm smart.'"

"A funny guy," said John. "Get it all off your chest," he said. "Talk it out, Virginia; it's the only way to kill the pain."

By and large, I was happy to oblige. Still I could not carry through about certain cruel remarks. It was like trying to move back into the dry mouth of a nightmare to remember that the last day I was happy was the middle of a week in March, when I told my husband I was going to have Linda. Barbara was five months old to the hour. The boys were three and four. I had to tell him. It was the last day with anything happy about it.

Later on he said, "Oh, you make me so sick, you're so goddamn big and fat, you look like a goddamn brownstone, the way you're squared off in front."

"Well, where are you going tonight?" I asked.

"How should I know?" he said. "Your big ass takes up the whole goddamn bed," he said. "There's no room for me." He bought a sleeping bag and slept on the floor.

I couldn't believe it. I would start every morning fresh. I couldn't believe that he would turn against me so, while I was still young and even his friends still liked me.

But he did, he turned absolutely against me and became no friend of mine. "All you ever think about is making babies. This place stinks like the men's room in the BMT. It's a fucking *pissoir.*" He was strong on truth all through the year. "That kid eats more than the five of us put together," he said. "Stop stuffing your face, you fat dumbbell," he said to Philip.

Then he worked on the neighbors. "Get that nosy old bag out of here," he said. "If she comes on once more with 'my son in the building trades' I'll squash her for the cat."

Then he turned on Spielvogel, the checker, his oldest friend, who only visited on holidays and never spoke to me (shy, the way some bachelors are). "That sonofabitch, don't hand me that friendship crap, all he's after is your ass. That's what I need—a little shitmaker of his using up the air in this flat."

And then there was no one else to dispose of. We were left alone fair and square, facing each other.

"Now, Virginia," he said, "I come to the end of my rope. I see a black wall ahead of me. What the hell am I supposed to do? I only got one life. Should I lie down and die? I don't know what to do anymore. I'll give it to you straight, Virginia, if I stick around, you can't help it, you'll hate me . . ."

"I hate you right now," I said. "So do whatever you like."

"This place drives me nuts," he mumbled. "I don't know what to do around here. I want to get you a present. Something."

"I told you, do whatever you like. Buy me a rat trap for rats."

That's when he went down to the House Appliance Store, and he brought back a new broom and a classy dustpan.

"A new broom sweeps clean," he said. "I got to get out of here," he said. "I'm going nuts." Then he began to stuff the duffel bags, and I went to the grocery store but was stopped by Mrs. Raftery, who had to tell me what she considered so beautiful—death—then he kissed and went to join some army somewhere.

I didn't tell John any of this, because I think it makes a woman look too bad to tell on how another man has treated her. He begins to see her through the other man's eyes, a sitting duck, a skinful of flaws. After all, I had come to depend on John. All my husband's friends were strangers now, though I had always said to them, "Feel welcome."

And the family men in the building looked too cunning, as though they had all personally deserted me. If they met me on the stairs, they carried the heaviest groceries up and helped bring Linda's stroller down, but they never asked me a question worth answering at all.

Besides that, Girard and Philip taught the girls the days of the week: Monday, Tuesday, Wednesday, Johnday, Friday. They waited for him once a week, under the hallway lamp, half asleep like bugs in the sun, sitting in their little chairs with their names on in gold, a birth present from my mother-in-law. At fifteen after eight he punctually came, to read a story, pass out some kisses, and tuck them into bed.

But one night, after a long Johnday of them squealing my eardrum split, after a rainy afternoon with brother constantly raising up his hand against brother, with the girls near ready to go to court over the proper ownership of Melinda Lee, the twenty-four-inch walking doll, the doorbell rang three times. Not any of those times did John's face greet me.

I was too ashamed to call down to Mrs. Raftery, and she was too mean to knock on my door and explain.

He didn't come the following Thursday either. Girard said sadly, "He must've run away, John."

I had to give him up after two weeks' absence and no word. I didn't know how to tell the children: something about right and wrong, goodness and meanness, men and women. I had it all at my fingertips, ready to hand over. But I didn't think I ought to take mistakes and truth away from them. Who knows? They might make a truer friend in this world somewhere than I have ever made. So I just put them to bed and sat in the kitchen and cried.

In the middle of my third beer, searching in my mind for the next step, I found the decision to go on "Strike It Rich." I scrounged some paper and pencil from the toy box and I listed all my troubles, which must be done in order to qualify. The list when complete could have brought tears to the eye of God if He had a minute. At the sight of it my bitterness began to improve. All that is really necessary for survival of the fittest, it seems, is an interest in life, good, bad, or peculiar.

As always happens in these cases where you have begun to help yourself with plans, news comes from an opposite direction. The doorbell rang, two short and two long—meaning John.

My first thought was to wake the children and make them happy. "No! No!" he said. "Please don't put yourself to that trouble. Virginia, I'm dog-tired," he said. "Dog-tired. My job is a damn headache. It's too much. It's all day and it scuttles my mind at night, and in the end who does the credit go to?"

"Virginia," he said, "I don't know if I can come anymore. I've been wanting to tell you. I just don't know. What's it all about? Could you answer me if I asked you? I can't figure this whole thing out at all."

I started the tea steeping because his fingers when I touched them were cold. I didn't speak. I tried looking at it from his man point of view, and I thought he had to take a bus, the tubes, and a subway to see me; and then the subway, the tubes, and a bus to go back home at 1 A.M. It wouldn't be any trouble at all for him to part with us forever. I thought about my life, and I gave strongest consideration to my children. If given the choice, I decided to choose not to live without him.

"What's that?" he asked, pointing to my careful list of troubles. "Writing a letter?"

"Oh no," I said, "it's for 'Strike It Rich.' I hope to go on the program."

"Virginia, for goodness' sakes," he said, giving it a glance, "you don't have a ghost. They'd laugh you out of the studio. Those people really suffer."

"Are you sure, John?" I asked.

"No question in my mind at all," said John. "Have you ever seen that program? I mean, in addition to all of this—the little disturbances of man"—he waved a scornful hand at my list—"they *suffer.* They live in the forefront of tornadoes, their lives are washed off by floods—catastrophes of God. Oh, Virginia."

"Are you sure, John?"

"For goodness' sake . . ."

Sadly I put my list away. Still, if things got worse, I could always make use of it.

Once that was settled, I acted on an earlier decision. I pushed his cup of scalding tea aside. I wedged myself onto his lap between his hard belt buckle and the table. I put my arms around his neck and said, "How come you're so cold, John?" He has a kind face and he knew how to look astonished. He said, "Why, Virginia, I'm getting warmer." We laughed.

John became a lover to me that night.

★ ★ ★

Mrs. Raftery is sometimes silly and sick from her private source of cheap wine. She expects John often. "Honor your mother, what's the matter with you, John?" she complains. "Honor. Honor."

"Virginia dear," she says. "You never would've taken John away to Jersey like Margaret. I wish he'd've married you."

"You didn't like me much in those days."

"That's a lie," she says. I know she's a hypocrite, but no more than the rest of the world.

What is remarkable to me is that it doesn't seem to conscience John as I thought it might. It is still hard to believe that a man who sends out the Ten Commandments every year for a Christmas card can be so easy buttoning and unbuttoning.

Of course we must be very careful not to wake the children or disturb the neighbors, who will enjoy another person's excitement just so far, and then the pleasure enrages them. We must be very careful for ourselves too, for when my husband comes back, realizing the babies are in school and everything easier, he won't forgive me if I've started it all up again—noisy signs of life that are so much trouble to a man.

We haven't seen him in two and a half years. Although people have suggested it, I do not want the police or Intelligence or a private eye or anyone to go after him to bring him back. I know that if he expected to stay away forever he would have written and said so. As it is, I just don't know what evening, any time, he may appear. Sometimes, stumbling over a blockbuster of a dream at midnight, I wake up to vision his soft arrival.

He comes in the door with his old key. He gives me a strict look and says, "Well, you look older Virginia." "So do you." I say, although he hasn't changed a bit.

He settles in the kitchen because the children are asleep all over the rest of the house. I unknot his tie and offer him a cold sandwich. He raps my backside, paying attention to the bounce. I walk around him as though he were a Maypole, kissing as I go.

"I didn't like the army much," he says. "Next time I think I might go join the Merchant Marine."

"What army?" I say.

"It's pretty much the same everywhere," he says.

"I wouldn't be a bit surprised," I say.

"I lost my cuff link, goddamnit," he says, and drops to the floor to look for it. I go down too on my knees, but I know he never had a cuff link in his life. Still I would do a lot for him.

"Got you off your feet that time," he says, laughing. "Oh yes, I did." And before I can even make myself half comfortable on that polka-dotted linoleum, he got onto me right where we were, and the truth is, we were so happy, we forgot the precautions.

GRACE PALEY

Goodbye and Good Luck

I was popular in certain circles, says Aunt Rose. I wasn't no thinner then, only more stationary in the flesh. In time to come, Lillie, don't be surprised—change is a fact of God. From this no one is excused. Only a person like your mama stands on one foot, she don't notice how big her behind is getting and sings in the canary's ear for thirty years. Who's listening? Papa's in the shop. You and Seymour, thinking about yourself. So she waits in a spotless kitchen for a kind word and thinks—poor Rosie. . . .

Poor Rosie! If there was more life in my little sister, she would know my heart is a regular college of feelings and there is such information between my corset and me that her whole married life is a kindergarten.

Nowadays you could find me any time in a hotel, uptown or downtown. Who needs an apartment to live like a maid with a dustrag in the hand, sneezing? I'm in very good with the bus boys, it's more interesting than home, all kinds of people, everybody with a reason.

And my reason, Lillie, is a long time ago I said to the forelady, "Missus, if I can't sit by the window, I can't sit." "If you can't sit, girlie," she says politely, "go stand on the street corner." And that's how I got unemployed in novelty wear.

For my next job I answered an ad which said "Refined young lady, medium salary, cultural organization." I went by trolley to the address, the Russian Art Theater of Second Avenue where they played only the best Yiddish plays. They needed a ticket seller, someone like me, who likes the public but is very sharp on crooks. The man who interviewed me was the manager, a certain type.

Immediately he said: "Rosie Lieber, you surely got a build on you!"

"It takes all kinds, Mr. Krimberg."

"Don't misunderstand me, little girl," he said. "I appreciate, I appreciate. A young lady lacking fore and aft, her blood is so busy warming the toes and the finger tips, it don't have time to circulate where it's most required."

Everybody likes kindness. I said to him: "Only don't be fresh, Mr. Krimberg, and we'll make a good bargain."

We did: Nine dollars a week, a glass of tea every night, a free ticket once a week for Mama, and I could go watch rehearsals any time I want.

My first nine dollars was in the grocer's hands ready to move on already, when Krimberg said to me, "Rosie, here's a great gentleman, a member of this remarkable theater, wants to meet you, impressed no doubt by your big brown eyes."

And who was it, Lillie? Listen to me, before my very eyes was Volodya Vlashkin, called by the people of those days the Valentino of Second Avenue. I took one look, and I said to myself: Where did a Jewish boy grow up so big? "Just outside Kiev," he told me.

How? "My mama nursed me till I was six. I was the only boy in the village to have such health."

"My goodness, Vlashkin, six years old! She must have had shredded wheat there, not breasts, poor woman."

"My mother was beautiful," he said. "She had eyes like stars."

He had such a way of expressing himself, it brought tears.

To Krimberg, Vlashkin said after this introduction: "Who is responsible for hiding this wonderful young person in a cage?"

"That is where the ticket seller sells."

"So, David, go in there and sell tickets for a half hour. I have something in mind in regards to the future of this girl and this company. Go, David, be a good boy. And you, Miss Lieber, please, I suggest Feinberg's for a glass of tea. The rehearsals are long. I enjoy a quiet interlude with a friendly person."

So he took me there, Feinberg's, then around the corner, a place so full of Hungarians, it was deafening. In the back room was a table of honor for him. On the tablecloth embroidered by the lady of the house was "Here Vlashkin Eats." We finished one glass of tea in quietness, out of thirst, when I finally made up my mind what to say.

"Mr. Vlashkin, I saw you a couple weeks ago, even before I started working here, in *The Sea Gull.* Believe me, if I was that girl, I wouldn't look even for a minute on the young bourgeois fellow. He could fall out of the play altogether. How Chekhov could put him in the same play as you, I can't understand."

"You liked me?" he asked, taking my hand and kindly patting it. "Well, well, young people still like me . . . so, and you like the theater too? Good. And you, Rose, you know you have such a nice hand, so warm to the touch, such a fine skin, tell me, why do you wear a scarf around your neck? You only hide your young, young throat. These are not olden times, my child, to live in shame."

"Who's ashamed?" I said, taking off the kerchief, but my hand right away went to the kerchief's place, because the truth is, it really was olden times, and I was still of a nature to melt with shame.

"Have some more tea, my dear."

"No, thank you, I am a samovar already."

"Dorfmann!" he hollered like a king. "Bring this child a seltzer with fresh ice!"

In weeks to follow I had the privilege to know him better and better as a person—also the opportunity to see him in his profession. The time was autumn; the theater full of coming and going. Rehearsing without end. After *The Sea Gull* flopped *The Salesman from Istanbul* played, a great success.

Here the ladies went crazy. On the opening night, in the middle of the first scene, one missus—a widow or her husband worked too long hours—began to clap and sing out, "Oi, oi, Vlashkin." Soon there was such a tumult, the actors had to stop acting. Vlashkin stepped forward. Only not Vlashkin to the eyes . . . a younger man with pitch-black hair, lively on restless feet, his mouth clever. A half a century later at the end of the play he came out again, a gray philosopher, a student of life from only reading books, his hands as smooth as silk. . . . I cried to think who I was—nothing—and such a man could look at me with interest.

Then I got a small raise, due to he kindly put in a good word for me, and also for fifty cents a night I was given the pleasure together with cousins, in-laws, and plain stage-struck kids to be part of a crowd scene and to see like he saw every single night the hundreds of pale faces waiting for his feelings to make them laugh or bend down their heads in sorrow.

The sad day came, I kissed my mama goodbye. Vlashkin helped me to get a reasonable room near the theater to be more free. Also my outstanding friend would have a place to recline away from the noise of the dressing rooms. She cried and she cried. "This is a different way of living, Mama," I said. "Besides, I am driven by love."

"You! You, a nothing, a rotten hole in a piece of cheese, are you telling me what is life?" she screamed.

Very insulted, I went away from her. But I am good-natured—you know fat people are like that—kind, and I thought to myself, poor Mama . . . it is true she got more of an idea of life than me. She married who she didn't like, a sick man, his spirit already swallowed up by God. He never washed. He had an unhappy smell. His teeth fell out, his hair disappeared, he got smaller, shriveled up little by little, till goodbye and good luck he was gone and only came to Mama's mind when she went to the mailbox under the stairs to get the electric bill. In memory of him and out of respect for mankind, I decided to live for love.

Don't laugh, you ignorant girl.

Do you think it was easy for me? I had to give Mama a little something. Ruthie was saving up together with your papa for linens, a couple knives and forks. In the morning I had to do piecework if I wanted to keep by myself. So I made flowers. Before lunch time every day a whole garden grew on my table.

This was my independence, Lillie dear, blooming, it didn't have no roots and its face was paper.

Meanwhile Krimberg went after me too. No doubt observing the success of Vlashkin, he thought, "Aha, open sesame . . ." Others in the company similar. After me in those years were the following: Krimberg I mentioned. Carl Zimmer, played innocent young fellows with a wig. Charlie Peel, a Christian who fell in the soup by accident, a creator of beautiful sets. "Color is his middle name," says Vlashkin, always to the point.

I put this in to show you your fat old aunt was not crazy out of loneliness. In those noisy years I had friends among interesting people who admired me for reasons of youth and that I was a first-class listener.

The actresses—Raisele, Marya, Esther Leopold—were only interested in tomorrow. After them was the rich men, producers, the whole garment center; their past is a pincushion, future the eye of a needle.

Finally the day came, I no longer could keep my tact in my mouth. I said: "Vlashkin, I hear by carrier pigeon you have a wife, children, the whole combination."

"True, I don't tell stories. I make no pretense."

"That isn't the question. What is this lady like? It hurts me to ask, but tell me, Vlashkin . . . a man's life is something I don't clearly see."

"Little girl, I have told you a hundred times, this small room is the convent of my troubled spirit. Here I come to your innocent shelter to refresh myself in the midst of an agonized life."

"Ach, Vlashkin, serious, serious, who is this lady?"

"Rosie, she is a fine woman of the middle classes, a good mother to my children, three in number, girls all, a good cook, in her youth handsome, now no longer young. You see, could I be more frank? I entrust you, dear, with my soul."

It was some few months later at the New Year's ball of the Russian Artists Club, I met Mrs. Vlashkin, a woman with black hair in a low bun, straight and too proud. She sat at a small table speaking in a deep voice to whoever stopped a moment to converse. Her Yiddish was perfect, each word cut like a special jewel. I looked at her. She noticed me like she noticed everybody, cold like Christmas morning. Then she got tired. Vlashkin called a taxi and I never saw her again. Poor woman, she did not know I was on the same stage with her. The poison I was to her role, she did not know.

Later on that night in front of my door I said to Vlashkin, "No more. This isn't for me. I am sick from it all. I am no home breaker."

"Girlie," he said, "don't be foolish."

"No, no, goodbye, good luck," I said. "I am sincere."

So I went and stayed with Mama for a week's vacation and cleaned up all the closets and scrubbed the walls till the paint came off. She was very grateful, all the same her hard life made her say, "Now we see the end. If you live like a bum, you are finally a lunatic."

After this few days I came back to my life. When we met, me and Vlashkin, we said only hello and goodbye, and then for a few sad years, with the head we nodded as if to say, "Yes, yes, I know who you are."

Meanwhile in the field was a whole new strategy. Your mama and your grandmama brought around—boys. Your own father had a brother, you never even seen him. Ruben. A serious fellow, his idealism was his hat and his coat. "Rosie, I offer you a big new free happy, unusual life." How? "With me, we will raise up the sands of Palestine to make a nation. That is the land of tomorrow for us Jews." "Ha-ha, Ruben, I'll go tomorrow then." "Rosie!" says Ruben. "We need strong women like you, mothers and farmers." "You don't fool me, Ruben, what you need is dray horses. But for that you need more money." "I don't like your attitude, Rose." "In that case, go and multiply. Goodbye."

Another fellow: Yonkel Gurstein, a regular sport, dressed to kill, with such an excitable nature. In those days—it looks to me like yesterday—the youngest girls wore undergarments like Battle Creek, Michigan. To him it was a matter of seconds. Where did he practice, a Jewish boy? Nowadays I suppose it is easier, Lillie? My goodness, I ain't asking you nothing—touchy, touchy . . .

Well, by now you must know yourself, honey, whatever you do, life don't stop. It only sits a minute and dreams a dream.

While I was saying to all these silly youngsters "no, no, no," Vlashkin went to Europe and toured a few seasons . . . Moscow, Prague, London, even Berlin—already a pessimistic place. When he came back he wrote a book, you could get from the library even today, *The Jewish Actor Abroad.* If someday you're interested enough in my lonesome years, you could read it. You could absorb a flavor of the man from the book. No, no, I am not mentioned. After all, who am I?

When the book came out I stopped him in the street to say congratulations. But I am not a liar, so I pointed out, too, the egotism of many parts—even the critics said something along such lines.

"Talk is cheap," Vlashkin answered me. "But who are the critics? Tell me, do they create? Not to mention," he continues, "there is a line in Shakespeare in one of the plays from the great history of England. It says, 'Self-loving is not so vile a sin, my liege, as self-neglecting.' This idea also appears in modern times in the moralistic followers of Freud. . . . Rosie, are you listening? You asked a question. By the way, you look very well. How come no wedding ring?"

I walked away from this conversation in tears. But this talking in the street opened the happy road up for more discussions. In regard to many things. . . . For instance, the management—very narrow-minded—wouldn't give him any more certain young men's parts. Fools. What youngest man knew enough about life to be as young as him?

"Rosie, Rosie," he said to me one day, "I see by the clock on your rosy, rosy face you must be thirty."

"The hands are slow, Vlashkin. On a week before Thursday I was thirty-four."

"Is that so? Rosie, I worry about you. It has been on my mind to talk to you. You are losing your time. Do you understand it? A woman should not lose her time."

"Oi, Vlashkin, if you are my friend, what is time?"

For this he had no answer, only looked at me surprised. We went instead, full of interest but not with our former speed, up to my new place on Ninety-fourth Street. The same pictures on the wall, all of Vlashkin, only now everything painted red and black, which was stylish, and new upholstery.

A few years ago there was a book by another member of that fine company, an actress, the one that learned English very good and went uptown—Marya Kavkaz, in which she says certain things regarding Vlashkin. Such as, he was her lover for eleven years, she's not ashamed to write this down. Without respect for him, his wife and children, or even others who also may have feelings in the matter.

Now, Lillie, don't be surprised. This is called a fact of life. An actor's soul must be like a diamond. The more faces it got the more shining is his name. Honey, you will no doubt love and marry one man and have a couple kids and be happy forever till you die tired. More than that, a person like us don't have to know. But a great artist like Volodya Vlashkin . . . in order to make a job on the stage, he's got to practice. I understand it now, to him life is like a rehearsal.

Myself, when I saw him in *The Father-in-law*—an older man in love with a darling young girl, his son's wife, played by Raisele Maisel—I cried. What he said to this girl, how he whispered such sweetness, how all his hot feelings were on his face . . . Lillie, all this experience he had with me. The very words were the same. You can imagine how proud I was.

So the story creeps to an end.

I noticed it first on my mother's face, the rotten handwriting of time, scribbled up and down her cheeks, across her forehead back and forth—a child could read—it said, old, old, old. But it troubled my heart most to see these realities scratched on Vlashkin's wonderful expression.

First the company fell apart. The theater ended. Esther Leopold died from being very aged. Krimberg had a heart attack. Marya went to Broadway. Also Raisele changed her name to Roslyn and was a big comical hit in the movies. Vlashkin himself, no place to go, retired. It said in the paper, "an actor without peer, he will write his memoirs and spend his last years in the bosom of his family among his thriving grandchildren, the apple of his wife's doting eye."

This is journalism.

We made for him a great dinner of honor. At this dinner I said to him, for the last time, I thought, "Goodbye, dear friend, topic of my life, now we part." And to myself I said further: Finished. This is your lonesome bed. A lady what they call fat and fifty. You made it personally. From this lonesome bed you will finally fall to a bed not so lonesome, only crowded with a million bones.

And now comes? Lillie, guess.

Last week, washing my underwear in the basin, I get a buzz on the phone. "Excuse me, is this the Rose Lieber formerly connected with the Russian Art Theater?"

"It is."

"Well, well, how do you, Rose? This is Vlashkin."

"Vlashkin! Volodya Vlashkin?"

"In fact. How are you, Rose?"

"Living, Vlashkin, thank you."

"You are all right? Really, Rose? Your health is good? You are working?"

"My health, considering the weight it must carry, is first-class. I am back for some years now where I started, in novelty wear."

"Very interesting."

"Listen, Vlashkin, tell me the truth, what's on your mind?"

"My mind? Rosie, I am looking up an old friend, an old warmhearted companion of more joyful days. My circumstances, by the way, are changed. I am retired, as you know. Also I am a free man."

"What? What do you mean?"

"Mrs. Vlashkin is divorcing me."

"What come over her? Did you start drinking or something from melancholy?"

"She is divorcing me for adultery."

"But, Vlashkin, you should excuse me, don't be insulted, but you got maybe seventeen, eighteen years on me, and even me, all this nonsense—this daydreams and nightmares—is mostly for the pleasure of conversation alone."

"I pointed all this out to her. My dear, I said, my time is past, my blood is as dry as my bones. The truth is, Rose, she isn't accustomed to have a man around all day, reading out loud from the papers the interesting events of our time, waiting for breakfast, waiting for lunch. So all day she gets madder and madder. By nighttime a furious old lady gives me my supper. She has information from the last fifty years to pepper my soup. Surely there was a Judas in that theater, saying every day, 'Vlashkin, Vlashkin, Vlashkin . . .' and while my heart was circulating with his smiles he was on the wire passing the dope to my wife."

"Such a foolish end, Volodya, to such a lively story. What is your plans?"

"First, could I ask you for dinner and the theater—uptown, of course? After this . . . we are old friends. I have money to burn. What your heart desires. Others are like grass, the north wind of time has cut out their heart. Of you, Rosie, I recreate only kindness. What a woman should be to a man, you were to me. Do you think, Rosie, a couple of old pals like us could have a few good times among the material things of this world?"

My answer, Lillie, in a minute was altogether. "Yes, yes, come up," I said. "Ask the room by the switchboard, let us talk."

So he came that night and every night in the week, we talked of his long life. Even at the end of time, a fascinating man. And like men are, too, till time's end, trying to get away in one piece.

"Listen, Rosie," he explains the other day. "I was married to my wife, do you realize, nearly half a century. What good was it? Look at the bitterness. The more I think of it, the more I think we would be fools to marry."

"Volodya Vlashkin," I told him straight, "when I was young I warmed your cold back many a night, no questions asked. You admit it, I didn't make no demands. I was softhearted. I didn't want to be called Rosie Lieber, a breaker up of homes. But now, Vlashkin, you are a free man. How could you ask me to go with you on trains to stay in strange hotels, among Americans, not your wife? Be ashamed."

So now, darling Lillie, tell this story to your mama from your young mouth. She don't listen to a word from me. She only screams, "I'll faint, I'll faint." Tell her after all I'll have a husband, which, as everybody knows, a woman should have at least one before the end of the story.

My goodness, I am already late. Give me a kiss. After all, I watched you grow from a plain seed. So give me a couple wishes on my wedding day. A long and happy life. Many years of love. Hug Mama, tell her from Aunt Rose, goodbye and good luck.

GRACE PALEY

A Conversation with My Father

My father is eighty-six years old and in bed. His heart, that bloody motor, is equally old and will not do certain jobs any more. It still floods his head with brainy light. But it won't let his legs carry the weight of his body around the house. Despite my metaphors, this muscle failure is not due to his old heart, he says, but to a potassium shortage. Sitting on one pillow, leaning on three, he offers last-minute advice and makes a request.

"I would like you to write a simple story just once more," he says, "the kind Maupassant wrote, or Chekhov, the kind you used to write. Just recognizable people and then write down what happened to them next."

I say, "Yes, why not? That's possible." I want to please him, though I don't remember writing that way. I *would* like to try to tell such a story, if he means the kind that begins: "There was a woman . . ." followed by plot, the absolute line between two points which I've always despised. Not for literary reasons, but because it takes all hope away. Everyone, real or invented, deserves the open destiny of life.

Finally I thought of a story that had been happening for a couple of years right across the street. I wrote it down, then read it aloud. "Pa," I said, "how about this? Do you mean something like this?"

> Once in my time there was a woman and she had a son. They lived nicely, in a small apartment in Manhattan. This boy at about fifteen became a junkie, which is not unusual in our neighborhood. In order to maintain her close friendship with him, she became a junkie too. She said it was part of the youth culture, with which she felt very much at home. After a while, for a number of reasons, the boy gave it all up and left the city and his mother in disgust. Hopeless and alone, she grieved. We all visit her.

"O.K., Pa, that's it," I said, "an unadorned and miserable tale."

"But that's not what I mean," my father said. "You misunderstood me on purpose. You know there's a lot more to it. You know that. You left everything out. Turgenev wouldn't do that. Chekhov wouldn't do that. There are in fact Russian writers you never heard of, you don't have an inkling of, as good as anyone, who can write a plain ordinary story, who would not leave out what you have left out. I object not to facts but to people sitting in trees talking senselessly, voices from who knows where. . . ."

"Forget that one, Pa, what have I left out now? In this one?"

"Her looks, for instance."

"Oh. Quite handsome, I think. Yes."

"Her hair?"

"Dark, with heavy braids, as though she were a girl or a foreigner."

"What were her parents like, her stock? That she became such a person. It's interesting, you know."

"From out of town. Professional people. The first to be divorced in their county. How's that? Enough?" I asked.

"With you, it's all a joke," he said. "What about the boy's father? Why didn't you mention him? Who was he? Or was the boy born out of wedlock?"

"Yes," I said. "He was born out of wedlock."

"For Godsakes, doesn't anyone in your stories get married? Doesn't anyone have the time to run down to City Hall before they jump into bed?"

"No," I said. "In real life, yes. But in my stories, no."

"Why do you answer me like that?"

"Oh, Pa, this is a simple story about a smart woman who came to N.Y.C. full of interest love trust excitement very up-to-date, and about her son, what a hard time she had in this world. Married or not, it's of small consequence."

"It is of great consequence," he said.

"O.K.," I said.

"O.K. O.K. yourself," he said, "but listen. I believe you that she's good looking, but I don't think she was so smart."

"That's true," I said. "Actually that's the trouble with stories. People start out fantastic. You think they're extraordinary, but it turns out as the work goes along, they're just average with a good education. Sometimes the other way around, the person's a kind of dumb innocent, but he outwits you and you can't even think of an ending good enough."

"What do you do then?" he asked. He had been a doctor for a couple of decades and then an artist for a couple of decades and he's still interested in details, craft, technique.

"Well, you just have to let the story lie around till some agreement can be reached between you and the stubborn hero."

"Aren't you talking silly, now?" he asked. "Start again," he said. "It so happens I'm not going out this evening. Tell the story again. See what you can do this time."

"O.K.," I said. "But it's not a five-minute job." Second attempt:

> Once, across the street from us, there was a fine handsome woman, our neighbor. She had a son whom she loved because she'd known him since birth (in helpless chubby infancy, and in the wrestling, hugging ages, seven to ten, as well as earlier and later). This boy, when he fell into the fist of adolescence, became a junkie. He was not a hopeless one. He was in fact hopeful, an ideologue and successful converter. With his busy brilliance, he wrote persuasive articles for his high-school newspaper. Seeking a wider audience, using important connections, he drummed into Lower Manhattan newsstand distribution a periodical called *Oh! Golden Horse!*
>
> In order to keep him from feeling guilty (because guilt is the stony heart of nine tenths of all clinically diagnosed cancers in America today, she said), and because she had always believed in giving bad habits room at home where one could keep an eye on them, she too became a junkie. Her kitchen was famous for a while—a center for intellectual addicts who knew what they were doing. A few felt artistic like Coleridge and others were scientific and revolutionary like Leary. Although she was often high herself, certain good mothering reflexes remained, and she saw to it that there was lots of orange juice around and honey and milk and vitamin pills. However, she never cooked anything but chili, and that no more than once a week. She explained, when we talked to her, seriously, with neighborly concern, that it was her part in the youth culture and she would rather be with the young, it was an honor, than with her own generation.
>
> One week, while nodding through an Antonioni film, this boy was severely jabbed by the elbow of a stern and proselytizing girl, sitting beside him. She offered immediate apricots and nuts for his sugar level, spoke to him sharply, and took him home.

She had heard of him and his work and she herself published, edited, and wrote a competitive journal called *Man Does Live by Bread Alone.* In the organic heat of her continuous presence he could not help but become interested once more in his muscles, his arteries, and nerve connections. In fact he began to love them, treasure them, praise them with funny little songs in *Man Does Live.* . . .

the fingers of my flesh transcend
my transcendental soul
the tightness in my shoulders end
my teeth have made me whole

To the mouth of his head (that glory of will and determination) he brought hard apples, nuts, wheat germ, and soybean oil. He said to his old friends, From now on, I guess I'll keep my wits about me. I'm going on the natch. He said he was about to begin a spiritual deep-breathing journey. How about you too, Mom? he asked kindly.

His conversion was so radiant, splendid, that neighborhood kids his age began to say that he had never been a real addict at all, only a journalist along for the smell of the story. The mother tried several times to give up what had become without her son and his friends a lonely habit. This effort only brought it to supportable levels. The boy and his girl took their electronic mimeograph and moved to the bushy edge of another borough. They were very strict. They said they would not see her again until she had been off drugs for sixty days.

At home alone in the evening, weeping, the mother read and reread the seven issues of *Oh! Golden Horse!* They seemed to her as truthful as ever. We often crossed the street to visit and console. But if we mentioned any of our children who were at college or in the hospital or dropouts at home, she would cry out, My baby! My baby! and burst into terrible, face-scarring, time-consuming tears. The End.

First my father was silent, then he said, "Number One: You have a nice sense of humor. Number Two: I see you can't tell a plain story. So don't waste time." Then he said sadly, "Number Three: I suppose that means she was alone, she was left like that, his mother. Alone. Probably sick?"

I said, "Yes."

"Poor woman. Poor girl, to be born in a time of fools, to live among fools. The end. The end. You were right to put that down. The end."

I didn't want to argue, but I had to say, "Well, it is not necessarily the end, Pa."

"Yes," he said, "what a tragedy. The end of a person."

"No, Pa," I begged him. "It doesn't have to be. She's only about forty. She could be a hundred different things in this world as time goes on. A teacher or a social worker. An ex-junkie! Sometimes it's better than having a master's in education."

"Jokes," he said. "As a writer that's your main trouble. You don't want to recognize it. Tragedy! Plain tragedy! Historical tragedy! No hope. The end."

"Oh, Pa," I said. "She could change."

"In your own life, too, you have to look it in the face." He took a couple of nitroglycerin. "Turn to five," he said, pointing to the dial on the oxygen tank. He inserted the tubes into his nostrils and breathed deep. He closed his eyes and said, "No."

I had promised the family to always let him have the last word when arguing, but in this case I had a different responsibility. That woman lives across the street. She's my knowledge and my invention. I'm sorry for her. I'm not going to leave her there in that house crying. (Actually neither would Life, which unlike me has no pity.)

Therefore: She did change. Of course her son never came home again. But right now, she's the receptionist in a storefront community clinic in the East Village. Most of the customers are young people, some old friends. The head doctor has said to her, "If we only had three people in this clinic with your experiences. . . ."

"The doctor said that?" My father took the oxygen tubes out of his nostrils and said, "Jokes. Jokes again."

"No, Pa, it could really happen that way, it's a funny world nowadays."

"No," he said. "Truth first. She will slide back. A person must have character. She does not."

"No, Pa," I said. "That's it. She's got a job. Forget it. She's in that storefront working."

"How long will it be?" he asked. "Tragedy! You too. When will you look it in the face?"

George Saunders (*1958–*),

born in Amarillo, Texas, and raised in Chicago, first got the idea to become a writer when his salesman father bought him books such as Upton Sinclair's The Jungle *and Machiavelli's* The Prince *but equally so when he listened to his father's "epic comic tales of the various hustlers and lunatics he ran into on his rounds." Saunders decided instead to become a geophysical engineer, graduating from the Colorado School of Mines and landing a job in Sumatra. After extensive travel thoughout Malaysia, Thailand, Russia, and Pakistan, Saunders contracted a virus that caused him to sleep fifteen hours a night; he quit his job, returned to the United States, and worked as a doorman in Beverly Hills, a roofer in Chicago, a musician, and a slaughterhouse laborer before returning to school and getting an MFA in creative writing from Syracuse University. He wrote his first collection of stories,* CivilWarLand in Bad Decline *(a finalist for the PEN/Hemingway Award), while working as a technical writer and engineer at an environmental engineering company in Rochester, New York. The stories were "little shouts," he says, "written when I was supposed to be writing technical reports or on the bus or late at night. The darkness and satire come, I guess, from the prevailing mode of storytelling on the south side of Chicago where, if you want to tell someone you love him, you generally pretend to knee him in the groin, then throw him in the pool while guffawing." He returned to Syracuse as a professor in the writing program, and in 2000 published his second collection,* Pastoralia; *every story in the book had been published in* The New Yorker. *That same year, he collaborated with illustrator Lane Smith on a children's book,* The Very Persistent Gappers of Frip.

INTRODUCTION BY **Aimee Bender**

George Saunders! George Saunders!

Those of us who love George Saunders (which is really a whole lot of people) love him with that kind of exclamation-pointed enthusiasm. Critics talk about how Saunders's world is so bleak and scarily American, but the heart is beating hard inside these stories, so that even inside our cubicles, lost in our theme parks, trapped in our lingo, beaten down by our plasticine shirts, we are crying out in there, somewhere, and dammit, he is going to flush our humanity out. In that way, his work is a kind of war cry against the freakish apathy and impotence that seem to be a signature for our times, an antidote to that modernistic alienation that Andrew Solomon talks about as one of the increasing sources of depression. Saunders puts this world—our world—under the most scathing of microscopes; he does not spare his characters, and his dialogue is heart-sinking and embarrassingly familiar. I talk like that. I know a million people who talk like that. I watch those shows. We are these people. And in the reflection, ugly as it may be, inside the wince, is a clarity.

How does he do it? He is able to *sustain* the inanity to reach depth. This is where he amazes. Saunders is one of those writers you want to imitate because he makes it look so easy! But only in the attempt to imitate does one realize how artful is the sustaining quality of his prose, how artful is his swift and biting characterization. In "Sea Oak," he throws hilarious conceptual ideas out there—the kid working at a strip lunch joint, the complex where they live—"no sea and no oak"—the aunt's job at DrugTown, but all of this could burn out in a page or two. That is, if you are another person. Saunders inserts the slow build of real characterization into the absurdity, and so each idea, which is so funny that it *seems* like enough, ends up delivering a wallop of depth. The strip job becomes our entryway into the narrator's emotional world, the apartment complex fuels the entire story's movement, the aunt's over-the-top martyrdom turns inside out. He wrings and uses what he has put out there, and this is what makes it go far beyond clever, and this is why a whole world of people want to imitate George Saunders but find that it is impossible. His literary fingerprint is real.

Here's another thing, and it contains some spoilers, so don't read it until you have first read "CivilWarLand in Bad Decline" unless you don't care. I remember the feeling, reading the story for the first time, that I knew what was going to happen. About three-quarters of the way through, I thought, "Oh, Sam is in the woods, he's going to shoot someone, and that'll be that." And truly, the minute I thought it, the minute the world of TV drama and plot savviness popped into my head, that's what happened in the story. I don't mean this as some kind of psychic moment; what I mean is that Saunders does not withhold from his reader. What I thought was the end was not the end, it was the near-end, which completely rearranged my readership. This allows for total unpredictability and a real sense of reader-writer trust, because Saunders knows, as we know, that we are a jaded audience and that if a plot move is looming, we will guess it. So he hands it right over and moves on from there. What freedom! What teaching in that!

In fact, his invented worlds are built on that trust, that inside knowledge. He knows that we know about the ridiculous slogans we live with, about the store chains and corporate TV-land rituals. He knows that we are sick of all of it but that we have become so accustomed to this world that we expect art to just slide into line. We are resigned to our world-weariness. So everything about Saunders's work—plot, character, and detail—addresses this reader proficiency and then moves beyond it. It's a tremendous gift because it is deeply funny, then, for a range of ages, and it can really save a bored fourteen-year-old reader from his own sense that all has been done and, dude, every famous story has been remade on TV anyway. That's modernistic depression for you. That's why we *need* Saunders. Exclamation point.

Aimee Bender is the author of The Girl in the Flammable Skirt *and* An Invisible Sign of My Own.

GEORGE SAUNDERS

CivilWarLand in Bad Decline

Whenever a potential big investor comes for the tour the first thing I do is take him out to the transplanted Erie Canal Lock. We've got a good ninety feet of actual Canal out there and a well-researched dioramic of a coolie campsite. Were our faces ever red when we found out it was actually the Irish who built the Canal. We've got no budget to correct, so every fifteen minutes or so a device in the bunkhouse gives off the approximate aroma of an Oriental meal.

Today my possible Historical Reconstruction Associate is Mr. Haberstrom, founder of Burn'n'Learn. Burn'n'Learn is national. Their gimmick is a fully stocked library on the premises and as you tan you call out the name of any book you want to these high-school girls on roller skates. As we walk up the trail he's wearing a sweatsuit and smoking a cigar and I tell him I admire his acumen. I tell him some men are dreamers and others are doers. He asks which am I and I say let's face it, I'm basically the guy who leads the dreamers up the trail to view the Canal Segment. He likes that. He says I have a good head on my shoulders. He touches my arm and says he's hot to spend some reflective moments at the Canal because his great-grandfather was a barge guider way back when who got killed by a donkey. When we reach the clearing he gets all emotional and bolts off through the gambling plaster Chinese. Not to be crass but I sense an impending sizable contribution.

When I come up behind him however I see that once again the gangs have been at it with their spray cans, all over my Lock. Haberstrom takes a nice long look. Then he pokes me with the spiny end of his cigar and says not with his money I don't, and storms back down the trail.

I stand there alone a few minutes. The last thing I need is some fat guy's spit on my tie. I think about quitting. Then I think about my last degrading batch of résumés. Two hundred send-outs and no nibbles. My feeling is that prospective employers are put off by the fact that I was a lowly Verisimilitude Inspector for nine years with no promotions. I think of my car payment. I think of how much Marcus and Howie love the little playhouse I'm still paying off. Once again I decide to eat my pride and sit tight.

So I wipe off my tie with a leaf and start down to break the Haberstrom news to Mr. Alsuga.

Mr. A's another self-made man. He cashed in on his love of history by conceptualizing CivilWarLand in his spare time. He started out with just a settler's shack and one Union costume and now has considerable influence in Rotary.

His office is in City Hall. He agrees that the gangs are getting out of hand. Last month they wounded three Visitors and killed a dray horse. Several of them encircled and made fun of Mrs. Dugan in her settler outfit as she was taking her fresh-baked bread over to the simulated Towne Meeting. No way they're paying admission, so they're either tunneling in or coming in over the retaining wall.

Mr. Alsuga believes the solution to the gang problem is Teen Groups. I tell him that's basically what a gang is, a Teen Group. But he says how can it be a Teen Group without an adult mentor with a special skill, like whittling? Mr. Alsuga whittles. Once he gave an Old Tyme Skills Seminar on it in the Blacksmith Shoppe. It was poorly attended. All he got was two widowers and a chess-club type no gang would have wanted anyway. And myself. I attended. Evelyn called me a bootlicker, but I attended. She called me a bootlicker, and I told her she'd better bear in mind which side of the bread her butter was on. She said whichever side it was on it wasn't enough to shake a stick at. She's always denigrating my paystub. I came home from the Seminar with this kind of whittled duck. She threw it away the next day because she said she thought it was an acorn. It looked nothing like an acorn. As far as I'm concerned she threw it away out of spite. It made me livid and twice that night I had to step into a closet and perform my Hatred Abatement Breathing.

But that's neither here nor there.

Mr. Alsuga pulls out the summer stats. We're in the worst attendance decline in ten years. If it gets any worse, staff is going to be let go in droves. He gives me a meaningful look. I know full well I'm not one of his key players. Then he asks who we have that might be willing to fight fire with fire.

I say: I could research it.

He says: Why don't you research it?

So I go research it.

Sylvia Loomis is the queen of info. It's in her personality. She enjoys digging up dirt on people. She calls herself an S&M buff in training. She's still too meek to go whole hog, so when she parties at the Make Me Club on Airport Road she limits herself to walking around talking mean while wearing kiddie handcuffs. But she's good at what she does, which is Security. It was Sylvia who identified the part-timer systematically crapping in the planters in the Gift Acquisition Center and Sylvia who figured out it was Phil in Grounds leaving obscene messages for the Teen Belles on MessageMinder. She has access to all records. I ask can she identity current employees with a history of violence. She says she can if I buy her lunch.

We decide to eat in-Park. We go over to Nate's Saloon. Sylvia says don't spread it around but two of the nine can-can girls are knocked up. Then she pulls out her folder and says that according to her review of the data, we have a pretty tame bunch on our hands. The best she can do is Ned Quinn. His records indicate that while in high school he once burned down a storage shed. I almost die laughing. Quinn's an Adjunct Thespian and a world-class worry-wart. I can't count the times I've come upon him in Costuming, dwelling on the gory details of his Dread Disease Rider. He's a failed actor who won't stop trying. He says this is the only job he could find that would allow him to continue to develop his craft. Because he's ugly as sin he specializes in roles that require masks, such as Humpty-Dumpty during Mother Goose Days.

I report back to Mr. Alsuga and he says Quinn may not be much but he's all we've got. Quinn's dirt-poor with six kids and Mr. A says that's a plus, as we'll need someone between a rock and a hard place. What he suggests we do is equip the Desperate Patrol with live ammo and put Quinn in charge. The Desperate Patrol limps along under floodlights as the night's crowning event. We've costumed them to resemble troops who've been in the field too long. We used actual Gettysburg photos. The climax of the Patrol is a re-enacted partial rebellion, quelled by a rousing speech. After the speech the boys take off their hats and put their arms around each other and sing "I Was Born Under a Wandering Star." Then there's fireworks and the Parade of Old-Fashioned Conveyance. Then we clear the place out and go home.

"Why not confab with Quinn?" Mr. A says. "Get his input and feelings."

"I was going to say that," I say.

I look up the Thespian Center's SpeedDial extension and a few minutes later Quinn's bounding up the steps in the Wounded Grizzly suit.

"Desperate Patrol?" Mr. A says as Quinn sits down. "Any interest on your part?"

"Love it." Quinn says. "Excellent." He's been trying to get on Desperate Patrol for years. It's considered the pinnacle by the Thespians because of the wealth of speaking parts. He's so excited he's shifting around in his seat and getting some of his paw blood on Mr. A's nice cane chair.

"The gangs in our park are a damn blight," Mr. A says. "I'm talking about meeting force with force. Something in it for you? Oh yes."

"I'd like to see Quinn give the rousing speech myself," I say.

"Societal order," Mr. A says. "Sustaining the lifeblood of this goddamned park we've all put so much of our hearts into."

"He's not just free-associating," I say.

"I'm not sure I get it," Quinn says.

"What I'm suggesting is live ammo in your weapon only," Mr. A says. "Fire at your discretion. You see an unsavory intruder, you shoot at his feet. Just give him a scare. Nobody gets hurt. An additional two bills a week is what I'm talking."

"I'm an actor," Quinn says.

"Quinn's got kids," I say. "He knows the value of a buck."

"This is acting of the highest stripe," Mr. A says. "Act like a mercenary."

"Go for it on a trial basis," I say.

"I'm not sure I get it," Quinn says. "But jeez, that's good money."

"Superfantastic," says Mr. A.

Next evening Mr. A and I go over the Verisimilitude Irregularities List. We've been having some heated discussions about our bird-species percentages. Mr. Grayson, Staff Ornithologist, has recently recalculated and estimates that to accurately approximate the 1865 bird population we'll need to eliminate a couple hundred orioles or so. He suggests using air guns or poison. Mr. A says that in his eyes, in fiscally troubled times, an ornithologist is a luxury, and this may be the perfect time to send Grayson packing. I like Grayson. He went way overboard on Howie's baseball candy. But I've got me and mine to think of. So I call Grayson in. Mr. A says did you botch the initial calculation or were you privy to new info. Mr. Grayson admits it was a botch. Mr. A sends him out into the hall and we confab.

"You'll do the telling," Mr. A says. "I'm getting too old for cruelty."

He takes his walking stick and beeper and says he'll be in the Great Forest if I need him.

I call Grayson back in and let him go, and hand him Kleenexes and fend off a few blows and almost before I know it he's reeling out the door and I go grab a pita.

Is this the life I envisioned for myself? My God no. I wanted to be a high jumper. But I have two of the sweetest children ever born. I go in at night and look at them in their fairly expensive sleepers and think: There are a couple of kids who don't need to worry about freezing to death or being cast out to the wolves. You should see their little eyes light up when I bring home a treat. They may not know the value of a dollar but it's my intention to see that they never need to.

I'm filling out Grayson's Employee Retrospective when I hear gunshots from the perimeter. I run out and there's Quinn and a few of his men tied to the cannon. The gangs took Quinn's pants and put some tiny notches in his penis with their knives. I free Quinn and tell him to get over to the Infirmary to guard against infection. He's absolutely shaking and can hardly walk, so I wrap him up in a Confederate flag and call over a hay cart and load him in.

When I tell Mr. A he says: Garbage in, garbage out, and that we were idiots for expecting a milquetoast to save our rears.

We decide to leave the police out of it because of the possible bad PR. So we give Quinn the rest of the week off and promise to let him play Grant now and then, and that's that.

When visitors first come in there's this cornball part where they sit in this kind of spaceship and supposedly get blasted into space and travel faster than the speed of light and end up in 1865. The unit's dated. The helmets we distribute look like bowls and all the paint's peeling off. I've argued and argued that we need to update. But in the midst of a budget crunch one can't necessarily hang the moon.

When the tape of space sounds is over and the walls stop shaking, we pass out the period costumes. We try not to offend anyone, liability law being what it is. We distribute the slave and Native American roles equitably among racial groups. Anyone is free to request a different identity at any time. In spite of our precautions, there's a Herlicher in every crowd. He's the guy who sued us last fall for making him hangman. He claimed that for weeks afterwards he had nightmares and because he wasn't getting enough sleep botched a big contract by sending an important government buyer a load of torn pool liners. Big deal, is my feeling. But he's suing us for fifty grand for emotional stress because the buyer ridiculed him in front of his co-workers. Whenever he comes in we make him sheriff but he won't back down an inch.

Mr. A calls me into his office and says he's got bad news and bad news, and which do I want first. I say the bad news. First off, he says, the gangs have spraypainted a picture of Quinn's notched penis on the side of the Everly Mansion. Second, last Friday's simulated frontier hunt has got us in hot water, because apparently some of the beef we toughen up to resemble buffalo meat was tainted, and the story's going in the Sunday supplement. And finally, the verdict's come in on the Herlicher case and we owe that goofball a hundred grand instead of fifty because the pinko judge empathized.

I wait for him to say I'm fired but instead he breaks down in tears. I pat his back and mix him a drink. He says why don't I join him. So I join him.

"It doesn't look good," he says, "for men like you and I."

"No it doesn't," I say.

"All I wanted to do," he says, "was to give the public a meaningful perspective on a historical niche I've always found personally fascinating."

"I know what you mean," I say.

At eleven the phone rings. It's Maurer in Refuse Control calling to say that the gangs have set fire to the Anglican Church. That structure cost upwards of ninety thousand to transport from Clydesville and refurbish. We can see the flames from Mr. A's window.

"Oh Christ!" Mr. A says. "If I could kill those kids I would kill those kids. One shouldn't desecrate the dream of another individual in the fashion in which they have mine."

"I know it," I say.

We drink and drink and finally he falls asleep on his office couch.

On the way to my car I keep an eye out for the ghostly McKinnon family. Back in the actual 1860s all this land was theirs. Their homestead's long gone but our records indicate that it was located near present-day Information Hoedown. They probably never saw this many buildings in their entire lives. They don't realize we're chronically slumming, they just think the valley's prospering. Something bad must have happened to them because their spirits are always wandering around at night looking dismayed.

Tonight I find the Mrs. doing wash by the creek. She sees me coming and asks if she can buy my boots. Machine stitching amazes her. I ask how are the girls. She says Maribeth has been sad because no appropriate boy ever died in the valley so she's doomed to loneliness forever. Maribeth is a homely sincere girl who glides around mooning and pining and reading bad poetry chapbooks. Whenever we keep the Park open late for high-school parties, she's in her glory. There was one kid who was able to see her and even got a crush on her, but when he finally tried to kiss her near Hostelry and found out she was spectral it just about killed him. I slipped him a fifty and told him to keep it under wraps. As far as I know he's still in therapy. I realize I should have come forward but they probably would have nut-hutted me, and then where would my family be?

The Mrs. says what Maribeth needs is choir practice followed by a nice quilting bee. In better times I would have taken the quilting-bee idea and run with it. But now there's no budget. That's basically how I finally moved up from Verisimilitude Inspector to Special Assistant, by lifting ideas from the McKinnons. The Mrs. likes me because after she taught me a few obscure 1800s ballads and I parlayed them into Individual Achievement Awards, I bought her a Rubik's Cube. To her, colored plastic is like something from Venus. The Mr. has kind of warned me away from her a couple of times. He doesn't trust me. He thinks the Rubik's Cube is the devil's work. I've brought him lighters and *Playboys* and once I even dragged out Howie's little synth and the mobile battery pak. I set the synth for carillon and played it from behind a bush. I could tell he was tickled, but he stonewalled. It's too bad I can't make an inroad because he was at Antietam and could be a gold mine of war info. He came back from the war and a year later died in his cornfield, which is now Parking. So he spends most of his time out there calling the cars Beelzebubs and kicking their tires.

Tonight he's walking silently up and down the rows. I get out to my KCar and think oh jeez, I've locked the keys in. The Mr. sits down at the base of the A3 lightpole and asks did I see the fire and do I realize it was divine retribution for my slovenly moral state. I say thank you very much. No way I'm telling him about the gangs. He can barely handle the concept of women wearing trousers. Finally I give up on prying the window down and go call Evelyn for the spare set. While I wait for her I sit on the hood and watch the stars. The Mr. watches them too. He says there are fewer than when he was a boy. He says that even the heavens have fallen into disrepair. I think about explaining smog to him but then Evelyn pulls up. She's wearing her bathrobe and as soon as she gets out starts with the lip. Howie and Marcus are asleep in the back. The Mr. says it's part and parcel of my fallen state that I allow a woman to speak to me in such a tone. He suggests I throttle her and lock her in the woodshed. Meanwhile she's going on and on so much about my irresponsibility that the kids are waking up. I want to get out before the gangs come swooping down on us. The Parking Area's easy pickings. She calls me a thoughtless oaf and sticks me in the gut with the car keys.

Marcus wakes up all groggy and says: Hey, our daddy.

Evelyn says: Yes, unfortunately he is.

Just after lunch next day a guy shows up at Personnel looking so completely Civil War they immediately hire him and send him out to sit on the porch of the old Kriegal place with a butter churn. His name's Samuel and he doesn't say a word going through Costuming and at the end of the day leaves on a bike. I do the normal clandestine New Employee Observation from the O'Toole gazebo and I like what I see. He seems to have a passable knowledge of how to pretend to churn butter At one point he makes the mistake of departing from the list of Then-Current Events to discuss the World Series with a Visitor, but my feeling is, we can work with that. All in all he presents a positive and convincing appearance, and I say so in my review.

Sylvia runs her routine check on him and calls me at home that night and says boy do we have a hot prospect on our hands if fucking with the gangs is still on our agenda. She talks like that. I've got her on speakerphone in the rec room and Marcus starts running around the room saying fuck. Evelyn stands there with her arms crossed, giving me a drop-dead look. I wave her off and she flips me the bird.

Sylvia's federal sources indicate that Samuel got kicked out of Vietnam for participating in a bloodbath. Sylvia claims this is oxymoronic. She sounds excited. She suggests I take a nice long look at his marksmanship scores. She says his special combat course listing goes on for pages.

I call Mr. A and he says it sounds like Sam's our man. I express reservations at arming an alleged war criminal and giving him free rein in a family-oriented facility. Mr. A says if we don't get our act together there won't be any family-oriented facility left in a month. Revenues have hit rock bottom and his investors are frothing at the mouth. There's talk of outright closure and liquidation of assets.

He says: Now get off your indefensible high horse and give me Sam's home phone.

So I get off my indefensible high horse and give him Sam's home phone.

Thursday after we've armed Samuel and sent him and the Patrol out, I stop by the Worship Center to check on the Foley baptism. Baptisms are an excellent revenue source. We charge three hundred dollars to rent the Center, which is the former lodge of the Siala utopian free-love community. We trucked it in from downstate, a redbrick building with a nice gold dome. In the old days if one of the Sialians was overeating to the exclusion of others or excessively masturbating, he or she would be publicly dressed down for hours on end in the lodge. Now we put up white draperies and pipe in Stephen Foster and provide at no charge a list of preachers of various denominations.

The Foleys are an overweight crew. The room's full of crying sincere large people wishing the best for a baby. It makes me remember our own sweet beaners in their little frocks. I sit down near the wood-burning heater in the Invalid area and see that Justin in Prep has forgotten to remove the mannequin elderly couple clutching rosaries. Hopefully the Foleys won't notice and withhold payment.

The priest dips the baby's head into the fake marble basin and the door flies open and in comes a racially mixed gang. They stroll up the aisle tousling hair and requisition a Foley niece, a cute redhead of about sixteen. Her dad stands up and gets a blackjack in the head. One of the gang guys pushes her down the aisle with his hands on her breasts. As she passes she looks right at me. The gang guy spits on my shoe and I make my face neutral so he won't get hacked off and drag me into it.

The door slams and the Foleys sit there stunned. Then the baby starts crying and everyone runs shouting outside in time to see the gang dragging the niece into the woods. I panic. I try to think of where the nearest pay phone is. I'm weighing the efficiency of running to Administration and making the call from my cubicle when six fast shots come from the woods. Several of the oldest Foleys assume the worst and drop weeping to their knees in the churchyard.

I don't know the first thing about counseling survivors, so I run for Mr. A.

He's drinking and watching his bigscreen. I tell him what happened and he jumps up and calls the police. Then he says let's go do whatever little we can for these poor people who entrusted us with their sacred family occasion only to have us drop the ball by failing to adequately protect them.

When we get back to the churchyard the Foleys are kicking and upbraiding six gang corpses. Samuel's having a glass of punch with the niece. The niece's dad is hanging all over Sam trying to confirm his daughter's virginity. Sam says it wasn't even close and goes on and on about the precision of his scope.

Then we hear sirens.

Sam says: I'm going into the woods.

Mr. A says: We never saw you, big guy.

The niece's dad says: Bless you, sir.

Sam says: Adios.

Mr. A stands on the hitching post and makes a little speech, the gist of which is, let's blame another gang for killing these dirtbags so Sam can get on with his important work.

The Foleys agree.

The police arrive and we all lie like rugs.

The word spreads on Sam and the gangs leave us alone. For two months the Park is quiet and revenues start upscaling. Then some high-school kid pulls a butter knife on Fred Moore and steals a handful of penny candy from the General Store. As per specs, Fred alerts Mr. A of a Revenue-Impacting Event. Mr. A calls Security and we perform Exit Sealage. We look everywhere, but the kid's gone. Mr. A says what the hell, Unseal, it's just candy, profit loss is minimal. Sam hears the Unseal Tone on the PA and comes out of the woods all mad with his face painted and says that once the word gets out we've gone soft the gangs will be back in a heartbeat. I ask since when do gangs use butter knives. Sam says a properly trained individual can kill a wild boar with a butter knife. Mr. A gives me a look and says why don't we let Sam run this aspect of the operation since he possesses the necessary expertise. Then Mr. A offers to buy him lunch and Sam says no, he'll eat raw weeds and berries as usual.

I go back to my Verisimilitude Evaluation on the Cimarron Brothel. Everything looks super. As per my recommendations they've replaced the young attractive simulated whores with uglier women with a little less on the ball. We were able to move the ex-simulated whores over to the Sweete Shoppe, so everybody's happy, especially the new simulated whores, who were for the most part middle-aged women we lured away from fast-food places via superior wages.

When I've finished the Evaluation I go back to my office for lunch. I step inside and turn on the fake oil lamp and there's a damn human hand on my chair, holding a note. All around the hand there's penny candy. The note says: Sir, another pig disciplined who won't mess with us anymore and also I need more ammo. It's signed: Samuel the Rectifier.

I call Mr. A and he says Jesus. Then he tells me to bury the hand in the marsh behind Refreshments. I say shouldn't we call the police. He says we let it pass when it was six dead kids, why should we start getting moralistic now over one stinking hand?

I say: But sir, he killed a high-schooler for stealing candy.

He says: That so-called high-schooler threatened Fred Moore, a valued old friend of mine, with a knife.

A butter knife, I say.

He asks if I've seen the droves of unemployed huddled in front of Personnel every morning.

I ask if that's a threat and he says no, it's a reasonable future prognostication.

"What's done is done," he says. "We're in this together. If I take the fall on this, you'll eat the wienie as well. Let's just put this sordid ugliness behind us and get on with the business of providing an enjoyable living for those we love."

I hang up and sit looking at the hand. There's a class ring on it.

Finally I knock it into a garbage sack with my phone and go out to the marsh.

As I'm digging, Mr. McKinnon glides up. He gets down on his knees and starts sniffing the sack. He starts talking about bloody wagon wheels and a boy he once saw sitting in a creek slapping the water with his own severed arm. He tells how the dead looked with rain on their faces and of hearing lunatic singing from all corners of the field of battle and of king-sized rodents gorging themselves on the entrails of his friends.

It occurs to me that the Mr.'s a loon.

I dig down a couple feet and drop the hand in. Then I backfill and get out of there fast. I look over my shoulder and he's rocking back and forth over the hole mumbling to himself.

As I pass a sewer cover the Mrs. rises out of it. Seeing the Mr. enthralled by blood she starts shrieking and howling to beat the band. When she finally calms down she comes to rest in a tree branch. Tears run down her see-through cheeks. She says there's been a horrid violent seed in him since he came home from the war. She says she can see they're going to have to go away. Then she blasts over my head elongate and glowing and full of grief and my hat gets sucked off.

All night I have bad dreams about severed hands. In one I'm eating chili and a hand comes out of my bowl and gives me the thumbs-down. I wake up with a tingling wrist. Evelyn says if I insist on sleeping uneasily would I mind doing it on the couch, since she has a family to care for during the day and this requires a certain amount of rest. I think about confessing to her but then I realize if I do she'll nail me.

The nights when she'd fall asleep with her cheek on my thigh are certainly long past.

I lie there awhile watching her make angry faces in her sleep. Then I go for a walk. As usual Mr. Ebershom's practicing figure-skating moves in his foyer. I sit down by our subdivision's fake creek and think. First of all, burying a hand isn't murder. It doesn't say anywhere thou shalt not bury some guy's hand. By the time I got involved the kid was dead. Where his hand ended up is inconsequential.

Then I think: What am I saying? I did a horrible thing. Even as I sit here I'm an accomplice and an obstructor of justice.

But then I see myself in the penitentiary and the boys waking up scared in the night without me, and right then and there with my feet in the creek I decide to stay clammed up forever and take my lumps in the afterlife.

Halloween's special in the Park. Our brochure says: Lose Yourself in Eerie Autumnal Splendor. We spray cobwebs around the Structures and dress up Staff in ghoul costumes and hand out period-authentic treats. We hide holograph generators in the woods and project images of famous Americans as ghosts. It's always a confusing time for the McKinnons. Last year the Mr. got in a head-to-head with the image of Jefferson Davis. He stood there in the woods yelling at it for hours while the Mrs. and the girls begged him to come away. Finally I had to cut power to the unit.

I drive home at lunch and pick the boys up for trick-or-treating. Marcus is a rancher and Howie's an accountant. He's wearing thick fake lips and carrying a ledger. The Park's the only safe place to trick-or-treat anymore. Last year some wacko in a complex near our house laced his Snickers with a virus. I drove by the school and they were CPRing this little girl in a canary suit. So forget it.

I take them around to the various Structures and they pick up their share of saltwater taffy and hard tasteless frontier candy and wooden whistles and toy soldiers made of soap.

Then just as we start across the Timeless Green a mob of teens bursts out of the Feinstein Memorial Conifer Grove.

"Gangs!" I yell to the boys. "Get down!"

I hear a shot and look up and there's Samuel standing on a stump at tree line. Thank God, I think. He lets loose another round and one of the teens drops. Marcus is down beside me whimpering with his nose in my armpit. Howie's always been the slow one. He stands there with his mouth open, one hand in his plastic pumpkin. A second teen drops. Then Howie drops and his pumpkin goes flying.

I crawl over and beg him to be okay. He says there's no pain. I check him over and check him over and all that's wrong is his ledger's been shot. I'm so relieved I kiss him on the mouth and he yells at me to quit.

Samuel drops a third teen, then runs yipping into the woods.

The ambulance shows up and the paramedics load up the wounded teens. They're all still alive and one's saying a rosary. I take the boys to City Hall and confront Mr. A. I tell him I'm turning Sam in. He asks if I've gone daft and suggests I try putting food on the table from a jail cell while convicts stand in line waiting to have their way with my rear.

At this point I send the boys out to the foyer.

"He shot Howie." I say. "I want him put away."

"He shot Howie's ledger," Mr. A says. "He shot Howie's ledger in the process of saving Howie's life. But whatever. Let's not mince hairs. If Sam gets put away, we get put away. Does that sound to you like a desirable experience?"

"No," I say.

"What I'm primarily saying," he says, "is that this is a time for knowledge assimilation, not backstabbing. We learned a lesson, you and I. We personally grew. Gratitude for this growth is an appropriate response. Gratitude, and being careful never to make the same mistake twice."

He gets out a Bible and says let's swear on it that we'll never hire a crazed maniac to perform an important security function again. Then the phone rings. Sylvia's cross-referenced today's Admissions data and found that the teens weren't a gang at all but a bird-watching group who made the mistake of being male and adolescent and wandering too far off the trail.

"Ouch," Mr. A says. "This could be a serious negative."

In the foyer the kids are trying to get the loaches in the corporate tank to eat bits of Styrofoam. I phone Evelyn and tell her what happened and she calls me a butcher. She wants to know how on earth I could bring the boys to the Park knowing what I knew. She says she doesn't see how I'm going to live with myself in light of how much they trusted and loved me and how badly I let them down by leaving their fates to chance.

I say I'm sorry and she seems to be thinking. Then she tells me just get them home without putting them in further jeopardy, assuming that's within the scope of my mental powers.

At home she puts them in the tub and sends me out for pizza. I opt for Melvin's Pasta Lair. Melvin's a religious zealot who during the Depression worked five jobs at once. Sometimes I tell him my troubles and he says I should stop whining and count my blessings. Tonight I tell him I feel I should take some responsibility for eliminating the Samuel problem but I'm hesitant because of the discrepancy in our relative experience in violence. He says you mean you're scared. I say not scared, just aware of the likelihood of the possibility of failure. He gives me a look. I say it must have been great to grow up when men were men. He says men have always been what they are now, namely incapable of coping with life without the intervention of God the Almighty. Then in the oven behind him my pizza starts smoking and he says case in point.

He makes me another and urges me to get in touch with my Lord personally. I tell him I will. I always tell him I will.

When I get home they're gone.

Evelyn's note says: I could never forgive you for putting our sons at risk. Goodbye forever, you passive flake. Don't try to find us. I've told the kids you sent us away in order to marry a floozy.

Like an idiot I run out to the street. Mrs. Schmidt is prodding her automatic sprinkler system with a rake, trying to detect leaks in advance. She asks how I am and I tell her not now. I sit on the lawn. The stars are very near. The phone rings. I run inside prepared to grovel, but it's only Mr. A. He says come down to the Park immediately because he's got big horrific news.

When I get there he's sitting in his office half-crocked. He tells me we're unemployed. The investors have gotten wind of the bird-watcher shootings and withdrawn all support. The Park is no more. I tell him about Evelyn and the kids. He says that's the least of his worries because he's got crushing debt. He asks if I have any savings he could have. I say no. He says that just for the record and my own personal development, he's always found me dull and has kept me around primarily for my yes-man capabilities and because sometimes I'm so cautious I'm a hoot.

Then he says: Look, get your ass out, I'm torching this shithole for insurance purposes.

I want to hit or at least insult him, but I need this week's pay to find my kids. So I jog off through the Park. In front of Information Hoedown I see the McKinnons cavorting. I get closer and see that they're not cavorting at all, they've inadvertently wandered too close to their actual death site and are being compelled to act out again and again the last minutes of their lives. The girls are lying side by side on the ground and the Mr. is whacking at them with an invisible scythe. The Mrs. is belly-up with one arm flailing in what must have been the parlor. The shrieking is mind-boggling. When he's killed everyone the Mr. walks out to his former field and mimes blowing out his brains. Then he gets up and starts over. It goes on and on, through five cycles. Finally he sits down in the dirt and starts weeping. The Mrs. and the girls backpedal away. He gets up and follows them, pitifully trying to explain.

Behind us the Visitor Center erupts in flames.

The McKinnons go off down the hill, passing through bushes and trees. He's shouting for forgiveness. He's shouting that he's just a man. He's shouting that hatred and war made him nuts. I start running down the hill agreeing with him. The Mrs. gives me a look and puts her hands over Maribeth's ears. We're all running. The Mrs. starts screaming about the feel of the scythe as it opened her up.

The girls bemoan their unborn kids. We make quite a group. Since I'm still alive I keep clipping trees with my shoulders and falling down.

At the bottom of the hill they pass through the retaining wall and I run into it. I wake up on my back in the culvert. Blood's running out of my ears and a transparent boy's kneeling over me. I can tell he's no McKinnon because he's wearing sweatpants.

"Get up now," he says in a gentle voice. "Fire's coming."

"No," I say. "I'm through. I'm done living."

"I don't think so," he says. "You've got amends to make."

"I screwed up." I say. "I did bad things."

"No joke," he says, and holds up his stump.

I roll over into the culvert muck and he grabs me by the collar and sits me up.

"I steal four jawbreakers and a Slim Jim and your friend kills and mutilates me?" he says.

"He wasn't my friend," I say.

"He wasn't your enemy," the kid says.

Then he cocks his head. Through his clear skull I see Sam coming out of the woods. The kid cowers behind me. Even dead he's scared of Sam. He's so scared he blasts straight up in the air shrieking and vanishes over the retaining wall.

Sam comes for me with a hunting knife.

"Don't take this too personal," he says, "but you've got to go. You know a few things I don't want broadcast."

I'm madly framing calming words in my head as he drives the knife in. I can't believe it. Never again to see my kids? Never again to sleep and wake to their liquid high voices and sweet breaths?

Sweet Evelyn, I think, I should have loved you better.

Possessing perfect knowledge I hover above him as he hacks me to bits. I see his rough childhood. I see his mother doing something horrid to him with a broomstick. I see the hate in his heart and the people he has yet to kill before pneumonia gets him at eighty-three. I see the dead kid's mom unable to sleep, pounding her fists against her face in grief at the moment I was burying her son's hand. I see the pain I've caused. I see the man I could have been, and the man I was, and then everything is bright and new and keen with love and I sweep through Sam's body, trying to change him, trying so hard, and feeling only hate and hate, solid as stone.

George Saunders

Sea Oak

At six Mr. Frendt comes on the P.A. and shouts, "Welcome to Joysticks!" Then he announces Shirts Off. We take off our flight jackets and fold them up. We take off our shirts and fold them up. Our scarves we leave on. Thomas Kirster's our beautiful boy. He's got long muscles and bright-blue eyes. The minute his shirt comes off two fat ladies hustle up the aisle and stick some money in his pants and ask will he be their Pilot. He says sure. He brings their salads. He brings their soups. My phone rings and the caller tells me to come see her in the Spitfire mock-up. Does she want me to be her Pilot? I'm hoping. Inside the Spitfire is Margie, who says she's been diagnosed with Chronic Shyness Syndrome, then hands me an Instamatic and offers me ten bucks for a close-up of Thomas's tush.

Do I do it? Yes I do.

It could be worse. It is worse for Lloyd Betts. Lately he's put on weight and his hair's gone thin. He doesn't get a call all shift and waits zero tables and winds up sitting on the P-51 wing, playing solitaire in a hunched-over position that gives him big gut rolls.

I Pilot six tables and make forty dollars in tips plus five an hour in salary.

After closing we sit on the floor for Debriefing. "There are times," Mr. Frendt says, "when one must move gracefully to the next station in life, like for example certain women in Africa or Brazil, I forget which, who either color their faces or don some kind of distinctive headdress upon achieving menopause. Are you with me? One of our ranks must now leave us. No one is an island in terms of being thought cute forever, and so today we must say good-bye to our friend Lloyd. Lloyd, stand up so we can say good-bye to you. I'm sorry. We are all so very sorry."

"Oh God," says Lloyd. "Let this not be true."

But it's true. Lloyd's finished. We give him a round of applause, and Frendt gives him a Farewell Pen and the contents of his locker in a trash bag and out he goes. Poor Lloyd. He's got a wife and two kids and a sad little duplex on Self-Storage Parkway.

"It's been a pleasure!" he shouts desperately from the doorway, trying not to burn any bridges.

What a stressful workplace. The minute your Cute Rating drops you're a goner. Guests rank us as Knockout, Honeypie, Adequate, or Stinker. Not that I'm complaining. At least I'm working. At least I'm not a Stinker like Lloyd.

I'm a solid Honeypie/Adequate, heading home with forty bucks cash.

At Sea Oak there's no sea and no oak, just a hundred subsidized apartments and a rear view of FedEx. Min and Jade are feeding their babies while watching *How My Child Died Violently.* Min's my sister. Jade's our cousin. *How My Child Died Violently* is hosted by Matt Merton, a six-foot-five blond who's always giving the parents shoulder rubs and telling them they've been sainted by pain. Today's show features a ten-year-old who killed a five-year-old for refusing to join his gang. The ten-year-old strangled the five-year-old with a jump rope, filled his mouth with baseball cards, then locked himself in the bathroom and wouldn't come out until his parents agreed to take him to FunTimeZone, where he confessed, then dove screaming into a mesh cage full of plastic balls. The audience is shrieking threats at the parents of the killer while the parents of the victim urge restraint and forgiveness to such an extent that finally the audience starts shrieking threats at them too. Then it's a commercial. Min and Jade put down the babies and light cigarettes and pace the room while studying aloud for their GEDs. It doesn't look good. Jade says "regicide" is a virus. Min locates Biafra one planet from Saturn. I offer to help and they start yelling at me for condescending.

"You're lucky, man!" my sister says. "You did high school. You got your frigging diploma. We don't. That's why we have to do this GED shit. If we had our diplomas we could just watch TV and not be all distracted."

"Really," says Jade. "Now shut it, chick! We got to study. Show's almost on."

They debate how many sides a triangle has. They agree that Churchill was in opera. Matt Merton comes back and explains that last week's show on suicide, in which the parents watched a reenactment of their son's suicide, was a healing process for the parents, then shows a video of the parents admitting it was a healing process.

My sister's baby is Troy. Jade's baby is Mac. They crawl off into the kitchen and Troy gets his finger caught in the heat vent. Min rushes over and starts pulling.

"Jesus freaking Christ!" screams Jade. "Watch it! Stop yanking on him and get the freaking Vaseline. You're going to give him a really long arm, man!"

Troy starts crying. Mac starts crying. I go over and free Troy no problem. Meanwhile Jade and Min get in a slap fight and nearly knock over the TV.

"Yo, chick!" Min shouts at the top of her lungs. "I'm sure you're slapping me? And then you knock over the freaking TV? Don't you care?"

"I care!" Jade shouts back. "You're the slut who nearly pulled off her own kid's finger for no freaking reason, man!"

Just then Aunt Bernie comes in from DrugTown in her DrugTown cap and hobbles over and picks up Troy and everything calms way down.

"No need to fuss, little man," she says. "Everything's fine. Everything's just hunky-dory."

"Hunky-dory," says Min, and gives Jade one last pinch.

Aunt Bernie's a peacemaker. She doesn't like trouble. Once this guy backed over her foot at FoodKing and she walked home with ten broken bones. She never got married, because Grandpa needed her to keep house after Grandma died. Then he died and left all his money to a woman none of us had ever heard of, and Aunt Bernie started in at DrugTown. But she's not bitter. Sometimes she's so nonbitter it gets on my nerves. When I say Sea Oak's a pit she says she's just glad to have a roof over her head. When I say I'm tired of being broke she says Grandpa once gave her pencils for Christmas and she was so thrilled she sat around sketching horses all day on the backs of used envelopes. Once I asked was she sorry she never had kids and she said no, not at all, and besides, weren't we her kids?

And I said yes we were.

But of course we're not.

For dinner it's beanie-wienies. For dessert it's ice cream with freezer burn.

"What a nice day we've had," Aunt Bernie says once we've got the babies in bed.

"Man, what an optometrist," says Jade.

Next day is Thursday, which means a visit from Ed Anders from the Board of Health. He's in charge of ensuring that our penises never show. Also that we don't kiss anyone. None of us ever kisses anyone or shows his penis except Sonny Vance, who does both, because he's saving up to buy a FaxIt franchise. As for our Penile Simulators, yes, we can show them, we can let them stick out the top of our pants, we can even periodically dampen our tight pants with spray bottles so our Simulators really contour, but our real penises, no, those have to stay inside our hot uncomfortable oversized Simulators.

"Sorry fellas, hi fellas," Anders says as he comes wearily in. "Please know I don't like this any better than you do. I went to school to learn how to inspect meat, but this certainly wasn't what I had in mind. Ha ha!"

He orders a Lindbergh Enchilada and eats it cautiously, as if it's alive and he's afraid of waking it. Sonny Vance is serving soup to a table of hairstylists on a bender and for a twenty shoots them a quick look at his unit.

Just then Anders glances up from his Lindbergh.

"Oh for crying out loud," he says, and writes up a Shutdown and we all get sent home early. Which is bad. Every dollar counts. Lately I've been sneaking toilet paper home in my briefcase. I can fit three rolls in. By the time I get home they're usually flat and don't work so great on the roller but still it saves a few bucks.

I clock out and cut through the strip of forest behind FedEx. Very pretty. A raccoon scurries over a fallen oak and starts nibbling at a rusty bike. As I come out of the woods I hear a shot. At least I think it's a shot. It could be a backfire. But no, it's a shot, because then there's another one, and some kids sprint across the courtyard yelling that Big Scary Dawgz rule.

I run home. Min and Jade and Aunt Bernie and the babies are huddled behind the couch. Apparently they had the babies outside when the shooting started. Troy's walker got hit. Luckily he wasn't in it. It's supposed to look like a duck but now the beak's missing.

"Man, fuck this shit!" Min shouts.

"Freak this crap you mean," says Jade. "You want them growing up with shit-mouths like us? Crap-mouths I mean?"

"I just want them growing up, period," says Min.

"Boo-hoo, Miss Dramatic," says Jade.

"Fuck off, Miss Ho," shouts Min.

"I mean it, jagoff, I'm not kidding," shouts Jade, and punches Min in the arm.

"Girls, for crying out loud!" says Aunt Bernie. "We should be thankful. At least we got a home. And at least none of them bullets actually hit nobody."

"No offense, Bernie?" says Min "But you call this a freaking home?"

Sea Oak's not safe. There's an ad hoc crackhouse in the laundry room and last week Min found some brass knuckles in the kiddie pool. If I had my way I'd move everybody up to Canada. It's nice there. Very polite. We went for a weekend last fall and got a flat tire and these two farmers with bright-red faces insisted on fixing it, then springing for dinner, then starting a college fund for the babies. They sent us the stock certificates a week later, along with a photo of all of us eating cobbler at a diner.

But moving to Canada takes bucks. Dad's dead and left us nada and Ma now lives with Freddie, who doesn't like us, plus he's not exactly rich himself. He does phone polls. This month he's asking divorced women how often they backslide and sleep with their exes. He gets ten bucks for every completed poll.

So not lucrative, and Canada's a moot point.

I go out and find the beak of Troy's duck and fix it with Elmer's.

"Actually you know what?" says Aunt Bernie. "I think that looks even more like a real duck now. Because sometimes their beaks are cracked? I seen one like that downtown."

"Oh my God," says Min. "The kid's duck gets shot in the face and she says we're lucky."

"Well, we are lucky," says Bernie.

"Somebody's beak is cracked," says Jade.

"You know what I do if something bad happens?" Bernie says. "I don't think about it. Don't take it so serious. It ain't the end of the world. That's what I do. That's what I always done. That's how I got where I am."

My feeling is, Bernie, I love you, but where are you? You work at DrugTown for minimum. You're sixty and own nothing. You were basically a slave to your father and never had a date in your life.

"I mean, complain if you want," she says. "But I think we're doing pretty darn good for ourselves."

"Oh, we're doing great," says Min, and pulls Troy out from behind the couch and brushes some duck shards off his sleeper.

Joysticks reopens on Friday. It's a madhouse. They've got the fog on. A bridge club offers me fifteen bucks to oil-wrestle Mel Turner. So I oil-wrestle Mel Turner. They offer me twenty bucks to feed them chicken wings from my hand. So I feed them chicken wings from my hand. The afternoon flies by. Then the evening. At nine the bridge club leaves and I get a sorority. They sing intelligent nasty songs and grope my Simulator and say they'll never be able to look their boyfriends' meager genitalia in the eye again. Then Mr. Frendt comes over and says phone. It's Min. She sounds crazy. Four times in a row she shrieks get home. When I tell her calm down, she hangs up. I call back and no one answers. No biggie. Min's prone to panic. Probably one of the babies is puky. Luckily I'm on FlexTime.

"I'll be back," I say to Mr. Frendt.

"I look forward to it," he says.

I jog across the marsh and through FedEx. Up on the hill there's a light from the last remaining farm. Sometimes we take the boys to the adjacent car wash to look at the cow. Tonight however the cow is elsewhere.

At home Min and Jade are hopping up and down in front of Aunt Bernie, who's sitting very very still at one end of the couch.

"Keep the babies out!" shrieks Min. "I don't want them seeing something dead!"

"Shut up, man!" shrieks Jade. "Don't call her something dead!"

She squats down and pinches Aunt Bernie's cheek.

"Aunt Bernie?" she shrieks. "Fuck!"

"We already tried that like twice, chick!" shrieks Min. "Why are you doing that shit again? Touch her neck and see if you can feel that beating thing!"

"Shit shit shit!" shrieks Jade.

I call 911 and the paramedics come out and work hard for twenty minutes, then give up and say they're sorry and it looks like she's been dead most of the afternoon. The apartment's a mess. Her money drawer's empty and her family photos are in the bathtub.

"Not a mark on her," says a cop.

"I suspect she died of fright," says another. "Fright of the intruder?"

"My guess is yes," says a paramedic.

"Oh God," says Jade. "God, God, God."

I sit down beside Bernie. I think: I am so sorry. I'm sorry I wasn't here when it happened and sorry you never had any fun in your life and sorry I wasn't rich enough to move you somewhere safe. I remember when she was young and wore pink stretch pants and made us paper chains out of DrugTown receipts while singing "Froggie Went A-Courting." All her life she worked hard. She never hurt anybody. And now this.

Scared to death in a crappy apartment.

Min puts the babies in the kitchen but they keep crawling out. Aunt Bernie's in a shroud on this sort of dolly and on the couch are a bunch of forms to sign.

We call Ma and Freddie. We get their machine.

"Ma, pick up!" says Min. "Something bad happened! Ma, please freaking pick up!"

But nobody picks up.

So we leave a message.

Lobton's funeral parlor is just a regular house on a regular street. Inside there's a rack of brochures with titles like "Why Does My Loved One Appear Somewhat Larger?" Lobton looks healthy. Maybe too healthy He's wearing a yellow golf shirt and his biceps keep involuntarily flexing. Every now and then he touches his delts as if to confirm they're still big as softballs.

"Such a sad thing," he says.

"How much?" asks Jade. "I mean, like for basic. Not superfancy."

"But not crappy either," says Min. "Our aunt was the best."

"What price range were you considering?" says Lobton, cracking his knuckles. We tell him and his eyebrows go up and he leads us to something that looks like a moving box.

"Prior to usage we'll moisture-proof this with a spray lacquer," he says. "Makes it look quite woodlike."

"That's all we can get?" says Jade. "Cardboard?"

"I'm actually offering you a slight break already" he says, and does a kind of push-up against the wall. "On account of the tragic circumstances. This is Sierra Sunset. Not exactly cardboard. More of a fiberboard."

"I don't know," says Min. "Seems pretty gyppy."

"Can we think about it?" says Ma.

"Absolutely," says Lobton. "Last time I checked this was still America."

I step over and take a closer look. There are staples where Aunt Bernie's spine would be. Down at the foot there's some writing about Folding Tab A into Slot B.

"No freaking way," says Jade. "Work your whole life and end up in a Mayflower box? I doubt it."

We've got zip in savings. We sit at a desk and Lobton does what he calls a Credit Calc. If we pay it out monthly for seven years we can afford the Amber Mist, which includes a double-thick balsa box and two coats of lacquer and a one-hour wake.

"But seven years, jeez," says Ma.

"We got to get her the good one," says Min. "She never had anything nice in her life."

So Amber Mist it is.

We bury her at St. Leo's, on the hill up near BastCo. Her part of the graveyard's pretty plain. No angels, no little rock houses, no flowers, just a bunch of flat stones like parking bumpers and here and there a Styrofoam cup. Father Brian says a prayer and then one of us is supposed to talk. But what's there to say? She never had a life. Never married, no kids, work work work. Did she ever go on a cruise? All her life it was buses. Buses buses buses. Once she went with Ma on a bus to Quigley, Kansas, to gamble and shop at an outlet mall. Someone broke into her room and stole her clothes and took a dump in her suitcase while they were at the Roy Clark show. That was it. That was the extent of her tourism. After that it was DrugTown, night and day. After fifteen years as Cashier she got demoted to Greeter. People would ask where the cold remedies were and she'd point to some big letters on the wall that said Cold Remedies.

Freddie, Ma's boyfriend, steps up and says he didn't know her very long but she was an awful nice lady and left behind a lot of love, etc. etc. blah blah blah. While it's true she didn't do much in her life, still she was very dear to those of us who knew her and never made a stink about anything but was always content with whatever happened to her, etc. etc. blah blah blah.

Then it's over and we're supposed to go away.

"We gotta come out here like every week," says Jade.

"I know I will," says Min.

"What, like I won't?" says Jade. "She was so freaking nice."

"I'm sure you swear at a grave," says Min.

"Since when is freak a swear, chick?" says Jade.

"Girls," says Ma.

"I hope I did okay in what I said about her," says Freddie in his full-of-crap way, smelling bad of English Navy. "Actually I sort of surprised myself."

"Bye-bye, Aunt Bernie," says Min.

"Bye-bye, Bern," says Jade.

"Oh my dear sister," says Ma.

I scrunch my eyes tight and try to picture her happy, laughing, poking me in the ribs. But all I can see is her terrified on the couch. It's awful. Out there, somewhere, is whoever did it. Someone came in our house, scared her to death, watched her die, went through our stuff, stole her money. Someone who's still living, someone who right now might be having a piece of pie or running an errand or scratching his ass, someone who, if he wanted to, could drive west for three days or whatever and sit in the sun by the ocean.

We stand a few minutes with heads down and hands folded.

Afterward Freddie takes us to Trabanti's for lunch. Last year Trabanti died and three Vietnamese families went in together and bought the place, and it still serves pasta and pizza and the big oil of Trabanti is still on the wall but now from the kitchen comes this very pretty Vietnamese music and the food is somehow better.

Freddie proposes a toast. Min says remember how Bernie always called lunch dinner and dinner supper? Jade says remember how when her jaw clicked she'd say she needed oil?

"She was a excellent lady," says Freddie.

"I already miss her so bad," says Ma.

"I'd like to kill that fuck that killed her," says Min.

"How about let's don't say fuck at lunch," says Ma.

"It's just a word, Ma, right?" says Min. "Like pluck is just a word? You don't mind if I say pluck? Pluck pluck pluck?"

"Well, shit's just a word too," says Freddie. "But we don't say it at lunch."

"Same with puke," says Ma.

"Shit puke, shit puke," says Min.

The waiter clears his throat. Ma glares at Min.

"I love you girls' manners," Ma says.

"Especially at a funeral," says Freddie.

"This ain't a funeral," says Min.

"The question in my mind is what you kids are gonna do now," says Freddie. "Because I consider this whole thing a wake-up call, meaning it's time for you to pull yourselfs up by the bootstraps like I done and get out of that dangerous craphole you're living at."

"Mr. Phone Poll speaks," says Min.

"Anyways it ain't that dangerous," says Jade.

"A woman gets killed and it ain't that dangerous?" says Freddie.

"All's we need is a dead bolt and a eyehole," says Min.

"What's a bootstrap," says Jade.

"It's like a strap on a boot, you doof," says Min.

"Plus where we gonna go?" says Jade. "Can we move in with you guys?"

"I personally would love that and you know that," says Freddie. "But who would not love that is our landlord."

"I think what Freddie's saying is it's time for you girls to get jobs," says Ma.

"Yeah right, Ma," says Min. "After what happened last time?"

When I first moved in, Jade and Min were working the info booth at HardwareNiche. Then one day we picked the babies up at day care and found Troy sitting naked on top of the washer and Mac in the yard being nipped by a Pekingese and the day-care lady sloshed and playing KillerBirds on Nintendo.

So that was that. No more HardwareNiche.

"Maybe one could work, one could baby-sit?" says Ma.

"I don't see why I should have to work so she can stay home with her baby," says Min.

"And I don't see why I should have to work so she can stay home with her baby," says Jade.

"It's like a freaking veece versa," says Min.

"Let me tell you something," says Freddie. "Something about this country. Anybody can do anything. But first they gotta try. And you guys ain't. Two don't work and one strips naked. I don't consider that trying. You kids make squat. And therefore you live in a dangerous craphole. And what happens in a dangerous craphole? Bad tragic shit. It's the freaking American way—you start out in a dangerous craphole and work hard so you can someday move up to a somewhat less dangerous craphole. And finally maybe you get a mansion. But at this rate you ain't even gonna make it to the somewhat less dangerous craphole."

"Like you live in a mansion," says Jade.

"I do not claim to live in no mansion," says Freddie. "But then again I do not live in no slum. The other thing I also do not do is strip naked."

"Thank God for small favors," says Min.

"Anyways he's never actually naked," says Jade.

Which is true. I always have on at least a T-back.

"No wonder we never take these kids out to a nice lunch," says Freddie.

"I do not even consider this a nice lunch," says Min.

For dinner Jade microwaves some Stars-n-Flags. They're addictive. They put sugar in the sauce and sugar in the meat nuggets. I think also caffeine. Someone told me the brown streaks in the Flags are caffeine. We have like five bowls each.

After dinner the babies get fussy and Min puts a mush of ice cream and Hershey's syrup in their bottles and we watch *The Worst That Could Happen,* a half-hour of computer simulations of tragedies that have never actually occurred but theoretically could. A kid gets hit by a train and flies into a zoo, where he's eaten by wolves. A man cuts his hand off chopping wood and while wandering around screaming for help is picked up by a tornado and dropped on a preschool during recess and lands on a pregnant teacher.

"I miss Bernie so bad," says Min.

"Me too," Jade says sadly.

The babies start howling for more ice cream.

"That is so cute," says Jade. "They're like, *Give it the fuck up!*"

"We'll give it the fuck up, sweeties, don't worry," says Min. "We didn't forget about you."

Then the phone rings. It's Father Brian. He sounds weird. He says he's sorry to bother us so late. But something strange has happened. Something bad. Something sort of, you know, unspeakable. Am I sitting? I'm not but I say I am.

Apparently someone has defaced Bernie's grave.

My first thought is there's no stone. It's just grass. How do you deface grass? What did they do, pee on the grass on the grave? But Father's nearly in tears.

So I call Ma and Freddie and tell them to meet us, and we get the babies up and load them into the K-car.

"Deface," says Jade on the way over. "What does that mean, deface?"

"It means like fucked it up," says Min.

"But how?" says Jade. "I mean, like what did they do?"

"We don't know, dumbass," says Min. "That's why we're going there."

"And why?" says Jade. "Why would someone do that?"

"Check out Miss Shreelock Holmes," says Min. "Someone done that because someone is a asshole."

"Someone is a big-time asshole," says Jade.

Father Brian meets us at the gate with a flashlight and a golf cart.

"When I saw this," he says. "I literally sat down in astonishment. Nothing like this has ever happened here. I am so sorry. You seem like nice people."

We're too heavy and the wheels spin as we climb the hill, so I get out and jog alongside.

"Okay, folks, brace yourselves," Father says, and shuts off the engine.

Where the grave used to be is just a hole. Inside the hole is the Amber Mist, with the top missing. Inside the Amber Mist is nothing. No Aunt Bernie.

"What the hell," says Jade. "Where's Bernie?"

"Somebody stole Bernie?" says Min.

"At least you folks have retained your feet," says Father Brian. "I'm telling you I literally sat right down. I sat right down on that pile of dirt. I dropped as if shot. See that mark? That's where I sat."

On the pile of grave dirt is a butt-shaped mark.

The cops show up and one climbs down in the hole with a tape measure and a camera. After three or four flashes he climbs out and hands Ma a pair of blue pumps.

"Her little shoes," says Ma. "Oh my God."

"Are those them?" says Jade.

"Those are them," says Min.

"I am freaking out," says Jade.

"I am totally freaking out," says Min.

"I'm gonna sit," says Ma, and drops into the golf cart.

"What I don't get is who'd want her?" says Min.

"She was just this lady," says Jade.

"Typically it's teens?" one cop says. "Typically we find the loved one nearby? Once we found the loved one nearby with, you know, a cigarette between its lips, wearing a sombrero? These kids today got a lot more nerve than we ever did. I never would've dreamed of digging up a dead corpse when I was a teen. You might tip over a stone, sure, you might spray-paint something on a crypt, you might, you know, give a wino a hotfoot."

"But this, jeez," says Freddie. "This is a entirely different ballgame."

"Boy howdy," says the cop, and we all look down at the shoes in Ma's hands.

Next day I go back to work. I don't feel like it but we need the money. The grass is wet and it's hard getting across the ravine in my dress shoes. The soles are slick. Plus they're too tight. Several times I fall forward on my briefcase. Inside the briefcase are my T-backs and a thing of mousse.

Right off the bat I get a tableful of MediBen women seated under a banner saying BEST OF LUCK, BEATRICE, NO HARD FEELINGS. I take off my shirt and serve their salads. I take off my flight pants and serve their soups. One drops a dollar on the floor and tells me feel free to pick it up.

I pick it up.

"Not like that, not like that," she says. "Face the other way so when you bend we can see your crack."

I've done this about a million times, but somehow I can't do it now.

I look at her. She looks at me.

"What?" she says. "I'm not allowed to say that? I thought that was the whole point."

"That is the whole point, Phyllis," says another lady "You stand your ground."

"Look," Phyllis says. "Either bend how I say or give back the dollar. I think that's fair."

"You go, girl," says her friend.

I give back the dollar. I return to the Locker Area and sit awhile. For the first time ever, I'm voted Stinker. There are thirteen women at the MediBen table and they all vote me Stinker. Do the MediBen women know my situation? Would they vote me Stinker if they did? But what am I supposed to do, go out and say Please ladies, my aunt just died, plus her body's missing?

Mr. Frendt pulls me aside.

"Perhaps you need to go home," he says. "I'm sorry for your loss. But I'd like to encourage you not to behave like one of those Comanche ladies who bite off their index fingers when a loved one dies. Grief is good, grief is fine, but too much grief, as we all know, is excessive. If your aunt's death has filled your mouth with too many bitten-off fingers, for crying out loud, take a week off, only don't take it out on our Guests, they didn't kill your dang aunt."

But I can't afford to take a week off. I can't even afford to take a few days off.

"We really need the money," I say.

"Is that my problem?" he says. "Am I supposed to let you dance without vigor just because you need the money? Why don't I put an ad in the paper for all sad people who need money? All the town's sad could come here and strip. Good-bye. Come back when you feel halfway normal."

From the pay phone I call home to see if they need anything from the FoodSoQuik.

"Just come home," Min says stiffly. "Just come straight home."

"What is it?" I say.

"Come home," she says.

Maybe someone's found the body. I imagine Bernie naked, Bernie chopped in two, Bernie posed on a bus bench. I hope and pray that something only mildly bad's been done to her, something we can live with.

At home the door's wide open. Min and Jade are sitting very still on the couch, babies in their laps, staring at the rocking chair, and in the rocking chair is Bernie. Bernie's body.

Same perm, same glasses, same blue dress we buried her in.

What's it doing here? Who could be so cruel? And what are we supposed to do with it?

Then she turns her head and looks at me.

"Sit the fuck down," she says.

In life she never swore.

I sit. Min squeezes and releases my hand, squeezes and releases, squeezes and releases.

"You, mister," Bernie says to me, "are going to start showing your cock. You'll show it and show it. You go up to a lady if she wants to see it, if she'll pay to see it, I'll make a thumbprint on the forehead. You see the thumbprint, you ask. I'll try to get you five a day, at twenty bucks a pop. So a hundred bucks a day Seven hundred a week. And that's cash, so no taxes. No withholding. See? That's the beauty of it."

She's got dirt in her hair and dirt in her teeth and her hair is a mess and her tongue when it darts out to lick her lips is black.

"You, Jade," she says. "Tomorrow you start work. Andersen Labels, Fifth and Rivera. Dress up when you go. Wear something nice. Show a little leg. And don't chomp your gum. Ask for Len. At the end of the month we take the money you made and the cock money and get a new place. Somewhere safe. That's part one of Phase One. You, Min. You baby-sit. Plus you quit smoking. Plus you learn how to cook. No more food out of cans. We gotta eat right to look our best. Because I am getting me so many lovers. Maybe you kids don't know this but I died a freaking virgin. No babies, no lovers. Nothing went in, nothing came out. Ha ha! Dry as a bone, completely wasted, this pretty little thing God gave me between my legs. Well I am going to have lovers now, you fucks! Like in the movies, big shoulders and all, and a summer house, and nice trips, and in the morning in my room a big vase of flowers, and I'm going to get my nipples hard standing in the breeze from the ocean, eating shrimp from a cup, you sons of bitches, while my lover watches me from the veranda, his big shoulders shining, all hard for me, that's one damn thing I will guarantee you kids! Ha ha! You think I'm joking? I ain't freaking joking. I never got nothing! My life was shit! I was never even up in a freaking plane. But that was that life and this is this life. My new life. Cover me up now! With a blanket. I need my beauty rest. Tell anyone I'm here, you all die. Plus they die. Whoever you tell, they die. I kill them with my mind. I can do that. I am very freaking strong now. I got powers! So no visitors. I don't exactly look my best. You got it? You all got it?"

We nod. I go for a blanket. Her hands and feet are shaking and she's grinding her teeth and one falls out.

"Put it over me, you fuck, all the way over!" she screams, and I put it over her.

We sneak off with the babies and whisper in the kitchen.

"It looks like her," says Min.

"It is her," I say.

"It is and it ain't," says Jade.

"We better do what she says," Min says.

"No shit," Jade says.

All night she sits in the rocker under the blanket, shaking and swearing.

All night we sit in Min's bed, fully dressed, holding hands.

"See how strong I am!" she shouts around midnight, and there's a cracking sound, and when I go out the door's been torn off the microwave but she's still sitting in the chair.

In the morning she's still there, shaking and swearing.

"Take the blanket off!" she screams. "It's time to get this show on the road."

I take the blanket off. The smell is not good. One ear is now in her lap. She keeps absentmindedly sticking it back on her head.

"You, Jade!" she shouts. "Get dressed. Go get that job. When you meet Len, bend forward a little. Let him see down your top. Give him some hope. He's a sicko, but we need him. You, Min! Make breakfast. Something homemade. Like biscuits."

"Why don't you make it with your powers?" says Min.

"Don't be a smartass!" screams Bernie. "You see what I did to that microwave?"

"I don't know how to make freaking biscuits," Min wails.

"You know how to read, right?" Bernie shouts. "You ever heard of a recipe? You ever been in the grave? It sucks so bad! You regret all the things you never did. You little bitches are gonna have a very bad time in the grave unless you get on the stick, believe me! Turn down the thermostat! Make it cold. I like cold. Something's off with my body. I don't feel right."

I turn down the thermostat. She looks at me.

"Go show your cock!" she shouts. "That is the first part of Phase One. After we get the new place, that's the end of the first part of Phase Two. You'll still show your cock, but only three days a week. Because you'll start community college. Pre-law. Pre-law is best. You'll be a whiz. You ain't dumb. And Jade'll work weekends to make up for the decrease in cock money See? See how that works? Now get out of here. What are you gonna do?"

"Show my cock?" I say.

"Show your cock, that's right," she says, and brushes back her hair with her hand, and a huge wad comes out, leaving her almost bald on one side.

"Oh God," says Min. "You know what? No way me and the babies are staying here alone."

"You ain't alone," says Bernie. "I'm here."

"Please don't go," Min says to me.

"Oh, stop it," Bernie says, and the door flies open and I feel a sort of invisible fist punching me in the back.

Outside it's sunny. A regular day. A guy's changing his oil. The clouds are regular clouds and the sun's the regular sun and the only nonregular thing is that my clothes smell like Bernie, a combo of wet cellar and rotten bacon.

Work goes well. I manage to keep smiling and hide my shaking hands, and my midshift rating is Honeypie. After lunch this older woman comes up and says I look so much like a real Pilot she can hardly stand it.

On her head is a thumbprint. Like Ash Wednesday only sort of glowing.

I don't know what to do. Do I just come out and ask if she wants to see my cock? What if she says no? What if I get caught? What if I show her and she doesn't think it's worth twenty bucks?

Then she asks if I'll surprise her best friend with a birthday table dance. She points out her friend. A pretty girl, no thumbprint. Looks somehow familiar.

We start over and at about twenty feet I realize it's Angela.

Angela Silveri.

We dated senior year. Then Dad died and Ma had to take a job at Patty-Melt Depot. From all the grease Ma got a bad rash and could barely wear a blouse. Plus Min was running wild. So Angela would come over and there'd be Min getting high under a tarp on the carport and Ma sitting in her bra on a kitchen stool with a fan pointed at her gut. Angela had dreams. She had plans. In her notebook she pasted a picture of an office from the J. C. Penney catalogue and under it wrote, *My (someday?) office.* Once we saw this black Porsche and she said very nice but make hers red. The last straw was Ed Edwards, a big drunk, one of Dad's cousins. Things got so bad Ma rented him the utility room. One night Angela and I were making out on the couch late when Ed came in soused and started peeing in the dishwasher.

What could I say? He's only barely related to me? He hardly ever does that?

Angela's eyes were like these little pies.

I walked her home, got no kiss, came back, cleaned up the dishwasher as best I could. A few days later I got my class ring in the mail and a copy of *The Prophet.*

You will always be my first love, she'd written inside. *But now my path converges to a higher ground. Be well always. Walk in joy. Please don't think me cruel, it's just that I want so much in terms of accomplishment, plus I couldn't believe that guy peed right on your dishes.*

No way am I table dancing for Angela Silveri. No way am I asking Angela Silveri's friend if she wants to see my cock. No way am I hanging around here so Angela can see me in my flight jacket and T-backs and wonder to herself how I went so wrong etc. etc.

I hide in the kitchen until my shift is done, then walk home very, very slowly because I'm afraid of what Bernie's going to do to me when I get there.

Min meets me at the door. She's got flour all over her blouse and it looks like she's been crying.

"I can't take any more of this," she says. "She's like falling apart. I mean shit's falling off her. Plus she made me bake a freaking pie."

On the table is a very lumpy pie. One of Bernie's arms is now disconnected and lying across her lap.

"What are you thinking of!" she shouts. "You didn't show your cock even once? You think it's easy making those thumbprints? You try it, smartass! Do you or do you not know the plan? You gotta get us out of here! And to get us out, you gotta use what you got. And you ain't got much. A nice face. And a decent unit. Not huge, but shaped nice."

"Bernie, God," says Min.

"What, Miss Priss?" shouts Bernie, and slams the severed arm down hard on her lap, and her other ear falls off.

"I'm sorry, but this is too fucking sickening," says Min. "I'm going out."

"What's sickening?" says Bernie. "Are you saying I'm sickening? Well, I think you're sickening. So many wonderful things in life and where's your mind? You think with your lazy ass. Whatever life hands you, you take. You're not going anywhere. You're staying home and studying."

"I'm what?" says Min. "Studying what? I ain't studying. Chick comes into my house and starts ordering me to study? I freaking doubt it."

"You don't know nothing!" Bernie says. "What fun is life when you don't know nothing? You can't find your own town on the map. You can't name a single president. When we go to Rome you won't know nothing about the history. You're going to study the World Book. Do we still have those World Books?"

"Yeah right," says Min. "We're going to Rome."

"We'll go to Rome when he's a lawyer," says Bernie.

"Dream on, chick," says Min. "And we'll go to Mars when I'm a stockbreaker."

"Don't you dare make fun of me!" Bernie shouts, and our only vase goes flying across the room and nearly nails Min in the head.

"She's been like this all day," says Min.

"Like what?" shouts Bernie. "We had a perfectly nice day."

"She made me help her try on my bras," says Min.

"I never had a nice sexy bra," says Bernie.

"And now mine are all ruined," says Min. "They got this sort of goo on them."

"You ungrateful shit!" shouts Bernie. "Do you know what I'm doing for you? I'm saving your boy. And you got the nerve to say I made goo on your bras! Troy's gonna get caught in a crossfire in the courtyard. In September. September eighteenth. He's gonna get thrown off his little trike. With one leg twisted under him and blood pouring out of his ear. It's a freaking prophecy. You know that word? It means prediction. You know that word? You think I'm bullshitting? Well I ain't bullshitting. I got the power. Watch this: All day Jade sat licking labels at a desk by a window. Her boss bought everybody subs for lunch. She's bringing some home in a green bag."

"That ain't true about Troy, is it?" says Min. "Is it? I don't believe it."

"Turn on the TV!" Bernie shouts. "Give me the changer."

I turn on the TV. I give her the changer. She puts on *Nathan's Body Shop.* Nathan says washboard abs drive the women wild. Then there's a close-up of his washboard abs.

"Oh yes," says Bernie. "Them are for me. I'd like to give those a lick. A lick and a pinch. I'd like to sort of straddle those things."

Just then Jade comes through the door with a big green bag.

"Oh God," says Min.

"Told you so!" says Bernie, and pokes Min in the ribs. "Ha ha! I really got the power!"

"I don't get it," Min says, all desperate. "What happens? Please. What happens to him? You better freaking tell me."

"I already told you," Bernie says. "He'll fly about fifteen feet and live about three minutes."

"Bernie, God," Min says, and starts to cry. "You used to be so nice."

"I'm still so nice," says Bernie, and bites into a sub and takes off the tip of her finger and starts chewing it up.

Just after dawn she shouts out my name.

"Take the blanket off," she says. "I ain't feeling so good."

I take the blanket off. She's basically just this pile of parts: both arms in her lap, head on the arms, heel of one foot touching the heel of the other, all of it sort of wrapped up in her dress.

"Get me a washcloth," she says. "Do I got a fever? I feel like I got a fever. Oh, I knew it was too good to be true. But okay. New plan. New plan. I'm changing the first part of Phase One. If you see two thumbprints, that means the lady'll screw you for cash. We're in a fix here. We gotta speed this up. There ain't gonna be nothing left of me. Who's gonna be my lover now?"

The doorbell rings.

"Son of a bitch," Bernie snarls.

It's Father Brian with a box of doughnuts. I step out quick and close the door behind me. He says he's just checking in. Perhaps we'd like to talk? Perhaps we're feeling some residual anger about Bernie's situation? Which would of course be completely understandable. Once when he was a young priest someone broke in and drew a mustache on the Virgin Mary with a permanent marker, and for weeks he was tortured by visions of bending back the finger of the vandal until he or she burst into tears of apology.

"I knew that wasn't appropriate," he says. "I knew that by indulging in that fantasy I was honoring violence. And yet it gave me pleasure. I also thought of catching them in the act and boinking them in the head with a rock. I also thought of jumping up and down on their backs until something in their spinal column cracked. Actually I had about a million ideas. But you know what I did instead? I scrubbed and scrubbed our Holy Mother, and soon she was as good as new. Her statue, I mean. She herself of course is always good as new."

From inside comes the sound of breaking glass. Breaking glass and then something heavy falling, and Jade yelling and Min yelling and the babies crying.

"Oops, I guess?" he says. "I've come at a bad time? Look, all I'm trying to do is urge you, if at all possible, to forgive the perpetrators, as I forgave the perpetrator that drew on my Virgin Mary. The thing lost, after all, is only your aunt's body, and what is essential, I assure you, is elsewhere, being well taken care of."

I nod. I smile. I say thanks for stopping by I take the doughnuts and go back inside.

The TV's broke and the refrigerator's tipped over and Bernie's parts are strewn across the living room like she's been shot out of a cannon.

"She tried to get up," says Jade.

"I don't know where the hell she thought she was going," says Min.

"Come here," the head says to me, and I squat down. "That's it for me. I'm fucked. As per usual. Always the bridesmaid, never the bride. Although come to think of it I was never even the freaking bridesmaid. Look, show your cock. It's the shortest line between two points. The world ain't giving away nice lives. You got a trust fund? You a genius? Show your cock. It's what you got. And remember: Troy in September. On his trike. One leg twisted. Don't forget. And also. Don't remember me like this. Remember me like how I was that night we all went to Red Lobster and I had that new perm. Ah Christ. At least buy me a stone."

I rub her shoulder, which is next to her foot.

"We loved you," I say.

"Why do some people get everything and I got nothing?" she says. "Why? Why was that?"

"I don't know," I say.

"Show your cock," she says, and dies again.

We stand there looking down at the pile of parts. Mac crawls toward it and Min moves him back with her foot.

"This is too freaking much," says Jade, and starts crying.

"What do we do now?" says Min.

"Call the cops," Jade says.

"And say what?" says Min.

We think about this awhile.

I get a Hefty bag. I get my winter gloves.

"I ain't watching," says Jade.

"I ain't watching either," says Min, and they take the babies into the bedroom.

I close my eyes and wrap Bernie up in the Hefty bag and twistie-tie the bag shut and lug it out to the trunk of the K-car. I throw in a shovel. I drive up to St. Leo's. I lower the bag into the hole using a bungee cord, then fill the hole back in.

Down in the city are the nice houses and the so-so houses and the lovers making out in dark yards and the babies crying for their moms, and I wonder if, other than Jesus, this has ever happened before. Maybe it happens all the time. Maybe there's angry dead all over, hiding in rooms, covered with blankets, bossing around their scared, embarrassed relatives. Because how would we know?

I for sure don't plan on broadcasting this.

I smooth over the dirt and say a quick prayer: If it was wrong for her to come back, forgive her, she never got beans in this life, plus she was trying to help us.

At the car I think of an additional prayer: But please don't let her come back again.

When I get home the babies are asleep and Jade and Min are watching a phone-sex infomercial, three girls in leather jumpsuits eating bananas in slo-mo while across the screen runs a constant disclaimer: "Not Necessarily the Girls Who Man the Phones! Not Necessarily the Girls Who Man the Phones!"

"Them chicks seem to really be enjoying those bananas," says Min in a thin little voice.

"I like them jumpsuits though," says Jade.

"Yeah them jumpsuits look decent," says Min.

Then they look up at me. I've never seen them so sad and beat and sick.

"It's done," I say.

Then we hug and cry and promise never to forget Bernie the way she really was, and I use some Resolve on the rug and they go do some reading in their World Books.

Next day I go in early. I don't see a single thumbprint. But it doesn't matter. I get with Sonny Vance and he tells me how to do it. First you ask the woman would she like a private tour. Then you show her the fake P-40, the Gallery of Historical Aces, the shower stall where we get oiled up, etc. etc. and then in the hall near the rest room you ask if there's anything else she'd like to see. It's sleazy. It's gross. But when I do it I think of September. September and Troy in the crossfire, his little leg bent under him etc. etc.

Most say no but quite a few say yes.

I've got a place picked out at a complex called Swan's Glen. They've never had a shooting or a knifing and the public school is great and every Saturday they have a nature walk for kids behind the clubhouse.

For every hundred bucks I make, I set aside five for Bernie's stone.

What do you write on something like that? LIFE PASSED HER BY? DIED DISAPPOINTED? CAME BACK TO LIFE BUT FELL APART? All true, but too sad, and no way I'm writing any of those.

BERNIE KOWALSKI, it's going to say: BELOVED AUNT.

Sometimes she comes to me in dreams. She never looks good. Sometimes she's wearing a dirty smock. Once she had on handcuffs. Once she was naked and dirty and this mean cat was clawing its way up her front. But every time it's the same thing.

"Some people get everything and I got nothing," she says. "Why? Why did that happen?"

Every time I say I don't know.

And I don't.

George Saunders

Winky

Eighty people waited in a darkened meeting room at the Hyatt, wearing mass-produced paper hats. The White Hats were Beginning to Begin. The Pink Hats were Moving Ahead in Beginning. The Green Hats were Very Firmly Beginning, all the way up to the Gold Hats, who had Mastered Living and were standing in a group around the Snack Table, whispering and conferring and elbowing one another whenever someone in a lesser hat walked by.

Trumpets sounded from a concealed tape deck. An actor in a ripped flannel shirt stumbled across the stage with a sign around his neck that said "You."

"I'm lost!" You cried. "I'm wandering in a sort of wilderness!"

"Hey, You, come on over!" shouted a girl across the stage, labeled "Inner Peace." "I bet you've been looking for me your whole life!"

"Boy, have I!" said You. "I'll be right over!"

But then out from the wings sprinted a number of other actors, labeled "Whiny" and "Self-Absorbed" and "Blames Her Fat on Others" and so on, who draped themselves across You and began poking him in the ribs and giving him noogies.

"Oh, I can't believe you love Inner Peace more than you love me, You!" said Insecure. "That really hurts."

"Frankly, I've never been so disappointed in my life," said Disappointed.

"Oh God, all this arguing is giving me a panic attack," said Too High-Strung to Function.

"I'm waiting, You," said Inner Peace. "Do you want me or not?"

"I do, but I seem to be trapped!" You shouted. "I can't seem to get what I want!"

"You and about a billion other people in this world," said Inner Peace sadly.

"Is there no hope for me?" asked You. "If only someone had made a lifelong study of the roadblocks people encounter on their way to Inner Peace!"

"And yet someone has," said Inner Peace.

Another fanfare sounded from the tape deck, and a masked Gold Hat, whose hat appeared to be made of actual gold, bounded onto the stage, flexed his muscles, and dragged Insecure to a paper jail, on which was written: "Pokey for Those Who Would Keep Us from Inner Peace." Then the Gold Hat dragged Chronically Depressed and Clingy and Helpless and the rest across the stage and shoved them into the Pokey.

"See what I just did?" said the Gold Hat. "I just liberated You from those who would keep him from Inner Peace. So good for You! Question is, is You going to be able to stay liberated? Maybe what You needs is a repeated internal reminder. A mantra. A mantra can be thought of as a repeated internal reminder, can't it? Does anyone out there have a good snappy mantra they could perhaps share with You?"

The crowd was delighted, because they knew the mantra. Even the lowly White Hats knew the mantra—even Neil Yaniky, who sat spellbound and insecure in the first row, sucking his mustache, knew the mantra, because it was on all the TV commercials and also on the front cover of the Orientation Text in big bold letters.

"Give it to me, folks!" shouted the Gold Hat. "What time is it?"

"Now Is the Time for Me to Win!" the crowd shouted. "You got that right, baby!" said the Gold Hat exultantly, ripping off his mask to reveal what many already suspected: This was not some mere Gold Hat but Tom Rodgers himself, founder of the Seminars.

"What fun!" he shouted. "To have something to give, and people who so badly need what I have to offer. Here's what I have to offer, folks, although it's not much, really, just two simple concepts, and the first one is: oatmeal."

From out of his suit he pulled a bowl and a box of oatmeal, and filled the bowl with the oatmeal and held the bowl up.

"Simple, nourishing, inexpensive," he said. "This represents your soul in its pure state. Your soul on the day you were born. You were perfect. You were happy. You were good.

"Now, enter Concept Number Two: crap. Don't worry, folks, I don't use actual crap up here. Only imaginary crap. You'll have to supply the crap, using your mind. Now, if someone came up and crapped in your nice warm oatmeal, what would you say? Would you say: 'Wow, super, thanks, please continue crapping in my oatmeal'? Am I being silly? I'm being a little silly. But guess what, in real life people come up and crap in your oatmeal all the time—friends, co-workers, loved ones, even your kids, especially your kids!—and that's exactly what you do. You say 'Thanks so much!' You say 'Crap away!' You say, and here my metaphor breaks down a bit, 'Is there some way I can help you crap in my oatmeal?'

"Let me tell you something amazing: I was once exactly like you people. A certain someone, a certain guy who shall remain nameless, was doing quite a bit of crapping in my oatmeal, and simply because he'd had some bad luck, simply because he was in some pain, simply because, actually he was in a wheelchair, this certain someone expected me to put my life on hold while he crapped in my oatmeal by demanding round-the-clock attention, this brother of mine, this Gene, and whoops, there goes that cat out of the bag, but does this maybe sound paradoxical? Wasn't he the one with the crap in his oatmeal, being in a wheelchair? Well, yes and no. Sure, he was hurting. No surprise there. Guy drops a motorcycle on a gravel road and bounces two hundred yards without a helmet, yes, he's going to be somewhat hurting. But how was that my fault? Was I the guy riding the motorcycle too fast, drunk, with no helmet? No, I was home, studying my Tacitus, which is what I was into at that stage of my life, so why did Gene expect me to consign my dreams and plans to the dustbin? I had dreams! I had plans! Finally—and this is all in my book, *People of Power*—I found the inner strength to say to Gene, 'Stop crapping in my oatmeal, Gene, I'm simply not going to participate.' And I found the strength to say to our sister, Ellen, 'Ellen, take the ball that is Gene and run with it, because if I sell myself short by catering to Gene, I'm going to be one very angry puppy, and anger does the mean-and-nasty on a person, and I for one love myself and want the best for me, because I am, after all, a child of God.' And I said to myself, as I describe in the book, 'Tom, now is the time for you to win!' That was the first time I thought that up. And do you know what? I won. I'm winning. Today we're friends, Gene and I, and he acknowledges that I was right all along. And as for Ellen, Ellen still has some issues, she'd take a big old dump in my oatmeal right now if I gave her half a chance, but guess what folks, I'm not giving her that half a chance, because I've installed a protective screen over my oatmeal—not a literal screen, but a metaphorical protective screen. Ellen knows it, Gene knows it, and now they pretty much stay out of my hair and away from my oatmeal, and they've made a nice life together, and who do you think paid for Gene's wheelchair ramp with the money he made from a certain series of Seminars?"

The crowd burst into applause. Tom Rodgers held up his hand.

"Now, what about you folks?" he said softly. "Is now the time for you to win? Are you ready to screen off your metaphorical oatmeal and identify your own personal Gene? Who is it that's screwing you up? Who's keeping you from getting what you want? Somebody is! God doesn't make junk. If you're losing, somebody's doing it to you. Today I'll be guiding you through my Three Essential Steps: Identification, Screening, Confrontation. First, we'll Identify your personal Gene. Second, we'll help you mentally install a metaphorical Screen over your symbolic oatmeal. Finally we'll show you how to Confront your personal Gene and make it clear to him or her that your oatmeal is henceforth off-limits."

Tom Rodgers looked intensely out into the crowd.

"So what do you think, guys?" he asked, very softly. "Are you up for it?"

From the crowd came a nervous murmur of assent.

"All right, then," he said. "Let's line up. Let's line up for a change. A *dramatic* change."

He crisply left the stage, and a spotlight panned across five Personal Change Centers, small white tents set up in a row near the fire door.

Neil Yaniky rose with the rest and checked his Line Assignment and joined his Assigned Line. He was a tiny man, nearly thirty, balding on top and balding on the sides, and was still chewing on his mustache and wondering if anyone or everyone else at the Seminar could tell that he was a big stupid faker, because he had no career, really, and no business, but only soldered little triangular things in his basement, for forty-seven cents a little triangular thing, for CompuParts, although he had high hopes for something better, which was why he was here.

The flap of Personal Change Center 4 flew open and in he went, bending low.

Inside were Tom Rodgers and several assistants, and a dummy in a smock sitting in a chair.

"Welcome, Neil," said Tom Rodgers, glancing at Yaniky's name tag. "I'm honored to have you in my Seminar, Neil. Now. The way we'll start, Neil, is for you to please write across the chest of this dummy the name of your real-life personal Gene. That is, the name of the person you perceive to be crapping in your oatmeal. Do you understand what I'm saying?"

"Yes," said Yaniky.

Tom Rodgers was talking very fast, as if he had hundreds of people to change in a single day, which of course he did. Yaniky had no problem with that. He was just happy to be one of them.

"Do you need help determining who that person is?" said Tom Rodgers. "Your oatmeal-crapper?"

"No," said Yaniky.

"Excellent," said Tom Rodgers. "Now write the name and under it write the major way in which you perceive this person to be crapping in your oatmeal. Be frank. This is just between you and me."

On an erasable markerboard permanently mounted in the dummy's chest Yaniky wrote, "Winky: Crazy-looking and too religious and needs her own place."

"Super!" said Tom Rodgers. "A great start. Now watch what I do. Let's fine-tune. Can we cut 'crazy-looking'? If this person, this Winky, were to get her own place, would the fact that she looks crazy still be an issue? Less of an issue?"

Yaniky pictured his sister looking crazy but in her own apartment.

"Less of an issue," he said.

"All right!" said Tom Rodgers, erasing "crazy-looking." "It's important to simplify so that we can hone in on exactly what we're trying to change. Okay. At this point, we've determined that if we can get her out of your house, the crazy-looking can be lived with. A big step forward. But why stop there? Let me propose something: if she's out of your hair, what the heck do you care if she's religious?"

Yaniky pictured Winky looking crazy and talking crazy about God but in her own apartment.

"It would definitely be better," he said.

"Yes, it would," said Tom Rodgers, and erased until the dummy was labeled "Winky: needs her own place."

"See?" said Tom Rodgers. "See how we've simplified? We've got it down to one issue. Can you live with this simple, direct statement of the problem?"

"Yes," Yaniky said. "Yes, I can."

Yaniky saw now what it was about Winky that got on his nerves. It wasn't her formerly red curls, which had gone white, so it looked like she had soaked the top of her head in glue and dipped it in a vat of cotton balls; it wasn't the bald spot that every morning she painted with some kind of white substance; it wasn't her shiny-pink face that was always getting weird joyful looks on it at bad times, like during his dinner date with Beverly Amstel, when he'd made his special meatballs to no avail, because Bev kept glancing over at Winky in panic; it wasn't the way she came click-click-clicking in from teaching church school and hugged him for too long a time while smelling like flower water, all pumped up from spreading the word of damn Christ; it was simply that they were too old to be living together and he had things he wanted to accomplish and she was too needy and blurred his focus.

"Have you told this person, this Winky, that her living with you is a stumbling block for your personal development?" said Tom Rodgers.

"No I haven't," Yaniky said.

"I thought not," said Tom Rodgers. "You're kindhearted. You don't want to hurt her. That's nice, but guess what? You are hurting her. You're hurting her by not telling her the truth. Am I saying that you, by your silence, are crapping in her oatmeal? Yes, I am. I'm saying that there's a sort of reciprocal crapping going on here. How can Winky grow on a diet of lies? Isn't it true that the truth will set you free? Didn't someone once say that? Wasn't it God or Christ, which would be ironic, because of her being so religious?"

Tom Rodgers gestured to an assistant, who took a wig out of a box and put it on the dummy's head.

"What we're going to do now is act this out symbolically," Tom Rodgers said. "Primitive cultures do this all the time. They might throw Fertility a big party say, or paint their kids white and let them whack Sickness with palm fronds and so forth. Are we somehow smarter than primitive cultures? I doubt it. I think maybe we're dumber. Do we have fewer hemorrhoids? Were Incas killed on freeways? Here, take this."

He handed Yaniky a baseball bat.

"What time is it, Neil?" said Tom Rodgers.

"Time to win?" said Yaniky. "Time for me to win?"

"Now is the time for you to win," said Tom Rodgers, clarifying, and pointed to the dummy.

Yaniky swung the bat and the dummy toppled over and the wig flew off and the assistant retrieved the wig and tossed it back into the box of wigs, and Tom Rodgers gave Yaniky a big hug.

"What you have just symbolically said," Tom Rodgers said, "is: 'No more, Winky. Grow wings, Winky. I love you, but you're killing me, and I am a good person, a child of God, and don't deserve to die. I deserve to live, I demand to live, and therefore, get your own place, girl! Fly and someday thank me!' This is to be your submantra, Neil, okay? *Out you go!* On your way home today I want you to be muttering, not angrily muttering but sort of joyfully muttering, to center yourself, the following words: 'Now Is the Time for Me to Win! Out you go! Out you go!' Will you do that for me?"

"Yes," said Yaniky, very much moved.

"And now here is Vicki," said Tom Rodgers, "One of my very top Gold Hats, who will walk you through the Confrontation step. Neil! I wish you luck, and peace, and all the success in the world."

Vicki had a face that looked as if it had been smashed against a steering wheel in a crash and then carefully reworked until it somewhat resembled her previous face. Several parallel curved indentations ran from temple to chin. She led Yaniky to a folding table labeled "Confrontation Center" and gave him a sheet of paper on which was written, "Gentle, Firm, Loving."

"These are the characteristics of a good Confrontation," she said, a bit mechanically. "Now flip it over."

On the other side was written, "Angry, Wimpy, Accusatory."

"These are the characteristics of a bad Confrontation," said Vicki. "A destructive Confrontation. Okay. So let's say I'm this person, this Winky person, and you're going to tell me to hit the road. Gentle, Firm, Loving. Now begin."

And he began telling Vicki to her damaged face that she was ruining his life and sucking him dry and that she had to go live somewhere else, and Vicki nodded and patted his hand, and now and then stopped him to tell him he was being too severe.

Neil-Neil was coming home soon and Winky was way way behind.

Some days she took her time while cleaning, smiling at happy thoughts, frowning when she imagined someone being taken advantage of, and sometimes the person being taken advantage of was a frail little boy with a scar on his head and the person taking advantage was a big fat man with a cane, and other times the person being taken advantage of was a kindly friendly British girl with a speech impediment and the person taking advantage was her rich, pushy sister who spoke in perfect diction and always got everything she wanted and went around whining while sucking little pink candies. Sometimes Winky asked the rich sister in her mind how she'd like to have the little pink candies slapped right out of her mouth. But that wasn't right.

That wasn't Christ's way! You didn't slap the little pink candies out of her mouth, you let her slap your mouth, seventy times seven times, which was like four hundred times, and after she'd slapped you the last time she suddenly understood it all and begged your forgiveness and gave you some candy, because that was the healing power of love.

For crying out loud! What was she doing? Was she crazy? It was time to get going! Why was she standing in the kitchen thinking?

She dashed up the stairs with a strip of broken molding under her arm and a dirty sock over her shoulder.

Halfway up she paused at a little octagonal window and looked dreamily out, thinking, In a way, we own those trees. Beyond the Thieus' was the same old gap in the leaning elms showing the same old meadow that would soon be ToyTowne. But for now it still reminded her of the kind of field where Christ with his lap full of flowers had suffered with the little children, which was a scene she wanted them to put on the cover of the singing album she was going to make, the singing album about God, which would have a watercolor cover like *Shoulder My Burden,* which was a book though but anyways it had this patient donkey piled high with crates and behind it this mountain, and the point of that book was that if you take on the worries and cares of others, Lord Jesus will take on your cares and worries, so that was why the patient donkey and why the crates, and why she prided herself on keeping house for Neil-Neil and never asked him for help.

Holy cow, what was she doing standing on the landing! Was she crazy? Today she was rushing! She was giving Neil-Neil a tea! She burst from the landing, taking two stairs at once. The molding had to go to the attic and the dirty sock to the hamper. While she was up, she could change her top. Because on it was some crusty soup. The wallpaper at the top of the stairs showed about a million of the same girl whacking a smiling goose with a riding crop. Hello, girls! Hello, girls! Ha ha! Hello, geese! Not to leave you out!

From a drawer in her room she took the green top, which Neil-Neil liked. Once when she was wearing it he'd asked if it was new. When had that been? At the lunch at the Beef Barn, when he paid, when he asked would she like to leave Rustic Village Apartments and come live with him. Oh, that sweetie. She still had the matchbook. Those had been sad days at Rustic Village, with every friend engaged but Doris, who had a fake arm, and boy those girls could sometimes say mean things, but now it was all behind her, and she needed to send poor Doris a card.

But not today, today she was rushing!

Down the stairs she pounded, still holding the molding, sock still over her shoulder.

In the kitchen she ripped open the cookie bag but there were no clean plates, so she rinsed a plate but there was no towel, so she dried the plate with her top. Hey she still had on the yellow top. What the heck? Where was the green top? Hadn't she just gotten it out of her drawer? Ha ha! That was funny She should send that in to *ChristLife.* They liked cute funny things that happened, even if they had nothing to do with Jesus.

The kitchen was a disaster! But first things first. Her top sucked. Not sucked, sucked was a bad word, her top was yugly Dad used to say that, yugly. Not about her. He always said she was purty. Sometimes he said things were purty yugly But not her.

He always said she was purty purty, then lifted her up. Oh Dad, Daddy Poppy-Popp! Was Poppy-Popp one with the Savior? She hoped so. Sometimes he used to swear and sometimes he used to drink, and once he swore when he fell down the stairs when he was drunk, but when she ran to him he hopped up laughing, and oh, when he sang "Peace in the Valley" you could tell he felt things would be better beyond, which had been a super example for a young Christian kid to witness.

She flew back up the stairs to change her top. Here was the green top, on the top step! Bad top! I should spank! She gave the green top a snap to undust it and discipline it and, putting the strip of molding and the dirty sock on the step, changed tops right then and there, picked up the molding, threw the dirty sock over her shoulder, and pounded back down the stairs.

There were so many many things to do! Not only now, for the tea, but in the future! It was time to get going! Now that she was out of that lonely apartment she could finally learn to play the piano, and once she learned to play and write songs, she could write her songs about God, then find out about making a record, her record about God, about how God had been good to her in this life, because look at her! A plain girl in a nice home! Oh, she knew she was plain, her legs were thick and her waist was thick and her hair, oh my God—oh my gosh, rather—her hair, what kind of hair was that to have, yugly white hair, and many was the time she had thought, This is not hair, this is a test. The test of white sparse hair, when so many had gorgeous manes, and that was why, when she looked in a mirror by accident and saw her white horrible hair, she always tried to think to herself, Praise God!

Neil-Neil was the all-time sweetie pie. Those girls were crazy! Did they think because a man was small and bald he had no love? Did they think bad things came in small packages? Neil-Neil was like the good brother in the Bible, the one who stayed home with his dad on the farm and never got even a small party. Except there was no bad brother, it was just the two of them, so no party although she'd get her party, a big party in Heaven, and was sort of even having her party now, on earth, because when she saw that little man all pee-stained at Rexall Drug, not begging but just saying to every person who went in that he or she was looking dapper, she knew that he was truly the least of her brothers. The world was a story Christ was telling her. And when she told the pee-man at the Rexall that he was looking dapper himself and he said loudly that she was too ugly to f——, she had only thought to herself, Okay, praise God, he's only saying that because he's in pain, and had smiled with the lightest light in her eyes she could get there by wishing it there, because even if she was a little yugly she was still beautiful in Christ's sight, so for her it was all a party, a little party before a bigger party, the biggest, but what about Neil-Neil, where was his party?

She would do what she could! This would be his party, one tiny installment on the huge huge party he deserved, her brother, her pal to the end, the only loving soul she had yet found in this world.

The bell rang and she threw open the door, and there was Neil-Neil.

"Welcome home!" she said grandly, and bowed at the waist, and the sock fell off her shoulder.

Yaniky had walked home in a frenzy, gazing into shop windows, knowing that someday soon, when he came into these shops with his sexy wife, he'd simply point out items with his riding crop and they would be loaded into his waiting Benz, although come to think of it, why a riding crop? Who used a riding crop? Did you use a riding crop on the Benz? Ho, man, he was stoked! He wanted a Jag, not a Benz! Golden statues of geese, classy vases, big porcelain frogs, whatever, when his ship came in he'd have it all, because when he was stoked nothing could stop him.

If Dad could see him now walking home in a suit from a seminar at the freaking Hyatt! Poor Dad, not that he was bashing Dad, but had Dad been a seeker? Well, no, Dad had been no seeker, life had beaten Dad. Dad had spent every evening with a beer on the divan, under a comforter, and he remembered poor Ma in her Sunday dress, which had a rip, which she'd taped because she couldn't sew, and Dad in his too big hat, recently fired again, all of them on the way to church, dragging past a crowd of spick hoods on the corner, and one spick said something about Ma's boobs, which were big, but all of Ma was big, so why did the hood have to say something about her big boobs, as if they were nice? When they all knew they weren't nice, they were just a big woman's boobs in a too tight dress on a rainy Sunday morning, and on her head was a slit-open bread bag to keep her gray hair dry. The hood said what he said because one look at Dad told him he could. Dad, with his hunched shoulders and his constant blinking, just took Ma's arm and mumbled to the hood that a comment like that did more damage to the insulter than to the insulted, etc. etc. blah blah blah. Then the hood made a sound like a cow, at Ma, and Neil, who was nine, tried to break away and take a swing at the hood but Ma had his hand and wouldn't turn him loose and secretly he was glad, because he was scared, and then was ashamed at the relief he felt on entering the dark church, where the thin panicked preacher who was losing his congregation exchanged sly biblical quotes with Dad while Winky stood beaming as if none of it outside had happened, the lower half of her body gone psychedelic in the stained-glass light.

Oh man, the world had shit on Dad, but it wasn't going to shit on him. No way. If the world thought he was going to live in a neighborhood where spicks insulted his wife's boobs, if the world thought he was going to make his family eat bread dragged through bacon grease while calling it Hobo's Delight, the world was just wrong, he was going to succeed, like the men described in *People of Power,* who had gardens bigger than entire towns and owned whole ships and believed in power and power only. Were thirty horse-drawn carts needed to save the roses? The call went out to the surrounding towns and at dusk lanterns from the carts could be seen approaching on the rocky, bumpy roads. Was a serving girl found attractive? Her husband was sent away to war. Those guys knew how to find and occupy their Power Places, and he did too, like when he sometimes had to solder a thousand triangular things in a night to make the rent, and drink coffee till dawn and crank WMDX full blast to stay psyched. On those nights, when Winky came up making small talk, he boldly waved her away, and when he waved her away, away she went, because she sensed in his body language that he was king, that what he was doing was essential, and when she went away he felt good, he felt strong, and he soldered faster, which was the phenomenon the book called the Power Boost, and the book said that Major Successes tended to be people who could string together Power Boost after Power Boost, which was accomplished by doing exactly what you felt like doing at any given time, with certainty and joy, which was what, he realized, he was about to do, by kicking out Winky!

Now was the time for him to win! Why the heck couldn't he cook his special meatballs for Beverly and afterward make love to her on the couch and tell her his dreams and plans and see if she was the one meant to be his life's helpmate, like Mrs. Thomas Alva Edison, who had once stayed up all night applying labels to a shipment of chemicals essential for the next day's work? But no. Bev was dating someone else now, some kind of guard at the mall, and he remembered the meatball dinner, Winky's pink face periodically thrusting into the steam from the broccoli as she trotted out her usual B.S. on stigmata and the amount of time necessary for an actual physical body to rot. No wonder her roommates had kicked her out, calling him in secret, no wonder her preacher had demanded she stop volunteering so much—another secret call, people had apparently been quitting the church because of her. She was a nut, a real energy sink, it had been a huge mistake inviting her to live with him, and now she simply had to go.

It was sad, yes, a little sad, but if greatness were easy everyone would be doing it.

Yes, she'd been a cute kid and, yes, they'd shared some nice moments, yes yes yes, yes she'd brought him crackers and his little radio that time he'd hid under the steps for five straight hours after Dad started weeping during dinner, and yes, he remembered the scared look in her eyes when she'd come running up to him after taking a hook in the temple while fishing with the big boys, and yes, he'd carried her home as the big boys cackled, yes, it was sad that she sang so bad and thought it was good and sad that her panties were huge now when he found them in the wash, but like it said in the book, a person couldn't throw himself across someone else's funeral pyre without getting pretty goddamned hot.

She had his key so he rang the bell.

She appeared at the door, looking crazy as ever.

"Welcome home!" she said, and bowed at the waist, and a sock fell off her shoulder, and as she bent to pick it up she banged her head against the storm window, the poor dorky thing.

Oh shit, oh shit, he was weakening, he could feel it, the speech he'd practiced on the way home seemed now to have nothing to do with the girl who stood wet-eyed in the doorway, rubbing her bald spot. He wasn't powerful, he wasn't great, he was just the same as everybody else, less than everybody else, other people got married and had real jobs, other people didn't live with their fat, clinging sisters, he was a loser who would keep losing for the rest of his life, because he'd never gotten a break, he'd been cursed with a bad dad and a bad ma and a bad sister, and was too weak to change, too weak to make a new start, and as he pushed by her into the tea-smelling house the years ahead stretched out bleak and joyless in his imagination and his chest went suddenly dense with rage.

"Neil-Neil," she said. "Is something wrong?"

And he wanted to smack her, insult her, say something to wake her up, but only kept moving toward his room, calling her terrible names under his breath.

John Updike (1932–)

was born in Shillington, Pennsylvania, the only child of an algebra teacher (his father) and an aspiring short story writer (his mother). For much of his childhood, he lived on his mother's parents' farm (a place not unlike the farm in "Pigeon Feathers" and "A Sandstone Farmhouse"). He was a straight-A student and received a full scholarship to Harvard University. There, he studied English and was president of the Harvard Lampoon, *a humor magazine to which he regularly contributed cartoons and poems. He graduated* summa cum laude, *spent a year studying art at the Ruskin School of Design in Oxford, England, then returned to the United States to take a staff position at* The New Yorker, *the magazine to which he would eventually contribute more pages than any other writer in its history. In 1959, he published his first novel,* The Poorhouse Fair, *and moved to Massachusetts, where he has lived ever since. Winner of nearly every major American literary award (two Pulitzer Prizes, the National Book Award, the National Book Critics Circle Award, and almost countless others), Updike is perhaps best known for his tetralogy of novels that chronicle the life of Harry "Rabbit" Angstrom, a Pennsylvanian suburbanite, from young adulthood though middle age and to death. But Updike has also written more than two hundred short stories and has said that his stories "more closely . . . hold my life's incidents, predicaments, crises, joys. Furthermore, they made my life possible, for I depended when young upon their sale to supply my livelihood." His prodigious achievement in the form led to his selection as the editor for* The Best American Short Stories of the Century.

INTRODUCTION BY **Brock Clarke**

One of the many things John Updike can teach us—and there are too many things to list here, and the things themselves are too significant to be merely listed or to be called "things," for that matter—is that in short fiction, something must be *off.* This is not to say that something must be horribly, obviously wrong: There are no car wrecks or men hurling themselves from skyscrapers in these three stories—one from early in his career, one from the middle, and one from a decade ago. Updike is not a short story writer who is interested in disasters, but rather a writer whose eye turns to what is slightly amiss—furniture where it shouldn't be, girls in bathing suits where "proper attire" is required—and much of the terror and sadness and pleasures (sometimes mean, sometimes not) of Updike's work come from watching these small wrongs turn larger and larger until there is no longer any way to ignore them, until the world we thought we knew becomes something slightly off itself. In "Pigeon Feathers," Updike's protagonist, David, flips through his parents' books and, "As he bent over the pages, yellow at the edges, they seemed rectangles of dusty glass through which he looked down into unreal and irrelevant worlds." If we take out the words "and irrelevant," this is a pretty fair description of what it's like to read Updike himself.

It seems silly to introduce "A & P," certainly Updike's most anthologized story and possibly the most anthologized story ever, but then again there is a reason this story is so widely read, a reason we keep coming back, no matter how well we think we know it. Like Updike's other two stories in this anthology, this one begins with a sense of what makes this day different from other days: Three girls in bathing suits walk into a grocery store. At the same time, we're introduced to the narrator, Sammy, and his voice, which is the other thing that truly matters in the story: "She's one of those cash-register-watchers, a witch about fifty with rouge on her cheekbones and no eyebrows." Sammy's voice, a variation on the familiar tough guy, full of what is obviously false bravado, distinguishes "A & P" from the latter two stories in this anthology (both of which are told in the third person and are quiet, contemplative). Despite these differences, Updike does at the beginning of "A & P" what he does in "Pigeon Feathers" and "A Sandstone Farmhouse": There is something that doesn't belong (the three girls), and we see what doesn't belong through the eyes of someone who might or might not belong himself. What will these girls cause Sammy to do? What is his own deviance? There is always a strong sense of mystery in Updike's short fiction, and that comes from the promise that we will learn exactly what is off—for instance, even though the town is nominally a beach town, the A & P is five miles from the beach, and "there's people in this town haven't seen the ocean in twenty years"—and the price to be paid for this aberrance. Indeed, one of the reasons writers can still learn from this story is that Sammy's defense of the girls against the small-mindedness of the store manager should be triumphant but isn't: "my stomach kind of fell as I felt how hard the world was going to be to me hereafter." There is no release, no rising above in Updike, but the world of his fiction is so interesting, so compelling in its offness that we shouldn't want to rise above it anyway.

Indeed, this is one of the rules that guide Updike's two later stories, "Pigeon Feathers" and "A Sandstone Farmhouse": The writer must know better than his characters, but he cannot *be* better. "Pigeon Feathers" begins with a family's move, and "things were upset, displaced, rearranged." David, Updike's young protagonist, tries to find order in God and in books, and Updike places enough distance between himself (and us) and David that we know this is a doomed enterprise; but it is familiar enough to us and it is rendered so carefully that we cannot *entirely* distance ourselves from it, so that we feel about the story as David's father feels about all this religious talk: "he . . . dug into his ear with a match miserably . . . to get at the thing inside his head." And speaking of distance, the Updike of these two later stories is chilly—he is sometimes like David, who "saw his position with a certain strategic coldness"—but the coldness is never a safety device, never a pose, never a barrier that the writer places between himself and what might pain him, but rather the thing the story seeks to overcome. And as Updike teaches us, the writer must overcome the coldness with loving, careful descriptions—of the dog and the pigeons in "Pigeon Feathers," of the mother and the house in "A Sandstone Farmhouse" (which in many ways is a sequel to "Pigeon Feathers"). The terrifying thing, of course, is that once the chilliness is overcome, once Updike creates objects and people worthy of love, then those people die, or those objects are revealed to be somewhat less than ideal, or they become meaningful in all the wrong ways, and then we end up longing for that coldness, that distance. But by then it's too late, and that's just another Updikean tactic from which we can learn, for which we should feel grateful.

There are, of course, other things worth mentioning here: Updike's terrific sense of humor and trickily profound insights—what is not to love about a writer who points out that "The dead are so feeble they can't even telephone"?—but the riches herein are so great that some of them, in this kind of introduction, are inevitably lost, just like the job in

"A & P," God and the pigeons in "Pigeon Feathers," the mother in "A Sandstone Farmhouse," and everything else Updike makes us finally love and relish, just before he takes them from us.

Brock Clarke is the author of the novel The Ordinary White Boy *(2001) and the short story collection* What We Won't Do *(2002). He is an assistant professor of English and Creative Writing at the University of Cincinnati.*

John Updike

A & P

In walks these three girls in nothing but bathing suits. I'm in the third checkout slot, with my back to the door, so I don't see them until they're over by the bread. The one that caught my eye first was the one in the plaid green two-piece. She was a chunky kid, with a good tan and a sweet broad soft-looking can with those two crescents of white just under it, where the sun never seems to hit, at the top of the backs of her legs. I stood there with my hand on a box of HiHo crackers trying to remember if I rang it up or not. I ring it up again and the customer starts giving me hell. She's one of these cash-register-watchers, a witch about fifty with rouge on her cheekbones and no eyebrows, and I know it made her day to trip me up. She'd been watching cash registers for fifty years and probably never seen a mistake before.

By the time I got her feathers smoothed and her goodies into a bag—she gives me a little snort in passing, if she'd been born at the right time they would have burned her over in Salem—by the time I get her on her way the girls had circled around the bread and were coming back, without a pushcart, back my way along the counters, in the aisle between the checkouts and the Special bins. They didn't even have shoes on. There was this chunky one, with the two-piece—it was bright green and the seams on the bra were still sharp and her belly was still pretty pale so I guessed she just got it (the suit)—there was this one, with one of those chubby berry-faces, the lips all bunched together under her nose, this one, and a tall one, with black hair that hadn't quite frizzed right, and one of these sunburns right across the eyes, and a chin that was too long—you know, the kind of girl other girls think is very "striking" and "attractive" but never quite makes it, as they very well know, which is why they like her so much—and then the third one, that wasn't quite so tall. She was the queen. She kind of led them, the other two peeking around and making their shoulders round. She didn't look around, not this queen, she just walked straight on slowly, on these long white prima-donna legs. She came down a little hard on her heels, as if she didn't walk in her bare feet that much, putting down her heels and then letting the weight move along to her toes as if she was testing the floor with every step, putting a little deliberate extra action into it. You never know for sure how girls' minds work (do you really think it's a mind in there or just a little buzz like a bee in a glass jar?) but you got the idea she had talked the other two into coming in here with her, and now she was showing them how to do it, walk slow and hold yourself straight.

She had on a kind of dirty-pink—beige maybe, I don't know—bathing suit with a little nubble all over it and, what got me, the straps were down. They were off her shoulders looped loose around the cool tops of her arms, and I guess as a result the suit had slipped a little on her, so all around the top of the cloth there was this shining rim. If it hadn't been there you wouldn't have known there could have been anything whiter than those shoulders. With the straps pushed off, there was nothing between the top of the suit and the top of her head except just *her,* this clean bare plane on the top of her chest down from the shoulder bones like a dented sheet of metal tilted in the light. I mean, it was more than pretty.

She had sort of oaky hair that the sun and salt had bleached, done up in a bun that was unravelling, and a kind of prim face. Walking into the A & P with your straps down, I suppose it's the only kind of face you *can* have. She held her head so high her neck, coming up out of those white shoulders, looked kind of stretched, but I didn't mind. The longer her neck was, the more of her there was.

She must have felt in the corner of her eye me and over my shoulder Stokesie in the second slot watching, but she didn't tip. Not this queen. She kept her eyes moving across the racks, and stopped, and turned so slow it made my stomach rub the inside of my apron, and buzzed to the other two, who kind of huddled against her for relief, and then they all three of them went up to the cat-and-dog-food-breakfast-cereal-macaroni-rice-raisins-seasoning-spreads-spaghetti-soft-drinks-crackers-and-cookies aisle. From the third slot I look straight up this aisle to the meat counter, and I watched them all the way. The fat one with the tan sort of fumbled with the cookies, but on second thought she put the packages back. The sheep pushing their carts down the aisle—the girls were walking against the usual traffic (not that we have one-way signs or anything)—were pretty hilarious. You could see them, when Queenie's white shoulders dawned on them, kind of jerk, or hop, or hiccup, but their eyes snapped back to their own baskets and on they pushed. I bet you could set off dynamite in an A & P and the people would by and large keep reaching and checking oatmeal off their lists and muttering "Let me see, there was a third thing, began with A, asparagus, no, ah, yes applesauce!" or whatever it is they do mutter. But there was no doubt, this jiggled them. A few houseslaves in pin curlers even looked around after pushing their carts past to make sure what they had seen was correct.

You know, it's one thing to have a girl in a bathing suit down on the beach, where what with the glare nobody can look at each other much anyway, and another thing in the cool of the A & P, under the fluorescent lights, against all those stacked packages, with her feet paddling along naked over our checkerboard green-and-cream rubber-tile floor.

"Oh Daddy," Stokesie said beside me. "I feel so faint."

"Darling," I said. "Hold me tight." Stokesie's married, with two babies chalked up on his fuselage already, but as far as I can tell that's the only difference. He's twenty-two, and I was nineteen this April.

"Is it done?" he asks, the responsible married man finding his voice. I forgot to say he thinks he's going to be manager some sunny day, maybe in 1990 when it's called the Great Alexandrov and Petrooshki Tea Company or something.

What he meant was, our town is five miles from a beach, with a big summer colony out on the Point, but we're right in the middle of town, and the women generally put on a shirt or shorts or something before they get out of the car into the street. And anyway these are usually women with six children and varicose veins mapping their legs and nobody, including them, could care less. As I say, we're right in the middle of town, and if you stand at our front doors you can see two banks and the Congregational church and the newspaper store and three real-estate offices and about twenty-seven old freeloaders tearing up Central Street because the sewer broke again. It's not as if we're on the Cape; we're north of Boston and there's people in this town haven't seen the ocean for twenty years.

The girls had reached the meat counter and were asking McMahon something. He pointed, they pointed, and they shuffled out of sight behind a pyramid of Diet Delight peaches. All that was left for us to see was old McMahon patting his mouth and looking after them sizing up their joints. Poor kids, I began to feel sorry for them, they couldn't help it.

Now here comes the sad part of the story, at least my family says it's sad, but I don't think it's sad myself. The store's pretty empty, it being Thursday afternoon, so there was nothing much to do except lean on the register and wait for the girls to show up again. The whole store was like a pinball machine and I didn't know which tunnel they'd come out of. After a while they come around out of the far aisle, around the light bulbs, records at discount of the Caribbean Six or Tony Martin Sings or some such gunk you wonder they waste the wax on, sixpacks of candy bars, and plastic toys done up in cellophane that fall apart when a kid looks at them anyway. Around they come, Queenie still leading the way, and holding a little gray jar in her hand. Slots Three through Seven are unmanned and I could see her wondering between Stokes and me, but Stokesie with his usual luck draws an old party in baggy gray pants who stumbles up with four giant cans of pineapple juice (what do these bums *do* with all that pineapple juice? I've often asked myself) so the girls come to me. Queenie puts down the jar and I take it into my fingers icy cold. Kingfish Fancy Herring Snacks in Pure Sour Cream: 49¢. Now her hands are empty, not a ring or a bracelet, bare as God made them and I wonder where the money's coming from. Still with that prim look she lifts a folded dollar bill out of the hollow at the center of her nubbled pink top. The jar went heavy in my hand. Really, I thought that was so cute.

Then everybody's luck begins to run out. Lengel comes in from haggling with a truck full of cabbages on the lot and is about to scuttle into that door marked MANAGER behind which he hides all day when the girls touch his eye. Lengel's pretty dreary, teaches Sunday school and the rest, but he doesn't miss that much. He comes over and says, "Girls, this isn't the beach."

Queenie blushes, though maybe it's just a brush of sunburn I was noticing for the first time, now that she was so close. "My mother asked me to pick up a jar of herring snacks." Her voice kind of startled me, the way voices do when you see the people first, coming out so flat and dumb yet kind of tony too, the way it ticked over "pick up" and "snacks." All of a sudden I slid right down her voice into her living room. Her father and the other men were standing around in ice-cream coats and bow ties and the women were in sandals picking up herring snacks on toothpicks off a big glass plate and they were all holding drinks the color of water with olives and sprigs of mint in them. When my parents have somebody over they get lemonade and if it's a real racy affair Schlitz in tall glasses with "They'll Do It Every Time" cartoons stencilled on.

"That's all right," Lengel said. "But this isn't the beach." His repeating this struck me as funny, as if it had just occurred to him, and he had been thinking all these years the A & P was a great big dune and he was the head lifeguard. He didn't like my smiling—as I say he doesn't miss much—but he concentrates on giving the girls that sad Sunday-school-superintendent stare.

Queenie's blush is no sunburn now, and the plump one in plaid, that I liked better from the back—a really sweet can—pipes up. "We weren't doing any shopping. We just came in for one thing."

"That makes no difference," Lengel tells her, and I could see from the way his eyes went that he hadn't noticed she was wearing a two-piece before. "We want you decently dressed when you come in here."

"We *are* decent," Queenie says suddenly, her lower lip pushing, getting sore now that she remembers her place, a place from which the crowd that runs the A & P must look pretty crummy. Fancy Herring Snacks flashed in her very blue eyes.

"Girls, I don't want to argue with you. After this come in here with your shoulders covered. It's our policy." He turns back. That's policy for you. Policy is what the kingpins want. What the others want is juvenile delinquency.

All this while, the customers had been showing up with their carts but, you know, sheep, seeing a scene, they all bunched up on Stokesie, who shook open a paper bag as gently as peeling a peach, not wanting to miss a word. I could feel in the silence everybody getting nervous, most of all Lengel, who asks me, "Sammy, have you rung up their purchase?"

I thought and said "No" but it wasn't about that I was thinking. I go through the punches, 4, 9, GROC, TOT—it's more complicated than you think, and after you do it often enough, it begins to make a little song, that you hear words to, in my case "Hello *(bing)* there, you *(gung)* hap-py pee-pul *(splat)!*"—the splat being the drawer flying out. I uncrease the bill, tenderly as you may imagine, it just having come from between the two smoothest scoops of vanilla I had ever known were there, and pass a half and a penny into her narrow pink palm, and nestle the herrings in a bag and twist its neck and hand it over, all the time thinking.

The girls, and who'd blame them, are in a hurry to get out, so I say "I quit" to Lengel quick enough for them to hear, hoping they'll stop and watch me, their unsuspected hero. They keep right on going, into the electric eye; the door flies open and they flicker across the lot to their car. Queenie and Plaid and Big Tall Goony-Goony (not that as raw material she was so bad), leaving me with Lengel and a kink in his eyebrow.

"Did you say something, Sammy?"

"I said I quit."

"I thought you did."

"You didn't have to embarrass them."

"It was they who were embarrassing us."

I started to say something that came out "Fiddle-de-doo." It's a saying of my grandmother's, and I know she would have been pleased.

"I don't think you know what you're saying," Lengel said.

"I know you don't," I said. "But I do." I pull the bow at the back of my apron and start shrugging it off my shoulders. A couple customers that had been heading for my slot begin to knock against each other, like scared pigs in a chute.

Lengel sighs and begins to look very patient and old and gray. He's been a friend of my parents for years. "Sammy, you don't want to do this to your Mom and Dad," he tells me. It's true, I don't. But it seems to me that once you begin a gesture it's fatal not to go through with it. I fold my apron, "Sammy" stitched in red on the pocket, and put it on the counter, and drop the bow tie on top of it. The bow tie is theirs, if you've ever wondered. "You'll feel this for the rest of your life," Lengel says, and I know that's true, too, but remembering how he made that pretty girl blush makes me so scrunchy inside I punch the No Sale tab and the machine whirs "pee-pul" and the drawer splats out. One advantage to this scene taking place in summer, I can follow this up with a clean exit, there's no fumbling around getting your coat and galoshes, I just saunter into the electric eye in my white shirt that my mother ironed the night before, and the door heaves itself open, and outside the sunshine is skating around on the asphalt.

I look around for my girls, but they're gone, of course. There wasn't anybody but some young married screaming with her children about some candy they didn't get by the door of a powder-blue Falcon station wagon. Looking back in the big windows, over the bags of peat moss and aluminum lawn furniture stacked on the pavement, I could see Lengel in my place in the slot, checking the sheep through. His face was dark gray and his back stiff, as if he'd just had an injection of iron, and my stomach kind of fell as I felt how hard the world was going to be to me hereafter.

John Updike

Pigeon Feathers

When they moved to Firetown, things were upset, displaced, rearranged. A red cane-back sofa that had been the chief piece in the living room at Olinger was here banished, too big for the narrow country parlor, to the barn, and shrouded under a tarpaulin. Never again would David lie on its length all afternoon eating raisins and reading mystery novels and science fiction and P. G. Wodehouse. The blue wing chair that had stood for years in the ghostly, immaculate guest bedroom, gazing through the windows curtained with dotted swiss toward the telephone wires and horse-chestnut trees and opposite houses, was here established importantly in front of the smutty little fireplace that supplied, in those first cold April days, their only heat. As a child, David had been afraid of the guest bedroom—it was there that he, lying sick with the measles, had seen a black rod the size of a yardstick jog along at a slight slant beside the edge of the bed and vanish when he screamed—and it was disquieting to have one of the elements of its haunted atmosphere basking by the fire, in the center of the family, growing sooty with use. The books that at home had gathered dust in the case beside the piano were here hastily stacked, all out of order, in the shelves that the carpenters had built along one wall below the deep-silled windows. David, at fourteen, had been more moved than a mover; like the furniture, he had to find a new place, and on the Saturday of the second week he tried to work off some of his disorientation by arranging the books.

It was a collection obscurely depressing to him, mostly books his mother had acquired when she was young: college anthologies of Greek plays and Romantic poetry, Will Durant's *Story of Philosophy,* a soft-leather set of Shakespeare with string bookmarks sewed to the bindings, *Green Mansions* boxed and illustrated with woodcuts, *I, the Tiger,* by Manuel Komroff, novels by names like Galsworthy and Ellen Glasgow and Irvin S. Cobb and Sinclair Lewis and "Elizabeth." The odor of faded taste made him feel the ominous gap between himself and his parents, the insulting gulf of time that existed before he was born. Suddenly he was tempted to dip into this time. From the heaps of books piled around him on the worn old floorboards, he picked up Volume II of a four-volume set of *The Outline of History,* by H. G. Wells. Once David had read *The Time Machine* in an anthology; this gave him a small grip on the author. The book's red binding had faded to orange-pink on the spine. When he lifted the cover, there was a sweetish, attic-like smell, and his mother's maiden name written in unfamiliar handwriting on the flyleaf—an upright, bold, yet careful signature, bearing a faint relation to the quick scrunched backslant that flowed with marvellous consistency across her shopping lists and budget accounts and Christmas cards to college friends from this same, vaguely menacing long ago.

He leafed through, pausing at drawings, done in an old-fashioned stippled style, of bas-reliefs, masks, Romans without pupils in their eyes, articles of ancient costume, fragments of pottery found in unearthed homes. He knew it would be interesting in a magazine, sandwiched between ads and jokes, but in this undiluted form history was somehow sour. The print was determinedly legible, and smug, like a lesson book. As he bent over the pages, yellow at the edges, they seemed rectangles of dusty glass through which he looked down into unreal and irrelevant worlds. He could see things sluggishly move, and an unpleasant fullness came into his throat. His mother and grandmother fussed in the kitchen; the puppy, which they had just acquired, for "protection in the country," was cowering, with a sporadic panicked scrabble of claws, under the dining table that in their old home had been reserved for special days but that here was used for every meal.

Then, before he could halt his eyes, David slipped into Wells's account of Jesus. He had been an obscure political agitator, a kind of hobo, in a minor colony of the Roman Empire. By an accident impossible to reconstruct, he (the small *h* horrified David) survived his own crucifixion and presumably died a few weeks later. A religion was founded on the freakish incident. The credulous imagination of the times retrospectively assigned miracles and supernatural pretensions to Jesus; a myth grew, and then a church, whose theology at most points was in direct contradiction of the simple, rather communistic teachings of the Galilean.

It was as if a stone that for weeks and even years had been gathering weight in the web of David's nerves snapped them and plunged through the page and a hundred layers of paper underneath. These fantastic falsehoods—plainly untrue; churches stood everywhere, the entire nation was founded "under God"—did not at first frighten him; it was the fact that they had been permitted to exist in an actual human brain. This was the initial impact—that at a definite spot in time and space a brain black with the denial of Christ's divinity had been suffered to exist; that the universe had not spit out this ball of tar but allowed it to continue in its blasphemy, to grow old, win honors, wear a hat, write books that, if true, collapsed everything into a jumble of horror. The world outside the deep-silled windows—a rutted lawn, a white-washed barn, a walnut tree frothy with fresh green—seemed a haven from which he was forever sealed off. Hot washrags seemed pressed against his cheeks.

He read the account again. He tried to supply out of his ignorance objections that would defeat the complacent march of these black words, and found none. Survivals and misunderstandings more farfetched were reported daily in the papers. But none of them caused churches to be built in every town. He tried to work backwards through the churches, from their brave high fronts through their shabby, ill-attended interiors back into the events at Jerusalem, and felt himself surrounded by shifting gray shadows, centuries of history, where he knew nothing. The thread dissolved in his hands. Had Christ ever come to him, David Kern, and said, "Here. Feel the wound in My side"? No; but prayers had been answered. What prayers? He had prayed that Rudy Mohn, whom he had purposely tripped so he cracked his head on their radiator, not die, and he had not died. But for all the blood, it was just a cut; Rudy came back the same day, wearing a bandage and repeating the same teasing words. He could never have died. Again, David had prayed for two separate war-effort posters he had sent away for to arrive tomorrow, and though they did not, they did arrive, some days later, together, popping through the clacking letter slot like a rebuke from God's mouth: *I answer your prayers in My way, in My time.* After that, he had made his prayers less definite, less susceptible of being twisted into a scolding. But what a tiny, ridiculous coincidence this was, after all, to throw into battle against H. G. Wells's engines of knowledge! Indeed, it proved the enemy's point: Hope bases vast premises on foolish accidents, and reads a word where in fact only a scribble exists.

His father came home. Though Saturday was a free day for him, he had been working. He taught school in Olinger and spent all his days performing, with a curious air of panic, needless errands. Also, a city boy by birth, he was frightened of the farm and seized any excuse to get away. The farm had been David's mother's birthplace; it had been her idea to buy it back. With an ingenuity and persistence unparalleled in her life, she had gained that end, and moved them all here—her son, her husband, her mother. Granmom, in her prime, had worked these fields alongside her husband, but now she dabbled around the kitchen futilely, her hands waggling with Parkinson's disease. She was always in the way. Strange, out in the country, amid eighty acres, they were crowded together. His father expressed his feelings of discomfort by conducting with Mother an endless argument about organic farming. All through dusk, all through supper, it rattled on.

"Elsie, I *know,* I know from my education, the earth is nothing but chemicals. It's the only damn thing I got out of four years of college, so don't tell me it's not true."

"George, if you'd just walk out on the farm you'd know it's not true. The land has a *soul.*"

"Soil, has, no, soul," he said, enunciating stiffly, as if to a very stupid class. To David he said, "You can't argue with a femme. Your mother's a real femme. That's why I married her, and now I'm suffering for it."

"*This* soil has no soul," she said, "because it's been killed with superphosphate. It's been burned bare by Boyer's tenant farmers." Boyer was the rich man they had bought the farm from. "It used to have a soul, didn't it, Mother? When you and Pop farmed it?"

"Ach, yes; I guess." Granmom was trying to bring a forkful of food to her mouth with her less severely afflicted hand. In her anxiety she brought the other hand up from her lap. The crippled fingers, dull red in the orange light of the kerosene lamp in the center of the table, were welded by paralysis into one knobbed hook.

"Only human indi-vidu-als have souls," his father went on, in the same mincing, lifeless voice. "Because the Bible tells us so." Done eating, he crossed his legs and dug into his ear with a match miserably; to get at the thing inside his head he tucked in his chin, and his voice came out low-pitched at David. "When God made your mother, He made a real femme."

"George, don't you read the papers? Don't you know that between the chemical fertilizers and the bug sprays we'll all be dead in ten years? Heart attacks are killing every man in the country over forty-five."

He sighed wearily; the yellow skin of his eyelids wrinkled as he hurt himself with the match. "There's no connection," he stated, spacing his words with pained patience, "between the heart - and chemical fertilizers. It's alcohol that's doing it. Alcohol and milk. There is too much - cholesterol - in the tissues of the American heart. Don't tell me about chemistry, Elsie; I majored in the damn stuff for four years."

"Yes and I majored in Greek and I'm not a penny wiser. Mother, put your waggler away!" The old woman started, and the food dropped from her fork. For some reason, the sight of her bad hand at the table cruelly irritated her daughter. Granmom's eyes, worn bits of crazed crystal embedded in watery milk, widened behind her cockeyed spectacles. Circles of silver as fine as thread, they clung to the red notches they had carved over the years into her little white beak. In the orange flicker of the kerosene lamp her dazed misery seemed infernal. David's mother began, without noise, to cry. His father did not seem to have eyes at all; just jaundiced sockets of wrinkled skin. The steam of food clouded the scene. It was horrible but the horror was particular and familiar, and distracted David from the formless dread that worked, sticky and sore, within him, like a too large wound trying to heal.

He had to go to the bathroom, and took a flashlight down through the wet grass to the outhouse. For once, his fear of spiders there felt trivial. He set the flashlight, burning, beside him, and an insect alighted on its lens, a tiny insect, a mosquito or flea, made so fine that the weak light projected its X-ray onto the wall boards: the faint rim of its wings, the blurred strokes, magnified, of its long hinged legs, the dark cone at the heart of its anatomy. The tremor must be its heart beating. Without warning, David was visited by an exact vision of death: a long hole in the ground, no wider than your body, down which you are drawn while the white faces above recede. You try to reach them but your arms are pinned. Shovels pour dirt into your face. There you will be forever, in an upright position, blind and silent, and in time no one will remember you, and you will never be called. As strata of rock shift, your fingers elongate, and your teeth are distended sideways in a great underground grimace indistinguishable from a strip of chalk. And the earth tumbles on, and the sun expires, and unaltering darkness reigns where once there were stars.

Sweat broke out on his back. His mind seemed to rebound off a solidness. Such extinction was not another threat, a graver sort of danger, a kind of pain; it was qualitatively different. It was not even a conception that could be voluntarily pictured; it entered him from outside. His protesting nerves swarmed on its surface like lichen on a meteor. The skin of his chest was soaked with the effort of rejection. At the same time that the fear was dense and internal, it was dense and all around him; a tide of clay had swept up to the stars; space was crushed into a mass. When he stood up, automatically hunching his shoulders to keep his head away from the spider webs, it was with a numb sense of being cramped between two huge volumes of rigidity. That he had even this small freedom to move surprised him. In the narrow shelter of that rank shack, adjusting his pants, he felt—his first spark of comfort—too small to be crushed.

But in the open, as the beam of the flashlight skidded with frightened quickness across the remote surfaces of the barn and the grape arbor and the giant pine that stood by the path to the woods, the terror descended. He raced up through the clinging grass pursued, not by one of the wild animals the woods might hold, or one of the goblins his superstitious grandmother had communicated to his childhood, but by spectres out of science fiction, where gigantic cinder moons fill half the turquoise sky. As David ran, a gray planet rolled inches behind his neck. If he looked back, he would be buried. And in the momentum of his terror, hideous possibilities—the dilation of the sun, the triumph of the insects, the crabs on the shore in *The Time Machine*—wheeled out of the vacuum of make-believe and added their weight to his impending oblivion.

He wrenched the door open; the lamps within the house flared. The wicks burning here and there seemed to mirror one another. His mother was washing the dishes in a little pan of heated pump-water; Granmom fluttered near her elbow apprehensively. In the living room—the downstairs of the little square house was two long rooms—his father sat in front of the black fireplace restlessly folding and unfolding a newspaper as he sustained his half of the argument. "Nitrogen, phosphorus, potash: these are the three replaceable constituents of the soil. One crop of corn carries away hundreds of pounds of"—he dropped the paper into his lap and ticked them off on three fingers—"nitrogen, phosphorus, potash."

"Boyer didn't grow corn."

"*Any* crop, Elsie. The human animal—"

"You're killing the *earth*worms, George!"

"The human animal, after thousands and thousands of years, learned methods whereby the chemical balance of the soil may be maintained. Don't carry me back to the Dark Ages."

"When we moved to Olinger the ground in the garden was like slate. Just one summer of my cousin's chicken dung and the earthworms came back."

"I'm sure the Dark Ages were a fine place to the poor devils born in them, but I don't want to go there. They give me the creeps." Daddy stared into the cold pit of the fireplace and clung to the rolled newspaper in his lap as if it alone were keeping him from slipping backwards and down, down.

Mother came into the doorway brandishing a fistful of wet forks. "And thanks to your DDT there soon won't be a bee left in the country. When I was a girl here you could eat a peach without washing it."

"It's primitive, Elsie. It's Dark Age stuff."

"Oh what do *you* know about the Dark Ages?"

"I know I don't want to go back to them."

David took from the shelf, where he had placed it this afternoon, the great unabridged Webster's Dictionary that his grandfather had owned. He turned the big thin pages, floppy as cloth, to the entry he wanted, and read

> soul . . . I. An entity conceived as the essence, substance, animating principle, or actuating cause of life, or of the individual life, esp. of life manifested in psychical activities; the vehicle of individual existence, separate in nature from the body and usually held to be separable in existence.

The definition went on, into Greek and Egyptian conceptions, but David stopped short on the treacherous edge of antiquity. He needed to read no further. The careful overlapping words shingled a temporary shelter for him. "Usually held to be separable in existence"—what could be fairer, more judicious, surer?

His father was saying, "The modern farmer can't go around sweeping up after his cows. The poor devil has thousands and *thousands* of acres on his hands. Your modern farmer uses a scientifically-arrived-at mixture, like five-ten-five, or six-twelve-six, or *three*-twelve-six, and spreads it on with this wonderful modern machinery which of course we can't afford. Your modern farmer can't *afford* medieval methods."

Mother was quiet in the kitchen; her silence radiated waves of anger.

"No now Elsie; don't play the femme with me. Let's discuss this calmly like two rational twentieth-century people. Your organic farming nuts aren't attacking five-ten-five; they're attacking the chemical fertilizer crooks. The monster firms."

A cup clinked in the kitchen. Mother's anger touched David's face; his cheeks burned guiltily. Just by being in the living room he was associated with his father.

She appeared in the doorway with red hands and tears in her eyes, and said to the two of them, "I knew you didn't want to come here but I didn't know you'd torment me like this. You talked Pop into his grave and now you'll kill me. Go ahead, George, more power to you; at least I'll be buried in good ground." She tried to turn and met an obstacle and screamed, "Mother, stop hanging on my *back!* Why don't you go to *bed?*"

"Let's all go to bed," David's father said, rising from the blue wing chair and slapping his thigh with a newspaper. "This reminds me of death." It was a phrase of his that David had heard so often he never considered its sense.

Upstairs, he seemed to be lifted above his fears. The sheets on his bed were clean. Granmom had ironed them with a pair of flatirons saved from the Olinger attic; she plucked them hot off the stove alternately, with a wooden handle called a goose. It was a wonder, to see how she managed. In the next room, his parents grunted peaceably; they seemed to take their quarrels less seriously than he did. They made comfortable scratching noises as they carried a little lamp back and forth. Their door was open a crack, so he saw the light shift and swing. Surely there would be, in the last five minutes, in the last second, a crack of light, showing the door from the dark room to another, full of light. Thinking of it this vividly frightened him. His own dying, in a specific bed in a specific room, specific walls mottled with wallpaper, the dry whistle of his breathing, the murmuring doctors, the nervous relatives going in and out, but for him no way out but down into the funnel. *Never touch a doorknob again.* A whisper, and his parents' light was blown out. David prayed to be reassured. Though the experiment frightened him, he lifted his hands high into the darkness above his face and begged Christ to touch them. Not hard or long: the faintest, quickest grip would be final for a lifetime. His hands waited in the air, itself a substance, which seemed to move through his fingers; or was it the pressure of his pulse? He returned his hands to beneath the covers uncertain if they had been touched or not. For would not Christ's touch *be* infinitely gentle?

Through all the eddies of its aftermath, David clung to this thought about his revelation of extinction: that there, in the outhouse, he had struck a solidness qualitatively different, a rock of horror firm enough to support any height of construction. All he needed was a little help; a word, a gesture, a nod of certainty, and he would be sealed in, safe. The assurance from the dictionary had melted in the night. Today was Sunday, a hot fair day. Across a mile of clear air the church bells called, *Celebrate, celebrate.* Only Daddy went. He put on a coat over his rolled-up shirtsleeves and got into the little old black Plymouth parked by the barn and went off, with the same pained hurried grimness of all his actions. His churning wheels, as he shifted too hastily into second, raised plumes of red dust on the dirt road. Mother walked to the far field, to see what bushes needed cutting. David, though he usually preferred to stay in the house, went with her. The puppy followed at a distance, whining as it picked its way through the stubble but floundering off timidly if one of them went back to pick it up and carry it. When they reached the crest of the far field, his mother asked, "David, what's troubling you?"

"Nothing. Why?"

She looked at him sharply. The greening woods crosshatched the space beyond her half-gray hair. Then she showed him her profile, and gestured toward the house, which they had left a half-mile behind them. "See how it sits in the land? They don't know how to build with the land any more. Pop always said the foundations were set with the compass. We must try to get a compass and see. It's supposed to face due south; but south feels a little more *that* way to me." From the side, as she said these things, she seemed handsome and young. The smooth sweep of her hair over her ear seemed white with a purity and calm that made her feel foreign to him. He had never regarded his parents as consolers of his troubles; from the beginning they had seemed to have more troubles than he. Their confusion had flattered him into an illusion of strength; so now on this high clear ridge he jealously guarded the menace all around them, blowing like a breeze on his fingertips, the possibility of all this wide scenery sinking into darkness. The strange fact that though she came to look at the brush she carried no clippers, for she had a fixed prejudice against working on Sundays, was the only consolation he allowed her to offer.

As they walked back, the puppy whimpering after them, the rising dust behind a distant line of trees announced that Daddy was speeding home from church. When they reached the house he was there. He had brought back the Sunday paper and the vehement remark, "Dobson's too intelligent for these farmers. They just sit there with their mouths open and don't hear a thing the poor devil's saying."

"What makes you think farmers are unintelligent? This country was made by farmers. George Washington was a farmer."

"They are, Elsie. They are unintelligent. George Washington's dead. In this day and age only the misfits stay on the farm. The lame, the halt, the blind. The morons with one arm. Human garbage. They remind me of death, sitting there with their mouths open."

"My *father* was a farmer."

"He was a frustrated man, Elsie. He never knew what bit him. The poor devil meant so well, and he never knew which end was up. Your mother'll bear me out. Isn't that right, Mom? Pop never knew what hit him?"

"Ach, I guess not," the old woman quavered, and the ambiguity for the moment silenced both sides.

David hid in the funny papers and sports section until one-thirty. At two, the catechetical class met at the Firetown church. He had transferred from the catechetical class of the Lutheran church in Olinger, a humiliating comedown. In Olinger they met on Wednesday nights, spiffy and spruce, in the atmosphere of a dance. Afterwards, blessed by the brick-faced minister from whose lips the word "Christ" fell like a burning stone, the more daring of them went with their Bibles to a luncheonette and smoked. Here in Firetown, the girls were dull white cows and the boys narrow-faced brown goats in old men's suits, herded on Sunday afternoons into a threadbare church basement that smelled of stale hay. Because his father had taken the car on one of his endless errands to Olinger, David walked, grateful for the open air and the silence. The catechetical class embarrassed him, but today he placed hope in it, as the source of the nod, the gesture, that was all he needed.

Reverend Dobson was a delicate young man with great dark eyes and small white shapely hands that flickered like protesting doves when he preached; he seemed a bit misplaced in the Lutheran ministry. This was his first call. It was a split parish; he served another rural church twelve miles away. His iridescent green Ford, new six months ago, was spattered to the windows with red mud and rattled from bouncing on the rude back roads, where he frequently got lost, to the malicious satisfaction of many. But David's mother liked him, and, more pertinent to his success, the Haiers, the sleek family of feed merchants and innkeepers and tractor salesmen who dominated the Firetown church, liked him. David liked him, and felt liked in turn; sometimes in class, after some special stupidity, Dobson directed toward him out of those wide black eyes a mild look of disbelief, a look that, though flattering, was also delicately disquieting.

Catechetical instruction consisted of reading aloud from a work booklet answers to problems prepared during the week, problems like, "I am the __________, the __________, and the __________, saith the Lord." Then there was a question period in which no one ever asked any questions. Today's theme was the last third of the Apostles' Creed. When the time came for questions, David blushed and asked, "About the Resurrection of the Body—are we conscious between the time when we die and the Day of Judgment?"

Dobson blinked, and his fine little mouth pursed, suggesting that David was making difficult things more difficult. The faces of the other students went blank, as if an indiscretion had been committed.

"No, I suppose not," Reverend Dobson said.

"Well, where is our soul, then, in this gap?"

The sense grew, in the class, of a naughtiness occurring. Dobson's shy eyes watered, as if he were straining to keep up the formality of attention, and one of the girls, the fattest, simpered toward her twin, who was a little less fat. Their chairs were arranged in a rough circle. The current running around the circle panicked David. Did everybody know something he didn't know?

"I suppose you could say our souls are asleep," Dobson said.

"And then they wake up, and there is the earth like it always is, and all the people who have ever lived? Where will Heaven be?"

Anita Haier giggled. Dobson gazed at David intently, but with an awkward, puzzled flicker of forgiveness, as if there existed a secret between them that David was violating. But David knew of no secret. All he wanted was to hear Dobson repeat the words he said every Sunday morning. This he would not do. As if these words were unworthy of the conversational voice.

"David, you might think of Heaven this way: as the way the goodness Abraham Lincoln did lives after him."

"But is Lincoln conscious of it living on?" He blushed no longer with embarrassment but in anger; he had walked here in good faith and was being made a fool.

"Is he conscious now? I would have to say no; but I don't think it matters." His voice had a coward's firmness; he was hostile now.

"You don't."

"Not in the eyes of God, no." The unction, the stunning impudence, of this reply sprang tears of outrage in David's eyes. He bowed them to his book, where short words like Duty, Love, Obey, Honor, were stacked in the form of a cross.

"Were there any other questions, David?" Dobson asked with renewed gentleness. The others were rustling, collecting their books.

"No." He made his voice firm, though he could not bring up his eyes.

"Did I answer your question fully enough?"

"Yes."

In the minister's silence the shame that should have been his crept over David: the burden and fever of being a fraud were placed upon *him,* who was innocent, and it seemed, he knew, a confession of this guilt that on the way out he was unable to face Dobson's stirred gaze, though he felt it probing the side of his head.

Anita Haier's father gave him a ride down the highway as far as the dirt road. David said he wanted to walk the rest, and figured that his offer was accepted because Mr. Haier did not want to dirty his bright blue Buick with dust. This was all right; everything was all right, as long as it was clear. His indignation at being betrayed, at seeing Christianity betrayed, had hardened him. The straight dirt road reflected his hardness. Pink stones thrust up through its packed surface. The April sun beat down from the center of the afternoon half of the sky; already it had some of summer's heat. Already the fringes of weeds at the edges of the road were bedraggled with dust. From the reviving grass and scruff of the fields he walked between, insects were sending up a monotonous, automatic chant. In the distance a tiny figure in his father's coat was walking along the edge of the woods. His mother. He wondered what joy she found in such walks; to him the brown stretches of slowly rising and falling land expressed only a huge exhaustion.

Flushed with fresh air and happiness, she returned from her walk earlier than he had expected, and surprised him at his grandfather's Bible. It was a stumpy black book, the boards worn thin where the old man's fingers had held them; the spine hung by one weak hinge of fabric. David had been looking for the passage where Jesus says to the one thief on the cross, "Today shalt thou be with me in paradise." He had never tried reading the Bible for himself before. What was so embarrassing about being caught at it, was that he detested the apparatus of piety. Fusty churches, creaking hymns, ugly Sunday-school teachers and their stupid leaflets—he hated everything about them but the promise they held out, a promise that in the most perverse way, as if the homeliest crone in the kingdom were given the Prince's hand, made every good and real thing, ball games and jokes and pert-breasted girls, possible. He couldn't explain this to his mother. There was no time. Her solicitude was upon him.

"David, what are you doing?"

"Nothing."

"What are you doing at Grandpop's Bible?"

"Trying to read it. This is supposed to be a Christian country, isn't it?"

She sat down on the green sofa, which used to be in the sun parlor at Olinger, under the fancy mirror. A little smile still lingered on her face from the walk "David, I wish you'd talk to me."

"What about?"

"About whatever it is that's troubling you. Your father and I have both noticed it."

"I asked Reverend Dobson about Heaven and he said it was like Abraham Lincoln's goodness living after him."

He waited for the shock to strike her. "Yes?" she said, expecting more.

"That's all."

"And why didn't you like it?"

"Well; don't you see? It amounts to saying there isn't any Heaven at all."

"I don't see that it amounts to that. What do you want Heaven to be?"

"Well, I don't know. I want it to be something. I thought he'd tell me what it was. I thought that was his job." He was becoming angry, sensing her surprise at him.

She had assumed that Heaven had faded from his head years ago. She had imagined that he had already entered, in the secrecy of silence, the conspiracy that he now knew to be all around him.

"David," she asked gently, "don't you ever want to rest?"

"No. Not forever."

"David, you're so young. When you get older, you'll feel differently."

"Grandpa didn't. Look how tattered this book is."

"I never understood your grandfather."

"Well I don't understand ministers who say it's like Lincoln's goodness going on and on. Suppose you're not Lincoln?"

"I think Reverend Dobson made a mistake. You must try to forgive him."

"It's not a *question* of his making a mistake! It's a question of dying and never moving or seeing or hearing anything ever again."

"But"—in exasperation—"darling, it's so *greedy* of you to want more. When God has given us this wonderful April day, and given us this farm, and you have your whole life ahead of you—"

"You think, then, that there is God?"

"Of course I do"—with deep relief, that smoothed her features into a reposeful oval. He had risen and was standing too near her for his comfort. He was afraid she would reach out and touch him.

"He made everything? You feel that?"

"Yes."

"Then who made Him?"

"Why, Man. Man." The happiness of this answer lit up her face radiantly, until she saw his gesture of disgust. She was so simple, so illogical; such a femme.

"Well that amounts to saying there is none."

Her hand reached for his wrist but he backed away. "David, it's a mystery. A miracle. It's a miracle more beautiful than any Reverend Dobson could have told you about. You don't say houses don't exist because Man made them."

"No. God has to be different."

"But, David, you have the *evidence.* Look out the window at the sun; at the fields."

"Mother, good grief. Don't you see"—he rasped away the roughness in his throat—"if when we die there's nothing, all your sun and fields and what not are all, ah, *horror?* It's just an ocean of horror."

"But David, it's not. It's so clearly not that." And she made an urgent opening gesture with her hands that expressed, with its suggestion of a willingness to receive his helplessness, all her grace, her gentleness, her love of beauty, gathered into a passive intensity that made him intensely hate her. He would not be wooed away from the truth. *I am the Way, the Truth . . .*

"No," he told her. "Just let me alone."

He found his tennis ball behind the piano and went outside to throw it against the side of the house. There was a patch high up where the brown stucco that had been laid over the sandstone masonry was crumbling away; he kept trying with the tennis ball to chip more pieces off. Superimposed upon his deep ache was a smaller but more immediate worry; that he had hurt his mother. He heard his father's car rattling on the straightaway, and went into the house, to make peace before he arrived. To his relief, she was not giving off the stifling damp heat of her anger, but instead was cool, decisive, maternal. She handed him an old green book, her college text of Plato.

"I want you to read the Parable of the Cave," she said.

"All right," he said, though he knew it would do no good. Some story by a dead Greek just vague enough to please her. "Don't worry about it, Mother."

"I *am* worried. Honestly, David, I'm sure there will be something for us. As you get older, these things seem to matter a great deal less."

"That may be. It's a dismal thought, though."

His father bumped at the door. The locks and jambs stuck here. But before Granmom could totter to the latch and let him in, he had knocked it open. He had been in Olinger dithering with track meet tickets. Although Mother usually kept her talks with David a confidence, a treasure between them, she called instantly, "George, David is worried about death!"

He came to the doorway of the living room, his shirt pocket bristling with pencils, holding in one hand a pint box of melting ice cream and in the other the knife with which he was about to divide it into four sections, their Sunday treat. "Is the kid worried about death? Don't give it a thought, David. I'll be lucky if I live till tomorrow, and I'm not worried. If they'd taken a buckshot gun and shot me in the cradle I'd be better off. The *world*'d be better off. Hell, I think death is a wonderful thing. I look forward to it. Get the garbage out of the way. If I had the man here who invented death, I'd pin a medal on him."

"Hush, George. You'll frighten the child worse than he is."

This was not true; he never frightened David. There was no harm in his father, no harm at all. Indeed, in the man's steep self-disgust the boy felt a kind of ally. A distant ally. He saw his position with a certain strategic coldness. Nowhere in the world of other people would he find the hint, the nod, he needed to begin to build his fortress against death. They none of them believed. He was alone. In that deep hole.

In the months that followed, his position changed little. School was some comfort. All those sexy, perfumed people, wisecracking, chewing gum, all of them doomed to die, and none of them noticing. In their company David felt that they would carry him along into the bright, cheap paradise reserved for them. In any crowd, the fear ebbed a little; he had reasoned that somewhere in the world there must exist a few people who believed what was necessary, and the larger the crowd, the greater the chance that he was near such a soul, within calling distance, if only he was not too ignorant, too ill-equipped, to spot him. The sight of clergymen cheered him; whatever they themselves thought, their collars were still a sign that somewhere, at some time, someone had recognized that we cannot, *cannot,* submit to death. The sermon topics posted outside churches, the flip, hurried pieties of disc jockeys, the cartoons in magazines showing angels or devils—on such scraps he kept alive the possibility of hope.

For the rest, he tried to drown his hopelessness in clatter and jostle. The pinball machine at the luncheonette was a merciful distraction; as he bent over its buzzing, flashing board of flippers and cushions, the weight and constriction in his chest lightened and loosened. He was grateful for all the time his father wasted in Olinger. Every delay postponed the moment when they must ride together down the dirt road into the heart of the dark farmland, where the only light was the kerosene lamp waiting on the dining-room table, a light that drowned their food in shadow and made it sinister.

He lost his appetite for reading. He was afraid of being ambushed again. In mystery novels people died like dolls being discarded; in science fiction enormities of space and time conspired to crush the humans; and even in P. G. Wodehouse he felt a hollowness, a turning away from reality that was implicitly bitter, and became explicit in the comic figures of futile clergymen. All gaiety seemed minced out on the skin of a void. All quiet hours seemed invitations to dread.

Even on weekends, he and his father contrived to escape the farm; and when, some Saturdays, they did stay home, it was to do something destructive—tear down an old henhouse or set huge brush fires that threatened, while Mother shouted and flapped her arms, to spread to the woods. Whenever his father worked, it was with rapt violence; when he chopped kindling, fragments of the old henhouse boards flew like shrapnel and the ax-head was always within a quarter of an inch of flying off the handle. He was exhilarating to watch, sweating and swearing and sucking bits of saliva back into his lips.

School stopped. His father took the car in the opposite direction, to a highway construction job where he had been hired for the summer as a timekeeper, and David was stranded in the middle of acres of heat and greenery and blowing pollen and the strange, mechanical humming that lay invisibly in the weeds and alfalfa and dry orchard grass.

For his fifteenth birthday his parents gave him, with jokes about him being a hillbilly now, a Remington .22. It was somewhat like a pinball machine to take it out to the old kiln in the woods where they dumped their trash, and set up tin cans on the kiln's sandstone shoulder and shoot them off one by one. He'd take the puppy, who had grown long legs and a rich coat of reddish fur—he was part chow. Copper hated the gun but loved the boy enough to accompany him. When the flat acrid crack rang out, he would race in terrified circles that would tighten and tighten until they brought him, shivering, against David's legs. Depending upon his mood, David would shoot again or drop to his knees and comfort the dog. Giving this comfort to a degree returned comfort to him. The dog's ears, laid flat against his skull in fear, were folded so intricately, so—he groped for the concept—*surely.* Where the dull-studded collar made the fur stand up, each hair showed a root of soft white under the length, black-tipped, of the metal-color that had lent the dog its name. In his agitation Copper panted through nostrils that were elegant slits, like two healed cuts, or like the keyholes of a dainty lock of black, grained wood. His whole whorling, knotted, jointed body was a wealth of such embellishments. And in the smell of the dog's hair David seemed to descend through many finely differentiated layers of earth: mulch, soil, sand, clay, and the glittering mineral base.

But when he returned to the house, and saw the books arranged on the low shelves, fear returned. The four adamant volumes of Wells like four thin bricks, the green Plato that had puzzled him with its queer softness and tangled purity, the dead Galsworthy and "Elizabeth," Grandpa's mammoth dictionary, Grandpa's Bible, the Bible that he himself had received on becoming a member of the Firetown Lutheran Church—at the sight of these, the memory of his fear reawakened and came around him. He had grown stiff and stupid in its embrace. His parents tried to think of ways to entertain him.

"David, I have a job for you to do," his mother said one evening at the table.

"What?"

"If you're going to take that tone perhaps we'd better not talk."

"What tone? I didn't take any tone."

"Your grandmother thinks there are too many pigeons in the barn."

"Why?" David turned to look at his grandmother, but she sat there staring at the burning lamp with her usual expression of bewilderment.

Mother shouted, "Mom, he wants to know why!"

Granmom made a jerky, irritable motion with her bad hand, as if generating the force for utterance, and said, "They foul the furniture."

"That's right," Mother said. "She's afraid for that old Olinger furniture that we'll never use. David, she's been after me for a month about those poor pigeons. She wants you to shoot them."

"I don't want to kill anything especially," David said.

Daddy said, "The kid's like you are, Elsie. He's too good for this world. Kill or be killed, that's my motto."

His mother said loudly, "Mother, he doesn't want to do it."

"Not?" The old lady's eyes distended as if in horror, and her claw descended slowly to her lap.

"Oh, I'll do it, I'll do it tomorrow," David snapped, and a pleasant crisp taste entered his mouth with the decision.

"And I had thought, when Boyer's men made the hay, it would be better if the barn doesn't look like a rookery," his mother added needlessly.

A barn, in day, is a small night. The splinters of light between the dry shingles pierce the high roof like stars, and the rafters and crossbeams and built-in ladders seem, until your eyes adjust, as mysterious as the branches of a haunted forest. David entered silently, the gun in one hand. Copper whined desperately at the door, too frightened to come in with the gun yet unwilling to leave the boy. David stealthily turned, said "Go away," shut the door on the dog, and slipped the bolt across. It was a door within a door; the double door for wagons and tractors was as high and wide as the face of a house.

The smell of old straw scratched his sinuses. The red sofa, half-hidden under its white-splotched tarpaulin, seemed assimilated into this smell, sunk in it, buried. The mouths of empty bins gaped like caves. Rusty oddments of farming—coils of baling wire, some spare tines for a harrow, a handleless shovel—hung on nails driven here and there in the thick wood. He stood stock-still a minute; it took a while to separate the cooing of the pigeons from the rustling in his ears. When he had focused on the cooing, it flooded the vast interior with its throaty, bubbling outpour: there seemed no other sound. They were up behind the beams. What light there was leaked through the shingles and the dirty glass windows at the far end and the small round holes, about as big as basketballs, high on the opposite stone side walls, under the ridge of the roof.

A pigeon appeared in one of these holes, on the side toward the house. It flew in, with a battering of wings, from the outside, and waited there, silhouetted against its pinched bit of sky, preening and cooing in a throbbing, thrilled, tentative way. David tiptoed four steps to the side, rested his gun against the lowest rung of a ladder pegged between two upright beams, and lowered the gunsight into the bird's tiny, jauntily cocked head. The slap of the report seemed to come off the stone wall behind him, and the pigeon did not fall. Neither did it fly. Instead it stuck in the round hole, pirouetting rapidly and nodding its head as if in frantic agreement. David shot the bolt back and forth and had aimed again before the spent cartridge had stopped jingling on the boards by his feet. He eased the tip of the sight a little lower, into the bird's breast, and took care to squeeze the trigger with perfect evenness. The slow contraction of his hand abruptly sprang the bullet; for a half-second there was doubt, and then the pigeon fell like a handful of rags, skimming down the barn wall into the layer of straw that coated the floor of the mow on this side.

Now others shook loose from the rafters, and whirled in the dim air with a great blurred hurtle of feathers and noise. They would go for the hole; he fixed his sight on the little moon of blue, and when a pigeon came to it, shot him as he was walking the ten inches of stone that would have carried him into the open air. This pigeon lay down in that tunnel of stone, unable to fall either one way or the other, although he was alive enough to lift one wing and cloud the light. It would sink back, and he would suddenly lift it again, the feathers flaring. His body blocked that exit. David raced to the other side of the barn's main aisle, where a similar ladder was symmetrically placed, and rested his gun on the same rung. Three birds came together to this hole; he got one, and two got through. The rest resettled in the rafters.

There was a shallow triangular space behind the cross beams supporting the roof. It was here they roosted and hid. But either the space was too small, or they were curious, for now that his eyes were at home in the dusty gloom David could see little dabs of gray popping in and out. The cooing was shriller now; its apprehensive tremolo made the whole volume of air seem liquid. He noticed one little smudge of a head that was especially persistent in peeking out; he marked the place, and fixed his gun on it, and when the head appeared again, had his finger tightened in advance on the trigger. A parcel of fluff slipped off the beam and fell the barn's height onto a canvas covering some Olinger furniture, and where its head had peeked out there was a fresh prick of light in the shingles.

Standing in the center of the floor, fully master now, disdaining to steady the barrel with anything but his arm, he killed two more that way. He felt like a beautiful avenger. Out of the shadowy ragged infinity of the vast barn roof these impudent things dared to thrust their heads, presumed to dirty its starred silence with their filthy timorous life, and he cut them off, tucked them back neatly into the silence. He had the sensation of a creator; these little smudges and flickers that he was clever to see and even cleverer to hit in the dim recesses of the rafters—out of each of them he was making a full bird. A tiny peek, probe, dab of life, when he hit it, blossomed into a dead enemy, falling with good, final weight.

The imperfection of the second pigeon he had shot, who was still lifting his wing now and then up in the round hole, nagged him. He put a new clip into the stock. Hugging the gun against his body, he climbed the ladder. The barrel sight scratched his ear; he had a sharp, garish vision, like a color slide, of shooting himself and being found tumbled on the barn floor among his prey. He locked his arm around the top rung—a fragile, gnawed rod braced between uprights—and shot into the bird's body from a flat angle. The wing folded, but the impact did not, as he had hoped, push the bird out of the hole. He fired again, and again, and still the little body, lighter than air when alive, was too heavy to budge from its high grave. From up here he could see green trees and a brown corner of the house through the hole. Clammy with the cobwebs that gathered between the rungs, he pumped a full clip of eight bullets into the stubborn shadow, with no success. He climbed down, and was struck by the silence in the barn. The remaining pigeons must have escaped out the other hole. That was all right; he was tired of it.

He stepped with his rifle into the light. His mother was coming to meet him, and it tickled him to see her shy away from the carelessly held gun. "You took a chip out of the house," she said. "What were those last shots about?"

"One of them died up in that little round hole and I was trying to shoot it down."

"Copper's hiding behind the piano and won't come out. I had to leave him."

"Well don't blame me. *I* didn't want to shoot the poor devils."

"Don't smirk. You look like your father. How many did you get?"

"Six."

She went into the barn, and he followed. She listened to the silence. Her hair was scraggly, perhaps from tussling with the dog. "I don't suppose the others will be back," she said wearily. "Indeed, I don't know why I let Mother talk me into it. Their cooing was such a comforting noise." She began to gather up the dead pigeons. Though he didn't want to touch them, David went into the mow and picked up by its tepid, horny, coral-colored feet the first bird he had killed. Its wings unfolded disconcertingly, as if the creature had been held together by threads that now were slit. It did not weigh much. He retrieved the one on the other side of the barn; his mother got the three in the middle and led the way across the road to the little southern slope of land that went down toward the foundations of the vanished tobacco shed. The ground was too steep to plant and mow; wild strawberries grew in the tangled grass. She put her burden down and said, "We'll have to bury them. The dog will go wild."

He put his two down on her three; the slick feathers let the bodies slide liquidly on one another. He asked, "Shall I get you the shovel?"

"Get it for yourself; *you* bury them. They're your kill. And be sure to make the hole deep enough so he won't dig them up." While he went to the tool shed for the shovel, she went into the house. Unlike her, she did not look up, either at the orchard to the right of her or at the meadow on her left, but instead held her head rigidly, tilted a little, as if listening to the ground.

He dug the hole, in a spot where there were no strawberry plants, before he studied the pigeons. He had never seen a bird this close before. The feathers were more wonderful than dog's hair, for each filament was shaped within the shape of the feather, and the feathers in turn were trimmed to fit a pattern that flowed without error across the bird's body. He lost himself in the geometrical tides as the feathers now broadened and stiffened to make an edge for flight, now softened and constricted to cup warmth around the mute flesh. And across the surface of the infinitely adjusted yet somehow effortless mechanics of the feathers played idle designs of color, no two alike, designs executed, it seemed, in a controlled rapture, with a joy that hung level in the air above and behind him. Yet these birds bred in the millions and were exterminated as pests. Into the fragrant open earth he dropped one broadly banded in slate shades of blue, and on top of it another, mottled all over in rhythms of lilac and gray.

The next was almost wholly white, but for a salmon glaze at its throat. As he fitted the last two, still pliant, on the top, and stood up, crusty coverings were lifted from him, and with a feminine, slipping sensation along his nerves that seemed to give the air hands, he was robed in this certainty: that the God who had lavished such craft upon these worthless birds would not destroy His whole Creation by refusing to let David live forever.

JOHN UPDIKE

A Sandstone Farmhouse

Joey's first glimpse of the house was cloudy in his memory, like an old photo mottled by mildew. During the Second World War, his family owned no car, and renting one, for their infrequent excursions out of the compact brick city where his father worked, embarrassed the twelve-year-old boy to the point that he didn't see clearly through the windows, or was not conscious of much beyond his internal struggle not to be carsick. He fought the swaying, jiggling motion, which was mixed with the warm confluent smells of rubber floor mat and petroleum combustion, and the patient pale veiny look of his father's hand on the gear-shift knob. Farm country, miles of it, poured past. Depressing, monotonous fields moved up and down beneath their hazy burden of crops. A winding asphalt highway climbed a hill, passed a lumpy stone church, then settled into a flat stretch where they slowed to turn left down a dirt washboard road that shook the car sickeningly. Not a building in sight. No sign of civilization but telephone poles carrying a single wire. Another turn, right this time, down an even smaller dirt road, and they stopped, and in the sudden flood of fresh air as Joey opened the car door, the green of the grass rose waxy and bright to greet his giddiness, his nausea. In his cloudy memory, they went up to the house and there were people in it, farm people, wearing cotton and thick muddy shoes, shyly trying to get out of their way, like animals. There was a front porch, he remembered that much. With a banister upheld by boards jigsawed into an ornamental shape, and a secret space underneath, of weeds and pebbly dirt. A space where chickens could scratch and dogs could lie and pant during hot weather, the kind of space that is friendly and inviting to a boy of the age he was just outgrowing.

By the time they had bought the house with its surrounding eighty acres and moved in, he was thirteen, and the front porch had vanished, leaving a space between the front of the house and the cement walk where they eventually planted crocuses and tulips and erected a grape arbor. Joey as an adult could not remember how or when it had happened, their tearing down the rotten old porch. Pieces of it remained in the barn—segments of banister with the ornamental balusters cut of inch-thick pine. Once he even took a baluster home with him, back to New York City, as some kind of memento, or sample of folk art. The pattern held a circle in the center, a circle with a hole, between two shapes jigsawed into the wood, one like an arrow and one like a fish. Different-colored flakes fell dryly from it, brittle layers of old-time lead paint. The object, not quite of art, rested sideways on the black marble mantel of his apartment for a while, then found its way to the back of a closet, with broken squash rackets and college textbooks and table lamps that might someday be made to glow again. Like his mother, he had trouble throwing anything away.

If he and his father and grandfather had torn the porch down themselves, he would have remembered so heroic a labor, as he did the smashing of the lath-and-plaster partition that separated the two small parlors downstairs, making one big living room, or the tearing out of the big stone kitchen fireplace and its chimney, right up into the attic. Joey remembered swinging the great stones out the attic window, he and his grandfather pushing, trying not to pinch their fingers, while his father, his face white with the effort, held the rope of a makeshift pulley rigged over a rafter. Once clear of the sill, the heavy stones fell with a ghostly slowness, seen from above, and accumulated into a kind of mountain it became Joey's summer job to clear away. He learned a valuable lesson, that first summer on the farm, while he turned fourteen: even if you manage to wrestle only one stone into the wheelbarrow and sweatily, staggeringly trundle it down to the swampy area this side of the springhouse, eventually the entire mountain will be taken away. On the same principle, an invisible giant, removing only one day at a time, will eventually dispose of an entire life.

When, over forty years later, his mother died, and the at last uninhabited house yielded up its long-buried treasures, he came upon a photograph of her at the age of ten, posing in front of the porch. Someone in pencil, in a flowing handwriting not his mother's—hers was tiny, and cramped, and back-slanted—had marked on the back "Taken August 1914. Enlarged August 1917." Someone had loved this snapshot enough to have it enlarged and mounted on thick gray cardboard: who?

His mother, wearing a low-waisted dress, dark stockings, and black shoes with big, thick heels, her hair done up in a long braid that hangs over one shoulder, is holding the collar of a young medium-sized dog, part collie. Both the child and the dog are looking straight into the camera with similar half-smiles and wide-spaced, trusting eyes. They are standing on a cement walk that is still there, uncracked; behind them the porch balusters repeat their simple artful pattern and a small rosebush blooms. The long-dead dog, the recently dead human female look identically happy. Joey would hardly have recognized his mother but for the thick abundance of her hair—a chestless cheerful little girl in old woman's shoes. Beyond the edge of the barn to her right, ghostly in the enlargement, are fences and trees of which no trace remains and, just barely visible, an entire building that has vanished—a tobacco shed, perhaps. The lawn is edged around the walk, and the fences look trim. This was the private paradises then, to which she attempted to return, buying back the old sandstone farmhouse that her parents, feeling full enough of tobacco profits to retire, had sold while she was innocently off at normal school. Precocious, she had been skipped, and was sent off at the age of twelve, and hated it, hated it all, including the hour-long trolley ride to Kutztown. The swaying, the ozone, the drunk men who sat down beside her made her sick.

She loved the old house; she loved the *idea* of it. For most of her life, except for the twenty years of exile in her young womanhood, when she went to normal school, then to college, and married a man she met there, and traveled with him until the Depression cost him his traveling job, and bore him a son, in the heart of the Depression, while they were all living with her parents in the brick city house—except for these twenty years, she happily inhabited an idea. The sandstone house was built, her fond research discovered, in 1812. In that era, teams of masons and stonelayers roamed the countryside, erecting these Pennsylvania farmhouses on principles of an elegant simplicity. Their ground plan was square, set square to the compass. The south face basked in the maximum of sunshine; the east windows framed the sunrise, and the west the sunset. The cornerstones were cut at a slightly acute angle, to emphasize the edge. The stout scaffolding was rooted in holes in the thirty-inch walls as they rose, and these holes were plugged with stones four inches square as the masonry was pointed, and the scaffolding dismantled, from the top down. In the mortar, lime from the lime kiln was mixed with sand from creek beds, to match the stones. Though the size of the stones raised and fitted into place was prodigious, the real feats of leverage occurred in the quarrying. Sandstone exposed in an outcropping was rendered useless by weather, but underneath the earth the sound stone slept, to be painstakingly split by star drills and wedges and "feathers" of steel, and then hauled out by teams of horses, on wagons or sleds. Sometimes the wagons shattered under the load of a single great stone. But this vast hauling and lifting continued, a tidal movement like that of the glaciers which here and there had deposited huge moraines, acres frightening in their sheer stoniness, in the middle of the forests—heaped-up depths of boulders in which no tree could take root, barren geological deposits fascinating and bewildering to nineteenth-century minds, so eager to see God's hand everywhere.

For sensitive, asthmatic Joey, removed from a brick semidetached city house where he had felt snug, where he could hear through his bedroom walls the neighbors stirring as he awoke, and the milk being delivered on the porch, and the trolley cars clanging at the corner a block away, the silent thickness of stones just behind the old plaster and wallpaper, and the rough hearths and fireplaces visible within the country house, seemed to harbor nature's damp and cold. A sullen held breath dwelled in the walls. The summer's heat brought swarms of wasps, millipedes, carpenter ants, and silverfish out from the crannies. That first winter in the house, before an oil furnace was installed in the basement, a kerosene-burning stove in the living room provided the only heat. Joey remembered the stove clearly; it was painted chocolate brown, and stood on little bent legs on an asbestos sheet papered with imitation wood grain. He spent days huddled in blankets next to this stove, on a grease-spotted sofa that had been brought close. With his constant cold, he missed days of school, and hated to, for it was warm at school, and there was running water, and flush toilets. And girls in long pleated skirts and fuzzy sweaters and bobby socks, who belonged to the modern era, to civilization. He clung to civilization by reading; huddled in the brown stove's aura of coal oil, he read anything—P. G. Wodehouse, Ellery Queen, John Dickson Carr, Thorne Smith—that savored of cities and took him out of this damp, cold little stone house.

His mother remembered that first winter with rueful pleasure, as a set of tribulations blithely overcome. "It was really very hard, I suppose, on everybody—you were *so* sick, and your father had to struggle so to get to work in that old Chevrolet that was all we could afford, and for my parents it was a terrible defeat, to come back to the farm when they had gotten away; they would hide together in the corner just like children—but I was so happy to be here I hardly noticed. The movers had broken the large pane of glass in the front door, and for some reason that whole first winter we never managed to replace it; we lived with a sheet of cardboard wedged over the hole. It's incredible that we survived." And she would laugh gaily, remembering. "We tried to light fires in the living-room fireplace, but all the wood the Schellenbargers had left us in the basement was moldy elm, and that fireplace never did draw well, even when the swifts' nests weren't plugging it up. Smoke leaks out into the room, I've never understood why. If you look up the flue with a flashlight, the stonework has a twist."

Joey seemed to remember, though, waking upstairs and putting his feet onto the bare wood floor and grabbing his school clothes and hurrying in his pajamas down the narrow stairs—the treads worn in two troughs by generations of footsteps, the nail-heads protruding and shiny and dangerous—to dress in front of the fireplace, where logs were crackling. The freezing upstairs air would lick at his skin like flame, like the endless conversations between his mother and her parents, incessant flowing exchanges that would ripple into quarrel and chuckle back again into calm while he focused, when he was home, into the pages of his book. His grandfather had a beautiful, patient, elocutionary voice; his grandmother spoke little, in guttural responses. His mother, unlike most adults, hadn't parted from her parents, and clung to them with old tales and grievances, like someone adding up the same set of figures day after day and always expecting a different answer. As Joey huddled by the stove, heated conversations were in his ears as the smell of coal oil was in his nostrils, but always, those five years (only five!) that he lived in the sandstone house with four adults, his attention was aimed elsewhere—on schoolwork, on the future. He tried to ignore what was around him. The house, even when plumbing and central heating and a telephone were installed, and new wallpaper made the repainted rooms pretty, embarrassed him.

He was never more embarrassed than in that summer before they moved in, before they owned even the erratic old Chevrolet. Several times, his mother made him travel with her by bus out to the farm they already owned. She had a vision of a windbreak of pines rimming the big field, along the road, and she and Joey carried seedlings in boxes, and shovels, and pruners, and a watering can—all this humiliating apparatus dragged onto a city bus by a red-faced middle-aged woman and a skinny boy with ears that stuck out and dungarees that were too short. His mother wore a checked shirt like a man's and a straw sun hat and a pair of light-blue overalls with a bib; she looked like a farmer in a Hollywood musical comedy. There was no space inside the bus for the shovels; the driver had to store them in the luggage compartment and then stop and get out in the middle of nowhere to hand the tools over. It was a relief when the bus, headed south toward Washington, D.C., disappeared around a bend in the highway.

Joey and his mother walked down the dirt washboard road in the heat, carrying their equipment. He had never been so humiliated, so ridiculous, and vowed never to be again. He couldn't blame his mother, he still needed her too much, so he blamed the place—its hazy, buggy fields, its clouds of blowing pollen that made him sneeze and his eyes water, its little sandstone house like a cube of brown sugar melting in the heat, in a little dip of hillside beneath an overgrown, half-dead apple orchard. All through noon and into the afternoon they cleared little spaces at the edge of the field, where the Schellenbargers' last crop of field corn was pushing up in limp green rows, and cut away burdock and poison ivy and honeysuckle, and dug holes, and set in each hole a little six-inch puff of pine tree, and sprinkled water over the socket of sandy red earth. Moving a few paces farther on to plant the next tree, Joey could no longer see the last one amid the weeds and wild grass. The work seemed hopeless. Yet when the afternoon breeze came up, he felt a purity of silence—perhaps one car an hour passed, the people staring at this woman and boy in clothes neither country nor city—that didn't exist in his beloved street of semidetached houses. And there was a kind of heroism to his periodic trudge, with the empty sprinkling can, the half-mile along the edge of the cornfields to the empty house, with its rusty iron pump on the back porch, and then the long haul back, the sloshing can as heavy as a stone.

He felt heroic to himself. Space for heroism existed out here. He was determined to impress his mother—to win her back, since here on this farm he for the first time encountered something she apparently loved as much as she loved him.

At last, the weeds threw feathery long shadows upon one another and the tiny pines were all planted in the hopeless roadside jungle and it was time to walk back up the dusty washboard road to wait for the bus from Washington to round the corner. Having gone and come so far, the bus could be as much as an hour late, and their eyes would sting, staring down the gray highway for it, and his stomach would sink at the thought that they had missed it and were stranded. But not even this possibility daunted him, for he had forged a mood of defiant collusion in which he was numbed to humiliation and played a role both stoic and comic, costarring with his heavy mother in her straw sun hat and his lanky, sharp-faced sidekicks, the clippers and the shovel. Years later, he could even laugh with her about it, those awkward hot trips to plant a line of trees most of which never thrived, choked by thistles and bindweed or severed by a too zealous mower. Yet a few of the pines, perhaps six or seven, did live to tower along the road bank—shaggy-headed apparitions taller than a ship's mast, swaying in the wind. By this time, the dirt road was macadamized and hummed with traffic, and the bus route to Washington had long ago been abandoned as unprofitable.

Five years after the September when they had moved, Joey went to college and, essentially, never returned. He married in his senior year, and after graduation moved to New York City. Another of his mother's visions, along with that of the farm as paradise, was of him as a poet; he fulfilled this heroic task as best he could, by going to work for an ad agency and devoting himself to the search for the arresting phrase and image, on the edge of the indecent, that incites people to buy—that gives them permission, from the mythic world above, to buy. The business was like poetry in that you needed only a few lucky hits, and he had his share, and couldn't complain. He never again had to get on a bus with a shovel.

The numbers attached to the years and decades slowly changed, and with them the numbers in his bank account and on his apartment building. His first marriage took place in three different apartments, his turbulent second in four, his short-lived third in only one, and now he wondered if women had not quite been his thing all along. He had always felt most at ease, come to think of it, in the company of men, especially those who reminded him of his father. But it was the AIDS-conscious eighties by then, and his hair had passed through gray into virtual white, and he found the personalities of young men an effective barrier to thinking about their bodies, and he was content to share his life with his books, his CDs (compact disks, certificates of deposit), his modest little art collection mixed of watery commercialism and icy minimalism. On the other side of the white walls of his apartment he could hear the mumble and thump of his neighbors, and he liked that. He was home.

Three hours away, his widowed mother lived alone in the sandstone house. Joey had been the first to depart, and then a few years later his grandfather died, suddenly, with a stroke like a thunderclap, and then, after a bedridden year, his grandmother. This created an extra room upstairs, so Joey and his first wife and young children, when they came to visit in the sixties, no longer had to camp out downstairs, on cots and the sofa spotted by the peanut-butter crackers he used to eat when sick and consigned to reading the days away. The upstairs had two real bedrooms, to which the doors could be closed, and a kind of hallway beside the head of the stairs where he had slept for five years, listening to the four adults rustle and snore and creak while girls and prayers and the beginnings of poems all ran together in his brain. His grandfather, on his way downstairs in the early morning, would ruffle the hair on the sleeping boy's head, and the gathering sounds of family breakfast, as Joey's grandmother and parents followed, would rise under him with the smell of toast, a doughy warmth of life rising beneath the cold bare floorboards. There was a fourth room, a small room in the northwest corner, where his mother had once been born, in a long agony of labor—a rural calvary, as Joey imagined it, with flickering lamps and steaming kettles and ministering cousins arriving by horse and buggy—that shaped her relations with her own mother into, it seemed, a ferocious apology, a futile undying adhesion in an attempt to make amends. She nursed her mother in the old woman's long paralyzed agony of dying, but not always patiently, or tenderly, and when the ordeal at last was over she was left with additional cause for self-blame, more sorry images. "I spent my whole life," she concluded, "trying to please my mother, and never did."

Joey would ask, irritated by these pat surges of self-dramatization, "Did she ever say so?"

"No, but you knew her. She never said anything."

"Unlike *my* mother," he said, with an ironic pretense of gallantry.

She heard the irony. "Yes, I inherited Pop's gift of gab," she said. "It's been a curse, really. If you talk enough, you don't feel you have to *do* anything."

This fourth room had become the bathroom, with a tub but no shower, a basin but no cabinet. Toothpaste, sun lotion, hand creams, razors, dental floss, slivers of soap thriftily stuck together all accumulated on the deep sill overlooking the blackening shingles of the back-porch roof. After his father died, in the early seventies, the house gradually lost the power to purge itself of accumulation. Their occupancy, which had begun with removal of the porch and the chimney stones, now silted the attic and cellar and windowsills full with souvenirs of his mother's lengthening residence. On the theory that it would save the wild birds from being eaten, she had fed a stray cat that came to the back porch; this cat then became several, and the several became as many as forty. The kitchen became choked with stacked cases of cat food, and a site in the woods, at the end of a path overgrown with raspberry canes, became a mountain of empty cat-food cans. Tin Mountain, Joey's children called it. Magazines and junk mail and church pamphlets sat around on tables and chairs waiting to be bundled and taken to the barn, to wait there for the Boy Scouts' next paper drive. Photographs of Joey and his children, Christmas cards and valentines from relations and neighbors, piled up on available spaces like a kind of moss. Even the table where his mother ate had room eventually for only one plate and cup and saucer, her own. The house was clogging up, Joey felt, much as her heart—coronary angiography had revealed—was plugging with arteriosclerosis, and her weakly pumped lungs were filling with water.

His arrivals, as the years went on, seemed to accumulate. He would park his car by the barn and pick his way across the line of steppingstones that in the decades since they were laid (even Granny, stiff and bent over, helping with the crowbar) had been silted over by the sandy soil and its crabgrass. On the back porch there would be a puddle of cats and kittens mewing to be fed. Entering the back door with his suitcase was like stepping into a quicksand smelling of cat food and damp cardboard. His mother saved, in separate sections of the floor, the plastic bags the supermarket bagged her groceries in, and slippery stacks of mail-order catalogues, and a bucketful of maddeningly snarled baling twine, to make bundles for the barn with. He recognized in this accumulation a superstition he had to fight within himself—the belief that everything has value. The birds in the trees, the sunflower at the edge of the orchard, the clumsily pasted-up valentine received years ago from a distant grandchild—all have a worth that might at any moment be called into account. It was a way of saying that one's own life was infinitely precious.

There would be a peck of a kiss at the door, and he would carry the suitcase upstairs, past the whirling, nipping mongrel bitch, who was thrilled to have a man in the house. The guest room had been his parents' old room. When she became a widow, his mother had moved into her parents' old room, closer to the room in which she had been born. The move was part, Joey felt, of an obscure religious system that had nothing to do with Christianity. He remembered how, in a surprising rite of that system, his parents the day after his grandmother died, took her stained, urine-soaked mattress outdoors and burned it, down near the stones he had dumped, darkening the sky all morning with the smoke.

Here, in this guest room, at night, without a wife to distract and comfort him, he would begin to fight for his breath. The bed sagged so that his back hurt. The pillow felt heavy and dense. The sandstone hearth of the never-used fireplace in the room would emit an outdoor dampness. Birds and bats and mice would stir in the porous walls, and his mother's motions would make her bed beyond the thin wall creak. Was she awake, or asleep? He could relax deeply only in the early morning, when the dog would wake her, scrabbling on the bare boards with her claws, and the two of them would slowly, noisily head downstairs, and the can opener would rhythmically begin to chew through the first installment of cat-food cans.

The guest room for some reason had no curtains; in the dead of the night the moon burned on the wide sills as if calling to him, calling him back to a phase his whole adult life had been an effort to obliterate. The asthma, the effect of inner tightening and complication, wasn't so bad, usually, the first two nights; he might manage five or six hours of sleep each if he could then get away, back to cozy, salubrious New York. But on long holiday weekends he would struggle through the whole third night with the accumulated house dust and pollen in his lungs, and the damp hard pillow, and the obdurate moonlight, so accusatory in its white silence.

He was aware of his mother and himself, lying each in bed, as survivors of the larger party that had once occupied this house. It was as if, on a snowy pass, they had killed and eaten the others, and now one of the two remaining must perish next. She, too, in her eighties, had breathing problems, and slept with her head up on two pillows. One night she woke him with the soft words, "Joey. I'm not doing so well. Put on your daddy's old overcoat and come downstairs with me."

He was awake, his head clear as moonlight, in an instant. "Shall we call the hospital?"

"No, I just need to sit up. You know which overcoat, it hangs at the foot of the stairs."

It had hung there for years. one of those curious comforting rags his father would acquire in thrift shops or outlet stores. Joey had often seen it on him, in the last year of the old man's life, when his legs turned white and phlebitic and his nose turned blue with poor circulation and his eyes sank deeper and deeper into his head and his deafness worsened. But to the end his father had held his head high, and took a lively interest in the world. Once a social-science teacher, he continued to read fat history books, and wrote Joey, in one of his rare letters, in his patient, legible schoolteacher's hand, that being deaf made it easier for him to concentrate.

Joey wondered why his mother was being so insistent about the coat, but obediently put it on. It had a fuzziness unusual in dark overcoats, and was big for him, since his father had been bigger than he. She was right; once it was on, over his pajamas, he became a child again, and calm, and trusting. They went downstairs and turned up the thermostat and sat in the dark living room together, he on the sofa and she in her television-watching chair, and he watched her struggle for breath, in little sudden shuddering gasps like the desperate heaves of a bird caught in the chimney.

"Do you hurt?" he asked.

She had little breath for speaking, and shook her head no, and her head underwent again the convulsion, as if trying to keep above water. "It's like," she gasped, "a squeezing."

"Sure you wouldn't like to drive to the hospital?"

A vigorous headshake again. "What can they do, but torture you?"

So he sat there, in his father's overcoat, fighting sleepiness, wondering if his mother would die before his eyes. The dog, agitated at first by this predawn rising, wheezed and resettled on the floor. The moonlight weakened on the sills across the room, with their potted geraniums and violets and a night-blooming cereus that had been allowed to grow grotesquely long, so that its stem filled the window. His mother's shudders lessened, and eventually she told him to go upstairs, she would sit here a while longer. In her old age she had become almost grafted onto this chair of hers. On a previous visit, she had shocked him by refusing, when the evening run of television comedies that she faithfully watched was over, to come upstairs at all; morning found her still sitting there, in her clothes. This irritated him, along with her television watching. "Why do you watch all these idiots?" he once asked her. "They seem realer to you than I am."

She did not deny it. "Well," she had answered, "they're always here."

Now, her crisis past, he accepted her dismissal gratefully and yet reluctantly. He went upstairs feeling that this hour had been the most purely companionable he had ever spent with her in this house. To Joey in his father's fuzzy, overlarge coat, as he silently watched his mother struggle and the dog stir and doze and the night-blooming cereus cast its gawky shadow in the deep window recess beyond the tasseled bridge lamp and the upright piano. it had been like one of those scenes we witness in childhood, from under the table or over the edge of the crib, understanding nothing except that large forces are moving around us—that there is a heavy dynamism from which we are, as children, sheltered.

When she had her next attack of breathlessness, he was not there, and she called the neighbors, and they called the township ambulance, which came at five in the morning. For all her talk of "torture," she seemed to settle gratefully into the hospital's ministrations. "They said I was quite blue, the oxygen in my blood was down to nothing." Rather gaily, she described the emergency-room doctors thrusting some violent sucking instrument down her throat and into her lungs.

Her bathrobe was turquoise with a maroon hem; she ordered her clothes from catalogues now and was attracted to decisive colors. With her white hair all about her on the pillow, and the baby-blue tubes of oxygen making a mustache, and the identification bracelet looped on her wrist, she looked festive and hectic and feminized. All day, young men in antiseptic garb came and tended to her, cutting her toenails, interrogating her bowels. Her bowels, to Joey's embarrassment, had become a topic of supreme fascination to her. Her insides in general were brought uncomfortably close to the surface by the wearing away of her body. His father's method of coping with what seemed to Joey her unaccountable whims, including moving them all to the farm, had been to say, "She's a femme. Your mother's a real femme. What can you do?" He would shrug, and sometimes add, "I should have put her on the burleycue stage."

This had seemed one of the man's lofty, pained jokes; but now her femininity, which Joey's father and succession of wives had shielded him from, was upon him. In her slightly disheveled, revealing gowns, in her gracefully accepted helplessness and fragility, in this atmosphere of frank bodily event, his mother had her sex on her mind. She told him, remembering the first years of her marriage in Pittsburgh, "There was this young doctor, Dr. Langhorne over on Sixth Street, who when I went to him with these pains on my chest I couldn't understand told me to take off my clothes. Well, I trusted him, and did, and he looked me over for the longest time, and then told me, 'You're not obese.' That was all he said."

His own birth, her conviction that she couldn't do such a normal thing as conceive and bear a child, recurred in her self-accounting; old Dr. Berthoff, who kept brusquely calming her fears, who treated her as a normal woman and not as the monstrous product of her own mother's agony, emerged as a kind of erotic hero, and Joey suddenly saw that his own self, which he had imagined she cherished for qualities all his own, was lovable to her above all as a piece of her body, as a living proof of her womanhood.

And she recalled, of those straitened Depression days when he was an infant, how she left him in the care of his grandparents and went off on the trolley car to work in the drapes department of the department store downtown. She had lost a tooth, a bicuspid, and the upper partial plate containing its replacement was uncomfortable, and one day she didn't wear it to work and was chastised by the department manager, Mr. Wirtheimer, for not wearing it. The image of her missing tooth, this tidy black hole leaping up within her young woman's smile, seemed erotic, too, along with the thought of his then-slender mother's charm as a saleswoman. "On my good days," she said, "I could sell anything. But then the people would bring it all back for exchange on Monday. As if I had bewitched them. Mr. Wirtheimer said there was such a thing as being *too* good."

But not all her days were good days, she told Joey. She took her periods too hard, they knocked her flat for thirty-six, forty-eight hours; and this brought the conversation back to her body, her body arching over his life like a firmament, and he would leave the hospital building and find relief in the reality of the city, Alton, with its close-packed suburbs, which he loved as his mother loved her farm, because it had formed his first impressions, when the wax was soft. He ate at aluminum diners, shopped at hardware stores for parts and tools the sandstone farmhouse in its long decrepitude needed, and bought a new vacuum cleaner, since his mother's old Hoover had hardly been used for years. He even got himself a haircut in a front-parlor barbershop—the kind of shop, with a radio playing and a baby crying in rooms out of sight, and a spiral pole out front, that he thought had disappeared, because such shops had disappeared in New York. A small child of his, years ago, had knocked the porcelain lid off the toilet water tank and it had shattered. Now, between visits to his mother, he went about the city with the cardboard box of fragments, dusty and cobweb-ridden after years in the attic, to plumbing-supply houses, where overweight, hard-smoking, not quite sardonic men would return from digging in their cavernous storerooms and give him, free, old spare lids that did not, it would turn out, quite fit. He kept trying. Alton had lost factories and population since he was a boy, and appeared in smaller letters on the maps of Pennsylvania, but it was still a place where things were made and handled, where brute matter got its honest due, and he recognized as still alive in himself the city's blue-collar faith in hardware and industry and repair, a humble faith that had survived all his heady traffic in imagery.

Life was a series of plumbing problems. After a week, the hospital had cleared out his mother's lungs, and now the cardiologists wanted to operate on the malfunctioning heart that had let the pulmonary edema occur. The angiography had revealed coronary arteries stenosed almost shut. "Oh, Joey—I could go any day," she blurted to him after the test results had been described to her. She showed him with a forefinger and thumb how small the lumen had become. "Worse than they thought." She was sitting on the bed with her hair wild and one shoulder bared by a loose tie in the hospital johnny, and her facial expression was girlish, womanhood's acquired composure all dissolved. Their intermittently shared life was being lifted into new octaves, and they seemed in these moments of hospital conference simply a man and a woman, both with more white hairs than dark, taking counsel because no one else who mattered was left. They were it.

To his relief she did not want the open-heart operation, sparing him the trouble, the expense, the tests, the trips to Philadelphia. He tried to suppress his relief and to argue for the coronary bypass that was recommended. She said, making a wryly twisted mouth just as her father used to when discussing the county's politicians, "Of course *they* recommend it. It's what they have to sell. They're in business, just like their fathers, only peddling different things. They pass me around, one to another; I've yet to see a Christian."

In the frankness that her closeness to death allowed, as her composed womanhood melted, an anti-Semitism was one of the things that emerged, shockingly. She could not see the doctors as saviors and allies but only as opportunists and exploiters. She even developed with one solemn young cardiologist a banter that cast her as a Palestinian: "You've taken me away from my village," she said. Joey was dismayed; his third wife, the briefest one, had been Jewish, and she and his mother had seemed especially friendly, and as he imagined now his mother's suppressed feelings in those years it was like seeing silverfish tumble out of old books. On her less lucid days, she seemed to think that the doctors and their allies ("One big fella, looked just like Danny Thomas, came and cut my toenails; now how much do you think *that's* going to add to the bill?") were scheming to do her out of her house and its priceless eighty acres—that she was territory they wanted to seize and develop. Each day she spent in the hospital, the little sandstone house pulled at her harder. "Get me home," she begged Joey.

"And then what?"

"Then we'll take what comes." Her eyes widened, watching his, and her mouth as it clamped shut over "what comes" was very like a child's, stubborn in its fright. For, however close their consultation and their agreements, both were aware that she was the star and he merely the prompter: though his turn would come, the spotlight burned upon her.

When, six months later, she died—instantly, it seemed to the coroner—in the kitchen, just under the room where she had been born, the neighbors, who were patient Mennonites and Lutherans, took a day to find her and another twelve hours to find him in at his apartment telephone number. It was midnight when he let himself into the house. The door keys had been lost long ago, in that distant, fabulous era after they had moved. When his mother would be away for more than a day, she would lock the doors from the inside and go out through the cellar bulkhead. Her neighbors knew this and had left the house that way after her body was removed. Joey had brought no flashlight; after parking the car by the barn, he walked to the slanted cellar doors by moonlight, and within the dark cellar was guided by memory. A Lally column here, a pyramid of paint cans there. His father and he had laid this cement floor one frantic long day when three cubic yards of ready-mix concrete were delivered in a giant gob by a truck. He would have been fifteen or so, his father in his late forties. The cellar floor of these old farmhouses was typically dirt, the red clay of the region packed more or less hard, except when the foundation walls wept in the spring and it turned to mud. His father had talked with construction men, and set out boards to frame the platform for the furnace, and dug a clay pipe into the dirt for drainage, and stretched strings here and there to determine the level and pitch, but none of these preparations encompassed the alarming dimensions of the slowly hardening concrete when it arrived early that Saturday morning. With rakes and shovels and boards and trowels they pushed and tugged the sluggish stuff level, into the far corners, around the furnace and the mouth of the drainage pipe. His father's face went white with effort, as it had when struggling with the chimney stones several years before, and the ordeal went on and on, by the light of a few bare bulbs, this panicky race with time and matter, as the concrete grew stiffer and stiffer, and in drying pushed its water toward the surface, and exuded its sonorous underground smell, its inexorable stony scent. The floor had come out surprisingly well, out of that day's sweaty panic—smooth and gray and delicately sloped so that hardly a puddle lingered after a flooding. It sometimes seemed, in the mottled perspectives of hindsight, that there had been a third man in the cellar with them, something of a professional, for it seemed unlikely that he and his father, a history teacher and a would-be poet, could have made such a satisfactory cellar floor. But if there had been such a man, Joey had mentally erased him, jealous of this arduous day at his father's side fending off disaster, doing a man's job. He was just becoming a man, and his father was wearying of being one; this was the last project so ambitious that he tackled around the house.

In the blackness, Joey's city shoes slithered on the smooth cement, and then thumped on the echoing wooden cellar stairs; he pushed the door open into the moon-striped kitchen, and a warm whimpering hairy body hurtled up against him, and he thought that his mother had not died after all. But it was the dog, who took his hand in her mouth and unstoppably whimpered and whined as if telling him a long story, the story of her hours alone in the house with her mistress, with the body, with her hunger and bafflement.

Things work out. One of his former wives, who had remarried into the Connecticut suburbs, agreed to take the dog. The cats a man from the county Humane Society came and trapped and carried away to be gassed, a few each day. Joey stacked the magazines and catalogues and Christmas cards and tied them with baling twine from the bucket and carried them to the barn to be trucked to a landfill. The Boy Scouts no longer collected paper and bottles; nothing was precious anymore. As his family assembled, Joey impressed them with his efficiency, portioning out the furniture and heirlooms among his children, his ex-wives, the local auctioneer, the junkman.

For himself he kept little but odd small items that reached back into his boyhood in the brick house they moved to the farm from—a brass tiger that sat on the piano there, when he still took piano lessons, and a curved leather-backed brush he remembered his grandfather using on his black hightop shoes before setting off to the Lutheran church. He kept some of his father's college notebooks, preserved in the attic, penned in a more rounded version of his legible schoolteacherish hand. A set of Shakespeare, with limp red covers, of which the silverfish had nibbled some pages into lace. His mother's sun hats—these were hard to throw away, though none of the assembled females wanted them. His daughters sorted through the clothes for him. He couldn't bear to touch and sort the dresses hanging in the closet, dozens of garments pressed together in an anthology of past fashions, all the way back to a fox-trimmed spring coat whose collar he remembered close to his face, its tingling black-tipped red-brown hairs. In the toolhouse, where his father had left a pathetic legacy of rusty screws and nails neatly arranged in jars, and oily tools, half of them broken, mounted on pegboard, there were also antique implements worn like prehistoric artifacts: an ancient oblong pink whetstone pointed at either end and soapily warped by all its use, and an old-fashioned square hoe worn into a lopsided metal oval, its edges had struck so many stones. Such wear couldn't have occurred in the merely forty years they were here, but must have been the work of generations; these tools had traveled back and forth across the county, surviving many moves, to end in his impatient hands. They seemed sacred—runes no one else could decipher. He was the last of his line to have ever hoed a row of carrots or sharpened a scythe.

Relatives and neighbors spoke to him with a curious soft gravity, as if he were fragile in grief. He knew he and his mother were regarded as having been unusually, perhaps unnaturally close; when in fact between themselves the fear was that they were not close enough. Why grieve? She was old, in pain, worn-out. She was too frail in her last half-year to walk to the mailbox or lift a case of cat food or pull a clump of burdock: it was time; dying is the last favor we do the world, the last tax we pay. He cried only once, during the funeral, quite unexpectedly, having taken his seat at the head of his raggedly extended family, suddenly free, for the moment, of arrangements and decisions, and seeing an arm's reach away the gleaming cherry-wood casket he had picked out in the undertaker's satiny showroom three days before. The lustrous well-joined wood, soon to be buried; the sumptuous waste of it; and the image of his mother as he first remembered her, a young slim woman dressed in a navy-blue suit, with white at her throat, to go off to her job at the downtown department store, hurrying to catch the trolley car. She had once reminisced, "Oh, how you'd run, and if you just missed it, there wouldn't be another for twenty minutes, and you wanted to cry." She had laughed, remembering.

His tears came and kept coming, in a kind of triumph, a breakthrough, a torrent of empathy and pity for that lost young woman running past the row houses, under the horse-chestnut trees, running to catch the trolley, the world of the thirties shabby and solid around her, the porches, the blue midsummer hydrangeas, this tiny well-dressed figure in her diminishing pocket of time, her future unknown, her death, her farm, far from her mind. This was the mother, apparently, he had loved, the young woman living with him and others in a brick semidetached house, a part of the world, youthfully finding her way. During the war she worked in a parachute factory, wearing a bandanna on her head like the other women, plump like them by this time, merging with them and their chatter one lunch break when he, somehow, had bicycled to the side entrance to see her. She was not like them, the tough other women, he knew, but for the moment had blended with them, did a job alongside them, and this too renewed his tears, his naive pride in her then, when he was ten or eleven. She had tried to be a person, she had lived. There was something amazing, something immortal to him in the image of her running. He remembered, from their first years on the farm, a crisis with the roof; it was being reshingled by a team of Amishmen and they had left it partially open to the weather on the night of a thunderstorm. Crashes, flashes. Joey's parents and grandparents were all awake, and he, boy though he still was, was expected now to wake and help too; they rushed up and down the attic stairs with buckets, to save the plaster of the walls and ceilings below. There was a tarpaulin in the barn that might help; he found himself outdoors, in the downpour, and he had retained an image of his mother running across the lawn in a flash of lightning that caught the white of her legs. She would not have been much over forty, and was still athletic; perhaps his father was included in this unsteady glimpse; there was a hilarity to it all, a violent health. Working his way, after her death, through all the accumulated souvenirs of her life, Joey was fascinated by the college yearbooks that preserved her girlish image above a line or two of verse:

She's blest with temper, whose unclouded ray
Can make tomorrow cheerful as today.

Group photographs showed his mother as part of the hockey team, the hiking club. With a magnifying glass he studied her unsmiling, competitive face, with her hair in two balls at her ears and a headband over her bangs. Her face seemed slightly larger than the other girls', a childlike oval broadest at the brow, its defenses relatively unevolved. As he sat there beside the cherry casket crying, his former wives and adult children stealing nervous peeks at him, the young woman ran for the trolley car, her breath catching, her panting mixed with a sighing laughter at herself, and the image was as potent, as fertile, as a classic advertisement, which endlessly taps something deep and needy within us. The image of her running down the street, away from him, trailed like a comet's tail the maternal enactments of those misty years when he was a child—crayoning with him on the living-room floor, sewing him Halloween costumes in the shape of Disney creatures, having him lift what she called the "skirts" of the bushes in the lawn while she pushed the old reel mower under them—but from her point of view; he seemed to feel from within his mother's head the situation, herself and this small son, this defenseless gurgling hatched creature, and the tentative motions of her mind and instincts as she, as new to mothering as he was to being a child, explored the terrain between them. In the attic he had found a padded baby-blue scrapbook, conscientiously maintained, containing his first words, the date of his first crawl, and his hospital birth certificate imprinted with his inky day-old feet. The baths. The cod-liver oil. Trying to do the right thing, the normal thing, running toward her farm, her death. In his vision of her running she was bright and quick and small, like an animal in a trap. This was the mother he had loved, the mother before they moved, before she betrayed him with the farm and its sandstone house.

Ruthlessly, vengefully, weekend by weekend, he cleaned the place out—disconnecting the phone, giving the auctioneer the run of the attic, seeing the refrigerator and stove hauled off for a few dollars each, by a truck that got stuck in the muddy winter lawn. With his new vacuum cleaner Joey attacked the emptying rooms, sucking up the allergen-laden dust from the cracks between the floorboards, sweeping the walls and ceilings clean of their veils of cobwebs upon cobwebs. How satisfying this was, one room after another that he would not have to do again. Joey discovered that his mother had been far from alone in the house; while the cats mewed and milled outside on the porch, a tribe of mice, year after year, ancestors and descendants, had been fed sunflower seeds, whose accumulated stored husks burst forth by the bucketful from behind where the stained-pine corner cupboard had stood, and the back of the dishtowel drawer of the kitchen sink. He set traps for the mice. He set out d-Con, and the next weekend tossed their small stiff bodies, held gingerly by the tail, down into the swamp, where the rocks were, and the ashes of his grandmother's mattress.

The old house had curious small cabinets built into the stone thickness, and they disgorged packets of his father's index cards, riddled with anxious, harried reminder notes to himself, and pads of old high-school permission slips, and small boxes of dull pencils and hardened erasers, and playing cards from the remote days when he and his parents played three-handed pinochle at the dining table. At first, he could scarcely hold the cards, sixteen fanned in one little hand, and would stifle tears when his meld was poor and he lost. Once at the farm, they never played cards again. There were animals of petrified Play-Doh made by Joey's children, and useless pretty vases and bowls sent distractedly as seasonal gifts, and plush-bound old-fashioned albums, with little mildewed mirrors on the covers, of stiffly posed ancestors he could not identify. His mother had offered, over the years, to teach him their names and relation to him, but he had not been interested, and now she was not there to ask, and his ancestors floated free and nameless like angels.

There were things she had offered to tell him he had not wanted to hear. "What didn't you like about him?" he had once asked her—a bit impatiently, wearying of her voice—about his father.

Sitting in her television-watching chair, her weight and strength so wasted that only her mouth and mind could move, she had been telling him about her youthful romantic life. She had gone to a one-room country school—when she was dead, he came upon a photograph of the student body and its corpulent mustachioed instructor, his mother's broad little face squinting toward the camera under a ponderous crown of wound braids. Among the other children there had been a dark-haired, dark-eyed boy she had fancied, and who had fancied her. But her parents had disapproved of the boy's "people," and of several other dark-eyed substitutes that over the years she had offered them. But no, not until Joey's blondish, pale-eyed father did she bring home a suitor they could endorse. "They liked him, and he liked them. I'll say this for your father, not every man could have lived with his in-laws that cheerfully all those years. He really admired my mother, that style of little woman. He loved energetic little women. He thought they could make money for him. It's true, Mother was a money-maker. She was the one who got up in the dark to drive the cart into Alton to market. The tobacco they retired on had been her project. But admiring Mother was no reason to marry me. I was *big.* It was a mistake, and we both knew it. We knew it the first day of our honeymoon." Joey had often heard his mother's views on little women, how they have the best of it, and take the men from the big women like herself, big women who have tortured their little mothers in the birthing. Behind these formulations there was something—about sex, he believed—that he didn't want, as a boy or a man, to hear. *A real femme.* Even as a very small child he had been aware of a weight of anger his mother carried; he had quickly evolved—first word, first crawl—an adroitness at staying out of her way when she was heavy with it, and a wish to amuse her, to keep her light. But now as they were nearing the end, and her flesh was dissolving, and her inner self rising to the surface, he had become more daring, less catering, even challenging. Her own blue eyes, that had never needed a cataract operation, widened at his question as if she were seeing ghosts over his shoulder. "Oh, Joey," she said, "don't ask. It was un*speak*able."

He had to smile at the old-fashioned concept. "Unspeakable? Daddy?"

A bit of flush had crept into her colorless creased cheeks. She was getting angry, once again. She kept staring, not so much at him as at the space in his vicinity. She knew from watching television what the talk shows permitted people to say these days. "Well, maybe you're old enough. Maybe I *should* speak it."

"Oh, no, no thanks, that's all right," he said, jumping up from his chair and heading into the kitchen, much as his father used to in the middle of a marital exchange. *Poor Daddy,* was his thought. Let the dead alone. Now she too was dead, and there were many things Joey would never know. Though he grew used to the sandstone house without her in it, he still found it strange, back in his Manhattan apartment, that she never called on Saturday mornings the way she used to, with her playful, self-mocking account of her week. The dead can't even telephone. The phone's silence more than any other conveyed the peace of the dead, their absolute and, as it were, hostile withdrawal.

The real-estate appraiser, an old high-school classmate, stood in his gray suit in the cobwebbed cellar, next to the rickety furnace, among the paint cans and rusty hot-air ducts, and said to Joey, "Seventeen years here alone. It took a lot of guts." Yes, she had been brave, he could now afford to see, all those years alone, alone but for the animals she fed, and the ghosts on television. Over the telephone, even when reporting an insomniac night of breathlessness and terror, she had tried to keep it light for his sake, and mocked herself, mocking her very will, at the age of eighty-five, to live. "It's strange, but I really don't intend to die. Though a lot of people would like me to."

"Really? Who?"

"The real-estate developers. The neighbors. They think it's time for this old lady to move over and make some room."

"Do they really?" He was grateful she had not included him among the many who wished her dead.

"*Really,*" she mocked. "But I have a responsibility here. The place still needs me."

"We all need you," Joey said, sighing, giving up. The fate of the place was another unspeakable matter. She wanted the place to go on and on, as it was in her idea of it.

He had scanned her in vain for some sign of sunset resignation. She had choked down her pills and vitamins to the end, and her fear of life's sensations ceasing had seemed as pure as a child's. The last time he had visited, on a cool fall day, she came outdoors to supervise his planting, in two arcs by a curve of the cement walk, two dozen tulip bulbs she had ordered from a catalogue. At first he had arranged the bulbs point down, and then realized that the point was what would grow upward, toward the sun. His mother had stood there on her unsteady feet, in her gaudy bathrobe, looking down; the sight of the fat cream-white bulbs nested in the turned red earth startled a kind of grunt out of her. "Oh, how dear they look," she said. To Joey she added, "How nicely you do things."

In all of her leavings that came to light he was most touched by her accounts—her tax forms and used checkbooks, meticulously kept, even though her tiny backward-slanting hand had become spasmodic and shaky. (Could that big penciled handwriting on the back of the enlarged photograph have been hers after all, at the age of thirteen?) She had kept, on a large pad of green paper, spreadsheets of her monthly expenses, ruled off by hand at the beginning of each month. The last entries had been made the day before the morning of her death. This financial and mathematical niceness of hers was something quite unpredictable, like a musical passion in a banker. Among the stored sheets of figures were several drawn up before they moved, with lists of expenses side by side, taxes, heating, utilities, upkeep—absurdly small amounts they now seemed, from that frozen wartime world. By her calculations, their reduced costs in the little sandstone house, and the projected rentals of their eighty acres to the neighboring farmers, would save them five hundred dollars—a third of her husband's salary. It had never really occurred to Joey that their move here had had a practical side. When he came to sheets showing how the money for his college education could be squeezed out among their other expenses, he couldn't bear to keep reading.

Gradually, through the stark months of a winter that was, according to the forecasters, unseasonably cold, and then unseasonably warm, he reduced the house to its essence, removing every trace, even a rusty pencil sharpener screwed to a windowsill, of his life and the four lives that had ended. Here on this patch of now uncarpeted wood his grandfather had fallen, having convulsively leaped from the bed where, a year later, his widow would breathe her last. Here, in the bedroom adjacent, his father had sat up with such pains in his chest that he told his wife to call the ambulance. He had died in the ambulance. Here in this same space Joey had lain sleepless, wondering how to tell his mother of his next divorce. Here on the other side of the wall he would lie after a date, his head still whirling with cigarette smoke and the perfume-counter smell of the girl. Here on the worn linoleum his mother had died, at the base of a wall she had had the Amish carpenters make of old chestnut boards, boards left in the barn from the era before the blight, to cover the rough stones exposed when the big kitchen chimney had been removed. The rooms had a soft beauty, empty. The uncovered floorboards drank the sunlight. Joey looked through the curtainless windows, seeing what his mother had seen—the sloping old orchard to the north, the barn and road and fields to the east, the lilac bushes and bird feeder and meadow to the south, the woods and the tall blue spruce to the west.

On his final cleanup visit, Joey found something devil-like—a small dark stiff shape, in size between a mouse and a rat, its legs attached by webs—floating in the bathroom toilet. A flying squirrel. It had come down from the attic and drowned, sick and thirsty from the d-Con. Joey remembered watching at twilight, that summer he moved the stones, a pair of flying squirrels sail, as if sliding swiftly on a wire, from the attic window over to the blue spruce. The house had stood empty before his family had moved in the previous fall, and this pair had moved in ahead of them.

He had bought a padlock for the cellar bulkhead, and closed the house with a key, having installed new locks. The house was ready for sale in the spring. But in the meantime, as he lay awake in his apartment three hours away, its emptiness called to him. It needed him. Suppose a fire, or local vandals, jealous of the price the place would fetch. . . Housing developments were all around, and even Philadelphians were moving into the area. His mother had made a shrewd investment, buying back paradise.

Those weekends alone in the house, sorting, cleaning, staying away from the motel until moonlight had replaced sunlight on the floors, he had discovered himself talking aloud, as if in response to a friendly presence just behind the dry old wallpaper, in the thick sandstone walls. His own uncluttered rooms, suspended above Manhattan's steady roar, with an ornamental piece of porch banister hidden at the back of a closet, felt as if they were flying somewhere. He felt guilty, anxious, displaced. He had always wanted to be where the action was, and what action there was, it turned out, had been back there.

Eudora Welty *(1909–2001)*

was born in Jackson, Mississippi, the daughter of an insurance executive from Ohio and a mother who had been a teacher in West Virginia. The Weltys instilled in their daughter their love of books and learning, and she checked out the two-book limit daily from the Andrew Carnegie library. She attended the Mississippi State College for Women and went on to earn her bachelor's degree from the University of Wisconsin. Welty took advertising courses at the Columbia University School of Business but disliked the field and soon returned to Jackson, where she would spend the rest of her life. During the Depression, she worked for the Works Progress Administration and traveled throughout Mississippi, taking hundreds of snapshots (later shown in several exhibitions and published in book form). In the late 1930s, she began to get her short stories published, including "A Worn Path" and "Why I Live at the P.O." in The Atlantic Monthly. *(A half-century later, the latter story was the first thing software developer Steven Dorner thought of when he was trying to come up with a name for his new post office protocol e-mail program, which is to this day called Eudora.) She went on to win eight O. Henry Awards and the Pulitzer Prize (for her novel* The Optimist's Daughter*). She won Lifetime Achievement Awards from the American Association of University Women, the National Endowment for the Arts, the National Endowment for the Humanities, and the National Book Foundation. The publication in 1980 of the career-spanning* The Collected Stories of Eudora Welty *is widely credited (along with the publication a little more than a year earlier of* The Stories of John Cheever*) with triggering a broader readership for the American short story.*

Introduction by **Lee Smith**

Like swallows from a Mississippi stubble field, Eudora Welty's luminous stories rise up from the commonplace. She has said that these are "stories written from within. They come from living here—they were *part* of living here, of my long familiarity with the thoughts and feelings of those around me, in their many shadings and variations and contradictions." Many of her earliest stories, such as "A Worn Path" (first published in *The Atlantic Monthly* in 1941), came out of her "response to the Depression."

Yet "A Worn Path" does not *feel* like an attempt to document the Depression; it does not arouse the kind of emotions we feel when we look at Walker Evans's photographs, for instance. The initial description of the "bright frozen day" followed by Phoenix Jackson's lively incantation—"Out of my way, all you foxes, owls, beetles, jack rabbits, coons and wild animals! . . . Keep out from under these feet, little bobwhites. . . . Keep the big wild hogs out of my path. Don't let none of those come running my direction. I got a long way."—heralds a mythic journey through an almost-magic landscape, a pilgrimage. Old Phoenix travels "up through pines. . . . Now down through oaks;" she is "caught in the thorny bush"; must cross the creek on a log, "creep and crawl" through a barbed-wire fence, and walk through a swamp. She is knocked over by a black dog and saved by a young hunter before—finally—"There ahead was Natchez shining." Silver is everywhere in this enchanted land: We find a "wagon track where the silver grass blew between the red ruts"; "little strings of trees silver in their dead leaves"; the lady with the "red-, green-, and silver-wrapped presents." This winter landscape has been transformed by Phoenix Jackson's love for her little grandson, who "sits up there in the house all wrapped up, waiting by himself. . . . He got a sweet look. He's going to last. . . . I could tell him from all the others in creation." The simplicity of this story adds to its mythic dimension. Miss Welty's plain yet poetic language also serves to lift Phoenix Jackson's journey into the realm of the timeless as she describes, for instance, those "cabins silver from weather, with the doors and windows boarded shut, all like old women under a spell sitting there. 'I walking in their sleep,' she said, nodding her head vigorously." Miss Welty's gentle humor leavens but does not diminish Phoenix Jackson's tragic situation.

By contrast, "Why I Live at the P.O." is flat-out hilarious. Famous for Sister's ratchety, self-satisfied, first-person narrative voice, this story has spawned countless clichéd imitations. But remember: This one was *first.* Sister's determined martyrdom is exceeded only by her paranoia: "Stella-Rondo hadn't done a thing but turn (Mama) against me from upstairs while I stood there helpless over the hot stove. So that made Mama, Papa-Daddy and the baby all on Stella-Rondo's side. . . . There I was with the whole entire house on Stella-Rondo's side and turned against me." Any unreliable narrator—such as Sister here—gets the reader immediately involved. We know what she knows, but we also understand more than she understands; we have become complicit in the story. We understand, for instance, the sexual jealousy Sister feels because Stella-Rondo, after all, did manage to catch Mr. Whitaker in the first place. We know that Sister's last statement is a lie, we know damn well that she is just *dying* to hear all "the incidents" of Stella-Rondo's life with Mr. Whitaker even though she would never admit it, not even to herself. Comedy also resides in Miss Welty's quick throwaway lines, such as "You ought to see Mama, she weighs two hundred pounds and has real tiny feet," and in her use of specific details such as those bluebird wall vases or the trip to Mammoth Cave, "with all expenses paid."

In the mysterious "No Place for You, My Love," two strangers, a man and a younger woman, leave a New Orleans luncheon together and, on impulse, start driving south into the hot and foreign bayou country, where they end up dancing together in a seedy riverside bar. The "extremity of this place" calls forth their own corresponding emotional response. Though anything at all could happen to them, it does not; in the end, he drives her safely back and deposits her at her New Orleans hotel. "Something that must have been with them all along suddenly, then, was not. In a moment, tall as panic, it rose, cried like a human, and dropped back." Whatever the mode (tragedy, comedy) or the mood of Eudora Welty's fiction, the reader always senses a deeper meaning, an unspoken revelation or unseen presence, an immanence beneath her graceful writing and the shining surface of the story.

Lee Smith is the author of many books, including the novels Fair and Tender Ladies *and* Saving Grace *and the story collections* Me and My Baby View the Eclipse *and* News of the Spirit, *both New York Times Notable Books. Her awards include the Lila Wallace–Reader's Digest Writer's Award and the 1999 Academy Award for fiction from the American Academy of Arts and Letters. She grew up in Grundy, Virginia; graduated from Hollins University; and lives now in Hillsborough, North Carolina.*

Eudora Welty

A Worn Path

It was December—a bright frozen day in the early morning. Far out in the country there was an old Negro woman with her head tied in a red rag, coming along a path through the pinewoods. Her name was Phoenix Jackson. She was very old and small and she walked slowly in the dark pine shadows, moving a little from side to side in her steps, with the balanced heaviness and lightness of a pendulum in a grandfather clock. She carried a thin, small cane made from an umbrella, and with this she kept tapping the frozen earth in front of her. This made a grave and persistent noise in the still air, that seemed meditative like the chirping of a solitary little bird.

She wore a dark striped dress reaching down to her shoe tops, and an equally long apron of bleached sugar sacks, with a full pocket: all neat and tidy, but every time she took a step she might have fallen over her shoelaces, which dragged from her unlaced shoes. She looked straight ahead. Her eyes were blue with age. Her skin had a pattern all its own of numberless branching wrinkles and as though a whole little tree stood in the middle of her forehead, but a golden color ran underneath, and the two knobs of her cheeks were illuminated by a yellow burning under the dark. Under the red rag her hair came down on her neck in the frailest of ringlets, still black, and with an odor like copper.

Now and then there was a quivering in the thicket. Old Phoenix said, "Out of my way, all you foxes, owls, beetles, jack rabbits, coons and wild animals! . . . Keep out from under these feet, little bob-whites. . . . Keep the big wild hogs out of my path. Don't let none of those come running my direction. I got a long way." Under her small black-freckled hand her cane, limber as a buggy whip, would switch at the brush as if to rouse up any hiding things.

On she went. The woods were deep and still. The sun made the pine needles almost too bright to look at, up where the wind rocked. The cones dropped as light as feathers. Down in the hollow was the mourning dove—it was not too late for him.

The path ran up a hill. "Seem like there is chains about my feet, time I get this far," she said, in the voice of argument old people keep to use with themselves. "Something always take a hold of me on this hill—pleads I should stay."

After she got to the top she turned and gave a full, severe look behind her where she had come. "Up through pines," she said at length. "Now down through oaks."

Her eyes opened their widest, and she started down gently. But before she got to the bottom of the hill a bush caught her dress.

Her fingers were busy and intent, but her skirts were full and long, so that before she could pull them free in one place they were caught in another. It was not possible to allow the dress to tear. "I in the thorny bush," she said. "Thorns, you doing your appointed work. Never want to let folks pass, no sir. Old eyes thought you was a pretty little *green* bush."

Finally, trembling all over, she stood free, and after a moment dared to stoop for her cane.

"Sun so high!" she cried, leaning back and looking, while the thick tears went over her eyes. "The time getting all gone here."

At the foot of this hill was a place where a log was laid across the creek.

"Now comes the trial," said Phoenix.

Putting her right foot out, she mounted the log and shut her eyes. Lifting her skirt, leveling her cane fiercely before her, like a festival figure in some parade, she began to march across. Then she opened her eyes and she was safe on the other side.

"I wasn't as old as I thought," she said.

But she sat down to rest. She spread her skirts on the bank around her and folded her hands over her knees. Up above her was a tree in a pearly cloud of mistletoe. She did not dare to close her eyes, and when a little boy brought her a plate with a slice of marble-cake on it she spoke to him. "That would be acceptable," she said. But when she went to take it there was just her own hand in the air.

So she left that tree, and had to go through a barbed-wire fence. There she had to creep and crawl, spreading her knees and stretching her fingers like a baby trying to climb the steps. But she talked loudly to herself: she could not let her dress be torn now, so late in the day, and she could not pay for having her arm or her leg sawed off if she got caught fast where she was.

At last she was safe through the fence and risen up out in the clearing. Big dead trees, like black men with one arm, were standing in the purple stalks of the withered cotton field. There sat a buzzard.

"Who you watching?"

In the furrow she made her way along.

"Glad this not the season for bulls," she said, looking sideways, "and the good Lord made his snakes to curl up and sleep in the winter. A pleasure I don't see no two-headed snake coming around that tree, where it come once. It took a while to get by him, back in the summer."

She passed through the old cotton and went into a field of dead corn. It whispered and shook and was taller than her head. "Through the maze now," she said, for there was no path.

Then there was something tall, black, and skinny there, moving before her.

At first she took it for a man. It could have been a man dancing in the field. But she stood still and listened, and it did not make a sound. It was as silent as a ghost.

"Ghost," she said sharply, "who be you the ghost of? For I have heard of nary death close by."

But there was no answer—only the ragged dancing in the wind.

She shut her eyes, reached out her hand, and touched a sleeve. She found a coat and inside that an emptiness, cold as ice.

"You scarecrow," she said. Her face lighted. "I ought to be shut up for good," she said with laughter. "My senses is gone. I too old. I the oldest people I ever know. Dance, old scarecrow," she said, "while I dancing with you."

She kicked her foot over the furrow, and with mouth drawn down, shook her head once or twice in a little strutting way. Some husks blew down and whirled in streamers about her skirts.

Then she went on, parting her way from side to side with the cane, through the whispering field. At last she came to the end, to a wagon track where the silver grass blew between the red ruts. The quail were walking around like pullets, seeming all dainty and unseen.

"Walk pretty," she said. "This the easy place. This the easy going."

She followed the track, swaying through the quiet bare fields, through the little strings of trees silver in their dead leaves, past cabins silver from weather, with the doors and windows boarded shut, all like old women under a spell sitting there. "I walking in their sleep," she said, nodding her head vigorously.

In a ravine she went where a spring was silent flowing through a hollow log. Old Phoenix bent and drank. "Sweet-gum makes the water sweet," she said, and drank more. "Nobody know who made this well, for it was here when I was born."

The track crossed a swampy part where the moss hung as white as lace from every limb. "Sleep on, alligators, and blow your bubbles." Then the track went into the road.

Deep, deep the road went down between the high green-colored banks. Overhead the live-oaks met, and it was as dark as a cave.

A black dog with a lolling tongue came up out of the weeds by the ditch. She was meditating, and not ready, and when he came at her she only hit him a little with her cane. Over she went in the ditch, like a little puff of milkweed.

Down there, her senses drifted away. A dream visited her, and she reached her hand up, but nothing reached down and gave her a pull. So she lay there and presently went to talking. "Old woman," she said to herself, "that black dog come up out of the weeds to stall you off, and now there he sitting on his fine tail, smiling at you."

A white man finally came along and found her—a hunter, a young man, with his dog on a chain.

"Well, Granny!" he laughed. "What are you doing there?"

"Lying on my back like a June-bug waiting to be turned over, mister," she said, reaching up her hand.

He lifted her up, gave her a swing in the air, and set her down. "Anything broken, Granny?"

"No, sir, them old dead weeds is springy enough," said Phoenix, when she had got her breath. "I thank you for your trouble."

"Where do you live, Granny?" he asked, while the two dogs were growling at each other.

"Away back yonder, sir, behind the ridge. You can't even see it from here."

"On your way home?"

"No sir, I going to town."

"Why, that's too far! That's as far as I walk when I come out myself, and I get something for my trouble." He patted the stuffed bag he carried, and there hung down a little closed claw. It was one of the bob-whites, and its beak hooked bitterly to show it was dead. "Now you go home, Granny!"

"I bound to go to town, mister," said Phoenix. "The time come around."

He gave another laugh, filling the whole landscape. "I know you old colored people! Wouldn't miss going to town to see Santa Claus!"

But something held old Phoenix very still. The deep lines in her face went into a fierce and different radiation. Without warning, she had seen with her own eyes a flashing nickel fall out of the man's pocket onto the ground.

"How old are you, Granny?" he was saying.

"There is no telling, mister," she said, "no telling."

Then she gave a little cry and clapped her hands and said, "Git on away from here, dog! Look! Look at that dog!" She laughed as if in admiration. "He ain't scared of nobody. He a big black dog." She whispered, "Sic him!"

"Watch me get rid of that cur," said the man. "Sic him, Pete! Sic him!"

Phoenix heard the dogs fighting, and heard the man running and throwing sticks. She even heard a gunshot. But she was slowly bending forward by that time, further and further forward, the lids stretched down over her eyes, as if she were doing this in her sleep. Her chin was lowered almost to her knees. The yellow palm of her hand came out from the fold of her apron. Her fingers slid down and along the ground under the piece of money with the grace and care they would have in lifting an egg from under a setting hen. Then she slowly straightened up, she stood erect, and the nickel was in her apron pocket. A bird flew by. Her lips moved. "God watching me the whole time. I come to stealing."

The man came back, and his own dog panted about them. "Well, I scared him off that time," he said, and then he laughed and lifted his gun and pointed it at Phoenix.

She stood straight and faced him.

"Doesn't the gun scare you?" he said, still pointing it.

"No, sir, I seen plenty go off closer by, in my day, and for less than what I done," she said, holding utterly still.

He smiled, and shouldered the gun. "Well, Granny," he said, "you must be a hundred years old, and scared of nothing. I'd give you a dime if I had any money with me. But you take my advice and stay home, and nothing will happen to you."

"I bound to go on my way, mister," said Phoenix. She inclined her head in the red rag. Then they went in different directions, but she could hear the gun shooting again and again over the hill.

She walked on. The shadows hung from the oak trees to the road like curtains. Then she smelled wood-smoke, and smelled the river, and she saw a steeple and the cabins on their steep steps. Dozens of little black children whirled around her. There ahead was Natchez shining. Bells were ringing. She walked on.

In the paved city it was Christmas time. There were red and green electric lights strung and criss-crossed everywhere, and all turned on in the daytime. Old Phoenix would have been lost if she had not distrusted her eyesight and depended on her feet to know where to take her.

She paused quietly on the sidewalk where people were passing by. A lady came along in the crowd, carrying an armful of red-, green- and silver-wrapped presents; she gave off perfume like the red roses in hot summer, and Phoenix stopped her.

"Please, missy, will you lace up my shoe?" She held up her foot.

"What do you want, Grandma?"

"See my shoe," said Phoenix. "Do all right for out in the country, but wouldn't look right to go in a big building."

"Stand still then, Grandma," said the lady. She put her packages down on the sidewalk beside her and laced and tied both shoes tightly.

"Can't lace 'em with a cane," said Phoenix. "Thank you, missy. I doesn't mind asking a nice lady to tie up my shoe, when I gets out on the street."

Moving slowly and from side to side, she went into the big building, and into a tower of steps, where she walked up and around and around until her feet knew to stop.

She entered a door, and there she saw nailed up on the wall the document that had been stamped with the gold seal and framed in the gold frame, which matched the dream that was hung up in her head.

"Here I be," she said. There was a fixed and ceremonial stiffness over her body.

"A charity case, I suppose," said an attendant who sat at the desk before her.

But Phoenix only looked above her head. There was sweat on her face, the wrinkles in her skin shone like a bright net.

"Speak up, Grandma," the woman said. "What's your name? We must have your history, you know. Have you been here before? What seems to be the trouble with you?"

Old Phoenix only gave a twitch to her face as if a fly were bothering her.

"Are you deaf?" cried the attendant.

But then the nurse came in.

"Oh, that's just old Aunt Phoenix," she said. "She doesn't come for herself—she has a little grandson. She makes these trips just as regular as clockwork. She lives away back off the Old Natchez Trace." She bent down. "Well, Aunt Phoenix, why don't you just take a seat? We won't keep you standing after your long trip." She pointed.

The old woman sat down, bolt upright in the chair.

"Now, how is the boy?" asked the nurse.

Old Phoenix did not speak.

"I said, how is the boy?"

But Phoenix only waited and stared straight ahead, her face very solemn and withdrawn into rigidity.

"Is his throat any better?" asked the nurse. "Aunt Phoenix, don't you hear me? Is your grandson's throat any better since the last time you came for the medicine?"

With her hands on her knees, the old woman waited, silent, erect and motionless, just as if she were in armor.

"You mustn't take up our time this way, Aunt Phoenix," the nurse said. "Tell us quickly about your grandson, and get it over. He isn't dead, is he?"

At last there came a flicker and then a flame of comprehension across her face, and she spoke.

"My grandson. It was my memory had left me. There I sat and forgot why I made my long trip."

"Forgot?" The nurse frowned. "After you came so far?"

Then Phoenix was like an old woman begging a dignified forgiveness for waking up frightened in the night. "I never did go to school, I was too old at the Surrender," she said in a soft voice. "I'm an old woman without an education. It was my memory fail me. My little grandson, he is just the same, and I forgot it in the coming."

"Throat never heals, does it?" said the nurse, speaking in a loud, sure voice to old Phoenix. By now she had a card with something written on it, a little list. "Yes. Swallowed lye. When was it?—January—two, three years ago—"

Phoenix spoke unasked now. "No, missy, he not dead, he just the same. Every little while his throat begin to close up again, and he not able to swallow. He not get his breath. He not able to help himself. So the time come around, and I go on another trip for the soothing medicine."

"All right. The doctor said as long as you came to get it, you could have it," said the nurse. "But it's an obstinate case."

"My little grandson, he sit up there in the house all wrapped up, waiting by himself," Phoenix went on. "We is the only two left in the world. He suffer and it don't seem to put him back at all. He got a sweet look. He going to last. He wear a little patch quilt and peep out holding his mouth open like a little bird. I remembers so plain now. I not going to forget him again, no, the whole enduring time. I could tell him from all the others in creation."

"All right." The nurse was trying to hush her now. She brought her a bottle of medicine. "Charity," she said, making a check mark in a book.

Old Phoenix held the bottle close to her eyes, and then carefully put it into her pocket.

"I thank you," she said.

"It's Christmas time, Grandma," said the attendant. "Could I give you a few pennies out of my purse?"

"Five pennies is a nickel," said Phoenix stiffly.

"Here's a nickel," said the attendant.

Phoenix rose carefully and held out her hand. She received the nickel and then fished the other nickel out of her pocket and laid it beside the new one. She stared at her palm closely, with her head on one side.

Then she gave a tap with her cane on the floor.

"This is what come to me to do," she said. "I going to the store and buy my child a little windmill they sells, made out of paper. He going to find it hard to believe there such a thing in the world. I'll march myself back where he waiting, holding it straight up in this hand."

She lifted her free hand, gave a little nod, turned around, and walked out of the doctor's office. Then her slow step began on the stairs, going down.

Eudora Welty

Why I Live at the P.O.

I was getting along fine with Mama, Papa-Daddy and Uncle Rondo until my sister Stella-Rondo just separated from her husband and came back home again. Mr. Whitaker! Of course I went with Mr. Whitaker first, when he first appeared here in China Grove, taking "Pose Yourself" photos, and Stella-Rondo broke us up. Told him I was one-sided. Bigger on one side than the other, which is a deliberate, calculated falsehood: I'm the same. Stella-Rondo is exactly twelve months to the day younger than I am and for that reason she's spoiled.

She's always had anything in the world she wanted and then she'd throw it away. Papa-Daddy gave her this gorgeous Add-a-Pearl necklace when she was eight years old and she threw it away playing baseball when she was nine, with only two pearls.

So as soon as she got married and moved away from home the first thing she did was separate! From Mr. Whitaker! This photographer with the popeyes she said she trusted. Came home from one of those towns up in Illinois and to our complete surprise brought this child of two.

Mama said she like to made her drop dead for a second. "Here you had this marvelous blonde child and never so much as wrote your mother a word about it," says Mama. "I'm thoroughly ashamed of you." But of course she wasn't.

Stella-Rondo just calmly takes off this *hat,* I wish you could see it. She says, "Why, Mama, Shirley-T.'s adopted, I can prove it."

"How?" says Mama, but all I says was, "H'm!" There I was over the hot stove, trying to stretch two chickens over five people and a completely unexpected child into the bargain, without one moment's notice.

"What do you mean—'H'm!'?" says Stella-Rondo, and Mama says, "I heard that, Sister."

I said that oh, I didn't mean a thing, only that whoever Shirley-T. was, she was the spit-image of Papa-Daddy if he'd cut off his beard, which of course he'd never do in the world. Papa-Daddy's Mama's papa and sulks.

Stella-Rondo got furious! She said, "Sister, I don't need to tell you you got a lot of nerve and always did have and I'll thank you to make no future reference to my adopted child whatsoever."

"Very well," I said. "Very well, very well. Of course I noticed at once she looks like Mr. Whitaker's side too. That frown. She looks like a cross between Mr. Whitaker and Papa-Daddy."

"Well, all I can say is she isn't."

"She looks exactly like Shirley Temple to me," says Mama, but Shirley-T. just ran away from her.

So the first thing Stella-Rondo did at the table was turn Papa-Daddy against me.

"Papa-Daddy," she says. He was trying to cut up his meat. "Papa-Daddy!" I was taken completely by surprise. Papa-Daddy is about a million years old and's got this long-long beard. "Papa-Daddy, Sister says she fails to understand why you don't cut off your beard."

So Papa-Daddy l-a-y-s down his knife and fork! He's real rich. Mama says he is, he says he isn't. So he says, "Have I heard correctly? You don't understand why I don't cut off my beard?"

"Why," I says, "Papa-Daddy, of course I understand, I did not say any such of a thing, the idea!"

He says, "Hussy!"

I says, "Papa-Daddy, you know I wouldn't any more want you to cut off your beard than the man in the moon. It was the farthest thing from my mind! Stella-Rondo sat there and made that up while she was eating breast of chicken."

But he says, "So the postmistress fails to understand why I don't cut off my beard. Which job I got you through my influence with the government. 'Bird's nest'—is that what you call it?"

Not that it isn't the next to smallest P.O. in the entire state of Mississippi.

I says, "Oh, Papa-Daddy," I says, "I didn't say any such of a thing, I never dreamed it was a bird's nest, I have always been grateful though this is the next to smallest P.O. in the state of Mississippi, and I do not enjoy being referred to as a hussy by my own grandfather."

But Stella-Rondo says, "Yes, you did say it too. Anybody in the world could of heard you, that had ears."

"Stop right there," says Mama, looking at *me.*

So I pulled my napkin straight back through the napkin ring and left the table.

As soon as I was out of the room Mama says, "Call her back, or she'll starve to death," but Papa-Daddy says, "This is the beard I started growing on the Coast when I was fifteen years old." He would of gone on till nightfall if Shirley-T. hadn't lost the Milky Way she ate in Cairo.

So Papa-Daddy says, "I am going out and lie in the hammock, and you can all sit here and remember my words: I'll never cut off my beard as long as I live, even one inch, and I don't appreciate it in you at all." Passed right by me in the hall and went straight out and got in the hammock.

It would be a holiday. It wasn't five minutes before Uncle Rondo suddenly appeared in the hall in one of Stella-Rondo's flesh-colored kimonos, all cut on the bias, like something Mr. Whitaker probably thought was gorgeous.

"Uncle Rondo!" I says. "I didn't know who that was! Where are you going?"

"Sister," he says, "get out of my way, I'm poisoned."

"If you're poisoned stay away from Papa-Daddy," I says. "Keep out of the hammock. Papa-Daddy will certainly beat you on the head if you come within forty miles of him. He thinks I deliberately said he ought to cut off his beard after he got me the P.O., and I've told him and told him and told him, and he acts like he just don't hear me. Papa-Daddy must of gone stone deaf."

"He picked a fine day to do it then," says Uncle Rondo, and before you could say "Jack Robinson" flew out in the yard.

What he'd really done, he'd drunk another bottle of that prescription. He does it every single Fourth of July as sure as shooting, and it's horribly expensive. Then he falls over in the hammock and snores. So he insisted on zigzagging right on out to the hammock, looking like a half-wit.

Papa-Daddy woke up with this horrible yell and right there without moving an inch he tried to turn Uncle Rondo against me. I heard every word he said. Oh, he told Uncle Rondo I didn't learn to read till I was eight years old and he didn't see how in the world I ever got the mail put up at the P.O., much less read it all, and he said if Uncle Rondo could only fathom the lengths he had gone to get me that job! And he said on the other hand he thought Stella-Rondo had a brilliant mind and deserved credit for getting out of town. All the time he was just lying there swinging as pretty as you please and looping out his beard, and poor Uncle Rondo was *pleading* with him to slow down the hammock, it was making him as dizzy as a witch to watch it. But that's what Papa-Daddy likes about a hammock. So Uncle Rondo was too dizzy to get turned against me for the time being. He's Mama's only brother and is a good case of a one-track mind. Ask anybody. A certified pharmacist.

Just then I heard Stella-Rondo raising the upstairs window. While she was married she got this peculiar idea that it's cooler with the windows shut and locked. So she has to raise the window before she can make a soul hear her outdoors.

So she raises the window and says, "*Oh!*" You would have thought she was mortally wounded.

Uncle Rondo and Papa-Daddy didn't even look up, but kept right on with what they were doing. I had to laugh.

I flew up the stairs and threw the door open! I says, "What in the wide world's the matter, Stella-Rondo? You mortally wounded?"

"No," she says, "I am not mortally wounded but I wish you would do me the favor of looking out that window there and telling me what you see."

So I shade my eyes and look out the window.

"I see the front yard," I says.

"Don't you see any human beings?" she says.

"I see Uncle Rondo trying to run Papa-Daddy out of the hammock," I says. "Nothing more. Naturally, it's so suffocating-hot in the house, with all the windows shut and locked, everybody who cares to stay in their right mind will have to go out and get in the hammock before the Fourth of July is over."

"Don't you notice anything different about Uncle Rondo?" asks Stella-Rondo.

"Why, no, except he's got on some terrible-looking flesh-colored contraption I wouldn't be found dead in, is all I can see," I says.

"Never mind, you won't be found dead in it, because it happens to be part of my trousseau, and Mr. Whitaker took several dozen photographs of me in it," says Stella-Rondo. "What on earth could Uncle Rondo *mean* by wearing part of my trousseau out in the broad open daylight without saying so much as 'Kiss my foot,' *knowing* I only got home this morning after my separation and hung my negligee up on the bathroom door, just as nervous as I could be?"

"I'm sure I don't know, and what do you expect me to do about it?" I says. "Jump out the window?"

"No, I expect nothing of the kind. I simply declare that Uncle Rondo looks like a fool in it, that's all," she says. "It makes me sick to my stomach."

"Well, he looks as good as he can," I says. "As good as anybody in reason could." I stood up for Uncle Rondo, please remember. And I said to Stella-Rondo, "I think I would do well not to criticize so freely if I were you and came home with a two-year-old child I had never said a word about, and no explanation whatever about my separation."

"I asked you the instant I entered this house not to refer one more time to my adopted child, and you gave me your word of honor you would not," was all Stella-Rondo would say, and started pulling out every one of her eyebrows with some cheap Kress tweezers.

So I merely slammed the door behind me and went down and made some green-tomato pickle. Somebody had to do it. Of course Mama had turned both the niggers loose; she always said no earthly power could hold one anyway on the Fourth of July, so she wouldn't even try. It turned out that Jaypan fell in the lake and came within a very narrow limit of drowning.

So Mama trots in. Lifts up the lid and says, "H'm! Not very good for your Uncle Rondo in his precarious condition, I must say. Or poor little adopted Shirley-T. Shame on you!"

That made me tired. I says, "Well, Stella-Rondo had better thank her lucky stars it was her instead of me came trotting in with that very peculiar-looking child. Now if it had been me that trotted in from Illinois and brought a peculiar-looking child of two, I shudder to think of the reception I'd of got, much less controlled the diet of an entire family."

"But you must remember, Sister, that you were never married to Mr. Whitaker in the first place and didn't go up to Illinois to live," says Mama, shaking a spoon in my face. "If you had I would of been just as overjoyed to see you and your little adopted girl as I was to see Stella-Rondo, when you wound up with your separation and came on back home."

"You would not," I says.

"Don't contradict me, I would," says Mama.

But I said she couldn't convince me though she talked till she was blue in the face. Then I said, "Besides, you know as well as I do that that child is not adopted."

"She most certainly is adopted," says Mama, stiff as a poker.

I says, "Why, Mama, Stella-Rondo had her just as sure as anything in this world, and just too stuck up to admit it."

"Why, Sister," said Mama. "Here I thought we were going to have a pleasant Fourth of July, and you start right out not believing a word your own baby sister tells you!"

"Just like Cousin Annie Flo. Went to her grave denying the facts of life," I remind Mama.

"I told you if you ever mentioned Annie Flo's name I'd slap your face," says Mama, and slaps my face.

"All right, you wait and see," I says.

"I," says Mama, "*I* prefer to take my children's word for anything when it's humanly possible." You ought to see Mama, she weighs two hundred pounds and has real tiny feet.

Just then something perfectly horrible occurred to me.

"Mama," I says, "can that child talk?" I simply had to whisper! "Mama, I wonder if that child can be—you know—in any way? Do you realize," I says, "that she hasn't spoken one single, solitary word to a human being up to this minute? This is the way she looks," I says, and I looked like this.

Well, Mama and I just stood there and stared at each other. It was horrible!

"I remember well that Joe Whitaker frequently drank like a fish," says Mama. "I believed to my soul he drank *chemicals.*" And without another word she marches to the foot of the stairs and calls Stella-Rondo.

"Stella-Rondo? O-o-o-o-o! Stella-Rondo!"

"What?" says Stella-Rondo from upstairs. Not even the grace to get up off the bed.

"Can that child of yours talk?" asks Mama.

Stella-Rondo says, "Can she what?"

"Talk! Talk!" says Mama. "Burdyburdyburdyburdy!"

So Stella-Rondo yells back, "Who says she can't talk?"

"Sister says so," says Mama.

"You didn't have to tell me, I know whose word of honor don't mean a thing in this house," says Stella-Rondo.

And in a minute the loudest Yankee voice I ever heard in my life yells out, "OE'm Pop-OE the Sailor-r-r-r Ma-a-an!" and then somebody jumps up and down in the upstairs hall. In another second the house would of fallen down.

"Not only talks, she can tap-dance!" calls Stella-Rondo, "Which is more than some people I won't name can do."

"Why, the little precious darling thing!" Mama says, so surprised. "Just as smart as she can be!" Starts talking baby talk right there. Then she turns on me. "Sister, you ought to be thoroughly ashamed! Run upstairs this instant and apologize to Stella-Rondo and Shirley-T."

"Apologize for what?" I says. "I merely wondered if the child was normal, that's all. Now that she's proved she is, why, I have nothing further to say."

But Mama just turned on her heel and flew out, furious. She ran right upstairs and hugged the baby. She believed it was adopted. Stella-Rondo hadn't done a thing but turn her against me from upstairs while I stood there helpless over the hot stove. So that made Mama, Papa-Daddy and the baby all on Stella-Rondo's side.

Next, Uncle Rondo.

I must say that Uncle Rondo has been marvelous to me at various times in the past and I was completely unprepared to be made to jump out of my skin, the way it turned out. Once Stella-Rondo did something perfectly horrible to him—broke a chain letter from Flanders Field—and he took the radio back he had given her and gave it to me. Stella-Rondo was furious! For six months we all had to call her Stella instead of Stella-Rondo, or she wouldn't answer. I always thought Uncle Rondo had all the brains of the entire family. Another time he sent me to Mammoth Cave, with all expenses paid.

But this would be the day he was drinking that prescription, the Fourth of July.

So at supper Stella-Rondo speaks up and says she thinks Uncle Rondo ought to try to eat a little something. So finally Uncle Rondo said he would try a little cold biscuits and ketchup, but that was all. So *she* brought it to him.

"Do you think it wise to disport with ketchup in Stella-Rondo's flesh-colored kimono?" I says. Trying to be considerate! If Stella-Rondo couldn't watch out for her trousseau, somebody had to.

"Any objections?" asks Uncle Rondo, just about to pour out all the ketchup.

"Don't mind what she says, Uncle Rondo," says Stella-Rondo. "Sister has been devoting this solid afternoon to sneering out my bedroom window at the way you look."

"What's that?" says Uncle Rondo. Uncle Rondo has got the most terrible temper in the world. Anything is liable to make him tear the house down if it comes at the wrong time.

So Stella-Rondo says, "Sister says, 'Uncle Rondo certainly does look like a fool in that pink kimono!'"

Do you remember who it was really said that?

Uncle Rondo spills out all the ketchup and jumps out of his chair and tears off the kimono and throws it down on the dirty floor and puts his foot on it. It had to be sent all the way to Jackson to the cleaners and re-pleated.

"So that's your opinion of your Uncle Rondo, is it?" he says. "I look like a fool, do I? Well, that's the last straw. A whole day in this house with nothing to do, and then to hear you come out with a remark like that behind my back!"

"I didn't say any such of a thing, Uncle Rondo," I says, "and I'm not saying who did, either. Why, I think you look all right. Just try to take care of yourself and not talk and eat at the same time," I says. "I think you better go lie down."

"Lie down my foot," says Uncle Rondo. I ought to of known by that he was fixing to do something perfectly horrible.

So he didn't do anything that night in the precarious state he was in—just played Casino with Mama and Stella-Rondo and Shirley-T. and gave Shirley-T. a nickel with a head on both sides. It tickled her nearly to death, and she called him "Papa." But at 6:30 A.M. the next morning, he threw a whole five-cent package of some unsold one-inch firecrackers from the store as hard as he could into my bedroom and they every one went off. Not one bad one in the string. Anybody else, there'd be one that wouldn't go off.

Well, I'm just terribly susceptible to noise of any kind, the doctor has always told me I was the most sensitive person he had ever seen in his whole life, and I was simply prostrated. I couldn't eat! People tell me they heard it as far as the cemetery, and old Aunt Jep Patterson, that had been holding her own so good, thought it was Judgment Day and she was going to meet her whole family. It's usually so quiet here.

And I'll tell you it didn't take me any longer than a minute to make up my mind what to do. There I was with the whole entire house on Stella-Rondo's side and turned against me. If I have anything at all I have pride.

So I just decided I'd go straight down to the P.O. There's plenty of room there in the back, I says to myself.

Well! I made no bones about letting the family catch on to what I was up to. I didn't try to conceal it.

The first thing they knew, I marched in where they were all playing Old Maid and pulled the electric oscillating fan out by the plug, and everything got real hot. Next I snatched the pillow I'd done the needlepoint on right off the davenport from behind Papa-Daddy. He went "Ugh!" I beat Stella-Rondo up the stairs and finally found my charm bracelet in her bureau drawer under a picture of Nelson Eddy.

"So that's the way the land lies," says Uncle Rondo. There he was, piecing on the ham. "Well, Sister, I'll be glad to donate my army cot if you got any place to set it up, providing you'll leave right this minute and let me get some peace." Uncle Rondo was in France.

"Thank you kindly for the cot and 'peace' is hardly the word I would select if I had to resort to firecrackers at 6:30 A.M. in a young girl's bedroom," I says back to him. "And as to where I intend to go, you seem to forget my position as postmistress of China Grove, Mississippi," I says. "I've always got the P.O."

Well, that made them all sit up and take notice.

I went out front and started digging up some four-o'clocks to plant around the P.O.

"Ah-ah-ah!" says Mama, raising the window. "Those happen to be my four-o'clocks. Everything planted in that star is mine. I've never known you to make anything grow in your life."

"Very well," I says. "But I take the fern. Even you, Mama, can't stand there and deny that I'm the one watered that fern. And I happen to know where I can send in a box top and get a packet of one thousand mixed seeds, no two the same kind, free."

"Oh, where?" Mama wants to know.

But I says, "Too late. You 'tend to your house, and I'll 'tend to mine. You hear things like that all the time if you know how to listen to the radio. Perfectly marvelous offers. Get anything you want free."

So I hope to tell you I marched in and got that radio, and they could of all bit a nail in two, especially Stella-Rondo, that it used to belong to, and she well knew she couldn't get it back, I'd sue for it like a shot. And I very politely took the sewing-machine motor I helped pay the most on to give Mama for Christmas back in 1929, and a good big calendar, with the first-aid remedies on it. The thermometer and the Hawaiian ukulele certainly were rightfully mine, and I stood on the step-ladder and got all my watermelon-rind preserves and every fruit and vegetable I'd put up, every jar. Then I began to pull the tacks out of the bluebird wall vases on the archway to the dining room.

"Who told you you could have those, Miss Priss?" says Mama, fanning as hard as she could.

"I bought 'em and I'll keep track of 'em," I says. "I'll tack 'em up one on each side the post-office window, and you can see 'em when you come to ask me for your mail, if you're so dead to see 'em."

"Not I! I'll never darken the door to that post office again if I live to be a hundred," Mama says. "Ungrateful child! After all the money we spent on you at the Normal."

"Me either," says Stella-Rondo. "You can just let my mail lie there and *rot,* for all I care. I'll never come and relieve you of a single, solitary piece."

"I should worry," I says. "And who you think's going to sit down and write you all those big fat letters and postcards, by the way? Mr. Whitaker? Just because he was the only man ever dropped down in China Grove and you got him—unfairly—is he going to sit down and write you a lengthy correspondence after you come home giving no rhyme nor reason whatsoever for your separation and no explanation for the presence of that child? I may not have your brilliant mind, but I fail to see it."

So Mama says, "Sister, I've told you a thousand times that Stella-Rondo simply got homesick, and this child is far too big to be hers," and she says, "Now, why don't you all just sit down and play Casino?"

Then Shirley-T. sticks out her tongue at me in this perfectly horrible way. She has no more manners than the man in the moon. I told her she was going to cross her eyes like that some day and they'd stick.

"It's too late to stop me now," I says. "You should have tried that yesterday. I'm going to the P.O. and the only way you can possibly see me is to visit me there."

So Papa-Daddy says, "You'll never catch me setting foot in that post office, even if I should take a notion into my head to write a letter some place." He says, "I won't have you reachin' out of that little old window with a pair of shears and cuttin' off any beard of mine. I'm too smart for you!"

"We all are," says Stella-Rondo.

But I said, "If you're so smart, where's Mr. Whitaker?"

So then Uncle Rondo says, "I'll thank you from now on to stop reading all the orders I get on postcards and telling everybody in China Grove what you think is the matter with them," but I says, "I draw my own conclusions and will continue in the future to draw them." I says, "If people want to write their inmost secrets on penny postcards, there's nothing in the wide world you can do about it, Uncle Rondo."

"And if you think we'll ever *write* another postcard you're sadly mistaken," says Mama.

"Cutting off your nose to spite your face then," I says. "But if you're all determined to have no more to do with the U.S. mail, think of this: What will Stella-Rondo do now, if she wants to tell Mr. Whitaker to come after her?"

"Wah!" says Stella-Rondo. I knew she'd cry. She had a conniption fit right there in the kitchen.

"It will be interesting to see how long she holds out," I says. "And now—I am leaving."

"Good-bye," says Uncle Rondo.

"Oh, I declare," says Mama, "to think that a family of mine should quarrel on the Fourth of July, or the day after, over Stella-Rondo leaving old Mr. Whitaker and having the sweetest little adopted child! It looks like we'd all be glad!"

"Wah!" says Stella-Rondo, and has a fresh conniption fit.

"*He* left *her*—you mark my words," I says. "That's Mr. Whitaker. I know Mr. Whitaker. After all, I knew him first. I said from the beginning he'd up and leave her. I foretold every single thing that's happened."

"Where did he go?" asks Mama.

"Probably to the North Pole, if he knows what's good for him," I says.

But Stella-Rondo just bawled and wouldn't say another word. She flew to her room and slammed the door.

"Now look what you've gone and done, Sister," says Mama. "You go apologize."

"I haven't got time, I'm leaving," I says.

"Well, what are you waiting around for?" asks Uncle Rondo.

So I just picked up the kitchen clock and marched off, without saying "Kiss my foot" or anything, and never did tell Stella-Rondo good-bye.

There was a nigger girl going along on a little wagon right in front.

"Nigger girl," I says, "come help me haul these things down the hill, I'm going to live in the post office."

Took her nine trips in her express wagon. Uncle Rondo came out on the porch and threw her a nickel.

And that's the last I've laid eyes on any of my family or my family laid eyes on me for five solid days and nights. Stella-Rondo may be telling the most horrible tales in the world about Mr. Whitaker, but I haven't heard them. As I tell everybody, I draw my own conclusions.

But oh, I like it here. It's ideal, as I've been saying. You see, I've got everything cater-cornered, the way I like it. Hear the radio? All the war news. Radio, sewing machine, book ends, ironing board and that great big piano lamp—peace, that's what I like. Butter-bean vines planted all along the front where the strings are.

Of course, there's not much mail. My family are naturally the main people in China Grove, and if they prefer to vanish from the face of the earth, for all the mail they get or the mail they write, why, I'm not going to open my mouth. Some of the folks here in town are taking up for me and some turned against me. I know which is which. There are always people who will quit buying stamps just to get on the right side of Papa-Daddy.

But here I am, and here I'll stay. I want the world to know I'm happy.

And if Stella-Rondo should come to me this minute, on bended knees, and *attempt* to explain the incidents of her life with Mr. Whitaker, I'd simply put my fingers in both my ears and refuse to listen.

Eudora Welty

No Place for You, My Love

They were strangers to each other, both fairly well strangers to the place, now seated side by side at luncheon—a party combined in a free-and-easy way when the friends he and she were with recognized each other across Galatoire's. The time was a Sunday in summer—those hours of afternoon that seem Time Out in New Orleans.

The moment he saw her little blunt, fair face, he thought that here was a woman who was having an affair. It was one of those odd meetings when such an impact is felt that it has to be translated at once into some sort of speculation.

With a married man, most likely, he supposed, slipping quickly into a groove—he was long married—and feeling more conventional, then, in his curiosity as she sat there, leaning her cheek on her hand, looking no further before her than the flowers on the table, and wearing that hat.

He did not like her hat, any more than he liked tropical flowers. It was the wrong hat for her, thought this Eastern businessman who had no interest whatever in women's clothes and no eye for them; he thought the unaccustomed thing crossly.

It must stick out all over me, she thought, so people think they can love me or hate me just by looking at me. How did it leave us—the old, safe, slow way people used to know of learning how one another feels, and the privilege that went with it of shying away if it seemed best? People in love like me, I suppose, give away the short cuts to everybody's secrets.

Something, though, he decided, had been settled about her predicament—for the time being, anyway; the parties to it were all still alive, no doubt. Nevertheless, her predicament was the only one he felt so sure of here, like the only recognizable shadow in that restaurant, where mirrors and fans were busy agitating the light, as the very local talk drawled across and agitated the peace. The shadow lay between her fingers, between her little square hand and her cheek, like something always best carried about the person. Then suddenly, as she took her hand down; the secret fact was still there—it lighted her. It was a bold and full light, shot up under the brim of that hat, as close to them all as the flowers in the center of the table. Did he dream of making her disloyal to that hopelessness that he saw very well she's been cultivating down here? He knew very well that he did not. What they amounted to was two Northerners keeping each other company. She glanced up at the big gold clock on the wall and smiled. He didn't smile back. She had that naive face that he associated, for no good reason, with the Middle West—because it said "Show me," perhaps. It was a serious, now-watch-out-everybody face, which orphaned her entirely in the company of these Southerners. He guessed her age, as he could not guess theirs: thirty-two. He himself was further along.

Of all human moods, deliberate imperviousness may be the most quickly communicated—it may be the most successful, most fatal signal of all. And two people can indulge in imperviousness as well as in anything else. "You're not very hungry either," he said.

The blades of fan shadows came down over their two heads, as he saw inadvertently in the mirror, with himself smiling at her now like a villain. His remark sounded dominant and rude enough for everybody present to listen back a moment; it even sounded like an answer to a question she might have just asked him. The other women glanced at him. The Southern look—Southern mask—of life-is-a-dream irony, which could turn to pure challenge at the drop of a hat, he could wish well away. He liked naïveté better.

"I find the heat down here depressing," she said, with the heart of Ohio in her voice.

"Well—I'm in somewhat of a temper about it, too," he said.

They looked with grateful dignity at each other.

"I have a car here, just down the street," he said to her as the luncheon party was rising to leave, all the others wanting to get back to their houses and sleep. "If it's all right with—Have you ever driven down south of here?"

Out on Bourbon Street, in the bath of July, she asked at his shoulder, "South of New Orleans? I didn't know there was any south to here. Does it just go on and on?" She laughed, and adjusted the exasperating hat to her head in a different way. It was more than frivolous, it was conspicuous, with some sort of glitter or flitter tied in a band around the straw and hanging down.

"That's what I'm going to show you."

"Oh—you've been there?"

"No!"

His voice rang out over the uneven, narrow sidewalk and dropped back from the walls. The flaked-off, colored houses were spotted like the hides of beasts faded and shy, and were hot as a wall of growth that seemed to breathe flower-like down onto them as they walked to the car parked there.

"It's just that it couldn't be any worse—we'll see."

"All right, then," she said. "We will."

So, their actions reduced to amiability, they settled into the car—a faded-red Ford convertible with a rather threadbare canvas top, which had been standing in the sun for all those lunch hours.

"It's rented," he explained. "I asked to have the top put down, and was told I'd lost my mind."

"It's out of this world. *Degrading* heat," she said and added, "Doesn't matter."

The stranger in New Orleans always sets out to leave it as though following the clue in a maze. They were threading through the narrow and one-way streets, past the pale violet bloom of tired squares, the brown steeples and statues, the balcony with the live and probably famous black monkey dipping along the railing as over a ballroom floor, past the grillework and the lattice-work to all the iron swans painted flesh color on the front steps of bungalows outlying.

Driving, he spread his new map and put his finger down on it. At the intersection marked Arabi, where their road led out of the tangle and he took it, a small Negro seated beneath a black umbrella astride a box chalked "Shou Shine" lifted his pink-and-black hand and waved them languidly good-by. She didn't miss it, and waved back.

Below New Orleans there was a raging of insects from both sides of the concrete highway, not quite together, like the playing of separated marching bands. The river and the levee were still on her side, waste and jungle and some occasional settlements on his—poor houses. Families bigger than housefuls thronged the yards. His nodding, driving head would veer from side to side, looking and almost lowering. As time passed and the distance from New Orleans grew, girls ever darker and younger were disposing themselves over the porches and the porch steps, with jet-black hair pulled high, and ragged palm-leaf fans rising and falling like rafts of butterflies. The children running forth were nearly always naked ones.

She watched the road. Crayfish constantly crossed in front of the wheels, looking grim and bonneted, in a great hurry.

"How the Old Woman Got Home," she murmured to herself.

He pointed, as it flew by, at a saucepan full of cut zinnias which stood waiting on the open lid of a mailbox at the roadside, with a little note tied onto the handle.

They rode mostly in silence. The sun bore down. They met fishermen and other men bent on some local pursuits, some in sulphur-colored pants, walking and riding; met wagons, trucks, boats in trucks, autos, boats on top of autos—all coming to meet them, as though something of high moment were doing back where the car came from, and he and she were determined to miss it. There was nearly always a man lying with his shoes off in the bed of any truck otherwise empty—with the raw, red look of a man sleeping in the daytime, being jolted about as he slept. Then there was a sort of dead man's land, where nobody came. He loosened his collar and tie. By rushing through the heat at high speed, they brought themselves the effect of fans turned onto their cheeks. Clearing alternated with jungle and canebrake like something tried, tried again. Little shell roads led off on both sides; now and then a road of planks led into the yellow-green.

"Like a dance floor in there." She pointed.

He informed her, "In there's your oil, I think."

There were thousands, millions of mosquitoes and gnats—a universe of them, and on the increase.

A family of eight or nine people on foot strung along the road in the same direction the car was going, beating themselves with the wild palmettos. Heels, shoulders, knees, breasts, back of the heads, elbows, hands, were touched in turn—like some game, each playing it with himself.

He struck himself on the forehead, and increased their speed. (His wife would not be at her most charitable if he came bringing malaria home to the family.)

More and more crayfish and other shell creatures littered their path, scuttling or dragging. These little samples, little jokes of creation, persisted and sometimes perished, the more of them the deeper down the road went. Terrapins and turtles came up steadily over the horizons of the ditches.

Back there in the margins were worse—crawling hides you could not penetrate with bullets or quite believe, grins that had come down from the primeval mud.

"Wake up." Her Northern nudge was very timely on his arm. They had veered toward the side of the road. Still driving fast, he spread his map.

Like a misplaced sunrise, the light of the river flowed up; they were mounting the levee on a little shell road.

"Shall we cross here?" he asked politely.

He might have been keeping track over years and miles of how long they could keep that tiny ferry waiting. Now skidding down the levee's flank, they were the last-minute car, the last possible car that could squeeze on. Under the sparse shade of one willow tree, the small, amateurish-looking boat slapped the water, as, expertly, he wedged on board.

"Tell him we put him on hub cap!" shouted one of the numerous olive-skinned, dark-eyed young boys standing dressed up in bright shirts at the railing, hugging each other with delight that that last straw was on board. Another boy drew his affectionate initials in the dust of the door on her side.

She opened the door and stepped out; and, after only a moment's standing at bay, started up a little iron stairway. She appeared above the car, on the tiny bridge beneath the captain's window and the whistle.

From there, while the boat still delayed in what seemed a trance—as if it were too full to attempt the start—she could see the panlike deck below, separated by its rusty rim from the tilting, polished water.

The passengers walking and jostling about there appeared oddly amateurish, too—amateur travelers. They were having such a good time. They all knew each other. Beer was being passed around in cans, bets were being loudly settled and new bets made, about local and special subjects on which they all doted. One red-haired man in a burst of wildness even tried to give away his truckload of shrimp to a man on the other side of the boat—nearly all the trucks were full of shrimp—causing taunts and then protests of "They good! They good!" from the giver. The young boys leaned on each other thinking of what next, rolling their eyes absently.

A radio pricked the air behind her. Looking like a great tomcat just above her head, the captain was digesting the news of a fine stolen automobile.

At last a tremendous explosion burst—the whistle. Everything shuddered in outline from the sound, everybody said something—everybody else.

They started with no perceptible motion, but her hat blew off. It went spiraling to the deck below, where he, thank heaven, sprang out of the car and picked it up. Everybody looked frankly up at her now, holding her hands to her head.

The little willow tree receded as its shade was taken away. The heat was like something falling on her head. She held the hot rail before her. It was like riding a stove. Her shoulders dropping, her hair flying, her skirt buffeted by the sudden strong wind, she stood there, thinking they all must see that with her entire self all she did was wait. Her set hands, with the bag that hung from her wrist and rocked back and forth—all three seemed objects bleaching there, belonging to no one; she could not feel a thing in the skin of her face; perhaps she was crying and not knowing it. She could look down and see him just below her, his black shadow, her hat, and his black hair. His hair in the wind looked unreasonably long and rippling. Little did he know that from here it had a red undergleam like an animal's. When she looked up and outward, a vortex of light drove through and over the brown waves like a star in the water.

He did after all bring the retrieved hat up the stairs to her. She took it back—useless—and held it to her skirt. What they were saying below was more polite than their searchlight faces.

"Where you think he come from, that man?"

"I bet he come from Lafitte."

"Lafitte? What you bet, eh?"—all crouched in the shade of trucks, squatting and laughing.

Now his shadow fell partly across her; the boat had jolted into some other strand of current. Her shaded arm and shaded hand felt pulled out from the blaze of light and water, and she hoped humbly for more shade for her head. It had seemed so natural to climb up and stand in the sun.

The boys had a surprise—an alligator on board. One of them pulled it by a chain around the deck, between the cars and trucks, like a toy—a hide that could walk. He thought, Well they had to catch one sometime. It's Sunday afternoon. So they have him on board now, riding him across the Mississippi River. . . . The playfulness of it beset everybody on the ferry. The hoarseness of the boat whistle, commenting briefly, seemed part of the general appreciation.

"Who wants to rassle him? Who want to, eh?" two boys cried, looking up. A boy with shrimp-colored arms capered from side to side, pretending to have been bitten.

What was there so hilarious about jaws that could bite? And what danger was there once in this repulsiveness—so that the last worldly evidence of some old heroic horror of the dragon had to be paraded in capture before the eyes of country clowns?

He noticed that she looked at the alligator without flinching at all. Her distance was set—the number of feet and inches between herself and it mattered to her.

Perhaps her measuring coolness was to him what his bodily shade was to her, while they stood pat up there riding the river, which felt like the sea and looked like the earth under them—full of the red-brown earth, charged with it. Ahead of the boat it was like an exposed vein of ore. The river seemed to swell in the vast middle with the curve of the earth. The sun rolled under them. As if in memory of the size of things, uprooted trees were drawn across their path, sawing at the air and tumbling one over the other.

When they reached the other side, they felt that they had been racing around an arena in their chariot, among lions. The whistle took and shook the stairs as they went down. The young boys, looking taller, had taken out colored combs and were combing their wet hair back in solemn pompadour above their radiant foreheads. They had been bathing in the river themselves not long before.

The cars and trucks, then the foot passengers and the alligator, waddling like a child to school, all disembarked and wound up the weed-sprung levee.

Both respectable and merciful, their hides, she thought, forcing herself to dwell on the alligator as she looked back. Deliver us all from the naked in heart. (As she had been told.)

When they regained their paved road, he heard her give a little sigh and saw her turn her straw-colored head to look back once more. Now that she rode with her hat in her lap, her earrings were conspicuous too. A little metal ball set with small pale stones danced beside each square, faintly downy cheek.

Had she felt a wish for someone else to be riding with them? He thought it was more likely that she would wish for her husband if she had one (his wife's voice) than for the lover in whom he believed. Whatever people liked to think, situations (if not scenes) were usually three-way—there was somebody else always. The one who didn't—couldn't—understand the two made the formidable third.

He glanced down at the map flapping on the seat between them, up at his wristwatch, out at the road. Out there was the incredible brightness of four o'clock.

On this side of the river, the road ran beneath the brow of the levee and followed it. Here was a heat that ran deeper and brighter and more intense than all the rest—its nerve. The road grew one with the heat as it was one with the unseen river. Dead snakes stretched across the concrete like markers—inlaid mosaic bands, dry as feathers, which their tires licked at intervals that began to seem clocklike.

No, the heat faced them—it was ahead. They could see it waving at them, shaken in the air above the white of the road, always at a certain distance ahead, shimmering finely as a cloth, with running edges of green and gold, fire and azure.

"It's never anything like this in Syracuse," he said.

"Or in Toledo, either," she replied with dry lips.

They were driving through greater waste down here, through fewer and even more insignificant towns. There was water under everything. Even where a screen of jungle had been left to stand, splashes could be heard from under the trees. In the vast open, sometimes boats moved inch by inch through what appeared endless meadows of rubbery flowers.

Her eyes overcome with brightness and size, she felt a panic rise, as sudden as nausea. Just how far below questions and answers, concealment and revelation, they were running now—that was still a new question, with a power of its own, waiting. How dear—how costly—could this ride be?

"It looks to me like your road can't go much further," she remarked cheerfully. "Just over there, it's all water."

"Time out," he said, and with that he turned the car into a sudden road of white shells that rushed at them narrowly out of the left.

They bolted over a cattle guard, where some rayed and crested purple flowers burst out of the vines in the ditch, and rolled onto a long, narrow, green, mowed clearing: a churchyard. A paved track ran between two short rows of raised tombs, all neatly white-washed and now brilliant as faces against the vast flushed sky.

The track was the width of the car with a few inches to spare. He passed between the tombs slowly but in the manner of a feat. Names took their places on the walls slowly at a level with the eye, names as near as the eyes of a person stopping in conversation, and as far away in origin, and in all their music and dead longing, as Spain. At intervals were set packed bouquets of zinnias, oleanders, and some kind of purple flowers, all quite fresh, in fruit jars, like nice welcomes on bureaus.

They moved on into an open plot beyond, of violent-green grass, spread before the green-and-white frame church with worked flower beds around it, flowerless poinsettias growing up to the windowsills. Beyond was a house; and left on the doorstep of the house a fresh-caught catfish the size of a baby—a fish wearing whiskers and bleeding. On a clothesline in the yard, a priest's black gown on a hanger hung airing, swaying at man's height, in a vague, trainlike, ladylike sweep along an evening breath that might otherwise have seemed imaginary from the unseen, felt river.

With the motor cut off, with the raging of the insects about them, they sat looking out at the green and white and black and red and pink as they leaned against the sides of the car.

"What is your wife like?" she asked. His right hand came up and spread—iron, wooden, manicured. She lifted her eyes to his face. He looked at her like that hand.

Then he lit a cigarette, and the portrait, and the right-hand testimonial it made, were blown away. She smiled, herself as unaffected as by some stage performance; and he was annoyed in the cemetery. They did not risk going on to her husband—if she had one.

Under the supporting posts of the priest's house, where a boat was, solid ground ended and palmettos and water hyacinths could not wait to begin; suddenly the rays of the sun, from behind the car, reached that lowness and struck the flowers. The priest came out onto the porch in his underwear, stared at the car a moment as if he wondered what time it was, then collected his robe off the line and his fish off the doorstep and returned inside. Vespers was next, for him.

After backing out between the tombs he drove on still south, in the sunset. They caught up with an old man walking in a sprightly way in their direction, all by himself, wearing a clean bright shirt printed with a pair of palm trees fanning green over his chest. It might better be a big colored woman's shirt, but she didn't have it. He flagged the car with gestures like hoops.

"You're coming to the end of the road," the old man told them. He pointed ahead, tipped his hat to the lady, and pointed again. "End of the road." They didn't understand that he meant, "Take me."

They drove on. "If we do go any further, it'll have to be by water—is that it?" he asked her, hesitating at this odd point.

"You know better than I do," she replied politely.

The road had for some time ceased to be paved; it was made of shells. It was leading into a small, sparse settlement like the others a few miles back, but with even more of the camp about it. On the lip of the clearing, directly before a green willow blaze with the sunset gone behind it, the row of houses and shacks faced out on broad, colored, moving water that stretched to reach the horizon and looked like an arm of the sea. The houses on their shaggy posts, patchily built, some with plank runways instead of steps, were flimsy and alike, and not much bigger than the boats tied up at the landing.

"Venice," she heard him announce, and he dropped the crackling map in her lap.

They coasted down the brief remainder. The end of the road—she could not remember ever seeing a road simply end—was a spoon shape, with a tree stump in the bowl to turn around by.

Around it, he stopped the car, and they stepped out, feeling put down in the midst of a sudden vast pause or subduement that was like a yawn. They made their way on foot toward the water, where at an idle-looking landing men in twos and threes stood with their backs to them.

The nearness of darkness, the still uncut trees, bright water partly under a sheet of flowers, shacks, silence, dark shapes of boats tied up, then the first sounds of people just on the other side of thin walls—all this reached them. Mounds of shells like day-old snow, pink-tinted, lay around a central shack with a beer sign on it. An old man up on the porch there sat holding an open newspaper, with a fat white goose sitting opposite him on the floor. Below, in the now shadowless and sunless open, another old man, with a colored pencil bright under his hat brim, was late mending a sail.

When she looked clear around, thinking they had a fire burning somewhere now, out of the heat had risen the full moon. Just beyond the trees, enormous, tangerine-colored, it was going solidly up. Other lights just striking into view, looking farther distant, showed moss shapes hanging, or slipped and broke matchlike on the water that so encroached upon the rim of ground they were standing on.

There was a touch at her arm—his, accidental.

"We're at the jumping-off place," he said.

She laughed, having thought his hand was a bat, while her eyes rushed downward toward a great pale drift of water hyacinths—still partly open, flushed and yet moonlit, level with her feet—through which paths of water for the boats had been hacked. She drew her hands up to her face under the brim of her hat; her own cheeks felt like the hyacinths to her, all her skin still full of too much light and sky, exposed. The harsh vesper bell was ringing.

"I believe there must be something wrong with me, that I came on this excursion to begin with," she said, as if he had already said this and she were merely in hopeful, willing, maddening agreement with him.

He took hold of her arm, and said, "Oh, come on—I see we can get something to drink here, at least."

But there was a beating, muffled sound from over the darkening water. One more boat was coming in, making its way through the tenacious, tough, dark flower traps, by the shaken light of what first appeared to be torches. He and she waited for the boat, as if on each other's patience. As if borne in on a mist of twilight or a breath, a horde of mosquitoes and gnats came singing and striking at them first. The boat bumped, men laughed. Somebody was offering somebody else some shrimp.

Then he might have cocked his dark city head down at her; she did not look up at him, only turned when he did. Now the shell mounds, like the shacks and trees, were solid purple. Lights had appeared in the not-quite-true window squares. A narrow neon sign, the lone sign, had come out in bright blush on the beer shack's roof: "Baba's Place." A light was on on the porch.

The barnlike interior was brightly lit and unpainted, looking not quite finished, with a partition dividing this room from what lay behind. One of the four cardplayers at a table in the middle of the floor was the newspaper reader; the paper was in his pants pocket.

Midway along the partition was a bar, in the form of a pass-through to the other room, with a varnished, second-hand fretwork overhang. They crossed the floor and sat, alone there, on wooden stools. An eruption of humorous signs, newspaper cutouts and cartoons, razor-blade cards, and personal messages of significance to the owner or his friends decorated the overhang, framing where Baba should have been but wasn't.

Through there came a smell of garlic and cloves and red pepper, a blast of hot cloud escaped from a cauldron they could see now on a stove at the back of the other room. A massive back, presumably female, with a twist of gray hair on top, stood with a ladle akimbo. A young man joined her and with his fingers stole something out of the pot and ate it. At Baba's they were boiling shrimp.

When he got ready to wait on them, Baba strolled out to the counter, young, black-headed, and in very good humor.

"Coldest beer you've got. And food—What will you have?"

"Nothing for me, thank you," she said. "I'm not sure I could eat, after all."

"Well, I could," he said, shoving his jaw out. Baba smiled. "I want a good solid ham sandwich."

"I could have asked him for some water," she said, after he had gone.

While they sat waiting, it seemed very quiet. The bubbling of the shrimp, the distant laughing of Baba, and the slap of cards, like the beating of moths on the screens, seemed to come in fits and starts. The steady breathing they heard came from a big rough dog asleep in the corner. But it was bright. Electric lights were strung riotously over the room from a kind of spider web of old wires in the rafters. One of the written messages tacked before them read, "Joe! At the boyy!!" It looked very yellow, older than Baba's Place. Outside, the world was pure dark.

Two little boys, almost alike, almost the same size, and just cleaned up, dived into the room with a double bang of the screen door, and circled around the card game. They ran their hands into the men's pockets.

"Nickel for some pop!"

"Nickel for some pop!"

"Go 'way and let me play, you!"

They circled around and shrieked at the dog, ran under the lid of the counter and raced through the kitchen and back, and hung over the stools at the bar. One child had a live lizard on his shirt, clinging like a breast pin—like lapis lazuli.

Bringing in a strong odor of geranium talcum, some men had come in now—all in bright shirts. They drew near the counter, or stood and watched the game.

When Baba came out bringing the beer and sandwich, "Could I have some water?" she greeted him.

Baba laughed at everybody. She decided the woman back there must be Baba's mother.

Beside her, he was drinking his beer and eating his sandwich—ham, cheese, tomato, pickle, and mustard. Before he finished, one of the men who had come in beckoned from across the room. It was the old man in the palm-tree shirt.

She lifted her head to watch him leave her, and was looked at, from all over the room. As a minute passed, no cards were laid down. In a far-off way, like accepting the light from Arcturus, she accepted it that she was more beautiful or perhaps more fragile than the women they saw every day of their lives. It was just this thought coming into a woman's face, and at this hour, that seemed familiar to them.

Baba was smiling. He had set an opened, frosted brown bottle before her on the counter, and a thick sandwich, and stood looking at her. Baba made her eat some supper, for what she was.

"What the old fellow wanted," said he when he came back at last, "was to have a friend of his apologize. Seems church is just out. Seems the friend made a remark coming in just now. His pals told him there was a lady present."

"I see you bought him a beer," she said.

"Well, the old man looked like he wanted *something.*"

All at once the juke box interrupted from back in the corner, with the same old song as anywhere. The half-dozen slot machines along the wall were suddenly all run to like Maypoles, and thrown into action—taken over by further battalions of little boys.

There were three little boys to each slot machine. The local custom appeared to be that one pulled the lever for the friend he was holding up to put the nickel in, while the third covered the pictures with the flat of his hand as they fell into place, so as to surprise them all if anything happened.

The dog lay sleeping on in front of the raging juke box, his ribs working fast as a concertina's. At the side of the room a man with a cap on his white thatch was trying his best to open a side screen door, but it was stuck fast. It was he who had come in with the remark considered ribald; now he was trying to get out the other way. Moths as thick as ingots were trying to get in. The cardplayers broke into shouts of derision, then joy, then tired derision among themselves; they might have been here all afternoon—they were the only ones not cleaned up and shaved. The original pair of little boys ran in once more, with the hyphenated bang. They got nickels this time, then were brushed away from the table like mosquitoes, and they rushed under the counter and on to the cauldron behind, clinging to Baba's mother there. The evening was at the threshold.

They were quite unnoticed now. He was eating another sandwich, and she, having finished part of hers, was fanning her face with her hat. Baba had lifted the flap of the counter and come out into the room. Behind his head there was a sign lettered in orange crayon: "Shrimp Dance Sun. PM." That was tonight, still to be.

And suddenly she made a move to slide down from her stool, maybe wishing to walk out into that nowhere down the front steps to be cool a moment. But he had hold of her hand. He got down from his stool, and, patiently, reversing her hand in his own—just as she had had the look of being about to give up, faint—began moving her, leading her. They were dancing.

"I get to thinking this is what we get—what you and I deserve," she whispered, looking past his shoulder into the room. "And all the time, it's real. It's a real place—away off down here. . . ."

They danced gratefully, formally, to some song carried on in what must be the local patois, while no one paid any attention as long as they were together, and the children poured the family nickels steadily into the slot machines, walloping the handles down with regular crashes and troubling nobody with winning.

She said rapidly, as they began moving together too well, "One of those clippings was an account of a shooting right here. I guess they're proud of it. And that awful knife Baba was carrying . . . I wonder what he called me," she whispered in his ear.

"Who?"

"The one who apologized to you."

If they had ever been going to overstep themselves, it would be now as he held her closer and turned her, when she became aware that he could not help but see the bruise at her temple. It would not be six inches from his eyes. She felt it come out like an evil star. (Let it pay him back, then, for the hand he had stuck in her face when she'd tried once to be sympathetic, when she'd asked about his wife.) They danced on still as the record changed, after standing wordless and motionless, linked together in the middle of the room, for the moment between.

Then, they were like a matched team—like professional, Spanish dancers wearing masks—while the slow piece was playing.

Surely even those immune from the world, for the time being, need the touch of one another, or all is lost. Their arms encircling each other, their bodies circling the odorous, just-nailed-down floor, they were, at last, imperviousness in motion. They had found it, and had almost missed it: they had had to dance. They were what their separate hearts desired that day, for themselves and each other.

They were so good together that once she looked up, and half smiled. "For whose benefit did we have to show off?"

Like people in love, they had a superstition about themselves, almost as soon as they came out on the floor, and dared not think the words "happy" or "unhappy," which might strike them, one or the other, like lightning.

In the thickening heat they danced on while Baba himself sang with the mosquito-voiced singer in the chorus of "*Moi pas l'aimez ça,*" enumerating the *ça's* with a hot shrimp between his fingers. He was counting over the platters the old woman now set out on the counter, each heaped with shrimp in their shells boiled to iridescence, like mounds of honeysuckle flowers.

The goose wandered in from the back room under the lid of the counter and hitched itself around the floor among the table legs and people's legs, never seeing that it was neatly avoided by two dancers—who nevertheless vaguely thought of this goose as learned, having earlier heard an old man read to it. The children called it Mimi, and lured it away. The old thatched man was again drunkenly trying to get out by the stuck side door; now he gave it a kick, but was prevailed on to remain. The sleeping dog shuddered and snored.

It was left up to the dancers to provide nickels for the juke box; Baba kept a drawerful for every use. They had grown fond of all the selections by now. This was the music you heard out of the distance at night—out of the roadside taverns you fled past, around the late corners in cities half asleep, drifting up from the carnival over the hill, with one odd little strain always managing to repeat itself. This seemed a homey place.

Bathed in sweat, and feeling the false coolness that brings, they stood finally on the porch in the lapping night air for a moment before leaving. The first arrivals of the girls were coming up the steps under the porch light—all flowered fronts, their black pompadours giving out breathlike feelers from sheer abundance. Where they'd resprinkled it since church, the talcum shone like mica on their downy arms. Smelling solidly of geranium, they filed across the porch with short steps and fingers joined, just timed to turn their smiles loose inside the room. He held the door open for them.

"Ready to go?" he asked her.

Going back, the ride was wordless, quiet except for the motor and the insects driving themselves against the car. The windshield was soon blinded. The headlights pulled in two other spinning storms, cones of flying things that, it seemed, might ignite at the last minute. He stopped the car and got out to clean the windshield thoroughly with his brisk, angry motions of driving. Dust lay thick and cratered on the roadside scrub. Under the now ash-white moon, the world traveled through very faint stars—very many slow stars, very high, very low.

It was a strange land, amphibious—and whether water-covered or grown with jungle or robbed entirely of water and trees, as now, it had the same loneliness. He regarded the great sweep—like steppes, like moors, like deserts (all of which were imaginary to him); but more than it was like any likeness, it was South. The vast, thin, wide-thrown, pale, unfocused star-sky, with its veils of lightning adrift, hung over this land as it hung over the open sea. Standing out in the night alone, he was struck as powerfully with recognition of the extremity of this place as if all other bearings had vanished—as if snow had suddenly started to fall.

He climbed back inside and drove. When he moved to slap furiously at his shirtsleeves, she shivered in the hot, licking night wind that their speed was making. Once the car lights picked out two people—a Negro couple, sitting on two facing chairs in the yard outside their lonely cabin—half undressed, each battling for self against the hot night, with long white rags in endless, scarflike motions.

In peopleless open places there were lakes of dust, smudge fires burning at their hearts. Cows stood in untended rings around them, motionless in the heat, in the night—their horns standing up sharp against that glow.

At length, he stopped the car again, and this time he put his arm under her shoulder and kissed her—not knowing ever whether gently or harshly. It was the loss of that distinction that told him this was now. Then their faces touched unkissing, unmoving, dark, for a length of time. The heat came inside the car and wrapped them still, and the mosquitoes had begun to coat their arms and even their eyelids.

Later, crossing a large open distance, he saw at the same time two fires. He had the feeling that they had been riding for a long time across a face—great, wide, and upturned. In its eyes and open mouth were those fires they had had glimpses of, where the cattle had drawn together: a face, a head, far down here in the South—south of South, below it. A whole giant body sprawled downward then, on and on, always, constant as a constellation or an angel. Flaming and perhaps falling, he thought.

She appeared to be sound asleep, lying back flat as a child, with her hat in her lap. He drove on with her profile beside his, behind his, for he bent forward to drive faster. The earrings she wore twinkled with their rushing motion in an almost regular beat. They might have spoken like tongues. He looked straight before him and drove on, at a speed that, for the rented, overheated, not at all new Ford car, was demoniac.

It seemed often now that a barnlike shape flashed by, roof and all outlined in lonely neon—a movie house at a crossroads. The long white flat road itself, since they had followed it to the end and turned around to come back, seemed able, this far up, to pull them home.

A thing is incredible, if ever, only after it is told—returned to the world it came out of. For their different reasons, he thought, neither of them would tell this (unless something was dragged out of them): that, strangers, they had ridden down into a strange land together and were getting safely back—by a slight margin, perhaps; but margin enough. Over the levee wall now, like an aurora borealis, the sky of New Orleans, across the river, was flickering gently. This time they crossed by bridge, high above everything, merging into a long light-stream of cars turned cityward.

For a long time afterward he was lost in the streets, turning almost at random with the noisy traffic until he found his bearings. When he stopped the car at the next sign and leaned forward frowning to make it out; she sat up straight on her side. It was Arabi. He turned the car, right round.

"We're all right now," he muttered, allowing himself a cigarette.

Something that must have been with them all along suddenly, then, was not. In a moment, tall as panic, it rose, cried like a human, and dropped back.

"I never got my water," she said.

She gave him the name of her hotel, he drove her there, and he said good night on the sidewalk. They shook hands.

"Forgive . . ." For, just in time, he saw she expected it of him.

And that was just what she did, forgive him. Indeed, had she waked in time from a deep sleep, she would have told him her story. She disappeared through the revolving door, with a gesture of smoothing her hair, and he thought a figure in the lobby strolled to meet her. He got back in the car and sat there.

He was not leaving for Syracuse until early in the morning. At length, he recalled the reason; his wife had recommended that he stay where he was this extra day so that she could entertain some old, unmarried college friends without him underfoot.

As he started up the car, he recognized in the smell of exhausted, body-warm air in the streets, in which the flow of drink was an inextricable part, the signal that the New Orleans evening was just beginning. In Dickie Grogan's, as he passed, the well-known Josefina at her organ was charging up and down with "*Clair de Lune.*" As he drove the little Ford safely to its garage, he remembered for the first time in years when he was young and brash, a student in New York, and the shriek and horror and unholy smother of the subway had its original meaning for him as the lilt and expectation of love.

Tobias Wolff (1945–)

was born in Alabama and grew up in Washington's Skagit River Valley. His father (whose life is detailed in The Duke of Deception, *by Tobias's older brother Geoffrey, also an accomplished fiction writer) was a charismatic con man, forger, check-kiter, car thief, and all-purpose liar who claimed to be an Episcopalian (he was Jewish) graduate of Yale and Oxford (he'd been expelled from several boarding schools) who had been a fighter pilot for the Royal Air Force (he'd been rejected because of his bad teeth). Tobias Wolff's parents divorced, and he was raised by his mother, whose entanglements with various subsequent abusive men are chronicled in Wolff's memoir* This Boy's Life. *To escape, Wolff, still in high school, forged transcripts and letters of recommendation and was accepted by the prestigious Hill School. He spent four years in Vietnam as a Green Beret (recounted in his memoir* In Pharaoh's Army*), graduated from Oxford University and got his master's degree from Stanford, and worked briefly at* The Washington Post *as a police reporter. Wolff taught for several years at Syracuse University and now teaches at Stanford. He is the author of three highly acclaimed collections of short stories:* In the Garden of the North American Martyrs, Back in the World, *and* The Night in Question. *He has won the 1985 PEN/Faulkner Award (for his novella* The Barracks Thief*), the Rea Award for the Short Story, and three O Henry Prizes. His first novel,* Old School, *was published in 2003.*

INTRODUCTION BY **Adam Johnson**

After high school, I worked construction for a few years. I was a peon on crews that built things like parking garages. When I finally made it to college, I was older than other undergraduates. They talked about things I'd never heard of—like Kurosawa movies and Coltrane albums. Working construction had taught me how to spot a bad burrito wagon and how to fake the ability to read blueprints. I needed an easy "A," so I took a creative writing class. For my first story, I typed up something I'd witnessed on a job site: a one-gallon jug of urine falling twenty-two stories from a tower crane to explode at the feet of an ironworker, a guy who happened to have a pistol in his lunchbox. I wrote it as if I was the ironworker with the gun instead of the kid rubbernecking from the shoring deck. The real ironworker did climb twenty-two stories with a gun but collapsed from exhaustion when he finally reached the top—he was a smoker—and had to be helped down by paramedics. Someone said his wife had left him. My version, however, ended with gunfire and blood dripping to the sawdust below.

Then my professor handed out Tobias Wolff's "The Rich Brother." Reading it gave me the kind of Joycean epiphany that most new writers are in for: My story suddenly seemed overly dramatic, self-centered, born of a spirit to impress people rather than to understand them. Writers, like doctors, have specialties, and Wolff is a delusionologist. He studies characters who have cultivated the small sets of lies people need in order to live with bad decisions. These characters are basically decent people who took a wrong turn, then told themselves a little story to help them live with their moral compromises. We all have these false stories within us, and by necessity, they grow. Like extra appendages, they become bulky, useless grafts that weigh us down. In the case of Tub, the protagonist of

"Hunters in the Snow," his internal contradictions swelled him to twice normal size. Wolff's trademark procedure, however, is the delusionectomy: He places his characters in situations of self-confrontation. Here, they must make a choice: Give name and body to this appendage—or cut it free.

By focusing on moral compromises, Wolff's stories feel both intimate and grand in scope. This personal-yet-universal scale imbues his stories with an ancient feeling, a sense that Tub from "Hunters in the Snow" could have been trouncing through the wintry woods outside Czarist St. Petersburg, that Anders in "Bullet in the Brain" might as easily have been critiquing the ceiling of a Medici bank, or that Pete from "The Rich Brother" could have given Donald a lift in his new Bavarian carriage. What emerges is a mythic, fablelike authority that puts the reader on notice that wisdom is around the corner. Reading these stories, you'll notice a Chekovian directness to the prose. You might also feel a Sherwood Anderson–like sense of patience and note a wry, dark humor reminiscent of Flannery O'Connor. What's all Wolff is his devotion to the history of a character. Each person comes on stage with a long shadow, a Doppler that suggests origin, direction, and velocity. The result is a story whose characters feel long observed as they negotiate situations people have faced forever; Wolff makes you care enough about them to understand their choices, even as a nagging doubt tells you those choices are wrong. I always get the feeling that Wolff knows the secret way out for his characters, that he could whisper the right sequence of decisions that would allow Pete and Anders and Tub to transcend their self-made traps.

I always remember Wolff's stories as longer and more elaborate than they are. "Bullet in the Brain," with the arc of a whole human life, holds the space of a novel in my mind. How can it be only a few pages long? Returning to them again, I'm struck by how simple and focused these stories are. Wolff talks about characters as if he has been studying them for a thousand years. Reading "The Rich Brother" a dozen years ago illuminated my own case of delusionitis. The second story I turned in to my writing class was just as bad as my first. But this time, I'd tried to write a "true" story, rather than a "great" story, and it failed only because I was a beginner and I had a lot to learn.

Adam Johnson teaches creative writing at Stanford University. His short stories have appeared in Harper's, Esquire, *and* The Paris Review. *He is the author of* Emporium, *a short story collection, and* Parasites Like Us, *a novel.*

TOBIAS WOLFF

Hunters in the Snow

Tub had been waiting for an hour in the falling snow. He paced the sidewalk to keep warm and stuck his head out over the curb whenever he saw lights approaching. One driver stopped for him but before Tub could wave the man on he saw the rifle on Tub's back and hit the gas. The tires spun on the ice.

The fall of snow thickened. Tub stood below the overhang of a building. Across the road the clouds whitened just above the rooftops, and the street lights went out. He shifted the rifle strap to his other shoulder. The whiteness seeped up the sky.

A truck slid around the corner, horn blaring, rear end sashaying. Tub moved to the sidewalk and held up his hand. The truck jumped the curb and kept coming, half on the street and half on the sidewalk. It wasn't slowing down at all. Tub stood for a moment, still holding up his hand, then jumped back. His rifle slipped off his shoulder and clattered on the ice, a sandwich fell out of his pocket. He ran for the steps of the building. Another sandwich and a package of cookies tumbled onto the new snow. He made the steps and looked back.

The truck had stopped several feet beyond where Tub had been standing. He picked up his sandwiches and his cookies and slung the rifle and went up to the driver's window. The driver was bent against the steering wheel, slapping his knees and drumming his feet on the floorboards. He looked like a cartoon of a person laughing, except that his eyes watched the man on the seat beside him. "You ought to see yourself," the driver said. "He looks just like a beach ball with a hat on, doesn't he? Doesn't he, Frank?"

The man beside him smiled and looked off.

"You almost ran me down," Tub said. "You could've killed me."

"Come on, Tub," said the man beside the driver. "Be mellow. Kenny was just messing around." He opened the door and slid over to the middle of the seat.

Tub took the bolt out of his rifle and climbed in beside him. "I waited an hour," he said. "If you meant ten o'clock why didn't you say ten o'clock?"

"Tub, you haven't done anything but complain since we got here," said the man in the middle. "If you want to piss and moan all day you might as well go home and bitch at your kids. Take your pick." When Tub didn't say anything he turned to the driver. "Okay, Kenny, let's hit the road."

Some juvenile delinquents had heaved a brick through the windshield on the driver's side, so the cold and snow tunneled right into the cab. The heater didn't work. They covered themselves with a couple of blankets Kenny had brought along and pulled down the muffs on their caps. Tub tried to keep his hands warm by rubbing them under the blanket but Frank made him stop.

They left Spokane and drove deep into the country, running along black lines of fences. The snow let up, but still there was no edge to the land where it met the sky. Nothing moved in the chalky fields. The cold bleached their faces and made the stubble stand out on their cheeks and along their upper lips. They stopped twice for coffee before they got to the woods where Kenny wanted to hunt.

Tub was for trying someplace different; two years in a row they'd been up and down this land and hadn't seen a thing. Frank didn't care one way or the other, he just wanted to get out of the goddamned truck. "Feel that," Frank said, slamming the door. He spread his feet and closed his eyes and leaned his head way back and breathed deeply. "Tune in on that energy."

"Another thing," Kenny said. "This is open land. Most of the land around here is posted."

"I'm cold," Tub said.

Frank breathed out. "Stop bitching, Tub. Get centered."

"I wasn't bitching."

"Centered," Kenny said. "Next thing you'll be wearing a nightgown, Frank. Selling flowers out at the airport."

"Kenny," Frank said, "you talk too much."

"Okay," Kenny said. "I won't say a word. Like I won't say anything about a certain babysitter."

"What babysitter?" Tub asked.

"That's between us," Frank said, looking at Kenny. "That's confidential. You keep your mouth shut."

Kenny laughed.

"You're asking for it," Frank said.

"Asking for what?"

"You'll see."

"Hey," Tub said, "are we hunting or what?"

They started off across the field. Tub had trouble getting through the fences. Frank and Kenny could have helped him; they could have lifted up on the top wire and stepped on the bottom wire, but they didn't. They stood and watched him. There were a lot of fences and Tub was puffing when they reached the woods.

They hunted for over two hours and saw no deer, no tracks, no sign. Finally they stopped by the creek to eat. Kenny had several slices of pizza and a couple of candy bars; Frank had a sandwich, an apple, two carrots, and a square of chocolate; Tub ate one hard-boiled egg and a stick of celery.

"You ask me how I want to die today," Kenny said, "I'll tell you, burn me at the stake." He turned to Tub. "You still on that diet?" He winked at Frank.

"What do you think? You think I like hard-boiled eggs?"

"All I can say is, it's the first diet I ever heard of where you gained weight from it."

"Who said I gained weight?"

"Oh, pardon me. I take it back. You're just wasting away before my very eyes. Isn't he, Frank?"

Frank had his fingers fanned out, tips against the bark of the stump where he'd laid his food. His knuckles were hairy. He wore a heavy wedding band and on his right pinky another gold ring with a flat face and an "F" in what looked like diamonds. He turned the ring this way and that. "Tub," he said, "you haven't seen your own balls in ten years."

Kenny doubled over laughing. He took off his hat and slapped his leg with it.

"What am I supposed to do?" said Tub. "It's my glands."

★ ★ ★

They left the woods and hunted along the creek. Frank and Kenny worked one bank and Tub worked the other, moving upstream. The snow was light but the drifts were deep and hard to move through. Wherever Tub looked the surface was smooth, undisturbed, and after a time he lost interest. He stopped looking for tracks and just tried to keep up with Frank and Kenny on the other side. A moment came when he realized he hadn't seen them in a long time. The breeze was moving from him to them; when it stilled he could sometimes hear Kenny laughing but that was all. He quickened his pace, breasting hard into the drifts, fighting away the snow with his knees and elbows. He heard his heart and felt the flush on his face but he never once stopped.

Tub caught up with Frank and Kenny at a bend of the creek. They were standing on a log that stretched from their bank to his. Ice had backed up behind the log. Frozen reeds stuck out, barely nodding when the air moved.

"See anything?" Frank asked.

Tub shook his head.

There wasn't much daylight left and they decided to head back toward the road. Frank and Kenny crossed the log and they started downstream, using the trail Tub had broken. Before they had gone very far Kenny stopped. "Look at that," he said, and pointed to some tracks going from the creek back into the woods. Tub's footprints crossed right over them. There on the bank, plain as day, were several mounds of deer sign. "What do you think that is, Tub?" Kenny kicked at it. "Walnuts on vanilla icing?"

"I guess I didn't notice."

Kenny looked at Frank.

"I was lost."

"You were lost. Big deal."

They followed the tracks into the woods. The deer had gone over a fence half buried in drifting snow. A no hunting sign was nailed to the top of one of the posts. Frank laughed and said the son of a bitch could read. Kenny wanted to go after him but Frank said no way, the people out here didn't mess around. He thought maybe the farmer who owned the land would let them use it if they asked. Kenny wasn't so sure. Anyway, he figured that by the time they walked to the truck and drove up the road and doubled back it would be almost dark.

"Relax," Frank said. "You can't hurry nature. If we're meant to get that deer, we'll get it. If we're not, we won't."

They started back toward the truck. This part of the woods was mainly pine. The snow was shaded and had a glaze on it. It held up Kenny and Frank but Tub kept falling through. As he kicked forward, the edge of the crust bruised his shins. Kenny and Frank pulled ahead of him, to where he couldn't even hear their voices any more. He sat down on a stump and wiped his face. He ate both the sandwiches and half the cookies, taking his own sweet time. It was dead quiet.

When Tub crossed the last fence into the road the truck started moving. Tub had to run for it and just managed to grab hold of the tailgate and hoist himself into the bed. He lay there, panting. Kenny looked out the rear window and grinned. Tub crawled into the lee of the cab to get out of the freezing wind. He pulled his earflaps low and pushed his chin into the collar of his coat. Someone rapped on the window but Tub would not turn around.

He and Frank waited outside while Kenny went into the farmhouse to ask permission. The house was old and paint was curling off the sides. The smoke streamed westward off the top of the chimney, fanning away into a thin gray plume. Above the ridge of the hills another ridge of blue clouds was rising.

"You've got a short memory," Tub said.

"What?" Frank said. He had been staring off.

"I used to stick up for you."

"Okay, so you used to stick up for me. What's eating you?"

"You shouldn't have just left me back there like that."

"You're a grown-up, Tub. You can take care of yourself. Anyway, if you think you're the only person with problems I can tell you that you're not."

"Is something bothering you, Frank?"

Frank kicked at a branch poking out of the snow. "Never mind," he said.

"What did Kenny mean about the babysitter?"

"Kenny talks too much," Frank said. "You just mind your own business."

Kenny came out of the farmhouse and gave the thumbs-up and they began walking back toward the woods. As they passed the barn a large black hound with a grizzled snout ran out and barked at them. Every time he barked he slid backwards a bit, like a cannon recoiling. Kenny got down on all fours and snarled and barked back at him, and the dog slunk away into the barn, looking over his shoulder and peeing a little as he went.

"That's an old-timer," Frank said. "A real graybeard. Fifteen years if he's a day."

"Too old," Kenny said.

Past the barn they cut off through the fields. The land was unfenced and the crust was freezing up thick and they made good time. They kept to the edge of the field until they picked up the tracks again and followed them into the woods, farther and farther back toward the hills. The trees started to blur with the shadows and the wind rose and needled their faces with the crystals it swept off the glaze. Finally they lost the tracks.

Kenny swore and threw down his hat. "This is the worst day of hunting I ever had, bar none." He picked up his hat and brushed off the snow. "This will be the first season since I was fifteen I haven't got my deer."

"It isn't the deer," Frank said. "It's the hunting. There are all these forces out here and you just have to go with them."

"You go with them," Kenny said. "I came out here to get me a deer, not listen to a bunch of hippie bullshit. And if it hadn't been for dimples here I would have, too."

"That's enough," Frank said.

"And you—you're so busy thinking about that little jailbait of yours you wouldn't know a deer if you saw one."

"Drop dead," Frank said, and turned away.

Kenny and Tub followed him back across the fields. When they were coming up to the barn Kenny stopped and pointed. "I hate that post," he said. He raised his rifle and fired. It sounded like a dry branch cracking. The post splintered along its right side, up towards the top. "There," Kenny said. "It's dead."

"Knock it off," Frank said, walking ahead.

Kenny looked at Tub. He smiled. "I hate that tree," he said, and fired again. Tub hurried to catch up with Frank. He started to speak but just then the dog ran out of the barn and barked at them. "Easy, boy," Frank said.

"I hate that dog." Kenny was behind them.

"That's enough," Frank said. "You put that gun down."

Kenny fired. The bullet went in between the dog's eyes. He sank right down into the snow, his legs splayed out on each side, his yellow eyes open and staring. Except for the blood he looked like a small bearskin rug. The blood ran down the dog's muzzle into the snow.

They all looked at the dog lying there.

"What did he ever do to you?" Tub asked. "He was just barking."

Kenny turned to Tub. "I hate you."

Tub shot from the waist. Kenny jerked backward against the fence and buckled to his knees. He folded his hands across his stomach. "Look," he said. His hands were covered with blood. In the dusk his blood was more blue than red. It seemed to belong to the shadows. It didn't seem out of place. Kenny eased himself onto his back. He sighed several times, deeply. "You shot me," he said.

"I had to," Tub said. He knelt beside Kenny. "Oh God," he said. "Frank. Frank."

Frank hadn't moved since Kenny killed the dog.

"Frank!" Tub shouted.

"I was just kidding around," Kenny said. "It was a joke. Oh!" he said, and arched his back suddenly. "Oh!" he said again, and dug his heels into the snow and pushed himself along on his head for several feet. Then he stopped and lay there, rocking back and forth on his heels and head like a wrestler doing warm-up exercises.

Frank roused himself. "Kenny," he said. He bent down and put his gloved hand on Kenny's brow. "You shot him," he said to Tub.

"He made me," Tub said.

"No no no," Kenny said.

Tub was weeping from the eyes and nostrils. His whole face was wet. Frank closed his eyes, then looked down at Kenny again. "Where does it hurt?"

"Everywhere," Kenny said, "just everywhere."

"Oh God," Tub said.

"I mean where did it go in?" Frank said.

"Here." Kenny pointed at the wound in his stomach. It was welling slowly with blood.

"You're lucky," Frank said. "It's on the left side. It missed your appendix. If it had hit your appendix you'd really be in the soup." He turned and threw up onto the snow, holding his sides as if to keep warm.

"Are you all right?" Tub said.

"There's some aspirin in the truck," Kenny said.

"I'm all right," Frank said.

"We'd better call an ambulance," Tub said.

"Jesus," Frank said. "What are we going to say?"

"Exactly what happened," Tub said. "He was going to shoot me but I shot him first."

"No sir!" Kenny said. "I wasn't either!"

Frank patted Kenny on the arm. "Easy does it, partner." He stood. "Let's go."

Tub picked up Kenny's rifle as they walked down toward the farmhouse. "No sense leaving this around," he said. "Kenny might get ideas."

"I can tell you one thing," Frank said. "You've really done it this time. This definitely takes the cake."

They had to knock on the door twice before it was opened by a thin man with lank hair. The room behind him was filled with smoke. He squinted at them. "You get anything?" he asked.

"No," Frank said.

"I knew you wouldn't. That's what I told the other fellow."

"We've had an accident."

The man looked past Frank and Tub into the gloom. "Shoot your friend, did you?"

Frank nodded.

"I did," Tub said.

"I suppose you want to use the phone."

"If it's okay."

The man in the door looked behind him, then stepped back. Frank and Tub followed him into the house. There was a woman sitting by the stove in the middle of the room. The stove was smoking badly. She looked up and then down again at the child asleep in her lap. Her face was white and damp; strands of hair were pasted across her forehead. Tub warmed his hands over the stove while Frank went into the kitchen to call. The man who had let them in stood at the window, his hands in his pockets.

"My friend shot your dog," Tub said.

The man nodded without turning around. "I should have done it myself. I just couldn't."

"He loved that dog so much," the woman said. The child squirmed and she rocked it.

"You asked him to?" Tub said. "You asked him to shoot your dog?"

"He was old and sick. Couldn't chew his food any more. I would have done it myself but I don't have a gun."

"You couldn't have anyway," the woman said. "Never in a million years."

The man shrugged.

Frank came out of the kitchen. "We'll have to take him ourselves. The nearest hospital is fifty miles from here and all their ambulances are out anyway."

The woman knew a shortcut but the directions were complicated and Tub had to write them down. The man told them where they could find some boards to carry Kenny on. He didn't have a flashlight but he said he would leave the porch light on.

It was dark outside. The clouds were low and heavy-looking and the wind blew in shrill gusts. There was a screen loose on the house and it banged slowly and then quickly as the wind rose again. They could hear it all the way to the barn. Frank went for the boards while Tub looked for Kenny, who was not where they had left him. Tub found him farther up the drive, lying on his stomach. "You okay?" Tub said.

"It hurts."

"Frank says it missed your appendix.'

"I already had my appendix out."

"All right," Frank said, coming up to them. "We'll have you in a nice warm bed before you can say Jack Robinson." He put the two boards on Kenny's right side.

"Just as long as I don't have one of those male nurses," Kenny said.

"Ha ha," Frank said. "That's the spirit. Get ready, set, *over you go,*" and he rolled Kenny onto the boards. Kenny screamed and kicked his legs in the air. When he quieted down Frank and Tub lifted the boards and carried him down the drive. Tub had the back end, and with the snow blowing in his face he had trouble with his footing. Also he was tired and the man inside had forgotten to turn the porch light on. Just past the house Tub slipped and threw out his hands to catch himself. The boards fell and Kenny tumbled out and rolled to the bottom of the drive, yelling all the way. He came to rest against the right front wheel of the truck.

"You fat moron," Frank said. "You aren't good for diddly."

Tub grabbed Frank by the collar and backed him hard up against the fence. Frank tried to pull his hands away but Tub shook him and snapped his head back and forth and finally Frank gave up.

"What do you know about fat," Tub said. "What do you know about glands." As he spoke he kept shaking Frank. "What do you know about me."

"All right," Frank said.

"No more," Tub said.

"All right."

"No more talking to me like that. No more watching. No more laughing."

"Okay, Tub. I promise."

Tub let go of Frank and leaned his forehead against the fence. His arms hung straight at his sides.

"I'm sorry, Tub." Frank touched him on the shoulder. "I'll be down at the truck."

Tub stood by the fence for a while and then got the rifles off the porch. Frank had rolled Kenny back onto the boards and they lifted him into the bed of the truck. Frank spread the seat blankets over him. "Warm enough?" he asked.

Kenny nodded.

"Okay. Now how does reverse work on this thing?"

"All the way to the left and up." Kenny sat up as Frank started forward to the cab. "Frank!"

"What?"

"If it sticks don't force it."

The truck started right away. "One thing," Frank said, "you've got to hand it to the Japanese. A very ancient, very spiritual culture and they can still make a hell of a truck." He glanced over at Tub. "Look, I'm sorry. I didn't know you felt that way, honest to God I didn't. You should have said something."

"I did."

"When? Name one time."

"A couple of hours ago."

"I guess I wasn't paying attention."

"That's true, Frank," Tub said. "You don't pay attention very much."

"Tub," Frank said, "what happened back there, I should have been more sympathetic. I realize that. You were going through a lot. I just want you to know it wasn't your fault. He was asking for it."

"You think so?"

"Absolutely. It was him or you. I would have done the same thing in your shoes, no question."

The wind was blowing into their faces. The snow was a moving white wall in front of their lights; it swirled into the cab through the hole in the windshield and settled on them. Tub clapped his hands and shifted around to stay warm, but it didn't work.

"I'm going to have to stop," Frank said. "I can't feel my fingers."

Up ahead they saw some lights off the road. It was a tavern. Outside in the parking lot there were several jeeps and trucks. A couple of them had deer strapped across their hoods. Frank parked and they went back to Kenny. "How you doing, partner," Frank said.

"I'm cold."

"Well, don't feel like the Lone Ranger. It's worse inside, take my word for it. You should get that windshield fixed."

"Look," Tub said, "he threw the blankets off." They were lying in a heap against the tailgate.

"Now look, Kenny," Frank said, "it's no use whining about being cold if you're not going to try and keep warm. You've got to do your share." He spread the blankets over Kenny and tucked them in at the corners.

"They blew off."

"Hold on to them then."

"Why are we stopping, Frank?"

"Because if me and Tub don't get warmed up we're going to freeze solid and then where will you be?" He punched Kenny lightly in the arm. "So just hold your horses."

The bar was full of men in colored jackets, mostly orange. The waitress brought coffee. "Just what the doctor ordered," Frank said, cradling the steaming cup in his hand. His skin was bone white. "Tub, I've been thinking. What you said about me not paying attention, that's true."

"It's okay."

"No. I really had that coming. I guess I've just been a little too interested in old number one. I've had a lot on my mind. Not that that's any excuse."

"Forget it, Frank. I sort of lost my temper back there. I guess we're all a little on edge."

Frank shook his head. "It isn't just that."

"You want to talk about it?"

"Just between us, Tub?"

"Sure, Frank. Just between us."

"Tub, I think I'm going to be leaving Nancy."

"Oh, Frank. Oh, Frank." Tub sat back and shook his head.

Frank reached out and laid his hand on Tub's arm. "Tub, have you ever been really in love?"

"Well—"

"I mean *really* in love." He squeezed Tub's wrist. "With your whole being."

"I don't know. When you put it like that, I don't know."

"You haven't then. Nothing against you, but you'd know it if you had." Frank let go of Tub's arm. "This isn't just some bit of fluff I'm talking about."

"Who is she, Frank?"

Frank paused. He looked into his empty cup. "Roxanne Brewer."

"Cliff Brewer's kid? The babysitter?"

"You can't just put people into categories like that, Tub. That's why the whole system is wrong. And that's why this country is going to hell in a rowboat."

"But she can't be more than—" Tub shook his head.

"Fifteen. Shell be sixteen in May." Frank smiled. "May fourth, three twenty-seven p.m. Hell, Tub, a hundred years ago she'd have been an old maid by that age. Juliet was only thirteen."

"Juliet? Juliet Miller? Jesus, Frank, she doesn't even have breasts. She doesn't even wear a top to her bathing suit. She's still collecting frogs."

"Not Juliet Miller. The real Juliet. Tub, don't you see how you're dividing people up into categories? He's an executive, she's a secretary, he's a truck driver, she's fifteen years old. Tub, this so-called babysitter, this so-called fifteen-year-old has more in her little finger than most of us have in our entire bodies. I can tell you this little lady is something special."

Tub nodded. "I know the kids like her."

"She's opened up whole worlds to me that I never knew were there."

"What does Nancy think about all of this?"

"She doesn't know."

"You haven't told her?"

"Not yet. It's not so easy. She's been damned good to me all these years. Then there's the kids to consider." The brightness in Frank's eyes trembled and he wiped quickly at them with the back of his hand. "I guess you think I'm a complete bastard."

"No, Frank, I don't think that."

"Well, you *ought* to."

"Frank, when you've got a friend it means you've always got someone on your side, no matter what. That's the way I feel about it, anyway."

"You mean that, Tub?"

"Sure I do."

Frank smiled. "You don't know how good it feels to hear you say that."

Kenny had tried to get out of the truck but he hadn't made it. He was jack-knifed over the tailgate, his head hanging above the bumper. They lifted him back into the bed and covered him again. He was sweating and his teeth chattered. "It hurts, Frank."

"It wouldn't hurt so much if you just stayed put. Now we're going to the hospital. Got that? Say it—I'm going to the hospital."

"I'm going to the hospital."

"Again."

"I'm going to the hospital."

"Now just keep saying that to yourself and before you know it we'll be there."

After they had gone a few miles Tub turned to Frank. "I just pulled a real boner," he said.

"What's that?"

"I left the directions on the table back there."

"That's okay. I remember them pretty well."

The snowfall lightened and the clouds began to roll back off the fields, but it was no warmer and after a time both Frank and Tub were bitten through and shaking. Frank almost didn't make it around a curve, and they decided to stop at the next roadhouse.

There was an automatic hand-dryer in the bathroom and they took turns standing in front of it, opening their jackets and shirts and letting the jet of hot air breathe across their faces and chests.

"You know," Tub said, "what you told me back there, I appreciate it. Trusting me."

Frank opened and closed his fingers in front of the nozzle. "The way I look at it, Tub, no man is an island. You've got to trust someone."

"Frank—"

Frank waited.

"When I said that about my glands, that wasn't true. The truth is I just shovel it in."

"Well, Tub—"

"Day and night, Frank. In the shower. On the freeway." He turned and let the air play over his back. "I've even got stuff in the paper towel machine at work."

"There's nothing wrong with your glands at all?" Frank had taken his boots and socks off. He held first his right, then his left foot up to the nozzle.

"No. There never was."

"Does Alice know?" The machine went off and Frank started lacing up his boots.

"Nobody knows. That's the worst of it, Frank. Not the being fat, I never got any big kick out of being thin, but the lying. Having to lead a double life like a spy or a hit man. This sounds strange but I feel sorry for those guys, I really do. I know what they go through. Always having to think about what you say and do. Always feeling like people are watching you, trying to catch you at something. Never able to just be yourself. Like when I make a big deal about only having an orange for breakfast and then scarf all the way to work. Oreos, Mars Bars, Twinkies. Sugar Babies. Snickers." Tub glanced at Frank and looked quickly away. "Pretty disgusting, isn't it?"

"Tub. Tub." Frank shook his head. "Come on." He took Tub's arm and led him into the restaurant half of the bar. "My friend is hungry," he told the waitress. "Bring four orders of pancakes, plenty of butter and syrup."

"Frank—"

"Sit down."

When the dishes came Frank carved out slabs of butter and just laid them on the pancakes. Then he emptied the bottle of syrup, moving it back and forth over the plates. He leaned forward on his elbows and rested his chin in one hand. "Go on, Tub."

Tub ate several mouthfuls, then started to wipe his lips. Frank took the napkin away from him. "No wiping," he said. Tub kept at it. The syrup covered his chin; it dripped to a point like a goatee. "Weigh in, Tub," Frank said, pushing another fork across the table. "Get down to business." Tub took the fork in his left hand and lowered his head and started really chowing down. "Clean your plate," Frank said when the pancakes were gone, and Tub lifted each of the four plates and licked it clean. He sat back, trying to catch his breath.

"Beautiful," Frank said. "Are you full?"

"I'm full," Tub said. "I've never been so full."

Kenny's blankets were bunched up against the tailgate again.

"They must have blown off," Tub said.

"They're not doing him any good," Frank said. "We might as well get some use out of them."

Kenny mumbled. Tub bent over him. "What? Speak up."

"I'm going to the hospital," Kenny said.

"Attaboy," Frank said.

The blankets helped. The wind still got their faces and Frank's hands but it was much better. The fresh snow on the road and the trees sparkled under the beam of the headlight. Squares of light from farmhouse windows fell onto the blue snow in the fields.

"Frank," Tub said after a time, "you know that farmer? He told Kenny to kill the dog."

"You're kidding!" Frank leaned forward, considering. "That Kenny. What a card." He laughed and so did Tub. Tub smiled out the back window. Kenny lay with his arms folded over his stomach, moving his lips at the stars. Right overhead was the Big Dipper, and behind, hanging between Kenny's toes in the direction of the hospital, was the North Star, Pole Star, Help to Sailors. As the truck twisted through the gentle hills the star went back and forth between Kenny's boots, staying always in his sight. "I'm going to the hospital," Kenny said. But he was wrong. They had taken a different turn a long way back.

Tobias Wolff

The Rich Brother

There were two brothers, Pete and Donald.

Pete, the older brother, was in real estate. He and his wife had a Century 21 franchise in Santa Cruz. Pete worked hard and made a lot of money, but not any more than he thought he deserved. He had two daughters, a sailboat, a house from which he could see a thin slice of the ocean, and friends doing well enough in their own lives not to wish bad luck on him. Donald, the younger brother, was still single. He lived alone, painted houses when he found the work and got deeper in debt to Pete when he didn't.

No one would have taken them for brothers. Where Pete was stout and hearty and at home in the world, Donald was bony, grave, and obsessed with the fate of his soul. Over the years Donald had worn the images of two different Perfect Masters around his neck. Out of devotion to the second of these he entered an ashram in Berkeley, where he nearly died of undiagnosed hepatitis. By the time Pete finished paying the medical bills Donald had become a Christian. He drifted from church to church, then joined a pentecostal community that met somewhere in the Mission District to sing in tongues and swap prophecies.

Pete couldn't make sense of it. Their parents were both dead, but while they were alive neither of them had found it necessary to believe in anything. They managed to be decent people without making fools of themselves, and Pete had the same ambition. He thought that the whole thing was an excuse for Donald to take himself seriously.

The trouble was that Donald couldn't content himself with worrying about his own soul. He had to worry about everyone else's, and, especially Pete's. He handed down his judgments in ways that he seemed to consider subtle: through significant silence, innuendo, looks of mild despair that said, *Brother, what have you come to?* What Pete had come to, as far as he could tell, was prosperity and Donald did not prosper.

At the age of forty Pete took up sky diving. He made his first jump with two friends who'd started only a few months earlier and were already doing stunts. They were both coked to the gills when they jumped but Pete wanted to do it straight, at least the first time, and he was glad that he did. He would never have used the word *mystical,* but that was how Pete felt about the experience. Later he made the mistake of trying to describe it to Donald, who kept asking how much it cost and then acted appalled when Pete told him.

"At least I'm trying something new," Pete said. "At least I'm breaking the pattern."

Not long after that conversation Donald also broke the pattern, by going to live on a farm outside of Paso Robles. The farm was owned by several members of Donald's community, who had bought it and moved there with the idea of forming a family of faith. That was how Donald explained it in the first letter he sent. Every week Pete heard how happy Donald was, how 'in the Lord.' He told Pete he was praying for him, he and the rest of Pete's brothers and sisters on the farm.

"I only have one brother," Pete wanted to answer, "and that's enough." But he kept this thought to himself.

In November the letters stopped. Pete didn't worry about this at first, but when he called Donald at Thanksgiving Donald was grim. He tried to sound upbeat but he didn't try hard enough to make it convincing. "Now listen," Pete said, "you don't have to stay in that place if you don't want to."

"I'll be all right," Donald answered.

"That's not the point. Being all right is not the point. If you don't like what's going on up there, then get out."

"I'm all right," Donald said again, more firmly. "I'm doing fine."

But he called Pete a week later and said that he was quitting the farm. When Pete asked him where he intended to go, Donald admitted that he had no plan. His car had been repossessed just before he left the city, and he was flat broke.

"I guess you'll have to stay with us," Pete said.

Donald put up a show of resistance. Then he gave in. "Just until I get my feet on the ground," he said.

"Right," Pete said. "Check out your options." He told Donald he'd send him money for a bus ticket, but as they were about to hang up Pete changed his mind. He knew that Donald would try hitchhiking to save the fare. Pete didn't want him out on the road all alone where some head case could pick him up, where anything could happen to him.

"Better yet," he said, "I'll come and get you."

"You don't have to do that. I didn't expect you to do that," Donald said. He added, "It's a pretty long drive."

"Just tell me how to get there."

But Donald wouldn't give him directions. He said that the farm was too depressing, that Pete wouldn't like it. Instead, he insisted on meeting Pete at a service station called Jonathan's Mechanical Emporium.

"You must be kidding," Pete said.

"It's close to the highway," Donald said. "I didn't name it."

"That's one for the collection," Pete said.

The day before he left to bring Donald home, Pete received a letter from a man who described himself as 'head of household' at the farm where Donald had been living. From this letter Pete learned that Donald had not quit the farm, but had been asked to leave. The letter was written on the back of a mimeographed survey form asking people to record their response to a ceremony of some kind. The last question said:

What did you feel during the liturgy?

a) Being
b) Becoming
c) Being and Becoming
d) None of the Above
e) All of the Above

Pete tried to forget the letter. But of course he couldn't. Each time he thought of it he felt crowded and breathless, a feeling that came over him again when he drove into the service station and saw Donald sitting against a wall with his head on his knees. It was late afternoon. A paper cup tumbled slowly past Donald's feet, pushed by the damp wind.

Pete honked and Donald raised his head. He smiled at Pete then stood and stretched. His arms were long and thin and white. He wore a red bandanna across his forehead, a T-shirt with a couple of words on the front. Pete couldn't read them because the letters were inverted.

"Grow up," Pete yelled. "Get a Mercedes."

Donald came up to the window. He bent down and said, "Thanks for coming. You must be totally whipped."

"I'll make it." Pete pointed at Donald's T-shirt. "What's that supposed to say?"

Donald looked down at his shirt front. "Try God. I guess I put it on backwards. Pete, could I borrow a couple of dollars? I owe these people for coffee and sandwiches."

Pete took five twenties from his wallet and held them out the window.

Donald stepped back as if horrified. "I don't need that much."

"I can't keep track of all these nickels and dimes," Pete said. "Just pay me back when your ship comes in." He waved the bills impatiently. "Go on—take it."

"Only for now." Donald took the money and went into the service station office. He came out carrying two orange sodas, one of which he gave to Pete as he got into the car. "My treat," he said.

"No bags?"

"Wow, thanks for reminding me," Donald said. He balanced his drink on the dashboard, but the slight rocking of the car as he got out tipped it onto the passenger's seat, where half its contents foamed over before Pete could snatch it up again. Donald looked on while Pete held the bottle out the window, soda running down his fingers.

"Wipe it up," Pete told him. "Quick!"

"With what?"

Pete stared at Donald. "That shirt. Use the shirt."

Donald pulled a long face but did as he was told, his pale skin puckering against the wind.

"Great, just great," Pete said. "We haven't even left the gas station yet."

Afterwards on the highway, Donald said, "This is a new car, isn't it?"

"Yes. This is a new car."

"Is that why you're so upset about the seat?"

"Forget it, OK? Let's just forget about it."

"I said I was sorry."

Pete said, "I just wish you'd be more careful. These seats are made of leather. That stain won't come out, not to mention the smell. I don't see why I can't have leather seats that smell like leather instead of orange pop."

"What was wrong with the other car?"

Pete glanced over at Donald. Donald had raised the hood of the blue sweatshirt he'd put on. The peaked hood above his gaunt, watchful face gave him the look of an inquisitor.

"There wasn't anything wrong with it," Pete said. "I just happened to like this one better."

Donald nodded.

There was a long silence between them as Pete drove on and the day darkened toward evening. On either side of the road lay stubble-covered fields. A line of low hills ran along the horizon, topped here and there with trees black against the grey sky. In the approaching line of cars a driver turned on his headlights. Pete did the same.

"So what happened?" he asked. "Farm life not your bag?"

Donald took some time to answer, and at last he said, simply, "It was my fault."

"What was your fault?"

"The whole thing. Don't play dumb, Pete. I know they wrote to you." Donald looked at Pete, then stared out the windshield again.

"I'm not playing dumb."

Donald shrugged.

"All I really know is they asked you to leave," Pete went on. "I don't know any of the particulars."

"I blew it," Donald said. "Believe me, you don't want to hear the gory details."

"Sure I do," Pete said. He added, "Everybody likes the gory details."

"You mean everybody likes to hear how someone messed up."

"Right," Pete said. "That's the way it is here on Spaceship Earth."

Donald bent one knee onto the front seat and leaned against the door so that he was facing Pete instead of the windshield. Pete was aware of Donald's scrutiny. He waited. Night was coming on in a rush now, filling the hollows of the land. Donald's long cheeks and deep-set eyes were dark with shadow. His brow was white. "Do you ever dream about me?" Donald asked.

"Do I ever dream about you? What kind of a question is that? Of course I don't dream about you," Pete said, untruthfully.

"What do you dream about?"

"Sex and money. Mostly money. A nightmare is when I dream I don't have any."

"You're just making that up," Donald said.

Pete smiled.

"Sometimes I wake up at night," Donald went on, "and I can tell you're dreaming about me."

"We were talking about the farm," Pete said. "Let's finish that conversation and then we can talk about our various out-of-body experiences and the interesting things we did during previous incarnations."

For a moment Donald looked like a grinning skull; then he turned serious again. "There's not that much to tell," he said. "I just didn't do anything right."

"That's a little vague," Pete said.

"Well, like the groceries. Whenever it was my turn to get the groceries I'd blow it somehow. I'd bring the groceries home and half of them would be missing, or I'd have all the wrong things, the wrong kind of flour or the wrong kind of chocolate or whatever. One time I gave them away. It's not funny, Pete."

Pete said, "Who did you give the groceries to?"

"Just some people I picked up on the way home. Some fieldworkers. They had about eight kids with them and they didn't even speak English—just nodded their heads. Still, I shouldn't have given away the groceries. Not all of them, anyway. I really learned my lesson about that. You have to be practical. You have to be fair to yourself." Donald leaned forward, and Pete could sense his excitement. "There's nothing actually wrong with being in business," he said. "As long as you're fair to other people you can still be fair to yourself. I'm thinking of going into business, Pete."

"We'll talk about it," Pete said. "So, that's the story? There isn't any more to it than that?"

"What did they tell you?" Donald asked.

"Nothing."

"They must have told you something."

Pete shook his head.

"They didn't tell you about the fire?" When Pete shook his head again Donald regarded him for a time, then said, "I don't know. It was stupid. I just completely lost it." He folded his arms across his chest and slumped back into the corner. "Everybody had to take turns cooking dinner. I usually did tuna casserole or spaghetti with garlic bread. But this one night I thought I'd do something different, something really interesting." Donald looked sharply at Pete. "It's all a big laugh to you, isn't it?"

"I'm sorry," Pete said.

"You don't know when to quit. You just keep hitting away."

"Tell me about the fire, Donald."

Donald kept watching him. "You have this compulsion to make me look foolish."

"Come off it, Donald. Don't make a big thing out of this."

"I know why you do it. It's because you don't have any purpose in life. You're afraid to relate to people who do, so you make fun of them."

"Relate," Pete said softly.

"You're basically a very frightened individual," Donald said. "Very threatened. You've always been like that. Do you remember when you used to try to kill me?"

"I don't have any compulsion to make you look foolish, Donald—you do it yourself. You're doing it right now."

"You can't tell me you don't remember," Donald said. "It was after my operation. You remember that."

"Sort of." Pete shrugged. "Not really."

"Oh yes," Donald said. "Do you want to see the scar?"

"I remember you had an operation. I don't remember the specifics, that's all. And I sure as hell don't remember trying to kill you."

"Oh yes," Donald repeated, maddeningly. "You bet your life you did. All the time. The thing was, I couldn't have anything happen to me where they sewed me up because then my intestines would come apart again and poison me. That was a big issue, Pete. Mom was always in a state about me climbing trees and so on. And you used to hit me there every chance you got."

"Mom was in a state every time you burped," Pete said. "I don't know. Maybe I bumped into you accidentally once or twice. I never did it deliberately."

"Every chance you got." Donald said. "Like when the folks went out at night and left you to baby-sit. I'd hear them say good night, and then I'd hear the car start up, and when they were gone I'd lie there and listen. After a while I would hear you coming down the hall, and I would close my eyes and pretend to be asleep. There were nights when you would stand outside the door, just stand there, and then go away again. But most nights you'd open the door and I would hear you in the room with me, breathing. You'd come over and sit next to me on the bed—you remember, Pete, you have to—you'd sit next to me on the bed and pull the sheets back. If I was on my stomach you'd roll me over. Then you would lift up my pajama shirt and start hitting me on my stitches: You'd hit me as hard as you could, over and over. And I would just keep lying there with my eyes closed. I was afraid that you'd get mad if you knew I was awake. Is that strange or what? I was afraid that you'd get mad if you found out that I knew you were trying to kill me." Donald laughed. "Come on, you can't tell me you don't remember that."

"It might have happened once or twice. Kids do those things. I can't get all excited about something I maybe did twenty-five years ago."

"No maybe about it. You did it."

Pete said, "You're wearing me out with this stuff. We've got a long drive ahead of us and if you don't back off pretty soon we aren't going to make it. You aren't, anyway."

Donald turned away.

"I'm doing my best," Pete said. The self-pity in his own voice made the words sound like a lie. But they weren't a lie! He was doing his best.

The car topped a rise. In the distance Pete saw a cluster of lights that blinked out when he started downhill. There was no moon. The sky was low and black.

"Come to think of it," Pete said, "I did have a dream about you the other night." Then he added, impatiently, as if Donald were badgering him, "A couple of other nights too. I'm getting hungry," he said.

"The same dream?"

"Different dreams. I only remember one of them well. There was something wrong with me, and you were helping out. Taking care of me. Just the two of us. I don't know where everyone else was supposed to be."

Pete left it at that. He didn't tell Donald that in this dream he was blind.

"I wonder if that was when I woke up," Donald said. He added, "I'm sorry I got into that thing about my scar. I keep trying to forget it but I guess I never will. Not really. It was pretty strange, having someone around all the time who wanted to get rid of me."

"Kid stuff," Pete said. "Ancient history."

They ate dinner at a Denny's on the other side of King City. As Pete was paying the check he heard a man behind him say, "Excuse me, but I wonder if I might ask which way you're going?" and Donald answer, "Santa Cruz."

"Perfect," the man said.

Pete could see him in the fish-eye mirror above the cash register: a red blazer with some kind of crest on the pocket, little black moustache, glossy black hair combed down on his forehead like a Roman emperor's. A rug, Pete thought. Definitely a rug.

Pete got his change and turned. "Why is that perfect?" he asked.

The man looked at Pete. He had a soft ruddy face that was doing its best to express pleasant surprise, as if this new wrinkle were all he could have wished for, but the eyes behind the aviator glasses showed signs of regret. His lips were moist and shiny. "I take it you're together," he said.

"You got it," Pete told him.

"All the better, then," the man went on. "It so happens I'm going to Santa Cruz myself. Had a spot of car trouble down the road. The old Caddy let me down."

"What kind of trouble?" Pete asked.

"Engine trouble," the man said. "I'm afraid it's a bit urgent. My daughter is sick. Urgently sick. I've got a telegram here." He patted the breast pocket of his blazer.

Pete grinned. Amazing, he thought, the old sick daughter ploy, but before he could say anything Donald got into the act again. "No problem," Donald said, "We've got tons of room."

"Not that much room," Pete said.

Donald nodded. "I'll put my things in the trunk."

"The trunk's full," Pete told him.

"It so happens I'm traveling light," the man said. "This leg of the trip anyway. In fact I don't have any luggage at this particular time."

Pete said, "Left it in the old Caddy, did you?"

"Exactly," the man said.

"No problem," Donald repeated. He walked outside and the man went with him. Together they strolled across the parking lot, Pete following at a distance. When they reached Pete's car Donald raised his face to the sky, and the man did the same. They stood there looking up. "Dark night," Donald said.

"Stygian," the man said.

Pete still had it in mind to brush him off, but he didn't do that. Instead he unlocked the door for him. He wanted to see what would happen. It was an adventure, but not a dangerous adventure. The man might steal Pete's ashtrays but he wouldn't kill him. If Pete got killed on the road it would be by some spiritual person in a sweatsuit, someone with his eyes on the far horizon and a wet Try God T-shirt in his duffel bag.

As soon as they left the parking lot the man lit a cigar. He blew a cloud of smoke over Pete's shoulder and sighed with pleasure. "Put it out," Pete told him.

"Of course," the man said. Pete looked into the rear-view mirror and saw the man take another long puff before dropping the cigar out the window. "Forgive me," he said. "I should have asked. Name's Webster, by the way."

Donald turned and looked back at him. "First name or last."

The man hesitated. "Last," he said finally.

"I know a Webster," Donald said. "Mick Webster."

"There are many of us," Webster said.

"Big fellow, wooden leg," Pete said.

Donald gave Pete a look.

Webster shook his head. "Doesn't ring a bell. Still, I wouldn't deny the connection. Might be one of the cousinry."

"What's your daughter got?" Pete asked.

"That isn't clear," Webster answered. "It appears to be a female complaint of some nature. Then again it may be tropical." He was quiet for a moment, and added: "If indeed it *is* tropical, I will have to assume some of the blame myself. It was my own vaulting ambition that first led us to the tropics and kept us in the tropics all those many years, exposed to every evil. Truly I have much to answer for. I left my wife there."

Donald said quietly, "You mean she died?"

"I buried her with these hands. The earth will be repaid, gold for gold."

"Which tropics?" Pete asked.

"The tropics of Peru."

"What part of Peru are they in?"

"The lowlands," Webster said.

Pete nodded. "What's it like down there?"

"Another world," Webster said. His tone was sepulchral. "A world far better imagined than described."

"Far out," Pete said.

The three men rode in silence for a time. A line of trucks went past in the other direction, trailers festooned with running lights, engines roaring.

"Yes," Webster said at last, "I have much to answer for."

Pete smiled at Donald, but Donald had turned in his seat again and was gazing at Webster. "I'm sorry about your wife," Donald said.

"What did she die of?" Pete asked.

"A wasting illness," Webster said. "The doctors have no name for it, but I do." He leaned forward and said, fiercely, "*Greed.*" Then he slumped back against his seat. "My greed, not hers. She wanted no part of it."

Pete bit his lip. Webster was a find and Pete didn't want to scare him off by hooting at him. In a voice low and innocent of knowingness, he asked, "What took you there?"

"It's difficult for me to talk about."

"Try," Pete told him.

"A cigar would make it easier."

Donald turned to Pete and said, "It's OK with me."

"All right," Pete said. "Go ahead. Just keep the window rolled down."

"Much obliged." A match flared. There were eager sucking sounds.

"Let's hear it," Pete said.

"I am by training an engineer," Webster began. "My work has exposed me to all but one of the continents, to desert and alp and forest, to every terrain and season of the earth. Some years ago I was hired by the Peruvian government to search for tungsten in the tropics. My wife and daughter accompanied me. We were the only white people for a thousand miles in any direction, and we had no choice but to live as the Indians lived—to share their food and drink and even their culture."

Pete said, "You knew the lingo, did you?"

"We picked it up." The ember of the cigar bobbed up and down. "We were used to learning as necessity decreed. At any rate, it became evident after a couple of years that there was no tungsten to be found. My wife had fallen ill and was pleading to be taken home. But I was deaf to her pleas, because by then I was on the trail of another metal—a metal far more valuable than tungsten."

"Let me guess," Pete said. "Gold?"

Donald looked at Pete, then back at Webster.

"Gold," Webster said. "A vein of gold greater than the Mother Lode itself. After I found the first traces of it nothing could tear me away from my search—not the sickness of my wife nor anything else. I was determined to uncover the vein, and so I did—but not before I laid my wife to rest. As I say, the earth will be repaid."

Webster was quiet. Then he said, "But life must go on. In the years since my wife's death I have been making the arrangements necessary to open the mine. I could have done it immediately, of course, enriching myself beyond measure, but I knew what that would mean—the exploitation of our beloved Indians, the brutal destruction of their environment. I felt I had too much to atone for already." Webster paused, and when he spoke again his voice was dull and rushed, as if he had used up all the interest he had in his own words. "Instead I drew up a program for returning the bulk of the wealth to the Indians themselves. A kind of trust fund. The interest alone will allow them to secure their ancient lands and rights in perpetuity. At the same time, our investors will be rewarded a thousandfold. Two-thousandfold. Everyone will prosper together."

"That's great," Donald said. "That's the way it ought to be."

Pete said, "I'm willing to bet that you just happen to have a few shares left. Am I right?"

Webster made no reply.

"Well?" Pete knew that Webster was on to him now, but he didn't care. The story had bored him. He'd expected something different, something original, and Webster had let him down. He hadn't even tried. Pete felt sour and stale. His eyes burned from cigar smoke and the high beams of road-hogging truckers. "Douse the stogie," he said to Webster. "I told you to keep the window down."

"Got a little nippy back here."

Donald said, "Hey, Pete. Lighten up."

"Douse it!"

Webster sighed. He got rid of the cigar.

"I'm a wreck," Pete said to Donald. "You want to drive for a while?"

Donald nodded.

Pete pulled over and they changed places.

Webster kept his counsel in the back seat. Donald hummed while he drove, until Pete told him to stop. Then everything was quiet.

Donald was humming again when Pete woke up. Pete stared sullenly at the road, at the white lines sliding past the car. After a few moments of this he turned and said, "How long have I been out?"

Donald glanced at him. "Twenty, twenty-five minutes."

Pete looked behind him and saw that Webster was gone. "Where's our friend?"

"You just missed him. He got out in Soledad. He told me to say thanks and good-bye."

"Soledad? What about his sick daughter? How did he explain her away?" Pete leaned over the seat: Both ashtrays were still in place. Floor mats. Door handles.

"He has a brother living there. He's going to borrow a car from him and drive the rest of the way in the morning."

"I'll bet his brother's living there," Pete said. "Doing fifty concurrent life sentences. His brother and his sister and his mom and his dad."

"I kind of liked him," Donald said.

"I'm sure you did," Pete said wearily.

"He was interesting. He'd been places."

"His cigars had been places, I'll give you that."

"Come on, Pete."

"Come on yourself. What a phony."

"You don't know that."

"Sure I do."

"How? How do you know?"

Pete stretched. "Brother, there are some things you're just born knowing. What's the gas situation?"

"We're a little low."

"Then why didn't you get some more?"

"I wish you wouldn't snap at me like that," Donald said.

"Then why don't you use your head? What if we run out?"

"We'll make it," Donald said. "I'm pretty sure we've got enough to make it. You didn't have to be so rude to him," Donald added.

Pete took a deep breath. "I don't feel like running out of gas tonight, OK?"

Donald pulled in at the next station they came to and filled the tank while Pete went to the men's room. When Pete came back, Donald was sitting in the passenger's seat. The attendant came up to the driver's window as Pete got in behind the wheel. He bent down and said, "Twelve fifty-five."

"You heard the man,"Pete said to Donald.

Donald looked straight ahead. He didn't move.

"Cough up," Pete said. "This trip's on you."

Donald said, softly, "I can't."

"Sure you can. Break out that wad."

Donald glanced up at the attendant, then at Pete. "Please," he said. "Pete, I don't have it anymore."

Pete took this in. He nodded, and paid the attendant.

Donald began to speak when they left the station but Pete cut him off. He said, "I don't want to hear from you right now. You just keep quiet or I swear to God I won't be responsible."

They left the fields and entered a tunnel of tall trees. The trees went on and on. "Let me get this straight," Pete said at last. "You don't have the money I gave you."

"You treated him like a bug or something," Donald said.

"You don't have the money," Pete said again.

Donald shook his head.

"Since I bought dinner, and since we didn't stop anywhere in between, I assume you gave it to Webster. Is that right? Is that what you did with it?"

"Yes."

Pete looked at Donald. His face was dark under the hood but he still managed to convey a sense of remove, as if none of this had anything to do with him.

"Why?" Pete asked. "Why did you give it to him?" When Donald didn't answer, Pete said, "A hundred dollars. Gone. Just like that. I worked for that money, Donald."

"I know, I know," Donald said.

"You don't know! How could you? You get money by holding out your hand."

"I work too," Donald said.

"You work too. Don't kid yourself, brother."

Donald leaned toward Pete, about to say something, but Pete cut him off again.

"You're not the only one on the payroll, Donald. I don't think you understand that. I have a family."

"Pete, I'll pay you back."

"Like hell you will. A hundred dollars!" Pete hit the steering wheel with the palm of his hand. "Just because you think I hurt some goofball's feelings. Jesus, Donald."

"That's not the reason," Donald said. "And I didn't just *give* him the money."

"What do you call it, then? What do you call what you did?"

"I *invested* it. I wanted a share, Pete." When Pete looked over at him Donald nodded and said again, "I wanted a share."

Pete said "I take it you're referring to the gold mine in Peru."

"Yes," Donald said.

"You believe that such a gold mine exists?"

Donald looked at Pete, and Pete could see him just beginning to catch on. "You'll believe anything," Pete said. "Won't you? You really will believe anything at all."

"I'm sorry," Donald said, and turned away.

Pete drove on between the trees and considered the truth of what he had just said—that Donald would believe anything at all. And it came to him that it would be just like this unfair life for Donald to come out ahead in the end, by believing in some outrageous promise that would turn out to be true and that he, Pete, would reject out of hand because he was too wised up to listen to anybody's pitch anymore except for laughs. What a joke. What a joke if there really was a blessing to be had, and the blessing didn't come to the one who deserved it, the one who did all the work, but to the other.

And as if this had already happened Pete felt a shadow move upon him, darkening his thoughts. After a time he said, "I can see where all this is going, Donald."

"I'll pay you back," Donald said.

"No," Pete said. "You won't pay me back. You can't. You don't know how. All you've ever done is take. All your life."

Donald shook his head.

"I see exactly where this is going," Pete went on. "You can't work, you can't take care of yourself, you believe anything anyone tells you, I'm stuck with you, aren't I?" He looked over at Donald. "I've got you on my hands for good."

Donald pressed his fingers against the dashboard as if to brace himself. "I'll get out," he said.

Pete kept driving.

"Let me out," Donald said. "I mean it, Pete."

"Do you?"

Donald hesitated. "Yes," he said.

"Be sure," Pete told him. "This is it. This is for keeps."

"I mean it."

"All right. You made the choice." Pete braked the car sharply and swung it to the shoulder of the road. He turned off the engine and got out. Trees loomed on both sides, shutting out the sky. The air was cold and musty. Pete took Donald's duffel bag from the back seat and set it down behind the car. He stood there, facing Donald in the red glow of the taillights. "It's better this way," Pete said.

Donald just looked at him.

"Better for you," Pete said.

Donald hugged himself. He was shaking. "You don't have to say all that," he told Pete. "I don't blame you."

"Blame me? What the hell are you talking about? Blame me for what?"

"For anything," Donald said.

"I want to know what you mean by blame me."

"Nothing. Nothing, Pete. You'd better get going. God bless you."

"That's it," Pete said. He dropped to one knee, searching the packed dirt with his hands. He didn't know what he was looking for; his hands would know when they found it.

Donald touched Pete's shoulder. "You'd better go," he said.

Somewhere in the trees Pete heard a branch snap. He stood up. He looked at Donald, then went back to the car and drove away. He drove fast, hunched over the wheel, conscious of the way he was hunched and the shallowness of his breathing, refusing to look at the mirror above his head until there was nothing behind him but darkness.

Then he said, "A hundred dollars," as if there were someone to hear.

The trees gave way to fields. Metal fences ran beside the road, plastered with windblown scraps of paper. Tule fog hung above the ditches, spilling into the road, dimming the ghostly halogen lights that burned in the yards of the farms Pete passed. The fog left beads of water rolling up the windshield.

Pete rummaged among his cassettes. He found Pachelbel's Canon and pushed it into the tape deck. When the violins began to play he leaned back and assumed an attentive expression as if he were really listening to them. He smiled to himself like a man at liberty to enjoy music, a man who has finished his work and settled his debts, done all things meet and due.

And in this way, smiling, nodding to the music, he went another mile or so and pretended that he was not already slowing down, that he was not going to turn back, that he would be able to drive on like this, alone, and have the right answer when his wife stood before him in the doorway of his home and asked, Where is he? Where is your brother?

TOBIAS WOLFF

Bullet in the Brain

Anders couldn't get to the bank until just before it closed, so of course the line was endless and he got stuck behind two women whose loud, stupid conversation put him in a murderous temper. He was never in the best of tempers anyway, Anders—a book critic known for the weary, elegant savagery with which he dispatched almost everything he reviewed.

With the line still doubled around the rope, one of the tellers stuck a "POSITION CLOSED" sign in her window and walked to the back of the bank, where she leaned against a desk and began to pass the time with a man shuffling papers. The women in front of Anders broke off their conversation and watched the teller with hatred. "Oh, that's nice," one of them said. She turned to Anders and added, confident of his accord, "One of those little human touches that keep us coming back for more."

Anders had conceived his own towering hatred of the teller, but he immediately turned it on the presumptuous crybaby in front of him. "Damned unfair," he said. "Tragic, really. If they're not chopping off the wrong leg, or bombing your ancestral village, they're closing their positions."

She stood her ground. "I didn't say it was tragic," she said. "I just think it's a pretty lousy way to treat your customers."

"Unforgivable," Anders said. "Heaven will take note."

She sucked in her cheeks but stared past him and said nothing. Anders saw that the other woman, her friend, was looking in the same direction. And then the tellers stopped what they were doing, and the customers slowly turned, and silence came over the bank. Two men wearing black ski masks and blue business suits were standing to the side of the door. One of them had a pistol pressed against the guard's neck. The guard's eyes were closed, and his lips were moving. The other man had a sawed-off shotgun. "Keep your big mouth shut!" the man with the pistol said, though no one had spoken a word. "One of you tellers hits the alarm, you're all dead meat. Got it?"

The tellers nodded.

"Oh, bravo," Anders said. "*Dead meat.*" He turned to the woman in front of him. "Great script, eh? The stern, brass-knuckled poetry of the dangerous classes."

She looked at him with drowning eyes.

The man with the shotgun pushed the guard to his knees. He handed the shotgun to his partner and yanked the guard's wrists up behind his back and locked them together with a pair of handcuffs. He toppled him onto the floor with a kick between the shoulder blades. Then he took his shotgun back and went over to the security gate at the end of the counter. He was short and heavy and moved with peculiar slowness, even torpor. "Buzz him in," his partner said. The man with the shotgun opened the gate and sauntered along the line of tellers, handing each of them a Hefty bag. When he came to the empty position he looked over at the man with the pistol, who said, "Whose slot is that?"

Anders watched the teller. She put her hand to her throat and turned to the man she'd been talking to. He nodded. "Mine," she said.

"Then get your ugly ass in gear and fill that bag."

"There you go," Anders said to the woman in front of him. "Justice is done."

"Hey! Bright boy! Did I tell you to talk?"

"No," Anders said.

"Then shut your trap."

"Did you hear that?" Anders said. "'Bright boy.' Right out of 'The Killers.'"

"Please be quiet," the woman said.

"Hey, you deaf or what?" The man with the pistol walked over to Anders. He poked the weapon into Anders' gut. "You think I'm playing games?"

"No," Anders said, but the barrel tickled like a stiff finger and he had to fight back the titters. He did this by making himself stare into the man's eyes, which were clearly visible behind the holes in the mask: pale blue and rawly red-rimmed. The man's left eyelid kept twitching. He breathed out a piercing, ammoniac smell that shocked Anders more than anything that had happened, and he was beginning to develop a sense of unease when the man prodded him again with the pistol.

"You like me, bright boy?" he said. "You want to suck my dick?"

"No," Anders said.

"Then stop looking at me."

Anders fixed his gaze on the man's shiny wing-tip shoes.

"Not down there. Up there." He stuck the pistol under Anders' chin and pushed it upward until Anders was looking at the ceiling.

Anders had never paid much attention to that part of the bank, a pompous old building with marble floors and counters and pillars, and gilt scrollwork over the tellers' cages. The domed ceiling had been decorated with mythological figures whose fleshy, toga-draped ugliness Anders had taken in at a glance many years earlier and afterward declined to notice. Now he had no choice but to scrutinize the painter's work. It was even worse than he remembered, and all of it executed with the utmost gravity. The artist had a few tricks up his sleeve and used them again and again—a certain rosy blush on the underside of the clouds, a coy backward glance on the faces of the cupids and fauns. The ceiling was crowded with various dramas, but the one that caught Anders' eye was Zeus and Europa—portrayed, in this rendition, as a bull ogling a cow from behind a haystack. To make the cow sexy, the painter had canted her hips suggestively and given her long, droopy eyelashes through which she gazed back at the bull with sultry welcome. The bull wore a smirk and his eyebrows were arched. If there'd been a bubble coming out of his mouth, it would have said, "Hubba hubba."

"What's so funny, bright boy?"

"Nothing."

"You think I'm comical? You think I'm some kind of clown?"

"No."

"You think you can fuck with me?"

"No."

"Fuck with me again, you're history. *Capiche?*"

Anders burst out laughing. He covered his mouth with both hands and said, "I'm sorry, I'm sorry," then snorted helplessly through his fingers and said, "*Capiche*—oh,

God, *capiche,*" and at that the man with the pistol raised the pistol and shot Anders right in the head.

The bullet smashed Anders' skull and ploughed through his brain and exited behind his right ear, scattering shards of bone into the cerebral cortex, the corpus callosum, back toward the basal ganglia, and down into the thalamus. But before all this occurred, the first appearance of the bullet in the cerebrum set off a crackling chain of ion transports and neuro-transmissions. Because of their peculiar origin these traced a peculiar pattern, flukishly calling to life a summer afternoon some forty years past, and long since lost to memory. After striking the cranium the bullet was moving at 900 feet per second, a pathetically sluggish, glacial pace compared to the synaptic lightning that flashed around it. Once in the brain, that is, the bullet came under the mediation of brain time, which gave Anders plenty of leisure to contemplate the scene that, in a phrase he would have abhorred, "passed before his eyes."

It is worth noting what Anders did not remember, given what he did remember. He did not remember his first lover, Sherry, or what he had most madly loved about her, before it came to irritate him—her unembarrassed carnality, and especially the cordial way she had with his unit, which she called Mr. Mole, as in, "Uh-oh, looks like Mr. Mole wants to play," and, "Let's hide Mr. Mole!" Anders did not remember his wife, whom he had also loved before she exhausted him with her predictability, or his daughter, now a sullen professor of economics at Dartmouth. He did not remember standing just outside his daughter's door as she lectured her bear about his naughtiness and described the truly appalling punishments Paws would receive unless he changed his ways. He did not remember a single line of the hundreds of poems he had committed to memory in his youth so that he could give himself the shivers at will—not "Silent, upon a peak in Darien," or "My God, I heard this day," or "All my pretty ones? Did you say all? O hell-kite! All?" None of these did he remember; not one. Anders did not remember his dying mother saying of his father, "I should have stabbed him in his sleep."

He did not remember Professor Josephs telling his class how Athenian prisoners in Sicily had been released if they could recite Aeschylus, and then reciting Aeschylus himself, right there, in the Greek. Anders did not remember how his eyes had burned at those sounds. He did not remember the surprise of seeing a college classmate's name on the jacket of a novel not long after they graduated, or the respect he had felt after reading the book. He did not remember the pleasure of giving respect.

Nor did Anders remember seeing a woman leap to her death from the building opposite his own just days after his daughter was born. He did not remember shouting, "Lord have mercy!" He did not remember deliberately crashing his father's car into a tree, or having his ribs kicked in by three policemen at an anti-war rally, or waking himself up with laughter. He did not remember when he began to regard the heap of books on his desk with boredom and dread, or when he grew angry at writers for writing them. He did not remember when everything began to remind him of something else.

This is what he remembered. Heat. A baseball field. Yellow grass, the whirr of insects, himself leaning against a tree as the boys of the neighborhood gather for a pickup game. He looks on as the others argue the relative genius of Mantle and Mays. They have been worrying this subject all summer, and it has become tedious to Anders: an oppression, like the heat.

Then the last two boys arrive, Coyle and a cousin of his from Mississippi. Anders has never met Coyle's cousin before and will never see him again. He says hi with the rest but takes no further notice of him until they've chosen sides and someone asks the cousin what position he wants to play. "Shortstop," the boy says. "Short's the best position they is." Anders turns and looks at him. He wants to hear Coyle's cousin repeat what he's just said, but he knows better than to ask. The others will think he's being a jerk, ragging the kid for his grammar. But that isn't it, not at all—it's that Anders is strangely roused, elated, by those final two words, their pure unexpectedness and their music. He takes the field in a trance, repeating them to himself.

The bullet is already in the brain; it won't be outrun forever, or charmed to a halt. In the end it will do its work and leave the troubled skull behind, dragging its comet's tail of memory and hope and talent and love into the marble hall of commerce. That can't be helped. But for now Anders can still make time. Time for the shadows to lengthen on the grass, time for the tethered dog to bark at the flying ball, time for the boy in right field to smack his sweat-blackened mitt and softly chant, *They is, they is, they is.*

Richard Yates (1926–1992)

was born in Yonkers, New York. He served in World War II and spent the rest of his life in and out of hospitals as he dealt with a near-debilitating chronic pleurisy. He worked for many years as a financial reporter and a public relations flack for Remington Rand before he started to get his fiction published. Stories from his collections Eleven Kinds of Loneliness *and* Liars in Love *appeared regularly in such magazines as* Ploughshares *and* The Atlantic Monthly. *His best-known and most highly regarded novel is* Revolutionary Road, *which Kurt Vonnegut called* "The Great Gatsby *of my time." He worked as a screenwriter (his most noteworthy project was a never-filmed adaptation of his friend William Styron's novel* Lie Down in Darkness*) and held several teaching positions, including many years at the Iowa Writers' Workshop. In the 1960s, Yates worked as a speechwriter for Robert Kennedy, and Yates was working on a novel about that experience—called* Uncertain Times—*at the time of his death in Birmingham, Alabama. The book remains unfinished and unpublished. In the late 1990s, Yates's entire body of work fell out of print, but the efforts of contemporary writers such as Stewart O'Nan, Richard Ford, and Richard Russo helped to bring the books back in new editions.* The Collected Stories of Richard Yates, *which includes all the stories in the two previous collections plus nine others that had never appeared in a book, was published in 2001.*

INTRODUCTION BY **Stewart O'Nan**

In his novels and stories, Richard Yates paints an unsparing, antiheroic picture of American life. Yates's subject, like his idol Fitzgerald's, is failure, but unleavened by either Fitzgerald's linguistic brilliance or his preoccupation with the romance of luxury. Yates's people are working-class with hopes of rising higher, hopes spurred on by society's constant broadcasting of what seems a reachable if materialistic American Dream: love, family, professional accomplishment, financial security. Just how brutally reality disposes of their hopes provides the story line.

Though Yates wrote well into the 1980s, his finest work chronicles the uneasy transition from the World War II years through the mid-1950s. In that age of affluence and anxiety, his vision of young and insecure Americans coming to grips with their less-than-ideal lives presages the fiction of Raymond Carver, Tobias Wolff, and Andre Dubus (the last a student of his at the Iowa Writers' Workshop).

Yates is most at home with unexceptional characters, people on the fringes still aspiring to conventional success—lonely shopgirls and troubled kids, tubercular patients and disgruntled vets. No matter how downtrodden his people are, they want to believe in their own unrecognized promise. Yates lays out the bitterness that follows their losses and reveals their complicity in those disappointments, their most cherished pretensions leading them astray. His little characters dream big, all the time fearing that they are impostors, terrified of being found out. And the world does strip them of their illusions, again and again, sometimes cruelly. Middle-class life is spiritually vacant and economically precarious, the promises America makes are hollow, yet Yates's people still chase after their impossible, often secondhand ideals.

In his signature piece, "The Best of Everything," two young lovers realize that their impending marriage won't solve their problems—in all probability, it will only add to them. Yates's language is stripped down, his tone—like their lives—flat and emotionless: "She tried to sound excited, but it wasn't easy." "Somehow, he'd expected more of the Friday before his wedding." That vague sense of letdown colors the story a dingy gray. The characters' mix of hope and resignation is unsettling yet rings true.

The worn-down characters, ping-pong dialogue, and flattened narration in "No Pain Whatsoever" could be lifted from a Raymond Carver story except for the sense of a long, unspoken history behind Myra's visit to the TB ward. This is the hard-luck world of Carver but without his goofy grim humor. It's a world that is purposefully not quirky or picturesque, just plain and sad and inescapable, and in the very end, rather than editorializing on Myra's situation, Yates wisely lets her last line of dialogue speak for itself.

"Oh, Joseph, I'm So Tired" is a later story, written in the mid-1970s, and finds Yates uncharacteristically using a first-person narrator looking back on his prewar childhood. The effect is warmer as well as more complex than his typical third-person omniscience. Here Yates deals with the same basic broken family unit that he features in several of his later novels—the dreamy, unreliable divorcee and her trapped and unhappy children—though the focus is still on the discrepancy between reality and the false promises of Wall Street and Hollywood and the consequences when people fall for the fleeting illusions of romantic love and money and fame.

Though Yates's work is always realistic, he despised the realist label that critics hung on him. In the experimental 1960s and 1970s, when metafiction and its formalist tricks were in vogue, hip critics and readers considered him old-fashioned, hopelessly behind the times, only to hail him in the 1980s as the father of the new realism (though the similarities between his work and the then-reigning minimalists are cosmetic at best). All the while, Yates had been writing the same lucid, straight-ahead prose, staying close to his people in their movement from innocence through hard experience to disillusion. Deceptively conservative in style, his work remains subversive, casting doubt, as it does, on our own most intimate hopes.

Stewart O'Nan's story collection In The Walled City *was chosen for the 1993 Drue Heinz Prize by Tobias Wolff. His many novels include* Snow Angels, A Prayer for the Dying, *and* Wish You Were Here.

RICHARD YATES

The Best of Everything

Nobody expected Grace to do any work the Friday before her wedding. In fact, nobody would let her, whether she wanted to or not.

A gardenia corsage lay in a cellophane box beside her typewriter—from Mr. Atwood, her boss—and tucked inside the envelope that came with it was a ten-dollar gift certificate from Bloomingdale's. Mr. Atwood had treated her with a special shy courtliness ever since the time she necked with him at the office Christmas party, and now when she went in to thank him he was all hunched over, rattling desk drawers, blushing and grinning and barely meeting her eyes.

"Aw, now, don't mention it, Grace," he said. "Pleasure's all mine. Here, you need a pin to put that gadget on with?"

"There's a pin that came with it," she said, holding up the corsage. "See? A nice white one."

Beaming, he watched her pin the flowers high on the lapel of her suit. Then he cleared his throat importantly and pulled out the writing panel of his desk, ready to give the morning's dictation. But it turned out there were only two short letters, and it wasn't until an hour later, when she caught him handing over a pile of Dictaphone cylinders to Central Typing, that she realized he had done her a favor.

"That's very sweet of you, Mr. Atwood," she said, "but I do think you ought to give me all your work today, just like any oth—"

"Aw, now, Grace," he said. "You only get married once."

The girls all made a fuss over her too, crowding around her desk and giggling, asking again and again to see Ralph's photograph ("Oh, he's *cute!*"), while the office manager looked on nervously, reluctant to be a spoilsport but anxious to point out that it was, after all, a working day.

Then at lunch there was the traditional little party at Schrafft's—nine women and girls, giddy on their unfamiliar cocktails, letting their chicken à la king grow cold while they pummeled her with old times and good wishes. There were more flowers and another gift—a silver candy dish for which all the girls had whisperingly chipped in.

Grace said "Thank you" and "I certainly do appreciate it" and "I don't know what to say" until her head rang with the words and the corners of her mouth ached from smiling, and she thought the afternoon would never end.

Ralph called up about four o'clock, exuberant. "How ya doin', honey?" he asked, and before she could answer he said, "Listen. Guess what I got?"

"I don't know. A present or something? What?" She tried to sound excited, but it wasn't easy.

"A bonus. Fifty dollars." She could almost see the flattening of his lips as he said "fifty dollars" with the particular earnestness he reserved for pronouncing sums of money.

"Why, that's lovely, Ralph," she said, and if there was any tiredness in her voice he didn't notice it.

"Lovely, huh?" he said with a laugh, mocking the girlishness of the word. "Ya *like* that, huh Gracie? No, but I mean I was really surprised, ya know it? The boss siz, 'Here, Ralph,' and he hands me this envelope. He don't even crack a smile or nothin', and I'm wonderin', what's the deal here? I'm getting fired here, or what? He siz, 'G'ahead, Ralph, open it.' So I open it, and then I look at the boss and he's grinning a mile wide." He chuckled and sighed. "Well, so listen, honey. What time ya want me to come over tonight?"

"Oh, I don't know. Soon as you can, I guess."

"Well listen, I gotta go over to Eddie's house and pick up that bag he's gonna loan me, so I might as well do that, go on home and eat, and then come over to your place around eight-thirty, nine o'clock. Okay?"

"All right," she said. "I'll see you then, darling." She had been calling him "darling" for only a short time—since it had become irrevocably clear that she was, after all, going to marry him—and the word still had an alien sound. As she straightened the stacks of stationery in her desk (because there was nothing else to do), a familiar little panic gripped her: she couldn't marry him—she hardly even knew him. Sometimes it occurred to her differently, that she couldn't marry him because she knew him too well, and either way it left her badly shaken, vulnerable to all the things that Martha, her roommate, had said from the very beginning.

"Isn't he funny?" Martha had said after their first date. "He says 'terlet.' I didn't know people really said 'terlet.'" And Grace had giggled, ready enough to agree that it *was* funny. That was a time when she had been ready to agree with Martha on practically anything—when it often seemed, in fact, that finding a girl like Martha from an ad in the *Times* was just about the luckiest thing that had ever happened to her.

But Ralph had persisted all through the summer, and by fall she had begun standing up for him. "What don't you *like* about him, Martha? He's perfectly nice."

"Oh, everybody's perfectly nice, Grace," Martha would say in her college voice, making perfectly nice a faintly absurd thing to be, and then she'd look up crossly from the careful painting of her fingernails. "It's just that he's such a little—a little *white worm.* Can't you see that?"

"Well, I certainly don't see what his *complexion* has to do with—"

"Oh God, *you* know what I mean. Can't you see what I *mean?* Oh, and all those friends of his, his Eddie and his Marty and his George with their mean, ratty little clerks' lives and their mean, ratty little. . . . It's just that they're all *alike,* those people. All they ever say is 'Hey, wha' happen t'ya Giants?' and 'Hey, wha' happen t'ya Yankees?' and they all live way out in Sunnyside or Woodhaven or some awful place, and their mothers have those damn little china elephants on the mantelpiece." And Martha would frown over her nail polish again, making it clear that the subject was closed.

All that fall and winter she was confused. For a while she tried going out only with Martha's kind of men—the kind that used words like "amusing" all the time and wore small-shouldered flannel suits like a uniform; and for a while she tried going out with no men at all. She even tried that crazy business with Mr. Atwood at the office Christmas party. And all the time Ralph kept calling up, hanging around, waiting for her to make up her mind. Once she took him home to meet her parents in

Pennsylvania (where she never would have dreamed of taking Martha), but it wasn't until Easter time that she finally gave in.

They had gone to a dance somewhere in Queens, one of the big American Legion dances that Ralph's crowd was always going to, and when the band played "Easter Parade" he held her very close, hardly moving, and sang to her in a faint, whispering tenor. It was the kind of thing she'd never have expected Ralph to do—a sweet, gentle thing—and it probably wasn't just then that she decided to marry him, but it always seemed so afterwards. It always seemed she had decided that minute, swaying to the music with his husky voice in her hair:

"I'll be all in clover
And when they look you over
I'll be the proudest fella
In the Easter Parade. . . ."

That night she had told Martha, and she could still see the look on Martha's face. "Oh, Grace, you're not—surely you're not *serious.* I mean, I thought he was more or less of a *joke*—you can't really mean you want to—"

"Shut up! You just shut up, Martha!" And she'd cried all night. Even now she hated Martha for it; even as she stared blindly at a row of filing cabinets along the office wall, half sick with fear that Martha was right.

The noise of giggles swept over her, and she saw with a start that two of the girls—Irene and Rose—were grinning over their typewriters and pointing at her. "*We* saw ya!" Irene sang. "*We* saw ya! Mooning again, huh Grace?" Then Rose did a burlesque of mooning, heaving her meager breasts and batting her eyes, and they both collapsed in laughter.

With an effort of will Grace resumed the guileless, open smile of a bride. The thing to do was concentrate on plans.

Tomorrow morning, "bright and early," as her mother would say, she would meet Ralph at Penn Station for the trip home. They'd arrive about one, and her parents would meet the train. "Good t'see ya, Ralph!" her father would say, and her mother would probably kiss him. A warm, homely love filled her: *they* wouldn't call him a white worm; *they* didn't have any ideas about Princeton men and "interesting" men and all the other kinds of men Martha was so stuck-up about. Then her father would probably take Ralph out for a beer and show him the paper mill where he worked (and at least Ralph wouldn't be snobby about a person working in a paper mill, either), and then Ralph's family and friends would come down from New York in the evening.

She'd have time for a long talk with her mother that night, and the next morning, "bright and early" (her eyes stung at the thought of her mother's plain, happy face), they would start getting dressed for the wedding. Then the church and the ceremony, and then the reception (Would her father get drunk? Would Muriel Ketchel sulk about not being a bridesmaid?), and finally the train to Atlantic City, and the hotel. But from the hotel on she couldn't plan any more. A door would lock behind her and there would be a wild, fantastic silence, and nobody in all the world but Ralph to lead the way.

"Well, Grace," Mr. Atwood was saying, "I want to wish you every happiness." He was standing at her desk with his hat and coat on, and all around here were the chattering and scraping-back of chairs that meant it was five o'clock.

"Thank you, Mr. Atwood." She got to her feet, suddenly surrounded by all the girls in a bedlam of farewell.

"All the luck in the world, Grace."

"Drop us a card, huh Grace? From Atlantic City?"

"So long, Grace."

"G'night, Grace, and listen: the best of everything."

Finally she was free of them all, out of the elevator, out of the building, hurrying through the crowds to the subway.

When she got home Martha was standing in the door of the kitchenette, looking very svelte in a crisp new dress.

"Hi, Grace. I bet they ate you alive today, didn't they?"

"Oh no," Grace said. "Everybody was—real nice." She sat down, exhausted, and dropped the flowers and the wrapped candy dish on a table. Then she noticed that the whole apartment was swept and dusted, and the dinner was cooking in the kitchenette. "Gee, everything looks wonderful," she said. "What'd you do all this for?"

"Oh, well, I got home early anyway," Martha said. Then she smiled, and it was one of the few times Grace had ever seen her look shy. "I just thought it might be nice to have the place looking decent for a change, when Ralph comes over."

"Well," Grace said, "it certainly was nice of you."

The way Martha looked now was even more surprising: she looked awkward. She was turning a greasy spatula in her fingers, holding it delicately away from her dress and examining it, as if she had something difficult to say. "Look, Grace," she began. "You do understand why I can't come to the wedding, don't you?"

"Oh, sure," Grace said, although in fact she didn't, exactly. It was something about having to go up to Harvard to see her brother before he went into the Army, but it had sounded like a lie from the beginning.

"It's just that I'd hate you to think I—well, anyway, I'm glad if you do understand. And the other thing I wanted to say is more important."

"What?"

"Well, just that I'm sorry for all the awful things I used to say about Ralph. I never had a right to talk to you that way. He's a very sweet boy and I—well, I'm sorry, that's all."

It wasn't easy for Grace to hide a rush of gratitude and relief when she said, "Why, that's all right, Martha, I—"

"The chops are on fire!" Martha bolted for the kitchenette. "It's all right," she called back. "They're edible." And when she came out to serve dinner all her old composure was restored. "I'll have to eat and run," she said as they sat down. "My train leaves in forty minutes."

"I thought it was *tomorrow* you were going."

"Well, it was, actually," Martha said, "but I decided to go tonight. Because you see, Grace, another thing—if you can stand one more apology—another thing I'm sorry for is that I've hardly ever given you and Ralph a chance to be alone here. So tonight I'm going to clear out." She hesitated. "It'll be a sort of wedding gift from me, okay?" And then she smiled, not shyly this time but in a way that was more in character—the eyes subtly averted after a flicker of special meaning. It was a smile that Grace—through stages of suspicion, bewilderment, awe, and practiced imitation—had long ago come to associate with the word "sophisticated."

"Well, that's very sweet of you," Grace said, but she didn't really get the point just then. It wasn't until long after the meal was over and the dishes washed, until Martha had left for her train in a whirl of cosmetics and luggage and quick goodbyes, that she began to understand.

She took a deep, voluptuous bath and spent a long time drying herself, posing in the mirror, filled with a strange, slow excitement. In her bedroom, from the rustling tissues of an expensive white box, she drew the prizes of her trousseau—a sheer nightgown of white nylon and a matching negligee—put them on, and went to the mirror again. She had never worn anything like this before, or felt like this, and the thought of letting Ralph see her like this sent her into the kitchenette for a glass of the special dry sherry Martha kept for cocktail parties. Then she turned out all the lights but one and, carrying her glass, went to the sofa and arranged herself there to wait for him. After a while she got up and brought the sherry bottle over to the coffee table, where she set it on a tray with another glass.

When Ralph left the office he felt vaguely let down. Somehow, he'd expected more of the Friday before his wedding. The bonus check had been all right (though secretly he'd been counting on twice that amount), and the boys had bought him a drink at lunch and kidded around in the appropriate way ("Ah, don't feel too bad, Ralph—worse things could happen"), but still, there ought to have been a real party. Not just the boys in the office, but Eddie, and *all* his friends. Instead there would only be meeting Eddie at the White Rose like every other night of the year, and riding home to borrow Eddie's suitcase and to eat, and then having to ride all the way back to Manhattan just to see Gracie for an hour or two. Eddie wasn't in the bar when he arrived, which sharpened the edge of his loneliness. Morosely he drank a beer, waiting.

Eddie was his best friend, and an ideal best man because he'd been in on the courtship of Gracie from the start. It was in this very bar, in fact, that Ralph had told him about their first date last summer: "Ooh, Eddie—what a paira *knockers!*"

And Eddie had grinned. "Yeah? So what's the roommate like?"

"Ah, you don't want the roommate, Eddie. The roommate's a dog. A snob, too, I think. No, but this *other* one, this little Gracie—boy, I mean, she is *stacked.*"

Half the fun of every date—even more than half—had been telling Eddie about it afterwards, exaggerating a little here and there, asking Eddie's advice on tactics. But after today, like so many other pleasures, it would all be left behind. Gracie had promised him at least one night off a week to spend with the boys, after they were married, but even so it would never be the same. Girls never understood a thing like friendship.

There was a ball game on the bar's television screen and he watched it idly, his throat swelling in a sentimental pain of loss. Nearly all his life had been devoted to the friendship of boys and men, to trying to be a good guy, and now the best of it was over.

Finally Eddie's stiff finger jabbed the seat of his pants in greeting. "Whaddya say, sport?"

Ralph narrowed his eyes to indolent contempt and slowly turned around. "Wha' happen ta you, wise guy? Get lost?"

"Whaddya—in a hurry a somethin'?" Eddie barely moved his lips when he spoke. "Can't wait two minutes?" He slouched on a stool and slid a quarter at the bartender. "Draw one, there, Jack."

They drank in silence for a while, staring at the television.

"Got a little bonus today," Ralph said. "Fifty dollars."

"Yeah?" Eddie said. "Good."

A batter struck out; the inning was over and the commercial came on. "So?" Eddie said, rocking the beer around in his glass. "Still gonna get married?"

"Why not?" Ralph said with a shrug. "Listen, finish that, willya? I wanna get a move on."

"Wait awhile, wait awhile. What's ya hurry?"

"C'mon, willya?" Ralph stepped impatiently away from the bar. "I wanna go pick up ya bag."

"Ah, bag schmagg."

Ralph moved up close again and glowered at him. "Look, wise guy. Nobody's gonna *make* ya loan me the goddamn bag, ya know. I don't wanna break ya *heart* or nothin'—"

"Arright, arright, arright. You'll getcha bag. Don't worry so much." He finished the beer and wiped his mouth. "Let's go."

Having to borrow a bag for his wedding trip was a sore point with Ralph; he'd much rather have bought one of his own. There was a fine one displayed in the window of a luggage shop they passed every night on their way to the subway—a big, tawny Gladstone with a zippered compartment on the side, at thirty-nine ninety-five—and Ralph had had his eye on it ever since Easter time. "Think I'll buy that," he'd told Eddie, in the same offhand way that a day or so before he had announced his engagement ("Think I'll marry the girl"). Eddie's response to both remarks had been the same: "Whaddya—crazy?" Both times Ralph had said, "Why not?" and in defense of the bag he had added, "Gonna get married, I'll *need* somethin' like that." From then on it was as if the bag, almost as much as Gracie herself, had become a symbol of the new and richer life he sought. But after the ring and the new clothes and all the other expenses, he'd found at last that he couldn't afford it; he had settled for the loan of Eddie's, which was similar but cheaper and worn, and without the zippered compartment.

Now as they passed the luggage shop he stopped, caught in the grip of a reckless idea. "Hey wait awhile, Eddie. Know what I think I'll do with that fifty-dollar bonus? I think I'll buy that bag right now." He felt breathless.

"Whaddya—crazy? Forty bucks for a bag you'll use maybe one time a year? Ya crazy, Ralph. C'mon."

"Ah—I dunno. Ya think so?"

"Listen, you better *keep* ya money, boy. You're gonna *need* it."

"Ah—yeah," Ralph said at last. "I guess ya right." And he fell in step with Eddie again, heading for the subway. This was the way things usually turned out in his life; he could never own a bag like that until he made a better salary, and he accepted it—just as he'd accepted without question, after the first thin sigh, the knowledge that he'd never possess his bride until after the wedding.

The subway swallowed them, rattled and banged them along in a rocking, mindless trance for half an hour, and disgorged them at last into the cool early evening of Queens.

Removing their coats and loosening their ties, they let the breeze dry their sweated shirts as they walked. "So what's the deal?" Eddie asked. "What time we supposed to show up in this Pennsylvania burg tomorra?"

"Ah, suit yourself," Ralph said. "Any time in the evening's okay."

"So whadda we do then? What the hell can ya do in a hillbilly town like that, anyway?"

"Ah, I dunno," Ralph said defensively. "Sit around and talk, I guess; drink beer with Gracie's old man or somethin'; I dunno."

"Jesus," Eddie said. "Some weekend. Big, big deal."

Ralph stopped on the sidewalk, suddenly enraged, his damp coat wadded in his fist. "Look, you bastid. Nobody's gonna *make* ya come, ya know—you or Marty or George or any a the rest of 'em. Get that straight. You're not doin' *me* no favors, unnastand?"

"Whatsa matta?" Eddie inquired. "Whatsa matta? Can'tcha take a joke?"

"Joke," Ralph said. "You're fulla jokes." And plodding sullenly in Eddie's wake, he felt close to tears.

They turned off into the block where they both lived, a double row of neat, identical houses bordering the street where they'd fought and loafed and played stickball all their lives. Eddie pushed open the front door of his house and ushered Ralph into the vestibule, with its homely smell of cauliflower and overshoes. "G'wan in," he said, jerking a thumb at the closed living-room door, and he hung back to let Ralph go first.

Ralph opened the door and took three steps inside before it hit him like a sock on the jaw. The room, dead silent, was packed deep with grinning, red-faced men—Marty, George, the boys from the block, the boys from the office—everybody, all his friends, all on their feet and poised motionless in a solid mass. Skinny Maguire was crouched at the upright piano, his spread fingers high over the keys, and when he struck the first rollicking chords they all roared into song, beating time with their fists, their enormous grins distorting the words:

"Fa he's a jally guh fella
Fa he's a jally guh fella
Fa he's a jally guh fell-ah
That nobody can deny!"

Weakly Ralph retreated a step on the carpet and stood there wide-eyed, swallowing, holding his coat. *"That nobody can deny!"* they sang, *"That nobody can deny!"* And as they swung into the second chorus Eddie's father appeared through the dining-room curtains, bald and beaming, in full song, with a great glass pitcher of beer in either hand. At last Skinny hammered out the final line:

"That—no—bod—dee—can—dee—nye!"

And they all surged forward cheering, grabbing Ralph's hand, pounding his arms and his back while he stood trembling, his own voice lost under the noise. "Gee, fellas—thanks. I—don't know what to—thanks, fellas. . . ."

Then the crowd cleaved in half, and Eddie made his way slowly down the middle. His eyes gleamed in a smile of love, and from his bashful hand hung the suitcase—not his own, but a new one: the big, tawny Gladstone with the zippered compartment on the side.

"Speech!" they were yelling. *"Speech! Speech!"*

But Ralph couldn't speak and couldn't smile. He could hardly even see.

At ten o'clock Grace began walking around the apartment and biting her lip. What if he wasn't coming? But of course he was coming. She sat down again and carefully smoothed the billows of nylon around her thighs, forcing herself to be calm. The whole thing would be ruined if she was nervous.

The noise of the doorbell was like an electric shock. She was halfway to the door before she stopped, breathing hard, and composed herself again. Then she pressed the buzzer and opened the door a crack to watch for him on the stairs.

When she saw he was carrying a suitcase, and saw the pale seriousness of his face as he mounted the stairs; she thought at first that he knew; he had come prepared to lock the door and take her in his arms. "Hello, darling," she said softly, and opened the door wider.

"Hi, baby." He brushed past her and walked inside. "Guess I'm late, huh? You in bed?"

"No." She closed the door and leaned against it with both hands holding the doorknob at the small of her back, the way heroines close doors in the movies. "I was just—waiting for you."

He wasn't looking at her. He went to the sofa and sat down, holding the suitcase on his lap and running his fingers over its surface. "Gracie," he said, barely above a whisper. "Look at this."

She looked at it, and then into his tragic eyes.

"Remember," he said, "I told you about that bag I wanted to buy? Forty dollars?" He stopped and looked around. "Hey, where's Martha? She in bed?"

"She's gone, darling," Grace said, moving slowly toward the sofa. "She's gone for the whole weekend." She sat down beside him, leaned close, and gave him Martha's special smile.

"Oh yeah?" he said. "Well anyway, listen. I said I was gonna borrow Eddie's bag instead, remember?"

"Yes."

"Well, so tonight at the White Rose I siz, 'C'mon, Eddie, let's go home pick up ya bag.' He siz, 'Ah, bag schmagg.' I siz, 'Whatsa matta?' but he don't say nothin', see? So we go home to his place and the living-room door's shut, see?"

She squirmed closer and put her head on his chest. Automatically he raised an arm and dropped it around her shoulders, still talking. "He siz, 'G'ahead, Ralph, open the door.' I siz, 'Whatsa deal?' He siz 'Never mind, Ralph, open the door.' So I open the door, and oh Jesus." His fingers gripped her shoulder with such intensity that she looked up at him in alarm.

"They was all there, Gracie," he said. "All the fellas. Playin' the piana, singin', cheerin'—" His voice wavered and his eyelids fluttered shut, their lashes wet. "A big surprise party," he said, trying to smile. "Fa me. Can ya beat that, Gracie? And then—and then Eddie comes out and—Eddie comes out and hands me this. The very same bag I been lookin' at all this time. He bought it with his own money and he didn't say nothin', just to give me a surprise. 'Here, Ralph,' he siz. 'Just to let ya know you're the greatest guy in the world.'" His fingers tightened again, trembling. "I cried, Gracie," he whispered. "I couldn't help it. I don't think the fellas saw it or anything, but I was cryin'." He turned his face away and worked his lips in a tremendous effort to hold back the tears.

"Would you like a drink, darling?" she asked tenderly.

"Nah, that's all right, Gracie. I'm all right." Gently he set the suitcase on the carpet. "Only, gimme a cigarette, huh?"

She got one from the coffee table, put it in his lips and lit it. "Let me get you a drink," she said.

He frowned through the smoke. "Whaddya got, that sherry wine? Nah, I don't like that stuff. Anyway, I'm fulla beer." He leaned back and closed his eyes. "And then Eddie's mother feeds us this terrific meal," he went on, and his voice was almost normal now. "We had *steaks;* we had French-fried *potatas*"—his head rolled on the sofa-back with each item of the menu—"lettuce-and-tomata *salad, pickles, bread, butter*—everything. The works."

"Well," she said. "Wasn't that nice."

"And afterwards we had ice cream and coffee," he said, "and all the beer we could drink. I mean, it was a real spread."

Grace ran her hands over her lap, partly to smooth the nylon and partly to dry the moisture on her palms. "Well, that certainly was nice of them," she said. They sat there silent for what seemed a long time.

"I can only stay a minute, Gracie," Ralph said at last. "I promised 'em I'd be back."

Her heart thumped under the nylon. "Ralph, do you—do you like this?"

"What, honey?"

"My negligee. You weren't supposed to see it until—after the wedding, but I thought I'd—"

"Nice," he said, feeling the flimsy material between thumb and index finger, like a merchant. "Very nice. Wudga pay fa this, honey?"

"Oh—I don't know. But do you like it?"

He kissed her and began, at last, to stroke her with his hands. "Nice," he kept saying. "Nice. Hey, I like this." His hand hesitated at the low neckline, slipped inside and held her breast.

"I do love you, Ralph," she whispered. "You know that, don't you?"

His fingers pinched her nipple, once, and slid quickly out again. The policy of restraint, the habit of months was too strong to break. "Sure," he said. "And I love you, baby. Now you be a good girl and get ya beauty sleep, and I'll see ya in the morning. Okay?"

"Oh, Ralph. Don't go. Stay."

"Ah, I promised the fellas, Gracie." He stood up and straightened his clothes. "They're waitin' fa me, out home."

She blazed to her feet, but the cry that was meant for a woman's appeal came out, through her tightening lips, as the whine of a wife: "Can't they wait?"

"Whaddya—*crazy?*" He backed away, eyes round with righteousness. She would *have* to understand. If this was the way she acted before the wedding, how the hell was it going to be afterwards? "Have a *heart,* willya? Keep the fellas waitin' *tonight?* After all they done fa *me?*"

After a second or two, during which her face became less pretty than he had ever seen it before, she was able to smile. "Of course not, darling. You're right."

He came forward again and gently brushed the tip of her chin with his fist, smiling, a husband reassured. "'At's more like it," he said. "So I'll see ya, Penn Station, nine o'clock tomorra. Right, Gracie? Only, before I go—" he winked and slapped his belly. "I'm fulla beer. Mind if I use ya terlet?"

When he came out of the bathroom she was waiting to say goodnight, standing with her arms folded across her chest, as if for warmth. Lovingly he hefted the new suitcase and joined her at the door. "Okay, then, baby," he said, and kissed her. "Nine o'clock. Don't forget, now."

She smiled tiredly and opened the door for him. "Don't worry, Ralph," she said. "I'll be there."

Richard Yates

No Pain Whatsoever

Myra straightened herself in the backseat and smoothed her skirt, pushing Jack's hand away.

"All right, baby," he whispered, smiling, "take it easy."

"You take it easy, Jack," she told him. "I mean it, now."

His hand yielded, limp, but his arm stayed indolently around her shoulders. Myra ignored him and stared out the window. It was early Sunday evening, late in December, and the Long Island streets looked stale; dirty crusts of snow lay shriveled on the sidewalk, and cardboard images of Santa Claus leered out of closed liquor stores.

"I still don't feel right about you driving me all the way out here," Myra called to Marty, who was driving, to be polite.

"'S all right," Marty grumbled. Then he sounded his horn and added, to the back of a slow truck, "Get that son of a bitch outa the way."

Myra was annoyed—why did Marty always have to be such a grouch?—but Irene, Marty's wife, squirmed around in the front seat with her friendly grin. "Marty don't mind," she said. "It's good for 'm, getting out on a Sunday insteada laying around the house."

"Well," Myra said, "I certainly do appreciate it." The truth was that she would much rather have taken the bus, alone, as usual. In the four years she had been coming out here to visit her husband every Sunday she had grown used to the long ride, and she liked stopping at a little cafeteria in Hempstead, where you had to change buses, for coffee and cake on the way home. But today she and Jack had gone over to Irene and Marty's for dinner, and the dinner was so late that Marty had to offer to drive her out to the hospital, and she had to accept. And then of course Irene had to come along, and Jack too, and they all acted as if they were doing her a favor. But you had to be polite. "It certainly is nice," Myra called, "to be riding out here in a car, instead of a—*don't* Jack!"

Jack said, "*Sh-h-h,* take it easy, baby," but she threw off his hand and twisted away. Watching them, Irene put her tongue between her teeth and giggled, and Myra felt herself blushing. It wasn't that there was anything to be ashamed of—Irene and Marty knew all about Jack and everything; most of her friends did, and nobody blamed her (after all, wasn't it almost like being a widow?)—it was just that Jack ought to know better. Couldn't he at least have the decency to keep his hands to himself now, of all times?

"There," Marty said. "Now we'll make some time." The truck had turned off and they were picking up speed, leaving the streetcar tracks and stores behind as the street became a road and then a highway.

"Care to hear the radio, kids?" Irene called. She clicked one of the dial tabs and a voice urged everyone to enjoy television in their own homes, now, tonight. She clicked another and a voice said, "Yes, your money buys more in a Crawford store!"

"Turn that son of a bitch off," Marty said, and sounding the horn again, he pulled out into the fast lane.

When the car entered the hospital grounds, Irene turned around in the front seat and said, "Say, this is a beautiful place. I mean it, isn't this a beautiful place? Oh, look, they got a Christmas tree up, with lights and all."

"Well," Marty said, "where to?"

"Straight ahead," Myra told him, "down to that big circle, where the Christmas tree is. Then you turn right, out around the Administration Building, and on out to the end of that street." He made the turn correctly, and as they approached the long, low TB building, she said, "Here it is, Marty, this one right here." He drew up to the curb and stopped, and she gathered together the magazines she had brought for her husband and stepped out on the thin gray snow.

Irene hunched her shoulders and turned around, hugging herself. "Oo-oo, it's *cold* out there, isn't it? Listen, honey, what time is it you'll be through, now? Eight o'clock, is it?"

"That's right," Myra said, "but listen, why don't you people go on home? I can just as soon take the bus back, like I always do."

"Whaddya think I am, crazy?" Irene said. "You think I want to drive all the way home with Jack moping there in the back seat?" She giggled and winked. "Be hard enough just trying to keep him happy while you're inside, let alone driving all the way home. No, listen, we'll cruise around a little, honey, maybe have a little drink or something, and then we'll come back here for you at eight o'clock sharp."

"Well okay, but I'd really just as soon—"

"Right here," Irene said. "We'll see you right here in front of the building at eight o'clock sharp. Now hurry up and shut the door before we all freeze to death."

Myra smiled as she slammed the door, but Jack, sulking, did not look up to smile back, or wave. Then the car rolled away and she walked up the path and the steps to the TB building.

The small waiting room smelled of steam heat and wet overshoes, and she hurried through it, past the door marked NURSES' OFFICE—CLEAN AREA and into the big, noisy center ward. There were thirty-six beds in the center ward, divided in half by a wide aisle and subdivided by shoulder-high partitions into open cubicles of six beds each. All the sheets and the hospital pajamas were dyed yellow, to distinguish them from uncontaminated linen in the hospital laundry, and this combined with the pale green of the walls made a sickly color scheme that Myra could never get used to. The noise was terrible too; each patient had a radio, and they all seemed to be playing different stations at once. There were clumps of visitors at some of the beds—one of the newer men lay with his arms around his wife in a kiss—but at other beds the men looked lonely, reading or listening to their radios.

Myra's husband didn't see her until she was right beside his bed. He was sitting up, cross-legged, frowning over something in his lap. "Hello, Harry," she said.

He looked up. "Oh, hi there, honey, didn't see you coming."

She leaned over and kissed him quickly on the cheek. Sometimes they kissed on the lips, but you weren't supposed to.

Harry glanced at his watch. "You're late. Was the bus late?"

"I didn't come on the bus," she said, taking off her coat. "I got a ride out. Irene, the girl that works in my office? She and her husband drove me out in their car."

"Oh, that's nice. Whyn't you bring 'em on in?"

"Oh, they couldn't stay—they had someplace else to go. But they both said to give you their regards. Here, I brought you these."

"Oh, thanks, that's swell." He took the magazines and spread them out on the bed: *Life, Collier's* and *Popular Science.* "That's swell, honey. Sit down and stay awhile."

Myra laid her coat over the back of the bedside chair and sat down. "Hello there, Mr. Chance," she said to a very long Negro in the next bed who was nodding and grinning at her.

"How're you, Mrs. Wilson?"

"Fine, thanks, and you?"

"Oh, no use complaining," Mr. Chance said.

She peered across Harry's bed at Red O'Meara, who lay listening to his radio on the other side. "Hi there, Red."

"Oh, hi, Mrs. Wilson. Didn't see you come in."

"Your wife coming in tonight, Red?"

"She comes Saturdays now. She was here last night."

"Oh," Myra said, "well, tell her I said hello."

"I sure will, Mrs. Wilson."

Then she smiled at the elderly man across the cubicle whose name she could never remember, who never had any visitors, and he smiled back, looking rather shy. She settled herself on the little steel chair, opening her handbag for cigarettes. "What's that thing on your lap, Harry?" It was a ring of blond wood a foot wide, with a great deal of blue knitting wool attached to little pegs around its edge.

"Oh, this?" Harry said, holding it up. "It's what they call rake-knitting. Something I got from occupational therapy."

"*What*-knitting?"

"Rake-knitting. See, what you do, you take this little hook and kind of pry the wool up and over each peg, like that, and you keep on doing that around and around the ring until you got yourself a muffler or a stocking cap—something like that."

"Oh, *I* see," Myra said. "It's like what we used to do when I was a kid, only we did it with a regular little spool, with nails stuck in it? You wind string around the nails and pull it through the spool and it makes sort of a knitted rope, like."

"Oh, yeah?" Harry said. "With a spool, huh? Yeah, I think my sister used to do that too, now that I think of it. With a spool. You're right, this is the same principle, only bigger."

"What're you going to make?"

"Oh, I don't know, I'm just fooling around with it. Thought I might make a stocking cap or something. I don't know." He inspected his work, turning the knitting-rake around in his hands, then leaned over and put it away in his bed stand. "It's just something to do."

She offered him the pack and he took a cigarette. When he bent forward to take the match the yellow pajamas gaped open and she saw his chest, unbelievably thin, partly caved-in on one side where the ribs were gone. She could just see the end of the ugly, newly healed scar from the last operation.

"Thanks, honey," he said, the cigarette wagging in his lips, and he leaned back against the pillows, stretching out his socked feet on the spread.

"How're you feeling, Harry?" she said.

"Feeling fine."

"You're looking better," she lied. "If you can gain a little weight now, you'll look fine."

"Pay up," said a voice over the din of the radios, and Myra looked around to see a little man coming down the center aisle in a wheelchair, walking the chair slowly with his feet, as all TB patients did to avoid the chest strain of turning the wheels with their hands. He was headed for Harry's bed, grinning with yellow teeth. "Pay up," he said again as the wheelchair came to a stop beside the bed. A piece of rubber tubing protruded from some kind of bandage on his chest. It coiled across his pajama top, held in place by a safety pin, and ended in a small rubber-capped bottle which rode heavily in his breast pocket. "Come on, come on," he said. "Pay up."

"Oh, yeah!" Harry said, laughing. "I forgot all about it, Walter." From the drawer of his bed stand he got out a dollar bill and handed it to the man, who folded it with thin fingers and put it in his pocket, along with the bottle.

"Okay, Harry," he said. "All squared away now, right?"

"Right, Walter."

He backed the wheelchair up and turned it around, and Myra saw that his chest, back and shoulders were crumpled and misshapen. "Sorry to butt in," he said, turning the sickly grin on Myra.

She smiled. "That's all right." When he had gone up the aisle again, she said, "What was that all about?"

"Oh, we had a bet on the fight Friday night. I'd forgotten all about it."

"Oh. Have I met him before?"

"Who, Walter? Sure, I think so, honey. You must've met him when I was over in surgery. Old Walter was in surgery more'n two years; they just brought him back here last week. Kid's had a rough time of it. He's got plenty of guts."

"What's that thing on his pajamas? That bottle?"

"He's draining," Harry said, settling back against the yellow pillows. "Old Walter's a good guy; I'm glad he's back." Then he lowered his voice, confidentially. "Matter of fact, he's one of the few really good guys left in this ward, with so many of the old crowd gone now, or over in surgery."

"Don't you like the new boys?" Myra asked, keeping her own voice low so that Red O'Meara, who was relatively new, wouldn't hear. "They seem perfectly nice to me."

"Oh, they're all right, I guess," Harry said. "I just mean, well, I get along better with guys like Walter, that's all. We been through a lot together, or something. I don't know. These new guys get on your nerves sometimes, the way they talk. For instance, there's not one of them knows anything about TB, and they all of them think they know it all; you can't tell them anything. I mean, a thing like that can get on your nerves."

Myra said she guessed she saw what he meant, and then it seemed that the best thing to do was change the subject. "Irene thought the hospital looked real pretty, with the Christmas tree and all."

"Oh, yeah?" Very carefully, Harry reached over and flicked his cigarette into the spotless ashtray on his bed stand. All his habits were precise and neat from living so long in bed. "How're things going at the office, honey?"

"Oh, all right, I guess. Remember I told you about that girl Janet that got fired for staying out too long at lunch, and we were all scared they'd start cracking down on that half-hour lunch period?"

"Oh, yeah," Harry said, but she could tell he didn't remember and wasn't really listening.

"Well, it seems to be all blown over now, because last week Irene and three other girls stayed out almost two hours and nobody said a word. And one of them, a girl named Rose, has been kind of expecting to get fired for a couple of months now, and they didn't even say anything to her."

"Oh, yeah?" Harry said. "Well, that's good."

There was a pause. "Harry?" she said.

"What, honey?"

"Have they told you anything new?"

"Anything new?"

"I mean, about whether or not you're going to need the operation on the other side."

"Oh, *no,* honey. I told you, we can't expect to hear anything on that for quite some time yet—I thought I explained all that." His mouth was smiling and his eyes frowning to show it had been a foolish question. It was the same look he always used to give her at first, long ago, when she would say, "But when do you *think* they'll let you come home?" Now he said, "Thing is, I've still got to get over this *last* one. You got to do one thing at a time in this business; you need a long postoperative period before you're really in the clear, especially with a record of breakdowns like I've had in the last—what is it, now—four years? No, what they'll do is wait awhile, I don't know, maybe six months, maybe longer, and see how this side's coming along. Then they'll decide about the other side. Might give me more surgery and they might not. You can't count on anything in this business, honey, you know that."

"No, of course, Harry, I'm sorry. I don't mean to ask stupid questions. I just meant, well, how're you feeling and everything. You still have any pain?"

"None at all, any more," Harry said. "I mean, as long as I don't go raising my arm too high or anything. When I do that it hurts, and sometimes I start to roll over on that side in my sleep, and that hurts too, but as long as I stay—you know—more or less in a normal position, why, there's no pain whatsoever."

"That's good," she said, "I'm awfully glad to hear that, anyway."

Neither of them spoke for what seemed a long time, and in the noise of radios and the noise of laughing and coughing from other beds, their silence seemed strange. Harry began to riffle *Popular Science* absently with his thumb. Myra's eyes strayed to the framed picture on his bed stand, an enlarged snapshot of the two of them just before their marriage, taken in her mother's back yard in Michigan. She looked very young in the picture, leggy in her 1945 skirt, not knowing how to dress or even how to stand, knowing nothing and ready for anything with a child's smile. And Harry—but the surprising thing was that Harry looked older in the picture, somehow, than he did now. Probably it was the thicker face and build, and of course the clothes helped—the dark, decorated Eisenhower jacket and the gleaming boots. Oh, he'd been good-looking, all right, with his set jaw and hard gray eyes—much better looking, for instance, than a too stocky, too solid man like Jack. But now with the loss of weight there had been a softening about the lips and eyes that gave him the look of a thin little boy. His face had changed to suit the pajamas.

"Sure am glad you brought me this," Harry said of his *Popular Science.* "They got an article in here I want to read."

"Good," she said, and she wanted to say: Can't it wait until I've gone?

Harry flipped the magazine on its face, fighting the urge to read, and said, "How's everything else, honey? Outside of the office, I mean."

"All right," she said. "I had a letter from Mother the other day, kind of a Christmas letter. She sent you her best regards."

"Good," Harry said, but the magazine was winning. He flipped it over again, opened it to his article and read a few lines very casually—as if only to make sure it was the right article—and then he lost himself in it.

Myra lighted a fresh cigarette from the butt of her last one, picked up the *Life* and began to turn the pages. From time to time she looked up to watch him; he lay biting a knuckle as he read, scratching the sole of one socked foot with the curled toe of the other.

They spent the rest of the visiting hour that way. Shortly before eight o'clock a group of people came down the aisle, smiling and trundling a studio piano on rubber-tired casters—the Sunday night Red Cross entertainers. Mrs. Balacheck led the procession; a kindly, heavy-set woman in uniform, who played. Then came the piano, pushed by a pale young tenor whose lips were always wet, and then the female singers: a swollen soprano in a taffeta dress that looked tight under the arms and a stern-faced, lean contralto with a briefcase. They wheeled the piano close to Harry's bed, in the approximate middle of the ward, and began to unpack their sheet music.

Harry looked up from his reading. "Evening, Mrs. Balacheck."

Her glasses gleamed at him. "How're you tonight, Harry? Like to hear a few Christmas carols tonight?"

"Yes, ma'am."

One by one the radios were turned off and the chattering died. But just before Mrs. Balacheck hit the keys a stocky nurse intervened, thumping rubber-heeled down the aisle with a hand outstretched to ward off the music until she could make an announcement. Mrs. Balacheck sat back, and the nurse, craning her neck, called, "Visiting hour's over!" to one end of the ward and, "Visiting hour's over!" to the other. Then she nodded to Mrs. Balacheck, smiling behind her sterilized linen mask, and thumped away again. After a moment's whispered counsel, Mrs. Balacheck began to play an introductory "Jingle Bells," her cheeks wobbling, to cover the disturbance of departing visitors, while the singers retired to cough quietly among themselves; they would wait until their audience settled down.

"Gee," Harry said, "I didn't realize it was that late. Here, I'll walk you out to the door." He sat up slowly and swung his feet to the floor.

"No, don't bother, Harry," Myra said. "You lie still."

"No, that's all right," he said, wriggling into his slippers. "Will you hand me the robe, honey?" He stood up, and she helped him on with a corduroy VA bathrobe that was too short for him.

"Good night, Mr. Chance," Myra said, and Mr. Chance grinned and nodded. Then she said good night to Red O'Meara and the elderly man, and as they passed his wheelchair in the aisle, she said goodnight to Walter. She took Harry's arm, startled at its thinness, and matched his slow steps very carefully. They stood facing each other in the small awkward crowd of visitors that lingered in the waiting room.

"Well," Harry said, "take care of yourself now, honey. See you next week."

"Oo-oo," somebody's mother said, plodding hump-shouldered out the door, "it is cold tonight." She turned back to wave to her son, then grasped her husband's arm and went down the steps to the snow-blown path. Someone else caught the door and held it open for other visitors to pass through, filling the room with a cold draft, and then it closed again, and Myra and Harry were alone.

"All right, Harry," Myra said, "you go back to bed and listen to the music, now." He looked very frail standing there with his robe hanging open. She reached up and closed it neatly over his chest, took the dangling belt and knotted it firmly, while he smiled down at her. "Now you go on back in there before you catch cold."

"Okay. Goodnight, honey."

"Goodnight," she said, and standing on tiptoe, she kissed his cheek. "Goodnight, Harry."

At the door she turned to watch him walk back to the ward in the tight, high-waisted robe. Then she went outside and down the steps, turning up her coat collar in the sudden cold. Marty's car was not there; the road was bare except for the dwindling backs of the other visitors, passing under a street lamp now as they made their way down to the bus stop near the Administration Building. She drew the coat more closely around her and stood close to the building for shelter from the wind.

"Jingle Bells" ended inside, to muffled applause, and after a moment the program began in earnest. A few solemn chords sounded on the piano, and then the voices came through:

"Hark, the herald angels sing,
Glory to the new-born King . . ."

All at once Myra's throat closed up and the street lights swam in her eyes. Then half her fist was in her mouth and she was sobbing wretchedly, making little puffs of mist that floated away in the dark. It took her a long time to stop, and each sniffling intake of breath made a high sharp noise that sounded as if it could be heard for miles. Finally it was over, or nearly over; she managed to control her shoulders, to blow her nose and put her handkerchief away, closing her bag with a reassuring, businesslike snap.

Then the lights of the car came probing up the road. She ran down the path and stood waiting in the wind.

Inside the car a warm smell of whiskey hung among the cherry-red points of cigarettes, and Irene's voice squealed, "Oo-oo! Hurry up and shut the *door!*"

Jack's arms gathered her close as the door slammed, and in a thick whisper he said, "Hello, baby."

They were all a little drunk; even Marty was in high spirits. "Hold tight, everybody!" he called, as they swung around the Administration Building, past the Christmas tree, and leveled off for the straightaway to the gate, gaining speed. "Everybody hold tight!"

Irene's face floated chattering over the back of the front seat. "Myra, honey, listen, we found the most adorable little place down the road, kind of a roadhouse, like, only real inexpensive and everything? So listen, we wanna take you back there for a little drink, okay?"

"Sure," Myra said, "fine."

"'Cause I mean, we're way ahead of you now anyway, and anyway I want you to see this place . . . Marty, will you take it *easy!*" She laughed. "Honestly, anybody else driving this car with what he's had to drink in him, I'd be scared to death, you know it? But you never got to worry about old Marty. He's the best old driver in the world, drunk, sober, I don't care *what* he is."

But they weren't listening. Deep in a kiss, Jack slipped his hand inside her coat, expertly around and inside all the other layers until it held the flesh of her breast. "All over being mad at me, baby?" he mumbled against her lips. "Wanna go have a little drink?"

Her hands gripped the bulk of his back and clung there. Then she let herself be turned so that his other hand could creep secretly up her thigh. "All right," she whispered, "but let's only have one and then afterwards—"

"Okay, baby, okay."

"—and then afterwards, darling, let's go right home."

RICHARD YATES

Oh, Joseph, I'm So Tired

When Franklin D. Roosevelt was President-elect there must have been sculptors all over America who wanted a chance to model his head from life, but my mother had connections. One of her closest friends and neighbors, in the Greenwich Village courtyard where we lived, was an amiable man named Howard Whitman who had recently lost his job as a reporter on the *New York Post.* And one of Howard's former colleagues from the *Post* was now employed in the press office of Roosevelt's New York headquarters. That would make it easy for her to get in—or, as she said, to get an entrée—and she was confident she could take it from there. She was confident about everything she did in those days, but it never quite disguised a terrible need for support and approval on every side.

She wasn't a very good sculptor. She had been working at it for only three years, since breaking up her marriage to my father, and there was still something stiff and amateurish about her pieces. Before the Roosevelt project her specialty had been "garden figures"—a life-size little boy whose legs turned into the legs of a goat at the knees and another who knelt among ferns to play the pipes of Pan; little girls who trailed chains of daisies from their upraised arms or walked beside a spread-winged goose. These fanciful children, in plaster painted green to simulate weathered bronze, were arranged on homemade wooden pedestals to loom around her studio and to leave a cleared space in the middle for the modeling stand that held whatever she was working on in clay.

Her idea was that any number of rich people, all of them gracious and aristocratic, would soon discover her: they would want her sculpture to decorate their landscaped gardens, and they would want to make her their friend for life. In the meantime, a little nationwide publicity as the first woman sculptor to "do" the President-elect certainly wouldn't hurt her career.

And, if nothing else, she had a good studio. It was, in fact, the best of all the studios she would have in the rest of her life. There were six or eight old houses facing our side of the courtyard, with their backs to Bedford Street, and ours was probably the showplace of the row because the front room on its ground floor was two stories high. You went down a broad set of brick steps to the tall front windows and the front door; then you were in the high, wide, light-flooded studio. It was big enough to serve as a living room too, and so along with the green garden children it contained all the living-room furniture from the house we'd lived in with my father in the suburban town of Hastings-on-Hudson, where I was born. A second-floor balcony ran along the far end of the studio, with two small bedrooms and a tiny bathroom tucked away upstairs; beneath that, where the ground floor continued through to the Bedford Street side, lay the only part of the apartment that might let you know we didn't have much money. The ceiling was very low and it was always dark in there; the small windows looked out underneath an iron sidewalk grating, and the bottom of that street cavity was thick with strewn garbage. Our roach-infested kitchen was barely big enough for a stove and sink that were never clean, and for a brown wooden icebox with its dark, ever-melting block of ice; the rest of that area was our dining room, and not even the amplitude of the old Hastings dining-room table could brighten it. But our Majestic radio was in there too, and that made it a cozy place for my sister Edith and me: we liked the children's programs that came on in the late afternoons.

We had just turned off the radio one day when we went out into the studio and found our mother discussing the Roosevelt project with Howard Whitman. It was the first we'd heard of it, and we must have interrupted her with too many questions because she said "Edith? Billy? That's enough, now. I'll tell you all about this later. Run out in the garden and play."

She always called the courtyard "the garden," though nothing grew there except a few stunted city trees and a patch of grass that never had a chance to spread. Mostly it was bald earth, interrupted here and there by brick paving, lightly powdered with soot and scattered with the droppings of dogs and cats. It may have been six or eight houses long, but it was only two houses wide, which gave it a hemmed-in, cheerless look; its only point of interest was a dilapidated marble fountain, not much bigger than a birdbath, which stood near our house. The original idea of the fountain was that water would drip evenly from around the rim of its upper tier and tinkle into its lower basin, but age had unsettled it; the water spilled in a single ropy stream from the only inch of the upper tier's rim that stayed clean. The lower basin was deep enough to soak your feet in on a hot day, but there wasn't much pleasure in that because the underwater part of the marble was coated with brown scum.

My sister and I found things to do in the courtyard every day, for all of the two years we lived there, but that was only because Edith was an imaginative child. She was eleven at the time of the Roosevelt project, and I was seven.

"Daddy?" she asked in our father's office uptown one afternoon. "Have you heard Mommy's doing a head of President Roosevelt?"

"Oh?" He was rummaging in his desk, looking for something he'd said we might like.

"She's going to take his measurements and stuff here in New York," Edith said, "and then after the Inauguration, when the sculpture's done, she's going to take it to Washington and present it to him in the White House." Edith often told one of our parents about the other's more virtuous activities; it was part of her long, hopeless effort to bring them back together. Many years later she told me she thought she had never recovered, and never would, from the shock of their breakup: she said Hastings-on-Hudson remained the happiest time of her life, and that made me envious because I could scarcely remember it at all.

"Well," my father said. "That's really something, isn't it." Then he found what he'd been looking for in the desk and said, "Here we go; what do you think of these?" They were two fragile perforated sheets of what looked like postage stamps, each stamp bearing the insignia of an electric light bulb in vivid white against a yellow background, and the words "More light."

My father's office was one of many small cubicles on the twenty-third floor of the General Electric building. He was an assistant regional sales manager in what was then called the Mazda Lamp Division—a modest job, but good enough to have allowed him to rent into a town like Hastings-on-Hudson in better times—and these "More light" stamps were souvenirs of a recent sales convention. We told him the stamps were neat—and they were—but expressed some doubt as to what we might do with them.

"Oh, they're just for decoration," he said. "I thought you could paste them into your schoolbooks, or—you know—whatever you want. Ready to go?" And he carefully folded the sheets of stamps and put them in his inside pocket for safekeeping on the way home.

Between the subway exit and the courtyard, somewhere in the West Village, we always walked past a vacant lot where men stood huddled around weak fires built of broken fruit crates and trash, some of them warming tin cans of food held by coat-hanger wire over the flames. "Don't stare," my father had said the first time. "All those men are out of work, and they're hungry."

"Daddy?" Edith inquired. "Do you think Roosevelt's good?"

"Sure I do."

"Do you think all the Democrats are good?"

"Well, most of 'em, sure."

Much later I would learn that my father had participated in local Democratic Party politics for years. He had served some of his political friends—men my mother described as dreadful little Irish people from Tammany Hall—by helping them to establish Mazda Lamp distributorships in various parts of the city. And he loved their social gatherings, at which he was always asked to sing.

"Well, of course, you're too young to remember Daddy's singing," Edith said to me once after his death in 1942.

"No, I'm not; I remember."

"But I mean really remember," she said. "He had the most beautiful tenor voice I've ever heard. Remember 'Danny Boy'?"

"Sure."

"Ah, God, that was something," she said, closing her eyes. "That was really—that was really something."

When we got back to the courtyard that afternoon, and back into the studio, Edith and I watched our parents say hello to each other. We always watched that closely, hoping they might drift into conversation and sit down together and find things to laugh about, but they never did. And it was even less likely than usual that day because my mother had a guest—a woman named Sloane Cabot who was her best friend in the courtyard, and who greeted my father with a little rush of false, flirtatious enthusiasm.

"How've you been, Sloane?" he said. Then he turned back to his former wife and said "Helen? I hear you're planning to make a bust of Roosevelt."

"Well, not a bust," she said. "A head. I think it'll be more effective if I cut it off at the neck."

"Well, good. That's fine. Good luck with it. Okay, then." He gave his whole attention to Edith and me. "Okay. See you soon. How about a hug?"

And those hugs of his, the climax of his visitation rights, were unforgettable. One at a time we would be swept up and pressed hard into the smells of linen and whiskey and tobacco; the warm rasp of his jaw would graze one cheek and there would be a quick moist kiss near the ear; then he'd let us go.

He was almost all the way out of the courtyard, almost out in the street, when Edith and I went racing after him.

"Daddy! Daddy! You forgot the stamps!"

He stopped and turned around, and that was when we saw he was crying. He tried to hide it—he put his face nearly into his armpit as if that might help him search his inside pocket—but there is no way to disguise the awful bloat and pucker of a face in tears.

"Here," he said. "Here you go." And he gave us the least convincing smile I had ever seen. It would be good to report that we stayed and talked to him—that we hugged him again—but we were too embarrassed for that. We took the stamps and ran home without looking back.

"Oh, aren't you excited, Helen?" Sloane Cabot was saying. "To be meeting him, and talking to him and everything, in front of all those reporters?"

"Well, of course," my mother said, "but the important thing is to get the measurements right. I hope there won't be a lot of photographers and silly interruptions."

Sloane Cabot was some years younger than my mother, and strikingly pretty in a style often portrayed in what I think are called Art Deco illustrations of that period: straight dark bangs, big eyes, and a big mouth. She too was a divorced mother, though her former husband had vanished long ago and was referred to only as "that bastard" or "that cowardly son of a bitch." Her only child was a boy of Edith's age named John, whom Edith and I liked enormously.

The two women had met within days of our moving into the courtyard, and their friendship was sealed when my mother solved the problem of John's schooling. She knew a Hastings-on-Hudson family who would appreciate the money earned from taking in a boarder, so John went up there to live and go to school, and came home only on weekends. The arrangement cost more than Sloane could comfortably afford, but she managed to make ends meet and was forever grateful.

Sloane worked in the Wall Street district as a private secretary. She talked a lot about how she hated her job and her boss, but the good part was that her boss was often out of town for extended periods: that gave her time to use the office typewriter in pursuit of her life's ambition, which was to write scripts for the radio.

She once confided to my mother that she'd made up both of her names: "Sloane" because it sounded masculine, the kind of name a woman alone might need for making her way in the world, and "Cabot" because—well, because it had a touch of class. Was there anything wrong with that?

"Oh, Helen," she said. "This is going to be wonderful for you. If you get the publicity—if the papers pick it up, and the newsreels—you'll be one of the most interesting personalities in America."

Five or six people were gathered in the studio on the day my mother came home from her first visit with the President-elect.

"Will somebody get me a drink?" she asked, looking around in mock helplessness. "Then I'll tell you all about it."

And with the drink in her hand, with her eyes as wide as a child's, she told us how a door had opened and two big men had brought him in.

"Big men," she insisted. "Young, strong men; holding him up under the arms, and you could see how they were straining. Then you saw this *foot* come out, with these awful metal braces on the shoe, and then the *other* foot. And he was sweating, and he was panting for breath, and his face was—I don't know—all bright and tense and horrible." She shuddered.

"Well," Howard Whitman said, looking uneasy, "he can't help being crippled, Helen."

"Howard," she said impatiently, "I'm only trying to tell you how *ugly* it was." And that seemed to carry a certain weight. If she was an authority on beauty—on how a little boy might kneel among ferns to play the pipes of Pan, for example—then surely she had earned her credentials as an authority on ugliness.

"*Anyway,*" she went on, "they got him into a chair, and he wiped most of the sweat off his face with a handkerchief—he was still out of breath—and after a while he started talking to some of the other men there; I couldn't follow that part of it. Then finally he turned to me with this smile of his. Honestly, I don't know if I can describe that smile. It isn't something you can see in the newsreels; you have to be there. His eyes don't change at all, but the corners of his mouth go up as if they're being pulled by puppet strings. It's a frightening smile. It makes you think: This could be a dangerous man. This could be an evil man. Well anyway, we started talking, and I spoke right up to him. I said 'I didn't vote for you, Mr. President.' I said 'I'm a good Republican and I voted for President Hoover.' He said 'Why are you here, then?' or something like that, and I said 'Because you have a very interesting head.' So he gave me the smile again and he said 'What's interesting about it?' And I said 'I like the bumps on it.'"

By then she must have assumed that every reporter in the room was writing in his notebook, while the photographers got their flashbulbs ready; tomorrow's papers might easily read:

GAL SCULPTOR TWITS FDR
ABOUT "BUMPS" ON HEAD

At the end of her preliminary chat with him she got down to business, which was to measure different parts of his head with her calipers. I knew how that felt: the cold, trembling points of those clay-encrusted calipers had tickled and poked me all over during the times I'd served as model for her fey little woodland boys.

But not a single flashbulb went off while she took and recorded the measurements, and nobody asked her any questions; after a few nervous words of thanks and good-bye she was out in the corridor again among all the hopeless, craning people who couldn't get in. It must have been a bad disappointment, and I imagine she tried to make up for it by planning the triumphant way she'd tell us about it when she got home.

"Helen?" Howard Whitman inquired, after most of the other visitors had gone. "Why'd you tell him you didn't vote for him?"

"Well, because it's true. I *am* a good Republican; you know that."

She was a storekeeper's daughter from a small town in Ohio; she had probably grown up hearing the phrase "good Republican" as an index of respectability and clean clothes. And maybe she had come to relax her standards of respectability, maybe she didn't even care much about clean clothes anymore, but "good Republican" was worth clinging to. It would be helpful when she met the customers for her garden figures, the people whose low, courteous voices would welcome her into their lives and who would almost certainly turn out to be Republicans too.

"I believe in the aristocracy!" she often cried, trying to make herself heard above the rumble of voices when her guests were discussing communism, and they seldom paid her any attention. They liked her well enough: she gave parties with plenty of liquor, and she was an agreeable hostess if only because of her touching eagerness to please; but in any talk of politics she was like a shrill, exasperating child. She believed in the aristocracy.

She believed in God, too, or at least in the ceremony of St. Luke's Episcopal Church, which she attended once or twice a year. And she believed in Eric Nicholson, the handsome middle-aged Englishman who was her lover. He had something to do with the American end of a British chain of foundries: his company cast ornamental objects into bronze and lead. The cupolas of college and high-school buildings all over the East, the lead-casement windows for Tudor-style homes in places like Scarsdale and Bronxville—these were some of the things Eric Nicholson's firm had accomplished. He was always self-deprecating about his business, but ruddy and glowing with its success.

My mother had met him the year before, when she'd sought help in having one of her garden figures cast into bronze, to be "placed on consignment" with some garden-sculpture gallery from which it would never be sold. Eric Nicholson had persuaded her that lead would be almost as nice as bronze and much cheaper; then he'd asked her out to dinner, and that evening changed our lives.

Mr. Nicholson rarely spoke to my sister or me, and I think we were both frightened of him, but he overwhelmed us with gifts. At first they were mostly books—a volume of cartoons from *Punch,* a partial set of Dickens, a book called *England in Tudor Times* containing tissue-covered color plates that Edith liked. But in the summer of 1933, when our father arranged for us to spend two weeks with our mother at a small lake in New Jersey, Mr. Nicholson's gifts became a cornucopia of sporting goods. He gave Edith a steel fishing rod with a reel so intricate that none of us could have figured it out even if we'd known how to fish, a wicker creel for carrying the fish she would never catch, and a sheathed hunting knife to be worn at her waist. He gave me a short axe whose head was encased in a leather holster and strapped to my belt—I guess this was for cutting firewood to cook the fish—and a cumbersome net with a handle that hung from an elastic shoulder strap, in case I should be called upon to wade in and help Edith land a tricky one. There was nothing to do in that New Jersey village except take walks, or what my mother called good hikes; and every day, as we plodded out through the insect-humming weeds in the sun, we wore our full regalia of useless equipment.

That same summer Mr. Nicholson gave me a three-year subscription to *Field & Stream,* and I think that impenetrable magazine was the least appropriate of all his gifts because it kept coming in the mail for such a long, long time after everything else had changed for us: after we'd moved out of New York to Scarsdale, where Mr. Nicholson had found a house with a low rent, and after he had abandoned my mother in that house—with no warning—to return to England and to the wife from whom he'd never really been divorced.

But all that came later; I want to go back to the time between Franklin D. Roosevelt's election and his Inauguration, when his head was slowly taking shape on my mother's modeling stand.

Her original plan had been to make it life-size, or larger than life-size, but Mr. Nicholson urged her to scale it down for economy in the casting, and so she made it only six or seven inches high. He persuaded her too, for the second time since he'd known her, that lead would be almost as nice as bronze.

She had always said she didn't mind at all if Edith and I watched her work, but we had never much wanted to; now it was a little more interesting because we could watch her sift through many photographs of Roosevelt cut from newspapers until she found one that would help her execute a subtle plane of cheek or brow.

But most of our day was taken up with school. John Cabot might go to school in Hastings-on-Hudson, for which Edith would always yearn, but we had what even Edith admitted was the next best thing: we went to school in our bedroom.

During the previous year my mother had enrolled us in the public school down the street, but she'd begun to regret it when we came home with lice in our hair. Then one day Edith came home accused of having stolen a boy's coat, and that was too much. She withdrew us both, in defiance of the city truant officer, and pleaded with my father to help her meet the cost of a private school. He refused. The rent she paid and the bills she ran up were already taxing him far beyond the terms of the divorce agreement; he was in debt; surely she must realize he was lucky even to have a job. Would she ever learn to be reasonable?

It was Howard Whitman who broke the deadlock. He knew of an inexpensive, fully accredited mail-order service called The Calvert School, intended mainly for the homes of children who were invalids. The Calvert School furnished weekly supplies of books and materials and study plans; all she would need was someone in the house to administer the program and to serve as a tutor. And someone like Bart Kampen would be ideal for the job.

"The skinny fellow?" she asked. "The Jewish boy from Holland or wherever it is?"

"He's very well educated, Helen," Howard told her. "And he speaks fluent English, and he'd be very conscientious. And he could certainly use the money."

We were delighted to learn that Bart Kampen would be our tutor. With the exception of Howard himself, Bart was probably our favorite among the adults around the courtyard. He was twenty-eight or so, young enough so that his ears could still turn red when he was teased by children; we had found that out in teasing him once or twice about such matters as that his socks didn't match. He was tall and very thin and seemed always to look startled except when he was comforted enough to smile. He was a violinist, a Dutch Jew who had emigrated the year before in the hope of joining a symphony orchestra, and eventually of launching a concert career. But the symphonies weren't hiring then, nor were lesser orchestras, so Bart had gone without work for a long time. He lived alone in a room on Seventh Avenue, not far from the courtyard, and people who liked him used to worry that he might not have enough to eat. He owned two suits, both cut in a way that must have been stylish in the Netherlands at the time: stiff, heavily padded shoulders and a nipped-in waist; they would probably have looked better on someone with a little more meat on his bones. In shirtsleeves, with the cuffs rolled back, his hairy wrists and forearms looked even more fragile than you might have expected, but his long hands were shapely and strong enough to suggest authority on the violin.

"I'll leave it entirely up to you, Bart," my mother said when he asked if she had any instructions for our tutoring. "I know you'll do wonders with them."

A small table was moved into our bedroom, under the window, and three chairs placed around it. Bart sat in the middle so that he could divide his time equally between Edith and me. Big, clean, heavy brown envelopes arrived in the mail from The

Calvert School once a week, and when Bart slid their fascinating contents onto the table it was like settling down to begin a game.

Edith was in the fifth grade that year—her part of the table was given over to incomprehensible talk about English and History and Social Studies—and I was in the first. I spent my mornings asking Bart to help me puzzle out the very opening moves of an education.

"Take your time, Billy," he would say. "Don't get impatient with this. Once you have it you'll see how easy it is, and then you'll be ready for the next thing."

At eleven each morning we would take a break. We'd go downstairs and out to the part of the courtyard that had a little grass. Bart would carefully lay his folded coat on the sidelines, turn back his shirt cuffs, and present himself as ready to give what he called airplane rides. Taking us one at a time, he would grasp one wrist and one ankle; then he'd whirl us off our feet and around and around, with himself as the pivot, until the courtyard and the buildings and the city and the world were lost in the dizzying blur of our flight.

After the airplane rides we would hurry down the steps into the studio, where we'd usually find that my mother had set out a tray bearing three tall glasses of cold Ovaltine, sometimes with cookies on the side and sometimes not. I once overheard her telling Sloane Cabot she thought the Ovaltine must be Bart's first nourishment of the day—and I think she was probably right, if only because of the way his hand would tremble in reaching for his glass. Sometimes she'd forget to prepare the tray and we'd crowd into the kitchen and fix it ourselves; I can never see a jar of Ovaltine on a grocery shelf without remembering those times. Then it was back upstairs to school again. And during that year, by coaxing and prodding and telling me not to get impatient, Bart Kampen taught me to read.

It was an excellent opportunity for showing off. I would pull books down from my mother's shelves—mostly books that were the gifts of Mr. Nicholson—and try to impress her by reading mangled sentences aloud.

"That's wonderful, dear," she would say. "You've really learned to read, haven't you."

Soon a white-and-yellow "More light" stamp was affixed to every page of my Calvert First Grade Reader, proving I had mastered it, and others were accumulating at a slower rate in my arithmetic workbook. Still other stamps were fastened to the wall beside my place at the school table, arranged in a proud little white-and-yellow thumb-smudged column that rose as high as I could reach.

"You shouldn't have put your stamps on the wall," Edith said.

"Why?"

"Well, because they'll be hard to take off."

"Who's going to take them off?"

That small room of ours, with its double function of sleep and learning, stands more clearly in my memory than any other part of our home. Someone should probably have told my mother that a girl and boy of our ages ought to have separate rooms, but that never occurred to me until much later. Our cots were set foot-to-foot against the wall, leaving just enough space to pass alongside them to the school table, and we had some good conversations as we lay waiting for sleep at night. The one I remember best was the time Edith told me about the sound of the city.

"I don't mean just the loud noises," she said, "like the siren going by just now, or those car doors slamming, or all the laughing and shouting down the street; that's just close-up stuff. I'm talking about something else. Because you see there are millions and millions of people in New York—more people than you can possibly imagine, ever—and most of them are doing something that makes a sound. Maybe talking, or playing the radio, maybe closing doors, maybe putting their forks down on their plates if they're having dinner, or dropping their shoes if they're going to bed—and because there are so many of them, all those little sounds add up and come together in a kind of hum. But it's so faint—so very, very faint—that you can't hear it unless you listen very carefully for a long time."

"Can you hear it?" I asked her.

"Sometimes. I listen every night, but I can only hear it sometimes. Other times I fall asleep. Let's be quiet now, and just listen. See if you can hear it, Billy."

And I tried hard, closing my eyes as if that would help, opening my mouth to minimize the sound of my breathing, but in the end I had to tell her I'd failed. "How about you?" I asked.

"Oh, I heard it," she said. "Just for a few seconds, but I heard it. You'll hear it too, if you keep trying. And it's worth waiting for. When you hear it, you're hearing the whole city of New York."

The high point of our week was Friday afternoon, when John Cabot came home from Hastings. He exuded health and normality; he brought fresh suburban air into our bohemian lives. He even transformed his mother's small apartment, while he was there, into an enviable place of rest between vigorous encounters with the world. He subscribed to both *Boys' Life* and *Open Road for Boys,* and these seemed to me to be wonderful things to have in your house, if only for the illustrations. John dressed in the same heroic way as the boys shown in those magazines, corduroy knickers with ribbed stockings pulled taut over his muscular calves. He talked a lot about the Hastings high-school football team, for which he planned to try out as soon as he was old enough, and about Hastings friends whose names and personalities grew almost as familiar to us as if they were friends of our own. He taught us invigorating new ways to speak, like saying "What's the diff?" instead of "What's the difference?" And he was better even than Edith at finding new things to do in the courtyard.

You could buy goldfish for ten or fifteen cents apiece in Woolworth's then, and one day we brought home three of them to keep in the fountain. We sprinkled the water with more Woolworth's granulated fish food than they could possibly need, and we named them after ourselves: "John," "Edith," and "Billy." For a week or two Edith and I would run to the fountain every morning, before Bart came for school, to make sure they were still alive and to see if they had enough food, and to watch them.

"Have you noticed how much bigger Billy's getting?" Edith asked me. "He's huge. He's almost as big as John and Edith now. He'll probably be bigger than both of them."

Then one weekend when John was home he called our attention to how quickly the fish could turn and move. "They have better reflexes than humans," he explained. "When they see a shadow in the water, or anything that looks like danger, they get away faster than you can blink. Watch." And he sank one hand into the water to make a grab for the fish named Edith, but she evaded him and fled. "See that?" he asked. "How's that for speed. Know something? I bet you could shoot an arrow in there, and they'd get away in time. Wait." To prove his point he ran to his mother's apartment and came back with the handsome bow and arrow he had made at summer camp (going to camp every summer was another admirable thing about John); then he knelt at the rim of the fountain like the picture of an archer, his bow steady in one strong hand and the feathered end of the arrow tight against the bowstring in the other. He was taking aim at the fish named Billy. "Now, the velocity of this arrow," he said in a voice weakened by his effort, "is probably more than a car going eighty miles an hour. It's probably more like an airplane, or maybe even more than that. Okay; watch."

The fish named Billy was suddenly floating dead on the surface, on his side, impaled a quarter of the way up the arrow with parts of his pink guts dribbled along the shaft.

I was too old to cry, but something had to be done about the shock and rage and grief that filled me as I ran from the fountain, heading blindly for home, and half-way there I came upon my mother. She stood looking very clean, wearing a new coat and dress I'd never seen before and fastened to the arm of Mr. Nicholson. They were either just going out or just coming in—I didn't care which—and Mr. Nicholson frowned at me (he had told me more than once that boys of my age went to boarding school in England), but I didn't care about that either. I bent my head into her waist and didn't stop crying until long after I'd felt her hands stroking my back, until after she had assured me that goldfish didn't cost much and I'd have another one soon, and that John was sorry for the thoughtless thing he'd done. I had discovered, or rediscovered, that crying is a pleasure—that it can be a pleasure beyond all reckoning if your head is pressed in your mother's waist and her hands are on your back, and if she happens to be wearing clean clothes.

There were other pleasures. We had a good Christmas Eve in our house that year, or at least it was good at first. My father was there, which obliged Mr. Nicholson to stay away, and it was nice to see how relaxed he was among my mother's friends. He was shy, but they seemed to like him. He got along especially well with Bart Kampen.

Howard Whitman's daughter Molly, a sweet-natured girl of about my age, had come in from Tarrytown to spend the holidays with him, and there were several other children whom we knew but rarely saw. John looked very mature that night in a dark coat and tie, plainly aware of his social responsibilities as the oldest boy.

After a while, with no plan, the party drifted back into the dining-room area and staged an impromptu vaudeville. Howard started it: he brought the tall stool from my mother's modeling stand and sat his daughter on it, facing the audience. He folded back the opening of a brown paper bag two or three times and fitted it onto her head; then he took off his suit coat and draped it around her backwards, up to the chin; he went behind her, crouched out of sight, and worked his hands through the coatsleeves so that when they emerged they appeared to be hers. And the sight of a smiling little girl in a paper-bag hat, waving and gesturing with huge, expressive hands, was enough to make everyone laugh. The big hands wiped her eyes and stroked her chin and pushed her hair behind her ears; then they elaborately thumbed her nose at us.

Next came Sloane Cabot. She sat very straight on the stool with her heels hooked over the rungs in such a way as to show her good legs to their best advantage, but her first act didn't go over.

"Well," she began, "I was at work today—you know my office is on the fortieth floor—when I happened to glance up from my typewriter and saw this big old man sort of crouched on the ledge outside the window, with a white beard and a funny red suit. So I ran to the window and opened it and said 'Are you all right?' Well, it was Santa Claus, and he said 'Of course I'm all right; I'm used to high places. But listen, miss: can you direct me to number seventy-five Bedford Street?'"

There was more, but our embarrassed looks must have told her we knew we were being condescended to; as soon as she'd found a way to finish it she did so quickly. Then, after a thoughtful pause, she tried something else that turned out to be much better.

"Have you children ever heard the story of the first Christmas?" she asked. "When Jesus was born?" And she began to tell it in the kind of hushed, dramatic voice she must have hoped might be used by the narrators of her more serious radio plays.

". . . And there were still many miles to go before they reached Bethlehem," she said, "and it was a cold night. Now, Mary knew she would very soon have a baby. She even knew, because an angel had told her, that her baby might one day be the saviour of all mankind. But she was only a young girl"—here Sloane's eyes glistened, as if they might be filling with tears—"and the traveling had exhausted her. She was bruised by the jolting gait of the donkey and she ached all over, and she thought they'd never, ever get there, and all she could say was 'Oh, Joseph, I'm so tired.'"

The story went on through the rejection at the inn, and the birth in the stable, and the manger, and the animals, and the arrival of the three kings; when it was over we clapped a long time because Sloane had told it so well.

"Daddy?" Edith asked. "Will you sing for us?"

"Oh, well, thanks, honey," he said, "but no; I really need a piano for that. Thanks anyway."

The final performer of the evening was Bart Kampen, persuaded by popular demand to go home and get his violin. There was no surprise in discovering that he played like a professional, like something you might easily hear on the radio; the enjoyment came from watching how his thin face frowned over the chin rest, empty of all emotion except concern that the sound be right. We were proud of him.

Some time after my father left a good many other adults began to arrive, most of them strangers to me, looking as though they'd already been to several other parties that night. It was very late, or rather very early Christmas morning, when I looked into the kitchen and saw Sloane standing close to a bald man I didn't know. He held a trembling drink in one hand and slowly massaged her shoulder with the other; she seemed to be shrinking back against the old wooden icebox. Sloane had a way of smiling that allowed little wisps of cigarette smoke to escape from between her almost-closed lips while she looked you up and down, and she was doing that. Then the man put his drink on top of the icebox and took her in his arms, and I couldn't see her face anymore.

Another man, in a rumpled brown suit, lay unconscious on the dining-room floor. I walked around him and went into the studio, where a good-looking young woman stood weeping wretchedly and three men kept getting in each other's way as they tried to comfort her. Then I saw that one of the men was Bart, and I watched while he outlasted the other two and turned the girl away toward the door. He put his arm around her and she nestled her head in his shoulder; that was how they left the house.

Edith looked jaded in her wrinkled party dress. She was reclining in our old Hastings-on-Hudson easy chair with her head tipped back and her legs flung out over both the chair's arms, and John sat cross-legged on the floor near one of her dangling feet. They seemed to have been talking about something that didn't interest either of them much, and the talk petered out altogether when I sat on the floor to join them.

"Billy," she said, "do you realize what time it is?"

"What's the diff?" I said.

"You should've been in bed hours ago. Come on. Let's go up."

"I don't feel like it."

"Well," she said, "I'm going up, anyway," and she got laboriously out of the chair and walked away into the crowd.

John turned to me and narrowed his eyes unpleasantly. "Know something?" he said. "When she was in the chair that way I could see everything."

"Huh?"

"I could see everything. I could see the crack, and the hair. She's beginning to get hair."

I had observed these features of my sister many times—in the bathtub, or when she was changing her clothes—and hadn't found them especially remarkable; even so, I understood at once how remarkable they must have been for him. If only he had smiled in a bashful way we might have laughed together like a couple of regular fellows out of *Open Road for Boys,* but his face was still set in that disdainful look.

"I kept looking and looking," he said, "and I had to keep her talking so she wouldn't catch on, but I was doing fine until you had to come over and ruin it."

Was I supposed to apologize? That didn't seem right, but nothing else seemed right either. All I did was look at the floor.

When I finally got to bed there was scarcely time for trying to hear the elusive sound of the city—I had found that a good way to keep from thinking of anything else—when my mother came blundering in. She'd had too much to drink and wanted to lie down, but instead of going to her own room she got into bed with me. "Oh," she said. "Oh, my boy. Oh, my boy." It was a narrow cot and there was no way to make room for her; then suddenly she retched, bolted to her feet, and ran for the bathroom, where I heard her vomiting. And when I moved over into the part of the bed she had occupied my face recoiled quickly, but not quite in time, from the slick mouthful of puke she had left on her side of the pillow.

For a month or so that winter we didn't see much of Sloane because she said she was "working on something big. Something really big." When it was finished she brought it to the studio, looking tired but prettier than ever, and shyly asked if she could read it aloud.

"Wonderful," my mother said. "What's it about?"

"That's the best part. It's about us. All of us. Listen."

Bart had gone for the day and Edith was out in the courtyard by herself—she often played by herself—so there was nobody for an audience but my mother and me. We sat on the sofa and Sloane arranged herself on the tall stool, just as she'd done for telling the Bethlehem story.

"There is an enchanted courtyard in Greenwich Village," she read. "It's only a narrow patch of brick and green among the irregular shapes of very old houses, but what makes it enchanted is that the people who live in it, or near it, have come to form an enchanted circle of friends.

"None of them have enough money and some are quite poor, but they believe in the future; they believe in each other, and in themselves.

"There is Howard, once a top reporter on a metropolitan daily newspaper. Everyone knows Howard will soon scale the journalistic heights again, and in the meantime he serves as the wise and humorous sage of the courtyard.

"There is Bart, a young violinist clearly destined for virtuosity on the concert stage, who just for the present must graciously accept all lunch and dinner invitations in order to survive.

"And there is Helen, a sculptor whose charming works will someday grace the finest gardens in America, and whose studio is the favorite gathering place for members of the circle."

There was more like that, introducing other characters, and toward the end she got around to the children. She described my sister as "a lanky, dreamy tomboy," which was odd—I had never thought of Edith that way—and she called me "a sad-eyed, seven-year-old philosopher," which was wholly baffling. When the introduction was over she paused a few seconds for dramatic effect and then went into the opening episode of the series, or what I suppose would be called the "pilot."

I couldn't follow the story very well—it seemed to be mostly an excuse for bringing each character up to the microphone for a few lines apiece—and before long I was listening only to see if there would be any lines for the character based on me. And there were, in a way. She announced my name—"Billy"—but then instead of speaking she put her mouth through a terrible series of contortions, accompanied by funny little bursts of sound, and by the time the words came out I didn't care what they were. It was true that I stuttered badly—I wouldn't get over it for five or six more years—but I hadn't expected anyone to put it on the radio.

"Oh, Sloane, that's marvelous," my mother said when the reading was over. "That's really exciting."

And Sloane was carefully stacking her typed pages in the way she'd probably been taught to do in secretarial school, blushing and smiling with pride. "Well," she said, "it probably needs work, but I do think it's got a lot of potential."

"It's perfect," my mother said. "Just the way it is."

Sloane mailed the script to a radio producer and he mailed it back with a letter typed by some radio secretary, explaining that her material had too limited an appeal to be commercial. The radio public was not yet ready, he said, for a story of Greenwich Village life.

Then it was March. The new President promised that the only thing we had to fear was fear itself, and soon after that his head came packed in wood and excelsior from Mr. Nicholson's foundry.

It was a fairly good likeness. She had caught the famous lift of the chin—it might not have looked like him at all if she hadn't—and everyone told her it was fine. What nobody said was that her original plan had been right, and Mr. Nicholson shouldn't have interfered: it was too small. It didn't look heroic. If you could have hollowed it out and put a slot in the top, it might have made a serviceable bank for loose change.

The foundry had burnished the lead until it shone almost silver in the highlights, and they'd mounted it on a sturdy little base of heavy black plastic. They had sent back three copies: one for the White House presentation, one to keep for exhibition purposes, and an extra one. But the extra one soon toppled to the floor and was badly damaged—the nose mashed almost into the chin—and my mother might have burst into tears if Howard Whitman hadn't made everyone laugh by saying it was now a good portrait of Vice President Garner.

Charlie Hines, Howard's old friend from the *Post* who was now a minor member of the White House staff, made an appointment for my mother with the President late on a weekday morning. She arranged for Sloane to spend the night with Edith and me; then she took an evening train down to Washington, carrying the sculpture in a cardboard box, and stayed at one of the less expensive Washington hotels. In the morning she met Charlie Hines in some crowded White House anteroom, where I guess they disposed of the cardboard box, and he took her to the waiting room outside the Oval Office. He sat with her as she held the naked head in her lap, and when their turn came he escorted her in to the President's desk for the presentation. It didn't take long. There were no reporters and no photographers.

Afterwards Charlie Hines took her out to lunch, probably because he'd promised Howard Whitman to do so. I imagine it wasn't a first-class restaurant, more likely some bustling, no-nonsense place favored by the working press, and I imagine they had trouble making conversation until they settled on Howard, and on what a shame it was that he was still out of work.

"No, but do you know Howard's friend Bart Kampen?" Charlie asked. "The young Dutchman? The violinist?"

"Yes, certainly," she said. "I know Bart."

"Well, Jesus, there's *one* story with a happy ending, right? Have you heard about that? Last time I saw Bart he said 'Charlie, the Depression's over for me,' and he told me he'd found some rich, dumb, crazy woman who's paying him to tutor her kids."

I can picture how she looked riding the long, slow train back to New York that afternoon. She must have sat staring straight ahead or out the dirty window, seeing nothing, her eyes round and her face held in a soft shape of hurt. Her adventure with Franklin D. Roosevelt had come to nothing. There would be no photographs or interviews or feature articles, no thrilling moments of newsreel coverage; strangers would never know of how she'd come from a small Ohio town, or of how she'd nurtured her talent through the brave, difficult, one-woman journey that had brought her to the attention of the world. It wasn't fair.

All she had to look forward to now was her romance with Eric Nicholson, and I think she may have known even then that it was faltering—his final desertion came the next fall.

She was forty-one, an age when even romantics must admit that youth is gone, and she had nothing to show for the years but a studio crowded with green plaster statues that nobody would buy. She believed in the aristocracy, but there was no reason to suppose the aristocracy would ever believe in her.

And every time she thought of what Charlie Hines had said about Bart Kampen—oh, how hateful; oh, how hateful—the humiliation came back in wave on wave, in merciless rhythm to the clatter of the train.

She made a brave show of her homecoming, though nobody was there to greet her but Sloane and Edith and me. Sloane had fed us, and she said "There's a plate for you in the oven, Helen," but my mother said she'd rather just have a drink instead. She was then at the onset of a long battle with alcohol that she would ultimately lose; it must have seemed bracing that night to decide on a drink instead of dinner. Then she told us "all about" her trip to Washington, managing to make it sound like a success. She talked of how thrilling it was to be actually inside the White House; she repeated whatever small, courteous thing it was that President Roosevelt had said to her on receiving the head. And she had brought back souvenirs: a handful of note-size White House stationery for Edith, and a well-used briar pipe for me. She explained that she'd seen a very distinguished-looking man smoking the pipe in the waiting room outside the Oval Office; when his name was called he had knocked it out quickly into an ashtray and left it there as he hurried inside. She had waited until she was sure no one was looking; then she'd taken the pipe from the ashtray and put it in her purse. "Because I knew he must have been somebody important," she said. "He could easily have been a member of the Cabinet, or something like that. Anyway, I thought you'd have a lot of fun with it." But I didn't. It was too heavy to hold in my teeth and it tasted terrible when I sucked on it; besides, I kept wondering what the man must have thought when he came out of the President's office and found it gone.

Sloane went home after a while, and my mother sat drinking alone at the dining-room table. I think she hoped Howard Whitman or some of her other friends might drop in, but nobody did. It was almost our bedtime when she looked up and said "Edith? Run out in the garden and see if you can find Bart."

He had recently bought a pair of bright tan shoes with crepe soles. I saw those shoes trip rapidly down the dark brick steps beyond the windows—he seemed scarcely to touch each step in his buoyancy—and then I saw him come smiling into the studio, with Edith closing the door behind him. "Helen!" he said. "You're back!"

She acknowledged that she was back. Then she got up from the table and slowly advanced on him, and Edith and I began to realize we were in for something bad.

"Bart," she said, "I had lunch with Charlie Hines in Washington today."

"Oh?"

"And we had a very interesting talk. He seems to know you very well."

"Oh, not really; we've met a few times at Howard's, but we're not really—"

"And he said you'd told him the Depression was over for you because you'd found some rich, dumb, crazy woman who was paying you to tutor her kids. Don't interrupt me."

But Bart clearly had no intention of interrupting her. He was backing away from her in his soundless shoes, retreating past one stiff green garden child after another. His face looked startled and pink.

"I'm not a rich woman, Bart," she said, bearing down on him. "And I'm not dumb. And I'm not crazy. And I can recognize ingratitude and disloyalty and sheer, rotten viciousness and *lies* when they're thrown in my face."

My sister and I were halfway up the stairs jostling each other in our need to hide before the worst part came. The worst part of these things always came at the end, after she'd lost all control and gone on shouting anyway.

"I want you to get out of my house, Bart," she said. "And I don't ever want to see you again. And I want to tell you something. All my life I've hated people who say 'Some of my best friends are Jews.' Because *none* of my friends are Jews, or ever will be. Do you understand me? *None* of my friends are Jews, or ever will be."

The studio was quiet after that. Without speaking, avoiding each other's eyes, Edith and I got into our pajamas and into bed. But it wasn't more than a few minutes before the house began to ring with our mother's raging voice all over again, as if Bart had somehow been brought back and made to take his punishment twice.

" . . . And I said '*None* of my friends are Jews, or ever will be . . .'"

She was on the telephone, giving Sloane Cabot the highlights of the scene, and it was clear that Sloane would take her side and comfort her. Sloane might know how the Virgin Mary felt on the way to Bethlehem, but she also knew how to play my stutter for laughs. In a case like this she would quickly see where her allegiance lay, and it wouldn't cost her much to drop Bart Kampen from her enchanted circle.

When the telephone call came to an end at last there was silence downstairs until we heard her working with the ice pick in the icebox: she was making herself another drink.

There would be no more school in our room. We would probably never see Bart again—or if we ever did, he would probably not want to see us. But our mother was ours; we were hers; and we lived with that knowledge as we lay listening for the faint, faint sound of millions.

Credits

This page constitutes an extension of the copyright page. We have made every effort to trace the ownership of all copyrighted material and to secure permission from copyright holders. In the event of any question arising as to the use of any material, we will be pleased to make the necessary corrections in future printings. Thanks are due to the following authors, publishers, and agents for permission to use the material indicated.

Sherman Alexie. 3: "The Lone Ranger and Tonto Fistfight in Heaven" from THE LONE RANGER AND TONTO FISTFIGHT IN HEAVEN by Sherman Alexie. Copyright © 1993 by Sherman Alexie. Used by permission of Grove/Atlantic, Inc. **8:** "This Is What It Means to Say Phoenix, Arizona" from THE LONE RANGER AND TONTO FISTFIGHT IN HEAVEN by Sherman Alexie. Copyright © 1993 by Sherman Alexie. Used by permission of Grove/Atlantic, Inc. **16:** "The Toughest Indian in the World" by Sherman Alexie from THE TOUGHEST INDIAN IN THE WORLD. Copyright © 2000 by Sherman Alexie. Used by permission of Grove/Atlantic, Inc.

Margaret Atwood. 26: "Happy Endings" from GOOD BONES AND SIMPLE MURDERS by Margaret Atwood, copyright © 1983, 1992, 1994, by O.W. Toad Ltd. A Nan A. Talese Book. Used by permission of Doubleday, a division of Random House, Inc. and McClelland & Stewart Ltd., The Canadian Publishers. **29:** "Death by Landscape" from WILDERNESS TIPS by Margaret Atwood, copyright © 1991 by O.W. Toad Limited. Used by permission of Doubleday, a division of Random House, Inc. **43:** "True Trash" from WILDERNESS TIPS by Margaret Atwood, copyright © 1991 by O.W. Toad Limited. Used by permission of Doubleday, a division of Random House, Inc. and McClelland & Stewart, The Canadian Publishers. **43:** "Wilderness Tips" from WILDERNESS TIPS by Margaret Atwood, copyright © 1991 by O.W. Toad Limited. Used by permission of Doubleday, a division of Random House, Inc. and McClelland & Stewart, The Canadian Publishers.

James Baldwin. 62: "Sonny's Blues" © 1957 by James Baldwin was originally published in Partisan Review. Copyright renewed. Collected in GOING TO MEET THE MAN, published by Vintage Books. Reprinted by arrangement with the James Baldwin Estate. **83:** "Going to Meet the Man" by James Baldwin is collected in GOING TO MEET THE MAN © 1965 by James Baldwin. Copyright renewed. Published by Vintage Books. Reprinted by arrangement with the James Baldwin Estate. **95:** From "Exodus," in GO TELL IT ON THE MOUNTAIN by James Baldwin, copyright © 1952, 1953 by James Baldwin. Used by permission of Doubleday, a division of Random House, Inc.

Toni Cade Bambara. 103: "My Man Bovanne," copyright © 1971 by Toni Cade Bambara from GORILLA, MY LOVE by Toni Cade Bambara. Used by permission of Random House, Inc. **107:** "The Lesson," copyright © 1972 by Toni Cade Bambara, from GORILLA, MY LOVE by Toni Cade Bambara. Used by permission of Random House, Inc. **113:** "The Organizer's Wife" from THE SEA BIRDS ARE STILL ALIVE by Toni Cade Bambara, copyright © 1974, 1976, 1977 by Toni Cade Bambara. Used by permission of Random House, Inc.

Andrea Barrett. 126: "The Behavior of the Hawkweeds" from SHIP FEVER AND OTHER STORIES by Andrea Barrett. Copyright © 1996 by Andrea Barrett. Used by permission of W. W. Norton & Company, Inc. **139:** "Birds With No Feet" from SHIP FEVER AND OTHER STORIES by Andrea Barrett. Copyright © 1996 by Andrea Barrett. Used by permission of W. W. Norton & Company, Inc. **150:** "Servants of the Map." Copyright © 2000 by Andrea Barrett, from SERVANTS OF THE MAP by Andrea Barrett. Used by permission of W. W. Norton & Company, Inc.

Donald Barthelme. 181: "A City of Churches" from 60 STORIES by Donald Barthelme. Copyright © 1982 by Frederick Barthelme printed with the permission of the Wylie Agency, Inc. **184:** "The School" from 60 STORIES by Donald Barthelme. Copyright © 1982 by Frederick Barthelme printed with the permission of the Wylie Agency, Inc. **186:** "Robert Kennedy Saved from Drowning" from 60 STORIES by Donald Barthelme. Copyright © 1982 by Frederick Barthelme printed with the permission of the Wylie Agency, Inc.

Richard Bausch. 196: "The Man Who Knew Belle Star" from THE STORIES OF RICHARD BAUSCH by Richard Bausch. Copyright © 2003 by Richard Bausch. Reprinted by permission of HarperCollins Publishers Inc. **211:** "What Feels Like the World" from THE STORIES OF RICHARD BAUSCH by Richard Bausch. Copyright © 2003 by Richard Bausch. Reprinted by permission of HarperCollins Publishers Inc. **222:** "Tandolfo the Great" from THE

STORIES OF RICHARD BAUSCH by Richard Bausch. Copyright © 2003 by Richard Bausch. Reprinted by permission of HarperCollins Publishers Inc.

Charles Baxter. 234: "Gryphon" from THROUGH THE SAFETY NET by Charles Baxter. Courtesy of Darhansoff, Verrill, Feldman Literary Agents. 245: "Westland" from THROUGH THE SAFETY NET by Charles Baxter. Courtesy of Darhansoff, Verrill, Feldman Literary Agents. 259: "Shelter" from A RELATIVE STRANGER by Charles Baxter. Copyright © 1990 by Charles Baxter. Used by permission of W. W. Norton & Company, Inc.

Ann Beattie. 274: "Janus" reprinted with the permission of Simon & Schuster from YOU'LL FIND ME AND OTHER STORIES by Ann Beattie. Copyright © 1986 by Irony & Pity, Inc. 278: "The Burning House," copyright © 1979 by Irony & Pity, Inc., from THE BURNING HOUSE: SHORT STORIES by Ann Beattie. Used by permission of Random House, Inc. 288: "Park City" by Ann Beattie from PARK CITY: NEW AND SELECTED STORIES by Ann Beattie, copyright © 1998 by Irony & Pity, Inc. Used by permission of Alfred A. Knopf, a division of Random House, Inc.

Robert Olen Butler. 317: "A Good Scent from a Strange Mountain" from A GOOD SCENT FROM A STRANGE MOUNTAIN by Robert Olen Butler. Copyright © 1992 by Robert Olen Butler. Reprinted by permission of Henry Holt and Company, LLC. 325: "Jealous Husband Returns in Form of Parrot" from TABLOID DREAMS by Robert Olen Butler. Reprinted by permission of the author. 330: "This is Earl Sandt" by Robert Olen Butler. Reprinted by permission of the author.

Raymond Carver. 342: "Are These Actual Miles?" from WHERE I'M CALLING FROM by Raymond Carver. Used by permission of Grove/Atlantic, Inc. 348: "What We Talk About When We Talk About Love" from WHAT WE TALK ABOUT WHEN WE TALK ABOUT LOVE by Raymond Carver, copyright © 1981 by Raymond Carver. Used by permission of Alfred A. Knopf, a division of Random House, Inc. 357: "Cathedral" from CATHEDRAL by Raymond Carver, copyright © 1983 by Raymond Carver. Used by permission of Alfred A. Knopf, a division of Random House, Inc.

John Cheever. 370: "Goodbye, My Brother" from THE STORIES OF JOHN CHEEVER by John Cheever, copyright © 1978 by John Cheever. Used by permission of Alfred A. Knopf, a division of Random House, Inc. 384: "The Country Husband" from THE STORIES OF JOHN CHEEVER by John Cheever, copyright © 1978 by John Cheever. Used by permission of Alfred A. Knopf, a division of Random House, Inc. 401: "The Swimmer" from THE STORIES OF JOHN CHEEVER by John Cheever, copyright © 1978 by John Cheever. Used by permission of Alfred A. Knopf, a division of Random House, Inc.

Junot Diaz. 411: "Ysrael" from DROWN by Junot Diaz. Copyright © 1996 by Junot Diaz. Used by permission of Riverhead Books, an imprint of Penguin Group (USA) Inc. 419: "Fiesta 1980" from DROWN by Junot Diaz. Copyright © 1996 by Junot Diaz. Used by permission of Riverhead Books, an imprint of Penguin Group (USA) Inc. 428: "The Sun, the Moon, the Stars" by Junot Diaz. Reprinted by permission of the author, Junot Diaz and Aragi Inc. First published in THE NEW YORKER.

Chitra Banerjee Divakaruni. 440: "Mrs. Dutta Writes a Letter" from THE UNKNOWN ERRORS OF OUR LIVES by Chitra Banerjee Divakaruni, copyright © 2001 by Chitra Banerjee Divakaruni. Used by permission of Doubleday, a division of Random House, Inc. 453: "The Lives of Strangers" from THE UNKNOWN ERRORS OF OUR LIVES by Chitra Banerjee Divakaruni, copyright © 2001 by Chitra Banerjee Divakaruni. Used by permission of Doubleday, a division of Random House, Inc. 466: "The Blooming Season of Cacti" from THE UNKNOWN ERRORS OF OUR LIVES by Chitra Banerjee Divakaruni, copyright © 2001 by Chitra Banerjee Divakaruni. Used by permission of Doubleday, a division of Random House, Inc.

Louise Erdrich. 485: "The Red Convertible" from LOVE MEDICINE: New and Expanded Version by Louise Erdrich, © 1984, 1993 by Louise Erdrich. Reprinted by permission of Henry Holt and Company, LLC. 492: "Saint Marie" from LOVE MEDICINE: New and Expanded Version by Louise Erdrich, © 1984, 1993 by Louise Erdrich. Reprinted by permission of Henry Holt and Company, LLC. 502: "Satan: Hijacker of a Planet" by Louise Erdrich. Copyright © 1997 by Louise Erdrich, reprinted with the permission of The Wylie Agency, Inc.

Richard Ford. 512: "Rock Springs" from ROCK SPRINGS by Richard Ford. Copyright © 1987 by Richard Ford. Used by permission of Grove/Atlantic, Inc. 526: "Communist" from ROCK SPRINGS by Richard Ford. Copyright © 1987 by Richard Ford. Used by permission of Grove/Atlantic, Inc. 537: "Issues" from A MULTITUDE OF SINS by Richard Ford. Copyright © 2001 by Richard Ford. Used by permission of Alfred A. Knopf, a division of Random House, Inc.

Barry Hannah. 547: "Testimony of Pilot" from AIRSHIPS by Barry Hannah. Copyright © 1978 by Barry Hannah. Used by permission of Grove/Atlantic, Inc. 564: "Water Liars" from AIRSHIPS by Barry Hannah. Copyright © 1978 by Barry Hannah. Used by permission of Grove/Atlantic, Inc. 567: "Constant Pain in Tuscaloosa" from AIRSHIPS by Barry Hannah. Copyright © 1978 by Barry Hannah. Used by permission of Grove/Atlantic, Inc. 567: "Nicodemus Bluff" from BATS OUT OF HELL. Copyright © 1993 by Barry Hannah. Reprinted by permission of Houghton Mifflin Company/Seymour Lawrence. All rights reserved.

Gish Jen. 584: "The Water Faucet Vision" by Gish Jen copyright © 1987 by Gish Jen. First published in NIMROD. Reprinted by permission of the author. "The Water Faucet Vision" is included in the collection WHO'S IRISH by Gish Jen, published by Alfred A. Knopf in 1999. All rights reserved. 590: "Birthmates" by Gish Jen copyright © 1994 by Gish Jen. First published in PLOUGHSHARES. Reprinted by permission of the author. "Birthmates" is included in the collection WHO'S IRISH by Gish Jen, published by Alfred A. Knopf in 1999. All rights reserved. 601: "Who's Irish" by Gish Jen copyright © 1998 by Gish Jen. First published in THE NEW YORKER. Reprinted by permission of the author. "Who's Irish" is included in the collection WHO'S IRISH by Gish Jen, published by Alfred A. Knopf in 1999. All rights reserved.

Jamaica Kincaid. 611: "Girl" from AT THE BOTTOM OF THE RIVER by Jamaica Kincaid. Copyright © 1983 by Jamaica Kincaid. Reprinted by permission of Farrar, Straus & Giroux, LLC. 612: "Figures in the Distance" from ANNIE JOHN by Jamaica Kincaid. Copyright © 1985 by Jamaica Kincaid. Reprinted by permission of Farrar, Straus & Giroux, LLC. 616: Excerpt from THE AUTOBIOGRAPHY OF MY MOTHER by Jamaica Kincaid. Copyright © 1996 by Jamaica Kincaid. Reprinted by permission of Farrar, Straus & Giroux, LLC.

Bernard Malamud. 632: "The Magic Barrel" from A MALAMUD READER by Bernard Malamud. Copyright © 1967 by Farrar, Straus & Giroux. Reprinted by permission of Farrar, Straus & Giroux, LLC. 644: "The Last Mohican" from A MALAMUD READER by Bernard Malamud. Copyright © 1967 by Farrar, Straus & Giroux. Reprinted by permission of Farrar, Straus & Giroux, LLC. 659: "The Jewbird" from A MALAMUD READER by Bernard Malamud. Copyright © 1967 by Farrar, Straus & Giroux. Reprinted by permission of Farrar, Straus & Giroux, LLC.

Rick Moody. 667: "The Grid" from THE RING OF BRIGHTEST ANGELS AROUND HEAVEN by Rick Moody. Copyright © 1995 by Rick Moody. By permission of Little, Brown and Company (Inc). 672: "The Apocalypse Commentary of Bob Paisner" from THE RING OF BRIGHTEST ANGELS AROUND HEAVEN by Rick Moody. Copyright © 1995 by Rick Moody. By permission of Little, Brown and Company (Inc). 686: "Demonology" from DEMONOLOGY by Rick Moody. Copyright © 2001 by Rick Moody. By permission of Little, Brown and Company (Inc).

Lorrie Moore. 696: "How to Become a Writer" from SELF-HELP by Lorrie Moore, copyright © 1985 by M.L. Moore. Used by permission of Alfred A. Knopf, a division of Random House, Inc. 701: "You're Ugly, Too" from LIKE LIFE by Lorrie Moore, copyright © 1990 by Lorrie Moore. Used by permission of Alfred A. Knopf, a division of Random House, Inc 715: "People Like That Are the Only People Here" from BIRDS OF AMERICA by Lorrie Moore, copyright © 1998 by Lorrie Moore. Used by permission of Alfred A. Knopf, a division of Random House, Inc.

Alice Munro. 739: "Walker Brothers Cowboy" by Alice Munro from SELECTED STORIES by Alice Munro, Copyright © 1996 by Alice Munro. Used by permission of Alfred A. Knopf, a division of Random House, Inc. and McClelland & Stewart Ltd., The Canadian Publishers. 749: "Friend of My Youth" by Alice Munro from SELECTED STORIES by Alice Munro, Copyright © 1996 by Alice Munro. Used by permission of Alfred A. Knopf, a division of Random House, Inc. and McClelland & Stewart Ltd., The Canadian Publishers. 763: "Save the Reaper" from THE LOVE OF A GOOD WOMAN by Alice Munro, Copyright © 1998 by Alice Munro. Used by permission of Alfred A. Knopf, a division of Random House, Inc. and McClelland & Stewart Ltd., The Canadian Publishers.

Antonya Nelson. 784: "The Control Group" reprinted with the permission of Scribner, an imprint of Simon & Schuster Adult Publishing Group, from IN THE LAND OF MEN by Antonya Nelson. Copyright © 2002 by Antonya Nelson. 794: "Naked Ladies" from FAMILY TERRORISTS by Antonya Nelson. Copyright © 1994 by Antonya Nelson. Reprinted by permission of Houghton Mifflin Company. All rights reserved. 806: "Female Trouble" reprinted with the permission of Scribner, an imprint of Simon & Schuster Adult Publishing Group, from FEMALE TROUBLE by Antonya Nelson. Copyright © 2002 by Antonya Nelson.

Joyce Carol Oates. 826: "Where Are You Going, Where Have You Been?" by Joyce Carol Oates. Published in 1970. Published by Vanguard. Copyright © 1970 by Ontario Review. Reprinted by permission of John Hawkins & Associates, Inc. 838: "Life After High School" by Joyce Carol Oates. Published in 1991. Published by Ontario Review. Copyright © 1991 by Ontario Review. Reprinted by permission of John Hawkins & Associates, Inc. 849: "Ghost Girls" by Joyce Carol Oates. Published in 1995. Published by American Short Fiction. Copyright © 1995 by Ontario Review. Reprinted by permission of John Hawkins & Associates, Inc.

Tim O'Brien. 862: "The Things They Carried" from THE THINGS THEY CARRIED by Tim O'Brien. Copyright © 1990 by Tim O'Brien. Reprinted by permission of Houghton Mifflin Company. All rights reserved. 874: "Sweetheart of the Song Tra Bong" from THE THINGS THEY CARRIED by Tim O'Brien. Copyright © 1990 by Tim O'Brien. Reprinted by permission of Houghton Mifflin Company. All rights reserved. 887: "Half Gone" from JULY, JULY by Tim O'Brien. Copyright © 2002 by Tim O'Brien. Reprinted by permission of Houghton Mifflin Company. All rights reserved.

Flannery O'Connor. 898: "A Good Man Is Hard to Find" from A GOOD MAN IS HARD TO FIND AND OTHER STORIES, copyright © 1953 by Flannery O'Connor and renewed 1981 by Regina O'Connor, reprinted by permission of Harcourt, Inc. 909: "Everything That Rises Must Converge" from THE COMPLETE STORIES by Flannery O'Connor. Copyright © 1971 by the Estate of Mary Flannery O'Connor. Reprinted by permission of Farrar, Straus & Giroux, LLC. 920: "Good Country People" from A GOOD MAN IS HARD TO FIND AND OTHER STORIES, copyright © 1955 by Flannery O'Connor and renewed 1983 by Regina O'Connor, reprinted by permission of Harcourt, Inc.

Grace Paley. 937: "An Interest in Life" from THE LITTLE DISTURBANCES OF MAN by Grace Paley, copyright © 1956, 1957, 1958, 1959 by Grace Paley. Used by permission of Penguin Group (USA) Inc. 947: "Goodbye and Good Luck" from THE LITTLE DISTURBANCES OF MAN by Grace Paley, copyright © 1956, 1957, 1958, 1959 by Grace Paley. Used by permission of Penguin Group (USA) Inc. 954: "A Conversation with My Father" from THE COLLECTED STORIES by Grace Paley, copyright © 1994 by Grace Paley. Reprinted by permission of Farrar, Straus & Giroux, LLC.

George Saunders. 960: "CivilWarLand in Bad Decline" from CIVILWARLAND IN BAD DECLINE by George Saunders, copyright © 1996 by George Saunders. Used by permission of Random House, Inc. 972: "Sea Oak" from PASTORALIA by George Saunders, copyright © 2000 by George Saunders. Used by permission of Riverhead Books, an imprint of Penguin Group (USA) Inc. 988: "Winky" from PASTORALIA by George Saunders, copyright © 2000 by George Saunders. Used by permission of Riverhead Books, an imprint of Penguin Group (USA) Inc.

John Updike. 1000: "A & P" from PIGEON FEATHERS AND OTHER STORIES by John Updike, Copyright © 1962 and renewed 1990 by John Updike. Used by permission of Alfred A. Knopf, a division of Random House, Inc. 1005: "Pigeon Feathers" from PIGEON FEATHERS AND OTHER STORIES by John Updike, Copyright © 1962 and renewed 1990 by John Updike. Used by permission of Alfred A. Knopf, a division of Random House, Inc. 1021: "A Sandstone Farmhouse" from THE AFTERLIFE: AND OTHER STORIES by John Updike, Copyright © 1994 by John Updike. Used by permission of Alfred A. Knopf, a division of Random House, Inc.

Eudora Welty. 1040: "A Worn Path" from A CURTAIN OF GREEN AND OTHER STORIES, copyright © 1941 and renewed 1969 by Eudora Welty, reprinted by permission of Harcourt, Inc. 1046: "Why I Live at the P.O." from A CURTAIN OF GREEN AND OTHER STORIES, copyright © 1941 and renewed 1969 by Eudora Welty, reprinted by permission of Harcourt, Inc. 1055: "No Place for You, My Love" from THE BRIDE OF THE INNISFALLEN AND OTHER STORIES, copyright © 1952 and renewed 1980 by Eudora Welty, reprinted by permission of Harcourt, Inc.

Tobias Wolff. 1070: "Hunters in the Snow" from IN THE GARDEN OF THE NORTH AMERICAN MARTYRS by Tobias Wolff. Copyright © 1981 by Tobias Wolff. Reprinted by permission of HarperCollins Publishers Inc. 1081: "The Rich Brother" from BACK IN THE WORLD by Tobias Wolff. Copyright © by Tobias Wolff. Reprinted by permission of International Creative Management, Inc. 1093: "Bullet in the Brain" from THE NIGHT IN QUESTION: STORIES by Tobias Wolff. Copyright © 1996 by Tobias Wolff. Used by permission of Alfred A. Knopf, a division of Random House, Inc.

Richard Yates. 1099: "The Best of Everything" from THE COLLECTED STORIES OF RICHARD YATES. Copyright © 1957, 1961, 1962, 1974, 1976, 1978, 1980, 1981, 2001 by the Estate of Richard Yates. Reprinted by permission of Henry Holt and Company, LLC. 1109: "No Pain Whatsoever" from THE COLLECTED STORIES OF RICHARD YATES. Copyright © 1957, 1961, 1962, 1974, 1976, 1978, 1980, 1981, 2001 by the Estate of Richard Yates. Reprinted by permission of Henry Holt and Company, LLC. 1117: "Oh, Joseph, I'm So Tired" from THE COLLECTED STORIES OF RICHARD YATES. Copyright © 1957, 1961, 1962, 1974, 1976, 1978, 1980, 1981, 2001 by the Estate of Richard Yates. Reprinted by permission of Henry Holt and Company, LLC.

Index